ABU-0013

W9-AEQ-323

ABU-0013

ENCYCLOPEDIA OF

Violence, Peace, & Conflict

VOLUME 2   F – Pe

EDITOR-IN-CHIEF
LESTER KURTZ
University of Texas, Austin

ASSOCIATE EDITOR
JENNIFER TURPIN
University of San Francisco

EXECUTIVE ADVISORY BOARD

NACHMAN BEN-YEHUDA
Hebrew University of Jerusalem

ALFRED BLUMSTEIN
National Consortium on Violence Research
Carnegie Mellon University

ELISE BOULDING
Dartmouth University (Emerita)

JAMES CALLEJA
International Peace Research Association, Malta

YUAN-HORNG CHU
Tunghai University, Taiwan

ED DONNERSTEIN
University of California, Santa Barbara

RIANE EISLER
Center for Partnership Studies
Pacific Grove, California

ROBERT ELIAS
University of San Francisco

MELVIN EMBER
President, Human Relations Area Files
New Haven, Connecticut

KAI ERIKSON
Yale University

NANCY HORNSTEIN
University of Illinois, Chicago

S. JEYAPRAGASAM
Madurai Kamaraj University, India

HANS JOAS
Free University of Berlin

MICHAEL KLARE
Hampshire College

RAJNI KOTHARI
Professor Emeritus, United Nations University

LOUIS KRIESBERG
Syracuse University

CREUZA MACIEL
International Committee
Service for Peace and Justice in Latin America

MITSUO OKAMOTO
Hiroshima Shudo University

DEBORAH PROTHROW-STITH
Harvard University School of Public Health

ALBERT J. REISS, JR.
Yale University (Emeritus)

ALISON DUNDES RENTELN
University of Southern California

J. DAVID SINGER
University of Michigan, Ann Arbor

METTA SPENCER
Erindale College, University of Toronto

MAJID TEHRANIAN
Harvard University

CHARLES TILLY
Columbia University

ENCYCLOPEDIA OF

Violence, Peace, & Conflict

VOLUME 2 F–Pe

ACADEMIC PRESS

SAN DIEGO   LONDON   BOSTON   NEW YORK   SYDNEY   TOKYO   TORONTO

This book is printed on acid-free paper.

Copyright © 1999 by ACADEMIC PRESS

All Rights Reserved.
No part of this publication may be reproduced or transmitted in any form or by any means, electronic or mechanical, including photocopy, recording, or any information storage and retrieval system, without permission in writing from the publisher.

Requests for permission to make copies of any part of the work should be mailed to: Permissions Department, Harcourt Brace & Company, 6277 Sea Harbor Drive, Orlando, Florida, 32887-6777

Academic Press
A Harcourt Science and Technology Company
525 B Street, Suite 1900, San Diego, California 92101-4495, USA
http://www.apnet.com

Academic Press
24-28 Oval Road, London NW1 7DX, UK
http://www.hbuk.co.uk/ap/

Library of Congress Catalog Card Number: 99-60408

International Standard Book Number: 0-12-227010-X (set)
International Standard Book Number: 0-12-227011-8 (Volume 1)
International Standard Book Number: 0-12-227012-6 (Volume 2)
International Standard Book Number: 0-12-227013-4 (Volume 3)

PRINTED IN THE UNITED STATES OF AMERICA
99   00   01   02   03   04   MM   9   8   7   6   5   4   3   2   1

Contents

Contents of Other Volumes

Contents by Subject Area

Contributors

Mimi Ajzenstadt
Women, Violence Against
    Hebrew University
    Jerusalem, Israel

Peter Almquist
Economic Conversion
    US Arms Control and Disarmament Agency
    Washington, DC, USA

Randall Amster
Power and Deviance
    Arizona State University
    Tempe, Arizona, USA

Kristin L. Anderson
Child Abuse
    Drew University
    Madison, New Jersey, USA

Kauko Aromaa
Victimology
    National Research Institute of Legal Policy
    Helsinki, Finland

Sidney Axinn
Moral Judgments and Values
    Temple University
    Philadelphia, Pennsylvania, USA

Kerri Lynn Bates
Urban and Community Studies
    University of British Columbia
    Vancouver, British Columbia, Canada

Hugo Adam Bedau
Death Penalty
    Tufts University
    Medford, Massachusetts, USA

Nancy Bell
Power, Alternative Theories of
    University of Texas
    Austin, Texas, USA

Robert D. Benford
Peace Movements
    University of Nebraska
    Lincoln, Nebraska, USA

Chawki Benkelfat
Biochemical Factors
    McGill University
    Montreal, Quebec, Canada

Nachman Ben-Yehuda
Assassinations, Political
    Hebrew University
    Jerusalem, Israel

Jacob Bercovitch
Mediation and Negotiation Techniques
    University of Canterbury
    Christchurch, New Zealand

Leonard Berkowitz
Aggression, Psychology of
    University of Wisconsin
    Madison, Wisconsin, USA

Irwin S. Bernstein
Animal Behavior Studies, Primates
    University of Georgia
    Athens, Georgia, USA

Mike Berry
Communication Studies, Overview
    University of California, Santa Barbara
    Santa Barbara, California

Vincent Boudreau
Political Theories
    City University of New York
    New York, NY, USA

Elise Boulding
Peace Culture
    Dartmouth College (emerita)
    Hanover, New Hampshire, USA

Janet Welsh Brown
Environmental Issues and Politics
Nongovernmental Actors in International
    Politics
Trade and the Environment
    World Resources Institute
    Washington, DC, USA

Lisa Brown
Ethnicity and Identity Politics
University of Florida
Gainesville, Florida, USA

Arden Bucholz
Militarism
State University of New York
Brockport, New York, USA

James Burk
Military Culture
Texas A&M University
College Station, Texas, USA

Gabriella Cagliesi
Trade Wars (Disputes)
Rutgers University
Newark, New Jersey, USA

Deborah Cai
Interpersonal Conflict, History of
University of Maryland
College Park, Maryland, USA

James Calleja
Aged Population, Violence and Nonviolence
toward
International Institute on Aging
United Nations, Malta

Jesus Casquette
Draft, Resistance and Evasion of
Universidad del Pais Vasco
Leioa, Spain

Victor D. Cha
Collective Security Systems
Georgetown University
Washington, DC, USA

Paul Chevigny
Police Brutality
New York University Law School
New York, NY, USA

Stephen J. Cimbala
Nuclear Weapons Policies
Pennsylvania State University, Delaware County
Media, Pennsylvania, USA

Murray Code
Reason and Violence
University of Guelph
Toronto, Ontario, Canada

Irwin Cohen
Torture (State)
Simon Fraser University
Burnaby, British Columbia, Canada

Noé Cornago-Prieto
Diplomacy
University of the Basque Country
Bilbao, Spain

Raymond R. Corrado
Torture (State)
Simon Fraser University
Burnaby, British Columbia, Canada

Alex E. Crosby
Public Health Models of Violence and Violence Prevention
Centers for Disease Control
Atlanta, Georgia, USA

S. Cumner
Peacekeeping
Pearson Peacekeeping Centre
Clementsport, Nova Scotia, Canada

G. David Curry
Gangs
Law and Violence
University of Missouri, St. Louis
St. Louis, Missouri, USA

Thomas C. Daffern
Peacemaking and Peacebuilding
International Institute of Peace Studies
London, UK

Linda L. Dahlberg
Public Health Models of Violence and Violence Prevention
Centers for Disease Control
Atlanta, Georgia, USA

James C. Davies
Human Nature, Views of
University of Oregon (Emeritus)
Eugene, Oregon, USA

Angela Davis
Crime and Punishment, Changing Attitudes toward
University of California, Santa Cruz
Santa Cruz, California, USA

Scott H. Decker
Gangs
University of Missouri, St. Louis
St. Louis, Missouri, USA

Paul F. Diehl
Territorial Disputes
University of Illinois
Urbana, Illinois, USA

Edward Donnerstein
Mass Media, General View
University of California, Santa Barbara
Santa Barbara, California, USA

William Donohue
Interpersonal Conflict, History of
Michigan State University
East Lansing, Michigan, USA

Steven Dubin
Peace and the Arts
State University of New York
Purchase, New York, USA

Antulio J. Echevarria
Warfare, Modern
U.S. Army Training and Doctrine Command
Fort Monroe, Virginia, USA

Riane Eisler
Family Structure and Family Violence and
Nonviolence
Carmel, California, USA

Robert Elias
Violence as Solution, Culture of
University of San Francisco
San Francisco, California, USA

Leonard D. Eron
Television Programming and Violence, U.S.
University of Michigan
Ann Arbor, Michigan, USA

Paul Lawrence Farber
Evolutionary Theory
Oregon State University
Corvallis, Oregon, USA

David N. Farnsworth
International Relations, Overview
Wichita State University
Wichita, Kansas, USA

Gordon Fellman
Enemy, Concept and Identity of
Brandeis University
Waltham, Massachusetts, USA

Juanita M. Firestone
Warfare and Military Studies, Overview
University of Texas
San Antonio, Texas, USA

Dietrich Fischer
Economics of War and Peace, Overview
Pace University
Pleasantville, New York, USA

Virginia Floresca-Cawages
Institutionalization of Nonviolence
University of Alberta
Edmonton, Alberta, Canada

Linda Rennie Forcey
Feminist and Peace Perspectives on Women
Binghamton University
Binghamton, New York, USA

Nicholas G. Fotion
Warfare, Trends in
Emory University
Atlanta, Georgia, USA

Karen Franklin
Homosexuals, Violence toward
University of Washington
Seattle, Washington, USA

Marvin D. Free
Minorities as Perpetrators and Victims
of Crime
University of Wisconsin
Madison, Wisconsin, USA

David Noel Freedman
Religious Traditions, Violence and Nonviolence
University of California, San Diego
San Diego, California, USA

William C. French
Ecoethics
Loyola University
Chicago, Illinois, USA

Gregory Fried
Critiques of Violence
Boston University
Boston, Massachusetts, USA

Robert Friedmann
Policing and Society
Georgia State University
Atlanta, Georgia, USA

Douglas P. Fry
Aggression and Altruism
Peaceful Societies
University of Abo
Helsinki, Finland

Theodore Gabriel
Ethical and Religious Traditions, Eastern
Cheltenham and Gloucester College
Gloucester, UK

James Garbarino
Long-Term Effects of War on Children
Cornell University
Ithaca, New York, USA

William Gay
Language of War and Peace, The
University of North Carolina
Charlotte, North Carolina, USA

George Gerbner
Mass Media and Dissent
Temple University
Philadelphia, Pennsylvania, USA

Douglas M. Gibler
Alliance Systems
Stanford University
Stanford, California, USA

Howard Giles
Communication Studies, Overview
University of California, Santa Barbara
Santa Barbara, California, USA

William Gissy
Political Economy of Violence and Nonviolence
Morehouse College
Atlanta, Georgia, USA

Nils-Petter Gleditsch
Peace and Democracy
International Peace Research Institute
Oslo, Norway

Mark Gold
Drugs and Violence
University of Florida College of Medicine
Gainesville, Florida, USA

Ralph M. Goldman
Political Systems and Conflict Management
San Francisco State University
San Francisco, California, USA

Janine Goldman-Pach
Sexual Assault
University of Arizona
Tucson, Arizona, USA

Jeff Goodwin
Revolutions
New York University
New York, NY, USA

Deborah Gorman-Smith
Urban Violence, Youth
University of Illinois
Chicago, Illinois, USA

F. Lincoln Grahlfs
Veterans in the Political Culture
National Association of Radiation Survivors
St. Louis, Missouri, USA

Adam Green
Revolutions
New York University
New York, NY, USA

Allen D. Grimshaw
Genocide and Democide
Indiana University
Bloomington, Indiana, USA

Linda Groff
Religion and Peace, Inner-Outer Dimensions of
California State University
Dominguez Hills, California, USA

David Grossman
Behavioral Psychology
Psychological Effects of Combat
Weaponry, Evolution of
Arkansas State University
Jonesboro, Arkansas, USA

Barrie Gunter
Television Programming and Violence, International
University of Sheffield
Sheffield, UK

Brien Hallett
Just-War Criteria
University of Hawaii
Honolulu, Hawaii, USA

Fen Osler Hampson
Peace Agreements
Carleton University
Ottawa, Ontario, Canada

Michael Hanagan
Industrial vs. Preindustrial Forms of Violence
New School for Social Research
New York, NY, USA

Ian M. Harris
Peace Education: Colleges and Universities
University of Wisconsin, Milwaukee
Milwaukee, Wisconsin, USA

John Hartman
Psychoanalysis
University of Michigan
Ann Arbor, Michigan, USA

Akira Hattori
Economics of War and Peace, Overview
Fukuoka University
Fukuoka, Japan

Mark Haugaard
Power, Social and Political Theories of
University College, Galway
Galway City, Ireland

Ira Heilveil
Violence Prediction
Ojai, California
USA

Errol A. Henderson
Civil Wars
Ethnic Conflicts and Cooperation
University of Florida
Gainesville, Florida, USA

Gregory Herek
Homosexuals, Violence toward
University of California, Davis
Davis, California, USA

Marjorie Hogan
Popular Music
Hennepin County Medical Center
Minneapolis, Minnesota, USA

Gregory Hooks
Military-Industrial Complex, Organization and History
Washington State University
Pullman, Washington, USA

Brenda Horrigan
Security Studies
Vineyard Haven, Massachusetts, USA

Michael W. Hovey
Conscientious Objection, Ethics of
Iona College
New Rochelle, New York, USA

L. Rowell Huesmann
Television Programming and Violence, U.S.
Institute for Social Research, University of Michigan
Ann Arbor, Michigan, USA

Paul K. Huth
Military Deterrence and Statecraft
University of Michigan
Ann Arbor, Michigan, USA

Larry W. Isaac
Class Conflict
Florida State University
Tallahassee, Florida, USA

James M. Jasper
Animals, Violence toward
New York University
New York, NY, USA

Ho-Won Jeong
Conflict Management and Resolution
Theories of Conflict
George Mason University
Fairfax, Virginia, USA

Hans Joas
Social Theorizing about War and Peace
Free University of Berlin
Berlin, Germany

Anthony James Joes
Guerrilla Warfare
St. Joseph's University
Philadelphia, Pennsylvania, USA

Hubert C. Johnson
Warfare, Strategies and Tactics of
University of Saskatchewan
Saskatoon, Saskatchewan, Canada

Theodore Karasik
Security Studies
University of California, Los Angeles
Los Angeles, California, USA

Robert W. Kentridge
Behavioral Psychology
University of Durham
Durham, UK

James R. Kerin, Jr.
Combat
United States Military Academy
West Point, New York, USA

Wolfgang Knöbl
Social Control and Violence
Free University of Berlin
Berlin, Germany

Edward Kolodziej
Arms Control
University of Illinois
Urbana, Illinois, USA

Fiona M. Kay
Urban and Community Studies
University of British Columbia
Vancouver, British Columbia, Canada

Mary Koss
Sexual Assault
Arizona Prevention Center
Tucson, Arizona, USA

Rajini Kothari
Institutionalization of Violence
Center for the Study of Developing Societies
Delhi, India

Louis Kriesberg
Conflict Transformation
Syracuse University
Syracuse, New York, USA

Mitsuru Kurosawa
Arms Control and Disarmament Treaties
Osaka School of International Public Policy
Osaka, Japan

John Kydd
Violence to Children, Definition and Prevention of
Child VIP—Child Violence Identification and
Prevention Project
Seattle, Washington, USA

Christos N. Kyrou
Cultural Anthropology Studies of Conflict
Syracuse, New York, USA
Syracuse University

Linda Lantieri
Peace Education: Youth
Educators for Social Responsibility
New York, NY, USA

Pat Lauderdale
Power and Deviance
Arizona State University
Tempe, Arizona, USA

Colin Wayne Leach
Ethnicity and Identity Politics
Swarthmore College
Swarthmore, Pennsylvania, USA

David LeMarquand
Biochemical Factors
McGill University
Montreal, Quebec, Canada

David Lester
Suicide and Other Violence toward the Self
Center for the Study of Suicide
Blackwood, New Jersey, USA

Amy Leventhal
Urban Violence, Youth
University of Illinois
Chicago, Illinois, USA

Howard S. Levie
Chemical and Biological Warfare
War Crimes
U.S. Naval War College
Newport, Rhode Island, USA

Jack Levin
Hate Crimes
  Northeastern University
  Boston, Massachusetts, USA

Sheldon G. Levy
Conformity and Obedience
Cooperation, Competition, and Conflict
Mass Conflict and the Participants, Attitudes toward
  Wayne State University
  Detroit, Michigan, USA

Elliott Leyton
Serial and Mass Murderers
  Memorial University of Newfoundland
  St. John's, Newfoundland, Canada

Daniel G. Linz
Mass Media, General View
  University of California
  Santa Barbara, California, USA

David Loye
Evil, Concept of
  Center for Partnership Studies
  Carmel, California, USA

Derek F. Lynch
Balance of Power Relationships
  University of Huddersfield
  Queensgate, Yorkshire, UK

Graeme MacQueen
Spirituality and Peacemaking
  McMaster University
  Hamilton, Ontario, Canada

Esther Madriz
Criminology, Overview
  University of San Francisco
  San Francisco, California, USA

Sanja Magdalenic
Folklore
  Stockholm University
  Stockholm, Sweden

Kevin Magill
Justification for Violence
  University of Wolverhampton
  Dudley, UK

Neil Malamuth
Pornography
  University of California, Los Angeles
  Los Angeles, California, USA

Brian Martin
Technology, Violence, and Peace
  University of Wollongong
  Wollongong, Australia

Peter B. Mayer
Militarism and Development in Underdeveloped
  Societies
  University of Adelaide
  Adelaide, Australia

Alfred McAlister
International Variation in Attitudes toward Violence
  University of Texas
  Austin, Texas, USA

Laura Ann McCloskey
Family Structure and Family Violence and
  Nonviolence
  University of Arizona
  Tucson, Arizona, USA

Michael J. McClymond
Religious Traditions, Violence and Nonviolence
  University of California, San Diego
  San Diego, California, USA

Jack McDevitt
Hate Crimes
  Northeastern University
  Boston, Massachusetts, USA

Gregory McLauchlan
Military-Industrial Complex, Contemporary Significance
  University of Oregon
  Eugene, Oregon, USA

Eduardo Mendieta
Ethical Studies, Overview
  University of San Francisco
  San Francisco, California, USA

James A. Mercy
Public Health Models of Violence and Violence Prevention
  Centers for Disease Control
  Atlanta, Georgia, USA

Thomas Mieczkowski
Drug Control Policies
  University of South Florida
  St. Petersburg, Florida, USA

Dinshaw Mistry
Arms Control
  University of Illinois
  Urbana, Illinois, USA

Alex Morrison
Peacekeeping
  Pearson Peacekeeping Centre
  Clementsport, Nova Scotia, Canada

C. David Mortensen
Linguistic Constructions of Violence, Peace, and Conflict
  University of Wisconsin
  Madison, Wisconsin, USA

Kenneth R. Murray
Behavioral Psychology
  Armiger Police Training Institute
  Ottawa, Ontario, Canada

Hanna Newcombe
World Government
  Peace Research Institute
  Dundas, Ontario, Canada

Roderick Ogley
Conflict Theory
  University of Sussex
  Brighton, UK

Tamayo Okamoto
Means and Ends
  Hiroshima Prefectural College of Health
    and Welfare
  Hiroshima, Japan

Marie Olson
Arms Trade, Economics of
  Center for Peace and Conflict Studies
  Wayne State University
  Detroit, Michigan, USA

Keith F. Otterbein
Clan and Tribal Conflict
  State University of New York
  Buffalo, New York, USA

Jan Pakulski
Social Equality and Inequality
  University of Tasmania
  Hobart, Tasmania, Australia

Edward L. Palmer
Children, Impact of Television on
  Davidson College
  Davidson, North Carolina, USA

Martin Palous
Totalitarianism and Authoritarianism
  Charles University
  Prague, Czech Republic

Hanbin Park
Peacekeeping
  Pearson Peacekeeping Centre
  Clementsport, Nova Scotia, Canada

Janet Patti
Peace Education: Youth
  Hunter College of the City of New York
  New York, NY, USA

Frederic S. Pearson
Arms Trade, Economics of
  Center for Peace and Conflict Studies, Wayne State
  University
  Detroit, Michigan, USA

Jordan B. Peterson
Neuropsychology and Mythology of Motivation for Group
Aggression
  Harvard University
  Cambridge, Massachusetts, USA

Robert O. Pihl
Biochemical Factors
  McGill University
  Montreal, Quebec, Canada

Solomon W. Polachek
Trade, Conflict, and Cooperation among Nations
  State University of New York
  Binghamton, New York, USA

Kenneth Powell
Public Health Models of Violence and Violence Prevention
  Centers for Disease Control
  Atlanta, Georgia, USA

Jason Pribilsky
Cultural Anthropology Studies of Conflict
  Syracuse, New York, USA
  Syracuse University

Anatol Rapoport
Decision Theory and Game Theory
Peace, Definitions and Concepts of
  University of Toronto
  Toronto, Ontario, Canada

David C. Rapoport
Terrorism
  University of California, Los Angeles
  Los Angeles, California, USA

Alison Dundes Renteln
Human Rights
  University of Southern California
  Los Angeles, California, USA

Claire Renzetti
Criminal Behavior, Theories of
  St. Joseph's University
  Philadelphia, Pennsylvania, USA

Patricia Richards
Effects of War and Political Violence on Health Services
Health Consequences of War and Political Violence
  London School of Hygiene and Tropical Medicine
  London, UK

Marc Riedel
Homicide
  Southern Illinois University
  Carbondale, Illinois, USA

John Robst
Trade, Conflict, and Cooperation among
  Nations
  State University of New York
  Binghamton, New York, USA

Robert A. Rubinstein
Cultural Anthropology Studies of Conflict
  Syracuse University
  Syracuse, New York, USA

Gordon W. Russell
Sports
  University of Lethbridge
  Lethbridge, Alberta, Canada

Andrew Sanders
Warriors, Anthropology of
  University of Ulster
  Coleraine, Northern Ireland, UK

Joanna Santa Barbara
Childrearing, Violent and Nonviolent
  McMaster University
  Hamilton, Ontario, Canada

Robert K. Schaeffer
Secession and Separatism
San Jose State University
San Jose, California, USA

Thomas J. Scheff
Collective Emotions in Warfare
University of California, Santa Barbara
Santa Barbara, California, USA

Christian P. Scherrer
Structural Prevention and Conflict Management, Imperatives of
Copenhagen Peace Research Institute
Copenhagen, Denmark

Brigitte H. Schulz
Cold War
Trinity College
Hartford, Connecticut, USA

John Paul Scott
Animal Behavior Studies, Nonprimates
Bowling Green University
Bowling Green, Ohio, USA

Leslie Sebba
Punishment of Criminals
Hebrew Institute of Jerusalem
Jerusalem, Israel

Daniel M. Segesser
World War I
Universiy of Berne
Berne, Switzerland

Carlos Seiglie
Economic Costs and Consequences of War
Rutgers University
Newark, New Jersey, USA

Gene Sharp
Nonviolent Action
Albert Einstein Institution
Cambridge, Massachusetts, USA

Martin Shaw
Civil Society
University of Sussex
Brighton, UK

James F. Short, Jr.
Youth Violence
Washington State University
Pullman, Washington, USA

Bruce K. Siddle
Psychological Effects of Combat
Executive Director, PPCT Management
Millstadt, Illinois, USA

Thomas R. Simon
Public Health Models of Violence and Violence Prevention
Centers for Disease Control
Atlanta, Georgia, USA

J. David Singer
Correlates of War
University of Michigan
Ann Arbor, Michigan, USA

Simon I. Singer
Juvenile Crime
State University of New York
Buffalo, New York, USA

John Sislin
Arms Trade, Economics of
Center for International Studies, University of Missouri
St. Louis, Missouri, USA

Elisabeth Skons
Arms Production, Economics of
Stockholm International Peace Research Institute
Stockholm, Sweden

Jackie Smith
Transnational Organizations
State University of New York at Stony Brook
Stony Brook, NY, USA

Philip Smith
Cultural Studies, Overview
Ritual and Symbolic Behavior
University of Queensland
Queensland, Australia

Paul Smoker
Religion and Peace, Inner-Outer Dimensions of
Antioch College
Yellow Springs, Ohio, USA

H. F. (Rika) Snyman
Organized Crime
Technikon SA
Florida, South Africa

Metta Spencer
Sociological Studies, Overview
University of Toronto
Toronto, Ontario, Canada

Carolyn M. Stephenson
Peace Studies, Overview
University of Hawaii at Manoa
Honolulu, Hawaii, USA

Pamela J. Stewart
Anthropology of Violence and Conflict, Overview
University of Pittsburgh
Pittsburgh, Pennsylvania, USA

Victor C. Strasburger
Popular Music
University of New Mexico School of Medicine
Albuquerque, New Mexico

Andrew Strathern
Anthropology of Violence and Conflict, Overview
University of Pittsburgh
Pittsburgh, Pennsylvania, USA

Mira Sucharov
Collective Security
Georgetown University
Washington, DC, USA

Keith Suter
Peace Organizations, Nongovernmental
United Nations Association of Australia and Wesley Mission
Sydney, Australia

Jukka-Pekka Takala
Evolutionary Factors
Victimology
National Research Institute of Legal Policy
Helsinki, Finland

Kenneth Tardiff
Mental Illness
Cornell University Medical School, New York Hospital
New York, NY, USA

Frank O. Taylor IV
Peace Movements
Dana College
Blair, Nebraska, USA

Bryan Teixeira
Nonviolence Theory and Practice
Camosun College
Victoria, British Columbia, Canada

Charles Thomas
World War II
U.S. Naval War College
Newport, Rhode Island, USA

David Tindall
Urban and Community Studies
University of British Columbia
Vancouver, British Columbia, Canada

Swee-Hin Toh
Institutionalization of Nonviolence
University of Alberta
Edmonton, Alberta, Canada

Patrick Tolan
Urban Violence, Youth
University of Illinois
Chicago, Illinois, USA

Jennifer Turpin
Women and War
University of San Francisco
San Francisco, California, USA

Bernard Udis
Economic Conversion
University of Colorado
Boulder, Colorado, USA

Antonio Ugalde
Effects of War and Political Violence on Health Services
Health Consequences of War and Political Violence
University of Texas
Austin, Texas, USA

Debra Umberson
Child Abuse
University of Texas
Austin, Texas, USA

Sheldon Ungar
Total War, Social Impact of
University of Toronto
Toronto, Ontario, Canada

Alonzo Valentine
Ethical and Religious Traditions, Western
Earlham College and School of Religion
Richmond, Indiana, USA

Peter van den Dungen
Peace Education: Peace Museums
Peace Prizes
University of Bradford
West Yorkshire, UK

Paul Viotti
Professional versus Citizen Soldiery
University of Denver
Denver, Colorado, USA

Joseph Vorrasi
Long-Term Effects of War on Children
Cornell University
Ithaca, New York, USA

Dierk Walter
Colonialism and Imperialism
University of Berne
Berne, Switzerland

Kathleen Maas Weigert
Structural Violence
University of Notre Dame
Notre Dame, Indiana, USA

Reinhilde Weidacher
Arms Production, Economics of
Stockholm International Peace Research Institute
Stockholm, Sweden

Peter Weiss
Legal Theories and Remedies
Center for Constitutional Rights
New York, NY, USA

Michael G. Wessells
Psychology, General View
Randolph-Macon College
Ashland, Virginia, USA

Dean A. Wilkening
Nuclear Warfare
Center for International Security and Cooperation
Stanford University
Stanford, California, USA

Angie Williams
Communication Studies, Overview
Cardiff University
Cardiff, Wales, UK

Franke Wilmer
Indigenous Peoples' Responses to Conquest
Montana State University
Bozeman, Montana, USA

Jon D. Wisman
Economic Causes of War and Peace
American University
Washington, DC, USA

Lynne Woehrle
Gender Studies
Wilson College
Chambersburg, Pennsylvania, USA

Gordon C. Zahn
Conscientious Objection, Ethics of
University of Wisconsin
Milwaukee, Wisconsin, USA

Kristeva A. Zoë
Peacekeeping
Pearson Peacekeeping Centre
Clementsport, Nova Scotia, Canada

Anthony Zwi
Effects of War and Political Violence on Health Services
Health Consequences of War and Political Violence
London School of Hygiene and Tropical Medicine
London, UK

Guide to the Encyclopedia

The *Encyclopedia of Violence, Peace, and Conflict* is a complete source of information within the covers of a single unified work. It is the first reference book to address a full range of topics in the field of violence, peace, and conflict studies, with coverage of issues as disparate as peace education, trends in warfare, mental illness, and violence toward animals. It also includes many topics of concern to contemporary society, such as ethnic conflict, hate crimes, drug control policies, and child abuse.

The Encyclopedia consists of three volumes and includes 196 separate full-length articles, all prepared especially for this publication. It includes not only entries on the leading theories and concepts of violence, peace, and conflict, but also a vast selection of entries on applied topics in areas such as criminology, politics, economics, communications, and biomedicine. Each article provides a detailed overview of the selected topic to inform a broad spectrum of readers, from research professionals to students to the interested general public.

In order that you, the reader, will derive maximum benefit from your use of the Encyclopedia, we have provided this Guide. It explains how the work is organized and how the information within it can be located.

ORGANIZATION

The *Encyclopedia of Violence, Peace, and Conflict* is organized to provide the maximum ease of use for its readers. All of the articles are arranged in a single alphabetical sequence by title. So that they can be easily located, article titles generally begin with the key word or phrase indicating the topic, with any descriptive terms following. For example, "Criminal Behavior, Theories of" is the article title rather than "Theories of Criminal Behavior" because the specific phrase *criminal behavior* is the key term rather than the more general term *theories*.

Similarly, "Criminology, Overview" is the article title rather than "Overview of Criminology" and "Warfare, Trends in" is the title rather than "Trends in Warfare."

TABLE OF CONTENTS

A complete alphabetical table of contents for the Encyclopedia appears at the front of each volume of the set, beginning on page v of the Introduction. This list includes not only the articles that appear in that particular volume but also those in the other two volumes.

The list of article titles represents topics that have been carefully selected by the Editor-in-Chief, Prof. Lester Kurtz of the University of Texas, Austin, in collaboration with the members of the Editorial Board.

In addition to the alphabetical table of contents, the Encyclopedia also provides a second table of contents at the front of each volume, listing all the articles according to their subject area. The Encyclopedia provides coverage of 15 specific subject areas within the overall field of violence, peace, and conflict, as indicated below:

- **Anthropological Studies**
- **Biomedical Studies**
- **Communications**
- **Criminology**
- **Cultural Studies**
- **Economic Studies**
- **Ethical Studies**
- **Historical Studies**
- **International Relations**
- **Peace and Conflict Studies**
- **Political Studies**
- **Psychological Studies**
- **Public Policy Studies**
- **Sociological Studies**
- **Warfare and Military Studies**

OUTLINE

Each article in the Encyclopedia begins with an Outline that indicates the general content of the article. This outline serves two functions. First, it provides a brief preview of the article, so that the reader can get a sense of what is contained there without having to leaf through the pages. Second, it highlights important subtopics that are discussed within the article. For example, the article "Youth Violence" includes among its subtopics "The Age/Crime Connection" and "Understanding and Controlling Youth Violence."

The Outline is intended as an overview and thus it lists only the major headings of the article. In addition, extensive second-level and third-level headings will be found within the article.

GLOSSARY

The Glossary contains terms that are important to an understanding of the article and that may be unfamiliar to the reader, or that may need clarification as to their specific use in the article. Each term is defined in the context of the particular article in which it is used. Thus the same term may appear as a Glossary entry in two or more articles, with the details of the definition varying slightly from one article to another. The Encyclopedia includes more than 1,000 glossary entries.

The following example is a glossary entry that appears with the article "Aged Population."

Dementia An acquired, ongoing impairment of general intellectual abilities to such a degree as to seriously interfere with social and occupational functioning, including memory loss and failures of abstract thinking and judgment, as well as personality changes; an age-related condition and especially associated with Alzheimer's disease.

DEFINING STATEMENT

The text of each article in the Encyclopedia begins with a single introductory paragraph that defines the topic under discussion and summarizes the content of the article. For example, the article "Ecoethics" begins with the following statement:

ECOETHICS is an emerging discipline that in recent decades has been prompted by alarm about increasing environmental degradation and its impact on human and nonhuman life.

CROSS-REFERENCES

Virtually all of the articles in the Encyclopedia have cross-references to other articles. These cross-references appear at the end of the article, following the conclusion of the text. They indicate related articles that can be consulted for further information on the same topic, or for other information on a related topic. For example, the article "Guerrilla Warfare" contains cross references to the articles "Civil Wars," "Colonialism and Imperialism," "Revolutions," "Terrorism," "Warfare, Modern," and "Warfare, Strategies and Tactics of." The Encyclopedia contains about 1,150 cross-references in all.

BIBLIOGRAPHY

The Bibliography appears as the last element in an article. It lists recent secondary sources to aid the reader in locating more detailed or technical information. Review articles and research papers that are important to an understanding of the topic are also listed.

The bibliographies in this Encyclopedia are for the benefit of the reader, to provide references for further reading or research on the given topic. Thus they typically consist of a limited number of entries. They are not intended to represent a complete listing of all the materials consulted by the author in preparing the article.

INDEX

The Subject Index in Volume 3 contains more than 10,000 entries. The entries indicate the volume and page number where information on this topic will be found. The Index serves, along with the alphabetical Table of Contents, as the starting point for information on a subject of interest.

INTERNET RESOURCES

The *Encyclopedia of Violence, Peace, and Conflict* maintains its own editorial Web Page on the Internet at:

http://www.apnet.com/violence/

This site gives information about the Encyclopedia project. It also features a link to the Academic Press Reference Works home page, which has information about related titles, such as the *Encyclopedia of Applied Ethics* and the *Encyclopedia of Human Behavior.*

Preface

The problem of violence poses such a monumental challenge at the end of the 20th century that it is surprising we have addressed it so inadequately. We have not made much progress in learning how to cooperate with one another more effectively or how to conduct our conflicts more peacefully. Instead, we have increased the lethality of our combat through revolutions in weapons technology and military training. The *Encyclopedia of Violence, Peace, and Conflict* is designed to help us to take stock of our knowledge concerning these crucial phenomena.

Most people have a profound ambivalence about violence, a simultaneous abhorrence of and reliance upon it; consequently we engage what policy makers use to guide their discourse and decisions. The relationship between knowledge and practice is complex, of course; many Moderns seem to have something like an addiction to violent solutions that is much like any dependency and escapes rational analysis. Knowledge of dire consequences does not automatically promote constructive action or deter destructive behavior; like the smoker who wants to quit but cannot, we sometimes move ahead consciously along a destructive path. Many of the articles in this encyclopedia, while remaining rooted in academic research, attempt to explore the policy implications of those investigations.

The study of violence—especially war—is as ancient as our religious texts, from the reflective insights of the Mahabharata and Sun Tzu in the East to the Torah and Thucydides in the West, and has an overwhelming advantage over the study of peace when it comes to research funding. The conduct of war is so significant to those in power that its study has a privileged place in the production of knowledge. A large proportion of public expenditures on all research in both the natural and social sciences is, in fact, controlled by military establishments. In the United States, for example, the Army Research Bureau's annual budget exceeds the total combined funding for every other federally funded social science research program including such agencies as the National Science Foundation, the National Institutes of Health, and the National Institute for Mental Health.

As a consequence of massive data-gathering we have, in recent decades, learned a great deal about a wide range of violent behaviors from war to patterns of crime. In these volumes readers can find summaries of those findings; e.g., David Singer's "Correlates of War" project, criminological investigations and cross-cultural anthropological studies of violence, psychological studies of combat and aggressive behavior, case studies of urban and youth violence, UN investigations of the causes of war, and so forth. We have gained a great deal of insight into specific types of violence and have some reasonable theories about what causes people to engage in them. We are still uncertain, however, about how to construct social institutions that provide secure neighborhoods and nations or how to nurture peaceful cultures.

The academic study of peace—a poor cousin to the science of war—is a relatively recent development. This encyclopedia encompasses both enterprises, along with an array of academic disciplines in neither camp that can deepen our understanding of violence. Most of the Enlightenment philosophers—in the same intellectual movement that gave birth to the modern encyclopedia—incorrectly speculated that war would gradually disappear as human society became more rational and civilized. It was not until the 20th century—in response to the horrors of modern warfare—that empirical research and systematic study oriented toward the construction of peace became a part of the academy. Indeed, the field called "peace studies" remains marginal to the academy despite its remarkable growth worldwide since the 1960s with formal programs in hundreds of universities and professional associations such as the International Peace Research Association, the Peace Studies Association, and the Consortium on Peace Research, Education, and Development (COPRED), as well as organized groups of conflict resolution professionals and sections devoted to peace studies in disciplinary societies.

The purpose of this encyclopedia is to bring together in one place a broad range of information and perspectives on violence, peace, and conflict in order to enhance our understanding of these crucial phenomena and to stimulate new research, insights, and better public policies. The encyclopedia's most significant contribution is its addressing the problem of intellectual compartmentalization by including scholarship from diverse disciplines from around the world, from military and peace sciences, to the social and biological sciences, as well as the humanities.

What Do We Know?

It is impossible to summarize briefly the information contained in these three volumes; I would, however, like to highlight some of the themes that emerge. First of all, it is salient that we do not even have a consensus on how to define these three concepts. Rather than impose one on the authors, we include a variety of approaches and a discussion of the debates. Some perceive conflict as a broader phenomenon that encompasses the other two: one can engage in either violent or peaceful conflict. Others perceive peace as something that reflects the absence of conflict. These conflicting definitions reflect salient domain assumptions and produce different theories and policies regarding how to manage the conflicts that seem to be an inevitable part of social life.

Similarly, violence is defined in several markedly different ways. Whereas some contend that the term should refer only to the deliberate infliction of physical harm, others insist that psychological harm must be included as well. Still others claim that we must include the injury caused by inequality (what Johan Galtung calls "structural violence") if the definition is to be sufficiently inclusive. Indeed, the holocaust-like deaths caused by contemporary malnutrition can scarcely be seen as anything but violent, especially by its victims, although usually not inflicted deliberately. UNICEF estimates that six million children under the age of five die annually from malnutrition—as many each year as were murdered in all the German death camps. How violence is defined is an issue with profound policy implications, as demonstrated in the elaborate taxonomy provided in the article "Violence to Children, Definition and Prevention of."

An adequate definition of peace seems almost as elusive as peace itself. The most basic concept, of course, is the absence of war, or more broadly the mitigation of violence. Some would insist, however, that one cannot have peace without justice. Whereas some, following Thomas Hobbes, view peace as something that must be imposed from the top, others claim that it will result only from the grassroots mobilization of common people demanding policy changes from the elites. Some contend that it is something that one must first find within oneself; for others, inner peace comes from living within a peaceful culture. As Linda Groff and Paul Smoker note, peace has many dimensions and understandings of it vary over time and across cultures.

Differing perceptions of peace within the academy reflect the participation of different groups involved in its study. Whereas scholars in the military sciences tend to see peace as primarily the absence of war, for example, many Third World students of peace will emphasize justice as a crucial component of peace; those in religious and cultural studies, as well as many psychologists, may include inner peace as a necessary condition for peace. We have included a range of these positions in this collection.

A second central theme that emerges in these volumes is that conflict has always been part of the human experience, but that the way in which it is carried out varies substantially across time and space, in different eras and cultures. Radical changes in our technologies and strategies of conflict in the 20th century, moreover, distinguish our conflicts from those of past eras. Because they are more destructive in their scale and scope, some age-old wisdom may become inappropriate, whereas other elements of our shared ethical and cultural heritage may be revived.

Conflict can be carried out in a variety of ways from war and violence on one end of the spectrum to nonviolent struggle on the other. In recent decades the means of violent conflict have changed so radically as to transform the very character of violence; dual revolutions in weapons technology and military training have made violence increasingly deadly in both interpersonal and large-scale conflicts. Warfare has been relatively limited until quite recently in scale and scope. Despite widespread destruction bordering on genocide reported in ancient scriptures, premodern combat was relatively inefficient compared to contemporary warfare, and it occurred infrequently. David Grossman observes that a significant majority of soldiers in World War II combat were reportedly not firing directly at the enemy. Modern training thus incorporates operant conditioning to help recruits to the military and police overcome what appears to be a natural resistance to killing.

A growing body of evidence suggests that violent television programs, movies, and interactive video games are providing the sort of psychological conditioning for violence previously reserved for the military and police, whose behavior is usually bounded by strict rules of discipline that are missing from the lay version of the process. Consequently, although it is too early to tell what the larger impact of video games might be on various cultures, the evidence suggests strongly that homicide rates and aggressive behavior—at least among males—increase with the introduction of violent entertainment media into a culture. What is less clear is the nature of human nature with regard to propensities to violence.

A final theme of this compilation is that our understanding of peace and of nonviolent conflict has undergone a revolution that (not accidentally) parallels the transformation of violent conflict in the 20th century. Whereas the change in combat is symbolized by the atomic bomb, the revolution in nonviolence is symbolized by Mahatma Gandhi, Martin Luther King, Jr., and the mobilization of nonviolent social movements. As with warfare, the basic strategies and tactics of nonviolent struggle have been used throughout human history but were transformed in scale and scope in the 20th century. People in many cultures have employed methods of nonviolent direct action and conflict resolution over the millennia, but their development and elaboration in recent decades is unprecedented. Nonviolent struggles are not always successful (nor are violent ones) but they have been remarkably effective in country after country, especially in toppling unpopular dictatorships through mass mobilization and nonviolent tactics of resistance from the people-power movements that toppled U.S.-backed dictatorships in the Philippines and Chile to the Velvet Revolution in Czechoslovakia and the Solidarity movement in Poland that overthrew Soviet-backed regimes.

Scholarly studies of both nonviolence and military combat converge in a surprising possibility, something perhaps never fully verifiable empirically but certainly suggested by the evidence: that human beings—like other species—have not only a capacity for aggression but also a natural resistance to killing their own kind. They may also inherit an inclination toward nonviolent behaviors such as cooperation, affection, and so forth. How else could one explain the remarkable successes of nonviolent social movements in recent decades and the resistance to killing in combat addressed by modern military training? Human genetics seem to provide relatively broad parameters for potential behavioral choices, allowing for a strong influence by culture. The question of the inherent aggressiveness or tendency toward violence in human nature remains a key unanswered question at the turn of the century, one that has profound policy implications and poses complicated methodological dilemmas for students of violence.

Nature versus Nurture

Are humans inherently violent and condemned to periodic and increasingly destructive warfare? A review of our knowledge may produce more questions than answers. We do know that violent behavior is not universal among animal species (see J. P. Scott's article "Animal Behavior Studies, Nonprimates"). We also know that humans exhibit a wide range of behaviors and that their language and tool-making abilities set them somewhat apart from other species in their use of violence and the extent to which their lives are limited by biological parameters. Certainly some individuals and cultures engage in more violence than others; is that because of biological or cultural differences, or is the variation a result of some complex interaction between the two? Most of the violence caused by humans is carried out by the males of the species; is that a direct result of genetic differences or does it come from gender socialization that promotes the use of force by males in solving problems while females are taught to create less violent solutions?

Is war inevitable, given our biological makeup? This question was addressed recently at a conference organized by the Spanish office of the United Nations Educational, Social, and Cultural Organization (UNESCO). An interdisciplinary group of scientists participating from around the world endorsed "The Seville Statement of Violence" that calls into question much popular wisdom about the inherently violent nature of humanity. In their evaluation of the available scientific literature on violence they concluded that it is scientifically incorrect to say that:

- we have inherited a tendency to make war from our animal ancestors;
- war or any other violent behavior is genetically programmed into our human nature;
- in the course of human evolution there has been selection for aggressive behavior more than for other kinds of behavior;
- humans have a "violent brain";
- war is caused by "instinct" or any single motivation.

They conclude that "biology does not condemn humanity to war, and that humanity can be freed from the bondage of biological pessimism" that prevents it from seeking peace. "The same species that invented war," they contend, "is capable of inventing peace." Although the nature–nurture debate will probably not be solved, at least in the near future, one interesting development is recent attention—especially by UNESCO—to cultures of peace in human social organization.

Cultures vary dramatically in the extent to which they promote violent behavior; indeed, many societies can be characterized as having cultures of peace. An ongoing UNESCO project initiated in 1995 analyzes the elements of peaceful cultures in hopes that they might be incorporated elsewhere, such as in war-torn societies attempting to rebuild their civil societies. A pioneer in this field of peace culture, Elise Boulding, outlines some of those characteristics in her article "Peace Culture," noting that humans have a natural tendency to respond to other humans. They are capable of conducting their conflicts peacefully and developing cultures that nurture cooperation, democratic decision making, and nonviolent conflict. Comparative studies of conflict resolution demonstrate that human cultures can organize social life on a peaceful basis. In many communities, children are socialized to conduct their conflicts nonviolently, to cooperate with and respect others, and to create social environments that are not free of conflict but have relatively little coercion or violence.

If humans may not be genetically programmed for violence and war, but are capable of developing cultures of peace, why then is there so much carnage in human life? Although the evidence is far from conclusive, and there is clearly a biological component—especially in extreme sociopathic cases—current studies of violence seem to suggest that it is a consequence primarily of the way in which we instruct our youth, construct our values and beliefs about violence, and structure our options for carrying out conflict. In short, levels of violence probably have more to do with cultural values and social institutions than with the biological parameters within which we operate.

Violence, Culture, and Society

Many of the articles in this encyclopedia outline aspects of the way in which societies are organized within what Robert Elias calls a "culture of violent solutions." The underlying assumption in such a culture is that violence must be used to solve serious problems, including the problem of violence itself. Consequently, we often declare war upon those who commit acts of violence,

using "legitimate" violence to put an end to their "illegitimate" use of force. A great deal of time, energy, and money in modern societies and governments is invested in a sort of war over impression management, a struggle to gain the upper hand in how one's use of violence is defined so that ours is viewed as legitimate and necessary, whereas our adversary's is illegitimate and despicable.

This framing process often involves an effort to obtain hegemony in public discourse about violence, as states, social movements, and various interest groups all struggle to have the situation defined in their favor. The ruling ideas about violence in any given social context are, of course, profoundly influenced by the ideas of those who have the most power in that context. In cultures that emphasize the use of violence in their conflicts, the narratives used to differentiate between legitimate and illegitimate violence usually reflect the social structure: violence by the state and elites is considered legitimate. The poor and marginalized are scapegoated and blamed for the violence in their society even if they actually perpetrate a small proportion of it.

Even in societies where there is relatively free public discourse, a limited range of options for defining violence and its use are enforced, setting up boundaries around what is considered viable. This aspect of framing varies dramatically from culture to culture. In some societies the use of violence is so soundly condemned that it is seldom considered as a serious option for conflict management. In other contexts, the failure to use violence is condemned as weak and ineffective. Control over the narrative process defining these norms thus becomes crucial in determining whose violence is accepted and whose is rejected, which modes of conflict are considered useful and which ineffective. St. Augustine understood this when he laid the groundwork for Just War theory in the fourth century, just as did Clausewitz when he founded modern military science centuries later. The nature of those narratives and who controls them has varied widely over time and across cultures.

In most preagricultural and even preindustiral societies, religious elites and institutions tend to control the defining narratives. The legends and stories of oral traditions and sacred scriptures provide the standards by which particular acts of violence or modes of conflict are evaluated. From the Hebrew Torah to the Bhagavad Gita and the Qur'an, stories told around the campfire by village storytellers and recited in places of worship, people learn which styles of conflict are considered ethical with regard to the use of force. The violence of nature, as well as that of foreign peoples, is often explained as an "act of God," and remedies that can be applied to problematic situations are provided in the narratives.

In modern cultures, authoritative storytelling—like many other social functions—is wrested from religious institutions and given to the state in an effort to democratize political authority. Giving the state authority does offer some remedies to earlier abuses, but modern political elites claim a monopoly of violence for the state and use force so widely to back up their claims that state violence has caused an unprecedented number of deaths by war, genocide, and democide in the 20th century, as Alan Grimshaw observes.

Now a new force is moving to center stage, the commercialization of storytelling, so that the narratives that have the most impact on popular culture are written by professionals, told in the media of the age—television, movies, and interactive video games, etc.—and sponsored by multinational corporations.

These new myths and legends regarding the appropriate use of force continue to reflect the interests of those in power and have three major themes. First, we find the age-old maxim that force is often necessary for serious problem solving. This idea is presented repeatedly in narrative form in the popular media and recounted by people who discuss the latest television shows and movies: a crime is committed and the police track down the criminals and drag them off to jail. They are brought to trial, convicted, and justice prevails. In the international arena parallel narratives unfold as criminal heads of state and marginal groups lacking states are apprehended and brought to justice. Terrorists operating on behalf of a dictator or religious fanatic are hunted down and punished, and so on. We all know the stories and their various reincarnations—how security is threatened by criminals and then reestablished by proper authorities using necessary force within a framework of laws.

Embedded within these entertaining narratives are lessons to be drawn about how people are to solve their problems and to recognize the necessity for legitimate authorities to use violence, thus raising the second theme, i.e., that some violence is legitimate and other force is not. As with the first theme, a social problem emerges, a struggle ensues, and sooner or later the problem is solved by force. Erich Fromm once observed that when individuals behave like nations do, we put them in an institution, either a prison or a mental hospital. When states kill, maim, or appropriate property, we hear stories about the honor of such acts. When the same acts are committed by individuals or groups not sanctioned by the state, or by enemy states, they are condemned as horrific.

The difference between the two kinds of violence is determined, of course, by the power of those who use it. The mechanism by which the violence employed by those in power is defined as legitimate is the cultural process embedded in the narratives of the culture. The monopoly of legitimacy still lies with the state even in postmodern culture, but it is not taken for granted; even well-established and popular regimes must now hire professional storytellers to frame their use of violence as legitimate and to counter the critics of their war-fighting, crime-fighting policies.

These for-profit stories about the necessity of fighting bad violence with good are not the only frame provided by modern culture. The major alternative to the good-versus-bad-violence frame is the innovative idea of the industrial age that consumerism can be used to solve problems as well, as told explicitly in advertisements and more subtly in the story lines of other genres. The paradigm here appears in fast food advertisements: within a 60-second story an entire drama unfolds. A problem disrupts the routine of social life but is quickly and efficiently solved by having everyone buy fast food. Everyone sits around smiling and eating; conflicts are resolved and order is restored.

This example seems to have taken us far afield from the initial problem of violence. It is, however, extremely salient: the consumer alternative to brute force seems less violent, certainly, than the use of guns, and many claim that a peaceful future will result from world trade, the free market, and the creation of an affluent lifestyle for everyone. This vision, others argue, is only superficially benign. Hidden behind the smiling consumer faces, they claim, is a very elaborate story of structural violence and destruction. The apparently positive search for happiness through material consumption is globally seductive, the critics argue. It promises more than it delivers because the satisfaction it brings is elusive and temporary, and the process creates a global social system with the hidden violence of mass poverty held in place by a system of overt violence in the form of a military–industrial complex that protects the interests of the rich and powerful. This sort of violence is the object of more recent research, and we know little about its mechansims because it is subtle, complex, and global, and its investigation often marginalized or politicized.

A final set of narratives in the postmodern era is also examined in this encyclopedia: those of nonviolent resistance from Gandhi and the Indian Freedom Movement to Martin Luther King, Jr. and the U.S. civil rights movement, as well as the prodemocracy and other non-violent movements for social change that they inspired. These stories challenge much conventional wisdom but have their roots in ancient cultures and have taken their place in the dominant culture of the late 20th century, legitimating what Czech president Vaclav Havel calls the power of the powerless. From this perspective, violence accentuates and forces hierarchy and embellishes inequality, whereas nonviolence facilitates equality and empowers democratic movements.

We know much less about how to mobilize Gandhi-style nonviolent struggles than we do about training and employing military forces. After all, we have not been doing it very long. The strategies and tactics of nonviolent action have been examined historically and explicitly only in the 20th century and are summarized here by the most prominent student of modern nonviolent action, Gene Sharp, as well as in Bryan Teixeira's broader discussion of nonviolence in theory and practice. We know even less about how individuals, families, and nations might be organized nonviolently, but that too is a subject of analysis that will persist into the next century. The future of nonviolence remains problematic, of course, especially given the domain assumptions of prevailing realpolitik theories of conflict and current structures for militarizing international conflict, but some remarkable changes have occurred in recent decades that are explored in this encyclopedia. These volumes attempt to bring into clearer focus the options before us and the consequences of our collective choices, as we evaluate these debates and study our policies.

Our hope is that this work will provide us with a more comprehensive picture of our current state of knowledge about violence, peace, and conflict. This collection is broader in its coverage than any other currently available resource, but we cannot claim to raise all of the right questions, let alone provide the necessary answers to them. It is not as comprehensive as one might hope, however, and some caveats are in order.

First, despite our best efforts to broaden the authorship of the encyclopedia, the majority of the contributors are Western, notably North American. Although this does in some sense reflect the current state of scholarship (because of Western dominance and resources), it does not necessarily reveal our best knowledge.

Second, the very genre of the Encyclopedia—with its nonadversarial standpoint and objective tone—may ironically exclude some of our best insights into the subject matter. Indeed, articles by two people, each knowing more about violence and peace (in my opinion) than some entire university faculties put together, were not included because their articles were inappropriate for the genre because they were too argumentative. Another piece was edited substantially but in the end was deemed too pejorative in tone. One prominent Latin American scholar declined our invitation up front, suggesting that if we wanted an objective article on the topic we had asked the wrong person.

Finally, the publication of this sort of resource—which we hope will be relevant for some time—can give the misleading notion that knowledge about a topic is fixed and definitive. On the contrary, the truth about any topic—and especially our understanding of the truth—changes dramatically over time so that it can be misleading to interpret the contents of these volumes in a reified manner. Although this work reviews our current state of knowledge about violence, peace, and conflict, it is a snapshot of a rapidly changing area of inquiry into a constantly shifting set of phenomena.

Thank you for joining us in this ongoing investigation. I would be happy to hear from you if you have comments, criticisms, or information about ongoing research or perspectives that are not adequately represented here.

Lester R. Kurtz
University of Texas at Austin

Family Structure and Family Violence and Nonviolence

Laura Ann McCloskey
University of Arizona

Riane Eisler
Center for Partnership Studies

GLOSSARY

Dominator Model Social organization based primarily on rigid rankings, with hierarchies of domination ultimately backed up by the institutionalization of the power to threaten or inflict pain and the selective suppression of empathy. Family structure is generally patriarchal, though it can also be matriarchal. Violence or the threat of violence is integral to childrearing.

Kinship Relationship by blood or descent.

Matriarchal Governed by women or mothers.

Matrilineal Inheritance of goods and status through the mother's lineage.

Matrilocal Family units residing near the wife's or mother's kin.

Partnership Model Social organization based primarily on linkings maintained by the exchange of mutual benefits as well as hierarchies of actualization in which power is informed by empathy and caring. Family structure is egalitarian and norm for childrearing is nonviolent.

Patriarchal Governed by men or fathers.

Patrilineal Inheritance of goods and status through the father's lineage.

Patrilocal Family units residing near the husband's or father's kin; this feature of family geography usually involves uprooting women away from their family.

THIS ARTICLE examines evidence from a number of studies relating to the question of what kinds of family structures promote or inhibit either violent or nonviolent relations. Families provide the universal building blocks of human communities, governing reproduction and childrearing. Definitions of the family vary, and include many different forms. For purposes of this article we will use the term family to designate those social units that assume the primary responsibility for reproducing or adopting and raising children. Some of the variants of family structure that will be addressed include the nuclear family (with both biological parents); the stepfamily (with two parents, one of whom is biologically unrelated); the single mother-headed household; coresidential extended or joint families; and, finally, spanning the range of these different structures, families orienting primarily to what one of the authors (Eisler) identifies as a dominator or partnership model of organization. Our discussion of family violence will focus mainly on those intentional acts that inflict serious physical or long-lasting psychological injury either by men to women, or by adults to the biologically or non-biologically related children within their household.

Copyright © 1999 by Academic Press.
All rights of reproduction in any form reserved.

I. OVERVIEW

A. Family Violence

We will use the term family violence to encompass several forms of identified and categorized maltreatment: from severe psychological to physical to sexual, perpetrated by a range of family members, most typically husbands toward wives, and parents toward children. These are the two most salient and prevalent forms of family violence. In local social science and political parlance, family violence is a term that describes the harm, injury, or death inflicted between family members, typically in a hegemonic cascade from more powerful to least. Serious physical abuse by women against men, although sometimes highly publicized, has been found to be rare. Although American surveys have shown that women hit men, it is usually in self-defense, and rarely carries the threat of injury inherent in men's assaults against women. Violence by children against their parents is also rare.

The study of family violence is a relatively new field, only a few decades old. Even in this short period it has become evident that family violence—more specifically, violence against women and children—is a deeply entrenched and worldwide practice. That work in this area is so recent reflects the fact that for most of recorded history until recent times parental violence against children and men's violence against their wives was either explicitly or implicitly condoned. In the West, the tradition of parents beating their children and men beating women has been legally challenged only recently. Parents were not subject to what was generally considered interference in family affairs at the same time that the biblical dictum "spare the rod and spoil the child" was still very strong. Men who beat their spouses were also usually exempt from criminal prosecution. In fact, under the earlier British common law imported during the 1700's into many North American colonies, the husband had a legal right to "physically chastise" his wife, since her body and her services were his legal property. Moreover, if a wife killed her husband, it was a crime punishable by the same terrible torture as the killing of a king by his "subject."

The recent research dedicated to explaining family violence reflects major changes in cultural values and beliefs and in the structure of social institutions, including the family. Much of the impetus for the study of violence against women has come from organized action by women, particularly during the United Nations Decade for Women (1975–1985) and through subsequent national and international meetings such as the 1993 United Nations World Conference on Human Rights in Vienna and the 1995 United Nations Conference of Women in Beijing. As a result, we now have a growing number of statistical studies on rates of abuse of women in intimate relationships from countries in Asia, Latin America, Africa, Europe, and North America (see, e.g., U.N. Report on Status of Women 1995). These studies show the extraordinary cultural and economic ranges of violence against women in intimate relations.

There are fewer studies comparing internationally different rates of child abuse. However, there are studies of specific forms of child abuse that reveal how pervasive the problem is, and how often female children are targets. For example, the 1997 United Nations State of World Population Report estimates that 120 million girls have undergone some form of female genital mutilation, with another two million at risk each year, particularly in regions of Africa and Asia where this practice is performed under the mantle of religious or ethnic tradition. There are data on selective female infanticide and medical neglect—a neglect that can be so severe that in India's Punjab state girls aged 2 to 4 die at nearly twice the rate of boys. There are also studies on the huge number of girl children enslaved through sale by members of their families to the large sex industry in places such as Thailand, India, and elsewhere, with the United Nations estimating that two million girls between ages 5 and 11 are introduced into the commercial sex market each year.

B. Family Structure and Violence

Family structure can mean many things. It can mean something as apparently straightforward and quantifiable as number and ages of children in the home or single vs two parent families. It might also refer to how marital power relations play out in subtle ways—whether these are based on the domination of one spouse or are egalitarian partnerships—and, accordingly, on the social, political, educational, and economic macrostructure underlying the valuing and distributions of resource contributions within families. The definition of family boundaries, identification of people as kin, rituals surrounding family formation and maintenance, and related subjects have occupied generations of cultural anthropologists. Perhaps the only universal feature of families in human communities is that they are identifiable in virtually every long-term community that biologically reproduces.

In spite of current discourse about the rights to privacy of family members, the control of reproductive contexts is among the oldest objects of the state, often functioning in tandem with religion. Aspects of family structure and functioning such as marriage and financial commitments, inheritance, and paternal obligation to offspring were the objects of state regulation through well-implemented policies since the beginning of state formation. For instance, the establishment of foundling homes in 18th-century Russia or 19th-century Italy, as well as other regions of Europe, was a state-initiated effort at control of perceptibly rising births of unwed mothers. Infant mortality rates in these institutions were typically as high as 90%. However, the government-sponsored rhetoric surrounding the institutions was one of charity, often paired with punitive attitudes towards the unwed mothers and forced servitude as wet-nurses.

The state's neglect of the use of physical tactics of control and punishment toward both wives and children is also indicative of a policy, albeit usually unproclaimed. The contemporary enactment and better enforcement of laws to protect women and children from family violence are the result of organized efforts to change policies of nonintervention.

Family violence is found in cultures with family structures ranging from nuclear to extended families. It occurs across affluent and poor countries and is also observed across social classes within a nation's borders, although there appear to be social class differences in the rates within the United States, with poor families more at risk. The translation of family structure into family practice, therefore, is complex and relies on beliefs about gender and parent–child relationships. Beliefs about violence, aggression, and privileges of men to dominate women are central to the perpetuation of domestic violence. And since through much of recorded history these beliefs have been supported by various institutions, family violence or nonviolence is not only related to family structure, but to the large social structure and the prevailing systems of values and beliefs of a particular culture. Specifically, the family embodies and perpetuates broader societal norms and the political economy. Moreover, the family is not only influence by, but in turn also influences, the larger social structure and culture of which it is a part. In short, what we view between families and culture is a transactive process.

Cultural beliefs and laws have gradually changed, as women's and children's rights become part of the cultural and legal discourse. Although the state has had an important role throughout the world in protecting patriarchal rights of male family heads, often seen as including the right to dominate and beat wives and children, the endorsement of violence in marriage is not a universal feature of all state ideologies.

In this article we explore what social conditions and changes in family structure serve to shield or expose women and children to abuse. A major tenet of this article is that we can better understand what causes wife and child abuse if we juxtapose the study of pacifism with the study of violence. The research on family violence focuses on the harm people do to one another rather than the potential support they provide. Families reveal the best and the worst of human social potential, and our chapter will explore what family structure variables contribute to these dynamics. Cooperative and mutually supportive families have been achieved despite ideologies that construct adversarial sexual relations and men's domination as the chief organizing principle. Close and trusting relationships between the sexes have surfaced in even the most inhospitable social climates; just as relationships between members of different races within a racist society, living side by side, sometimes give way to the humanity of that relationship. Still, if the dominant culture is rooted in a set of beliefs of women's inferiority the walls are well mortared against intimacy and communication across strict gender boundaries. Such contact might even be stigmatized, as can be seen in attitudes toward friendship or talk between men and women in some Bedouin societies.

As we will detail, there are various factors that contribute to, enhance, or diminish the risk of recurrent family violence. For example, patterns of family composition can pose a risk or buffer for wife or child abuse. However, quantifiable features of family structure cannot explain the presence or absence of interpersonal physical abuse per se. The response and norms of the broader community and the cultural ideology governing attitudes toward sexual relationships and equality, childrearing practices, and violence all make central contributions to the expectations shaping sexual and family relationships.

II. VIOLENT DYADS: WIFE ABUSE

Women who are abused by their husbands are often controlled in myriad ways. These forms of control impose a policy of "patriarchal terrorism," terrorizing the wives and often keeping them from staying in jobs, visiting with friends, or maintaining normal social connections.

Wife abuse of varying forms occurs across cultures and geographic regions (see Table I). In Mexico City, one in three women reported violence from a spouse or partner. Another study shows that one of every five Colombian women were beaten by a partner. In Kenya

TABLE I
Societies with Wife Abuse Worldwide

Country	Proportion of women
Developed regions	
Belgium	25
Canada	25
Japan	59[a]
Netherlands	21
New Zealand	17
Norway, Trondheim	25
United States	28
Africa	
Kenya, Kissi District	42
Zambia	40[b]
Uganda, Kampala	46
United Republic of Tanzania, Dar es Salaam and 3 districts	60
Latin America and the Caribbean	
Antigua	30
Barbados	30
Chile, Santiago	26
Costa Rica	54[c]
Colombia	20
Ecuador, Quito	60
Guatemala	36
Mexico, Mexico City	34
Jalisco State, urban	57[d]
Jalisco State, rural	44[d]
Suriname	35
Asia and the Pacific	
India, southern Karnataka (3 villages)	22
Jullundur District, Punjab (1 village)	
Scheduled lower caste	75
Higher caste	22
Korea, Republic of	38[e]
Malaysia	39[e]
Papua New Guinea, urban	58
Papua New Guinea, rural (19 villages)	67
Sri Lanka, Colombo	60

Note. Based on survey results on percentage of adult women who have been physically assaulted by an intimate partner compiled and published in the *United Nations Report on the Status of Women,* 1995; New York: Author.
[a] Based on a limited (17%) return on questionnaires distributed nationally, through women's groups, adult education classes and the media.
[b] Based on a sample of women from shanty compounds.
[c] Based on a sample of women attending child welfare clinics.
[d] Women on "DIF" (social welfare) register.
[e] Percentage beaten within the last year.

42% of women admitted that they were regularly beaten by their husbands. In Papua New Guinea 67% of rural women and 56% of urban women have been abused by partners. A study from Lima, Peru, shows that one out of every three women in the city's emergency rooms were victims of domestic violence. According to estimates by the former U.S. Surgeon General C. Everett Koop in 1989, three to four million women are battered in the United States each year.

Hitting and battering are only one dimension of wife abuse. Wife abuse can also take the form of marital rape, stalking, harassing, and ultimately even homicide. In Bangladesh, for example, uxoricide, or the husband's murder of his wife, accounts for half of all homicides. In Canada 62% of women murdered in 1987 died as a result of domestic violence. In Bombay, India, one out of every five deaths among women 15 to 44 was found to be due to "accidental burns"—that is, infamous "bride-burnings" or "dowry deaths".

In short, violence against women by men in intimate relationships is not only a major cause of injury to women, but all too often results in a woman's death. Often these killings are not prosecuted, as in the so-called "honor" killings of wives (and sometimes daughters and sisters) in parts of the Middle East. Violence against women accounts in many world regions for the reversal of the longer life span for women, since so many women die from violent causes.

One question that arises is whether this violence is more frequent or less frequent outside or inside of marriage. As we shall see, the studies do not indicate that the structure of the relationship is a consistent key factor. Violence can surface as a tactic of control under virtually any set of relationship conditions.

Abuse can surface immediately in a new relationship. It can also surface after courtship and during marriage. Because of the variability in the timing and expression of domestic violence, it is difficult to determine whether women are more at risk in new sexual relationships without commitment or ties, or in marriage when the men have more freedom to exercise masculine prerogatives of ownership. On the one hand, men who bear little commitment to the woman and little familiarity with her family might be more inclined to use physical abuse as a tactic of control because (1) the woman still has the freedom to leave and physical coercion might induce her to stay; (2) the man is uncommitted to the relationship and is unconcerned with the long-term impact of abuse. In this case the network of financial, social and reproductive commitments have yet to develop, and both parties are more likely to end the relationship sooner when conflict and violence surfaces.

On the other hand, marriage provides a less penetrable cover for men's behavior. When young children are involved, the woman might find herself in a unique state of economic and emotional dependency that makes it difficult to leave, and she might be more likely to tolerate abuse for want of exit options. Marriage usually extends the duration of suffering for a battered woman, and in those families within American society, or cultures throughout the world, that keep marriages nearly impossible to dissolve, or keep a woman yoked for economic survival to her husband, beatings and cruelty are endured for a lifetime. Marriage, therefore, is no source of protection from battering, and short-term liaisons also carry their risk. In fact, across studies it has been found that men who are violent are as violent while the woman is pregnant.

While the length and level of commitment in sexual relationships—whether during coutrship, common law liaisons, brief relationships, or marriage—probably has little bearing on whether a woman will be exposed to violent behavior, the social and legal construction of these relations will largely determine whether the woman has the freedom to leave an abusive situation. Across cultures, as a general rule women who are unmarried have more ostensible freedom to leave an abusive relationship than women who are married. Freedom is of course relative, since part of the battering involves restriction and in some cases virtual imprisonment by the partner. For instance, some men who control and abuse their wives restrict their access to telephones, keep them homebound and without transportation, and isolate them from friends, family, and the community.

There is some evidence indicating that violence against women in relationships escalates *after* marriage. In one East African society, it is a ritual of the wedding night that the husband beats his new bride, establishing what subsequently becomes habitual abuse. In the United States, as in many other countries, penalties for rape or violence against women diminish after marriage if the perpetrator is the husband. Rape within marriage is still only recognized as a crime in a small number of nations, and is rarely prosecuted even in those states where it is criminal. Beatings, too, are not criminal offenses in most nations, despite the 1994 United Nations Declaration on the Elimination of Violence Against Women. Since most governments still fail to prohibit or circumscribe the use of force in marital or filial relationships, they tacitly allow these violations of women's and children's human rights to persist—and to date many human rights organizations have still not taken a strong stand on this issue. In addition, extended family members or the community often force women to remain with abusive husbands after marriage, and cultural norms still accept a husband's abuse of his wife as normal. Moreover, on the most basic survival level, women often have no other economic alternative.

Under such circumstances, particularly if there are children, some women might decide to remain with the abusive partner because of their own past extensive commitment of emotional and material resources, as well as time and reproductive investment. There appears to be empirical support for such a decision-making process. Women in longer term marriages, with more children by the abusive partner, and less years of education or employment (accumulated human capital) tend to remain in violent relationships more often than women with fewer ostensible commitments. In other words, the combination of increased commitments to the partnership, aversive as it is, and a lack of options deters women from leaving. This finding would suggest that in male-dominated societies violence against women in intimate relations is more enduring after marriage than during premarital phases. Men who dominate and coerce their wives generally escalate their tactics over time, usually with relative impunity because they have proprietary claims to the residence, to the children, and ultimately to the woman herself.

In those cultures where a material exchange occurs between families to seal the marital union, as in the case of dowries paid from the bride's family to the groom's in India, or brideprice in Papua New Guinea, paid from the groom's kin to the bride's, the bride's extended family has a material investment in keeping their female kin married. In the case of brideprice if the vows are broken and the newly married woman returns to her family of origin, even as a response to abuse, the family is obligated to repay the groom. Unfortunately, the inverse is not applied to dowry exchanges; grooms are rarely obligated to return the dowry, even if the wife has died after a brief residence with her new husband's family (even when the groom is suspected of homicide, as in the case of the recent and widely publicized wave of dowry-motivated killings in India, wherein the groom and his extended family plot to kill the new wife, in order to remarry and amass further dowries and fortune). Implicit in this situation is the belief that ownership of a daughter transfers from parents, or her father, to her husband. After this "property transfer" has taken place, accompanied both by the husband's commitment to financially support this woman and the wife's commitment to respect his authority, his use of force is subsequently viewed as justified because force is a sanctioned means in the society to control subordinates—whether they be children, wives, or workers. The privilege of beating one's wife proceeds from the father's privilege to beat his daughter. This cycle persists across time and generations.

A characteristic feature of battering husbands is that they willfully isolate their wives, often cutting off contact with her nascent family of origin or other means of support, and discouraging her from employment or activities out of the home. These households are typically unwelcoming and isolated. This fact alone indicates if social and family connections were strong in a woman's life, her husband would be deterred from abusing her, since such ties are obviously viewed as a threat to the abusive husband's autonomous control of his wife. Women's social support does present barriers to men's domination of women, which is exactly the reason those men try to eliminate it.

No studies to date have explicitly tested the role of networks and extended families in protecting women from relationship violence. Although there is little direct evidence indicating that, for instance, matrilocal societies have lower rates of marital violence than patrilocal ones, or that the presence of extended family members inhibits men's abusive behavior toward their wives, it is certainly plausible that such a mechanism operates in some cultures. The proximity of extended family, especially of brothers or a father within patriarchal societies, might intimidate violence-prone husbands. We know that among nonhuman primate societies, close female liaisons and coresidential groups offer protection to allied females from male aggression. Among humans, this protection is only likely for women when their family is both willing and free to enforce societal proscriptions against wife abuse.

In some societies, the husband's family might actually enforce nonviolence in marriage because of economic and social relationships they maintain with the wife's extended family. This situation would be most typical in a small interconnected village, for instance, as opposed to more anonymous urban settings. India illustrates a notable exception, however, and the husband's family typically defends his right to dominate his wife. Moreover, in India, abuse by mothers-in-law toward their daughters-in-law remains common. In China until the beginning of this century, well-to-do "first wives" exercised supreme domestic control, and participated in oppressing subsequent wives in these historically polygynous households.

In short, violence against women spans a wide spectrum of relationships and family structures, the comon denominator being socially approved hierarchies of domination, with force or the threat of force used as a means of maintaining the domination of one member of the family over another. In male-dominated societies violence against women has generally been considered a prerogative of men. However, abuse of wives has also been perpetrated by women who are either mothers-in-law or higher ranking wives in extended patriarchal families. Both custom and law have had an important role throughout the world in protecting patriarchal rights of male family heads.

III. NONVIOLENT DYADS

The endorsement of violence in marriage is not universal. For example, as Eisler (1987) has documented in her analysis of the Minoan society of ancient Crete, within this stable and nonviolent society, where responsibility rather than hegemony characterized political leadership, men and women appeared to have far more equal roles and power. Accordingly, woman-directed violence was not idealized and hence probably also infrequent. Similarly, a pattern of violence against women has not been found in the present century among such societies as the Balinese of Asia or the Amish of Lancaster County, Pennsylvania—cultures that vary considerably in family size and marriage arrangements.

As noted earlier, comparative studies of different social structures and attendant cultural values strongly suggest that family violence or nonviolence and family structure can best be understood in their larger social and cultural context. In his review of nonviolent cultures across the world Bonta isolates a factor that might explain heightened levels of male-to-male violence and male violence against women: socially expected and extolled competition between men. Those societies that reward competition, particularly competitive displays between men, exhibit higher levels of violence than those that discourage competitive displays. An emphasis on competition, therefore, appears to engender, or at least accompany, aggression both between men and toward women.

Gender roles, then, and especially the construction of masculinity are implicated in the expression of violence against women. When men participate more fully in childrearing, breaking out of some of the rigid restrictions of their masculine gender role, some authors have argued that tension between the sexes diminishes. In fact, in those societies that enable men to participate extensively in childrearing, women enjoy a higher social status and there is less violence than in societies that strictly exclude men from childcare. There are important questions yet to be answered in the study of social structure, gender role beliefs, and violence. For instance, it is unclear whether the high value placed on masculine competition is a cause or a result of other factors, including the socialization of men to perceive male identity as the capacity to control or win through violence. Are there unique human social structures that foster the ideology of "heroic" masculinity and male family control? It remains uncertain whether there would be a large-scale social impact on rates of domestic violence if men were to share more in caretaking, and to participate less in activities fostering aggression and domination. Much more research is needed on potential ways to end violence within families, even without major social changes in patriarchal belief systems.

Although family configuration fails to predict relationship violence or nonviolence, there are indications that extended family connections promote cooperative and nonviolent partnerships. Various studies of Mexican immigrant families, for instance, have revealed that immigrant men are less likely to abuse their wives than second-generation Mexican American men. One possible explanation of this finding is that when immigrant families come to the United States they typically come "en masse," with in-laws and relatives on both sides of the spouses' families. The experience of poverty and immigration intensifies interdependency, and the marriage itself may serve as a nexus for various close in-law relationships involving employment and work opportunities for men. Close economic interdependency discourages marital conflict and violence in these immigrant cultures. Similar pressures to cooperate have been observed among other cultural groups such as the Arctic Inuit aboriginals, who have to survive in a physically hostile environment through close interdependency. There are strong proscriptions against even the expression of anger among the Inuit, as Briggs has documented in her ethnography. Here again we see the interconnection between cultural norms and whether human relationships, including spousal and other forms of intimate sexual relations, are violent or nonviolent.

IV. VIOLENT PARENTING: CHILD ABUSE

Like violence against wives, violence against children is often practiced with tacit and even explicit social approval. For instance, according to some surveys, 95% of American parents approve of and admit to spanking their children. Although parents are less likely to approve of their child being spanked by someone outside of the family, there remain many communities in the United States where corporal punishment continues to be used in the schools. Most people would not place spanking in the same class of behaviors as child abuse, but there is research to indicate that the more corporal punishment is used against a child, the more mental health symptoms and behavior problems that child will display. In addition, it should be kept in mind that escalated forms of physical abuse—for example, beatings resulting in injuries—start with a single slap or spank. When spanking is widely practiced, the gate is left open for more extreme expressions of parental anger.

Both fathers and mothers who use corporal punishment believe that it is their responsibility to discipline their children, and they are in most cases well-intentioned. However, physical coercion is actually the least effective tactic for socializing children to be cooperative and other-oriented. In fact, such coercive tactics often backfire to make children defiant, noncompliant, and aggressive. Straus has campaigned vigorously against corporal punishment of all kinds in American families, pointing out that even "common spanking" results in elevated symptoms of psychopathology among children, in contrast to verbal cricism or other forms of discipline (e.g., "time out"). Unfortunately, the large body of evidence that has amassed in child socialization research demonstrating problems with coercive parenting has yet to reach most popular channels or to widely alter parental practices.

Violence against children can take many forms—from systematic beatings of children of both sexes to more female-directed forms of abuse such as the foot-binding of girl children in prerevolutionary China or the ongoing infanticide of female children in parts of China, Bangladesh, and India. The sexual mutilation of female children is still legal in many world regions, despite overwhelming evidence that it is extremely harmful to girls' and women's physical and mental health. As with other forms of family violence, the genital mutilation of girls is a traditional means of controlling women, and is practiced in societies where women's sexuality is considered male property. But, as with many other forms of family violence, it is justified on religious or traditional grounds. Children of both sexes throughout the world are also targeted for severe sexual abuse and exploitation.

Once again, the circumstances under which different family configurations elicit nurturant or abusive patterns of behavior toward children can vary extensively. More telling is the society's system of cultural beliefs and organizational frameworks, especially in relation to matters such as laws or customs abridging or denying female inheritance rights or inheritance for some male children; beliefs that women's sexuality is male property; beliefs about female inferiority and consequent male preference; lack of access by females to earning or control over property; and legal, economic, religious, and social factors leading to the view that some children are less valuable than others.

Birth order, for instance, can be the determining factor for infanticide in cultures with inheritance rules of primageniture (where only first-born male children inherit property), as in 18th-century Austria and other Alpine regions. Still today, the child's female sex is the basis in some cultures for infanticide or systematic neglect, as in the pattern of allocating resources primarily to male children in some parts of India. Hypergamy, or the custom of arranging marriages for females up the social caste ladder, places higher caste female children at unique risk, since their marriage prospects will necessarily be dim. Large numbers of children in a family and economic stress also pose a risk for child maltreatment.

In the United States there has been a virtual revolution in family structure, however, and within this society certain elements of family composition can place children more at risk. Below is a review of these different configurations of family, and the risks and benefits they offer to children.

A. Nuclear or Two-Parent Families

Most American families, regardless of family structure, use physical punishment to control children's behavior. In some families this cultural license to spank escalates to the equivalent of beatings, and also makes frequent slapping and spanking a potential problem when the parents are under stress. When mothers report knowing few other strategies of discipline or control, living in a cultural climate (such as Mexico) that promotes the use of physical punishment, child abuse can escalate. Again, cultural ideology (reflecting and reinforcing what Eisler calls the dominator model of social and family organization) seems to carry the most influence in a parent's decision to use physical punishment. Once physical abuse is employed as a regular tactic there is always the danger that it can escalate in severity.

There is no evidence that children are more likely to be spared from frequent spankings or beatings by the mother in intact families as opposed to single-mother families. Mothers are the principal disciplinarians within all forms of American families, particularly with young children. Fathers usually have less exposure to

the children, and are in most families on the periphery of childrearing. Various studies indicate, however, that mothers and fathers both use similar means of punishment and that mothers are as likely to spank children as fathers.

Despite the apparent equity between parents in spanking, fathers pose more of a seious physical threat when they do take over the corporal punishment of the children. Fathers are typically larger, stronger, and more imposing disciplinarians in children's eyes. They are also implicated in 75% of the cases when punishment escalates to homicide, according to a recent study in Los Angeles (Sorenson & Peterson, 1994). Other studies of child homicide in Canada over the past decade indicate that when mothers are perpetrators of homicide the children are typically under the age of 3, and fathers are more likely to be the perpetrators of children over this age (Daly & Wilson, 1988). Fathers, both biological and unrelated, therefore, are more likely to escalate abuse to homicide than mothers in intact families, and this effect is strongest among older children. Although lethal child abuse is rare, it is nevertheless among the five most common reasons for child mortality among children under 10 in the United States, according to recent Center for Disease Control statistics (Center for Disease Control, 1997).

Children are also at risk for physical abuse when their mothers are battered. They can be hurt if they try to intervene or are even present during violent marital disputes, and they are psychologically damaged by witnessing the abuse of their mothers. Violence against wives, therefore, places children at heightened physical and psychological risk even when they are not the intentional target. Those features of extended family life and community that restrict men's abuse of women within marriage simultaneously protect children.

B. The Changing Structure of Families: Single and Divorced

The United States family has undergone rapid changes in structure because of both rising divorce rates and the rising birth rate to unmarried mothers, the latter being most pronounced among urban African Americans. As a result of these trends, the United States has the highest proportion of mother-headed households in the industrial world (38%). It also has the highest rate of teenage pregnancies, even though adolescents in some other countries are also equally sexually active. In the United States, mother-headed families are poorer than either father-headed or two-parent families. Unmarried women with young children face unique economic struggles and poverty because of sex-based discrimination in employment and wage-earning prospects and because fathers often avoid financial responsibilities to their offspring.

Poverty is neither a sufficient nor necessary condition for abuse within families. Various studies conducted in Chicago (Garbarino & Sherman, 1982), for example, showed that poverty per se failed to account for child abuse after examining other neighborhood risk factors. The social environment that families live in—with high crime rates and abuse rates in neighboring families—account for maltreatment within families more than family income alone. Nevertheless, the link between child abuse and poverty has been determined across a range of national studies (Goerge & Lee, 1997). What specific features of poor families contribute to raised levels of domestic violence, both wife and child abuse, remains uncertain.

In most single-mother headed households throughout the world maternal child abuse is no more likely than in intact families. For instance, among the African Ashanti single motherhood is widespread, with traditional roots, and children are well cared for. It is also the case that among the Ashanti resources in single-mother headed households are often sufficient to raise the children, since there is a long-standing history of such family structures. In Brazil, among poor women in the north coastal areas, children are virtually never beaten, and physical child abuse is extremely rare. In these same mother-headed families infanticide within the first few weeks or months of a newborn's life is common, essentially as a form of birth control, but subsequent violence or even corporal punishment toward those offspring who survived is unusual. However, in studies conducted in the United States, when single-motherhood is combined with early age onset of childbearing, especially under the age of 16, the risk of child maltreatment and removal of children to foster care placements is several times higher than when the mothers are 22 or older.

One risk factor for children of mother-headed households is the likelihood that an unrelated male partner will coreside with them. Children appear to be at greater risk for both physical and sexual abuse when there are stepfathers in the home. The presence of stepfathers greatly increases the likelihood of child sexual abuse, especially of girls. In one college student survey conducted in California, 17% of the freshmen girls reported sexual abuse experiences with their mother's partners or their stepfathers, in contrast to only 2% of girls who lived in intact families with their biological fathers (Russell, 1986).

No heightened risk for abuse has been documented with stepmothers. One reason for the absence of such findings is that children usually remain in their mothers' custodial care following divorce or separation, and therefore a new man in the home has more extensive daily contact with the children than a stepmother would have through occasional or even regular visitations when children see their fathers. However, sexual abuse in particular is rarely perpetrated by women. When it does occur, it is usually in collusion with an adult male.

C. The Extended Family

Extended families composed of grandparents, aunts, and uncles can be protective of children, given a non-abusive ideology. If there is an abusive ideology, however, the extended family can pose as much a risk as a buffer to children and women. Simple generalizations, therefore, about features of family structure and their role in child maltreatment cannot be made.

There are widespread beliefs that the presence of grandparents is a buffer for children, and probably inhibits abuse. However, research findings on the support provided by grandparents to young children are mixed. For instance, in one series of studies the positive contributions African American grandmothers made to the welfare and adjustment of their grandchildren in mother-headed and intact families were examined (Taylor, Casten, & Flickinger, 1993; Taylor & Roberts, 1995). The researchers found that children in two-parent families did not appear to benefit from the co-residence of a grandmother. Children within single or divorced mother-headed households, however, did show signs of better adjustment when a grandmother lived with them. However, this effect did not seem due to the grandmother's parenting skills or direct care to the child, but to the support these grandmothers provided their daughters. The daughters, therefore, became more effective and less stressed during their own parenting tasks, and the children subsequently benefited. In the United States, therefore, the nuclear family relationships remain the most critical for the children's health and outcome. When single mothers are nested in supportive extended family contexts, the children benefit from the direct aid offered the mother.

IV. NONVIOLENT PARENTING

There have been some studies on what kinds of skills foster nonviolent and nurturant parenting. For example, researchers in child development found that mothers who are able to develop higher levels of attunement or synchrony when interacting with toddlers, and who are able to establish a mutual focus with the child on some activity or thought, have children who are more compliant and happier than mothers who are less attuned, so to speak, to their young children. Flowing with the child rather than against her or him seems to be the best policy for socializing cooperativeness and stability.

Finally, the quality of the relationship between parents has a profound impact on children's coping and mental health. Studies on the impact of divorce revealed that children suffer more directly before parental separation than after the divorce, suggesting that interparental conflict rather than separation per se was most disturbing to the child (Emery, 1982). Even verbal conflict, then, has an adverse effect on children's sense of wellbeing. The relationship of adult women and men in a household sets a climate of stability or conflict in the home for children.

Once again, the indicators of nonviolent parenting seem to be more lodged within parenting beliefs than in the structure of the family. Coercive parenting engenders aggression in children, either through modeling parental aggression or through the development of an internal mental script or "working model" of antagonistic interpersonal relationships. Although there have been few direct studies to date, it appears that parents who espouse a "partnership model" with each other, are more likely to raise children to do the same, and to develop mutual respect for boundaries, opinions, and interests that will benefit the child as well as the parents. The "dominator model" or traditional patriarchal family is a problematic environment for successful childrearing, and can diminish children's own self-esteem and ability to forge intimate relationships.

V. CONCLUSIONS: CULTURAL IDEOLOGY AND FAMILY VIOLENCE

As we have seen, in many cultures family violence has been, and continues to be, considered normal, and even desirable. Even now, the study of family violence or nonviolence still focuses primarily on statistical information, on the gathering of data. Only gradually is this area beginning to be the subject of intensive study in its larger social context. One important aspect that has begun to receive attention, thanks to feminist research and more recently to "men's studies" is the study of the relationship between stereotypical gender roles and violence. An area that is also beginning to receive more attention in these quarters is the interaction between family violence or nonviolence, personality formation, and social structure. One of the earliest studies in this area was accomplished by the psychologist Else Frenkel-Brunswick (Adorno et al., 1964). This pioneering work showed that children brought up in what Brunswick termed authoritarian families (the dominator model) where corporal punishment and other forms of abuse as well as rigid gender stereotypes were considered normal tended to harbor extreme prejudices and beliefs about the "rightness" of violence from "superiors" to "inferiors." More recently, the work of one of the authors (Eisler) has extended this area of inquiry, focusing on the interaction between intimate relations in the private sphere and economic or political relations in the public sphere. Eisler's work suggests that if a society, or family, orients strongly to the dominator model—in which relations are based primarily on rankings of domination—patterns of violence will be necessary to maintain these rankings. By contrast, in families and societies orienting primarily to the partnership model—where relations are based primarily on linking, with herarchies of actualization maintained by enabling rather than disabling power—the teaching of empathy, caring, and the exchange of mutual benefits can be central in the socialization process.

There have been a number of different approaches to ending violence against women and children. While at one time acceptance of corporal punishment was featured in most theories of pedagogy, today in the United States there are scientific and political movements against the use of physical punishment with children. Changes in legislation, due to the pressure of organized women's rights, children's rights, and other human rights supporting groups, are also of great significance. United Nations Conventions, such as the United Nations Convention on the Elimination of All Forms of Discrimination Against Women, the United Nations Convention on the Rights of the Child, and the United Nations Declaration on the Elimination of Violence Against Women, are also extremely important developments. Most important is the continuing grassroots actions of groups all over the world—from groups working to stop the sex trade of women and girls to groups working against rape, battering of women, child abuse, genital mutilation of female children, and other human rights violations.

One of the most serious and continuing threats to women and children—especially girl children—is the higher valuation of males over females. This feature of so many cultures is also characteristic of cultures orienting to the "dominator" model. In fact, female offspring are so devalued that according to a recent United Nations report in 1997 at least 60 million girls who would otherwise be expected to be alive are "missing" from various populations as a result of sex-selective neglect and abortions (UNDP Report, 1997).

Family violence occurs across different cultures and family structures. The common denominators are the cultural attitudes and the social structure that the family both shapes and is shaped by. It would seem that only fundamental cultural changes and changes in these entrenched social structures—in Eisler's terms, a shift from the dominator to a partnership model family and social orientation—will make it possible to deal with family violence in a systemic way and to move to nonviolence as the norm in both families and societies worldwide.

Also See the Following Articles

CHILD ABUSE • CHILDREARING, VIOLENT AND NONVIOLENT • FEMINIST AND PEACE PERSPECTIVES ON WOMEN • GENDER STUDIES • HUMAN RIGHTS • INSTITUTIONALIZATION OF VIOLENCE • PEACEFUL SOCIETIES • SEXUAL ASSAULT • SOCIAL CONTROL AND VIOLENCE • WARRIORS, ANTHROPOLOGY OF

Bibliography

Bonta, B. D. (1997). Cooperation and competition in peaceful societies. *Psychological Bulletin, 121*, 299–320.

Coltrane, S. (1988). Father-child relationships and the status of women. *American Journal of Sociology, 93*, 1060–1095.

Counts, D. A., Brown, J. K., & Campbell, J.C. (Eds.). (1992). *Sanctions and sanctuary: Cultural perspectives on the beating of wives.* Boulder and Oxford: Westview Press.

Das Gupta, M. (1987). Selective discrimination against female children in rural Punjab, India. *Population and Development Review* 13, 55–70.

Dobash, R. E., & Dobash, R. P. (1980). *Violence against wives: A case against the patriarchy.* London: Open Books.

Eisler, R. (1987). *The chalice and the blade: Our history, our future.* San Francisco: Harper & Row.

Eisler, R. (1995). *Sacred pleasure: Sex, myth, and the politics of the body.* San Francisco: HarperCollins.

Eisler, R., Loye, D., & Norgaard, K. (1995). *Women, men and the global quality of life.* Pacific Grove, CA: Center for Partnership Studies.

Frias-Armenta, M., & McCloskey, L. A. (1998). Psychosocial determinants of harsh parenting in Mexico. *Journal of Abnormal Child Psychology, 26*, 129–139.

Gelles, R., & Cornell, C. (1990). *Intimate violence in families.* Newbury Park: Sage Publications.

Levinson, D. (1989). *Family violence in cross-cultural perspective.* Newbury Park, CA: Sage.

McCloskey, L. A. (1996). Socioeconomic and coercive power in families. *Gender and Society, 10*, 449–463.

Smuts, B. (1992). Male aggression against women: An evolutionary perspective. *Human Nature, 3*, 1–44.

Straus, M. A. (1994). *Beating the devil out of him: Corporal punishment in American families.* New York: Lexington.

United Nations Report on the Status of Women (1995). New York: United Nations.

Feminist and Peace Perspectives on Women

Linda Rennie Forcey

Binghamton University

GLOSSARY

Ecofeminism An approach that opposes the domination of nature by Western industrial culture, and the domination of women by Western industrial man. Ecofeminists see this as part of the same process of devaluation and destruction oddly characterized in masculinist history as the "enlightenment."

Essentialism An approach that takes gender division as given and monolithic. This means, in the parlance of feminist theory, an argument that women are *essentially* different from men.

Feminism Acknowledgment of women's oppression and exploitation and of the need to do something about it.

Peace Studies An interdisciplinary field of study, first emerging in the aftermath of World War I, which seeks to understand all threats to global security and human survival.

Postmodernism An approach, based on borrowings from the humanities, that attacks the methodological assumptions of modern science, on the one hand, and that questions the status of all knowledge on the other. It is providing a major challenge to the essentialist standpoint in the fields of international relations and peace studies.

Structural Violence A form of violence that is more insidious and indirect than physical violence. It is built into the structure of social and cultural institutions, often denying people basic human rights.

MANY CONTEMPORARY FEMINISTS challenge the notion that there is an assumed relationship between women and peace. This article briefly summarizes the contributions of feminist theorizing to peace studies and research in the United States. It alerts readers to the feminist debate and resulting tensions within the fields as to the very nature of women. Many feminist peace researchers and educators now seek a finely tuned appreciation of a variety of approaches to the study of gender and of human differences and commonalties. Understanding of the historical and social specificity of peace making and reconsideration of the role of human agency are now reflected in the work of contemporary feminist peace researchers.

I. INTRODUCTION

This end-of-the-century decade is one of global transformation and destabilization. Twentieth-century history has not been kind to many of the world's peoples, particularly its women and children in developing

Copyright © 1999 by Academic Press.
All rights of reproduction in any form reserved.

countries. The gap between rich and poor has widened virtually everywhere, placing mothers and children in increasingly precarious economic positions, allowing each day tens of thousands of children to die to preventable causes. For the past 50 years and more militarism has shaped many of our economic priorities. Its use of the resources and capital of this country have helped to deplete medical, educational, and social programs. Its violent effects have shaped the contours of the political agendas of both peace advocates and feminists.

The most fundamental tenet of feminism, acknowledgment of women's oppression and exploitation and of the need to do something about it, is now woven into peace studies, an interdisciplinary field of study that first emerged in the aftermath of World War I. The field has been moving steadily since then toward the "positive peace" approach, one articulated by the influential peace researcher Johan Galtung, who asks us to understand that global security encompasses many more threats than war to human survival. Both peace studies and women's studies (feminism's academic incarnation) share basic assumptions about the more peaceful nature of women and the more violent nature of men.

Violence and war have historically been associated with the making of masculinity; hence, this concordance of peace with women's studies is not surprising. The public domain has long been, for men, the place that calls on them to sacrifice their lives for their country. K. von Clausewitz, a 19th-century Prussian army officer best known for his work *On War*, wrote that there was no better way to educated the spirit of people than by war. "By it alone can the effeminacy of feeling be counteracted, that propensity to seek for the enjoyment of comfort, which causes degeneracy in a people...."

While man's participation in war in the name of the state has been his highest calling, for woman the parallel duty has been service to family. Nonviolence and peace are, of course, the hallmarks of the private world where women serve. Hegel, in *The Philosophy of Right*, wrote:

> Man has his actual substantive life in the state, in learning, and so forth, as well as in labour and struggle with the external world and with himself so that it is only out of his diremption that he fights his way to self-subsistent unity with himself.... Woman, on the other hand, has her substantive destiny in the family, and to be imbued with family piety is her ethical frame of mind.

This gendered view of the public/private spheres is a dominant theme of Western political thought. As political scientist Jean Elshtain argues, we are "the heirs of a tradition that assumes an affinity between women and peace, between men and war, a tradition that consists of culturally constructed and transmitted myths and memories."

By and large, peace studies has been quite comfortable with an approach that takes this gender dichotomy as a given, with "women as women" representing "an ethic of care" as suggested by Carol Gilligan, Betty Reardon, Birgit Brock-Utne, Sara Ruddick, and others. On the other hand, while there remains a common core of beliefs for feminists centering around women's oppression, subordination, and exploitation, there has arisen a serious tension about what is meant by the very term "women." Some feminists go so far as to argue that *any* idea of women as women is empty. Women's studies as a whole, in fact, has become extremely skeptical of universalist ideas that discourage us from thinking about how distinct and different people are. The field now encompasses a variety of theories of gender and strategies for change. Many feminists assert that in these times of multiply contested oppressions gender cannot be considered the most salient basis of oppression.

II. ESSENTIALISM AND ITS CRITICS

As noted, peace studies, entwined with feminism in many ways for the past several decades, has been generally comfortable with an approach that takes gender division as given and monolithic. This means, in the parlance of feminist theory, an argument that women are *essentially* different from men. Pragmatically speaking, this essentialism is not necessarily a bad thing. Given the needs of all oppressed groups, essentialism can be a powerful consciousness-raising tool for women's solidarity and for collective action. To argue that women are *essentially* different is thus to valorize women's experiences as caretakers and peacemakers, and thereby to encourage women's activism. And, ethically speaking, humanist aspirations for a more peaceful world, where peace must include an ethic of caring and of valuing caring labor for both women and men, are and must remain at the heart of the peace studies endeavor. The essentialists' call to action is quite simple: men must become kinder, nicer, gentler—more like peaceful women.

Until the publication of Betty Reardon's and Birgit Brock-Utne's monographs there had been only a most tenuous relationship between feminist and peace research. Most peace researchers were neither women nor feminists, and many feminists considered peace studies a diversion from the main task of liberating women. It was left primarily to a few feminist scholars (most of whom would not have called themselves "peace researchers") to acknowledge the role of earlier pioneers such as Bertha von Suttner, Jane Addams, Emily Greene Balch, and members of the Women's Peace Party and the Women's International League for Peace and Freedom (WILPF). Their major objective was to show that some women did play a role in social and political history and could be counted among men for equal citizenship.

Reardon and Brock-Utne called for a new definition of peace that included such structural forms of violence as inequality of rights and oppression of women. Reflecting the thinking of Nancy Chodorow, Jean Baker Miller, and especially Carol Gilligan, Reardon and Brock-Utne saw a separate female world, one in which women are essentially different from men (by and large for psychological and sociological rather than biological reasons)—more caring, more cooperative, more peaceful. They called for an integration of feminist scholarship with peace research to draw attention to the fundamental relationship between sexism and militarism.

Betty Reardon's monograph, *Sexism and the War System*, grew out of her experiences with the World Policy Institute and the World Order Models Program in the 1970s and early 1980s. Reardon sees an unhealthy imbalance toward male principles in modern society, leading to war, aggression, greed, and other embodiments of "manly" aspects, rather than the more conciliatory and constructive "womanly" aptitudes. She argues that "the war system" (which she defines very broadly and loosely as "our competitive social order") has brought us to the brink of global annihilation, leaving in its wake a society "paralyzed by the masculine suppression of emotion." Even peace research and world order studies are closed out to "the world of feeling and the repositories of that world, feminine values and women."

Contending that within the field of peace studies most researchers have viewed women's issues as secondary or collateral to the central concerns of peace, Reardon calls for an integration of feminist scholarship with peace research whereby the need for inner psychic transformation on a personal level is appreciated as much as the need for global political and economic change. She develops a feminist peace paradigm focused on the Yin and Yang aspects of being, contrasting such characteristics as gentleness and strength, receptivity and dominance, caring and competing. One of Reardon's central metaphors is mothering: conception, labor, birth, and nurture. She writes of humane and

fulfilling human relationships, personal change, vulnerability, and pastoral images of peace, and ultimately transformation.

Norwegian feminist Birgit Brock-Utne's *Feminist Perspectives on Peace and Peace Education* begins with a broad positive definition of peace, similar to that implicit in Reardon's *Sexism and the War System*: the elimination of structural violence ("all types of repression and exploitation") as well as war. Her central themes are (1) that women's concerns are defined in terms of interpersonal relationships and they hence find it more difficult to condone acts of violence; (2) that individuals can be educated to eschew violent and aggressive behavior; (3) that doing away with sex role socialization is essential to this effort; and (4) that for peace educators there may be light at the end of the dark tunnel.

Histories of peace-loving and peace-promoting women continue to abound. Harriet Hyman Alonso gives us an historical study of the peace movement's evolution from a wing of the woman's suffrage movement with the focus on motherhood and caring. Margaret Kamester's and Jo Vellacott's edited collection of World War I writings on early pacifist feminism by Catherine Marshall, C.K. Ogden, and Mary Sargent Florence illustrate ways in which men were categorized as militaristic and women innately peaceful and mothering. Pam McAllister's most recent chronicle of women's nonviolent protests for social change, *This River of Courage: Generations of Women's Resistance and Action*, makes women's commitment to nonviolent actions for social change a stirring challenge for her readers. Amy Swerdlow's historical account of the Women's Strike for Peace movement of the 1960s and early 1970s shows how 50,000 women, all of them still espousing the traditional female pursuits of motherhood and domesticity, attempted to rein in the power of the Pentagon.

Among the more recent forms of essentialist female political activity are ecofeminist interpretations of efforts to save the environment. The Chipko movement of the Himalayan foothill regions of Tehri Carwhal in Uttar Pradesh was the most famous of India's new social movements and plays an important part in most peace studies curricula. Widespread forest destruction had caused a great deal of economic hardship for the local people who drew their sustenance from the trees. The effect was particularly hard on women who did the work of cultivating the soil and gathering fodder, fuel, and water. Under the leadership of C.P. Bhatt and others Sarvodaya workers organized the Movement. The famous 1974 struggle developed when the forest department granted permission to fell ash trees and the people, mostly women influenced by Gandhian workers, turned to "tree-hugging" to prevent the felling.

Indian ecofeminist Vandana Shiva argues that this movement is part of the women's movement because of gender interests in the forest economy. In the worldview of the women of the Chipko Movement, according to Vandana Shiva, nature is Prakriti, the creator and source of wealth. Rural women, peasants and indigenous peoples who live in, and derive sustenance from, nature thus have a systematic and deep knowledge of nature's processes of reproducing wealth. Nature and women do not acquire value through their domination by modern Western man; both lose through this process of subjugation. The domination of nature by Western industrial culture, and the domination of women by Western industrial man, is part of the same process of devaluation and destruction oddly characterized in masculinist history as the "enlightenment." A recent UN report by the International Labor Organization also echoes these radical ecofeminists' views: "Women tend to speak with a different voice, [it reads] which as a rule lays stress on the social ethos of development, that is to say education, dialogue and peace."

Such arguments have had tremendous appeal among peace and women's studies readers. Questioning these essentialist assumptions, therefore, becomes a delicate business. Nevertheless, there have been critics who argue this line of theorizing placed an exaggerated focus on the differences between men and women, dangerously distorting any real portrait of woman as woman. Important aspects of women's lives such as anger, frustration, aggression, sexuality, jealousy, and envy, reliving of one's childhood, conflict between demands of a child, one's mate, other children and other work are missing. British feminist Lynne Segal, striking a central theme as to the inadequacy of polarized thinking about men and women, writes: "This has meant a minimal interest in conflicts and contradictions as they are experienced within feminine identity, a false universalizing of our own gender categories and a disregard for other social practices (outside mother–daughter bonding) as they impinge upon gender identity." Segal points out that, "the weight of one's own children can mean a contradiction of social vision, an envy and resentment of the welfare of others;e;. While it may be true that women are more concerned about peace and a better world ;e; this does not necessarily mean that women are any less nationalistic, racist, or committed to class privilege than men."

A recent collection of essays entitled *Not June Cleaver: Women and Gender in Postwar America, 1945–1960*, edited by historian Joanne Meyerowitz, is a fur-

ther good example of the revisionist effort to document the complexity and diversity of women and their multifarious identities and activities. The collection also documents what many White Western feminists in the 1970s and 1980s were unable or unwilling to see—that women's identities included not only gender but also their class, racial, ethnic, sexual, religious, and political senses of themselves.

In the public sphere, as most peace researchers now acknowledge, the record of women's resistance to national wars is problematic at best, and certainly no candidate for universalization. Many women, in fact, encourage their sons to join the military in the hope that its institutions will make their sons more mature, less prone to addictive drugs, better able to earn a living. African American sociologist Barbara Omolade points out that African American women have a legacy of support of war because the military represents economic opportunity and social status for Black men and now for Black women too. She writes, "every day black women encourage our men, especially our sons, to enlist as an alternative to unemployment and street crime.... Few black women can live outside the dilemmas posed by this predicament. Which war zone does she protect her son from: the military or the street?"

The more radical ecofeminist and "deep ecology" positions, which argue that the earth is inviolate and women and nature are especially coterminous, often face the charge of being too essentialist. Feminist international relations theorists V. Spike Peterson and Anne Sisson Runyan argue that although ecofeminism makes a strong case about the relationship between the abuse of nature and the abuse of women, its approach is highly problematic. It makes women so coterminous with nature, the authors argue, that it can lead to justifications for keeping women out of decision-making positions that would enable them to have an impact on how nature is best used by human beings. Furthermore, ecofeminists' call for low low-technology strategies to protect women and nature can conflict with women's interests both to gain access to resources to meet their families' needs, and to participate as equals in modern, high-technology, male-dominated institutions that control, manage, and distribute resources.

Many feminist peace researchers now argue that a different set of questions needs to be asked. How else can we explain diverse historical and cultural forms of femininity and masculinity? How else can we explain mothers who send their sons to war? How else can we explain women's behavior that does not conform to maternal thinking? How else can we understand the lives of women who do not wish to be mothers? Or of others who wish to be military heroes? Clearly, in the late 1990s, any notion of a unified female experience must be treated cautiously.

More significant for feminist discourse is the kind of essentialist danger many feminists see lurking in any claim about "women" that implies a homogeneous group. As political theorist Jean Elshtain points out, feminists who privilege women over men because of their female nature, are guilty of "paradigmatic linkages" that "dangerously overshadow other voices, other stories: of pacific males; of bellicose women; of cruelty incompatible with just-war fighting; of martial fervour at odds—or so we choose to believe—with maternalism in women." Clearly, feminist peace researchers can never again unabashedly accept Betty Friedan's homogenized and universalized account of women's experiences in the postwar decades in the United States.

III. POSTMODERNISM AND ITS CRITICS

While it remains clear that men throughout the world continue to have greater access to power, wealth, and privilege than do women, it also has become clear that feminists are having increasing difficulty coming to agreement on the theories and strategies needed to explain and challenge these inequities. Feminist peace theorizing now fluctuates ambivalently around a standpoint (one increasingly supported by men in the field) that focuses on the identification of essential psychological/sociological differences between men and women and another that acknowledges the distortion and disadvantages of this very stance. It grapples with this difference-versus-equality debate both on theoretical and strategic levels. The tension, writes Anne Phillips, is "built into the feminist project. Men and women are different; they are also unequal; feminists will continue to debate and disagree over how far the inequality stems from the difference, and how far the difference can or should be eliminated."

That it is time to move beyond the difference versus equality debate is the emerging consensus, at least outside the peace studies field. As long as women find themselves in the political context of these present times, comments historian Ruth Milkman, "feminist scholars must be aware of the real danger that arguments about "difference" or "women's culture" will be put to uses other than those for which they were originally developed." Joan Scott, taking Milkman's point further, argues that the equality-difference debate can be an intellectual trap, one out of which feminists must

move. "When equality and difference are paired dichotomously, they structure an impossible choice. If one opts for equality, one is forced to accept the notion that difference is antithetical to it. If one opts for difference, one admits that equality is unattainable." How then, Scott asks, "do we recognize and use notions of sexual difference and yet make arguments for equality?" The only response, she answers, is a double one: "the unmasking of the power relationship constructed by posing equality as the antithesis of difference, and the refusal of its consequent dichotomous construction of political choices." In other words, feminists need to recognize that the antithesis of difference is not equality but rather sameness; and the antithesis of equality is not difference, but rather inequality.

The analytic perspective Scott and many contemporary feminist social scientists find most valuable for moving beyond the difference versus equality debate is postmodernism (and its variant known as poststructuralism). This approach, based on borrowings from the humanities that attack the methodological assumptions of modern science, on the one hand, and that question the status of all knowledge on the other, is providing a major challenge to the essentialist standpoint in the fields of international relations and peace studies. In this context, it is referred to as "the third debate"—a loosely defined and evolving cluster of attitudes toward theory and practice that takes into account a whole range of analytical approaches and "for all its heterogeneity has a number of thematic connections that help to identify it and explain its over arching critical purpose."

Postmodernism does not have one fixed meaning; rather, it is applied to a wide range of theoretical positions derived from the work of Derrida, Lacan, Kristeva, Althusser, and Foucault. In its myriad aspects, it can be defined as a broadly interdisciplinary approach that disputes the underlying assumptions of most social sciences—epistemological foundations, the Enlightenment heritage (faith in the idea of progress and rationality), and a social science methodology modeled after the hard sciences with its search for generalizations, simplifications, and verifications. Rather than focusing on personality, behavior, attitudes, goals, and choices, it turns attention to language, symbols, alternative discourses, and meaning. It holds that knowledge is grounded in language and language does not reflect "reality." And it is language itself that creates and reproduces a world that is never definitive but always in transition. Having said so much, we can admit that it is really easier to say what postmodernism is not, than what it is. This is partly because it resists definition on empirical grounds and partly because it, still in its infancy, remains undefined. Postmodernism's positive identity has yet to be formed. Its proponents, however, do agree that it aims to destabilize and render open to question all claims to an absolute foundation.

In her discussion of the contribution postmodernism can offer contemporary feminism, linguist Chris Weedon articulates a specific version that is able to address the questions of how social power is exercised and how social relations of gender, class, and race might be transformed. This is not to say that the differences among forms of postmodernism are not important; but rather, that they are not equally productive for feminism. Postmodernists, according to Weedon, deny the assumption that women and men have essential natures. They refuse to "fall back on general theories of the feminine psyche or biologically based definitions of femininity which locate its essence in processes such as motherhood or female sexuality." This does not, however, "rule out the specificity of women's experiences and their difference from those of men, since, under patriarchy, women have differential access to the discursive field which constitutes gender, gendered experience and gender relations of power in society."

Political scientist Christine Sylvester defines the project of postmodernism as:

> a form of critical theory which questions secure knowledges and practices and seeks to open up policy processes to those who have been spoken for and "protected" by purveyors of certitude and security. It is a community—of radical doubters, tolerant dissenters, neo-anarchists, seekers of knowledge at the hyphens of lived experience. Unabashedly pro-women, it also is alert to other groups historically silenced within the master discourses of andocentric modernity.

From this position, Sylvester challenges the theses of essentialists like Brock-Utne, Reardon, Chodorow, and Ruddick, arguing that women are not naturally opposed to war and for peace, and that peace and war are all of a piece, rather than negations of each other. At this moment in time, she argues, that piece, as it were, has its substance in patriarchy. It is patriarchy itself that damages and distorts women's perspectives as well as those of men: women may be embracing (and calling our own) peacemaker images that reflect and serve the prevailing gender order, leading to a denial that liberation brings pain, confusion, and loss. Sylvester questions the value of what she calls "establishment-supporting gender expectations" for bringing an end to patriarchal society as we now know it. It is inappropri-

ate, she concludes, to draw sharp conclusions about interrelationships of women, peace-lovingness, women warriors, and strategies for tipping patriarchal war-peace pieces in more feminist directions. This thinking, very much in process, is, it might be said, also healthfully incoherent. It encourages us to examine carefully claims that war and peace are negations of each other, and that women are unified in a natural or conditioned opposition to men.

In a recent collection of essays entitled *Feminism and the Politics of Difference*, contributors highlight the point that feminism's days of exclusionary solidarity and its universalizing of women as women are long gone. The editors, Anna Yeatman and Sneja Gunew, with contributors from Australia, New Zealand, Canada, and the United States, reject (1) the assumption that women and men have essential natures; (2) the Kantian notion of the "categorical imperative" as producing universally self-evident values; and (3) the existence of any universalism except in its interested and particularized context. This interdisciplinary collection raises several key questions for peace studies: how and where do race and ethnicity intersect; who is authorized to speak for whom; which voice is authentic; what are the structures of legitimization for minorities; and how can feminists set up nonexclusive cultural and gendered positions? For U.S. peace researchers, the centering of this analysis on the politics of difference in Australia, New Zealand, and Canada is especially informative and challenging.

A growing number of dissenting voices to postmodernism have arisen, however, particularly among women of color. Professor of African-American Studies Barbara Christian deplores feminists' emphasis on theory "with its linguistic jargon, its emphasis on quoting its prophets, its tendency towards 'Biblical' exegesis, its refusal even to mention specific works of creative writers, far less contemporary ones, its preoccupations with mechanical analyses of language, graphs, algebraic equations, its gross generalizations about culture." The acknowledgment of differences among women, must not be so exaggerated as to negate feminist discourse, many other feminists are now arguing. "Skepticism of universalist ideas encourages us to think about how distinct and different people are," argues Sondra Farganis "but by taking this track, there is the chance that moral indifference and uncertainty will undermine the very basis on which a feminist politics is founded—that is, the shared status of women who want to overcome what they see as oppressive conditions and establish their human authenticity." Farganis, trained in both political and social theory, outlines the major themes and contentions within feminist thought and argues for a multicultural approach that embraces common humanity while taking into account diversity of people's lives.

Maxine Sheets-Johnstone, a philosopher, provides a further alternative to currently dominant language/text-oriented and social-constructionist theories by arguing that power and of power relations are rooted in bodily life, in animate form. Sheets-Johnstone's critique of contemporary feminist social constructionists and postmodernists is so unequivocal that she opens up some new questions and approaches for feminist scholarship. In this provocative interdisciplinary work, she argues that power is rooted in bodily life. This view is not a comfortable one for feminists who have subsumed it with "essentialism," and have claimed, for very good reason, that power differences as symbolized by "anatomy equals destiny" arguments are by and large social constructions that have served men well and oppressed women. Maxine-Johnstone's objective is to demonstrate that in corporeal matters of fact lie dimensions of ourselves that are at once both personal and political. She insists that we acknowledge the ties that make us part of a common evolutionary humanity.

IV. CONCLUSION

Because of the activist nature of the field of peace studies, feminists believe there is a special urgency, poignancy, if you will, to this debate about the nature of women. To argue that women are *essentially* different because they are more nurturing, more caring, they argue, is to valorize many women's experiences as peacemakers in the home. Who among us can say that there could ever be too much CARING in this violent world? Furthermore, peace studies can be seen as a critique of one of the most male-dominated of the social sciences fields, international relations. Feminist peace research that focuses on caring, nurturing, feeling, intuiting, empathizing, relating remains an important catalyst to challenge militarism. This contribution of essentialist thinking to the field of international relations and the peace endeavor is refreshing, comforting, energizing, and affirming for women. It poses a very different set of questions than those traditionally asked by practitioners (mostly male) in both international relations and peace studies.

In retrospect, however, it now seems inevitable to most feminist scholars that understandings of what it means to be "women" would be contested, and that feminism's days of exclusionary solidarity and univer-salized women are long gone. Peace studies can no longer accept a strict dualism between feminine and masculine development. Much of feminists' early observations about women now seem naive at best, dangerous at worst. Their exaggeration of sexual differences, their belief in an intrinsic female pacifism, and their lack of adequate analysis of the modern war system is troubling for postmodern feminist theorists and should be troubling for peace educators.

Clearly, any notion of a unified female experience must be treated cautiously as we approach the end of the 20th century. The question as to whether women are *essentially* different from men—that is, have a distinctively "women's point of view"—is now easily read as a biologically essentialist claim compatible with conservative discourse as to the proper roles for women and men. More significant is the kind of essentialist danger many feminists see lurking in any claim about "women" that implies a homogeneous group. As recent feminist theorists remind us, contested understandings of what it meant to be "women" must include our evolutionary history and an appreciation of both the diversity and commonality of women's lived experiences.

Interdisciplinary in its boundaries, the new feminist scholarship raises two key internal questions: Is feminism itself built on the "othering" of some women because of feminists' tendency to believe that they have privileged access to gender truths? And who is authorizing whom to speak? As Australian sociologist Anna Yeatman writes, "It is a salutary and uncomfortable experience for … white, Western and middle-class women … [to] have been challenged as voices privileged by the discursive economies of feminism by those whom these same economies disprivilege: women who are not white, Western, middle-class."

The challenge for feminist peace researchers and educators is to recognize the dilemmas inherent in the feminist debate. It is to recognize both the power of universalizing women as women in the name of solidarity for social change, and the danger of such a denial or suppression of differences among women. It is to learn how politically to manage fragmentation in ways that do not deny women's differences or interdependence. Clearly, there must be an accommodation between what Edward Said regards as an ominous position involving the "fetishization and relentless celebration of 'difference' and 'otherness'" that ultimately undermines all feminist discourse, and, on the other hand, "a hegemonic white western feminist intellectuals' universal civilizing mission to extend to their less fortunate sisters their embracing voices that speak for *all* women." In granting each and every one a separate identity we need not lose the essence of the human community of which we as women and men are a part.

As feminist Rosemary Tong points out, "[Feminists] need a home in which everyone has a room of her own, but one in which the walls are thin enough to permit a conversation." For feminists to feel unable to speak out for women from a variety of cultures "only further reinforces the voices of those who have constructed approaches ;e; out of the experiences of men." This is to say, the facts of women's unequal power in most cultures of the world and the violence inflicted upon women across all cultures and socioeconomic groups must be addressed in all their complexity without grossly oversimplifying women as women. The trick, it now seems to many contemporary feminist peace researchers, is to honor the differences but also to acknowledge at the outset what Edward Said calls "the massively knotted and complex histories of special but nevertheless overlapping and interconnected experiences—of women, of Westerners, of Blacks, of national states and cultures." In granting each and every one a separate identity we need not lose the essence of the human community of which we as women and men are a part.

Also See the Following Articles

ENVIRONMENTAL ISSUES AND POLITICS • GENDER STUDIES • MILITARY CULTURE • PEACE CULTURE • PEACE STUDIES, OVERVIEW • SOCIAL CONTROL AND VIOLENCE • STRUCTURAL VIOLENCE • WARRIORS, ANTHROPOLOGY OF • WOMEN AND WAR

Bibliography

Alonso, H. H. (1993). *Peace as a women's issue: A history of the U.S. movement for world peace and women's rights*. Syracuse, NY: Syracuse University.

Brock-Utne, B. (1989). *Feminist perspectives on peace and peace education*. New York: Pergamon.

Elshtain, J. B. (1987). *Women and war*. Brighton: Harvester Books.

Forcey, L. R. F. (1995). Women's studies, peace studies, and the difference debate. *Women's Studies Quarterly*, Vol. XXIII, No. 3 & 4.

Gilligan, Carol. (1982). *In a different voice*. Cambridge: Harvard University Press.

Gunew, S., & Yeatman, A. (1993). *Feminism and the politics of difference*. Boulder: Westview.

Harris, A., & King, Y. (1989). *Rocking the ship of state: Toward a feminist peace politics*. Boulder: Westview.

Peterson, V. S., & Runyan, A. S. (1993). *Global gender issues*. Boulder: Westview.

Reardon, B. (1985). *Sexism and the war system*. New York: Teachers College.

Ruddick, S. (1989). *Maternal thinking: Toward a politics of peace*. Boston: Beacon.

Segal, L. (1987). *Is the future female?* London: Virago.

Shiva, V. (1988). *Staying alive: Women ecology and survival in India*. New Delhi: Kali for Women.

Swerdlow, A. (1993). *Women's strike for peace: Traditional motherhood and radical politics in the 1960s*. Chicago: University of Chicago Press.

Sylvester, C. (1994). *Feminist theory and international relations in a postmodern era*. Cambridge: Cambridge University.

Folklore

Sanja Magdalenic

Stockholm University

GLOSSARY

Art Distinctive creative acts in the form of products, processes, or behavior, through which folklorists analyze the complexity of cultural communication within and among groups.

Context A frame of reference that influences agents of cultural production.

Genre Traditionally, a system for the classification of folklore material, in recent perspectives orienting framework for the production and interpretation of discourse.

Group A customary network of interactions with a shared identity and its own repertoire of traditions.

Performance Repeated aesthetic practices that shape individual and group identity.

Tradition A continuous process in which individuals and groups construct their future by reference to past experiences.

I. WHAT IS FOLKLORE?

Although there is no consensus among folklorists on how to define folklore nor how to explain the issues of the meaning and the function of it, folklore generally refers to cultural expressions, such as narratives, music, dance, beliefs, and festivals, through which groups shape and transmit a shared identity. The problem with the definition is closely related to the historical as well as geographical development of this academic discipline.

The interest in folklore emerged primarily out of the Romantic nationalism of the early 19th century. In 1846 William Thoms coined the term "folklore", substituting it for popular antiquities, and therewith named an emerging field of study for the English-speaking world. Close equivalents of the term were used in other languages, such as *Volkskunde* in German, or *traditions populaires* in French. The first folklore societies emerged in Europe and the United States during the 19th century: the Finnish Literature Society in 1831, the British Folk-Lore Society in 1878, the American Folklore Society in 1888, and the Hungarian Ethnographic Society in 1889. Enthusiastic European intellectuals, amateurs, and artists started to collect different kinds of folklore material in order to be able to study various aspects of "the folk" and folklife. During this early period, folklore was viewed as "the lore"—the materials of folklore—of "the folk"—the people who utilize the materials. The discoverers of folklore identified the "folk" as peasant

Copyright © 1999 by Academic Press.
All rights of reproduction in any form reserved.

society or rural groups, regarding them as the main carriers of distinct traditions that were slowly dying out due to urbanization and industrialization during the transition to modernity. The bourgeois nostalgia for the "paradise lost" motivated the efforts to examine and preserve different aspects of folklife. In some countries, for example, in Scandinavia, the rising interest in folklore studies was also motivated by the 18th-century Enlightenment. Within this perspective, the folk and their traditions were regarded as primitive and therefore had to be studied in order to be transformed. Early folklorists focused primarily on oral traditions, such as ballads, folktales, epics, and sagas, disseminated within rural communities.

During the 1960s, a paradigm shift occurred in the theory and methods of folklore study. Not surprisingly, this paradigm shift was most conspicuous in the United States, for it was difficult to study American folklore using more traditional European concepts. For example, while peasants formed a common class in Europe, no such class existed in the United States. Folklorists became aware of and made attempts to get rid of the class bias as well as the national bias implicit in the old concept of folklore. Moreover, contrary to earlier research that approached folklore as ahistorical and homogeneous, it was pointed out that folklore was always situated within some particular space and time. The emphasis on space, time, and society as the most important elements of folk culture was stressed by Scandinavian and German folklorists. Different emerging schools of folklore tried to improve the definition of folklore in order to avoid the shortcomings of the earlier distinction between "folk" and "lore." Folklore was approached as process-centered, context-sensitive, and performance-oriented. According to a contemporary influential conception of folklore, "folk" refers to any group of people who share some common grounds, such as occupation, language, religion, or ethnicity. The objects of study of the discipline of folklore are different forms or genres of "lore": dance, music, songs, drama, costume, legends, myths, beliefs, curses, folk medicine, jokes, proverbs, festivals, and so on. In other words, all people, not only peasants, belong to folk groups. Most people are members of several and not just one folk group. In the interaction of everyday life, the members of each and every group create their particular traditions and make sure that these are transmitted among them. Consequently, folklore can be seen as a kind of established code that serves as a mode of cultural production on the intragroup level as well as an indicator of distinction on the intergroup level. The change of the definition allowed the expansion of folklore study

into new areas of inquiry that previously received little attention.

The paradigm shift was paralleled by the emergence of feminist folklore studies. Feminist folklorists shed light on the existence of the conscious or unconscious gender biases along with the nationalist bias in the concept of folklore. They wanted to challenge folklore scholarship by directing attention to women performers and women's genres that previously had been mostly neglected. In traditional folklore research, as feminist studies indicated, women were described in male terms and most of women folklore genres were accorded attention only if they were compatible with the existing image of women. The aim of feminist folklore studies is to integrate the issue of gender with folkloristics and thus open new perspectives for the study of folklore.

Folklore as a discipline continues to struggle for its place in the academic world, where it rarely has achieved an autonomous status. In most countries, folklore is studied within the neighboring fields of ethnology, anthropology, cultural studies, literature, or history. Folklore material is primarily collected through fieldwork, participant observation, and interviews. Various kinds of secondary sources, such as archival materials, diaries and autobiographies, letters, and in modern time even photography, serve as excellent sources of folkloric imagination. Collections of folklife items for everyday use are also available in folk museums. The quality of sources, however, varies both geographically and chronologically. Inasmuch as "folk culture" was long considered to be of low status and was defined in opposition to "high culture," records of it sometimes exist only as selected and filtered by the latter. When folkloristics as a scholarly endeavor emerged in the West, it was primarily oriented toward documenting Western folklore. Collecting folklore from other parts of the world was done occasionally by missionaries, travelers, and anthropologists. Thus British missionaries founded the Malagasy Folk-lore Society in 1877, a year before its British counterpart. Yet, there are also examples that colonial powers not only actively discouraged but even banned native scholars from collecting folklore expressions, as was done by the British in Bengal in 1903. Gradually, however, folklore research became institutionalized even in non-Western countries, and it started to fill in the knowledge gap and to correct the Western bias in folkloristics. The inevitable language barriers only add to the difficulties in obtaining information about the similarities and differences in folklore traditions. In recent discussions on the state of folklore scholarship, there have emerged claims that contemporary folklorists must direct attention even toward the political aspect of folklore research in order to be aware of who is studying whose traditions and on what terms.

Some folklorists believe that the use of folklore almost invites its abuse. There are numerous examples within folklore scholarship of folklore being employed for commercial or political purposes. In the 1950s, Richard Dorson coined the term "fakelore" to direct attention to the abuse of folklore for commercial purposes. Concerning the ideological manipulation of folklore, two of the most known and most extreme cases are those of Nazi folklore scholarship in Hitler's Germany and Soviet folklore during the Stalin era. In Nazi Germany, some of the folklorists actively took part in supporting Hitler's imperialist policies and ideas of racial superiority. The notion of "romantic primitivism" and its emphasis on nation, race, and the purity of blood provided folklorists with a standpoint from which to idealize rural life and peasants as opposed to the perceived decadence of urban life. Folklore, in particular, oral genres such as tales, proverbs, and speech, was used as a powerful instrument for promoting Nazi ideology and for transmitting racist and hateful attitudes.

Around the same time period, the 1930s, a cult of folklore was created in Stalinist Russia. As the officials considered whether the development of folklore should and could be controlled, folklorists and performers worked together to create lore that addressed contemporary subjects through traditional expressive forms. By deliberately choosing the subjects of prosperity and happiness, the creators of folklore attempted to promote the political doctrine of socialism. Heroic poetry was also an important part of the folklore production. It praised the heroes of the Revolution and the Civil War as well as the soldiers of the Red Army who were willing to give their lives for their country. The protests of folklorists who repudiated doing such pseudofolklore became more open after Stalin's death. The recently published collections of politically incorrect folklore genres of the Stalin era, such as critical political anecdotes and songs, only confirm that the attempts to control the development of folklore are bound to fail.

II. IDENTIFYING THEMES OF VIOLENCE, PEACE, AND CONFLICT IN FOLKLORE RESEARCH

Recent research approaches tend to view folklore as a system in which and through which individuals and groups interact. The assumption underlying this perspective inspired by sociology is that folklore takes shape within groups and is strengthened in communication with other groups. Folklorists have shown that the group's image of itself as well as its images of other groups are often reflected in its folklore repertoire. Folklore acts as an integrative force and as a framework for defining and expressing identity on both intra- and intergroup level. Folklorists have been predominantly concerned with documenting traditions that result in social consensus, while neglecting the negative aspects of social life. Even though folklore archives contain such material, entries such as aggression, conflict, violence, and war are seldom found in folklore journals and monographs. Some folklorists have suggested that the fact that such studies are rare is to a great extent related to the two perspectives that influenced the development of folklore scholarship. The perspective of Romantic nationalism considered folklore to represent the best of a given national culture. Such a point of view, however, hindered folklorists from acknowledging that the folk, the idealized object of their study, could even have destructive thoughts and traditions. The political perspective of the Enlightenment, on the other hand, perceived folklore as a primitive culture that had to be studied in order to be changed. From this perspective, it was justifiable to collect destructive elements if the aim was to condemn them and eliminate them through social reforms. Even though these two perspectives were opposed to each other, they created a similar outcome: folklorists experienced considerable difficulties when confronted with the violent behavior and aggressive ideas of their informants. This in turn created the remarkable avoidance of such topics and placed them on the margins in folklore research. The absence of these issues is also explained with reference to the character of knowledge production in folkloristics as well as the lack of funding support. Comparative research, in particular, cross-cultural research in this area, has been uncommon. During recent years, however, the interest in the dark side of folklore, in aggressive and violent actions about which groups invent traditions, seems to have found its way onto the research agenda. The change of paradigm in folklore research brought to light an awareness that not only peace, conflict, and violence are an inherent part of human existence, but also that folklore can be as much a mechanism of social cohesion and identity affirmation as of conflict and violence. The focus of this article is on examples of folklore research that consider issues along the continuum from symbolic aggression to excessive violence.

A. Verbal Assaults

A common characteristic of the wide variety of ways in which people express verbal aggression is the underlying presence of conflict. Such actions, however, do not necessarily lead to violence. What is at issue is a kind of symbolic aggression between different groups and individuals who participate in the mutual exchange of stereotype attitudes so as to define their identity and establish their place in an imagined social hierarchy. Sociocentrism and boundary work are some of the conceptual tools that folklorist utilize when studying "the will to differentiate."

Some folklorists believe that people need hate figures in order to be able to project onto outsiders the hostilities and tensions that exist within the community. Projection is a type of psychological defense mechanism that is defined as the unconscious ascription of one's own feelings and qualities to a source in the environment. Some of the common examples in folklore of how attitudes of suspicion and hate can be projected toward outsiders include projections on witches and scapegoating. Manifesting indifference and/or feelings of superiority are used as a device in practices that facilitate the formation of individual and group identity. From time to time, folklore can act as a channel through which people are able to express attitudes and behavior that otherwise might be considered socially unacceptable.

Examples from the area of folklore research on humor and jokes reveal the existence of a complex hierarchy among folk groups and their subgroups. Groups employ different strategies to regulate joking so that it does not get out of hand and become a destructive force. Regulation of joking, for instance, is easily observed in gender differences in joke-telling traditions. Contemporary folkloristics emphasizes the importance of collecting context in the study of jokes, claiming that variations in text and structure of jokes are related to the particular situation within which jokes are told as well as that variation in context offers multiple interpretations of jokes. The person telling the joke and the audience listening to it are identified as two of the most vital constituents of contextual structure. A joke often reflects a concern of society. Thus the existence of racist jokes is seen as an indication of the society's racist attitudes. In a comparative study of ethnic jokes, Christie Davies has examined jokes as a means of ascribing different traits to other groups in a comical manner. According to her findings, the most popular and universally spread are ethnic jokes in which groups either are depicted as stupid, inept, and ignorant, or are portrayed as canny, calculating, and craftily stingy. Every country has its own repertoire of ethnic jokes about "stupid" and "canny" groups. By means of telling ethnic jokes, people strengthen their own identity. Davies also emphasizes that joke-telling patterns and patterns of social stratification are strongly related to each other in an asymmetrical manner. The members of the dominant ethnic group in a given society never make jokes about their own group but only about others. The joke patterns of subordinate and marginal groups, on the other hand, include their own group but are even more directed toward superior groups in the hierarchy.

How people construct the category of otherness and use it as a boundary device can be observed in another folklore genre: narrative. Abraham-Van der Mark collected stories told by the older residents of a predominantly working class neighborhood in Amsterdam, the Netherlands, about their encounters with members of ethnic minorities. In the narratives, the native Dutch group is concerned that their "traditional" lifestyle is being threatened by newcomer ethnic groups. Because it is aware of its own low and unfavorable status compared with the rest of the society, the Dutch group places the emphasis on being born in the Netherlands as the basis for perceived superiority. To indicate distinction toward the newcomers, the Dutch residents emphasize the traditional norms and values of the host society, which they believe the newcomers should assimilate to. The stories about different experiences with members of other ethnic minorities told by the Dutch group have an identifiable structure. Most often they begin with a description of the setting in which the event takes place and then proceed with making accusations about various communication difficulties. The end of the story gives the evaluation of the event and provides a possible solution to the problem. Narratives become a way for people to express the perceived strangeness of the culture and behavior of the members of other ethnic communities, which the dominant group defines as cultural "others," through disapproving comments on language, clothing, food, mentality, point of view, attitudes, and temperament. Some of the themes of the collected stories, such as slaughtering sheep in the shower, are known to folklorists as a part of the classical repertoire of stories and urban legends about ethnic groups. In folklorist view, the collected stories reveal more about the Dutch tellers than about members of ethnic minorities. Such narratives are considered one of the aspects of a xenophobic nationalism that is on the rise in many parts of the world.

Folkloristic collections include numerous examples of how cultural and ethnic stereotypes as well as racial prejudices are transmitted through proverbs. Proverbs are among the most universal expressions within the genre of traditional verbal folk art. They are found in all human cultures, and they display similar structural features across languages and societies. A proverb is a saying that is assumed to express a general truth, a wisdom of the elders, that everyone can approve of as important and useful to recall. Folklorists have indicated that proverbs often reflect the norms and values of some particular society in which they circulate. In this view, a complete interpretation of a proverb has to take into account what is being promoted and in which context. One classical example in point is the incorporation of proverbial expressions aimed at degrading the undesirable members of the population, the Jews and Gypsies in particular, into the propagandistic vocabulary that supported the political program in Nazi Germany. Wolfgang Mieder has explored the mechanisms of how proverbs are created and transmitted, and how they often continue to be used in daily communication with the analysis of the American proverb "The only good Indian is a dead Indian." He has found that the origins of this particular proverb date back to the middle of the 19th century. Even though it is not certain who was the first to use this proverbial slur, its appearance in documents and speeches suggest that by 1886 its use was already well established. This proverb was used as a battle slogan in the massive campaign that started after the American Civil War with a purpose to physically and culturally exterminate the Native Americans. Even today this proverb is widely spread in the United States and continues to transmit the negative image of Native Americans. Moreover, Mieder has noticed that an internationalization of the basic proverbial pattern "The only good X is a dead X" has occurred. This essentially racist saying has been practiced against military enemy in many "national" variants. For example, during the first and second World Wars, the original pattern was adequately adapted and utilized as a slogan against the German enemy. The same motto was also found during early Spanish conquests in South America. There seem to be no limits for how this particular proverb can be modified as a national stereotype or be used as a generalization about any racial minority. Hence, the study of proverbs can significantly increase the awareness of the psychological and ethical implications of the strategies for transmitting prejudices in everyday verbal interaction.

B. Folklore and Violence

Some folklorists tend to view violence as a continuation of sociocentrism. This section considers how folklorists examine ritualized or festive canalization of inter-community and intracommunity violence as well as how they refer to circumstances in which ritualized aggression turns into real aggression and violence. Many analyses show that the mechanisms for control of violence are closely related to the outbursts of it. Folklorists indicate that mock battles, football matches, or festivals often are accompanied with ritualized and real violence. Various studies also report of Spanish, Peruvian, and Trinidadian festive violence. Carnival is one example of ritualized canalization of festive violence. The tradition of carnival—an annual festival held in days preceding Ash Wednesday—has European origins and is particularly strong in the Mediterranean and Central European area. Of the three main themes of Carnival festivities—food, sex, and violence—that folklorists have distinguished, violence—especially the relationship between ritualized aggression and real aggression—seems to have attracted the least scholarly attention. Folklorists view carnival as a cultural performance that allows social roles to be temporarily inverted. Carnival is a time of institutionalized disorder, when adults and children dress in costumes and are encouraged to insult others and criticize authorities under controlled forms. There are folklorists who believe that festive violence has a meaning, and that it should not be understood simply as an unintended consequence of festive behavior or alcohol consumption. In an inquiry on carnival in a Brazilian city, Daniel Touro Linger has observed that people even tend to judge carnival by its level of violence and they see it as a disturbing indication of the community's underlying anxieties. Carnival violence often takes form of *briga*, a physical fight between two individuals, and *entrudo*, a practice of throwing various substances, such as mud, urine, sewer water, and rotten eggs, at other members of the carnival procession. In Linger's view, there is an apparent class component in violent carnival actions: people always attack either their social equals or social inferiors, never those in a superior position within the internal social hierarchy of the given community.

Violence can also take a form of a ritual combat over an imagined territory. Within the analysis of rituals in public places in Sweden, attention was directed to the ritual of honoring the anniversary of death of Charles XII (1682–1718), the warrior king of Sweden. This ritual occurs on November 30, and was organized for the first time in 1853 by students in Lund, Sweden. Since then, it has become an annual tradition in several Swedish cities. During the 1930s, the performance of this ritual was taken over by members of National Socialist groups. Since the mid-1980s, one of the places for this ceremony was around the statue of Charles XII in Kungsträdgården, a square at the center of Stockholm, Sweden. In the beginning of the 1990s, celebrating the death of Charles XII often escalated into violent conflicts that required police intervention. The ritual scenario brings together a series of events in which two opposing groups take part. One group consists of nationalists and skinheads, who march together in a procession toward the square, determined to place a wreath at the king's statue. They see the statue and its surroundings as their own symbolic territory. The opposing group is formed by antiracists and members of immigrant groups. At the moment when the first group approaches the square, they are confronted by the opposing group, which attempts to prevent them from achieving their plan. At this point, the manifestation evolves into a conflict about conquering and defending an imagined territory around the statue. The celebrators of Charles XII assume that they have to reconquer this particular territory and defend the right to pay tribute to their national symbol. Moreover, they accuse members of the opposing group of being traitors and non-Swedes. Although they differ in ideological standpoints, both sides in the conflict sing the national anthem, yet two different versions of it, and both use the flag as their main symbol. Folklorists have observed that the media used war rhetoric and words such as front line, attack, and war scenario when reporting this ritual conflict. In media accounts, the conflict came to symbolize an annual struggle between good and evil forces in the given society and was described on the basis of polarization between racist and antiracist groups. Members of the Nazi, skinhead, and racist groups were portrayed as representatives of xenophobic ideas and chauvinistic nationalism in the society and a discussion was raised about the extent to which these groups have the right to publicly promote fascist and xenophobic values. An interesting detail is that the 30th of November, the day of death of Charles XII, coincides with the day of birth of Arthur Hazelius, the creator of Skansen, an open-air museum in Stockholm, which was built to represent Swedish nature and folk culture. During a short period after World War II, on November the 30th, homage to both Charles XII and Arthur Hazelius was paid in Skansen. In the view of the celebrators of Charles XII, Skansen continues to stand for genuine Swedish values and culture, which, they believe, are being threatened by foreign influence. These groups tend to romanticize the peasantry, mythologize the past, promote the ideas of cultural purity—which originate from the ideas of racial purity—and see themselves as keepers of the ancient traditions.

The folkloristic study of gangs focuses on particular aspects of a phenomenon that can be observed in the larger cities throughout the world. Poor social and economic conditions, loosening of family ties, domination of female heads of households, lack of male adult identification, and spatial segregation from the rest of the society are usually indicated as the main reasons behind the formation of a gang subculture. Most gangs recruit their members from racial or ethnic minorities, for whom membership in gangs becomes an important source of identity. In a study of African-American oral tradition, based on fieldwork carried out at the end of the 1950s in what at that time was a lower-class Black neighborhood in Philadelphia, Abrahams referred to distinctive characteristics of gang formation and gang behavior. This folkloristic inquiry into traditional oral performances of the people from the ghetto contains numerous insights into gang patterns in the neighborhood. For the youngsters living on the streets, the gang becomes one of the main forces of socialization. Organized as a loosely formed grouping, the gang gives the individual, who is generally male, the sense of belonging to a particular neighborhood and it offers protection from aggression by other similar groups. Obscene rough talk, a distinctive, colorful dress style, a characteristic way of walking and hair style have been indicated as parts of the image of gang members. A Gang lifestyle emphasizes and promotes manliness in both words as well as actions, ranging from general toughness, roughness, and mistrust toward women, via choices of profession and favorite heroes, to actual physical violence. In this context, folklore—in the form of proverbs, jokes, taunts, toasts, or catches—is used as a weapon in verbal battles and provides an important channel for control of expressions and anxieties. Winning verbal contests affirms the masculinity of the winner and demonstrates the femininity of the defeated. Such verbal battles generally follow specific rules by which the boundaries of the game are strictly predetermined so as to provide the means for the control of aggression.

In a 1988 study of Chicano gang subculture in Southern California, James Diego Vigil employs the concept of multiple marginality to explain why some members of this particular ethnic minority join and identify with gangs. He has observed a characteristic style of appearance called "cholo," a particular street identity required by everyday life in the street. Cholo, which actually appears marginal to both Mexican and American culture, consists of: (a) cholo front: dress, forms of speech, gestures, and body language; (b) street rituals: initiation and exit rites, gang warfare; and (c) symbols: tattoos and graffiti. According to this study, this particular image becomes a source of identification with the gang and with the territory that is under its control. Affiliation with gang style may be of varying duration: from short to lifelong membership. In Vigil's view, the difference among regular, peripheral, temporary, and situational gang members is central to an explanation of gang behavior, since it influences not only gang entrance and exit but even the likelihood of engaging in violent behavior. Scarcity of resources, discrimination, drugs, delinquency, and frustrations that result from an awareness of the inescapable cycle of poverty are listed as the main generators of violent behavior. Even though the presence of conflict is found in many aspects of gang life, Vigil's analysis points out that manifestation of conflict and violence within some particular gang formation is regulated and restricted. For example, a member who too often causes confrontation within the group runs the risk of being expelled from it. On the other hand, violence is considered obligatory when it is directed toward nonmembers of the gang, especially when it is used to defend the territory claimed by the gang, the boundaries of which are symbolically marked out by graffiti. The inquiry confirms that fighting between gangs is the main reason behind most contemporary gang violence. Such conflicts are increasing and they create numerous problems, especially in the large cities. A rivalry between gangs often has a long tradition that tends to be reproduced by group solidarity based on perceived differences in gang organization and culture.

One of the ways in which people cope with the increasing rate of violence in urban areas is by transforming their experiences into narratives. Particularly in the United States, folklore about crime in general, and narratives that deal with violence and criminal behavior in particular, have been identified as a part of the common cultural heritage. Eleanor Wachs collected and analyzed crime-victim stories that circulated in New York, a city that occupies a special place in American folklore as regards the issues of crime and violence. Crime-victim stories fall within the genre of urban folklore. Some of these stories are versions of urban legends. Mugging, murder, and rape are three types of narratives that have been distinguished. The stories focus on three characters: the victim (hero/heroine), the offender, and the occasional witness to the event. The pattern of resolution is predictable and appears in three forms: the offender manages to flee the scene, the victim somehow sneaks away from his/hers pursuers, or the police are called to intervene. Unlike the media reports on crime, the tellers of crime-victim stories are highly reluctant to talk about violence in concrete terms and tend to

use euphemisms instead. To a certain extent, however, these narratives transmit racial prejudices, since the offender in stories most often is Black. Crime-victim stories have several functions. They are used to transmit attitudes about life in New York, they provide information about required cultural and social codes for living, or they are told as cautionary tales to warn women, who make up the majority of victims, about how to protect themselves as well as how to avoid dangerous situations. It is believed that the wish to show others how not to become a crime victim is one of the main reasons that these stories continue to circulate.

The analysis of political violence—or state-sponsored violence—is probably one of the most complex research areas, folklore studies included. A special term "culture of fear" was created to direct scholarly attention to everyday experience of human rights violation. Originally, this term described the circumstances in Argentina, but in an extended meaning, it referred to the authoritarian regimes of several South American states that during the 1960s and the 1970s applied various forms of terror actions with purpose to eliminate political opponents. Organized state violence, which was supported by the control of media, as well as a permanent feeling of fear, deeply affected political, social, and cultural life in a variety of respects. When these regimes were transformed to nonauthoritarian, it became possible to analyze the mechanisms of the "culture of fear" and to examine the strategies people used to overcome pervasive powerlessness and anxiety produced by systematic state violence. For example, it was observed that silence and withdrawal to inward everyday life were the main ways of self-protection and survival. Victims of torture even described the significance of the gender dimension in torture sessions. The torturers, whose own perceived manliness was reinforced by the power to give suffering, had a tendency to humiliate men by feminizing them during torture. The humiliation was made more intensive by the use of jokes, music, and various sadistic acts. The torturers often chose animal nicknames for themselves, such as tiger, jaguar, puma, or gorilla, in order to emphasize their dominant position. Folklorists have otherwise indicated that cruel rituals used for creating bonds within male groups by emphasizing masculinity, such as rites of passage in the military, exist even in democratic societies. However, in the death camps of South America these were institutionalized and justified even by state religion.

In his 1991 ethnography, Alan Feldman studied the case of Northern Ireland and the cultural construction of political violence during the period between 1969 and 1986. He used oral histories to identify the types of spaces of violent exchange in the conflict between Catholic and Protestant communities. The analysis revealed a hierarchical continuum of such spaces, ranging from the individual body and extending to the confessional community, the state, and the imagined community of United Ireland and British Ulster. Each of these spaces was constituted around some specific shared cultural codes that reproduced the existing ideological and ethnic antagonisms. The interrelation among the spaces was accomplished through ideology and violence. The study has indicated that Protestant and Catholic communities demarcate their territory through specific historical and spatial arrangements, such as kinship and residence ties, ceremonial parades, or creation of myths. Rioting, commemorative parades, as well as ceremonial marching were identified as some of the mechanisms for establishing and extending territorial boundaries. By means of a calendric organization of the parades, people can channel ethnic violence into controlled forms, times, and spaces.

C. Folklore and War

Folklore collections contain reminiscences of war in various forms of folklore material. War is a context of extreme and unpredictable violence. It is characterized by chaos, terror, dehumanization, but even by creativity in developing strategies for coping with the situation. In a study published 1995, Kathleen Stokker has shown how jokes that ridiculed the Germans helped the Norwegian people who were opposed to Nazism to develop a sense of solidarity and resistance mentality during Norway's World War II Nazi occupation. Folklore studies on war primarily deal with different aspects of military folklore. The existence of a soldier subculture and its masculinity as manifested in clothes, songs, dance, slang, and various kinds of rituals, was observed already during the early modern period. It was not unusual among ordinary people at that time to have warriors and soldiers, whom they probably considered a form of protection, painted on cupboards. In the analysis of female warrior ballads, songs about heroines who were disguised in men's clothes in order to participate in war, Dianne Dugaw has directed attention to the often missing female perspectives on war. This study demonstrates how changes in social and historical contexts influence the gender dimension of aggressive behavior. Folklorists have not systematically analyzed wars. In studies on war, they usually examine some traditional folklore topic within the context of war. Collecting folklore material seems to be the main interest and the context of war is seldom problematized in these studies.

Some analyses of folklore material have pointed out the existence of taboos within the context of war. Taboo, the principle of social prohibition or the method of social control, is found in most cultures. It can appear in diverse forms, such as actions, words, names, sexual relationships, food, or social contacts. Chinome observed that practicing various kinds of taboos was common among both the guerrilla soldiers and peasants in Zimbabwe during the War of National Liberation. The taboos regulated different kinds of actions. For example, it was forbidden for combatants to eat certain kind of food, to mate, to sleep in houses, as well as to allow anyone not engaged in combat to carry weapons. It was even prohibited for menstruating girls to make food and enter the military base. Since the taboos had their origins in the precolonial era, they helped to establish a sense of homogeneity among the combatants.

In many parts of the world warriors prepared for battle or celebrated victory by ritually performing the conflict. War dance is a highly specialized form of folk dance with great variation in form and style. It can be classified on the basis of whether it is performed by men, women, or men and women together. In some parts of the world, such as in the Far East, dance performances include acrobatic scenes with weapons, or, as in some countries of South America, require specific masks. One of the most common forms of war dance is a stylized combat mime usually performed with weapons. Various types of sword dances still performed in Europe are some of the examples of ritualized reminiscence of conflict and war. The origin of sword dances, as folklorists believe, derives from ancient victory dances or military training exercises. Sword dances are today only performed during festivals and the original meaning of these performances has been completely transformed. *Moreska*, a sword dance that reflects rivalry between the Turks and the Arabs, can at present only be observed on the island of Korcula, Croatia. Professional folkdancers are dressed in rich costumes and their performance is interpreted as a symbolic struggle for freedom. *Moros y Cristianos* is another sword dance whose theme is the conflict between the Moors and Christians. Since the 15th century it has been performed annually on festival occasions in numerous Spanish cities. Folklore studies emphasize that one of the main purposes of this kind of dance today is to reinforce the integrity of the particular community within which the performance takes place.

Folk songs are considered another important means for establishing a sense of belonging and homogeneity among group members. Collections of folksongs performed during war consist mainly of military occupational folk songs, but still provide a specific inside perspective on the war. In the War of National Liberation in Zimbabwe, folk songs were an important part of oral traditions used by the liberation movement in the armed confrontation with the White colonial regime. According to folklorist analysis, the *Chimurenga* (Uprising) songs helped the combatants to emotionally cope with the war situation and raised their fighter spirit as well as their awareness of oppression. At the same time, folk songs documented and preserved the radical social transformation Zimbabwe was passing through.

Folk songs, together with the rock and roll music of the '60s, had an important role among American soldiers in the Vietnam War as well. Even references to popular music found their way into the language of the war: "rock and roll" meant fire from an M-16 on full automatic. Some of the collected folk songs were created especially for Vietnam and both the words and music were original. Otherwise, it was more common to set new lyrics to the already existing folk, country, or popular tunes. Most of the songs, however, were actually a part of the traditional military folklore of earlier wars: the First and the Second World Wars, the Korean War, and even RAF and British Army songs. These songs display traditional themes of the military folksong: praise of the great leader, celebration of heroic deeds, laments for the death of comrades, disparagement of other units, and complaints about incompetent officers. The civilians serving in Vietnam developed their own traditions and had a different song repertoire. It is interesting to note that the majority of folk songs from Vietnam were not collected by a professional folklorist, but by an air force general stationed in Vietnam. His collection of occupational folk songs provides folklorists with an inside perspective on the ways in which soldiers expressed emotions and the strategies they developed in order to cope with violence, fear, and frustration during the war.

Marching chants, a particular military tradition, have attracted minor attention among folklorists. This part of military training programs circulates not only from company to company but even from war to war. In time of war, marching chants make the recruits adopt the role of front-line soldiers, whereas in peacetime, they make them remember their predecessors. Folklorists who have studied the lyrics of this particular form of military folklore have indicated that marching chants provide valuable information about how some traditions and attitudes characteristic for military life are transmitted to new recruits. Offensiveness, whether in the form of insult to a superior, slaughter of innocents, or sexist objectification of women, has been identified

as the main characteristic of the chants. The chants assist the transition from civilian to military life through the verses that celebrate the displacement of sexual energy from the female left behind to the enemy waiting on the battlefield. The existence of particular projective folk characters was indicated in the lyrics of marching chants during the Vietnam War: "Jody," a reference to a trainee's nonprofessional life, the trainee's car, his girl, or his sister; "Charlie," a personification of the military/civilian enemy, "Slippery Sam," a marine soldier who fights against "Charlie," and "Mama," a character who is addressed to approve the use of violence. To a great extent, marching chants are used by soldiers as a way of controlling emotions, of establishing group cohesion, and of easing the strain caused by the demands of military training. Recently, some efforts have been made to prohibit the transmission of the most sadistic versions.

During the Gulf War, folklorists observed that many houses and public places in the United States were decorated with yellow ribbons and American flags. Two related traditions merged in this custom: the public assemblage and the symbolism of yellow ribbon. The custom of decorating public and private spaces with assemblage has become quite common in the country during recent decades. The old tradition of displaying a yellow ribbon as a sign of remembering the absence of a dear person emerged anew during the 1970s crisis with Iran. During that period, many Americans tied yellow ribbons to trees, on doors, and on facades of buildings. Two meanings of this custom were identified: showing absence and expressing welcome. During the Gulf War, the yellow ribbon became a patriotic symbol. During the calendrical holidays that occurred at the time of war, holiday decorations were combined with war symbols, which made the signification of assemblage even stronger. By displaying flags and yellow ribbons people not only declared their support for American troops but also found a way to cope with uncertainty and their inability to control and influence the war situation. Moreover, putting up war-related assemblage was an expression of a community-based unity.

Even individual creativity based on experiences during the Vietnam War has attracted folklorists' attention. One of the examples is the analysis of dioramas created by a disabled Vietnam veteran, in which he portrayed scenes of battle and military experiences, such as firefights, POW camps, torture pits, and ambushes. Three types of dioramas were identified: those dealing with situations familiar to most Vietnam veterans, those reflecting personal memories, and those based on stories told by other veterans. For folklorists, this work is an interesting example of folk creativity that is directly related to such narrative forms as war stories and ballads. The fact that dioramas are not for sale makes them characteristic of folk art. This example shows how personal war traumas can be dealt with creatively through artistic expression.

Everyday life in war is an issue seldom addressed in folklore studies. During the war in Croatia, scholars and folklorists found themselves within the war. Their accounts on war from an insider position provide a number of exceptional insights on how the war transforms everyday life and about the strategies that people use to deal with the everyday life in the context of war. Two main strategies were observed: (a) rituals, on the group level; and (b) routines, on the individual level. By performing a number of specific rituals in the form of nonviolent protests against the war, such as calls for peace, lighting candles, and mass gatherings in town squares, people were able to control their emotions and regulate their expressions during the time of stress. These rituals created a sense of solidarity among people who suddenly found themselves in similar extreme circumstances. For example, with the outbreak of war, the intellectuals as a group were confronted with a dilemma of what to write and whether to write at all during the war, or whether their position ought to be on the front line instead. For some of them, this dilemma resulted in an intense need to write about war and to inform others about the situation. An important part of the activity that emerged included sending letters and appeals to existing or symbolic addresses in foreign countries, which was meant to give the war an international dimension and provide a Croatian perspective on the evaluation of events. The sending of appeals was most intensive at the very beginning of the war, when it was thought that the confusion in international scientific and media reports was a result of a lack of information. Since most of the appeals received little attention abroad, this activity slowly died out. The existing image of the Balkans as the "other" in Western press and academic reports, of the war as a tribal conflict, was difficult to change. Routines, such as going to work and doing ordinary duties, became a way of coping with the situation on the individual level. The war even made necessary a redefinition of values: survival, family, home and the nation emerged as central values. An absence of humor was one of the indications that people were living in fear. The war context made the soldiers become visible as a subgroup. Folklorists observed a particular dress style, music, and speech. Some of the soldiers transmitted warrior images from films and television series. For example, this tendency can be ob-

served in the names given to a small number of military formations: The Turtles, The Terminators, The Hawks, The Gladiators, The Khmers, The Phantoms, The Daltons, The Garfields, Battalion Mickey Mouse, The Black Widows, The Ninja Mutant Turtles, or The Calamity Men. Even in this war, music had an important role in the front-line folklore: rock and rap were the dominant style. Songs were emitted through loudspeakers as a means of provoking fear in enemy troops as well as outvoicing their own songs. One of the most popular war songs was "Battalion Cavoglave," which communicates a resolute decision to defend Croatian territory from Serbian attacks. This song was composed by an amateur and recorded at the frontline. For a while, its release in the official media was forbidden, until it gained popularity among soldiers and ordinary people through alternative radio programs. The rituals of commemorating Croatian soldiers killed in the war were important for preserving the integrity of the particular community in which they took place. As the analysis indicates, the war transformed many of these rituals. For example, civilian occupation was no longer mentioned in obituary notices. Instead it was indicated that the deceased soldier was a Croatian guardsman, a member of the Croatian armed forces. Funerals changed into soldierly funerals, with uniformed soldiers in the funeral procession, the coffin covered with the Croatian flag, the decorations often in shape of the Croatian coat of arms, and the Croatian national anthem at the end of the ceremony. Folklorists analyzed the phenomena related to a commemorative board with photographs of soldiers that was placed at the central square in a small Croatian town. When one of the photographs was taken down, rumors started to circulate about the event. The commemorative board became a cult place that was visited not only by relatives and friends of dead soldiers but also by the official delegations that came to town. The board was decorated on the name-day of soldiers with wreaths, flowers, and candles. Even the annual holidays, such as Christmas, Palm Sunday, and Easter, were marked by placing ribbons or decorations characteristic for the holiday underneath the board. Through these rituals of compassion, the community, which experienced the war only indirectly through death of its young men, managed to preserve and strengthen its integrity.

Researchers also collected narratives and letters of refugees from Eastern Slavonia, a part of Croatia that was occupied by Serbian troops during the war. The potential of these documents is significant, inasmuch as they provide accounts of personal experiences of violence and fear as well as raising awareness about the human tragedy of the war. A plastic bag in which refugees carried their belongings, which they usually were ordered to pack in 15 minutes, became a symbol of the war. A large number of refugees gave birth to a folklore comparison with the Kurds. On the basis of personal narratives, researchers were able to analyze the issue of nutrition, a traditional research topic in folklore study, in the context of war. Personal narratives revealed how everyday life during the shellings turned into everyday struggle for survival in food shortages and chaos. People baked bread in ashes, as they had seen in an educational program on Australian aborigines. Many started smoking—mint tea leaves and corn leaves because of a lack of cigarettes—to be able to cope with tensions caused by constant bombings and life in shelters. To prepare food was an even greater problem than finding it. Women and children risked their lives to prepare meals between or during the shellings. These documents also have the potential to show how refugees keep or change their cultural tradition. However, researchers emphasized that the study of refugees, from all other possible war themes, caused the greatest moral and scientific dilemmas.

III. THE DILEMMAS OF FOLKLORISTS REGARDING RESEARCH ON VIOLENCE AND CONFLICT

Many folklorists who have studied violence and related themes in folklore have pointed out serious personal as well as professional dilemmas in connection with such research efforts. The mentioned dilemmas, however, do not seem to be as apparent among folklorists who study archival material as they are among those who personally encounter their informants during fieldwork. An issue that has been discussed concerns the potential effects of publishing studies that deal with material that can be viewed as delicate or provocative. There is always the risk that such publications will be perceived as sensational. Doing folklore research on political violence and on war in particular raises a number of ethical issues. Researchers also must be extremely cautious when interviewing refugees in war conditions or other victims of violence to carefully protect their anonymity. The researcher also has to be able to cope with his/her own emotions when confronted with the traumas of others. Studying violent topics may in some cases even involve personal danger. Finally, there is a dilemma as to whether researchers should collect folklore material without questioning the circumstances in which some of the informants or groups of informants live. On the whole, doing folklore research about conflict and violence is a complex and demanding effort that raises important ethical, methodological, as well as theoretical problems.

IV. PROSPECTS FOR FUTURE RESEARCH

During recent decades, the awareness that the dark side of folklore often has been neglected and left out of the research agenda has created a growing interest in the mutual relationship between identity-affirming folklore and its opposite destructive component. There is a trend toward studying the issues of conflict and violence from within the location in which they take place. Like other scholars who deal with similar issues, folklorists will have to solve problems connected with dangerous fieldwork, emotional dilemmas, or veracity of data. Having realized that comparative studies are necessary for mapping the historical and geographical distribution of folklore items as well as for their interpretation, many folklorists now call for the exchange of scholarly information across cultural and disciplinary borders. In this contemporary vision of folklore as transdisciplinary and integrative, folklorists will have to be prepared to accept multiple interpretations and to capture the interplay between national and international influences brought about by processes of globalization. Understanding folklore as partly universal and partly embedded into some particular cultural context benefits the systematic field research necessary to elaborate a conceptual framework within which to study and explain different aspects of the interrelation among peace, conflict, and violence. The existing folklore studies form a solid foundation for future research.

Also See the Following Articles

COLLECTIVE EMOTIONS IN WARFARE • ETHNICITY AND IDENTITY POLITICS • GANGS • MILITARY CULTURE • RITUAL AND SYMBOLIC BEHAVIOR

Bibliography

Abraham-Van der Mark, E. E. (1989). I don't discriminate, but . . . Dutch Stories about Ethnic Minorities. *Ethnologia Europaea. Journal of European Ethnology.* XIX,2,169–184.

Abrahams, R. D. (1970). *Deep down in the jungle. Negro narrative folklore from the streets of Philadelphia.* Chicago: Aldine Publishing Company.

Cale Feldman, L., Prica, I., and R. Senjkovic, R. (1993). *Fear, death* and resistance. *An ethnography of war: Croatia 1991–1992.* Institute of Ethnology and Folklore Research. Matrix Croatica. Zagreb: X-Press.

Chinome, E. (1990). The role of oral traditions in the War of National Liberation in Zimbabwe: Preliminary Observations. *Journal of Folklore Research,* Vol 27 (3).

Davies, C. (1990). *Ethnic humor around the world. A comparative analysis.* Bloomington: Indiana University Press.

Dugaw, D. (1989). *Warrior women and popular balladry 1650–1850.* Cambridge: Cambridge University Press.

Dundes, A. (1997). *From game to war and other psychoanalytic essays on folklore.* Lexington: The University Press of Kentucky.

Feldman, A. (1991). *Formations of violence. The narrative of the body and political terror in Northern Ireland.* Chicago: The University of Chicago Press.

Klein, B. (Ed.). (1995). *Gatan är vår! Ritualer på offentliga platser* (The street is ours: Rituals in public places). Stockholm: Carlssons.

Linger, D. T. (1992). *Dangerous encounters. Meanings of violence in a Brazilian city.* Stanford: Stanford University Press.

Mieder, W. (1995). The only good Indian is a dead Indian. History and meaning of a proverbial stereotype. *De Proverbio.* An Electronic Journal of International Proverb Studies. Vol 1. Nr 1.

Mitchell, T. (1988). *Violence and piety in Spanish folklore.* Philadelphia: University of Pennsylvania Press.

Stokker, K. (1995). *Folklore fights the Nazis. Humor in occupied Norway, 1940-1945.* London: Associated University Press.

Tower Hollis, S., Pershing, L., and Young, M. J. (Eds.). (1993). *Feminist theory and the study of folklore.* Urbana and Chicago: University of Illinois Press.

Vigil, J. D. (1988). *Barrio gangs. Street life and identity in Southern California.* Austin: University of Texas Press.

Vietnam. (1989). *Journal of American Folklore,* 102 (406).

Wachs, E. (1988). *Crime-victim stories. New York City's urban folklore.* Bloomington: Indiana University Press.

Gangs

G. David Curry and Scott H. Decker
University of Missouri—St. Louis

GLOSSARY

Gang (Malcolm W. Klein) Any denotable group of youngsters who are (a) generally perceived as a distinct aggregation by others in their neighborhood, (b) recognize themselves as a denotable group (almost invariably with a group name), and (c) have been involved in a sufficient number of delinquent incidents to call forth a consistent negative response from neighborhood residents and/or enforcement agencies.

Gang (James F. Short, Jr.) Groups of young people who meet together with some regularity, over time, on the basis of group-defined criteria of membership and group-defined organizational characteristics. In the simplest terms, gangs are unsupervised (by adults), self-determining groups that demonstrate continuity over time.

REASON FOR TWO DEFINITIONS The operational definition of what constitutes a gang is one of the major debates in research on gangs. Both sides in the debate agree that gangs are groups and are recognized as such by their members and those outside the group. The controversy is over whether the definition of gangs should include participation in delinquent or criminal behavior as part of the definition. Among senior gang researchers, James F. Short and Joan Moore are among those favoring the exclusion of delinquency criteria from the definition of a gang. They argue that discussions of the relationship between gangs and delinquency become tautological when the definition of gang requires such a relationship. On the other hand, a larger number of researchers, including Walter Miller, Malcolm Klein, and Irving Spergel, argue that the exclusion of delinquent or antisocial behavior from the definition of gang diffuses any study of the phenomenon beyond practicality. Since this definitional issue is far from resolved, one of each kind of definition is offered.

I. GANGS IN HISTORY

At least one biographer of Napoleon described his youthful participation as a leader in gang fights. The Sons of Liberty were described by British sympathizers as no more than a gang of delinquent youth. Accounts of the American Civil War include the threats against Lincoln made by a Baltimore gang and the effort of Jefferson Davis to intervene in a dispute between rival adolescent gangs in Richmond. Urban industrial development in the latter part of the 19th century brought

Copyright © 1999 by Academic Press.
All rights of reproduction in any form reserved.

a large influx of European immigrants into American cities. The children and adolescents of these immigrants became members of groups identified as gangs. In the late 1800s, youth gangs emerged in New York, Philadelphia, Boston, Chicago, St. Louis, and Pittsburgh. In those decades, Italians and Irish immigrants were overrepresented in the ranks of gang members. These gangs roamed the streets of their neighborhoods engaging in petty forms of property crime and conflict with members of rival gangs. As with today's gang members, these youth represented what were regarded as the lowest levels of the economic strata of their communities.

There was an apparent decline in gang activity between the last decades of the 19th century and the 1920s. This was the first such increase and decline to be recorded. This and subsequent rises and declines in gang activity have led some researchers to hypothesize that gang activity in the United States follows decades-long cyclical patterns. While the youth gangs were very different organizationally from the adult gangs of the prohibition era, it is worth noting that Al Capone and a number of his peers were members of delinquent youth gangs before moving into organized crime in adulthood. One of the most important of all gang researchers, Frederic Thrasher, did his work on the gangs of this period. Based on his observations of Chicago gangs, Thrasher concluded that gangs developed out of the spontaneous play groups of children and adolescents and were strengthened by conflict with other groups and community adults. The major activity of gangs, he noted, was the search for thrills and excitement. Fighting was the predominant activity, and fights with members of one's own gang were as likely as those with members of rival gangs.

During the depression and World War II, the United States again experienced a decline in gang activity. The postwar gangs differed from the gangs of the late 19th and early 20th centuries. For the first time, large numbers of African American, Puerto Rican, and Mexican American youths were involved in gangs. Also, levels of violence were higher than in previous periods of gang activity. This increased lethality has been attributed to guns and automobiles, a condition that would be magnified in the next great wave of gang activity.

The most recent wave of gang activity emerged in the 1980s. At the beginning of that decade, gang problems were recognized in only a few large cities, particularly Chicago, Detroit, New York City, Philadelphia, and Los Angeles. By the end of the decade, gangs taking on the symbols and names of the Blood and Crip "nations" from Los Angeles and the People and Folk "nations" from Chicago were appearing in large- and me-

dium-sized cities across the nation. Levels of violence were much higher than during any previous wave of gang problems, perhaps corresponding with even more widespread availability of automobiles and firearms. The spread of gangs in this most current wave of activity has been attributed on the one hand to the emergence of an urban underclass hopelessly separated from available economic opportunities and on the other to a youth culture that makes gang symbols, clothing, and language commodities available in large and small cities.

II. THE MAGNITUDE OF CONTEMPORARY GANG PROBLEMS

National surveys of law enforcement agencies have served to provide the most widely accepted assessment of the magnitude of the U.S. gang problem. In 1988, Irving Spergel and his colleagues found that 76% of 98 cities screened indicated the presence of organized gangs and gang activities. From reports from 35 of these jurisdictions, 1439 gangs and 120,636 gang members were tabulated. In 1994, the Office of Juvenile Justice and Delinquency Prevention established the National Youth Gang Center (NYGC) in Tallahassee, Florida. In 1995, the NYGC conducted its first assessment survey of the national gang problem. Of 3440 responding agencies, 2007 reported youth gang problems. The survey's total of 23,388 youth gangs and 664,906 gang members suggested that the most recent wave of gang activity is the largest ever experienced in the nation's history.

III. THEORIES OF GANG INVOLVEMENT

A. Cultural Theories

Two major bodies of theory have most frequently been offered as explanations of gang activity. The first of these are cultural theories. Subcultural theory has been characterized by two very different kinds of explanations. In one view, lower class youths find that they are failing to measure up to "middle class measuring rods." As a result these youths undergo what has been called a "reaction formation" and turn middle class values "upside down" to create subcultural norms. Youth gangs become repositories and mechanisms for transmitting these antisocial subcultural values. A very different perspective suggests that gang behavior reflects preexisting focal concerns of lower class culture. Hence, lower class youth who join gangs are not rebelling against the values of the adults in their lives but are simply taking on the values of lower class adults.

B. Social Disorganization Theories

Of the two major types of theories, social disorganization theories has the longer history. From Thrasher's research on 1920s gangs, he concluded that gangs were interstitial in the sense that they filled gaps in the institutional fabric in which youths grew into adulthood. Where families or schools were weak or ineffective in socializing a youngster, the gang took their place. In this earlier form, social disorganization theory placed its emphasis on interpersonal ties between members of a community. This led to a powerful critique of social disorganization theory as an explanation of gangs, because gangs existed in many comparatively poor communities where interpersonal ties were strong. Systemic control theory has been offered by Robert Bursik and Harold Grasmick as an enhancement to classic social disorganization theory. Under systemic control theory, interpersonal ties between community residents are only one level of social control. Two other levels are also important. These are control of parochial institutions such as schools and businesses and public resources such as government and police protection. Gangs then can emerge in communities where interpersonal ties are strong, but parochial or public control are weak.

C. Levels of Explanation

Gangs are collectivities. In terms of social organization, gangs fall somewhere between their individual members and their greater community context. Most studies of gangs have treated individuals gang members or communities as the level of analysis. Very few studies have incorporated differences in individual gangs into the analysis. In his 1997 presidential address to the American Society of Criminology, James F. Short called upon social scientists to attempt to include all three levels of explanation into their research on gangs.

IV. CORRELATES OF GANG INVOLVEMENT

A. Ethnicity and Gangs

Ever since the post-World War II resurgence of gangs, law enforcement records have indicated an overrepresentation of minority youth among the ranks of gang members. A national survey of police departments conducted by the National Institute of Justice supported this overrepresentation especially for African Americans and Latinos. According to that study 48% of gang members were African Americans, 43% Latinos, 5% Asian Americans, and 4% white. It has been argued, however, that police, and thereby police data, overly criminalize the activities of minorities. Survey research projects conducted in Denver, Colorado, and Rochester, New York, have reported far more White gang members than were found in surveys of police departments.

B. Gender and Gangs

From a study of police records conducted in the late 1970s, Walter Miller suggested that 10% of gang members were females. Several studies suggested that police departments have consistently underestimated gang involvement by females, at least until recently. A number of surveys based on different community contexts have reported that as many as 30% of all self-reported gang members are females. Her study of female gang members in New York City led Ann Campbell to suggest that female gang members were becoming more independent of males in their gang involvement. Joan Moore and Meda Chesney-Lind have challenged the perspective that gang involvement by females can be a "liberating" experience. From their separate research efforts in Los Angeles and Hawaii, they have argued that gang involvement for females results in levels of social injury sufficient to overshadow any level of personal actualization. A view that accepts both the findings of Campbell and those of Moore and Chesney-Lind suggests that gang involvement can provide females some level of agency in coping with the deprivations of their day-to-day existence, yet still result in social injury and enhanced risk of victimization.

C. Gangs and Community

As noted above, gangs can be considered as interstitial groups that are able to develop to the degree that other community institutions are weak. For this reason, one strategy for understanding gangs places them in the broader social context of other community institutions. Five social institutions that have been shown to have an impact on gangs are (1) families, (2) schools, (3) the criminal justice system, (4) politics, and (5) the labor market.

The family or household is the primary institution in community life and particularly in the lives of children and adolescents. The proposed connection between the emerging urban underclass and the most recent increase in gang activity is very important, since the institution most affected by the emergence of the underclass is the family. Where families were once the key socializing and supervising institutions for young people, families where they still exist are preoccupied by the struggle to survive. As a consequence, many young children grow up with little or no direction, and the need for socialization and order in their lives is often found on the streets. In many instances, gangs filled the void in juveniles' lives. Another factor linking families to gangs is the growing intergenerational character of gangs in some locales. When gang members and former gang members become parents, their children are at increased risk for gang membership.

After the family, schools are the most powerful socializing agent in the lives of adolescents. As is the case with families, the strength and stability of inner-city schools have suffered as a result of national-level changes in the economy over the last two decades. Just as strong families produce strong communities, strong communities have historically been associated with effective schools. This principle has an obvious converse. Weakened communities with struggling households produce schools that have a tenuous place in those communities and a limited capacity to prepare students for participation in mainstream society. The relationship between school and gangs has been conceived in two ways by researchers. In one perspective, gang involvement in schools drive students to skip school or to drop out in fear of gang violence. There is limited empirical support for this view. The more likely scenario is that it is gang members themselves who are pushed or pulled away from schools. Gang members are usually poor academic performers and are more likely than other students to violate school discipline codes. Administrators and teachers facing such unpromising and disruptive charges may do everything possible to force them out of school. On the other hand, the gang and its thrills and excitement may have a greater appeal to the student gang member than anything that the school can offer.

Another important institution, particularly in the lives of gang-involved youths, is the juvenile justice system. Research suggests that while most adolescents engage in some level of risk-taking or delinquent behavior, sanctions are more likely to be leveled against the minority youths most likely to be involved in gangs identified as such by law enforcement. In communities where families and schools are stronger, youths who do get in trouble with the juvenile justice system have more resources available to them with which to recover

from the stigma of a delinquent label. There is a great deal of evidence that incarceration may be an extremely important factor in increasing a youth's ties to gangs. In some juvenile facilities, gangs are extremely active. The incarcerated youth must choose between taking care of himself or relying on a gang for some margin of safety and protection. At the same time, being incarcerated can provide gang members with additional status when they return to the streets.

In the past, researchers have viewed gang involvement as a transitional phenomenon filling the gap between childhood and adulthood. The primary mechanism by which the transition was effected was through the young adult getting a job and eventually forming a family. A predominant feature of the urban underclass is the absence of linkages to the mainstream economy. Under the dramatic economic restructuring of the last two decades, there are few if any jobs to motivate a gang member to leave the gang. When there is no prospect for a job, there is even less likelihood of stable family formation. From family to labor market and back to family, the dearth of opportunities result in community conditions that foster the emergence and continuity of gang activity.

V. THE DYNAMICS OF GANG INVOLVEMENT

A. Gangs and Delinquency

One consistent research finding has been that gang youths engage in more delinquency than nongang youths. Surprisingly enough these findings come not from law enforcement data, but from surveys where both gang membership and delinquency are self-reported. Both cross-sectional and longitudinal surveys conducted in a variety of social settings have shown that youth who report being gang members also report higher levels of delinquency. In studies conducted in Chicago, Los Angeles, San Diego, Rochester (New York), and Denver, males were found to report more frequent and a wider range of delinquency than girls. Male gang members surpassed female gang members, but female gang members surpassed male nonmembers. Across all of these studies, gang members reported approximately three times as many delinquent offenses as did nongang members. Longitudinal studies have shown that levels of self-reported delinquency go up after youths join gangs and decline again after youths leave their gangs.

1. Gangs and Violence

In a national survey conducted in the late seventies, Walter Miller found that by far the most common defining characteristic of gangs offered by representatives of agencies dealing with gangs was violent behavior. Field researchers in the decades since have reached a similar conclusion. In a study of Milwaukee gang members, John Hagedorn reported that gang members were well-armed and have unactualized potential for engaging in violence. From another field study in St. Louis, Scott Decker described how gang members' lives were permeated with thoughts and actual incidents of violence. Many gang members report joining their gangs out of fear of gang violence only to discover that their risk of violent victimization is actually increased. Violence serves as a method of initiation for many gangs through "beating in" rituals or requirements to commit an act of violence against members of rival gangs. The day-to-day activities of gang members were characterized by violence, and even gang members' own proposed solutions for gang problems were violent in nature. Of the 99 gang members included in Decker's study which was published in 1996, 16 were dead by New Year's Eve 1998. In order to explain cycles of gang violence at the community level, a contagion model has been suggested. In such a model, subsequent acts of violence are directly linked to preceding acts of violence through an expanding network of retaliation. The central role of violence in gang life is evident in recent patterns in gang homicide rates. Between 1987 and 1992, the number of gang-motivated homicides in Chicago increased five times. In Los Angeles County, the number doubled in that same period of time. Most large cities with gang problems reported that in the early 1990s a larger and larger proportion of their city's homicide victims involved gang members. Some cities such as Chicago and St. Louis report that about one in four homicide victims are gang members. In Los Angeles County, authorities claim that nearly half of homicide deaths are gang members.

2. Gangs and Drugs

There are two very different opinions among researchers about the role of gangs in drug sales. The first argues that gangs run well-organized narcotics distribution operations. The other presents the contrary view that while individual gang members may engage in drug sales and especially drug use, organized drug-selling operations by gangs as organizations is comparatively rare. Interestingly enough, both of these very different perspectives originated from studies of crack distribution in California. One study was based on interviews with prison inmates and representatives of law enforcement agencies. Its authors concluded that many gangs are organized solely for the purpose of selling drugs. They characterized involvement of gangs in drug distribution as disciplined and structured. A principal conclusion was that many gangs in California effectively controlled the drug markets in their territory. The second study analyzed the official records on drug-related crimes in Los Angeles and several other jurisdictions. The authors of this study concluded that gangs did not control a significant portion of crack distribution and that drug-related crimes involving gang members were no less likely to involve violence than those that did not involve gang members. Subsequent studies of drug sales by gang members in other cities have supported one or the other of the two perspectives.

The key question underlying gang involvement in drug markets revolves around the nature of gang organization. In order for gangs to participate in drug distribution with any kind of organizational effectiveness, a stable leadership structure, member roles, shared goals, mechanisms for consistently disciplining members, and the ability to manage collective resources would all be required. Few studies of gangs have substantiated the existence of any of these features in contemporary gangs. In an extensive report issued in 1992, the District Attorney's Office of Los Angeles County concluded that gangs did not control drug sales in that jurisdiction because of their disorganized and loosely confederated structures.

B. Entering and Leaving Gangs

Gang members have been said to both "pulled" and "pushed" into gang membership. Those pulled into gang membership are attracted by the camaraderie and excitement promised by membership. In many communities, especially Latino and Hispanic, gangs represent a source of cultural pride and identification. A number of studies also quote gang members as stating their motivation for joining the gang to be profits from drug sales and other crimes. There is a general distrust of such professed gains from gang-related criminal activity among most researchers. Youths are pushed into gangs by the perceived threat of violence from other gangs and by the lack of other alternatives. As noted above, the supposed security provided by gang membership often is accompanied by greater risk of victimization. The lack of other alternatives can be represented by both a lack of economic opportunities and deficits in what James S. Coleman called social capital.

Whether a member is pulled or pushed into joining the gang, becoming a member is agreed by most researchers to be a gradual process requiring an extended period of trust-building and progressive participation. Most gangs do, however, have a recognized initiation process to mark the point at which a gang associate makes the transition to gang member. Most often this initiation involves violence. The most widespread procedure is being "beaten in." In the beating in process, the new initiate usually experiences a brief infliction of violence by current members. The next most common ritual is a requirement to inflict some kind of harm on a member of a rival gang or at least issue through some action a challenge to a rival gang's sovereignty. Such challenges usually involve assault on a rival gang member or committing an act of vandalism or a robbery in the rival gang's territory. Any initiation requirement is, however, likely to be waived for a younger sibling or cousin of a current member with some level of prestige.

Several incidents given attention in the media involve the initiation of female members by male gang members in mixed-sex gangs through a process described as "sexing in." The veracity of the most highly publicized incidents of this type have been subsequently challenged. In most cases, female gang members enter the gang in initiations similar to those required of males, most often being "beaten in" or required to perform a violent act against a rival gang. Most often the initiation of females is the responsibility of other females. In some incidents recorded by researchers, female gang members have "set up" females whom they did not really intend to include in their group for group rape or other abuse by male gang members.

There exists considerable mythology about leaving the gang among gang members. Media reports and gang members have attested that it is simply impossible to leave the gang. In some gangs, there is a myth that the member must kill a parent in order to leave the gang without experiencing the gang's wrath. The truth is that no such exit from a gang has ever been recorded. In some gangs, there is a ritual "beating out" comparable to the ritual "beating in." Based on studies from a number of cities, though, it is a very simple matter for members to leave their gangs. The major problem is that former gang members find little else to do outside of the gang. Gang members who try to leave too often find themselves hanging out with the same old associates and engaging in many of the same activities that they did as a gang member. The gang is where the former members friends are, and there are few opportunities, social or otherwise, to take their place.

VI. RESPONDING TO GANGS

A. Types of Response

Irving Spergel led a team of researchers in conducting a 1988 national study of promising gang intervention programs. From this study, four basic strategic responses to gangs were identified. These were suppression, social intervention, community organization, and economic opportunities.

Suppression was the most common reaction to gang problems in the 1980s. On one hand, it involved traditional criminal justice efforts to identify and incapacitate serious offenders. On the other, it involved enhanced networks between criminal justice agencies and the implementation of sophisticated intelligence-gathering techniques. The rise of suppression as the dominant response to gang crime problems in the 1980s may have been a function of growing political conservatism, or suppression may have simply been the easiest and most rapid response to implement in reaction to increased levels of gang violence. In most cases, the institutional instrument of suppression strategies has been police department gang crime units, many modeled after Los Angeles Police Department's CRASH (Community Resources Against Street Hoodlums) program. A 1992 national survey reported specialized police gang units in 53 of the 79 largest city police departments. Of these units, a majority were created after 1986.

The second most common strategy used as a response to gangs in the past has been social intervention. Social intervention strategies primarily have taken one of two forms—agency-based service programs and street outreach programs. In the agency-based programs, youth centers usually offer adolescents a secure setting in which to participate in structured recreational activities while receiving other kinds of services. One of the oldest and without question the most widespread agency-based program involved in gang response is the Boys and Girls Clubs of America. Frederic Thrasher evaluated a gang intervention program at a New York "Boys Club" in 1928. In a typical Boys and Girls Club in St. Louis, a gang prevention and intervention program is provided to specifically targeted youth at high risk of gang involvement. At the same time, the club offers water recreation activities (including kayaking), organized sports programs, music and art lessons, and even a free dental clinic. The other kind of social intervention program is street outreach. These programs have been called detached worker or street worker programs. In street outreach programs, workers approach and interact with youths on the streets of their neighborhoods where risk of gang involvement and youth violence is greatest. On the street, the worker provides counseling. From the street, the worker makes referrals to agency-based social intervention programs. Social intervention programs were the most common response to gangs in the 1950s, 1960s, and early 1970s. A study published by Malcolm Klein in 1971 on his research in Los Angeles questioned the effectiveness of social intervention strategies. When such strategies dealt with gangs members within the context of their gangs, Klein concluded that programs could increase the cohesion of the gangs.

The first large-scale gang response program was implemented under the leadership of Clifford Shaw, a University of Chicago professor, who had conducted extensive research on gangs in 1929. The Chicago Area Project was in its philosophy and structure a community organization strategy. Residents were empowered to elect the leaders of the Chicago Area Projects, of which the major goal was the strengthening of interpersonal ties within the community and greater community control over key institutions such as police, schools, and government. Subsequent community organization strategies were implemented in Boston, New York, and Philadelphia. A major criticism of these earlier community organization programs has been their inadequate or inconclusive evaluations.

The fourth response strategy to gangs has been opportunities provision. This response strategy is based on the importance of access to legitimate opportunities for avoiding and ending gang involvement. Opportunities provision strategies are financially costly and difficult to implement. Under this response strategy fall programs that provide job preparation, training, and placement for gang involved youths, as well programs that reintegrate younger gang members back into schools or alternative educational programs that can enhance their future employability. The 1988 national survey found that opportunities provision strategies were the least common of all strategies.

B. Major Gang Initiatives

In 1982, Walter Miller advised that any significant reduction in collective youth crime would require major federal initiatives. In the 1990s more federal and local initiatives responding to gangs were in place than ever before. In 1988, under the Omnibus Anti-Drug Abuse Act, the Youth Gang Drug Prevention Program under the Administration on Children, Youth, and Families (ACYF), U.S. Department of Health and Human Services (DHHS), was implemented. Between 1989 and 1996, this program established gang program consortiums in 16 cities and a diversity of single-agency gang prevention and intervention programs (including programs designed specifically for females, new immigrant youth gang members, and intergenerational gang families). Each year between 1991 and 1994, ACYF sponsored an annual conference designed to build skills, communication, and understanding among representatives of funded projects and other agencies with shared goals. Although the Youth Gang Drug Prevention Program was eventually phased out, it provided a model for a number of the programs that would follow.

Programmatic responses to gangs have emerged in conjunction with an unprecedented level of federally funded research on gangs. The Office of Juvenile Justice and Delinquency Prevention undertook a longitudinal research program in four cities to identify the causes and correlates of delinquency. The first wave of data was gathered in 1990. In 1991, an initiative on research on gangs was undertaken by the National Institute of Justice. Many of the findings cited in this article were generated by these research efforts. In addition to longitudinal research on gang involvement in Rochester, New York, and Denver, and the national surveys of law enforcement agencies about record-keeping and levels of gang activity, research was conducted on gang activity in correctional facilities, patterns of gang migration, and other topics with relevance for policy. In 1995, the Office of Juvenile Justice and Delinquency Prevention established the National Youth Gang Center in Tallahassee, Florida. The Center is responsible for maintaining updated information on the level of gang problems nationwide and serving as a clearing house for current information on gangs.

At least three major gang program initiatives with strictly defined evaluation guidelines were in place in 1997. The first was the Comprehensive Community-Wide Approach to Gangs implemented by the Office of Juvenile Justice and Delinquency in five cities. The Community-Wide Approach is generally known as the "Spergel model" because it was developed by Irving Spergel from his surveys and program analyses conducted between 1988 and 1992. The Spergel Model is primarily a community organization strategy with integrated social intervention, opportunities provision, and suppression components. As described in a set of 10 implementation manuals, the Spergel Model must at minimum involve law enforcement and grass roots agencies. Training manuals are also available for schools, youth service agencies, prosecution, the court, probation, and corrections. Once the mobilization is underway, any of the component agencies can be the lead or mobilizing agency. The model was designed to be tailored to the special needs of each individual community. The program's flexibility encourages local program planners to assess the special features of local gang problems and take advantage of local agency strengths. The guidelines for community mobilization are intended to facilitate interagency cooperation and minimize interagency conflict.

At the same time that the Spergel model was being developed, the Causes and Correlates Program was developing a systematic response to serious, chronic, and violent offending by juveniles. The model was based on a social development model emphasizing protective and risk factors and focusing on the influences of family, school, and community. A key principle of this response model (called the "Comprehensive Strategy") required the juvenile justice system to become part of a comprehensive continuum of services and sanctions for youth. Officials at the Office of Juvenile Justice and Delinquency Prevention have become convinced that the problems of serious, violent, and chronic offending and gang-related crime are related. In their most commanding initiative to date, the agency has undertaken the implementation of a combined program called Safe Futures in four urban sites, one rural site, and one Indian reservation. The Safe Futures Program combines both the Spergel Model and the Comprehensive Strategy. Initiated in 1996, funding for Safe Futures projects was larger and extended over a longer period of time (5 years) than funding for previous comparable efforts. Each program was required to incorporate a local evaluation and cooperate with a national evaluation.

In addition to community organization initiatives, two other kinds of gang response programs were implemented in the 1990s. A law enforcement strategy that ties suppression to community organization is community orienting policing. In 1996, the Community Oriented Policing Services (COPS) office in the Department of Justice launched a 15-city Anti-Gang Initiative. The 15 target cities were selected on the basis of their consistency in providing gang-related crime statistics to na-

tional surveys in the preceding decade. The local programs were encouraged to choose among a number of community policing strategies, including the improvement of data collection, the integration of law enforcement agencies into community-wide responses to gangs, and the provision of a safer setting in which less suppressive response programs could be given a chance to develop. The COPS office is coordinating the efforts of local evaluators from each site.

The final contemporary gang response program of note is school-based. Gang Resistance Educational Assistance and Training (GREAT) was modeled after the Drug Abuse Resistance Education (DARE) program. Under GREAT, uniformed police officers provide in-class training to fourth and seventh-grade students. GREAT is funded by the Bureau of Alcohol, Tobacco, and Firearms (ATF) of the U.S. Treasury Department. Initial evaluation results of GREAT suggest that the program has been successful in reducing gang participation by middle school children.

Also See the Following Articles

DRUGS AND VIOLENCE • ETHNICITY AND IDENTITY POLITICS • JUVENILE CRIME • MINORITIES AS PERPETRATORS AND VICTIMS OF CRIME • RITUAL AND SYMBOLIC BEHAVIOR

Bibliography

Curry, G. D., & Decker, S. H. (1998). *Confronting gangs: Crime and community*. Los Angeles: Roxbury.

Decker, S. H., & Van Winkle, B. (1996). *Life in the gang: Family, friends, and violence*. New York: Cambridge University Press.

Huff, C. R. (1996). *Gangs in America*. (Second Edition.) Thousand Oaks: Sage.

Klein, M. W. (1995). *The American street gang*. New York: Oxford University Press.

Moore, J. W. (1991). *Going down to the Barrio: Homeboys and homegirls in change*. Philadelphia: Temple University Press.

Spergel, I. A. (1995). *The youth gang problem: A community approach*. New York: Oxford University Press.

Gender Studies

Lynne Woehrle
Wilson College

GLOSSARY

Gender One's socially constructed identity as male or female. May or may not be identical to one's biological sex characteristics.

Essentialism Assumes that all in some social category (e.g., gender) are the same and therefore have a shared experience. Failure to take into account the multiplicity of social identities.

Feminism Theories and practices that challenge male dominance and privilege. Critiques patriarchal power relations.

Intersectionality A theoretical perspective that analyzes social structures and relations from and at the points where various categories (e.g., race, class, gender, etc.) intersect. Argues that oppression is not an additive model (e.g., race+class+gender) but a dialectical model.

Marginalization Placing a person, group, theory, or practice to the edge of society. Includes exclusion from institutions and social relations. May include silencing, severe disempowerment, and the exclusion from participation in the creation of dominant knowledges.

Patriarchy A hierarchical system of power relations that is based on male privilege.

Privilege Access to or control over social power and resources that provide power. Often its presence seems invisible.

Womanist Theoretical and activist perspective of women of color that critiques male privilege and White privilege. Points out the essentializing nature of White feminism.

GENDER STUDIES is a multifaceted field of inquiry into social structures and social relations that has important implications for the study of violence, peace, and conflict. In gender, analyses are tools that are applicable to a wide range of social concerns. This article summarizes the field of gender studies in order to consider the contributions that gender analysis brings to inquiries into violence, peace, and conflict. An area in its own right, gender studies focuses on the implications of values, actions, and systems formed on the basis of definitions of and beliefs about masculinity and femininity. Suppositions in the theories of gender mesh well with the normative approach of peace and conflict studies. This essay considers the influence that gender studies has and can have on thinking about violence, nonviolence, war and peace, communication, and mediation.

Copyright © 1999 by Academic Press.
All rights of reproduction in any form reserved.

I. OVERVIEW

Gender studies does not offer a single, unified approach to understanding the phenomenon of gender. The very interdisciplinary nature of the topic and the variety of areas from which gender analysis has emerged means that there are various and at times conflicting streams of thought about gender and its meaning and origins. One point of discussion revolves around whether role theory and socialization theory adequately explain the emergence and perpetuation of the basic concept of gender.

A related discussion revolves around to what extent gender emerges from nature or nurture. While there seems to be a general sense that both nature and nurture contribute to the creation and reification of gender and gender differences, there is little agreement over how much to attribute to one explanation or the other.

A third area of discussion evolved in recent years around the relationship of gender to other social categories that can be coupled with privilege and hierarchy to create systems of inequality. Most often discussed are the relationships of race, class, and gender. Some theorists also add sexuality and ability as important categories through which processes of differentiation, "othering," and therefore inequality can be rationalized by those with the privilege of power. Although processes of sexism, racism, classism, heterosexism, and ableism vary in the specific ways in which they operate in social structures, each shares a dependence on a hierarchical system of power relations for continued existence. Identifying the operation and effects of those power relations is a central component of gender studies.

For this reason, gender studies cannot merely analyze gender but it must also case a critical eye to the larger systemic nature of social inequality—power and privilege. Of particular interest to those doing the critical work of gender analysis should be those points of intersection with other systems of inequality. It is those points that help us to realize that the root of inequality is not simply gender differentiation, but that larger system of the protection of privilege for a small elite of the world's citizens. While research often focuses on the problems of the oppressed, recent writing in gender studies has opened a discussion of the importance of identifying the role of privilege (the access to and power over social power and economic capital and the ability or recognized "right" to invoke that power) in perpetuating systems of inequality.

Thus while the very creation of a category such as "gender studies" serves to encourage us to notice how gender operates in social relations (an important insight) it also serves to discount the very power of privilege in its ability to combine multiple levels of exclusion and oppression. Therefore if we think of a gender analysis as narrowly focused on differences between men and women, we make invisible the important variances in experience and power brought by being a *White* woman or a *Black* woman (or working class vs. middle class). And we may miss that Black men do not carry the same social or economic power as do White men, yet their gender does shape their life chances as different from Black *women*. For this reason many scholars now encourage a multifaceted view of inequalities. To miss working at the intersections is to reinforce the idea that there is an essential concept of "woman" or "man" that can be applied regardless of the other social categories in which one may be entrapped. Recognizing the multiplicity of power relations and that inequality is not just about a "lack of" but also about overconsumption gives clearer insight into how systems of inequality are maintained and enforced and this can assist the project of emancipation. It also points to the responsibility the "haves" hold in creating social change and reminds us that the categories of "have" and "have not" are a false dichotomy that oversimplifies the complex web of relations of power.

In this article I attempt to keep the intersectionality of gender analysis consistently present. This is not easy for many reasons. My personal social location is one of White privilege and the educated elite. Although I have visited cultures different from my own, I cannot begin to claim to be a voice of expertise in anything beyond my own historical experience and current social location. In writing this I am offering an interpretation of the concept of gender studies grounded in the work of many academics and activists, but still seen through my own particular lens.

The relevance of gender to the study of violence, peace, and conflict is significant. My intent is to show how the analysis of gender has over time opened new insights into each of these areas. I work from the understanding that the dominance of White, male, heterosexual, middle- and upper-class privilege is the primary point from which most analyses of violence, peace, and conflict emerge. Invoking the process of gender analysis suggests a beginning means for showing just how multidimensional these issues really are when studied in a global context. I introduce approaches to gender analysis and some of the major contributions that emerge from the use of a gendered lens to view topics as diverse as war, social movements, nonviolence, and national politics.

II. WHAT IS GENDER?

A. Theoretical Explanations of Gender

One place to enter gender studies is through the discussion of "What is gender?" According to Myra Marx Ferree and Elaine J. Hall, theoreticians suggest three different ways to understand gender. One perspective, the "sex differences approach," assumes a natural and biological differentiation of male and female at the base of gender development and tries to measure the importance of these differences by removing and ignoring the influences of socialization. A second perspective that they suggest is the "sex roles approach" (others call it the socialization model), which argues that there are masculine and feminine roles that are "quasi-permanent" and that males and females take on early in childhood through a process of socialization. Both of these models emphasize an individual level of causality rather that the influence of social structures on the daily basis. Critics of these two approaches suggest that they make gender look as if it happens naturally or, equally problematic, as a matter of individual choice. The pressures and constraints operating in society and throughout our lives are virtually ignored.

A third model explored by Ferree and Hall is the newest, the "gender as a system of stratification approach." This theory argues that gender is constantly produced and reproduced as a means of maintaining a system of inequality. Socialization thus becomes a means for maintaining gender difference rather than an analytic end. This approach connects the microlevel to the mesolevel of groups and the macrolevel of social structures of the political economy to help understand the creation and maintenance of gender. The establishment of a gendered sense of society creates the potential for systems of inequality.

If we actually believed that sex was a continuum rather than a dichotomy, it would be much more difficult to establish membership in distinct groups and to create a hierarchical ordering of society. This perception is similar to the argument that race is a system of artificial categories that allows for the perpetuation of inequality. Gender analysis points out the ways in which we have taken a series of rather discrete variations and developed categories that make it possible to use those categories to reify the hierarchical systems of power.

B. "Doing Gender"

In a 1987 article (a classic in the field) West and Zimmerman make a persuasive argument to view gender as "an achieved property of situated conduct" (p. 126). This means that while we as individuals "do" gender, or act out what we understand to be appropriate behavior for the gender category to which we believe we belong, that doing of gender must be understood in its social context. When we act as a gender, it is to convince other members of society that we are either male or female. Thus gender emerges from social situations. It was this argument that laid the groundwork for more recent analyses that understand gender as a product of social systems rather than of individual conduct. Once you see your gender as an action rather than as a static role, it makes it possible to understand how gender can be the basis for enforcing a system of privilege and oppression.

One way to notice the social construction of gender is to look for points of resistance to gender roles. Transvestite, transgendered, and transsexual communities are often raised by theorists as an example of the process of doing gender. These communities show that it is possible to be biologically in one sex category while doing the gender activities of the other sex. In this case the biological appearance and how the person was raised as either male or female does not coincide with how he or she actually identifies. This process of convincing others of your gender is highlighted by the public presence of these communities. However, it is important to understand how traumatic it is for the individual who must transgress social codes and risk stigmatization to be what he or she believes himself or herself to be regardless of his or her biological makeup. Listening to these communities can help us perceive how central the gender dichotomy is to the structure of society. If I cannot tell whether you are male or female, how am I supposed to act toward you? We have such deeply embedded structures of gender in society that we will risk everything to fit "properly" into one group or the other. And those who transgress strict gendered social codes are marginalized and stigmatized.

C. Cultural Comparisons

I acknowledged in the beginning of this essay that my social context shapes the purview of my analysis. Culture operates in a similar way on gender. Gender seems to play a role of categorization throughout history and across cultures, but the importance of those categories varies with time and place. Over time, patriarchal societies have been quite common and today we know little else. Those cultures where male dominance is not a primary value are marginalized and in some cases nearly extinct in the world today. One of the dictates of the patriarchal system that has so much economic and political power is that competing systems of power sharing are destabilizing. To continue to be seen as a natural social order patriarchy must make sure that other alternatives are unattractive at best. Many global inhabitants have little idea of what alternatives are possible and have existed throughout history. For example, little is known by the average person about cultures that are fighting to keep matriarchal structures and traditions alive. Early colonial powers and missionaries expected all cultures they encountered to be patriarchal and dealt in those terms. If patriarchy was not already the ruling system of power, than some semblance of patriarchy was introduced.

D. Media and Cultural Representations

One way of showing how gender operates in society is to turn a critical eye to the media and cultural representations of gender. There are many ways in which the media serves to reinforce gender identities and inequalities but one of the most explicit is in advertising. Most advertisements have some direct or indirect reference to the masculine cowboy motif or to the feminine, thin, sexy, and vulnerable motif. Advertising reinforces the belief that men rescue and women are rescued. It also reinforces a false norm of heterosexuality. Through advertising we get hundreds of messages each day about the gender standards of our particular society and images of how to "do gender" in a successful way. Popular television shows (and even the news) and successful advertising campaigns have found that without a little sex and lots of violence (often sexist and racist violence) it is hard to sell a show or a product. Since on average we watch between 5 and 7 hours of television a day it is clear that this inundation of ideas must impact how we understand the world.

Moreover we might argue that media is the modern-day colonizer. The disproportionate affluence of White Western societies is portrayed in the media as is the "proper" means for succeeding at catching the "golden ring" or achieving the mythical "American Dream." A clear message is that acting in so-called "gender appropriate" ways is an important part of achieving wealth and privilege. This is yet another way of focusing on the individual rather than on social systems as the cause of failure or success.

Beauty contests are another concrete example of gender analysis of colonization and violence. Beauty has very different meanings from one society to the next. However, anthropological studies of beauty *contests* suggest that there is another level at which beauty operates and that it has important sociopolitical implications. Beauty *contests* predominantly (although not exclusively) focus on conceptions of female beauty. The international structure of beauty contests that have emerged in the last 40 years is not about a multicultural definition of beauty. These contests have come to represent the transference of White Western definitions of beauty. Regardless of local conceptions of beauty, these contests are often about looking like the Hollywoodized images of super models that help supply the images used to socially construct femininity and female beauty in places such as the United States. Images of beauty in these contests provide artificial and mostly unreachable goals and demand constant work on women's part to maintain the status of beautiful. The mono-definition of beauty offered by contests such as Miss World and Miss Universe helps to perpetuate the marginalization and domination of cultures that are not White and Western. These contests reflect and reinforce through gender dichotomies the social inequalities of the global political economy. And perhaps more disturbing is the link between the international scope of these contests and the industry of sex tourism. The contests create a globally dominant definition of beauty that is white and western, protected and desexualized. Held in contrast to this is the "forbidden" or "exotic" sexualized beauty of indigenous women who would never win a contest but are fair game for commodification through sex tourism and as prostitutes around military bases. Representations of beauty become a link in the global chain of misogynistic violence.

III. VIOLENCE AND MASCULINITY

A. Male Power and Privilege

Gender studies, which grew out of feminist social critique and the feminist movement to end sexism, concerns much more than studying the ways in which women are oppressed in various social conditions. Recognizing the way in which gender operates in a society demands that we understand the experience of males. This is not a singular experience because other sources of categorization, such as race, class, and sexuality, enter into the larger picture of male experiences. The naming of "male privilege" hides important adjectives that go along with that expression. When we look more closely at the intersections of race, class, and gender, we can see that the privilege of being male is a different experience for White, middle/upper-class males than it is for other groups of men.

This can affect men's relations with women. The most privileged men may view their advantage as natural and can justify it based on the rationale that they are better and more prepared than are women and other men. It is to their benefit to exclude women on the basis of gender and to view the power that they have as a failure on women's part to be strong enough or masculine enough to compete. Thus men's power over the so-called "weaker sex" is justified in biological and historical terms, and the social structures of oppression and exclusion are ignored. Male power is often reinforced with physical violence, an arena in which men generally have a clear advantage over women.

Men who are not in the most privileged categories may have more of a sense of inferiority and thus have a different and more complex relationship with women's oppression. As author bell hooks suggests, men in the traditionally oppressed and underrepresented groups can be an ally for social change if they embrace the goal of ending sexist oppression. On the other hand these men can also contribute to perpetuating sexist oppression if they believe that exercising their physical power over women is a means for joining the club of the elite privileged male. In this way, Manning Marable in his essay in Messner and Kimmel's book, *Men's Lives,* suggests that men of color and with lower incomes manipulate women in order to try to make up for the disempowerment that they feel elsewhere in their lives. Perhaps controlling women or the family as a whole is their one means of feeling good about themselves.

Studying the impact of cultural assumptions about masculinity and the intersections of gender with other categories is an important strategy for understanding violence and nonviolence, and conflict and peace and the various experiences of these social interactions. Studying "domestic violence" as an important issue in peace studies means unpacking the complex layers of gender in which it is embedded. If we can see beyond a sense of isolated victims and bad individuals we can explore the ways in which gender, race, and class structures of inequality are an integral part of violence that happens on a seemingly personal level.

B. Sports and the Military

Two important areas for the study of how masculinity is socially constructed are competitive sports and the military. In many societies competitive sports, particu-larly those that operate at a professional level and actu-ally pay players for their efforts are very much male dominated. The major lesson about masculinity that boys/men learn from participating in sports is that strength and competitiveness equals power. Studies of sport, such as the research done by Michael Messner in his 1992 book, *Power at Play,* suggest that boys/men have to be taught to endure and accept the physical pain that comes with sports. Moreover, those who play over a period of years integrate the image of self-as-athlete and therefore strong and dominant directly into their sense of identity. To stop playing sports then becomes devastating because the loss of sports means the loss of masculinity.

Messner also suggests that for many men sports is a primary means for forming bonds with other men. These bonds are formed on the basis of the exclusion and often the ridicule of women or of the concept of being female. In both sports and in the military, boys/men are pushed to try harder by a fear of becoming "the other" and being ridiculed as having female-like characteristics. To call a boy a "girl" or a man a "woman" is to threaten his sense of self. Through the socialization of the "tough guy" in sports and the military, men learn to hate and fear femininity and to see it as a loss of privilege. In this way both institutions (sports and the military) help perpetuate misogyny.

This apparent association of female with weak and male with strong and successful is rife throughout military organizations and the history of modern warfare. An excellent analysis of the embedded masculinity in military organizations appears in the work of Carol Cohn, writing in her 1987 article in *Signs,* "Sex and Death in the Rational World of Defense Intellectuals," about her firsthand observations of "nukespeak" among military leaders and strategists. This, coupled with accounts of misogynist training rituals in the preparation of military recruits and the barring of women from positions of power and honor in the military, suggests means by which we can do a structural analysis of gender inequality and its relationship to masculinity.

IV. PATRIARCHAL GENDER RELATIONS AND VIOLENCE

A. Violence against Women

Violence against women by men is a means of controlling women and maintaining or enforcing male privilege. Male privilege is the mainstay of a patriarchal system. Violence against women is linked to all other forms of violence that are perpetuated by the model of dominant and dominated that is basic to Western models of hierarchical rule. Thus it is a system of rule and not a biological function to dominate. As bell hooks argues, there are many ways in which women also use this system to dominate others, including other women. As children we are consistently exposed to the idea that violence is the most effective way to deal with conflict.

However, blatant violence against women happens so often because it is accepted as a means of enforcing patriarchal rule. Violence against women is evident in social institutions beyond those discussed above (competitive sports and the military), and beyond the domestic scene, which is where most violence against women is thought to exist. Across many cultures violence against women is a means of channeling female sexuality. In some cultures it is believed that women's sexuality is very strong and men fear its release. For example in the United States when a woman is raped, often one of the first questions is "What was she wearing?" Probably more important in most patriarchal systems is whether men can be sure of paternity in the birth of their sons.

Violence against women can enter into struggles to maintain culture against outside influences. Women are often pawns in the practice of state politics. And women as a group seldom have much say in the processes of foreign relations. Sometimes women are the victims of violence used in the resistance of external influences. Two examples of this are explored in Moghadam's work, including *sati*, the tradition of wife-immolation in India, which has been revived in recent years by religious traditionalists in resistance to the introduction of values perceived to be Western and the increasing influence of modernity. Also the sometimes violent enforcement of *hijab* and seclusion is argued by some to be a resistance to the cultural colonialism of Western economic and military powers.

Women also feel the violence of state politics in wartime. There are plenty of examples throughout history where the rape of women is a conscious strategy of warfare and cultural genocide. Perhaps most vividly in our mind in recent years is the use of rape in the Bosnian war as documented in Beverly Allen's 1996 book *Rape Warfare*. But this is not a new concern; perhaps more surprising is that it is still used as a strategy in the late 20th century despite a clear exposure of its basis in power rather than in sexuality.

The use of rape in warfare reminds us that in a patriarchal social structure women are viewed as property. Many historical precedents in Western legal code are based on this objectification of women's bodies as property of men. We still have not shaken patriarchal roots that pass a woman from her father to her husband to her son. It is this objectification of women as property that makes it possible to believe that violence against women is a plausible means for gaining power over women or over other men related to the women against whom the violence is directed.

There is a parallel practice that shores up White privilege. The view of Blacks as property was the basis of the slave trade and it is not completely erased from contemporary social relations. In the modern world we have pervasive racism. We also have female sexual slavery, a common practice among White men visiting and working in other cultures. We have seriously underpaid women workers who live in poverty but work more than full-time jobs and will not resist because they are dependent on the small wages they receive. These women are employed by multinational corporations, a majority of which are based in the wealthy, economically dominant countries of the world. It is the depersonalization of women historically that makes it possible for such relations to continue.

Perhaps the most vivid example of backlash violence against movements to end sexist oppression is the murder of 14 women at the University of Montreal's Ecole Polytechnique in Montreal, Canada, on December 6, 1989. As the women sat among approximately 60 of their fellow engineering students in a classroom, 25-year-old Marc Lepine entered the room with a semiautomatic rifle and fired two shots at the ceiling while yelling "You're all a bunch of feminists, and I hate feminists." He told all the men to leave and despite the attempts of the women to calm him he shot 6 of them dead. He then visited the cafeteria and other classrooms. In the end 27 men and women (mostly women) were shot; 14 of them, all women, died. He then shot himself.

They were by no means the first or the last women or men to pay a high price for the cause of social change. What was so stunning about this particular crime was that the 14 women killed were not in the process of doing any specific feminist work that day. They were killed because they were women and because they happened to be present at the time when the killer decided to take revenge on a world that he felt had unfairly treated him because he was a man. It is unusual for the work of ending sexist oppression to bring such direct violence, but the 1989 incident highlights the deep anger that can be felt by those who stand to lose their privileges should patriarchal relations be eliminated from our social structures.

B. Homophobic Violence

An important part of the patriarchal gender system is the privileging of heterosexual intimate relations. The social construction of heterosexual as the norm is achieved in a number of ways, one of which is the repression of homosexuality through homophobic violence. Many people are surprised to learn that with the increasing public presence of homosexuals in social institutions and throughout daily life, violence against homosexuals has increased. Besides ridicule, discrimination, and general social exclusion, homosexuals are constantly faced with threats and acts of physical violence if they make their sexuality public knowledge.

V. FROM HISTORY TO THEORY: INTEGRATION OF GENDER

Utilizing gender analysis can happen at several levels. Women's studies theorists have long argued that there are three stages of taking the integration of women seriously; this three-part model is relevant to gender analysis as well. In the first stage the history of participation of the silenced actor or concept is reclaimed, named, and included. Feminist movements over the years have left a wake of books and articles about women's contributions. In the second stage women are included in the larger picture, and books written by women may be part of the course, or a cited reference. A study may include a more diverse sample. In research terms being a woman or the category of gender becomes a variable for analysis. This stage is often referred to as "add-and-stir" gender studies.

In the third stage, which expresses the highest level of integration, gender or female is not merely a variable but it becomes a paradigm of analysis. So, for example, in studying social inequality one would not just control for gender, but rather the larger social context of patriarchal systems would guide the development of the analysis. Two books written in the 1980s help guide the emergence of the third stage in U.S. gender studies: Carol Gilligan, *In A Different Voice* (1982), and Mary Field Belenky and colleagues, *Women's Ways of Knowing* (1986). Perhaps a more important influence, however, is the theories of intersectionality that have been generated by womanist theorists writing about feminism from the margins of society. It is these African American, Latina, African, and Asian scholars and activists who chart the way for seeing the multidimensions of gender and oppres-sion. In the two sections that follow I give examples of the potential for integration of gender analysis into two areas of peace and conflict studies.

A. Gender, Conflict, and Conflict Resolution

For centuries women have played central roles in conflict and in resolving conflict. As discussed above women's bodies have been violently abused as a strategy of escalation in conflict. Women have filled the wartime industries, making it possible for more men to join combat. Women in significant numbers have joined revolutionary armies, particularly in colonial and post-colonial societies. On another point in the spectrum women have participated in and led nonviolent confrontations throughout the world, documented at least as far back as when Hebrew women hid their sons in the bulrushes to protect them from the Pharaoh.

Carrying the precepts of gender studies into research on conflict demands that gender (and thereby other relevant social categories as discussed earlier) be introduced into the analysis. In studies of conflict and conflict resolution, gender is currently introduced primarily as a variable rather than as a social paradigm. Therefore, most study of gender in conflict has tended to look at the influences of sex category differences in behavior rather than in the way in which gender operates in conflict and conflict resolution. Exceptions to the "variable approach" are evident in work that views conflict and conflict resolution as situated in a particular social system, such as patriarchy. This research then considers how a woman's identity as female and her experience growing up as a female in a system of male dominance impact on her attitudes and approaches to conflict. There is also comparison in this approach of male and female views toward conflict situations and toward the possible range of solutions. A further step is to see that the very conflicts and any possible resolutions themselves are embedded in the system of power relations in a particular social structure. In many cases power is controlled mostly by men, by Whites, by heterosexuals, and by the upper and middle classes.

The ways in which dominant systems of gender shape our experiences of conflict are also apparent in research on communication. It is argued that in the process of learning how to be masculine or feminine we also learn different styles of communicating. Women and men also develop different expectations for when and how communication should happen. These differences are thought to be an important source of conflict between men and women. Conflict styles also seem to differ, not for biological reasons but because of social messages that encourage women to please and to submit (and thereby women practice conflict-avoiding behavior), and that teach men that conflict is a power of wills and that winning is what is ultimately important.

But how we conflict and communicate is not only about gender. It is also about race and class and the many other social categories that place us either in positions of power or of dominance. The work of bell hooks in *Feminist Theory from Margin to Center* highlights that there are alternatives to the two major White Western models of deling with power: (1) dominant/submissive relationships where someone must be on top, or (2) a separatist model in which the answer to power inequalities is for the submissive party to exclude the oppressor. As a woman who lives at intersections of race, class, and gender oppressions, she rejects the White feminist claim that gender oppression is the root of all other oppressions and calls for a multifacited understanding of power relations.

In the early 1980s an important contribution was made by feminist theoreticians to the field of conflict resolution. A series of critiques of mediation as an alternative to the court system emerged from the literature of feminist jurisprudence. The conversations that emerged broke down the dominance of male-centric theory and practice in the field. The critique held that mediation at times lacked the structure that disempowered women needed to negotiate fair outcomes. The very unstructured process of mediation, it was argued, could at times reify power imbalances that existed in relationships between men and women within the U.S. patriarchal culture. Moreover, as Deborah Kolb suggests in her 1988 book *Her Place at the Table*, having learned different negotiation styles and having different levels of power, women may be at a disadvantage in current practices of mediation and arbitration. Knowing what we do about cultural differences in handling conflict and the power implications of race and class it is likely that our options for negotiating and solving problems are really much wider than current literature and practice suggests. The study of how social categories (e.g., race, class, gender) and cultural factors may deeply change how we relate to, define, enact, and resolve conflicts is a desperately needed area of research.

Feminist critiques of conflict resolution opened a space for seeing gender and other categories of powerlessness and inequality as relevant to the mediation process. What had been seen as a neutral process to be used as a tool to reach fair solutions became problematic. In the years since that critique the field has paid increasing attention to the social structures behind and around both interpersonal and international conflicts.

While this means that theorists have had to struggle with the implications of admitting the process is not actually neutral (this is still a source of debate) there is increasing sensitivity to the importance of the context of the conflict and the layers of power relations that must be dealt with in seeking a resolution. It is also more widely accepted that there are situations in which severe power imbalances make mediation an inappropriate solution in and of itself. Moreover, in recent years critiques have turned toward the patriarchal and Western origins of the dominant models of mediation theory and practice. The latter issue is also emphasized in postcolonial feminist literatures that point to the control White Western theories have over academic explanations of conflict, social movements, and social change. There are important insights for theorists of conflict and mediation (who are still predominantly White and Western) in the work of postcolonial critiques such as Audre Lorde, bell hooks, Angela Davis, Chandra Mohanty, and Patricia Hill Collins, among others.

B. Gender Studies and Nonviolence

One of the more interesting debates to emerge from the intersection of gender analysis and the study of peace, violence, and conflict is whether women are more peaceful than men. Some writers have carved out a particular place in history for women as peacemakers. These theorists claim that by nature and through the experience of mothering women are more apt to oppose violent responses to conflict. In a sense peacemaking is a niche that women can claim. The question in gender analysis, however, is not a static association of women with peace or men with war; rather, it is to ask whether the gender system in any way shapes our relations to violence or nonviolence.

Looking at women's participation in nonviolence provides an example of moving through the levels of integrating gender analysis into the study of peace. The historical reclaiming of memories about women's nonviolent actions was one of the first rewritings of peace studies to be more gender inclusive. There are hundreds of books and articles that document the nonviolent actions of women around the world, throughout history. But there is minimal recognition of gender as a means of analyzing the philosophy of nonviolence or the specifics of nonviolent action. The small group that works on the latter project exists among the margins of theorists in the field.

In 1992, Susan French and I developed the concept that various life experiences brought on by the structures of gender meant that men and women approached participation in nonviolence from different points of origin. The system of gender assignment often teaches women to be passive and to solve conflicts by avoiding violence to others and by absorbing the consequences oneself. Because of this, women's passivity is often seen as nonviolence when we think it really is another form of violence. On the other hand, masculinity teaches the equation being male with strength and dominance, which is portrayed by being an actor (not passive) and thus being on the offense. In Figure 1 both the parallels and the differences of women's and men's socialization as they respond to situations of conflict with violence are portrayed. When men, whose voices dominate the discussions of philosophical nonviolence and nonviolent action, speak of learning nonviolence they must travel a different path than the one faced by women. For example, we found in studying women's nonviolent protests that often they include a stage of becoming rageful in an effort to move from a passive mode to a view of women as social actors. The energy of that rage is then carefully channeled in actions with a nonviolent strategy. In offering this crosscut view of the violence-nonviolence continuum we have essentially moved gender to be the paradigm within which we look at nonviolence, and this has shifted our analytic gaze away from merely adding women's nonviolent acts to the list of those led by men. Our analysis should also be made more multidimensional by considering what implications one's assigned racial category has for participation in nonviolence. And we should consider the ways in which racism may lead to human rights abuses that provoke the oppressed to respond violently (for example, the government infiltration of the Black Panther movement). Gender studies also asks questions such as: Through what systemic forces did Martin Luther King, Jr., become the leader of the Montgomery bus boycott rather than Rosa Parks? Why is Barbara Deming's work on the "two-hand" approach to conflict seldom remembered as her work or discussed using her terms?

There are many critiques of the "woman is peaceful" motif. Most of the concern over the failure of those who claim that women have an innate peacefulness is that the analysis stays in the first two stages mentioned above, and never fully integrates a gender paradigm into the discussion. Critics point out that historically women have played all sorts of roles in society and many of them have perpetuated violence. Another problem with the "woman as peaceful" analysis is that it marginalizes women who participate in violence, such as members of liberation armies, into the category of bad women. It makes essential a particular approach and experience of being a woman. And that approach

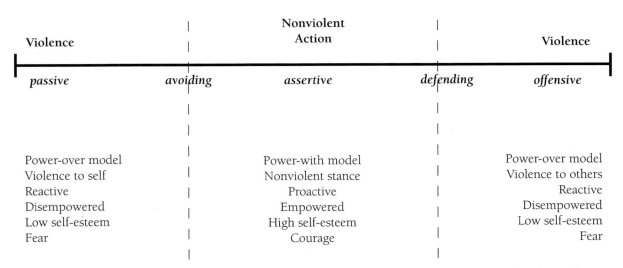

FIGURE 1   Nonviolence continuum. (From Lynne Woehrle and Susan French, 1992, "Unlocking the Paradox of Nonviolence and Self-Defense: A Feminist Analysis." Paper presented at the Annual Meeting of the Consortium on Peace Research and Education, Atlanta.)

emerges predominantly from the experiences of the colonizers rather than the colonized.

A somewhat different analysis views the act of gendering war and peace as a product of a partriarchal system. Assigning certain activities to each gender helps to establish a sense of difference between male and female. That sense of difference is exploited into definitions of masculinity and femininity. So rather than attributing women's participation in peacemaking to the fact that they have the resources and the power to make that their life's work, it is instead attributed to their gender. At the same time the violence of men is made more acceptable because it is argued that it is in the nature of the male to solve problems in this way. In her 1995 *Women's Studies Quarterly* article, "Riding the Hyphens of Feminism, Peace, and Place in Four (or more) Part Cacophony" Christine Sylvester argues that one perspective is to see that the war system and the peace system are really two halves of a whole. To affix a gender association to war and to peace is to reify patriarchal definitions of world politics and systems of power relations.

VI. CONCLUSION

Bringing gender studies into research on violence, peace, and conflict is essential. A gender analysis helps to show that even the most basic systems that we may assume are "natural" are in actuality socially con-

structed and culturally embedded, and serve to perpetuate larger systemic values. In the case of gender analysis it makes the institutional structures of patriarchy more apparent. If gender is approached from a view of the intersectionality of privileges and oppressions, then it also becomes apparent that male privilege connects to White privilege, to class privilege, and to heterosexual privilege. Noticing these intersection's may complicate analytic work, but it gives us a more complete view of the issues and events that we study.

A preliminary picture of how gender analysis might shape the work of the field of peace studies is charted in Table I. On a theoretical level, gender analysis requires that we renegotiate the meaning of several concepts: violence, power, justice, difference, and social movement theory. The typologies listed in Table I suggest that gender studies expands the traditional definition of violence studied in peace research. Thus, issues of personal violence and structures that perpetuate violence against women are defined as types of violence that are socially unacceptable in our vision of peace and justice. Table I also begins the project of de-centering Western experiences of violence and inequality by pointing to the connection of individual levels of gender inequality with global levels of social and economic inequality.

Feminist scholarship and experience offer several ways of altering our traditional definition of power as the ability to control and to have or to own. This traditional definition of power focuses on the tangible accumulation of symbols of wealth, including money,

TABLE I
Integrating Gender, Race, and Class into Peace and Conflict Studies

Sexism	Masculinity	Economic inequality	Education	Social change
		Personal/Local Level		
Discrimination and harassment	Competitive socialization	Underpaid/unemployed	Educational opportunity	Consciousness
Rape: stranger or date	War toys/TV	Poverty/hunger	Low wages and low status	Empowerment
Battering of women; different wage scales	Military training	Nat'l spending priorties	Economic draft	Activism and social movements
Wartime rape	Misogyny	Int'l labor market	Racism and sexism in criminal "justice"	NGOs and nonprofits
Female sexual slavery, tourism, military bases	Arms race; arms transfer	Global inequality	"Brain drain" and Western curriculum	Alternative structures
		Global/Transnational Level		

women, land, industry, food, shelter, and slaves/employees. However, we can alter power and who has it by redefining it to be based on competence, ability, and self-determination.

While the academic study of violence, peace, and conflict has tended to focus on the nation-state, a gender analysis demands that analytic work be done across levels. Moreover, the definition of politics is extended to cover those whom it effects, not just those who have a voice. A gender analysis can help point out where other analytic frames have privileged the male perspective on a particular subject such as nonviolence theory or mediation training. A gender analysis demands that we ask in each moment of theory building: In what ways is gender influencing what is happening here? The emphasis is on realizing that gender is not natural, objective, or neutral. Rather, gender is always a product of dominant cultural systems and of the structure of power relations in a given society.

Also See the Following Articles

CONFLICT MANAGEMENT AND RESOLUTION • FAMILY STRUCTURES, VIOLENCE AND NONVIOLENCE • FEMINIST AND PEACE PERSPECTIVES ON WOMEN • HOMOSEXUALS, VIOLENCE TOWARD • MILITARY CULTURE • NONVIOLENCE THEORY AND PRACTICE • PEACE CULTURE • SEXUAL ASSAULT • SOCIAL CONTROL AND VIOLENCE • SPORTS • WARRIORS, ANTHROPOLOGY OF

Bibliography

Andersen, M. L. & Collins, P. H. (1992). *Race, class, and gender.* Belmont, CA: Wadsworth, Inc.

Allen, B. (1996). *Rape Warfare.* Minneapolis: University of Minnesota Press.

Belenky, M. F., Clinchy, B. M., Goldberger, N. R., & Tarule, J. M. (1986). *Women's Ways of Knowing.* NY: Basic Books.

Cohn, C. (1987). Sex and death in the rational world of defense intellectuals. *Signs.* V.12, n.4:687–719.

Ferree, M. M., & Hall, E. J. (1996). Gender, race, and class in mainsteam textbooks. *American Sociological Review, 61,* 6.)

Forcey, L. R. & Swerdlow, A. (Eds.). (1995). Rethinking women's peace studies. Special Issue of *Women's Studies Quarterly, 23* (3 & 4).

Gilligan, C. (1982). *In A Different Voice.* Cambridge, MA: Harvard University Press.

Hooks, B. (1984). *Feminist theory from margin to center.* Boston, MA: South End Press.

Kimmel, M., & Messner, M. (Eds.). (1995). *Men's lives* (3rd Ed.). Needham Heights, MA: Allyn and Bacon.

Kolb, D. (1988). *Her Place at the Table.* Cambridge, MA: Harvard Law School.

Lorber, J. (1994). *Paradoxes of gender.* New Haven: Yale University Press.

Messner, M. (1992). *Power at Play.* Boston, MA: Beacon Press.

Moghadam, V. (Ed.). (1994). *Identity politics and women.* Boulder, CO: Westview Press.

West, C., & Zimmerman, D. (1987). Doing gender. *Gender and Society, 1,* (2).

Genocide and Democide

Allen D. Grimshaw

Indiana University

THERE IS PROBABLY no area of contemporary scholarly research in the social historical and social sciences that generates more bitter contention over facts, such emotional turmoil over theorizing on causes, motives, and intentions, or such barrages of conflicting ideological claims as that addressing matters of state-sponsored or -condoned large-scale killing of groups or categories of domestic or foreign civilian populations. Different constituencies have stakes in inflating or minimizing estimates of numbers killed in historical instances of such killing; there have been denials that the Holocaust and the Armenian genocide ever actually occurred. There are students of the Holocaust who insist that *that* terrible event was unique; other scholars disagree. Experts who read various drafts of the following article have taken sharp issue with my version of reported facts and with my selection of sources. They have disagreed no less sharply with each other. Readers should keep in mind that the topic *is* profoundly controversial. I simply hope that they will be sufficiently stimulated/distressed by what I report that they will look closely at more comprehensive and better-documented sources.

I. INTRODUCTION

Rummel devoted nearly three decades to compiling documentation of numbers of victims of government killing in domestic and international democide (in their several manifestations) and internal and international war *and* to analysis of causes of these behaviors and their differential distribution across nation states. After tracking down estimates for these behaviors from the beginnings of record-keeping, Rummel concluded that for every period governments have killed more of their own subjects than they have foreign enemies *by substantial margins* (Table I). Even low-end estimates suggest close to 400 million victims of large-scale killings by governments, some estimates are considerably higher. Roughly four times as many people have been killed by their own governments (or in killing *sponsored* by their governments) as have died in war. The number of magnitudes of difference between democidal deaths and those in war has increased over time (three times as many in the earlier period and five times as many in the current century); it seems likely that this change reflects in part that democidal killings in 20th-century democracies are massively lower than those in totalitarian states in any

Copyright © 1999 by Academic Press.
All rights of reproduction in any form reserved.

TABLE I

Democidal and War Deaths, All Pre-20th Century and 20th Century

Period	Deaths by democide* (000s)	War deaths (000s)	Total killing by government (000s)
Pre-20th century	133,147	40,457	173,604
20th century	169,198	34,021	203,219
Total recorded history**	302,345	74,478	376,823

Source: Adapted from Rummel 1994 and 1997. Rummel's estimates are largely low to mid-range across multiple sources.

* Subsumes genocide and politicide, domestic and foreign.

** Extrapolated from 1900–1987 figures.

period. The numbers killed by governments must be massively greater than those murdered by individuals; there are no worldwide or over-time data on homicide.

The proportionate risks of dying by homicide or as a casualty of war, or as a victim of slaughter by the government to which one is subject are not reflected in public attention to different ways of dying. Perhaps in part because of the mind-boggling enormity of the facts of genocide and other democide, there has been much less research on them than on other varieties of violence which have taken fewer lives. The Oxford English Dictionary gives 180 inches to war, 80 to murder (plus another 10 to homicide), and two and a half to genocide and genocidal (the terms democide and politicide have yet to make their way into standard references). My local research library subject index lists fewer than 500 items under genocide, 1700 on murder, and 5000 on war. An international catalog has fewer than 2000 on genocide, 32,000 on murder and homicide, and well over half a million on war. Similar patterns exist in papers presented at professional meetings.

In the pages following I will: (1) discuss some problematic dimensions of labels and definitions for large-scale government killing and identify criteria that should be considered in such discussion; (2) provide a synthesis of some goal-oriented typologies and a sampling of historical and areal exemplars; (3) focus on some patterns in genocide and other state-sponsored large-scale killings; (4) direct attention to popular and scholarly interpretations of and explanations for genocidal and other democidal behaviors and to reports of official bodies about specific instances; (5) consider issues of forecasting and controlling democidal behaviors; and (6) comment very briefly on issues of morality and inevitability.

II. SOME COMPLEXITIES OF DEFINITION(S)

Social violence is violence directed against individuals or their property solely or primarily because of their membership in a social category, whether that category be age cohort, socioeconomic class, dependency status, educational attainment, ethnicity, nationality, native language, occupation, political affiliation, religion, veteran status, or a fan, or not, of a particular sports team. *Fatal social violence sponsored or condoned by states* is the topic of this article. For an initial working definition we can say that all murder of members of social categories by governments constitutes what Rudolph Rummel has called *democide*. Rummel includes in democide (1) mass murders and massacres such as reprisal, murder by quota, and the sack and rape of captured cities and (2) state terror such as death squads, purges, and "disappearances." Democide where the group or category assaulted is ethnic, national, or religious (or possibly linguistic) constitutes a special subcategory called *genocide. Politicide* (Harff and Gurr) is government murder of people because of their politics or class status or for political purposes and is manifested in assassinations as well as mass murder. (A government may be under attack, and both sides can be responsible for democide in civil wars, revolutions, uprisings, and so on.) It will be evident that conceptual boundaries are permeable.

While it seems likely that there has been large-scale killing of own populations by governments as long as there have been governments, terms for identifying different varieties of such slaughter are fairly recent (at least in English). The term genocide was coined by Lemkin, who writing for the Carnegie Endowment for Peace observed:

> New conceptions require new terms. By "genocide" we mean the destruction of a nation or ethnic group.... Generally speaking, genocide does not necessarily mean the immediate destruction of a nation, except when it is accomplished by mass killing of all members of a nation. It is intended rather to signify a coordinated plan of different actions aiming at the destruction of essential foundations of the life of national groups, with the aim of annihilating the groups themselves.... Genocide is directed against the national group as an entity, and the actions involved are directed against the individuals, not in their individual capacity, but as members of the national group. (1944)

Lemkin was writing about events in Europe during World War II, his term gained widespread currency during the post-WW II war criminal trials and in 1948 was incorporated into international law in the Convention on the Prevention and Punishment of the Crime of Genocide of the United Nations (UNGC). Article II of the Convention reads:

> ... genocide means any of the following acts committed with intent to destroy, in whole or in part, a national, ethnical, racial or religious group as such: (a) Killing members of the group; (b) Causing serious bodily or mental harm to members of the group; (c) Deliberately inflicting on the group conditions of life calculated to bring about its physical destruction in whole or in part; (d) Imposing measures intended to prevent births within the group; (e) Forcibly transferring children of the group to another group. (Cf. Levy, two of whose four conditions which will terminate the existence of a society are (1) the biological extinction or dispersion of the members and (2) the absorption of the society into another society.)

Fein (1993) reports that the initial draft of the Convention contained language that would have extended protection to political groups and that would have criminalized "cultural genocide" via destruction of languages, religions, or cultures. These protections were never enacted because of resistance from countries of quite different political structure and varying cultural diversity and a likely shared belief that they would not themselves practice genocide but that other countries might try to infringe their sovereign rights to restructure their political life or favor one or another language or religion.

A number of problems have contributed to dissatisfaction with the terminology of the UNGC (and therefore to the appearance of supplementary nomenclature) and disappointment with the UN's inability to do anything about genocide (or other varieties of democide). Many observers were unhappy with (1) gaps in coverage and (2) the ambiguity of the notion of destroying a group "as such." This vagueness along with a general unawareness of the pervasiveness of democidal phenomena historically and comparatively has contributed to both (1) the development of new terminology and typologies and (2) a contentious and continuing dispute over whether the Holocaust was a manifestation of a widespread phenomenon of the human species or whether, rather, the Nazi killings of the mid-twentieth century were somehow unique. This same vagueness,

along with the specification that only states can invoke the Convention and the inability to provide means of enforcement has meant that attempts to curb genocide and other democide in the 50 years since passage of the UNGC have been largely unsuccessful.

A. What Genocide Is *Not*

The term genocide is often used for behaviors and events that meet neither the formal definition of the UNGC nor the more global characterization that this article is intended to convey. Two usages are particularly problematic because they apply the term to behaviors or events that, however unsavory, cannot be accurately characterized as, "committed with intent to destroy, in whole or in part, a national, ethnical, racial or religious group as such." First, pogroms and punitive raids are not genocide, even though there may be large numbers of fatalities; their aim is not to destroy a group but rather to intimidate members or perhaps even to have some fun bullying the weak. (Such events *may* be democidal.) Self-destruction by cult members may be intended to destroy a "religious group"; it is not state-sponsored and thus does not meet the UNGC definition. Nor do government shootings of political protesters meet the *genocide* standard, the victims are not members of the kinds of groups listed.

Second, teaching immigrant or minority children in a majority language with the end enhancing their success in the majority-dominated society is *not* genocide. Nor is provision of birth control education and devices to poor women who are members of minorities. Nor is criminal law (for example, on drugs), which disproportionately imprisons members of a minority population. Nor is revocation of affirmative action. While such actions may make life more difficult for subordinated populations, their intent is at least putatively benign.

Uses of the term genocide for nongenocidal events allows publics to disattend reports of actual genocide/democide on grounds that many behaviors so characterized are either aberrations or not very significant or even benignly intended.

In the remainder of this section on definition, I will first comment briefly on (1) active and passive methods of democide, and (2) variations in killing by scope, a sort of scalar approach.

B. Active and Passive Democide

The most visible and obvious killing by governments is active killing (sometimes after assembling large numbers of victims) of known or identifiable members of target social categories. Killing is done by asphyxiation, beating, bombing, burning, burying alive, crucifixion, decapitation, defenestration and other pushing or throwing from high places (including aircraft), disembowelment, dismemberment, drowning, electrocution, explosion, exposure, gassing, hanging, impalement, lapidation (stoning or burying under stones), mines (land and other antipersonnel mines as well as marine mines), poisoning, "putting to the sword," shooting, strangling, torture, and various combinations of "punishments" from this unfortunately incomplete listing. Readers may think some of these methods are archaic; there is documentation that all are currently in use. Other methods, such as the large-scale use of "weapons of mass destruction," including biological, chemical, and nuclear weapons, are in only limited use at this writing, they are ready for use at any time. Some of these methods, such as the large-scale gassing associated with Nazi "death camps" require a substantial infrastructure; large numbers of people can be forced to cooperate in their own slaughter by having them dig their own mass graves, little more equipment is needed than shovels and firearms (or even axes and swords). Or, victims may simply be marched to the banks of swiftly flowing streams, murdered, and dumped in. Choice of methods of killing reflects the size of the job to be done, a few hundred indigenes ordinarily constitute a lesser logistic challenge than millions of members of racial, ethnic, or religious categories. All of these methods have been used for both genocide and politicide. Those responsible for killing may be more willing to acknowledge use of more "respectable" methods such as hanging or firing squads than others, but all are used. Large numbers have been killed without the benefits of modern technologies. Finally, some scholars consider as active genocidal or democidal behavior the sterilization or other prevention of births to members of social categories or rape of women members with intention of denying the group new members.

The active killing just described is clearly intentional. Government actions (including inaction) result in deaths of additional millions of their own subjects and those of other countries; the extent to which such deaths are intended outcomes of government policies is often unclear. Widespread death from starvation results from wartime blockades (Biafra, Bosnia, Congo, Eritrea, Somalia, and some of the post-Soviet states are late 20th century examples), from "scorched earth" tactics of retreating armies or armies in transit, and from government seizure of harvests, levies that include agricultural supplies, and collectivization or other reorganization of agriculture. Tens of millions died in the one-time Soviet Union and in the People's Republic of China as a consequence of governmental policies reorganizing agriculture; smaller numbers have died elsewhere. Millions have also died from famines in which governments have failed to move available food to where it was needed and the effects of famine and epidemic have been exacerbated by *withholding* of food, shelter, medical assistance, clothing, and so on. Millions of people have died "incidentally" as a result of forced labor (often with minimal sustenance) ranging from galley slavery to heavy toil in miasmic plantation swamps or always dark and noisome mines or dangerous factories. "Incidental," too, were at least some of the millions of deaths that resulted from fatigue and exposure of populations, particularly the very young or old and weak and disabled, and so on, on marches (or trips on densely crowded trains) of expulsion and forced relocation to Indian reservations in the United States or across Russia to Siberia or to defeated Germany (after World War II).

Countless additional millions have died as the result of usually unintended introduction of disease—or failure to control known causes of disease. Epidemics often followed initial contact with Europeans, populations in the Americas and in Pacific regions were particularly hard hit. Governments have often spent immense sums on arms instead of the provision of pure water, thereby ensuring continuing endemic status of cholera and other water-related diseases. The United States is a major exporter of tobacco products in spite of known linkages to mortality.

The extent to which these various causes of large-scale death can or should be considered as democide seems ultimately to come down to questions of intent. Four government perspectives can be identified: (1) the view that as many should die as needed to break a population's spirit and will to resist (blockades, sieges, embargoes, etc.); (2) a position parallel to depraved indifference or disregard for life or criminal negligence in criminal law (some forced labor, some relocation, some collectivization); (3) the orientation that costs are inevitable, some will die but "you can't make omelets without breaking eggs" (some collectivization, some relocation); and (4) some sort of fatalistic acceptance of impotence to prevent deaths (famine, environmental toxins, etc.). Individuals, bureaucracies, and entire governments may delude themselves; instances where massive killings are accompanied by the first two perspectives are candidates for characterization as (passive) democide.

Some count as genocide attempts to insulate children from their native culture through quarantine away from home, often in boarding schools where they are forbidden to speak their native languages or engage in native cultural practices—such action may constitute genocidal practice under the UNGC definition. Similarly, some members of minorities consider cross-racial adoption as genocidal. The practices may result in "culturecide"; they do not involve killing.

C. How Many at a Time, How Many Altogether

There have been times and places where a glimpse of a lone member of some category, or a small party, would set a hunt in motion. We associate such "hunts" (sometimes seen as "sport") with settlers hunting and killing indigenes in the Americas, in Australia, and in South Africa. Many American "Westerns" portrayed Indians as equally likely to track down and kill small parties or individual Whites. In more modern times sighting of members of minorities or stigmata associated with education or class (for example, glasses or soft hands) have set off similar chases and precipitated similar deadly outcomes. Individuals have also been selected and slain (periodically) as religious sacrifices or to assure the health and vigor of tyrants or in reprisal or simply to intimidate subject populations.

Many but not all *individuals* killed are nonanonymous and perhaps even known to their killers. (Goldhagen writes of men, women, and children and their German executioners marching two by two, side by side, into the woods where killing was to be done.) Anonymity is more likely when governments (or their agents or allies) kill people in "batches" in mass executions by gassing (as in Nazi Germany) or by firearms or sharp-edge weapons or in siege warfare and subsequent sacking and slaughter of inhabitants. Even more "distancing" from victims is involved when large numbers of anonymous people are killed by so-called strategic bombing or ship sinkings or the use of "weapons of mass destruction." It may seem that these last kinds of slaughter are behaviors associated only with war between foreign powers; it has been alleged that Iraq has both bombed and used chemical weapons against minority Kurds (attempted genocide?) and both sides used bombing in the Spanish and other civil wars.

There are, finally, killings on a grander scale. Extermination of peoples and of social categories have been stated (and published) goals of regimes through historical times. The Nazis wanted to destroy Jews (and possibly Gypsies); longtime accommodation of the handicapped and of homosexuals was not in the future of the Reich. The Soviet Communists wanted to extirpate old-style kulaks (a category for which they developed an extremely elastic definition) and other "enemies of the state"; Cossacks and other ethnic and nationality groups became defined as such enemies. The Romans hunted down Christians. There were United States Army officers who would have liked to slaughter not only all adult Indians but children and infants as well. Most Americans of European origin in both hemispheres grew up hearing some version of the "The only good Indian is a dead Indian" mantra attributed to General Philip Sheridan. The difference among these last cases is that the Soviet and Nazi democides were explicit government policy, while the government of the United States, however much its officials may have condoned genocidal actions against Indians, did not enunciate any such policy.

1. What Does "How Many" Mean?

More than 60 million people were killed in the Soviet Union in the 70 years after 1917, about 55 million by various regimes in China in the 70 years after 1923, and more than 21 million by Nazi Germany in the shorter period of 12 years ending in 1945. Only two million were killed in Cambodia in the 4-year Khmer Rouge regime (1975–1979). The Cambodian politicide was much greater *proportionally*, more than 8% of the entire Cambodian population was killed annually during the period. During the various communist regimes between 1917 and 1987 the *rate* of death in the USSR was less than one half of one per cent. In the USSR one person in 200 was being killed, in Cambodia one in about 11. The totals are staggering, the distinction between absolute and relative numbers should be kept in mind. Further variation is concealed in both absolute and relative figures; the percent of Jews who became victims varied across countries under Nazi influence or domain, and urban and rural Khmer had different likelihoods of victimization in Cambodia.

III. A GOAL-ORIENTED TYPOLOGY OF DEMOCIDE

In a later section I review a number of behavioral science perspectives that seek to explain social violence, whether manifested in atrocity, massacre, rioting, varieties of democide, or war. Most students of genocide have limited their explanatory efforts to eclectic invocation of elements of various general theories to account for specific genocidal events, or have developed classification schemes that try to make sense of these behaviors in terms of apparent goals of perpetrators. In the following classificatory scheme I draw on typologies developed by a number of students of genocide. The terms they use overlap, are sometimes contradictory, and vary, as does what gets included in a specific type.

A. Economic

There are at least three varieties of economically based democide. *Predatory* democide occurs when a victim population is in possession of valuable commodities (precious minerals of the Aztec, Maya, and Inca) or land (North American natives), or are themselves potentially valuable as slaves. *Developmental* democide occurs when conquerors convert land use or otherwise alienate resources necessary for indigenous ways of life. This has occurred everywhere colonial powers have initiated latifundiary economies. Related to this is *structural* democide, where similar disruptions occur to already established societies, as by the introduction of cotton culture and the subsequent desiccation of the Aral Sea or damage to Native American and Black populations in the United States through the presence of reservations and ghettoes.

B. Retributive

Retributive genocide occurs when a group which believes (frequently correctly) that it was victimized in the past gains power and moves to take revenge *or* when a dominant group visits massively disproportionate reprisals on minorities for delicts such as stock stealing or justified homicide by individual members of the group. Norton reports that during White settlement in Northern California in the 1850s entire bands of Native Americans were killed by Whites as punishment for what amounted to attempts by Indians to protect themselves. In the latter part of the 20th century such retribution has been visited by Serbs on Croats and Muslims, by Hutu on Tutu and the reverse, by Hindus and Muslims on each other in the Indian subcontinent, by Tamils on Sinhalese and Sinhalese on Tamils. Memories are long; Serbs punished Croats for events at the time of World War II—and Muslims for events that putatively occurred four centuries ago. While many events of the 1990s have involved ethnic and national groups, retributive politicide has also occurred, as when the Chinese Communists successfully ousted the Nationalists (Kuomintang), or peasants rebel against their masters. Again, in at least some of these

instances violence is certainly not official state policy and quite possibly not state-condoned.

C. Despotic/Hegemonic/Repressive

Subjects of despotic rulers are subject to abduction, enslavement, torture and death at the whim of the tyrant. Members of elites and of police and the military are no more insulated from risk than are slaves, peasants, merchants, or the intelligentsia. Villages or neighborhoods can be destroyed because of inconvenience suffered in passage through them, or extended families wiped out because of imagined plots, or individuals regularly forced to kill one another in fights to the death, and so on. Killing goes on not because of any specific concern to instill terror but because, as Acton says, "Absolute power corrupts absolutely." Ancient African and Asian empires and the USSR under Stalin and Hitler's Third Reich are classic examples of such regimes; Amin's Uganda and Haiti under Duvalier are among beter known examples in the second half of the 20th Century.

D. Strategic-Tactical: Dominance Maintaining/Intimidating/Threat Controlling

Other despotic and totalitarian regimes are reputed to employ terror more deliberately. Reports on the Mongol hordes frequently express the belief that Ghengis Khan slaughtered all the inhabitants of cities which dared resist to intimidate rulers and residents of cities yet to be attacked, so that the latter would surrender easily in hopes of being spared. Nazi forces in conquered areas of Europe and the Japanese in Asia slaughtered hostages and potential leaders to reduce resistance and facilitate control. This sort of pragmatic democide also differs from the despotic variety in that it is likely to be foreign rather than domestic.

E. Ideological

The potency of ideological belief in motivating behavior is well-established; three varieties of ideology closely associated with democide can be identified. *Political* ideologies often combine elements of idealism and self-interest as when it is anticipated that a new order of some sort will make everybodies' life better, including one's own, or where protecting one's position of privilege is equivalent to defending natural or god-ordained order.

"Manifest destiny," the "dictatorship of the proletariat," "death to the American imperialist infidels" and the "thousand year Reich" have all resonated, and have all been associated with democide. *Religious* ideologies have been major factors in genocide from the first emergence of coherent religions. Pagan Romans killed Christians and Christians killed pagans and animists the world over for centuries afterwards. Major democide occurred between Christians and Muslims, particularly during the Crusades. Shortly afterwards Protestant and Catholic Christians began killing each other. Hindus and Muslims engaged in mutual slaughter from the first appearance of Islam on the Indian sub-continent. *dīn* (religion in danger) and *jihad* (holy war) have been rallying calls for Islam for more than a millennium (there have also been long periods of both local and national amity). Similar slogans reflect other religious ideologies and have been similarly invoked in large-scale killing. *Racial* ideologies about the superiority of one or another group and the inferiority of others seem always to accompany contact between groups. In some cases, as in anti-Semitism, characterization of Jews as inferior has been comfortably accommodated with portrayals of them as successful schemers and exploiters. Slogans here include "final solution" and "only good Indians" and lead to colonialist open seasons on wogs and kaffirs, eliminationism in Nazi Germany and the "ethnic cleansing" of 1990s Yugoslavia in dissolution.

F. Habitual/Inertial/Institutionalized/ Traditional

There are many societies that have populations of minorities which constitute recognizable and more or less permanent underclasses. Blacks, Mexicans, and Native Americans constitute such categories in the late 20th century United States and Indians in some central and south American countries; even Western-educated Indians constituted such an underclass in British India along with Africans in British colonies in Africa and Filipinos in the American-controlled Phillippines. In such circumstances members of the underclass are subject to social, economic, and political discrimination *and* are more likely to be subject to police brutality, execution, and killings classified as "justifiable police homicide." While the killings are not large-scale in the short term, they are in the aggregate. While racial ideologies are likely to be invoked in explanation for democide of this variety, it is also likely to be explained, as just "what happens," in much the same sense that people have fights when they drink lots of alcohol—and kill one another when weapons are part of the scene (and culture).

G. Genocidal and Other Democidal Massacres

Massacres minimally require that armed military or paramilitary units of some sort be copresent with members of a target population, legitimated as such by governmental or subgovernmental authority. Sometimes massacres are the direct result of orders from higher authorities. In other instances the likelihood of massacre increases to the extent that there is fear on the part of the military (or quasi-military) units that they may themselves be attacked by the target population. The combination of arms and fear (and sometimes fatigue) and vulnerable populations can be a lethal one, whether killing actually occurs depends in part on actual policies and intentions of governments and military superiors and, particularly, on field commanders' perception of policies and wishes. Massacres occur in the course of war. Toward the end of World War II in Europe SS troops slaughtered unarmed prisoners at Malmédy, and during the war in Vietnam U.S. troops killed nearly all the Vietnamese of every age and gender in My Lai. While the Germans were engaged in the "Final Solution" there is no evidence that either the military or civil authorities intended the elimination of American captives. Nor, however some senior officers in Vietnam may have encouraged high "body counts," was there any American *policy* of genocide. The shooting of hundreds of unarmed Indians at Jallianwala Bagh by General Dyer's troops, which was a major impetus for the independence movement in India, did not reflect government policy, nor, again, did the shooting of Native American women and children at Wounded Knee reflect that of the U.S. government. It has sometimes been the case that governments or government officials have acquiesced in or even encouraged vigilante killings; there are instances where officials have joined mobs. All this to reiterate that genocidal massacres can occur that are *not* expressions of government policies intended to encourage democide.

IV. A SAMPLING OF CASES

Table II lists some of the major democides (including genocide but excluding war casualties) of the 20th century. Rummel, from whom the table is adapted, has detailed lists and tables of democides of varying size both for this century and for the previous three millennia or so of recorded history up to 1899. It will be seen from discussion elsewhere in this article that with the exception of efficiencies introduced by the availability

TABLE II
Twentieth-Century Democide (000)[a]

Regimes	Years	Total	Domestic	Genocide
Megamurderers	1900–1987	151,491	116,380	33,476
(10,000,000 and more)	1900–1987	128,168	100,842	26,690
USSR	1917–1987	61,991	54,769	10,000
China (PRC)	1949–1987	35,236	35,236	375
Germany	1933–1945	20,946	762	16,315
China (KMT)	1928–1949	10,075	10,075	nil
Lesser megamurderers	1900–1987	19,178	12,237	6,184
(under 10,000,000)				
Japan	1936–1945	5,964	nil	nil
China (Mao soviets)[b]	1923–1949	3,466	3,466	nil
Cambodia	1975–1979	2,035	2,000	541
Turkey	1909–1918	1,883	1,752	1,883
Vietnam	1945–1987	1,678	944	nil
Poland	1945–1948	1,585	1,585	1,585
Pakistan	1958–1987	1,503	1,503	1,500
Yugoslavia (Tito)	1944–1987	1,072	987	675
Suspected megamurderers	1900–1987	4,145	3,301	602
North Korea	1948–1987	1,663	1,293	nil
Mexico	1900–1920	1,417	1,417	100
Russia	1900–1917	1,066	591	502
Lesser murderers	1900–1987	14,918	10,812	4,071
(100,000 to 999,999)				
Top five lesser murderers	1900–1987	4,074	2,192	1,078
(China [warlords], Turkey [Ataturk], United Kingdom, Portugal [dictatorship], Indonesia)				
Lesser murderers	1900–1987	2,792	2,335	1,019
(under 100,000)				
World total	1900–1987	169,202	129,547	38,556

Source: Adapted from Rummel 1994.

[a] Includes genocide, politicide, and mass murder; excludes war dead. These are most probably mid-estimates in low to high ranges. Figures may not sum due to rounding.

[b] Guerrilla period.

of explosives and biological and chemical weapons, democide has not changed much over recorded history. Justification for killings is much the same, so are effects on victims, socialization of perpetrators, variations of responses from bystanders, and so on. It cannot be argued, even ironically, that civilization has humanized democidal practice.

There are, nonetheless, differences across cases of genocide, massacre, and other democide. Ten of the books included in the Bibliography (Andreopolous, Chalk and Jonassohn, Charny, 1988, Jongman, Markusen and Kopf, Rummel 1994, Rummel 1997b, Staub, Totten, Parsons and Charny, and Uekert) each contain

from modestly to quite detailed descriptions of four or more instances of democide; several additionally contain extensive bibliographies. Several of the books contain detailed personal and eyewitness accounts (as do others, particularly in this small selection, Goldhagen). Stiglmayer focuses primarily on mass rape in a single location, Bosnia-Herzegovina; there is more than enough detail in the book to provide a sense of the phenomenon and its many dimensions of pain.

It is not possible to convey the full diversity of democide over the millennia, or by world regions, or by characteristics of victims or offenders. I can do no more here than offer a sampling of democide varying on several dimensions and identifying features that make the instances chosen notable in some way. I list examples from each of three bounded time periods. The events occurred, documentation of particulars and even of general magnitudes is variably persuasive. For present purposes the descriptions illustrate the diversity of democidal events (excluding war).

A. Pre-20th Century

Documentation for the last four of five centuries is substantial. Surprisingly, a combination of archaeological records, of contemporary inscriptions by rulers, of complementary accounts by contemporaries with quite different stakes in event outcomes, and of religious or mythological renderings where a deity is credited with democidal destruction, has allowed historians to write with cautious confidence about a number of earlier events. In the earliest records, democide is known primarily from boasts from rulers who claim to have killed many people and to have terrorized many more.

1. Ancient Middle East

According to self-reports ancient rulers, particularly the Assyrians, slaughtered foreign civilians during times of war, tortured and mutilated captives whether military or civilians, raped, pillaged, destroyed. Quotas for slaughter were set, sliced off ears and noses constituted documentation. Captured nobles were thrown from towers, flayed alive, slow roasted. Populations were smaller, killing was sometimes near total (some observers note that only elites may have been eliminated with serfs simply continuing to labor for new masters).

Total destruction of cities and all within them was not limited to the Middle East, schoolchildren learn about the destruction and leveling of Carthage and the slaughter of all survivors of its siege by the Romans. Indeed, similar events accompanied the Crusades, particularly those directed against heretics in Europe itself

(Christian Crusaders also kept count with cut-off bits and pieces) and continued in European wars well into the late Middle Ages and occasionally later.

2. Melos

The Athenians led the Greeks in their successful wars against the Persians. They demanded not only credit for that success but tribute and allegiance as well. Late in the 5th century B.C. the Athenians demanded assistance from the Melians (descended from Spartan colonists) in the Peloponnesiann War against Sparta. They warned the Melians they would be annihilated if they did not cooperate. After debate between the parties the Melians declined the Athenian demand. The Athenians laid siege to Melos and after victory executed all the men on the island and enslaved the surviving women and children.

3. Mongol Hordes, 14th and 15th Centuries

While schoolchildren know little about democide, many remember tales about mounds of human heads/skulls outside of destroyed cities. Successive invasions of Mongol "hordes" brought terror to those in their paths; they are memorable both for their magnitude and their alleged cruelty. Saunders (quoted in Rummel 1994) reported that every resident of an ancient Persian capital was murdered, "and even cats and dogs were killed in the streets." Here and elsewhere, the few who escaped were tracked down and killed. Rummel estimates 30 million killed in successive sweeps across Asia, mostly killed one-at-a-time with hand weapons.

4. Native American Empires

Just a short time after the Mongols and just years before Europeans began the large-scale slaughter of Native Americans throughout the hemisphere, the Aztec and Maya empires were themselves engaged in democide, principally through widespread human sacrifice (Davies). Similar practices were common throughout the world. The Aztec sacrifices were notable both because of their numbers (claims were made that thousands would be sacrificed for a single ceremonial) and their method (hearts cut out and offered to the gods while still beating). The purpose of Aztec warfare was putatively to take prisoners for sacrifice; it has been asserted that it was because of this that a small number of Spanish soldiers with better weapons and with no interest in taking prisoners was able to defeat them. (One commentator disputes the religious explanation and asserts that the Aztec intensification of sacrifice was merely part of a strategy of rule by intimidation.) The Spaniards, at the time in the midst of the horrors of the Inquisition, justified their slaughter of the Aztecs on grounds of the necessity of stopping the un-Christian practice of human sacrifice.

5. "American Holocaust" (Stannard, Thornton)

Stannard cites sources that depict precontact population of the Americas as greater than those of Europe and Africa at the same time. He reports 8 million Native Americans had died from direct violence, disease, and despair within 21 years of Colombus' landing. He estimates that from more than 100 million inhabitants of the hemisphere at the end of the 15th century numbers had declined to about 5 million a few hundred years later. (Thornton reports late 20th century estimates for the earlier period as low as 15 million and as high as 112 million, his own estimate is around 79 million with the rest of the world numbering about 500 million.) Rummel's (1994) more cautious estimate is a bit below fourteen million deaths during the 16th–19th centuries. The small numbers of Europeans, at least initially, means that a substantial proportion of the millions of deaths were caused not by direct violence but by disease (and as Stannard says, by despair). There is no consensus on numbers. Almost certainly more deaths resulted from disease than from democide. Killing on a massive scale *did* occur, and Europeans (and their descendants) in many venues in the hemisphere continued to engage in mass killing, mutilation, torture and rape into the late 20th Century.

B. Twentieth Century through 1945

Rummel estimates four democides in which more than 10 million were killed in the millennia of recorded history before the 20th century. According to his calculations 34 million were killed in China between 221 B.C. and the end of the 19th century A.D., 34 million by the Mongols during the 14th and 15th centuries, 17 million as a result of African enslavement, and 14 million in the Western hemisphere between the arrival of Europeans and the end of the 19th century. These four democides alone accounted for close to 100 million deaths.

Between the end of the first World War and the end of the 20th century four democides began (two, those of Nazi Germany and of Kuomintang China, are over) in which more than 128 million people have already perished (Table II). Of all the democides between 1900 and the end of World War II those of Turkey (Armenia) and Nazi Germany are probably best known; reports in recent years have allowed people to become informed about the democides of Soviet and Chinese Communism and Japanese atrocities in Asia from 1936 onwards. Democide by the Nationalist Chinese (Kuomintang), by their antagonists (the Chinese Soviets), in Tsarist Russia, and in Mexico are largely unknown except for people whose lives were affected by them. I have chosen for brief description here two lesser known instances, one small and one massive: (1) the revolt of the Hereros (Bridgman) and (2) the multiple democides in China by warlords, the Nationalists, the Communists, and by the Japanese in the 1930s.

1. The Hereros of German South West Africa (Contemporary Namibia)

In 1903 there were 80,000 Herero (a Bantu tribe) and something under 5000 German settlers in the German colony. Two years later there were somewhere between 15 and 20 thousand surviving (but numbed) Herero and a growing colonial population. The scenario was a familiar one, increasing encroachment by Whites, unheeded indigene complaints, discriminatory treatment, including individual homicide and rape. Promises were made, shortly before the uprising, that if the Herero would surrender their weapons they would be protected from abuses they had recently suffered. They turned in their weapons, but abuses continued. In early 1904 they rose and attacked Germans, primarily farmers and settlers distant from German population centers and from German troops (they specifically told non-Germans that they intended them no harm). By late spring German troops were arriving in great numbers: in October the German commander published a ban of all Herero from the country on pain of being shot on sight (in a separate order he advised that German soldiers should not shoot at women and children—but only over their heads "to force them to run faster"). In the event, when Herero fleeing the country were caught they were shot and bayoneted with no recorded concern about age or gender. The German official historians remarked. "The Hereros ceased to exist as a tribe."

The Herero case is interesting primarily because the slaughter was neither ordered nor endorsed by the military high command in Berlin but was in large part the initiative of local commanders. Many Germans were temporarily embarrassed by the episode but no punitive action against the German military is recorded, and once over the episode was quickly forgotten. The combination of predatory and retributive democide was overshadowed by other events—in Europe.

2. 1930s China

While more than 60 million were killed in the USSR between 1917 and 1987 and while the absolute toll of Native Americans killed throughout the hemisphere *may* have been as large, the highest closely documented cumulative figure for democide in a single country is clearly that for China. Including pre- 20th century deaths along with those killed in the 20th century by warlords, the Nationalists, Mao (during the guerrilla period), the Communist regime, and the Japanese during their invasion, Rummel's estimates sum to somewhat more than 85 million killed, *exclusive of combatants*. During one span of two decades (1928–1949) 35 million died (this figure *does* include war dead), very roughly 40% the number of all the democides. Rummel (1994) succinctly summarizes what happened to these millions:

> They have been slaughtered because they happened to live where nationalists, warlords, communists, or foreign troops fought each other. They have been executed because they had the wrong beliefs or attitudes in the wrong place at the wrong time. They have been shot because they critized or opposed their rulers. They have been butchered because they resisted rape, were raped, or tried to prevent rape. They have been wiped out because they had food or wealth that soldiers or officials wanted. They have been assassinated because they were leaders, a threat, or potential antagonists. They have been blotted out in the process of building a new society. And they have died simply because they were in the way.
>
> These poor souls have experienced every manner of death for every conceivable reason: genocide, politicide, mass murder, massacre, and individually directed assassination; burning alive, burying alive, starvation, drowning, infecting with germs, shooting, stabbing. This for personal power, out of feelings of superiority, because of lust or greed, to terrorize others into surrendering, to keep subjects in line, out of nationalist ideals, or to achieve utopia. (92)

C. Twentieth Century after 1945

The USSR and the Peoples Republic of China, the two largest and most populous Communist dictatorships, continued to be major contributors to democide statistics after 1945. (Rates were declining in the USSR before the regime collapse and dissolution of the Union.) On a smaller scale, some states in the Americas continue to discriminate against, kill, rape, and torture, Native American populations; in some places Indians have been victimizers as well as victims. The highest rate of democide (primarily politicide but including some genocide) ever calculated, over 8% annually of the population, also occurred in this period, in Cambodia, also a Communist state. While inaccessibility has made democide (largely politicide) in North Korea (a fourth totalitarian Communist state) difficult to document, reports characterize the state as being high both in absolute numbers of dead and in annual rate. I have selected for brief description here post-1945 democidal episodes in Pakistan, and in Poland and other areas of Eastern Europe that had been occupied by the Germans before the defeat of the Nazis, because they are little known and somewhat surprising.

1. Previously Nazi-Occupied Eastern Europe

(This section draws heavily on de Zayas and Wiskemann for historical reviews and on Rummel 1994 and 1997b and his multiple sources for numerical estimates.) There were two waves of democidal actions in Eastern Europe at the end of World War II and immediately afterwards. First, as the Red army and its Polish allies drove toward Berlin they raped, tortured, mutilated, murdered, and pillaged Germans living in Nazi-occupied areas in the USSR, Poland, and other countries in Eastern Europe, both prewar residents and participants in the Nazi occupations. De Zayas estimates that four to five million Germans fled or were forced by the Nazis to evacuate and that as many as a million may have died. Some news of this filtered into the West; awareness was low.

After Germany fell many of those earlier displaced tried to return to their homes in the East. After the Potsdam agreement (July 1945) that Germans would be repatriated (humanely) they, along with millions who had not fled earlier were subjected to evictions and confiscation of property along with murder, rape, and beatings throughout the region. Germans were forced to wear identifying armbands, just as Jews had been earlier, and they were subjected to much of the same treatment that had been meted out by the Nazis. Former forced laborers, national and local committees, militias, remnants of national armies that had been fighting alongside the Soviets, partisans and partisan armies, local gangs, and sometimes groups of neighbors joined in assaults on and eviction of Germans (and others as well, including occasionally Jews and other recently released concentration camp inmates). Expellees were marched to existing or hastily constructed concentration camps and packed into railway cars and taken long distances without food, water, or heat. Columns of old men and boys, women, and disabled German soldiers were driven on long marches from the

Baltic States, Czechoslovakia, Hungary, Poland, Romania, and Yugoslavia, sometimes through frozen mountain passes. Adolescent boys and men were rounded up, held under life-threatening health conditions—and shot without justification. Rummel estimates roughly 15 million expelled in the second wave by postwar governments (or with tacit government assent) and somewhat less than two million killed; he notes that estimates for this genocide/democide are even more variable than most in an area of scholarship fraught with controversy.

Some of this could be labeled *retributive* genocide. Some in the new regimes tried to protect the victims or to at least provide due process. As elsewhere there were rescues by neighbors and protection accorded by individual officers and soldiers. Senior officials in the Allied military and diplomatic establishment were aware of these activities and there were protests, intervention, and rescue; there were limits to what they could (or would) do. Publics in the victorious countries were aghast at unfolding awareness of the Holocaust, concerned about their own recovery (and in western Europe, with pursuit and punishment of collaborators) and, in the United States, with the final agonies of the war with Japan. The reaction of distant observers if and when told about these events may well have been that imputed to American soldiers in Viet Nam when told about My Lai, "It never happened and besides they deserved it."

2. East Pakistan/East Bengal/Bangladesh

The Indian subcontinent has witnessed substantial democidal violence during the latter part of the 20th century. At the time of Independence and Partition in 1947 there were massive movements of population as Hindus sought safety in India, Muslims in the new state of Pakistan, and Sikhs with concentrations of their coreligionists. More than 15 million people became refugees and as many as a million may have been killed in communal violence in a short span, *notwithstanding efforts by the new Indian government to control the violence.* Violence continues on a smaller scale in the 1990s. The government of India has been embroiled in attempts at pacification of tribal peoples in Assam. Sri Lanka has had increasing violence between the Hindu Tamil minority and the Buddhist Sinhalese majority, Bihari-Pathan violence is endemic in Pakistan; beatings, bombings and riots are commonplace in the subcontinent (Tambiah).

The greatest sustained violence, however, and that of the greatest magnitude, was that of the government of West Pakistan and its army against the population of its so-called Eastern Wing—now, the country of Bangladesh (this account draws heavily on Payne. See, also, Chalk and Jonassohn and Totten *et al.*). During the two decades after Independence the Bengalis of East Pakistan became increasingly unhappy, and vocal, about their underrepresentation in government and the civil service and military, about denial of national status to the Bengali language, about what they considered unfair shares of national development funds. Even their piety as Muslims was questioned. When in 1970 East Bengal was struck by a major cyclone (and associated floods) in which as many as half a million may have died, help from West Pakistan was slow, and modest in extent. Outrage grew, and took the form of political action in which the Awami League of the dissident Easterners gained an absolute majority in the Pakistan National Assembly. The government postponed the Assembly, and Bengalis went on what amounted to a general strike. In 1971 West Pakistan moved to subdue the rebellious province.

Initial targets were police (and the East Pakistan units of the military) and intellectuals, including college teachers and students, writers, newspaper journalists and editors, cultural leaders, the entire political establishment of East Bengal, *and in many instances the families of these leaders.* Students at the University of Dacca who survived point-blank shelling by American-built tanks were forced to dig mass graves and were then themselves shot. A slum area in Dacca, occupied mostly by Hindus, was set on fire and thousands of its inhabitants shot. The industrial base was destroyed in order to assure the dependent status of the province. Rape, murder, beatings, mutilation, and torture spread from Dacca to outlying rural districts. There were death camps. Thousands of Bengalis were marched into a river, shot, and pushed into the current. By the time the blood bath was ended with the defeat of Pakistani forces by an intervening Indian army, about a million and a half were dead and 10 million Hindus had fled into India. A successful war of independence soon followed; victorious Bengalis killed about 150,000 Bihari residents in retributive genocide along with about 5000 suspected collaborators.

D. Summary

Democide and genocide have occurred on every inhabited continent and during every historical epoch into the present. Victims have included entire populations or categories within populations. Numbers of victims have ranged from a few thousands to tens of millions.

V. SOME PATTERNS IN GENOCIDE AND OTHER STATE-SPONSORED, LARGE-SCALE KILLING

With more than 300 million people killed it is reasonable to expect that there are differences in occurrences of genocide and other democide. There *are* differences. There are also patterns, both in democide itself and in differences from other varieties of social violence ranging from riot to war. In this section I identify some patterns in democide, looking particularly at aspects of large-scale killing not discussed in other sections.

A. Ecological Patterns

There are no particular venues in which democide is uniquely concentrated; there are few inhabited places where it has not occurred. It is neither an urban nor a rural phenomenon, for example, although some *types* of genocide, such as that of indigenous populations, most often occurs in areas far away from metropolitan centers. Jews were herded into urban ghettoes during the Nazi Holocaust, *Einsatzkommandos* went to towns and hamlets to kill Jews there. Indeed, one ecological pattern of democide has been the transport of victims to places where they are killed, often with stops at concentration camps or other collection centers—and of executioners to places where victims are located. Victims are also driven on forced marches to new locations, dying along the way. Unknown numbers have died in transport (Elkins calculated that only 5 of 15 million captured Africans survived the trip to slavery; see also Conquest on the USSR). Efforts may be made to collect victims at times and places where what is happening is less visible (for example, in the early morning hours and at unfrequented railway sidings); the principal consideration most often is to cope with logistical problems.

B. Temporal Patterns

Riots usually occur during daytime hours and in good weather. Political disappearances usually occur at night. Genocide, in contrast, occurs continuously once begun, postponed only because of shortages of killing space or personnel or because of weather so inclement that transport cannot move. When indigenous populations are targeted weather considerations may become important; killing is ordinarily limited only by technological and logistic constraints. Lifton has shown that there were stages in the Nazi genocide in the course of which the variety and number of victims increased; there is too much diversity in instances of genocide and democide to say with what frequency such temporal stages occur.

C. Participants

A very considerable amount is known about victims, perpetrators, and bystanders (Hilberg) and, somewhat more recently, rescuers (Fogelman) and refusers (Goldhagen). There are available detailed studies of killing professionals (Lifton, 1986, of medical doctors) and of professional executioners (Goldhagen), of rape victims (Stiglmayer) and of survivors (Lifton 1982 [1967]). (With the exception of Stiglmayer the books just listed focus on the Holocaust; there have not been specialized monographs on participants in other democides.) The numbing statistics of millions of casualties from contemporary democide (including genocide) are depressing; the eyewitness accounts and recountings of personal experiences (and occasional photographs) are truly unremittingly distressing. (Lifton, 1986, writes with clarity, honesty, and remembered pain about the personal costs of research at the individual level.)

1. Victims

When mass killing other than that of military combat occurs no category is spared by reason of weakness or age or handicap. (This is equally true, of course, of bombing in the course of so-called total war. See Markusen and Kopf.) Distinctions are made, however, as when healthy and strong individuals or those with needed technical skills or perhaps physical attractiveness are temporarily spared. Additional distinctions are neither cheering nor comforting. Are individuals or families or extended families or communities killed or transported? Are there warnings, or do prospective victims wait in terror for knocks on their doors or their names on lists? Are the criteria of selection predictable or not? Are all victims treated the same or can the rich, or the skilled, or the beautiful, or the sophisticated, or the simply determined buy time or even escape? What is the nature of assault? Immediate and efficient death? Arson with death coming as victims run from their burning homes? Incarceration in "camps" or churches or public schools with minimal or no food or water punctuated (or not) by beating, torture, and rape? Primarily physical restriction of movement and deprivation from starvation or assault or execution? Primarily physical harm or physical harm along with symbolic and psychological injury such as rape, forcing families to watch mothers and daughters and sisters raped, forcing males to rape or castrate one another, forcing par-

ents to watch their children sexually assaulted and then killed, cutting fetuses from their mothers' wombs and then slitting their throats? Stripping victims of all their possessions including, just before death, the clothing they wear? Cutting off their hair (or in the case of adult Jewish males, their beards)? Forced motherhood or forced prostitution and pornography followed by execution? All of these things and others have happened in the second half of the 20th century and many continue today.

One does not have to be particularly empathic to understand why so many surviving spectators of such activities withdraw into catatonic-like immobility, sitting motionless and only responding compliantly to orders, including those which lead them later to their own deaths. Among those who do survive many are overcome with guilt because of that very survival. Among those who survive rape, particularly that accompanied by forced motherhood, for many women, return to what remains of their communities has often meant rejection and divorce and pariah status for them and any resulting child.

An obvious question is, Why don't victims more often resist their attackers or, at the very least, attempt escape? There *are* variations here, critical considerations include the extent to which groups victimized are dispersed, how far individuals or families are from possible safe havens, past traditions of resistance in the attacked community, prospects for assistance from within the perpetrating or bystander communities and, importantly, psychological denial of the possibility of what is happening. Members of victimized groups often claim that reports are not true, or that law will prevail, or that they are not really members of the group being attacked. Others are simply immobilized by the enormity of ongoing events or are unwilling to abandon their families. In the case of ghetto Jews, particularly outside of Germany, community elders often discouraged resistance or escape on grounds that punishment would be visited on the rest of the community. For many, however, there are feelings of powerlessness very similar to those experienced by civilians after massive bombing (or nuclear bombing) or destruction of their homes and communities, by survivors of large-scale natural disasters, and by the bereaved. In some cases victims go beyond compliance and even cooperation to collaboration. Motivations are obviously complex. Escapees and resisters, and there are always some or some attempters, are overwhelmingly young, healthy, and without impediment in the persons of dependents; some older resisters engage in sabotage in camps and in factories where they are forced to work. Fein (1993) reviews studies of how victims attempted to cope and concludes that those able to recreate social bonds were most successful.

2. Perpetrators

Perpetrators are generally young postadolescent males. When there is full mobilization older males are recruited, some women become enthusiastic participants, and even children sometimes get into the act. There are numerous reports of training youth to engage in torture and mass killing and of gradual socialization from being punished, to watching torture, to participating in torture and execution. Perpetrators ordinarily are members of the dominant group engaged in democide; when the killing becomes international, volunteers are frequently found. In the case of the Holocaust, volunteers and their effectiveness varied sharply from one Nazi-occupied country to another (see Fein, 1979, on universes of obligation).

Participants in Nazi genocide have been most studied. Hilberg distinguishes among (my terms) reluctants (who approached their work with reservations and misgivings), evaders, volunteers (who sought participation in democide for personal advantage [sometimes because of hopes to punish particular Jews and/or acquire their property], because of hatred for victim categories, perhaps even because the "action" seemed exciting), vulgarians (essentially nonideological bullies and sadists), perfectionists (who set standards for others to follow), and zealots (who embraced both the ideology and its implied responsibilities). There are careerists and draftees. Responses to orders to kill included dutiful obedience, withdrawal and avoidance (sometimes permitted by superiors), enthusiasm, and frenzied overachievement.

There are few studies of the psychology or sociology of participation of perpetrators (see, however, the review in Fein, 1993). Lifton (1986) studied the recruitment, socialization, and accommodation of physicians who participated in the Nazi genocide, and Goldhagen studied executioners of various sorts. It appears that the defense "following orders" was not even germane in some cases, there *is* documentation that some perpetrators declined opportunities to avoid participation. The reasons for this are complex and apparently include a feeling of obligation to peers, fear of later reprisals, and a certain amount of opportunism. There are also reports, from both victims and perpetrators, of occasional kindnesses. Both Lifton and Goldhagen, studying quite different populations, reported that many years after their participation, many of their interviewees did not deny participation but justified it on ideological

(anti-Semitic) grounds. Similarly, ideology was invoked in characterization of "kulaks" in the USSR and the middle-class and intellectuals as enemies of revolutions (Melson). In the German and Turkish/Armenian cases there have been manifestations of denial, of guilt, of adherence to ideological justification.

Corporate bodies, such as manufacturers who employ slave labor or judicial bodies that confiscate the possessions of victims or hospitals that sterilize or "euthanize" are also perpetrators. So are legislative bodies that pass enabling laws.

3. Bystanders

Only individual homicide is likely to ever be completely anonymous and unwitnessed. Surely most democide, whether human sacrifice of individuals or the execution of all the educated people in a town or village, or the movement of as many as millions by march or transport to killing places will be witnessed by those who are neither victim nor perpetrator. Countries are bystanders to war and democide. Majority populations are bystanders to domestic democide. Domestic educational, health-providing, financial, information, and other institutions are witness to governmental actions. The governments, institutions, and people of other countries are to varying degrees witnesses and bystanders. Domestic and international bystanders at all levels play various roles. Some, discussed briefly below, become helpers or rescuers or even defenders. Some act opportunistically to obtain gain from the vulnerability and weakness of the victims. Just as there have been neighbors and pastors who have sought to protect victims there have been neighbors who have blackmailed victims and stolen their possessions and ministers who have closed their eyes. There have been at the most very few large-scale 20th century democides that have been secret from the world. The United States refused entrance to Jews, Swiss banks accepted Nazi deposits of Jewish gold and financial instruments, art stolen from Jews is in museums the world around, and the UN and major world powers looked on as Nigeria starved secessionist Biafra into submission (Jacobs). And, there are onlookers, bystanders much like the "sidewalk superintendents" who stop to watch buildings going up or passersby who stop to watch children's ball games.

The variety of responses reflects diversity in democidal events themselves, patterns of prejudice and racism in bystander societies, cultural traditions of helping and of privacy, socioeconomic characteristics of observers, perceptions of own danger and of potential economic advantage or disadvantage. Among the individual level responses to reports of democide are: approval ("It's about time"), cupidity, cynicism, denial, ennui, horror, hyperidentification, ignorance (for example, geographic), immobilization, impotence, inability to act because of legal constraints, and indifference. Institutional, national, and international (for example, the UN and the International Red Cross) reactions parallel a number of the individual responses, particularly those claiming inability to act.

4. Helpers and Rescuers

Some people give water to victims awaiting execution or transport, some do no more than give fleeing victims directions, some snatch children from the arms of dead family members and take them home to raise, some smuggle food to those being starved, some take strangers into their homes and hide them, some provide false papers, some smuggle those about to be arrested to safety abroad. Some help but are unable to save a single life, others save hundreds. Some help is transitory, surreptitious, and risk free. Some is perduring and riskier. Some is particularistic (only known others), some is universal. Some help is given only when requested and then perhaps reluctantly. Some is volunteered and even insistently so. Some is done by individuals, some is collective effort. Some helpers and rescuers are caught and become victims. (For a review, see, again, Fein, 1993.)

D. Causes of Genocide, Politicide, and Other Forms of Democide

While there are exponentially larger literatures on war, riots, lynching, and murder, there is no dearth of explanations for the occurrence of the social violence manifest in the variety of behaviors labeled democide. There is more literature on the Holocaust of WW II than on other genocide and probably more on genocide than on politicide. (There is a substantial literature on class violence in both capitalist and communist or socialist states [historical and contemporary].) The amount of attention given to various democidal events in the second half of the 20th century has covaried with their visibility to North American and European audiences; that visibility has been determined in part by actual physical remoteness and by perceived significance in terms of "national security" of far-off events. That perceived significance is substantially influenced by media coverage and policymaker's perceptions of interests and desires of electorates. There are popular interpretations of democide, explanations by behavioral scientists, and findings of investigative bodies of various sorts. While there are some common threads, the elements of popular explanations, behavioral science perspectives, and

postevent bodies, private, public, and judicial, have often been quite different in conclusions and in recommendations for solutions.

1. Popular Explanations

Popular explanations come from (1) individuals engaged in everyday interaction; (2) formal organizations of various sorts, for example, human rights and related activist groups across the political spectrum attempting to prevent or stop large-scale killing by governments, not-for-profit relief organizations, and some professional associations; (3) apologists of the political right and left; (4) emergent spokespersons or experts who have opinions, share them freely, and come to be asked as social violence continues; (5) representatives of affected corporations, governments, or populations, and other lobbyists; and (6) the print and electronic media. Immediately or potentially affected governments provide interpretations supportive of victims or of perpetrators. As democide has become both more commonplace and more widely reported toward the end of the 20th century, popular explanations have increasingly incorporated elements of behavior science theories and the conclusions of various investigative bodies. (And, to some extent, claims and interpretations of groups with interests in forming public opinion).

Folk explanations are variously favorable and/or sympathetic to victims or perpetrators. Perspectives appear to reflect social identities and location in the social structure, and to some degree, the extent to which individuals and groups themselves feel threatened ("It could [could never] happen here"); sympathies for victims in the abstract obviously affect some interpretations.

Space constraints allow me to do no more here than list some popular explanations and interpretations for large-scale killings by governments in the 20th century: (1) human nature; (2) victims deserved it or "brought it on themselves"; (3) denial (it never happened); (4) it never happened and besides they deserved it; (5) such events are the work of criminal groups, criminal states, and so on; (6) such behaviors are the result of prejudice and hate; (7) it's all economic; (8) progress has costs ("You can't make an omelet without breaking eggs"—a French proverb sometimes attributed to Lenin); (9) "what can you expect from such people?"; (10) God demands the destruction of the wicked, of dissenters, of unbelievers, and so on. Some find an explanation in (11) the wickedness of indivduals of great power (i.e., remarkable individuals) such as Genghis Khan, Hitler, Pol Pot, or Stalin.

The kinds of "theories" noted have appeared and reappeared over time, they have been applied in variant forms to the whole range of violent behaviors, and they have been invoked with widely varying sophistication (and similarly rejected) by the full range of involvement and noninvolvement in democide and at all levels of society.

2. Biological and Behavioral Science Perspectives

My coverage of biological perspectives will be perfunctory (for an excellent and accessible review see Barash). Given space limitations I will suggest that there are two major behavioral science perspectives on democide and its component behaviors: (1) those focusing on the individual, associated primarily with psychology and related disciplines, and (2) those focusing on groups and the social structure. Economic perspectives, including Marxist structuralism, are treated separately. Two excellent volumes, McPhail (1991) and Rule (1988), contain comprehensive discussions which together cover most of the theoretical perspectives mentioned below. Fein, Gamson, Kuper, du Preez, Rummel, Stannard (see, especially, Appendix II), and Staub, among others, (1) review explanations more specifically focused on large-scale killing, (2) address questions of whether specific instances they discuss constitute genocide (or politicide or democide, etc.), and occasionally (3) suggest their own explanatory frameworks.

a. Biological and Sociobiological Interpretations

Most scientists today deny that humans have an instinct for war, that humans are genetically programmed for war, or that human evolution has selected for aggressiveness. Some scientists find Wilson's more sophisticated version of sociobiology with its emphasis on *adaptive* behavior whereby aggressiveness might be optimal in the short term (for example, in driving other, genetically unrelated, humans from scarce land, or killing them and taking the land) more persuasive. Others question that war and democide can *ever* be adaptive for the species. None of this denies that there are humans who might not start wars or democide but who seem to enjoy destructiveness and slaughter once they get started. Nor that we can be socialized into aggressive behavior and our inhibitions against killing dampened. The ultimate argument against human nature explanations of war and democide, including genocide, is that even "warlike" societies have long periods of peace and some societies do not participate in wars at all.

b. Economic Explanations

There are essentially two economic interpretations of genocide and other large-scale killings. The first is that of pragmatism or what has been called "rational choice" theory, an interpretation which says that people (and groups) engage in behaviors perceived as optimal paths to preferred worlds, for example, worlds without a disvalued minority, or where land or other resources previously possessed by a collectivity becomes available, or where the previously downtrodden become masters. Homer-Dixon's perspective on environmental scarcity and violent conflict with its (unexplained) implications for democide is congenial with such an interpretation. The second view consists of a collection of sometimes disparate Marxist and neo-Marxist interpretations. From a Marxist perspective it would be consistent to say that large-scale killing associated with colonial expansion or from assaults on domestic minorities results from the greed of capitalists *and* that killings of internal ethnic minorities (for example, Cossacks or Ukrainians, or Jews in the erstwhile Soviet Union) or of class or occupational groups (nobility, kulaks, intelligentsia, and so on) are necessary for completion of the struggle of the proletariat against feudalism or capitalism. One Marxist scholar (Cox) enriched his interpretation of large-scale killings (and individual discrimination—or lynching) by incorporating a notion of race as caste into his identification of capitalism as culprit.

c. Individually Oriented Perspectives

These perspectives generally look for explanations of violence in the personality characteristics or past experiences of violent individuals or some dynamic combination of the two. I noted above a view that human nature is at least predispositionally aggressive. The psychoanalyst looks for violence proneness, rooted perhaps in early truamatic experiences but clearly the consequences of uniquely personal experiences in molding an individual psyche. Freud believed that all of us have aggressiveness in our make-ups as well as a predisposition to "narcissistic rage" and that whether or not we *act* aggressively depends on differential success in socialization for repression or control. Storr locates the propensity for mass outbreaks of cruelty in the imagination—as shaped by aggressive personality disorders, sadomasochism, and paranoid delusion. Lifton (1986) offers an explanation for individual participation in genocide as facilitated by "doubling"—a process through which individuals develop a second self capable of demoniacal behaviors while retaining an earlier, more humane self. Proponents of the notion of "authoritarian personality" assert that childhood socialization experiences transform relatively undifferentiated initial personalities so that some people become tolerant and others authoritarian and prejudiced. Authoritarian personalities are more likely to agree to and participate in democide. Other psychologists simply postulate prejudiced personalities and then look at differences in their behaviors from the nonprejudiced. Fromm developed a theory according to which exposure to functionally debilitating social conditions generated *individual* alienation and disconnectedness leading in turn to "malignant aggression," including, presumably, enhanced likelihood of participation in genocide and other large-scale killing.

Clinical psychologists focus less on the individual personality than on the dynamics of the individual's interaction with his/her environment. The frustration-aggression hypothesis has been attractive to both psychological and psychological political science investigators, particularly those of the quantitative persuasion. Social psychologists have looked for explanations of violence in constellations of individual attitudes and have attended particularly to structural features of society fostering one or another attitude. "Relative deprivation" or a "search for identity" become independent variables related to specific attitudes, for example, isolation, powerlessness, and anomie, which in turn are linked to participation in group violence. Other social psychologists and anthropologists have drawn attention to the differences in societal socialization for aggression that result in *societies* more or less prone to war and in which individuals are more or less prone to aggressive behavior. Some investigators, predicating a link between ideologies and behavior, note that we tend to share the ideologies of those around us and that some ideologies are more favorable to chauvinism or to democide of various sorts. Lifton (1986) discovers in the Turkish-Armenian and Nazi genocides national ideological narratives of diseased societies cured by purification (destruction of the disease source) and regeneration. Hayden argues that exclusionary ideological justifications for "ethnic cleansing" were written into the constitutions of the postdissolution republics of former Yugoslavia. Du Preez argues for an interaction between social events (wars, famines, and so on) and individual events (fear, insecurity, and so on), which serially and in parallel culminate in individual and collective readiness for social violence. Melson hypothesizes that democidal killing is often a consequence of successful labeling of victim groups as enemies of ideological revolutions. Staub has argued an *incremental* acceptance of evil, specifically including genocide. Part of such incremental acceptance results from processes of dehumanization, distancing, bureaucratization, and so on, persuasively described by Sanford and Comstock and their colleagues, and from "psychic numbing." Re-

lated too, are notions of "spirals of aggression" parallel to arms races.

Some studies of war have observed how participation is massively satisfying for some. Men may feel that in fighting for a just cause they are doing something truly worthwhile, they may be exhilarated by actual fighting, or feel their masculinity enhanced by control over powerful weapons—or the lives of others. Numerous investigators have documented the gratifications that result from bonding experiences in combat, and wartime experiences more generally. The obvious question is, are such positively valued outcomes likely from participation in genocide, politicide, and democide? Do mass murderers bond? Frenzied participation in slaughter of noncombatant men, women, and children in colonial assaults on natives, in Mongol devastation of medieval Asian cities, and the Japanese rape of Nanking suggest that the answer must minimally be, "at least to some degree."

Importantly, while early studies attempted to describe the attitudinal structure of violent or nonviolent individuals, more recent studies have seen sets of attitudes as characterizing members of categories rather than as individual attributes. Interpretations that focus on prejudice alone or that invoke concepts such as deindividuation or emotional contagion have waned; they have not sustained empirical test.

d. Structural and Processual Perspectives

In recent years research on social conflict has become increasingly interdisciplinary as behavioral scientists in anthropology, cultural and social geography, economics, political science, psychology, and sociology, along with historians and philosophers, have unabashedly borrowed from one another in their attempts to make sense out of social conflict and social violence. The resulting literature is too rich to even outline/summarize, let alone discuss, in a short encyclopedia piece.

These wide-ranging interpretive theories generally come in about a dozen (the number is essentially an arbitrary artifact of how notions are divided up) varieties, most of which were developed in studies of other varieties of social violence than democide and its constituent elements: (1) theories of the middle range or empirical generalizations based on empirical studies (for example, that social conflict and violence increase in intensity to the degree that societal cleavages are superimposed [Coleman on community conflict, Lambert on communalism in India, Williams, *et al.*, on race relations]); (2) theories that emphasize the explanatory utility of different versions of "culture" ranging from anthropological notions of class or regional "cultures of violence" to the Marxian use of the term as synonymous with ideology; (3) theories that find the roots of collective violence in the structural arrangements of hierarchy and social differentiation in societies (for example, Marx on exploiting and exploited classes, the Tillies on structures of urbanization, industrialization, and state authority, Gamson on the criterial structural relation between authorities and potential partisans, or Grimshaw on "accommodative" structures); (4) theories that focus on social *processes/forms of interaction* and/or social *acts/behaviors* (for example, Collins, Coser, Dahrendorf, and Simmel on conflict as a social form or process or Tilly on repertoires of collective action or of collective behavior) or on social control as a societal structure *and* process (for example, Janowitz); (5) perspectives that give special attention to social violence (usually rioting in incidents used as documentation) as rational (in the means-end sense of that term—or even in the special "rational-choice" sense) and intentional behavior *and* as a successful agent for social change; (6) what Rule has labeled "value integration theory," the quintessential exemplary of which is Smelser's "value-added" theory with its five stages of: (i) structural conduciveness; (ii) structural strain; (iii) growth and spread of a generalized belief; (iv) precipitating factors; and (v) mobilization of participants (see Mazian for an adaptation of Smelser focused specifically on genocide); (7) theories that focus on the nature of the state, for example, Andrzejewski on military organization and society or Rummel (1997a) on state power as a criterial variable in probabilties of participation in war or democide (cf. however, Krain's argument that opportunity better predicts genocide and politicide than level of power concentration), and Freeman on bureaucracy, modernization, and genocide; (8) Actonian theories on the availability of power and its corrosive effects (see, again, Rummel 1997a); (9) theories that weapons for large-scale murder, just as those for individual homicide, will be used if available; (10) collective behavior theories such as Turner and Killian's conceptualization of "structurally emergent collective definitions"; (11) McPhail's integration of Mead on purposive problem-solving with Powers' feedback perspective in which rational, autonomous, problem-solving individuals in difficult situations cooperate and coordinate their behaviors in attempts to achieve shared goals. Riots, or war, or lynchings, or democide, could all result from such a process.

(12) Donald Black is developing an ambitious theory that may have important explanatory implications for large-scale killing by governments. Black's premises for his "paradigm of pure sociology" for the field of conflict often differ sharply from those reviewed in the paragraphs above, including the principles that: (1) conflict is not a clash of interests but of right and wrong and a matter of morality and justice; (2) that understanding individuals qua individuals, or personalities, will not provide understanding of social conflict and violence; (3) that conflict relations are determined by *relations* of spatial, social, and cultural distance; and (4) that conflict relations can be propositionally specified *and* are susceptible to quantification.

All of these theoretical perspectives seem reasonable on first reading and all have been shown to be compatible with some facts of some events. Sorting out *which* theories are truly falsifiable and which most powerful will require considerable comparative research. The unfortunate likelihood is that there will continue to be opportunities for such research.

E. Judicial and Other Archives, Investigations, and Reports

There have probably been written reports on social violence, including large-scale killing, for as long as there have been written narrative reports of any sort. Large-scale killing in the name of maintaining the public order, or in retribution, or to put down revolt, has been employed by civil authority from its first establishment. Local officials and resident military commanders will have been asked to keep their superiors in metropolitan centers informed of local disruptions, particularly those that might be seen as harbingers of threats to the regime; it is reasonable to believe that private intelligence on democide of all sorts has an equivalently respectable antiquity. Accounts of pre- 20th century democide are based on government reports (often undistinguishable from myths and religious writing in earliest documents), biblical stories, despots' boasts inscribed on desert cliffs, and, in the last half millennium, increasingly on accounts of contemporaries and the scholarship of historians.

During the modern period official reports on wars and rebellions have become more or less routinized; in the second half of the 20th century the same has become true of democidal events. At the international level there have been reports by League of Nations and UN agencies and by organizations of victorious allies. There are reports by accused and accusing nations, Turkey defends its actions with its Armenian minority, the Vietnamese report on American atrocities. Neutral governments appoint bodies such as the British and Finnish Enquiry Commissions on Kampuchea. Organizations such as the International Red Cross report on their activities or, in some instances, defend themselves against accusations of neglect or timorousness (for example, against claims of abandonment of the people of Biafra during the Nigerian civil war). There are countless ad hoc and self-designated international commissions such as the East Timor Defense Committee or the Lawyers Committee on Human Rights. Organizations such as Amnesty International, Cultural Survival, and Human Rights Watch (initially Americas Watch Committee) publish regular and special reports on variously labeled manifestations of democide. Research institutes such as the Carnegie Endowment for International Peace and the American Enterprise Institute for Public Policy Research have counterparts in many other countries, as do university-based research centers. In the United States there have been Senate, House, State and Defense Department, Agency, and military commissions, boards, and reviews, at least part of whose findings are made public. These bodies, which sit from periods of weeks to periods of years or in some cases continuously, receive from no funding at all to millions of dollars. They are variously charged with finding facts of events (sometimes particular versions of facts), causal explanations, solutions, modes of prevention, and, assessing responsibility.

Factual details, interpretations, and recommendations in reports of these various bodies reflect (1) the factual and interpretive biases and the social and political agendas of appointing and sponsoring entities; (2) the political climate when investigating bodies are appointed; (3) the composition of the commissions (or other investigative bodies) and their staff; (4) the extent to which investigators are able to gain access to relevant documents, evidence, and witnesses; (5) the support, both moral and financial, provided; (6) the time allowed for the body's investigation and report writing; (7) whether or not there were open hearings, particularly hearings in which public participation was invited; and (8) what sort of dissemination of findings was projected. Curiously, reporting practices at one time may inflate the extent of democide "documented" in later investigations, as when military officers or bureaucrats inflate the number of enemy casualties or those of "enemies of the people" (for example, "body counts" in Vietnam and meeting of "quotas" in the course of democide in Stalin's USSR). More accurate accountings can be equally damning, of course, as in Nazi records of their large-scale killings of civilians. Also curious, perhaps, is the fact that later governments of countries that have practiced democide have in some instances documented, and apologized for, the slaughter.

At least tens of thousands of pages have been published (and perhaps millions written—see, for example, Goldhagen on his sources) about the extent, causes, and prevention of democide. Commissions, nongovernmental investigative bodies, and activist organizations have made basically two varieties of recommendations for prevention of genocide. The first set of recommendations aims at reducing the root causes of democidal phenomena by eradicating poverty and injustice and reducing prejudice. The second emphasizes social control through successful application of law or increasing the control capabilities of international social control agencies such as UN peace-keeping units *and* changing sovereignty law so that peacekeepers can intervene in domestic democide. Additional suggestions are sometimes made, such as bans on certain kind of weapons or the invention of governmental structures which will allow at least partial autonomy for minorities, none of these additional proposals have made much headway (see, *inter alia*, Damrosch, Fein 1992, Gottlieb).

VI. FORECASTING AND CONTROLLING GENOCIDAL/POLITICIDAL/DEMOCIDAL BEHAVIORS

Aside from the moral toll of large-scale killing for both perpetrators and bystanders, there are incalculable social and economic costs. Time, energy, and material resources are expended in killing, in some cases along with vast material wealth. When healthy humans are killed their productivity is lost and resources expended in raising them are wasted, to say nothing of lost creativity, inventiveness, and so on. The forecasting, prevention, and control of democide should be high priority goals. In this section I will say something about these goals—and about obstacles to their attainment.

A. Forecasting, Early Warning, and So On

Enough is known about democide and its subtypes so that it should be possible to specify necessary and sufficient causes if data can be obtained. Intelligence on social violence or new patterns of legal discrimination against domestic minorities can be gathered by individual monitoring by business men and women, journalists, missionaries, and diplomatic personnel, and can be reported by mail, electronic media (including e-mail), diplomatic pouch, and travelers, including refugees. Intelligence on troop movements, refugee flows, destruction of cities and hamlets or crops, can also be gathered by distance monitoring via satellite imagery. Governments publish a variety of series on topics ranging from education and health to crime and policing; many of these materials are assembled into statistical compendia and published by UNESCO and other UNO agencies, the World Bank and the International Monetary Fund and a variety of activist philanthropic and ameliorative organizations. The CIA, the U.S. Department of Defense, and the U.S. Disarmament Agency publish materials on foreign military establishments and the international arms trade. Ruth Sivard has for some years collected many of these statistics and used them to show, for example, relations between arms expenditures per capita and those on health and education or to discover relationships between per capita wealth, arms expenditures, and government repression of own people. Similar analyses could be employed to forecast probabilities of democide that could be used in conjunction with more qualitative assessments of same likelihoods.

B. Proposals for Prevention, Control, and Termination of Democide

There are perhaps five levels of activity that might be pursued in attempts to cope with democide. I list them in order of increasing potency and decreasing likelihood of occurrence: (1) dissemination of information, invocation of public opinion and grass roots letter-writing campaigns, public and private efforts at moral suasion; (2) sanctions short of intervention, for example, international law with cases tried in the world court or special tribunals (problem: who delivers alleged perpetrators to courts and who enacts punishments?), diplomatic sanctions ranging from letters of query to acts of censure (problem: what perpetrators are likely to be affected by such communications?), economic sanctions of various sorts ranging from blockades (problem: what keeps third parties from providing blockaded goods), boycotts (problem: what keeps other parties from purchasing boycotted goods), embargoes on strategic matériel (problem: who will police violators who persist in sending strategic matériel? Note, for example, failures of embargoes on China, Iraq, and Libya in the late 20th century) and, manipulation of foreign (including military) aid (problems: [a] donor governments may have competing policy goals and [b] military and other suppliers want to maintain markets); (3) intervention or credible threat of intervention and/or establishment of peacekeeping structures by the United Nations, or

regional security organizations, or by sovereign states (problems: [a] disagreement among potential peacekeeping sponsors or partners, for example, Russian disagreement re sanctions against Iraq and Serbia and [b] domestic concerns over danger to peacekeepers, for example, U.S. concern over danger to peacekeepers in Somalia and Bosnia); (4) changes in the worldwide patterns of distribution of wealth and poverty and injustice and justice that contribute to the occurrence of democide (problem: which rich and powerful countries will lead the procession in voluntarily divesting themselves of wealth and power?); (5) changes in governmental structures such as [a] spread and enhancement of democracy (problem: Rummel's solution *may* be occurring through evolutionary change, there is no obvious way in which force can be employed to change totalitarian states into democracies) or [b] creation of ethnic or other "nations" within states (Gottlieb) or invention of new forms of federalism (problem: thus far such solutions have received no visible support) or [c] a stronger United Nations (problem: a continuing goal continually running into resistance from sovereign states, particularly those of greatest power).

1. Some Problems Concerning the Implementation of Proposals for Control

A particularly instructive chapter in Kuper's (1985) pioneering and suggestive volume, *The Prevention of Genocide*, is devoted to the history of vicissitudes of antislavery action in the United Nations; many of the problems were continuations of earlier difficulties in the League of Nations. Three principal problems contributed to the lack of success in confronting the problem of world slavery; the same problems have been critical in difficulties in attaining consensus about coping with democide: (1) the central stumbling block has been and continues to be the issue of national sovereignty. No nation wants to give it up and all nations are reluctant to try to even nibble at that of other nations. (2) Every nation, even the most democratic, engages in behaviors which by some definitions and from some perspectives can be seen as unjust. Thus, nations are reluctant to push for protection of minorities elsewhere because of concern that there may be challenges to their own practices; And (3) a combination of popular indifference in nonaffected societies and occasional support of democidal practices by large sectors of populations in violator states. These matters have proved critical in efforts to curb genocide and other democide.

Slavery has not disappeared but it has substantially declined. There *are* instances of sustained peace among nations. Harmony among diverse populations *has* sometimes perdured for centuries. A world without democide should be possible.

Acknowledgments

Thanks for various sorts of collegial assistance are due Donald Black, Kai Erickson, Helen Fein, William Gamson, Polly Grimshaw, Barbara Harff, Albrecht Holschuh, Rudy Rummel, Barry Schwartz, Brad Smith, David Stannard, and Arthur Stinchcombe and are most gratefully given. I want also to thank Les Kurtz and Jennifer Turpin for making me think about these unhappy but important matters.

Also See the Following Articles

ENEMY, CONCEPT AND IDENTITY OF • ETHNIC CONFLICTS AND COOPERATION • PEACE AND DEMOCRACY • WARFARE, MODERN

Bibliography

Barash, D. P. (1991). *Introduction to peace studies.* Belmont, CA: Wadsworth.

Black, D. (1989). *The social structure of right and wrong.* New York: Academic.

Chalk, F., and Jonassohn, K. (1990). *The history and sociology of genocide: Analyses and case studies.* New Haven: Yale University Press.

Chang, I. (1997). *The rape of Nanking: The forgotten Holocaust of World War II.* New York: Basic Books.

Charny, I. W. (ed.). (1988), *Genocide: A critical bibliographic review.* New York: Facts On File Publications.

Charny, I. W. (ed.). (1991). *Genocide: A critical bibliographic review,* Volume Two. New York: Facts on File Publications.

Conquest, R. (1986). *The harvest of sorrow: Soviet collectivization and the terror-famine.* New York: Oxford University Press.

Cooney, M. (1997). From warre to tyranny: Lethal conflict and the state. *American Sociological Review, 62,* 316–338.

Cox, O. C. (1948). *Caste, class, and race: A study in social dynamics.* New York: Doubleday.

Damrosch, L. F. (ed.). (1993). *Enforcing restraint: Collective intervention in internal conflicts.* New York: Council on Foreign Relations Press.

Davies, N. (1981). *Human sacrifice in history and today.* New York: William Morrow.

Elkins, S. (1959). *Slavery: A problem in American institutional and intellectual life.* Chicago: University of Chicago Press.

De Zayas, A. (1994). *A terrible revenge: The ethnic cleansing of the East European Germans, 1944–1950.* Translated from the German by John A. Koehler. New York: St. Martin's Press. (Published in 1993 under title, *The German expellees: Victims in war and peace.*)

Fein, H. (1979). *Accounting for genocide: National responses and Jewish victimization during the Holocaust.* New York: Free Press.

Fein, H. (1993). *Genocide: A sociological perspective.* London: Sage.

Fein, H. (ed.). (1992). *Genocide watch.* New Haven: Yale University Press.

Fogelman, E. (1994). *Conscience and courage: Rescuers of Jews during the holocaust.* New York: Anchor.

Freeman, M. (1995). Genocide, civilization and modernity. *British Journal of Sociology, 46,* 207–225.

Fromm, E. (1941). *Escape from freedom.* New York: Rinehart.

Gamson, W. A. (1995). Hiroshima, the Holocaust, and the politics of exclusion. *American Sociological Review 60,* 1–20.

Goldhagen, F. J. (1996). *Hitler's willing executioners: Ordinary Germans and the holocaust.* New York: Knopf.

Gottlieb, G. (1993). *Nation against state: A new approach to ethnic conflicts and the decline of sovereignty.* New York: Council on Foreign Relations Press.

Grossman, D. A. (1995). *On killing: The psychological cost of learning to kill in war and society.* New York: Little, Brown and Company.

Hale, C. R. (1997). Consciousness, violence, and the politics of memory in Guatemala. With commentary by Arturo Arias, Ricardo Falla, Jorge Ramón González Ponciano, David McCreer and David Stoll. *Current Anthropology, 38,* 817–838.

Harff, B., and Gurr, T. R. (1996). Victims of the state: Genocides, politicides, and group repression from 1945 to 1995. In Jongman, 1996.

Hassig, R. (1988). *Aztec warfare: Imperial expansion and political control.* Norman: University of Oklahoma Press.

Hayden, R. M. (1996). Imagined communities and real victims: Self-determination and ethnic cleansing in Yugoslavia. *American Ethnologist, 23,* 783–801.

Hilberg, R. (1992). *Perpetrators, victims, bystanders: The Jewish catastrophe 1933–1945.* New York: Harper-Collins.

Hinton, A. L. (1996). Agents of death: Explaining the Cambodian genocide in terms of psychosocial dissonance. *American Anthropologist, 98,* 818–831.

Homer-Dixon, T. F. (1991). On the threshold: Environmental changes as causes of acute conflict. *International Security, 16,* 76–116.

Homer-Dixon, T. F. (1994). Environmental scarcities and violent conflict: Evidence from cases. *International Security 19,* 5–40.

Jacobs, D. (1988). *The brutality of nations.* New York: Paragon House.

Jongman, A. J. (ed.). (1996). *Contemporary genocides: Causes, cases, consequences.* Leiden: Interdisciplinary Research Program on Root Causes of Human Rights Violations.

Kaufman, S. J. (1996). Spiraling to ethnic war: Elites, masses, and Moscow in Moldova's Civil War. *International Security 21,* 108–138.

Kelman, H. C., and Hamilton, V. L. (1989). *Crimes of obedience: Toward a social psychology of authority and responsibility.* New Haven: Yale University Press.

Krain, M. (1993). State-sponsored mass murder: The onset and severity of genocides and politicides. *Journal of Conflict Resolution, 41,* 331–360.

Krausnick, H., Bucheim, H., Broszat, M., and Jacobsen, H. (1968). *Anatomy of the SS state.* Translated from the German by Richard Barry, Marian Jackson, and Dorothy Long. London: Collins.

Kressel, N. J. (1996). *Mass hate: The global rise of genocide and terror.* New York: Plenum Press.

Kuper, L. (1985). *The prevention of genocide.* New Haven: Yale University Press.

Lemkin, R. (1944). *Axis rule in occupied Europe.* Washington, DC: Carnegie Endowment for International Peace.

Levy, M. J. (1952). *The structure of society.* Princeton: Princeton University Press.

Lifton, R. J. (1982 [1967]). *Death in life: Survivors of Hiroshima.* New York: Random House.

Lifton, R. J. (1986). *The Nazi doctors: Medical killing and the psychology of genocide.* New York: Basic Books.

Markusen, E., and Kopf, D. (1995). *The holocaust and strategic bombing: Genocide and total war in the 20th century.* Boulder: Westview.

Mazian, F. (1990). *Why genocide? The Armenian and Jewish experiences in perspective.* Ames: Iowa State University Press.

McPhail, C. (1991). *The myth of the madding crowd.* New York: Aldine de Gruyter.

Melson, R. (1992). *Revolution and genocide: On the origins of the Armenian genocide and the Holocaust.* Chicago: University of Chicago Press.

Norton, J. (1979). *When our worlds cried: Genocide in Northwestern California.* San Francisco: The Indian Historian Press.

Payne, R. (1973). *Massacre.* New York: Macmillan.

du Preez, P. (1994). *Genocide: The psychology of mass murder.* London: Boyars/Bowerdean.

Reisman, W. M., and Antoniou, C. T. (eds.). (1994). *The laws of war: A comprehensive collection of primary documents of international law covering armed conflict.* New York: Vintage.

Rule, J. B. (1988). *Theories of civil violence.* Berkeley: University of California Press.

Rummel, R. (1990). *Lethal politics: Soviet genocide and mass murder since 1917.* New Brunswick: Transaction.

Rummel, R. (1991). *China's bloody century: Genocide and mass murder since 1900.* New Brunswick: Transaction.

Rummel, R. (1992). *Democide: Nazi genocide and mass murder.* New Brunswick: Transaction.

Rummel, R. (1994). *Death by government.* New Brunswick: Transaction.

Rummel, R. (1997a). *Power kills: Democracy as a method of nonviolence.* New Brunswick: Transaction.

Rummel, R. (1997b). *Statistics of democide: Genocide and mass murder since 1900.* Charlottesville: Center for National Security Law, University of Virginia.

Sanford, N., and Comstock, C. (eds.). (1971). *Sanctions for evil.* San Francisco: Jossey-Bass.

Sivard, R. L. (1991). *World military and social expenditures 1991.* Washington, DC: World Priorities.

Smith, R. (1994). Women and genocide: Notes on an unwritten history. *Holocaust and Genocide Studies, 8,* 315–334.

Stannard, D. E. (1992). *American holocaust: Columbus and the conquest of the new world.* New York: Oxford University Press.

Staub, E. (1989). *The roots of evil: The origins of genocide and other group violence.* Cambridge: Cambridge University Press.

Stiglmayer, A. (ed.). (1994). *Mass rape: The war against women in Bosnia-Herzegovina.* Lincoln: University of Nebraska Press.

Storr, A. (1991). *Human destructiveness.* New York: Grove Weidenfeld.

Totten, S., Parsons, W. S., and Charny, I. W. (1997). *Century of genocide: Eyewitness accounts and critical views.* New York: Garland Publishing.

Uekert, B. (1995). *Rivers of blood.* Westport CT: Praeger.

Wiskemann, E. (1956). *Germany's eastern neighbours: Problems relating to the Oder-Neisse Line and the Czech frontier regions.* London: Oxford University Press.

Guerrilla Warfare

Anthony James Joes

Saint Joseph's University

GLOSSARY

Guerrilla A term of Spanish origin; literally, "little war." First used in English to describe the local Spanish forces opposing Napoleon's effort to rule Spain, in the Peninsular War of 1808–1814. Now generally applied to any irregular military force carrying on a protracted conflict at the local level against a ruling or occupying government with superiority of conventional military forces.

Infrastructure Civilians within the society who provide active support to guerrillas operating outside the society.

Policy of Attraction A method of undermining the appeal of a guerrilla movement to the indigenous population by ameliorating the negative social conditions that create support for the guerrilla cause in the first place.

Pyrrhic Victory A victory achieved at great cost to the victor; a triumph that is a virtual defeat. (From *Pyrrhus,* an ancient Greek king who is said to have remarked after a costly defeat of the Romans, "Another such victory and I am ruined.")

Sanctuary A safe haven across an international border that may be used by guerrillas as a refuge or base of operations.

GUERRILLA WARFARE is a form of struggle carried on by those who seek to wage a protracted conflict against greatly superior forces. This article examines the general principles of guerrilla warfare as well as methods employed to defeat it, and then presents case studies illustrating those principles and methods.

I. HOW GUERRILLAS FIGHT

In the decades following World War II, the term "guerrilla" became widely associated with communism. Certainly, some of the most notable guerrilla movements, as those in China, Greece, and Vietnam, were communist-directed. But in Eritrea, Ukraine, Tibet, and most spectacularly Afghanistan, guerrillas fought *against* communist regimes. In those countries, as in the Vendean resistance to the French Revolution and the Spanish insurgency against Napoleon, guerrilla war was the instrument of popular movements of nationalist, religious, and/or conservative orientation.

By definition, guerrillas are the weaker party in a struggle. They lack the numbers, training, and equipment of a conventional army. That is precisely why they fight as guerrillas. Their first duty, therefore, is self-preservation; it is no disgrace for guerrillas to retreat in face of superior force, indeed it is mandatory.

Guerrillas must seek to protract the conflict: if it is quickly over, it will be because the guerrillas have been destroyed. A protracted conflict means that government forces cannot eliminate or disperse the guerrillas; this will weaken the morale of the government troops. It

Copyright © 1999 by Academic Press.
All rights of reproduction in any form reserved.

also provides time: for the guerrillas to train and test leaders, for foreign help to arrive, and most of all for the guerrillas to develop themselves into conventional forces, which is their true objective.

Well-led guerrillas are always on the tactical offensive, searching out opportunities for action: attacking small outposts, convoys, and patrols, or damaging bridges, railways, and roads. They will never attack except when they are certain to win. This requires that they greatly outnumber the enemy at the point of contact. And that in turn requires the ability to assemble, strike, withdraw, and disperse with great speed. Speed, in attack and in withdrawal, is the essence of guerrilla combat. Here the guerrillas' lightness of armament is an advantage (the Roman word for the equipment of a regular army was *impedimenta*). That is why the great philosopher of war Carl von Clausewitz advised guerrillas to operate in rough country.

Thus, guerrillas are combatants who seek to wage a protracted conflict against superior forces by emphasizing speed and deception, whereby they win small victories through their numerical superiority at a particular point.

To survive, guerrillas need high morale, accurate intelligence, and if possible, a secure base. Guerrilla life involves much physical hardship, and the taking of life and destruction of property. Hence maintaining good morale becomes essential. Morale can be kept high by recruiting only volunteers and by constantly winning small victories; but most of all, good morale requires a good cause. Sometimes the good cause is obvious, as in Afghan resistance to Soviet invasion; sometimes the cause needs to be explained through political indoctrination.

Intelligence—knowledge of the location, numbers, equipment, and morale of the enemy—is equally vital. Such intelligence can derive from penetration of the enemy police and armed forces. It can also come from sympathetic civilians (hence it is a good idea for guerrilla bands always to include at least some natives of the area in which they are operating). Besides high-quality intelligence, guerrillas need food, medicine, and recruits. These come from their organized civilian supporters, called the *infrastructure*. Guerrillas operate outside of settled life, the civilian infrastructure operates inside.

A secure base means an area where the guerrillas can store supplies, train members, nurse their wounded, and rest in safety. Normally that place will be in a remote or inaccessible part of the country, as was the case in Mao's China. Today, perhaps few if any areas are really inaccessible to a government equipped with helicopters and specialized aircraft. In substitution for, or in addition to, a secure base, guerrillas may possess a *sanctuary,* that is, a refuge across an international frontier, as the Viet Cong possessed in Laos and Cambodia. The main problem with a sanctuary is that the host country may withdraw its use, which happened to the Greek communist guerrillas of the late 1940s.

Well-led guerrillas can survive on human and material resources from inside the country of their operations. To win, however, they need foreign assistance, because almost certainly guerrillas cannot accumulate the kind of armament necessary for them to field conventional units if they lack outside aid. Experience strongly suggests that it is very difficult to defeat guerrillas who have an attractive cause and outside help. On the other hand, even if the guerrillas enjoy both foreign aid and a sanctuary, it will do them little good in the end if they pursue a bad strategy, as in the case of the Greek insurgents (see below).

Finally, operating in tandem with friendly conventional forces is immensely helpful to guerrillas, for this makes it dangerous for the enemy to maintain strongpoints and/or to send out small units to hunt guerrillas.

II. DEFEATING GUERRILLAS

An analysis of guerrilla conflicts both ancient and contemporary produces a set of principles by which a government can hope to defeat guerrillas. First and foremost, the government must control the conduct of its troops toward civilians. Brutality or looting in the villages legitimizes the guerrillas, makes recruits for them, and interferes with the government's gathering of intelligence. Even the most resource-poor government can make sure that the arrival of its troops in a village does not resemble the descent of a plague of locusts (or worse). *Rectitude* on the part of the authorities is worth many battalions. Confirming this principle in a negative sense are the experiences of the Japanese in China, the Germans in Yugoslavia, and the Soviets in Afghanistan, and in a positive sense the British in Malaya, the Americans against Aguinaldo, and Magsaysay against the Huks (see below). Two additional and quite effective means by which a government can undercut the appeal of guerrillas are (1) addressing some major peasant grievance(s), and (2) offering a peaceful road to change, in the form of honest elections or some sort of traditional assembly. It is often observed that the ballot box is the coffin of insurgencies. (For both of these approaches, see section "The Huks" below.)

Other inexpensive tactics for the government to pursue include: encouraging defection by the offer of amnesty and resettlement (surrendered or even captured guerrillas often provide valuable intelligence); buying up guns from civilians in or near guerrilla areas, no questions asked; offering large rewards for the apprehension of specific guerrilla leaders accused of specific criminal acts; and sending small, well-trained hunter groups into guerrilla territory on long-term patrols.

If the guerrillas have a sanctuary, great effort should be made to shut it down, through either diplomatic or military means. In the Algerian struggle, the French quite effectively closed off the Tunisian frontier, while during the Afghanistan war the Soviets utterly failed to deal effectively with the Pakistan border. If, however, the guerrillas are clearly losing, the sanctuary problem will probably solve itself.

In the last analysis, victory over guerrillas consists not in killing them (usually a difficult thing to do) but in separating them from civilians from whom they derive sustenance. Resolving some peasant grievance(s) is one effective way to accomplish this, because almost invariably peasants who support guerrilla movements do so for concrete and finite reasons, as contrasted to the often ideological and open-ended goals of the insurgent leadership. Another method is to gather scattered or nomadic populations into easily guarded settlements. This procedure requires a good deal of planning and money if it is not to thoroughly alienate the regrouped civilians; resettlement was successful in Malaya, but in general it is inadvisable. Better than removing the civilians is removing the guerrillas. This can be done through "clearing and holding": government forces inundate a given area, driving the guerrillas out and identifying their sympathizers (clearing); a local militia is trained and armed to prevent the return of the guerrillas (holding). Then a neighboring area is cleared, and so on until the guerrillas are pushed into remote and poorly inhabited areas. This is definitely a low-casualty strategy, but it requires time, patience, coordination, and well-disciplined troops.

One cannot wage successful counterinsurgency on the cheap. The country undertaking to defeat a serious guerrilla movement must be prepared to make a substantial commitment of troops, or else find some other way to deal (or not to deal) with the insurgency. Many authors have maintained that for a government to defeat guerrillas, the ratio of its forces to the guerrillas needs to be 10 : 1. In Malaya, the ratio of soldiers and paramilitary to guerrillas reached 29 : 1; in French Algeria, 18 : 1. In contrast, the ratio of French forces to the Viet Minh was 1.7 : 1; and for the Americans and South Vietnamese against the Viet Cong and North Vietnamese Army, 1.6 : 1. Yet wars are not won by favorable ratios alone: shortly before Fidel Castro's triumphant march into Havana, the regime's army overmatched the Fidelistas 15 : 1.

The role of geography in guerrilla warfare is complex. The British waged a successful counterinsurgency in far-off Malaya, as did the Americans in the far-off Philippines, while the Soviet debacle in Afghanistan and the Napoleonic disaster in Spain both took place just across the border. But geography is primary and decisive for the all-important question of foreign assistance to guerrillas.

III. SOME MAJOR GUERRILLA CONFLICTS

A. The American Revolution

Every American schoolchild once knew that the climax of the American Revolution was the surrender of General Charles Cornwallis at Yorktown. But why was Cornwallis there?

The army available to the British Crown during the Revolution was small; hence the notorious "Hessian mercenaries." This army enjoyed no great technological advantages over the troops of the Continental Congress. Much of its food and munitions had to come from Britain by sailing ship across the treacherous North Atlantic, with crossings taking up to 2 months. The Royal Navy had deteriorated since its victory in the Seven Years War, and the watchful French were ready to cause whatever mischief they could for their British rivals.

In October 1777, the battle of Saratoga (in New York) convinced the French to help the Americans. It also turned British strategy toward the southern colonies, supposedly rich in food and full of loyalists. Their plan was to conquer South Carolina and then proceed methodically northward. A large British force captured Charleston in May 1780 and then destroyed the last regular American army in the southern colonies. The British and their vengeful loyalist allies began burning private homes and Presbyterian churches, and the whole of Georgetown, South Carolina. These acts provoked the predictable response: guerrilla leaders like the Swamp Fox (Francis Marion) and the Gamecock (Thomas Sumter) kept the torch of resistance burning. Their well-mounted bands pushed small British outposts back to Charleston, harried communications between Charleston and Camden, and attacked British detachments trying to gather food. The Swamp Fox led bands varying in size between 50 and 250 men; the born guerrilla chieftain, "fertile in strategems, he struck unperceived."

Deciding that the true source of the South Carolina guerrilla war lay in North Carolina, in October 1780 Cornwallis led an army there. He soon fell victim to guerrillas operating symbiotically with the small, newly arrived American army of Nathanael Greene. If Cornwallis were to subdivide his army into numerous, fast-moving groups to hunt the guerrillas, they would be in danger from Greene's forces; but by concentrating on the pursuit of Greene, the British fell victim to harassment day and night by the guerrillas. Cornwallis's victory over Greene at Guilford Court House (March 1781) was Pyrrhic: of his force of 1900 he lost 500, which he could not replace. Meanwhile, guerrillas wore out his remaining troops with alarms and chases and sudden small encounters. Simply getting enough food became a major problem. In tacit admission that the Carolina enterprise had been a mistake from the beginning, Cornwallis crossed the line into Virginia, to keep his rendezvous with destiny at Yorktown.

B. The Vendée

In 1793 the French Revolution was entering its most radical phase. It would take the lives of the King and Queen and thousands of ordinary Frenchmen, assault the Church, and plunge France into war against all Europe. These policies evoked profound and widespread domestic opposition: revolt swept Brittany, Lyons, and the southern provinces. But the most famous of the uprisings against the radical regime in Paris took place in the Vendée, an Atlantic province the size of Connecticut, with a pre-Revolutionary population of 800,000.

Persecution of religion and the imposition of the draft upon the peasantry (from which town officials exempted themselves) were the principal grievances of the Vendeans. More than 120,000 of them, including women and youths, joined the insurgent forces. They captured several sizeable towns, notably Saumur. From there they might have marched to Paris, but did not, owing to their narrow regional perspective and the absence of both professional military leadership and strict discipline. But most of all they lacked good arms, because England, although nearby, declined to help.

The Paris regime employed the most extreme methods to crush the Vendean peasantry, including mass executions preceded by mass rape, the deliberate killing of children, the drowning of prisoners, the burning of villages, the poisoning of wells, even experiments with poison gas. It was "the first ideological genocide" in human history. The distinction between combatant and noncombatant disappeared; supporters of the regime were slaughtered along with its opponents. The regime overwhelmed the Vendée with 130,000 troops, compared to 180,000 fighting all of France's enemies on the northern and eastern frontiers. The war was brought to an end, for a while, by the young General Louis-Lazare Hoche. He isolated the Vendée by gridding its eastern section with little forts, moving slowly westward so that the insurgents would have no place to go. Civilian hostages were taken until weapons were handed over. But Hoche also strove to reestablish discipline among the government troops who had hitherto raped and burned at will; he also restored a measure of religious freedom. These latter policies went far to calm the desperate peasantry.

To suppress the guerrilla risings in the Vendée and neighboring Brittany cost 150,000 French lives, more than the disastrous Russian campaign of 1812. The once prosperous Vendée had been reduced to ruin. But the Vendeans had their revenge: in May 1815, at the return of Napoleon from Elba, they rose again in hostility to the heir of the Revolution. The 30,000 soldiers Napoleon sent to the Vendée would have made all the difference to him at Waterloo.

C. Spain

In 1808, Emperor Napoleon invaded Spain. It was this act, not the invasion of Russia a few years later, that was the real undoing of his precarious empire. The fundament of this Spanish disaster was the national uprising of the Spanish people, from which our word *guerrilla* derives. The invasion of their country, followed by French outrages—systematic rape, routine sacrilege, the looting of cathedrals and the burning of churches—aroused the fury of the Spanish people.

Economically underdeveloped, crossed by several mountain chains, Spain provided an ideal setting for guerrillas. With widespread popular support, the insurgents always enjoyed timely and abundant intelligence. Their rapidity of movement baffled, exhausted, and finally overwhelmed the French. The French government in Madrid often found itself isolated from France and even from the rest of Spain. Shipments of food and mail required large and expensive convoys, often as many as 2000 soldiers, as protection against guerrillas. French cavalry horses, overworked and underfed, died in droves. French generals behaved like independent powers, indifferent or hostile to the claims of neighboring commanders. British seapower brought guns and supplies to the insurgents. At the same time, Wellington's small Anglo-Portuguese army both supported and was supported by the insurgents, a symbiotic relationship between regular troops and guerrilla bands like the one in Revolutionary Carolina. And throughout the war the port of Cadiz remained in the hands of a regular Spanish army. French numbers in Spain proved inadequate to the multidimensional struggle, even though by the time of the Russian campaign they reached 230,000, including Polish and Italian allied units. They regrouped into large, immobile city garrisons, abandoning the countryside to guerrillas. By the summer of 1813, Napoleonic Spain had ceased to exist.

Their lost struggle in Spain cost French and Imperial forces between 200,000 and 300,000 casualties, of whom perhaps 180,000 died. By destroying the myth of French invincibility, the Spanish insurgency encouraged renewed European resistance to the French imperium. But even if the French had achieved victory in Spain it would have represented little more than a strategically irrelevant diversion of valuable forces from more important fronts. Napoleon himself grasped this strategic truth, saying "I am the heir of Charlemagne, not of Louis XIV," meaning that France's destiny lay across the Rhine, not the Pyrenees. But he ignored his own words, and in the end, the Spanish adventure must rank as Napoleon's greatest mistake.

D. The Boers

The Boer Republics of southern Africa were about the size of Kansas and Nebraska combined. Their inhabitants, today called Afrikaaners, were the descendants of religious refugees from 17th-century Europe. Fulfillment of the British grand design for an African empire stretching from the Cape to Cairo required the subjugation of the Boer Republics. Between October 1899 and June 1900, British forces easily defeated the regular Boer armies. But the Boers (literally "farmers") fought on as mounted guerrillas. In a pre-aircraft age, the vast spaces of southern Africa offered them shelter and scope. Civilian leaders emerged, displaying real talent for guerrilla war. But the contest grew ugly, as prisoner-killing and farm-burning became common on both sides.

To subdue these farmers-turned-guerrillas, the British sent an army of 450,000 men, the biggest British force in history to that time, far larger than anything they had fielded against Napoleon. Their commander, General Horatio Kitchener, deprived the Boers of their sheltering space: he chopped up the Veldt with 8,000 blockhouses connected by barbed wire, close enough to each other for mutual protection with searchlights and rifle fire. Beyond these blockhouse lines Kitchener flushed out guerrillas with huge drives, consisting of mounted soldiers, one every 10 yards, sometimes for 50 miles across. To isolate the guerrillas, he concentrated much of the scattered civilian population into huge camps.

By the beginning of 1902, although 20,000 Boer guerrillas were still in the field, it was clear that they had suffered irredeemable strategic defeat. They were hopelessly outnumbered, and foreign help (mainly from Kaiser Wilhelm's Germany) had evaporated. Under such conditions, and with the British offering amnesty, self-government, and compensation for damaged property, most of the Boer leaders signed peace accords in May 1902. Imperial losses, from battle and disease, totalled 22,000; 7000 Boers died in battle, and several thousand civilians perished from unsanitary conditions in the camps.

E. Aguinaldo

The Philippine Archipelago consists of 7000 islands, over 160,000 square miles, about the size of Arizona. Philippine guerrillas had been active against their Spanish rulers for 2 years before the Spanish-American War broke out. After Commodore Dewey smashed the Spanish fleet in Manila Bay (May 1, 1898), United States forces entered that city. Believing that the islands could not govern themselves and would soon fall prey to either German or Japanese imperialism, the McKinley administration decided to retain possession of the archipelago for the time being. But meanwhile Emilio Aguinaldo, a leader of the anti-Spanish insurgents, had proclaimed himself provisional president of the Republic of the Philippines. Armed clashes between Aguinaldo's followers and American troops began in February 1899.

With his forces soon dispersed, Aguinaldo reluctantly decided to carry on the struggle through guerrilla war. His men dug pits with sharpened stakes and arranged booby traps with poisoned arrows. Avoiding combat except when they had overwhelming superiority, at other times they assumed the guise of peaceable civilians. They also killed local officials who cooperated with the Americans, and set the torch to entire villages that were unenthusiastic for the insurgent cause.

American forces in the islands suffered from a variety of tropical diseases, which diminished their already inadequate numbers, only 20,000 in early 1899, 70,000 by early 1901. Nevertheless, the Americans embarked on a systematic program of social improvement in the backward islands. The U.S. Army built and staffed free schools, cleaned up the most unsanitary aspects of city life, reformed the benighted penal system, fought malaria, and provided free inoculation against smallpox. No Filipino could deny that American rule was incomparably better than that of the Spanish. This preemptive "policy of attraction" profoundly undermined the already limited appeal of Aguinaldo's movement.

At the same time, the Americans reduced guerrilla contact with the civilian population by gathering small settlements into large protected areas. They aggravated the weapons shortage among the insurgents by offering either cash or release of a prisoner of war to anyone who would turn in a gun, no questions asked.

Although they enjoyed much sympathy in Japanese naval circles, Aguinaldo's guerrillas had no real prospects of foreign assistance, thanks to the newly victorious U.S. Navy. Nor could they effectively raise the banner of nationalism: Philippine society encompassed many religious, linguistic, and ethnic groups, often living in mutual hostility, while most of the insurgent leaders were Tagalog. The Americans were able to take advantage of these internecine conflicts by recruiting among the minority peoples of Luzon; more than 5000 of these served as scouts or police, and eventually a 3000-man mounted Philippine Constabulary was operating under American officers. Aguinaldo's only real card to play was that of independence. Fewer and fewer Filipinos, however, were willing to risk death for that cause because the U.S. government had promised repeatedly and in writing that it too intended that the Philippines should one day be independent. And then in March 1901 American soldiers captured Aguinaldo himself. During March and April 1901 nearly 13,000 guerrillas surrendered. On July 4, 1902, the Americans proclaimed an amnesty for all remaining guerrillas except a few accused of specific felonies.

The suppression of Aguinaldo's insurgency cost 4200 Americans lives, more than in the Spanish-American War itself. The Americans were limited in numbers and culturally alien: very few could speak any Philippine language. They had neither aircraft nor tanks. But by combining effective small-unit tactics with astute political measures, they not only won the war but did it in a way that allowed all sides to live afterwards with each other and with themselves. Years later, Aguinaldo himself wrote that the American triumph had been to the advantage of the Philippine people.

F. Greece

The Communist insurgency in Greece was the first armed confrontation between the newly formed Communist bloc and the emerging Western alliance. It called forth the proclamation of the Truman Doctrine, and hence set out the basis of containment that would guide U.S. foreign policy for the next three decades.

German forces invaded Greece in April 1941. Eventually, several guerrilla resistance groups formed, the largest being the communist-dominated ELAS, which appeared in December 1942. The Germans did not engage in a vigorous repression of guerrillas, and ELAS wished to save its strength for the inevitable post-war struggle for power. With Soviet armies entering the Balkans, the Germans evacuated Greece in the latter half of 1944. While war raged across Europe, ELAS attempted an armed seizure of Athens in December 1944. British forces defeated this effort in heavy fighting. National elections took place in March 1946, which the communists boycotted. Shortly thereafter they launched a guerrilla war, under the name of the Democratic Army.

The communist insurgency enjoyed many advantages. Covered with mountains and crossed by few roads, Greece was ideal territory for guerrillas. The German occupation had left the country in a desperate economic condition. The Greek Royal Army was completely demoralized. The communists were linked to the prestige of the victorious, close, and powerful USSR. Most importantly, the communist governments of Greece's northern neighbors—Albania, Bulgaria, Yugoslavia—were ready and willing to furnish supplies and sanctuary to the guerrillas. And amidst these perils the parliamentarians in Athens devoted their time to political machinations and mutual hostilities.

In the spring of 1947 the British cabinet informed Washington that it could no longer afford to sustain the Greek government. Accordingly, in a memorable address to Congress, President Truman declared that the United States would henceforth assist Greece, and other countries threatened with communist subversion. The United States gave substantial financial help to the Greeks, which enabled them to enlarge their armed forces without unduly upsetting their economic recovery. And the Greek Royal Army received American military advisers, but no U.S. ground combat troops, due mainly to the opposition of the U.S. Chiefs of Staff.

In late 1948 the Democratic Army abandoned guerrilla tactics for conventional warfare, a conversion that it was not strong enough to sustain. It had also thoroughly alienated much of the peasantry, reflecting the predominantly urban petit bourgeois and non-Greek composition of the guerrilla movement. By 1949 the Greek government was deploying 150,000 regular troops and 75,000 paramilitary personnel. The guerrillas numbered about 25,000, an increasing proportion of whom consisted of Macedonian separatists and kidnapped civilians forced to fight under duress. In July 1949, Marshal Tito closed the Yugoslav border, the coup de grâce for the all-but-finished insurgents.

The defeat of the Greek guerrillas had several causes, but came because above all they had violated the two most important principles of guerrilla war: do not engage in combat unless certain to win, and do not make enemies of the rural population.

G. China

The Chinese revolutions of this century, Nationalist and Communist, have been attempts to bring China into the modern world, so that it could resist Western, Russian, and Japanese intrusion and aggression. Mao Tse-tung's rise to power was a symbol and consequence of these attempts.

During the 1920s, the Kuomintang (KMT) regime ruled China under Chiang Kai-shek, heir to Sun Yat-sen's republican revolution. In the eyes of contemporary observers, the KMT was making real progress in modernizing the country. In contrast, the Chinese Communist Party was in serious trouble. In 1934, after years of continuous and damaging attacks by the KMT, the communists had fled into the remote interior of the country in the disastrous Long March. The KMT was planning the final destruction of the communists when Japanese aggressions culminated in open war in 1937. The war brought domestic reform within KMT territory to a halt as attention shifted toward resisting the Japanese. It also gave new life to the Chinese Communist Party and its efforts at armed revolution. Having in the mid-1930s solidified his control over the Communist Party, Mao Tse-tung set forth the thesis that for a revolution to succeed in a peasant country like China, it must have peasant support; power would come as the result of protracted rural conflict, not a Petrograd-style coup. Now the Japanese would provide Mao the peasant support he needed.

Japanese forces in China had two key characteristics. First, they possessed neither the training, the discipline, the equipment, nor the numbers to bring the war to a successful conclusion or even to maintain order in occupied areas. Second, their behavior toward the Chinese was absolutely appalling; as a consequence, normally peaceful peasants were driven into the arms of Maoist guerrilla bands.

Mao placed great stress on the following points: maintaining guerrilla morale through ceaseless political indoctrination; building good relations with the peasantry (in marked contrast to every other army in China), because "the guerrilla moves among the people as fish move in the water"; treating prisoners well and then releasing them, to dissuade the enemy from resisting to the end; engaging in combat only when victory was assured by overwhelming numbers; achieving surprise through mobility; establishing secure bases, not difficult in a big country like China, rich in mountains and poor in communications.

After the surrender of Japan, the war between Chiang and the Communists became predominantly a conventional one. Of the many errors made by the KMT, perhaps the most significant was holding on to all the major cities of China, thus allowing the Communists to defeat their forces piecemeal. Preoccupied with the Marshall Plan, NATO, and the crisis in Greece, the U.S. Government regretted the slow defeat of Chiang but did not act to prevent it.

In considering Mao's rise to power the following points are very important. First, the Japanese severely mauled the armies and the prestige of Chiang Kai-shek to the supreme benefit of the communists. Second, it was the Americans who defeated Japan, not the Chinese. Third, Mao beat the KMT by deploying large conventional armies, not guerrilla bands. Thus the popular paradigm of Maoist "people's war"—hardy peasant guerrillas defeating first the Japanese and then the KMT—is quite false. That is mainly why most subsequent attempts to imitate it met disaster.

H. The Huks

During the Japanese occupation of the Philippines (1942–1945) several guerrilla groups appeared, some organized by the Americans and some by the Philippine Communist Party. The latter came to be known as the Huks (from the acronym *Hukbalahap*, People's Army Against Japan). By 1945 the Huks were well-armed with weapons taken from the Japanese or shipped in from the United States. In late 1946 open fighting flared between the Huks and the newly independent Philippine Republic. The Huk stronghold was on Luzon, the size of Kentucky, among the long-exploited sugar workers.

The Philippine Constabulary was poorly armed and poorly trained; abuse of civilians was common. The elections of 1949, which produced the reelection of President Quirino and the Liberal Party, were corrupt even by Philippine standards of the day, lending credibility to Huk claims that violent revolution offered the only path to change. By the time the Korean war broke out (June 1950), the Huks numbered 25,000 fighters, and were engaging in spectacular raids in the very outskirts of Manila.

Nevertheless, the tide was about to turn. The communist-dominated Huks failed to reach out to other alienated groups and form a broad front. The numerous common criminals among their ranks frightened the peasantry, and they suffered a public relations disaster from the murder of the daughter of former President Quezon. But the most important event of the conflict was the appointment, in September 1950, of Ramon Magsaysay, member of congress and former guerrilla, to be secretary of defense.

Magsaysay greatly improved the armed forces' treatment of civilians, flying around rural areas in a small plane to see that his orders were carried out. He sent the constabulary into Huk food-growing areas, forcing the guerrillas back into the swamps and cutting them off from the civil population. He sowed distrust among the Huks by offering fabulous rewards for the capture of specific Huk leaders accused of criminal acts. He began a program of resettlement for guerrillas who accepted amnesty. And he used troops to ensure the honesty of the 1951 congressional elections, reopening a peaceful road to reform.

The government forces waged a low-tech campaign that minimized civilian casualties. Meanwhile, the Huks obtained no help from abroad. And the return of honest elections undermined the appeal of violence. Nor could the Huks invoke nationalist sentiments: the Philippine Republic was already independent, and the United States, although emotionally involved with the Philippines, was preoccupied with events in Greece, Korea, and French Indochina. Besides, both the State Department and the Pentagon believed the fundamental problems in the Philippines were political, not military. Hence the Americans sent financial assistance to Manila, and a military advisory mission of 58 personnel, but no combat troops.

In May 1954 the military leader of the Huks, Luis Taruc, surrendered; for practical purposes the insurgency was over. From 1946 to 1954, 10,000 Huks had been killed, 4000 captured, and 16,000 surrendered.

I. Malaya

In Malaya, predominantly foreign forces waged a successful and inexpensive counterinsurgency against communist guerrillas.

In 1948, Malaya's area was 51,000 square miles, the size of Alabama, and contained 2.7 million Malayan Muslims, 2 million Chinese, and 700,000 Indians; the three communities lived in isolation from one another.

The Japanese occupation, which began in 1942, provided an opening for the small communist party to organize guerrilla bands. The Japanese troops in Malaya were not first quality, and the jungle was ideal terrain for the insurgents. Nevertheless, Japanese soldiers killed by communist guerrillas between 1942 and 1945 amounted to less than two per day; the guerrillas in fact killed more anticommunist Chinese. By December 1945, the guerrillas, calling themselves the Malayan People's Anti-Japanese Army, counted 10,000 members, with good weapons, many of which had been given to them by the Japanese-sponsored Indian National Army.

For obscure reasons the communists did not try to seize power in August 1945, their best opportunity. But by June 1948, in the face of growing terrorist attacks on civilians, the British administration proclaimed an Emergency. In homage to the Maoists, the insurgents changed their name to the Malayan Races Liberation Army. They attacked small police posts, ambushed civilian vehicles, damaged bridges, slashed rubber trees and burned the huts of rubber workers. They also killed their prisoners, especially if Chinese. The few half-hearted efforts by the almost exclusively Chinese leadership of the guerrillas to reach out to the Malays were not successful.

In summer 1950, General Sir Harold Briggs inaugurated closer coordination of the army and the police, and began methodically clearing the country province by province from south to north. But the centerpiece of the Briggs Plan was the resettlement of landless Chinese squatters: by 1954, 570,000 lived in new villages and received title to land. The British were draining the water in which the fish had to swim. All this formed part of a general food denial program: rice convoys were heavily guarded, canned goods were carefully controlled, and guerrilla food-growing areas were searched out and destroyed.

In February 1952 Sir Gerald Templer took overall command. He emphasized good intelligence, for which he offered impressive monetary rewards. Surrendered or captured guerrillas were excellent intelligence sources, often turning in their comrades for cash. The British used few aircraft, and rarely employed artillery; instead small, well-trained, jungle-fighting units harried the guerrillas ceaselessly.

In retrospect it is hard to see how the guerrillas could have won. The Malay half of the population was against them from the start; instead of the Chinese guerrillas reaching out to them, on the contrary the British successfully trained and armed a Chinese militia; and independence was clearly approaching. Militarily, the insurgent position was hopeless. They received no outside help: Malaya's only land border is with Thailand, whose government was hostile to the guerrillas. And the British assembled overwhelming force: by 1954 they had 40,000 regular troops (British, Gurkha, Commonwealth, and Malayan), plus 24,000 Federation police, 37,000 Special Constables, and 250,000 Home Guards (militia).

From 1946 to 1958, the guerrillas killed 512 government soldiers and 3000 civilians. More than 6700 guerrillas were killed, 1300 were captured, and 2700 surrendered.

J. Cuba, Castro, and Guevara

Some have described Fidel Castro's coming to power as the first communist revolution in the Western Hemisphere. This is erroneous: Castro did not come to power as a communist, nor had he led a revolution.

Cuba was a peculiar, invertebrate country. Those sinews of Latin American society—the Church, the army, and the landowning aristocracy—were either absent from Cuba, or present in a distorted form. The Batista regime that ruled Cuba in the 1950s was a mafia in khaki, antagonizing all segments of Cuban society.

On December 2, 1956, Fidel Castro, a law school graduate and landowner's son, came ashore in Cuba with 80 armed followers. Most were apprehended, but a few escaped with Castro into the Sierra Maestra. Batista's army of 15,000 should have been more than adequate to deal with this challenge. Its officers, however, owed their positions to favoritism and graft. The army had little counterguerrilla training and less desire to fight: during its 2-year conflict with Castro it suffered fewer than three casualties per week, and when Batista fled, most units had not fired a shot. The army used to take out its frustration on helpless peasants, under the eyes of the U.S. media. With Castro promising free elections, President Eisenhower imposed an arms embargo in May 1958, a fatal blow to Batista's prestige. In December the State Department withdrew recognition from his government. On New Year's Eve, Batista left the country. When the Fidelistas entered Havana, they numbered less than a thousand.

The isolated and reviled Batista regime had not been overthrown, it had collapsed. Thus the Castro "revolution" was a fatally misleading paradigm for other Latin American countries, and efforts to export it failed resoundingly. In the Sierra Maestra, Castro had presented himself as a democrat, but his latter-day imitators declared themselves Leninists or Maoists, alerting their intended victims and also the United States. The spectacle of hundreds of thousands of Cubans fleeing to Florida, and Castro's execution of many former Cuban officers, made a profound impression all over Latin America. And no other Latin American country had an army as grotesquely inadequate as Batista's. Thus Castro's regime, the first communist dictatorship in the New World, became one of the last anywhere at all.

The most famous would-be imitator of Castro was Ernesto "Che" Guevara, an Argentine physician. Determined to ignite "another Vietnam" in Bolivia, Guevara and a select group of Cubans and Argentines entered that country in November 1966, via the La Paz airport, without even having informed the Bolivian Communist Party of their arrival. Everything went wrong. The country had already had a popular revolution. The Bolivian Army consisted of peasant conscripts drawn from the very villages Guevara was trying to arouse. President René Barrientos was a popular leader of Indian heritage, who had come to power in national elections; Guevara was thus violating his own well-known dictum that revolution cannot be made against a democratic or quasi-democratic state. None of Guevara's band could speak Guarani, the language of the region. The Bolivian highlands were too rough for Guevara's urban compatriots, and he himself was an asthmatic. The would-be guerrillas did not know the terrain, became separated from one another, wandering lost for weeks, with little food and no medical supplies, under the disapproving eyes of the local Indians. A U.S. Special Forces team trained some Bolivian units, which in October 1967 killed Guevara and put his corpse on public display.

K. French Indochina

Before World War II the French had maintained their control of Vietnam with only 11,000 troops; after the War, 30 times that number would prove insufficient.

In 1941, Vietnam had a population of around 25 million. Eighty percent of that number was illiterate. Nevertheless, the French had built up an educated elite, whose members often found their aspirations for suitable positions in the government or the economy frustrated by French control of the good jobs.

The prestige of the French was shattered by their inability to prevent the Japanese occupation of Vietnam. The communist party formed a front organization called the League for the Independence of Vietnam (Viet Minh for short). Their leader, Ho Chi Minh (one of several aliases), born in 1890, had graduated from a good secondary school but had failed to obtain a position with the colonial government. He left Vietnam, went around the world, including the United States, and returned as the Moscow-appointed leader of Indochinese commu-nism. The Viet Minh military director was a Hanoi University law graduate, Vo Nguyen Giap.

The Viet Minh seized the leadership of the nationalist movement in Vietnam by downplaying their Leninist program, calling for a united patriotic struggle of all classes, and assassinating promising leaders of rival na-tionalist groups. The Japanese occupation was con-cerned with stopping supplies from reaching China and with sending foodstuffs to Japan, not chasing the Viet Minh. Hence the communists had time to build up their forces. When Japan unexpectedly surrendered to the United States, Ho and Giap's little army marched unop-posed into Hanoi and proclaimed independence, the so-called August Revolution.

When the French returned to Vietnam they recog-nized Ho's government as autonomous, with its own army and finances. This did not satisfy the Viet Minh; relations deteriorated, and sustained fighting broke out in December 1946. Unable to resist the French in Hanoi, the Viet Minh retreated to the bush and to guerrilla war.

By 1949 the conflict had reached a clear stalemate: the Viet Minh could not challenge French control of the cities, but the French, even with tens of thousands of Vietnamese soldiers, lacked the numbers and training to clear the countryside. This was mainly because parlia-ment in Paris forbade the use of French conscripts in Vietnam (and during the 8 years of the war the Paris politicians set up and pulled down no less than 16 different cabinets). But late in 1949 Communist Chi-nese forces reached the Vietnam border, providing the Viet Minh with sanctuary, supplies, and instructors. Giap began to wage both guerrilla and conventional warfare, while the French were losing officers at an unsustainable rate.

The French strategy of trying to hold on everywhere, through a system of outposts and convoys, was ill-advised, especially in view of the totally inadequate air power available to them. That is why the French decided to entice Giap to give battle at the isolated fortress of Dien Bien Phu. There, 13,000 French and Vietnamese were besieged by 100,000 Viet Minh and their Chinese advisers. The fall of the fortress was only a tactical defeat for the French, but it broke the will of the French government to continue the war. Vietnam was parti-tioned at the 17th parallel, into a communist North and a noncommunist South.

French losses included 22,000 killed from metropol-itan France (100 of them women), 22,000 Foreign Legion and Colonial troops, plus 80,000 Vietnamese soldiers. Viet Minh losses are usually estimated at around 400,000.

The victory of the Viet Minh would have been incon-ceivable without both the Japanese occupation of Viet-nam and the arrival of Mao's forces on the border. After the surrender of Japan, the French neither sent sufficient troops from France, nor built a good, well-trained Vietnamese army, nor attacked the enemy polit-ically by addressing peasant grievances, nor pursued a strategy of concentrating their forces around Saigon and the populous Mekong Delta where the Viet Minh was relatively weak, nor closed the Chinese border through diplomatic or military means. And so they lost the war.

L. The Americans and Vietnam

In 1954, the newly installed communist regime in Hanoi expected that terrorism in the countryside against vil-lage officials and schoolteachers carried out by the southern wing of the Party, the Viet Cong, would soon cause the fall of South Vietnam (SVN). But by 1960, with SVN proving unexpectedly sturdy, under Hanoi's leadership the Viet Cong launched guerrilla war, as-sisted by units of the regular North Vietnamese Army entering SVN through Laos. In 1965, with SVN on the verge of collapse, President Johnson began a massive infusion of U.S. ground forces, to number almost 600,000 by early 1968.

By 1967, communist forces had suffered enormous casualties. Hanoi decided to launch the Tet Offensive of 1968 to break the South Vietnamese Army (ARVN) and provoke massive uprisings in the cities. This was an acknowledgement that guerrilla war had failed. The Tet Offensive was a tremendous shock, but ARVN held up well, the urban population did not rise, and the Viet Cong took a mortal mauling. Communist executions of civilians, especially in Hue, alarmed many South Vietnamese. The following year, with numerous Ameri-cans turning loudly against the war, President Nixon inaugurated "Vietnamization," which meant providing ARVN with good equipment and withdrawing U.S. forces. After Tet the war became mostly conventional, with regular North Vietnamese troops taking over from badly depleted Viet Cong units. The next great offensive after Tet was the Easter Offensive of 1972, involving a multifront invasion of SVN by the entire North Viet-namese regular army; it failed against an ARVN sup-ported by U.S. air power. By the fall of 1972, the last few U.S. ground combat troops remaining in SVN were withdrawn.

ARVN soldiers were drafted for the duration, were stationed far from home and were granted little leave; hence desertion rates were high (as they were in the

Viet Cong). During the long conflict ARVN suffered 200,000 killed, proportionally the equivalent of 2.5 million American deaths. Casualties in the SVN militia (the Regional Forces and Popular Forces) were much higher, but desertion was notably lower. Despite their many shortcomings, the SVN armed forces had withstood the best efforts of the Viet Cong (Tet 1968) and the North Vietnamese Army (Easter 1972). Major strata of the Southern population—Army officers and their families, Catholics, northern refugees, the powerful indigenous southern religious sects, the urban middle class—were determined to resist a Northern conquest.

The Paris peace accords of January 1973 provided for the removal of the few remaining U.S. military personnel from SVN and cessation of U.S. bombing of the North, but tacitly permitted Hanoi to keep a third of a million troops inside SVN. The U.S. Congress, where opinion had been turning against the South since the Tet Offensive, now began slashing aid to SVN; by spring 1975 ARVN soldiers were being issued 84 bullets per man per month. Deprived of American help, while Soviet and Chinese supplies poured into the North, SVN's President Thieu decided to pull ARVN out of the northern and central provinces and retrench in the heavily populated areas of Saigon and the Mekong Delta. Retrenchment in itself was an excellent idea, but it was attempted with little planning and less warning to ARVN units. Roads became clogged with civilians fleeing southward. Many soldiers left their units to search for their families. In these circumstances the North Vietnamese Army launched a massive offensive operation. Within weeks much of ARVN disintegrated. Nevertheless, Saigon and the Delta remained quiet and in ARVN hands. On April 30, 1975, however, the new president declared the surrender of SVN.

Neither a peninsula like Malaya or South Korea nor an archipelago like the Philippines, SVN fell victim above all to its geography. From the beginnings to the end of the conflict, the Hanoi regime used the Ho Chi Minh Trail, eventually a multilane, all-weather road through allegedly neutral Laos, to thrust troops and supplies into SVN. If all the troops and supplies that came down the Trail over a 15-year period had entered SVN on the same day, it would have looked bigger than the North Korean invasion of June 1950. Several proposals for closing the Trail by holding a line from Vietnam to Thailand (about the distance from Washington, D.C., to Philadelphia) were rejected by the Johnson Administration; the American bombing of North Vietnam and the so-called attrition strategy (trying to kill more North Vietnamese soldiers than Hanoi could replace) were some of the consequences of leaving the Trail open. After the fall of Saigon, many in Hanoi identified the Trail as their most valuable weapon.

But perhaps the most important lesson of the entire conflict was that Maoist guerrilla war had failed: the conquest of SVN had required the largest conventional invasion Asia had seen since World War II, by one of the best armies on the continent.

M. Algeria

Algeria provides a textbook case study on military victory turning into political defeat.

Larger in area than all of Western Europe, Algeria in the mid-1950s had a population of nine million Arabs and Berbers, and one million Europeans, called *colons*. Fighting broke out in October 1954 when the Muslim National Liberation Front (FLN) attacked 50 military posts and police stations throughout Algeria. This insurgency closely followed the end of the fighting in Indochina, where the French Army believed it had been betrayed by the politicians. The soldiers in Algeria were determined that this time, there would be no defeat, and no betrayal.

The French Army evolved three primary weapons against the insurgents. First, unlike in Vietnam, they deployed large numbers; by 1956, 450,000 French troops were in Algeria, enough both to hold all the cities and large towns and to field mobile strike forces. Second, they closed off FLN sanctuaries in Tunisia and Morocco by building barrier lines hundreds of miles long. The most spectacular of these was the Morice Line along the Tunisian border, with electrified wire fences, watchtowers, and minefields on both sides; artillery and aircraft would immediately respond to any break in the fence line. The French had 80,000 troops along this Morice Line. Third, the army regrouped two million Muslim peasants into new settlements.

By the end of 1957, only 15,000 guerrillas remained inside Algeria. But rumors of torture of captured terrorists, the unpopularity of the draft, the agitation of the still-large French Communist Party, the unattractive attitudes of the *colons*, and the spread of Muslim-on-Muslim terrorism to Paris itself, all undermined French willingness to pursue the struggle. In the spring of 1958 the Paris politicians were ready to negotiate with the FLN. Fearing another Vietnam-style betrayal, the French Army in Algeria threatened to invade France. The terrified politicians summoned General De Gaulle to office, and the army backed down. But De Gaulle soon disappointed the army as well as the *colons*. Believing that France's future lay across the Rhine, not across the Mediterranean, he moved toward negotiations with the FLN. Elements of the army attempted another revolt in April 1961, but this much smaller affair was faced down by De Gaulle. July 4, 1962, became Algerian Independence Day.

French forces, including *Harkis* (Muslim troops in French uniform) suffered 18,000 deaths. European civilian casualties of various degrees numbered 10,000. Among Muslim civilians, 16,000 had been killed and 50,000 were missing. Of the insurgents, 141,000 had been killed by the French and another 12,000 in internecine fighting. After the war the government of independent Algeria began killing *Harkis*; estimates of their deaths run from 30,000 to 150,000.

N. Afghanistan

Located at the intersection of the Middle East and East Asia, Afghanistan is the size of Illinois, Indiana, Ohio, Michigan, and Wisconsin combined. Covered by forbidding mountains, it has very few all-weather roads, and no railways. A traditional buffer state between the Czarist and British empires, it is a patchwork of numerous linguistic, ethnic, and religious minorities.

After a confused and bloody coup d'état in April 1978, the tiny local communist party, the People's Democratic Party of Afghanistan (PDPA), emerged in nominal control of the country. In a short time the new regime executed thousands of political prisoners, attacked Islam (the religion of the overwhelming majority) and outlawed age-old peasant family customs. On the eve of the Soviet invasion, 23 of Afghanistan's 28 provinces were under rebel control.

Seeking to prevent the embarrassing collapse of a pro-Moscow regime, the Soviets invaded on December 24, 1979. Against what was believed to be the mightiest land power in history, the Afghan resistance possessed few modern weapons. What they did have, however, was a land suited to guerrilla war, a priceless sanctuary in Pakistan and, above all, excellent morale: fighting for the holiest of causes, these *mujahideen* ("warriors of God") were convinced of their inevitable victory.

By 1985 the guerrillas numbered between 80,000 and 150,000. Against them were the 30,000 troops of the PDPA regime, 50,000 local militia more or less purchased, and 115,000 Soviet troops (the standard 10 to 1 ratio would have required from 720,000 to 1.2 million Soviet troops). The insurgents ambushed convoys and mined roads; they isolated major cities so effectively that the Soviets had to supply them by aircraft. Government officials and collaborators were assassinated in the very streets of the capital. The guerrillas had clearly stalemated the war.

The PDPA army proved unreliable: desertion, defection, mass surrenders, and handing over of weapons to insurgents were common. Rival PDPA factions engaged in murderous infighting. Thus the Soviets had to shoulder almost the entire burden of the unexpectedly long and bitter war. Lacking not only numbers but also experience of fighting guerrillas, the Soviets embarked on the systematic destruction of the countryside: crops, orchards, animals, homes. They sought especially to empty the provinces bordering the Soviet Union and Pakistan, a program labelled "migratory genocide." Eventually there were 4 million refugees and 1.3 million civilian dead, equivalent to the deaths of 20 million Americans.

Air power was the Soviets' most effective weapon, but in 1983 the insurgents began receiving surface-to-air missiles; by 1986 the United States was sending in via Pakistan the very useful Stinger missile, which neutralized Soviet air power. Help was coming in also from Saudi Arabia, Egypt, China, and Iran; meanwhile the military inadequacies of the once-vaunted Soviet Army became ever more apparent. Deciding to cut his losses, Soviet leader Gorbachev in April 1988 forced the PDPA to reach an accord with Pakistan. A month later the Soviets begin their UN-monitored withdrawal.

Afghanistan was not "Russia's Vietnam": Afghanistan was right over the Soviet border, while Washington was closer to the South Pole than to Saigon; there were no intrusive media, no public congressional investigations into the Soviet war; the Soviet force commitment never approached that of the U.S. in Vietnam; and the Afghan guerrillas, however brave, were simply not comparable to the North Vietnamese Army.

Nevertheless, the incredible suffering and successful resistance of the Afghan people contributed mightily to the forces of disintegration gathering within the Soviet empire. One day the cries of battle in the Afghan mountains would be echoed in the shouts of freedom at the Berlin Wall.

O. The American Civil War

Confederate guerrillas played a prominent role in the American Civil War, notably in Missouri and Virginia. Even after Lee surrendered at Appomattox, 100,000 Confederates remained under arms. Upon the defeat of their regular armies, the American colonials, the Spanish and the Boers had all resorted to guerrilla resistance. But a similar eruption in the defeated Confederacy, so feared by Lincoln and Grant, did not occur. The reasons for this nonoccurrence provide many insights into what guerrilla war requires.

Many Southerners had had deep misgivings about secession. Then, the war turned out to be much longer and much harder than predicted. The Confederate conscription law aroused widespread bitterness. Furious quarrels between the President and Congress and between the Richmond government and the states wracked the Confederacy. Nor was there any stirring ideology to sustain the rebellion: at bottom, secession had been about holding millions of human beings in slavery, an institution condemned in most of the civilized world. The moral problem of slavery weighed heavily on the consciences of many Confederates, and besides, 90% of White Southerners owned no slaves. And in the war's last hour, the Confederate Congress had authorized the enrolling of 300,000 slave soldiers, promising them freedom at war's end.

In any event, by early 1865 all could see that the Confederates had been thoroughly and irredeemably beaten. If Confederates turned to guerrilla war, what were the prospects for success? They could not realistically hope for outside aid: no foreign state had openly helped the Confederacy in its flower, and none was likely to do so after its defeat. And what, indeed, would the fearsome destructiveness of guerrilla struggle be for? Slavery was finished. The leaders and soldiers of the Union were not foreigners committing systematic sacrileges (as the Spanish guerrillas faced). They indulged in no mass rapes and mass murders (as occurred in the Vendée). Confederates faced no prospect of concentration camps, firing squads, mass expulsions; on the contrary, with malice toward none, Lincoln and Grant were offering an easy peace. The embodiment of the Southern Cause, Robert E. Lee himself, advised his people to take the path of reconciliation. Thus, after Appomattox, guerrilla conflagration did not consume the prostrate South.

P. And the Future

Guerrilla warfare has a very long history; one finds instances of it recorded in the Bible. And even during the height of the Cold War, at least one major guerrilla struggle (in Algeria) raged totally outside the schemata of that global ideological contest. It should therefore be no surprise that the end of the Cold War has not meant the end of guerrilla conflicts. On the contrary, many factors make guerrilla warfare more rather than less likely in the 21st century. The very breakup of the Soviet Empire, for one example, has permitted long-suppressed ethnic and religious tensions to surface in its former satrapies; an unusually large percentage of the population of the Third World is young and poor; certain Islamic groups have completely and angrily rejected the contemporary world; in many societies no peaceful road to change exists; and high-quality weapons are easily obtainable.

An additional—and ominous—element in the contemporary guerrilla picture is the international drug trade. Peru's *Sendero Luminoso* guerrillas supported themselves for years through arrangements with drug traffickers. Today drug lords are using their vast funds to subsidize guerrilla movements and may actually launch their own; under a veil of ethnic or religious populism, international criminal organizations may take possession of a weak or disintegrating state and create a haven for their activities.

These conditions all but guarantee that for many of the oppressed, the marginalized, the frustrated, the ambitious, the vengeful and the greedy, the widely known techniques of guerrilla warfare will continue to be available and attractive options.

Also See the Following Articles

CIVIL WARS • COLONIALISM AND IMPERIALISM • REVOLUTIONS • TERRORISM • WARFARE, MODERN • WARFARE, STRATEGIES AND TACTICS OF

Bibliography

Beckett, I., & Pimlott, J. (Eds.). (1985). *Armed forces and modern counterinsurgency*. New York: St. Martin's.
Callwell, C. (1976). *Small wars*. Wakefield, UK: EP Publishing.
Haycock, R. (Ed.) (1979). *Regular armies and insurgency*. London: Croom, Helm.
Joes, A. (1992). *Modern guerrilla insurgency*. Westport, CT: Praeger.
Joes, A. (1996). *Guerrilla insurgency before the Cold War*. Westport, CT: Praeger.
Joes, A. (1996). *Guerrilla warfare: A historical, biographical and bibliographical sourcebook*. Westport, CT: Greenwood.
Laqueur, W. (1979). *Guerrilla: A historical and critical study*. Boston: Little, Brown.
Manwaring, M. (1991). *Uncomfortable wars: Toward a new paradigm of low-intensity conflict*. Boulder, CO: Westview.
Mao Tse-tung. (1966). *Basic tactics*. New York: Praeger.
Mockaitis, T. (1990). *British counterinsurgency, 1919–1960*. New York: St. Martin's.

Hate Crimes

Jack Levin and Jack McDevitt

Northeastern University

GLOSSARY

Defensive Hate Crimes Hate offenses aimed against particular "outsiders" who are regarded as posing a challenge to a perpetrator's neighborhood, workplace, school, or physical well-being.

Ethno-violence Acts of hate that do not necessarily rise to the legal standard of a crime, but contain an element of prejudice.

Hate Crimes (also known as Bias Crimes) Criminal offenses motivated either entirely or in part by the fact or perception that a victim is different from the perpetrator.

Mission Hate Crimes Hate offenses committed as an act of "war" against any and all members of a particular group of people.

Modern Racism Subtle and institutionalized forms of bigotry based on the race of the victim.

Prejudice A negative attitude toward individuals based on their perceived group membership.

Thrill Hate Crimes Hate offenses typically committed by youngsters who are motivated by the desire for excitement.

HATE CRIMES are criminal offenses motivated either entirely or in part by the fact or perception that a victim is different from the perpetrator. As used by the FBI and a number of other law enforcement agencies across the United States, this definition has three important elements that have been widely accepted: first, it involves actions that have already been defined as illegal in state or federal statutes. Thus, the vast majority of hate crime laws do not criminalize any new behavior; instead, they increase the penalty for behaviors that are already against the law. Second, the definition specifies the motivation for committing the offense; it requires that a racial, religious, ethnic, or some other identified difference between victim and offender play at least some role in inspiring the criminal act. For example, an individual who seeks money to buy illicit drugs may decide to rob only Asians because of some stereotype he holds regarding this group of people. If part of the motivation for the robbery involves the victim's Asian identity, then the offense can be regarded as a hate crime. Third, the definition of hate crimes provided here does not identify a particular set of protected groups to which the hate crime designation can be exclusively

Copyright © 1999 by Academic Press.
All rights of reproduction in any form reserved.

applied. Unlike statutes in many states in which protected racial, religious, and ethnic groups are specified, this definition includes any group difference that separates the victim from the offender in the offender's mind. This broad definitional standard undoubtedly introduces much ambiguity in deciding whether or not any particular case fits, but it also allows for inclusion of important cases that might not come up very frequently; for example, attacks on homeless men that have occurred from time to time in various cities across the United States. The use of an open-ended standard also allows for the possibility that other groups can be added to the list protected by hate crime legislation. Some have argued, for example, that gender-motivated crimes of violence (e.g., rape) should be considered a hate crime in order to place them "on equal legal footing with analogous deprivations based on race, national origin, religion, and sexual orientation" (Weisburd and Levin, 1994, p 42). Some 13 American states now treat gender-motivated offenses as hate crimes.

The term hate crime first appeared in the late 1980s as a way of understanding a racial incident in the Howard Beach section of New York City, in which a Black man was killed while attempting to evade a violent mob of White teenagers who were shouting racial epithets. Although widely used by the federal government of the United States, the media, and researchers in the field, the term is somewhat misleading because it suggests incorrectly that hatred is invariably a distinguishing characteristic of this type of crime. While it is true that many hate crimes involve intense animosity toward the victim, many others do not. Conversely, many crimes involving hatred between the offender and the victim are not "hate crimes" in the sense intended here. For example an assault that arises out of a dispute between two White, male co-workers who compete for a promotion might involve intense hatred, even though it is not based on any racial or religious differences between them. Similarly, a love triangle resulting in manslaughter may provoke intense emotions, but may have nothing at all to do with race or religion.

Hate crimes are also known by other names. The most commonly employed of such terms is *bias crime*, perhaps because it accurately emphasizes that such offenses often arise out of prejudice toward another group of individuals. In addition, Howard Ehrlich, director of the Prejudice Institute at Towson State University, has coined the term *ethno-violence* to include acts that do not rise to the legal standard of a crime, but contain an element of prejudice. These hate incidents may, for example, include the use of ethnic slurs or the exclusion of members of targeted groups from social activities at the workplace.

I. LEGAL DISTINCTIONS

At present there is no U.S. federal statute that prohibits hate crimes. The Congress of the United States in 1990 passed the Hate Crime Statistics Act, which requires the reporting of statistics on hate crimes, but did not dictate that the commission of a hate crime be regarded as a violation of federal law.

In the United States, it has been left up to the states to formulate hate crime legislation. While 39 states presently have some form of hate crime statute, there exists a wide variation among states in the specifics of their laws. For example, in the area of protected groups (i.e., particular groups are designated as protected in the statute), most states list crimes targeted toward individuals because of their race, religion, or ethnicity as prohibited. However, a number of states also include sexual orientation, disability, and age. The implication of this lack of uniformity is that members of a particular group may be protected by a hate crime statute in one community but not protected in a neighboring community in an adjacent state.

A second area of legal distinctions involves the penalty structure of the statute. In some states, a separate statute exists that prohibits hate crime behavior. In other states the hate crime statute is a "penalty enhancement." This means that if an existing crime is committed and it is motivated by bias, the penalty on the existing crime may be increased. Penalty enhancements have been enacted in other areas as well. For example, they have been applied to crimes committed with a gun, crimes committed by individuals with long criminal histories, and crimes committed against vulnerable victims such as children.

The United States has chosen not to follow the lead of many European countries, where anti-hate speech legislation has been passed. Countries including Canada, France, Great Britain, and Germany have all passed laws prohibiting at least some forms of hate speech. In Germany, these forms of prohibition have been applied most broadly, particularly in the area of Nazi propaganda and symbols, which are illegal to own or display. Consistent with its long tradition of free speech protections, the United States has, except on college campuses, decided not to develop similar legislation. Even in the area of campus speech codes, moreover, the American efforts to control offensive speech have been met with significant resistance and debate.

II. HATE CRIMES AND PREJUDICE

From a psychological perspective, "prejudice" refers to a negative attitude toward individuals based on their perceived group membership—for example, their race, religion, ethnicity, or sexual orientation. Although as a form of discriminatory behavior, hate crimes often have an attitudinal dimension, the relationship between prejudice and criminal behavior tends to be complex. There is reason to believe that certain hate offenses *result from* some personal bias or hatred. Perpetrators may act out of prejudicial beliefs (i.e., stereotypes) or emotions (e.g., envy, fear, or revulsion) concerning people who are different. In the extreme case, a hatemonger may join an organized group in order to devote his life to destroying a group of people he considers "inferior."

Where it is cultural, a particular prejudice may even become a widely shared and enduring element in the normal state of affairs of the society in which it occurs. As such, it may be learned from an early age through parents, friends, teachers, and the mass media. Individuals separated by region, age, social class, and ethnic background all tend to share roughly the same stereotyped images of various groups. In the United States, for example, some degree of anti-Black racism can be found among substantial segments of Americans—males and females, young and old, rich and poor—from New York to California. In Germany, the same might be said of anti-Semitism as well as anti-Turkish immigrant sentiment. In fact, a recent analysis of anti-Jewish attitudes in east and west Germany found that strong anti-Semitism remained in west Germany even after "four decades of re-education ... and a nearly total taboo on public expressions of anti-Semitism" (Watts, 1997, p. 219).

It is not, however, always necessary for the prejudice to precede the criminal behavior. In fact, from the literature in social psychology, we know that prejudices often develop or at least become strengthened in order to justify *previous* discriminatory behavior.

This is probably true of hate crimes as well. For example, a White teenager may assault someone who is Black because his friends expect him to comply, not because he personally feels intense hatred toward his victim. If he views the target of his attack as a flesh-and-blood human being with feelings, friends, and a family, the offender may feel guilty. By accepting a dehumanized image of the victim, however, the perpetrator may actually come to believe that his crime was justified. After all, the rules of civilized society apply only to human beings, not to demons or animals. Simi-

larly, an individual may initially commit an act of violence against an individual for economic reasons (e.g., because he believes that the presence of Blacks in his neighborhood reduces property values) and subsequently becomes totally convinced that all Blacks are rapists and murderers. Who would want a rapist living next door?

Such negative images are often seen in warfare. The underlying causes of a conflict may be economic, but stereotyping facilitates bloodshed. In Northern Ireland, for example, civil strife seems to be reinforced by a set of stereotypes of Catholics and Protestants that might be expected to describe racial differences alone—for example, that Catholics have shorter foreheads and less space between their eyes than their Protestant neighbors.

At times, certain prejudices become narrowly targeted. During the 1800s and early 1900s, when they came to the United States and competed for jobs with native-born citizens, Irish-American newcomers were stereotyped by political cartoonists of the day as apes and crocodiles. During the same period, as soon as they began to compete with native-born landowners and merchants, Italian immigrants settling in New Orleans were widely depicted as members of organized crime.

Similarly, the term "gook" was employed by the allies during World War II to characterize the Japanese enemy, during the Korean conflict to refer to North Koreans, and during the Vietnam war to refer to North Vietnamese and Vietcong. In the mid-1970s, as large numbers of newcomers arrived in the United States, the term "gook" became a racial slur with which to discredit all southeast Asian immigrants.

Thus, although some hate crimes may be committed out of a profound sense of hatred toward the members of a victim's group, others may be committed for conformist or economic reasons and subsequently reinforced by the development of prejudice. As a result, it is important to operationally define hate crimes, based not on an offender's initial bias motivation alone, but on the fact that victims are chosen because they are different in terms of their race, religion, ethnic identity, or sexual orientation.

Since the 1960s, social scientists have increasingly downplayed the importance of individual-level prejudice. To a growing extent, the thinking in behavioral science has been that racist attitudes (or at least their public expression) are on the decline and that discrimination is more or less independent of prejudice. In 1974, for example, 55 journal articles in psychology and 32 journal articles in sociology dealt directly with the concept of prejudice; in 1984, these figures declined somewhat to 41 articles in psychology and 26 in sociology. By 1994, only 30 psychology articles and 13 sociology articles were concerned with the topic of prejudice.

Rather than focus on individual prejudices, researchers in the behavioral sciences have during recent decades turned more of their attention to investigate institutional and structural forms of discrimination: in college applications, for example, the manner in which SATs indirectly favor White applicants, whether or not individual admissions officers hold racist attitudes; in real estate transactions, how real estate associations, as a matter of policy, "steer" Black homebuyers from White neighborhoods, regardless of the racial biases of particular agents (Pearce, 1979). Because behavioral scientists have enthusiastically examined such structural issues, they may have been surprised when advocacy groups suggested that hate violence was on the rise. The so-called "new" or "modern" racism emphasized subtle and institutionalized forms of bigotry; it failed to recognize the possibility that policies and programs directed at reducing structural forms of discrimination (e.g., affirmative action and compulsory busing) might also provoke increasing numbers of hate crimes committed by members of traditionally advantaged groups in society.

III. WHY TREAT HATE CRIMES DIFFERENTLY?

Since hate crimes by definition involve behavior that is already prohibited by state or federal statutes (e.g., assault, threats, vandalism), the question is frequently posed as to why we need additional penalties. Are these crimes truly different?

We believe that a number of characteristics of hate incidents make them different from other types of offenses. First, hate crimes are directed symbolically at large groups of people, not at a single individual. If youths decide that they do not want Blacks living on their block, they may decide to throw a rock through the window of a home owned by a new neighbor who is Black. Their intention is to send a message not just to that neighbor but to all Blacks, informing them that their presence in the neighborhood will not be tolerated.

Thus, not unlike acts of terrorism, hate crimes are about messages. Offenders use a criminal event to put the members of an entire group on notice, by example, that they are not welcome in a community, in a workplace, on a college campus, or at school. By contrast, if a window is broken in a simple act of vandalism,

the offenders typically have no desire to communicate anything in particular to the property owner; in fact, they frequently do not even know anything about the victim they have targeted.

Another characteristic that differentiates hate crimes from most other offenses is that the victim characteristic motivating the attack (e.g., race or ethnicity) is in most cases ascribed and immutable. A person cannot modify her or his race, ethnicity, age, gender, or disability status. Even a religious identity or a sexual orientation cannot be modified without causing an individual to make dramatic and painful changes in lifestyle. Consequently, if a woman is attacked because she is a Latina, there is little that individual can do to become "de-Latinized" and thus reduce the likelihood of her future victimization. This is also true of perceived characteristics. If a man becomes a hate crime victim because he is perceived by a group of youths to be gay, he is also powerless to change the offenders' perception of him. The feeling on the part of victims that they lack control over the characteristic that motivated their victimization causes most hate crime victims to feel extremely vulnerable to future bias-motivated attacks.

A third characteristic of hate crimes that makes them different from many other offenses is that the individual victim typically did nothing to provoke the attack and is therefore interchangeable, at least from the perpetrator's standpoint. To a group of youths waiting outside a gay bar to attack someone whom they believe might be gay, it does not matter which individual comes through the door next. Whoever comes out is likely to become a victim, because all bar patrons are identical in the mind of the perpetrator.

Indeed, the interchangeability of victims tends to apply as well across groups of victims. If offenders cannot locate the members of one racial group to terrorize, they are likely to target members of another racial group. This aspect of hate crimes suggests that they are often motivated by an offender's psychological need to feel superiority at the expense of his victims.

In order to collect data about hate crimes in a large city, we examined records compiled over a 16-month period by the Community Disorders Unit of the Boston Police Department. The final sample totaled 169 hate crimes-all such offenses reported to the Boston Police during the 1991–1992 period under study where the offenders were known.

With regard to the lack of victim precipitation in hate offenses, most of the victims we studied in Boston were simply walking down the street when they were attacked. Regarding incidents in which they did do something that could be seen as precipitating, victims were most often engaged in some constitutionally protected right; for example, moving into a house in a previously all-White neighborhood or worshiping in a church or synagogue.

In Boston, 66% of the hate crimes we studied were committed by strangers to their victims. When generalized to cities and towns across the nation, this finding, along with the fact that victims seldom do anything to precipitate the attack, makes victims of these incidents incredibly nervous. Criminologists have long known that random acts of violence-for example, serial killings and airplane bombings-generate disproportionate levels of anxiety in most people. Unable to distance themselves from the incident, they fear that they could be next. Similarly, victims of most hate crimes believe they can do little to reduce the potential of future victimization. They typically feel helpless in the face of random attacks.

Deputy Superintendent William Johnston, formerly commander of the Boston Police Department's hate crime-investigation unit, observes that hate crime offenders are typically "cowards" because they need to feel that they outnumber the victim before they can attack. It is true that most hate crimes seem to involve multiple offenders assaulting a single victim. In Boston, for example, 73% of the incidents reported to the police involved more than one offender, and frequently several of them. Clearly, any attack by a group against an individual is more threatening than an attack by only one person.

Hate crimes can be grouped according to their targets. In sending a message to their victims, some hate crimes are aimed at property through vandalism, while others are directed at individuals in the form of violence. In an escalating cycle, those victims who are assaulted may have received earlier threats to their property or perhaps less serious personal abuse.

Some research suggests that attacks against individuals can be incredibly violent. According to Levin (1992–1993), hate offenses are more likely than other serious crimes to include a physical assault. Moreover, when hate crimes involve assaultive behavior, they tend to be especially brutal. In Boston, for example, victims of hate-motivated assaults were three times more likely to need hospital treatment than were other assault victims. The especially brutal nature of hate violence may be due to the depersonalization that many hate crime offenders employ in justifying their offenses. Hatemongers frequently view members of targeted groups as less that human. They reason, therefore, that it is appropriate to treat their victims in the manner in which they might treat a wild animal or a demon.

IV. PROBLEMS IN COLLECTING HATE CRIME DATA

During the 1980s researchers, journalists, and government officials increasingly turned their attention to questions regarding the extent and nature of hate crimes in the United States. At that time there were no national data gathered on the incidence and character of such offenses. The FBI, that agency responsible for collecting and reporting national data on crime, did not collect information separately for offenses motivated by bias. For example, a hate-motivated assault reported by the local police to the FBI would be grouped together with other assaults, regardless of their motivation. As a result, it was impossible to distinguish which offenses were hate motivated and which were not.

Even though no national data on hate crimes existed during this period, some public information began to be collected at the state and local levels. As early as 1979, Maryland became the first state to collect hate crime data; several other states—for example, Rhode Island and Connecticut—followed Maryland's lead. At the local level a number of large cities, including Boston, Baltimore, and New York City, began collecting information about the hate crimes incidents their police had investigated. Even though such state and local jurisdictions provided important information about the extent and character of hate crimes, legal and procedural differences between them prevented them from making any meaningful comparisons across state and city lines. In addition, a recent report by the Office of Juvenile Justice and Delinquency Prevention (1996) found that only 6 of 30 responding states could provide any information on the age of hate crime offenders.

Also during the 1980s, a small number of private organizations collected data on hate crime incidents in the United States. The Anti-defamation League (ADL) has been collecting and reporting data on anti-Semitic incidents since 1981. In 1990 the ADL was the only public or private organization engaged in an ongoing national hate crime data collection effort. Other organizations such as the national Gay Lesbian Task Force collected information about incidents of antigay violence. While their evidence may be somewhat unreliable as a national data string, the Task Force did provide a basis for some very important studies of antigay violence.

In April 1990, Congress passed and the president signed the Hate Crime Statistics Act (28 USC 534). Although it did not criminalize any particular behavior, the Act required the attorney general of the United

States to publish an annual report about crimes that "manifest evidence of bias based upon race, religion, sexual orientation, or ethnicity." This act authorized the first national data collection effort undertaken by any public agency to be targeted specifically at hate crimes. The Uniform Crime Reporting Section of the FBI has been designated as the federal agency empowered to collect and tabulate these data.

Although charging the attorney general with the responsibility for collecting information and publishing an annual report about hate crimes, the Hate Crime Statistics Act did not require that local law enforcement agencies report to the FBI. Historically, crime reporting has been voluntary with most but not all major law enforcement agencies agreeing to participate.

Hate crime reporting was initially a different story. Many agencies had not separated hate crimes data from other offenses in their collection procedures. As a result, retrieving hate crime data was not an easy task. In addition, many law enforcement agencies resisted the new national emphasis on hate crime investigation. For these reasons, few agencies participated in the original effort. In 1991, 2771 agencies submitted hate crime data to the FBI, which represented only 20% of the agencies participating in the UCR program. Through significant training efforts of the UCR section of the FBI and support from local advocacy groups, however, by 1996 the participation rate had increased to 11,355 agencies representing approximately 60% of all agencies submitting information to the FBI.

V. TYPES OF HATE CRIMES

When they read newspaper accounts of an assault or vandalism based on race, sexual orientation, or ethnicity, many Americans immediately assume that an organized hate group was involved. Early reports of church burnings in the South almost invariably attempted to implicate the Ku Klux Klan in some sort of far-reaching conspiratorial plan to destroy the fabric of life for Black Americans, especially those who reside in rural areas of the South. After more careful study, however, the situation appeared much more complex. Although a few cases involved the Klan, it turned out that most of the racially inspired church burnings had little if anything to do with White supremacist groups. In South Carolina, for example, two-thirds of them were instead perpetrated by teenagers and young adults looking for a good time. Some of the young perpetrators had tenuous links with the KKK, if only because they enjoyed their symbols of power or Klan propaganda.

But most of the youthful offenders operated on their own, without being directly guided by the members of any organized group, including the KKK.

Like church burnings, hate crimes in general are typically committed by individuals without links to any organized groups. With this in mind, we propose a typology in which hate crimes can be classified in terms of their offenders' motivations. In our view, there are three distinct types, which we identify as thrill, defensive, and mission.

A. Thrill Hate Crimes

Based on Boston Police Department reports, we found that nearly three out of five hate crimes in that city were committed for the thrill. More than 53% of these thrill offenses were committed by two or more offenders looking for trouble in the victim's neighborhood. Perpetrators were predominantly White teenage males, the vast majority of whom—some 91%—did not know the person they were attacking. Latinos and Asians had the highest victimization rates; Whites had the lowest. One surprising finding was the extent of the violence associated with thrill hate attacks. We found that fully 70% of the thrill offenses were assaults, sometimes brutal attacks that put the victim in the hospital.

Thrill hate crimes are committed by offenders who are looking for excitement. In the same way that some young men get together on a Saturday night to play a game of cards, youthful hatemongers gather to destroy property or to bash minorities. They look merely to have some fun and stir up a little excitement . . . but at someone else's expense. In a thrill-seeking hate crime, there need not be a precipitating incident. The victim does not necessarily "invade" the territory of the assailant by walking through his neighborhood, moving onto his block, or attending his school. On the contrary, it is the assailant or group of assailants, looking to harass those who are different, who searches out locations where the members of a particular group regularly congregate. The payoff for the perpetrators is psychological as well as social: In addition to gaining a sense of importance and control, the youthful perpetrators also receive a stamp of approval from their friends who regard hatred as "hip" or "cool."

B. Defensive Hate Crimes

Not all hate offenses are motivated by thrill or excitement; not every hate crime is committed by groups of teenagers. In defensive hate crimes, the hatemongers seize on what they consider as a precipitating or triggering incident to serve as a catalyst for the expression of their anger. They rationalize that by attacking an outsider they are in fact taking a protective posture, a defensive stance against intruders. Indeed, they often cast the outsiders in the role of those actively threatening them, while they regard themselves as pillars of the community.

As with thrill hate attacks, most defensive hate offenses in our study of incidents reported to the Boston police involved White offenders who did not know their Asian, Latino, or Black victims. In defensive crimes, however, the majority were committed by a single offender.

Whereas in thrill-motivated hate crimes a group of teenagers travels to another area to find victims, the perpetrators in defensive hate crimes typically never leave their own neighborhood, school, or workplace. From the point of view of the perpetrators, it is their community, means of livelihood, or way of life that has been threatened by the mere presence of members of some other group. The hatemongers therefore feel justified, even obligated, to go on the "defensive." Characteristically, they feel few, if any, pangs of guilt even if they savagely attack an outsider.

In thrill hate crimes, almost any member of a vulnerable group will usually "do" as a target. In contrast, the perpetrators of defensive hate crimes tend to target a particular individual or set of individuals who are perceived to constitute a personal threat—the Black family that has just moved into the all-White neighborhood, the White college student who has begun to date her Asian classmate, or the Latino who has recently been promoted at work.

Just as in thrill hate crimes, the offenders in defensive attacks are not necessarily associated with any organized hate group. Typically, the perpetrators have no prior history of either crime or overt bigotry. Their reaction may have an economic basis—they fear losing property value or opportunities for advancement at work. Sometimes they react instead to a symbolic loss of "turf" or "privilege"—for example, when "our women" begin to date "them" or when "they" come into our neighborhood and begin to "take over."

According to a survey conducted by the Klanwatch Project, a unit of the Southern Poverty Law Center in Birmingham, Alabama, about half of all racially inspired acts of vandalism and violence are directed at Blacks moving into previously all-White neighborhoods. Typical of such hate crimes is the case of Purnell Daniels, a 41-year-old Black engineer whose house was located in a mostly White section of Newark, Delaware. In May

1989 he discovered a cardboard containing the raised letters KKK glued to the front door of his home.

The escalation of violence that often occurs in such attacks can also be illustrated. In 1997, a group of Whites in Grayson, Georgia, shouted racial epithets at a Black couple as they moved their belongings into their new home in a previously all-White neighborhood. A week later, when it was clear that the couple had no intention of leaving, assailants sprayed gunfire at their home. At least four bullets struck the house, one missing the man's head by a few inches. This time, the Black couple seriously considered moving out of the neighborhood.

Given the competitive nature of the workplace, it should come as no surprise that many defensive hate crimes also occur on the job. In their study of "ethnoviolence at work," sociologists Joan Weiss, Howard Ehrlich, and Barbara Larcom interviewed a national sample of 2078 Americans. These researchers found that 27% of all respondents who reported "prejudice-based" episodes experienced them while at work. These incidents included break-ins, property damage, robbery, harassing language, physical assaults, sexual harassment, or rapes.

C. Mission Hate Crimes

Defensive hate crimes are generally aimed against particular "outsiders"—those who are regarded as posing a personal challenge to a perpetrator's workplace, neighborhood, or physical well-being. The attack tends to be narrowly focused. Once the threat is perceived to subside, so does the criminal behavior.

On occasion, hate crimes go beyond what their perpetrators consider reaction, at least in the narrow sense. Rather than direct their attack at those individuals involved in a particular event or episode—moving into the neighborhood, taking a job at the next desk, attending the same party—the perpetrators are ready to wage "war" against any and all members of a particular group of people. No precipitating episode occurs; none is necessary. The perpetrator is on a moral mission: His assignment is to make the world a better place to live.

Those who perpetrate a mission crime are convinced that all out-group members are subhumans who are bent on destroying <u>our</u> culture, <u>our</u> economy, or the purity of <u>our</u> racial heritage. The offender therefore is concerned about much more than simply eliminating a few Blacks or Latinos from his job, his neighborhood, or his school. Instead, he believes that he has a higher order purpose in carrying out his crime. He has been instructed by God or, in a more secular version, by the

Imperial Wizard or the Grand Dragon to rid the world of evil by eliminating <u>all</u> Blacks, Latinos, Asians, or Jews; and he is compelled to act before it is too late. Mission hate crime offenders are likely to join an organized group such as the KKK or the White Aryan Resistance.

In our study of hate crimes reported to the Boston police, we uncovered only one mission hate offense among our 169 cases (Levin and McDevitt, 1995b). This result is consistent with recent estimates that no more than 5% of all hate crimes in the United States involve organized hate groups.

A few perpetrators of mission hate crimes operate alone and typically suffer from a profound mental illness that may cause hallucinations, impaired ability to reason, and withdrawal from contact with other people. What is more, he believes that he must get even for the horrific problems that he has suffered. In his paranoid and delusional way of thinking, he sees a conspiracy of some kind for which he seeks revenge. His mission is in part suicidal. Before taking his own life, however, he must attempt to eliminate the *entire category* of people he is absolutely convinced is responsible for his personal frustrations. There are rare cases in which a depressed and frustrated gunman has opened fire with the objective of eliminating *all* women, Asians, or White racists.

VI. ORGANIZED HATE GROUPS

According to the Southern Poverty Law Center's Klanwatch project, there may be 20,000 and almost certainly no more than 50,000 members of White supremacist groups across the United States—a country whose residents number more than 265 million. Membership in citizens' militias has been estimated at between 15,000 and 100,000. Klanwatch (1997) suggests that these militia groups number 370 and are only loosely connected to one another. It should also be pointed out that the militia movement in the United States is diverse. Some members are clearly racist in their beliefs, but there are also Jewish and Black militia members. The constitutionality of militia activities has, however, been challenged by observers who regard them as illegal private armies. In addition, there seems to be some degree of overlap in the memberships of White supremacy groups and militias.

The growing presence of hate groups is hardly confined to the United States, but has occurred around the world. In Germany, for example, the Federal Office for the Protection of the Constitution reported in 1991 that there were 4400 neo-Nazis in Germany, most of whom were skinheads. By adding in all other right-wing extremist and Nazi groups in the country, this figure swells to approximately 40,000—an increase of nearly 20% over the 1990 figures for Germany.

But numbers alone do not tell the full story of the impact of organized hate. In total, it is not only their revolutionary activism, but the growing sophistication of such organized hate groups in reaching the young people around the world—their apparent finesse and respectability—that represents the real cause for alarm. White supremacy groups encourage, and in certain cases even train, the 3500 racist skinheads who have been responsible for perpetrating violence against people of color, Jews, gays, and other vulnerable people. Known for their "uniforms" consisting of shaved heads, black jackets, and steel-toed boots, most skinheads have been at best loosely organized. Most have no formal ties with White supremacy groups, although they may be inspired by such organizations.

It should also be noted that hundreds of thousands of individuals in many different countries agree to some extent, if not wholeheartedly, with the principles of White supremacy, even if they would never join a hate group. White supremacist groups represent a fringe element among those who commit hate crimes. In statistical terms alone, the membership of all organized hate groups combined constitutes a tiny fraction of the population, most of whom would not consider burning a cross or wearing a swastika. Even so, the influence of White supremacist groups such as Posse Comitatus, White Aryan Resistance, Aryan Nations, and the Ku Klux Klan may be considerably greater than their numbers might suggest. It takes only a small band of dedicated extremists to make trouble for a large number of apathetic middle-of-the-roaders. Even in this age of activism, there are many solid citizens who have neither the time nor the inclination for political action. In Europe, this popular sentiment has taken the form of growing support for far-right political parties. Le Pen and his National Front in France, the Flemish block in Belgium, the Free Party in Austria, and MSI in Italy have all experienced increasing support in recent years. In addition, Le Pen holds an influential position in French government.

Most Americans are at least somewhat acquainted with the objectives of White hate groups like the Ku Klux Klan and neo-Nazis. Those who are familiar with American history know that the Klan has risen and fallen time and time again in response to challenges to the advantaged position of the White majority. During a short period of post-Civil War reconstruction, for example, many Whites were challenged by newly freed slaves who sought some measure of political power and began to compete for jobs with White working-class southerners. Thus, the Klan, responding with a campaign of terror and violence, lynched many Blacks. Klan-initiated violence increased again during the 1920s, as native-born Americans sought "protection" from an unprecedented influx of immigration from Eastern and Southern Europe. During the 1950s and 1960s, uniformed members of George Lincoln Rockwell's American Nazi Party gave the Nazi salute and shouted "Heil Hitler." During the same period, Klansmen in their sheets and hoods marched in opposition to racial desegregation in schools and public facilities.

By contrast, the newer organized hate groups of the 1980s and 1990s do not always come so easily to mind for their bizarre uniforms or rituals. Followers of such White supremecy groups as John and Tom Metzger's White Aryan Resistance (WAR) have shed their sheets and burning crosses in favor of more conventional attire. They often disavow the Klan and the Nazi movement in favor of a brand of "American patriotism" that plays better among the working people of America. In France, one of the original organizing slogans of Le Pen's right-wing party was the utterly respectable idea: "Two million foreigners, two million Frenchmen out of work."

Moreover, White supremacist organizations now often cloak their hatred in the aura and dogma of Christianity. Followers of the religious arm of the hate movement, the Identity Church, are only "doing the work of God." At Sunday services, they preach that White Anglo-Saxons are the true Israelites depicted in the Old Testament, God's chosen people, while Jews are actually the children of Satan. They maintain that Jesus was not a Jew, but an ancestor of the White, northern European peoples. In their view, Blacks are "pre-Adamic," a species lower than Whites. In fact, they claim that Blacks and other non-White groups are at the same spiritual level as animals and therefore have no souls.

Members of the movement also believe in the inevitability of a global war between the races that only White people will ultimately survive. The survivalists among Identity followers prepare for war by moving to communes where they can stockpile weapons, provide paramilitary training, and pray. According to a recent Identity directory, there are Identity churches in 33 American states, Canada, England, South Africa, and Australia.

The particularly depressed economic conditions in rural areas of the United States since the early 1980s have provided a fertile breeding ground for organized hate. Playing on a theme that has special appeal to downtrodden farmers and small town residents, members of Posse Comitatus (latin for "power of the county") argue that all government power should be focused at the county, not the federal level. From this perspective, IRS agents and federal judges are mortal enemies of the White race, and the county sheriff constitutes the one and only form of legitimate government. Many members of the Posse refuse to pay taxes. They charge that Jews create recessions and depressions and control the Federal Reserve.

Consistent with its emphasis on maintaining local control, Posse Comitatus has no nationally recognized leadership and consists of a number of decentralized and loosely affiliated groups of vigilantes and survivalists. But, from time to time, the Posse has attracted national attention.

VII. ARE HATE CRIMES ON THE RISE?

Due to the inadequacy of the hate crime data to date, we cannot know with certainty whether the number of hate crimes in the United States has increased, decreased, or remained stable over time. Because legal definitions are in flux and additional law enforcement agencies are constantly being added to those who report to the FBI, the data from one year to the next frequently are not comparable. In addition, much of the data collected on an annual basis have been reported by advocacy groups such as the Anti-Defamation League and the Gay and Lesbian Alliance, making them subject to the criticism that such organizations have a vested interest in generating inflated figures. Indeed, some observers have even suggested that those who argue that hate offenses have increased are creating a "social construction" without any basis in reality.

With such limitations in mind, however, it is still possible to gain some perspective as to changes in the prevalence of hate crimes over time. Based on data collected by various advocacy groups such as the ADL, the Southern Poverty Law Center, and the Gay and Lesbian Alliance, it is likely that hate crimes in the United States increased throughout the 1980s and into the early 1990s.

First, this conclusion is in agreement with evidence gathered by independent research organizations concerning hate incidents generally. The National Institute Against Prejudice and Violence in Baltimore found, for example, a dramatic upsurge in 1989 in racial and anti-Semitic incidents on college campuses. At the same time, sociologist Gary Spencer reported a growth of JAP ("Jewish-American Princess") baiting on his campus,

Syracuse University, as well as on other campuses around the United States (Anti-Defamation League, 1988). Spencer's observations coincided with those of Keough, a professor of English whose research suggested that a new form of "attack comedy" aimed at the most downtrodden and least fortunate members of American society was on the rise. Finally, antigovernment militias and survivalists—groups almost totally unheard of before 1980—have made their presence increasingly known throughout the 1980s and into the 1990s. Although many militia members disavow any connection with hatemongers, there is at least some overlap between militia groups and White supremacists in the United States.

Global reports of ethnic violence also lend support to the suggestion that hate crimes have been on the rise. Although claims as to the increasing presence of hate crimes in the United States may be controversial, reports of escalating violence directed against Jews and immigrant groups in the early 1990s remains essentially undisputed for many European countries, including France, Germany, England, Poland, Italy, Russia, and Hungary. In these countries, there were dramatic increases in violent skinhead and neo-Nazi demonstrations or in the prevalence of political bigotry. In Germany, for example, the Federal Office for the Protection of the Constitution reported that "xenophobic and violent" acts monitored by this government agency increased dramatically from 1989 through 1992, and since then have begun to decline.

During 1991 alone, for example, there were almost 1500 attacks against foreigners in Germany. In April 1991, a 28-year-old Mozambican was killed by a gang of neo-Nazi eastern German youths who pushed him from a moving trolley in the city of Dresden. In September, 1991, 600 right-wing German youths firebombed a home for foreigners and then physically assaulted 200 Vietnamese and Mozambicans in the streets of Hoyerswerde. In August 1992, there were seven nights of organized violence in the streets of the eastern German seaport town of Rostock. Armed with gasoline bombs and stones, 1000 Nazi youths attempted to force out foreigners who were seeking asylum in Germany. First, the mob firebombed a 10-story hostel in which Romanian gypsies were housed. Then they stormed the building next door, a residence for Vietnamese "guest workers," and set it on fire. Within days, the attacks in Rostock had touched off a massive wave of antiforeign violence in at least 20 cities around eastern Germany.

A second factor in evaluating the validity of the argument that hate crimes have been on the increase in-

volves the issue of bias. It is obvious that all data about social and political phenomena are collected either by individuals or by organizations consisting of individuals who come to the research situation with their own personal biases and preconceptions. If there is a social construction among those who have observed an increase, then there may also be a social construction among those who deny it. Very few conclusions based on social science research are clear-cut. After amassing incredible amounts of evidence as to the harmful nature of television programming on children, for example, there continue to be observers who deny that television violence is the least bit harmful. Those who are eager to criticize those researchers who have argued that hate crimes are on the rise must be careful not to expect more rigorous evidence of their adversaries than they expect of themselves.

Reports of increased hate offenses are supported also by studies that show intergroup hostility escalating as a result of increasing intergroup contact, especially in the form of competition. Research conducted by *The Chicago Reporter* (1997) suggests that Chicago-area suburbs with growing minority populations have recently experienced increasing numbers of hate offenses against Blacks and Latinos. In many previously all-White suburban communities, minorities have reached a critical mass, causing White residents to feel threatened by the influx of newcomers. This seems to be the point at which hate crimes escalate.

Those who argue that hate crimes have been increasing also note that intergroup competition has been on the rise. Whether or not economically based, growing threats to the advantaged majority group since the early 1980s may have inspired a rising tide of hate incidents directed against members of challenging groups. Over the last 15 or 20 years, there have been dramatic increases in interfaith and interrace dating and marriage, migration especially from Latin America and Asia, newly integrated neighborhoods, schools, college dormitories, and workplaces, and gay men and lesbians coming out (and, in many cases, organizing on behalf of their shared interests). Donald Green and his associates (1997) have shown that hate crimes occur most frequently in "defended" White neighborhoods—that is, in predominantly White areas that have experienced an in-migration of minorities.

As for the contention that advocacy groups inflate their estimates of hate crimes, it is interesting to note that the ADL has recently reported decreases in skinhead activity and in the overall level of hate crimes. Their more recent conclusions concerning the downward trend in hate offenses are consistent with evidence collected by the FBI indicating that serious crime in general has declined since 1992.

Regardless of the reality, the question of whether hate crimes have been increasing or decreasing overall may not be as useful a question as it might appear. Hate crimes are relatively rare and often result from a particular incident or a set of conditions in a local area. We have seen increases in hate crimes in local communities, as a result of court orders to desegregate public housing (Boston), after a highly publicized death (Howard Beach, NY), or in response to some large-scale external situation (attacks on Arab Americans during the Gulf War). In addition, demographic shifts within a metropolitan region can cause hate crime incidents to rise and fall. In the Chicago area, many suburban communities in which the proportion of Black and Latino residents has recently increased now have higher hate crime rates than the city of Chicago.

Thus, the question of changes in the number of hate crimes might most reasonably be posed in the most disaggregated fashion possible, at a state or community level. Attempts to aggregate hate crime data to a national estimate may mask counteracting trends as one community's incidents go down and another's increases.

VIII. RESPONSES TO HATE CRIMES

Interviews with victims of hate violence indicate that the aftermath of the victimization is characterized by a pervasive feeling of fear. As indicated earlier, the victims of these incidents generally did nothing to bring this violence upon them and thus do not know what to do to reduce their chance of future victimization. Their fear may be based on threats by the offender or friends of the offender but often it is simply based on the random nature of the crime.

In order to reduce fear in victims of hate crimes, it is important to offer them some form of protection from future violence and a degree of reassurance that they are valued members of the community. First of all, community leaders must speak out, condemning the attack. This is important because it sends two essential messages: to the victims, that local residents want them to remain members of that community and, to the offenders, that most people in the community do not support their illegal behavior.

Interviews with hate crime offenders indicate that they frequently believe that most of the community shares their desire to eliminate the "outsider." The offenders often see themselves as heroes or at least as "cool" in the eyes of their friends, because they have

the courage to act on what they believe to be commonly held beliefs. Public statements by local community leaders challenge this idea and send a message to offenders that their actions are not supported.

As noted earlier, many hate crimes are perpetrated by young people who do not yet have a profound commitment to bigotry and therefore may be dissuaded from repeating their offense. It is important, therefore, to apprehend youthful hate crime perpetrators at this point, especially in light of the possibility that many property offenders who go undetected may later graduate to hate crimes directed against people. Because what the perpetrators derive from committing such crimes is so minimal in a practical sense, they may be very influenced by a strong statement from society at large that demonstrates that this type of behavior will not be tolerated.

The local police play an essential role in responding to hate crimes. Advocacy groups can offer support and encouragement, and political leaders can offer reassurance, but the police are the only group that can legitimately promise to protect the victim in any future attack. Before law enforcement personnel can effectively offer this protection to victims of hate crimes, however, they must be trained to identify and investigate these difficult cases. The UCR section of the FBI has developed an outstanding training program for local law enforcement that teaches officers how to identify and effectively prosecute hate crimes.

In the past, judges were likely to respond to hate crimes committed by youthful first offenders by giving them a "slap on the wrist" consisting of a stern warning and little more than a sentence of probation. More recently, however, as the seriousness of hate offenses has received greater recognition by the courts, more and more judges have responded to such offenses with creative alternative sentencing including components of education, community service, and victim restitution. It is unfortunate that some youthful perpetrators have instead received a prison sentence that, in many cases, seems only to increase their hatred and slow their rehabilitation. Many American prisons now have organized hate groups—for example, Aryan Brotherhood—from which White supremacy groups recruit their members. Anyone convicted of committing a hate crime will be tempted to join an organized hate group in prison, if only for the protection he will need to survive. Incarceration serves an important purpose, but should be reserved for recidivist hatemongers or for individuals who have committed especially heinous crimes.

Finally, the most important response to a hate crime, as reported by its victims, is the reaction of those closest to them—their neighbors, co-workers, or fellow students. When a hate crime occurs, victims quite realistically wonder just how widespread is the hatred directed toward them. Do all their neighbors agree with the person who attacked them? Therefore, the most significant reaction for most victims is when members of the *perpetrator's* group come forward to assure the victim that they do not agree with the offenders and to urge the victims to remain in the neighborhood.

IX. CONCLUSION

Even if they were not labeled hate crimes, offenses committed against individuals because they are different have undoubtedly occurred throughout the history of humankind. Moreover, depending on prevailing economic and political circumstances at any given time and place, there have been important changes in the incidence of such offenses as well. In particular, hate crimes seem to rise whenever one group in a society feels that its advantaged position is being threatened by the presence of another. This was true in Nazi Germany; it was also true in the United States during Reconstruction, the Great Depression of the 1930s, and the civil rights movement of the 1960s. Even large-scale ethnic conflicts such as those in Bosnia and Northern Ireland seem to be based on intergroup competition for scarce resources.

Recent behavioral science research aimed at understanding the causes and characteristics of hate crimes may in part reflect a worsening of intergroup relations during the 1980s and early 1990s, as traditionally disadvantaged groups begin to make claims for equal treatment. In addition, however, such efforts to explain hate crimes probably also reflect a heightened sensitivity to violence perpetrated against vulnerable members of society—especially women, gays, and people of color. Because of the recent convergence of new social movements involving civil rights, women, gays and lesbians, and victims in general, we are strengthening our efforts to confront the destructive consequences of hate crimes especially for the most vulnerable among us.

Also See the Following Articles

ENEMY, CONCEPT AND IDENTITY OF • ETHNIC CONFLICTS AND COOPERATION • HOMOSEXUALS, VIOLENCE TOWARD • WOMEN, VIOLENCE AGAINST

Bibliography

Anti-Defamation League. (1988). "JAP baiting": When sexism and anti-semitism meet. *Special Education of ADL Periodic Update.* New York: ADL.

Anti-Defamation League. (1995). *The skinhead international.* New York: ADL.

Anti-Defamation League. (1997). *Vigilante justice: Militias and common law courts wage war against the government.* New York: ADL.

Berrill, K. (1992). Anti-gay violence and victimization in the United States: An overview. In G. Herek, K. Berrill (Eds.), *Hate crimes: Confronting violence against lesbians and gay men.* Newbury Park, CA: Sage Publications.

Bureau of Justice Assistance. (1997). *A policy makers guide to hate crimes.* Washington DC: U.S. Government Printing Office.

Delgado, L. (1992, July 31). Black family in North End is met with racist graffiti. *Boston Globe,* p. 17.

Ehrlich, H. (1972). *The social psychology of prejudice.* New York: Wiley.

Ehrlich, H. (1990). *Ethno-violence on college campuses.* Baltimore: National Institute Against Prejudice and Violence.

Fox, J., & Levin, J. (1996). *Overkill: Mass murder and serial killing exposed.* New York: Dell.

Freeman, S. (1993). Hate crime laws: Punishment which fits the crime. *Annual Survey of American Law,* pp. 581–585. New York: New York University School of Law.

Gambino, R. (1977). *Vendetta.* New York: Doubleday.

Gordon, D., & Pardo, N. (1997, September). Hate crimes strike changing suburbs. *The Chicago Reporter,* p. 1.

Green, D. P., Strolovitch, D. Z., & Wong, J. S. (1997). *Defended neighborhoods, integration, and hate crime.* Unpublished manuscript, Institution for Social and Policy Studies, Yale University.

Gunshots aimed at home of Black family. Associated Press. (June 6, 1997).

Halpern, T., & Levin, B. (1996). *The limits of dissent: The constitutional status of armed civilian militias.* Amherst, MA: Aletheia Press.

Hamm, M. S. (1994). *Hate crime: International perspectives on causes and control.* Cincinnati: Anderson.

Jacobs, J. B., & Henry, J. S. (1996, Winter). The social construction of a hate crime epidemic. *The Journal of Criminal Law and Criminology,* 366–391.

Jacobs, J., B., & Potter, K. A. (1997). Hate crimes: A critical perspective. *Crime and Justice: A Review of Research,* M. Tonry, Ed. Chicago: University of Chicago Press.

Jenness, V., & Broad, K. (1997). *Hate crimes: New social movements and the politics of violence.* New York: Aldine De Gruyter.

Karl, J. (1995). *The right to bear arms.* New York: Harper.

Keen, S. (1988). *Faces of the enemy.* New York: Harper and Row.

Keough, W. (1990). *Punchlines.* New York: Paragon House.

Klanwatch Intelligence Report (1997, Spring). Two years after: The patriot movement since Oklahoma City. pp. 18–20.

Lamy, P. (1996). *Millennium rage.* New York: Plenum Press.

Langer, E. (1990, July 16/23). The American Neo-Nazi movement today. *The Nation,* pp. 82–107.

Levin, B. (1992–1993, Winter). Bias crimes: A theoretical and practical overview. *Stanford Law and Policy Review,* pp. 165–171.

Levin, J. (1996, December 12). Teenagers burn churches. *Boston Globe, Focus Section.*

Levin, J. (1997, March 1). Visit to a patriot potluck. *USA Today,* 6A.

Levin, J. (1997, July 13). N. Irish racialize "The Troubles." *The Boston Herald.*

Levin, J., & Levin, W. J. (1982). *The functions of discrimination and prejudice.* New York: Harper and Row.

Levin, J., & McDevitt, J. (1993). *Hate crimes: The rising tide of bigotry and bloodshed.* New York: Plenum.

Levin, J., & McDevitt, J. (1995a, August 4). The research needed to understand hate crime. *Chronicle of Higher Education,* pp. B1–2.

Levin, J., & McDevitt, J. (1995b, August). Landmark study reveals hate crimes vary significantly by offender motivation. *Klanwatch Intelligence Report,* pp. 7–9.

Martin, S. (1995). A cross-burning is not just an arson: Police social construction of hate crimes in Baltimore County. *Criminology, 33*(3), 303–330.

Not in Our Town II. (1996). Public Broadcasting System.

Office of Juvenile justice and Delinquency Prevention. (1996). *Report to Congress on juvenile hate crime.* Washington, DC: U.S. Government Printing Office.

Olzak, S., Shanahan, S., & McEneaney, E. H. (1996, August). Poverty, segregation, and race riots: 1960 to 1993. *American Sociological Review,* 590–613.

Paulsen, M. (1996, July 6). Fires come in different shades of hate. *The State,* 1A.

Pearce, D. M. (1979, February). Gatekeepers and homeseekers: Institutional patterns in racial steering. *Social Problems,* 325–342.

Schuman, H., Steeh, C., & Lawrence Bobo, L. (1988). *Racial attitudes in America.* Cambridge: Harvard University Press.

Sherif, M., & Sherif, C. (1961). *Intergroup conflict and cooperation: The Robbers cave experiment.* Norman, OK: University of Oklahoma.

Stossen, N. (1993, May). Special penalties should apply to hate crimes. *American Bar Association Journal.*

Watts, M. (1997). *Xenophobia in united Germany.* New York: St. Martin's Press.

Weisburd, S. B., & Levin, B. (1994, Spring). "On the basis of sex": Recognizing gender-based bias crimes. *Stanford Law and Policy Review,* 21–43.

Weiss, J. Ehrlich, H., & Barbara Larcom, B. (1991/1992, Winter). Ethnoviolence at work. *Journal of Intergroup Relations,* 21–33.

Health Consequences of War and Political Violence*

Antonio Ugalde and Patricia L. Richards
University of Texas, Austin

Anthony Zwi
London School of Hygiene and Tropical Medicine

GLOSSARY

Biological Weapons According to the United Nations, biological weapons are those that depend for their effects on multiplication within the target organism, and are intended for use in war to cause disease or death in man, animals, or plants.

Dirty Wars Systematic acts of repression, including torture, disappearance, executions, and exile, carried out by states against their own citizens for purposes of destroying any opposition to the regime's policies.

Genocide According to the Convention on the Prevention and Punishment of the Crime of Genocide (UN 1946) genocide means any of the following acts committed with the intent to destroy, in whole or in part, a national, ethnic, racial, or religious group, such as: killing members of the group; causing serious bodily or mental harm to members of the group; deliberately inflicting on the group conditions of life calculated to bring about the physical destruction in whole or in part; imposing measures intended to prevent births within the group; forcibly transferring children of the group to another group.

Incidence The proportion of people in a defined population who develop a particular state of health or illness over a defined period of time.

Internally Displaced Populations Internally displaced populations are persons who may have been forced to flee their homes for the same reasons as refugees (see definition of refugee), but have not crossed an internationally recognized border.

Low-Intensity Warfare A total war at the grassroots level: commonly includes political, economic, and psychological warfare, along with a less direct involvement, often, of military forces. There are three types of low-intensity warfare: classic counterinsurgency, active defense against potential insurgencies, and pro-insurgency, carried out through proxy armies.

Militarism An increasing propensity by states and significant groups within states to rely on force as a normal political tactic; it is manifested in the violent attitudes and behavior of such groups.

Post-Traumatic Stress Disorders (PTSD) A defined state of mental health that may occur in people who

---

* Several parts of this article borrow from previous work by the authors, in particular from A. Zwi and A. Ugalde, 1989, 1991; A. Ugalde and R. Vega, 1989; A. Zwi and A. J. Cabral (Eds.), 1991; J. Macrae, A. Zwi, and H. Birungi, 1993; A. Ugalde and A. Zwi (Eds.), 1994, 1995; J. Macrae and A. Zwi (Eds.), 1994; A. Zwi 1996; A. Ugalde *et al.*, 1996.

Copyright © 1999 by Academic Press.
All rights of reproduction in any form reserved.

have experienced particularly traumatic exposures to horrific or near-death experiences. Initially applied to soldiers exposed to traumatic conditions in wartime, the term has now begun to be applied much more widely. PTSD is common among victims of manmade and natural disasters, military activities (for both soldiers and civilians), violence, ethnic cleansing, and genocide, torture, and repression, as well as among refugees. Typical symptoms include flashbacks and dreams of the traumatic event, insomnia, numbness, detachment from other people, and an avoidance of activities and situations than can reawaken painful memories.

Prevalence The proportion of people who exhibit a particular health outcome (state of health or illness or disease) within a defined population at a particular point in time.

Refugee According to the United Nations High Commission for Refugees, persons who flee from war and war-related conditions and whose state is unwilling to protect them, are in need of international protection and should be considered refugees. A refugee is a person who "owing to a well-founded fear of being persecuted for reasons of race, religion, nationality, membership in a particular social group, or political opinion, is outside the country of his nationality, and is unable to or, owing to such fear, is unwilling to avail himself of the protection of that country" (Convention Relating to the Status of Refugees, 1951).

Torture The United Nations define torture as an act by which severe pain or suffering, whether physical or mental, is intentionally inflicted by or at the instigation of a public official or a person for such purposes as obtaining from him/her or a third person information or confession, punishing him/her for an act he/she has committed, or intimidating him/her or other persons.

I. HISTORICAL BACKGROUND

From the first recorded historical documents we are aware of the human propensity to violence as a means of resolving conflict. The quest for discovering ever-more destructive technologies is also an ongoing feature of human history. Almost 3000 thousand years ago, after its conquest the city of Shechem was covered by salt to ensure its final and total destruction, a technique also used by the Romans against their enemies. Chemical nerve poisons such as curare have also been used

for centuries, and crop destruction as a military tactic has been documented since early days. Biological "weapons" were successfully used hundreds of centuries ago when Romans contaminated their enemies' drinking water with corpses. The Tartars prevailed in the siege against Caffa in the Black Sea by catapulting into the city bubonic plague-infested corpses.

Massive destruction for military purpose also has a long history. Toward the end of the 17th century, the Dutch military destroyed dikes and flooded its own country to stop the French invading army. A more drastic version of this tactic was used in 1938 against Japanese invaders when the Chinese blew up a dam in the Yellow River. Several thousand villages were flooded and thousands of enemy soldiers were killed, effectively stopping the advance of the Japanese force on one front. In the process, hundreds of thousands of rural Chinese died, millions were left homeless, and the flooding of millions of acres caused enormous crops losses.

A. Communicable Diseases

Communicable diseases and conflict are closely related. Conflict may disrupt normal environmental controls and health services that normally assist in keeping communicable diseases in check. It is well documented that almost until World War II more soldiers were killed by communicable diseases than by battle-related causes. Maintaining sanitary conditions for a large number of soldiers living in crowded conditions, difficulties in ensuring access to hygienic food and water, and exposure of invading armies to communicable diseases to which they had not been previously exposed, such as malaria, are all part of the explanation.

It is believed that the malaria that Hannibal's African troops brought to Europe was more deadly than their military prowess. In 1489 during the siege of Granada in Spain, King Ferdinand and Queen Isabella lost 17,000 soldiers from typhus, which was also responsible for many of the 300,000 deaths in Russia, more than half of Napoleon's 1812 invading army. It is estimated that in the Spanish-American War at the turn of the 19th century the ratio of deaths from disease to deaths from battle-related causes was about five to one. Public health developments reduced the ratio to one in World War I. To some extent, the development of public health has been a response to the needs of the colonial powers to protect their armies overseas. The creation in the nineteenth century of the first schools of public health with their emphasis on tropical diseases attests to the colonial military demands for sanitation and communicable disease control.

B. Twentieth Century Changes

1. Development of Weapons of Mass Destruction

The scientific development and refinement of weapons of mass destruction has taken place during the 20th century. In Dresden, Germany, during the Second World War, more than 100,000 civilians died in the fire-bombing of the city. The 20th century has also witnessed the creation of the most destructive weapon in the history of mankind: the nuclear weapon.

Chemical weapons, including mustard gas, chlorine, and phosgene, were produced and used for the first time during World War I. More recently, in violation of the 1925 Geneva Protocol that outlawed a first-use of chemical and biological weapons, chemical weapons have been used against human populations in the Iraq-Iran war and against the Kurds. Massive amounts of herbicides (about 19 million gallons) were used in Vietnam; more than five million acres were sprayed to deprive the enemy of coverage and of food crops. The health consequences are discussed later.

The Japanese tested biological weapons, including agents of anthrax, cholera, and plague on prisoners of war, and it has been alleged that during the Japanese invasion of China 11 cities were attacked with biological weapons.

It is estimated that on August 6, 1945, the explosion of the nuclear bomb in Hiroshima killed instantly about 40,000 civilians. By 1945, the combined death toll in Hiroshima and Nagasaki from the two nuclear explosions was 210,000 persons. The delayed effects are more difficult to assess. Increases in the incidence of several types of cancer such as breast, lung, and thyroid cancer have been established, as well as increases in chromosome abnormalities and microcephaly with mental retardation. It is believed that exposure to nuclear radiation contributed to the increase of incidence of other types of cancer, for example skin, urinary tract, and esophagal cancers, salivary gland tumors, and malignant lymphomas.

2. Civilians as Targets of War

In contrast to traditional wars of the past, in recent wars civilians have been the main target of violence. More than 107 million people have died in wars this century alone; where earlier in the century 90% of all casualties were military, in recent wars 90% are civilians. UNICEF's finding that at the end of the 20th century wars are killing more children than soldiers is particularly disturbing. The shift from military to civilian targeting has coincided with the development of military technologies that can, in a few days, cause massive damage to humans and the environment. Automatic weapons, aerial bombings, missiles, powerful armored tanks and vehicles, and antipersonnel mines are able to cause massive devastation among civilian populations and their habitats, and they create millions of refugees and internally displaced populations.

C. War and Public Health

Among social scientists and public health experts there is a growing recognition of the health impact of armed conflicts and political violence. Political violence and war have become identified as a major public health problem, not only because of the deaths and disability they cause, but also because of their longer term and more indirect effects on the health, well-being, and livelihoods of individuals, families, and communities.

In addition, wars and political violence shift large amounts of scarce resources from social and health services to the military. Third world countries spent more than $400 billion on arms between 1960 and 1987.

Wars and political violence have become an important health issue because they:

- cause much morbidity and mortality among civilians;
- have important and long-lasting negative health effects on the population;
- disrupt the provision and organization of health services; and
- do not seem to decrease with the passing of time; as soon as some conflicts are resolved, new violence explodes elsewhere.

II. EXTENT AND TYPES OF POLITICAL VIOLENCE

A. Extent of Political Violence

Even the most basic data from war-torn countries are notoriously faulty (an issue to be discussed in Section III). Table I presents estimates of casualties and displaced populations—the only statistics systematically published cross-nationally—by war and political violence from 1985 to 1995. Other basic data, such as war-caused physical disability, have been estimated only for a few conflicts.

In spite of the difficulties of obtaining accurate data, Table I is suggestive of the magnitude of the problem.

TABLE I

Casualties, Externally and Internally Displaced by Political Violence 1985–1995*

Country	Nature of conflict	Years	Casualties	Refugees & externally displaced 1994**	Internally displaced 1994*
Africa					
Algeria	Civil war/religious	1992–95	50,000 (b)	n/a	n/a
Angola	Civil War/East-West confrontation	1975–94	800,000	344,000	2 million
Burundi (l)	Ethnic	decades long	40–70,000 since 1988	330,000	400,000
Chad (h,k,j,l)	Ethnic/civil war Libyan conflict	1964–93? 1987–89	33,800	27,000	50,000 (at start of 94)
Djibouti (l)	Ethnic	1991–94	n/a	10,000	50,000
Eritrea (j,l)	Independence from Ethiopia	1962–91	500,000	380,000	n/a
Ethiopia (c,l)	Civil War Continuing ethnic clashes	1975–91 1991–95	n/a	190,000	400,000
Ghana (l)	Ethnic/regional	1994–95	2,000	5,000	20,000
Kenya (l)	Ethnic (Rift Valley)	1991–92, 1994–95 (sporadic)	1,500+	8,000	210,000
Liberia	Civil war/local lords	1989–95	150,000 (b)	784,000	1.1 million
Mali (l)	Ethnic/regional autonomy	1991–95	n/a	45,000	n/a
Mauritania (l)	Ethnic (Blacks expelled by Moors)	1989–91	n/a	75,000	n/a
Morocco (i)	Western Sahara: regional autonomy	1975–92	10–13,000	n/a	n/a
Mozambique (d,l)	Civil War	1975–92	1 million	325,000	500,000
Namibia (k,n)	Independence from South Africa	1967–90	12,800 (1989)	46,000	n/a
Rwanda	Ethnic	1990–94	1/2–1 million	1.7 million	1.2 million
Senegal (l)	Regional autonomy	1991–93	n/a	17,000	2,700
Sierra Leone (b,l)	Civil war	1992–95	14,000	260,000	700,000
Somalia	Ethnic/local lords	1991–95	300,000+	458,700	500,000
South Africa (g,k,l)	Anti-apartheid	1961–94 (intensified 84–89)	18,900 (1984–93)	40,000	4 million
Sudan	Regional autonomy/religious	past 4 decades	1 million+	510,000	4 million
Togo (l)	Political warloads	1991–95	n/a	140,000	100,000
Uganda (i,k,l)	Civil war Ethnic conflict	1981–86 1987–91	n/a 112,000	15,000	n/a
Regional Totals			4.5–5 million	5.7 million	15.2 million
Asia					
Afghanistan	Civil war/East–West confrontation	1978–95	1 million+	2.8 million	1 million
Bangladesh	Territory/religious in Chittagong Hill Tract	1975–95	3,000–3,500 (f)	48,000	n/a
Bhutan (l)	Ethnic	1990–92	n/a	132,000	n/a
Cambodia	Civil War Continued skirmishes	1975–78 1979–95	1 million+ (f)	30,300	113,000
India	1. Kashmir: territory 2. Punjab: ethnic conflict 3. NE: regional independence	1990–95 1993–95, ?–95	9,000 (f) 336,000+ n/a	n/a	250,000 Kashmir only)
Indonesia	East Timor independence	1975–95	15,000–16,000 (military) (f)	9,900	n/a
Myanmar	Territory/ethnic/democracy	1988–95	5,000–9,000 (f)	203,300	1/2–1 million

TABLE I (*continued*)

Country	Nature of conflict	Years	Casualties	Refugees & externally displaced 1994**	Internally displaced 1994*
Philippines	Religious/social class	1969–95	25,000+	n/a	n/a
Sri Lanka	Ethnic/regional autonomy	1983–95 (a)	11,000	104,000	525,000
Tajikistan	Civil War	1992–93	36,000	165,000	n/a
	Continued regional fighting (a)	1993–95	n/a		
Tibet	Independence from China	1959–95	n/a	139,000	n/a
Regional Totals			2.4 million	831,500	1.4–1.9 million
Latin America					
Colombia	Social class	past 3 decades	30,000+ (f)	200	600,000
El Salvador	Civil war/social class	1980–92	80,000	1–1.5 million	n/a
Guatemala	Civil war/social class	1967–95	150,000+	45,050	200,000
Nicaragua (k,o)	Civil war/social class	1979–89	30,000+ (military)	400,000– 500,000	50,000
Peru	Social class	1981–95	17,500+ (through the 1980s)	450	600,000
Regional Totals			307,500	1.4–2 million	1.65 million
Europe					
Azerbaijan	Ethnic/territory	1988–95	10,000+	374,000	630,000
Bosnia-Herzegovina	Ethnic	1992–95	200,000+	864,000	1.3 million
Russia (a,e)	Regional independence (Chechnya)	1994–95	10–40,000	n/a	220,000
Croatia	Ethnic (Croatian Serb War)	1991	10,000+	136,900+	290,000
Georgia	Regional independence	1992–95	3,000	106,800	260,000
Romania (k,n)	Democracy/ethnic	1989–90	750–1,000	n/a	n/a
Regional Totals			234,000–264,000	1.48 million	2.7 million
Middle East					
Iran	1. Regional autonomy (Kurds)	1970s–95	800 since 1991	54,500	n/a
	2. War/(border conflict) with Iraq	1980–88 (1995)	n/a		
Iraq	1. Regional autonomy (Kurds)	1984–95	100,000 (Kurds)	635,900	1 million
	2. Regional (Shiite)	1991–95	n/a		
	3. Gulf War and repercussions	1991	n/a		
	4. War/(border conflict with Iran)	1980–88	n/a		
	5. Fighting between Iraqi Kurds and Turkey	(1995)	n/a		
	6. Fractional ethnic (Kurds)	1992–95?	n/a		
Israel/Palestine	Territory/religious	1948–96	100,000+	3,136,800 (Palestinians)	n/a
Lebanon (j,n)	Civil war	1975–90	150,000	n/a	800,000
Turkey	Regional autonomy (Kurds)	1984–93?	10,000+	13,000	2 million
Regional Totals			360,800	3.8 million	3.8 million
World Totals			7.9–8.4 million	13.2–13.8 million	24.8–25.3 million

continues

TABLE I (*continued*)

* Includes conflicts started before 1985. Some conflicts with a 1995 ending date were still raging at that time. All information from *State of World Conflict Report 1994–1995* by The Carter Center, Atlanta, unless otherwise noted. Numbers in the casualties column represent total casualties at the end of the conflict (or up until 1995), unless otherwise noted. Blank cells indicate that no information was available.

** All externally and internally displaced figures are for totals up to the end of 1994, except in the cases of Nicaragua, where the figures are for 1986, Lebanon (1990), Namibia (1989), and South Africa, where the externally displaced figure represents the number of exiles before 1993. Figures for Bosnia-Herzegovina and Croatia include the former Yugoslavia. These figures must be read with caution, since displaced populations are in constant flux and are difficult to count. The various groups and states that count displaced populations may use different definitions. In addition, refugees in different countries may be livig in very different conditions. For instance, most refugees in Ghana are settled into communities rather than into camps. Furthermore, it is important to stress that the 1994 figures simply represent the total number of people who were displaced at the end of 1994. As such, they often do not represent the maximum population displaced by a given conflict. For example, the peak of Mozambique's conflict, the total number of internally and externally displaced people exceeded 5.7 million, while by 1994 only 825,000 were displaced. Clearly, displaced populations rise and fall as a conflict intensifies and wanes. As in the case of Mozambique, most displaced populations eventually return home, but counts may also be altered by displaced individuals who die or resettle in another country. Finally, repatriation efforts vary in their efficiency. In Eritrea, for example, 380,000 people remained externally displaced in 1994 even though that country's war for independence ended in 1991

(a): United Nations High Commissioner for Refugees. (1996). *REFWorld*. UNHCR website (www.unhcr.ch/refworld/refworld.htm).

(b): *Country Reports on Human Rights Practices for 1995*. (1996, March). U.S. Department of State website (www.usis.usemb.se/human/index.htm).

(c): *Country Reports on Human Rights Practices for 1993*. (1994). U.S. Department of State. Washington, DC: U.S. Government Printing office.

(d): *Country Reports on Human Rights Practices for 1992*. (1993). U.S. Department of State. Washington, DC: U.S. Government Printing Office.

(e): *Sipri Yearbook 1996*. Stockholm International Peace Research Institute. New York: Oxford University Press.

(f): *Sipri Yearbook 1995*. Stockholm International Peace Research Institute. New York: Oxford University Press.

(g): *Sipri Yearbook 1994*. Stockholm International Peace Research Institue. New York: Oxford University Press.

(h): *Sipri Yearbook 1993*. Stockholm International Peace Research Institute. New York: Oxford University Press.

(i): *Sipri Yearbook 1992*. Stockholm International Peace Research Institute. New York: Oxford University Press.

(j): *Sipri Yearbook 1991*. Stockholm International Peace Research Institute. New York: Oxford University Press.

(k): *Sipri Yearbook 1990*. Stockholm International Peace Research Institute. New York: Oxford University Press.

(l): *World Refugee Survey, 1995*. Washington, DC: US Committee for Refugees.

(m): *World Refugee Survey, 1993*. Washington, DC: US Committee for Refugees.

(n): *World Refugee Survey, 1991*. Washington, DC: US Committee for Refugees.

(o): *World Refugee Survey, 1986*. Washington, DC: US Committee for Refugees.

Between 1985 and 1995 there were about 8 million deaths caused by ongoing wars (this figure includes deaths that took place before 1985 in wars that continued after this year), and almost 25 million internally and 10 million externally displaced populations. If we add to these figures those from wars that ended before 1985, we have a total of 19 million refugees, and possibly as many as 38 million internally displaced people.

The geographic patterns of conflict are changing: from the Second World War until the end of the Cold War, almost all major conflicts, with very few exceptions, occurred in the Third World. Since the demise of the Soviet Union, conflicts have erupted with great ferocity in the former Yugoslavia, in Chechneya, Nagorno-Karabakh, Azerbaijan, and in a variety of other previously unaffected areas.

B. Types of Political Violence

Table I also provides an attempt to classify the main types of wars. It is acknowledged that frequently more than one cause is present but observers are not always in agreement about the leading cause. By and large, in Latin America most conflicts result from an inequitable distribution of societal resources, and the military has sided with the dominant class. Some conservative observers downplayed the social class origins of the conflicts and considered the East-West confrontation as the main cause of political violence in this region. In Africa, ethnic conflicts and the Cold War have fueled much of the fighting between factions led by native strongmen. However, in Africa, the Middle East, and in many Asian countries most analysts trace the majority of ethnic, civil, religious, and territorial wars back to colonial and decolonization policies. In Europe and the former Soviet Union, most recent conflicts can be classified as territorial or ethnic confrontations. After WW II, the few generally short-lived international wars responded to the needs of the military to legitimize itself or the need to generate nationalistic support for politically ambitious generals. Attempts to summarize with a label the nature of a conflict is at best simplistic. Political violence has complex historical and international dimensions, and as a result, multicausal explanations.

1. Dirty Wars

It is perhaps useful to explain the characteristics of two types of political violence, the political repression that has been known as dirty war, and low-intensity warfare. Since times immemorial tyrants and dictators have used the power of the state to destroy their opponents and those considered for any reason undesirable. As applied today, the concept of dirty war goes beyond the annihilation of individuals and groups. Dirty wars, in which the victory over the enemy (ethnic groups, the poor, or opposition political parties) is considered to justify the use of any means, are an extreme application of the concept of total war. The concept of total war was originally formulated by Erich von Lundendorff, a World War I German general, who argued that during a war all political and economic resources of a nation should be under the control of the armed forces and used according to military needs. Military regimes in third world countries have transformed the concept of total war and applied it to fight internal enemies. Once the achievement of an end justifies the means there is no limit to human barbarism and the perpetrators succeed in achieving their goal of creating a permanent and complete state of fear among the population: fear to demand justice, fear to express one's ideas, fear to know the political activities and ideas of neighbors, relatives, and friends, fear of being betrayed by family members and friends, and even fear of being fearful.

The case of the Argentinean military is a good illustration of the nature of violence in dirty wars. The 1976–1983 military junta used all resources under their control to institute a state of terror, including coercing judges, intimidating and threatening members of the press, and demanding assistance from medical practitioners to increase the effectiveness of torture. The junta did not discriminate: victims included children and infants, pregnant women, the blind, the handicapped, bishops, priests, and nuns, and even members of the military. If the target victim could not be found, his/her relatives were held hostage until the victim was apprehended. At times, children and spouses were forced to witness the torture of their loved ones. Every oppressive act committed by the Argentinean military aimed at creating intense fear among family members of the victim and the rest of the community. Studies of other dirty wars in Chile, Uruguay, and Brazil confirm the intense forms of brutalities and violations of most basic human rights.

In South Africa, the apartheid regime conducted a total war against the perceived threat of communism and majority rule. The apartheid regime destabilized surrounding states, routinely engaged in the torture of political opponents, engaged in political killings, supported factions that undermined peace and security, and sought to control every aspect of society in responding to threats against the apartheid regime.

2. Low-Intensity Warfare

The conflicts in Central America, Mozambique, and Angola have been characterized as low-intensity warfare. In low-intensity wars, guerilla-style tactics are used by the military, frequently with the tactical support of foreign armed forces, against the insurgency. In a low-intensity war, the insurgency may aim to destabilize the government by terrorist acts and by the destruction of vital economic assets. One of the military tactics in low-intensity war is to remove the support that the insurgency receives from the local population in the form of food supplies, hiding places, and information. Terror is commonly used to stop local dwellers from aiding the insurgency. The objective can be achieved by forcing civilian populations out of their hamlets into new isolated villages under the surveillance of the military, a policy first used by the British in Malaysia with the rural Chinese population.

In some conflicts, once the local population has been removed, the military follows the scorched earth policy in which villages are razed, crops and food supplies are burned, animals are slaughtered, roads and fields are mined, and bridges are destroyed. When the construction of new settlements or the displacement of the dwellers to new settlements is not feasible, the military includes in the total destruction of the countryside the brutal annihilation of its inhabitants, including children, women, and the elderly. In low-intensity warfare civilians become military targets, and in the process, the most hideous crimes and violations of basic human rights, including medical neutrality, occur. Large numbers of civilian casualties, mass displacement of the peasantry to urban centers, neighboring countries, and new villages, and environmental degradation of the countryside are characteristics of low-intensity warfare.

Foreign participation in low-intensity warfare has occurred through:
- financial assistance to the military including the provision of food for the armed forces;
- strategic tactical military and security information;
- training of personnel;
- transfers of military equipment and munitions

(tanks, helicopters, antipersonnel mines, communication equipment); and

- economic assistance to reduce the impact of the war on the country's economy.

On several occasions low-intensity warfare was supported in violation of the foreign country's own laws, but violators have seldom been brought to court because necessary legal disclosures can be avoided by invoking the principle of national security. As a result, the manufacturers of illness and death, an expression used by McKinlay (1986), are never identified, and the impunity sets an example for future violators.

C. Health Effects by Types of Political Conflict

The characteristics of a war influence the nature and the magnitude of its impact. While the number of victims in dirty wars is relatively small compared to other wars, the mental health consequences could be very severe and affect the victims, their families, and entire communities. In contrast, ethnic wars, "ethnic cleansing," and genocide seek to annihilate the opposing groups and lead to a very large number of casualties and many brutalities. Large mass executions and rape are routinely reported in ethnic wars. Today, wars between independent nations are few and, with rare exceptions, short in duration, but because international wars use advanced military technologies the number of victims can be very high.

The destruction of the country's physical infrastructure and the environment tends to be minimal in dirty wars but large in civil, ethnic wars and in international

wars except in the cases of border disputes. The impact on the environment has severe health implications, although it also varies by type of conflict. Table II attempts to summarize the above discussion.

III. MEASURING THE IMPACT AND HIDDEN COSTS

A. Limitations

Before undertaking an analysis of the health impact of wars we need to emphasize and discuss the limitations in quantifying the impact. The constraints respond to one or a combination of the following:

- methodological and theoretical shortcomings;
- inconsistencies in the definition of some terms such as refugees and displaced populations;
- restricted access to areas of conflict and sources of information;
- massiveness and swiftness of events;
- political manipulation of data;
- economic limitations; and
- hidden or indirect nature of the impact.

One common limitation is inaccurate population and sociodemographic data. Among refugee populations data are not routinely collected by age and sex, which greatly undermines their use in identifying key health problems and responding to them. Without demographic data, it is impossible to estimate age specific rates of morbidity and mortality, a requirement for

TABLE II
Types of Wars and Health Effects: Tendencies

Health effects	International wars		Civil wars				Independence wars	Dirty wars
	Border disputes	Other types (territorial etc.)	Religious	Ethnic	Class	Warlords		
deaths	few	high	small/medium	high	high	variable	high	few
destruction sanitary/health infrastructure	small	high	small/medium	high	high	small/medium	variable	negligible
displaced populations	small	variable	variable	very high	high	variable	small/medium	small
mental health	small	variable	variable	very high	high/very high	variable	small/medium	high
environment	small	medium/high	variable	high	high	small/medium	variable	negligible

many epidemiological decisions and interventions. For example, age-specific data among Mozambican refugees in Zimbabwe were unknown; most deaths were reported anecdotally to have occurred in children under 5 years of age.

1. Methodological and Theoretical Limitations

One frequent methodological limitation is the lack of reliable prewar health data. Without it, it is not possible to assess how much wars add to existing malnutrition, mental health disorders, infectious diseases, sexually transmitted diseases, other diseases or disability, all of which will be affected by war. Furthermore, the war itself disrupts whatever surveillance and information systems operated previously.

Health conditions of populations respond to multiple causes such as health services interventions, changes in the national and global economies, epidemics, weather conditions, and natural disasters. When one or several of these events occur at the same time as a war it is theoretically difficult to ascertain with any precision how much of the health condition is attributable to the war or to the other causes. For example, effective primary care interventions such as the use of rehydration salts, immunizations, food fortification and supplementation programs, and simple sanitation interventions are very inexpensive and efficient in improving health conditions of populations. It may be possible in many conflict-affected settings to continue and even increase the delivery of these services: this may lead to improved health indices (e.g., declining child and infant mortality) despite the ongoing effects of war. Obviously, had it not been for the war, health conditions would have improved more rapidly, but estimating by how much is somewhat circumstantial and imprecise.

2. Inconsistencies in the Definitions Used

Lack of consistency in the definitions of terms also makes it difficult to know with accuracy the number of persons affected by war. The UN High Commissioner for Refugees (UNHCR) at times includes in its definition of refugees only persons who suffer persecution or have a well-founded fear of being persecuted and are outside of their country of nationality. In other instances the definition is broader and includes also those who leave their countries of nationality because their safety is threatened by events seriously disturbing the public order. Other institutions may also use the term refugee—even if it has no legal implications under international law—to refer to persons who flee their place of residence because they fear for their safety due to wars.

In this case the difference between displaced and refugees tends to disappear.

3. Massiveness and Swiftness of Events

The extermination of ethnic rivals in Rwanda, for example, was so massive that it was impossible for any party to provide an approximate number of deaths. To date estimates of immediate deaths in the genocide range from 500,000 to one million people. There are many examples of massive population movements in very short periods of time. Thus, between May and December of 1990 the estimated number of Liberian refugees in Guinea increased from 80,000 to 600,000 people. Such massive movements present considerable challenges in terms of providing services, but also make difficult the presentation of accurate estimates of the incidence and prevalence of disease.

4. Political Motivation to Alter Information

According to their political interests, parties at war increase or decrease the stated number of casualties and displaced populations. Neither the Iraqi nor the U.S. governments were willing to provide accurate data on Gulf War casualties. The U.S. government fired a Census Bureau civil servant for releasing an estimate of Iraqi casualties because the figure was too high and would have contradicted the official image of the war as a highly technical operation limited to the destruction of military targets. For the Iraqi regime the deaths of more than 100,000 and injuries of 300,000 soldiers, plus the deaths of more than 7000 civilians would have been embarrassing and humiliating, and perhaps would have weakened popular support and incited desertions among the army's rank and file.

In addition to skewing death and injury figures, governments have different interpretations of why persons seek refugee status. The U.S. Immigration and Naturalization Service argues that many displaced populations from third world countries who claim political refugee status in the United States are economic refugees. In fact, political refugees are frequently also economic refugees. The decision to classify migrants escaping from war and political violence as economic migrants instead of political refugees is itself a political decision. Many who leave their country of origin because of safety concerns are aware of governments' tendency to deny refugee status and they decide to enter the country of asylum illegally. In Costa Rica there were 30,780 registered refugees in 1986 but the government estimated that there were an additional 200,000 undocumented refugees.

5. Hidden and Indirect Effects

Often the impact of war on health is indirect, is not immediately observable, and may only surface some time later, even in subsequent generations. We refer to these consequences as the hidden health costs of war.

Different types of hidden health costs caused by wars and political violence can be summarized as follows (examples are given in Sections IV and V):

- additional human suffering caused by deterioration of quality and availability of health services and health services organization (scarcity of medicines, delays of surgical interventions and complications resulting from the delays, increased problems of referrals, reduction of physical and human resources, etc);
- mental health disorders from rapes and from exposure to horrors and brutalities;
- negative impact on nutrition produced by reductions of arable land because of the destruction of physical infrastructure, antipersonnel land mines, and degradation of the environment;
- delayed effects from exposure to biological and chemical agents, and from radiation;
- indirect effects from war-induced violent behavior, alcoholism, and drug abuse; and
- indirect health effects, which cannot be measured with precision, from the contamination of air, water, and soil.

B. Overcoming the Data Limitations

Emergency and relief services pressed by the need to provide rapid assistance have developed methodologies to overcome data deficiencies. In the absence of information, rapid assessment methods such as community questionnaires, verbal autopsies, monitoring of grave sites, structured morbidity interviews, focus groups, and rapid anthropological procedures have been used to estimate the health needs of the populations. Many reports agree that the application of these techniques is easier among refugees than among displaced populations. A practice that is increasingly used and perfected is the identification of the most important and common diseases that could be expected to occur in the region, at a particular time of the year, taking into account the characteristics of the camp or settlement, the demographics of the population, and weather conditions. The diseases are defined by symptoms to facilitate rapid intervention by lay health workers.

IV. PHYSICAL HEALTH CONSEQUENCES

A. Diversity of Effects

War and political violence characteristics, differences in levels of economic and health services of the war-afflicted countries, epidemiological conditions, and conditions of refugee camps are so different that it is impossible to provide a picture of war-produced morbidity and mortality applicable to most settings. In many situations, drugs to treat diseases, including noncommunicable diseases such as diabetes or asthma, become unavailable with consequent negative impacts on community health.

B. Communicable Diseases

The destruction of clinics, the reduction of health personnel, and the difficulties of maintaining the cold chain to preserve the potency of vaccines tends to reduce immunization coverage and increase the incidence of communicable diseases. During the war, fewer that 35% of children were being immunized in Bosnia, compared with 95% before the war. An outbreak of measles in Nicaragua during the contra war was caused by the inability of health services to immunize in the war zones. The reduction of malaria control programs during wars has been associated with epidemic outbreaks in many countries. In Ethiopia, epidemics of louse-borne typhus and relapsing fever were attributed to crowded army camps, prisons, and refugee camps, as well as the sale of infected blankets and clothes to civilians by retreating soldiers.

Wars and political conflict present high-risk situations for the transmission of sexually transmitted diseases including HIV infection. HIV infection is high among many armies, particularly in Africa. There are various ways in which war predisposes to STD and HIV transmission: population movement may be widespread, increased crowding occurs, normal societal structures that inhibit aggressive behavior or prevent the violation of women may be weakened, women may be separated from their partners who normally provide a degree of protection, and military personnel or others with power may specifically use such power to obtain sexual favors or simply to violate others. In addition, access to barrier contraceptives, treatment for sexually transmitted diseases, the conditions for maintaining personal hygiene, and health promotion advice are all compromised in conflict situations.

Rape is common during wars and victims of rape

seldom talk about their victimization. A study in Uganda found that many women had hardly spoken with other people about their ordeals during the civil war. Treatment of victims and control of sexually transmitted diseases is hampered by the victims' silence. Rape, sexual violence, and exploitation may also be widespread in refugee camps although the extent of its recognition is limited. "I have walked around camps and seen doctors who have said 'no problems,' says Marie Lobol, UNHCR's Senior Social Services Officer, "I have then gone into tents, and found women who have been raped" (cited in Marshall, 1995:4). In Rwanda, during the 1994 genocide the Foundation de France reported that ". . . virtually every adult woman or girl past puberty who was spared from massacre by the militia had been raped. There are estimates that 2,000–5,000 children may have been born to rape, many immediately abandoned" (ibid.:4–5).

C. Disability

Numbers and types of war-disabled are not well known; only a few countries such as Zimbabwe, El Salvador, and Tigray have taken censuses of war-related disability. In Zimbabwe, 13% of all disability was war-related, and in El Salvador the census identified 12,041 war-disabled, 82% of whom were combatants and the rest civilians. About one-third of the 300,000 soldiers returning from the front at the end of the war in Ethiopia had been injured or disabled. By 1984, well before the end of the war in 1991, more than 40,000 people had lost one or more limbs in the conflict.

Estimates of mine-caused disabilities are staggering: 36,000 in Cambodia (one in every 236 persons has lost at least one limb), 20,000 in Angola, 8000 in Mozambique, and 15,000 in Uganda. Many of the severely disabled will require permanent medical and social services, and strain the health resources of the country for many years. UNICEF estimates that there are about four to five million war-disabled children.

Experts guess that there are more than 100 million antipersonnel landmines scattered over more than 60 countries. For years to come the antipersonnel landmine and munitions will constitute a health hazard and contribute to thousands of deaths and severe disabilities, including those of many children. It has been estimated that one person will die and two will be injured for every 5000 inactivated mines. As the Soviets withdrew in defeat in Afghanistan it is alleged that a Soviet officer told the Mujahideen forces "we are leaving but our mines will kill your grand-children"(McGrath, 1994:156).

D. Displaced and Refugee Populations

Among those fleeing violence, death rates tend to be very high when the exodus is precipitous and the number of persons on the move high. Under these conditions, crude mortality rates during the first days of displacement have been reported to be in some locations 60 times higher than in the country of origin. Communicable-preventable diseases such as upper respiratory infections, diarrheal diseases, malaria, and measles have been identified as the main causes of mortality among displaced populations.

Health conditions in most refugee camps are very precarious and change rapidly. Examples from Kurdish and Rwandan refugees illustrate that information about health conditions is time and place specific. The epidemiological surveillance of 25,000 Kurdish refugees in Iran from June 6 to September 1, 1991 (more than 720,000 crossed the Iraq-Iran boarder) revealed rapid shifts in disease incidence rates and the explosive onset of some epidemic outbreaks (Babille et al., 1994). According to this and other studies, increases or reduction of crowding in the camps, changes in camp management, seasonal climatic changes, health interventions, and variations of food and water availability accounted for the rapid and significant morbidity rate changes. Among the refugee Kurds, between May and September 1991, the most frequently reported causes of morbidity were diarrheal diseases, acute respiratory infections, skin infections (scabies and bacterial infections were rampant), eye diseases, and typhoid fever. During the postemergency, crude mortality rates were 9 times higher than in Iraq (in one of the camps in Turkey the crude mortality rate among Kurdish refugees was reported to be 45 times higher than among nonrefugees).

In Burundi, in May 1994, the crude mortality rate experienced significant daily variations among the different camps with Rwandan refugees. In some camps it was zero, in others 80 per 10,000 population. By July, mortality rates had declined to zero and 2 per 10,000. The most common cause of mortality was diarrheal diseases, and the main causes of morbidity were malaria, bloody diarrhea, and acute respiratory infections (rates were not available), and there was an outbreak of meningococcal meningitis. In 1994 in Zaire, deaths of Rwanda refugees were recorded by counting the number of bodies found on roadsides and in mass graves, and camp hospital deaths. During the period between August 8th and 21st, the crude mortality rate was estimated to be between 34.1 to 54.5 per 10,000 per day depending on the population figures used; by September 29 the rate was 2.5, and by November 30 it was 0.2. An outbreak of cholera caused approximately 37,500 cases, many of which were fatal, largely due to the unavailability of safe water. The incidence of malaria was unknown because it was not possible to confirm through laboratory tests the nature of the fevers. The incidence of fevers of unknown origin varied between 15.8 and 21.0 per 10,000 persons, depending on the population figures used.

E. Populations Not Directly Exposed to Wars

In recent years information from industrial nations shows that during peacetimes large numbers of civilians have been exposed to health hazards from the release of chemicals into the environment at military bases, weapon manufacturing plants and storage facilities, and test sites.

In addition, a few studies have examined the health effects of political violence and war on populations not directly exposed to enemy attacks or combat. A study carried out in West Beirut in 1987 looked at the health impact on such persons during the civil war by assessing the effects on mental and physical health of other war-related life events common in most civil wars, such as damage to property, armed clashes in the neighborhood, change of residence, injury of a family member, kidnaping of a family member, daily stresses (including water shortages, electricity cuts, crossing the dividing line between the fighting factions), economic deterioration, and the breakdown of the family network. Because prewar health data were not available the only way to assess the impact of the war was linking the degree of stress—assumed to be caused by other-than-combat war-related events—and levels of somatization. The findings suggest a high level of somatization with symptoms such as pharyngitis, headaches, muscle pain, lower back or neck pain, shortness of breath, faintness/dizziness, and nausea. As will be discussed in the next section, these populations also suffered from war-related mental health disorders.

F. Impact on Nutritional Status

The use of herbicides, antipersonnel land mines, the targeting of markets, and the destruction of the rural infrastructure greatly reduce the availability of arable land, food production, and food distribution. In low-income nations, the reduction of food availability is frequently accompanied by large protein, calorie, and micronutrient deficiencies, and these deficiencies can produce severe malnutrition. In the presence of disease, nutritional intake is lowered and malnutrition diminishes the body's ability to fight infection. The symbiotic interaction between disease and malnutrition often lead to high levels of mortality, especially in the early phases of complex emergencies.

Wars may cause malnutrition by increasing food prices, which reduces food accessibility. For example, during the 1943–1944 Bengal famine more than two million Indians starved to death; there was no food scarcity in India but World War II had caused food price increases and many Indians, who because of floods were unemployed, could not afford it.

Refugees frequently suffer from malnutrition: a survey of 25,000 Kurdish refugees in Iran in 1991 found that wasting and stunting accounted for 2.7% of all consultations, and between 10 and 12% of children under 5 suffered severe malnutrition. Protein deficiencies were common among women, and 90 percent of malnourished women also suffered from anemia. A nutritional survey of 115,000 Somali refugees in a Kenya camp showed that in 1997 the levels of wasting was very severe ranging between 26 and 33%. Nutritional surveys are routinely carried out in refugee camps and the conditions are reported by the United Nations Administrative Committee on Coordination/Sub-Committee on Nutrition.

The use of food as a weapon operates through the commission of acts that destroy food supplies or productive capacity, the provision of food selectively to certain areas or groups but not to others, and through omissions in allowing food supplies to reach certain target groups. It is increasingly recognized that the delivery of humanitarian aid, including food supplies, can be controlled by competing factions in their effort to manage the conflict and undermine their opponents. In the refugee camps in Zaire after the Rwandan genocide, the *interahamwe*, the Hutu militia, continued to control the refugee camps and their populations through control over the provision of food and other resources, and the siphoning off of such resources for sale in exchange for arms.

G. Health Consequences of Environmental Degradation

1. Military Readiness and Environmental Degradation

In recent years in industrial nations, reports have drawn attention to the environmental impact of the production, testing, and stockpiling of arms, and the environmental damage caused by maintaining armies in combat readiness. Few studies have, however, assessed the health consequences of these exposures.

The experimentation, testing, and production of weapons has had a heavy toll on human health. For example, in the United States, radioactive fallout from 90 open-air nuclear weapons tests between 1952 and 1957 may have caused between 10,000 to 75,000 cases of thyroid cancer. In the former Soviet Union, thousands of workers at Kyshtym's nuclear production plant were exposed to radiation doses of more than 100 rems (one rem is equivalent to seven or eight X-rays).

According to Renner (1997), the maintenance of the military during peacetimes also has negative consequences for health. In the United States by 1989 contamination problems had been identified in 1579 military installations and the situation might be worse in other countries. In some areas of Cape Cod in Massachusetts higher rates of breast cancer than expected have been attributed to underground water contamination caused by large spills of aviation fuels, solvents, and other chemicals at the Massachusetts Military Reservation. At this site alone, it is estimated that three to eight million gallons of drinking water are contaminated daily. In Cape Cod some wells have solvent concentrations hundreds of times higher than the recommended safe drinking water standard, and in 1996 solvents surfaced in a Hatchville cranberry bog. Only recently Russians and Eastern Europeans are discovering the health costs of their military build-up during the Cold War.

Unfortunately, governments have made few efforts to increase our knowledge of the health risks posed by the presence in the environment of the many chemicals and radiative materials released by the military, but it is suspected that "human exposure (to fuels, paints, solvents, heavy metals, pesticides, polychlorinated byphenyls, cyanides, phenols, acids, alkalies, propellants, and explosives) through drinking, skin absorption, or inhalation may cause cancer, birth defects, and chromosome damage, or may seriously impair the function of the liver, kidneys, blood, and central nervous system" (Renner, 1997:124).

In sum, during peaceful times, the armed forces' negative effects on health are the result of:

- accidental releases of chemicals and radiation:
  - ▶ during weapon production and testing
  - ▶ at storage facilities of arms and of by-products from arms production;
- accidents during war games and training;
- releases of chemicals during destruction and disposal of weapons; and,
- releases of chemicals during regular operations of the armed forces.

2. Wars and Environmental Degradation

There are not too many studies that examine the health consequences produced by the environmental degradation caused by wars. Some efforts have been made in Vietnam. During the Vietnam War (1961–1975) more chemicals were used than in any other war in human history. More than 90 million kilograms of herbicides (Agents Orange, White, and Blue), and three million kilograms of the pesticide malathion were sprayed by the United States. Several authors have assessed the impact of these chemicals on the environment but the impact on human health continues to be tentative and incomplete. It has been estimated that the spraying of herbicides by the United States caused the immediate destruction of 300 million kilograms of food, but impact on nutrition has not been measured. Persons exposed to herbicides manifested diarrhea, vomiting, dizziness, headaches, coughing, and shortness of breath. However, some authors have indicated that the symptomatology could also be attributed to other causes such as malnutrition, poor health conditions, and mental problems resulting from the war itself.

The Institute of Medicine of the U.S. National Academy of Science has associated Agent Orange with soft-tissue sarcoma, non-Hodgkin's lymphoma, Hodgkin's disease, and limited evidence of some respiratory cancers, prostate cancer, multiple myeloma, and spina bifida.

Measuring long-term health effects is further complicated due to the difficulties of determining levels of exposure, poor hospital records, and scientific limitations on separating the contribution that other risk factors have on a disease. There is some relatively well-established evidence that as a result of exposure to war chemicals the Vietnamese experienced higher rates than expected of chronic weakness, nausea, gastrointestinal problems, recurrent headaches, depression, anxiety, and lack of libido. There is some inconclusive evidence in regard to increases in the number of liver cancers, chronic hepatitis, and spontaneous abortions.

With the passing of time, some types of antipersonnel land mines break down before exploding; when this is the case rains and floods spread the toxic chemicals over large tracts of land, contaminating rivers, aquifers, and soil. The environmental problem posed by the mines is so grave that authors consider it to be a "major ecological disaster." According to McGrath (1994:121) the mines left in the fields after conflicts are denying not only "vital land to farmers, pastoralists and returning refugees, but have covered large tracts of the earth's surface with non-biodegradable and toxic garbage."

An understudied impact of war is its effect on animal and plant life: the 1997 Zairian civil war destroyed national parks and reserves, placing some endangered species in an extremely critical situation.

V. MENTAL HEALTH CONSEQUENCES

A. Influencing Factors

War and political violence have mental health consequences for victims, relatives, neighbors and communities. The severity and type of mental health disorders caused by war and political violence respond to:

- the nature and intensity of the violence endured or witnessed (torture, acts of terror, rape, detention, persecution, exile, displacement, forced relocation, bombings, and multiple trauma);
- the nature of the physical disability suffered, for example, tetraplegia, physical disfiguration, and blindness;
- the type and location of refugee camp or new settlement, for example, UN, government, private;
- the relationship of the witness to the victims;
- the number of relatives and friends killed, tortured, disappeared, detained, exiled, and displaced;
- the sociopsychological characteristics of the patient such as sex, age, and personality traits;
- type of participation in the production of violence (combatant, victimizer, terrorist).

National surveys of mental health disorders produced by wars are not available. Even if postconflict surveys would be done, it would be necessary—in order to measure the impact of the conflict—to have preconflict data, information that is not available in most countries. With the exception of research on U.S. veterans of the Vietnam War and studies of victims of dirty wars, little is known about the mental health problems caused by wars. There are only small clinical studies of victims, including victims of torture, studies of some communities in a few countries, and descriptive and at times anecdotal information obtained in some refugee camps. The lacunae in this field are large: little is known about the etiology of the symptoms of multiple trauma, the mental health consequences suffered by those who vic-

timize, and the role of coping mechanisms. On the other hand, the literature indicates that the effects of some forms of extreme violence such as torture and rape may be long lasting; for example, among tortured women it has been confirmed that some continue to experience sexual anxiety and feelings of evasion for many years.

In addition to the above difficulties, a number of mental health workers are beginning to question the adequacy of Western mental health constructs to understand and treat non-Western patients.

B. Torture

Torture is a common practice in many wars and conflicts. Because victims tend to hide the trauma and because there are political pressures to conceal the use of torture it is difficult to provide an approximate number of victims. The purpose of torture may be to extract information, to harass the victim, to engender a feeling of worthlessness in those detained, or to frighten their families and the rest of the community. In dirty wars, it is used as a means of attempting to maintain, through fear and intimidation, the exploitation of workers in the presence of a social struggle that threatens the existence of the status quo.

Mental health workers have identified disintegration as one of the consequences of torture. Disintegration means the destruction of the person as an autonomous subject with norms and values that inspired his/her political and social activities. This is achieved by the methodical induction of devastation and madness during detention and torture. Expressions by patients in therapy provide a sense of the meaning of personality's destruction: "After that, everything changed for me," "I do not recognize myself. Before, I was not like this," "I have the feeling that I have been marked forever."

C. Combatants

Combatants who perform or witness brutal acts in situations over which they have limited control may suffer mental disorders as a result of their engagement in violence. Posttraumatic stress disorder (PTSD), a recognized mental health condition following exposure to massive stress, has been diagnosed among Vietnam veterans in a general community survey conducted in the United States. Among wounded veterans, up to 20% had the full blown PTSD syndrome, while 60% had one or more of the associated symptoms. It is estimated that 700,000 combatants suffered severe PTSD, and 1.5 million may in time be in need of mental care. It has been estimated that about 20,000 U.S. Vietnam War veterans committed suicide.

Combatants who engaged in horrific acts, and torturers are also traumatized by their own actions, but little is known about the trauma suffered by the perpetrators of these crimes.

D. Refugee and Displaced Populations

Conditions of uncertainty, fear, lack of knowledge about relatives left behind, and the monotony of life at refugee camps are conditions conducive to stress, anxiety, and severe depression among camp dwellers. Studies from Kampuchea, Vietnam, Sudan, Uganda, Guatemala, Indonesia, El Salvador, and other countries suggest that those displaced within their own country suffer more intense trauma than the externally displaced.

Mental conditions of persons who moved to other countries or are exiled vary according to specific circumstances. The small percentages of political refugees who are given asylum in industrialized nations have access to comprehensive health care, some assistance, and counseling, but at times they encounter severe cultural and language barriers. Uncertainty and guilt for relatives left behind, legal restrictions to employment, and ethnic discrimination are common causes of mental disorders among exiles in advanced industrial nations.

E. Family of the Disappeared

Families of the disappeared present a unique situation because they suffer from ongoing fear. The family does not know whether the relative is dead or alive, and the authorities do not acknowledge the disappearance. Relatives of the disappeared and of the executed exhibit different symptomatologies. The former experience a depression marked by confusion and a denial of mourning, whereas the latter endure a long-term mourning characterized by horror and fear: horror because of the tragic and premature way in which the relative was murdered and fear of experiencing the same fate. Repressive situations common in dirty wars do not allow a normal mourning. The loss of the beloved has to be considered in the context of other losses such as the loss of economic stability, of membership in organizations, in reference groups, of sociopolitical roles, and of friends who have been executed.

Families of the disappeared, tortured, and executed frequently experience social evasion. They consider the world outside to be hostile, a feeling that can last many years. Studies of families of torture victims confirm an increase of intrafamily conflict, the reproduction of the trauma within the family, insomnia, repressive reactions, loss of appetite, rejection, and other psychosomatic symptoms.

F. Children

Rates higher than expected of anxiety, aggression, phobias, and enuresis have been found among Palestinian children in the occupied West Bank and Gaza strip. Similarly, among Lebanese children who were exposed to the civil war, researchers reported rates higher than normal of submissiveness, overdependency, withdrawal symptoms, overaggressive and violent behaviors, as well as general unhappiness.

There is disagreement in the literature regarding the effects of the repression suffered by adults on family children. Some therapists have noted sleep and appetite alterations, speech and development disorders, and affective and behavioral alterations and disorders among children of Chilean disappeared who also witnessed their parents' torture, assassination, rape, or imprisonment. Among preschoolers in South Africa, researchers detected sleep alterations and nightmares, bed wetting, irritability, overdependency, moodiness, and psychosomatic disorders such as headaches and abdominal pains. Among Filipino children, investigators found rates higher than normal of anxiety, attention-seeking behavior, dependency, oversensitivity, and low self-esteem. Other authors have suggested that mental consequences of torture can be detected even among grandchildren.

In contrast, in a comparative study of children of Latin American refugees whose parents had experienced some type of repression (such as imprisonment, detention, persecution, and torture) and those whose parents had not, the Division of Transcultural Psychiatry of the Toronto Western Hospital found no differences in mental health status and social behavior.

G. Other Noncombat Populations

Persons who have not been exposed to combat may suffer mental health disorders from wars. A mental health study in El Salvador compared mental health problems in three communities: one had not been exposed to combat and the other two had experienced different levels of war intensity. The study found that 3 years after the conclusion of the war persons in the three communities suffered from anxiety, depression, sleep disturbances, suicidal tendencies, trembling, dizziness, fears, flashbacks, and other symptoms of posttraumatic stress, as well as somatic and emotional conditions such as migraines, nausea, headaches, back pain, and stomach problems. The number of persons affected by the symptoms varied according to the level of intensity of the exposure to war, but even in the community that had not experienced directly any combat there were persons who showed severe mental health problems.

H. Indirect Effects

There is some evidence to suggest that wars and political violence contribute to increases of violent behavior, alcoholism, and drug abuse. A postconflict, multimillion dollar assessment of the health sector of El Salvador sponsored by the U.S. government identified but did not quantify a number of war-related sequelae: household and street violence, alcoholism, and drug addiction. In 1997, 5 years after the signing of the peace agreement, El Salvador had one of the highest rates of homicides in the world. Obviously, not all cases of violence and substance abuse were a sequelae of the armed conflict but it can be suggested that the war left its mark in the culture of violence. Studies of U.S. Vietnam War veterans have also found higher than expected levels of drug and alcohol abuse, divorce rates, broken families, and violent and antisocial behavior.

I. Summary of Symptoms and Disorders

By way of concluding this section, it can be said that clinical studies have shown that state repression, exposure to war violence, forced exile, and displacement can cause the following bio-psychosocial disorders among victims and families:

- psychosomatic disorders: general aches, headaches, nervousness, nocturnal panics and nightmares, insomnia, night myoclonia, sweats, trembling, weakness, dizziness, diarrhea, gastrointestinal ulcers, allergies, disorders of the respiratory system, and chronic pains of the joints (arthralgia);
- affective disorders: severe depressions, which at times include behavioral disorders, anxiety, fears and phobias of electricity, hospitals, injections, dentists (due to torture applied to gums), and guilt;
- behavioral disorders: aloofness, irritability, aggressiveness, impulsiveness, sexual disorders such as inhibitions, evasion, difficult or painful intercourse (dyspareunia), and painful spasms of the muscular fibers inside the vagina (vaginismus), suicidal tendencies, and drug addiction;

- mental disorders: confusion, disorientation, loss of memory, and loss of concentration.

VI. CONCLUSIONS

Never before in the world's history have there been so many persons exposed to wars and political violence. In addition to the millions of persons who were killed and disabled in wars during the 20th century, there is an unprecedented figure, perhaps as many as 60 million persons, who in the last few decades have been displaced internally and externally by political violence, and in the process, suffered severe physical and mental health disorders. The literature suggests that persons who have engaged in political violence as combatants and civilians who have been directly and indirectly exposed to political violence may also have suffered health disorders as a result of the engagement and exposure. No author has offered an estimate of how many persons fall into these categories. Death, disability, infectious diseases such as malaria, cholera, HIV, tuberculosis, gastrointestinal diseases, respiratory disorders, severe malnutrition, micronutrient deficiencies, and mental health disorders such as severe depression, anxiety, and PTSD represent only a small part of the health toll produced by political violence. The health risks posed by the stockpiles of thousands of nuclear missiles and tons of chemical and biological weapons, and an estimated 100 million antipersonnel land mines scattered over the territory of 60 countries should be added to the list.

A. Improved Data

A first effort for social epidemiologists of political violence should be to obtain more accurate knowledge of the number of persons affected by political violence and the nature of the health problems they experience. Better definitions of concepts such as political refugees, internally and externally displaced, postconflict mental health surveys, and censuses of war disability, orphans, and the elderly whose children may have been killed, disappeared, or gone into exile may lead to more accurate information of the impact and health needs. Mental health surveys need to be carried out by trained lay personnel utilizing instruments whose reliability has been tested in multicultural settings. During peacetimes the instruments should be tested in as many countries as possible in order to have instruments in native languages ready to be used when the need arises. In this context, the training of primary mental health care personnel is urgently needed.

B. Medical Care Improvements

Health practitioners and researchers strive to provide care, to prevent disease, and to promote healthy behaviors. Improving relief assistance has been very slow. Many deaths and much illness could be prevented by more efficient responses to emergency situations, basic improvements to the extremely precarious conditions in refugee camps, and removing legal obstacles for asylum seekers. Health workers and agencies are so overwhelmed with attending—with few resources—the exhausting exigencies of displaced populations that they seldom have the opportunity to carry out in-depth post-event analysis of the limitations and successes experienced. Funding systematic research of relief assistance efforts could make future programs more efficient, less costly, and more importantly, they could reduce human suffering and deaths.

In the area of medical care provision, in addition to supporting the further development of effective emergency and relief NGOs, the international community should move quickly to establish a rapid strategic health corps under the U.N. and/or other international organizations with supplies (portable hospitals, food, vaccines, medicines, tents) that could be mobilized as the need arises. Deployment of the corps in strategic locations in countries that historically have shown low levels of violence such as Costa Rica, Tunisia, and Singapore could reduce the time between the request and the response. Warning signals (breakdowns of political institutions, increases of militarism or state repression, formation of guerrilla groups) could place the corps in a state of alert and readiness for immediate action.

Surveillance systems have made significant advances to reduce the impact of epidemic outbreaks. In comparison, little has been done to care for the disabled, reverse the negative human development effects of malnutrition, and treat mental disorders. The latter has been entirely neglected by assistance efforts; for example, the European Union supported in Central America a modest program to assist the war-disabled to cope psychologically with their disability, but the program was not intended to treat their mental health disorders caused by exposure to war brutalities.

C. Prevention Interventions

Prevention is an early intervention aimed at averting or at least reducing the potential health damage by risk factors. Unfortunately, the eradication of political violence is not in sight, but much can be done to reduce it and its negative health consequences. Former colonial powers share a heavy responsibility for postcolonization violence. Quite frequently, former colonial powers have supported and armed brutal third world dictatorial regimes. Development assistance by former colonial power and other economically advanced nations could have helped former colonies to find solutions to their political, social, and economic problems, but, with rare exceptions, the assistance has been guided to create a neocolonialism, that is, economic exploitation without direct political control. Neocolonialism commonly requires militarism or the tendency by states and significant groups to rely on violence as a political tool. Militarism has been frequently supported by foreign powers, and civil wars, state repression, and/or low-intensity warfare have followed militarism.

The following list summarizes ways through which foreign powers have promoted militarism in the third world:

- training large numbers of military and police forces;
- helping to prepare the military coup (subverting the political process, logistic support and intelligence gathering, and precoup assurances of early diplomatic recognition after the coup);
- providing the military government with economic and security assistance after the coup;
- providing logistic support, intelligence gathering, training, and equipment, and technologies to be used in the repression (armored tanks, training security forces in riot controls, torture, and repression);
- garnering international support for the military government; and
- acts of omission.

At the end of the 20th century the United States is the largest trader of arms. The U.S. total amounts to about $8.4 billion per year, a sum larger than the combined sales of arms by Russia, Germany, France, and England, and represents three-fourths of the world trade to the third world. Much of the political violence in third world nations will decrease the moment industrial nations stop exporting it. In most countries it would be difficult for elites and the military to maintain repressive regimes, state terrorism, and low-intensity warfare without outside support. As indicated, international policies of hegemonic powers, and colonial and decolonization policies are to a great extent responsible for low-intensity and dirty wars, and ethnic and territorial wars in many parts of the world. It should fall upon these nations to assist in the reversal of the policies, to undo to the extent possible the health damage, and to reimburse victims for the costs of the health care required.

Public awareness within the countries promoting militarism and low-intensity warfare abroad, and in the international community at large, of the mechanisms though which political violence is promoted and of its destructive health results would facilitate the building of pressures against exporting violence.

In many countries after peace and democracy have been restored the military and conservative forces have enacted amnesty laws that, under the excuse of reconciliation, leave perpetrators of hideous crimes free and even occupying high positions in government and the armed forces. Amnesties such as those passed in South Africa, Argentina, Chile, and Central America may not foster the prevention of political violence or national reconciliation; on the contrary, they may create precedents for committing the same crimes in the future. Amnesties have a second undesirable health consequence: they do not allow victims and their families to experience the catharsis required for restoring mental health. This is a topic that has been given little attention by researchers and needs to be more fully documented as soon as possible. Governments should be deprived by international convention of the power to pardon by amnesty crimes such as torture, mass executions, executions without trials, violations of international war codes, unwanted assaults on civilian populations, recruitment of children for combat, and violations of medical neutrality.

The international community has made very slow progress in banning the use of and research on most abhorrent weapons: nuclear, biological, and chemical. In addition to renewing efforts of banning, ways to enforce the bans need to be found. One of the few recent positive achievements has been the widespread consensus that antipersonnel land mines be banned. Although the majority of the world's countries have signed the recent Ottawa Treaty, key nations such as the United States, China, and Russia have so far refused to do so.

To advocate more international conventions might sound futile since the ones already in existence have been consistently violated. Perhaps, a preventive priority should be to call for interdisciplinary studies by legal, health, and social science experts to review the reasons for the inability of the international community to enforce legislation that has been signed by the majority of nations. These efforts could lead to the globaliza-

tion of justice through revision of definitions, international codes, and new ideas for enforcement.

Imperfect as they are, international institutions need to be given an increasing role in peace promotion and international law enforcement. Reforms of international bodies should go along with additional roles and support. The world will never be a perfect one, but if there is a hope for survival, humans have to discover ways of enforcing international justice and its laws without decreasing cultural diversity.

The following listing summarizes preventive actions:

- reducing militarism by removing the international assistance that supports it;
- helping to reverse the consequences of colonial and decolonization policies;
- creating public awareness regarding the relationship between the promotion of militarism and low-intensity warfare and their tragic negative health effects;
- redefining the concept of national security and removing the possibility of exporting violence under such a concept;
- defining and periodically redefining war crimes;
- denying governments the right to pardon certain war crimes by amnesties;
- banning research on and use of nuclear, chemical, biological weapons, and antipersonnel mines;
- removing antipersonnel mines left in the fields;
- supporting research to find ways to enhance compliance with international conventions.
- supporting research to assess environmental degradation caused by wars and the military during peace times.

The task ahead is immense. Postponing changes and interventions to improve the provision of care to victims of political violence and the prevention of violence only delays the construction of a more peaceful and healthy world.

Also See the Following Articles

CHEMICAL AND BIOLOGICAL WARFARE • CIVIL WARS • EFFECTS OF WAR AND POLITICAL VIOLENCE ON HEALTH SERVICES • GUERRILLA WARFARE • LONG-TERM EFFECTS OF WAR ON CHILDREN • NUCLEAR WARFARE • TORTURE • WARFARE, MODERN

Bibliography

Allukian, M., & Atwood, P. L. (1997). Public health and the Vietnam War. In S. B. Levy & V. W. Sidel (Eds.), *War and public health*, pp. 215–237. Oxford: Oxford University Press.

APHA (American Public Health Association). (1993). The health of refugees and displaced persons: A public health priority (Position Paper). *American Journal of Public Health, 83,* 463–468.

Babille, M., de Colombani, P., Guerra, R., Zagaria, N., & Zanetti, C. (1994). Post-emergency epidemiological surveillance in Iraqi-Kurdish refugee camps in Iran. *Disaster, 18,* 58–75.

Barudy, J. (1989). A programme of mental health for political refugees: dealing with the invisible pain of political exile. *Social Science and Medicine, 28,* 715–727.

Bendfeldt-Zachrisson, F. (1988). Torture as intensive repression in Latin America: the psychology of its methods and practice. *International Journal of Health Services, 18,* 301–310.

CODEPU (1989). The effects of torture and political repression in a sample of Chilean families. *Social Science and Medicine, 28,* 735–740.

Farhood, L., Zurayk, H., Chaya, M., Saadeh, F., Meshefedjian, G., & Sidani, T. (1993). The impact of war on the physical and mental health of the family: The Lebanese experience. *Social Science and Medicine, 36,* 1555–1567.

Garfield, R. M. (1989). War-related changes in health and health services in Nicaragua. *Social Science and Medicine, 28,* 669–676.

Hill, J. (1944). *Silent Enemies.* New York: G. P. Putnam's Sons.

Marshall, R. (1995). Refugee, feminine plural. *Refugees, 2,* 3–9.

Macrae, J., & Zwi, A. (Eds.). (1994). *War and hunger. Rethinking international responses to complex emergencies.* London: Zed Books.

Macrae, J., Zwi, A., & Birungi, H. (1993). *A healthy peace?: Rehabilitation and development of the health sector in a post-conflict situation* (unpublished report). London: Health Policy Unit, London School of Hygiene and Tropical Medicine.

McGrath, R. (1994). Landmine: the global problem. In P. Davies & N. Dunlop (Eds.), *War of the Mines. Cambodia, Landmine and the Impoverishment of a Nation,* pp. 121–126. London: Pluto Press.

McGrath, R. (1994). The reality of the present use of mines by military forces. In P. Davies & N. Dunlop (Eds.), *War of the mines. Cambodia, landmine and the impoverishment of a nation,* pp. 55–157. London: Pluto Press.

McKinlay, J. (1986). A case for refocussing upstream: the political economy of illness. In P. Conrad & R. Kern (Eds.), *The sociology of health and illness. Critical perspectives,* pp. 484–500. New York: St. Martin Press.

Renner, M. (1997). Environmental and health effects of weapons production, testing, and maintenance. In S. B. Levy & V. W. Sidel (Eds.), *War and public health,* pp. 117–133. Oxford: Oxford University Press.

Ugalde, A., Selva-Sutter, E., Castillo, C., Paz, C., Cañas, S., Oakes, M., & Solas, S. (1996). *Reconstruction and development of the health sector in El Salvador after the 1981–1992 war* (unpublished report prepared for the European Union). TSA-CT94-0305 (DG 12 HSMU), San Salvador.

Ugalde, A., & Zwi, A (Eds.). (1994). *Violencia política y salud en América Latina.* Mexico City: Nueva Imagen.

Ugalde, A., & Zwi, A. (1995). Violencia política. In G. Vidal (Ed.), *Enciclopedia Ibero Americana de Psiquiatría.* Buenos Aires: Fundación Acta Fondo para la Salud Mental.

Ugalde, A., & Vega, R. R. (1989). Review essay: State terrorism, torture, and health in the Southern Cone. *Social Science and Medicine, 28,* 759–765.

UNHCR (1996). Morbidity and mortality surveillance in Rwanda refugees. Burundi and Zaire, 1994. *MMWR, 45,* 104–107.

UNHCR (1993a). Mortality among newly arrived Mozambican refugees. Zimbabwe and Malawi, 1992. *MMWR, 42,* 468–477.

Walker, J. I., & Cavenar, J. O. (1982). Vietnam veterans: their problems continue. *Journal of Nervous and Mental Disease, 170,* 174–180.

Westing, A. H. (Ed). (1984). *Herbicides in war. The long-term ecological and human consequences.* London: Taylor and Francis.

Yokoro, K., & Kamada, N. (1997). The public health effects of the use of nuclear weapons. In B. S. Levy & V. W. Sidel (Eds.), *War and public health,* pp. 65–83. Oxford: Oxford University Press.

Zwi, A. (1996). Numbering the dead: counting the casualties of war. In Bradby H. (Ed.), *Defining violence: Understanding the causes and effects of violence,* pp. 99–124. Aldershot: Avebury.

Zwi, A. & Ugalde, A. (1991). Political violence and health in the Third World—a public health issue. *Health Policy and Planning 6,* 203–217.

Zwi, A., & Cabral, A. J. (1991). Identifying 'high risk situations' for preventing AIDS. *British Medical Journal, 303,* 1527–1529.

Zwi, A., & Ugalde, A. (1989). Towards an epidemiology of political violence in the third world. *Social Science and Medicine, 28,* 633–642.

Additional Sources

Cahill, K. M. (Ed). (1995). *Clearing the fields: Solutions to the global land mine crisis.* New York: Basic Books.

Levy, B. S., & Sidel, V. W. (Eds.). (1997). *War and public health.* Oxford: Oxford University Press.

United Nations Administrative Committee on Coordination/Sub-Committee on Nutrition. Refugee Nutrition Information System. *Occasional reports.* Geneva: World Health Organization. ACCSC-N@WHO.CH.

United Nations High Commissioner for Refugees (yearly reports). *The state of the world's refugees.* Geneva: UNHCR.

The following periodical publications contain information on the impact of war on health:

Disasters, published by Basil Blackwell Ltd.

Journal of Refugee Studies, published by Oxford University Press.

Mortality and Morbidity Weekly Report (MMWR), published by U.S. Center for Disease Control (Atlanta).

Refugees, published by United Nations High Commissioner for Refugees.

Homicide

Marc Riedel

Southern Illinois University

GLOSSARY

Clearance Clearing crimes is a police task. Crimes are cleared or "solved" by legally charging an offender or offenders. Cleared by arrest means that offenders are apprehended and charged. Offenses are "exceptionally cleared" where there is enough evidence to effect an arrest, but the offender or offenders are not available for a variety of reasons.

Crime Rate Number of crimes divided by the population at risk, the result being multiplied by a constant (usually 100,000). Both the numerator and denominator refer to the same geographical area and time span.

Criminal Homicide Purposely, knowingly, recklessly, or negligently causing the death of another. Criminal homicide is murder, manslaughter, or negligent homicide.

Homicide The killing of one human being by the act, procurement, or omission of another.

Justifiable Homicide Homicide committed intentionally but without any evil design and under such circumstances of necessity or duty as render the act proper and which relieve the party from any shadow of blame.

Murder Criminal homicide that is committed purposely or knowingly or committed recklessly under circumstances manifesting extreme indifference to the value of human life.

Primary Prevention Focuses on eliminating conditions that lead to or cause criminal behavior. Also called "corrective prevention."

THE KILLING of others generally carries penal sanctions, which may include the imposition of the death penalty. This article presents a cross-cultural review of legal definitions, data sources, trends, rates, and the use of homicide statistics. It also reviews current research on age, race, ethnicity, and gender of participants. Other elements of the homicide event, including firearms, alcohol and drugs, and prior relationships, are also examined. The final section focuses on violence prevention approaches.

Copyright © 1999 by Academic Press.
All rights of reproduction in any form reserved.

I. HOMICIDE AND CRIMINAL HOMICIDE

Generally defined, homicide is the act of killing another person. Cross-culturally, it is impossible to succinctly take account of the legal variations that characterize one of the oldest criminal laws. Most countries treat premeditated killings as crime. In many countries, criminal homicide and murder are distinguished from homicide by the element of culpability or intent. Criminal homicide is an act judged by legal authorities to be culpable: the offender set out to kill the victim and succeeded. Hence, homicide may not be a crime, while criminal homicide always is.

Difficulties emerge when considering what kinds of killings should be culpable and how to establish the relationship between the subjective element of intent or blame and the behavior. Laws in different countries vary as to the kinds of killings regarded as culpable. If a woman kills her newborn child, it is a culpable killing in the U.S. and Canada but not in some developing countries. Where survival conditions are harsh, infanticide may be viewed as an appropriate or altruistic act.

A major source of cross-cultural variation is in the establishment of the nexus between the subjective cause and the objective effect. If the person driving the getaway car in a robbery murder does not enter the store that is being robbed and did not participate in any planning of the murder, should he or she be criminally liable? Many states in the U.S. answer positively. If a person intentionally wounds another and the victim later dies of his or her wounds, is the offender open to a charge of murder, as happens in the United States, or a charge of aggravated assault, as is true for Japan?

Generally, homicide law includes provisions for killings that would be called justifiable or excusable homicides in the United States, that is, killings for which there are no criminal penalties. Examples include police who kill felons in the line of duty, soldiers following orders in combat, people who lack the mental capacities to understand the nature of their act, and self-defense.

II. A NOTE ON CRIMINOLOGY AND LAW

Legal definitions are important not only because they guide the behavior of medical and criminal justice personnel but because their records are data sources for criminological research. In short, for researchers, criminal homicide is what law enforcement, medical personnel, judges, and juries say it is. However, it is important to consider how homicide researchers "process" this data to reflect social science purposes.

First, homicide researchers are interested in using data as close to the event as possible, which means using law enforcement records and/or mortality statistics. One problem posed by this approach is the variations between what is collected by agencies and the terms used by researchers. Mortality statistics use the term "homicide," making it difficult, even impossible, to separate criminal homicides from the broader category of homicides in cross-cultural data. Law enforcement agencies collect data on all forms of homicides, but most researchers focus on criminal homicides or murders. In this article, we use the term "homicide"; when citing the work of others, we attempt to use the term provided by the researcher. It is generally true that most homicide statistics refer to criminal homicides; justifiable homicides are a very small proportion of all homicides.

Another problem posed by using data as close to the event as possible is the difficulty of studying offenders. In the U.S., about one-third of murder offenders are not arrested, which means there are no data about them. Further, the more homicides are "processed" through various legal decisions and distinctions, the more selective the resulting set of cases may be. Hence, generalizations based on offenders convicted of murder may not represent all offenders.

Second, although most homicide research is based on criminal justice and medical records, researchers do not feel constrained to limit inquiry to legal categories. Researchers select and combine this material in an explicit manner to address scientific hypotheses. For example, in the United States, homicides and aggravated assaults are very similar with respect to the behavior and circumstances of victims and offenders. Behaviorally, differences turn on fortuitous factors such as bad aim or poor-quality firearms, types of weapons, and proximity to emergency medical facilities. Legally, an assault becomes a criminal homicide when the victim dies. Although there are substantial differences in legal processing, behaviorally, they may be considered a form of violence with similar causes.

Third, because of substantial variations in legal definitions of killing, cross-cultural studies are limited to homicides rather than subtypes and use data series that apply a consistent definition. Similarly, in a search for causes, other cross-cultural commonalities, such as age, gender, social services, unemployment, or number of marriages, are used. While the latter contribute to a general understanding of homicides, they provide little understanding of the different cultural contexts in which homicides occur.

III. SOURCES OF DATA

Nationally, most countries collect homicide data from law enforcement agencies. For example, criminal statistics in Canada are collected by Statistics Canada, a government agency; in France, the source of criminal statistics is known as *Compte general de l'administration de la justice criminelle*; in England, criminal statistics are published in *Home Office: Criminal Statistics, England and Wales*. *Crime in the United States: Uniform Crime Reports* (UCR) is published annually by the Federal Bureau of Investigation.

A second source of homicide data are medical cause-of-death statistics that are drawn from the files of officials such as coroners or medical examiners. In the U.S., statistics drawn from death certificates are gathered and distributed by the National Center for Health Statistics, National Institutes of Health.

Finally, researchers compile and archive national data sets drawn from official records and contact with criminal justice agencies. In the United States, the most extensive data file on homicides, which has been updated several times, has been compiled by Richard and Carolyn Rebecca Block. It consists of detailed data on nearly 23,000 homicides in Chicago from 1965 through 1994.

Researchers also compile and archive data sets on homicide and violence for many countries. The best known is the 110-nation Comparative Crime Data File, compiled by Dane Archer and Rosemary Gartner, and the 14-nation crime file by Ted Robert Gurr and Erika Gurr. Both contain data on murder, assault, robbery, and rape.

There are three readily available sources of homicide data compiled by international agencies: United Nations Surveys, crime data from the International Criminal Police Organization (INTERPOL), and mortality statistics from the World Health Organization.

A. International Data Sources

1. United Nations

The United Nations has collected information from member nations since 1946. Beginning in 1974, the UN began a series of surveys covering crime trends and operations of criminal justice systems. The first survey covered the years 1970 through 1974, with 56 member and nonmember states responding. The most recent survey, the fifth, covers the years 1990 through 1994; 65 nations provided information on homicides in 1994. The surveys are collections of data on officially reported crimes, including intentional homicides (death purposely inflicted by another, including infanticide and attempts), assaults, sex crimes, robberies, and kidnappings, with the data broken down by age and gender. They also provide information on prosecutions, convictions, and penal sanctions.

2. International Criminal Police Organization

INTERPOL has collected and published crime data from national police forces since 1950. It collects data on homicide, which it defines as "any act performed with the purpose of taking human life, no matter under what circumstances." This definition excludes manslaughter and abortion, but includes infanticide (the killing of newborns), sex offenses, larceny, fraud, counterfeiting, and drug offenses. The data are presented by yearly quarters, and statistics are given on the number of crimes solved by police. Each category of offense is broken down by gender and specifies whether the offenders are adults or minors. The nations reporting vary. For example, from 1980 to 1984, 145 countries were listed as members of INTERPOL, but no more than 85 countries reported crime data in a single year.

3. World Health Organization

Generally believed to be the best data source, WHO has collected mortality statistics, categorized by cause of death, from national health organizations since 1948. The definition of homicide used by WHO (death due to injuries purposely inflicted by others) has varied, at times including deaths due to legal intervention and war. Raw data and rates are provided only on victims of homicide. Classifications are given for age and gender. Data are available for between 40 and 55 nations each year.

4. Evaluation

Generally, cross-national data on homicide is more reliable than data on crimes such as rape, robbery, and assault. Limitations on cross-national homicide research are design specific: time-series studies of homicide are more reliable than cross-sectional comparisons of national rates. Ultimately, however, researchers that rely on official statistics of national agencies must use what is available; there are few opportunities to learn the over- or underreporting or misclassification of events.

Cross-national homicide statistics provide few variables and limited detail: the data consist of total homicides and are classified by age and gender. Data on whether the homicide involved robbery, originated in domestic conflict, or involved weapons are absent, as is race/ethnicity information. While such information would provide valuable insights, variations in cultural definitions make it difficult to collect this kind of cross-national data.

Finally, available cross-national data are biased toward more developed countries that have sufficient resources and political stability to develop an adequate reporting system. Some countries are involved in devastating civil wars and civil unrest, which provides little opportunity for government to function, control crime, or count it. Afghanistan, Croatia, Bosnia-Herzegovina, and Somalia fall into this category. Other countries, such as Zaire (Democratic Republic of Congo) and Albania, have had, or are undergoing, profound political changes in which the government's capacity to report crime is nonexistent.

IV. USING HOMICIDE STATISTICS

A. Describing Reality: Rates and Trends

Homicide rates in the United States are substantially higher than homicide rates in comparably developed countries. Figure 1 shows that homicide rates in the United States range from more than 11 times (1986, 1988) to more than 30 times higher (1976) rates for Ireland (excluding Northern Ireland). Homicide rates in the United States are two (1970) to three times (1980) higher than those in Finland.

It is important to understand how Fig. 1 was con-

structed: the trends for Finland and Ireland "bracket" the trends for 13 other countries. Statistics and mean rates for 16 countries were obtained to find the highest and lowest homicide rates. Excluding the United States, Finland had the highest rate and Ireland the lowest, with the remaining 13 countries (Australia, Austria, Canada, Denmark, England and Wales, France, Italy, Japan, the Netherlands, New Zealand, Norway, Sweden, and Switzerland) falling somewhere between the two. These countries were chosen because they are economically and socially developed democracies with well-developed statistical reporting systems.

Based on socioeconomic factors, it is certainly appropriate to include the United States in the above group of countries. Unfortunately, the generally high rates of homicide in the U.S. are actually more comparable to those of some of the poorest and least economically developed countries in the world. Homicide rates for 84 countries were taken from the 1994 United Nations Demographic Yearbook and ranked. Table I indicates that, among the countries reporting homicide victimization rates to the United Nations, the United States ranked 17 among the top 20.

One perspective explains transnational homicide rates by suggesting that societies at different stages of modernization will show different crime patterns reflecting differences in criminal motivations, controls, and opportunities. A major prediction of modernization theory is that property crimes will be higher and violent crimes lower in modernized societies, with the reverse true for developing countries.

Rosemary Gartner has suggested that sociocultural contexts are important in explaining crime. Societies that enjoy low rates of violence have strong systems of informal social control and highly consensual normative systems, strong networks of communal obligation,

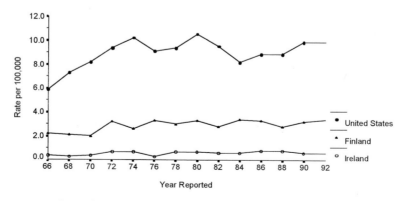

FIGURE 1   Homicide trends in three countries. (Source: World Health Organization Statistics Annuals.)

TABLE I
Homicide Victimization Rates in Selected Countries (1994)

Rank	Year	Country	Rate per 100,000
1	1991	Colombia	89.6
2	1993	Russian Federation	30.3
3	1990	El Salvador	28.1
4	1993	Estonia	25.8
5	1992	Armenia	25.3
6	1993	Latvia	24.7
7	1992	Puerto Rico	23.8
8	1989	Brazil	20.2
9	1992	Mexico	18.5
10	1993	Kazakhstan	17.6
11	1990	Kyrgyzstan	13.9
12	1993	Lithuania	12.5
13	1989	Venezuela	12.1
14	1992	Ukraine	11.3
15	1992	Singapore	11.2
16	1987	Bahamas	10.8
17	1991	United States	10.4
18	1993	Belarus	10.4
19	1990	Ecuador	10.3
20	1991	Trinidad and Tobago	7.7

Source. Demographic Yearbook of the United Nations (1994).

and cultural orientations that discourage interpersonal aggression. Such societies are characterized by collectivist rather than individualistic principles.

B. Creating Reality: Serial Murders

While homicide statistics are generally used to describe a social problem in ways that are useful to practitioners and policy-makers, it is also true that statistics have been constructed to bring a social issue to public attention. In countries where political leaders have to remain sensitive to the demands of a voting public, the process of constructing statistics to support and enhance a social problem is not always sensitive to traditional scientific concerns of reliability, validity, and the relationships between concepts and measures. This was illustrated during the 1980s, when there was widespread public concern over serial murders that occurred in the U.S.

Serial murderers kill repeatedly over a long period, whereas mass murderers kill several people at one time. Serial murderers are not exclusively a current or a U.S. phenomenon. Reliable reports of serial killing have been reported for Canada, Germany, and England at least as far back as the 19th century. "Jack the Ripper," an

inhabitant of London, is probably the most familiar example of a serial killer.

Serial murder became a popular topic in the 1980s, resulting in an outpouring of books and television and newspaper stories. Besides Congressional hearings, a large variety of nonprofit service agencies took up the banner to protect people, especially women and children, against what was perceived as a demonic menace.

To give the problem threatening proportions, numbers are needed and not just any kind of numbers. Joel Best describes three principles that are important in promoting a social issue: "big numbers are better than little numbers; official numbers are better than unofficial numbers; and big, official numbers are best of all." For serial murders, the big, official numbers were promoted by the Behavioral Sciences Unit of the FBI.

Philip Jenkins explains how the statistic that 20% of all murders involved serial killers was generated, how the view of a social problem was promoted through Congressional hearings, and how various organizations took sociological ownership of the issue to promote their agendas.

In fact, Jenkins points out that it is difficult to find evidence that serial murders comprise any more than 1% of all murders. It is worth considering what might have been accomplished had the resources spent on serial murders been allocated to reducing the other 99%.

Further, Jenkins describes how organizations capitalized on and promoted stereotypes of serial murder offenders. A predominant stereotype is that the serial murderer is a lone white male. However, one reliable estimate is that 10 to 20% of serial murders involve group activity. In addition, in one study, at least 15% of offenders were women.

Nor are serial murderers exclusively white. In one study of 163 serial offenders, 13% were African American, 1% were Hispanic, and 1% were Asian.

Another stereotype is that serial murderers rape their victims and engage in a variety of other sadistic behaviors. However, this overlooks the substantial contribution of "medical murderers." For example, Genene Jones, a nurse, was suspected of killing 47 babies and children by injection.

Finally, most serial killers do not travel wantonly across the country looking for victims. About two-thirds of serial killers operate within a state or urban area.

V. AGE AND GENDER

Homicide is predominantly a young (ages 15–24) male offense. Generally, females have low rates of homicides

TABLE II

Male and Female Homicide Victimization Rates (15–24):
Selected Countries (1992)

Country	Rate per 100,000		
	All ages	Males	Females
United States	9.9	36.8	6.4
Australia	1.8	2.3	2.1
Austria	1.3	1.9	1.3
Canada	1.8	3.3	1.5
Denmark	1.2	1.6	0.8
England	0.6	0.7	0.6
Finland	3.4	5.2	3.2
France	1.0	1.3	0.5
Ireland	0.6	1.9	0.3
Italy	2.2	4.4	0.6
Japan	0.6	0.4	0.4
Netherlands	1.3	1.9	1.2
New Zealand	2.4	3.6	1.5
Norway	1.1	1.9	0.3
Sweden	1.3	1.7	0.7
Switzerland	1.5	2.2	0.9

Source: World Health Organization Statistics Annuals

and the killings involve family members or spouses, an issue that will be considered in a later section. Table II gives homicide rates for young homicide victims in selected countries.

Table II shows very high victimization rates for 15- to 24-year-old males in the United States in comparison to the rates in other countries. The rate for this group is more than seven times that of the country with the next highest rate of Finland.

The United States has experienced an enormous increase in homicide among young males. From 1985 through 1991, the rates for all homicides increased by 25%. However, the homicide rate for persons ages 15–34 increased 50%, the rate for 15- to 19-year-old males increased an impressive 154%, and the rate for 20- to 24-year-old males increased by 76%.

While homicide is predominantly a young man's offense, the role of age in homicide is not as pronounced in other countries. Table II indicates that, although young male rates are higher, there are substantial variations among countries. While Italy's young male rate is twice that of the rate for all ages, Japan's young male rate is *less* than the rate for all ages. Consistent with this view is Rosemary Gartner's finding that, across 18 high-income nations over a 30-year span, the percentage of those ages 15–29 had little effect on homicide.

Fred Pampel and Rosemary Gartner have shown that shifts in the age structure may be counteracted by collectivist institutions. Thus, among 18 similar high income countries over 36 years, the authors found that corporatist arrangements for bargaining among social classes, types of class compromise, coalition cabinets, left-of-center political rule, universality of benefits, and governability of a country serve to reduce the effects of homicide in young age groups.

VI. RACE AND ETHNICITY

There are racial and ethnic groups in many countries characterized by poverty, unemployment, little education, unstable families, frequently being the targets of prejudice and discrimination, and disproportionately high homicide rates. This section examines African Americans and Latinos in the U.S. and Canadian Indians.

A. African Americans

Except for Native Americans, the oldest minority group in the United States is African Americans. Although civil rights legislation has had ameliorative effects, African Americans are still characterized by many social and economic disadvantages. As a result, African Americans run an extremely high risk of homicide victimization.

Table III shows particularly high rates of homicide victimization among both males and females in the 15-

TABLE III

Homicide Victimization Rates by Racial Groups, Gender, and
Age (1994)

Age	African Americans			Whites		
	Male	Female	Both	Male	Female	Both
<1	23.2	16.9	20.1	5.9	5.0	5.4
1–4	8.4	6.4	7.4	2.3	1.9	2.1
5–9	2.1	1.5	1.8	0.5	0.7	0.6
10–14	9.0	4.6	6.8	1.7	0.9	1.3
15–24	156.2	18.7	87.4	17.0	3.6	10.6
25–34	110.3	23.1	64.3	13.8	4.2	9.0
35–44	66.9	15.6	39.5	10.0	3.2	6.6
45–54	38.9	7.8	21.9	6.9	2.2	4.5
55–64	23.9	4.7	13.1	5.1	1.6	3.3
>64	21.7	4.4	12.9	3.6	1.8	2.6

Source: http://wonder.cdc.gov

to 24-year age group. The homicide victimization rate for African-American males (156.2) is more than nine times higher than the rate for White males (11.5). For African-American females in the same age group, the homicide rate (18.7) is more than five times higher than it is for White females (3.6).

It is also important to note from Table III that homicide rates for African-American males and females remain higher throughout their life spans. In 1987, the lifetime risk of being a homicide victim for African-American males was 4.16 per 100. For African-American females, it was 1.02 per 100. For white males, the risk was 0.46 per 100 and for white females only 0.26 per 100. Thus, while the risk of homicide victimization is extremely high for young African-American males, it is very high for African-American males of *all* ages.

The ranking of race and gender groups in Table III have been confirmed by other research since the 1940s. The ranking of rates for race and gender groups begins with African-American males as highest by a wide margin, followed by African-American females, White males, and White females.

Finally, most homicides involve victims and offenders of the same race. According to FBI statistics, 86% of White victims and 93% of African-American victims are slain by members of the same racial group.

B. Latino Homicides

Until comparatively recently, the epidemiology of Latino homicides has often been ignored. Latino homicides are not distinguished in racial classifications in the United States because they are an ethnic, not a racial, category. Despite the sparse research, Latino homicides are important to understand there has been a dramatic increase in the Latino population in recent decades. Since the late 1960s the largest number of Latinos have come from Mexico and have settled mainly in California and Texas. Recent government reports suggest that by 2006, Latinos will be the largest minority group in the U.S., surpassing the African-American population. Because of the increasing size and influence of this group, it is important to examine the limited research available on Latino homicides.

Drawing on the author's unpublished research, Fig. 2 represents race-/ethnic-specific rates for African Americans, Latinos, and Whites in Los Angeles County.

Comparisons of the three race/ethnic groups show that African Americans have the highest risk of homicide victimization, followed by Latinos and Whites. After 1990, the Latino rates decline slightly while White rates show little variation throughout the series. African-American homicides peaked in 1993 and declined the last 2 years of the series.

Martinez's research in Miami supports the preceding. Using race/ethnic specific rates, he found African Americans had a rate of 73.49, Latinos had 21.66, and Whites had 19.83 for homicides reported for 1990 through 1995.

There are three other characteristics of Latino homicides. First, as Martinez suggests, Latino female victimization is similar to Whites. Using the Los Angeles County data, the 9-year means of race/ethnic gender-specific rates were 3.6 for White females, 5.0 for Latino females, and 19.6 for African-American females.

Second, the mean rates of victimization among older age categories were similar for Whites and Latinos. The mean race/ethnic age-specific rates (65–75) were 4.1 for Whites, 4.3 for Latinos, and 24.6 for African Americans.

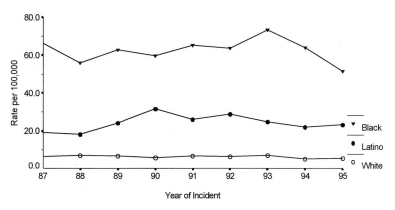

FIGURE 2   Race/ethnic specific murder rates: Los Angeles County, 1987–1995.

Finally, Carolyn Rebecca Block found in her study of Latino homicides in Chicago that gang-related homicides are particularly high among Latino youths. From 1982 through 1989, 34% of Latino male victims were killed in street gang confrontations.

C. Canadian Indians

Conditions of poverty, lack of opportunities, and prejudice associated with minorities in the U.S. also exist for Canadian Indians. Canadian Indians represent only 2–3% of the Canadian population, but account for 17% of the murder incidents. The total murder rate in Canada for 1961 through 1989 was never above 3.5 per 100,000. The rate for Canadian Indians increased from about 10.0 per 100,000 in 1961 to 30.0 in 1978 and 1979 and then declined to about 23.0 by 1989.

Robert Silverman and Leslie Kennedy report in their book *Deadly Deeds* that most (20.9%) murder incidents involving Canadian Indians occur in nonmetropolitan areas in contrast to metropolitan areas (5.7%). The experiences of Canadian Indians, with respect to the conditions of urban centers, that lead to lethal violence vary by city. For example, Toronto had a murder rate of 12.3 for the period from 1977 through 1981; Saskatoon, Saskatchewan, on the other hand, had a rate of 57.4.

Homicide in Canada, like the United States, is predominantly an intraracial offense. Among Canadian Indian victims, 80.3 were killed by offenders of the same race; for Whites, the intraracial percentage was 96.5%.

VII. ALCOHOL AND PSYCHOACTIVE DRUGS

It is well established that violent behavior is related to alcohol consumption. In *Drugs in American Society*, Erich Goode states the relationship unequivocally:

> Of all drugs, nationally, internationally, and cross-culturally, alcohol is *by far* the one most likely to be implicated in violent crimes. The empirical evidence is overwhelming. More individuals who commit violent offenses are under the influence of alcohol than of any other single drug. [Italics in the original]

The research supports a strong association between alcohol consumption and homicide. While study results vary, between one-third and one-half of homicide participants have blood-alcohol concentrations above 0.1.

The difficulty with much of the research on alcohol and homicide is that, as is well known, association is not causation. Increased alcohol consumption results in a corresponding decline in sensorimotor coordination, but that is only one part of the causal issue.

Many homicides arise out of situational conflicts; they originate in disputes between two people who come to play the roles of victim and offender. The topics of such disputes may include anything over which people can disagree, ranging from serious and substantive issues to the most trivial. Many of us have been involved in such disputes that tend to escalate with claims, counterclaims, and even insults and name-calling until one actor leaves the situation or a third party intervenes. With respect to homicide, the difference is that disputes continue to escalate until one party resorts to physical force or the use of a weapon.

Sometimes a fatal conflict turns on issues such as money or marital fidelity; other times, with disturbing frequency, homicides result from conflicts over the performance of opposing sports teams, ownership of a can of beer, or a parking space. What is common to these topics is not the content but that one actor sees the other's behavior as an attempt to compel or prevent a certain behavior or achieve a favorable self-image at the actor's expense. The actor counters with behavior to protect his or her own sense of self. This can take the form of refusing to do what is demanded, insisting that the person justify his or her demand, or retaliating with insults, all of which set the stage for a possible violent resolution. Unlike sensorimotor activity, this is a highly symbolic activity where the effect of alcohol is least understood.

The effects of alcohol in social situations are mediated by set and setting. Set refers to the psychic, mental, and emotional state of the actors. For example, after a few drinks, some people engage in witty and animated conversations, tell jokes, talk to strangers, and so on. Others become sullen, withdrawn, and hostile.

Setting refers to the social and physical environment in which drug use takes place. Different effects from alcohol consumption occur depending upon where the alcohol is consumed, whether it is consumed among strangers or friends, and whether the actors are comfortable in the setting.

Cultural definitions of drug and alcohol use play an important role in whether violent behavior is related to alcohol. Craig MacAndrew and Robert Edgerton, in their anthropological study *Drunken Comportment*, show that alcohol is not a universal "releaser of inhibitions." For example, beer is consumed in South African tribal villages without causing rancor and physical aggression. However, when beer is drunk by the same tribespeople in South African urban slums, there are arguments, fights, brawls, and stabbings. In rural Okinawa, Japanese men and women drink sake together without drunken aggression. However, when the same men drink by themselves, they become quarrelsome and often physically violent. Obviously, alcohol plays a role in violent behavior, but it is unclear how it interacts with the complexities of psychological functioning and social interaction.

A. Psychoactive Drugs

Illegal psychoactive drug use is implicated in a substantial share of urban homicides. National estimates of drug related homicides range between 8 and 10%.

The research seems most consistent regarding the effects of cocaine and marijuana. James Inciardi compared homicide trends and cocaine arrests in six U.S. cities and found no simple aggregate relationships between the two. Chronic use of cocaine in powdered or smokable forms ("crack") sometimes leads to mental states in which aggressive and violent behavior is expressed. One hospital study showed that 6% of all cocaine-related emergency admissions involved violent behavior; another showed no difference in the frequency of violence between institutionalized cocaine users and other in-patients. Homicides arising from the pharmacological effects of cocaine are rare, although its use accelerates violent behavior in settings where violence is common.

A recent report of the National Research Council summarizes the effects of marijuana on violent crime:

> During the past two decades, five major scientific reviews of the research literature have concluded that violent human behavior is either decreased or unaffected by cannabis use. Similarly, studies of many animal species demonstrate that acute does of THC, the psychoactive ingredient in marijuana, promote submissive and flight responses and, at least in large doses, inhibit attack and threat behavior. These effects persist during chronic administration to animals.

Studies of prevalence and dosage do not tell the whole story. Drug use and its violent effects can be attributed to individual differences such as long-term patterns of drug use, dosage levels, and even genetic mechanisms. Further, such differences interact with group, social, and cultural factors in ways that are not understood with the most familiar drug, alcohol. We have just begun to understand the intricate interrelationships that characterize other drugs and homicide.

B. Economic and Systemic Violence

The process of obtaining and distributing illegal drugs makes possible two kinds of violence, according to Paul Goldstein and his colleagues. The first, economic violence, occurs when some drug users obtain money to buy drugs by committing robberies. The second, systemic violence, occurs in disputes over marketing practices. Since illegal markets are not subject to legal dispute resolution mechanisms, violence may result.

While violence is clearly part of obtaining money to buy drugs, the type of violence is primarily robbery. Burglaries are also frequent and can become violent if the burglar encounters an occupant of the property. Heroin users prefer nonviolent alternatives such as burglaries.

Two important forms of systemic violence are related to organizations and transactions. Processing, importing, and distributing illegal drugs is a complicated organizational task. Violence and homicide are used to enforce organizational rules, such as abstaining from drug use while selling or trafficking, resolving territorial disputes, punishing informers, protecting sellers, and battling police.

Transaction-related violence is used in robberies of drugs and money from sellers to resolve disputes over the quantity or quality of drugs and to resolve disputes over how much money low-level sellers pay higher-level sellers. Robberies of dealers and assaults to collect debts are the most common.

VIII. FIREARMS

About 60% of the homicides in the United States involve firearms. While there is no precise count of the number of privately owned firearms in the United States, the most recent estimate by the Bureau of Alcohol, Tobacco, and Firearms places the figure at 200 million. The percentage of all households owning a firearm has remained stable at about 50% for at least 3 decades. However, the percentage of handguns increased from 13% in 1959 to 24% in 1978, and has since remained stable.

Gun ownership and gun use in homicide is predominantly a United States problem. The Centers for Disease Control conducted a study of firearms-related deaths among young children from 1990 to 1995, comparing the United States with 25 other industrialized countries. For firearms-related homicides for ages 0–4, the ratio of U.S. rates to the pooled rates of 25 other countries was 8.6 to 1. For 5- to 14-year-old victims, the ratio was 17.4 to 1 and for 0- to 14-year-old victims, it was 15.7 to 1.

Among adolescents, other research indicates that the risk of homicide victimization by gun in the United States is very high among African-American males. The gun homicide rate in 1988 was 8 per 100,000 for teenagers and 6 for the total population. For African-American males ages 15–19, the firearms homicide death rate was 83.4. For White males of the same ages, it was 7.5 per 100,000.

The pervasiveness of firearms and their disproportionate use by teenagers have been the subject of a survey by Joseph Sheley and James Wright. For their book *In the Line of Fire*, they surveyed 758 male students in 10 inner-city high schools and 835 male inmates in six correctional institutions in four states. The more important findings from the survey of males in inner-city schools include the following.

The social environment of the students was such that 37% had males in their families who carried guns; 42% had friends who carried guns. When asked if it was okay to shoot someone to get something they wanted, 10% of the student sample responded affirmatively. The percentage increased if the scenario included a person from another neighborhood and who also injured or insulted them.

Twelve percent of the student sample carried a gun all or most of the time. Automatic and semiautomatic sidearms and large caliber revolvers were the weapons of preference. Students preferred weapons that were well-made, accurate, easy to shoot, and not easily traced; cheap, poorly manufactured imports (Saturday Night Specials) play a very small role in teenage use of firearms.

Forty-one percent of the students surveyed felt that they could easily obtain a gun. Most felt that they could buy one from family or friends; only 28% of the students would purchase one from a gun shop. Where gun shop purchases were made, respondents typically had someone over 21 make the purchase for them.

Most amazing was the cost of handguns. For the majority (53%) of purchases reported by students, the cost was between $50 and $100. Legally purchased firearms are priced substantially higher: $300 or more. From the perspective of supply and demand, the low price indicated an ample supply of handguns, many of which were stolen. Given this informal network of peo-

ple who can provide firearms, legislation and regulation of legal firearms is likely to have little effect.

Finally, while there was an association between guns, drug dealing, and violent crime, more important is the finding that most of the students purchased guns to protect themselves. As Albert Blumstein has indicated, among students who are involved in drug dealing, guns are obtained because they are the tools of the trade. This results in an "arms race" in which other teenagers feel compelled to carry weapons for self protection. The presence of lethal weapons leads to a major escalation of violence that frequently characterizes teenage males.

IX. THE MISSING OFFENDER

Much of what is known about homicide is based on data about victims. What is said about victims is generally applicable to offenders because it is an offense where victims and offenders are often of the same race, ethnicity, gender, and/or age. In addition, data on victims are more comprehensive than data on offenders. This section discusses the declining availability of offender information and its impact on criminal justice.

A. The Decline in Arrest Clearances

When a homicide that occurs in the United States is investigated and results in the arrest of one or more offenders, it is considered "cleared by arrest." Figure 3 gives the percentage of murders and nonnegligent manslaughters cleared by arrest as a percentage of all homicides reported.

Figure 3 indicates that, nationally, arrest clearances have been decreasing steadily since 1961, except for a slight increase in 1983. In 1961, the percentage of murders and nonnegligent manslaughters cleared by arrest was 93%. By 1995, the figure had declined to 65%. Variations in national murder rates do not account for the decline in arrest clearances.

Robert Silverman and Leslie Kennedy have examined arrest clearances in Canada and note that in 1961 the U.S. and Canada had identical clearance rates (93%). The results by Silverman and Kennedy show that the highest *uncleared* homicide rate in Canada is

barely 0.6 per 100,000 (1983) while in the United States the peak rate is more than three per 100,000 (higher than Canada's homicide rate). While the homicide rate in the United States is three to four times that of Canada, the uncleared

FIGURE 3 Arrest clearances for murder: 1961–1995. (Source: Annual Editions of Uniform Crime Reports.)

homicide rate is closer to six times as high in the United States.

The decline in arrest clearances is important because arrests are the entry point to the criminal justice system. If a substantial proportion of offenders are not arrested, it is not possible for criminal justice processes to have any significant deterrent or punishment effect.

The decline in arrest clearances has other negative effects. The fact that over one-third of the people who kill other people remain at-large raises questions about public safety and increases fears of victimization. Felony-related homicides are more likely to be repeated than those that do not involve a concomitant felony and these are the offenses most difficult to clear by arrest.

Further, because arrest clearances are used as a measure of police performance, the decline in clearances has led to a decline in morale and effectiveness among law enforcement personnel. In a 1994 article in *U.S. News and World Report*, a veteran Washington detective commented:

> I can honestly say this is the first time in my career I don't enjoy this stuff any more. And I'm in the process of looking for another job. We're losing the war. We're not even winning battles anymore.

In addition, the trauma experienced by the families of murder victims is only compounded when no suspects are arrested. The available research indicates that victims' families undergo stress and trauma for long periods and that children are especially vulnerable.

Finally, uncleared murders are important because what represents uncleared murders to law enforcement represents missing data to researchers. On the surface,

it is important to consider whether research that reports on offender-related variables, when over one-third of the data are missing, can avoid serious problems of bias.

There are three possible causes for the decline in arrest clearances. First, it is customary to look to changes in police activity or organization to explain variations in arrest behavior. Unfortunately, the large amount of research on the topic, plus evaluations of programs to increase arrests, point to only modest positive effects.

Second, over the time discussed, there have been changes in the types of homicide committed. As will be discussed subsequently, there has been a decline in family-related killings, which are also the offenses most easily cleared by arrest. This leaves a higher proportion of felony-related crimes, which are more difficult to clear.

Finally, Albert Reiss noted 25 years ago, "There is no feasible way to solve most crimes except by securing the cooperation of citizens to link a person to the crime." In homicide investigations, community cooperation is essential. Without information about the offender and the circumstances of the offense, law enforcement is unable to effect arrests. Where police investigators face hostility and fear, clearances may be difficult. Although the relationship to arrest clearances is unknown, it is likely that where there are large numbers of gang killings, area inhabitants fear retaliation for cooperation with police.

X. PRIOR RELATIONSHIPS BETWEEN VICTIMS AND OFFENDERS

A. Friends and Gangs

It is frequently said that the average person stands a greater chance of being killed by someone they know than by a stranger. While this is true, the generalization is circumscribed by the limits of the data: among homicide victim/offender relationships on which information is available, the largest percentage involve prior relationships. However, there are many cases for which the relationships are unknown.

According to the FBI's 1995 *Uniform Crime Reports*, 11.6% of murders involved family members and 33.9% involved friends, acquaintances, and such relationships as boyfriends, employees, neighbors, and so on; thus, 45.5% of murder victims had prior relationships with their killers. In 15.1% of cases, the victims were strangers to their offenders. However, information on victim/offender relationships was missing for 39.4% of the cases, nearly all of which were uncleared homicides. Since it is not known what types of relationships are contained in cases with missing data, the claim that murder victims are likely to know their killers is limited by what is known about victim/offender relationships.

Information about prior relationships between victims and offenders is obtained from friends, family members, or associates of the victim or from offenders upon arrest. Since homicides involving intimate relationships frequently occur in the presence of family members or in private locations where witnesses observe either the homicide or events leading up to it, homicides involving intimates are reported with a reasonable degree of accuracy.

In a conflict situation, the presence of third parties whose good opinion is valued by the actors contributes to a lethal outcome. Such third parties as friends, spouses, and gang members more often encourage violence rather than mediate or reduce it. When the initiating insult represents an attack on male identities, the presence of other male third parties results in more severe violence.

However, the importance of peer influence extends beyond the immediate situation with respect to gangs and motivation for homicide. Determining the number of gang homicides presents a problem because counting rules depend on the definitions of gangs and gang involvement. Law enforcement agencies take two approaches.

Los Angeles law enforcement officials follow a broad gang-member definition: a gang homicide is one in which either victims or offenders are gang members. Chicago police, on the other hand, use a narrower gang-motive definition, requiring that a homicide be directly linked to a gang function. There must be some positive evidence that gang activity or membership was the motive for the encounter. Examples include quarrels over territory, retaliation, recruitment, and "representing"

(graffiti, shouting gang slogans, wearing gang colors). Therefore, the killing of a convenience store clerk by a gang member during a robbery would be a gang homicide in Los Angeles, but may not be in Chicago.

The difference in definition also results in a difference in the number of gangs and gang-related homicides. Maxson and Klein note that, using the Los Angeles gang-member definition, 44% of all homicides occurring in the city in 1994 were gang homicides. For the same year in Chicago, using the gang-motive definition, 32% of all homicides were gang related.

Definitions make a difference in terms of *prevalence* because the number of gang homicides plays a powerful role in motivating public opinion and resources; an equally important issue is whether the two definitions make a difference in the *patterns* of gang homicide. Comparisons of the two definitions to nongang homicide in Los Angeles, using many variables related to homicides, show few differences, at least at the bivariate level. In other words, gang-member or gang-motive homicides are more similar to each other than to nongang homicides.

Among the characteristics that distinguish gang from nongang homicides are the presence of firearms. Nearly all (95%) of gang homicides involved guns while this was true for 75% of nongang homicides. Males are victims in 90% of gang-related homicides, but only 77% of nongang homicides. Males are also more prominent (93%) as offenders in gang in comparison to nongang (83%) homicides.

While there are differences among gangs, the research does not support media reports of high levels of drug-motivated homicides among gangs. Patrick Meehan and Patrick O'Carroll found that 5% of gang-motivated homicides in Los Angeles involved narcotics compared with 23% for other homicides. Just 2.2% of Chicago street gang-related homicides between 1965 and 1974 involved drug motives. At least with respect to what is found in law enforcement records, drug-related homicides do not occur with a high frequency among gangs.

B. Intimate Partners and Family

Most prior relationships between victims and offenders involve limited knowledge of another: "acquaintances" are the single largest category of victim/offender relationships tabulated by the FBI. Among gang homicides, victims and offender may know little more than that the other is a member of an opposing gang.

Intimate partner and family homicides are different; they involve continuing relationships and repeated violent victimization commonly occurs before the actual homicide. For example, Browne, in her classic study of women who kill, documents frequent serious violent acts, many of which resulted in permanent injury to the woman, stretching over several years before the actual killing.

Intervention and research are hampered because victims are vulnerable and relatively powerless against offenders. This means that offenders can threaten victims with additional violence if incidents are disclosed to others. Victims may also refrain from disclosure for fear of stigmatization and denigration. Finally, much of the domestic violence, short of homicide, occurs in private places where it is not visible to others and less likely to be detected and reported to police.

Violence between family members and intimate partners is a serious problem, but family-related homicides, primarily homicides involving spouses, have been declining. According to the UCR, in 1977, family-related murders accounted for 19.4% of all homicides. By 1995, they had declined to 11.6%.

In Canada, intimate murders (family and spouses) accounted for 40% of all murders during the 1980s. As a *proportion* of all murders, murders involving spouses and lovers have been declining, although at about 25% in 1990, the rate is higher in Canada than in the United States. The *rate* of spousal murders has remained stable since the late 1960s.

Richard Rosenfeld examined the decline in spousal homicides by studying intimate partner homicides. Marital intimate partners are those victims who have been married to, separated from, or divorced from their killers and those in common-law relationships. Nonmarital intimate relationships include boyfriends, ex-boyfriends, girlfriends, and ex-girlfriends.

Using homicide data from St. Louis, Rosenfeld found that total intimate partner homicide rates declined for African-American females from 1970 to 1990. African-American males, White males, and White females showed a decline from 1980.

Marital intimate homicide rates declined for African-American males and females from 1970 to 1990 and for White males and females from 1980. Nonmarital intimate partner homicide rates decreased for all race and gender groups from 1980 to 1990.

Much of the decline in intimate partner homicide is a consequence of changes in marriage patterns among the young adult population, which is at greatest risk for homicide victimization. In 1970, 55% of U.S. males between the ages of 20 and 24 had never married; by 1992, this percentage had increased to 80%. Rosenfeld reports a decrease in percentage married in St. Louis,

especially among African Americans. Between 1970 and 1990, the percentage of African-American women never married dropped from 58 to 43%.

There are two additional factors that may contribute to a decline in intimate partner homicides. First, in the past few decades, there has been a shift away from the view that homicides, particularly those between intimates, are crimes that cannot be prevented. Nothing can be done, it was said, when a man or woman suddenly kills their intimate partner "for no apparent reason." What is slowly sifting into public consciousness is the recognition that few spouses or intimate partners kill "for no apparent reason." The public is becoming increasingly aware that intimate partner homicides are frequently the culmination of a long history of extremely violent abuse. Homicides are the result of battering or a last desperate attempt by abused women to free themselves from their tormentors. This awareness shifts the burden of social concern to the prevention of violence preceding the homicide. Doing something to prevent less serious forms of violence may also contribute to preventing lethal forms.

Second, consensus about norms and values in a society are typically given formal shape and substance by law. For example, the immorality of murder is given expression by legislation, criminal justice processes, and penal sanctions. But the reverse is also true: legal formalization strengthens norms. With changes in legislation, wife-battering is no longer a minor irritant for police and the source of gossip, but a crime with substantial penalties.

There have been a variety of legislative changes besides making abuse a criminal offense. These include making restraining orders more readily available, creating statutes permitting warrantless arrests based on probable cause in domestic violence cases, providing funds for family violence shelters, and developing abuse programs that offer counseling. In Canada, the battered-wife syndrome is now a defense against homicide. While these steps do not eliminate the problem of domestic violence, they may contribute to preventing its most serious expression.

XI. PREVENTING HOMICIDES AND VIOLENCE

A. Punishment and Deterrence

The obvious approach to reducing the number of homicides is to arrest, convict, incarcerate, and/or impose the death penalty on offenders. This politically popular approach is justified as a general and specific deterrent.

Arrests are a general deterrent, that is, they teach by example that others should not commit the same crime. But it is difficult to argue for a general deterrent effect when no offender is arrested in more than one-third of murder and nonnegligent manslaughter cases in the United States.

Further winnowing of the number of offenders takes place after arrest. Persons arrested for a killing may or may not be charged with murder, those charged may plead guilty to a less serious charge (plea bargain) or be acquitted, and those convicted may or may not be incarcerated in state institutions.

While incapacitation limits the number of crimes committed by felons, the effect on the crime levels in society is negligible. Research shows a 31% or more decrease in violent crimes among offenders with a 5-year mandatory sentence. However, the general effect on crime levels in society is less than 14% and may be as small as 0.8%.

B. The Death Penalty

One of the most controversial sanctions for homicide in the United States is the death penalty. At the end of 1994, 34 states and the federal jurisdiction held 2890 prisoners under sentence of death. Comparison to other industrialized countries indicates that the U.S. is among the few nations that use capital punishment: 28 European countries have abolished the death penalty either in law or in practice. Countries that continue to use it (China, Iraq, Iran, South Africa, and the former Soviet Union) are known for their disregard for human rights.

A much smaller percentage of those incarcerated are sentenced to death. Without taking into account uncleared offenses, only 2% of persons convicted of criminal homicide are sentenced to death—hardly an argument for a deterrent effect.

Further, it appears that prison sentences are more effective with murder offenders than with other kinds of violent offenders. For 6835 males released on parole, Sellin found only 21 (0.3%) were returned because they had committed another murder. These persons were less likely to commit murder while on parole than persons originally sentenced for armed robbery or forcible or aggravated assault.

The most persistent argument advanced for the death penalty is that it is a specific deterrent: once the offender is executed, it is certain that he or she will not commit any additional homicides. But would this offender have committed more homicides if he or she had been sentenced to life and eventually released? One way to answer that question is to examine the behavior of offenders who were sentenced to death but allowed to live.

In 1972, the U.S. Supreme Court concluded in *Furman v. Georgia* that the existing form of the death penalty was unconstitutional. As a result, over 600 offenders under sentence of death were resentenced. Some of these offenders were eventually released on parole.

In a study of 47 offenders in Texas taken off death rows by *Furman*, none were implicated in a prison homicide. Among those released into the community, only one offender committed another murder. In another study of 272 *Furman* offenders, there were two additional murders of correctional workers and one of an inmate. Among the 185 offenders released on parole, there were three additional murders. Whether the six additional murders represent an acceptable level of risk requires comparison to the reincarceration records of comparable offenders not sentenced to death. From that perspective, the imposition of the death penalty appears *not* to prevent significantly more murders.

C. Primary Prevention

Another approach focuses on the broader problem of preventing violent behavior. Two facts support that approach. First, as was noted earlier, homicide often emerges from interactional escalation in a social situation. This suggests that it takes two or more people to perform the interaction sequence that leads to homicide; homicides do not occur unless someone responds aggressively in a conflict situation. When the potential victim is not responsive or leaves the setting, homicide does not occur. This suggests that we need to examine the social and cultural commonalities of victims and offenders that lead them to escalate conflicts to a violent end.

Second, many homicide offenders have a prior record of violent behavior, although there are people who commit homicide with no previous record of violence. For example, Edwin Megargee noted that overcontrolled persons may suddenly erupt in a violent episode. But we have noted than many spousal killings involve a record of prior violence, and this is true for other homicides as well. This suggests we also need to examine developmental patterns that contribute to violence.

1. Social and Cultural Factors

Homicide victims and offenders are not randomly distributed through the population. Descriptions of the social and demographic variables that contribute to homicide show what groups and strata in society are most at risk of homicide. In the United States, the highest risk is found among young African-American males and females and Latino males. Knowing something about the social and economic conditions faced by young people in these categories leads to explanations and prevention programs.

The extent of poverty, racism, lack of opportunity in inner-city neighborhoods, and prevention programs have been discussed in many other publications. In their study of gun ownership and use in inner-city neighborhoods, Sheley and Wright paint a compelling picture of inner-city life in which gun ownership seems a very reasonable response to the dangerous conditions of daily life.

There is much talk these days about family values and the importance of family in socializing children against the use of violence. What seems to be forgotten is that many families function in communities and neighborhoods that undermine their efforts to inculcate values opposing violence. The presence of gangs, availability of drugs and guns, and daily exposure to violence in the neighborhood mean that many families in inner-city neighborhoods face insuperable difficulties in raising children to avoid violent victimization.

For example, I became very good friends with a well-educated professional African-American woman who came from a very close family in an inner-city neighborhood of Houston. Over the years, I met her family and many people with whom she had grown up. Very frequently, when I would ask her about the background of the people I met, she would relate stories of violence and crime: one or both parents became drug addicts, the mother killed the father, brothers were imprisoned for dealing drugs, murders or robberies, sisters were prostitutes, and so on. I once asked her if she knew any conventional people, that is, people who grew up in families in which the most traumatic event was getting the mumps. She said she did not, which says a great deal about the impact of neighborhood and community. Unfortunately, this anecdote has an even sadder ending: after moving back to Houston to take another job, my friend was stabbed to death during a burglary by a 15-year-old African-American male.

Criminologists, such as Marvin Wolfgang and Franco Ferracuti, have suggested the existence of shared clusters of beliefs about the use of violence. These beliefs characterize a subculture of violence that is most prevalent among young males, African Americans, and lower-income persons. These beliefs predis-

pose actors to respond to certain behaviors, such as insults, with force. Because they believe that violence is a way of solving interpersonal problems, they are more likely to escalate a verbal conflict and use violence to resolve the dispute.

2. Developmental Factors

There is a significant relationship between childhood aggression and violence: aggressive children tend to become violent teenagers and violent adults. Farrington has shown that aggressive children at ages 8–10 and 12–14 tended to have later convictions for violence and be violent at age 32. Predictors and correlates of violence include low IQ, low school attainment, high impulsivity, and poor concentration. Family factors include low income, large family size, parents with criminal convictions, harsh discipline, poor supervision, and parental separations.

Cognitive-behavioral theories have resulted in prevention programs. Huesman and Eron have developed a cognitive model of aggression development in which the expression of aggression is controlled by "scripts" learned during early development. These scripts suggest what events are about to occur, the expected reaction, and what the outcome will be. These scripts are retrieved with appropriate environmental cues and guide behavior. In this theory, a repeatedly aggressive child is one who consistently retrieves and uses aggressive scripts that are learned, in part, from the behavior of parents.

The prevention of violence focuses on changing these scripts to foster nonviolence. Social skills training can have positive effects in changing aggressive behavior in children. The Earlscourt Social Skills Group Program attempts to improve self-control and social skills of aggressive children. The program teaches such social skills as problem-solving, knowing one's own feelings, using self-control, responding to teasing, and avoiding fights. An evaluation of the program showed improvement in dealing with aggression, and these improvements were maintained over a 3-month follow-up.

Poor parental training techniques predict delinquency and may have an effect in reducing violence. Parental intervention programs, aimed at families with delinquent and predelinquent children, focus on noticing what the child is doing, monitoring his or her behavior over long periods, clearly stating and standing by house rules, making rewards and punishment consistently contingent on behavior, and negotiating disagreements so that conflicts and crises do not escalate. Many parent training programs have been evaluated and shown to be effective in reducing aggression in children.

XII. SUMMARY

While comparisons to other countries have of necessity been limited and selective, what we have shown is that homicide is a U.S. problem—in many ways, uniquely so. There is little doubt that among technologically advanced countries, the United States has the highest homicide rates; its rates are more comparable to developing and third world countries than advanced industrial ones. The major contributors to this high rates are young African-American males, gangs, and the prevalence of lethal weapons. The ability of police to clear or arrest offenders has declined to where approximately one-third of offenders are not arrested.

On the positive side, marital homicides have declined as a proportion of total homicides largely as a result of increased concern and resources. These include programs designed to prevent the long-term escalation of violence such as counseling and women's shelters. In addition, changes in legislation have convinced offenders and public alike that spousal violence is no longer a minor offense.

Transnational research has been useful in suggesting that institutional arrangements have a bearing in reducing homicides. The research by Pampel and Gartner indicate that social institutions that encourage negotiation and compromise play a role in reducing homicides among high-risk age groups.

Arguments to promote "family values" as a way or reducing homicides overlook that such values are not generated from urban conditions that include impoverished families, poor educational opportunities, drugs, and gangs. There seems little hope that these conditions will be changed in any significant way in most countries. What does show greater promise are programs that focus on teaching parenting skills and programs that teach children to interact with others that do not include violence.

Also See the Following Articles

DEATH PENALTY, OVERVIEW • DRUGS AND VIOLENCE • EVOLUTIONARY FACTORS • FAMILY STRUCTURES, VIOLENCE AND NONVIOLENCE • GANGS • MINORITIES AS PERPETRATORS AND VICTIMS OF CRIME • URBAN VIOLENCE, YOUTH

Bibliography

Best, J. (1988). Missing children: Misleading statistics. *The Public Interest, 92,* 84–92.

Blumstein, A. (1995). Youth violence, guns, and the illicit drug industry. *Journal of Criminal Law and Criminology, 86,* 10–36.

Browne, A. (1987). *When battered women kill.* New York: Free Press.

Browne, A., & Williams, K. R. (1993). Gender, intimacy, and lethal violence. *Gender & Society, 7,* 78–98.

Gartner, R. (1993). Methodological issues in cross-cultural large-survey research on violence. *Violence and Victims, 8,* 199–215.

Gartner, R. (1997). Crime: Variations across cultures and nations. In C. Ember & M. Ember (Eds.), *Cross-cultural research for social science.* Englewood Cliffs, NJ: Prentice–Hall.

Harries, K. D. (1989). Homicide and assault: A comparative analysis of attributes in Dallas neighborhoods, 1981–1985. *The Professional Geographer, 41,* 29–38.

Jenkins, P. (1994). *Using murder: The social construction of serial homicide.* New York: Aldine de Gruyter.

Klein, M. W., Maxson, C. L., & Miller, J. (Eds.) (1995). *The modern gang reader.* Los Angeles: Roxbury.

Martinez, R. (1997). Homicide among Miami's ethnic groups: Anglos, blacks, and latinos in the 1990s. *Homicide Studies, 1,* 17–34.

Pampel, F. C., & Gartner, R. (1995). Age structure, socio-political institutions, and national homicide rates. *European Sociological Review, 11,* 243–260.

Riedel, M. (1999). Sources of homicide data: A review and comparison. In M. D. Smith & M. Zahn (Eds.), *Homicide studies: A sourcebook of social research.* Newbury Park, CA: Sage.

Riedel, M., & Rinehart, T. A. (1996). Murder clearances and missing data. *Journal of Crime and Justice, 19,* 83–102.

Reiss, A. J., & Roth, J. A. (Eds.). (1993). *Understanding and preventing violence.* Washington, DC: National Academy Press.

Rosenfeld, R. (1997). Changing relationships between men and women: A note on the decline in intimate partner homicide. *Homicide Studies, 1,* 72–83.

Silverman, R., & Kennedy, L. (1993). *Deadly deeds: Murder in Canada.* Scarborough, Ontario: Nelson Canada.

Silverman, R. A., & Kennedy, L. W. (1997). Uncleared homicides in Canada and the United States. In M. Riedel & J. Boulahanis (Eds.), *Lethal Violence: Proceedings of the 1995 Meeting of the Homicide Research Working Group* (pp. 81–85). Washington, DC: U.S. Government Printing Office.

Homosexuals, Violence toward

Karen Franklin
University of Washington, Seattle

Gregory M. Herek
University of California, Davis

GLOSSARY

Bisexuals Persons with sexual, romantic, and affectional attractions to both men and women.

Hate Crimes Actions intended to harm or intimidate a person because of her or his race, sexual orientation, religion, or other comparable group identification. In the United States, many states have enacted so-called hate crimes legislation that increases legal penalties for crimes based on group identity. The term has met with criticism because of its assumption that individuals who commit certain acts are necessarily motivated by hatred. The term is used synonymously with "bias crime."

Heterosexism An ideological system that denies, denigrates, and stigmatizes nonheterosexual forms of behavior, identity, relationships, or community. Heterosexism is manifested in societal customs and institutions as well as in individual attitudes and behaviors.

Heterosexuals Individuals whose primary sexual, romantic, and affectional attractions are to people of the other sex.

Homosexuals Individuals whose primary sexual, romantic, and affectional attractions are to people of the same sex. In Western cultures, people who have developed identities as homosexuals typically refer to themselves as gay, with many women preferring the term lesbian.

VIOLENCE AGAINST HOMOSEXUALS is a significant social problem in many parts of the world. On a global level, its primary manifestation is in state-sanctioned violence by law enforcement officials. In some countries, extralegal violence—committed primarily by young males—is also widespread. The violence has been documented in institutional settings—such as prisons, militaries, and schools—and within families. Forms of victimization include assault, beating, rape, torture, and murder. Probably the most frequent victims, due to their visibility and their violation of traditional gender norms, are men who assume the dress or characteristics associated with women. Efforts to combat the violence are being waged on legislative, public policy, and educational fronts.

Copyright © 1999 by Academic Press.
All rights of reproduction in any form reserved.

I. HISTORY OF VIOLENCE AGAINST HOMOSEXUALS

Human beings have probably engaged in homosexual behavior in all cultures throughout history. Ritualized homosexuality has been documented in various nonindustrial societies in Africa, Papua New Guinea, and barbarian Europe. Ancient Arabic poetry is replete with homoerotic poetry and literature. Some forms of homosexuality also held a respected position in ancient Greece and Rome. A flourishing homosexual subculture—with its own literature, art, and slang—appears to have arisen in Europe during the rapid urban expansion of the 11th and 12th centuries. In other cultures, homosexuality remained invisible or was conflated with long-standing, gender-linked traditions, such as adoption of the dress and mannerisms of the other sex.

All societies have rules governing sexuality and gender. Anthropologists and historians have located examples from many time periods and geographic settings of individuals being punished for violating the gender and sexual norms of their particular culture. Widespread institutionalized violence against homosexuals appears to be a relatively recent historical phenomenon, however, emerging in Europe in the 13th and 14th centuries during the rise of the modern nation-state. The Christian Crusades and the Holy Inquisition of this period saw unprecedented vilification and persecution of homosexuals and other previously tolerated social groups including Jews, Muslims, religious dissidents, witches, lepers, money-lenders, and the poor. Women, too, lost significant social power during this period.

Public antagonism during this period was exacerbated by homosexuality's linkage with both Islamic cultures and religious heretics. Trials of heretics frequently mentioned their alleged practice of sodomy, and Muslims were accused during the Crusades of sodomy, effeminacy, transvestitism, and the sexual corruption of Christian youth. Indeed, the earliest legislation against homosexual behavior during the High Middle Ages, proscribing death by burning for sodomites, was enacted by Europeans attempting to wrest Jerusalem from the Muslims.

During the latter half of the 13th century, the pendulum regarding homosexuality swung from complete legality to punishment by death in most of Europe. In Spain, the new law proscribed castration followed by death by hanging from the legs. In France, male sodomites were punishable by castration for the first offense, dismemberment for the second, and burning for the

third, whereas women were punishable by dismemberment for the first and second offenses and burning for the third.

The extent to which these laws were actually enforced is difficult to determine. Contemporaneous records suggest that accusations of homosexuality were widely used during religious and political crusades. The Church accused wealthy noblemen of homosexuality in order to seize their lands. Pagans who practiced ritualized homosexuality and cross-dressing were executed at so-called "witch" trials; these antiwitch campaigns continued until the end of the 18th century, with estimates of the number of people killed ranging from several hundred thousand to several million.

The legal persecution of homosexuals continued for several centuries in Europe and North America. Records from 17th and 18th century England, France, and the Netherlands reveal that gatherings of homosexual men in parks and taverns were met with arrests, torture, and executions. In colonial New England, executions for sodomy occurred as early as 1646. A statute passed in 1655 by the New Haven colony mandated the death penalty for lesbianism as well as male homosexuality. Antihomosexual epithets such as *faggot, fairy, punk,* and *bugger* date back to this repressive era, which set the stage for contemporary violence toward homosexuals.

Although laws in Europe and the United States proscribing the death penalty for homosexuality were largely abolished by the end of the 19th century, anecdotal accounts suggest that extralegal violence against gay men and lesbians was common in the early 1900s. Contemporary accounts describe the dangers of frequenting gay and lesbian bars, where sailors lurked outside waiting to pounce. As today, groups of urban teenage boys stalked cruising locations in search of gay men to verbally harass, beat, and rob.

Hostility toward homosexuality reached a tragic climax in Nazi Germany. An estimated 50,000 to 63,000 suspected male homosexuals were convicted of homosexuality under the infamous Paragraph 175 between 1933 and 1944. Between 5,000 and 15,000 are thought to have died in concentration camps. Gay men were forced to wear a pink triangle or letter "A" (for *Arschficker*) as a badge of identity, and were singled out for violence including beating, rape, castration, and medical experimentation. (Although a small number of lesbians were ensnared in the Nazi juggernaut, lesbianism was not illegal under Paragraph 175.) At the war's end, other surviving prisoners were liberated but the homosexuals were not; Germany's antihomosexual law remained in effect until 1969.

In the United States, the end of World War II signaled

the emergence of the homosexual subculture as a definable, self-conscious social minority in the United States. The birth of modern gay culture coincided with the anticommunist hysteria of the McCarthy era, which ushered in a resurgence of antihomosexual discrimination through legal codes, military regulations, mass firings, and arrests. As early as 1950, the Republican National Chairman announced that "the sexual perverts who have infiltrated our government" were "perhaps as dangerous as the actual communists." By April of that year, 91 alleged homosexuals had been fired from the State Department alone. The branding of homosexuals as traitors and security risks led to an upsurge of antigay violence as police across the United States routinely engaged in bar raids, blackmail, entrapment, and other abuses.

II. A CONTEMPORARY OVERVIEW

Although scholars debate the origins of contemporary social categories based on sexuality, there is widespread agreement that numerous cultural and historical factors have shaped the individual experience of sexual orientation, the formation of identities based on it, and the development of communities of people who share similar identities. Consequently, comparisons across cultures and historical periods are inherently problematic. However, the increasingly transnational nature of local cultures has contributed to the spread of Western notions of gay and lesbian identity throughout the globe. The emergence of gay and lesbian subcultures, in turn, has been accompanied in many places by widespread violence against men and women suspected of homosexual behavior or identity.

The serial torture-murder of suspected homosexuals is an extreme manifestation of this violence. For example, in Chiapas, Mexico, more than a dozen gay men were killed between 1991 and 1993 by death squads targeting the local gay community. In Bahia, Brazil, more than 320 murders of gay men and lesbians were reported in the early 1990s. And in Colombia, human-rights groups documented the torture-murders of 298 homosexuals and other "undesirables" during one 8-month period as part of so-called "clean-up operations" by police-backed death squads.

Laws prescribing dismemberment or death for homosexual acts represent another facet of violence against homosexuals. These punishments are on the books in only a small minority of countries, including Iran and Saudi Arabia. Although they are rarely imposed, their existence sets a tone of tolerance for police and extralegal violence.

Globally, state-sanctioned violence by law enforcement authorities appears to be the most prevalent form of violence experienced by homosexuals. In many countries, the police routinely raid gay and lesbian meeting places. Suspected homosexuals are rounded up and detained, frequently without formal charges. These detentions are often marked by beatings, torture, attempted blackmail, and other forms of abuse. Examples include a June 1996, discotheque raid in Halle, Germany, in which patrons were beaten with batons and bar stools by 160 masked police, and mass roundups around Bulgaria in July 1996 at gay beaches, magazine offices, and bars. Routine police beatings and torture of arrested homosexuals have been reported in numerous other countries. Countries garnering extensive international attention due to such incidents in the 1990s included Albania, Greece, and Romania.

Extralegal violence against homosexuals is prevalent in many countries, including the United States, Australia, Germany, South Africa, and Russia. In the former German Democratic Republic, for example, the rise of neofascist, nationalist movements during the 1990s led to a sharp increase in antihomosexual violence. In Australia, both Sydney and Melbourne experienced rashes of "poofter-bashings" in the 1990s, with six murders in Melbourne during one 12-month period. In Russia, young gangs called *remonti* (repairmen) seek out homosexuals to beat and rob. Similarly, many adolescent males in the United States participate in group assaults on homosexuals as a way to mark their passage to heterosexual manhood.

Probably more than any other group, cross-dressers—individuals who assume the dress and characteristics traditionally associated with the other sex—are particular targets of sexuality related violence. In Istanbul, Turkey, in June 1996, for example, ax-wielding police staged a series of raids on a street inhabited by about 70 male cross-dressers. The police allegedly burned down homes, destroyed property, and beat and tortured those who were taken into custody. In Chiapas, Mexico, at least half of the homosexual men murdered by death squads in the early 1990s (discussed earlier) were cross-dressers. And in Buenos Aires, Argentina, police sweeps resulted in the arrests of an estimated 50 cross-dressing men every night in August 1995; widespread public outrage led to the repeal of the law under which these arrests were conducted.

Also particularly targeted in many countries are boys and girls who do not conform to cultural gender norms. For example, a Turkish man testified at a United Nations tribunal in 1995 that due to his childhood effeminacy he was constantly taunted, beaten, stalked, robbed, and sexually assaulted by other schoolboys. His terror became so extreme that he—like other effeminate boys he knew—tied his penis in an attempt to avoid having to urinate and thus enter the school bathroom. The extreme and continuous abuse experienced by children who do not conform to dominant gender roles forces many of them ultimately to drop out of school.

Violence against lesbians is less well documented than that against gay men, probably due in large part to the social invisibility of lesbians within both the dominant culture and homosexual subcultures. In many places, women are not permitted to establish communities or participate in public life, and the very existence of lesbians is denied. Lesbians most typically are victimized when their behaviors interfere with male privileges or property rights. For example, women who will not marry, who request divorces, or who refuse to terminate same-sex love affairs face punishment by male suitors, husbands, or family members. Frequent forms of punishment are rape and beating. For example, a Zimbabwean woman reported that when her parents learned of her lesbianism, they locked her in a room with an older man who raped her daily, in order that she become pregnant and be forced to marry. Similarly, an Iranian woman who refused to curtail her lesbian relationship was severely beaten by her father and brothers and then repeatedly raped by the man whom they forced her to marry. In addition to physical abuse, one of the most severe punishments faced by lesbians is state-sanctioned theft of their children based on judicial decisions that their sexuality makes them unfit parents.

The emergence of fundamentalist religious movements has brought with it an upsurge of violence against homosexuals in some regions of the world. This is primarily due to the extreme hostility with which these movements regard homosexuality; extremists in both the Islamic and Christian religions have called for the execution of homosexuals. Thus, homosexuals are much more negatively regarded in fundamentalist Iran than in the traditionally Islamic nation of Morocco. And in the Australian island-state of Tasmania, a 1990s campaign to eradicate laws against sodomy was met with mass protest rallies by Christian fundamentalists and distribution of a poster depicting two dead men and captioned, "Stop AIDS now: execute homos." (After a 7-year effort, the sodomy law was overturned in early 1997.)

Another late-20th century phenomenon that is blamed for violence against homosexuals is the AIDS epidemic. The unprecedented increase in media attention to gay and lesbian issues that coincided with the AIDS epidemic—especially in the United States and Western Europe—may have simultaneously increased public acceptance as well as antigay violence by the most extreme opponents of homosexuality. The double-edged nature of increased visibility was illustrated in Zimbabwe in 1996, when a government-inspired crackdown against a local gay organization distributing AIDS literature at an international book fair led to mob harassment and threats of physical violence but, at the same time, an outpouring of international support and a doubling of membership in the gay organization.

In cultures that lack social roles and identities based on sexual orientation, legal and extralegal violence against homosexuals is typically less common. Antihomosexual violence is also less common in some Buddhist-dominated countries that were never colonized by European powers, such as Thailand and Japan. In these countries, traditional same-sex behaviors are not equatable with Western gay identity, most homosexuals are not public about their sexuality, and violence is not an officially sanctioned response. Compared to countries with high rates of antihomosexual violence, those with low rates of antihomosexual violence also tend to have generally lower rates of violent crime.

III. PATTERNS OF VICTIMIZATION

The primary targets of antihomosexual violence are individuals who are perceived as gay men or lesbians because of their attire, mannerisms, interactions with a same-sex partner, or presence in gay-identified settings. Thus, victims include not only gay men, lesbians, and bisexuals, but also heterosexuals who attend gay events and establishments or who fit popular stereotypes of a homosexual. As mentioned earlier, people who cross-dress are frequent targets of antihomosexual violence, whether or not they are homosexual. In addition, boys who do not conform to the dominant cultural norm of appropriate masculine behavior or appearance are often ridiculed and assaulted as "sissies" and "fags." Similarly, women who decline men's sexual advances are subject to being attacked as "dykes" and "lezzies."

Although efforts have been made to document violence against homosexuals in Australia, Germany, and a few other industrialized nations, the best documentation has come from the United States, where interest in the phenomenon increased dramatically among political groups and policymakers during the 1980s and 1990s. Thus, the following section focuses on research conducted in the United States.

A. Forms of Victimization

The National Gay and Lesbian Task Force (NGLTF) in Washington, D.C., began collecting annual statistics from local victim service agencies in 1984. They classified incidents as antihomosexual based on a set of standardized criteria, including: (a) use of antihomosexual or AIDS-related language; (b) history of similar antihomosexual incidents in an area; and (c) evidence that victims were targeted due to homosexual appearance or behavior (e.g., gay slogans on apparel or same-sex hand-holding). The NGLTF recorded significantly more incidents than did law enforcement agencies in the same cities and during the same time period, probably due to a combination of factors. These include victim reluctance to report to police, police indifference or hostility when victims do seek help, and police failure to classify crimes as bias-related.

Of the 2064 incidents collected by the NGLTF from nine local agencies in 1995, 43% involved physical assaults or attempted assaults, resulting in injuries to about one in four victims. Slightly less than half of assaults were committed with weapons, most commonly bats, clubs, bottles, bricks, rocks, and knives. Other incidents involved harassment, intimidation, police abuse, robbery, sexual assault, bombings of gay establishments, and other property offenses.

Homicides in which the victim's sexuality is determined to be a factor frequently manifest extreme brutality or "forensic overkill"—gratuitous violence involving multiple lethal methods, mutilation, dismemberment, or more than three gunshot or stab wounds. Gay men who frequent secluded cruising spots are at particular risk of being murdered by serial killers and robbers. In one study of 151 sexuality-related homicides between 1992 and 1994, half of the killings involved a "pickup" at a gay bar or cruising area. More than one-fourth of the incidents involved robbery, and 16% were committed by serial murderers who prey on gay men. The number of middle-aged victims contrasted sharply with general crime statistics; 30% of victims were between 45 and 64 years of age, compared with 12% of all U.S. homicide victims. Killers of lesbians appear more likely than those of gay men to know their victims. For example, in 1997 a popular track star and wrestler was beaten with a claw hammer and stabbed with four kitchen knives by her husband, who suspected a lesbian affair.

Verbal harassment is by far the most frequent form of victimization experienced by lesbians and gay men. Because it is not illegal in most cases, it is rarely reported. However, because it is often a prelude to violence, with victims usually unable to know whether a particular verbal incident will escalate to violence, verbal harassment constitutes a routine reminder of ever-present threat and, thus, may be considered a symbolic form of violence.

In addition to pervasive verbal harassment and the constant threat of physical violence, sexual minorities face a number of less visible but equally injurious forms of oppression. These include arbitrary arrest, involuntary psychiatric treatment, revocation of parental rights, forced marriages, and immigration restrictions. Homosexuals are routinely subjected to discrimination in employment, housing, public accommodations, and other services. In addition, societal invisibility and the denial of homosexuals' relationships take a deep psychological toll.

B. Prevalence Rates

Crime prevalence rates in the United States are derived from police report data and from national surveys of the general population. Relying on such methods to determine the prevalence of violence against homosexuals is problematic, however.

Police report data are unreliable because law enforcement agencies in many communities do not routinely track crimes based on the victim's sexual orientation. Moreover, many victims do not reveal their sexual orientation to police—or do not even report their victimization—because they fear secondary victimization, such as abuse by police or public exposure that might jeopardize employment, housing, or family relations if their homosexuality is publicly revealed. As homosexuality becomes less stigmatized and as law enforcement agencies take affirmative steps to combat the violence and to reach out to gay communities, gay men and lesbians may become more willing to report crimes committed against them because of their sexual orientation.

The other sources of prevalence data—national victimization surveys based on large probability samples—historically have not included questions about sexual orientation. Consequently, estimates of the prevalence of antihomosexual violence have necessarily been based on findings from surveys conducted with nonrepresentative samples. Although the findings from such samples cannot be generalized to the entire U.S. gay and lesbian population, they indicate that being homosexual—like belonging to a historically oppressed racial, ethnic, or religious group—places one at significantly greater risk than the general population for verbal harassment, vandalism, physical assault, sexual assault, and murder. Most gay men and lesbians who are surveyed report having experienced verbal abuse based on their sexual orientation. Although physical assault is less common, it is a significant problem, experienced by approximately one-fifth of the respondents to community surveys.

Due to the nonrepresentative nature of existing victimization data, it is unclear whether victimization rates differ by racial group. Anecdotal evidence suggests that racial differences do exist in at least some parts of the world. For example, aboriginal Australians and U.S. African Americans who are gay or lesbian may be at greater risk for police assault, in particular.

Many law enforcement officials, victim-service workers, and gay and lesbian activists believe that violence against homosexuals increased during the 1980s in the United States. They base this conclusion on an observed increase in the number of incidents reported to victim assistance groups and to police bias crime units, as well as data from longitudinal studies conducted by academic researchers. Various explanations have been offered for this apparent increase, including the growing visibility of gay and lesbian people during this period, increasing polarization of heterosexuals' attitudes toward gay people, and greater willingness of gay victims to report their experiences to the criminal justice system. The advent of the AIDS epidemic and its early perception as a "gay plague" in the United States has frequently been cited as a factor in the escalating violence. Indeed, victim service agencies recorded many antigay incidents during the 1980s that involved verbal references to AIDS or attacks on people with AIDS. However, AIDS may be less a cause of antigay sentiment than a new justification for violence by already-biased individuals.

Whether or not the violence is increasing, research with perpetrators themselves confirms that the problem is endemic in the United States. In a 1995 survey of noncriminal young adults in the San Francisco Bay area, almost 1 in 5 men admitted to physically assaulting or threatening people whom they believed were homosexual, with much larger percentages of both men and women admitting antigay name-calling. Reflecting the socially normative nature of these behaviors among U.S. youth, particularly males, 1 in 10 respondents reported that their male friends had "hit, kicked, or beaten" homosexuals.

C. Settings

Violence against gay men and lesbians occurs in a variety of venues, ranging from private residences to public settings (e.g., streets, nightclubs, workplaces, sports events) and institutions (e.g., schools, penal institutions, the military). Assaults committed within institutional and family settings are rarely reported to police, although by some estimates they form the large bulk of the violence.

Stranger-on-stranger violence in public settings is the most visible and publicized form of the violence. It is typified by assaults committed by young males, often in groups, as well as beatings by police. The emergence of specifically gay districts in major cities, as well as public events such as gay pride parades and celebrations, have made it increasingly easy for would-be assailants to locate homosexual targets. In addition, men who pursue anonymous sex with other men are easy targets for opportunistic muggings in public "cruising" locations. If they have public identities as heterosexuals, men victimized in these latter settings are especially unlikely to report assaults to the police.

Violence against homosexuals is commonplace in institutional settings, such as prisons, workplaces, and military forces. In male prisons, the most common form of assault is rape. Although in the United States an estimated one-fifth of all male inmates are sexually abused during confinement, the rate of victimization is significantly higher for homosexual men, as well as for inmates who are particularly youthful or effeminate. Prison administrators historically have ignored the problem or attributed it to inmates' openness about being gay.

Violence and harassment are endemic in elementary and secondary schools. Surveys have found that teenagers react more negatively to homosexuals than to any other minority group, and even make gratuitous threats of antigay violence in their survey responses. Homosexual students often do not report abuse out of fear of retribution by their tormentors. Instead, constant bullying and beatings by classmates force many visibly homosexual youths to leave school. In a landmark 1996 civil rights case, a young Wisconsin man received $900,000 from his former school district after a federal jury ruled that school administrators had knowingly allowed other students to harass and assault him over a 5-year period. He had quit school and attempted suicide after he was urinated on, repeatedly beaten, and subjected to a mock rape during which 20 students looked on and jeered. School administrators had ignored multiple pleas by the victim and his parents and had told him he should expect such treatment for being openly gay.

Effeminate boys are particularly likely to face violence in their homes. Retrospective research with adult male homosexuals indicates they were significantly more likely to have been physically abused by their parents than were comparable heterosexual controls, particularly if they engaged in feminine behaviors as children or in gay sex as adolescents.

D. Sex Differences in Victimization

Compared with gay men, lesbians appear to experience fewer beatings and attacks with weapons but higher rates of sexual harassment, rape, verbal abuse, and victimization by family members. Although antilesbian violence is widespread, it frequently goes unreported. Gay men are consistently more likely than lesbians to report their bias-related victimization to police and community agencies.

Patterns of specifically anti-lesbian assault include: (a) assaults on women leaving lesbian bars; (b) attacks on lesbian couples in which the women are forced to watch each other's victimization; (c) assaults in which heterosexual men pose as gay men to befriend lesbians, often in settings such as mixed-sex gay bars; (d) assaults by former husbands or male lovers on women who reveal their lesbianism; and (e) assaults on women who enter certain male domains, such as traditionally all-male work forces. Men are overwhelmingly responsible for antilesbian attacks. Some evidence also suggests that assailants of lesbians tend to be older and more socially powerful than assailants of gay men.

A notable feature of violence against lesbians is the extreme difficulty in separating it from harassment of women in general. This is in marked contrast to attacks on gay men, since men typically are not attacked because of their sex. Lesbians often report that attacks begin as antiwoman and then escalate to antilesbian when a woman responds in what is perceived as a nonfeminine manner, such as by answering back to her attacker. Indeed, some lesbian assault victims have expressed doubt that their assailants even knew they were lesbians, conjecturing that the assailants used antilesbian accusations as the ultimate insult. Lesbian-baiting effectively controls the social behavior of women, particularly in traditionally all-male domains such as the armed forces.

IV. PSYCHOLOGICAL AND SOCIAL CONSEQUENCES

Gay men and lesbians face unique psychological and social challenges when they are victimized because of their sexual orientation. One risk is that they may associate their sexuality with the heightened sense of vulnerability that typically follows criminal victimization, feeling that they were justifiably punished for being gay and experiencing their sexuality as a source of danger and punishment. Lesbian and gay male bias crime victims exhibit higher rates of psychological distress—including depression, stress, and anger—compared to those who experience crimes not based on their sexuality. Heterosexuals who are mistakenly perceived as gay in a bias crime attack are also at risk for psychological problems, such as self-doubts about their sexuality.

Bias crimes also have other consequences. As noted earlier, reporting an attack places the victim at risk for secondary victimization by police or family members. Furthermore, gay men and lesbians who had not publicly disclosed their sexual orientation prior to the attack may subsequently lose employment, housing, or child custody if they are exposed. Relentless harassment and violence in certain settings may also make life unbearable, forcing targeted individuals to terminate school, employment, or military posts and to seek alternative housing.

Violence also has potential environmental consequences. Just as the threat of rape has a repressive effect on all women, violence against individual homosexuals pressures lesbians and gay men as a group to restrict their day-to-day activities and conceal their sexual identities. To reduce their own feelings of vulnerability, some homosexuals may blame victims of violence for being too open about their sexuality, thus reinforcing the prescription that men and women must conform to highly restrictive norms of gender-appropriate behavior. The endemic nature of antihomosexual harassment in elementary and secondary schools also teaches heterosexuals at a young age that they must conform to stereotypical gender roles and restrict their expressions of physical affection for members of their own sex.

V. CULTURAL CONTEXT

Because heterosexism has been promulgated by major societal institutions such as the courts, medicine, religion, and the mass media, it is ubiquitous in most parts of the world. This cultural climate of denigration allows widespread violence against homosexuals to go largely unpunished, clearly conveying the message that gay people do not deserve full legal protection and justice.

The legal tradition of heterosexism was cogently expressed in *Bowers v. Hardwick,* the 1986 U.S. Supreme Court decision permitting states to outlaw homosexual behavior, which held that condemnation of homosexuality "is firmly rooted in Judeo-Christian moral and ethical standards." In 1997, approximately 84 countries and nearly half of the U.S. states had laws on the books prohibiting sex between two men and, in many cases, two women. By defining homosexuals as criminals and deviants, these laws provided moral justification for violence against gay men and lesbians.

Judicial disdain for homosexual victims also encourages perpetrators to believe they will face no significant consequences if caught. The so-called "homosexual panic defense," in which assailants claim they acted in self-defense against homosexual overtures, has resulted in lenient sentences and even acquittals in U.S. courts. By shifting responsibility from the perpetrator to the victim, this defense appeals strongly to the cultural stereotype of gay people as sexually predatory. Judges have often perpetuated this victim-blaming. In a Florida murder trial, for example, the judge joked, "That's a crime now, to beat up a homosexual?" And in a Texas case the judge explained his light sentence for the killing of two gay men by saying, "I put prostitutes and queers at about the same level . . . and I'd be hard put to give somebody life for killing a prostitute."

In the field of medicine, homosexuals have been victimized since the 19th century by attempted "cures" such as castration, hysterectomy, lobotomy, drug therapies, and shock treatment. Although homosexuality was removed from the Diagnostic and Statistical Manual of the American Psychiatric Association in 1973, the International Classification of Diseases has continued to label homosexuality as a mental illness, and many medical practitioners outside of the United States continue to regard homosexual behavior as pathological. Homosexuals—especially adolescents—are still disproportionately hospitalized in mental institutions, where they are often physically and emotionally abused due to their sexuality.

In religion, luminaries in both Christian and Jewish faiths have vociferously condemned homosexuality for centuries. Although some denominations began to express more tolerance during the 1980s and 1990s, others maintained a strong antigay stance. In 1986, for example, a Roman Catholic proclamation opposing civil rights protections for homosexuals was widely interpreted as condoning antigay violence.

Most virulent among modern religious institutions are the fundamentalist movements of the late 20th century. Both Christian and Islamic fundamentalist leaders have publicly advocated execution of homosexuals.

Christian fundamentalists in particular have used homosexuality as a primary organizing issue. Casting civil rights for homosexuals as "special rights" for perverts and child molesters, they have warned that homosexual proselytizers are "on the advance" against heterosexuals. Their militaristic rhetoric thus coats antihomosexual violence with a moralistic veneer. The Internet provides a far-reaching forum for dissemination of inflammatory propaganda through World Wide Web sites with titles such as "Homosexuals: A Clear and Present Danger to Our Children," "AIDS and God's Wrath," and "The True Objective of 'Gay Rights': Total Domination!"

Inseparable from the Christian fundamentalists in their virulent opposition to homosexuality have been right-wing political extremists, who are particularly active in parts of Europe, the United States, Canada, and the former Soviet Union. While most violence against homosexuals is not directly committed by organized extremists, their rhetoric—part of a larger ideology of racism, xenophobia, anti-Semitism, and anti-feminism—has undoubtedly encouraged potential perpetrators. In the United States during the 1990s, for example, temporary and dramatic upswings in regional violence consistently accompanied conservative campaigns for laws barring civil rights protections for homosexuals.

During most of the 20th century, media portrayals mirrored the heterosexist ideologies of the churches and courtrooms, providing almost universally negative portrayals of homosexuality. In cinema, homosexual characters were depicted through negative stereotypes and were inordinately likely to die through suicide or murder. In children's cartoons, implicitly homosexual characters were set up for ridicule and violence. On the radio, "shock jocks" intensified popular sentiments against homosexuality through inflammatory rhetoric, for example advertising special offers for "beating up queers" and advocating the castration of "fags" to stop AIDS. Several popular songs of the 1980s and 1990s advocated beating or shooting "sissy" gays, and "White power" music such as Berserkr's "Crush the Weak" and Nordic Thunder's "Born to Hate" unabashedly promoted violence.

By the mid-1990s, however, a trend toward more positive depiction of homosexuals had gained sway in the media, particularly on television. During the 1990s, the number of homosexual characters in U.S. television network series increased steadily. Heralded as a major turning point was the 1997 "coming out" of "Ellen" on the TV situation comedy of the same name, marking the first openly homosexual leading character on network television. Meanwhile, the popular daytime soap opera *All My Children* directly tackled the issue of antigay violence when it depicted a gay teacher who acknowledged his sexuality while teaching about World War II and the Holocaust; violence subsequently erupted when one of his students told a heterosexist brother that he too was gay.

VI. PERPETRATORS

Perpetrators come from all economic classes and racial groups, and most do not have serious criminal records or known psychiatric disorders. The profile of a typical assailant as described in victim reports is a young male, usually acting in concert with other young males, all of them strangers to the victims. Due to the nature of crime reporting, this profile underrepresents violence within families and institutions.

It has not yet been established whether the same types of individuals attack homosexuals and members of racial, ethnic, or religious minorities. Nor is it known whether the same motivations underlie bias-driven crimes against different minority groups. One study of Boston-area hate crimes found little distinction among perpetrators based on victim category. Minority-group victims were selected by thrill-seeking adolescents based primarily on perceived vulnerability and included homosexuals as well as Latinos, Asians, African Americans, and Jews.

However, crime statistics and assailant interviews suggest at least two discontinuities among victim groups. First, homosexual victims report a significantly greater proportion of crimes against persons (rather than property) than do racial and religious minorities. Second, assailants themselves report less fear of consequences when assaulting homosexuals than other minorities, based on their beliefs that homosexuals are universally despised and are unlikely to fight back. Indeed, a 1988 statewide survey of public school students in New York showed that an alarming number of teenagers viewed homosexuals as legitimate targets that can be openly attacked.

Although the term *hate crime* conjures up images of swastikas, burning crosses, bigoted zealots, and a right-wing fringe far removed from America's more socially tolerant center, many assailants express relatively little animosity toward homosexuals. The everyday nature of so-called "gay-bashings" by young males suggests that it is a type of transient offense committed primarily as a result of environmental rather than internal psychological factors.

Like much other violence, violence against homosexuals can be distinguished by whether it is primarily *instrumental* or *symbolic*. Instrumental violence is aimed chiefly at achieving a utilitarian goal. In symbolic violence, individuals are attacked based on the symbolic meanings of the social category to which they belong.

A. Instrumental Motivations

Instrumental motivations—most chiefly robbery—are particularly prevalent in crimes against gay men. Robbers seek out gay men due to three factors: (a) the stereotype that they are wealthy; (b) the belief that they are low-risk adversaries because they are unlikely to fight back or to report assaults; and (c) the expectation that men cruising for sex can be lured to deserted locations where victimization is relatively easy. The proportion of violence against gay men that is at least partially driven by instrumental motivations is difficult to determine from victimization data, as many victims do not report such crimes. However, it appears that robbery is a factor in a significant minority of gay-related homicides and other crimes, suggesting that instrumental motivations are commonplace.

B. Symbolic Motivations

Symbolically motivated assailants can be divided into two primary types—one whose primary aim is to express heterosexist values and the other driven more by developmental, social, and environmental factors than by their belief systems, with cultural heterosexism providing a perceived sense of permission to assault homosexuals. Among both types, cultural gender-norm stereotypes and expectations appear to be more influential than individual hostility toward gay men and lesbians. In addition, ego-defensive motivations appear to drive a minority of assailants.

1. Value-Expressive Violence

Value-expressive assailants view themselves as social norms enforcers who are punishing homosexuals for moral transgressions. The four most common transgressions of which they accuse homosexuals are violation of gender norms, violation of religious or natural law, sexual predation, and—in the case of lesbians—failure to obey men.

As discussed earlier, religious and political extremists frequently invoke religious or natural law in their antihomosexual rhetoric. Thus, assailants may cite the Bible as proof that homosexuality is "unnatural" or evil.

In this way, they justify their law-breaking as in the service of higher moral authority.

Many value-expressive assailants also express vehement objection not so much to homosexuality itself but to visible challenges to essential gender norms, such as public "flaunting" of sexual nonconformity or male effeminacy. Indeed, until the past few decades, homosexuality was popularly viewed in many Western countries more as a deviant *gender identity* than a matter of sexual attraction. Homosexuals were assumed to be effeminate men and masculine women who rejected their socially proscribed sex roles. The conflation of homosexuality with deviant gender behavior explains the disproportionate victimization of individuals who do not conform to gender roles, regardless of whether they are homosexual or heterosexual. Gender-norm enforcers often make calculated use of antigay epithets such as "faggot" and "cocksucker" to assess masculinity, with contempt and ridicule leveled at men who do not respond physically to such provocation, in much the same way as these terms are deployed in hypermasculine sports culture.

Two patterns of specifically antilesbian violence—one in the private sphere and one in the public—suggest that presumed lesbians are often victimized in order to punish them for defying patriarchal control. In one pattern, husbands and boyfriends assault women who reveal their lesbianism. In the other pattern, women who answer back to male catcalls or other intimidating behavior are attacked as lesbians. The more patriarchal a particular society or subculture, the more pervasive these patterns appear to be.

A dramatic example of how these value-expressive themes may work in tandem was the 1994 murder of 20-year-old Teena Brandon and two friends in Nebraska. Brandon, a woman who had passed as a man in a small town, was beaten and raped by two former male friends when they learned of her biological sex. When the local sheriff refused to arrest the pair, they returned to Brandon's house, stabbed and shot her to death, and then murdered her girlfriend and a male friend. Brandon was attacked to punish her for violating gender norms by presenting herself as a man; her girlfriend was murdered for eschewing male control by dating Brandon. These punishments are understood and sanctioned in popular culture; commenting on the case, one television comedian joked that the victims "deserved to die."

Many individuals who engage in physical confrontations with homosexuals later perceive their actions as justified self-defense against sexual aggression. They interpret the words, actions, and demeanors of presumed homosexuals based on the cultural stereotype of homosexuals as sexual predators. Any glance, smile, or conversation by an individual believed to be homosexual is interpreted as sexual flirtation. Their underlying cognitive schema are (a) that homosexuals are solely—and indiscriminately—sexual beings; (b) that homosexuality is based on predation, that is, aggressive attempts to seduce heterosexual victims; and (c) that violence is the appropriate response to any type of sexual advance from a person of one's same sex. These schema are constantly reinforced through the subjectivity involved in interpreting eye contact and casual banter. Even heterosexuals who have never assaulted or harassed a homosexual may feel that doing so would be justified in response to a flirtation or sexual proposition. The sense of cultural permission to engage in antigay violence was exemplified in 1995 when a heterosexual man murdered a gay man who had verbally disclosed a long-standing attraction to him on a television talk show. Particularly revealing in that case was the popular perception that the television show's producers had humiliated the heterosexual man and thus were responsible for the murder.

2. Social-Expressive Violence

Membership in a social group is often a central component of one's identity. Attacking a social outgroup can help individuals to feel more positive about their own group and, consequently, about themselves. In the case of violence against gay men and lesbians, this type of social-expressive motivation is exemplified in adolescent rites of passage, thrill-seeking by the disenfranchised, and increased gay-bashing during periods of economic or social unrest.

In the first instance, assaults on homosexuals provide an ideal means for adolescent males to prove their masculine identity to their peers. Through assaulting homosexuals, young men prove that they are heterosexual, tough, and dominant over everything feminine, all prerequisites for masculine identity. In addition, group assaults on homosexuals can foster camaraderie and cohesion within the peer group, which is particularly important during adolescence.

Adolescents who assault homosexuals in peer-group circumstances frequently deny personal antagonism toward homosexuals. They acknowledge the harm visited upon victims, but minimize their own roles and freedom of choice. This pattern is consistent with a body of delinquency research indicating that much group criminality results from collective processes in which individual participants feel little sense of personal control.

A related contributor to assaults on homosexuals

is adolescent boredom and social alienation. Lacking constructive roles in society and feeling powerless and uncertain about their futures, teenagers may focus their fears and anxieties on a socially ostracized scapegoat. Both male and female assailants who reflect this pattern typically minimize the level of harm to their victims and depict incidents as amusing, describing their goals as having fun and excitement.

Vilification of social outgroups is typically exacerbated by economic and social downturns. Homosexuals have long functioned as an ideal scapegoat in such circumstances. As discussed earlier, homosexuality was used as an excuse for the persecution of Muslims, witches, and others during the Middle Ages. A contemporary example of this context for violence is in Bulgaria, where government officials incited confrontations against homosexuals and other social groups in 1997 in order to deflect public opinion from a ballooning inflation rate, floundering banking system, and shortages of basic foodstuffs. Similarly, in U.S. cities, economically and socially marginalized individuals are especially resentful of a minority that is widely portrayed not only as sinful but also as rich and privileged.

3. Ego-Defensive Violence

The folkloric explanation of antigay violence as an externalization of internal homosexual impulses appears to play a role in a minority of assaults committed by both males and females. In this motivation, homosexuals are attacked as symbols of unacceptable aspects of an assailant's own personality, such as homoerotic feelings or effeminate tendencies. For example, ego-defensiveness may be a factor in assaults by young males who are uncertain of their ability to meet cultural standards for masculinity. By attacking someone whom they perceive to symbolize the antithesis of masculinity (a homosexual man), they may be unconsciously attacking an unacceptable part of themselves.

The ego-defensive motivation is particularly relevant to understanding sexual assaults and assaults committed subsequent to sexual relations. It may explain the extreme brutality, or "forensic overkill," found in many homicides committed by heterosexually identified hustlers against gay male victims. It may also explain male-male rapes in which the rapist externalizes his homosexual arousal as caused by the victim's seductiveness and then punishes the victim through sexual assault.

VII. PREVENTION STRATEGIES

The 1980s and 1990s saw a dramatic upswing in organizing efforts by lesbians and gay men against vio-

lence. These efforts took a number of forms, including legislative drives, educational outreach, community mobilizations, and increased data collection and research efforts.

A. International Campaigns

Internationally, efforts to reduce violence and public hostility toward homosexuals have focused on legislative drives for anti-discrimination laws, repeal of sodomy statutes, and efforts to publicize and put an end to basic human rights violations. Considerable progress has been made in all three areas. In 1996, for example, the new government of South Africa took the historic step of becoming the first country in the world to ban all forms of discrimination against homosexuals. An international campaign for the repeal of sodomy laws—which have set a social tone of tolerance for both legal and extralegal violence against homosexuals—met with significant success during the 1990s. And increasing scrutiny by international human rights agencies helped to curtail some of the more extreme cases of mass arrests, torture, and police abuse of suspected homosexuals during the 1990s. In the wake of this heightened international focus, several countries—including Australia, Canada, and the United States—began granting refugee status to homosexuals attempting to escape violence and other types of persecution in their home countries.

On the local and national levels, gay and lesbian activists in several countries have mounted direct-action responses to violence. In East Berlin, thousands of gay men and lesbians marched through a neighborhood known as a neo-Nazi stronghold in response to a rash of neo-Nazi and skinhead violence targeting gay coffee shops and parties. In New South Wales, Australian activists' telephone survey of violence led to the establishment in 1990 of a joint government–community program called Streetwatch, aimed at documenting and reducing the violence. Police participation in this project was especially remarkable, given the historical enmity between police and homosexual communities in most parts of the world. The New South Wales police even conducted their own survey of lesbians in order to remedy the overemphasis on violence against men in Streetwatch statistics.

B. U.S. Efforts

In the United States, a combination of local and national efforts led to dramatic legislative and public policy changes, combined with significant changes in public opinion, during the 1990s.

In response to the perception of a significant rise in violence during the early 1980s, gay and lesbian activists established victim service agencies in more than a dozen U.S. cities. These agencies collect statistics, assist victims in reporting attacks to police, and monitor cases as they go through the criminal justice system. In the mid-1990s, many of these local agencies joined together in a collaborative project with a uniform reporting procedure.

Intensive lobbying by antiviolence activists, civil rights organizations, and concerned professionals led to the inclusion of homosexuals in the 1990 Hate Crimes Statistics Act, a modest law that encouraged local law enforcement agencies to voluntarily report hate crimes to the Federal Bureau of Investigation. Subsequent federal and state laws mandated enhanced sentencing for a variety of hate crimes, including those based on sexual orientation. By 1997, 16 U.S. states required stiffer penalties for crimes committed on the basis of sexual orientation. At the same time, efforts to include sexual orientation in hate crimes legislation were rebuffed in some states.

Academic researchers also paid increasing attention to the problem in the 1990s. Research in the behavioral and social sciences focused on various aspects of violence against homosexuals, including patterns in victimization, psychological effects on survivors, and the attitudes and motivations of perpetrators.

Other innovative responses to the violence have included the establishment of schools and street patrols. One early effort was the establishment in 1985 of the Harvey Milk School in New York City as a haven for gay and lesbian adolescents who had been driven out of traditional schools by relentless persecution. Street patrols, with names such as the Pink Panthers and the Q Patrol, walked the streets in gay districts, discouraging would-be assailants by recording automobile license numbers and distributing whistles that victims could use to call for help. Although many of the patrols were short-lived, due to the high degree of labor and organization required, they increased gay community awareness and resistance to violence.

Many lesbian and gay activists believe that the most effective long-term method of reducing violence is to change the cultural stereotypes that make homosexuals a socially permissible target, especially for adolescents and young adults. With this in mind, they have launched public opinion campaigns in the schools and the mass media. Efforts to teach school children about homosexuality have been introduced into larger anti-bias curriculums in several school districts around the United States. Teachers lead discussions aimed at correcting inaccurate beliefs, and gay and lesbian speakers are brought into classrooms to answer questions and counteract negative stereotypes. "Gay/Straight Student Alliances" and support groups for gay and lesbian youth also have been established in dozens of schools across the country. Research indicating that antigay assailants are more influenced by peers' opinions than parents' opinions about homosexuality suggests that such school-based interventions have utility. However, these programs have not been established on a widespread basis, largely due to vehement opposition by antigay individuals, political organizations, and religious groups.

One effect of school-based interventions is that they frequently encourage gay and lesbian teachers in those schools to be more open about their identities. Research indicating that personal contact with gay men and lesbians is correlated with more tolerant attitudes toward homosexuality suggests that the increasing public visibility of gay and lesbian teachers—and indeed homosexuals more generally—may ultimately contribute to a decrease in antigay violence.

Perceiving that mass media are often more influential than personal contacts in contemporary society, activists have turned significant attention to media portrayals of homosexuality. They have campaigned to end negative stereotypes that encourage violence and, simultaneously, to increase positive images of lesbians and gay men. The media watchdog group Gay and Lesbian Alliance Against Defamation has confronted film industry executives over movies that promote antigay violence or ridicule homosexuals and has targeted radio stations that broadcast antihomosexual slurs.

The combination of efforts on legislative, educational, and media levels appears to be dramatically changing public attitudes. Although most Americans in 1996 still believed that homosexuality was morally wrong, national surveys showed overwhelming support for equal employment rights. According to Gallup polls, for example, the percentage of Americans who supported equal job rights for homosexuals had skyrocketed in a two-decade period, from 56% in 1977 to 84% in 1996.

VIII. Conclusion

Antihomosexual violence is not always based on individual heterosexuals' animosity toward gay men and lesbians. People who assault homosexuals typically do not recognize themselves in the stereotypical image of the hate-filled extremist. Rather, the roots of such violence are complex and multidetermined, shaped by a variety of individual motivations and cultural factors. For this reason, the term "hate crime"—although potentially useful in the legal arena—can be misleading when applied to individual assailants. Indeed, violence against homosexuals is appropriately viewed as a hate crime not because of the motivations of individual assailants, but because it reinforces a climate of cultural hostility and effectively terrorizes all homosexual people, as well as heterosexuals who do not conform to societal gender norms. Understanding the complex causes of antigay violence is critical for reaching assailants and potential assailants with clinical and educational interventions.

Also See the Following Articles

GENDER STUDIES • HATE CRIMES • INSTITUTIONALIZATION OF VIOLENCE • POLICE BRUTALITY • SEXUAL ASSAULT • WOMEN, VIOLENCE AGAINST • YOUTH VIOLENCE

Bibliography

Boswell, J. (1980). *Christianity, social tolerance, and homosexuality.* Chicago: University of Chicago Press.

Cohen, H. S. (Producer), & Chasnoff, D. (Producer/Director). (1996). *It's Elementary: Talking about gay issues in school.* [Film]. (Available from Women's Educational Media, 2180 Bryant Street, Suite 203, San Francisco, CA 94110)

Comstock, G. D. (1991). *Violence against lesbians and gay men.* New York: Columbia University Press.

Dong, A. (Producer/Director). (1997). *Licensed to Kill.* [Film]. (Available from Deep Focus Productions, c/o Film Arts Foundation, 346 Ninth Street, San Francisco, CA 94103)

Franklin, K. (1996). Hate crime or rite of passage? Assailant motivations in antigay violence. Unpublished doctoral dissertation, California School of Professional Psychology.

Franklin, K. (1998). Unassuming motivations: Contextualizing the narratives of antigay assailants. In G. M. Herek (Ed.), *Stigma and sexual orientation: Understanding prejudice against lesbians, gay men, and bisexuals* (pp. 1–23). Thousand Oaks, CA: Sage.

Herek, G. M., & Berrill, K. T. (1992). *Hate crimes: Confronting violence against lesbians and gay men.* Newbury Park, CA: Sage.

Herek, G. M., Gillis, J. R., Cogan, J. C., & Glunt, E. K. (1997). Hate crime victimization among lesbian, gay, and bisexual adults: Prevalence, psychological correlates, and methodological issues. *Journal of Interpersonal Violence, 12,* 195–215.

Pharr, S. (1988). *Homophobia: A weapon of sexism.* Inverness, CA: Chardon Press.

Plant, R. (1986). *The pink triangle: The Nazi war against homosexuals.* New York: Henry Holt.

Rosenbloom, R. (1995). *Unspoken rules: Sexual orientation and women's human rights.* San Francisco, CA: International Gay and Lesbian Human Rights Commission.

Note: For additional international information, the World Wide Web is a good source. Search the web sites and links of Amnesty International, the International Gay and Lesbian Human Rights Commission, and the International Lesbian and Gay Association. For U.S. information, contact the National Gay and Lesbian Task Force, 1734 14th St., N.W., Washington, DC 20009.

Human Nature, Views of

James Chowning Davies

University of Oregon

I. INTRODUCTION

A general definition of human nature helps to appraise the wide variety of such definitions. Some of the views of human nature discussed here either state or imply that human nature is violent or at least intends to be. That is, humankind are naturally aggressive. Other views are more benign. Like beliefs about religion and politics, those about human nature vary widely but are held closely. Millions of people are Christian or Muslim or Confucian or Buddhist, and few of them ever move from one of these religions to another. The same is the case in ideological and partisan orientation in politics. And so it is also, in views of human nature.

Its discussion need no longer be left to philosophers or to theorists in psychology. Because it is possible to learn more about human nature by scientific investiga-

tion, it is possible to diminish the use of violence as a last-resort means of accomplishing ends that are naturally desired and that provide inherent satisfaction. The problem is akin to that facing global explorers and navigators in the 15th century: if you no longer suppose the earth is flat, it is much easier to get around the globe. The problem is also akin to cosmic navigation: if you no longer suppose that space and time are independent factors, it is much easier to understand and move around in the universe.

Before proposing a general definition of human nature, along with such definitions of the concepts violence and aggression, a statement of the great difficulty in establishing consensus is appropriate. Viewing human nature is like viewing the weather. In reality, sometimes it is warm and sunny and in reality sometimes it is one raging hurricane after another. Few people take themselves or others seriously when they say the weather is always benign or always malign. It is not quite so with views of human nature, or of the innateness of violence and aggression. The following discussion is not likely to end such preconceptions, but it may help understand them.

So *human nature* is defined here as those tendencies to behave whose roots are in the organism as it is programmed by the genes and as the innate, genetic potential is realized in the processes of human evolution (phylogenesis) and of individual development (ontogenesis).

Violence is here defined as behavior whose effect is to injure real human beings or to destroy material objects. The term violence is best used rather strictly. To

Copyright © 1999 by Academic Press.
All rights of reproduction in any form reserved.

attribute violent tendencies to a person simply because of nationality, skin color, wealth, religion, and so on, is confusing. To define violence so broadly establishes a catch-all bag of unpleasant or wrongful acts, and it grossly reduces the ability for people not only to agree but to agree as to what they are talking about. It is like saying a person who takes one drink is a drunk; or who drives one mile per hour over the speed limit a driving maniac.

Aggression is defined as the deliberate, intended effort to harm people or destroy property. Again, it is well to define rather narrowly. When Person A attacks Person B because B threatened A—or at least A thought B did—it is a little easier to sort things out and establish responsibility if we say that A started the dispute and was the first aggressor. A initiated the first harmful act, and B was the second aggressor, initiating the responsive harmful act. That is, both A and B are aggressors: each intended to harm the other and we cannot determine who is culpable by declaring only one the aggressor.

The same goes for nations: when Nation A launches a surprise ground or missile attack on Nation B, charging that B threatened A, it muddles analysis to say that A was not acting aggressively. This is to say that both attack and defense can be aggressive, and one is jumping to a moral conclusion to say that defensive acts are never aggressive.

Aggressiveness is the underlying general tendency. It is easy and treacherous to conflate the tendency and the act: that is, both individuals and nations attack because they think their adversary is aggressive, even though the adversary has not engaged in aggression. Aggression and aggressiveness are two percepts that remain hard to distinguish, even verbally.

Agonistic is sometimes employed to objectify and neutralize the negative connotation of aggressive. Some writers have said the set is aggression and agonism is the subset; some have said just the opposite. But either substituting or adding the term agonistic does not lessen the difficulty of making clear just what is the subject of discussion. Attempting to neutralize analysis by using the term agonistic may blur the distinction between positive and negative intention but it does not eliminate it. So the term *assertive* is used here to denote interaction that is positive, and *aggressive* is used as negative interaction, the kind that aims to do harm or injury. *Assertive* and *aggressive* are regarded here as equal and parallel categories of analysis.

Experiences—far more critically than formal learning—establish the general attitudes that people have about each other as human beings and therefore about human nature. The experiences that produce elemental orientations begin at birth and continue through childhood, adolescence, and at least early maturity. One's attitudes toward his or her fellow beings are very stable, like one's religion and one's political orientation. Theorists who deal with human nature as a concept tend not to appreciate the role of experience, direct and indirect, as it establishes enduring values and attitudes.

Experience can be either direct and interpersonal or indirect and vicarious. Perhaps usually it is both. In the latter, individuals use the speaking and writing of others to interpret direct experience. If individuals start life in families and neighborhoods that are high in violence and later experience nonviolent interactions in solving problems, they may change to a less violent view of human nature. If individuals start life with minimal domestic violence and later experience violent interactions, they may more easily retain or reestablish a less violent view of human nature. Nevertheless, individuals from a stable, relatively nonviolent culture may go to war and kill. These killers are not usually dangerous when they return to civilian life nor are they so regarded. They are often treated as heroes. Violence is often a life-or-death matter, and the wrong attitude can be deadly.

Writers, readers, speakers, and listeners alike are inclined to regard their own views as objective, without considering the subjective role of experience in forming them. Both tend to believe that their views of moral right and wrong are based solely on an abstract and absolute truth, on precepts that are canonical and that are formed without subjective evaluation.

It may seem insulting to say that great writers are more influenced by their own experience than by what they have read. On the contrary, if writers or anyone else were more influenced by what they read than by what they experience, knowledge would become static and ever further divorced from reality. The assumption that the world was the center of the universe and God made it so was passed on for centuries before direct investigations by Copernicus in the mid-16th century and by Galileo in the 17th century asserted that it was not.

II. SOME EARLIER, MOSTLY PHILOSOPHICAL VIEWS OF HUMAN NATURE

Not all the writers considered here described themselves as philosophers. Indeed some of them—notably

Hobbes and Freud—scorned the term. Nonetheless, they are here included as philosophers rather than as scientists, on the assumption that their preconceptions and observations rose mainly from their individual experience rather than from systematic, scientific investigation, experimentation, and validation. This is not to say that these viewers of human nature were wrong because they are scientists but that, in their views of human nature, they were not acting as scientists. Because of his enormous prestige as a theorist in nuclear physics, Albert Einstein was credited with being an authority on the nature of man, in the joint essay he wrote with Sigmund Freud (1933). Such association has perhaps been less harmful than was the practice in the Soviet Union of crediting Stalin with omniscience.

Plato, more than two millennia before Hobbes, proposed government by the guardians, by vesting total power in the active intellectual elite. Like his successor Hobbes, Plato did not adequately address the problem of who governs the governors: both philosophers avoided logically facing the fact that rulers also are human beings and so much appraise their own violent tendencies. Plato seemed to believe that those who were not guardians did not want power; Hobbes said everybody wanted power and fought for it incessantly.

Aristotle, Plato's protégé, used somewhat different language than is used today, and he looked at violence causally. He concluded that revolution is caused by subjective inequality:

When inferior, people enter into strife in order that they may be equal, and when equal, in order that they may be greater." And he added that "the motives of gain and honor also stir men up against each other, . . . and when men in office show insolence and greed, people rise in revolt against one another. . . . (Aristotle, *Politics*, pp. 379–381).

He was the tutor of one of the most successfully violent rulers of all time: Alexander the Great. More than two millennia later George Orwell produced the succinct aphorism about life in the very unjust *Animal Farm*. In that anti-Utopia, the ruling elite had total control of both power and ideology: everyone is equal, the elite said, but some are more equal than others. It is perhaps more accurate to describe Aristotle and Orwell not as prescient but as intuitively basic in their analyses. They both said that human beings naturally expect to be regarded as equals, if not more so: as it would now be expressed, and as Lasswell put it, people want dignity and power.

Thomas Hobbes provides an example of environmental influences that profoundly affected his view of violence. He was in exile from the persistent and frightful civil war of the Protestant Reformation in 17th-century England, during which England for a time became a republic under Oliver Cromwell's domination. Hobbes fled England, to avoid persecution because of his outspoken antagonistic position on contested political issues. He was thus a participant-observer in this very violent century in England's history.

His experience led him to view human nature as inherently, innately violent and he said this tendency is controllable only if people surrendered their power of self-rule to the sovereign. Hobbes generally shared the view of many people in the 20th century regarding humankind as creatures who were survivalists and if they could be tamed, should be socialized like sheep in a flock. Unlike Aristotle before him and Lasswell in the 20th century, Hobbes did not work into his system a recognition that people want other things in addition to power. The inevitable implication of his conclusion is that self-rule is impossible, and, in the English Reformation, he did not consider that people who lacked power were forcibly demanding it and—if they won enough battles—taking it. Like many observers of wars and violence in the 20th century, Hobbes did not consider that people want anything besides power, and turn violent when they are denied it. From such a starting point, it is easy to say that violence is an innate drive.

Views of human nature in the late-18th and 19th centuries heavily emphasized the environment as a determinant of behavior. In the writings of John Locke, Rousseau, and Marx two assumptions were dominant. One is that people are naturally good and get damaged by harmful experience. The other is that the mind is pretty much a blank sheet, on which the environment can write pretty much what it wants. That is, Locke, Rousseau, and Marx are credited also with making the moral judgment that it is institutions, both social and political, that are responsible for failing to let human beings achieve what they naturally want to achieve. This basic assumption, supposedly objective, was regarded as amoral: that is, it dealt with the *is*. But it spilled over into the *ought* and became the basis for moral principle: people's natural virtue, natural goodness, was the natural condition of human interaction. It was damaged, even destroyed by social and political practices and institutions that made constructive, supportive interaction difficult, if not impossible. The good, the peaceful society could be achieved by opening up or destroying institutions that were harmful, or that society could be achieved by deliberate conditioning of people to virtuous action.

Early in the 20th century, perhaps partly because of the strong and pervasive influence of Marx, environmentalism flourished. Ivan Pavlov did brilliant new work in conditioning responses in dogs, making them drool when they had established a relationship between a bell ringing or a light turning on when they were rewarded with food. This work was elementally consistent with the Marxist assumptions of the revolutionary government after 1917 in Russia and got strong support from the Communist regimes. Similar work was established in the United States, first by J. B. Watson, who said that if he were given an infant, he could make out of him virtually any kind of skilled human being— butcher, baker, candlestick maker. B. F. Skinner extended the work of Pavlov by getting pigeons to respond to a conditioning stimulus of light or whatever. Extrapolating from pigeons to human beings, he proposed establishing a good society by operant conditioning, which was the responsibility of psychologists. It was not clear whether Skinner was influenced by Plato's proposal to put the intellectual elite of guardians in control, but the implication was clear: that a small group of specialists could manipulate the bulk of humankind in the best interests of both the specialists and humankind. Again, this was a matter not simply of objective observation but of moral necessity, and if psychologists can condition pigeons, they can condition human beings.

Heavy emphasis on environment not only frees individuals of responsibility for the existence and the development of institutions. It also produces a dead end in scientific pursuit of understanding: if genes and human nature do not generate needs, demands, expectations, then from where comes the energy and direction that make people behave in destructive ways? Is the human organism, the human being, a passive product of active conditioning? Logically, the problem is like that in which Plato and others believing in a suprahuman aristocracy did not face: who guards the guardians? What institutions spontaneously generate which internal tensions in human nature? The model of humankind implicit in strict environmentalists would have to say that there are indeed some needs, some tensions, in human beings that are not shared by lower vertebrates, unless human beings are to be regarded as having no innate demands beyond those shared with lower vertebrates: self-preservation and species perpetuation. If Buddha, Jesus, and Muhammad taught dignity and respect for everyone was it just an accident that they got so many millions of adherents, and just an accident that Plato

did not? It seems more reasonable to suppose that the appeal for dignity was attractive because people *naturally* wanted it. Highly articulate people, like Plato and many later philosophers and scientists, want recognition and respect: they want dignity. They seem to assume that ordinary people do not.

Sigmund Freud's greatest contribution to the science of human behavior was his insistence that unconscious influences not only exist but also are very powerful. He brilliantly applied and used his contribution mainly in the analysis of childhood experiences as they affected adult sexual behavior. He was less successful in applying his study of the unconscious to nonsexual behavior (and he tended to sexualize the nonsexual). In 1922 he wrote, "the nucleus of what we mean by love naturally consists . . . in sexual love with sexual union. But we do not separate from this . . . on the one hand self-love and one the other, love for parents and children, friendship, and love for humanity in general, and also devotion to concrete objects and to abstract ideas" (Freud, 1922: pp. 37–38).

Freud experienced the First World War, the meatgrinder of millions of soldiers on both sides, from the viewpoint of Germany and the Central Powers. Two of his sons saw military service. His early reaction during that war was to say that as German victories extended, they would spread German culture more broadly throughout the world.

Later during the war he observed with growing horror the enormous violence and concluded that violence is an innate tendency. He elevated it in his theoretical system so that in addition to the positive, life-producing (i.e., the sex) instinct in his earlier theorizing, there was a murderous death instinct that produced destruction of not only others but of self. He collaborated with Albert Einstein in an exchange published in 1933. In it he chided some presumptions of Einstein, noting that "All this [speculation regarding instincts] may give you the impression that our theories amount to a species of mythology and a gloomy one at that! But does not every natural science lead ultimately to this—a sort of mythology? Is it otherwise today with your physical science?" (*Why War*, pp. 49–50) In terms used in the social sciences, Freud perhaps assumed that the war was simply a struggle for power, and he did not examine his own assumptions.

The here-significant fact is that Freud was influenced by his (adult) experience and that this colored, indeed determined, the construction of his basic orientation. If the World War served only as a reminder and not a determinant, it speaks ill of Freud that he was unable to include a death instinct before the war. It was as much an oversight as it would have been to overlook the sex instinct, the bonding instinct, during the war. Freud did not view humankind holistically through time and space, but only episodically. And, like Plato, he was an elitist. In the exchange with Einstein he wrote: "That men are divided into leaders and the led is but another manifestation of their inborn and irremediable inequality. The second class constitutes the vast majority; they need a high command to make decisions for them, to which decisions they usually bow without demur.... men should be at greater pains to form a superior class of independent thinkers, unamenable to intimidation and fervent in the quest for truth, whose function it would be to guide the masses dependent on their lead" (Einstein and Freud, pp. 46–47).

Investigators have tended to focus on only the most primitive parts of human nature. Behavioral science for the most part has recognized that human beings share with all other life forms a desire to be fed and to associate. Ignoring Aristotle and Lasswell, behavioral science has shied away from considering that human beings have a natural desire for deference and respect or any other nonphysical need that is unassociated with the need for food and for sex regarded solely as a means of self- and species-perpetuation.

Working mainly with insects, E. O. Wilson established a novel way of looking at behavior. He found that in the interests of perpetuating if not the species, at least the colony, ants were quite willing to sacrifice themselves. Without falling into a trap of saying that human beings should sacrifice themselves to perpetuate the species, Wilson clearly broadened the assumption of many investigators who have followed Darwin's views even more strictly than Darwin did. Wilson said that there was, in addition to the innate desire of individuals to survive, a desire of individuals to participate in making the species survive. In a later theoretical book, Wilson backed off from the elementary premises presented in his treatise on sociobiology, but his underlying frame of reference has evolved in the trend called "evolutionary psychology." Its premises are much like Wilson's initial ones.

Richard Wright, an articulate spokesman of evolutionary psychology, has moved a step beyond Wilson's implicit view of human nature, basing his views not on ant societies but on the work of game theorists like Dawkins, Trivers, and Axelrod. They view altruistic behavior as instrumental to self-interest and leave quite unexplained not only the human pursuit of self-fulfillment but also the growth of civilization itself. And they do not directly consider violence and aggression. These often-destructive actions are not readily apparent to

investigators who generate formulas, equations, and manipulate their data in front of computers.

Arthur Koestler developed an explanation for public violence that is somewhat akin to E. O. Wilson's self-sacrificing ants. Koestler moved intellectually beyond his belief in the Marxist system as it developed in the Soviet Union to a disillusion with it as a means of effecting progressive change. He explained the resort to violence as the consequence of a natural tendency people have to sacrifice themselves in the name of causes—in a sense to self-immolate.

A great pioneer in political behavior, Harold Lasswell (1951, p. 474), listed among the goal values of people "power, respect, affection, rectitude, well-being, wealth, skill, enlightenment"—a more inclusive list than E. O. Wilson's. He repeatedly wrote that there was a common need among human beings for deference and that governments had to address that need. The implications for democratic as distinct from aristocratic or plutocratic government are obvious. And behind Lasswell's positing of a natural need for deference lie the "self-evident" truths of Jefferson about human beings: that they are created equal—that is, have the genetically determined attribute of wanting to be treated equally. Jefferson's assumptions have origins in Locke and possibly in a near contemporary of Jefferson: Rousseau. In 1755 he published his *Discourse on the Origin of Inequality*, arguing that people naturally were unequal in competence but unequal in society as the result of institutions which gave legal force to differences in competence. Rousseau's two principal works, *The Social Contract* and *Emile*, were published in 1762, 14 years before Jefferson composed the Declaration of Independence. He may have read one or all three of these crucial works. It is interesting to speculate whether, like Hobbes, Rousseau would have regarded violence as a part of human nature if he had lived to experience the French Revolution, which began a decade after his death. To reiterate, experience seems to be a more powerful influence than abstract ideas, and it is fortunate for the advancement of knowledge that abstract ideas do not take precedence.

III. BEYOND SURVIVAL AND ASSOCIATION

The preoccupation of social scientists with self- and species-preservation was not always present. The preoccupation is understandable: the 20th century is perhaps the most violent since the 125 years of the wars of the Protestant Reformation that ended in 1648 with the

Treaties of Westphalia—and ended in England about the time that Hobbes was writing. But the lineage on human motivation is there: perhaps William James was the earliest to produce a systematic model of human nature that included metasurvival needs. Freud, who met James when visiting the United States, in the 1920s broadened his definition of "sex" or "Eros" so that it came to include the tenderness and altruism connotations of "love."

And after Freud came Henry Alexander Murray with a long list of human needs. He established two categories—"viscerogenic" and "psychogenic." Among the former are food, sex, and "harmavoidance." Among the latter are dominance, deference, "blamavoidance," nurturance, aggression, cognizance, and autonomy. He avoided classifying needs as being innate or involving early conditioning.

After Murray, Abraham Maslow developed a rather rigorous set of elemental needs and placed them in a hierarchy. He said that after the physical needs for food, good health, and so on, people wanted security, love, self-esteem, and self-actualization—and they wanted them pretty much in that order. Like Murray, Maslow avoided classifying them as innate.

There has been resistance and indifference to the idea of positing some elemental needs that are beyond survival and sex, and resistance to the idea of establishing any priority among elemental needs. Some investigators have acknowledged that human beings have innate physical and love needs, but are not so confident that they also naturally want dignity and freedom to do their thing.

In social science there is some acceptance of the idea that (equal) dignity is innate, but skepticism about its naturalness may be related to the fact that prevailing opinion among psychologists—aside from James, Murray, and Maslow—saw only philosophers as calling dignity an innate human need. In any event, dignity has not been very systematically or deliberately subjected to psychological analysis. Despite this neglect, it is difficult to suppose that the need for (equal) dignity is generated by—that is, originates in—childhood experience and in the long-term conditioning to values provided by moralists and religious leaders.

Environmental determinism, which limits innate drives to survival, does not explain how metasurvival values get generated in the first place. They certainly are not the first needs to emerge in infancy. But very early on, infants get upset if they are laughed at: their dignity is hurt. Founders of great religions, including Jesus, Buddha, and Mohammed, heavily emphasized the right of all people to be respected, to be dignified.

Their success was not in contriving a wish for human beings but in striking a natural chord among their billions of adherents.

Such speculations are perhaps unnecessarily argumentative. Rather than continuing a discussion that can be endless, it seems more appropriate to pursue experimentation in which determinants that are innate can be more clearly separated from those that purely products of conditioning or are at least contaminated by it.

IV. SOME CASUAL DEFINITIONS OF AGGRESSION

There has been critical vagueness in defining aggression, even by its longtime students. *Agonism* is used by writers such as Konrad Lorenz, J. P. Scott, and others. It means forceful action against some part of the environment. Using the term avoids saying whether violence, as a kind of agonistic behavior, may be harmful and whether human beings are naturally violent. Lorenz believed that they are; Scott that they are not. The question of motive is sidestepped: to restore and to take life become indistinguishable: a surgeon wielding a scalpel and a thug lugging a long knife are judged the same. That is, they are not judged. Perpetrators of violence intend to do harm, and we cannot avoid judging whether actions are harmful.

The term *aggression* is often paired with *defense*, as though they are opposites, when the purpose of either kind of behavior is to do harm. Analysis is muddled if we suppose that a person defending him- or herself against another who is bent on homicide is not as aggressive as the attacker. If the defender is successful against the attacker, the defender will survive and the attacker may die.

After the Second World War, the United Nations started to define aggression and in 1975 finally adopted a definition. It altogether avoided the issue of intent to do harm. Perhaps a reason was that no nation was willing to admit to harmful intent, and every nation wants to consider its violent action to be defensive. The UN General Assembly declared aggression to be "the use of armed force by a state against the sovereignty, territorial integrity or political independence of another state." If using armed force against the sovereignty of another nation is the critical criterion, the UN definition would condemn several actions that have been considered necessary, before and after the UN was organized. Germany did not attack the sovereignty, territorial integrity, or political independence of the United States in either the First or the Second World War, but Germany did attack American shipping. In the Balkans in the 1990s, the Yugoslav government did not attack the sovereignty, territorial integrity, or political independence of the Nato nations, but it at least threatened its Balkan neighbors and did engage in genocide; the NATO nations did then attack Yugoslavia. The moral issue is more relevant than who uses force first. It is not aggression but rather the imposition of dictatorship, the long-term threat to democratic government, and genocide that are critical to the justification or the condemnation of aggression. Unfortunately the moral aspects are seen antithetically by democracies and dictatorships and both sides claim moral superiority: Either side can start the fighting without establishing moral consensus.

The problem is that aggression—as in fighting off an attacker—may be and usually is harmful. Furthermore, a passive, nonviolent response to aggression may also be harmful. Watching a helpless person being attacked when one can stop the attack is harmful. Saying that one party is aggressor and therefore harmful and the other party is victim and therefore harmless does not resolve the issues between them. Saying that one's subhuman adversaries are the aggressors does not resolve the issues, either. If one regards all humans or only one's subhuman adversaries to be violent, one is almost predicting the outcome: violent confrontation. And if violence is an innate tendency, like eating, then the very least that can satisfy the tendency is a diet of bread and circuses—and violence on television. On the other hand, if violence is not innate but is instrumental to tendencies that are innate, then it does not occur if these natural needs are met.

In 1939 a group of psychologists and a behavioral neurologist at Yale University (J. Dollard *et al.*, 1939) composed a book around the theory that aggression is a product of frustration. Appearing on the eve of the Second World War, it was depreciated or ignored when it was easier to assume that nations were filled with people who enjoyed killing and to presume that aggression is innate. A look at real-life conflict suggests the utility of the frustration–aggression hypothesis.

Even the interindividual aggression that occurs within families and neighborhoods involves prior frustration. And when needs beyond self- and species-survival are frustrated, violence may happen. A child denied food or affection within its family may in consequence turn violent, but food and affection are not everything. A child who is denied social acceptance and respect may turn violent. Urban gangs may be well fed

and have a solidary gang. Joining a gang may provide recognition to individual members, but the group that is formed may seek recognition and respect from the community outside the gang. But if they are denied dignity, they may turn violent. The gang may encourage violence, in the interest of getting money for food and drugs, but if the gang is denied recognition, the innate drive in all individuals for dignification remains unfulfilled. Thousands of individuals have done so: they identify themselves and are identified as minorities and are depreciated by the majority. Millions of individuals have also been depreciated, as members of a nation that is denied equal dignity, as Germany was in the 1919 Versailles treaty and Japan was in the 1922 naval conference.

V. INNATE, THAT IS, NATURAL SOURCES OF TENSION

The need for equal dignity has been a major basis for the foundation and endurance of major religions. As a characteristic of individuals, the need becomes social when denied to neighborhood groups. It becomes international when this individual need is shared by groups large enough to be called nations that threaten each other with violence they call defensive.

Partly as a result of the preoccupation with self- and species-survival, broad analyses of social and political behavior have often not established or have severed connections with analysis of interindividual behavior. Awesome weapons, biological and nuclear, divert attention from the individual human psyche. That is, studies of violence in a family and violence in a neighborhood get detached from analysis of causes of aggression involving impersonalized violence among large populations. We may say that individuals become alienated, humiliated, or otherwise frustrated and say the same thing about socioeconomic classes, ethnic and religious groups, and nations. What we need to look at more closely is the evidence that the dynamics of these frustrations is generated in the individual human psyche and ultimately the individual human gene plasm. High-powered firearms and deadly missiles divert attention from the individual psyche.

Detachment of physical from mental needs diminishes the ability to resolve social and political conflict. The internalization of values that recognize individuals will fight—will aggress—if the ideologies and values expressed by social and political leaders recognize these values. Individuals and nations will not fight long for values unrelated to the full range of individual needs.

It is very, very difficult to separate out, to abstract, innate determinants for at least two reasons: the genetically established organism is influenced even before birth by several neurochemicals that pass through not only the placenta but also the fetal blood-brain barrier. These prenatal influences, perhaps the earliest experiences, cannot be regarded as innate, but they so affect the developing fetus that they quite surely are permanent. Infants whose mothers while gestating took heavy doses of alcohol and narcotics like heroin are likely to be mentally damaged for life.

Such prenatal influences may be called second nature because they remain permanent determinants of behavior. Research in lower vertebrates suggests the process. When a pregnant monkey was injected with testosterone, its female offspring became more aggressive than females not subjected to infusion of abnormal, unnatural amounts of prenatal testosterone. When newborn rats were injected with testosterone, the injected female pups later, as adults, fought more than those not injected, both with other female rats and with male rats.

In addition to such prenatal influences, there is the steady stream of experience mentioned earlier that commences with the first contacts with mothers, fathers, family, neighborhood, and so on, and continues throughout life. Even though they may seem natural, they also can be accurately described as second nature.

This detachment does not take advantage of the fact that individuals will not fight well if they have not internalized the ideologies and the values expressed by social and political leaders. And even this internalization is overridden by more intimate interindividual reactions. Analyses of cooperation of individual soldiers in the Second World War have indicated that the most immediately powerful motivator was the identity, the solidarity, that individual soldiers had with their buddies in the same small military unit: the other fellow in the foxhole, the squad, or the company. The slaughter of millions in the Japanese investment of Nanking in 1937 was undertaken in person-to-person combat, and so was the destruction by individual American soldiers of civilians in Vietnam in the 1970s.

Interdisciplinary analogies are not always good argument, particularly when the number of variables is vastly increased. A child that is humiliated by its parents is acted upon by a relatively small number of forces, in the family and in the cultures' practices of child-rearing. An adult citizen of a nation that is humiliated by other nations may act in part like a child humiliated by parents, but the loyalties and identifications that an adult has to his nation have much broader origins and much longer histories. Russian soldiers defending the Soviet Union against German invasion in 1941 could not escape the memory of their motherland being invaded during the First World War, and during the Napoleonic Wars a century before. Germans in the 1930s responded eagerly and angrily to Hitler's emphases on the humiliations of the Versailles Treaty of 1919, and he enjoyed in June 1940 taking the French surrender at the site where Germany had recognized in November 1918 its defeat in the First World War by signing the armistice. Humiliation in 1918 was erased by exaltation twelve years later.

Analysis of violent human behavior is deficient if it does not look deeply at historical and contemporary context. Violence can be understood only as an interactive process: a product of interaction between individuals, groups, and nations whose natural, innate needs are frustrated by an indifferent or hostile environment. Nuclear physicists cannot understand the behavior of subatomic particles, like protons, neutrons, and electrons, without observing their interaction with other particles. The behaviors of both these particles and of far more complex human beings (with their natural, inherent tendencies) are observable only in interactions.

VI. SOME RESEARCH IN THE NEUROPHYSIOLOGY OF ASSERTIVE AND VIOLENT BEHAVIOR

The unique complexity of the human brain warns us that any findings about it can at best be only partial and tentative. A 1996 collection of research writings about aggression presents both conflicting and tentative findings by scores of neuroscientists (Stoff and Cairns, 1996). That mushrooming segment of natural science is discussed elsewhere in this encyclopedia. Nonetheless, complexity need not deter us any more than it does natural scientists faced with the considerably simpler interaction of the universe and elemental, subatomic particles. Astro- and nuclear-physicists have progressed enormously on the foundations of Newton, Einstein, and other fundamentalists. We can quite confidently say that time and space are so intertwined that we cannot explain elemental phenomena if we consider them separately. We can say that light travels at a certain speed, but only for practical purposes such as establishing just how long is an hour, a day, a century, and a millennium. We can accept as fact that energy has mass, although the difference in mass between energy and more palpable forms of mass such as plutonium, lead, or water vapor is truly enormous. As Einstein put it, energy equals mass times the square of the speed of light.

Correlatively, we can say that behaviors such as a search for food or affection or for dignity have innate components, without thereby settling the dispute over the innateness of aggression, violence, dominance, or subservience. Freud, Lorenz, and Ardrey build their basic theses on the assumption that aggression is innate. Other writers, notably Locke, Rousseau, and Jefferson, supposed that it is not. We can get at better bases for addressing the question if we look systematically at the way brain researchers organize their less certain, less definitive conclusions about human nature.

VII. THE TRIUNE BRAIN

A physiologist, Paul MacLean, has divided the brain into three basic parts: the reptilian, paleomammalian, and neomammalian. The reptilian part is so named by MacLean because in it are contained behavioral functions that humans share with reptiles. That is, reptiles have been found to manifest these and other behaviors: (1) the establishment and marking of territory; (2) defense of territory; (3) fighting; (4) the formation of groups; (5) the establishment of social hierarchy; (6) courtship; (7) mating; (8) the breeding and sometimes the care of offspring. We need to note that fighting may be involved in pursuit of each of the other reptilian behaviors that MacLean lists. An anthropocentric view would describe these behaviors of reptiles as humanoid. MacLean's nomenclature reminds us better of the evolutionary continuity between the behavior of human beings and those of some of the lowest vertebrates.

Between the most primitive, reptilian part and the most advanced, neomammalian part of the brain (otherwise called the neocortex, the "new" cortex, where information is processed and decisions are made) lies the part which is most critical for our analysis: the limbic system, the emotional brain.

The limbic system (Isaacson, 1974) was "discovered" by Paul Broca, in France in 1878. Its major parts are the hypothalamus, amygdala, hippocampus, and the septal area. In size, in reptiles it is most of the brain. In Homo sapiens, it is proportionally much smaller, and the very large neocortex, the thinking and feeling brain, wraps around and envelops the limbic system. There are many big neural pathways between particular parts of the neocortex and particular parts of the limbic system.

Following Broca and Papez, MacLean, Delgado, and many others have done extensive research within the limbic system. To the extent that conflict behavior involves emotion, the limbic system is involved, and it is hard to conceive of emotion-free conflict behavior. However, it must always be borne in mind that bundles of nerves connect the limbic system not just with the neocortex but also with the most primitive, "reptilian" parts of the brain. One implication of these interties is that, physiologically speaking, there are probably few behaviors that are quite free of either the information-processing and decision-making functions of the neocortex or the most primitive "instincts" of the sort that MacLean listed for reptiles. Another implication is that, to the extent that the primitive brain and the limbic systems "dominate" overt behavior, people may not be totally in control of their behavior and not fully aware why they act as they do, notably in times of stress that attend conflict.

VIII. RESEARCH IN NERVES

The brain's activity is so complex and so interactive, both internally and with the environment, that the role of various factors can best be looked at by categories. Nerves and hormones interact continuously in the brain and in parts of the rest of the body that are directly under the brain's control, such as the heart and the adrenal glands, which sit on top of the kidneys. A pinch or a stab wound may produce an immediate and violent response against the person who pinched or stabbed: this is primarily a neural response. The same stimuli also involve activation of hormonal response: the person pinched or stabbed experiences a surge of noradrenaline and adrenaline, and this surge may cause the whole organism, the whole person, to respond violently. The neural part of the brain's activity does not act alone; neither does the hormonal part. The master gland, most widely involved in controlling the function of other glands, is in the brain: the pituitary, the hypophysis. It is the size of a pea. The pituitary is physically divided into a part that is composed of a tiny set of nerves, the neurohypophysis, and another part consisting of a tiny sac of hormones, the adenohypophysis. Functionally, the pituitary's two separate parts themselves are in continuous interaction.

First, a look at some early but classical research in which emphasis has been on nerves. One of the great early investigators was Walter Cannon. In the 1920s he did experiments with dogs, cutting away different parts of the brain or cutting connections between them.

He found that when a main trunk of nerves high in the brain (connecting the neocortex with the limbic system) was cut, the animals became veritable engines of destruction, sizing up in a coordinated way whomever was near and waiting for the first opportunity to strike. The neocortex no longer controlled the limbic system or even inhibited a rage response. When the cut was made lower, the animals became snarling, growling, uncoordinated, and *un*dangerous animals—perhaps like a human being about to pass out from alcohol. That is, the less the neocortex was involved, the less controlled the response behavior. We ask whether the aggression, controlled as it is by the neocortex, an innate drive. The position of Cannon's cuts facilitates distinctions hard to make in normal human beings, particularly in stressful circumstances: is the *potential* for aggressive action the same as aggressive action? If the neocortex can control the aggressive potential, is the individual person innately aggressive?

Electrodes implanted in the brains of various vertebrates have again helped map the paths involved in violence. When electrodes were put in the brainstems (part of the "reptilian" brain) of chickens and an electrical charge was fed into the electrode, the chickens, which previously had been friendly with their human attendants, pecked viciously at them. It is well to note that the chickens were not naturally, normally, hostile but the electrical charge made them so. It served the same function as ablation and cutting in the brains of Cannon's dogs.

Reis and colleagues implanted electrodes in nine gentle cats, in a part of the brain immediately adjacent to the limbic system. When a current of 40 μA was introduced, the cats merely became alert. When it was increased to 50 μA, the cats started to groom themselves. When it was increased to 60 μA, five of the nine cats started to eat. When the current was increased to 70 μA, seven of the nine cats savagely attacked a rat placed in their cages. When the current was turned off, they stopped their attacks, and when it was turned on again they attacked again.

In an experiment with a group of monkeys housed in a single cage, Delgado noted unsurprisingly that the alpha male monkey, the top monkey, was if not aggressive, at least assertive. He was the first to eat and sat wherever he wanted to. Delgado implanted an electrode in the caudate nucleus, a part of the limbic system, and on the cage wall he put an electrical switch that could send a current to the implanted electrode by remote control. The switch could be operated by any of the monkeys. One of the female monkeys discovered that by pressing the switch, she could stop the alpha's dominant behavior. After pressing

the switch, she could do what no subordinate monkey would dare do to an alpha: she looked him straight in the eye. After the effect had worn off, the alpha male was boss again. There is no evidence that the clever female had read the Declaration of Independence, but clearly she preferred equal deference and equal power.

An idiosyncratic case emphasizes the role of the emotional brain in determining behavior. A mentally healthy attorney started to take offense at others' actions that for him became major crises: he got very angry in discussion at cocktail parties. He pursued and tried to punish drivers on freeways who were rude or careless. He was getting short-tempered with his wife. Persistence and intensity of symptoms led to brain surgery. A tumor surrounded his hypothalamus, a major part of the limbic system. He died in the hospital.

A young woman who had stabbed someone in the heart with a knife was put in hospital. She attacked a nurse with scissors. Brain surgery took the form of cauterizing and thus destroying the amygdala, another major part of the limbic system. It can confidently be said that the behavior of both the attorney and the young woman was violent: at least on the surface, overt evidence indicated conscious attacks on objects these two people considered appropriate. And it cannot be said with any confidence that either the attorney or the girl was responsible for his or her behavior: their brains were not normal and the neocortex could not exercise its normal control.

IX. RESEARCH IN HORMONES

There are dozens of hormones—neurochemicals or endocrines—that interact with the nervous system in controlling behavior. Their interaction is so reciprocal that one cannot confidently say that nerves control hormonal secretions or vice versa. But there are two categories of hormones that most directly relate to aggressive and violent behavior: the catecholamines and the steroids.

The principal *catecholamines* relevant to aggressive behavior are noradrenaline or norepinephrine (NE) and adrenaline or epinephrine (E). The sequence of production (the metabolism) of these hormones is from dopamine to NE to E. The sequence of production has distinct significance for the kind of behavior each helps produce. Dopamine tends to produce assertive interaction rather basically and positively: nurses administering dopamine have been the objects of amorous advances from old patients being treated with dopamine. Noradrenaline tends to produce broad, unspecified response to protect the organism from threat: destroy that attacker or get me out of here (fight or flight). Adrenaline, the metabolite of noradrenaline, tends to produce specific, deliberated response: the best way to destroy that attacker is to put him on trial, convict him or her, and then hang him or her.

The ratio of noradrenaline varies from species to species. In chickens, lions, and whales, there is more NE than E. In human beings, the ratio of NE to E is about 1 to 3. That is, human beings have more of the deliberative kind than other vertebrates—more of it than of the unmetabolized kind.

The *steroids*, which are also involved in aggressive behavior, are the sex hormones. The two kinds of steroids are the estrogens and androgens. Both males and females have both kinds: females have more estrogens than androgens and more estrogens than males, who have more androgens than estrogens. Both are metabolites of cholesterol. Estrogen is associated with many kinds of overt behavior, but one of them is nurturance. Androgen is similarly complicated in producing overt behavior, but a principal one is assertive and aggressive behavior.

Among both males and females, the production of the steroids increases at puberty and at menopause the proportions change as between males and females. According to some research, women after menopause have less estrogen than androgen and have less estrogen than men. One indicator of these changes is that women often have more facial hair than they ever had before menopause. One indicator in men: as they age they may get less aggressive and more nurturant. That is, more nurturant than they were—and in some instances more nurturant than women.

It is perhaps more difficult to separate out the behavioral consequences of different catecholamines than, perhaps, to isolate the effect of ingesting too much or too little salt or too much fatty food or too little. But, without attributing physiological wisdom to the Roman Stoics, with their prescription, nothing to excess, it does appear that there is a normal range of amounts of catecholamines that, when it is exceeded, produces abnormal behavior, some of which is clearly assertive and may be aggressive. Furthermore, variation in amounts of catecholamines may be partly under conscious control of the individual human being. And they can take various drugs to control the effect of catecholamines and steroids: among the most common are alcohol, cocaine, and heroin. People do not need to know the physiology to enjoy or suffer from the effects of drugs on the natural production and effect of hormones.

Serotonin has been the object of so much research in the 1990s that it is hard to recall that the steroids have such a central role in aggressive behavior. Serotonin is a neurotransmitter, like the catecholamines and the steroids, but does not belong in either category. Extensive research has found that levels of serotonin tend to be higher among dominant individuals (both vervet monkeys and humans) than among subordinates, and when an individual loses dominance, his serotonin level goes down. Serotonin does not act by itself but in conjunction with other hormones, such as the androgens and estrogens, to help produce aggressive behavior, but so do alcohol and some drugs, sometimes. It is hard to resist reductionism when studying the functions of various parts of the brain and the functions of different kinds of stimulus from the pre- and postnatal environment.

Brain research has hitherto been neglected. It is hard to realize that this neglected organ is not at all a passive recipient of stimuli in the form of class-status, nationality, religion, and "race." The brain is not an empty dish in which anyone can mix a soup of his or her own concoction. Not only are the forces operating within the brain, whether natural or implanted, very largely unconscious, as Freud took the courage to show. Additionally, these forces operating unconsciously cover the entire spectrum of activity—not just sexual but all other kinds, among writers and readers and among all other categories of humanity. Broca, Papez, MacLean, and many others have pioneered physiologically the way Freud did psychologically. But one of the first steps is an appreciation of the exciting interactivity in the brain's neural and endocrine structures. Another first step is an awareness that all of its parts have been operating with fair regularity and success for many millennia, without the knowledge or consent of either natural or social scientists.

Research in neural and endocrine phenomena is indeed developing explosively and promises to help in the understanding and treatment of violent individuals. This research has not yet been much applied to broad social and political phenomena. The set of cultural variables that separately contribute to behavior greatly complicates the task of integrating neuroscientific with social-scientific research. And applying the ever-increasing knowledge to political violence raises a set of formidable and threatening moral issues.

Generally, neuroscientists have avoided discussing human nature and they tend to leave to the reader the task of defining just what it is they are writing about. The advantage is that they avoid taking the usual ideological stances of those who do write about human nature. Avoiding definition, they also avoid relating causes and correlates of violence in individuals to political violence.

X. NONDEFINITIVE VIEWS OF HUMAN NATURE

It is not possible to make definitive appraisals of such a broad array of views of the human essence. Along with such concepts as democracy, revolution, and violence, the term human nature will likely continue to be used and used as loosely as it has been for more than two thousand years. People, even in the large aggregates that are called nations have fought and died over such terms. Christianity has for two thousand years witnessed wars waged between nations whose inhabitants were adherents to the Roman and Greek Orthodox Catholic churches. The same violence occurred during the European Reformation, between Protestants and Roman Catholics. In the American Civil War of 1861–1865, ministers in heavily Calvinist New England were urging force against Southern slave owners. The former were convinced that the Bible condemned slavery; the latter insisted that the Bible justified their peculiar institution.

There is a perpetual contest over the meaning of words, especially those dealing with elemental concepts. In *Alice in Wonderland* the Queen of Hearts said that a word means what she wants it to mean. In America, many have said that the Constitution is what the Supreme Court says it is. In the Soviet Union, Communism was what Stalin said it was. In no major part of the world is there any real consensus yet about such concepts as democracy and God.

What can help diminish the rhetorical use of the term human nature is to look frankly at the way it has been used by people who are well recognized for their competence as philosophers, writers, and scientists, natural or social. The competence of the individuals discussed here is high. But their use of such abstractions as human nature, violence, and aggression—like the more common use of the terms democracy and God—remains little if any more judicious and helpful than views on the same abstractions by less specialized observers of self and society.

Also See the Following Articles

AGGRESSION AND ALTRUISM • ANIMAL BEHAVIOR STUDIES, NONPRIMATES • BEHAVIORAL PSYCHOLOGY • BIOCHEMICAL FACTORS • EVIL, CONCEPT OF • EVOLUTIONARY FACTORS • NEUROPSYCHOLOGY OF MOTIVATION FOR GROUP AGGRESSION • PSYCHOLOGY, GENERAL VIEW

Bibliography

Aristotle. (1932). *Politics*. H. Rackham, transl. London: William Heinemann.

Bronson, F. H., & Desjardins, C. (1968). Aggression in adult mice: Modification by neonatal injection of gonadal hormones. *Science*, 161, 705–706 (16 August 1968).

Davies, J. C. ([1963] 1977). *Human nature in politics*. Westport, CT, Greenwood Press.

Davies, J. C. (Ed.). ([1971] 1997). *When men revolt and why*. New Brunswick, NJ, Transaction Publishers.

Davies, J. C. (1967). Aggression: Some definition and some physiology. *Politics and the Life Sciences*, 6 (1):27–57.

Delgado, Jose M. R. (1969). *Physical control of the mind*. New York: Harper and Row.

Dollard, J., L. Doob, N. E. Miller, O. H. Mowrer, & Sears, R. R. (1939). *Frustration and aggression*. New Haven: Yale University Press.

Einstein, A., & Freud, S. (1933). *Why war?* Paris: International Institute of Intellectual Cooperation.

Freud, S. (1922). *Group psychology and the analysis of the ego*. London: The Hogarth Press.

Gay, P. (1989). *Freud: A life for our time*. New York: Doubleday Anchor Books.

Goy, R. M. (1970). Early hormonal experiences and the development of sexual and sex-related behavior. In F. O. Schmitt *et al.*, (Eds.), *The neurosciences: Second study program*. New York: Rockefeller University Press.

Isaacson, R. L. (1974). *The limbic system*. New York: Plenum Press.

James, W. (1890). *The principles of psychology*. New York: Henry Holt and Co.

Lasswell, H. D. (1951). *The political writings of Harold D. Lasswell*. Glencoe, IL: The Free Press.

Koestler, A. (1967). *The ghost in the machine*. New York: The Macmillan Co.

MacLean, P. (1967). The brain in relation to empathy and medical education. *Journal of Nervous and Mental Disease*, 144:374–382.

MacLean, P. (1972). Cerebral evolution and emotional processes: New findings on the striatal complex. *Annals of the New York Academy of Sciences*.

Maslow, A. H. (1943). A theory of human motivation. *Psychological Review*, 50:370–396.

Maslow, A. H. (1954). *Motivation and personality*. New York: Harper and Bros.

McGuire, M. (1982). Social dominance relationships in male vervet monkeys. *International Political Science Review*, 3:11–32.

Montagu, M. F. A. (1973). *Man and aggression*. London: Oxford University Press.

Murray, H. A. (1938). *Explorations in personality*. New York: Oxford University Press.

Papez, J. W. (1937). A proposed mechanism of emotion. *Archives of Neurology and Psychiatry*, 38:725–743.

Skinner, B. F. (1971). *Beyond freedom and dignity*. New York: Alfred A. Knopf.

Stoff, D. M., & Cairns, R. B. (1996). *Aggression and violence: Genetic, neurobiological, and biosocial perspectives*. Mahwah, NJ: Lawrence Erlbaum Associates.

Von Holst, & von St. Paul (1960). Vom Wirkungsgefüge der Triebe. *Die Naturwissenschaften*, 18:409–422.

Von Holst, & von St. Paul (1962). Electrically controlled behavior, *Scientific American*. 206(3):50–59. A less complete report of the research originally published in 1960.

Watson, J. B. ([1924] 1961). *Behaviorism*. Chicago: University of Chicago Press.

Wilson, E. O. (1975). *Sociobiology*. Cambridge: Belknap-Harvard University Press.

Wright, Richard (1994). *The moral animal: Evolutionary psychology and everyday life*. New York: Pantheon Books.

Human Rights

Alison Dundes Renteln

University of Southern California

I. Introduction
II. Principal Human Rights Instruments
III. Human Rights Machinery
IV. Human Rights and Violence
V. New Developments
VI. Conclusion

GLOSSARY

Customary International Law Unwritten norms that are, by definition, binding on all states. Such a norm is identified by the behavior and attitude of the state or state practice and *opinio juris*.

Derogation Refers to the ability of a state to suspend temporarily its international legal obligations, usually because of a national emergency.

Human Rights The rights that individuals have simply by virtue of being human.

Ius Cogens A fundamental right that is nonderogable.

Opinio Juris Refers a state's belief that it is legally obligated to comply with specific international laws.

Reservation A state can enter a reservation indicating that while it ratified the treaty, it will not be bound by a particular article. This is allowed unless the provision is central to the "object and purpose" of the convention or is proscribed by the treaty itself.

Treaty A written document that must be ratified by states before entering into force, i.e., becoming legally enforceable.

HUMAN RIGHTS are rights that individuals have simply by virtue of being human. These rights are considered to be universal, nonconditional rights that states, governments, and private actors are required to respect. There are various types of rights, generally classified under the rubric of "generations" of civil and political rights, economic, social and cultural rights, and solidarity rights. As the rights have become codified in various international instruments, this has resulted in the clarification of the norms and has led to the establishment of enforcement techniques.

I. INTRODUCTION

A. Historical Background

The idea of human rights is an ancient one, dating back centuries. It is essentially the notion that there are higher laws that supersede human-made laws. The basic premise is that every human being has inalienable rights that cannot be denied by any regime, regardless of the justification. These rights are not conditional in any way. The precursor to human rights was natural law, a higher law that superseded government law. The

Copyright © 1999 by Academic Press.
All rights of reproduction in any form reserved.

conflict between higher law and positive law is illustrated in the famous play *Antigone* in which the heroine has to decide whether or not to bury a brother who violated the positive law by fighting against the city; to deny him a burial would violate a higher law.

Prior to the post-WWII international campaign for human rights, the struggle for the protection of human rights was limited to national documents such as the Magna Carta, the American Declaration of Independence and Bill of Rights, the French Declaration of the Rights and Man and of Citizens, and national constitutions. The term human rights replaced "natural rights." Many associate human rights with the rationalistic thinking of the Age of Enlightenment. Eighteenth-century philosophers relied on notions comparable to human rights to challenge political absolutism.

Some historical antecedents to the modern human rights machinery deserve mention. The international system had some mechanisms whose purpose was the protection of rights, prior to the establishment of the UN system. Of particular note was the League of Nations Mandates system and the International Labor Organization (ILO). Although the Covenant of the League of Nations did not explicitly mention human rights, two provisions had implications for human rights. Article 22 established the Mandates System, which governed former colonies of states that lost in World War I (territories taken from the German and Ottoman Empires). (The UN replaced this system with the UN Trusteeship System). Article 23 dealt with ensuring proper labor conditions. The ILO helped to develop further international human rights standards pertaining to the workplace.

Despite the absence of any minority rights provisions in its Covenant (a lacuna shared by the UN Charter), the League of Nations sponsored an international system for the protection of minorities, though the standards were applied almost exclusively within Europe. Although most of the system disappeared with the demise of the League, it is historically significant that some parts served as precursors to present-day human rights institutions.

The idea of individual rights was presaged by a body of law concerning state responsibility for injuries to aliens according to which state treatment of aliens had to be consistent with a minimum standard of justice. States were held liable if aliens or their property were harmed within their borders. The fiction was that the state of the alien suffered the injury because traditionally only states were subjects of international law. The notion that a state could be held internationally responsible for its treatment of aliens was expanded in human rights law, so that states could also be sanctioned for

the manner in which they treated their own citizens. With the emergence of human rights law, individuals became subjects of international law.

The modern development of human rights occurred in the aftermath of World War II when there was a strong desire to establish international standards to prevent the sorts of atrocities witnessed during the Holocaust. The experience at the Nuremberg tribunal persuaded leaders that it would be necessary to develop international standards to prevent gross violations of human rights. In 1945 a group of delegates from various countries met in San Francisco to draft the United Nations Charter, at which time many states and nongovernmental organizations (NGOs) lobbied for the inclusion of an international "bill of rights" in the Charter. Instead, the group decided to create a Human Rights Commission, whose purpose would be to establish international human rights standards. Latin American states wanted stronger language included in the UN Charter stating that the UN would "safeguard and protect" human rights, but the language adopted requires members of the UN system, by virtue of ratifying the UN Charter, to "promote" human rights.

The Human Rights Commission convened for the first time in early 1947 with Eleanor Roosevelt as chair. By mid-1947 they began work on the Universal Declaration of Human Rights (UDHR), the centerpiece of what would eventually be known as the International Bill of Rights. The Draft Committee drew on many different sources, including various national constitutions. They examined draft proposals submitted by the United States and the United Kingdom, as well as various (mainly U.S.) NGOs, including the American Jewish Committee, the American Law Institute, the American Federation of Labor, the Commission to Study the Organization of the Peace, the World Government Association, the International Law Association. The Organization of American States and H.G. Wells proposed drafts.

The draft declaration of the UDHR was debated over a period of several months in the Third Committee of the General Assembly on Social and Humanitarian issues. After making only slight changes, the committee forwarded the UDHR to the General Assembly, which adopted it on December 10, 1948, with 48 votes in favor and 8 abstentions. The communist bloc abstained, as did South Africa and Saudi Arabia. Saudi Arabia appealed to cultural and religious differences as the basis for objecting to part of the UDHR. One objection was to Article 14, which provides for the equal rights to marriage for men and women of full age, and was intended to discourage child marriage, and another was to Article 16's guarantee of the right to change one's religion. With 30 articles, the UDHR was the first attempt to establish universal standards meant to serve as a "common standard of achievement for all peoples and all nations." It is remarkable that despite their differences, the vast majority of countries agreed to support a declaration that contains different types of rights.

The UDHR is a document that has acquired significant juridical status in the world. In contrast to a treaty, a declaration is ordinarily nonbinding. But it is often argued that the UDHR is legally binding, for three reasons: (1) it provides the authoritative interpretation of Articles 55 and 56 of the U.N. Charter (its human rights provisions); (2) it has been followed so faithfully that it has become part of customary international law (see below); and (3) it has been incorporated into many domestic legal systems.

Because the UDHR was not viewed as legally binding at the time of its drafting, the international community subsequently drafted several human rights treaties which were intended to have the force of law. These were the International Covenant of Civil and Political Rights (ICCPR) and the International Covenant of Economic, Social and Cultural Rights (IESCR). These covenants as well as the human rights provisions of the U.N. Charter, the UDHR, and the Optional Protocol to the ICCPR, are referred to collectively as the "International Bill of Rights."

B. Philosophical Foundations

The debate as to whether human rights are Western or Eurocentric has recurred throughout the history of UN human rights institutions. Proponents contend that, despite its "Western imprint," the notion of human rights is universally applicable, or that it is possible to forge a consensus through cross-cultural dialogue. Opponents argue that the extraordinary diversity in moral systems may preclude any sort of agreement as to the universal applicability of human rights standards. Although this argument is usually advanced under the heading of "cultural relativism," some cultural relativists believe that cross-cultural research may reveal human rights equivalents in other cultures.

The most fundamental human rights are called *ius cogens* or peremptory norms. They are at the pinnacle of the human rights normative hierarchy. Any policy or treaty that conflicts with a *ius cogens* is presumptively invalid. A *ius cogens* can only be superseded by another *ius cogens*. To date there is only agreement with respect to a few rights such as the right against slavery and the right against genocide. The challenge for the international community has been how to go about identifying these fundamental human rights in a world of diverse cultures.

II. PRINCIPAL HUMAN RIGHTS INSTRUMENTS

A. Sources of Human Rights: Treaties and Custom

Because significant ideological differences existed, a decision was made to create two distinct human rights instruments, the International Covenant of Civil and Political Rights and the International Covenant of Economic, Social, and Cultural Rights. The Western nations favored civil and political rights whereas the socialist nations emphasized economic rights. The two covenants were completed in 1966 but did not enter into force, that is, become legally enforceable until 1976.

The logic of having different sets of rights has endured. So-called first generation rights refer to civil and political rights, second generation rights to economic, social and cultural rights, and third generation rights to solidarity rights. Many contend that the first two sets of rights are interdependent. With respect to third generation rights, there is debate as to whether they exist at all. Although there is not a consensus on this point, some believe that there is an implicit hierarchy in the generational scheme with first generation rights as the most important.

In the past few decades many other human rights treaties have been drafted. Some instruments are concerned with the prevention of discrimination, for example, the Convention on the Elimination of All Forms of Racial Discrimination, and the Convention on the Elimination of All Forms of Discrimination Against Women. Other important ones include the Slavery Convention, the Convention on the Prevention and Punishment of the Crime of Genocide, the Convention against Torture and Other Cruel, Inhuman or Degrading Treatment of Punishment, and the Convention on the Rights of the Child. Treaties are only binding on those parties that have ratified them, unless the treaties represent the codification of customary international law.

Many instruments are, in fact, based on the other major source of international law norms besides treaties, namely custom. It turns out that the most fundamental human rights norms emerged as part of customary international law. Indeed, many of the norms embedded in the treaties were originally customary and were subsequently codified in the conventions. For a norm to be designated as customary international law, two requirements have to be met. First, state practice must demonstrate that states adhere to the norm in question. Second, the states must comply with the standard because of a sense of legal obligation known as *opinio juris,* otherwise their prior compliance may be merely coincidental rather than reflective of an underlying legal commitment.

Each requirement has its own difficulties. State practice is problematic for human rights norms because states generally violate the human rights standards; hence if a state practice of respecting human rights standards is necessary, it may seldom, if ever, be possible to proclaim that a given norm is part of customary international law. Consequently, Philip Alston and Bruno Simma argue that state practice should be interpreted as the public pronouncements of state officials regarding state practice, rather than actual practice.

The concept of *opinio juris* is somewhat murky and leads to a temporal paradox. If a norm is part of customary international law, that is because there is *opinio juris,* but prior to the moment when a legal obligation is recognized, the state was adhering to the norm that it mistakenly presumed to be legally binding (but it was not yet).

Despite the challenge of identifying customary international law norms, some human rights are considered to be part of this corpus of law, namely, the right against genocide, the right against slavery, and the right against piracy. Other rights are said to be emerging, for example, the right against torture.

Whereas treaties are only binding on those states that have ratified them, customary international law has the advantage of being binding on all states, by definition. When a treaty represents the codification of customary international law, the human rights norms are technically both conventional as well as customary. States may try to avoid being bound by human rights standards in the case of treaties, by entering reservations to provisions that they find unacceptable. This is allowed as long as the article in question is not central to the "object and purpose" of the treaty. In the case of customary international law states may try to evade human rights standards by being what is known as a "persistent objector." If the international community accepts a state's frequent protestations that it will not be bound, the state may be permitted not to respect a particular standard that would normally be considered binding on all states.

The United Nations plays a crucial role in the progressive development of new international human rights instruments. For instance, the International Law Commission (ILC) drafts new conventions. Human rights treaty committees (see below) develop interpretation of norms through issuance of general comments on particular articles in the treaties they enforce. For example, because there has been a concern that states have entered too many reservations to human rights treaties, the Human Rights Committee, which enforces the provisions of the ICCPR, issued a general comment that recommends that the use of such reservations be minimized to the greatest extent possible.

III. HUMAN RIGHTS MACHINERY

A. UN Institutions

Nation-states dominate the international system. This makes it exceedingly difficult for individuals to challenge violations of human rights because the state plays a dual role as both the protector and the violator of human rights. Since only states may submit disputes to the International Court of Justice and most often states violate the human rights of their own citizens, it is unrealistic to expect them to enforce human rights standards. Consequently, the emergence of human rights institutions that review petitions from individuals whose human rights have allegedly been violated is a remarkable and important development.

The main international human rights institutions are based on either Charter provisions or specific human rights treaty provisions. UN Charter Article 68 mandated that the Economic and Social Council establish commissions designed to promote human rights. In 1947 the Human Rights Commission was created. Originally consisting of 18 members, by the 1990s it had fifty three members. The gradual expansion reflected the need to have equitable geographical distribution. It is noteworthy that the individuals on the Commission on Human Rights are government representatives, meaning that they serve as officials of their governments and not in an independent capacity.

Since its beginning the Commission on Human Rights played a crucial standard-setting role by drafting new international instruments. Although it suffered a self-inflicted wound in 1947 when it concluded that it lacked the power to investigate human rights violations, it has gradually acquired the ability to engage in monitoring functions. After 20 years the position of the Commission that it had "no power to take any action in regard to any complaints concerning human rights" was questioned.

Two procedures were established: ECOSOC Resolution 1235 authorized the consideration of violations in public debate before the Commission. The other, ECOSOC Resolution 1503 created a confidential procedure that permitted private consideration of situations that appeared to reveal "a consistent pattern of gross and reliably attested violations of human rights" in consultation with the governments concerned. Since the 1970s it has met annually to consider complaints filed by individuals alleging specific violations of human rights. "Thematic" procedures evolved as well that permit careful study of specific types of human rights abuses.

The Sub-Commission on the Prevention of Discrimination and the Protection of Minorities also meets annually to ascertain which complaints should be referred to the Commission. It consists of 27 members elected by the Commission from a list of nominees submitted by member states of the United States. Because these individuals serve in their personal capacity, independent of their governments, this is the human rights institution most likely to be sympathetic to human rights issues. The Sub-Commission has had many functions including sponsoring research, standard-setting, and creating procedures for investigating human rights abuses. Technically, it is subordinate to the parent body, the Commission on Human Rights, and it has had a complicated relationship with the Commission over the years. The Sub-Commission studies human rights problems and also helps determine UN responses to them. It devotes most of its time to reviewing allegations of violations.

The Sub-Commission has working groups that evaluate particular issues such as communications (complaints), contemporary forms of slavery, the rights of indigenous peoples, traditions harmful to children, judicial independence, and detention. In addition to these thematic studies, the Sub-Commission has undertaken country-specific research as well, though this has often proven to be controversial.

As the name would suggest, the Sub-Commission has consistently focused on the rights of minorities. In 1971 it appointed Francesco Capotorti as Special Rapporteur to write a report on the implications of Article 27 of the ICCPR, which is the main human rights provision concerning minority rights. It provides that: "Persons belonging to ethnic, religious, and linguistic minorities shall not be denied the right, in community with other members of their group, to enjoy their own culture, to profess and practice their own religion, or to use their own language." Subsequently, the Commission asked the Sub-Commission to define the term "minority." Jules Deschenes proposed in 1985

that the term exclude indigenous people, noncitizens, and oppressed majorities. No consensus on the precise definition emerged, but all concerned agreed that one ought to distinguish between indigenous and ethnic groups. A separate effort to develop standards for indigenous peoples resulted in the Draft Declaration of the Rights of Indigenous Persons. Religious minorities also have the Declaration on the Elimination of All Forms of Religious Intolerance. In 1992 the Sub-Commission helped draft the Declaration of the Rights of Persons Belonging to National or Ethnic, Religious and Linguistic Minorities.

Each human rights treaty has its own committee that considers complaints filed under the instrument. This is sometimes only possible when the state being accused of the violation has ratified the Optional Protocol to the substantive treaty, giving the treaty committee the power to review the complaints about its conduct. The committee also reviews periodic reports filed by states in which they detail the extent to which their policies are in compliance with each of the articles in the treaty. It is within the purview of the committee, when problems are found, to work with states to make changes needed to improve human rights conditions. Despite the small size of a treaty committee, it has the potential to effect significant change. For instance, in 1992 the Economic, Social and Cultural Rights Committee prevented the eviction of 19,000 families from their homes in the Dominican Republic. The committees also generate decisions which have jurisprudential significance.

Another key international institution is the UN High Commissioner for Human Rights newly established in 1994. The Commissioner, appointed by the Secretary-General to a four-year term, is subject to confirmation by the General Assembly. The Commissioner, who has the rank of Under-Secretary-General of the UN, is responsible for supervising the Geneva-based Human Rights Center, coordinating all the UN human rights activities, and promoting international human rights. In 1998 the Commissioner had a budget of approximately $73 million and a staff of 300 employees. The first commissioner was Jose Ayala Lasso from Ecuador and the second, Mary Robinson, former president of Ireland. The UN High Commissioner has been asked to intervene in trouble spots around the world. Because it is such a new institutional development, it is premature to assess its effectiveness.

B. Regional Institutions

Regional human rights institutions have developed their own jurisprudence. The Council of Europe set up the system that relies on two major texts, the European Convention of Human Rights (entered into force in 1953 and ratified by 40 states) and the European Social Charter, which contains economic rights. This catalogue of rights has been expanded by protocols.

The European system originally operated with a Commission, which engaged in fact-finding, and a Court, which heard appeals by states or the Commission. Although the Court at first had no power to issue advisory opinions, a limited power to do so was added by Protocol 2. When Protocol 11 entered into force in 1998, the Commission and Court were merged into a single court. The arrangement consists of a chamber and a Grand Chamber with somewhat complex jurisdictional rules.

The European human rights system is considered to be the most well-established system, having decided more than 400 cases since it was created. Most of its early cases concerned due process, such as pretrial detention, and the right to privacy. It has rendered decisions on many topics, such as terrorism, sexual orientation, freedom of expression, freedom of association, and torture. The first case to reach the Court was the Lawless Case, which involved the question of state derogations during national emergencies. Although the Court found that states parties had a "margin of appreciation," it was not an unlimited power. The margin of appreciation doctrine in the European system has generated controversy. It involves a significant question: to what extent should nation-states have latitude to interpret provisions in the European human rights system so that they do not have to comply with the standards?

Whereas the right of individual petition was originally optional for states parties to the European Convention, signatories are automatically bound by the inter-state complaint process. Article 24 provides for an inter-state procedure according to which a state can refer a breach of the Convention to the Commission. This means that State A, by ratifying the European Convention, agrees to be subject to investigation by the system if State B files a complaint accusing State A of human rights violations under the Convention. By 1995 all parties to the European Convention had also accepted both the right of individual petition and the jurisdiction of the Court, Articles 25 and 46, respectively. Under Article 25 the Commission could process complaints from an individual, nongovernmental organization, or group alleging violations of the Convention, provided the State in question had formally accepted the competence of the Commission to review applications. Although initially the Convention did not permit peti-

tioners before the Commission to take their cases to the Court, when Protocol 9 came into force in 1994, it enabled individuals in a minority of states to do so.

The relationship between the European human rights machinery in Strasbourg and the European Court of Justice of the European Union is evolving. The European Court of Justice has rendered some decisions that have human rights implications, and relies on cases decided in the Strasbourg system. Furthermore, Member States of the European Union have ratified the European Convention of Human Rights and have accepted the Court's jurisdiction, which should minimize conflict between the two systems.

Created by the Organization of American States (OAS) 50 years ago, the Inter-American human rights system is based on the OAS Charter and the American Convention on Human Rights (entered into force in 1978 and ratified by 26 states). It differs from the European human rights system in important respects. In this system the individual petitions process is mandatory, but the interstate complaint procedure is optional. It has always had the power to issue advisory opinions (the European system acquired a limited power only recently). Perhaps most significant is that the Inter-American system has had to contend with governments hostile to its human rights work. Whereas states of emergency are rare in the European context, they have been frequent in Latin America. The Inter-American human rights system is known for having the most impressive fact-finding techniques. Among its most significant decisions is the *Velasquez Rodriguez* case (1988), which involved the disappeared in Honduras. The Inter-American Court held that a state is responsible if it fails to take steps to prevent human rights violations. This suggests that nonaction or omission by the state, that is, if a state fails to protect individuals within its borders from actions by private parties that violate their human rights, can also give rise to liability under international law.

In addition to the European and Inter-American human rights systems, there is an African Commission on Human and People's Rights that was created by the Organization for African Unity in 1981. The [Banjul] African Charter of Human and Peoples Rights (ratified by 49 states) contains some rights not enumerated in the other regional and international human rights instruments, and the formulations of rights in the Banjul Charter differ somewhat. The main criticism of the African system has been that it lacks a serious enforcement mechanism, and, therefore, many believe it should establish a court. Since the creation of the African human rights system, it has not promoted human rights as energetically as some had hoped. The reports filed by states parties, for example, contain only formal law and not any accounts of how laws are put into practice. There is also a dormant Arab human rights apparatus and a proposal for an Asian human rights system. Neither has, as of yet, contributed much to the promotion of international human rights.

There is serious debate about the desirability of regional human rights institutions. Those in favor argue that their normative principles are more likely to resonate with local cultures, that the enforcement will seem less imperialistic, and that investigation of alleged abuses is facilitated by regional institutions. Those opposed argue that the existence of multiple regional bodies will likely give rise to conflicting interpretations of human rights and that it will not be a trivial matter to harmonize divergent interpretations of specific human rights norms.

C. Domestic Courts

Domestic courts are another important institution for the enforcement of human rights. This method avoids some of the difficulties associated with enforcement of international law. Human rights law is used in national courts either as the basis of the decision or as an interpretive guide for domestic norms, for example, invoking human rights norms to clarify the meaning of the 8th Amendment prohibition of "cruel and unusual punishment." In the United States treaty law has seldom been used because (1) the United States only ratified some of the major treaties in the 1990s, (2) the U.S. adheres to the non-self-executing treaty doctrine according to which ratified treaties do not come into effect until enabling legislation is enacted, and (3) the United States objects to the idea that Americans would be subject to international law in tribunals abroad. Instead of using treaties, U.S. courts have successfully invoked customary international law.

The landmark case in the United States that established the propriety of relying on customary international human rights law was *Filartiga v. Pena-Irala* (1980). The former chief of police in Paraguay tortured the son of a prominent doctor to death. Dr. Filartiga and his daughter, assisted by the Center for Constitutional Rights, filed a lawsuit against the torturer, Pena-Irala, in federal district court in New York. The court ruled that it had jurisdiction under the Alien Tort Claims Act (ATCA), which gives U.S. federal courts the authority to hear aliens' tort claims involving a violation of the law of nations if it has jurisdiction over the defendant. The court awarded $10 million to Dr. Filartiga and his

daughter. Although they were unable to collect this sum, the decision conveyed the symbolic message that human rights violations will not be tolerated. It paved the way for hundreds of other human rights lawsuits. In subsequent litigation, new issues have emerged, such as whether sovereign immunity bars lawsuits, whether nonstate actors can be held liable under international law, and whether this activity potentially interferes with the executive branch by threatening to undermine diplomacy.

After the *Filartiga* decision there was some question as to whether the Alien Tort Claims Act authorized human rights lawsuits of this kind. Federal Court of Appeals Judge Robert Bork, in *Tel-Oren v. Libyan Arab Republic* (1984), specifically challenged the idea that the statute permitted them. Congress clarified this matter when it passed the Torture Victim Protection Act (TVPA) of 1992, which gives federal courts jurisdiction over human rights lawsuits involving torture, summary execution, and similar abuses. It empowers both aliens and also U.S. citizens to bring suit. The TVPA is narrower than the ATCA with regard to the types of violations it covers, but it is broader because it allows U.S. citizens to file suit.

Sovereign immunity has been held to bar lawsuits against leaders who have allegedly violated the human rights of their citizens. The problem in the United States is that the Foreign Sovereign Immunities Act (FSIA) does not include *ius cogens* violations as one of the exceptions for the application of immunity. The Court of Appeals for the Ninth Circuit held in *Siderman v. Argentina* (1992) that because the U.S. Supreme Court explicitly stated in *Amerada Hess* (1989) that the only permissible exceptions to sovereign immunity are those listed in the FSIA, immunity applies even when governments stand accused of gross violations of human rights.

In the 1990s plaintiffs have filed suit against private parties, alleging that their human rights were violated. For instance, in *Kadic v. Karadzic* (1992), the district court dismissed allegations of torture, summary execution, genocide, and war crimes because it found no state action. But in 1995 the U.S. Court of Appeals reversed, because the court found that he was the leader of a "de facto" regime and therefore met the state action requirements for torture and summary execution and because the court held that the crimes of genocide and war crimes do not require state action. A dilemma that exists is that if the court considers a person to be a "de facto" leader in order to hold him responsible for conduct that must be state-sponsored, the court thereby enshrouds the defendant with immunity. In *John Doe I. et al. v. Unocal*, (1997) a federal judge held that a

U.S. company, Unocal, was responsible for gross violations of international human rights committed by a foreign partner, in this case a state-owned oil and gas company in Myanmar, the former Burma. If nonstate actors are held responsible under international law, that will represent an important development in the field. This type of litigation may depend on the sort of human rights violations alleged, as some like genocide are defined in such a way that nonstate actors are clearly liable, whereas other abuses like torture have to be state-sponsored.

D. NGOs

Nonstate actors are often the most serious champions of human rights. Indeed, nongovernmental organizations play a critical role in raising consciousness about human rights. The largest global Human Rights NGO is Amnesty International, which is headquartered in London. It concentrates on civil and political rights, primarily the rights of freedom of expression and assembly. A grassroots organization, Amnesty relies heavily on chapters' letter-writing campaigns designed to pressure governments to release political prisoners from incarceration. The largest U.S. NGO is Human Rights Watch, which is based in New York. Human Rights Watch is run by professional staff organized in different geographical and subject-matter units, such as Asia Watch, Middle East Watch, the Children's Rights Project, Arms Control Project, and the Women's Rights project. Some other human rights organizations include the Minority Rights Group, Anti-Slavery International (formerly the Anti-Slavery Society for the Protection of Human Rights), the International Committee of Jurists, Cultural Survival, the International Committee of the Red Cross, and many others. They differ in the scope of their mandates, the nature of their collective actions, and the extent of their influence with governments.

Despite differences of opinion about the proper role of Human Rights NGOs, there is no question that their research often affects decision-making by governments, the United Nations, and regional human rights institutions. Their reports are read widely by these institutions, their staff members give testimony in legislatures, and they try to generate public support for human rights. They may also file *amicus curiae* briefs in court cases. For example, Amnesty International filed one in *Stanford v. Kentucky*, the U.S. Supreme Court decision on juvenile executions.

Another important method of promoting human rights is through the foreign policy of nation-states. When states are displeased with the actions of others,

they may impose economic sanctions, either bilateral or multilateral ones. This can be a desirable approach inasmuch as it avoids the use of force. It can, however, be unattractive if the sanctions end up hurting the individuals whose human rights are in question. Some commentators thought this was the case in South Africa.

Some governments collect human rights data to aid the foreign policy decision-making process. For instance, the Country Reports on Human Rights Practices, which the U.S. Department of State has compiled since 1977, are submitted to the Congress as required by law. In 1977 the reports were only for the 82 countries receiving U.S. aid, but 20 years later, in 1997, 194 reports were submitted to Congress. In the United States responsibility for human rights data gathering in embassies was handled by the Bureau of Human Rights and Humanitarian Affairs. In 1994 the Bureau was renamed the Bureau of Democracy, Human Rights, and Labor. The data is compiled by the embassies and subsequently corroborated by State Department officers. The reports contain useful overviews of human rights conditions across the globe, although there are claims that the measures used to assess violations are politicized.

IV. HUMAN RIGHTS AND VIOLENCE

A. Humanitarian Intervention

Many rules of international human rights law were designed to limit violence. Norms pertaining to humanitarian intervention, the law of war, and rules governing national emergencies show the logic of the international system with regard to the proper management of conflict.

A perennial question is when is intervention by one state in the territory of another justified in order to protect human rights. Most scholars prefer multilateral intervention to unilateral intervention because they consider it less susceptible to abuse. Indeed, the debate about whether customary international law permits humanitarian intervention has been contentious. The International Court of Justice addressed the legitimacy of humanitarian intervention to protect human rights in its 1986 Judgment in the *Case Concerning Military and Paramilitary Activities in and Against Nicaragua*. The World Court stated that the use of force to protect human rights, in the context of that case, could not be justified under international law. The entire premise seemed illogical: "... the protection of human rights, a strictly humanitarian objective, cannot be compatible with the mining of ports, the destruction of oil installations, or again with the training, arming and equipping of the contras. The Court concludes that the argument derived from the preservation of human rights in Nicaragua cannot afford a legal justification for the conduct of the U.S. . . ."

As for treaty-based justification, the United Nations Charter stipulates in Article 2(7) that the UN shall not intervene in "matters which are essentially within the jurisdiction of any state" but makes no mention of a similar prohibition for member states. Article 2(4) prohibits the threat or use of force against the territorial integrity or political independence of any state. It does not mention intervention per se. The United Nations can intervene if a situation poses a "threat to the peace" within the meaning of Article 39 of the United Nations Charter. Article 42 specifies what steps the UN Security Council may take, such as demonstrations, blockade, and other operations by air, sea, or land forces, in order to restore international peace and security. The Security Council invoked these powers when it imposed economic sanctions against Southern Rhodesia in 1968, and an arms embargo against South Africa in the early 1970s. In the Gulf War, the Security Council relied on Resolution 688 (1991), which made a reference to Chapter VII of the UN Charter, the Council's obligation to maintain international peace and security.

B. The Law of War

There is some degree of overlap between humanitarian international law and international human rights law. The main difference between the two is that whereas humanitarian law only applies during wartime, international human rights law is always in effect. The law of war consists of customary international law norms dating back centuries. After WWII, states codified the law when they adopted the four Geneva Conventions of August 12, 1949. Initially, some argued that the rules should apply to both civil and international conflicts, but in the end it was decided that they would not apply to "internal" armed conflicts. Some states were concerned that if the rules applied to internal conflicts, this would give rebels *de facto* status as belligerents and possibly even *de jure* legal recognition. Basically, states did not want to create a mechanism that would confer legitimacy on rebels. Since these same states were opposed to giving rebels prisoner of war status partly because they wanted to discourage rebellion, they persuaded the diplomatic conference to make the rules applicable only to international armed conflicts.

The compromise, which became known as the "Common Article Three" (because it is in all four Geneva Conventions), protects combatants and civilians during "non-international conflicts." It sets forth a bill of rights for noninternational armed conflicts, and, at the time of its adoption, was considered to be a significant development. Because it is not clear precisely what constitutes "non-international armed conflict" and because states worried that rebels will gain international legal status as belligerents if Common Article Three is applied to their internal conflicts, the provision has not had the practical success desired.

In the late 1970s there was an attempt to expand Common Article Three through two Additional Protocols (1977). Protocol I dealt with the phenomenon of anticolonial conflicts, so-called wars of national liberation. It was designed to recognize the international character of wars of national liberation based on the right of self-determination, a right so vital that it appears as Article 1 in both the ICCPR and the ICECSR. Western nations abstained when the final vote was taken, with only Israel voting against. Article 4 was controversial because it seemed to accept the notion of "just wars." Protocol II (Protocol Additional to the Geneva Conventions of 12 August 1949, and Relating to the Protection of Victims of Non-International Conflicts), expands protections concerning medical personnel, judicial guarantees, and human treatment. A question about Protocol II has been what level of conflict triggers its application.

C. Human Rights during Civil Strife: Derogations

When there is domestic turmoil and the law of war does not apply, the international law of human rights concerning states of emergency is used. Under these circumstances states will claim that they must suspend or "derogate from" international human rights standards. Article 4 of the ICCPR, concerning the issue of when a public emergency threatens the life of the nation, permits derogation for some human rights, but not for fundamental ones such as the right to life, the right against genocide, the right against torture, the right against slavery, and the right against arbitrary arrest and detention. Article 15 of the European Convention on Human Rights also allows for derogations "to the extent strictly required by the exigencies of the situation" in the case of public emergency or in time of war. The American Convention on Human Rights contains Article 27. Suspension of Guarantees, which permits derogation "in time of war, public danger, or other emergency that threatens the independence or security of a State Party." While its formulation seems to provide the easiest means of justifying derogation, the drafting history (*travaux preparatoires*) suggests otherwise.

All three treaties include the key concept of proportionality, permitting derogations only to the extent "strictly required by the exigencies of the situation." All three also require formal notification of authorities who can monitor the implementation of the derogation policies. Where they differ is in the rights that they define as absolute rights that can never be suspended, that is, nonderogable rights.

V. NEW DEVELOPMENTS

A. Permanent International Criminal Court

For decades there have been proposals on the table to establish a permanent international criminal court. In the aftermath of the genocides in the former Yugoslavia and in Rwanda, a perceived need to have a permanent institution to prosecute violators of these norms led to renewed efforts to establish such a tribunal. The arguments for its creation include: deterring future atrocities, avoiding the conflict of interest inherent in domestic court martials, and obviating the need to kidnap defendants to put them on trial, as in the *Eichman* and *Alvarez-Machain* cases, or to go through the cumbersome process of extradition, as in the *Soering* case. In July 1998 a preparatory conference met in Rome to finalize a statute for the proposed permanent international tribunal. 120 states voted to approve the final document, and the International Criminal Court will be established when 60 states have ratified the treaty (58 have signed it, but ratification requires additional steps on the part of governments).

Although the completion of the statute was a victory, human rights advocates had some serious criticisms. First, the jurisdiction of the tribunal remained unclear because the conference did not interpret some of the crimes. Although crimes of aggression appear in the Statute, they are not defined. A concession to Security Council members wielding nuclear power resulted in defining war crimes so that they did not include any reference to nuclear weapons. In addition, landmines were excluded from the Statute, due to opposition by the United States, Russia, China, and Britain. Although the statute mentions "enforced disappearances of persons" as a crime against humanity, there was an unfortunate stipulation that the disappearances may be prosecuted only if they occur for a "prolonged period of time."

Another controversy revolved around the child soldier provisions. Article 8(2)(e)vii of the Statute holds that it is a war crime to conscript or enlist children under the age of 15 in armed forces or groups or to use them in armed conflict, even though most human rights activists argued strongly for raising the age limit to 18. The United States led the campaign to lower the age to 15 because of its practice of recruiting 17 year olds. Despite the 15 year rule, the Statute specifies that the ICC will not have jurisdiction over children who were under 18 at the time of the alleged commission of crimes (Article 26).

Another major criticism is that the Statute accepts the defense of superior orders in Article 33, even though this defense has never been recognized in international law and was rejected at the Nuremberg and Tokyo tribunals. The rationale for the defense is that soldiers should not be held responsible for crimes committed when they are following the orders of their superior officers.

A potential inequity may result because the international tribunal, like the Yugoslav and Rwandan tribunals, will not have the power to impose the death penalty, even though domestic courts may wield this power. Consequently, the more senior officials, if prosecuted in the international criminal court, will face less severe punishment than would junior officers tried in national courts.

It is noteworthy that there were earlier efforts to formulate a code of international crimes. Inspired by the Nuremberg principles, the International Law Commission (ILC) worked on a Draft Code of Crimes Against the Peace and Security of Mankind. In 1954 the ILC forwarded the document to the UN General Assembly, which took 27 years before sending it back to the ILC for elaboration. Another version was finished in 1991. It applies only to individuals, and not to states. A separate instrument, the Draft Articles on State Responsibility, includes a provision indicating that the prosecution of individuals for crimes against the peace and security of mankind does not relieve the state of responsibility under international law.

B. Other Developments

Human rights institutions have begun to address rights against discrimination based on gender, disability, and sexual orientation, which had previously been ignored because of their controversial nature. Although women's rights were traditionally relegated to the Commission on the Status of Women, which was set up at the same time as the Commission on Human Rights, in the 1990s human rights institutions embraced women's rights as well. In the 1990s there has been a movement to focus attention on the experience of women. The World Conference in Beijing in conjunction with the publication of major works on women's rights as human rights challenged the marginalization of women.

At the same time, international institutions began to place more emphasis on violence against women. In 1993 the General Assembly adopted a Declaration on the Elimination of Violence against Women. Pressure was brought to include gender-specific violence such as mass rapes in the statutes of the ad hoc tribunals for the former Yugoslavia and for Rwanda and in the statute for the Permanent International Criminal Court. The UN appointed a Special Rapporteur, Radhika Coomaraswamy, a Sri Lankan jurist, to document the global trends in violence against women, and she issued several reports on this subject.

In national contexts, because of increased awareness about the plight of women, Canada and the United States changed their immigration policies to permit women to seek political asylum on the basis of gender persecution. In the past political persecution was construed as deliberate acts to harm women. In the 1990s the failure of government to protect women from cultural traditons such as female genital cutting began to be considered grounds for political asylum. The landmark case in the United States that prompted the policy change was that of Fausiya Kasinga from Togo. The U.S. government expanded its measure of human rights in the country reports to include violence against women, requiring amassing data on gender-specific violence.

In the past, the predicament of women was that the violations of their rights took place in the "private" realm of family, religion, or culture and thus were beyond the reach of the law. The trend toward holding governments accountable for the failure to protect women from harm perpetrated by private actors has helped break down the "public/private" distinction.

Another issue that the human rights community embraced was human rights and the environment, even though ecological issues had usually been handled by the U.N. Commission on Sustainable Development. In the 1990s Fatma Zohra Ksentini, the UN Special Rapporteur, conducted research on the relationship between Human Rights and the Environment. Her final report was an important contribution in many ways because of its documentation of phenomena such as "environmental refugees" (individuals forced to move because of environmental degradation), its compilation of 50 national constitutional provisions guaranteeing a right to a clean environment, and an appendix, "A Draft Declaration of Principles on Human Rights and the Environment."

Another human rights movement underway is an international campaign to abolish the death penalty. This is evidenced by the completion of the Second Optional Protocol to the ICCPR, aiming at the abolition of the death penalty, the Protocol to the American Convention on Human Rights to Abolish the Death Penalty, Protocol 6 to the European Convention on Human Rights, and the abolition of the death penalty for juveniles in most legal systems across the globe. At present, the death penalty is not *per se* a violation of international human rights law, but through the progressive development of international norms, it may eventually be.

VI. CONCLUSION

The notion of human rights has become a well-accepted idea across the globe. Human rights advocates have had notable success at both standard-setting and enforcement. One of the major tasks which lies ahead is that of harmonizing human rights, given the conflicting interpretations of particular norms in a multicultural world. Where there is a clear consensus on human rights, governments will not be able to circumvent those standards which have been universally embraced.

Also See the Following Articles

CIVIL SOCIETIES • COLLECTIVE SECURITY SYSTEMS • ENVIRONMENTAL ISSUES AND POLITICS • MORAL JUDGMENTS AND VALUES • PEACE ORGANIZATIONS • WAR CRIMES

Bibliography

Alston, P. (Ed.). (1992). *The United Nations and human rights: A critical appraisal.* Oxford: Clarendon Press.

Bozeman, A. B. (1971). *The future of law in a multicultural world.* Princeton, NJ: Princeton University Press.

Bruno, S., & Alston, P. (1992). The Sources of Human Rights Law: Custom, *Jus Cogens,* and General Principles. *Australian Year Book of International Law* 23, 82–108.

Caportorti, F. (1979). *Study on the rights of persons belonging to ethnic, religious and linguistic minorities.* UN Sales NO. E78.XIV.1.

Cook, R. J. (Ed.). (1994). *Human rights of women: National and international perspectives.* Philadelphia: University of Pennsylvania Press.

Dallmeyer, D. G. (Ed.). (1993). *Reconceiving reality: Women and international law.* Washington, DC: American Society of International Law.

Danieli, Y., Stamatopoulou, E., & Dias, C. J. (Eds.). (1999). *The universal declaration of human rights: Fifty Years and Beyond.* Amityville, New York: Baywood Publishing Company, Inc.

Degener, T., & Koster-Dreese, Y. (Eds.). (1995). *Human rights and disabled persons: Essays and relevant human rights instruments.* Dordrecht, Boston, and London: Martinus Nijhoff Publishers.

Donnelly, J. (1982). Human rights and human dignity: An analytic critique of non-Western conceptions of human rights. *American Political Science Review* 76.

Eide, A., *et al.* (Eds.). (1993). *The universal declaration of human rights: A commentary.* Norway: Scandanavian University Press.

Hannum, H. (1990). *Autonomy, sovereignty, and self-determination: The accommodation of conflicting rights.* Philadelphia: University of Pennsylvania Press.

Henkin, L., & Hargrove, J. L. (Eds.). (1994). *Human rights: An agenda for the next century.* Washington, DC: American Society of International Law.

Hersh, J. (1969). *Birthright of man: A selection of texts.* New York: UNESCO.

Human Rights Committee (1994). General Comment on issues relating to reservations made upon ratification or accession to the Covenant or the Optional Protocols, or in relations to declarations under Article 41 of the Covenant. 34 *International Legal Materials (I.L.M.)* 839 (1995).

Humphrey, J. (1984). *Human rights and the United Nations: A great adventure.* Dobbs Ferry, NY: Transnational Publishers.

Korey, W. (1998). *NGOS and the universal declaration of human rights: "A curious grapevine."* New York: St. Martin's Press.

Ksentini, F. Z. (1994). United Nations Economic and Social Council Final Report, Special Rapporteur, Annex I, Draft Principles on Human and the Environment, pp. 74–78, E/CN.4/Sub.2/1994/9.

Lauren, P. G. (1998). *The evolution of international human rights: Visions seen.* Philadelphia, Pennsylvania: University of Pennsylvania Press.

Laqueur, W., & Rubin, B. (Eds.). (1989). *The human rights reader* (revised edition). New York: New American Library.

McGoldrick, D. (1994). *The Human Rights Committee: Its role in the development of the International Covenant on Civil and Political Rights.* Oxford: Clarendon.

Panikkar, R. (1982). Is the notion of human rights a Western concept? *Diogenes* 120, 75–102.

Pollis, A. (1996). Cultural relativism revisited: Through a state prism. *Human Rights Quarterly* 18, 316–344.

Pollis, A., & Schwab, P. (Eds.). (1979). *Human rights: Cultural and ideological perspectives.* New York: Praeger.

Renteln, A. D. (1990). *International human rights: Universalism versus relativism.* Newbury Park: Sage Publications.

Stephens, B., & Ratner, M. (1996). *International human rights litigation in U.S. Courts.* Irvington-on-Hudson, NY: Transnational Publishers.

Tolley, H., Jr. (1987). *The U.N. Commission on Human Rights.* Boulder and London: Westview Press.

Roosevelt, E. (1958). *On my own.* New York: Harper and Brothers.

United Nations. (1994). *Human rights: A compilation of international instruments.* Volume 1 (Parts 1 and 2: Universal Instruments). New York and Geneva: United Nations.

UNESCO (1949). *Human rights: Comments and interpretations* (London: Allan Wingate).

Indigenous Peoples' Responses to Conquest

Franke Wilmer

Montana State University

I. INTRODUCTION

The past two and one-half decades have witnessed a burgeoning political movement among the world's indigenous peoples. Representatives of indigenous groups from every continent have been mobilizing in international, regional and national arenas. They protest, lobby, litigate, and in rare cases, resist with force the policies of states aimed at their assimilation, cultural destruction and expropriation from their traditional territories. (I distinguish between "acculturation," which entails adopting the cultural traits of another group and, in my opinion, has been a mutual process in indigenous contact and coexistence with nonindigenous and modernizing groups (as it has been among indigenous groups), and "assimilation" which involves a dominant group absorbing indigenous peoples as individuals into the cultural practices of the dominant group, in the process eliminating most or all of those practices, beliefs and values which would otherwise signify the cultural distinctiveness of the indigenous group as a collectivity. Assimilation has been the objective of settler and dominant modernizing groups vis-a-vis indigenous peoples in virtually all settings.) Whether such resistances are a continuation of struggles begun as long as five centuries ago in settler states (in the Americas, Australia, and New Zealand)) or in the face of state-building and modernization in the Third World (in India, Southeast Asia, and Africa), indigenous peoples have never remained passive in confrontations with those who seek their cultural or physical destruction through domination.

In 1993 the United Nations Working Group on Indigenous Populations produced a Draft Declaration on Discrimination Against Indigenous Peoples, the culmination of two decades of work prompted by indigenous activism. Following the completion of a report on the Problem of Discrimination Against Indigenous Populations, the UN Working Group initiated a series of yearly meetings in 1981 to develop a draft declaration, which would then provide the basis for an international convention, and therefore a legal instrument for the protection of indigenous peoples' rights. Hundreds of indigenous representatives and nongovernmental organizations interested in the protection of indigenous peoples' rights attended the yearly sessions, providing testimony, reports, and recommendations pursuant to the

Copyright © 1999 by Academic Press.
All rights of reproduction in any form reserved.

development of the final document. There was both consensus and dissent on a wide variety of issues, highlighting the commonalities in indigenous–state relations as well as the tremendous variety in the historical and political experience of indigenous peoples in industrialized and developing states. Like virtually all international human rights law, the assertion of indigenous peoples' rights seeks to impose on states' obligations to observe certain restraints in the exercise of their power and authority. What is particularly remarkable about these developments is that they flow directly from the nationally, regionally, and globally organized resistances of indigenous peoples to domination and conquest by states.

Just as nearly universal assent to basic international human rights covenants has not eliminated human rights violations in many parts of the world, neither would a Convention on Discrimination Against Indigenous Peoples in itself mark the end of indigenous peoples' struggles for physical and cultural survival. It would, however, acknowledge a shift in international norms, and secure a discursive space on the international agenda for continued attention to the need for change in indigenous–state relations. Before turning to an examination of international norms pertaining to the idea of conquest and indigenous peoples' responses, it will be helpful to clarify what is meant by "indigenous peoples."

II. WHO ARE INDIGENOUS PEOPLES?

In 1974 the National Indian Brotherhood in Canada organized and sponsored the first contemporary international meeting of indigenous peoples. For the purposes of the conference, indigenous peoples were defined as

> . . . people living in countries which have a population composed of differing ethnic or racial groups who are descendants of the earliest populations living in the area and who do not as a group control the national government of the countries within which they live (Sanders, 1980).

Because today there are between four and five thousand distinct ethnic groups living in fewer than 200 states, this definition could be applied to literally thousands of groups. Thus when the issue was raised within the United Nations, state and indigenous representatives tried to develop a narrower definition of indigenous peoples—or "American Indians and people like

that"—to include those who had previously been referred to as "tribal," "native," or "aboriginal" peoples living in states formed as a result of European colonization. Such a definition includes not only the native peoples of the Americas and the settler states (U.S., Canada, Australia, and New Zealand) but also tribal peoples such as the Masai (in Kenya), the Dani (in Indonesia), and the East Timorese, since they constitute distinct tribal peoples who were self-governing prior to colonization but whose political destiny is now controlled by a force (the postcolonial governments of Kenya and Indonesia) "outside" of the indigenous community. A definition contingent upon the creation of states as a result of colonization therefore includes indigenous peoples in Third World states, even though their postcolonial governments may now be controlled by individuals "indigenous" to the area. (Proceedings within the UN among indigenous representatives indicates that the definitional issue remains ambiguous and contentious. The discussion here should be taken as the author's position, not as a position on which there is universal agreement.)

In considering who is indigenous, it is the political significance of the term that emerged in relation to a specific political process of state-building that is important. Because state-building has proceeded on two implicit assumptions about the role of the state it *ipso facto* infringes on the self-determination of indigenous peoples. The first assumption is that the state exists largely as a mechanism for appropriating resources for industrialization (expanded in the First World) and development (in the Third World). This assumption holds that there is a coherent and unified "national" interest in industrialization, and that this interest is superior to other uses as well as to the claims of subnational groups to self-determine the use of any resources within the territory of the state. It is, of course, not only indigenous peoples who make claims to exempt certain resources from national industrialization programs, but environmental and conservation groups as well, and in some cases this has produced alliances between indigenous and environmental interests. It should be noted, however, that indigenous peoples do not necessarily oppose industrialization, nor do they necessarily support all environmental movements, but rather they claim a right to exercise self-determination over the use some portion of resources now "located" within the jurisdictional domain of the state. They may choose to incorporate these resources into national industrialization programs, or not.

The second assumption is that the state has a legitimate interest in articulating and promoting a national identity in whose name national economic programs are carried out. This is often associated with "modernization" schemes as well as in the nation-building process that accompanies state-building. Following from this assumption, the state is "justified" in making the assimilation of indigenous peoples a national priority, legitimating policies aimed at the destruction of indigenous peoples' cultural resources—language, religious practice, and version of history, for example. Indigenous peoples become the targets of state policies that not only expropriate indigenous resources, but directly and indirectly aim at their cultural destruction—the destruction of their existence and identity as a people.

In contemporary international politics, therefore, the concept of indigenousness does not simply refer to groups occupying an area prior to the arrival of other groups, for the present location of ethnic groups in the world is a result of centuries of migration, diasporas, imperial expansion and collapse, permanent settlements resulting from conquest, and the building of states. Rather it refers to that particular quality of modern state-building in which peoples who have lived as culturally distinct societies struggle to retain or reclaim the right of self-determination in the face of state-building and industrial expansion that seeks, one way or another, to destroy their existence as self-determining peoples.

The resistances of indigenous peoples "located" within the settler states of the Americas, Australia, and New Zealand span the widest band of modern history and are intimately tied to the peculiar instance of post-imperial settler states' conquest of indigenous occupants of these lands. But the Saami in northern Scandinavia face similar pressures as continued industrial expansion in, for example, Norway, led to a demand for increased exploitation of hydroelectric power in the north of the country where many Saami live. Other groups of indigenous peoples are found throughout the Third World in recently decolonized states. Here the pattern of state-building as a process of modernization which characterized the indigenous-settler relationship in the United States, Canada, New Zealand, and Australia, is reproduced by modernizing Third World elites. The "scheduled tribes" of India, the Maasi in Kenya, the Chittagong Hill tribes in Bangladesh, and the Iban, Penan, and others of Sarawak in Malaysia, are among the many indigenous groups resisting assimilation, expropriation and cultural and physical destruction as a result of postcolonial state-building and industrial development in the Third World.

The resistances of indigenous peoples are therefore resistances to conquest by states created through imperialism and decolonization. There are two general historical patterns that characterize indigenous peoples' political situation and relations with states today. The first is that of the settler state created as a result of European colonization in which a dominant population descended from European settlers now controls the political life of the state and the people within it. The obvious examples are those created as a result of British colonization—the United States, Canada, Australia, and New Zealand. The conquest of indigenous peoples in these states is a direct result of a settler population expanding its claim to territory and displacing indigenous peoples in the process. The conquest was accomplished by a combination of public violence, or war (often undeclared) and publicly (though often tacitly) sanctioned private violence as settlers were induced to move into indigenous territories and violent clashes between settlers and indigenous peoples ensued. The second pattern is the case of postcolonial states, where, after centuries of colonization, power was transferred from colonial governments to local elites who continued the "modernization" and "development" processes. These new "indigenous" elites reproduced the settler-indigenous relationship by characterizing those indigenous groups who remained unintegrated into or in a peripheral relationship to the modernization process as "backward," legitimating them as targets for forced assimilation, relocation and, as in the settler states, public and private forms of violence.

In the first case the conquest of indigenous peoples and their resistance to it has taken place over a period of several centuries. Their present struggles take place in the context of that history, which includes a period of initial contact during which there may have been treaties made between the colonial and indigenous peoples as well as violent confrontation of one sort or another, including the use of force by settler governments. These histories also typically include a period of forced assimilation and relocation programs. Indigenous peoples in these states today carry on their resistances mainly through legal and political channels. In the second case, many of the indigenous peoples involved were not the target of full-scale conquest, and they have only become the targets of official policies aimed at their assimilation and relocation within the past few decades. Yet they have joined with indigenous peoples of the First World to form a high degree of international solidarity and have often proceeded with their own resistances through legal and political means, where possible, in national and international arenas. The situation of indigenous peoples in Central and

South America represents something of a variation on these two patterns, for these states were also created as a result of colonial conquest. For a variety of reasons, however, such as geographic barriers, many indigenous peoples, such as the Yanomamo, remained unintegrated or peripheral to state-building here well into the second half of the 20th century, while others, in Guatemala and Ecuador, for example, became embroiled in a struggle characterized by both cultural and class cleavages.

The numbers and locations of indigenous peoples—approximately 300 million on every continent—render the topic much too large to cover comprehensively in one article (see Table 1).

There are a number of good sources providing more comprehensive historical and contemporary perspectives on indigenous political activism (Aga Khan and bin Talal, 1987; Burger, 1987; Moody, 1988; Wilmer, 1993; Van Cott, 1994; Anaya, 1996; Perry, 1996; Maybury-Lewis, 1997). This article will primarily focus on the experience of indigenous peoples in the First World in order to illustrate the commonalities in indigenous–state relations over the longer historical period. The pattern of contact, overt and covert conquest, expropriation and assimilation aimed at ending the distinct existence of indigenous peoples is the process indigenous peoples resist. There are two main differences between this pattern in the settlers states and its reproduction in postcolonial settings: (1) the time period in which is occurs, being several centuries in settler states and several decades elsewhere; and (2) the conquest was carried out by colonizing Westerners in settler states, whereas in postcolonial settings it is carried out by "modernizing elites," who are often themselves in some way "indigenous" and non-Western. The case of indigenous peoples in settler states, however, is instructive, for it also established norms that modernizing elites elsewhere implicitly and explicitly draw on as justification for their own policies aimed at the conquest and assimilation of indigenous peoples.

Following the more detailed case studies of indigenous peoples in settler states, this article will briefly discuss developments in Central and South America to indicate how and where the experience of indigenous peoples there, albeit within a different time frame, both parallels and differs from the patterns found in the settler states. Finally, it will provide a brief discussion of the experience of the indigenous peoples in the Sarawak region of Malaysia as case of indigenous resistance in the postcolonial setting, and conclude with some observations about indigenous resistance as a global process.

TABLE I

Indigenous Peoples: Locations and Approximate Numbers

		% of total pop.
Central America		
Belize	15,000	10
Costa Rica	20,000	1
El Salvador	960,000	21
Guatemala	5,400,000	60
Honduras	250,000	7
Mexico	10,500,000	12.5
Nicaragua	135,000	5
Panama	194,000	8
Total		(16.2 million)
South America		
Argentina	477,000	1.5
Bolivia	4,900,000	71.0
Brazil	325,000	.2
Chile	1,000,000	9.0
Colombia	708,000	1.0
Ecuador	3,750,000	37.0
French Guiana	4,000	4.0
Guyana	30,000	4.0
Paraguay	100,000	3.0
Peru	8,100,000	39.0
Surinam	11,000	2.9
Venezuela	290,000	1.5
Total		(19.7 million)
Asia		
Afghanistan		
(6.7 million Pathan, 300,000 Baluchis, 3 million Koochis)		
Bangladesh	600,000–1,500,000	1
Burma	11,000,000	30
India	51,000,000	7
Indonesia	1,500,000	1
Laos	800,000	23
Malaysia (East)	500,000	50
(peninsula)	71,000	4
Pakistan	7,700,000	8
Phillipines	6,500,000	16
Sri Lanka	2,000	
Taiwan	310,000	2
Thailand	500,000	1
Vietnam	800,000	2
Japan (Ainu)	50,000	
China	67,000,000 (55 minorities)	
Total		(142 million)
First World		
Australia	250,000	2.0
Canada	1,100,000	4.0
USA	1,900,000	.8
New Zealand	300,000	10.0
Pacific Colonies	500,000	
Inuit	112,000	
Saami	58,000	
Total		(4 million)
Indigenous Peoples in C.I.S.		
C.I.S.	1,000,000 northern peoples	
	6,000,000 Kazakhs	
	22,000,000 Turkick	
Total		(96 million)
Africa (Partial listing)		
Nomadic herders including: Maasai, Tuareg, Bororo Afar		
Somali herders—	14,000,000	
in Arabia	5,000,000	
San (Bushmen);		
Botswana	25,000	
Namibia	29,000	
Angola	8,000	
Mbut and forest peoples	200,000	
Total		(19.6 million)

Sources: Julian Burger, *Report from the Frontier* (London: Zed Books) 1987, and *Canada Year Book 1992*, and Franke Wilmer, *The Indigenous Voice in World Politics* (Sage, 1993). (The World Bank uses a total of 230 million while the I.L.O. uses a total of 300 million.)

III. INDIGENOUS PEOPLES AND CONQUEST

While *norms* of conquest have been asserted as the basis for the domination of indigenous peoples, in *practice* European colonization, at least through the late 19th century, was also accomplished in part by negotiating treaties with indigenous peoples. Treaty-making in practice was erratic, intermittent, arbitrary, and inconsistent. The first treaties in North America were negotiated between the Dutch and the Iroquois, and subsequently by the British and their successor settler states. An elaborate debate among 16th- and 17th-century Spanish theologians on the status of indigenous peoples in relation to the "law of civilized nations" produced a justification for the conquest and subjugation of indigenous peoples without treaty-making, while in the southwest United States native sovereignty "passed" from the Spanish to the Mexican and finally the U.S. governments—all, of course, without the consent of the indigenous peoples. In New Zealand the Treaty of Waitangi was viewed by the British as the abdication of native sovereignty, while for the Maori it was the basis for shared sovereignty and coequal coexistence. In Australia the British Privy Council concluded that the continent was *terra nullius* or "unoccupied" because the aboriginal peoples did not constitute "peoples" with discernible (to the British) governments capable of asserting proprietary rights to land and resources. (This claim was finally overturned by the Australian High Court in 1993, opening the door for the first time to indigenous land claims and initiating an indigenous-state dialogue on the prospect of negotiating a contemporary treaty on Aboriginal rights.) As the British, French, Belgians, Dutch, and Portuguese scrambled for dominance in Africa in the late 1800s, treaties of "friendship" and "tribute" were signed with African chiefs and headmen.

Surprisingly, conquest remained a justification for dominance over indigenous peoples until very recently. When representatives of the Hopi and Navajo nations appealed to the United Nations Human Rights Commission to uphold their sovereign rights to land and self-determination, representatives of the U. S. State Department in 1987 defended its claim that the United States was not accountable to recognize indigenous rights by asserting the applicability of the law of conquest. Although modern writers have been ambivalent toward the application of conquest to the contemporary law of nations, even the ancient Roman law of conquest on which any modern claims rest, holds that it can occur legitimately only after a "just" war between equals, such as nation-states. It could not be applied, according to 18th century international lawyer Emerich deVattel, to the relationship between European powers and the North American indigenous peoples. He even went so far as to argue that to assert conquest one must be the victor in a war fought in self-defense. In any event, two developments leave no doubt that a law of conquest has no validity in contemporary international law: the coming into force of the UN Charter, and the emergence of the principle of self-determination, which liberates peoples who were formerly subjugated to colonial and imperial power.

While in practice thus far the UN and the World Court have seemed reluctant to apply the principle of self-determination beyond the formerly colonized areas of the Third World, the spirit and intent of self-determination is to liberate peoples politically, socially, economically, and culturally subjugated by colonial practices. The 1960 General Assembly Declaration on the Granting of Independence to Colonial Countries and Peoples holds that "The subjection of peoples to outside domination and exploitation constitutes a denial of fundamental human rights," and that "All peoples have the right of self-determination; by virtue of that right they freely determine their political status and freely pursue their economic, social and cultural development." The Declaration, however, is also careful to balance the right of self-determination with the *a priori* rights of the state by prohibiting "Any attempt at the partial or total disruption of the national unity and the territorial integrity of a country," holding that such action "is incompatible with the purposes and principles of the Charter of the United Nations."

It seems clear within the normative framework of the present world system—state-centric as it is—that indigenous peoples nevertheless fall into a category of those entitled to self-determination. Hesitancy to secure this entitlement within international institutions flows not from any normative conflicts, but rather from the lack of political will on the part of states to do so. Indigenous assertions of sovereignty over land and resources—particularly in conjunction with existing treaties—in itself constitutes no threat to "national unity," although it may deny commercial interests and even the state itself access to certain territories and resources on the basis of aboriginal proprietary claims. The threat to territorial integrity is less ambiguous. The majority of indigenous peoples do not assert any desire to secede from the state. The few who do make such an assertion do not base their claims on a right of self-determination, but rather on the exercise of a continuous right of sovereignty predating the formation of contemporary states and that is supported by historical evidence indicating state recognition of their sovereignty. (The Maori claims to sovereignty do not constitute an aspiration to secession, but rather to the exercise of co-equal sovereignty with the New Zealand state.) In fulfilling the right to self-determination, there is an enormous degree of latitude to delineate the terms by which external sovereignty may be limited, while leaving internal sovereignty intact.

The central issue raised by indigenous peoples' political resistance in the form of activism in national and international forums is how to achieve social justice in indigenous-state relations, both in older states, such as the settler states and Scandinavia, given the history of domination and its legacy, as well as in Third World states that have only come into existence as states in the aftermath of colonization and whose boundaries often seem particularly artificial. Attempts to secure a legal and normative justification for the international protection of indigenous peoples are only part of the story of indigenous peoples' responses to conquest. Although for the most part, their sociopolitical systems were rarely organized for the large-scale use of force that characterize the dominant European states, they also at times resisted by means of military defense and rebellion. The history of indigenous responses to conquest, however, is primarily a history of political, legal, and rhetorical resistance, within states, in regional and in international arenas. The next two sections will trace some of these developments by focusing primarily on the case of indigenous peoples in settler states, highlighting developments in Central and South America, as well as in regional and international arenas.

IV. INDIGENOUS PEOPLES' RESPONSES IN SETTLER STATES

From the Anglo-Powhatan War in 1609, to the Maori-Pakeha Wars of the 1860s, the Plains Indian resistance culminating in the defeat of the U.S. army at the Battle of Little Bighorn in 1876, the Frog Lake and Louis Reil rebellions in Canada, numerous indigenous African rebellions such as that of the Sotho and Zulu peoples led by Chaka against colonial domination, the Huaorani use of violence to resist multinational and missionary encroachment in Ecuador in the 1990s, and the recent and more publicized conflict in Chiapas—indigenous peoples have never passively accepted their physical, social, and cultural destruction at the hands of Western colonists, settlers, and state expansionists. Their military defeat is explained not only by the more destructive technology of European weapons coupled with the devastating effects of alien disease, but also by the simple fact that the majority of indigenous societies were not and are not organized for large-scale military operations, either aggressive or defensive.

Yet in spite of military defeat and near physical decimation, indigenous peoples have never abandoned what for some has been a five centuries-long struggle for their cultural survival. The term "cultural survival" is used here because to survive as assimilated individuals is not to survive *as* indigenous peoples, and because indigenous peoples' cultural survival is linked to the perpetuation of culturally self-determined social, political, and economic systems. This is not to say that indigenous peoples do not and have not adapted their cultures as a result of contact and colonization. Both indigenous and settler cultures have changed as a result of their contact with one another. No culture is stagnant. But it has also been a *de facto* objective of state and nation-building projects to incorporate indigenous peoples into national populations as assimilated individuals rather than as culturally self-determining and unique peoples. Worldwide, indigenous resistance movements confront issues of land rights, forced relocation, and cultural, political and economic self-determination, as the examples in Table II illustrate.

By the far the most effective and persistent forms of resistance have been nonviolent: appeals to international and regional organizations, publicity, protests, litigation, and political participation, including grass-roots political organization and campaigns to alter the constitutional basis for indigenous–state relations. The scope of indigenous resistance today is truly global, as the participation of hundreds of indigenous organizations in the UN process of drafting principles for the protection of their rights, and local, national, and regional resistance movements indicates.

A. The United States

When the Europeans arrived in North America, hundreds of indigenous societies were living in a variety of sociopolitical arrangements (including a number of confederacies), practicing agricultural food production as well as hunting and gathering. Initially, the Dutch, French, and English engaged in treaty-making with North American indigenous nations, and there can be little doubt that during early colonization these treaties were viewed by both sides as agreements between equals. By the middle of the 18th century, however, the European and African slave population east of the

TABLE II

Examples of Grass Roots Indigenous-Controlled Political Movements

State	Movement	Goals/Issues
U.S.A.	American Indian Movement	End termination policy, sovereignty
Canada	North American Indian Brotherhood	Oppose external interference in indigenous self-government
Aotearoa (New Zealand)	Maori Unity Movement Maori Peoples Liberation Movement of Aotearoa Waitangi Action Committee	Recognition of Maori sovereignty
Australia	Federal Council for the Advancement of Aboriginals and Torres Strait Islanders	Land rights, resource rights
Malaysia	Residents Action Committee Sarawak Indigenous Peoples' Association	Halt Bakun Dam Construction Resist encroachment by logging companies
West Papua	Kanak Independence Movement	Self-determination
Pradesh, India	Chipko Movement	Protest to save forest homelands
Chotanogpur, India	Jharkhand Party	Call for creation of indigenous state
Philippines	Cordillera Peoples Alliance	Autonomy
Norway Finland Sweden	Nordic Saami Council Saami Union Saami Youth Council	Cultural rights, legal protection, language rights
Japan	Hakkaido Utari	Ainu language, land rights
Alaska, U.S.A.	Federation of Alaskan Natives	Land Settlement Act
Chile	ADMAPU (Mapuche)	Oppose allotment policy
Ecuador	CONFENIAE, ECUARUNARI, COISE, CONAIE	Resistance to encroachment by oil companies
El Salvador	Association Nacional Indigena del Salvador	Land, cultural rights

Source: Franke Wilmer, *The Indigenous Voice in World Politics* (Sage, 1993).

Mississippi vastly outnumbered the indigenous population, and as settlement and conquest pushed westward, alien-born diseases and settler violence was rapidly devastating the indigenous peoples west of the Mississippi as well. The period following the Civil War through the Ghost Dance massacre of over 300 people at Wounded Knee in 1890 is sometimes referred to as the period of the Plains Indian Wars.

Contemporary Native American political and legal activism was fueled both by a package of U.S. Federal Indian policies known as "termination" (aimed at "terminating" the collective, tribal existence of Native American Indian people and assimilating them as individuals into mainstream American society), and by the growing civil rights activism initiated by African Americans in the late 1950s and 1960s. By 1970, as a result

of Native American political opposition, the termination era was officially ended with many of the terminated tribes restored to their federally recognized status. The National Indian Youth Council (NIYC) was formed during a historic American Indian Conference in Chicago in 1961. Today it not only publicizes the sovereign rights of Native Americans, but it also conducts voter participation drives, job training, and youth leadership and internship programs, and it promotes cultural pride (Wilmer 1993). The NIYC also became involved in protests in support of Indian fishing rights which became known as "fish-ins" in the 1960s. The NIYC is one of 13 organizations with consultative status at the United Nations.

The American Indian Movement adopted more radical, though primarily nonviolent, strategies of resistance, leading to the 19-month occupation of Alcatraz Island in 1969 asserting a treaty right entitling Indians to the return of unused federal property; a week-long occupation of the Bureau of Indian Affairs following the "Trail of Broken Treaties" march to Washington, D.C. in 1972; and a two and a-half month stand-off at Wounded Knee, South Dakota, in 1973. The Wounded Knee protest served both to expose the highly questionable legitimacy of the U.S.-supported local tribal government and to heighten solidarity and pride for Indian identity. Some of the early founders of the American Indian Movement went on to form the International Indian Treaty Council, which received consultative status at the United Nations and is headed by an international board of indigenous representatives.

A number of factors converged—the Civil Rights movement, Red Power activism, more Native American students graduating from university and law school programs, and a federal policy allowing tribes to sue in federal court—to raise key indigenous issues in American courts beginning in the 1970s. A conflict over the Western Shoshone land and claims under the Treaty of Ruby Valley arose in the 1970s, was heard and appealed through U.S. courts. The Supreme Court upheld the U.S. position that aboriginal land rights for the Shoshone had been "extinguished" through settlement and through the Indian Claims Commission. The case centers on the rights of Carrie and Mary Dann to continue working the ranch that has been in their family for over 100 years, and before that was in the territory occupied by the 60,000 Shoshone indigenous peoples of the area. In 1993 the Indian Law Resource Center filed a complaint on behalf of the Danns in the Inter-American Commission for Human Rights. In 1993 the Danns received the Right Livelihood Award in Stockholm, Sweden, for their "courage and perseverance in asserting the rights of indigenous people to their land."

Though many battles are still being fought—over the Black Hills and the Western Shoshone land claims, for example—there have also been some gains. (In a 1980 decision, the Supreme Court upheld a decision that acknowledged the illegality of U.S. confiscation of the Black Hills. The Sioux, however, refused to acknowledge receipt of the monetary compensation, holding that only the return of land will satisfy their grievance.) The Blue Lake Lands taken from the Taos Pueblo by President Theodore Roosevelt in 1906 to be incorporated into National Forest lands was returned to them by a bipartisan congressional act strongly supported by President Nixon in 1970. Without a treaty-based claim, the Passamaquoddy instituted a suit in 1971 against the U.S. government for land lost that, through appeals, was eventually upheld in 1980. Fishing rights entitling indigenous peoples of the Pacific Northwest to one-half of the harvestable fish were upheld in a 1974 case. (Known as the "Boldt" decision, *U.S. v. State of Washington*, March 22, 1974, Indian fishing rights were upheld by the Supreme Court in *Washington v. Washington State Commercial Passenger Fishing Vessel Association, 443 U.S. Reports,* 658–708.) Indian sovereignty and tribes' immunity from suit was upheld by *Santa Clara Pueblo v. Martinez* in 1978.

Native American Indian activism also led to a series of legislative victories for Indian rights in the U.S.: the Indian Self-Determination and Educational Assistance Act in 1975; the American Indian Religious Freedom and Indian Child Welfare Acts in 1978; the Archaeological Resources Protection Act in 1979; and the Native American Graves Protection and Repatriation Act of 1990 (NAGPRA).

The strategy of protest and confrontation in the 1960s and 1970s has given way to an emphasis on litigation, lobbying and strengthening community-based self-determination.

B. Canada

In the 1870s the Canadian government began negotiating a series of 11 numbered treaties to "open" the western and northern provinces for Canadian expansion. The last was concluded in 1921. The Indian Act by which the Canadian government asserted "jurisdiction" over Indian affairs until the 1950s was so restrictive that Natives were required to have passes to leave their reserves, potlatch and other ceremonies were banned, and Indian women who married non-Indian men lost their status as Native people, as did their children. The

Act also provided for involuntary enfranchisement. Amendments to the Act in 1951 provided only modest improvements in the situation. Native ceremonies were no longer outlawed, but provisions pertaining to the status of Indian women and involuntary enfranchisement remained. Some improvement was also marked by the extension of national voting rights to Natives by 1960.

After consulting with Native leaders in 1968 and 1969 the Canadian government issued a White Paper on Indian Policy that, like termination policy in the United States, proposed ending the special status of Native nations in Canada by repealing the Indian Act and assimilating them as individuals into the dominant society. Canadian First Nations mobilized rapidly to oppose the policy. As a result, in 1969 Indian agents were removed from reserves, and thus began an era of restructuring in Canadian–Indian relations. The Act was amended in 1985 and 1988 to (1) end gender discrimination and restore Native status to indigenous women (and their children) who married non-Natives; (2) to give control over enrollment to the First Nations councils; and (3) to allow First Nations to develop bylaws and on-reserve taxing power. The 1982 Constitutional Act also recognizes the Aboriginal and treaty rights of Indians, Inuit and Metis, although some indigenous nations opposed their inclusion in the Canadian constitution at all, arguing that they remained sovereign nations and that inclusion in the Canadian constitution would compromise their sovereign status. (This was the position, for instance, of the Iroquois traditional chiefs and elders, even though it was not formally recognized by the Constitutional Act (from interviews with the author in June 1992).)

Shushwap leader George Manuel, then President of the National Indian Brotherhood of Canada (or NIBC, now the Assembly of First Nations) traveled to New Zealand where he met with Maori activists, attended the United Nations conference on the environment in Stockholm as a member of the Canadian delegation and connected with Saami there, and then went on to the International Labour Organization and World Council of Churches in Geneva, the International Work Group for Indigenous Affairs in Copenhagen and the Anti-Slavery Society and Survival International in London. These contacts led to a landmark international meeting of indigenous peoples in 1974, following which the NIBC was granted consultative NGO status at the United Nations.

In 1973 the Canadian government began to recognize the need to address Native claims, but it was not until 1991 that it lifted restrictions preventing consideration of pre-Confederation claims. Conflicts between Natives and the Canadian government over the James Bay hydroelectric project first arose in 1974 and 1975, leading to several agreements addressing land claims, aboriginal rights, and compensation settlements. The reversal of a 50-year-old policy barring Native peoples from raising funds to file claims without the permission of the Canadian government accelerated the use of litigation as resistance. By 1996 over 700 specific claims had been filed resulting in 151 settlements and 354 still being processed. Under agreements with the Gwich'in, Sahtu Dene, and Metis the DIAND (Department of Indian Affairs and Northern Development) in 1994 and 1995 collected $70 million in resource royalties. Agreements with the Yukon First Nations, Vuntut Gwitchin First Nation., First Nation Na-cho Ny'a'k Dun, Champagne, and Aishihik First Nations over land and monetary compensation have been concluded. Twenty-five First Nations in Saskatchewan have been awarded $450 million for land purchases to increase reserve territories. In 1992 a Treaty Commission was established in British Colombia, where the absence of treaties had complicated the claims issues. By 1996 70% of the First Nations in British Colombia had become involved in negotiating the first ever treaty with the Canadian government.

Conflicts in Mohawk communities in 1980 and 1990 led to violent confrontation between Native groups within Iroquois communities in disagreement over the legitimacy of tribal governments, and between Natives and the federal (Mounties) and provincial authorities. The 1990 standoff at Kanesatake/Oka, 30 miles northwest of Montreal, precipitated by plans to construct a municipal golf course in an area claimed to be a traditional burial site, lasted 78 days. When the provincial authorities dispatched a paramilitary unit armed with automatic weapons, grenades, and tear gas to disband the initially nonviolent protesters, the conflict turned violent, leaving one police officer dead. In solidarity with the Mohawks at Oka/Kanesatake, Kahnawake Mohawks blockaded the Mercy Bridge between Montreal and the outlying city of Chateauguay.

In the 1980s the Sheshatshiu and LaRomaine Innu in Labrador/Nitassinin initiated a nationwide campaign protesting the use of airspace over their territory for NATO training overflights, which they say are detrimental to their way of life and destructive of the wildlife that they continue to hunt for food. The Innu engaged in civil disobedience, initiated land claims and litigation, and aroused publicity to bring pressure on the Canadian government to end the overflights.

The Nisga'a and Nuxalk nations in British Colombia have vehemently opposed clear-cutting in territory under consideration in a land dispute. They emphasize that they do not oppose development, but seek Native-controlled, managed development. Protests and publicity accelerated in 1994, and in 1995 protest rallies were coordinated by the Forest Action Network in London, Ottawa, Los Angeles, Seattle, Victoria, and Vancouver, although some Nuxalk representatives were annoyed with the Network's "appropriation" of the issue for their own purposes. Three hereditary chiefs and 19 supporters were arrested in connection with a blockade against logging companies, with 21 of those arrested being found guilty of criminal contempt in June 1996. Another logging blockade organized by the Nuu-Chah-Nulth First Nations along with Friends of Clayquot and Greenpeace, followed in late June. In August Nuxalk Chief Quatsinas made a formal statement to the UN Subcommission on the Nuxalk Logging Dispute, explaining the nations' commitment to the use of nonviolent means of opposition, the creation story in which the area in question appears as a sacred site, and his view of the logging operation as an act of ethnocide and continuing genocide aimed at destroying Native peoples *as Native peoples*.

The process of political restructuring of indigenous–state relations continues in Canada. In 1994 the Canadian government and the First Nations in Manitoba agreed to dismantle the Department of Indian Affairs in the province. In 1995 a new round of negotiations were initiated to further amendments to the Indian Act. A number of self-government agreements have been signed between First Nations and the federal government, and in 1996, 13 First Nations signed a Framework Agreement on land management. The Royal Commission on Aboriginal Peoples was created in 1991 to evaluate the need for rebuilding the relationship between Canada's Aboriginal and non-Aboriginal societies. The final report recommends a new Royal Proclamation and companion legislation on treaty implementation, recognition of First Nations, a treaty tribunal, the creation of an Aboriginal Parliament, and reform of the federal agencies involved in Aboriginal Affairs.

In a landmark settlement between the Inuit of Nunavut and the Canadian government, not only was 350,000 square miles transferred to the Inuit, but a new territory of Nunavut was created. Beginning in 1999 and concluding in 2009 the government of the Northwest Territories will transfer responsibilities to the new Inuit-controlled Nunavut government. Finally, in the course of its search for a new constitutional foundation, the Canadian government has undertaken extensive studies on the question of electoral reform for

Aboriginal peoples. The Royal Commission on Electoral Reform and Party Financing considered in detail the question of Aboriginal electoral participation and alternatives for restructuring the basis of Aboriginal political participation. Among the alternatives considered, the Commission examined the New Zealand/Aotearoa model for Maori participation in the federal government and the possibility of adapting such a model to Canada.

C. New Zealand

As the English colonists in North America were preparing for a war with the British after two centuries of settlement, Captain James Cook made the first English landing in New Zealand. Between Cook's landing in 1769 and 1835, European settlement in New Zealand was sparse. Thirty-five raritanga met with James Busby in Waitangi in October, 1835, and signed a "Declaration of Independence" declaring a new "state" under the "United Tribes of New Zealand." They agreed to meet on a yearly basis, but as English settlers began to arrive in increasing numbers, Maori sovereignty and land rights affirmed by the 1835 Declaration were increasingly ignored. By 1840 there were both intertribal conflicts as well as conflicts between settlers and Maori. These conflicts—particularly the latter—would come to be known as the "land wars," and lasted over the next 20 years. In 1840 four Maori *rangatira* from the North signed the Treaty of Waitangi, which is now considered to be the foundational document of the New Zealand state.

During the 1850s, concern over continued *Pakeha* (European settler) ignorance of their sovereignty and land rights, Maori leaders began to meet and discuss the possibility of unifying through a confederation and name a single Maori leader in what came to be known as "The King Movement." In 1958 the first Maori king was named. The movement, however, did not resolve growing tensions between Maori and the English who were determined, as in North America and Australia, to conquer the land and people of New Zealand/Aotearoa by settlement and force.

When in 1863 conflicts arising over attempts by Maori to retain self-government erupted over a controversy involving British purchase of Maori land at Waitara, the British invaded Waikato. From a Maori perspective, the "invasion of Waikato by England [led] troops [was used] as a pretext to force Maori to defend themselves and then confiscate their land for being 'in rebellion' against the English crown" (Jones, 1997). In the aftermath of defeat, a pacifist Maori resistance known as Pai Marire formed and spread through the northern tribes. During this period a series of Land Acts were passed by the parliament in order to force the destruction of the Maori system of collective land tenure and authority in favor of individual title, which in turn made the transfer and sale of property from Maori to settlers much easier. As in the western United States, this period was marked both by the most severe decline in the indigenous population and the most widespread dispossession of them from their lands.

It is estimated that at the time the Treaty of Waitangi was signed—1840—Maori outnumbered settlers 100 to 1 (Waitangi Tribunal, 1997). Twenty years later the populations were roughly equal, but for the next four decades Maori population declined steadily. As with the indigenous peoples of the Americas and Australia, diseases against which they had no immunity, were devastating the Maori. As the settler population grew, their relationship with and view of the Maori were increasingly directed by an assimilationist policy. "Native" schools established in 1867 were a prime instrument for the destruction of Maori culture. In 1926, Maori visionary and spiritual leader T. W. Ratana travelled to England to appeal to the King, and to Geneva to address the League of Nations on behalf of the Maori and their grievances against the settlers. He was granted an audience with neither. He went on to become a political leader in New Zealand, serving in the Parliament along with several of his followers. Apirana Ngata, who has been called "the most able Maori leader of the century" became the Minister of Maori Affairs in 1928 and from there spearheaded a Maori cultural revival and land recovery.

The 1945 Maori Social and Economic Advancement Act promised help for tribal committees, assistance for Maori health, education, and welfare, and the creation of Marae (Maori community) administration. In 1967 a Maori Affairs Act made it still easier for Maoris to sell land to Europeans, leading to the loss of millions of acres of land formerly under Maori control, and a massive migration of Maori seeking work in the cities. The 1967 Act also evoked widespread Maori protest as a new generation of younger Maori leaders emerged. They demanded that their Maori names be properly pronounced in public arenas, began to establish bilingual programs, and celebrated pride in Maori culture. The 1960s and 1970s have been called the period of Maori Renaissance. The Nga Tamata or Young Warriors and the Maori Organization on Human Rights provided organizational structure from which to launch protest through picketing, petitioning, and publicity. In 1975 organizers of the Maori Land March collected over 60,000 signatures on a petition protesting the sale of

Maori land. In a 1977 land dispute at Bastion Point, Maori protesters occupied the area for 506 days in protest, although a court ruled in 1978 that the protesters were trespassing and had them removed.

In 1975 the Treaty of Waitangi Act established the Waitangi Tribunal and for the first time recognized the conflict over Maori and Pakeha interpretations, but it was not until the Act was amended in 1985 that the Maori text achieved statutory recognition. The original act, which allowed only for claims pertaining to grievances from 1975 on, was amended so that Maori grievances extending all the way back to 1840 could be considered by the Tribunal. The effect was dramatic—during the first 10 years of the Tribunal, only 24 claims were made, but during the first 2 years after the amended act was passed, the number of claims jumped to over 150. As of 1993, six major negotiated agreements were underway; one followed Tribunal hearings and two followed Tribunal mediation. A large claim was settled in 1995 when Queen Elizabeth II signed a parliamentary bill apologizing to the Tainui people for the British military invasion of their lands in 1863. The settlement returned 39,000 acres and awarded (US) $112 million to the Tainui tribe. The Queen's 1995 visit was also marked by protest when 60 Maori activists demonstrated against the Crown's continued involvement in Maori affairs.

D. Australia

Of the 1007 settlers arriving in Australia in 1788, three-fourths were convicts, and most of the rest were their wardens and caretakers. It is often alleged that the particularly ruthless treatment of Aboriginal peoples by European settlers in Australia is in part attributable to the callous treatment of convicts (who became settlers) by their wardens (who also became settlers). Richard Broome, for example, writes of 8- and 9-year-old Aboriginal girls being raped; of Tasmanian Aboriginals being "flogged, branded, castrated and mutilated by convicts;" the killing of between 100 and 300 people by 23 "troopers" on the Naomi River in 1838; at Mayall Creek six months later "about 30 [Aboriginal people] were roped together, shot, stabbed and their bodies burned by a party of 12 stockmen;" and 200 Aboriginals killed at Gravesend the same year (Broome, 1996:41–42). Aboriginal resistance often became a pretext for White brutality. From an estimated original population of 300,000, by 1930 there were only 60,000 Aboriginal people in Australia. The Aboriginal population today remains below the preconquest level. As elsewhere in the settler states, many Aboriginal Australians also died from contact with deadly alien diseases. In Victoria alone, an estimated 80% of the Aboriginal population died from violence and disease between 1820 and 1840—just 20 years.

Early Aboriginal resistance consisted mainly of raiding parties and what today would be called guerilla tactics. They were soon, however, vastly outnumbered, and resistance leaders were designated as "outlaws" and thus "liable to be shot on sight" (Broome, 1996:29). By some accounts, Aboriginals and settlers were embroiled in a bloody war for the land, a war in which the balance of inhumane killing without question went to the settlers, and which after all was begun by the settlers.

Two things have profoundly shaped the course of Aboriginal-White relations: (1) a growing Aboriginal reliance on the expanding pastoral economy, particularly in the north; and (2) the absence of Commonwealth or federal involvement in Aboriginal affairs until 1967. The history of Aboriginal work on the pastoral stations is a history of labor exploitation, and thus Aboriginal resistance has often been combined with issues of economic marginalization and labor struggles. Before World War II only about half of the Aboriginal cattle workers received any pay, and Aboriginal wages were still much lower than Whites received for the same work. These conditions provided the first occasion for nonviolent Aboriginal resistance in the form of labor strikes beginning in the 1940s, and continued mainly in the form of economic sabotage until the Federal Council for the Advancement of Aborigines and Torres Strait Islanders was created in the 1960s. The Federal Council began pressuring the labor movement and heavily lobbying the Australian Council of Trade Unions Congress meetings in 1950, 1961, and 1963. When a case involving Aboriginal laborers was sent by the North Australian Workers Union to arbitration in 1965, the Commission issued a landmark decision in favor of equal wages for Aboriginal workers. Although implementation was delayed for 3 years, by the late 1960s Aboriginal workers were paid an equal wage, but ironically this produced a backlash against hiring Aboriginal labor.

Worldwide the 1960s saw a tremendous increase in protest movements, freedom rides, student activism, pressures for voting rights, the return of reserve lands, and in Australia, petitions for Aboriginal citizenship. The Australian federal government in 1967 took over responsibility for Aboriginal affairs, granting citizenship to all Aboriginal people and shifting Aboriginal reserve policy from government control to self-determination. Yet even with the granting of citizenship, many Aboriginal people in the 1960s still found themselves unable, for instance, to obtain passports, since many Aboriginal births had been recorded in stock books. In 1972 Aboriginal protesters established a "tent embassy" in Canberra to publicize their plight. A youth leadership, employing strategies of direct action, emerged within a pan-Aboriginal movement that demanded publicity, accountability, and change. By the 1970s the Labour Party responded, and recognizing the political value of taking on the issue of Aboriginal equality, repealed most of the discriminatory legislation was repealed by the 1980s. Federal investigations into land rights were initiated, while Aboriginal leadership formed alliances with environmental interests, advancing their own concerns with land rights, mining rights, and restrictions on corporate development. Aboriginal peoples formed Land Councils to represent their interests, and in 1975 the Northern Territory passed an Aboriginal Land Rights Act, which included rights to royalties from mining and an Aboriginal veto over mining in the state. The first controversy between an Aboriginal Land Council and mining interests went to court in 1978. Thirty percent of the Northern Territory was acknowledged to be under Aboriginal ownership, and 20% of South Australia. Aboriginal activists began flying a pan-Aboriginal flag to symbolize their unity and right to self-determination.

In 1979 the National Aboriginal Commission called for a constitutional amendment allowing the government to negotiate a compact (treaty) for the first time with Aboriginal Australians. Parliament passed the Aboriginal and Torres Strait Islanders Commission bill in 1979. The Aboriginal Development Corporation (ADC), wholly controlled by Aboriginal people, was created in 1980. That same year Aboriginal activists in Victoria staged the occupation of a proposed mining site against the Alcoa corporation. Activists pressed for the establishment of Aboriginal Studies programs, the teaching of Aboriginal culture at all levels of education, the creation of Aboriginal health services programs, and progressive self-management of their own affairs.

Protests heated up as the Bicentenary approached, and a Royal Commission launched investigations into "deaths in custody"—the problem of a disproportionate number of Aboriginal people dying while in policy custody. The issue had become the subject of international criticism, from both the United Nations and Amnesty International. The Royal Commission on Aboriginal Deaths in Custody also began to publicize the need to address the problem of the "Lost Generation" on a national scale. (Aboriginal children were often forcibly removed from their families and placed either in White homes to learn "domestic skills" or in institutional

schools, creating what has recently become known as the "Lost Generation." In New South Wales, for example, one out of seven children had been removed between 1909 and 1969.) During the 1988 Bicentenary, Aboriginal activists "landed" on the cliffs of Dover and proclaimed England "discovered" by Aboriginal Australians. In 1981 the Northern Territory passed an Aboriginal Sacred Sites Act.

During the 1980s, housing, health, and education grants for Aboriginal programs increased by 80%. In 1988, Prime minister Hawke spoke to a crowd of more than 10,000 at the Barunga Festival, promising the negotiation of an Australian-Aboriginal Treaty. A Council for Aboriginal Reconciliation was created in 1991, made up of 12 Aboriginal members, 2 Torres Strait Islanders, and 11 "other" Australians.

The most significant event to follow from two decades of sustained pan-Aboriginal political activism occurred in 1993 when a court case brought by Eddie Mabo and the Torres Strait Islanders against the government of Queensland was settled as the court overturned the doctrine of *terra nullius* that underlaid Aboriginal dispossession from the land. According to *terra nullius,* the continent was "unoccupied" upon the arrival of the British because the Aboriginal peoples did not possess governments like European governments and therefore did not exercise ownership of the land. This doctrine had precluded any claim of native title under the Commonwealth or Australian governments for more than two centuries. Following the landmark *Mabo* ruling that Aboriginal people did exercise ownership of the land and sovereignty prior to settlement and retained a right to land title in the present, the entire foundation of Aboriginal-White relations crumbled. Land claims filled the courts. In December the Native Title Act was passed, reflecting a fragile balance between landholder, Aboriginal, and state interests. It outlined procedures for transfer to native title, provided funding for land acquisition, and promised additional steps toward social justice. Aboriginal peoples were awarded 250,000 square kilometers in the Kimberleys, the Wiradjuri claimed most of central New South Wales, claims were made in the Snowy Mountains, the Yorta Yorta claimed areas of the Barmah Forest on the Murray River, and the Martu claimed 200,000 square kilometers on the east Pilbara.

Recent struggles center on controversies and conflicts over mining, since many new mining projects seek access to Aboriginal lands and involve areas now subject to native title applications. A resources boom began in the 1970s, bringing a tremendous increase in both domestic and multinational mining activities in Australia. The Northern Territories passed legislation recognizing Aboriginal interests in mining and gave them the right to share in royalties that were previously paid to the Crown. Being forced to deal with the issue of native title has brought mining companies and governments into negotiations with Aboriginal Land Councils as representatives of Aboriginal interests. A 1991 Commonwealth Industry Commission report recommended federal recognition of Aboriginal title to minerals in their territories, direct negotiation between commercial interests and Aboriginal councils, and federal funding of Aboriginal councils.

V. INDIGENOUS RESISTANCE IN CENTRAL AND SOUTH AMERICA

As the British were successfully establishing colonial dominance in North America, Australia, and New Zealand, the Spanish proceeded unhindered with the colonization of Central and South America. However, unlike the British Commonwealth, Spanish and Portuguese colonization did not produce democratic settler states. Racially mixed births and a greater degree of acculturation produced a large Mestizo, mostly peasant population in most Central and South American countries, although the governments have for the past 5 centuries been predominantly controlled by descendants of European conquerors. Additionally, geographical factors made the Southern Hemisphere more difficult to penetrate, and many indigenous peoples were able to survive with very little or no contact with outsiders into the middle of the 20th century. Several states—Guatemala and Bolivia, for instance—today contain a majority indigenous population. As elsewhere, diseases also killed huge numbers of indigenous peoples during the earliest period of contact, and where contact has been more recent, continue to do so today. Within the past three decades, for example, as many as 85% of the Yanomami may have been killed by disease and violence at the hands of settlers.

Contemporary resistance in Central and South America is in part a response to increased pressure for industrial economic development since the 1960s. As governments, multinationals, and miners have attempted to penetrate dense tropical forests and mountain highlands, they have encountered numerous indigenous peoples who managed over the past 5 centuries to survive European conquest and colonization. But their resistance is not only a part of recent developments in indigenous activism, for much of the region's political history has involved indigenous opposition to domination and brutal government responses. A 1934 "upris-

ing" of "peasants" against the Salvadoran government, for example, met with the ruthless torture and murder of over 30,000 Indians. Recent activism has also on some occasions given rise to armed resistance. The Zapatista Army of National Liberation, for instance, was formed partly in response to the murder of Indian leader Sebastian Nunez Perez by a landowner in 1990. The Zapatista movement itself grew out of a resistance alliance formed in 1989 with widespread Indian support. That same year a less publicized armed uprising occurred along the Pichis River in Peru when some 50,000 Ashaninkas responded to a Tupac Amaru assassination of an Ashaninka leader.

The subject of indigenous resistance in Central and South America is too vast to cover here, but some highlights will serve to illustrate its seriousness and effectiveness, as well as the generally nonviolent nature of contemporary indigenous movements. In 1992, on the occasion of the Columbian Quincentenary, the Organization of Indigenous People of Pastaza organized a march to Quito, capital of Ecuador, to draw attention to the situation and demands of indigenous peoples. They called for government recognition of their legal right to land, for the reform of the Constitution to include indigenous rights, and for indigenous control over the remaining Amazon rainforests in Ecuador. Ten thousand Quichua, Shiwar, Zapara, and Achuar Indians, "Wearing feathered plumes and toucan headdresses, carrying spears, they marched, followed by thousands of highland Indians in their traditional ponchos (Veilleux, 1992). Ten thousand Indians protested the Mexican Columbian Quincentenary celebration in San Cristobal. In 1992, indigenous resistance and struggle for rights was internationally acknowledged when Guatemalan Indian human rights activist Rigoberta Menchu was awarded the Nobel Peace Prize.

Resistance movements in Central and South America over the past few decades have been aided by those indigenous peoples to the North whose struggles for cultural and physical survival in those more open and otherwise democratic states began 100 or more years earlier. They have also been aided by a growing global environmental movement, though they sometimes find their interests subverted or more patronized than defended by some environmental groups. Nongovernmental organizations (NGOs) allied with Yanomami leaders to combat invasions into Yanomami territory and advance indigenous rights have made the Yanomami a symbol of indigenous resistance in recent decades. In Venezuela, environmental activists and Pemon Indian groups have teamed up to oppose a government plan to open the Imataca rain forest reserve to gold, diamond, and emerald mining. In Brazil, the Tapajos Roadway-Waterway "megaproject" in the Munduruku Indigenous Area was suspended as a result of opposition by indigenous groups and environmentalists. In May 1997, in response to assassinations of indigenous leaders, indigenous activists staged a nonviolent protest at the Honduran capital as part of a continuing struggle for land rights. They were forcibly removed by Honduran armed forces, with reports of brutal beatings and disappearances accompanying the "removal."

One of the most successful and sustained contemporary indigenous resistances is the case of the Kayapo of the Xingu River in Brazil. To open the area to "development" in the 1970s, the Brazilian government attempted to relocate them to an "Indian Park." The Kayapo quickly learned how to effectively utilize the media in service to their cause over the next 15 years as they engaged in a struggle to resist territorial encroachment with violence when necessary, while emphasizing the violations of their rights that drove them to do so. They confronted the government in 1984 and 1988 in what became major media events, opposing a project in which 60 of 136 proposed dams would have flooded their lands. International human rights and environmental groups joined the protest. Kayapo leaders travelled to the World Bank to stop its financing. In 1989 they organized a meeting of investment bankers, government officials, environmentalists, and hundreds of representatives from 20 different Indian tribes. Environmental NGOs pressured international lending agencies to withdraw support for the project, and the dam projects were derailed.

The experience of the Huaorani and other indigenous peoples in Ecuador is also illustrative. A coalition of indigenous peoples and environmentalists called for a 15-year moratorium on new oil development projects so that the Ecuadoran government could assess the damages such development has caused already and devise plans to implement cultural and environmental safeguards against future damage. The government of Ecuador was anticipating some $3 billion in foreign oil investments by the year 2000, but environmental activists in the United States, including the New York-based Natural Resources Defense Council, and Europe protested so strenuously that the Ecuadorian government was compelled to cool relations with Conoco. Indigenous alliances—CONFENIAE, ECUARUNARI, COISE, and CONAIE—representing seven indigenous nations in the region have been spearheading opposition strategies. The "Declaration of Villano" was issued at a meeting among these groups in January 1994, calling on petroleum companies to withdraw from petroleum auctions. In March the Confederation of Indigenous Nations of Ecuador called for a United Nations mediation panel and an investigation into human rights violations as well as environmental damage. In addition to the National Resources Defense Council, the Sierra Club has also become involved, filing a petition on behalf of the Huaorani with the Inter-American Commission on Human Rights. In November 1993, indigenous organizations also filed a $1 billion damage suit in New York against Texaco, prompting Texaco to yield its exploration rights to other companies.

VI. RESISTANCE IN THE SARAWAK

The Malaysian states of Sarawak and Sabah are on the island of Kalamantan/Borneo, separated by the South China Sea from Peninsular Malaysia and sharing a land border with Indonesia. "Dayak" is a term that has been applied to the dozens of distinct indigenous peoples of the island, which in Sarawak and Sabah number several million. Malaysia's export-led development depends primarily on logging, accounting for as much as 60% of the global export of tropical lumber, much of it from Sarawak. Lumber exports have grown from 4.2 million cubic meters in 1971, to 18.8 cubic meters by 1990. More than 30 companies are today logging the forests in the traditional territory of the Kayan, Kenyah and Penan indigenous peoples.

In 1980 the Penan appealed to the government to restrict logging and protect their territories. Seven years later, with no government protection forthcoming, a delegation of Penan leaders issued a statement urging the government again to stop the logging, or face armed Penan defense. A month later—in March 1987—they implemented a blockade of the Tutoh River Basin, and by the end of the year several thousand people erected as many as 25 blockades from as many Penan villages. Between 1987 and 1992, more than three hundred native people had been arrested. Blockades continued into the 1990s, some lasting as long as 8 months, and involving as many as 4000 people.

Internationalization of Penan resistance began 1987 when the Malaysian affiliate of Friends of the Earth called for a moratorium on Sarawak logging. In 1988 the European Parliament introduced a (failed) motion to ban Sarawak imports. International support also came from Australian dock workers, the Japanese Tropical Forest Action Network, British furniture manufacturers, and local governments in the Netherlands who refused to license building projects using tropical timber. When the European Parliament took up the issue again in 1989, this time calling for the release of arrested indigenous protesters in Sarawak, the motion was unanimously supported.

Penan leaders undertook a strategy of international publicity, traveling to 13 countries, appearing on television, and meeting with government leaders in the United States, Netherlands, France, Canada, Belgium, attending the Earth Summit in Rio in 1992, and presenting their case to the UN Human Rights Commission in Geneva in 1991. Under an Internal Security Act, which made it illegal for anyone to block logging roads, the Malaysian government made numerous arrests, including a leader of the Sarawak Indigenous Peoples Association, whose case drew further international attention. Following his exile into Canada, he spoke before the General Assembly of the UN. In 1992 a resolution was introduced in the U.S. Congress calling for the protection of indigenous peoples rights in Sarawak.

Since then, the Malaysian government has stepped up its use of force to dismantle roadblocks and suppress indigenous activism. In a few rare cases, logging companies have negotiated directly with indigenous groups, quieting protests, although the agreements are regarded with skepticism by the indigenous groups. In 1992 an Alliance of Indigenous-Tribal Peoples of the Tropical Forests met in Penang and issued a 48-point statement outlining their cultural and land rights, decision-making procedures, and their policy positions on issues of development, forestry, intellectual property, education, conservation, and biodiversity. The statement was signed by 28 representatives from South Asia, India, and South America.

VII. CONCLUSION

One of the most striking features of contemporary indigenous resistance is the effectiveness of transnational and international mobilization as well as the speed with which it emerged. The formation of indigenous NGOs accelerated in tandem with increased United Nations activity during the 1970s and 1980s. During the 1990s, on average more than 100 indigenous NGOs have participated in the annual Working Group meetings. The Center for Human Rights in Geneva lists over two hundred indigenous NGOs. Indigenous issues have been raised within the Food and Agricultural Organization, the International Labour Organization, the United Nations Development Program, the United Nations Environmental Program, the United Nations High Commis-

sion on Refugees, the World Health Organization and the World Bank. Thirteen indigenous NGOs now have consultative status at the United Nations, and in 1992 an indigenous representative was invited for the first time ever to address an international UN-sponsored conference—the Rio "Earth" Summit. A workshop on the possible establishment of a permanent forum for indigenous peoples at the UN was scheduled for 1997.

Indigenous international and regional political activism has produced tangible results. In addition to the draft set of principles reported out of the Working Group and the ongoing efforts within the Organization of American States to develop a similar instrument, the World Bank has issued guidelines for the consideration of project impacts on indigenous peoples. In 1989 the International Labour Organization—the only international organization to have concluded a convention addressing the issue of indigenous peoples—was pressured into revising its 1957 convention (No. 107) Concerning Indigenous and Tribal Peoples in Independent Countries to eliminate its paternalistic tone and to reflect the concerns of indigenous peoples. The reconciliation processes in Australia and New Zealand were at least partly brought about in response to international indigenous activism, and a number of Central and South American states have undergone constitutional revisions to reflect the need to protect the special rights of indigenous peoples there. Colombia is considering special districting to increase indigenous electoral participation. The 60% Mayan majority in Guatemala has traded its political support for constitutional reform for the establishment of a special National Indigenous Fund. Regional activism has probably been more important for Central and South American indigenous peoples who live under more directly repressive governments than do their counterparts in settler states. Many groups, such as the Yanomami, traditionally occupy territories which are now divided among two or more states.

It is difficult to say whether indigenous peoples' resistances in democracies have generally been more effective than in nondemocracies, although that is what one would expect to find. There are at least two reasons for this. First, the democracies in which there are now indigenous peoples living are also states in which industrial development has been occurring longer, and thus the marginalization through dispossession and forced relocation and assimilation has a longer history than in the less democratic and less industrially developed Third World states. Second, the political and economic expansion of the state in these settler states took place mostly during the 19th century when the ideology of modernization as a rationalization for the displacement and destruction of indigenous peoples and cultures was less contestable, particularly in terms of the ethical and moral consequences for indigenous peoples. So while on the one hand, indigenous peoples living in democracies have had opportunities to engage in political and legal forms of resistance, they have done so for a much longer time, under much greater and sustained attack, and during an historical era when the notion of destroying indigenous peoples in the name of "progress" was much more widely and unquestionably accepted as a tenable goal of state policies. Thus while indigenous peoples in the Brazilian rainforest had survived with little outside contact and no direct assaults from various industrializing and "civilizing" influences until after World War II, in recent decades they have experienced as much as an 80% loss of population as a result of alien-born diseases, direct violence by miners and "settlers," and indirect violence in the form of economic and social displacement. On the other hand, political activism by and on behalf of indigenous peoples led to constitutional reform in Brazil in 1988, and in Ecuador in 1991, requiring for the first time demarcation of indigenous territories. (The process remains fraught with conflict as anti-Indian groups mobilize to contest the Indian land demarcation, which is far from complete or, from an indigenous view, satisfactory.)

The most significant aspect of indigenous political activism—"responses to conquest"—is its overwhelmingly nonviolent nature. Indigenous peoples possess virtually no international "capital," that is, resources associated with the ability to influence international political outcomes, such as weapons, resources or more correctly, sovereign control of resources. They do not even possess the most important form of international political capital—internationally recognized sovereignty. Thus their success in influencing national and international outcomes, and in utilizing international mechanisms to influence domestic outcomes, challenges conventional thinking about international relations as a political arena of anarchy or, at best, where might prevails over right, or justice claims. Indigenous peoples have fought for their survival and advanced toward their objectives using primarily the tools of rhetorical power, moral suasion, and nonviolent resistance, accompanied by a sophisticated understanding of nonindigenous politics. Indigenous political activism suggests that international politics bears a much greater resemblance to "normal" politics—struggles over interests, ideas and values carried on through political and legal institutions—than conventional accounts of international relations acknowledge.

Also See the Following Article

COLONIALISM AND IMPERIALISM

Bibliography

Abya Yala News. (1994, Fall). "Indian movements and the electoral process," *Abya Yala News.* Vol 8, No. 3.

Akwe:kon: A Journal of Indigenous Issues. (1994, Summer). *Chiapas: Challenging history.* Ithaca, NY: Cornell University Press.

Alfred, G. R. (1991, Spring). From bad to worse: Internal politics in the 1990 crisis at Kahnawake. *Northeast Indian Quarterly,* 23–31.

Anaya, S. J. (1996). *Indigenous peoples in international law.* New York: Oxford University Press.

Aparicio, T. (1992). The struggle of the Yanomami for their territory. *IWGIA Newsletter 1/92,* 24–30.

Benavides, M. (1992). Peru: Ashaninka self-defense in the central forest Region. *IWGIA Newsletter 2/92,* 36–45.

Berkey, C. (1992). The United States Indian Relations: The constitutional basis. In J. Mohawk *et. al.* (Eds.), *Exiled in the land of the free.* Sante Fe: Clear Light Publishers.

Broome, R. (1996). *Aboriginal Australians: Black response to White dominance.* Concord, MA: Paul and Co. Publishing Consortium.

Brown, D. (1970). *Bury my Heart at wounded knee: An Indian history of the American West.* New York: Holt, Rhinehart and Winston.

Burger, J. (1987). *Report from the frontier: The state of the world's indigenous peoples.* London: Zed Books.

Fenwick, C. G. (Ed.) (1916.) *The law of nations or the principles of Natural Law applied to the conduct and to the affairs of nations and of sovereigns.* Washington, DC: Carnegie Institute of Washington.

Griggs, R. (1992). Background on the term fourth world. *Occasional Paper No. 8.* Olympia, WA: Center for World Indigenous Studies.

Hornung, R. (1991). *One nation under the gun.* New York, NY: Pantheon Books.

Indian Law Resource Center. (1993). *Annual report.* Helena, MT: Indian Law Resource Center.

Indian Law Resource Center. (1994, Spring/Summer). Indigenous peoples, self-determination and the unfounded fear of secession. *Indian Law Resource Center Newsletter,* 2(3), 1–6.

Indian Law Resource Center. (1995, Spring). New draft OAS legal instrument on Indian rights slated for public review and indigenous consultation. *Indian Rights Human Rights,* 3(1), 7.

IWGIA. (1992). Statement of the international alliance of the indigenous-tribal peoples of the tropical forests, Penang, 1992. *IWGIA Newsletter 2/92,* 21–24.

Kane, J. (1995). *Savages.* New York: Alfred A. Knopf Publishers.

Kawharu, I. H. (Ed.). (1989). *Waitangi: Maori and Pakeha perspectives of the Treaty of Waitangi.* Auckland: Oxford University Press.

Maybury-Lewis, D. (1997). *Indigenous peoples, ethnic groups and the state.* Needham Heights, MA: Allyn and Bacon.

Milen, R. A. (Ed.). (1991). *Aboriginal peoples and electoral reform in Canada.* Toronto: Dundurn Press.

Moody, R. (1988). *The indigenous voice: Visions and realities.* London: Zed Books.

Nagel, J. (1996). *American Indian ethnic renewal: Red power and the resurgence of identity and culture.* New York: Oxford University Press.

Nicholas, C. (1992). Sarawak: The plight of the natives worsens, *IWGIA Newsletter ½,* 40–43.

Nietschmann, B. (1987). Militarization and indigenous peoples: The third world war, *Cultural Survival Quarterly,* 11(3), 1–6.

Perry, R. J. (1996). *From time immemorial: Indigenous peoples and state systems*. Austin: University of Texas Press.

Snipp, M. (1986). The changing political and economic status of American Indians: From captive nations to internal colonies, *American Journal of Economics and Sociology, 45*, 145–157.

UN Document A/51/493. (1996, October 14). Programme of activities of the international decade of the world's indigenous people: Review of the existing mechanisms, procedures and programmes within the United Nations concerning indigenous people. *Report of the Secretary-General*. General Assembly Fifty-first Session Agenda Item 107.

Van Cott, D. L. (1994). *Indigenous Peoples and Democracy in Latin America*. New York: St. Martin's Press.

Vielleux, P. G. (1992, July/August/September). Ecuador: 500 kilometers of resistance, *IWGIA Newsletter,* No. 3, 36–38.

Voz de la CONFENIAE. (1994, November/December/January). Declaration of the Quichua and Shuar Nations before the government, ARCOO, and international opinion. *Voz de la CONFENIAE, 10*(2).

Walker, R. (1987). *Nga Tau Tohetohe: Years of anger*. Victoria, Australia: Penguin Books.

Wilmer, F. (1993). *The indigenous voice in world politics: Since time immemorial*. Newbury Park, CA: Sage Publications.

Williams, R. A., Jr. (1990). *The American Indian in Western Legal Thought: The Discourses of Conquest*. New York: Oxford University Press.

Internet References

Colechester, M. (1993, July). Indigenous Peoples Fight Back. *Human Rights Coordinator,* on the internet at NATIVE-L at: http://bioc09.ethscsa.edu/natnet/archive/nl/ 9307/0166.html.

Innu Home Page. (1997). www.web.apc.org/~innu/index.html. Accessed 30 May 1997.

Jones, P. S. (1997). Frequently asked questions, Subject: B2 The people. On the internet soc.culture.new-zealand. Accessed June 1997.

Lonely Planet. (1997). Australian Aborigines. On the internet:http://www.lonelyplanet. com.au/dest/aust/abor.html. Accessed 8 June 1997.

Native-1 Archives. (1993–97). Day of Action for Innu, 1 March 1993; "Nuxalk Nation," 1 December 1994; "Nuxalk rally Oct 16," 10 October 1995; "Article about Nuxalk Blockade," 24 December 1995; "Nuxalk Nation Under Siege," 24 January 1996; "Re: BC: Nuxalk Arrests," 29 March 1996. http://bioc09.ethscsa.edu/natnet/archive/nl. Accessed 30 May 1997.

Nunavut Home Page. (1996). Nunavut: A territory of regions and communities. Internet site: http://nti.nunavut.ca/geninfo.htm. Accessed 6 June 1997.

Report of the Royal Commission on Aboriginal Peoples. (1997). Internet site: http://dsp-psd.pwgsc.gc.ca/publishing/titles/recent/rcap-e.html. Accessed 6 June 1997.

Reuter Information Service. (1995). Queen signs bill to compensate wronged maoris. Internet: http://www.nando.net/newsroom/ntn/world/110295/world946_5.html. Accessed 8 June 1997.

SAIIC. (1997) Urgent Action, May 9, 1992. *South and Meso American Indian Information Center Newsletter Online*. Accessed June 8, 1997.

Sanders, D. (1980). Background information on the World Council of Indigenous Peoples: The formation of the World Council of Indigenous Peoples. From the web site *Fourth World Documentation Project of the Center for World Indigenous Studies* http://www.halcyon.com/FWDP/ cwisinfo.html. Accessed 28 May 1997.

South and Meso American Indian Center (SAIIC). (1997). *South and Meso American Indian Inormation Center Newsletter* online. saiic.pc.org. Accessed July 7, 1997.

Waitangi Tribunal. (1997). Te Reo Maori Claims. On the internet: http://www.knowledge-basket.co.nz/topic4/waitr_db/text/wai011/doc009.html.Accessed 7 June 1997.

Industrial versus Preindustrial Forms of Violence

Michael Hanagan

New School for Social Research

GLOSSARY

Collective Violence Events in which groups of people take part in seizing or damaging persons or property.

Moral Economy The idea that there is a social and moral dimension to economic transactions. The Austrian scholar Karl Polanyi (1886–1964) argued that the distinguishing characteristic of modern capitalism was its repudiation of moral or social aspects of markets. Contemporary economic sociologists argue that modern markets remain embedded in social relations.

Nomadism A form of economic activity in which a social group moves through an annual cycle of economic and social activities in response to seasonal climatic changes. Not all pastoralists are nomads, many have a fixed abode and participate in migratory herding for only part of the year. Hunters, fishers and gatherers can be nomads but pastoralists have formed the great majority of nomads over the last several millennia.

Pastoralism An economic activity involving the care of herds of domesticated livestock. Instead of bringing food to their livestock, pastoralists bring livestock to their food.

Proletariat Those who work for wages, using means of production over whose disposition they have little or no control.

Timar A landholding system prevalent in parts of the Ottoman Empire in which state land was leased in return for military or other services. Often compared to European feudalism, Ottoman elites were never able to consolidate hereditary control over these lands as were Europeans, and the system itself declined in the seventeenth and eighteenth centuries, replaced by something more akin to private property subject to taxfarming.

Tribute Payments made by states or kinship groups to other states or kinship groups in order to avoid the outbreak of warfare. Tribute is sometimes used by conquered groups to preserve a degree of autonomy from their conquerors, sometimes by ruling groups that find tribute less costly than warfare.

Völkerwanderung Originally coined to describe the penetration of Germanic tribes into the Roman Em-

Copyright © 1999 by Academic Press.
All rights of reproduction in any form reserved.

pire in the fifth and sixth centuries C.E., the term has come to signify any armed migration of entire peoples. Ironically, research into the German migrations into the Roman world have increasingly deemphasized its violent aspects, stressing instead its gradual and negotiated character.

INDUSTRIAL COLLECTIVE VIOLENCE arises out of demonstrations or strikes, forms of protest sponsored by trade unions and social movements and carefully regulated by state authorities. Violence occurs when: (1) state authorities refuse to permit legally sanctioned protests; (2) confrontations emerge between protesting groups or between protestors and state authorities; or (3) protestors take advantage of their numbers to attack persons or objects of their anger. At the heart of industrial protest and, thus, of industrial violence are issues of economic justice and the rights of citizens.

In contrast, preindustrial violence emerges when: (1) states seek to solve problems of the distribution of wealth by external violence against neighbors; (2) those excluded from legal economic activity turn to violent illegal means of extracting revenues; or (3) groups protest economic policies by violently righting wrongs, only subsequently looking for state confirmation of their actions. As contrasted with witchhunts, pogroms, millenarian movements, feuding and vendettas, nationalist revolts, and ethnic cleansing, "preindustrial" and "industrial" violence are directly and immediately concerned with the distribution of economic resources. The crucial distinction is that preindustrial violence emerges when a state or a group seek to effect economic redistribution *outside the framework of the individual state* while industrial violence emerges from conflicts over policies of economic distribution pursued by *individual* states.

This article discusses preindustrial violence, the transition from preindustrial to industrial violence, industrial violence, and briefly considers post-industrial violence.

I. PREINDUSTRIAL VIOLENCE: PREDATORY WARFARE AND VÖLKERWANDERUNG

Three forms of preindustrial collective violence can be distinguished: predatory warfare, predatory violence, and violent protest.

While industrial violence emerges from disputes among citizens concerning the distribution of wealth within national economies, "predatory warfare" stems from states' efforts to solve quotidian economic problems by extracting wealth from neighboring populations. Of course late 20th-century rulers fight for privileged access to vital resources—witness the Gulf War of 1990–1991—but booty and tribute are no longer routine contributions to state budgets. The ideal climate for predatory warfare is where productivity is low, markets are rare, the climate is uncertain, and accumulation is concentrated in a few, highly visible hands.

Difficulties with communication or a scarcity of trained bureaucrats dictated the revenue-extracting strategies of some preindustrial states. Lacking an adequate system of transportation and bureaucratic techniques for provisioning troops at home, the only way of maintaining a powerful army was by annual plundering expeditions. Historians believe that annual military campaigns were necessary to Sargon of Akkad, who ruled in Mesopotamia 2500 B.C.E.; Sargon otherwise lacked the capacity to maintain his large army in peace time. Another means of extracting wealth without stationing garrisons and situating administrators in distant provinces was to accept regular tribute and periodic pledges of loyalty from subordinate rulers. The Aztecs, who used their vast tribute to redistribute wealth throughout society and to reward allied leaders, are paradigmatic here. The absence of wheeled vehicles and draft animals made long distance transportation difficult in Mesoamerica where narrow roads slowed the movement of Aztec armies while seasonal demand for agricultural labor restricted the length of the warmaking period; the gory sacrifices and elaborate rituals so frequent in the Aztec capital were intended to retain the allegiance of subordinate rulers by terror and awe.

Genghis Khan (r. 1206–1227 C.E.) built an irresistible army from dispossessed herdsman who had sworn personal loyalty to him but he was unable to construct anything more than an embryonic state because he could not reconcile steppe warriors' skills with administrative expertise; to escape the burdens of organizing empire, he preferred tribute. His successors, Ogödei Khan and Ghazan Khan faced with insubordination among tributary states and tempted by the prestige of empire, embraced the bureaucratic methods and political practices developed by antecedent Chinese and Iranian rulers.

Their belief in warfare as a means of production helps explain the Mongols' extraordinary violence. In China, Mongol leaders proposed to slaughter the remaining peasants of North China to open new horse pastures, until Yeh-lü Ch'u-ts'ai, Ogödei Khan's prime minister explained to skeptical warriors that if they set up a system of taxation he could produce annual revenues of a half million ounces of silver, 400,000 bags of grain, and 80,000 pieces of silk. They were astounded when he proved to be correct. Hereditary enemies of the peasant, nomad horseman did not realize that the intensive methods of cultivation the Chinese employed on the loess soil of the semiarid northern provinces were the secret of the vast wealth they found in its cities. The view of labor and arms as alternative ways of producing wealth was quite general among predatory warriors. In the 1920s, a Bedouin confided "Raids are our agriculture."

Predatory warfare was also one element of Europe's "new monarchies" and absolutist states. According to Machiavelli, "warfare is the only art expected of a ruler." Perry Anderson reminds us that "war was possibly the most *rational* and *rapid* single mode of expansion of surplus extraction available for any given ruling class under feudalism." Following Anderson, absolutist states of early modern Europe "were machines built overwhelmingly for the battlefield." (Anderson 1979: 31 & 32). Absolutist diplomacy was only a continuation of predatory warfare in which diplomats used military threats and pleaded strategic advantage so as to arrange marriages that brought land and revenues to the absolutist state.

Related to "predatory warfare" but less ongoing and connected with the routine reproduction of states is the violence associated with the mass migration of people. Völkerwanderung occurs outside the territorial framework of states when peoples abandon previously occupied territory and seek to acquire a new territorial basis. The most famous armed mass migration, that of the Germanic peoples in the fourth and fifth century C.E. was a gradual process in which Germanic tribes entered the Roman Empire slowly over several centuries, assimilating much of the Empire's culture in the process. More sudden and violent cases abound. In a classic example, in 58 B.C.E., the Gallic Helvetii, dissatisfied with the small size of their territory, purchased draft animals and wagons and burned their fortresses, their 400 villages, and all the grain except the three months supply they carried with them. They then preceded to look for land to conquer. Not so different is the entry of Bantu speakers into Zambia and southeastern Zaire around 500 C.E., driving the Khoi Khoi and Nan into desolate southeastern Africa. More ancient was the entry of the Hebrew people into the land of Canaan where, following Moses's instructions, they killed everyone.

II. PREINDUSTRIAL VIOLENCE: NOMADS, BANDITS, PIRATES, AND MAROONS

In preindustrial societies, when floods, famine, or tax increases threatened to deprive peasants of land, and wage labor was already oversupplied or unavailable, or when masters were too overbearing, many took desperate actions that broke with the routines of daily life. The options available differed greatly across regions and over time. In Ming China (1368–1644), men castrated themselves so that they could sell themselves as eunuchs; parents pawned children and husbands, wives; men joined imperially subsidized religious orders, people migrated, although this entailed begging and vagabondage. Except insofar as they involved self-mutilation, these terrible choices were relatively nonviolent. Others were not. Ordinary peasants and artisans could also choose nomadic raiding, banditry, and piracy.

When a significant section of the population turns to illegal, violence-prone occupations it poses a challenge to state authority. But where most successful, violent predators simultaneously challenge state sovereignty yet seek incorporation within the state on their own terms. One common and *potentially* violent form of abandoning mainstream preindustrial societies was nomadism. Historically, states distrust pastoralists whose flocks of sheep, goats, camels, cattle, and horses cross borders and seasonally escape their control. For good reason! Belying their image of fierce independence, nomads needed sedentary society far more than sedentary society needed nomads. Pastoral societies generally lacked the storage facilities and administrative structures that enabled peasant societies to survive periods of natural disaster, and sedentary societies are the only places where manufactured goods, grain, and luxury products can be obtained; the saying goes that, "the only pure nomad is a poor nomad."

When bad times hit the agricultural lands on the fringes of pastoral regions, the numbers of poor nomads tended to swell, as formerly settled peasant/pastoralists, driven from the land, became full-time nomads, and policing in sedentary society deteriorated. Under such circumstances, nomads, who were often affected by the same adverse climatic conditions as agriculturalists, turned from raiding one another's flocks to raiding settled communities. To reduce the nomadic threat, the Roman and Ottoman empires enforced mass compulsory sedentarization on their nomadic populations. To deal with rival nomadic groups, the Ottomans enrolled one group into their army, and used it to enforce sedentarization on its rivals. While incorporating nomadic bands wholesale into the state apparatus helped to preserve their collective identities, Ottoman strategy toward nomads was generally effective in preventing large-scale nomadic confederations; even in troubled times, nomadic raiding was generally confined to small bands who could do considerable damage to civilians but did not threaten the state. In contrast, Chinese emperors pursued a more ambitious and ultimately less rewarding strategy. Creating a rigid boundary, the Great Wall, between nomads and settled societies made it impossible to incorporate nomad leaders into society and did not prevent Chinese peasants and artisans from joining with the nomads during times of crisis when nomadic bands periodically overthrew Chinese dynasties.

Marauding nomadism is sometimes confused with endemic banditry but, while endemic banditry, like nomadism, usually requires a rugged terrain, banditry can occur without any ties to a pastoral economy. In many preindustrial societies, the division between bandits and state officials was extremely fluid. In troubled times, successful bandits stood a good chance of being pardoned and awarded office. In the Ottoman Empire, disbanded troops or military deserters were frequent recruits to banditry. At the end of the 16th century, bandit chiefs such as Deli Hasan were able to negotiate lucrative positions for themselves in the Ottoman administration; his men were just as happy plundering Ottoman Muslims in peacetime as Hapsburg Christians in war. Kalenderoglu, another Ottoman bandit who sought to negotiate an administrative position for himself, joked that "If we win over Kuyucu [the grand vizier], then we will have the Ottomans give up everything east of Scutari [i.e. Anatolia], if we do not we will be content being the heros of folk songs" (Barkey 1994: 208).

Like Turkish bandits, 16th-century pirates in the Mediterranean defied some states while benefitting from the toleration of others. After 1540, refugees from the Turkish conquest of Hungary and Croatia, the Uskok pirates emerged in the region around Fiume in the Adriatic. The word "Uskok" means "fugitive." Their attacks on Turkish vessels in the Adriatic imperiled the Venetians' treaty with the Ottoman empire but, as stalwart crusaders against Islam, the Uskoks were supported by the papacy as well as by the Hapsburgs, who resented the Venetian relationship with the Porte.

As in the case of the Uskoks, when pirates had their own autonomous communities, which often served as havens for poorly treated sailors, they were only a few steps from "marronage," which involves escape from unfree labor combined with efforts to establish societies composed of escapees. "Marronage" derives from the Spanish (*cimarron*) meaning wild; a classic example is that of the 16th-century Zaporozhian cossacks; "cossack" is derived from a Tatar word for free warrior or vagrant. The cossacks began as bandit gangs roaming the Ukrainian steppes; the Christian cossacks fought the Muslim Tatars for the right to plunder the native population. At the time, the Ukraine was the only part of eastern Europe where serfdom had not been reimposed. The real making of the cossacks came as the "second serfdom," the reimposition of unfree labor, came to the Ukraine, and many peasants fled with their families to join the cossack brotherhood; there they were joined by hunters, fisherman, nobles fleeing royal punishment, thieves, Christian religious sectarians, and other social outcasts. As they grew, the cossack communities inevitably increased their contact with encroaching Russian, Polish, and Ottoman states. Proclaiming their own right to self-government, the cossacks attempted to create leeway for themselves by playing off Polish king against Russian czar. (Sometimes marronage is decomposed into "petit-marronnage," meaning illegal absences of slaves for short periods, and "grand-marronage," referring to efforts to establish an autonomous society. The use of the term "marronage" in this essay is equivalent to grand-marronage.) Ultimately of course, the cossacks were forced to acknowledge the Russian czar and became the most feared of his repressive tools.

III. PREINDUSTRIAL VIOLENCE: PROTEST

Protest occurs in most societies but not always in the same ways. Performances that contemporaries readily identified as rebellious may easily seem either innocuous or criminal from the point of view of a modern-day observer. Charles Tilly observes that much preindustrial protest involves attempts to take action on the spot to put right a perceived violation of popular morality; violence was often an implicit or explicit element in such actions. In this analysis, preindustrial protest is typically bifurcated with vigorous popular action at the local level combined with humble appeals to powerful intermediaries to intercede at higher administrative levels (Tilly, 1995). The following are characteristic examples of protest in different societies.

In 1628, a terrible famine swept the northern Shaanxi province of China, where a group of rebellious soldiers were soon joined by hungry peasants and, then, by the inevitable contingents of bandits and Mongol tribesmen. The local administrator largely ignored the revolt, and subsequent efforts to pacify the rebels proved fruit-less. In the meantime, the rebel ranks grew as the imperial funds allocated to famine relief proved inadequate. Imperial decisions to save money by reducing the number of administrative centers led redundant officials to join the rebels, and raids by Manchu nomads from outside the Great Wall greatly complicated efforts at repression. The terrible death throes of the Ming dynasty had begun!

In 1702 in small Naganuma fief lands in the Fukushima region of Japan, peasants petitioned against the imposition of taxes on cotton spinning and cash crops used to supplement their farm income; their petitions were not only refused by their powerful lord, the *daimyo*, but the peasants were ordered to transport the tax rice to his warehouse in Edo. Two peasants, alleged to be on the verge of losing their land, called for a mass meeting and, a few days later, a large crowd assembled, marched to the fief administrative officer, and demanded that he accept their petition for the repeal of tax. Afterwards the lord did grant tax reductions but also executed the two peasants who had initiated the protest on the spot where the mass meeting had occurred.

In 1703 in Cairo the prices of basic commodities are rising, a crowd hurries to the Great Mosque and occupies the minarets, from which it launches calls to resistance. The Egyptian crowd forces stores to close and assembles in the great court, voicing its complaints to the religious authorities and pressuring them to convey their grievances to the rulers. A procession then marched from the Mosque to the Citadel, headed by religious leaders (*ulama*), who negotiated with the authorities. Concessions were announced and guaranteed by the religious authorities who calmed the crowd and dispersed it peacefully.

In 1765 in Quito, Viceroyalty of New Granada, an administrative official was sent by the Viceroy to reorganize the lax administration of the liquor monopoly and excise taxes. Hearing of these proposals, the Quito clergy petitioned the administration to hold a *cabildo abierto* (open municipal meeting), a traditional Spanish institution in which representatives of the urban community could express their views. In spite of petitions opposing the reform from the clergy, the creole elite, and the community (*vecindad*), the administration decided to implement the reforms. In response, on the night of May 22, parish bells rang an alarm and crowds of artisans, small shopkeepers, and small tradesmen, particularly the butchers, attacked the excise office and official distillery. Troops sent to disperse the crowd refused to fire, and patrols were attacked. In the end,

Jesuits were sent to mediate and local judges ratified the concessions. Such were the opening acts in a series of confrontations that a month later on St John's night, June 24, would climax in a massive urban rebellion.

IV. THE FORMS AND INTENSITY OF PREINDUSTRIAL VIOLENCE

Why did discontented peasants choose nomadic marauding or banditry in some regions and social protest in others? Why did protest repertoires involve violence against persons in some regions and not in others?

To put these questions in comparative perspective while providing temporal boundaries to our discussion, preindustrial violence under three very different regimes will be considered; ancien régime Bourbon France (1589–1792), the post-Süleyman Ottoman Empire (1566–1923), and Tokugawa Japan (1600–1868). Protest was frequent in Europe and Japan but, in contrast to Europe, Japanese violence was concentrated on property and seldom turned on persons. In the Ottoman Empire, where urban protests were many, peasant protests were few—although not unknown; the great Kisrawan rebellion broke out in Lebanon in 1858–1861. Rural unrest was much more likely to take the form of military uprisings, marauding nomadism, and endemic banditry. The form and intensity of preindustrial violence depend on several factors: (1) what sets of common interests are united by everyday ties of work, kinship or religion; (2) whether geography favors banditry, nomadism, or marronage; (3) whether actions by visible outsiders threatens groups' survival; (4) whether political entrepreneurs have organized a significant section of the rural population; (5) whether coalitions can be formed with groups that reduce the risks of collective actions; (6) the extent and continuity of military activity.

First, let us consider the questions of what group interests were informed by social ties that could alone give abstract interests meaning. In both France and Japan, a peasant identity emerged based on ties of work and administration; peasant communities were taxed collectively and had to apportion taxation within the community; they usually possessed some forms of common land, and, in some areas, made collective decisions about planting, crop selection, and pasturage. While both French and Japanese rulers sought to disarm the peasantry, they also took action against the most repressive forms of labor and, in both countries, the spread of commercialization and protoindustrialization promoted the growth of freeholding and leaseholding peasants living together in autonomous villages. Just as they were connected in work so peasant villages united together in protest and, as in the Pitaut rebellion of 1548 in France, "marched parish by parish, under the banner of each village." In contrast, village ties were weak among the Ottoman rural population. Individual household heads made the important decisions about production, and many taxes were assessed on individual timars; when villages did collectively pay taxes, the distribution was carefully policed by outside officials. Community ties also weakened as timar holders left their plots and offered their services elsewhere; considerable evidence of peasant mobility shows that this was a popular option.

Religious identity was more central in Ottoman communities, which lacked the close rural communities of the European and Japanese countryside as well as the secular corporate structures characteristic of European cities. The contrast between the presence of corporatism in Europe and its absence in the Ottoman Empire is important, particularly because Europeans took their urban corporate structures with them wherever they settled; in the 18th century, there were *échevins* and *prévôts* in Paris, selectmen and town meetings in Boston, and *cabildo abierto* in Quito. Within this urban framework, the secular idea of a moral economy emerged. Yet Ottoman urban dwellers did hold urban authorities morally responsible for controlling grain markets and preventing unjust taxes. Among Muslims, the equivalent of the moral economy was the idea of justice in society centered on the application of Muslim law (*Shari'ah*) by a vigilant Muslim ruler, including the regulation of the grain supply by the *muhtasib*, the official in charge of overseeing the marketplace and safeguarding public morals. While dispossessed Muslim peasants gravitated to the cities where they might join religious orders capable of pressuring rulers, non-Muslims lived in separate parts of the city, outside the moral consensus. And religious identity often divided the Islamic community internally as much as it united them externally. In desert and steppe areas, part-time pastoralists might be attracted by the Suffi brotherhoods so popular among nomads while fulltime cultivators inclined to a more traditionalist Islam.

Second, most people had no chance to become bandits, nomads, or maroons, for these depended on the availability of a nearby terrain that could support such activities. On the face of it, the Ottoman Empire surrounded on one side by the world's largest desert, on another side by the world's largest steppe, and on a third by extensive mountains possessed a more favorable environment for predatory violence than either France or the main Japanese islands, although each country had regions where rugged terrain straddled territorial borders or areas of contested sovereignty, making it hard for police authorities to coordinate efforts and illegal groups. But indigenous groups might limit recourse to banditry. In the poor isolated French Haute Auvergne in the first half of the 16th century, the great obstacle to endemic banditry was the presence of territorially based nobles who themselves often engaged in patently illegal property seizures and personal violence. There, nobles resembled brigands lucky enough to run their own law courts. They were generally left alone by monarchical authority, so long as they did not turn their violence against the state, other nobles, or powerful churchmen.

Third, while moving slowly to enforce law, even against local nobles, the French central state made its power more effective at the local level and thereby focused protestors' attention on the state. In the 18th-century the monarchy tightened tax collection, increased regulation of industry, took sterner measures against smugglers, and encouraged the shipping of grain outside local regions. Those who protested these policies were clearly attempting to change or moderate royal policy. In contrast, the relative decentralization of administration in Japan encouraged protestors to focus their attention on individual lords or government officials without challenging the Tokugawa regime. The Tokugawa ruled through an integrated but decentralized state structure within a pyramidal organization of power. Faced with tax increases they regarded as unjust, peasants might bypass the legal procedures for making complaints and demonstrate in the lord's castle town. While protest leaders were often severely punished, lords who became the objects of popular protest might be forced by the central government to concede to the peasants' demands. Again, compare the Ottoman Empire's evolution a century after Süleyman, when rapacious taxfarmers sent armed retainers, some of them former bandits, to collect taxes. The ease with which the state incorporated successful bandits into the administration weakened the state's legitimacy in the eyes of the mass of people and discouraged efforts to petition or appeal to the rulers' local representatives.

Fourth, the availability of groups that might help organize and coordinate protests was much greater in France than in the Ottoman Empire or Japan. By the late 18th century, French lawyers, merchants, artisans, and shopkeepers had constructed networks of political clubs that enabled them to circulate oppositional ideas throughout much of France; the backbone of these communications was the urban network tieing major urban centers to smaller towns and villages. In the Ottoman

Empire, too, mercantile networks bound together port cities of the empire, but these networks were controlled by Jews and Christian Armenians and Greeks; until 1839, non-Islamic groups could have little role in shaping or participating in reform debates. In Japan mercantile networks were far less developed than in France: Japan had three giant cities, centers of administration, but many fewer small and middle-sized commercial centers. Relations between villages and administrative cities were largely unmediated by mercantile networks. Also, Japanese merchants were cut off from politics and had little opportunity through marriage, education, or purchase of estates to mix with the political classes. Dress codes and their enforced humility in the presence of samurai created a profound gap between the two groups.

Fifth, there were variations in the availability of powerful protectors who might shield protesting peasants from the full force of possible state repression. In 16th-century France, peasants protesting increased royal taxation often found at least tacit support among local nobles and churchmen whose own landed income was threatened by the diversion of local resources to the monarch. Between 1500 and 1700, in England, France, and Spain, Brustein and Levy provide evidence that resident landlords, subsistence production, a common church and regional parliaments all encouraged peasant rebellions by increasing the opportunities for alliances between peasants and nobles and churchmen (Brustein and Levy, 1987).

In regard to the potential for landlord alliances, the contrast between Ottoman Empire and France is especially dramatic. All the more because both systems were originally based on a somewhat similar arrangement in which rulers gave villages to cavalrymen who used his revenues to ensure their livelihood and to raise a retinue for war. Ottoman rulers were sufficiently strong to enforce the connection between service and land, while European rulers were not. European knights took advantage by consolidating their position on the land by making it hereditary, adding adjacent lands, and increasing their local legal jurisdiction. In contrast, the villages that Ottoman cavalrymen controlled were often widely separated, and they were moved from timar to timar and frequently demoted or displaced; while a son might inherit his father's position and be granted timar lands, he would be unlikely to inherit the same lands as his father. Where the European nobility became local landlords with considerable stake in the region that they dominated, Ottoman warriors and the local religious judges who administered justice circulated throughout the Empire. Where disgruntled landlords were always an element in French peasant rebellions before 1650, malcontented timar holders were far more likely to join military uprisings.

One of the reasons for the non-violence of Japanese protest was the inability to form alliances that might have given protestors greater protection against repression. By disarming the common people, dissolving independent guilds and cities, and beginning to transform the samurai from landed warriors to stipendiary urbanites, Japanese rulers made cross-class coalitions difficult. The Tokugawa's insistence that samurai live in cities and seek approval before visiting their lands further isolated the samurai from their peasants. One of the few instances of samurai/commoner alliances was the Shimabara Rebellion of 1637–1638; its religious, Christian, character may have been one reason for its unusually harsh repression, but religious conversion was also accompanied by a potentially dangerous politics.

Finally, for all these contrasts, there remained a most important similarity between France and the Ottoman Empire that differentiated both from Japan. Both French and Ottoman rulers were forced to turn repeatedly to their population to raise money to wage war. Famine and flood were episodic, but in France and the Ottoman Empire warfare was nearly continual. The competitive European state system in which France played a leading role was inherently unstable, and Europeans menaced the Ottoman Empire by west and northwest, while Persians and steppe nomads threatened it east and northeast. The need to muster troops for war put a nearly continuous pressure on both France and the Ottoman Empire that was lacking in Japan. War forced France and the Empire to extract resources from peasants and from trade. In France, mercantile pressure forced kings to make concessions to its subjects. In the Ottoman Empire, the disbanding of armies after major military campaigns frequently produced rebellion or endemic banditry among soldiers who had no home to which they could return. To prevent bandit depredations the authorities encouraged the countryside to arm, and the militarization of the countryside, in turn, facilitated the recourse to banditry and military revolts.

In contrast, after the turbulent period of the Warring States, the first two centuries of Tokugawa rule in Japan was marked by considerable internal peace. Freed from the fear of war, the Tokugawa were not so reliant on mercantile loans as were French and Ottoman rulers. In fact, in 1649 the Tokugawa regime forbade almost all foreign contacts, dispensing with foreign trade that was a potential source of revenue, but also merchants powerful and difficult to control.

V. THE TRANSITION FROM PREINDUSTRIAL TO INDUSTRIAL VIOLENCE

Beginning more than two centuries ago and still not fully completed, the transition from preindustrial to industrial violence was the result of two interrelated revolutions. The first revolution was military. Between the 17th and 19th centuries the transformation of military technology required the bureaucratization and then the industrialization of warfare. War became a more capital-intensive enterprise, requiring substantial administrative organization and the application of up-to-date industrial technologies. The second revolution was economic; commercial and industrial revolutions dramatically increased productivity and created an industrial proletariat. Commerce yielded money with which military men could obtain the artillery, munitions, and, later, the steel battleships that were the latest products of industrial revolutions.

Together, industrial revolution and the industrialization of war depended on the creation of a new kind of state. Warmaking required money and, to obtain it, European war lords and political leaders had to come to terms with industrialists and bankers as well as with a nascent proletariat. The paradox of the 19th-century European state was that, while it could wage war on a unparalleled scale, actual involvement in war diminished. Partly it diminished because industrial growth was a less risky and more secure source of state revenues than predatory warfare and partly because the French Revolution served an unmistakable warning that continual warfare could produce internal revolution. While wars have become incredibly more murderous and destructive, a recent study confirms that "as societies become more industrialized their proneness to warfare decreases" (Cohen, 1986: 265).

To wage war in industrial fashion, particularly in the wake of the French Revolution, European states were forced to conscript an ever larger proportion of the civilian population. The new way of organizing war could make urban civilians into effective soldiers and marked the end of the long ages when nomadic bands of highly skilled light cavalrymen could topple urban-based societies, a prospect that had worried Edward Gibbon, historian of the fall of Rome, in the late 18th century. Although banditry persisted on Europe's peripheries and in its mountainous center, the increasing state penetration of the local economy by tax collectors and military recruiters left less and less room for endemic banditry or piracy and none at all for marronage.

In 18th- and 19th-century Europe, the penetration of state authorities and of markets into local areas met with popular resistance. Preindustrial protest crested just at the moment when conditions in industry were undercutting its roots, and new forms of protest were beginning to develop. The dominant themes of protest in late 18th- and early 19th-century Europe were not protests of newly created industrial proletarians but protests of peasants and artisans against the prospect of becoming proletarianized; they were not efforts to change state policy but resistance to states' claims to make policy in areas of regional or local concern. Yet at the very moment when preindustrial protest reached its peak, serious movement toward industrial protest occurred. British protestors began to accept the triumph of the state and factory, and they demanded that states take action to rectify the inequities of economic distribution. Within the world of industrial states, forms of protest emerged that were, as Tilly argues, more "cosmopolitan," in that they regularly exceeded a single locality, sometimes extending to a national scale, "modular" because standard forms served for a wide variety of claims, and "autonomous" because claimants took major initiatives in determining time and place of their action (Tilly, 1995). Cosmopolitanism, modularity, and autonomy all characterized industrial protest.

Between 1780 and 1832, as the Industrial Revolution progressed, protesting British workers increasingly directed their attention to the British state and addressed their demands to national government. Insofar as they did so, the means that they used included public meetings, petition drives, and mass demonstrations. Workers also began to express their dissatisfaction with wages or working conditions by organizing firm-by-firm strikes. But while social movements and trade unions were emerging, on every side, they kept company with donkeying renegade workers, Rough Music, taking sides at executions, collective seizures of food, smashing shops of merchants accused of unfair dealing, and attacks on Poor Houses. In Britain, liberal politicians were appalled by popular violence but identified the more stable and nonviolent sections of the population and allowed them to become citizens with voting rights.

Over the course of the 19th-century the growth of the industrial working class in Britain and France, then in Germany and the United States, and finally in Austria Hungary, Italy, and Scandinavia attracted worldwide attention. Its rapid growth, its concentration in large cities or industrial regions, and its speedy organization into trade unions and socialist or labor parties gave credibility to Marxist claims that it represented the future. This new industrial working class was first to embrace the new forms of industrial protest. Toward the end of the 19th century, industrial working classes began to acquire voting rights and to become full citizens. Organized into their own Second International (1889), socialist parties attempted to spread their ideas worldwide. Immigrants brought socialist ideas and trade unionism with them when they migrated to the Americas. Asian and African workers brought to Europe during the First World War came into contact with socialists and trade unionists in factories and battlefields. Forms of organization and strike tactics that developed in Europe over a century were spread round the world in a few short decades.

At the time when new forms of state organization and warfare were developing in Europe, contact with Western commercialization and military revolution produced a Walpurgis night of violence in a non-Western world lacking such centralized states and new technologies. The discovery of gold booty and silver mines in Spanish America underpinned the greatest of the tributary empires at the cost of untold blood and toil. The growth of sugar and tobacco production in the Caribbean and southern United States was no less terrible. Beginning in the 17th century, in west Africa, slave raiding was a driving force promoting predatory state formation. Founded in 1712, the state of Segu was described as "an enormous machine to produce slaves." (Klein 1992: 29). By providing muskets in exchange for slaves, merchants gave African chiefs a new source of power that enabled them to dominate both native elites and their neighbors; until their neighbors were forced to turn to slave trading to respond to the armed threat. In 17th-century North America, the drive to maintain an armed superiority over one's neighbors led in 1648–1650 to such violent slaughters as that of the Hurons by Iroquois seeking fur-hunting grounds. In 17th- and 18th-century North America, the mass migration of European farmers produced a new wave of violent Völkerwanderung; both the Dutch and Puritan colonists showed a taste for mass extermination of Indian tribes that sometimes shocked their Indian allies.

By 1815, save with a few minor exceptions such as the Balkan Wars, and one huge exception, World War II, predatory warfare was largely ended in Europe, but Europeans pursued it with great gusto elsewhere. Successive attacks by the Austrians (1683–1699 and 1714–1718) and the Russians (1768–1774 and 1828–1829) had demonstrated the military weakness of the Ottoman Empire. By 1833, a series of Western interventions in the Middle East brought the Ottoman empire to the brink of destruction; only the difficulty of dividing the plunder saved it. During the same period, Britain and Russia imposed humiliating treaties on the Kajar dynasty in Persia, which also lost territory to Russia. The Opium War of 1841–1842 kept a reluctant Chinese Empire open to British commerce, but seriously wasted the Empire's strength and opened it to challenges by internal opponents. The second half of the 19th century witnessed a final round of colonial expansionism but these colonies were more likely to add to government budgets than to reduce them.

The intensification of predatory warfare outside Europe also led to a dramatic resurgence of predatory violence. Wrecked by the loss of money and men, victims such as the Ottoman and Persian Empires weakened their hold on their desert peripheries, where nomadic groups began to reassert their strength and proclaim their commitment to Islamic fundamentalism. As the Ottoman hand weakened, Wahhabi, Sanusi, and Mahdist movements spread among resurgent nomads. In China, grain riots and anonymous violence were relatively rarely used in protests since the state gradually abandoned to local elites the maintenance of the government granaries for providing against famine. Some Chinese peasants turned to organized brigandage, forcing others, often richer peasants, to respond by organizing anti-brigandage societies; if initially successful, both the brigands and the anti-brigandage societies acquired large-scale means of violence and came into violent conflict with states.

As commercial activity advanced, groups pursuing occupations previously deemed legitimate or at least tolerated were labeled "bandits" and "pirates." In early 19th-century Venezuela, expanding commercialization made bandits out of the amalgam of African slaves escaping coastal sugar plantations, Arawak indians fleeing settlers, and free landless men who inhabited the Llanos, a plains region of Venezuela, a bit like the Eurasian steppe. At the end of the 18th century, the market for meat was growing, and the Caracas elite sought to cater to this demand by taking legal control of free-ranging cattle. This attempt conflicted with the time-honored view, rooted in colonial tradition and legislation, that everyone had rights to hunt plains wildlife. Although their claims to legal access to the plains were denied by the state, the Llaneros survived because of their collusion in cattle smuggling with local authorities, ranchers, and merchants.

Western military rivalries introduced piracy into the Caribbean and Indian Oceans on a heretofore unequaled scale as England and France commissioned private ships as "privateers" to attack Spanish and Dutch commerce during wartime. Tolerated by English and French authorities, pirates established their own independent communities in areas of disputed sovereignty such as Tortuga in Hispaniola and St. Marie in Madagascar; there they engaged in piracy, awaiting the return of war that would enable them to turn to legal, and more profitable, careers in privateering. The difference between Captain Kidd (ca. 1645–1702) and his distinguished 16th-century precursors such as Giovanni da Verrazano or Sir Francis Drake was one of context and luck. Kidd's fatal mistake was to attack a vessel owned by a close advisor of the Mogul Emperor at a time when the struggling East India Company sought to regularize commercial relationships between Britain and India.

To the degree that pirate colonies served as havens for mistreated sailors, there is a parallel with marronage, whose expansion in the Caribbean coincided with that of the pirate era. Escaped slaves established communities wherever desolate land adjoined slave plantations, for example, in Columbia, Cuba, Ecuador, Haiti, Surinam, and West Florida. However isolated and remote, such communities always required contact with larger societies to obtain basic tools and foodstuffs, and, since Maroon escapees tended to be predominantly male, to recruit or kidnap women. Colonial armies repeatedly mounted expeditions to destroy maroon societies. Colonial administrators often adapted the same strategy as the Czars employed toward the cossacks, recognizing established maroon communities in exchange for help in tracking down escaped slaves and preventing the further expansion of maroon communities.

As warfare and predatory violence accelerated outside Europe under the whip of commercialization and military aggression, so did resistance. On Europe's eastern periphery in Russia, peasant insurrections, led by cossacks, opposed the reimposition of serfdom on peasants that occurred as nobles responded to the growing international grain trade. Both great Russian peasant insurrections, those of Stenka Razin in 1667 and Emelyan Pugachev in 1773, involved coalitions of "cossacks, peasants, Old Believers, bandits and footloose wanderers" (Rude :57). Powerful rebellions, including mutinous soldiers, displaced elites, and peasants, occurred in the Tupac Amaru rebellion in southern Peru, 1780–1781, the Hidalgo uprising of 1810, the Java War of 1825–1830, and the Indian "Mutiny" of 1857–1859. Portrayals of these rebellions as embryonic nationalist movements are anachronistic; peasant participation was based on their discontent with the introduction of market-oriented landholding systems imposed by an elite that shared neither native tongue nor religion.

VI. PROTEST VIOLENCE IN THE AGE OF TRANSITION

The single most important feature of this transition is the manner in which industrial and preindustrial violence could interact to magnify the levels of violence. New methods of protest, such as strikes, demonstrations, and organized political parties, disseminated quickly to wherever an industrial proletariat developed. Under the right circumstances, organized social movements, particularly national industrial workers' movements, could provide important urban allies for protesting agriculturalists. By harnessing the village revolts and urban riots of preindustrial protestors to the cause of national social change, industrial protestors intensified levels of violence.

Let us look at some characteristic forms of protest in the age of transition.

Beginning on September 23, 1880, in Ballinrobe, County Mayo, Ireland, an unpopular minor landlord and land agent found himself shunned by the surrounding community for attempted eviction of Lord Erne's tenants after they had demanded rent abatements due to bad harvests. In response, a crowd of villagers had assembled and drove off his farm laborers, herdsmen, coachman, stableman, and serving girls, telling them never to work for him again. Local merchants refused his trade and, most important, day laborers refused to harvest his potato crop. Behind this display of community solidarity was the Irish National Land League whose supporters collected money for legal defense and attracted worldwide publicity to their cause. The new tactic took the name of the landlord against whom it had first been used, Captain Charles Cunningham Boycott.

In Moscow on January 22, 1905, hundreds of thousands of factory workers accompanied by their parents, wives and children converged on the Winter Palace, carrying religious standards and portraits of the czar. Organized by an Orthodox priest the purpose of the demonstration was to present the czar with a petition that requested everything from minor reforms to the convening of a Constituent Assembly. Suddenly the crowd was fired upon without warning by the czar's cossack troops. Hundreds were killed. In response to "Bloody Sunday," a great general strike was called, beginning the Revolution of 1905.

In Beijing on May 4, 1919, thousands of students poured into the streets to protest the concession of China's northern province of Shandong to Japan by the Versailles Peace Treaty. On June 5, when news of government violence against Beijing students reached Shanghai, merchants closed their shops, a general strike was called, and demonstrations spread nationwide; two students were killed and more than a thousand people arrested before the May 4 Movement was ended. The major organizers of the strike in Shanghai were the nascent Chinese Communist Party, Goumindang leftists, and the Green and Red gangs.

The characteristic features of the transition are its anomalies, the harnessing of peasant community solidarities to national political organizations, the transformation of the brutal suppression of humble imperial petitioners into a general strike, and the organization of strikes by a newly formed Communist party and traditional secret gangster organizations.

VII. THE FORMS AND INTENSITY OF PROTEST VIOLENCE IN THE AGE OF TRANSITION

Under what circumstances do preindustrial and industrial protest come together and produce intense violence? To get the elements of an answer, let us briefly examine China, Mexico, and Russia in the turbulent years between 1910 and 1925, using the same set of explanatory factors as before, quickly summarized as: common interests, geography, visible outsiders' threats, political entrepreneurs, coalitions, and war. In all three countries, preindustrial and industrial protest came together to produce situations of concentrated violence. Unlike in Mexico, in China and Russia labor movements played key roles in national protest. In the Russian Empire, labor mobilized rural populations against an unstable national government, while in China labor radicals were instrumental in negotiating broad-ranging coalitions between protesting peasants, bandits, and industrial workers.

In China, Mexico, and Russia work-based ties played an important role in identity formation. In all three countries, peasant communities were both an abstract social category and a lived identity. As we saw earlier, a peasant community was not an inevitable outcome in peasant societies; when the Ottoman state collapsed in the crisis years of 1918–1922, nomads seized control of Arabia, and military revolt installed a secular nationalist, Kemal Ataturk, as ruler of Turkey; lacking informal collective organization, peasants still remained on the sidelines. By this time, a peasant community was also absent from much of European agriculture; German agriculturalists were hard hit in the worldwide agrarian depression that followed World War I, but while Mecklenburg farmers may have been attracted by the romantic concept of community embodied in Naziism, class stratification had divided agriculturalists between rich and poor and sundered the bonds of community.

The peasant communities that engaged in violent action between 1910 and 1925 shared some general characteristics, but each was the product of different historical trajectories and had distinctive features. After emancipation, the Russian government had legally imposed collective fiscal responsibility on Russia's peasant communities as a way of preserving traditional loyalties. In some respects the evolution of Chinese peasants toward village community followed a logic independent of the West; since the early 18th century, Chinese commerce had tended to break up kin-based property structures and promote an individual conception of property. As kin ties weakened and the political order came under attack, villages became the nucleus for protection and self-defense. In Mexico, village communities were the central institutions in the more populous southern and central regions of Mexico, but the power of estates increased in the north; since Mexican independence, peasants had fought with some success to retain village common lands against the determined efforts of liberals to privatize them. Attempts of late 19th-century estate developers in the north to divide Ranchero common lands to promote cattle export resemble the struggles of the Venezuelan Llaneros in the early 1900s.

At turn of the 19th century China and Russia industrial workers played a more important role than in Mexico. In all three countries the working classes were quite small compared with the rest of the population, but in Russia and China they were heavily concentrated in strategically located cities such as St Petersburg, Moscow, and Shanghai, and had shown themselves capable of extraordinary militancy in the Russian Revolution of 1905 and in the mass strikes in Shanghai in 1919 and 1925. In Mexico, as in Russia and China, industrial workers were concentrated in the capital, Mexico City, but Mexican labor was deeply divided internally and courted by politicians within the dominant Constitutionalist camp.

All three countries possessed lands suitable for bandits, and in all three, banditry resurged during economic and political crises. Many Chinese peasants also chose banditry, but peasant bandits often retained contact with their villages and conflicts between bandits and richer villages where antibrigand societies flourished often overlaid village competitiveness. The Russian Civil War witnessed a major upsurge of banditry; bandit armies, such as that of Vakhulin, composed of deserters from the Red and White armies, raided Bolshevik-held towns and won peasant support by preventing Bolshevik efforts at requisitioning food. In times of tumult, in Mexico such as the decade between 1857 and 1867, banditry flourished and prominent bandit leaders were associated with either liberals or conservatives. Pancho Villa began as a cattle rustler in Durango, although by the time of the civil war he was a railroad construction foreman in Chihuahua. Banditry returned in full force during the civil war.

In all three countries, outsiders pulled peasant communities into the political arena and were instrumental in focusing their attention on national government. In Mexico, quarreling elites appealed to already angry peasants to support their candidate, Francisco Madero, who promised political democracy and a vague agrarian justice. Once mobilized, peasants remained involved in the struggle for agrarian justice long after Madero's assassination. In Russia, frightened by peasant support for the 1905 revolution, the Czarist government abandoned the peasant communities it had so long promoted, and a series of laws known as the Stolypin reforms sought to abolish common lands and commercialize peasant agriculture. At the very moment that the Imperial government was attacking peasant communities head on, the state conscripted peasants' sons for a murderous world war. In a China divided by warlords, forced to pay a huge indemnity to foreign powers, and subjected to the rule of Westerners in foreign enclaves in major seaports, the concession of portions of China to Japan by the Versailles conference brought home to everyone the consequences of their country's enfeebled state. In each country, issues of profound consequence for peasants could only be addressed at the national political level.

In Russia and particularly in China, there were political groups that sought to draw rural peoples into national politics and to coordinate their activities once they had entered the national scene. But national political parties could only extend their rural contacts when a network of contacts existed that tied large cities to market towns and then to the countryside. This was a great deal easier in centralizing empires such as Russia and China, that had built a transportation system and administrative networks to facilitate the penetration of the periphery by the center; in this context Mexico was less well integrated and the new railway network built in successive waves in the early 1880s and again at the turn of the century was less oriented toward tying the nation together than toward commercial uses. In Mexico commercialization and industrial change occurred most rapidly on the peripheries, in the

north and around Veracruz, and this made it difficult for rebels to cooperate during the civil war that began in 1910. The agrarian core of the revolution was clearly in the south with Zapata's Morelos and to a lesser extent Guerrero and Peubla, while Pancho Villa's northern movement was more diverse, including mine workers, railroad workers, and rancheros.

Also, left-wing parties centered in cities such as St Petersburg, Moscow, and Shanghai were able to serve as an important ally for rural protestors. In the wake of Russian defeat in the First World War, many radicalized soldiers deserted and returned to the countryside, where they encouraged their countrymen to seize the land and refuse to pay taxes. Following preindustrial patterns of protest, mass land seizures swept the kingdom without the prompting of Bolsheviks, Mensheviks, or Socialist Revolutionaries. The major contribution of the Bolshevik party was to demand legal sanction for these land seizures. The hesitations and refusals on the part of political parties, provoked by the bringing of the land question to the very front of the national political stage, was a fundamental engine driving the revolution in a radical direction—a movement that ended in the profound betrayal of its peasant supporters.

Political parties were also able to make alliances with bandits and to incorporate them into their organizations, just as rulers incorporated them into their states. Bandits were no less willing to ally with strong left-wing movements than with governments, and they sometimes had much to offer these movements. As mentioned before, in organizing the May 4 Movement (1919) in Shanghai, gangs were extremely important. Their role as the chief suppliers of unskilled Shanghai labor, from factory laborers to nightsoil collectors, beggars, and prostitutes, contributed support from groups that the Communists and Goumindang with their influence in artisanal and industrial worker trade unions were unable to reach; the gangs also often controlled access to factory employment, and the first successful Communist entry into the trade union movement was made through the influence of the Green gang. The gangs were deeply involved in local politics and their alliances with established officials as well as with Communists increased their ability to maneuver politically.

From its inception the Chinese Communist Party attempted to coopt bandit and antibrigandage societies, which sometimes had hundreds of thousands of members in the countryside. Chinese bandits did not confine themselves to small-scale raiding parties; in 1940 the Communist New Fourth Army joined with both bandit and antibrigandage groups such as the Big Swords and Red Spears to attack the Japanese; many Big Swords and Red Spear members were reorganized into the New Fourth Army. In Mexico no left-wing political group possessed the national standing of the Chinese Communist Party, which enabled it to negotiate alliances with bandit leaders; the anarcho-syndicalists who composed the left wing of the workers' movement in Mexico City had no orientation whatsoever toward national politics. No Mexican party was able to forge an agrarian program capable of uniting the disparate forces of the rebellion—this helps to explain the limits of its achievements—and no party was able to seize control of the revolution and shape it to its own purposes either.

Finally, war was crucial to the success of radical revolution in Russia. In the period under consideration, 1910–1925, it was less of a factor in China or Mexico. Certainly, in China the threat of Japanese imperialism and the conflicts of rival warlords were powerful forces that promoted social protest as were, in Mexico, the American occupation of Veracruz and the cross-border incursions by American troops. Villa's efforts to provoke American invasions were efforts to win popular support in Mexico, but had the United States been more deeply involved, the triumph of centrist liberalism would have been impossible. Ultimately, war would bring social revolution to China.

VIII. INDUSTRIAL VIOLENCE

Today, in the industrialized societies of the West, the routine use of violence in protest has declined. Outside of Western Europe and North America, industrial violence remains an important feature of protest, although in the second half of the 20th century, protest-based violence has been overshadowed by the unparalleled violence of war and "democide," that is, mass murder and genocide perpetrated by states against those subject to their authority.

In Western Europe and the United States the greater organization of industrial protest helps to explain the decline of industrial violence; both states and protesters developed more control over their members. The emergence of civilian police forces gave states a more sensitive tool for crowd control than did the regular army. The appearance of the organized social movement with formal membership and hierarchical structure enabled protesters to better discipline their own ranks. In the contemporary world, industrial violence is most likely to occur in nations where citizenship has not been fully extended to the working classes. One reason for the decline of violent protest is the growth of worker/citizenship, which raises the cost of repression for state

authorities and renders the use of violence politically undesirable for labor movements. Another reason is the declining percentage of the labor force in blue-collar jobs in Western Europe and North America and the falling percentage of trade-union membership in many European countries and in North America. The sense that labor represents the future is almost gone, and in many Western European countries labor is well on its way to becoming just another interest group—a position it has long held in the United States.

In Western Europe, where industrial violence began, it is now at fairly low levels although there remain important differences among European nations. In some European countries, referred to as "countries of consensus," strikes are actually rare events and accordingly strike-related violence almost never occurs. Such countries include Austria, Denmark, Germany, Holland, Norway, and Sweden. In other countries, workers strike much more frequently and violence sometimes occurs. Countries of confrontation include Belgium, Finland, France, Ireland, Italy, and the United Kingdom. Barricades briefly returned to the streets of Paris in May 1968 and students were attacked by the police. A large general strike began and ended with little violence in France in the summer of 1983; immigrant workers played an important role.

In recent decades industrial violence along with political general strikes have returned to Eastern Europe, where they originated in 1905. In Poland general strikes for higher wages turned into violent encounters in 1956, 1970–1971, 1976 and 1980–1982. While none of these strikes was successful in winning its demands, the strikes of the 1970s and early 1980s were decisive in weakening the Communist regime and preparing the way for its demise. Mass strikes were particularly damaging in Poland because Communist ideology stressed the leading role of workers in socialist society; if even the leading social group was dissatisfied with Communism, something was undoubtedly wrong. The sense of labor as the "leading social group" was, to some extent, also accepted by the leaders of the Polish Solidarity movement, who used their labor organization as a forum to articulate a larger vision of Polish society, to champion democracy, and to form coalitions with a variety of groups, including the Polish Catholic Church.

Something of the same sense of labor as the champion of a democratic society has flourished in some South American countries and in South Africa, where it has also been associated with higher levels of labor violence. A recent case is that of Brazil between 1977 and 1989, where labor movements, working with movements of students, left-wing Catholics, and moderate reformers, played an important role in returning the country to democracy after 17 years of military rule. In the early years of the struggle, the militancy of workers fighting to raise their wages contributed powerfully to the sense that the military regime was not all powerful, but as negotiations for the return to democracy got underway workers joined students, reformist politicians, and left-wing Catholics to campaign in favor of a constitutional amendment to restore the direct election of the president. A key element in the coalition's success was the labor movement's willingness to acknowledge the "relative autonomy" of its partners. After Brazil returned to democracy the independent struggles of social movements and workers, including a general strike of two million workers, was crucial in winning structural reforms that ensured that Brazilian democracy would bring higher standards of living and guarantees for political and civil rights.

Crucial to labor's rise in both Poland and Brazil was its commitment to democracy and a willingness to form coalitions and work with other social groups and mass movements. In these countries, labor has acted less as an interest group and more as a movement working with others for social change. Many voices have urged European and North American labor movements to establish closer links with contemporary social movements and to adopt a social movement orientation.

IX. CONCLUSION: POSTINDUSTRIAL VIOLENCE?

Today, we live on the edge of a new postindustrial world whose major trends are still far from clear. One of the foremost characteristics of claims for economic redistribution in the industrial era was their focus on individual states. In today's postindustrial global world, states have less and less control of access to their own markets, and the age may not be far off when transnational trade unions organize internationally against multinational corporations. More immediately, John Walton and David Seddon have claimed that the neoliberal economic policies of the mid-1970s and the imposition by the International Monetary Fund and the World Bank of austerity regimes produced a first wave of "global food riots" (Walton and Seddon, 1994). In the past, relatively small labor movements in predominantly peasant countries have been able to play a major role in protest, including violent protest, by coordinating the demands of preindustrial protestors, negotiating alliances between disparate groups, providing support

for their struggles, and articulating their demands on a national stage. One of the oldest traditions of the labor movement is internationalism, and one of the most important issues in the coming period is whether international labor movements may serve to project the concerns of the disenfranchised and oppressed portions of national populations on an international stage.

Also See the Following Articles

ECONOMIC CAUSES OF WAR AND PEACE • INSTITUTIONALIZATION OF VIOLENCE • WARFARE, TRENDS IN

Bibliography

Anderson, P. (1979). *Lineages of the absolute state.* London: Verso.

Barfield, T. J. (1994). The devil's horsemen: Steppe nomadic warfare in historical perspective. In (eds.) S. P. Reyna and R. E. Downs, *Studying war: Anthropological perspectives.* Langthorne, PA: Gordon and Breach Science Publishers. Pp. 157–184.

Barkey, K. (1994). *Bandits and bureaucrats: The Ottoman route to state centralization.* Ithaca: Cornell University Press.

Brustein, W., & Levy, M. (1987). The geography of rebellions: Rulers, rebellions and regions, 1500 to 1700. *Theory and Society* 16:4(July), 467–496.

Cohen, R. (1986). War and peace proneness in pre- and postindustrial states. In (Eds.) M. L. Foster and R. A. Rubenstein, *Peace and war: Cross-cultural perspectives.* New Brunswick, NJ: Transaction Books. Pp. 253–267.

Ikegami, E., & Tilly, C. (1997). State formation and contention in Japan and France. In (eds.) James L. McClain, John M. Merriman, and Ugawa Kaoru, *Edo and Paris: Urban life and the state in the early modern era.* Ithaca: Cornell University Press. Pp. 429–454.

Klein. M. A. (1992). The impact of the Atlantic slave trade on the societies of the western Sudan. In (eds.) J. E. Inikori and S. L. Engerman, *The Atlantic slave trade: Effects on economies, societies, and peoples in Africa, the Americas, and Europe.* Durham: Duke University Press. Pp. 25–42.

Magagna, V. V. (1991). *Communities of grain: Rural rebellion in comparative perspective* Ithaca: Cornell University Press.

Perry, E. J. (1993). *Shanghai on strike: The politics of Chinese labor.* Stanford: Stanford University Press.

Rummel, R. J. (1994). Power, genocide and mass murder. *Journal of Peace Research.* 1:31, 1–10.

Tilly, C. (1995). *Popular contention in Great Britain, 1758–1834.* Cambridge, MA: Harvard University Press.

Tong, J. W. (1991). *Disorder under heaven: Collective violence in the Ming Dynasty.* Stanford: Stanford University Press.

Tutino, J. (1986). *From insurrection to revolution in Mexico: Social Bases of agrarian violence 1750–1940.* Princeton: Princeton University Press.

Walton, J., & Seddon, D. (1994). *Free markets & food riots: The politics of global adjustment.* Oxford: Blackwell.

White, J. W. (1995). *Ikki: Social conflict and political protest in early modern Japan.* Ithaca: Cornell University Press.

Wolf, E. R. (1982). *Europe and the people without history.* Berkeley: University of California Press.

Womack, J. Jr. (1968). *Zapata and the Mexican Revolution.* New York: Vintage.

Institutionalization of Nonviolence

Toh Swee-Hin (S.H.Toh) and Virginia Floresca-Cawagas

University of Alberta

GLOSSARY

Cultural Solidarity The relationships and structures within, between, and among cultural groups and communities that promote values and principles of respect, understanding, justice, tolerance, dialogue, harmony, and solidarity.

Culture of Peace and Nonviolence The paradigm of values, attitudes, norms, and practices (personal, institutional, structural) that sustain nonviolent and peaceful living, enhance societal and global justice, uphold human rights, promote intercultural harmony, and nurture ecological sustainability.

Culture of War and Violence The paradigm of values, attitudes, norms, and practices (personal, institutional, structural) that sustain wars and other physical forms of violence and various nonphysical expressions of violence (economic, social, psychological, cultural) that destroy or diminish the quality of life of human beings and planet earth.

Ecological Nonviolence The relationships between human beings (as individuals, communities, organizations, nations, and global regimes) and the natural environment that are underpinned by principles of sustainability, social and economic justice, simplicity of lifestyles, and biodiversity.

Inner Peace Values, beliefs, and practices that promote spiritual growth, wisdom, and the development of the inner being to think and live nonviolently and peacefully with oneself and all other beings.

Institutionalization Processes of building the capacities of persons, institutions, communities, organizations, and even nations to reflect a set of preferred visions, values, policies, principles, and practices.

Peace Education Education for transforming consciousness and worldviews toward a culture of peace and nonviolence; rests on developing a critical understanding of root causes of conflicts and violence, and empowering learners to take personal and societal action to dismantle a culture of violence and to build a peaceful self and world; takes place across all modes (formal, nonformal, informal) and levels, relying on participatory, creative, and critical pedagogies.

Structural Violence Violence caused by social and economic injustices resulting in diminished access of marginalized groups to basic needs and humane quality of life; operates at local, national, international, and global levels, and requires varying degrees of political repression.

INSTITUTIONALIZATION OF NONVIOLENCE. A wide range of meanings of nonviolence has emerged in the theory and practice of peace research, education and action worldwide. As a philosophy, nonviolence advocates the non-use of ideas and strategies of violent force in the relationships of individuals, groups, organi-

Copyright © 1999 by Academic Press.
All rights of reproduction in any form reserved.

zations, and nation-states. While one application of this philosophy is in the nonparticipation in wars and violent revolutions, a more holistic approach opposes all other forms of violence, including social, economic, political, and cultural manifestations. It also recognizes the interconnectedness of types and sources of violence from micro to macro levels. The institutionalization of nonviolence focuses simultaneously on the elimination and/or reduction of physical as well as other multiple forms of violence and violent conflicts in multiple sites including domestic nation-states and international systems, local, national and global economic structures and relationships, social institutions at formal and informal levels, and interactions between human beings and their ecologies.

I. INTRODUCTION

As humanity approaches the next millennium, there are increasing signs of a paradigm shift in how nations, groups, communities, and individuals relate to each other. From the battlegrounds of large-scale wars and armed conflicts to more localized intergroup and interpersonal sites of violence (e.g., home, schools, communities), a greater understanding of and commitment to the theory and practice of nonviolence is clearly emerging. This is not to deny the ongoing ravages, destruction, and suffering of wars in various corners of the earth, as well as a general climate of violent relationships in everyday life in virtually all societies. But increasingly hope and inspiration have been generated by movements, groups, individuals, and some state agencies that seek nonviolent alternatives to the complex challenges of nurturing and maintaining life, and of living together in peace and harmony. Certainly the story of nonviolence is not a new one. Over the thousands of years of recorded human history, communities and leaders of wisdom and faiths have been urging fellow human beings, rulers, and governments to abandon violence in their ideas and actions. But often, such voices have usually been marginalized and overshadowed by the forces for and of violent disposition and dispensation. From current trends, the next century may well provide the critical spaces for the culture of nonviolence and peace to grow and replace the culture of violence and war.

The 1990s can be appropriately characterized as the decade of the "peace dividend." With the ending of the Cold War, the palpable tensions caused by nuclear-backed superpower rivalry have receded. Several significant contexts of long-standing militarized internal

conflict have been amenable to nonviolent conflict mediation and resolution, resulting in peace accords such as those in the Middle East, El Salvador, Mozambique, South Africa, Guatemala, the Philippines, and most recently, Northern Ireland. Yet the signing of peace accords and treaties is clearly only one step in the peace-building process—a crucial step in laying some key conditions for the ending of bitter armed struggle and conflict, but not necessarily sufficient for lasting and sustainable peace. As these cases indicate, the institutionalization of nonviolence is or will be a very complex and difficult journey.

The complexities embodied in efforts to institutionalize nonviolence are in turn rooted in the multifaceted and multidimensional realities of violence. No longer can "violence" have a restricted meaning and expression in physical forms (e.g., wars, bodily fighting, and abuse). In order to build a more peaceful world, all forms of violence must be addressed, including physical and nonphysical interactions from the psychological to the social and economic. The interconnectedness of types and sources of violence from micro/interpersonal to macro/global levels calls for a complementary and holistic integration of nonviolent principles, structures, and relationships in all institutions and systems of society. As the often-cited concept stresses, peace is not just the absence of war.

II. NONVIOLENCE: MEANINGS, VALUES, AND PRINCIPLES

In essence, nonviolence as a philosophy seeks to cultivate relationships and structures among all peoples, groups, organizations, and nation-states that do not use ideas and strategies of violent force. Many traditions and faiths worldwide over thousands of years have promoted this concept of nonviolence, from Christian teachings of pacifism to Hindu and Buddhist principles of ahimsa or noninjury and nonkilling. Among many indigenous peoples, a spirituality of nonviolence can also be found. In modern times, nonviolence has been considerably catalyzed by such inspirational role models as Mahatma Gandhi and Martin Luther King. While some pacifists have focused their resistance to violence on nonparticipation in wars or violent revolutions, a holistic approach to nonviolence also opposes all other forms of violence including social, economic, political, and cultural manifestations encapsulated by the notion of structural violence popularized by the pioneer in peace research, Johan Galtung.

Advocates of the theory and practice of nonviolence

are guided by several key principles (e.g., see Sharp, Burton). A central one affirms nonviolence as a moral, ethical, or spiritual truth, indeed a way of life. Furthermore, nonviolent efforts at reconciliation and persuasion are deemed more effective and in the long term more sustainable for resolving conflicts than the use of physical force. Another key principle in the philosophy of nonviolence links ends with means, so that it is vital to promote peace and nonviolence by the consistent means of nonviolence. Using violence only lays the basis for further violence, fueling a continuing cycle of violence and counterviolence. Nonviolence proponents also see the vital need for the "powerless" to recognize that the "power" of those in dominant positions is derived from their own "obedience" or "consent" to be so "dominated." Hence, if the ruled refuses to "obey," the powerful's basis for their rule will be weakened and can be challenged from below. However, in nonviolence action, those who oppress are viewed as human beings that are in part also victims of the system of oppression. Nonviolence chooses love over hate. Nonviolence calls on advocates to willingly sacrifice or suffer as a result of taking nonviolent action. Such suffering can help to educate and transform.

Finally, violence is often caused by the failure of ruling institutions and groups to adequately respond to human needs. Nonviolent transformation hence seeks to overcome behavioral and structural violence by facilitating the participation of the marginalized in fulfilling their needs. As another popular theme emphasizes, there can be no peace without justice. A major root cause of violence due to militarization and armed conflicts is the presence of structural injustices that underpin oppression and repression with subsequent resistance from the oppressed. For societies emerging from protracted armed conflicts to a state of nonviolence, there must be transformations in the economic, social, and political dimensions of life that overcome inequities and marginalization of certain groups.

Given the complexity and multidimensionality of nonviolence, the institutionalization of nonviolence is necessarily rooted in a great variety of sources of inspiration, role models, and practices increasingly evident across the world. While these exemplars have their own dynamics and sites of praxis, the challenge now is to see how they are interdependent struggles for the building of a culture of peace.

A. Uprooting War and Physical Violence

The efforts to bring about a cessation of war and armed conflicts in many parts of the world through mediation and conflict resolution strategies have clearly yielded positive outcomes. Governments and combatant parties at national and international levels have shown some willingness to negotiate peace settlements. However, the increasing role of citizen peacemakers in the peaceful resolution and transformation of conflicts needs to be acknowledged as inspiring role models. For example, in 1993, the Buddhist-inspired Walk for Peace and Reconciliation in Cambodia empowered citizens to work toward a peaceful post-civil war future. In the Philippines, the Coalition for Peace and other peacebuilding networks have worked with grassroots peoples initiatives in creating demilitarized peace zones as a microsite of institutionalized nonviolence. In South Africa and Nicaragua, people organizations and NGOs have participated in shaping the national peace accords. Hence, critical education and empowerment of ordinary citizens to be active in the peacebuilding process has been vital in the successful steps toward building nonviolent societies.

Furthermore, in postwar or post-armed conflict contexts, processes of national healing and reconciliation are strongly needed to overcome the legacies of enmity, distrust, and bitterness of victimization. The National Commission on Truth and Reconciliation in the new South Africa provides, for instance, a unique social experiment in building a multicultural society not fractured by deep "racial"/"ethnic" divides. In the Southern Philippines, groups such as the Bishops-Ullama Forum have sought to play a role in increasing understanding and trust among Christians and Muslims thereby helping to institutionalize the September 1997 peace accord between the government and the Moro National Liberation Front. Furthermore, healing in a post-armed conflict requires not just the physical rehabilitation of traumatized and scarred victims, especially children, but also their psychological and emotional healing. Worldwide, children rehabilitation centers are seeking to help the victims of war regain trust and faith in a culture of peace.

At the global level, apart from strengthening mechanisms and organizations for peacekeeping and peacebuilding (e.g., diplomatic peace initiatives, intervention of NGOs such as International Alert, Fellowship of Reconciliation, Peace Brigades), the work to delegitimize weapons of war and armed conflicts is very crucial. Project Ploughshares and other NGO-led campaigns to abolish the arms trade, including the recent advances in banning land mines, have educated and mobilized citizens in some arms-producing societies to demand policies from their governments and industries for reducing and eliminating the sale of weapons across borders. Rather than reinforce a culture of death and violence, countries should be investing in life and nonviolence (e.g., conversion of arms industries to civilian production; other arms reduction treaties; control of horizontal nuclear proliferation in the post-Cold War era; nonrecruitment of children as soldiers).

In many formal schooling systems, especially in North but also increasingly in South contexts, the integration of nonviolence principles in policies, programs, curricula, and teaching-learning environments has expanded in recent decades. Responding to heightened concerns over attitudes, conduct, and relationships among members of school communities (students, teachers, administrators) that sanction a culture of direct and other forms of violence (e.g., bullying, assaults, corporal punishment, "gang" fighting, teacher victimization, verbal put-downs, initiation rituals, intolerance, discrimination on the basis of sexual orientation, ethnicity, religion, appearance, or skin color, sexual harassment and drug addiction), these programs essentially promote values and practices of conflict resolution and violence-prevention (e.g., students skilled in peer mediation and conflict resolution interventions; school discipline, code of behavior, pedagogical and other institutional policies that uphold nonviolent relationships among students, teachers, and administrators; collaboration between schools, parents, and external agencies such as police, justice, legal, and social services; teacher intervention in domestic violence against children). Likewise, there is increasing attention in many societies over the entrenchment of physical violence within the family institution. For example, the Family Violence Prevention Fund (FVPF) is a national nonprofit organization in the United States that focuses on domestic violence education, prevention, and public policy reform. Throughout its history, the FVPF has developed pioneering prevention strategies in the justice, public education, and health fields. In South countries such as India, women's groups are speaking out against some traditional and even modern family and social-based practices that sponsor violence against women (e.g., female infanticide, dowry deaths).

These programs for violence prevention, reduction, and resolution show that building a nonviolent culture within schools needs to take into account the multiple parts, levels, relationships, and structures constituting a school community. Besides integrating appropriate knowledge, skills, and values into content and pedagogy in both formal and extra or co-curriculum (e.g., sports, play, and clubs), a surfacing or reforming where necessary of the hidden informal curriculum is crucial. Organizational and administrative principles, processes, and structures have to be implemented to sustain nonviolent relationships between administrators and teachers, administrators and students, teachers and students, students and students, and teachers and teachers. Likewise, a nonviolent school culture extends into school–community relationships between and among teachers, administrators, parents, students, community members, NGOs, business and social-cultural institutions or agencies (e.g., religious bodies, media, police, and social services). Last but not least, violence prevention calls on the integration and coordination of wider societal agencies, including educational system authorities, political bodies, and legal-judicial systems. Apart from the short-term outcome of schools becoming more peaceful and safe environments, the success of such school-based programs of education for nonviolence and conflict resolution in turn hold positive implications in the years ahead. Hopefully, children and youth will join the next generation of adults with internalized values and practices rooted in principles and norms of nonviolence.

The intersection of wider societal and institutional endeavors for dismantling a culture of war and violence is also seen in campaigns worldwide to transform the production and distribution of cultural, leisure, and recreation products/services (e.g., media, toys, entertainment). Through public and school-based critical literacy, adults and children are empowered to not consume media violence or war toys, while pressuring governmental and private sectors to enforce relevant policies and regulation. Another important extension of violence prevention programs in schools is to raise students' awareness and action on major problems of global militarization. These include reconsidering the value of war toys and campaigns to end the deadly arms trade. Recently, many school children in the Pacific region (e.g., Australia, New Zealand, Philippines, South Pacific Islands) participated in the protest against French nuclear testing as a serious undermining of the post-Cold War peace dividend and potential ecological destruction whose effects will weigh on future generations in the region.

B. Dismantling Structural Violence

One recognized root cause of militarized conflicts within societies is the presence of structural violence. The inequitable distribution of resources internally and globally, which inflicts much suffering on marginalized sectors, is usually underpinned by repressive state structures. Such structural violence in turn spawns the seeds of societal unrest, which can sprout into armed revolutionary struggles. Confronted with the realities of a structurally violent paradigm of "development," increasingly referred to as "development aggression," ordinary peoples, NGOs, people's organizations, social institutions (e.g., religious, education), global networks of advocates, and some critical political and governmental representatives have been mobilizing and implementing alternative development thinking and strategies. One acronym, PEACE, refers to this alternative as development that is participatory, equitable, appropriate (in values and technology), critically empowering (conscientizing), and ecologically sustainable. Such peaceful development has as its central priority the basic needs of all citizens and rethinks the goals of high consumerist technologically advanced "progress."

For example, through critical education and organizing projects, poor Filipino rice farmers and fisherfolk have empowered themselves via hundreds of NGOs and peoples organizations (POs) under the CODE-NGO (Caucus of Development NGOs) to substitute ecologically destructive farming or fishing methods and inequitable economic relationships with sustainable techniques and just sharing of benefits (e.g., organic inputs, mangrove reforestation, low-cost credit, cooperative production and marketing, advocacy to access deserved public social services). Since 1972, the Bangladesh Rural Advancement Committee (BRAC) has grown to become the largest NGO in the country, involving some 350,000 poor, landless rural peoples in 3200 villages. Through conscientization processes, BRAC has empowered its members to develop self-reliant income-generating projects, primary healthcare services and practices, functional adult literacy and nonformal primary education programs, paralegal skills, and credit cooperatives. Initially in Burkina Faso and later in Senegal and Togo, the Six S's(*Se Servir de la Saison Seche en Savanne et au Sahel*) NGO has educated and motivated poor farmers to draw on local and appropriate modern knowledge and resources to cooperate in developing small-scale irrigation, erosion control, fruit orchards, and village grain facilities. In India, the Working Women's Forum has facilitated more than 150,000 poor women workers to form a grassroots union to overcome moneylender and employer exploitation, as well as gender and caste discrimination. Using strategies of empowerment education, people-controlled credit and health services, mass demonstrations and political lobbying, the WWF presents a counter to top-down "development" strategies that often end up benefiting local and national elites, or males as a social group.

The institutionalization of nonviolence through the window of development also necessarily involves education and action directed toward the global level Thus, in the Philippines, the Freedom from Debt NGO has helped to raise consciousness of Filipino peoples to their nation's entrapment in the global debt machinery, including IMF structural adjustment programs, and to lobby for policies of debt cancellation or at least debt capping to free up the national budget for meeting the basic needs of Filipinos. Other networks of Filipino NGOs and POs (e.g., National Peace Conference, CODE-NGO) similarly educate and empower citizens to challenge the government and politicians to design and implement not just growth-first and globalization policies but also a "social reform agenda" that delivers social and economic justice to all marginalized sectors. In many North societies, a whole spectrum of aid and development NGOs have grown over the decades to promote links of solidarity with South peoples, NGOs and POs engaged in grassroots peace-oriented development; to advocate for alternative aid, trade and other foreign policies of their governments that would reverse North-South inequities; and to challenge global organizations and globalization forces (IMF, TNCs, WTO, trade blocs) that further marginalize poor and vulnerable majorities. The development/global education being undertaken by such North-based NGOs raise critical consciousness of North peoples about their responsibilities and accountabilities in world poverty and underdevelopment, including rethinking unsustainable consumerist lifestyles. In some cases, official aid agencies have also supported NGOs in development education work as well as grass-roots empowerment projects.

In formal educational systems worldwide, especially in North contexts, programs and projects have infused curricula and pedagogies with structural violence issues and problems to critically empower teachers and learners to participate in North-South solidarity activities and actions for building a just and sustainable world system. Recently a Canadian high school youth mobilized a campaign among peers against the increasing problem of child labor and urged North governments, businessmen, and consumers to stop encouragement of oppressive child labor practices through importation, investment, and consumption policies. Craig Kielburger's campaign is providing meaningful opportunities for Canadian youth to feel empowered to take social action on issues of structural violence and consequently deepening the level of peacebuilding in their schools. In the Philippines, some schools, notably in the private sector, integrate programs of immersion or outreach whereby their students personally experience the realities of marginalization and are catalyzed to reflect on injustices in Filipino society. A more peaceful world cannot be built on foundations of gross inequities and other manifestations of structural violence. Indeed, a major root cause of wars and physical violence can be traced to social and economic injustices, and therefore schools have a responsibility to enhance their students' capacity to build a culture of peace which directly face up to problems of structural violence a tall levels of human life.

C. Upholding Human Rights

Another long-standing expression of institutionalizing nonviolence is anchored in the concept of human rights. Although it faces continual elaboration, a significant theory-practice gap and frequent challenge as to its validity, humans rights received a strong affirmation of its universality at the 1993 Vienna world conference. While the Declaration noted the need to take into account specific social and cultural conditions, it is understood that cultural or social practices cannot justify human rights violations. Peace and nonviolence surely also mean that the rights, dignities and freedoms inherent in all human beings are respected and promoted.

Promoting and respecting human rights continue to pose enormous challenges despite the Universal Declaration and numerous covenants, conventions, and charters that have come into being since 1948. The power entrenched in structures of state, private interests, sociocultural systems, and global agencies still weigh heavily on the fulfillment of human rights and dignities. The risk-taking and dedicated work of human rights campaigners to educate and mobilize citizens and institutions to resist violations and to assert rights in all spheres and levels of life is surely a vital dimension of peace education. As ordinary peoples experience critical literacy and empower themselves to participate actively in building a strong civil society to which agencies of state and private power must be accountable in the spirit of authentic democracy, so will their human rights be better protected and promoted.

A proper recognition and affirmation of the role of human rights in peacebuilding needs, however, to acknowledge the evolving complexity and maturity in its theory and practice. Key themes in this emergent global consensus include the need to uphold the indivisibility and interrelatedness of all rights, thereby avoiding earlier emphases on individual civil and political rights to the neglect of social, economic, cultural, group, peoples', and solidarity rights; to move beyond legal or juridical dimensions of human rights teaching; to legiti-mize the role of NGOs and POs in promoting human rights; to accord equitable space to South interpretations and voices albeit within a universalist consensus; and to address root causes rather than symptoms of human rights violations.

For example, In Bicol, one of the poorest regions of the Philippines, a women-centered NGO-initiated project infused issues of women's human rights into income-generating activities, reproductive health education and services, and their domestic empowerment vis-a-vis traditional male-dominant gender roles and relationships. As the women's economic independence and health/reproductive literacy improved, they also developed confidence and assertiveness in building more equitable, less sexist domestic relationships in nonviolent ways. Similar experiences have been found among women's education and empowerment projects or programs in other South countries where the promotion of women's human rights have created more just, sustainable, and gender-fair development environments so fundamental to personal and societal peace. Often, women's NGOs (e.g., DAWN—Development Alternatives with Women for a New Era; AAWORD—Association for African Women for Research & Development; AWHRC—Asian Women's Human Rights Council) are assuming leadership in educating and acting for women's human rights.

In Asia, Latin America, and Africa, and increasingly in North contexts, the expanding numbers of child laborers and the streetchildren phenomenon has given impetus to the implementation of the historic Convention on the Rights of the Child. NGOs have engaged in critical education and empowerment of the child workers themselves, as well as of adult citizens, including parents and policymakers, to defend children against exploitation, marginalization, and violence (economic, sexual, cultural, social, domestic). As structural violence intensifies with globalization, these efforts will need to magnify as children increasingly fall below the social safety nets or are in greater economic and social exploitative demand. It is indeed inspiring and hopeful to see streetchildren acquiring alternative economic and social resources, or bonded child laborers organizing to assert their rights and freedoms.

In formal educational institutions, the advocacy for integrating human rights education into teaching and learning have borne fruit, not only in North states where political systems are more disposed to notions of rights and freedoms. No doubt, in some contexts, the ongoing debate over "universalism" versus "cultural relativism" poses a barrier for such formal programs given the need for official endorsement. Nevertheless, where possible, both formal and nonformal NGO-based educators have been able to justify spaces in various curricula for promoting student awareness of local, national, and global realities of human rights, and catalyzing empowered action to protect and respect human rights in their societies or abroad. From the role-modeling of human rights in their own school institution to advocating for release of political prisoners (e.g., Amnesty International campaigns), abolition of the death penalty, and improved rights of marginalized sectors (e.g., homeless poor suffering constant evictions; landless peasants; export processing workers; child laborers; indigenous peoples facing development aggression and the injustices of colonialism), students will hopefully embrace a culture of human rights that in turn positively contributes to a culture of peace and nonviolence. Indeed, significant dimensions of violence prevention are facilitated by a respect among all school members of each others' rights. The development of fair and appropriate policies and codes of conduct and interrelationships in school institutions necessarily integrate basic principles of human rights thinking and practices.

Promoting human rights at international and global levels also contributes to the institutionalization of nonviolence. There is emerging a critical mass of human rights workers and organizations that are collaborating in public education across regions and continents for a fuller implementation of human rights provisions that many governments have formally ratified. Whether calling into question the human rights accountability of agencies/regimes such as TNCs, IMF, APEC, and NAFTA in their aggressive "development" paradigm, or lobbying governments to protect human rights as in specific cases (e.g., East Timor, Myanmar, Chiapas, Tibet), such interregional or international education-cum-advocacy efforts also simultaneously contribute to local empowerment of their civil societies. One exemplar of work that tries to institutionalize nonviolence through promotion of human rights is shown in Peace Brigades International. This is a unique grassroots organization that on invitation sends teams of volunteers into areas of political conflict to provide protective international accompaniment for individuals and organizations at risk from repression. Thus, PBI helps to enhance nonviolent zones of action for local promoters of social justice and human rights. In the post-apartheid South African context, the National Commission on Truth and Reconciliation provides a unique societal experiment for recognizing the injustices of gross human rights violations while opening spaces for reconciliation between oppressors and oppressed and for healing on all sides.

D. Cultures in Solidarity

Conflicts between peoples of different cultures or ethnic/"racial" identities, while not new in human history, have posed or are posing major problems of peacelessness and tragic violence in the context of a militarized and structurally violent world. Bosnia, Rwanda, Sri Lanka, Myanmar, and the southern Philippine island of Mindanao are but some examples of conflicts involving different ethnic, "racial" or tribal groups within a society. In multicultural nations in the North (e.g., Canada, The United States, Australia, The United Kingdom, and other West European states), relationships between various ethnic or cultural groups have also seen their share of prejudices, discrimination, and racism, which on occasion have sparked direct confrontations and physical violence.

Often, contestation for resources and territories and for redressing historical injustices is the underlying cause of such conflicts rather than cultural differences per se. As earlier noted, the dominant modernization paradigm is further marginalizing indigenous or aboriginal peoples who are portrayed as standing in the way of "progress" as forests are logged, energy infrastructures are constructed, mining proliferates to meet industrialization and consumerism, and agribusinesses expands into the hinterlands.

The institutionalization of nonviolence therefore needs to grapple with the challenge of promoting cultural solidarity or what a Filipino-based interfaith educator and activist has called "active harmony." Through critical dialogue and collaborative activities, conflicting or divided cultural/ethnic/racial groups, communities, and nations are able to understand the root causes of their divisions, to cultivate respect of each other beliefs and traditions, and to seek reconciliation or healing of differences that may often harbor deep and violent feelings of bitterness, enmity, and revenge. In facilitating such intercultural respect and ties of solidarity, the challenge is not only to build societal and global harmony, but also to simultaneously promote culture-related provisions in the human rights conventions. This also contributes to a culture of nonviolence as it prevents cultural conflicts from escalating into violent "resolution."

For example, in many North multicultural societies, formal school curricula and institutional environments have been integrating principles, values, and strategies of intercultural education. Through a more inclusive perspective of their nation's and the world's history, consciousness raising on cultural differences, the need for all groups to receive equitable respect and nondiscrimination, and skills training to reconcile existing intercultural conflicts nonviolently, such programs demonstrate that a peaceful world is not feasible without the ability and willingness of all groups to live nonviolently in unity amid diversity.

The development of antiracist and a prejudice-reduction curriculum and school climate, including collaboration with community sectors, is a vital component of institutionalizing a culture of nonviolence in schools. The empowerment of minorities, excluded from mainstream processes and alienated or victimized by discrimination inside and outside school, needs to be facilitated. All students, regardless of heritage or ideology, need to develop values and skills for living with each other in a spirit of trust, respect, and sharing. It is important, however, to be critical of versions of multicultural education that merely "celebrate" cultural differences in superficial ways without promoting critical understanding of and solidarity in resolving root causes of intercultural disharmony (e.g., racism, discrimination, structural injustices, historical oppression). In this regard, First Nations or aboriginal educational movements also would not deem intercultural education valid if it does not actively promote their identity and wisdom traditions so crucial to their cultural survival in a world pushed by forces of global "cultural homogenization." Among First Nations schools themselves, there are serious challenges in integrating education for nonviolence that can effectively respond to the pervasive symptoms of internalized community violence amid cultural fragmentation and other social problems such as substance abuse/addiction and domestic violence, and the trauma and dysfunctions inherited from colonial oppression (e.g., residential schools, cultural denigration by colonizers). In this regard, the role of elders with strong memories of indigenous cultural frameworks is vital in institutionalizing a culture of nonviolence, in the same way that ongoing UNESCO-initiated national culture of peace programs emphasize drawing on traditional/indigenous forms of conflict resolution.

Increasingly, representatives of diverse faiths, religions, and spiritual traditions are also meeting to promote interfaith, interreligious, or ecumenical dialogue deemed crucial to developing greater active harmony of peoples within and across societies. Thus in the Philippines, the Silsilah NGO and the Catholic Bishops Conference have promoted dialogue between Muslims and Christians, including the religious as a way to complement the ongoing peace-building processes and the recently signed Government-Moro National Liberation Front peace accord. While the "Muslim-Christian" conflicts stem more from economic, political, and social causes of territorial conquest and structural violence, there is also today a need to build harmony from a faith perspective, so that religious beliefs do not become a motivating force for further violent divisions. Similar principles of institutionalizing intercultural nonviolence are also evident in the Arab-Jewish conflict in the Middle East and the long-standing conflict in Northern Ireland, which recently witnessed a negotiated settlement. Likewise, on a global level the World Conference on Religions and Peace provides an educational and empowering forum for diverse faith leaders and followers to work for nonviolent and just interfaith and intercultural relationships.

The institutionalization of nonviolence through intercultural harmony also means acknowledging the vital role of indigenous or traditional social-cultural ways of resolving conflicts. Kalinaw Mindanao, for example, promotes as part of its nonformal peace education activities in the Philippines a deep appreciation for indigenous or traditional strategies of nonviolent conflict resolution. In promoting respect among cultures, mutual learning and adaptation of indigenous values and strategies can be most constructive to building a culture of peace. In a parallel spirit, spokespersons of major faiths (e.g., Dalai Lama, Fr. Thomas Keating, Bro. Wayne Teasdale) have drafted a universal Declaration on Nonviolence to underpin a vision of civilization in which organized violence is no longer tolerated.

E. Living Nonviolently with the Earth

Through recognition that much of the modern era has endorsed human-led violence against our environment, the vigorous environmental movement since the 1970s has challenged all of humanity to live more peacefully with planet earth. Personal and social practices that inflict ecological destruction can only undermine human survival in the present and among future generations. Indeed, conflicts arising out of the competitive control, use, and distribution of environmental resources portent a new wave of peacelessness in the world today ruled by the logic of growth and globalized competition.

In the literature on violence prevention programs, it is still rare to see reference to the violence inflicted on the natural environment by human action. Yet, a critical and holistic understanding of such ecological violence will remind us that unless we learn to institutionalize nonviolence in our relations with planet Earth, there are and will be dire consequences for human survival. Indeed, the evidence mounts that conflicts over environmental resources and the outcomes of ecological destruction lead to other manifestations of peacelessness, including structural violence and human rights violations (e.g., displacement of peoples from ancestral lands; pollution hazards on health; depletion of subsistence resources) and even physical violence such as logging interests in the South resorting to armed repression of environmentalists and people's movements or nations contesting territories or resources for environmental wealth. Hence, programs to foster an environmentally friendly school are based on values, principles, and skills that are very complementary to institutionalizing a culture of nonviolence (e.g., respecting rights of everyone to a clean and safe environment; humane treatment of all species).

Environmental education also contributes to national and global cultures of peace, including the campaign to save the rainforests, anti-toxic waste dumping, recycling, moderating heavy-consumption lifestyles, and a sense of "green justice" between the North and South hemispheres. The social action that environmental education facilitates gives students empowerment skills and confidence that are applicable to all aspects of institutionalizing environmental nonviolence. On the other hand, if the often state-sanctioned version of "sustainable development" is conditioned to serve the unchanged goals of growth-centered globalization, the roots of the ecological crisis will remain unshaken.

For example, in Costa Rica, ASACODE (San Miguel Association for Conservation and development) was formed in 1988 to educate and mobilize poor peasants to keep forests under local control. By rejecting ecologically destructive timber firm logging, AASCODE provides knowledge and incentives for peasants to harvest and process their wood sustainably, using ecologically sound techniques and reaping higher prices. AASCODE has expanded into cooperative-managed native tree nurseries and educating neighboring villages on successful strategies for community-controlled and environmentally just development. In many African countries, women, who have borne the brunt of environmental degradation, have been empowered through critical education and organizing by NGOs and POs to save their local environments in order to better and more sustainably meet the basic needs of their families and communities. Examples such as the green belt movement in Kenya or ORAP (Organization of Rural Associations for Progress) in Zimbabwe have enabled women to reverse ecological destruction and to generate community-controlled resources for equitable sharing. Similar stories of how grass-roots-centered education and empowerment have drawn on women's indigenous resources and wisdom to link environment with just

development as well as women's human rights abound in all South regions.

In the Philippines, massive ecological destruction occurs through the greed and structural violence wielded by some economic and political elites, as seen in the rapid depletion of forests, illegal and overfishing, polluting industries, mining, transportation, and agribusiness operations, and coral reef and mangrove destruction. In recent years, NGOs and POs such as the Lianga Ecological Concerns Organization (LECO) in the southern island of Mindanao have emerged to challenge this unsustainable and unjust environmental exploitation. Having been conscientized through a basic ecclesial community seminar in ecology, the Lianga villagers organized LECO to educate and mobilize their communities in tree planting and public information campaigns (despite intimidation by paramilitary personnel), the monitoring of logging and illegal fishing activities (including gathering evidence for prosecuting offenders), lobbying for official closure of furniture firms that use a protected hardwood species, preventing the illegal conversion of mangroves into commercial fishponds, and introducing alternative sustainable agricultural methods. Underpinning LECO's energies and dedication was not just the people's assertion of their rights for just development, but a firm belief that they are stewards and caretakers of the "wholeness of creation." Parallel tales of peace-oriented environmental education and action can be told by the followers of ecological martyr Chico Mendes and the indigenous peoples of the Amazon forests, the Chipko-inspired movements in India, social Buddhist-led campaigns in Sri Lanka and Thailand, the severely repressed Ogoni peoples' struggles for protection and compensation from the oil TNCs in Nigeria, and the struggles of the First Nations and aboriginal peoples in the North context to save their ancestral domains.

In most Northern and increasingly in Southern formal educational systems, environmental education has become a regular theme in school curricula and pedagogy. While initial emphasis has been placed on educating children to be personally and socially green and for schools to be environmentally friendly (e.g., recycle, reuse, reduce, save animal and plant species), there is a recognition that a holistic perspective to environmental education must dig deep into the roots of the crisis. Hence, personal earth-caring must integrate principles of structural justice and rights between groups and nations, challenge modernization ideals of growth and consumerism, advocate voluntary simplicity in lifestyle, and promote the concept of Earth rights. The institutionalizing of nonviolence in our relations with the

Earth centrally demands the self-internalization of green principles and values as expressed in our lifestyles.

F. Cultivation of Inner Peace

Increasingly, as inspired by spiritual and religious elders and traditions, the institutionalization of nonviolence in societies also calls for the development of inner peace. There is much inner violence that human beings in interaction with societal forces inflict on themselves. While the multiple dimensions of institutionalization explored thus far focus on visible relationships and structures of human life, there is a growing consensus that the inner dimensions and sources of peaceful values and practices should not be ignored. In cultivating inner peace, peoples from diverse traditions, faiths, and cultures are better prepared ethically, emotionally, and spiritually to work for outer or societal peace. There is also a basic assumption here that core values and root principles of diverse cultures and/or faiths provide guidance and inspiration for developing a culture of inner peace. As reflected in the holy texts, doctrines, oral wisdom, and body of practices across many faiths, including indigenous spiritualities and "new age" conceptions, it is through a constant cultivation and renewal of such roots of inner peace that individuals can grow spiritually.

It is important, however, to raise concerns over some popular models of education for inner or personal peace that can limit individuals or groups to be primarily content with their progress in attaining personal peace. Whether through praying, meditating, or other faith or spirituality activities, the yardstick of this paradigm of peace education is an individual's or group's feeling of having attained greater personal peace, and of closer communion with one's creator or god. But from a holistic peace education framework, is it meaningful or authentic to feel inner peace divorced from the multifold problems of outer peacelessness and violence? Would this not then reduce inner peace to a self-centered over-individualistic satisfaction, instead of an inner peace that interacts dialogically with an aspiration to work simultaneously for societal and global peace? For instance, a sense of "inner peace" may motivate individuals in advantaged socioeconomic positions to feel "pity" for the marginalized and to engage in acts of "pity" (e.g., charity). But will this help to dismantle structures of violence and injustice? Education that renews the roots of inner peace, while indeed essential, needs to integrally link with empowerment for structural transformation.

For example, in the grassroots Basic Christian or Ecclesial Communities that have emerged largely in Southern contexts under the inspiration of "liberation theology," members are motivated to develop deeper interiorization of Christian values and principles so as to experience authentic inner transformation. At the same time, such interiorization goes hand in hand with critical social analysis that challenges members to work for more peaceful, just communities and the larger society. In Buddhist societies, there is a growing reinterpretation of the role of the clergy as well as Buddhist practices of inner peace or the search for personal "enlightenment." Thus while the central principles and purposes of prayer and meditation practices toward self-enlightenment remain vital, social Buddhism does not remain alienated from societal events, especially those promoting peacelessness. Thus in Cambodia the 1993 walk for peace and reconciliation was simultaneously an expression of inner peace development through prayer and meditation for compassion, nonviolence, nonhatred, forgiveness, and selflessness. In Thailand and Sri Lanka, Buddhist inner cultivation also leads monks and followers to reflect on the deviations of excessive materialism, consumerism, social injustices, and ecological destruction spawned by the modernization paradigm from Buddhist principles of nonattachment to things and power, moderation in lifestyle, and compassion for all beings.

In some programs of holistic peace education, the theme of inner peace is explored through exercises that challenge learners to examine meanings and implications of inner peace development across various levels of life: the very personal and interpersonal; one's work and institutional environment; and a citizen's place in society and the world. This approach reminds learners that the "inner" and the "personal" is infused with the social and structural, and vice versa, so that social action for peace draws deeply on inner peace values and spiritualities. As the Buddhist teacher Thich Nat Hanh aptly reminds us, we are not just "being"; we are "inter-being."

This theme also has significant implications for an effective institutionalization of nonviolence. The responsibility of each individual to cultivate a sense of equilibrium and inner peace is vital in sustaining everyone's contribution to a culture of peace at all levels of life. In Edmonton, for example, a world-renowned physician in alternative healing and medicine conducts *chiqong* relaxation exercises with high school students so that they are better equipped to maintain calm through their daily school and out-of-school life. One can think of other exercises to enhance reflection (e.g., *tai chi, yoga,* centering).

III. SIGNPOSTS FOR INSTITUTIONALIZATION

The processes and strategies for institutionalizing nonviolence, as reflected in the diverse exemplars in this article, are clearly complex and multidimensional. Without any claim that our synthesis rests on a comprehensive and systematic research effort, it seems possible to at least raise some signposts on the slow but hopeful journey toward the institutionalization of nonviolence in local, national, international, and global contexts.

To begin with, it is advocated here that a holistic paradigm of nonviolence is meaningfully built on the insights, analysis, practices, and role models that can be drawn from the diverse and increasingly convergent or at least consensus-building fields or movements of local, national, and global transformation. The institutionalization of nonviolence necessarily and urgently calls for simultaneous and complementary visioning, thinking, and action at multiple levels and contexts of life. These multiple sites of rethinking and practice must all be activated given that we are formed as human beings through a complex, interactive blend of socializing influences. From the family to formal or nonformal schooling, to the media and increasingly the information superhighway, the institutionalization of nonviolence is slowly but steadily gaining momentum. At the same time, nonviolence is being institutionalized in countless and inspiring struggles of grassroots movements and empowered civil society. These include community and adult education projects and programs; nongovernment and peoples' organizations for demilitarization, human rights, and grass-roots development; alternative media from newspapers to audiovisuals; children's play and toys; international solidarity groups; music and art; peace museums; basic Christian or ecclesial communities; religious or spiritual retreats; youth groups and movements; parenting for peace; Internet for solidarity; challenging hate and racist literature on the Internet; the critical education of prisoners subject to violent or dehumanizing punishment; and people's summits and networks to challenge powerful global and private regimes such as the IMF, WTO, MAI, APEC, TNCs, and the like—all of these reflect the enormous energies, sweat, courage, risks, tears, pain, and even sacrifices of countless human beings committed to a culture of peace.

A second signpost toward institutionalizing nonviolence rests on the bedrock of education in its deepest sense. Unless action for transformation of a culture of violence toward a culture of peace is consistently underpinned by educational processes that increase the conscience of and empower individuals, groups, organizations, nations, and transnational actors, the possibilities for cooptation, resorting to nonpeaceful methods, and unsustainability of action are very real. Institutionalization of nonviolence, of course, requires the implementation of appropriate institutional frameworks (e.g., laws, regulations, structures, and incentives). But all human beings need spaces for critical and democratic education, which builds a self-reliant, participatory, and open-minded commitment to transformation. Institutionalization imposed from above can only lay very shallow roots for the long-term process of building a culture of nonviolence.

In the third instance, the evidence of numerous exemplars in both Northern and Southern contexts suggest that institutionalization of nonviolence cannot and should not be seen as the primary responsibility of the marginalized sectors, the victims of violence and peacelessness. The willingness of nonmarginalized "privileged" individuals, groups, and not the least nations, and increasingly global actors, to critically challenge their own accountabilities and responsibilities, whether direct or indirect, is another crucial signpost for a paradigm shift. From such self-critical analysis, the journey moves for such relatively powerful actors toward a vision and praxis of solidarity. This reflection does not imply, however, a naive hope that those entrenched in the ways of repressive power and injustices easily converts to a culture of nonviolence. As the exemplars illustrate, personal and institutional conversion is always a difficult struggle. But the signpost tells us that some spaces for conversion and for building solidarity do exist within the more powerful and privileged sectors of local and global societies, and that these spaces need conscientious and critical engagement.

Finally, a profoundly challenging signpost that is becoming more visible in the processes of institutionalizing nonviolence points toward the wisdoms of the ancient sages, religious founders, and spiritual elders across diverse civilizations. While alternative institutions in the economic, political, social, and cultural spheres of life are certainly necessary to dismantle a culture of violence, the "inner" institution that we may generally refer to as spirituality plays a pivotal and catalytic role. A profoundly decentering displacement of "values," attitudes, and dispositions within ourselves as authentic human beings cannot be avoided as we strive to cultivate personal cultures of nonviolence that spiral and dialectically interact with family, community, national, and global cultures of nonviolence.

In conclusion, a sustainable institutionalization of

nonviolence explores all potential spaces for education and transformation, searching for links between formal, nonformal, and informal strategies, and mindful that building a peaceful world cannot start and end in only one segment of life. Likewise, it must constantly link the personal with the societal, and the inner with the outer expressions of nonviolence. As we stand before the doors of the next century, there are innumerable human beings as individuals and in communities following these signposts for institutionalizing nonviolence and/or planting these very signposts themselves through their praxis. Our challenge is to join this journey into a culture of nonviolence and peace.

Also See the Following Articles

CONFLICT MANAGEMENT AND RESOLUTION • ENVIRONMENTAL ISSUES • HUMAN RIGHTS • NONVIOLENT ACTION • PEACE CULTURE • PEACE EDUCATION • PEACEMAKING AND PEACEBUILDING • STRUCTURAL VIOLENCE

Bibliography

Adam, D. (Ed.). (1995). *UNESCO and a culture of peace*. Paris: UNESCO.

Alger, C., & Stohl, M. (Eds). (1988). *A just peace through transformation*. Boulder: Westview.

Archer, D., & Costello, P. (1990). *Literacy and power*. London: Earthscan.

Barrett, R. J., & Cavanagh, J. (1994). *Global dreams: Imperial corporations and the new world order*. New York: Simon & Schuster.

Bjerstedt, A. (Ed.). (1993). *Peace education: Global perspectives*. Stockholm: Almqvist & Wiksell International.

Bonta, B. D. (1993). *Peaceful peoples: An annotated bibliography*. Metuchen, NJ: Scarecrow

Boulding, E. (1988). *Building a global civic culture*. New York: Teachers College, Columbia University.

Burns, R. J., & Aspeslagh, R. (Eds.). (1996). *Three decades of peace education around the world*. New York: Garland.

Clark, J. (1991). *Democratizing development*. London: Earthscan.

Commission on Global Governance. (1995). *Our global neighborhood*. New York: Oxford University.

Dankelman, I., & Davidson, J. (1988). *Women and environment in the Third World*. London: Earthscan.

Elkins, P. (1992). *A new world order: Grassroots movements for global change*. London: Routledge.

Garcia, E. (Ed.). (1994). *Pilgrim voices: Citizens as peacemakers*. Quezon City: Gaston Z. Ortigas Peace Institute & Ateneo Center for Social Policy & Public Affairs and London: International Alert.

Haavelsrud, M. (Ed.). (1994). *Disarmament education*. Tromso: Arena.

Housemans peace Diary (Annual). London: Housemans

Korten, D. C. (1990). *Getting to the twenty-first century*. Manila: Bookmark.

Lakey, G. (1987). *Powerful peacemaking*. Philadelphia: New Society.

Miller, M. S. (Ed.). (1993). *State of the peoples*. Boston: Beacon.

Myers, N. (Ed.). (1993). *Gaia: An atlas of planet management*. New York: Doubleday.

Peters, J., & Wolper, A. (Eds.). (1995). *Women's rights, human rights*. New York: Routledge.

Reardon, B., & Nordland, E. (Eds.). (1994). *Learning peace*. Albany: SUNY.

Shor, I., & Freire, P. (1987). *A pedagogy for liberation*. South Hedland: Bergin & Garvey.

Tobias, M., Morrison, J., & Gray, B. (Eds.). (1995). *A parliament of souls*. San Francisco: KQED Books.

UNESCO. (1997). *Second International Forum on the Culture of Peace (The Manila Forum)* 26–30 November, 1995, Manila, Philippines. Manila: OPAPP & Paris: UNESCO.

Institutionalization of Violence

Rajni Kothari

Centre for the Study of Developing Societies, Delhi, India

GLOSSARY

Anomie A widespread attitude of discontent, unrest, and uncertainty stemming from a general breakdown in the structure and values of a society; moral instability.

Dacoities Physical attacks by a group of armed robbers. (From the *Dacoit* robber society that historically committed such crimes in India and Burma.)

Dalits A social group in India, including those who were formerly designated in the Hindu caste system as the untouchables; i.e., those completely beneath the main caste system and thus of lowest social status.

Global Commons The sum of the Earth and its plant and animal life, thought of as a commons, or common area, to be protected and conserved by all humans and shared with all other species.

Institutionalization A situation in which a certain behavior, condition, or phenomenon has become so established within a society that it can be considered an inherent aspect of the society rather than an incidental or subsidiary feature; e.g., violence, though not ordained by a society and perhaps even officially described as an aberration, may actually be so widespread as to have become institutionalized.

Polity The form or structure according to which the political system of a society is organized; the body politic.

INSTITUTIONALIZATION OF VIOLENCE generally refers to the process by which acts of violence or force are undertaken by an official group on behalf of, or at least with the tacit approval of, the society as a whole. Examples of such actions might include violence carried out by the society's police against criminals, warfare by the armed forces against external enemies, and repressive measures by security forces against the society's internal opponents, real or perceived.

In this way institutionalized violence is typically contrasted with noninstitutionalized violence; i.e., violent actions by individuals without any authorization or acceptance by the larger society, such as serial killings, gang violence, or spousal and child abuse. However, it can also be argued that these seemingly unsanctioned acts of violence are actually not the random behavior of deviant individuals, but an inevitable consequence of the inequities and pathologies of the society. In that sense the institutionalization of violence includes all types of violent acts that are prevalent within the soci-

Copyright © 1999 by Academic Press.
All rights of reproduction in any form reserved.

ety, not just those carried out collectively by official groups.

I. INTRODUCTION

With the world moving from an era of well laid out assumptions about the path of human "progress" and the institutional framework in which this was to take place to an age of growing uncertainty, ambivalence and groping towards a wholly unclear future, creating a growing sense of insecurity and anomie, violence seems to have become endemic to the state of human society. We are increasingly witnesses to a deepening of the social roots of violence and, at the other end of the spectrum, a growth of isolation and alienation of the individual. This tends to leave, in their wake, violent backlashes all the way from terrorist to neo-fascist responses to what many perceive as a decline in prospects for alternative futures.

We can identify many symptoms of the institutionalization of violence. There is an increasing sense of vulnerability at both the elite level and the level at which the common folk find themselves. There is a gradual erosion of the "state" that had at one time given a sense of security to both levels. That at any rate was the basic presumption underlying Hobbes's conception in his *Leviathan*. It is this sense of security that is, in the times we are living in, under siege. For today "security" appears to be taking on an increasingly defensive stance, for both the ruling classes and the large masses of the people. Ruling elites the world over are creating walls of security around them and signing joint declarations against violence, terrorism, and the like, at a time when the mass of the people are being exposed to both state repression and the violence unleashed by militants of various types. It is with this loss of a sense of security at both ends of the social spectrum that we are witness to an increasing resort to violence.

Other major symptoms widely observed include a growing role of corruption in human affairs which in turn is producing a culture of "mafia" rule at the very grassroots of societies, a considerable growth in violation of human rights in many parts of the world, including atrocities against the weaker sections of society, especially women and children, the minorities and the dispossessed, and the poor at large, much of which is increasingly taking on an organized and institutionalized form. Many of us have been brought up on a belief in the sanctity of life in all forms and have for long considered violation of all sentient life as an aberration. The reality that faces us today, however, is that most

nation-states and cultures tolerate oppression and rejection of basic rights and even endorse the institutionalization of such oppression and hence of violence. Violence is often hidden, especially violence against women but also violence against all beings that are victims of discrimination and exploitation. This is increasingly being brought out in investigations carried out by human-rights groups. (Women face violence all the way from family and neighborhood settings to arenas where modern technology is rendering them unwanted and forcing them into the highly vulnerable "unorganised sector" in which single women, child labor, involuntary immigrants and slum dwellers are huddled together.)

Paradoxical and ironic though it may sound, the more such reports get publicized, the more the mass media are showing an obsession with violence even while they profess to abhor violence in their own surroundings. Indeed this seems to be the case with so many of us. While we abhor violence, we find it attractive and enticing in the world of the mass media, of fiction, and of stories and gossip that we are getting accustomed to. Studies of violence in the media are demonstrating a strong affect on levels of violence in civil society. Films depicting violence in its most grueling forms seem to have a special attraction for us—for the younger generation, the bored and frustrated housewives, those seeking escapism from the realities of life, those dealt with harshly by society and seeking refuge in criminalized acts which they themselves often try to emulate.

Nor is this limited to the more criminalized aspects of modern life. We are being constantly threatened by the abuse of religion for economic and political power, giving rise to a phenomenal growth in ethno-religious conflicts and in religious fundamentalism, causing potential damage to our psyches. Minds may be enslaved by the stereotyping that we see on television as indeed by the myths about "others" that are perpetrated in the textbooks on which our children are brought up. In the meantime we find ourselves surrounded by pornography on the Internet.

II. SPECTER OF SECURITY AND THE CULT OF VIOLENCE

All in all we find ourselves surrounded by not just a growing scale of violence but in fact an emerging cult of violence that is spreading fast and may lie behind the growing sense of insecurity, especially in elite circles. Expenditures on the military, police, prisons, private security systems, and the upper strata are growing more and more fearful of the social reality that confronts them which they may have themselves to some extent given rise to but are unable to predict and deal with. It is this fear that lies behind what may be a pathological preoccupation with creating walls of "security" from one and all, the cult of violence giving rise to a cult of security. What has come to be known as a national security state is not merely a reflection of nation-states constantly preparing themselves against both real and imagined "enemies" (more the latter than the former) but also of the ruling class anticipating outbreaks of unanticipated violence resulting from growing turbulence and states of discontent and anomie in society at large. That bombs and explosives are blowing up here and there, that assassinations and political murders (including of people at the very top) have taken place, that more and more incidents of "indigenous terrorism" are taking place, cannot any longer be blamed on outsiders. Yet no matter how much security is provided to a whole phalanx of "leaders" and their large retinues and kins, and no matter how much diplomatic effort is expended to hold the forces of terrorism at bay (e.g., by designating some countries as "rogue states" and pressuring allies to cut trade and other relations with them), fear of violence, both from within and from without, appears to be a dominant strain in the mental makeup of those in command of diverse states and perhaps the state system as a whole.

As for the non-elite strata constituting more than 50 to 60 per cent of the world's population, the tendency is the opposite: rather than provide minimum security to them it is found more efficient to shove them out of the system, excluding millions from the institutional framework of the polity and the economy and treating them as dispensable. Poverty is increasingly ceasing to be seen as a problem to be resolved and perceived instead as an embarassment, especially as there seems to be a slow dawning on our consciousness that we may not for a very long time be able to eradicate it. This in itself and indeed above all is a most cruel manifestation of basic violence. Poverty is also a source of violence in reverse, as survival on the margins of society is becoming a breeding ground of a variety of violent acts—turning inward (hence the growing number of suicides among the poor as well as a growing resort to murders of one's own kin). Violence is thus premeating primary units like family and immediate neighborhoods, along secondary channels of social castes and classes, as well as in sudden outbursts of anger and aggression against those belonging to the upper reaches of the social order. Criminality and the violence associated with it are not merely a function of "criminaliza-tion" of the polity about which there is a lot of talk these days in a number of countries in which "antisocial elements" and people with a criminal record are gaining access to the portals of power. It is something much more corrosive and comprehensive and consists of a whole social order—nationally and internationally—becoming vulnerable to the growing virus of crime and corruption of all kinds, from the flimsiest to the most grotesque, all the way from financial scams to the destruction of religious sites and the destruction of the global commons, in which a large array of otherwise prestigious institutions are found to be involved. Closely aligned with all this is the violence that is taking hold of the state itself, with armed police, paramilitary units, and even the official armed forces allegedly indulging in it wantonly, as some suggest for the sheer pleasure of shooting down people, raping women, indeed simply letting themselves go. The paradox is striking: the very custodians of law and of people's safety, as well as the very segments that are expected to observe exemplary discipline in their behavior, are found to indulge in what appears to be a whole lifestyle of violence and disorder.

All this leads to another insight: perhaps the simplest forms of institutionalization of violence lie in its routinization—violence as a "daily affair", murders galore, incidents of rape of women, old and young and the very young among them on the increase, and a growing spate of shootouts in public places in metropolitan centers. We can also observe a growing incidence of inner violence in the form of suicides and suicide pacts, bands of ruffians from the upper classes carrying out massacres of segregated communities in rural areas and burning down their dwellings, hit and run killings of members of rival races and ethnic groups, sporadic as well as organized "riots" between rival religious sects, a growing spate of assassinations of political cadres belonging to rival political parties, robberies and dacoities followed by killing of the victims of the same, police firings on "mobs" and processions of protesting demonstrators. Governments themselves issue "shoot on sight" orders, and sanction "encounter" killings mounted by police and paramilitary personnel on extremist groups belonging to separatist and/or revolutionary causes. So much of this is taking place regularly and on an almost daily basis.

III. GLOBAL CONTEXT

All this is happening at time when it appears to many that the whole world is adrift. The 20th century has been a century of violence—of wars, revolutions, a fascist cult of destruction and all-out devastation, "liberation wars" gone awry in so many parts of the ex-colonial world, turning anti-people, repressive and particularly coercive toward the laboring classes, increasingly brutalized and dehumanized. Everywhere the state is found hand-in-glove with special interests at home and in concert with neocolonial interests globally, in turn forcing the victims to turn anarchistic and violent. It is this phenomenon of the rise of national-security states opposed by the victimized turning unruly and turbulent, suffering continuously but at the same time displaying bursts of anger and contempt against those wielding power and authority, often becoming available to movements of insurgency and terrorism, in all of which violence is becoming the new language of discourse between the wielders of coercive power and those run over by them.

IV. EMERGING SCENARIOS

To put it all in perspective, the reactions of surprise, despair, and intrigue at the various forms in which violence has surfaced and resurfaced in recent years needs to be seen in a general historical context. The point is that unless consciously checked and countered, violence often takes on an endemic state in a society so full of inequity and potential for basic protest and growing despair, extremes of both socioeconomic and cultural kinds, and political misuse of the power of the state in rich and diverse societies. As governments themselves increasingly feel threatened, they frequently resort to a "law-and-order" approach to deal with what are basically deep social and psychological issues. This pushes them to retain large retinues of armed forces which are no longer aimed at an "enemy" but rather at citizens who are found to engage in movements of protest, struggles for civil liberties, and generally in dissent against a system that is judged by them to be undemocratic and lacking in accountability. The result is often internal militarization in which since there is no longer any need to go to war with an outside enemy, an inner enemy has to be found and "crises" created within the society. Small social groups, activists and intellectuals, and those struggling for survival in situations of growing want and destitution often become the targets. Once this happens, violence grows by leaps and bounds (violence as well as counter-violence). As we have learned during the last decade and more, once violence takes root in a society full of divisions and schisms, it rarely vanishes. It grows, seeks new outlets, looks for new

enemies. As the basic principle of militaristic thinking is typically the suspension of all thought other than its own, those who dare to think become the ultimate enemy. The point is that one tyranny can face another tyranny. It can handle brute force. What it can not handle is creativity that resists control and refuses to fall in line. The result is that the violence which was justified at one time by pointing to an outside enemy may gradually turn against its own people, against minorities, against women activists, against generalists who dare to write independently, against artist, and thinkers. This is what happened under Hitler, Stalin, and Mao. For all of them a nuclear bomb in the possession of an enemy appeared less dangerous than a sketch drawn by an artist in one's own society, a sketch that exposes the ills of the regime. For this artist is the more immediate enemy. Violence, then, becomes endemic to a society when it reaches deeply into the social and cultural terrain. It is this that ultimately makes it truly institutionalized. In the foregoing I have deliberately laid out a broad synoptic statement on the larger issues that underlie the institutionalization of violence. I shall now proceed to take up the matter in different fields of human endeavor as structured by different agencies and institutions.

V. THE STATE AS A SOURCE OF VIOLENCE

Having dealt with the evidence for a gradual increase in the repressive nature of the modern state in the face of growing assertions based on class, on the one hand, and indigenous structures of civil society on the other, we may now examine how state violence has been institutionalized over time.

There is a historical background to this. The modern state since the Treaty of Westphalia was signed, has had an expansive streak to it (almost following the homocentric thrust of modern man). Culturally too, the modern divorce between the secular and the religious domains set the stage for the tendency of secular authority to expand outwards both vis-a-vis voluntaristic structures at home and vis-a-vis other peoples and cultures. This led to the spread of a geopolitical, militaristic, and technologically outward looking and colonizing character of the modern state, beginning with Europe and, by stages, engulfing practically the whole world. The growth of population movements, for example, (both from rural agricultural hinterlands to urban industrial enclaves following the enclosure movements in the industrializing countries and from high-density regions with overflowing populations to low-density regions) have led to ever new forms of conquests and wars (including civil wars). Also, the rise of linguistic nationalism and the proliferation of modern nation-states in Europe, in the wake of the decline of multicultural empires and the spread outward of these states towards distant lands, has led to the development of professionalized armies and advances in military technology. More recently this process has been taken further with the growth of ethnicity and diverse forms of sub-nationalism, again following the weakening of empire-like formations (including that of the Soviet Union). In short, both the *integrative* thrust based on superimposition of the expansionist drive of the European conception of the state and the *disintegrative* thrust following the rise of cultural nationalism have precipitated a simultaneous surge towards ethnic conflicts, interstate rivalries, geopolitical conquests, and local and regional wars, all of these involving a great deal of violence.

The current and latest phase of these developments occurs especially in post-colonial states created by the presence of artificial boundaries left behind by colonial regimes but lately also in the European region following the collapse of Cold War bipolarity. There has taken place a growth of armed militias fighting for capture of state power, the worst manifestations of which are to be found in Afghanistan, Bosnia, Rwanda, Burundi, Zaire, and Chechnya. Some of these struggles also involve religious fundamentalism. An extreme form is found in the Taliban in Afganistan. Almost all of them have taken highly explosive and bloody forms, often verging on genocide.

The scenario that is unfolding before us is hardly conducive to reducing the role of violence in human affairs. Indeed, as we move towards the end of the century we are witness to both a clash of cultures and ethnicities within nation-state boundaries and a clash of civilizations between and beyond nation-states and constellations thereof. Both forms of conflicts are also reinforced by counter-systemic movements, e.g. for self-determination, for human rights, and even for social justice and economic and regional equity. Indeed violence is often institutionalized even in the struggles for peace (conceived as resistance to violation of people's right and their struggles for justice, often termed as "just wars"), found especially in Africa. As has been expressed by one of the most seasoned statesmen of Africa, Julius Nyerere, "Peace can only be a product of justice; it is not simply the absence of violence." Even the processes associated with decolonization have produced a legacy of territorial disputes and brutal civil

wars sometimes fought out of personal hatreds, or on account of tribal and ethnic aggrandisement. As regards the behavior of major powers, the post-Cold War promise of peace, disarmament, and a radical change in the psychology of competing power blocs has been totally belied by the continued use of military force in the conduct of international conflict. A few intractable conflicts of the Cold War era, like those in Indochina, have been dealt with as a result of a worldwide movement of protest. The worst manifestations of inhuman governance, such as apartheid in South Africa, have been successfully put to an end, but we can hardly say we are out of the woods. Over fifty conflicts continue to rage even today, some of them putting on display humanity's basest instincts that many thought the march of human civilization would have brought under control.

VI. "DEVELOPMENT" AND VIOLENCE

Meanwhile, "development," which was once thought of as an antidote to war and violence, and even the struggle for justice, are riddled with both social conflicts and a culture of violence. The idea that economic well-being, achieved through planned development, would reduce exploitation of various types does not seem to be that clear any more. The same is apparently true of the idea that the growth of economic independence of different social strata, as for example of women or of tribal groups (and what we in India call the "Dalits," i.e., the ex-untouchables) will make them less vulnerable, e.g. to the male atrocities and vandalism against the deprived groups in society which are now on the rise. Violence against women, as against depressed ethnic racial groups, is on the increase in much of the world. And as gaps widen and inequality in access to power and decision making grows, vulnerability to atrocities and exploitation grows as well, and with that grows both violence of the system and counterviolence against it. For there is still a considerable lack of security for ordinary people who can be shot at and killed, or be tortured by the police to force a confession, or be arrested and jailed, or be at the mercy of gangsters and kidnappers, even quite often at the mercy of "militants" who are supposed to be waging a struggle on their behalf. In the meantime, the large hordes of migrants and refugees who come to the cities to escape persecution or social ostracism in the areas—even countries—they belonged to as well as tribal groups and other rural folk who resist being displaced and forciby evicted, as a result of the construction of large dams and nuclear and thermal plants, are branded as extremists and are pushed around, often arrested under some anti-terrorist act or subjected to the opposite end of state repression, namely handed over to the terrorist arms of the state, the police, the paramilitary, and even the armed forces.

VII. POLITICS OF IDENTITY AND THE GROWTH OF VIOLENCE

Then there is the phenomenon of sectarian violence, usually waged by ethnic and religious majorities against minorities but sometimes also by minorities. In both cases people claim to seek justice but adopt organizational modes involving violence. Indeed, violence is often used for both forging and sustaining sectarian identities; what has baffled social scientists for some time now is the unabated continuation of violence in creating a sense of belonging among those who are driven to the wall. According to one estimate, nearly 120 million people have been killed in the present century on the sites of collective identities. It appears as though "genocide" has become an integral part of many mass movements for self-definition. There is now taking place a phenomenal growth in the politics of identities which involve a growing recourse to violence.

While much of the focus of social-science studies and investigative reports is on the state and its repressive arms, these being seen as the main agents of genocidal acts, there is relative neglect of the selves of people—individuals—who also participate in such acts, of course for more complex reasons. People are found to kill themselves and are ready to kill others, engage in collective self-immolation, often backed by religious cults. Even the aspiration at leveling the differences between the rich and the poor, between the privileged and those left out of the system, is often conceived in forms that are violent. There is no space here to go into the manner in which sacrificial altars are created on which human beings commit both suicides and murders, the variety of occult activities that are on the rise, the inner recesses of a psychological kind in which some residual evil allegedly resides and various other rituals that are performed in which violence is seen not as an aberration but as a mode of self-expression. Suffice it to say that we are moving into an era in which violence is represented at so many levels and across so many institutional structures that it would be foolish to wish it away or simply engage in some naive and innocent or romantic utopian "vision". Violence is getting increasingly institutionalized, of course more against the

weak (especially women and children and the poor at large) but also against the rich and the powerful, in opposition to whom banners of revolt and revulsion are being raised.

VIII. COUNTERVAILING TENDENCIES

And yet the opposite tendency is also on the rise. There is evidence of growing exasperation with violence of both state-sponsored and militant varieties which is leading to a search for solutions that, if they succeed or even make slow headway, could lead to nonviolent ways of resolving conflicts and reconciling seeming opposites. There is of course still a long way to go on this path, but the process seems to have begun. We find this in the long beleaguered Middle East—the melting pot of two major Semitic cultures—of course in the apartheid-ridden South Africa, in the slow and painful but nonetheless continuing efforts in the former Yugoslavia (despite more recent aggressions as found in Kosovo), in the emerging way out of the long drawn out war of attrition based on an interface between bellicose religiosity and militarist confrontation in Northern Ireland, and even in the difficult and irrational dispute in the muddy terrains of hatred and suspicion in the Indian sub-continent. In each of these conflicts there are many hurdles to be crossed. In each of them new problems keep emerging. And in each of them not only the politics of military engagements but also the politics of ethnicities and identity formations, so often drawing upon deeply religious sentiments, are being tackled. But there seems to be no escape from continuing with the efforts that have already begun.

As the specter of violence keeps haunting us and as the human urge towards a more peaceful and civilized existence persists despite it, and in both cases through ever new institutionalized forms, we are also witness to the growth of institutional structures that go beyond violence and non-violence. This is occurring through the growing interface between state and civil society, the former being forced to become increasingly decentralized and the latter increasingly providing alternatives to mainstream politics, economics, and society, thereby returning to deeper roots of both human nature and human personality, and indeed also to a caring approach toward nature and toward diverse other species with whom the human species is bound in an organic way, both for sheer survival and for new flowering of potentialities and possibilities. This will not of course be realized merely on the basis of some naive hopes and some "grand vision" (which is of course vital, for without it we can not move out of the present crisis). Advocates of this alternative call for immense efforts to ensure that the rise of the poor and oppressed against the "system," after an early phase of violent backlash, both against it and from within its own dynamics, can provide a basis for a more integrated and negotiated framework to reconcile conflicts and bridge the wide gaps that exists in livelihood patterns, in access to political power, and in the structuring of civil society. And by doing this we will also defuse, through new institutionalized expressions, the violence that has of late accompanied the politics of protest and the culture of identity formations and the deeper roots in both nature and human nature—and the human psyche—that violence has acquired and that needs to be contained.

It may be no less necessary to collectively deal with the various disasters visited by floods and famines, ecological breakdowns, and the erosion of life-sustaining gases and the ozone layers in the atmosphere. The eco-logical challenge faced by humankind, including the challenge for restraining "development" from taking violent forms, calls for new institutional mechanisms that cut across nation-state boundaries, social identities, and political divisions of various kinds. Perhaps the struggle against violence might be waged by focusing first on these more basic challenges. Once that is done and a more balanced approach to cosmic issues is evolved, and human imagination moved along to deal with the same, and the earth is seen as not only an ecosystem but also a sociopolitical arena, then the scourge of violence might automatically start receding.

Also See the Following Articles

CLASS CONFLICTS • ENVIRONMENTAL ISSUES AND POLITICS • ETHNIC CONFLICTS AND COOPERATION • INSTITUTIONALIZATION OF NONVIOLENCE • SOCIOLOGICAL STUDIES, OVERVIEW • STRUCTURAL VIOLENCE • TERRORISM • TORTURE (STATE)

International Relations, Overview

David N. Farnsworth
Wichita State University

GLOSSARY

Balance of Power A system of dividing power among two or more coalitions of nation-states to prevent a dominance of power by any one coalition.

Bipolarity A two coalition system of nation-states in which each is seeking to obtain a dominance of power.

Collective Security A universal system in which all nation-states are committed to join together to punish a nation-state that commits an act of aggression.

Colonization The creation of overseas empires mainly by European powers during the 18th and 19th centuries.

Decolonization The movement following World War II that led to colonies gaining their independence and greatly expanding the nation-state system.

Diplomacy The protocol that regulates and the personnel that conducts negotiations and other forms of contact between nation-states for the purpose of protecting and presenting their nation's interests.

International Actors Nation-states and other organizations that participate in the international system for the purpose of defending and promoting their interests.

International Governmental Organizations (IGOs) Organizations made up of two or more nation-states for the purpose of regulating aspects of international behavior.

International Law Rules of conduct between nation-states that are a product of custom and treaties.

Multinational Corporations (MNCs) Corporations that have interests in several nation-states including natural resources, marketing facilities, manufacturing, and other forms of investment.

Nationalism The socialization of the populace of a nation-state that usually produces loyalty to the state and its government.

Nation-state The basic unit of organization for the international system that developed out of the 16th and 17th centuries.

Nongovernmental Organizations (NGOs) Organizations whose members come from several nation-states but are not representatives of the government of any nation-state.

Power The combination of various capabilities a nation-state possesses which contribute to its ability to achieve its international policy objectives.

Sovereignty The legal concept that places the highest authority in the government of the nation-state.

Copyright © 1999 by Academic Press.
All rights of reproduction in any form reserved.

Terrorism Acts of national or international violence committed by individuals or organizations to publicize their cause and punish their enemies.

Unipolarity An international system in which one nation-state is significantly more powerful than any other or coalition of other nation-states.

United Nations The single universal international organization presently operating in the international system. Its most significant organs are the General Assembly and the Security Council.

INTERNATIONAL RELATIONS pertains to the interaction that occurs between actors that make up the international system; a system that those actors developed for the purpose of promoting and protecting their interests in their relations with other actors. Since participating actors do not have the same interests, and cannot be expected to have such, this interaction often produces conflict, but when it is to the advantage of two or more actors to do so, it can also result in cooperation. Conflict is a relative term. It can range from routine disagreements that carry no threat of violence and are easily resolved to all-out warfare with all of the energies of the nations involved devoted to prosecution of that war.

The international system is not what is thought of commonly as a political system in the sense that institutions such as the U.S. Senate or the British House of Commons, which make decisions binding on the society that created them, do not exist. The purpose of such domestic institutions is, minimally, to contain conflict but, at best, to resolve it to the satisfaction of the major interests that are involved; the international system has no such institutions. For example, the United Nations General Assembly falls considerably short of being an international legislative body; its powers are limited when compared to national legislative bodies found in stable domestic political systems.

It does not follow, however, that procedures found in the international system are incapable of containing or resolving conflict or that domestic systems are necessarily more successful in resolving conflict than is the international system. In the late 1990s, considerably more violence is occurring within domestic political systems around the world than between nation-states. In Africa alone, Liberia, Sierra Leone, Rwanda, Burundi, both Congos, Sudan, and Algeria have, or recently had, internal violence that largely is domestic in origin. In South Asia, the Taliban in Afghanistan, a domestic movement, is attempting to take over the country. While India and Pakistan have occasional violent incidents along their common border, both countries have had more incidents of domestic violence. Even Europe, which avoided open warfare between nations for 45 years after World War II, produced major military conflict with the breakup of Yugoslavia in 1991.

The ethnic conflict that followed this breakup is difficult to categorize as domestic or international in origin. The violence was either the result of a domestic system collapsing—Yugoslavia—or ethnic groups within the new nation-states conducting ethnic cleansing within or across the borders of the new countries, an international act of violence. It clearly became international, however, when the United Nations sent in peacekeeping forces and, later, NATO and several other countries introduced an implementing force (IFOR) to carry out the Dayton Agreement. Whichever category the violence falls in is not as significant as that the conflict illustrates the range violence can take.

I. RELATIONSHIP OF INTERNATIONAL TO DOMESTIC

These examples of violence within and between nations illustrate two important characteristics of the international system. First, in the last years of the 20th century, and especially since the Warsaw Pact and the Soviet Union collapsed, domestic conflict has become increasingly apparent even if clear distinctions cannot be made between what is domestic and what is international. Second, an even more important point concerning an understanding of international relations, incidents of violence, war, cooperation, and peaceful settlement that occur at the international level have their origins at the domestic level. Often a distinction is made between domestic and international behavior especially by the media, when a more appropriate analysis is to see international events as an extension of what is going on domestically. The interests a domestic political system pursues and protects come from the domestic political system and then are projected to others as that country's foreign policy; domestic decision makers determine a nation's international behavior. International conflict occurs when the decision makers of one or more other nations find those interests in conflict with their own. The decision makers' purpose is to fulfill their nation's interests by whatever means is reasonable and at minimum cost. They determine when the cost of total success is too high and compromise is the better option. In some instances, if the cost seems too extravagant, a nation may postpone pursuit of an interest or abandon it altogether.

II. INTERNATIONAL ACTORS

Even though several categories of actors exist in the international system, clearly the category that has the greatest influence over how the system is organized and functions is the nation-state.

A. The Nation-State

Although states and empires existed for thousands of years, the nation-state is a relatively recent development. The earliest nation-states developed not much more than 3 centuries ago and nearly two-thirds of them gained their independence after World War II. Historians disagree as to when the first nation-states developed, probably in the 1500s, but domination of the international system by nation-states occurred sometime between the Peace of Westphalia in 1648, which ended the Thirty Years War, and the Peace of Utrecht in 1713. Regardless, by the early 18th century the nation-state was a strong international actor.

The conference at Westphalia dragged on for 2 years mainly because nation-states had not yet developed a means of dealing with one another. More time at Westphalia was devoted to the development of diplomatic protocol than was spent on negotiating the peace.

The expansion of the rules of diplomatic protocol was only one contribution of Westphalia to the international system. The peace treaty weakened the Holy Roman Empire, although its control over major European states had been in decline for some time. This development meant that a nation-state now owed allegiance to no higher authority—either internationally or within the nation-state—than its own central government. The concept of national sovereignty was not unknown before Westphalia, but the peace agreement certainly strengthened its importance. Nation-states were now independent of one another or any other authority.

Another development that coincided with the Peace of Westphalia was the growth of nationalism, the psychological underpinning of the nation-state. It was not that citizens did not have loyalties to some political entity earlier, but now that loyalty was directed toward an independent nation-state. The populace of any nation-state is socialized into being loyal to the nation-state in which they are born and reared. This socialization process is nearly always successful. Sovereignty and nationalism were essential to the establishment of the nation-state and were what made the nation-state different from political entities that came earlier. It must be pointed out, however, that these concepts existed only in Europe in the 17th century and not in all European countries at that.

Through the 18th and 19th centuries two opposing developments took place. New participants were added to the nation-state system as the Spanish empire collapsed and Latin America divided into 18 new nation-states. The United States took on the characteristics of a nation-state when it broke away from Great Britain. Only a scattering of Asian nation-states developed. In Europe, the nation-state system continued to expand.

As the concepts of sovereignty and nationalism spread, a second movement was resisting these developments. Several major European powers, as an expression of their nationalism, moved overseas to create empires. India came under British control during the 18th century and was the most populous colony any nation possessed. China suffered colonial pressures from several European nations but never formally became a colony or, for that matter, did not develop the characteristics of a nation-state until the 20th century. Japan was independent as was Thailand (Siam, at times), but the French colonized southeast Asia and the Netherlands made a colony of the East Indies, present-day Indonesia. Virtually all of Africa was colonized. Great Britain and France took the largest share and nearly went to war with each other in the process, but Spain, Portugal, Germany, Italy, and Belgium had their African empires as well. The Asian Middle East came under British and French control but not until after World War I; earlier the region was dominated by the Ottoman Empire. The United States had its empire as well but it was small by comparison with the British and French empires; the Philippines and Puerto Rico were the major possessions, both taken during the Spanish-American War. The status of Puerto Rico still is undecided. Technically it is a commonwealth of the United States but within the United Nations many developing nations want the United States to register it with the United Nations as a colony. Japan created an empire by taking Korea and various islands in the Pacific before occupying large sections of China when it went to war with that country in 1937.

After World War II, various colonies and mandates (former colonies usually administered by European powers under the authority of the League of Nations) resisted restoration of European control and the breakup of colonialism began. Although various colonies and mandates (Syria, Lebanon, and the Philippines) gained their independence near the end of the war or just after, the most notable decolonization came with the independence of India in 1947. Due to religious pressures within India, the country was split into a Hindu India and Moslem East and West Pakistan. In 1971, East Pakistan separated from West Pakistan and became independent as Bangladesh.

Various colonies gained their independence during the late 1940s and 1950s, but the breakup of empire in Africa did not gain momentum until 1960 and after (although Morocco, Tunisia, and Ghana gained their independence in the mid-to-late 1950s). The decolonization of Africa was not completed until the early 1990s when Namibia became independent and, if apartheid is seen as a form of colonialism, when South Africa granted voting rights to its Black citizens and held free elections. Latin America completed decolonization during the 1970s when several British islands in the Caribbean were granted their independence. At the close of the 20th Century, only a scattering of islands, mainly held by France and Great Britain, are not independent.

Shortly after World War I, the nation-state system had about 65 members—the status of some territories was difficult to determine—although during the 1920s and 1930s, the membership of the League of Nations never exceeded 61. The United States was one of those nations that chose not to join. The membership of the United Nations presently is 185 with virtually all nation-states belonging, except Switzerland.

In spite of this increase in the number of nation-states, the argument can be made that the nation-state's role in the international system is not as strong as it once was. Even though the concept of the nation-state is now accepted worldwide, two factors limit its activities. One is the spread of international organizations (IGOs). While no international organization has the capability to seriously challenge a country's sovereignty, with the possible exceptions of the European Union (EU) and the new World Trade Organization (WTO), nations that belong to an IGO, and most belong to several, must give up a certain amount of autonomy to function effectively within an international organization. Membership demands, in most cases, that a nation compromise some of its own interests in order to gain the advantages it incurs through the decisions of the IGO. Second, the world's economy has undergone an extensive revision since World War II. No nation can function effectively as an economic unit in the world economy without accepting the economic interdependence that now exists. Whether this interdependence is formalized through an economic IGO or through treaties a nation makes with other countries, no nation-state can claim to be without a degree of restraint resulting from economic interdependence.

B. International Organizations

Nation-states and IGOs are closely related actors in the international system as was illustrated in pointing out the restraints placed on countries in order to prosper economically. IGOs and nation-states are related in another manner as well. The membership of IGOs is made up of nation-states; therefore, the activities of an IGO and its members are inseparable. Since IGOs have nation-states as members, the development of international organizations necessarily came after the development of the nation-state. Nation-states first appeared in Europe, thus it was to be expected that the first IGO would develop there. The first IGO came into existence shortly after the Congress of Vienna in 1815; the second was negotiated nearly 40 years later.

Before creating an international organization, European nations had to find a situation that could better be handled on a multilateral basis to the benefit of participants. Both of these early organizations dealt with the navigation of rivers, the Rhine and the Danube, and was clearly a multilateral problem. Although the development of IGOs was off to a slow start, by World War I about 50 existed; by World War II about 90; and in the late 1990s, more than 400. Clearly, conditions after World War II strongly encouraged the development of IGOs.

Although IGOs have in common nation-states as members, they have a great diversity otherwise. The League of Nations after World War I and the United Nations after World War II were universal organizations in that theoretically any nation-state could belong and the organizations were given the broad responsibility of maintaining peace throughout the international system. Other IGOs are regional in nature such as the Organization of American States (OAS) and the Organization of African Unity (OAU), but are granted broad powers. Some have universal membership but are assigned a specific problem such as the Food and Agriculture Organization (FAO) and the International Atomic Energy Agency (IAEA). A number are economic in nature, the best known being the European Union (EU). In the United States one of the best known such IGOs is the North American Free Trade Association (NAFTA). In Latin America, Mercosur seems to have made the most progress as an economic IGO. Some IGOs require a special nonregional qualification in order to be a member such as the Arab League or the Organization of Petroleum Exporting Countries (OPEC). IGOs can also be military in nature such as the North Atlantic Treaty Organization (NATO) and, until 1991, the Warsaw Pact. Except for the League of Nations, all of these well-known organizations came into being after World War II.

C. The United Nations as an Actor

The impact of the United Nations on the international system has varied considerably during its first half-century. It is, undoubtedly, the best known IGO in existence, but what the UN has done and how it has affected conflict in the international system depends on what period of the UN's history is being analyzed. The 1990s have proved to be its most active decade.

The UN began in 1945 in the high state of optimism that followed World War II, but within a few years, that optimism collided with the political realities of the postwar world. The original design of the organization was a compromise among the war's victors as to what caused war and violence in the international system. If war was a result of colonialism, and many wars had been, then a Trusteeship Council would be established to oversee the dissolution of the colonial empires. Colonialism collapsed but the Trusteeship Council had little to do with it. If wars resulted from poor social and economic conditions found in many countries, then these problems would be handled by the Economic and Social Council (ECOSOC). Again, while more successful than the Trusteeship Council, ECOSOC has had a limited role in the changes that have taken place in the developing countries.

The International Court of Justice (ICJ) was the legal approach to solving the world's problems. Until the 1990s, cases brought before the ICJ were for the most part unimportant and, if a decision was handed down, unenforceable. In addition, the ICJ has not been busy. During one period of several years, the court handed down no decisions. Since the mid-1990s, however, an international war crimes tribunal has been established in the Hague which is also the headquarters of the ICJ. This tribunal is not a part of the ICJ but tends to strengthen the international law the ICJ enforces.

The two organs of the UN that became the most prominent are the General Assembly and the Security Council. The approach to peace of the General Assembly, the one major organ of the UN that contains all member states, was for it to serve as a forum for the world's problems. As a forum, however, it can pass only nonbinding recommendations.

The Security Council was designed to take a more hard-nosed approach to confronting the threat of conflict escalating into wars. Resolutions that passed the Security Council, in theory, were considered binding on the UN's membership but such is often not so in practice. From the beginning of the UN, the veto-bearing and permanent members of the Security Council were the United States, the United Kingdom, France, China, and the Soviet Union (Russia now has this veto). Possessing the veto meant that that country alone, by voting in the negative, could stop any further action by the Security Council. These five powers were the major victors of World War II and they intended to preserve their status in the postwar world through the veto.

The approach to peace of the Security Council was that if the major powers could agree, nothing could stop them, but, if one or more disagreed it was better that no action be taken for fear of expanding conflict among the major powers. The League of Nations had had no veto and the UN's founders did not want to repeat the splits, and subsequent conflict, that had occurred among the major powers in the League's Council.

The veto has been controversial from the UN's beginning; quite naturally it is attacked by virtually any nation that does not have it. Attempts to add nations to those already possessing the veto have thus far failed. In the late 1990s, one proposal would give the veto to Germany, Japan, and perhaps Brazil as a representative of the developing nations, although in Latin America there is support for Argentina having this seat instead. A variation on this plan is to make these nations permanent members of the Council but not grant them a veto. Yet another proposal is to give the European Union a veto in lieu of the United Kingdom's and France's veto rights. The British and French fear that the EU veto would be dominated by Germany. These issues thus far have prevented the UN from changing the original distribution of the veto or permanent membership on the Council.

International developments that occurred in the postwar world immediately affected the UN, especially the Security Council. During the late 1940s East-West relations deteriorated rapidly. By 1948 and the Berlin Airlift, the Cold War was developing rapidly. With the creation of NATO in 1949, a military standoff between East and West quickly developed. Within the UN these developments had considerable impact.

By 1955 the Soviet Union had cast more than 100 vetoes, which effectively deadlocked the Security Council as an arbiter of international conflict. Paradoxically, in later years, as the Soviets picked up support from the developing countries serving as members of the Security Council, Soviet vetoes fell dramatically in number. Due to this declining support for the West, in 1970 the United States cast its first veto, and from then on cast more than did the Soviet Union. In the 1990s, following the collapse of the Soviet Union, use of the veto has not been the issue it once was, although threat of its use occasionally occurs.

During the years when the Security Council was deadlocked by the Soviet use of the veto, the United States and other Western countries preferred the veto-free General Assembly to promote their policies. At that time, Latin America, Western Europe and the scattering of African and Asian countries in the UN supported the United States, which was sufficient for the United States to obtain the two-thirds vote necessary to pass a resolution. Bypassing the Soviet veto in this manner accomplished little because the General Assembly, no matter how large the majority, could not pass binding resolutions. Thus, as a result of the Soviet veto, the limited authority of the General Assembly and an ever-increasing number of developing nations in the General Assembly that were largely anti-Western, the UN went into a period of decline after 1960 as far as Western and U.S. policy was concerned.

The UN's political watershed came in 1989 after more than 20 years of being low on the foreign policy agendas of the major states. This change began when Gorbachev came to power in the Soviet Union in 1985. By 1988, Gorbachev had presented his policies of glasnost and perestroika as well as other policies more accomodating to the West. Initially, Western nations were suspicious of Gorbachev's motives, but implementation of these new approaches to the West resulted in a much closer relationship between the Cold War adversaries. The dismantling of the Berlin Wall in 1989 was followed by the collapse of the Warsaw Pact and, in December 1991, the dissolution of the Soviet Union. By 1989 the Soviet veto was no longer a threat and the major powers then revived the Security Council. Gorbachev went along with this change and China made no major objections. The UN was back to where its founding fathers had intended it to be when it began; an institution where the major powers had the potential to control world events.

Quickly the UN was called upon to send peacekeeping forces to various trouble spots around the world. The UN had had forces in Cyprus, the Golan Heights, and peace observers in Kashmir for many years. New operations included sending substantial peacekeeping forces to Cambodia and Somalia; overseeing elections in Namibia, El Salvador, and Nicaragua; sending forces to Rwanda, and attempting to assemble a peacekeeping force to go to Mozambique although sufficient forces were never found. The civil war in that country ended nevertheless. Security Council resolutions were also the basis on which the United States sent armed forces into Haiti. These forces were later replaced with armed forces from Canada and Pakistan. The UN also sent a small group to Angola to oversee the ceasefire ending that country's civil war and to accept the arms of the rebel groups. In all, the United Nations introduced 23 peacekeeping operations after 1989. Before 1989 the UN had had only 18 such operations since 1948, when it introduced its first peacekeeping operation.

During this period of expanded role for the Security Council, its most difficult assignment was in Croatia and Bosnia, but the peacekeeping force assigned there could not stop the fighting and genocide. NATO and several other countries replaced that force with their implementing force (IFOR) which was replaced at the end of 1996 with the stabilizing force (SFOR). The Security Council did, however, make the decisions that made these various operations possible. The success rate of UN peacekeeping missions was not high, but the Security Council was back in the middle of international diplomacy.

The biggest action brought on by Security Council resolutions was the Gulf War. None of the forces in that operation were designated UN forces (they were referred to as coalition forces), but the resolutions (14 in all) that those forces enforced were all passed by the Security Council. The coalition force carried out its mission first with air attacks and then by invading Kuwait and Iraq. Following the fighting, the UN left severe economic and weapons sanctions in place as well as unprecedented resolutions protecting the human rights of Kurds in northern Iraq and Shi'ite Moslems in the south until Iraq complied with all resolutions.

Little was heard from the General Assembly after 1989 and the decades of complaints against the West emanating from the developing countries there was greatly reduced. No longer could those countries play off the Western industrialized nations and the communist countries against one another in order to obtain aid; one set of players no longer existed. The failure of the Soviet model of development turned many developing countries away from central planning thus further reduced tensions in the General Assembly. The West became an economic ally of many developing countries that had once been so critical of it.

III. LESS TRADITIONAL ACTORS

While nation-states and IGOs are easily included among the actors found in the international system, other entities also play important roles although not necessarily positive ones. Three in particular deserve mention-multinational corporations. (MNCs), terrorist organizations, and nongovernmental organizations.

A. Role of Multinational Corporations

If a multinational corporation is defined as a corporation with major operations in more than one country, MNCs have been actors in the international system for some time. Illustrations of prewar MNCs would be Standard Oil (it began its operation in Saudi Arabia in the 1930s and in several other countries earlier) and United Fruit, with its products coming from plantations in several Latin American countries. But, as nations became increasingly economically interdependent following World War II, the role of MNCs increased greatly.

MNCs have become the single most important means for private capital to flow from the industrial nations to the economies of developing countries. Some of the receiving nations, such as Malaysia, Singapore, South Korea, and Taiwan, have benefited from these investments to the extent that they have become both competitors of and partners with the more advanced industrial countries. Although MNCs have nongovernmental organizations (NGOs) that unite them across international boundaries (virtually every raw material and product has some international NGO), their individual international activities are highly competitive in their struggle for overseas markets.

MNCs, at least the largest ones, exert more economic power than do the national economies of all but the strongest economies of the industrialized nations. No IGO is designed to control their activities and, at times, the international behavior of some MNCs is as if they had foreign policies independent of the countries in which they have their corporate headquarters.

The United States' attempts to control the activities of U.S.-based MNCs by applying the restrictions it places on the U.S. corporations domestically to those corporations' overseas branches. This has resulted in a number of disputes between the United States and the countries in which those branches are located. Most Western industrial nations are not as restrictive of their MNCs abroad as is the United States.

When comparing investments MNCs make in developing countries with the economic aid Western governments grant those countries, the investment from MNCs far exceeds that of the governments. Complaints do occasionally come from developing countries in which MNCs invest heavily that the influence of MNCs is so great that their governments run the risk of losing control of their countries' economies. This is heard less frequently than it once was now that the Soviet Union is no longer a possible alternative source of aid.

B. Terrorist Organizations

In the shadowy world of terrorism, it is not always possible to determine when a terrorist act is the product of an organization or that of an individual; but whoever carries out the act, it often has international implications. Although hundreds of terrorist organizations exist in name only or claim responsibility for a terrorist act when they probably were not involved, many well-organized terrorist organizations do commit acts of terrorism for what they feel are justifiable reasons. Unlike nation-states, IGOs, or MNCs, terrorist organizations have no official international standing. They are a part of the international system, nevertheless, because their acts of violence can do great physical and human damage thereby drawing considerable international attention to their cause.

Terrorism, perhaps best described as acts of violence carried out for political ends, is generally viewed as acts of desperation; terrorists feel they have no other means of making their cause known. The terrorists perspective is that only through a violent act can they promote their views, revenge an injustice and make the world know of their cause. Terrorists, particularly members of Hamas in Israel, often commit suicidal attacks to show the degree of commitment they have to their cause and to inflict maximum injury on their enemies.

One aspect of terrorism that has had a direct impact on international relations is that some of the most serious acts of terrorism have been state sponsored: some nation provided support to the terrorists. This has caused the states in which the terrorist act took place to retaliate against the states that support terrorism. The United States has branded Libya and Iran as state sponsors of terrorism and, in the case of Libya, launched an airstrike on that country in 1986 in retaliation for the deaths of American servicemen resulting from the bombing of a Berlin nightclub. Both countries are subject to economic sanctions as well. Iran, although it denies the charge, is seen by a number of countries, including the United States, as supporting Hamas and Hezbollah, organizations that have committed numerous terrorist attacks in the Middle East. The United States has also labeled Syria a state sponsor of terrorism, but retaliation has been more limited than that directed against Libya and Iran. In 1997, a German court found Iran responsible for a terrorist act committed in Germany. This was contrary to what had been Germany's more relaxed policy toward Iran and more in line with what is U.S. policy.

Terrorism has increased since the 1960s and as it has done so, it has become more organized and widespread. The hijacking of airliners once was a common means of calling the world's attention to a cause, but as security increased that act is now difficult to carry out. Terrorism now is most often carried out with explosives, the targets being commercial aircraft, buildings, or crowds of people.

The destruction of the Marine barracks in Lebanon by a suicide bomber in 1983 had the intended consequence when the United States withdrew its forces a short time later. The destruction of Pan Am Flight 103 over Scotland was a retaliatory act for a U.S. warship shooting down an Iranian civilian airliner over the Persian Gulf. The United States charges that those responsible for the Pan Am bombing have been given sanctuary in Libya; a further reason for U.S. sanctions against Libya. In recent years, the pattern of terrorism has changed; acts of terrorism are not as frequent as they once were, but when they do occur, the loss of life is greater.

A distinction should be made between domestic and international terrorism. A violent act need not be international in nature to be a terrorist act. In the United States, the destruction of the Murrah Federal Building in Oklahoma City was, from all evidence, a domestic act of violence directed against the U.S. government by a U.S. citizen with no international implications. The bombing of the World Trade Center in New York, on the other hand, was seen as international in nature. The 1996 bombing of the U.S. military barracks in Saudi Arabia was clearly an international act of terrorism. Terrorism has, for many nations including the United States, become both a domestic and international problem. Controlling such violence has proved to be extremely difficult.

C. Nongovernmental Organizations

The most rapid increase in numbers of international actors is undoubtedly the nongovernmental organization (NGO). These organizations are international in the sense that their membership comes from more than one country and are nongovernmental in that membership is not made up of representatives from any government. The number of NGOs (which number in the thousands) far exceeds the approximately 400 IGOs. The span of interests NGOs represent seems almost limitless. About any aspect of commerce, sports, human rights, business, academic disciplines, raw materials,

transportation, and so on has an NGO. While, by their very nature, they do not make society-binding decisions, they do carry out several functions in the international system.

Many NGOs serve as lobbyists at the international level. The United Nations and various other international organizations frequently hold conferences on a particular policy question. On most occasions NGOs show up in substantial numbers to make their positions known to the official representatives. A notable example was the United Nations conference on women's rights held in Beijing. NGOs were present in great numbers and, although they did not always agree with one another, were vocal in their positions. The UN conference on the environment held in Rio in 1992 also produced many NGO observers.

NGOs also serve as publicists for their cause. Amnesty International is an example. This NGO monitors political prisoners throughout the world and makes known to a wide international audience their plight. IGOs also have a special role to play in less than democratic societies. Where the opportunity for citizens to participate directly in the political process is limited, NGOs often provide an opportunity to make the NGO's membership views known at an international level.

IV. THE ROLE OF DIPLOMACY

With such a variety of actors in the international system, a means of communication between them is essential. The most commonly used means of contact between international actors are the rules and traditions of diplomacy. This means of communication is largely limited to nation-states and the IGOs they create in that MNCs are domestically controlled whereas terrorist groups, by definition, are rarely interested in peaceful communication. NGOs attempt to influence political behavior both domestically and internationally, although from outside of any political system.

Within the context of peaceful settlement of disputes, diplomatic channels allow a nation to express its position concerning a dispute and, if the parties involved are willing to do so, work out a reasonable compromise. Even if no settlement is forthcoming, the channels of diplomacy allow a nation to convey what its interests are in the matter at hand. Clarification of interests does not necessarily mean that a settlement is pending; rather it can mean that negotiating nations find that they have no common ground. This too can be beneficial. When nations are engaged in talks they are less apt to go to war; at least not until one or more of the actors becomes convinced that further negotiations are futile. The hope of any negotiations, unless they are entered into for purely propaganda purposes, is that through bargaining a compromise can be reached and violent conflict avoided.

It is also through the use of diplomacy that coalitions and alliances are formed among nation-states. Since joining an IGO generally means that each member must compromise some of its interests in order to become a member, this alone is an important step to the resolution of the conflicts that will come before the IGO.

Nations often engage in one-on-one negotiations, but if multilateral negotiations are chosen then an IGO is one means of carrying on such talks. IGOs are forums for diplomatic interchange either in a formal or informal setting. The latter is seen as one of the most important contributions of the United Nations; often more meaningful contact takes place outside the formal sessions of the organization during so-called hallway diplomacy.

Diplomacy thus is a complicated process. It is multipurposed and is intended to improve communication concerning the interests of nations; it is intended to manage, if not resolve, conflicts among nations and, if possible, to negotiate and bargain international agreements and treaties. It has day-to-day functions as well. A nation's embassies abroad keep in touch with the host government and by doing so keep minor issues low key, thus avoiding the escalation of many disputes. Another function of overseas diplomats is to serve as observers of the political situation in the host country and to evaluate how that situation affects the interests of the sending nation.

The use of diplomacy does, however, demand patience. In some instances diplomacy does not bring resolution to a conflict, but the dispute and talks about it go on for such a long time that the issue simply becomes moot: the ultimate positive result of patience in diplomacy. For major agreements, particularly those ending longstanding problems such as the war in Vietnam or arms control agreements, diplomatic discussions can go on for years before an agreement is forthcoming. Mention was made earlier that negotiations at Westphalia went on for two years, partly because diplomatic protocol was far from developed. During the Cold War agreements often took even longer although protocol was now developed.

Negotiating the end of U.S. participation in the Vietnam War took about 5 years. One problem was that the talks were taking place between the United States, a recognized member of the international community, and North Vietnam, which was not an accepted member. Protocol did not allow for this sort of situation. Major arms agreements, SALT I, SALT II, START I, START II, and the Conventional Forces in Europe (CFE) agreement, each took longer to negotiate than did the Treaty of Westphalia. Negotiations are often recessed. Although adding to their length, the pause in negotiation gives each side an opportunity to rethink its position and perhaps develop new proposals before reconvening; this was often successful in U.S.-Soviet talks. Patience is indeed important to successful diplomacy.

V. INTERNATIONAL LAW AND DIPLOMACY

International law and diplomacy are closely related in that diplomacy provides the means of contact between nation-states and international law is frequently the basis for resolving a conflict. International law is based on a wide variety of principles, norms, and rules that developed parallel to the development of the nation-state system. The origin of international law initially was customary practice between nation-states. If nations dealt with a problem in a certain manner long enough that they felt obligated to behave in that fashion, custom became international law. By the 19th century treaties became a far more important source of international law than was custom. Multilateral treaties could establish new principles of international law and, in turn, by custom, treaties were to be obeyed, a principle known as *Pacta Sunt Servanda*.

International law is not interpreted the same way by all countries. The Soviet Union had its own particular manner of applying international law and even minor differences exist between Anglo-American perspectives and those of continental European nation-states. Since international law grew out of the nation-state system in Europe, former colonies of European countries occasionally take exception to the principles developed by Europe. In spite of these differences and the impression many persons hold that international law is unenforceable and therefore useless, international law is used to settle a wide variety of disputes on a daily basis. It does not settle the sorts of disputes that may go on for years without resolution or prevent the outbreak of many wars, but it is useful in settling lesser disputes thus preventing them from becoming more serious ones. Principles of international law designed to prevent war exist, but often are not applied to a conflict.

Examples of the close relationship between diplomacy and international law include the protection of diplomats stationed abroad—diplomatic privileges and immunities. These principles, protected by both custom and treaty, leave diplomats free to represent the nation that sent them. The protocol of carrying on negotiations is also specified by international law. International law also covers the recognition of new governments and states, the rules for specifying boundaries between nations, the use of a nation's air space, extradition, and many other matters of importance. Yet another body of international law is concerned with the conduct of nations during wartime.

If the development of a set of rules and principles is accepted broadly enough and applied with near universality to a particular problem, this is known as a regime. Recent developments concerning Law of the Sea, a product of several United Nations-sponsored conferences, is often cited as a regime. The General Agreement on Tariffs and Trade (GATT), which developed into the World Trade Organizations (WTO), is another frequent example. Both examples, however, have necessary further development before they will have successfully provided the rules to cover major conflict in either subject area. A logical extension of this concept of regimes is that if they were sufficient in number, the international system would have available the means to resolve any outstanding conflict.

VI. POWER AND THE INTERNATIONAL SYSTEM

Nations engaged in diplomatic talks often do not negotiate as equal participants. Although it is valid to say that each state is sovereign, thus legally equal to any other, nations are vastly different in the power (or influence) they exert in the international system. The problem of using power to gauge a nation's position in the international pecking order is that it is difficult to measure; therefore nations often disagree as to how powerful one nation is relative to another. A coalition of nations opposing another coalition makes the task even more complicated.

A. The Elements of Power

A means of measuring a nation's power is to look at and attempt to measure various elements that are thought of as making up a nation's power. Although the process sounds simple, many miscalculations develop that can contribute to conflict among nations.

B. Military Capability

Comparison of a nation's armed forces with that of other nations is a commonly used means of assessing a nation's power; it is also a tangible element of power easily miscalculated. Comparisons usually are made by citing numbers—how many divisions of troops, how many combat naval vessels, how many wings of combat aircraft, and how many main battle tanks. Comparing quantities overlooks two important aspects of armed force. The first is the age and quality of the equipment. An example is which is the best main battle tank, the German Leopard II, the American M1A2, the French Leclerc, or the Russian T-72 or T-80? Each has its strengths and weaknesses. During the Gulf War, the Iraqis, using Soviet tanks, were badly defeated. Perhaps the tanks used by coalition forces were superior, but even if they were the tactics used by the Iraqis were poor, thus the war proved little about the quality of the tanks used. The same problems exist when comparing aircraft, especially fighters. Navies are also a problem in comparison. Russia has more combat naval ships than does the United States, but numbers mean little as most of the Russian navy is rusting in port due to a lack of money for maintenance.

Other aspects of miscalculation concerning armed forces are training and morale. If an army is poorly trained or if morale is low those forces will not perform well in combat. The Gulf War again provides a good example. In 1990, the Iraqi army was thought to have nearly one million men. The coalition forces were at about half that figure. Much of the Iraqi army was poorly trained and subsequently quickly captured. The better trained portion of that army retreated without a fight. Another example is the Chinese army, the People's Liberation Army (PLA), the largest army in the world. In 1979 it invaded Vietnam and was driven out by a much smaller force of Vietnamese militia. In the late 1990s China purchased some new equipment from Russia, mainly aircraft, and is expanding its arms industry, but the 1979 humiliation and the army's participation in the Tiananmen Square massacre continue to contribute to a lack of respect for the PLA by other countries. Estimating other countries' military capabilities, especially how their armed forces will behave in combat, is always difficult.

Another means of measuring a nations' military power, short of an all-out war, is to compare the size of military budgets. During the Cold War this measurement was commonly used even though the United States was unsure as to how much the Soviets were spending or even how to calculate their budget. Since the Cold War ended the United States clearly outspends Russia or any other nation. In 1997 the United States outspent the total budgets of the next seven highest nations' budgets.

Yet another measurement of military capabilities is nuclear weapons. Even in the post-Cold War era, large nuclear arsenals remain. The United States and Russia have several treaties designed to reduce their nuclear stockpiles, which lowers the threat somewhat. A remaining question, however, is the potential spread of nuclear weapons to nations that do not now possess them. An increase in the number of nations with nuclear weapons would further complicate the problem of how to measure military power.

C. State of the Economy as Power

As the 20th century nears an end, the state of a nation's economy has become not only the most frequently cited element of a nation's influence internationally, but also in some ways it is the easiest to measure; unlike military power, it does not take a war to measure the effectiveness of a nation's economy. Even so, complications arise because different means are used to measure economic power.

The size of a nation's economy cannot be taken alone as a reliable measure of economic power. China has a large economy, the seventh largest in the world, and India, as does China, has a high rate of economic growth. The two countries are not considered to be wealthy because their Gross Domestic Product (GDP) must be divided among large populations; their populations are number one and two, respectively. Before the collapse of the Soviet Union the United States had the largest GDP and either the Japanese or the Soviet economy was next in size. In the late 1990s the United States still has the largest economy with Japan now clearly second, but Japan's economic influence has declined. Japan suffered from a recession through most of the 1990s and its political leadership is weak compared to what it once was. The Russian economy is so chaotic that it is difficult to assess; ranking the present Russian economy is virtually impossible due to unreliable data.

The value of a nation's currency is another measure. The Japanese yen has fallen compared to the American dollar, but among the currencies of Western Europe, some have fallen and others have risen relative to the dollar. The relationship of currencies is an important influence on the flow of international trade.

Comparing per capita incomes between nations would seem to be a simple calculation—just divide a nation's GDP by its population—but the purchasing-power parity (PPP) of that income often changes the ranking of a nation's economy. PPP refers to how much a per capita income will purchase. The United States not only has the largest per capita income, its per capita income buys more dollar for dollar than does the per capita income of any other country. China, as mentioned, has the world's 7th largest economy, but in PPP terms it is 2nd and Japan slips to 3rd. India has the world's 15th largest economy, but in PPP ranks fifth.

D. Other Tangible Measures of Power

The size of a nation's population is not a reliable measure of power alone. A nation needs a well-educated and skilled population in proportion to its economy's ability to absorb its available workers into the national economy. A characteristic of developing countries is having too many people to keep employed, although developed nations have the same problem during periods of recession.

Population is a military factor as well, but less so than it once was. When warfare was based on massive armies, the larger the army the more power a nation possessed. Armies now are more often measured by the technological sophistication of their weaponry and a nation's ability to transport their armed forces over great distances than by the size of a nation's population or how many people are in their armed forces. The United States is estimated to have the sixth largest army in the world (after China, Russia, North Korea, Iraq, and Vietnam) but, due to its sophistication, is recognized to have the most powerful.

Natural resources are also a factor of power. The country most nearly self-sufficient in resources is Russia. But with the collapse of its economy, this is not nearly as important as when the Cold War was on. As long as a nation can import the natural resources it needs, as the United States does, their location is not important.

E. Intangible Measures of Power

Intangible elements of power also are considerations in assessing a nation's power. Among such elements is the quality of a nation's leadership, which varies considerably from nation to nation. A nation's morale and how the populace feels about its government are other intangibles. The success of a country's political system to protect and project the nation's interests internationally is yet another intangible element. Intangible elements of power are even more difficult to measure than tangible ones.

F. Measurement versus Perception

Pointing out that power is difficult to measure does not mean that power is not being measured. With all the difficulties of measuring one country's power and comparing it to that of other nations, nations must make such assessments in order to know where they stand in the international system. If nations are relatively close in their assessment of one another and of themselves, disputes are more easily settled through diplomacy. Danger exists when those assessments are off to the point that those involved in a dispute negotiate from inaccurate assessments of one another. Power may not be calculated easily, but perceptions of power are present and utilized nevertheless.

VII. ORGANIZING THE INTERNATIONAL SYSTEM

As described to this point the international system would appear to be one in which every nation must look out for itself; a self-help system in which diplomacy and, to a limited extent, international law can moderate somewhat the use of power, but power and the threat of force are what control the system. The system is not, however, international anarchy in that there is organization to the relationships among its members. These relationships change and as change takes place, the manner in which the system is organized alters; the system and the environment evolve together.

The international system has several alternative ways in which it can be organized, but each means of organization depends on the demands of the international environment. Each means of organization has different underlying assumptions about how to control power, the manner in which diplomacy will be utilized, and the role of major states and the extent to which smaller states are important. The result is an organization of the international system that is not made up of formal decision-making institutions so much as it is a number of informal understandings as to how the international system can minimize conflict among its actors. An important factor to keep in mind is that nations do not actively choose among alternative systems; international conditions dictate how the system will function. The possible exception to this is collective security, a means of organizing the system devised by the founders of the League of Nations.

A. Balance of Power

Historically, perhaps the most often referred to means of organizing the international system is that of balance of power. Common use of the term is in reference to two or more competing nations or coalitions as being about equal in power. Under these circumstances, balance of power describes little more than a condition or situation that exists at any given moment. As a means of organizing the international system, however, balance of power means more than a condition alone; it also includes how a balance can limit conflict and provide international stability.

Balance of power as a system was a regulator of European politics for nearly a century, and it never included any non-European major powers such as the United States and Japan. The political environment that made balance of power possible followed the Congress of Vienna in 1815 and lasted, intermittently, until the outbreak of World War I in 1914.

The view major European states took following the Napoleonic era was that there could not again be another dominant coalition in Europe. In place of such a situation, the major powers felt the best means of maintaining order was to have two coalitions of about equal power since no coalition could be trusted with dominant power. The minor powers could be part of either coalition, but the distribution of the major states' power was centrally important. At the time, Europe had several major powers including Great Britain, France, Prussia (a unified Germany later), Italy (after 1870), the Austro-Hungarian Empire, and Russia. This meant that each coalition needed two or three major powers in order to achieve the desired balance.

In addition to not trusting any country or coalition with dominant power, two conditions were important to the maintenance of balance. One was that since the coalitions were about equal in power, it was assumed that the major states would not go to war with one another since the result could be a devastating war of attrition. The second assumption was that if war did break out involving major powers, it must be a limited one. For the balance of power system to work no major power could suffer long-term injury, for if one was weakened it would make achieving a balance more difficult.

Important to the functioning of this system was agreement on when a balance had been achieved. In addition to power being difficult to measure, it is also a constantly changing condition. Although a balance of power would seem to have been achieved, the relationship could easily go out of balance. If this occurred, it would be the responsibility of one of the major powers to leave the stronger coalition and go to the weaker, thus reestablishing the semblance of balance.

The role of shifting between coalitions fell to Great Britain, although disagreement exists as to how much the British actually played that role. If minor powers shifted coalitions, this was of little consequence; only a major power could make a significant difference. When a major state chose to change coalitions in the name of maintaining balance, it meant that loyalty to the former coalition was abandoned; thus in a balance of power coalition loyalty was fleeting.

Shifts in coalition by major states placed special responsibilities on diplomacy. Changing coalitions would be difficult to achieve if a nation's public gained a sense of commitment to that nation's allies. In order to avoid such loyalty, diplomacy was often conducted in secret with treaties not only negotiated in secret, but remaining so after they were completed. A nation's public thus did not know what its government was committed to; only the leaders of the major states needed to know.

Although these were the understandings as to how balance of power would function, all were not carried out at any given time. However loosely the informal rules were applied, the system did seem to work. Europe did have two serious wars during the period of balance of power, the Crimean War and the Franco-Prussian War, but diplomacy prevented them from becoming European-wide with broad objectives.

The environment in Europe underwent important changes shortly after the turn of the century. An important diplomatic practice that had worked well until then was that when the list of disputes among the European powers accumulated, a conference would be called. The interval between conferences was irregular; the important factor was knowing when to call such a conference. The last such conference was at Algeciras in 1907. This conference did not go well. The coalitions had lost their flexibility in membership, and conditions were in place for a major European war, which came in 1914 with the beginning of the first World War.

B. Bipolarity

Bipolarity, or the Cold War as it was popularly known, was the organization of the international system that dominated international politics for more than 40 years after World War II. The conditions discussed earlier that had such a profound effect on the evolution of the United Nations from 1947 to 1989 were also descriptive of relations overall between the Western nations and the communist bloc; the UN reflected existing tensions in the world. The division of Europe between East and West as a consequence of the outcome of World War II and, later, divisions in other parts of the world produced two competing coalitions—bipolarity. The behavior of those coalitions, however, was considerably different than that expected of coalitions in a balance of power system.

Once World War II ended, the Western allies conducted a massive disarmament program, reducing their armed forces to a fraction of their wartime strength. The Soviet Union reduced its armed forces as well, but how much was a matter of considerable speculation in the West, although there was general agreement that Soviet reductions were not as extensive as those in the West. As tensions grew, NATO was created in 1949 in an attempt to counter Soviet military superiority. Military alliances in other parts of the world followed as Western nations surrounded the Soviet Union and—after the 1949 communist takeover—China, with anticommunist alliances. This policy was known in the West as containment; a policy opposed to further expansion of communism. The Soviets countered these moves by creating the Warsaw Pact in 1955.

Clearly these confrontational coalitions were not seeking a balance of power. Beyond both a balance of power and bipolarity having two competing coalitions, the two systems shared little in common. The objective of each bipolar coalition was to achieve superiority over the other; the coalitions were in an arms race, not a search for balance. The objective of each coalition was to gain an advantage in arms and to translate superior power into diplomatic pressure or, if war occurred, military victory.

Measuring the power of each coalition was, as with any measure of power, difficult, but particularly so with the Soviet Union being a closed society. In the West, because of uncertainty concerning communist power, defense budgets increased in an effort to keep up with only general estimates of Soviet power. When in doubt Western countries used the higher estimates of what was needed for defense.

Unlike coalitions in balance of power those of bipolarity were rigid in membership. Since balance was not the objective, no state, major or minor, was free to change sides. The Soviets intervened in Hungary in 1956 when that country attempted to leave the Warsaw Pact and occupied Czechoslovakia in 1968 when that country adopted policies the Soviets thought incompatible with their own. U.S. forces comprised 90% of the United Nations force that responded to North Korea's invasion of South Korea in 1950. The Korean War ended in 1953 in a stalemate near the line that divided the two countries when the war began. The only countries to successfully switch coalitions were when Castro introduced a communist government in Cuba in 1959 and the United States unsuccessfully resisted a communist takeover of South Vietnam. No major states shifted allegiances after China adopted communism.

In spite of tensions between the Cold War coalitions, understood practices in limiting the possibilities of a major war did exist. One was trying to avoid direct confrontations. When wars were fought or interventions conducted involving the armed forces of either the United States or the Soviet Union, the armed forces of the other country stayed out. Soviet interventions in Eastern Europe were not countered with a NATO or U.S. intervention. When the Soviets intervened in Afghanistan in 1979, the U.S. did not send forces. Soviet forces did not become directly involved in either the Korean War or the Vietnam War. Military confrontations between what were seen as the world's only superpowers were carefully avoided since both realized the possibility that a confrontation could lead to a nuclear exchange and all-out war. Both countries possessed substantial nuclear arsenals.

During the Cold War, the Cuban Missile Crisis in 1962 generally was seen as the closest the United States and the Soviet Union came to war. The lesson learned from the confrontation was that the risks were too great when a crisis involved an open confrontation between the superpowers. As the Cold War ended, decision makers from both countries participated in conferences in an effort to determine how close they came to war. A firm answer is yet to be determined.

While the term massive retaliation was considered a U.S. policy and meant that if war came the U.S. would place no limits on its attack, the Soviet Union apparently supported a similar policy. Although a limited nuclear exchange was promoted as an alternative to massive retaliation, few decision makers felt any use of nuclear exchange would result in anything but all-out war. Nuclear weapons were of such concern to the superpowers that most of their diplomatic efforts were devoted to the negotiation of nuclear arms treaties or related agreements.

The 19th century balance of power system was little concerned with arms control since balance was to be achieved by other means. Bipolarity had a more central role for arms control particularly when large stockpiles of nuclear weapons existed. The delivery of nuclear weapons could be carried out in three ways—submarine-launched ballistic missiles (SLBM), land-based intercontinental ballistic missiles (ICBM), and long-range manned bombers. Although the United States and the Soviet Union arrived at a limited nuclear test ban in 1963 and reached agreements to place no nuclear weapons in outer space, in the Antarctic, or on the seabed, and signed a Non-Proliferation Treaty, no treaties controlling delivery systems came until 1972 with SALT I. This agreement dealt only with ceilings, not reductions, and was limited to ICBMs and SLBMs. Limitations on warheads were to come later. SALT II was completed in 1979 and was more comprehensive. It included controls on all three delivery systems with some Soviet reductions since they had the larger number of delivery systems. Negotiations began late in the 1980s that resulted in START I and START II, both of which called for reductions in the number of warheads. By the late 1990s some reductions in warheads had taken place but both sides continued to have considerable nuclear stockpiles. Negotiations between Russia and the United States to extend these agreements further yet continue.

The longstanding system of bipolarity came to an end a decade before the 20th century ended. The manner in which it ended was a surprise to virtually everyone—decision makers, students of international politics, and average citizens alike. War or a gradually worked out settlement between the superpowers were seen as the only logical means of ending the Cold War; the collapse of the Soviet Union, if such were ever to occur, would be a possibility of the distant future. Due to internal bad management and leadership, the Soviet Union collapsed and bipolarity came to an end.

C. Collective Security

Collective security often is the label placed on any military alliance a group of nations negotiate, but it also has meaning as a manner in which the international system can be organized. Collective security was a key element in the Covenant of the League of Nations and, on a less central basis, in the Charter of the United Nations. But, like balance of power and bipolarity, collective security has certain prerequisites before it can successfully control international violence.

Unlike the other means discussed of organizing the international system, collective security was a system designed by diplomats, the founders of the League, and was not a direct outgrowth of the international environment. The control of power was vested in the universal actor, the League or the UN, not competing coalitions of nations. Under collective security all member nations had the responsibility to aid in the maintenance of world peace. In that sense peace was indivisible in that if the peace were broken anywhere all nations should act to restore it.

The assumption of collective security made about war was that it was a product of a nation committing an act of aggression. If the rest of the world united to punish this aggressor, overwhelming power could be brought to bear against any aggressor nation. Better yet, if a potential aggressor felt such power would be used against it if it committed aggression, no aggression would occur. All of these principles presented problems when attempts were made to implement them.

The first problem was in defining an act of aggression; the second was to devise a suitable punishment and have all nations collectively impose that punishment. Yet another problem was the assumption that aggression was the sole cause of wars and that when aggression took place, only a single country committed the act. When Japan invaded Manchuria in 1931, after a year's delay the League labeled Japan an aggressor but took no further action. Japan retaliated by withdrawing from the League and the occupation of Manchuria stood. When Italy invaded Ethiopia in 1935, the League labeled Italy an aggressor and imposed economic sanctions. A number of countries violated the sanctions and Ethiopia remained under Italian control. The UN's one effort at collective security followed North Korea's invasion of South Korea in 1950. The UN labeled North Korea the aggressor and sent in troops. Later, when China intervened, it too was labeled an aggressor. The UN force sent to Korea included contributions from only 16 nations out of the 60 UN members at the time.

Each of these operations failed for a different reason. In the case of Japan, the League took too long to act and no punishment was handed out. As for Italy, sanctions were not imposed effectively. When the Axis coalition was formed by Germany, Japan, Italy, and three smaller European nations, the world discovered that aggressors were not necessarily lone actors. The Korean War, where only about a quarter of the UN's membership participated in any way, was fought to a stalemate. Thus the aggressors were not punished. The UN has not attempted a collective security action since the Korean War. In no one of these examples were the underlying principles of collective security met.

D. Unipolarity

The obvious question of the late 1990s is what sort of international arrangement exists to maintain peace now that the Cold War has ended? Balance of power, bipolarity, and collective security are for various reasons inappropriate; balance of power because only one superpower remains, bipolarity for the same reason and collective security because it has never lived up to expectations. What remains is a central role for the United States and, when they can agree, the other Western states to join together to ensure peace. This would be unipolarity.

While president, George Bush referred to a New World Order; what he meant by this phrase is unclear and thus has been given broad interpretation. If he had in mind that the United States should take a leading role in maintaining world peace, then he was suggesting unipolarity. If the Western industrial states can form a common security bond, then perhaps unipolarity is on the horizon for the 21st century. Western leadership in the Security Council and the expansion of NATO into Eastern Europe is consistent with the concept of unipolarity because they expand the U.S.-led coalition. Disputes among the Western industrialized nations make unipolarity less likely, however.

VIII. THE INTERNATIONAL ENVIRONMENT

A number of significant changes have occurred in recent years that have had considerable effect on the international environment and determine the form the international system takes. The impact of both world wars is perhaps the most profound.

The allies won World War I in the sense that the opposing force, the Central Powers, signed an armistice. The war settled little and left the circumstances that led to World War II. World War II left the world divided into two powerful armed camps, the basis of the Cold War, which easily could have led to World War III. A third world war was avoided through the collapse of the Soviet Union.

A long-term result of the Soviet collapse was the need to integrate the former Soviet republics and East European satellite states into the Western economic and political system. These new countries went through uncertainty about their political systems (how to set up a democratic state), high inflation, and economic upheaval as they converted to free market economies. The 1990s, for these countries, were times of considerable uncertainty and confusion. Local wars were common such as those between Armenia and Azerbaijan, civil war in Uzbekistan, fighting in Moldova, and civil war in Georgia. The largest of the wars was in Chechnya, inside Russia. Yugoslavia's collapse also produced several new countries and contributed a similar chapter of fighting and confusion. The political and economic integration of these countries is still in progress and the outcome uncertain.

Several events outside Europe have changed the world's economic environment. An important economic development has been the changing relationship between the economically developed and developing nations. The developing countries (most of which were former colonies) once were virtually all dependent on the good will of the industrialized nations for aid and trade. This dependence is now moving toward interdependence.

Many of the dependent nations, particularly in Latin America and Asia, have experienced economic growth to the point that they now are strong economic trading partners. This has not only increased trade but it has also increased the number of trade agreements involving both developing and developed countries. International conferences on trade now often include the recently developed nations, especially those countries from the Pacific Rim.

Not only has the economic status of many developing countries changed, more of those countries are now democracies. Freedom House, a research organization, reports that 118 countries are democracies in 1997, up from 69 in 1987. The standard used to determine a country's political status is the extent of political and civil rights. A problem presented by some countries considered to be democracies a few years ago is that they recently have slipped to near-authoritarian countries and, at best, are only pseudo-democracies. Overall, however, the number of democracies has increased in the last 15 years, especially in Latin America.

One development in the international environment has caused concern. This pertains to the spread of Islam as the basis of some countries' governments. Iran has had an Islamic government since the late 1970s and Afghanistan is engaged in a civil war over that issue. Turkey, a secular state for more than 70 years, is in a struggle over the role of Islam in its public life. Algeria's government refuted the results of an election that an Islamic party won. The Egyptian government has been plagued for several years by Islamic terrorists demanding a role in that country's government. The gov-ernments of Libya and the Sudan also label themselves as Islamic. Most countries with an Islamic majority do not have this threat, however, but those that do present a disturbing condition to the international system.

These changes in the international environment illustrate that change is a constant factor; therefore, how the international system functions is also in constant change. Governments change, usually peacefully through an established procedure, but revolutions and coups d'etat are still common. Whether the world is more peaceful today than it was before 1989 is difficult to determine. The only certainty is that a massive nuclear exchange is not the threat it once was.

Also See the Following Articles

ALLIANCE SYSTEMS • BALANCE OF POWER RELATIONSHIPS • COLD WAR • DIPLOMACY • TERRORISM • WARFARE, MODERN

Bibliography

Baldwin, D. A. (ed.). (1993). *Neorealism and neoliberalism: The contemporary debate.* New York: Columbia University Press.

Betts, R. K. (1993). *Conflict after the Cold War: Arguments on causes of war and peace.* New York: Macmillan.

Cashman, G. (1993). *What causes war?* Lexington, MA: Lexington Books.

Garthoff, R. (1994). *The great transition: American–Soviet relations and the end of the Cold War.* Washington, DC: Brookings.

Gregg, R. W. (1993). *About face? The United States and the United Nations.* Boulder, CO: Lynne Rienner.

Holsti, K. J. (1991). *Peace and war: Armed conflicts and international order. 1648–1989.* Cambridge, U.K.: Cambridge University Press.

Huntington, S. P. (1996). *Clash of civilizations and the remaking of world order.* New York: Simon and Schuster.

Klare, M., & Thomas, D.C. (Eds.). (1994). *World security: Challenges for a new century.* New York: St. Martin's Press.

Mann, M. (1990). *The rise and decline of the nation state.* Cambridge, MA: Basil Blackwell.

Mueller, J. (1989). *Retreat from doomsday: The obsolescence of major war.* New York: Basic Books.

Ratner, S. R. (1995). *The new UN peacekeeping.* New York: St. Martin's Press.

Russett, B. (1993). *Grasping the democratic peace: Principles for a post-Cold War world.* Princeton, NJ: Princeton University Press.

Sullivan, M. P. (1990). *Power in contemporary international relations.* Columbia, SC: University of South Carolina.

International Variation in Attitudes toward Violence

Alfred McAlister
University of Texas, School of Public Health

Pamela Orpinas
University of Georgia

Luis Velez
Universidad de Valle, Colombia

I. INTRODUCTION

During the past decades, the region of the Americas has gone through many demographic and sociopolitical changes. Stable democracies have been established in most countries, and internal warfare has decreased. From a health perspective, deaths due to transmittable diseases have been decreasing, while homicides rates, as well as violence against children and partners, have increased in many countries. Faced with this reality, the Pan-American Health Organization (PAHO) has begun to develop programs to promote an accurate evaluation of prevalence and risk factors, as well as to prevent violence and injuries due to violence.

The prevention of violence lies at the intersection of diverse scientific disciplines, traditionally attracting different types of psychologists, sociologists, anthropologists, criminologists, and various experts in policy and urban studies. The scope of inquiry into the causes and control of violence is now being profoundly broadened as another field of science has joined the effort. Because the costs of violence are largely medical, including injuries and mental health problems, it is natural that the problem has come to the attention of specialists in preventive medicine and public health. Epidemiological research has identified multiple risk factors associated with violence, including personal, familial, cultural, and environmental factors that are now subjects of action for public health.

When epidemiologists seek to understand the origin of a disease, it has often been helpful to compare the culture of populations with different rates of that disease. The "seven country studies" of cardiovascular diseases provide an excellent example of this type of research, where surveys of nutrition practices and serum cholesterol levels were combined with data on national rates of heart disease. This study elucidated the role of dietary culture (unsaturated fats) and the value of the "Mediterranean" diet for prevention of cardiovascular disease.

In recent years, epidemiologists and social scientists have also begun to investigate international differences and trends in violent mortality, finding very large differences among and within nations of the Americas in homicide rates (Table I). The situation in Colombia has been thoroughly analyzed, revealing large differences between different cities. In U.S. groups, homicide rates are highest among persons of African origin. In Colombia, homicide rates are lowest in coastal cities with large African-origin populations and highest in the cities with predominantly non-African groups. Studies conducted within the U.S. have found that specific norms and attitudes are associated with different rates of aggressive behaviors in different regions of the U.S. Homicide rates among the dominant ethnic group (Anglo-Americans) are highest in the Southern states of the U.S., where surveys also find a high prevalence of attitudes support-

Copyright © 1999 by Academic Press.
All rights of reproduction in any form reserved.

TABLE I

Homicide Rates in the Region of the Americas

Countries and cities	Rate/100,000
Canada	2.3
Chile	2.8
Colombia	
Total	110.4
Bogota	62.0
Cali	90.9
Medellin	435.1
Cartagena	17.6
Costa Rica	3.9
Mexico	19.4
U.S.	
Total	8.5
White, selected New England cities	1.7
White, selected cities in South	4.8
Latinos in Dallas	31.5
African-Americans in Dallas	68.4

Sources: PAHO: Health Statistics for the Americas (1991, 1994); 1989 World Health Statistics Annual; Nisbett (1993); Gaitan and Diaz (1994); McAlister and Dozier (1995).

ing violence. Baron and Straus have found a relationship between homicide and an index of legitimate violence that reflects different cultural norms in different U.S. states.

According to Bandura, the infliction of suffering is excused or justified through processes of "moral disengagement." When some kind of reaction is deemed necessary by a dispute or grievance, the selection of response is influenced by the person's perceptions of their skills and resources and by their attitudes toward alternative violent on nonviolent means of conflict resolution. For example, even when a person has the skills and resources need to effectively use the legal justice system, they may not consider it to be an acceptable means for settling some disputes. Cohen and Nisbett found that persons from violent Southern cultures were more likely to malign the "manhood" of individuals who would not respond with illegal violence to some provocations (e.g., rape of a daughter). Even when a person considers a nonviolent alternative to be socially acceptable in a case like that, e.g., reporting it to the police, the person may rather seek personal revenge than legal prosecution if the trust in the police system is low. Trust and confidence ultimately depend upon the availability and quality of justice and mediation systems that are made available. When legal or political systems fail to resolve conflicts or satisfy grievances, forms of protest (e.g., violent versus peaceful) may

come to mirror the forms of reaction to that protest (e.g., violently oppressive versus conciliatory). On both sides if this exchange, the degree of forceful violence depend upon the attitudes and skills of the participants.

Attitudes, skills, and perceptions of institutions may also influence national responses to international conflict. The effectiveness of international mediation and diplomacy, while greatly aided by formal structures such as the UN, is dependent upon the "grassroots" attitudes and skills of the people who are experiencing and helping to resolve the conflict. In democracies, the propensity to make war and invest national product in military capability may depend upon public attitudes toward war and military as measured in opinion polls such as the General Social Survey.

To help understand the factors that lead to differences in rates of violence, further studies are needed to describe and analyze skills, attitudes, and cultural beliefs between and within different countries. Through this type of research, it may be possible to identify the specific beliefs and other factors that are most important in the social etiology of violence. The purpose of this paper is to examine and compare cultural norms regarding violence in nine cities: seven large metropolitan areas in Latin America, Madrid in Spain, and Houston/Austin, Texas, in the U.S. Results are based on Project ACTIVA: Cultural Norms and Attitudes toward Violence in Selected Cities of the Region of the Americas and Spain. Project ACTIVA, a regional initiative coordinated by the PAHO, was a multicenter project designed to evaluate violence and related cultural norms and attitudes in selected cities of the Region of the Americas and Spain. The study was an inter-American effort supported by technical cooperation provided by the Pan-American Sanitary Bureau and by research centers of excellence in the Region, with joint financing by both entities. The PAHO provided technical cooperation and financing for the development of the survey, meetings of investigators, revision and compilation of data sets, and dissemination of results. Investigators guaranteed financing from grants from their own country for data collection and analysis. This article presents selected national comparisons. More detailed reports were published by Orpinas in the *Pan American Journal of Public Health*.

II. METHODOLOGY

A. Design and Sample

ACTIVA researchers surveyed a sample of the population between 18 and 70 years of age living in households

TABLE II

Description of the Sample by City in Percentages

	Bahia, Brazil (n = 1384)	Cali Colombia (n = 2288)	Caracas, Venezuela (n = 1297)	Madrid, Spain (n = 1105)	Rio de Janeiro, Brazil (n = 1105)	San Jose, Costa Rica (n = 1131)	San Salvador, El Salvador (n = 1290)	Santiago, Chile (n = 1212)	Texas, USA (n = 1110)
Gender									
Men	45.7	46.4	39.0	38.8	43.4	42.4	44.7	46.8	47.0
Women	54.3	53.6	61.0	61.2	56.6	57.6	55.3	53.2	53.0
Age									
18–24	22.4	22.5	21.7	19.8	18.1	20.1	20.8	20.4	14.6
25–44	51.4	52.6	49.5	43.4	46.9	43.5	50.1	49.7	49.8
45–65	23.5	21.5	24.1	29.0	29.3	29.1	24.7	24.8	30.2
65+	2.7	3.3	4.8	7.7	5.7	7.3	4.5	5.1	5.4
Socioeconomic status									
High	8.2	9.9	2.3	19.8	14.5	13.6	12.6	13.9	—
Medium	36.6	41.5	24.2	59.8	27.2	51.0	35.4	28.8	—
Low	55.2	48.6	73.5	20.4	58.3	35.4	51.9	57.3	—
Education									
Elementary or less	24.1	23.2	13.7	26.4	34.9	19.4	26.7	11.9	5.3
Secondary	53.3	60.5	44.8	38.3	35.1	39.3	40.3	56.4	28.7
College or technical	22.7	16.3	41.5	35.3	30.0	41.3	33.0	31.7	66.0

in the metropolitan areas of selected cities. Between September, 1996 and March, 1997, representative samples were selected in each city through a multistage sampling procedure. The sample was stratified by clusters so as to be proportional in terms of socioeconomic condition and population density. Sample size was approximately 1,200 individuals per city. Individuals were selected within households by systematic sampling without substitution. Data were collected using a common questionnaire. A total of 10,821 adults were surveyed in their households in eight cities: El Salvador-Bahia (n = 1384) and Rio de Janeiro (n = 1114), Brazil; Santiago, Chile (n = 1212); Cali, Colombia (n = 2288); San José, Costa Rica (n = 1131); San Salvador, El Salvador (n = 1290); Madrid, Spain (n = 1105); and Caracas, Venezuela (n = 1297) (Table II). Due to sampling differences, in two cities, Santiago and Cali, the data from those cities was adjusted for socioeconomic status and gender to represent the distribution of the population. Women were slightly more represented in the sample than in the population. Survey response rates varied by city and socioeconomic status and were lowest in the high socioeconomic stratum and highest in the low stratum.

The U.S. survey in Texas (Harris County/Houston and Travis County/Austin) was conducted through telephone interviews of a random sample of adults between 18 and 70 years of age. The questionnaire contained approximately one-third of the questions of the ACTIVA common questionnaire. In Texas, 1110 persons (500 in Austin and 610 in Houston) between 18 and 70 years old were interviewed by phone (Table II).

B. Instrument

1. Instrument Development

In January, 1996, the Pan-American Health Organization, in collaboration with the WHO Collaborating Center at University of Texas–Houston, organized a meeting in Houston with Latin American investigators to design a common household survey of adults. During the next year, the survey was pilot-tested four times, manuals for data collection and data management were developed, and the survey and sampling methodology was specified. All the investigators involved in the project participated in reviewing and refining the protocol and the final design of the questionnaire to be used in the cities. Investigators agreed on standardized survey items to measure the attitudes, norms, and perceptions of social institutions.

The process of selection of the items was guided by theory, research on risk factors, and experience of the participating investigators. Albert Bandura's social cognitive learning theory provided the theoretical framework for the selection of variables to be measured. The central concepts in this model are attitudes and beliefs (based on outcome expectations) and self-efficacy (beliefs about one's own skills and abilities). Attitudes are measured by asking about specific behaviors and the person's agreement with evaluative adjectives about those behaviors (e.g., good–bad, necessary–unnecessary, approved–unapproved), while self-efficacy is measured by asking whether the person agrees that he or she would be able to perform the behavior in question. According to theory, behavior can be predicted by attitudes toward specific actions and by self-efficacy. Thus, for example, physical punishment of children can be predicted by attitudes toward punishment (e.g., the belief that it is necessary to raise children properly) and by self-efficacy for nonviolent alternatives (e.g., the ability to control a children's behavior by using rewards or reasoning with them). When people choose violence to resolve conflicts, their attitudes and abilities influence a process of "moral disengagement," which justifies or excuses the infliction of suffering.

The final questionnaire included, among other variables, perceptions of efficiency of the police system and attitudes toward democracy, war, family violence, homicide, and weapon-carrying. Self-efficacy measures included self-control, nonviolent discipline for children, and communication with spouse. The questionnaire consisted of items with closed-ended alternatives. Variables were measured by statements followed by a 3-point or a 5-point scale from which respondents were asked to choose alternatives. This article provides data only on selected items from the surveys, which are described below. A full report is published by PAHO.

One item evaluated respondents' perception of efficiency of the police in a 5-point scale ranging between "very good" and "very bad." One item measured attitude toward war: "War is necessary to settle differences between countries." Three items measured attitudes toward family violence: "Corporal punishment is necessary to bring up children properly," "There are situations in which a man is justified in slapping his wife in the face," and "There are situations in which a woman is justified in slapping her husband in the face." Four items measured respondent's attitudes toward personal violence and weapon-carrying: "A person has the right to kill to defend his/her family (or property)," "A weapon in the house makes the home safer," and "Carrying a gun makes a person safer." Another item concerning community violence contained the statement: "If authorities fail, people have the right to take justice in their own hands." Agreement with these items was rated on a 5-point scale ranging between "strongly agree" and "strongly disagree." Three additional items concerned approval of extra-legal killing in the community. Approval of the acts cited in these three items was measured in a 3-point scale: "would approve," "would not approve but understand," "would neither approve nor understand." The items were "If your community feels threatened by an individual and someone kills this

person, you ..." "Suppose a person kills someone who has raped his/her child, you ..." and "If a group of people begin to carry out 'social cleansings,' that is, to kill undesirable people, you ..." Another item evaluated perceptions of democracy. Respondents had to choose among three alternatives: "Democracy is the best political system under any circumstances," "In certain circumstances a dictatorship could be good," and "Whether we live in a democracy or in a dictatorship makes no difference to people like me."

C. Statistical Analyses

Data were analyzed for the selected items by city and gender. Percentages were weighted by gender to avoid the effect of differential gender distribution in the different samples. The precision of the proportion estimates depends on the frequency of the response and the sample size. For a city with a sample size of 1200, very frequent (90%) or infrequent responses (10%) were generally accurate within 2 percentage points. This means that the true score will be between 2 percentage points over or under the present findings 95 out of 100 times. Responses in the middle range (near 50%) were generally accurate within 3 percentage points. The Pearson correlation coefficient was used to evaluate the association between confidence in the police system and support for taking the law in their own hands.

III. RESULTS

Figure 1 shows that confidence in the police system was highest in Texas, followed by Santiago and Madrid,

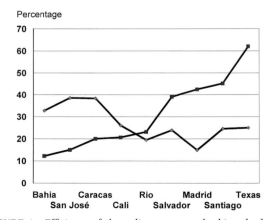

FIGURE 1 Efficiency of the police system and taking the law in own hands by city.

TABLE III

Frequencies of Agreement with Attitude Statements Regarding Democracy and Violence by City in Percentages

Attitude Statements	Salvador de Bahia, Brazil	Cali, Colombia	Caracas, Venezuela	Madrid, Spain	Rio de Janeiro, Brazil	San Jose, Costa Rica	San Salvador, El Salvador	Santiago, Chile	Austin/Houston Texas, USA
Democracy									
Democracy is the best political system	67.6	—	62.7	83.3	62.3	87.5	73.3	61.3	85.9
In some occasions, dictatorship is good	9.3	—	23.3	7.9	19.1	6.5	5.3	11.8	8.1
War[b]									
War is necessary to settle differences between countries	11.2	9.1	12.5	3.8	9.6	4.4	6.8	7.3	23.7
Gov. should negotiate with groups using violence	70.8	58.7	78.4	59.2	78.7	71.9	84.0	59.2	55.8
Justification of weapons and homicide									
Keeping a weapon makes the home safer[b]	23.7	23.7	24.5	14.1	19.3	24.4	18.1	24.6	34.7
Carrying a weapon makes a person safer[b]	12.9	20.1	24.0	17.3	11.3	28.9	14.4	21.1	21.4
Right to kill to defend family[b]	59.2	48.4	71.3	48.4	61.6	60.9	60.0	60.5	78.5
Right to kill to defend property[b]	38.8	35.0	61.7	18.0	45.9	43.9	42.8	49.8	42.9
OK to kill a person who threatens the community[c]	35.5	—	32.8	7.3	26.5	14.7	22.1	19.8	10.0
OK to kill an undesirable people ("social cleansing")	15.8	13.3	21.1	5.4	11.0	8.4	15.7	5.8	1.4
OK to kill rapist of child[b]	57.9	36.3	48.5	19.7	42.0	31.5	38.7	54.0	26.8
Justification of family violence[b]									
Corporal punishment is necessary for children	25.3	33.5	8.5	6.3	10.2	15.8	15.2	5.1	36.4
Sometimes is justified: men slap wife	5.6	11.0	8.3	4.9	5.0	3.4	4.9	6.9	—
Sometimes is justified: women slap husband	5.7	—	14.5	5.4	8.0	7.3	6.5	9.7	28.8

Note. To avoid the effect of differential gender distribution in the different samples, all percentages were weighted by gender.

[a] Percentage of respondents who staged "very good" or "good."

[b] Percentage of respondents who "strongly agree" or "agree."

[c] Percentage of respondents who "would approve."

TABLE IV

Support for War by City and Demographic Variables in Percentages[a]

	Bahia, Brazil	Cali, Colombia	Caracas, Venezuela	Madrid, España	Rio, Brazil	San Jose, Costa Rica	San Salvador, El Salvador	Santiago, Chile	Texas, USA
Total	11.0	8.8	11.5	3.3	9.2	4.2	6.7	7.3	23.4
Gender									
Men	12.7	12.7	17.0	5.9	12.4	5.8	7.8	9.0	27.9
Women	9.5	5.5	8.0	1.6	6.7	3.1	5.9	5.7	19.5
Age									
18–24	14.5	10.7	11.0	1.4	14.4	4.8	6.0	5.3	26.7
25–44	8.7	8.8	11.7	3.1	9.3	2.9	7.1	8.5	20.1
45–65	11.7	7.3	11.9	5.0	5.6	5.2	6.9	7.0	25.7
65+	18.9	6.7	9.7	2.4	10.9	7.2	5.2	3.2	32.8
Education									
Elementary or less	14.7	10.4	9.6	2.4	5.9	6.8	6.9	6.8	22.8
Secondary	10.7	8.4	10.8	2.5	10.0	2.3	7.2	6.3	26.0
College or technical	6.2	9.9	12.7	4.9	6.8	5.2	5.0	10.3	22.4

[a] Percentage that strongly agrees or somewhat agrees that "war is necessary."

and lowest in Venezuela. In Texas, almost two-thirds of the population rated the police system as "good" or "very good." In the rest of the cities, less than half of the respondents rated the police positively. Cities with lower confidence in the police tended to have a stronger support for taking the law in their hands. The Pearson correlation coefficient between these two lines was −0.58.

One-third of the respondents in Texas stated that keeping a weapon makes the home safer, however, less than a fourth of the population of the other cities believed that keeping weapons at home increased security. Surprisingly, the highest support for the belief that carrying weapons makes the person safer was in San José, Costa Rica (Table III). Over half of the respondents approved of killing to defend the family. The highest approval was in Texas, followed by Caracas. Approval of killing to defend property was less strong in all cities. One in five respondents in Madrid approved killing to defend the property, while two in three respondents in Caracas approved it. Justification of killing not in self-defense or to defend the family followed a different pattern. Justification of killing people who threaten the community and of "social cleansings" was highest in Cali, Caracas, and Bahia, and lowest in Madrid and Texas. Madrid and Texas also had the lowest approval of killing someone who has raped their child (Table III).

The strongest support for war as a way to solve international conflicts and the least support for the government to negotiate with groups that use violence was found in Texas. In Texas, almost one-fourth of the population (28% of the men and 20% of the women) stated that war was necessary, almost twice as high as the percentage of approval of the next highest city: Caracas (17% of the men and 8% of the women). The lowest support for war was in Madrid (6% of the men and 2% of the women), San José (6% of the men and 3% of the women), and Santiago (9% of the men and 6% of the women) (Table IV). In all cities, a stronger support for war was found among men than women. Support for war did not vary by educational level. Figure 2 shows that the U.S. stands alone both in national military spending and, in the Texas surveys, public support for wars to resolve international differences.

In spite of the strong support of Texans to use violence to defend the family, Texans also showed the strongest support for violence against the family. The strongest support for corporal punishment was found in Texas and Cali, where one-third of the population agreed that corporal punishment of children is necessary. Justification of partner violence was also highest in Texas and Cali. (Table V).

VI. CONCLUSIONS

This article shows that preliminary research and theorization is sufficient for the development of an approach to international measurement of important attitudes and other cultural factors across the entire spectrum of violence. The results clarified some international differences in levels of violence, e.g., high levels of extralegal

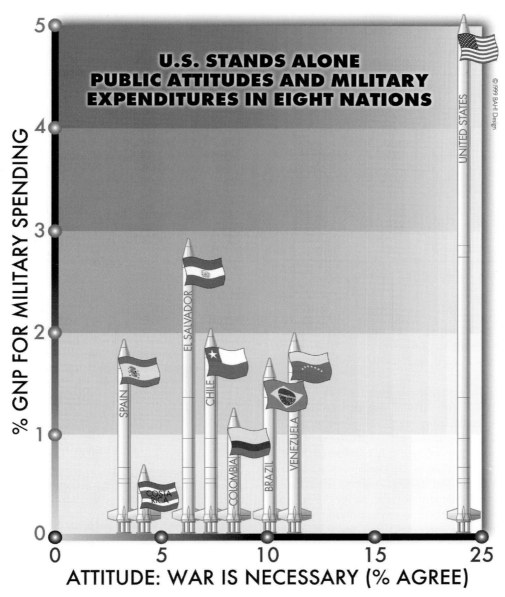

FIGURE 2 Surveys of attitudes (p = 1105 − 2288) and analyses of spending (Sivard, 1993) show highest support for war and military force in U.S. populations. Military spending is calculated as a proportion of GNP (gross net product).

execution in some Latin American cities. The ACTIVA surveys found that support for "social cleansing" and extralegal executions is strongly related to lack of confidence in police and justice institutions. The U.S. survey respondents in Texas expressed relatively high confidence in police and very little support for social cleansing. However, the Texas samples were consistently high in their support for other forms of violence, ranging from home defense to punishment of children.

This finding is consistent with numerous other studies of regional differences in the U.S. The Texas sample expressed the greatest support for war, a factor that is probably related to international differences in military spending. High levels of "moral disengagement" in U.S. support for war have also been found in recent surveys comparing young people in the U.S. and Europe. In a survey of adults in Texas during 1998, 39% agreed that "war is necessary" (44% of men and 34% of women).

TABLE V
The Item "Corporal Punishment Is Necessary for Children" by City and Demographic Variables (in Percentages)[a]

	Bahia, Brazil	Cali, Colombia	Caracas, Venezuela	Madrid España	Rio, Brazil	San Jose, Costa Rica	San Salvador, El Salvador	Santiago, Chile	Texas, USA
Total	25.0	33.6	8.7	6.0	10.5	15.7	15.2	5.0	36.2
Gender									
Men	28.4	31.8	7.3	8.2	7.6	16.3	15.3	6.0	39.6
Women	22.2	35.2	9.6	4.6	12.8	15.3	15.1	4.2	33.6
Age									
18–24	20.3	27.0	5.7	2.7	12.9	12.3	11.6	2.8	34.6
25–44	25.3	36.8	9.5	4.2	10.8	15.7	15.8	5.8	35.6
45–65	28.6	31.8	9.3	9.4	8.3	16.4	16.4	5.3	36.9
65+	28.9	37.8	11.3	11.8	12.5	22.9	19.0	4.8	43.3
Education									
Elementary or less	31.5	39.4	10.8	7.7	7.5	18.2	20.6	8.4	33.9
Secondary	20.3	32.4	6.6	4.2	8.3	15.2	12.5	3.9	39.0
College or technical	28.3	26.5	10.3	4.5	11.2	15.0	12.9	4.6	35.3

[a] Percentages that strongly agree or somewhat agree.

These studies, coordinated by the International Federation of Medical Students Associations, also show that general attitudes toward war predict opinions about specific military actions.

Despite the differences in manifestations and degrees of complexity, all forms of violence can probably be understood to result from measurable concepts that operate according to basic theoretical processes of social learning. Through survey research conducted from a public health perspective, it is possible to study and compare levels of cultural "risk factors" and, eventually, to develop international and population-level programs to reduce them. In addition to environmental changes such as better law enforcement and more equitable economic development, comprehensive prevention programs for the prevention of violence must include cultural change through the promotion of nonviolent attitudes, beliefs, and behaviors, i.e., a "culture of peace and conviviality" (Guerrero et al., 1994).

Also See the Following Articles

CULTURAL STUDIES, OVERVIEW • HOMICIDE • JUSTIFICATION FOR VIOLENCE

Acknowledgments

This research was partially funded by a grant from the PanAmerican Health Organization and the Carnegie Corporation. The views expressed here are those of the authors. Participating Investigators: Rebecca de los Rios (PAHO, Washington, D.C., USA), Rodrigo Guerrero (Universidad de Valle, Colombia), Leandro Piquet Carneiro (Universidade do Sao Paulo, Brazil), Ceci Vilar Noronha (Instituto de Saude Coletiva, Brazil), Enrique Oviedo (Sur Profesionales Consultores, Ltda., Santiago, Chile), Marco V. Fournier (Universidad de Costa Rica), Jose Miguel Cruz Alas (Instituto Universitario de Opinion Pública, El Salvador), Roberto Briceno-Leon (Universidad Central de Venezuela), Florentino Moreno (Universidad Complutense, Madrid, Spain).

Bibliography

Anderson, E. (1976). The social and cultural roots of political violence in Central America. *Aggressive Behavior, 2,* 249–256.

Anderson, E. (May, 1994). The code of the streets. *Atlantic Monthly,* 81–94.

Ayres, E. L. (1984). *Vengeance and justice.* New York: Oxford University Press.

Bandura, A. (1973). *Aggression: A social learning analysis.* Englewood Cliffs, NJ: Prentice–Hall.

Bandura, A. (1986). *Social foundations of thought and action: A social cognitive theory.* Englewood Cliffs, NJ: Prentice–Hall.

Bandura, A. (1990). Mechanisms of moral disengagement. In W. Reich (Ed.), *Origins of terrorism: Psychologies, ideologies, theologies, states of mind* (Ch. 9, pp. 161–191). New York: Woodrow Wilson International Center for Scholars/Cambridge University Press.

Bandura, A. (1991). Social cognitive theory of moral thought and action. In W. M. Kurtines & J. L. Gewirtz (Eds.), *Handbook of Moral Behavior and Development: Theory.* (Vol. I, Ch. 1, pp. 45–103). Hillsdale, NJ: Erlbaum.

Baron, L. (1989). Four theories of rape: A macrosociological analysis. *Social Problems, 34,* 467–489.

Baron, L., & Straus, M. A. (1988). Cultural and economic sources of homicide in the United States. *The Sociological Quarterly, 29(3),* 371–390.

Baron, L., Straus, M. A., & Jaffee, D. (1988). Legitimate violence, violent attitudes, and rape: A test of the cultural spillover theory. *Annals of the New York Academy of Sciences, 528,* 79–110.

Baron, R. A. (1977). *Human aggression.* New York: Plenum.

Berkowitz, L. (1964). The effects of observing violence. *Scientific American, 21,* 35–41.

Berkowitz, L. (1968). The study of urban violence: Some implications of laboratory studies of frustration and aggression. *American Behavioral Scientists, 2,* 14–17.

Berkowitz, L. (1989). Frustration-aggression hypothesis: Examination and reformulation. *Psychological Bulletin, 106*(1), 59–73.

Berkowitz, L., Parke, R. D., Leyens, J. P., & West, S. G. (1974). Reactions of juvenile delinquents to "justified" and "less justified" movie violence. *Journal of Research in Crime and Delinquency, 11,* 16–24.

Blackburn, H. (1983). Research and demonstration projects in community cardiovascular disease prevention. *Journal of Public Health Policy, 4*(4), 398–421.

Blumenthal, M. D., Kahn, R. L., Andrews, F. M., & Head, K. B. (1972). *Justifying violence: Attitudes of American men.* Ann Arbor, MI: Institute for Social Research.

Burton, J. W., & Sandole, D. J. D. (1987). Expanding the debate on generic theory of conflict resolution: A response to a critique. *Negotiation Journal, 3*(1), 97–99.

Cohen, D., & Nisbett, R. E. (1994). Self-protection and the culture of honor: Explaining southern violence. *Personality and Social Psychology Bulletin, 20*(5), 551–567.

Comstock, G., & Paik, H. (1991). *Television and the American child.* San Diego, CA: Academic Press.

Daly, M., & Wilson, M. (1988). *Homicide.* Hawthorne, NY: Aldine De Gruyter.

Daro, D. (1988). *Confronting child abuse: Research for effective program design.* New York: The Free Press.

de Roux, G. I. (1994). Ciudad y violencia en America Latina. In F. Carrion, A. Concha, & G. Cobo (Eds.), *Ciudad y violencias en America Latina: Programa de gestion urbana* (Vol. 2). PGU: Oficina Regional Para America Latina y El Caribe.

Deutsch, M. (1962). Psychological alternatives to war. *The Journal of Social Issues, 18*(2), 97–119.

Devine, P. H. (1989). When peacekeeping does not lead to peace: Some notes on conflict-resolution. *Bulletin of Peace Proposals, 18*(1), 47–53.

Eron, L. D. (1987). The development of aggressive behavior from the perspective of developing behaviorism. *American Psychologist, 42*(5), 435–442.

Espitia, V. E., Guerrero, Velasco, R., & Concha Eastman, A. (1994). Viligancia epidemiologica de los homicidios ocurridos en Cali. Enero a diciembre de 1993. La epidemiologia aplicada a la administracion publica. In A. Concha Eastman, F. Carrion, & G. Cobo (Eds.), *Ciudad y violencias en America Latina* (pp. 155–165). Quito, Ecuador: Programa de Gestion Urban.

Fagan, J., Piper, E. S., & Moore, M. (1986). Violent delinquents and urban youth. *Criminology, 24,* 439–472.

Fagan, J. (1990). Intoxication and aggression. In *Drugs and crime: Crime and justice: A review of research* (Vol. 13). University of Chicago.

Fondaraco, M. R., & and Heller, K. (1990). Attributional style in aggressive adolescent boys. *Journal of Abnormal Child Psychology, 18*(1), 75–89.

Fournier, M., de los Ríos, R., Orpinas, P., Piquet-Carneiro, L. (1999). Multicenter study on attitudes and cultural norms toward violence (Project ACTIVA): Methodology. [in Spanish]. *Pan American Journal of Public Health, 5*(4/5), 222–231.

Franco, S. (1990). La violencia: Un problema de salud publica que se agrava en la region. PAHO.

Gaitan Daza, F., & Diaz Moreno, J. (1994). La violencia Colombiana. Algunos elementos explicativos. In Fernando Carrion, Alberto Concha and German Cobo (Eds.), *Ciudad y violencias en America Latina: Programa de gestion urbana* (Vol. 2). PGU: Oficina Regional Para America Latina y El Caribe.

Guerrero, R., et al. (1994). Unpublished data, Cali, Colombia.

Guerrero, R., McAlister, A., Concha Eastman, A., & Espitia, V. E. (1995). Personal disarmament deters homicide in Cali, Colombia. Unpublished report.

Hammock, G. S., & Richardson, D. R. (1992). Aggression as one response to conflict. *Journal of Applied Social Psychology, 22*(4), 298–311.

Homer-Dixon, T. F. (February, 1993). Environmental change and violent conflict. *Scientific American,* 38–45.

Huesmann, L. R., & Eron, L. D. (1984). Cognitive processes and the persistence of aggressive behavior. *Aggressive Behavior, 10,* 243–251.

International Federation of Medical Students Associations (Standing Committee on Refugees and Peace) (1999). Attitudes toward war, killing and the punishment of children among young people in U.S., Finland, Russia, Estonia and Romania. Helsinki: National Public Health Institute, Department of Epidemiology.

Keegan, J. (1993). *A history of warfare.* London: Hutchinson.

Keen, S. (1986). *Faces of the enemy.* New York: Harper & Row.

Keys, A. (1970). Coronary heart disease in seven countries (Monograph No. 29). New York: American Heart Association.

Kleck, G., & Patterson, E. B. (1993). The impact of gun control and gun ownership levels on violence rates. *J. Quantitative Criminology, 9,* 249–87.

Koop, C., & Lundberg, G. (1992). Violence in America: A public health emergency. *Journal of the American Medical Association, 267*(22), 3075–3076.

McAlister, A. (1999). Moral disengagement and opinions on war with Iraq. Unpublished manuscript, University of Texas, School of Public Health.

McAlisiter, A., & Velez, L. (1999). Behavioral sciences concepts in research on the prevention of violence. *Pan American Journal of Public Health, 5*(4/5), 316–321.

McAlister, A., & Kopina, O. (October 1995). Opinions on war: Houston and Moscow. Attitudes toward international relations in public health research institutions in Houston and Moscow. *Houston Peace News.*

McAlister, A., & Velez, L. (1995). Measures and attitudes related to violence in Colombia: Pretest report unpublished. University of Texas.

McAlister, A., & Velez, L. (1995). Pretest of Colombian culture of violence survey. Unpublished manuscript, Center for Health Promotion Research and Development, University of Texas Houston Health Science Center.

McAlister, A., & Dozier, J. (1995). Epidemics of homicide in Texas counties. Unpublished manuscript, University of Texas, School of Public Health.

McAlister, A., Krosnick, J., & Milburn, M. (1984) Causes of adolescent cigarette smoking. *Social Psychology Quarterly, 47*(1), 24–36.

McAlister, A., Orlandi, M., Puska, P., Zbylot, P., & Bye, L. L. (1991). Behavior modification in public health: Principles and illustrations. In W. W. Holland, R. Detels, & E. G. Knox (Eds.), *Oxford textbook of public health.* London: Oxford Medical.

Nisbett, R. E. (1993). Violence and U.S. regional culture. *American Psychologist, 48*(4), 441–449.

National Research Council (1993). *Understanding and preventing violence.* Washington, DC: National Academy Press.

ONU (1989). *La violencia contra la mujer.* New York: ONU.

Orpinas, P. (1999). Who is violent? Factors associated with aggressive behaviors in Latin America and Spain. *Pan American Journal of Public Health, 5*(4/5), 232–244.

PAHO (1993a). La violencia contra las mujeres y las ninas: Analisis y propuestas desde la perspectiva de la salud publica. Documento MSD 13/6.

PAHO (1993b). Violencia y salud. Documento CE111/19.

PAHO Salud y Violencia: Plan de Accion Regional (Dto. PAHO/HPP/CIPS/).

Restrepo, H. (1993). Propuestas de accion para la reduccion de los factores de riesgo de accidentes y violencia. Documento presentado al Seminario Latinoamericano de Urgencias en Salud, Medellin.

Rosenberg, M., O'Carroll, P., & Powell, K. (1992). Let's be clear—Violence is a public health problem. *Journal of the American Medical Association, 267*(22), 3071–3072.

Sivard, R. L. World Military and Social Expenditures 1993. Washington DC: World Priorities, INC.

Slotkin, R. (1992). *Gunfighter nation: The myth of the frontier in twentieth-century America.* New York: Atheneum.

Smith, M. B. (1986). Kurt Lewin Memorial address, 1986: War, peace and psychology. *Journal of Social Issues, 42*(4), 23–38.

Straus, M. A. (1974). Leveling, civility and violence in the family. *Journal of Marriage and the Family, 36,* 13–29.

Straus, M. A., & Gelles, R. J. (1995). Physical violence in American families: Risk factors and adaptation to violence in 8,145 families. New Brunswick, NJ: Transaction.

Yunes, J. (1993). Tendencia de la mortalidad por causas violentas entre adolescentes y jovenes de la region de las Americas. Washington, DC: PAHO.

Yunes, J., & Rajas, D. (1993). Tendencia de la mortalidad por causas violentas entre adolescentes y jovenes de la region de las Americas. Washington, DC: PAHO.

Zylke, J. (1988). Violence increasingly being viewed as problem of public health: Prevention programs attempted. *Journal of the American Medical Association, 260*(18), 2621–2625.

Interpersonal Conflict, History of

William A. Donohue
Michigan State University

Deborah A. Cai
University of Maryland

GLOSSARY

Affiliation Messages Communicating to the receiver a sense of relational belonging and inclusion.

Communication Exchange Sequences Repetitive communication patterns observed in dialogue between two or more individuals.

Integrative Agreement An agreement that takes into account the needs and interests of both parties.

Organizational Climate Perceptions that organizational members have about the organization's conditions of communication openness, such as supportiveness and encouragement of employees to participate in the organization's decision making.

Relational Parameters The boundaries of the social relationship existing between two individuals.

Social Distance The degree of relational separateness felt by one individual toward another.

THE HISTORY OF INTERPERSONAL CONFLICT is fundamentally embedded within the history of interpersonal relationships. Sustained human social contact demands the formation of interpersonal relationships, and the inevitable and frequent changes demanded by those relationships surfaces conflict. For as long as history has reflected on interpersonal relationships, it has also reflected on conflicts associated with changes in relational parameters. For example, creation stories in all religions chronicle conflicts that emerged from changes in relational parameters among the characters, with Adam and Eve and Cain and Abel filling this role in the Judeo-Christian account. Thus, interpersonal conflict must be understood in the context of interpersonal relationships and how they function.

I. INTERPERSONAL RELATIONSHIPS AND CONFLICT

A. Defining Interpersonal Relationships

Interpersonal communication constitutes the production, transmission, and interpretation of symbols by relational partners. This definition focuses on relational partners, or individuals who have unique, personal knowledge of the other and base their production, transmission, and interpretation decisions on this personal knowledge. Interpersonal communication allows partners to exchange resources to help them coordinate their actions to produce the relational rewards necessary for relational maintenance and growth.

Copyright © 1999 by Academic Press.
All rights of reproduction in any form reserved.

According to Hinde, a relationship is a sequence of interchanges that is essentially dyadic, that occurs over an extended period of time, and that has specific cognitive and affective effects. The affective/cognitive relational parameters that partners create over time include goals, expectations, values, feelings, and understandings. Hinde contends that these cognitive and affective understandings are the key features affecting how individuals produce, transmit, and interpret symbols. For example, a number of studies find that negotiators who demonstrate a balanced power orientation, anticipate future interactions with one another, clarify their values on key points, and avoid prolonged periods of negative affect, are more likely to reach integrative, or win-win agreements.

Researchers have identified several key cognitive and affective relational parameters that significantly predict such outcome issues as satisfaction, intimacy, and commitment. A review by Burgoon and Hale finds that the central relational parameters guiding the study of interpersonal relationships include: dominance-submission (control), intimacy (affection, attraction, interest, inclusion), trust, depth, emotional arousal, composure, similarity, formality, and task-social orientation. Topics partners explore that include these kinds of themes, or include these kinds of issues as a subtext to the surface topic, can be considered to be relationally focused.

Hinde emphasizes that these cognitive/affective parameters are altered continuously through communication exchange sequences. Negotiators, for example, use communication tactics to continuously bargain such issues as power, solidarity, formality, and affiliation. Following the key insight by Ruesch and Bateson in 1951 that all communication contains content and relational information, Donohue and Roberto demonstrated how negotiators continuously bargain relational parameters as they interact. A move to interrupt displays power. A move to change the topic rejects the other's ability to control the agenda. A change to more formal language seeks to bolster the speaker's status. The use of humor or pun communicates decreased social distance and increased affiliation. This complex relational negotiation generally occurs underneath the substantive, content negotiations. But both interact so that the relational parameters that evolve out of the discussion serve to shape the kinds of content directions and agreements that are formed.

B. Defining Interpersonal Conflict

In 1973, Deutsch charged that "conflict exists whenever incompatible activities occur. An action that is incom-patible with another action prevents, obstructs, inter-feres, injures, or in some way makes the latter less likely or less effective" (p. 10). From this perspective, interpersonal conflict focuses on incompatible actions associated with the negotiation of relational parameters. Interpersonal conflict is not simply conflict about all incompatible actions in a relationship. Using an example provided by Morton Deutsch, a conflict between a husband and wife about how to treat their son's mosquito bites that does not involve the negotiation of such relational parameters as control, or trust, is not an interpersonal conflict. It is certainly a substantive conflict, but does not involve or even invoke relational issues. However, if the husband and wife begin negotiating relational parameters while discussing the mosquito problem, or arguing overtly about the status of their relationship, then the conflict focuses on relationship issues and qualifies as interpersonal conflict.

It may be possible to make the case that all substantive conflicts involve negotiations about relational parameters making all conflict in some sense interpersonal. For example, Kennedy and Khrushchev's exchange of letters during the Cuban Missile Crisis clearly involved intense negotiations on a relational level associated with status, respect, and control. As a result, this international negotiation over the substantive issues of missiles in Cuba between two adversaries was certainly an interpersonal conflict in addition to being an international conflict. This example illustrates that interpersonal conflict can evolve in any context in which individuals communicate, and in the course of their communication, exchange both relational and content information.

This definition limits our discussion to conflicts associated with the negotiation of relational parameters. As suggested previously, since relationships are an ancient topic, many philosophers have reflected on relational conflict.

II. HISTORICAL PERSPECTIVES

A. Ancient and Medieval Perspectives

Ancient religion and philosophy provide different cultural paradigms for understanding interpersonal conflict. For example, the Jewish Torah emphasizes righteous judgment against wrongdoers with "an eye for an eye" and the instruction by God to completely destroy the enemies of the people of Israel in the time of the patriarchs. In contrast, Christian religious teaching promotes forgiveness. "Turning the other cheek" and the

Golden Rule of "treating others as you would like to be treated" are the common themes toward interpersonal conflict in the New Testament. Across religions, interpersonal conflict is generally represented as being the opposite of loving and peaceful relationships.

Influential in Eastern cultures, Confucius taught that harmony should be valued highly and that a gentleman should have no contentions with others. In addition, Confucian tradition emphasizes the importance of understanding and enacting appropriate roles as a means of maintaining harmony. The "five relationships" of ruler to subject, father to son, elder brother to younger brother, husband to wife, and older to younger, were proposed on the basis that if individuals properly enact their roles with appropriate respect and relationship toward others, order and peace will be maintained within society and harmony will exist between individuals.

Within the ancient Greek and Roman philosophical traditions, management of conflict is at the level of the individual communicating to the audience. For example, Aristotle's emphasis on the effects of the persuader's ethos, logos, and pathos (ethics, logic, and emotion, respectively) on the audience points to the importance of the communicator's responsibility to prepare and deliver effective messages. Socrates and Plato similarly attended to the role of the communicator within the "conversation" as the focus for understanding conflict. Logic and character, in particular, play important roles among the ancient Romans and Greeks, with the emphasis on the communicator's ability to persuade through logical discourse and personal credibility. Thus, conflict is confronted with directness and appropriate argument, rather than avoided to preserve harmony as in Confucian philosophy.

B. Beginning of Modern Perspectives

The Magna Carta in 1215 marks an important development in Western thought as it relates to interpersonal conflict. With its emphasis on guaranteeing individuals rights and freedoms within society, Western thought related to conflict begins to follow a similar shift from considering public entities of government and community as the locus of conflict to beginning to consider the individual as responsible for and affected by conflict. Numerous theoretical and philosophical perspectives have since contributed to the development of Western cultural values toward interpersonal conflict. Darwin's theory of evolution, for example, upholds the value of competition in conflict, giving support to the belief that conflict is fundamental in all existence and those who are more fit to compete are more likely to survive.

Marxist theory similarly promotes the need for struggle and dominance in conflict. Freud further defined the individual and aggressive drives that are exhibited while Adler focused on the individual's drives for self-advancement. These few examples highlight the development of Western thinking about conflict, with the overall focus emphasizing the importance of the individual, and the value of dominance and competition as the individual struggles to survive in a competitive world. It is out of this pattern of thought that many of the developments in understanding interpersonal conflict emerge. Although non-Western cultures that emphasize the collective over the individual do not necessarily share Western views of the individual and may value more cooperative than competitive notions toward conflict, these differences are still, for the most part, not reflected in modern theories and models of interpersonal conflict. In fact, it is the incompatibility between Western and non-Western perspectives regarding the individual and the collective that is a common source of intercultural and international conflicts.

III. MODERN RESEARCH DOMAINS

A. Primary Theories and Models of Interpersonal Conflict

1. Motives-Based Theory

Perhaps the most productive way of beginning a coherent description of modern research domains associated with interpersonal conflict is to begin by focusing on individual, relationally centered motives to understand their impact on conflict. The early work on motives suggests that individuals are intrinsically driven to be included into social groupings, to achieve or accomplish tasks, and to affiliate, or receive some kind of affection from others. Winter's research on international conflict uses this framework to understand how leaders' expressions of these motives in speeches and other communications are precursors to war. Most of the case study material Winter uses are essentially interpersonal exchanges between leaders of states qualifying his research as both international and interpersonal. Interestingly, the research has discovered that as the ratio of power motives to affiliation motives increases, the likelihood of war increases. As these messages become more balanced in communication, the leaders tend to find more diplomatic solutions to their conflicts.

Using a similar research model, Donohue and Roberto examined power and affiliation motives in hostage negotiation. The research focused on the verbal exchanges of hostage takers and hostage negotiators as they constructed their interpersonal relationships. Similar to the Winter research, Donohue and Roberto discovered that when affiliation messages dominated the interaction regardless of whether the power messages were prevalent or not, parties were much more likely to build relational consensus and make progress toward a peaceful resolution of the hostage situation.

The interesting feature of these motives regarding conflict in interpersonal relationships is their role in forging or supporting individual identities. The concept of "face," which stems from traditional social interactionist perspectives (see work by Gottfredson and Hirschi), contends that individuals develop identities through their experiences in satisfying their needs for inclusion, control, and affection. If individuals have been successfully included into important groups, have experienced great success in asserting control in important situations, and have received positive affection from valued individuals, their social identities are likely to be relatively strong. Thus, when others threaten or attack these needs, individuals strive boldly to defend them because they comprise the core of their identity. As Cupach and Canary point out, conflict creates circumstances that are inherently face-threatening. Disagreement suggests rejection of group identity, and the potential loss of affection and control. Thus, when conflict in relationships tips toward relational issues centering on these identity needs, parties lose their focus on substantive issues.

2. Personality Theories

A theoretical staple of interpersonal conflict has been the focus on theories related to individual psychological orientations, often called personality traits. This discussion of traits follows a discussion of motives and needs because, like motives, personality theories seek to identify core individual factors that predispose individuals for conflict in relationships. While needs are more fundamentally tied to individual identities, traits focus more on orientations that do not necessarily define how individuals view themselves socially. Yet, these orientations affect the way in which individuals manage conflict in interpersonal relationships.

For example, one trait that has been researched extensively in the field of communication is the construct of argumentativeness, or a "generally stable trait which predisposes the individual in communication situations to advocate positions on controversial issues and to attack verbally the positions which other people take on these issues" (Infante & Rancer, 1982, p. 72). This trait focuses on predispositions to address issues and

not necessarily attack an individual's character, which is more of an act of aggression. Highly argumentative people are seen as very competent at managing conflict situations because they focus more on issues and avoid personal character or identity attacks. By steering clear of personal attacks, these argumentative individuals are more capable to creating constructive outcomes in conflict situations. Individuals lacking argumentation skills often turn to aggressive identity attacks pulling the focus of the discussion away from substantive issues and more toward relational struggles.

Hample and Dallinger identify another interesting personality trait focusing on the tendency to take conflict personally in which individuals possess a bias that encourages them to view all conflict as contributing to a negative emotional climate. These individuals feel threatened, anxious, damaged, devalued, and insulted whenever conflict arises in a relationship. Self-defense of face becomes the first priority forcing conflict into a more competitive situation. These authors would probably predict that individuals with this trait would display fewer argumentative skills and more aggressive behaviors toward partners in conflict since taking conflict personally encourages individuals to avoid conflict. However, when forced into conflict, these individuals would become aggressive to protect themselves from attack.

Locus of control is another personality trait that emerges in the research as a relatively stable orientation focusing on the issue of how individuals attribute their success or failure in achieving tasks. The difference in locus of control varies not only individually but also across cultures. Western cultures, and the United States in particular, tend to have a strong internal locus of control, where individuals attribute success or failure to their own skills and orientations. Eastern cultures, such as Taiwan and Korea, tend to have a stronger external locus of control, where individuals attribute outcomes to chance, fate, or the actions of powerful others. In relationships, internals have been found to be more able to resolve their marital problems productively than externals. Internals try harder to succeed because they believe they can control the outcome of the discussion and are more likely to rely on integrative, cooperative messages. In contrast, externals give up easily and withdraw taking conflict personally and resorting to more aggressive tactics when forced into conflict and report using more distributive, competitive messages and avoidance messages. Balancing internal and external orientations at the appropriate moments in conflict settings appears to yield more positive outcomes.

Gender is another individual difference that affects

responses to conflict. Gender refers to the social-psychological-cultural meanings attached to one's sex. In a review of research associated with gender differences in conflict, Cupach and Canary found that men and women engage in more similar behaviors than dissimilar behaviors in managing conflict. For example, men and women act in a similar manner in about 75% of the types of behaviors analyzed. The differences that do emerge are relatively counterintuitive. For example, women are more assertive and aggressive while men are more withdrawn and passive and both are equally likely to use cooperative behavior during conflict. Consistent with these findings, women tend to pursue the conflict topic and men tend to withdraw, depending on who wants change in the relationship, because the person resisting change will tend to withdraw regardless of gender. Women also tend to use more tears when they get angry while men view tears as a sign of weakness and capitulation.

3. Conflict Styles Theory

Consistent with the idea that individuals varied in how they approach conflict based on specific internal traits or orientations is the idea that individuals develop habits or general styles of handling conflict, as well. The work by Blake and Mouton is credited with providing the fundamental conceptual framework for this idea. They proposed that any distinct mode of interpersonal conflict management results from what they termed the dual concern model: concern for the production of results, and concern for people. The idea is that people develop a style that balances these dual concerns. The dual concerns have evolved into concern for satisfying one's own goals, and concern for helping the other satisfy their goals by Kilman and Thomas. When one concern dominates the other, or the concerns are equally high or equally low, then a particular conflict style emerges.

Crossing these two concerns yields five distinct styles: integrating (showing a high concern for own and other's goals), avoiding (low concern for own and other's goals), dominating (high concern for own goals), obliging (low concern for own and high concern for other's goals), and compromising (moderate concern for both own and other's goals). These styles are not fixed across situations. People can and do change to break out of destructive patterns of communication. This idea is important because this idea of change separates the styles research from the personality-based approaches to individual differences in managing conflict. The personality-based approaches assume relative stability across situations. The styles approach assumes

that individuals change based on the situations they confront in managing conflict. Researchers have shown that more competitive approaches work best when conflict must be brought out into the open and keep individuals motivated to confront it; more integrative approaches are best when parties are highly interdependent, must work together in the future, and can avoid power problems; and avoidance is best when the conflict is unimportant.

In intercultural comparisons, Confucian cultures such as China, Japan, Korea, Taiwan, and Hong Kong have been found to demonstrate more avoidance in handling interpersonal conflict. Further, Eastern cultures are motivated to avoid conflict because of the importance of avoiding shame. In contrast, Western cultures tend to be more motivated to avoid personal guilt. In conflict styles, the United States and Australia have been found to be more dominating. Further research comparing cultures suggests, however, that when individuals were compared by levels of high or low collectivism, higher collectivism was associated with a more integrative conflict style but low collectivism, or high individualism, did not associate with any one particular conflict style.

4. Attribution Theories

Another theory explaining how individuals react to conflict situations deals with attributions, or explanations that people have for the causes of social events. Individuals search for the causes of conflict to determine how they should respond to the situation. According to Fincham, Bradbury and Scott, people view causes in six different dimensions: a. globality—the extent to which the cause is specific to the situation or is transsituational; b. stability—the cause lasts a long time or is short term; c. locus—the cause is internal or external to the person and relationship; d. intent—the cause was deliberately created or beyond the person's control; e. selfishness—the cause was self serving for the individual; and f. blameworthiness—responsibility for the failure. In interpersonal relationships, individuals seek to protect their positive face or identity as a responsible, reasonable partner that conforms to role expectations. So, individuals tend to select a configuration of attributions that project this appropriate identity.

For example, in a conflict, one partner might accuse the other of being consistently insensitive and uncaring. Notice that this accusation proposes that the cause of the conflict is global (long lasting), demonstrates an external locus on the other's problems, is deliberate on the other's part, and is selfish and blameworthy. Sillars found that roommates who view the cause of the conflict as stable and internal to the partner were more likely than others to engage in more competitive communication styles using threats and sarcasm. When both partners continue to make these kinds of attributions designed to protect their respective relational identities, communication can turn quickly destructive to the relationship. In fact, this tendency to immediately link the cause of the conflict to the partner's internal, stable personality traits is a common attributional bias. Few partners look at themselves first in trying to understand the source of conflict. This bias encourages individuals to avoid conflict because if the source of the problem is external and stable, there is little point in trying to impact the situation. The other person simply has a problem that cannot be solved.

Notice how these theories interrelate to this point. In a relationally focused conflict, issues quickly center on key needs for inclusion, control, and affection that place the parameters of the relationship up for negotiation. This stressful event begins to evoke certain personality traits that are salient to this context. The person might take the conflict quite seriously, view the events from the lens of an external locus of control, and adopt a conflict style that is highly competitive. This person is likely to exhibit the attributional biases that accompany these characteristics and attribute the cause of the conflict to the other's personal problems in an attempt to protect their relational identity. This script, or consistent pattern of conflict handling practices typically leads to an initially competitive communication event from which parties must ultimately extricate themselves. If the parties are not particularly skilled at argumentation, then they will resort to aggressive tactics in an attempt to hurt the other. Thus, it is important to be aware that these orientations combine, and quickly emerge in any relationally sensitive conflict situation.

5. Facework and Identity Theories

This summary suggests that face, or one's situated identity, is an ever-present feature of interpersonal conflict. Research focusing on the area of politeness, such as the research done by Brown and Levinson in the 1980s, suggests that individuals have two kinds of face, or situated identities as they interact with their partners. Negative face refers to the desire to maintain one's freedom or autonomy, and positive face refers to the desire to be liked, or seen as doing the right thing. In any kind of conflict, many studies have found that individuals work hard to appear strong, or free to act as they feel necessary, and appropriate or right. They tend to vigorously defend their face from attacks. When conflict centers directly on such attacks, then substantive issues become quickly secondary. Since interpersonal conflict always exhibits relational challenges, face plays a very important role in the way in which conflict is managed in relationships.

The way communication is used to resolve conflict related to face issues varies across cultures. In low-context cultures, where the content of the message is verbalized and little meaning is left for interpretation, more direct means of defending face and restoring interpersonal relationships are used. Low-context cultures, including the United States, Australia, and most Western cultures, are more likely to rely on modes such as face-to-face negotiations or direct confrontation to resolve the conflict. In high-context cultures, however, message content is interpreted based on the context in which the message is given and the relationship between the communicators. More indirect means of communication are valued so that personal identities and interpersonal relationships are not put at risk. Therefore, in high-context cultures, including China, Japan, and most Eastern cultures, are more likely to rely on more indirect modes for managing interpersonal conflict such as using third parties intervention or simply avoiding the conflict issues altogether to preserve relational harmony.

Studies seeking to understand why individuals in interpersonal conflict resort to violence have focused on the need to manage face or impressions. Felson indicates that individuals resort to aggression to restore an identity that has been attacked. The extreme retaliation rebuilds an external impression of strength. Retaliation is particularly likely if third parties are present since face-saving concerns are heightened with the presence of an audience. Or, individuals can resort to violence if they need to bolster their identity even if the aggression is not a response to a prior attack. Perhaps not all violent acts can be explained using this theory of impression management, but it performs well in understanding ritualistic violence, particularly in a public domain.

In this kind of public domain using the impression management theory, it is easy to see how aggression can quickly escalate and become cyclical. Attack follows attack, with each escalating beyond the prior attack to restore face. Failing to escalate opens the individual to accusations of weakness and exploitation, particularly in cultures in which face is the primary social currency. Breaking the cycle requires resorting to communication to resolve the conflict in which both parties can present solutions that do not center on destroying the other party. Again, the mediation of a third party is often needed to initiate this communication approach.

6. Aggression Theories

Why do people often turn to aggression to solve their interpersonal problems? This question generates a considerable quantity of research and social commentary as social scientists and practitioners search for solutions to help people solve problems with dialogue and not physical or psychological intimidation. To help understand aggression, Felson and Tedeschi begin by categorizing violence into two domains: predatory and dispute related. Predatory violence usually involves acts of exploitation in which the target has done nothing provocative, but is used for some purpose such as demonstrating power, or forcing compliance. Robbery, rape, and bullying are examples of predatory acts. The current thinking is that predatory violence stems from being significantly detached from intimacy, and from membership in rewarding social groups. Predators also experience significant bouts of loneliness. Often the perpetrator sees the target as someone who represents a group that has contributed heavily to the perpetrator's social detachment, so committing violence upon the target helps even the score.

Dispute-related violence is conducted in response to some aggravating event such as a perceived personal attack. Perhaps the most useful theory explaining this kind of violence is by Felson, called a social interactionist approach. This approach holds that aggression is an instrumental behavior used for achieving certain values or goals. That is, aggression is a normal consequence of conflict in human relationships with aggression as one strategy that can be used to solve the problem as perceived by the aggressor. Violence is not "pushed out," or "compelled by" inner forces such as aggressive energy, instincts, hormones, or frustration. When the aggressor perceives that the target has violated an important norm or rule, then aggression is equivalent to punishment. Thus, situational and interpersonal factors are critical in instigating violence and aggression. The antagonists, the third parties watching, and the actor interconnect in a dynamic social exchange that occurs as aggressive incidents escalate.

For example, aggression is used to manage impressions or save face in response to some attack. Retaliation becomes the vehicle to prove strength, prevent future attacks, punish the other for some wrongdoing, or coerce the other into some action. The extensive literature on spouse abuse, rape, and other acts of relationship-based violence supports this interactive approach to aggression and violence. Violence is the tool individuals use, generally in response to some provocative act, to solve a problem. The husband may believe that the wife has not performed some prescribed duty and uses violence to dominate and punish the wife for the infraction.

Studies on urban and ethnic conflict have also sought to identify social and environmental factors that influence aggression such as urbanization, population density, oppressive heat, and competition over resources. In 1963, Hauser identified several features of folk communities that influence communication processes: strength of family bonds, homogeneity of the community, illiteracy, strong solidarity, and reliance on set conventions. In contrast, the heterogeneity, density, and size of cities does not impose the same expected norms on conflict behavior as in folk communities. Thus, the various contexts of cultural social structures affect communication processes and the acceptability of interpersonal conflict and the appropriate modes for handling conflict.

7. Communication Competence Theory

A final theory that has received considerable attention is the Communication Competence Theory, by Spitzberg, Canary, and Cupach. The basic idea is that partners in a relationship judge one another's competence in handling conflict, and this judgment is critical in determining whether the person is satisfied with the relationship. If both partners are competent in handling conflict, they are likely to assess the relationship as rewarding and continue to develop that relationship.

Individuals evaluate competence along two dimensions: effectiveness and appropriateness. Communication is effective when it accomplishes the goals of the communicators. Three kinds of goals are always present in any interpersonal situation: instrumental, self-presentational, and relational goals. Instrumental goals relate to the substantive objectives associated with the communication, like persuading someone to go to a movie. Self-presentational goals relate to saving face, or appearing strong or caring, or whatever impression is necessary to help support the instrumental goals. Relational goals deal with status and power, informality and formality, and attraction, trust, and intimacy. For example, asking someone out on a date (instrumental goal) is generally best accomplished if the person appears confident and caring (self-presentation goal), and is informal, approachable, attractive, and trustworthy (relational goal).

Appropriateness deals with the issue of how individuals accomplish their goals. Do they follow appropriate roles and expectations of others? Do individual strategies conform to appropriate rules for communication and social interaction? Individual partners in a relationship often develop unique roles and rules, and are expected to act within those rules when communicating. Individuals are judged as competent when they are effective and follow the rules.

Within this framework, conflict occurs when individuals demonstrate goals that are incompatible with one another, and/or break rules or role expectations in trying to accomplish goals. For example, an aggressive act is viewed as incompetent because, while it may be effective in accomplishing the individual's instrumental, self-presentational, and relational goals, it violates rules of appropriateness. If partners see one another as incompetent in handling conflict, they become much less invested in the relationship and turn to others who support their goals and their vision of appropriate ways of accomplishing those goals.

8. Summary

These seven theoretical perspectives provide a sample of the most current ways of thinking about conflict in interpersonal relationships. As suggested previously, they overlap a great deal in the following ways:

a. Interpersonal conflict generally revolves around goal and/or process incompatibilities, particularly in the area of relational and self-presentational goals.

b. Interpersonal conflict is often driven by internal needs and individual traits that predispose individuals to either escalate or deescalate the emphasis on relational and self-presentation goals.

c. Conflict is the product of intense social interaction, and must be viewed as a highly complex communicative accomplishment.

B. Marital Conflict

These three generalizations explaining how and why conflict evolves set the stage for better understanding how conflict evolves in various relational contexts. The one context that has received considerable attention is marriage. Since society has so much interest in the health of this institution, scientists have sought to understand how couples manage differences that threaten it. While research in marital conflict focuses specifically on couples who are legally married, the research probably applies broadly to intimate, heterosexual couples who have long-term relationships.

In general, work on marital conflict has moved within three primary domains. First, a number of scholars have expressed an interest in learning how intimate-partner (generally marital) relationships develop over the life span, dividing couples into three groups: young, midlife, and older couples. The young couples face the specific challenge of coping with the rapid pulse of family life, learning how to live with each other, how to respond to declines in relational satisfaction, and how to negotiate roles. Young couples respond to these considerable challenges by using more dynamic behaviors that are often confronting, analytical, and sometimes funny. In contrast, midlife couples have found their equilibrium and solved problems of autonomy and interdependence, which helps their conflict evolve into more analytical, and less confrontational forms. Older couples avoid intense analyses of relational issues and are quite passive in their conflict interactions. Across the life span, conflict becomes more problem centered and less relationally centered as key issues naturally fall away due to relational longevity.

The second domain of research in marital conflict deals with the issue of marital types, or the manner in which couples define and enact the nature of their interdependence. The research seeks to disclose the kinds of psychological and behavioral patterns couples exhibit in their marriages and the impact of those patterns on their conflict habits. The chief contributor to this line of research, Fitzpatrick, has identified three general marital (pure) types: traditionals (adhering to traditional marital roles with the male as the breadwinner and the woman assuming domestic duties), separates (couples detached from one another physically and emotionally), and independents (couples who form partnerships for mutual goal achievement, but reject traditional values). Traditionals avoid conflict over relational issues since those have been largely sorted out, and instead focus on larger substantive issues related to such problems as financial management. This group prefers to use cooperative conflict management strategies. Separates avoid conflict altogether, and even seek to constrain their partner's ability to raise issues of disagreement. Since conflict pulls people together, separates find this kind of behavior unrewarding. Independents move in the opposite direction by actively confronting differences and often prevent their partners from withdrawing from important conflicts.

The third area of marital conflict focuses on communication, or the messages that couples exchange and the manner in which these exchanges create contexts that are tied into couples' levels of martial satisfaction and functioning. For example, Gottman examined the kinds of communication patterns between couples who lived in unsatisfactory marriages. He discovered that these couples were not very mutually supportive, or skilled at negotiating differences when discussing their marital problems. They were less likely to actively listen to one another's positions on issues, and more likely to repeat their own positions and labeling the other person's feelings and intentions. In addition, these unhappy couples were more likely to enter a complaining loop at the beginning of their discussions that consisted of one party complaining, while the other ignored the issue surrounding the complaint. Nonverbally, these couples were also much more likely to reciprocate negative feelings about one another and much less likely to reciprocate positive feelings.

In another impressive program of research, Notarius and Markman also examined the nature of couple communication patterns. Their results contrasted sharply with prior research that relied heavily on psychological predictors of marital success. In general, their studies demonstrated very clearly that psychological compatibilities or incompatibilities were significantly less important in relationships than how couples managed conflict communicatively. For example, they learned that personality traits do not predict marital happiness or marital stability. Similarity and difference is much less important than how couples handle their differences. In fact, they even dismissed the issue of need compatibility and such cornerstone traits as relational intimacy as predictors of happiness. Couples who handle conflict poorly regardless of gender, personality, or need differences are significantly less likely to survive. For example, when couples enter a pursuit-withdrawal cycle, they tend to become relationally focused and ignore substantive issues. Traditionally, the woman pursues the issue and the man withdraws. These roles feed off each other because as the woman pursues more the man withdraws more, making meaningful conversation very difficult. Similar to the Gottman findings, when couples learn to step out of such roles and adopt more active listening strategies, the relational issues are taken off the table and parties are capable of focusing on substantive issues.

C. Family Conflict

Moving a step further into a more complex relational system is research dealing with family conflict. Understandably, this research views families as complex systems that deal with conflict in complex ways depending upon how the system functions. For example, in her synthesis of several systems perspectives on family functioning, Sieburg identifies four types of family systems and discusses how they deal with differences. A System One family demonstrates low familial involvement and indifference with weak connections and a limited capacity to deal with stress. When conflicting issues arise,

this family system avoids them. Feedback is generally lacking, and the use of conflict for system self-correction is limited because parties will not stay with it to resolve divisive issues.

System Two families are unresponsive to changes in its members, or changes in the environment. They rely on already-programmed behavioral patterns, applying old rules to new situations, using old information, and avoiding new information. Because this closed, inflexible system is dedicated to keeping things the way they are, conflict is more frequent than in the System One families because there is more communication. However, the conflict is still very limited and highly ritualistic. This family lives with the illusion of family togetherness, but excludes individual preferences requiring that individuals avoid authentic conflict, control the expression of spontaneous anger, and avoid any potential source of unpleasantness. Conflict often takes the form of ritualistic, pointless bickering in repetitive family quarrels.

System Three families are troubled with extreme instability and little or no structure. In this system, communication is very ambiguous so that there may be little disagreement, or turbulent disagreement. These families demonstrate a very fragmented, interruptive communication style with hints of underlying power struggles. The most notable characteristics of these disordered families are confusion and convolution, denial and manipulation. Individuals are invited to take the lead, then criticized; opinions are solicited then rejected. So, family members avoid personal blame by external attribution of cause. Parents speak in riddles, and children are not permitted to raise questions about these riddles. This ambiguity places great stress on relational issues because they are always at the forefront of every family interaction. This trait promotes a highly volatile environment.

System Four families are termed the open-facilitative families. Members are open to new information and interface freely outside the environment. They constantly seek to grow as opposed to preserve the status quo. Conflicts can be resolved in a number of different ways as rules for managing conflict are flexible. Members feel loved and supported, intimacy is present, and autonomy is respected and nurtured. In this environment, members can concentrate more on substantive issues since members grant one another's relational needs. Generational separation is maintained, leadership is stable, appropriate, and recognized, yet all have a voice in decision making.

While conflict frequency differs by system type, researchers suggest that the family conflict process evolves through five recognizable stages. The first is the prior conditions stage focusing on the situation and circumstances preceding the actual conflict such as role responsibilities, family rules, power struggles, negative experiences, and so on. The second is the frustration awareness stage in which a frustration surfaces that is focused on another member of the family. Sorting out these frustrations is difficult, which leads to the active conflict stage in which the conflict escalates into a full-blown discussion, both verbal and nonverbal. Depending upon the family system, this third stage can be very vociferous or very subdued. At the fourth stage, the solution stage, parties get past relational issues and focus on substantive matters, ultimately bargaining around a specific solution to the problem. The final stage is the follow-up stage in which family members review the conflict after it has been resolved to provide additional understanding about the implications of the conflict for family functioning.

D. Crisis Conflict

One area of interpersonal conflict that has a broad range of applications explores the area of crisis bargaining. In a series of studies, Donohue and his colleagues have sought to understand how hostage takers and police negotiators develop a relationship during a hostage negotiation incident, and how that relationship impacts outcomes. A theoretical framework for conceptualizing relationships is offered that functions across two dimensions: affiliation (trust, liking, acceptance) and interdependence (the mutual acceptance of rights and obligations). A coding system for verbal immediacy was developed that was used to track the relationship between the principle parties as it moved through different phases. The research found that those negotiations demonstrating more relational stability were more likely to yield cooperative agreements. Negotiations in which the phases were brief and volatile demonstrated less cooperation between parties. Also, the negotiators were more likely to vary their levels of interdependence since power struggles are an inherent part of hostage negotiations. But, they typically retained either consistently high or low levels of affiliation during the negotiations. Perhaps relational discussions tend to stabilize around such issues as trust and attraction, but vary in terms of power and control.

An important revision of this model is offered by Womack and Walsh in their recent discussion of hostage negotiation. These researchers contend that the extent to which the participants are genuine or deceptive affects the extent to which parties can develop a more cooperative or competitive relationship. Unde-

tected deception, or genuine communication can set the stage for increased affiliation and interdependence. However, if deception is detected or the issue is raised, then affiliation is certainly likely to decline, and perhaps a power struggle will ensue, as well.

The links between this work and research in aggression is worth noting. In dispute-related aggression, the parties focus on power and interdependence issues as forcing compliance becomes the objective. The extent to which parties like or trust one another should remain at a fairly low level throughout the interchange. Moving away from an aggressive format in a relationship requires bridge building at the affiliation level in advance of any other issues. If parties are sufficiently communicatively competent to articulate their positions, perhaps they can demonstrate more cooperative behavior that will permit the upward adjustment of their mutual affiliation.

IV. CONCLUSIONS

Three main lessons about interpersonal conflict emerge from this essay. First, interpersonal relationships are at the center of all conflicts. Even in large-scale conflict between social groups up to international conflicts between nation-states, conflicts are still managed through interpersonal relationships and affected by such matters as levels of trust, cooperation versus competition, use of distributive tactics and so on. The issues in contention may not center on relationships, and the relationship quality of the disputants may not be in jeopardy; still, the quality of the relationship shapes the strategies and tactics disputants select as they attempt to manage their conflict. Identity and face issues also enter into this mix suggesting that the relationship is always a very visible part of any conflict, and can quickly take over as the focus of the conflict if parties are not careful in resorting to tactics that can destroy the relationship.

Second, interpersonal conflict exists on a very precarious edge between negotiation and violence. The edge is often very narrow, making it easy for individuals to lose their balance and slip into violence. This is especially true in cultures such as the United States, where cultural context and availability of means to perform violent acts results in a higher likelihood for these acts deadly violence to occur. As issues begin to center more on interpersonal relationships, parties become more personally threatened. If those threats become sufficiently severe, individuals—especially in cultures that are less restrained in their verbal and emotional expression-may often cross the line into violence in an attempt to bring the situation back in control. Maintaining a focus on negotiation requires that individuals maintain the argumentation and communication skills that serve as the primary tool for controlling the conflict.

Third, an understanding of interpersonal conflict provides an important window into the social structure of the organization. Organizational climate issues that extend to such areas as support, decision-making structure, autonomy, and rewards tend to emerge quickly when parties are in conflict. As individuals play out their conflicts they reveal important information about the climate issues. For example, individuals typically become more direct in the course of seeking to "win" the conflict, encouraging them to edit less and say what they feel about climate issues. So, the assumptions underlying how individuals function as a social system become quickly apparent as that social system is stressed by the conflict. Thus, examining interpersonal conflict can be a very valuable exercise.

Also See the Following Articles

AGGRESSION, PSYCHOLOGY OF • FAMILY STRUCTURES, VIOLENCE AND NONVIOLENCE • MEDIATION AND NEGOTIATION, TECHNIQUES OF • RELIGIOUS TRADITIONS, VIOLENCE AND NONVIOLENCE • THEORIES OF CONFLICT

Bibliography

Bateson, G. W. (1951). Conventions of communications: Where validity depends on belief. In J. Ruesch & G. Bateson (Eds.), *Communication, the social matrix of society* (pp. 212–227). New York: Norton.

Blake, R. R., & Mouton, J. S. (1964). *The managerial grid.* Houston, TX: Gulf.

Brown, P., & Levinson, S. (1987). *Politeness: Some universals in language usage.* Cambridge: Cambridge University Press.

Burgoon, J. K., & Hale, J. L. (1984). The fundamental topoi of relational communication. *Communication Monographs, 51,* 193–214.

Cupach, W. R., & Canary, D. J. (1995). Managing conflict and anger: Investigating the sex stereotype hypothesis. In P. J. Kalbfleisch and M. J. Cody (Eds.), *Gender, power, and communication in human relationships* (pp. 233–252). Hillsdale, NJ: Erlbaum.

Cupach, W. R., & Canary, D. J. (1997). *Competence in interpersonal conflict.* New York: McGraw-Hill.

Deutsch, M. (1973). *The resolution of conflict.* New Haven, CT: Yale University Press.

Donohue, W. A., & Roberto, A. J. (1993). Relational development in hostage negotiation. *Human Communication Research, 20,* 175–198.

Donohue, W. A., Ramesh, C., & Borchgrevink, C. (1991). Crisis bargaining: Tracking relational paradox in hostage negotiation. *International Journal of Conflict Management, 2,* 257–274.

Felson, R. B., & Tedeschi, J. T. (1993). *Aggression and violence: Social interactionist perspectives.* Washington, DC: American Psychological Association.

Fincham, F. D., Bradbury, T. N., & Scott, C. K. (1990). Cognition in marriage. In F. D. Fincham & T. N. Bradbury (Eds.), *The psychology of marriage: Basic issues and applications* (pp. 118–149). New York: Guilford.

Fitzpatrick, M. A. (1988). *Between husbands and wives: Communication in marriage.* Newbury Park, CA: Sage.

Gottfredson, M. R., & Hirschi, T. (1993). A control theory interpretation of psychological research on aggression. In R. Felson & J. Tedeschi (Eds.), *Aggression and violence: Social interactionist perspectives* (pp. 47–68). New York: Academic Press.

Gottman, J. M. (1979). *Marital interactions: Experimental investigations.* New York: Academic Press.

Gottman, J. M. (1994). *What predicts divorce? The relationship between marital processes and marital outcomes.* Hillsdale, NJ: Erlbaum.

Hample, D., & Dallinger, J. M. (1995). A Lewinian perspective on taking conflict personally: Revision, refinement, and validation of the instrument. *Communication Quarterly, 43,* 297–319.

Hauser, P. M. (1968). Application of ideal-type constructs to the metropolis in the economically less-advanced areas. In S. F. Fava (Ed.), *Urbanism in world perspective* (pp. 93–97). New York: Crowell.

Hinde, R. A. (1979). *Towards understanding relationships.* New York: Academic Press.

Infante, D. A., & Rancer, A. S. (1982). A conceptualization and measurement of argumentativeness. *Journal of Personality Assessment, 46,* 72–80.

Kilmann, R. H., & Thomas, K. W. (1977). Developing a forced-choice measure of conflict-handling behavior: The "MODE" instrument. *Educational and Psychological Measurement, 37,* 309–325.

Sieburg, E. (1985). *Family communication: An integrated systems approach.* New York: Gardner Press.

Sillars, A. L. (1980). The sequential and distributional structure of conflict interactions as a function of attributions concerning the locus of responsibility and stability of conflicts. In D. Nimmo (Ed.), *Communication Yearbook 4* (pp. 217–235). New Brunswick, NJ: Transaction.

Spitzberg, B. H., Canary D. J., & Cupach, W. R. (1994). A competence-based approach to the study of interpersonal conflict. In D. D. Cahn (Ed.), *Conflict in personal relationships* (pp. 183–202). Hillsdale, NJ: Erlbaum.

Winter, D. G. (1993). Power, affiliation, and war: Three tests of a motivational model. *Journal of Personality and Social Psychology, 65,* 532–545.

Womack, D. F., & Walsh, K. (1997). A three-dimensional model of relationship development in hostage negotiations. In R. G. Rogan, M. R. Hammer, & C. R. Van Zandt (Eds.), *Dynamic processes of crisis negotiation* (pp. 57–76). Westport, CT: Praeger.

Justification for Violence

Kevin Magill

University of Wolverhampton

GLOSSARY

Communitarian Ethics Moral theories that view moral values and claims as grounded in the practices, rules, associations and ways of living of specific moral communities.

Consequentialism Moral theories or forms of ethical thinking in which actions or rules are thought to be right or wrong according to the value of their consequences.

Deontological Ethics Moral theories or forms of ethical reasoning in which certain acts are thought to be right or wrong in themselves, regardless of their consequences.

Moral Subjectivism Theory that moral values and judgments are a matter of subjective preference and that moral disagreements are akin to differences of taste.

Principle of Utility Utilitarian ethical principle, according to which actions, rules and states of affairs are good to the extent that their consequences include a greater overall balance of pleasure, happiness or well-being over pain or suffering.

Universalist Ethics Moral theories or forms of ethical thinking involving principles that are considered to be binding on all persons, regardless of community, national, political, family, or other associations and whatever limited moral obligations or loyalties are bound up with them.

VIOLENCE involves the infliction of harm or damage on persons and property, and for this reason its use calls for justification. The subject of justifications for violence in mainstream Anglo-American philosophy and political theory has conventionally focused on *political violence,* which usually refers to acts and strategies of violence for political ends excluding those carried out by states and including terrorism, guerrilla warfare and assassination, as well as riot and violence in demonstrations, protests and picket lines. Inquiry about the justifiability of state violence tends to fall under the headings of just-war theory and justifications for punishment. Whether the conventional distinction between the standing of state and nonstate violence, as subject matters, is defensible will not be addressed in this article, although it is a matter of argument in discussions of both. A justification for violence will urge that some or other violent action or campaign was or is the right thing to do, or anyhow permissible. Philosophical inquiries into the justifiability of violence typically focus on what general conditions must be satisfied by any defensible moral justification for violence.

Copyright © 1999 by Academic Press.
All rights of reproduction in any form reserved.

I. ETHICAL THEORY AND THE STANDARD JUSTIFICATIONS

Much philosophical discussion about political violence is taken up with argument about whether and to what extent acts of violence can be justified as means to good ends. According to deontological ethics there are limits on what may justifiably be done in pursuit of good or worthy ends. Although many actions can be justified by their beneficial consequences, some actions are simply wrong in themselves. Immanuel Kant famously argued that it is wrong to tell a lie, even to save a person's life. Many deontologists would accept that bad actions *can* sometimes be justified in extreme or catastrophic situations—Fried suggests that killing an innocent person would be justified if it will save a whole nation—while maintaining that in normal circumstances such actions are morally prohibited regardless of their consequences.

Deontologists typically take the view that, other than in circumstances of war, the only acceptable justification for violence is that of self-defense or defense of others from wrongful attack. Persons have moral rights not to be wrongfully injured or killed and, consequently, they have rights to defend themselves against wrongful physical attack. It is also sometimes argued that to violently attack someone who is not engaged in or threatening violence is akin to punishing someone who is innocent. Conversely, one who engages in wrongful violence against another may be said to have relinquished his normal rights not to be attacked. We can only be justified in using as much violence against an attacker, however, as is required to defend ourselves. Thus, according to Elizabeth Anscombe, a person could not be justified in poisoning someone they believe to be out to kill them. Defensive violence must be exactly that: if a state allows huge inequalities among its population or denies freedom to a colony, it may justly be opposed for doing so, but if it does not order or permit violent persecution by its police or armed forces, acts of political violence carried out by or on behalf of those it oppresses cannot be considered acts of defense.

For many deontologists, therefore, political violence is only likely to be justified where it is undertaken in defense against murderous states, police or militia. A campaign of political violence in which large numbers of activists are prepared to sacrifice their lives for national self-determination or religious expression is unlikely to be given a convincing or straightforward justification in such terms. Deontologists have also argued that violence can only justifiably be directed against those who are *directly* involved in it or *responsible* for it. Failure to prevent murder or injury, although it may be blameworthy in some circumstances, does not make one responsible for it. If, for example, members of an ethnic group are routinely tortured, beaten and murdered by soldiers and police, other citizens may be considered blameworthy for failing to protest or put pressure on their government, but they cannot be held responsible for the murders, tortures and beatings: they are *innocent* of those crimes. If they pay taxes and provide services to the army, their responsibility for death and injury is not increased by that. Bombs planted in order to kill such citizens, and thereby to terrorize the population, could not count as a defense against the actions of the army and police. To be responsible for a person's death requires that one has intentionally caused their death. Only those involved in carrying out murders and beatings and their political masters may properly be considered responsible for them and only they are legitimate targets for defensive violence.

While we may agree that there are limits to what can justifiably be done for good ends under normal circumstances, many might wonder how extreme or catastrophic circumstances need to be before political violence that is not strictly defensive can be justified. To take Fried's example: would only the saving of a whole nation be enough to justify the killing of one innocent person? In addition, if there is no justification for the intentional taking of innocent lives, what should we say about acts of terror that are intended to intimidate rather than take life, but with some foreseeable risk of causing death or injury? And what of explosions and acts of sabotage aimed at causing economic and political instability with, say, only a small foreseeable risk of causing death or injury?

A well-known and chilling hypothetical case in which many lives might be saved by the ending of one is described by Bernard Williams in *Utilitarianism: For and Against*. Williams tells a story about Jim who stumbles into a South American town in which twenty townspeople are about to be executed by the army as a warning against recent protests in the area. As an honored visitor Jim is offered the privilege of shooting one of the townspeople, and if he does so, as a mark of the occasion, the remaining nineteen will be spared. Both the captives and the other townspeople implore him to accept. What ought he to do? According to deontological ethics shooting the one cannot be justified, since it would involve intentional murder of an innocent person. It is true that whoever Jim chooses would be killed anyway, along with nineteen of his fellows, but that would not be an intentional act of

Jim's: the foreseeable villainy of the army cannot justify him in murdering once in order to prevent it.

William's example is employed as part of a critique of the chief competitor of deontological ethics in modern moral philosophy: utilitarianism. For utilitarians the right thing to do is obvious and straightforward: the lives of the many outweigh the life of the one. According to Williams, while many of us might agree with the utilitarian conclusion, we would not regard it as so obviously and straightforwardly the right thing to do as utilitarian thinking would have it. One reason why we would not, as deontologists have emphasized, is that we each have a sense of responsibility for what we *do*. Should Jim fail to take up the army's offer, the loss of nineteen lives will be a consequence of his inaction, but their murder will not be his doing. As Williams observes, it is difficult to see how any moral outlook could get by without treating the distinction between action and inaction as morally significant, but at the same time we do hold people responsible for things they could have prevented but chose not to. As things stand, at any rate, the question of whether taking lives can be justified if doing so will save more lives is given clear, unequivocal and opposing answers by deontological and utilitarian ethics, neither of which it is easy to embrace with conviction.

Consequentialist ethics, of which utilitarianism is a kind, holds that actions are not right or wrong because of their intrinsic characteristics, but because of their consequences. One should decide how to act according to whether one's actions are likely, on balance, to cause more good than harm or more right than wrong. In Jim's case, the consequences of his acting violently or of his refusing to do so are obvious, straightforward and considerable. In reality the consequences of acts of political violence, particularly in relation to their aims, are often far from obvious. By contrast, the immediate consequences of violent action tend to be all too clear and weigh against their justifiability. Most consequentialists take the view that the harms caused by acts of violence are only likely to be outweighed by their helping to bring an end to substantial evil or injustice. For consequentialists a justification for political violence should satisfy the following three conditions: (1) that it aims and can realistically be expected to rectify serious and remediable wrong; (2) that it does not bring about worse consequences than would occur without it; and (3) that there are no alternative means of securing its aims that would have better consequences.

Whether an act of violence will satisfy the first condition will depend among other things on one's view of what counts as a serious and remediable wrong.

According to the classical utilitarianism of Jeremy Bentham, good is identified with happiness and evil with suffering; happiness in turn is equated with pleasure. A serious and remediable wrong, on this view, would be any state of affairs involving needless and substantial suffering. Later utilitarians have rejected Bentham's equating of happiness with pleasure, and have variously identified it with well-being or satisfaction of desires. However they define good and evil, at any rate, all utilitarians accept some version of the *Principle of Utility,* according to which the rightness or wrongness of actions, social arrangements and rules depends on the extent to which their consequences maximize good and minimize evil. How one should act is therefore decided according to what is likely to produce the best overall balance of good over evil. A standard deontological criticism of utilitarianism is that it can routinely justify theft, deceit, violence and murder, provided that the harm they do is outweighed by the good they cause. A related set of criticisms, touched on in William's example, concerns the way in which utilitarian thinking conflicts with our ordinary notions about responsibility and agency. A person's liability to attack and to other kinds of harsh treatment such as punishment is standardly thought to follow from what she has done and from her responsibility, as an agent, for what she has done. The exclusive emphasis that utilitarianism places on the consequences of actions appears to conflict with this notion in two ways. In the first place, it rules out any principled distinction between a person's responsibility for what she does intentionally and what are foreseeable but unintended consequences of her actions or of her failure to act. In addition, it does not permit any principled basis for differential treatment of people according to what they have done and what they are responsible for. It therefore allows, in principle, that anyone might be a legitimate target of political violence, regardless of their responsibility for whatever evil or injustice the violence is aimed at ending. Utilitarians can argue that acts of violence against ordinary civilians are unlikely to be effective in achieving their aims, but this is debatable and many would regard the claim, in any case, as an inadequate basis for determining who may justifiably be attacked.

Some consequentialists (including some utilitarians) have responded to these difficulties by arguing that the rightness or wrongness of an action is not determined by the consequences of the action itself, but by whether it accords with rules of conduct whose general observance is productive of more good than harm or more right than wrong. Such *rule consequentialists* therefore aim for a kind of compromise between moral concerns about consequences and deontological claims that some actions are prohibited, under normal circumstances, whatever their consequences. Thus, although the assassination of a brutal police officer might realistically be expected to have more good consequences than bad, a rule consequentialist would argue that, in general, abiding by laws prohibiting murder has better consequences than if everyone were to decide whether or not to kill according to the likely consequences of doing so.

The rule consequentialist method of determining how to act does not, however, yield a general prohibition on the use of political violence. If, for example, the laws prohibiting violence in a particular state apply in practice only to the civilian population and are not enforced against the police or the army, observance of the law by civilians might have dire consequences for the population. A society's rules can be evaluated collectively and abiding by a law that might have beneficial consequences in a just society may be the wrong thing to do under a violent dictatorship.

One question that arises here is whether, in an unjust society, acts of political violence are to be assessed according to their consequences or according to general rules of conduct, such as the rules of engagement in wartime. If we think of political violence as a departure from normal rules of conduct, the idea that it might be justified according to some general rule of conduct will look like a contrivance. There have been political struggles in which rules about permissible uses of violence appear to have been followed, but it is implausible to think that all decisions about violence in such struggles either were or ought to have been carried out according to rules. There is no obvious contradiction, for example, in supposing that an act of violence carried out according to general rules of conduct that have consequentialist backing might lack such a justification when considered on its own. Moreover, the good consequences of normal rules of conduct, especially laws, depend on their being generally respected. It is difficult to see how the claim could be made for rules governing the uses of political violence.

II. ARGUMENTS AGAINST VIOLENCE

A. Duties to Support and to Oppose

In an ideally good or just society, we may suppose, violence for political ends will not satisfy the consequentialist conditions for the justification of violence mentioned above, either because such a society would not permit a serious and remediable wrong or because it would have effective legal and political alternatives to violence for remedying wrongs and injustices. Thus, for consequentialists, whether political violence is justified will depend to a large extent on how far short of good or just a given society's arrangements, practices and laws are thought to fall.

According to the Principle of Utility, a good society is one whose institutions, practices, and social arrangements maximize overall happiness and minimize overall suffering. Critics of utilitarianism have pointed out that a good society, understood in this way, is compatible with, and in some circumstances may positively require, unfair and unequal rules and social arrangements, even slavery. In *A Theory of Justice* John Rawls argues that the regulative principles according to which the consequences of rules and social arrangements should be assessed are those that embody the idea of *justice as fairness*. Against utilitarianism, Rawls argues that the right is prior to the good and cannot be reduced to or defined as that which will maximize the good. A just society, according to Rawls, must satisfy what he describes as the Principle of Liberty and the Principle of Difference. The Principle of Liberty stipulates that all members of society should have the maximum liberty consistent with equal liberty for all. The Principle of Difference calls for as much inequality as is required to make the worst-off members of society better off than they would be in a more equal state of affairs. The Principle of Liberty takes precedence over the Principle of Difference. This has the consequence that restrictions on liberties, which could include property rights, cannot be justified in order to make the worst-off better off.

For a Rawlsian consequentialist, therefore, what would qualify as serious and remediable wrong are rules, practices and social arrangements that seriously violate the two principles. Given the ordering of the principles, it is unlikely that serious violation of the Principle of Difference alone would be sufficient to justify political violence since it is difficult to see how any act of violence could fail to infringe someone's liberties. Thus, for a Rawlsian, political violence is only likely to be justified in states that seriously restrict freedom in a way that is not required by maximum equality of liberty for all (although, as Rawls notes, different conceptions of liberty provide considerable scope for disagreement about whether a given society satisfies the principle).

Egalitarian critics of Rawls, such as Ted Honderich, have suggested that while the two regulative principles are superior to the principle of utility, they would allow far more inequality than could properly be called fair. Honderich also argues that given the egregious history of claims about the benefits to the poor of various inequalities, the Principle of Difference, although formally acceptable, would be a poor or ineffective regulative principle by which to judge the fairness of existing societies. Egalitarian consequentialists such as Honderich therefore argue that a just or fair society must be governed by a Principle of Equality. There are difficulties in formulating what kinds of measures are called for by such a principle and how to judge to what extent existing societies have failed to satisfy it. According to Honderich, it requires that a priority be made of "leveling up" the worst off in society. Many egalitarians would argue that existing societies fail to satisfy the principle to such an extent that the justifiability of violence aimed at rectifying this state of affairs cannot be quickly dismissed.

All consequentialists would agree that we have a general *duty* to abide by and support those institutions, practices and arrangements that have good or just consequences, and also a duty to oppose those whose consequences are bad or unjust. If a state's institutions, practices and arrangements, taken collectively, have consequences that are decently close to good and just, we have a general duty to support it and abide by its laws. If, instead, the consequences are far from good and just, then that duty will be either lacking or reduced. Many would argue that contemporary Western societies, while certainly open to improvement, are close enough to good or just that their citizens have a duty to abide by their laws, and perhaps also to support their political institutions. Such societies would not, in that case, suffer from the kind of serious and remediable wrong that might justify political violence. Egalitarian consequentialists, as we have noted, have a less sanguine view about serious and remediable wrong in contemporary societies, including Western societies. In consequence, they are apt to be more sceptical about our supposed duties to abide by the laws and institutions of such societies. They also argue that Western societies have grave responsibilities for serious and remediable wrongs elsewhere in the world. While such wrongs might be enough to satisfy the first condition of political violence, however, the nature and sophistication of modern military and law enforcement technologies, taken together with a judgment about the lengths privileged elites will go to in order to defend their interests, has led some egalitarian consequentialists to the view that violence for egalitarian ends is unlikely to satisfy the second of the consequentialist conditions: that it should not make matters worse than they would be without it. In "Hierarchic Democracy and the Necessity of Mass Civil Disobedience," Ted Honderich comes to the dispiriting conclusion that attempts at large scale egalitarian redistribution by nonviolent and constitutional means are unlikely to satisfy it either. Radical egalitarians might have no intention or desire that their actions—violent or otherwise—should provoke violence in defense of entrenched interests, but if such violence were a foreseeable consequence of their actions it would count against a consequentialist justification for them. Honderich has also argued, however, that if egalitarian political violence is not justified, we may consider it less blameworthy than the intransigence of vested interests and governments that could do much to remedy inequality but who work instead to perpetuate it.

B. Obligations to Obey the Law

Setting aside questions about whatever duties we may be said to have to abide by the laws of existing societies, it is also argued that as beneficiaries of laws, of systems of law enforcement and, not least, of the law abiding behavior of others, we incur *obligations* to abide by laws. The benefits of living under laws are not restricted to protection from murder and injury, but this can certainly be counted among the principal benefits. Socrates famously argued that one who accepts and benefits from the protection of law is clearly obliged by that to obey the laws himself, even if, as with Socrates, he has been wrongfully, but legally, condemned to death. The notion that enjoying the protection of the law or the state places us under some obligation to abide by and support it has been urged and argued for in different ways by several political thinkers. It is sometimes expressed in the idea that properly constituted states and laws have an authority that gives them, within limits, a right to our obedience or compliance. The claimed authority is also thought to give the state a right to use violence, to whatever extent it is needed to enforce the law and to protect the country from its enemies. The lack of such authority has been claimed as part of what is meant by *political violence*. Political violence is unauthorized, and thus, some would argue, beyond justification.

There are several questions that may be asked about our obligations to obey the law and what moral weight they have. In the first place, if I have enjoyed or accepted the benefits that come with laws and their enforcement, does the obligation that arises from that take precedence over any other duties I may have? If I have reason to believe that others are less well protected by the law than me, does the protection I have received place an absolute limit on what steps I may take to help them? In addition, how do my obligations stand if my protectors engage in unjust violence toward others? And how do they stand if my protectors uphold a system that needlessly allows children to go hungry?

The benefits I derive from the law are not, it may be thought, owed solely, or as such, to the state that upholds it. We may think that our obligations to obey the law are, in a sense, obligations to those others whose law-abiding behavior we benefit by. If we consider our legal obligations in this way, further questions present themselves. For example, if I have reason to believe that the most law-abiding of my fellow citizens are those who would have most to lose if laws were not observed, do whatever benefits I derive from their law-abiding behavior place a limit on what I may justifiably do to help others who have much less to lose? Or if I believe that those with least to lose could have more if those with most to loose were prepared to have less, how much should I consider myself bound or obliged by the benefits I receive from the law-abiding behavior of the latter? We might also ask: what are my obligations to law-abiding citizens who, without threat of serious legal penalty, benefit from and deliberately allow factory conditions that cause physical ruin and death to those unfortunate enough to have to work in them?

Discussions about political obligation often assume that all are equal under the law: that all are equally protected. If, in a spirit of realism, we drop the assumption and consider the case of those who are relatively poorly served by the law, what should we take their obligations to be? Do they have legal obligations weighty enough to rule out their having a justification for engaging in illegal defensive or vigilante activity? And would they be wrong to engage in political violence aimed at creating a system of law enforcement that serves them as well as it currently does others?

None of the questions considered are such as to undermine the idea that people have obligations to obey the law, or to dismiss it as ideological contrivance. They do, however, call for careful consideration, especially if one is inclined to think that our legal obligations block all possibility of justified political violence. We might also wonder whether considerations about legal obligation, or the authority of state and law, do justice to what can be said *against* political violence. If, for example, we suppose that a terrorist has somehow managed not to avail himself of the benefits and protection afforded by the law, would his actions be considered much less blameworthy on that account?

C. Violence and Reason

Violence, according to some influential thinkers, is mostly irrational. Their claim is not, and could hardly be, that there are never circumstances in which a person might have good reasons for acting violently. There are, to mention one reason, violent and murderous people, in defense against whom violence is sometimes the only reasonable resort. The claim, as advanced by Karl Popper and others, is that to resort to violence as a means of settling disputes is irrational or unreasonable. Other things being equal, to settle a dispute by *reasoning* or arguing it through is evidently preferable to using violence to do so. If I reason with an opponent, I may persuade him by my arguments and get what I want without injury to either of us. Alternatively, I may be brought to see the force of his position and to give up my claims. That I should be open to either possibility is characteristic of what Popper takes to be the attitude of *reasonableness*: a commitment to give-and-take discussion. This, it will be noticed, is allowed for, indeed required, by the third of the consequentialist conditions for the justification of violence mentioned earlier. The point of Popper's claims may be to emphasize that condition against those who are too ready to conclude that reasoning and discussion will be ineffective or too ready to give vent to feelings such as anger and vengefulness. Perhaps many who have resorted to violence in pursuit of their political ends gave insufficient time and thought to reasoning with their opponents. It can scarcely be denied that had the outcomes of many violent struggles and wars been decided by reasoning, many people would have had longer lives, many people now dead would still be with us and many would have been spared grievous injury. Ought we therefore to conclude that, as Popper claims, violence is the *precise opposite* of *reason*?

Whether violently attacking someone is the precise opposite of reasoning with him, to do the one, undeniably, is not to do the other. Does it follow that violence, if not exactly an opposite, stands at some distance from reason or *rationality*? This would follow if it were a requirement of reason or rationality that we should always attempt to reason with someone with whom we are in disagreement or dispute. That it is not has been mentioned already and is insisted on by Popper himself: it may not be possible to reason with someone who would rather shoot you than reason with you. When faced with violence and intolerance, violence and intolerance can be reasonable responses, and presumably what makes them so, under those circumstances, is that the circumstances, coupled with an assumption that we do not wish to be injured or murdered, give us reason for using violence. Under those circumstances, violence, far from being the precise opposite of reason, may be rational: rational in the familiar sense of being the best means to our ends. Still, what would make violence rational, in that case, is the unreasonable violence of our opponent. The implication is that, were it not for the fact that some people behave unreasonably and intolerantly, there would never be a reason for violence. While this might not make violence exactly the opposite of reason, it does imply that the occurrence of violence always requires a lack of reason or rationality on someone's part.

The claim that violence always involves unreasonableness or irrationality on the part of at least one protagonist appears to be supported by what we have already noted about past wars and violent struggles: that if their outcomes had been decided by reasoning matters through, many people would have had longer or healthier lives. An obvious objection to putting the matter like this is that the outcomes of such struggles might have gone differently had they been carried out by reasoning. The concern expressed is that what good has been achieved through violent struggle might not have been achieved, or that less of it might have been achieved, had matters been decided by reasoning. The ready reply is that violence has no better claim as a means to justice than reasoning: if anything, it has most likely a poorer claim (although Georges Sorel and others have denied this).

A more telling objection is that in many disputes that have been brought to a conclusion by reasoning, give-and-take discussion, negotiation and the like, it took violence by party A to bring party B to the negotiating table. Let us suppose, then, that party A tries every reasonable means—petitions, lobbies, demonstrations, civil disobedience, and so forth—to get a hearing for its case before resorting to violence. If party B simply refuses to negotiate or to listen, but otherwise behaves peacefully, party A's violence would lack the justification of defense from attack. It would not follow, without further assumptions, that it lacked any justification or that it lacked reason. Ought we to say, instead, that it is party B that is behaving unreasonably in refusing to listen or negotiate, thereby leaving party A with no alternative means of getting a hearing for its case than resorting to violence? This might depend on the nature of party A's claims. Is it reasonable to negotiate with someone whose claims are unreasonable? The obvious difficulty facing us here is that what is judged to be reasonable is often linked to prior and arguable judgements about the fairness, propriety and reasonability of the status quo, as well as the legitimacy and moral standing of constitutions, property rights, freedoms and sovereignty. That we lack any means of resolving arguments about them that commands common agreement is a fact of social and political life.

Judgments about reasonability and about what should be given a hearing, moreover, are also colored by material interests. Judgements colored in this way are often described as "ideological," but such labeling does not come close to establishing truths on which all can agree. Suppose that party B's refusal to negotiate issues from a hard-headed refusal to relinquish established and valued advantages and interests: does it follow from this that its obduracy is irrational? According to Popper, when opposing interests are at stake the only alternatives are reasonable compromise or to attempt to destroy one's opponent. But violence in pursuit of interests may be directed at less extreme ends than outright destruction of an opponent. The intent of party A's violence, we can suppose, is to give party B a reason for ending its refusal to negotiate. If party B could have foreseen that party A would use violence to force it to the negotiating table, it would have been rational, other things being equal, for party B to begin negotiating without being forced. If party B's intelligence was that party A would not resort to violence, or that it lacked the means to use it effectively, its refusal would not have been obviously irrational.

What should also be noted here is that violence need not only be a means of bringing opponents to the negotiating table, but has often been a key element in negotiating. Supposing, again, that party B is committed to defending its established interests, what kind of argument would give it reasons to concede party A's claims? It is possible to think of arguments that try to show that selfishly pursuing only one's own interests is self-defeating or unfulfilling, and such arguments can be effective, but they typically fall short of conclusively proving the case. If party B is unmoved by such arguments, or by considerations of justice or sovereignty, then it may be that the only effective argument in favor of its meeting party A's claims will be one that demonstrates that it is in its interests to do so. The threat of violence, backed up by concrete demonstrations, is clearly relevant in calculations of material interest.

Just as judgments have to be made in disputes, about the strength and determination of opponents, likewise judgments must be made about what reasoning and negotiation are likely to achieve. If there are reasons for thinking that one's opponent's willingness to negotiate is a pretense, or that negotiations are being deliberately drawn out, this can also be weighed against alternative means. An occupying power, for example, might intend to negotiate with a national liberation movement only until world attention has been distracted elsewhere. And while negotiations are dragged out, injustices may persist and people may starve. Such considerations show that it is far from obvious that it is always rational to reason with an opponent who is willing to come to the negotiating table.

To be prepared to reason with our opponents, and to do so in a spirit of give-and-take, is doubtless a good general policy. Looking back on various wars and violent struggles we may judge that things would have gone better if the policy had been followed more often. But the judgment is based on a view of the outcomes of past struggles that was obviously unavailable to those involved. While it may be true that many violent struggles would have been better resolved by reasoning, it is, at any rate, no necessary truth that any occurrence of violence requires irrationality or lack of reason on the part of at least one of the protagonists. It can also be added, in line with our discussion of material interests, that violence and the threat of it cannot, by definition, be excluded from what can count as reasoning.

According to Hannah Arendt and others, even if not all violence is unreasonable, violence for revolutionary or large-scale egalitarian goals is: violence is only ever likely to succeed in achieving short-term concrete aims. Success of larger aims depends on many variables: entrenched interests, economics trends, balances of political forces and so forth. The variables are not such as to allow for sound prediction. Violence that aims at large scale change cannot, therefore, be based on a well-founded judgment that it will be successful. In that case, its use for such ends would be irrational.

The argument is clearly related to the first consequentialist condition for the justification of violence: that it can realistically be expected to meet its aims. Few would take issue with the argument: the various premises have much support from human experience and social science and the conclusion, if not exactly tight, is difficult to resist. But how relevant is it? It is hard to think of real examples of political violence that did not have short-term concrete ends. Indeed, it is difficult to think of any long-term political aim that would not require its supporters to have short- and medium-term aims and to consider what actions were required to realize them. Neither are short-term aims always just means to the long-term end. Violence might aim at the release of a group of political prisoners or an end to their torture. Should we consider such violence to be irrational because its concrete short-term aim will also serve a less predictable longer term aim? That would require more argument than has been given.

D. Violence and Democracy

Considerations about persuasion and give-and-take discussion have also featured in arguments that political violence is necessarily undemocratic. *Democracy* requires freedom to vote in accordance with one's beliefs and preferences and, arguably, the opportunity to persuade others, by argument, as well as the opportunity to be so persuaded by the arguments of others. Since violence necessarily involves force rather than reasoned persuasion, some have argued, it is incompatible with democratic process. Violence might be thought of as democratic if it is directed against undemocratic systems, but only in that sense. Our duties to uphold and support democratic systems and our obligations to abide by democratic decisions, it is claimed, rule out any justification for political violence in democratic states. It can be argued that since it is possible for democratic majorities to behave unjustly toward minorities, political violence aimed at rectifying democratic injustices might, in some circumstances, be justified. Many would argue, however, that such circumstances are rare or nonexistent in contemporary Western democracies, which have effective legal and constitutional channels for pursuing minority grievances.

By contrast, Ted Honderich has argued that if we set aside ideal notions of democracy, as involving free and open debate and in which representatives vote solely according to their assessments of reasoned arguments, and look instead to the actual operation of political decision making in Western democracies, we can consider political violence as a way of bringing persuasive pressure to bear on governments and legislative assemblies, which is akin to the pressures exerted by wealthy and powerful interest groups. Some political violence may be viewed, in that case, as helping to rectify the undemocratic influence of wealthy and powerful elites and as helping to achieve greater democracy. If an act of violence could properly be thought of as democratic in this way, it would not be enough to justify it, although it might certainly be relevant to its justifiability.

III. UNIVERSAL DUTIES AND MORAL PARTIALITY

The deontological and consequentialist models of ethical reasoning that have been considered, as well as the various subsidiary arguments about political duties and obligations, reason and democracy, are all universal in scope; which is to say, they appeal to principles and issue in judgments about the rightness and wrongness of actions that, according to their supporters, ought to be accepted by any person. For deontologists a person's rights not to be violently attacked or unjustly imprisoned are not dependent or mediated in any way by their membership of a nation or community or by that of a potential attacker. Likewise, for consequentialists, the principles according to which the consequences of institutions, rules or actions are to be evaluated are indifferent to gender, creed or association. Both kinds of moral reasoning can, within the terms set by their principles, allow some kinds of partiality toward others. Both can agree, for example, that parents have obligations to their own children that they do not have to children generally. Both can agree that to be a citizen of a country or a member of an organization entails obligations and duties to other members that do not extend to outsiders. Nevertheless, both kinds of ethical reasoning have been criticized for the ways in which their *universalism* has been thought to limit, unreasonably or immorally, the scope of affiliations, bonds, citizenship and material interests.

Imagine that the children of a community have died or suffered severe illness as a result of advertising, misinforming parents and health workers that a baby milk formula is better for their children than mother's milk. The manufacturers have also supplied free formula milk to maternity hospitals, causing newborn babies to become dependent on it. Community activists have explored all effective nonviolent means of putting an end to the advertising. They have protested to the manufacturers, to their own government and that of the manufacturers' country. They have, in addition, brought the matter to the attention of the international press and broadcasting media and international regulatory bodies and called for legislative changes. But the manufacturers have persisted in their practices, using inducements to secure the acquiescence of government, as well as counterpropaganda and manipulation of legal loopholes. The resources of local activists are negligible in comparison to what is available to the manufacturers. They have had some success in getting the dangers of the formula across to mothers and health workers, but this has been hampered by their limited resources, human gullibility in the face of sophisticated advertising, continuation of supplies of free milk to hospitals and legal challenges from the manufacturers. Having explored all realistic nonviolent alternatives without success and with children continuing to suffer and die, what are the activists to do?

While deontological ethical reasoning may recognize the immorality of the manufacturers' behavior, it rules out any justification for violence against them. The manufacturers may be behaving in a harmful way, but they are not engaged in violent attack and do nothing to force mothers to use their product. If the activists judge that only resorting to violence against the manufacturers, their directors, employees and collaborators is likely to bring them to mend their ways, especially if the violence intentionally causes death or injury, there can be no justification, on a strictly deontological view, for their doing so. The rights of, say, a company executive, whose own children are healthy, well fed and otherwise well cared for, not to be murdered or attacked must take precedence over the certain harm that will be caused to more of the community's children if drastic measures are not taken to stop it. Anti-universalist critics of deontological reasoning would argue that it is perverse to suggest that, in such a situation, concern for one's children, or the children of one's community, would be morally trumped by a duty to respect the rights of those whose behavior causes avoidable harm to them. Even if we suppose that the activists decide that it would be wrong to injure or murder, many would consider it strange or contrived—absurdly legalistic, even—to imagine that the force of the moral concerns that limit what they feel can justifiably be done to protect their community's children issues from a respect for the rights of members of the manufacturing company.

It might be thought that the objection to deontological reasoning is not, in a strict sense, anti-universalist. Much of the force of the example derives from concerns about the well-being of children: the special duties we have to children, a universalist might argue, are duties to *all* children. The example reminds us, moreover, that there are other ways of causing harm than what we may call (to forestall an unpromising argument about whether the company's actions constitute a kind of violence) *open violence*. In which case the implicit criticism of deontological reasoning is not directed at its universalism, but at its assumption that violence can only be justified in defense from open violence. While duties to children and defense against harm caused by other means than open violence do raise distinct problems for deontological reasoning, however, there is a further significant element in the example that concerns the special obligations we have toward our own children: obligations that are additional to any universal duties we may have to children as such. It is also worth noting that in communities living in circumstances that make mutual interdependence and loyalties strong, special obligations to protect and nurture children may extend to community members other than parents and relatives in ways that would not be true of most parts of Europe and the United States. Obligations to one's own children or those of one's community are partial in scope: they not only allow but positively require us to give partial consideration to the well-being of our own children. Such obligations may not always outweigh consideration or respect for the rights of others, but they do require what can be called a *moral partiality* in our actions toward our children.

In contrast to deontological ethical reasoning, consequentialism might allow that acts of violence against the company could be justified, providing that the consequences for overall happiness, justice or equality are best served by it. But consequentialist universalism requires that in reasoning about the right course of action, the consequences for the children should have no greater individual weight than those for company members. It is unlikely that such calculation would approximate closely to the moral reflections of the activists. A familiar consequentialist response to the likely dissonance between the activists' moral reflections and consequentialist calculation would be that judgments made according to ordinary moral concerns about, for example, loyalty and obligation do involve weighing up of consequences and will generally approximate those that would follow from consequentialist calculation. The approximation to consequentialist calculation, it is suggested, can be thought of as an approximation to an ideal moral calculation. Whether the claim is well founded in respect of ordinary moral reflection in general, however, there is certainly room for doubt about whether it can safely be made in respect of reasoning about violence. In addition, talk of approximation to an ideal moral calculation would appear to suggest that to whatever extent the activists' reflections depart from the model of consequentialist reasoning—for example, in showing partiality toward their children—it lacks moral authenticity.

The anti-universalist argument against both deontological and consequentialist thinking can be strengthened by drawing on other obligations and duties that present difficulties for their universalism. Ties and obligations to members of one's community, nation or class, based on mutual dependency, need or common oppression have all been cited in support of the claim that universalism not only places unrealistic requirements on moral agents, but that it is unrealistic about the nature and grounding of morality, moral claims and moral psychology. Philosophers such as Aristotle, Hegel and, more recently, *communitarian* theorists, have all argued that a person's rights, duties, obligations and moral values are always grounded in the practices, rules, associations and ways of living of the moral community to which she belongs, whether clan, city or state. If rights, duties and obligations are always grounded in a particular community and its way of life, they will be, to some extent, partial in their source and in their scope. Authentically moral judgments about what to do follow from one's commitments within and to a community, rather than from dispassionate assessment of universal rights or interests.

Another influential contemporary argument against both deontological and consequentialist universalism is that it is only within a community with well-established practices and traditions that we can take for granted the kind of shared ethical understanding that will allow us to agree about matters concerning well-being, justice and right and what they permit or require us to do or prohibit us from doing. It is a feature of modern life, according to thinkers such as Alasdair MacIntyre, that such agreement is increasingly stymied by the fragmentation and breakdown of community and tradition. A related attitude toward the possibility of common moral agreement can be seen in the writings of thinkers such as Marx and Frantz Fannon, who see moral rules and beliefs as reflecting class and group interests. Such thinkers, while being ready at times to engage in moral condemnation of exploitation, racism and dehumanization, are consequently sceptical about the efficacy of appeals to justice and morality in securing social change. While there may be agreement across classes, or between oppressors and oppressed, that, for example, poverty and squalor are evil, differences of material interest and social location, and consequent differences about moral priorities, rule out any possibility of agreement on what to do about them. For the same reasons, and for as long as existing forms of exploitation and oppression persist, no actions—violent or otherwise—taken in pursuit of political and social ends can hope to be given a justification that could, even in principle, command universal assent. At the same time, Marx and Fannon, and many who have shared their attitudes, acted and argued for action in ways that reflected clear moral commitments to those classes and peoples whose interests they championed. While both have been accused of amoralism, it is more likely that they believed that the actions and strategies they advocated had moral justifications (although, Marx's attitude to insurrectionary violence was markedly more sanguine than Fannon's), but justifications that were partial in scope, appeal and effectiveness.

A standard objection to arguments for moral partiality is that obligations and responsibilities to community, family and country must be limited by duties to respect the rights or interests of human beings in general, if we are not to be left with a moral indifference to those with whom we have no ties of kinship, citizenship or community. Rejection or downgrading of universal rights and duties would leave us with no basis for condemnation of imperialism or of xenophobic genocide. The arguments for and against anti-universalism on this point would take us beyond the subject matter of this essay, but it should be noted that the anti-universalist claims considered above do not entail any straightforward denial that we have duties to human beings as such (whatever the claims of anti-universalists such as Fannon and Sartre), or that universal duties are always trumped by the claims of community and kinship.

The case against universalist justifications or prohibitions of the use of political violence can roughly be summarized as follows: (1) that human beings have special responsibilities, obligations and duties that are partial in scope; (2) that these moral claims arise from associations and practices of kinship, community and citizenship, as well as common interests and mutual dependency, common endeavor and even love; (3) that they sometimes permit us, and to some extent require us, to override or disregard what duties we may have to respect the rights or interests of others, particularly those who are our enemies, aggressors and oppressors; and (4) that, given the grounding of moral claims mentioned in (2) there is no possibility of any justification for political actions, least of all violent actions, that can command universal assent.

IV. CONCLUSION

It has been argued that support for and opposition to campaigns of violence is necessarily rooted in ideological commitment, which is, perhaps, just a shorthand way of expressing the anti-universalist reflections already mentioned in relation to Marx and Fannon. In support of this it can be claimed that many of the arguments about political violence we have considered are, precisely because of their universality, so general and abstract as to offer no clear guidance about the justifiability of violence in particular and concrete circumstances. The point has already been made in respect of arguments about the comparative rationality of violence for short- and long-term ends. And how often, after all, has political violence been undertaken in order to remedy what its agents believed to be minor wrongs and injustices? or in the conviction that their ends would be better or less harmfully served by other means or by doing nothing? It is only when we move beyond the school room generalities of consequentialist trea-

tises, it may be argued, that any real and substantive argument about the justification of violence can begin; and the real and substantive is inevitably bedeviled by uncertainty about alternatives and their consequences and framed by the claims of ideological commitment and moral partiality. It has also been claimed that the moral outlook of those who place constraints about universal rights and absolute wrongs in the way of what may be done to achieve greater social justice and equality is typical of those who have little to benefit from greater social justice and equality: their principles, it is suggested, are as rooted in ideology as everyone else's.

If the claims about ideology, commitment and partiality are set against those of the standard deontological and consequentialist models of ethical reasoning, the obvious and familiar conclusion we may come to is that, as we would expect of any matter that touches on substantive concerns in morals, philosophy or politics, political violence and what may be said in justification of it is a matter of irreconcilable disagreement and unbridgeable division. The conclusion can be resisted. In the first place, it comes close to an endorsement of the claims of one of the disagreeing parties, since at least one intent of the claim that attitudes toward political violence are ideological is to say that it is a matter of practically irreconcilable disagreement. Moreover, none of the arguments and principles considered in this essay could properly be thought of as issuing from ideology *and nothing more*. Each of the claims we have considered, about rights and bad means to good ends, consequences and alternatives, rationality, political obligation and authority, community and moral partiality and, finally, about ideology and the efficacy of moral argument, has recommendations. The recommendations can be evaluated, disputed, made more precise and compared, which may take us beyond entrenched disagreement, assuming that is all we have in the first place. If none of us is entirely open to persuasion, there is nothing in any of the arguments we have considered that would place its adherents entirely beyond persuasion. It is unrealistic to hope that persuasion might bring all of our opponents to see matters as we do, or to entertain the idea that we, and those who think as we do, are, in principle, entirely open to persuasion. It is similarly unrealistic, and would presuppose a commitment to universalism, to think that we might, through argument and persuasion, come to a hitherto unelaborated position on which all might agree. But agreement on a general approach to political violence is, arguably, neither necessary nor sufficient for agreement about actual cases.

Debate and disagreement about violent and nonviolent means is not peculiar to political theory and philosophy: it has been a feature of many modern struggles against injustice. One large recommendation of philosophical reflection about political violence is that it supposedly enables us to disengage from party and ideological commitment, as well as the details and peculiarities of particular struggles, so that through dispassionate inquiry we may reach agreement about the general principles according to which violence can be justified. Such a procedure is also supposed to enable us to determine what constitutes an authentically moral justification for violence, freed from the amoral, political or merely pragmatic considerations that enter into the arguments and debates of political agents and their followers. It can be argued, however, that, far from disengagement, philosophical reflection introduces additional commitments and further possibilities for disagreement: about whether, for example, the moral status of actions or rules is to be assessed according to their consequences or whether certain actions are wrong in themselves. Moreover, despite the generality of philosophical and theoretical argument, it is often tacitly or explicitly conducted with an eye to the moral standing or legitimacy of existing states, institutions and social arrangements and what may legitimately be done within or against them. Wherever published philosophical and theoretical reflection about political violence may stand in relation to ideology, those who engage in it are certainly, as Honderich has argued, in the business of *advocacy*: their arguments are intended to issue in recommendations about the political ends we should seek and the means we may adopt in pursuit of them. This is not to say that philosophical and theoretical reflection about violence is a fruitless exercise: there are, after all, general issues or principles concerning political ends and the means used to achieve them, that can and should be considered, to some extent, in abstraction from particular cases. But there are grounds for scepticism about what special authority might, on account of its generality and disengagement, be claimed for such reflection and also for wariness about being drawn into arguments about general ethical theory. It might be thought that since justifications for violence must appeal to ethical first principles, general ethical theory must have a logical or reflective priority over ethical thinking about violence. What this overlooks, however, is that the standing of any ethical theory or reasoning about first principles can be, and often is, assessed according to its implications for particular subjects such as the moral status of acts of violence and what we would otherwise be inclined to think or say about them.

With this in mind, let us set aside commitments and arguments about first principles and consider what scope for agreement about political violence might be gained by doing so. Say that the community activists considered earlier reluctantly conclude, in light of their obligations to protect the children of their community, that they have no decent alternative but to resort to violence against the representatives of the baby milk manufacturers. If one takes the view that this is an unjustified violation of the rights of the company representatives, one might still consider that the intentions of the activists, albeit wrong or mistaken, do issue from genuinely ethical reasoning about the issues. It would be a mistake to think that their actions and intentions are on a par with violent robbery carried out for selfish gain and without thought to victims. Likewise, if a political movement allows the interests or rights of their own community, class or citizens to override those of their oppressors, or the citizens of a colonial occupier, their violent actions may lack the recommendation of either deontological or consequentialist reasoning, but if members of the movement act as they do in the belief that their obligations call for them to give preference to their own over others, we should judge their actions differently than if they are simply indifferent to the rights, interests or humanity of anyone else. Conversely, a member of the same group who hinders or endangers their actions in order to avoid harm to an innocent member of an occupying power may be condemned by his comrades, but they would be wrong to view his actions as of a piece with that of a quisling, a turncoat or a hired informer.

Where an agent's judgment about political violence is at odds with any of the standard lines of reflection we have considered, therefore, it does not follow from this that she must be indifferent to the concerns or principles they contain or that her judgment must somehow fall short of being genuinely moral. An agent may arrive at a judgment about political violence that differs from one or more of the standard models because of a different appreciation of the morally relevant considerations; in other words, that those considerations weigh differently with her than what is required by the standard model. If this is so, then philosophers and theorists who wish to have anything to say to such an agent must engage with her assessment of the relevant considerations, including the relevant facts. The relevant facts may include those about inequality; for example, that the gap in average life expectancy between the wealthiest in the wealthiest countries and the poorest in the poorest countries comes to what, according to Ted Honderich, can be described as a "species difference," and that the shorter lives contain far less of what makes life worth living. The relevant facts would also include those about violence and its effects: facts about who or what is attacked, about the scale of injury and death and about what is intended and what foreseen, as well as facts about the violence of governments. Facts are relevant, however, not simply as objects of an agent's thinking and judgments about means to political ends: rather her experiences of certain facts and the significance she attaches to them will affect and figure in her assessment of other relevant considerations. Whether one considers that moral rules and principles are universal and absolute or local and relative, one can accept that if someone has never owned and had security of property, she lacks a significant reason—arguably a necessary psychological condition—for respecting the property of others. Similarly, it may be argued, one who lives among the poorest tenth of the poorest countries, or who has strong sympathy with those who do, may be thought to lack a reason for giving equal weight to the rights of the wealthiest tenth in the wealthiest countries not to be attacked or killed.

As a proposal for the conduct of reflection and discussion about political violence and what may be said for or against it, some will reject the suggestion as a discreditable *moral subjectivism*. A person's duties and obligations, whatever they may be, and whatever their relationships to facts, are independent of her *experiences* of facts and of her subjective assessments of the morally relevant considerations. One can accept this, however, and one can hold to the view that only defensive violence can be justified or that morality requires that the interests of all agents who will be affected by an action must weigh equally in any justification of it, while recognizing that the bad or mistaken judgments of those who think differently may still issue from recognizably moral perspectives. If one thinks that an agent does not give due weight to the rights or interests of all persons, or, alternatively, if one thinks that she gives insufficient weight to her obligations to her own community, one must provide her with reasons for thinking differently and that will require some understanding of why she sees things as she does. It may also call for a rigorously Popperian openness to counterarguments about one's own moral assessments and how they relate to one's situation and experiences.

To adopt the proposal might be to go too far in the direction of substantive political argument, and also of moral psychology, than some philosophers believe to be proper for the discipline. Some may also be suspi-

cious of the claim that wrong or bad moral judgments may issue from authentically moral reasoning. But those who reject the proposal and continue to confine their inquiries to the general conditions for the justification of violence, ought, one might think, to have something to say about the point of the enterprise: providing the materials for well-argued endorsements or denunciations of acts of violence hardly seems enough.

Also See the Following Articles

JUST-WAR CRITERIA • LAW AND VIOLENCE • MEANS AND ENDS • TERRORISM • VIOLENCE AS SOLUTION, CULTURE OF

Bibliography

Anscombe, G. E. M. (1970). War and murder. In R. A. Wasserstrom (Ed.), *War and morality*. Belmont, CA: Wadsworth.

Arendt, H. (1970). *On violence*. London: Allen Lane.

Edgley, R. (1974). Reason and violence: A fragment of the ideology of liberal intellectuals. In Körner, S. (Ed.), *Practical reason*. Oxford: Blackwell.

Fannon, F. (1967). *The wretched of the earth*, with preface by J. P. Sartre. Harmondsworth: Penguin.

Fashima, O. (1989, Summer). Frantz Fannon and the ethical justification of anti-colonial violence. *Social Theory and Practice, 15*, 179–212.

Fried, C. (1978). *Right and wrong*. Cambridge MA: Harvard University Press.

French, P. A. (1974). Morally blaming whole populations. In V. Held, S. Morgenbesser, & T. Nagel (Eds.), *Philosophy, morality and international affairs*. New York: Oxford University Press.

Gomberg, P. (1990). Can a partisan be a moralist? *American Philosophical Quarterly, 27*, 1, 71–79.

Honderich, T. (1980). *Violence for equality: Inquiries in political philosophy*. Harmondsworth: Penguin.

Honderich, T. (1995). *Hierarchic democracy and the necessity of mass civil disobedience*. London: South Place Ethical Society.

Khatchadourian, H. (1991). Terrorism and morality. In B. Almond & D. Hill (Eds.), *Applied philosophy: Moral and metaphysics in contemporary debate*. London: Routledge.

MacIntyre, A. (1981). *After virtue*. London: Duckworth.

Margolis, J. (1974). War and Ideology. In V. Held, S. Morgenbesser, & T. Nagel (Eds.), *Philosophy, morality and international affairs*. New York: Oxford University Press.

Nielsen, K. (1972). On the choice between reform and revolution. In V. Held, K. Nielsen, & C. Parsons (Eds.), *Philosophy and political action*. New York: Oxford University Press.

Popper, K. R. (1972). Violence and utopia. In *Conjectures and refutations*. London: Routledge & Kegan Paul.

Rawls, J. (1955). Two concepts of rules. *Philosophical Review, 64*, 3–32.

Rawls, J. (1973). *A theory of justice*. New York: Oxford University Press.

Sorel, G. (1950). *Reflections on violence*. London: Collier Macmillan.

Williams, B., & Smart, J. J. C. (1973). *Utilitarianism: For and against*. Cambridge: Cambridge University Press.

Just-War Criteria

Brien Hallett

University of Hawaii—Manoa

GLOSSARY

Consequentialist Ethics The view that decisions should be based primarily on the consequences of action.
Deontological Ethics The view that decisions should be based primarily on principles of moral duty.
Jus ad bellum "The law or right *to* war," the criteria that should be debated before deciding *to* initiate a war.
Jus in bello "The law or right *in* war," the criteria that should be debated before deciding to use this or that strategy, tactic, or weapon during a war.

THE JUST-WAR CRITERIA organize discussions of war. Initially, the *jus ad bellum* criteria are used to organize the debate as to whether or not to begin a war. Subsequently, when the decision is for war, the *jus in bello* criteria are used to organize debates over appropriate actions during the war. The moral foundation of the criteria is the presumption that war is seldom, if ever, justified and, hence, that only the most compelling circumstances can overcome this presumption. The empirical foundation is the principle of double effect, the

principle that every action produces both good and bad, intended and unintended consequences. Because of this, decisions should be made only after a thorough investigation of all their consequences. It is the specific purpose of the criteria to ensure that this investigation is disciplined and thorough, none of the important perspectives or circumstances having been left out.

I. THE CRITERIA

The just-war criteria, as the three versions in Table 1 indicate, are not fixed and immutable. Through the millennia different authors have compiled different lists, shifting and changing the emphasis as their interests and circumstances demanded. For example, Thomas Aquinas was content with listing three of the *ad bellum* criteria in his *Summa Theologica*—competent authority, just cause, and right intention (IIa-IIae, q40)—and emphasizing the competent authority criterion as part of the effort to minimize and control private wars, which were a great problem during the Middle Ages. In 1983, the Catholic bishops listed only two *in bello* criteria, adding right intention to their list a decade later, in 1993. The only settled points are (1) that the criteria, whatever their number, are founded upon a strong presumption against war and the operation of the principle of double effect; and (2) that the question of war and peace divides into two distinct parts: The initial decision to begin a war, that is, the *jus ad bellum* criteria, and subsequent decisions on the conduct of the war, that is, the *jus in bello* criteria.

Copyright © 1999 by Academic Press.
All rights of reproduction in any form reserved.

TABLE I

Three Versions of the Just-War Criteria

Version 1:

A. Just causes to resort to war.

   1. To protect the innocent from unjust attack.

   2. To restore rights wrongfully denied.

   3. To reestablish an order necessary for a decent human existence.

B. Criteria for determining a just cause:

   1. Lawful authority

   2. Clear declaration of causes and aims

   3. Just intention

   4. Last resort

   5. Probability of success

   6. Proportionality of ends

   7. Maintenance of *jus in bello*

     a. Noncombatant immunity (Potter, 1970)

Version 2:

I. *Jus ad bellum* (Right *to* war)

   A. Just cause against a real and certain danger

   B. Competent authority

   C. Comparative justice

   D. Right intention

   E. Last resort

   F. Probability of success

   G. Proportionality of ends

II. *Jus in bello* (Right *in* war)

   A. Proportionality of means

   B. Discrimination, i.e., noncombatant immunity

   C. Right intention

     (United States Catholic Conference 1993)

Version 3:

In order to be fought justly.

1. War must be publicly declared.

2. War must be declared by a competent authority.

3. War must be fought with the right intention.

4. War must be fought for a just cause.

5. War must be fought for a proportionate reason.

6. War must be fought for a just peace.

7. War must be a last resort.

   (Johnson and Kelsay 1990, 58)

Inasmuch as the second version of the criteria in Table 1 is the most elaborate, it will be adopted for purposes of illustration. To add specificity to the discussion, the Declaration of Independence will be used to illustrate the *ad bellum* criteria, while the Allied carpet bombing of World War II will be used to question the *in bello* criteria. Sherman's march to the sea also raises interesting *in bello* questions.

A. Jus ad bellum

1. Just Cause

The purpose of the war must be to enhance and further peace and justice by righting some grievous public wrong. Private wars to correct private wrongs are, therefore, not justified. The traditional causes listed in the first version in Table 1 establish the general categories of legitimate purposes.

Given the importance of this criterion, more than half of the Declaration of Independence is devoted to arguing the colonists' just cause, presenting both philosophical and practical reasons. In terms of philosophy, the rebellion is justified because the Crown had frustrated the basic purpose of all government, denied the colonists their "inalienable rights," and thereby lost all legitimacy. In terms of practical politics, Jefferson listed 27 specific grievances, ranging for "He has forbidden his Governors to pass Laws of immediate and pressing Importance, . . ." to "He has abdicated Government here, by declaring us out of his Protection and waging War against us."

2. Competent (Legitimate or Lawful) Authority

This is first and foremost a prohibition against private war. Only properly constituted *public* authorities may decide for war. Not only must the public authority be competent in the general sense of being a legitimate sovereign, it (or its ally) must also be competent in the particular sense of being the legitimate sovereign over the territory under dispute in the war. For example, during the Opium Wars, Great Britain was a competent authority to wage war in the general sense of being an internationally recognized sovereign, but she was not competent in the particular sense of being the legitimate sovereign of China, and, therefore, able to legislate whether the Chinese would or would not import opium.

Until the 14th century, this criterion was used to disallow revolutionary wars because their leaders were not sovereign authorities. Under pressure from the Counter-Reformation, John Calvin developed his "Lesser Magistrates" doctrine (*Institutes* IV, xx, 31), which holds that duly constituted, but inferior, public authorities possess a duty to lead an oppressed people in revolt against obstinately tyrannical "Superior Magistrates." In line with Calvin's doctrine, the Declaration asserts the colonists competence to wage war in two different way: First, under natural law, it asserts in the very first sentence that, "When in the course of human events, it becomes necessary for one people to dissolve the political bands which have connected them with another, and to assume among the Powers of the earth, the separate and equal station to which the Laws of Nature and of Nature's God entitle them, ..."

Then, in the concluding paragraph, competence is based upon the rock of representative democracy, "We, therefore, the Representatives of the United States of America, in General Congress, Assembled, appealing to the Supreme Judge of the world for the rectitude of our intentions, do, in the Name, and by authority of the good People of these Colonies, solemnly publish and declare, That these United Colonies are, and of Right ought to be Free and Independent States; . . . ."

Calvin's Lesser Magistrate doctrine does not, however, extend to guerrilla wars or wars of national liberation, which, most frequently, possess the character of a private war. The clandestine nature of guerrilla wars and wars of national liberation makes it extremely difficult for their leaders to receive a public mandate, which is the essential characteristic of a "Lesser Magistrate."

3. Comparative Justice

In general, the justice of one's cause must be significantly greater than that of the adversary. This criterion forces each side to consider the position and perspective of the other side. The Declaration makes this comparison implicitly throughout, but, in the transition from the philosophical to the practical reasons for independence, it explicitly emphasizes the gross imbalance in comparative justice. While the Americans are seeking "Life, Liberty, and the pursuit of Happiness," "The history of the present King of Great Britain is a history of repeated injuries and usurpations, all having in direct object the establishment of an absolute Tyranny over these States. To prove this, let Facts be submitted to a candid world."

4. Right Intention

Despite the fact that the war will produce unintended evil consequences, one's own intentions must be good. This means not fighting out of a desire for revenge or to injure others, but only for a just cause, avoiding unnecessarily destructive acts or seeking unreasonable conditions such as unconditional surrender, and reconciling at the first opportunity. Implicit in a right intention is a public declaration of war. For, out of "a decent respect to the opinions of mankind" a clear public declaration of the war's causes and aims is required to show the rightfulness of one's intentions.

In the Declaration, the rectitude of the colonists' intentions are not only asserted formally in the concluding paragraph (cited above) but are also demonstrated by means of the colonists' prudence and long-suffering, "Prudence, indeed, will dictate that Governments long

established should not be changed for light and transient causes; and accordingly all experience hath shewn, that mankind are more disposed to suffer, while evils are sufferable, than to right themselves by abolishing the forms to which they are accustomed." But . . . prudence and long-suffering must eventually give way before a radical imbalance in the relative justice that separates each side's cause. Hence, the Declaration continues, ". . . when a long train of abuses and usurpations, pursuing invariably the same Object evinces a design to reduce them under absolute Despotism, it is their right, it is their duty, to throw off such Government, and to provide new Guards of their future security. Such has been the patient sufferance of these Colonies; and such is now the necessity which constrains them to alter their former Systems of Government."

5. Last Resort

Since war is, at best, the lesser of two evils, it should be chosen only as a last resort. Thus, the intended results of the war must be judged in relation to (1) the accumulating injustice if nothing is done; (2) the delayed arrival of justice if other less decisive options are chosen; and (3) the unintended harmful consequences (both known and unknown) of the war.

In the Declaration, last resort is shown not just by the "prudence" shown by the Colonists, but also by the fact that:

> In every stage of these Oppressions We have Petitioned for Redress in the most humble terms: Our repeated Petitions have been answered only by repeated injury. A Prince, whose character is thus marked by every act which may define a Tyrant, is unfit to be the ruler of a free people.
>
> Nor have We been wanting in attentions to our British brethren. We have warned them from time to time. . . . We have reminded them. . . . We have appealed to their native justice and magnanimity, and we have conjured them. . . .

But to no avail, "They too have been deaf to the Voice of Justice and of Consanguinity." Consequently, as a last painful resort, "We must, therefore, acquiesce in the Necessity, which denounces our Separation, and hold them, as we hold the rest of Mankind, Enemies in War, in Peace, Friends."

6. Probability of Success

This criterion is primarily an injunction against lost causes. Beyond prohibiting lost causes, this criterion, when combined with right intention, suggests that one should avoid the even greater evils that will result from defeat in war. This is the only criterion that the Declaration does not address.

7. Proportionality of Ends

The good to be realized must be greater than the evil inflicted. In a world of limited resources and limited effects, the ends never justify the means. Only a relatively few actions can be justified as proportional to and compatible with the ends sought.

The handling of this point in the Declaration is quite weak. The only explicit reference allows, "that mankind are more disposed to suffer, while evils are sufferable, than to right themselves by abolishing the forms to which they are accustomed." However, the entire Declaration is also suffused with a feeling that royal tyranny has become entirely unacceptable and, hence, that a return to good government is well worth the evils of war.

B. Jus in bello

Having organized a debate that led to a decision to wage war, new issues, questions and dilemma arise. During the course of the war, one must ensure that the means selected, for example, the carpet bombing of World War II, do not negate the ends sought:

1. Discrimination of Means

To minimize the war's evil consequences and maximize its good consequences, only military facilities and persons should be attacked, and these should be attacked with the minimum amount of force required to achieve the objectives of the attack. In other words, the principle of noncombatant immunity must be upheld. In this regard, did the carpet bombing of German and Japanese cities uphold the principle of noncombatant immunity within the limits of the principle of double effect? Did the bombing attack military targets?

2. Proportionality of Means

None of the acts of war may be so devastating as to render the whole war unjust by increasing the unintended evil effects to the point where they overwhelm the intended good effects. For example, was the destruction of German and Japanese cities disproportionate to the good produced by their destruction?

3. Right Intention

The aim of military operations must be to achieve reconciliation and peace as expeditiously as possible. Their aim cannot be vengeance or wanton destruction. Even during combat, individuals, units, and governments must keep their emotions under control. In this regard, how did the carpet bombing speed reconciliation?

II. EVALUATING THE CRITERIA

Four comments are in order: First, it should be clear that the criteria are designed to assist in making agonizing choices between the lesser of two evils. If any of the viable options were good, then there would be little need for such an elaborate and belabored debate. For example, when the options are between sending the military to intervene in Bosnia or standing by while the country is ethnically cleansed, the agony of the decision will force a full and detailed debate over each of the criteria before a final judgment is made.

Second, the indeterminate and controversial character of each of the criteria individually and all of them together should also be clear. The Declaration of Independence is an excellent example of this. However persuasive its reasoning may be, 20% of the colonialists were not persuaded and remained loyal to the British crown. A fifth of the population opposed the war as unjust, unneeded, and waged by unlawful authorities. This would appear to be about right: In even the justest of wars, approximately 20% of the population will disagree and condemn the war as unjust. In wars where the justice of the cause is less clear than during the American Revolution, the percentage will be even higher. This is one reason a public authority is the only competent authority to decided for war or peace. Only by conducting the debate widely and aggregating the final judgments of many people can any degree of confidence in the decision be obtained. A single person, or even a small group, debating these complex issues alone cannot presume to arrive at a sound judgement.

Third, it should be clear that all of the criteria are grounded simultaneously in ethical imperatives and empirical experience. The ethical grounds are the strong presumption against war. In order for circumstances to override this presumption, the cause must be just; the authorities, competent; justice, comparatively greater; intentions, right, both with respect to ends and means; and so forth. The empirical grounds are the principle of double effect. In order to minimize its bad and maximize its good effects, war must be the last resort; success must be probable; the value of ends sought must outweigh the harm inflicted, and, during the war, noncombatant immunity must be maintained by discriminate and proportional means; and so on.

Fourth, the common-sense quality of the criteria

should also be clear. When one sits down to discuss the decision to initiate a war, what else would one debate besides how right one's own cause was and how wrong was that of the other side? What else would one debate besides the probability of success; whether the last resort had arrived, and so forth? This common-sense quality is perhaps seen most clearly in the *in bello* criteria. Although they are clothed in an ethical language, they wear military uniforms equally well. That is, the principle of double effect and the call for noncombatant immunity are but another way to express the Pentagon's doctrine of minimizing "collateral damage."

The need to minimize the "collateral" or unintended damage done by military operations arises out of two reciprocal principles of war, the principle of mass and the principle of economy of force. In order to achieve victory, one must concentrate the mass of one's military forces at the decisive time in the decisive place. Massing forces in one place means that forces must be economized in every other place, allocating a minimum of the available forces to secondary efforts. In other words, one must make a discriminate and proportional uses of one's forces, so as not to waste limited military resources. And, of course, the greatest waste of military resources is to use them against nonmilitary people and facilities, a common-sense military observation that returns one to the ethical call for noncombatant immunity. Indeed, the only excuse for diverting military forces away from military objectives and against civilian people and facilities is a desire for vengeance and wanton destruction, which, not incidentally, is a violation of the *in bello* criterion of right intention.

III. ISSUES RAISED BY THE CRITERIA

The common-sense quality of the just-war criteria makes one wonder why other non-European cultures have not developed a similarly elaborate set of criteria. The response is paradoxical: On the one hand, all the major cultures of the world possess something similar to the European just-war criteria. They all recognize the principle of double effect. They all maintain a strong presumption against war. Hence, they all possess codes of chivalry and other customs and traditions to ameliorate the savagery of military operations. For the same reason, the initial decision to declare war is debated in all cultures in terms of its causes, its probability of success, whether the tools of diplomacy have been exhausted, and so forth.

On the other hand, only in Europe were the criteria

elaborated in such detail and so explicitly. In other cultures, they remain informal and not always explicitly stated in a formal and legalistic manner. For example, Sun-Tzu in his *Art of War* emphasizes that *dao* (moral influence) is the first factor to be considered before engaging in war, a thought that the commentator Chang Yu elaborates as, "When troops are raised to chastise transgressors, the temple council first considers the adequacy of the rulers' benevolence. . . ." (1963, p. 63). Next, the temple council considers the probability of success criterion, which Sun-Tzu interprets as consisting of four factors: weather, terrain, command (i.e., the abilities of the opposing generals), and doctrine (i.e., the organization and training of the opposing armies).

Early on, the criteria were treated informally in Europe as well. For example, scattered passages in the *Iliad* articulate a rudimentary set of just causes for war but no attempt at systematization: "to fight for Helen and her property" (III, 70), "[to] take vengeance on the men who break their oaths" (III, 279), "[for] injuring the host who entertained him" (III, 353). Homer recognizes that only the most compelling circumstances can override the presumption against war. He, therefore, provides not one, but three just causes. Still, there is no effort at further elaboration or systematization.

A. Systematization and Secularization in Europe

However, systematization and secularization of the criteria soon began. Aristotle, in his *Rhetorica ad Alexandrum* (1425ᵃ), outlines in rudimentary fashion the arguments that should be made when one wishes either to initiate or prevent war. In both cases, the justice of one's cause and the probability of success are the cardinal points. Thus, Aristotle advises Alexander that, "The pretexts for making war on another state are. . ." either to avenge past or present wrongs or to gain some advantage such as glory, resources, or strength, while the factors leading to success are the favor of the gods, the number of troops, an abundance of resources, the wisdom of the general, excellent allies, and superior position.

In the ancient world, the most sustained effort at articulating the criteria took place in early Republican Rome, where the issues of war and peace were submitted to sustained scrutiny and systematization in the *collegium fetiales,* the religious congregation that was responsible for sanctifying the ratification of treaties and declarations of war in accordance with the *jus fetiale.* The *jus fetiale* was a well-established tradition of law built upon the principle that, "Therefore the only justification for war is that peace and justice should afterwards prevail," as Cicero tells his son in *De Officiis* (I, xi, 35). The *jus fetiale* has since been lost; we know of it only through scattered references and a long passage in Livy (I, xxxii).

Still, the knowledge that legal criteria for a just war could be and had been articulated survived the fall of Rome and became the basis of Christianity's response to war. During the zenith of the Roman Empire, Christianity had been a marginal dissident religious sect that was often persecuted. Excluded from political power, the Church seldom took a position one way or another on political issues, in general, and on war, in particular. Whether this silence concerning war was motivated by indifference to all things secular or by religiously based pacifist principle is difficult to say. Considerable evidence exists to support both positions.

But whatever her motivation while excluded from political power, as the Empire in the west slowly disintegrated under repeated barbarian invasions, the Church was forced, first, to assume greater and greater political responsibilities and, eventually, to consider the issue of war in all its practical details. In response to repeated questions as to whether a good Christian prince could wage war or a good Christian soldier could kill in war, Augustine and others seized upon Cicero and the ancients to respond, yes, thereby drawing the ancient pagan thinking on just war into the Christian Church. However, the concern at this time was pastoral, not legal. Augustine and the Church were responding to the immediate concerns of the times and the laity. There was as yet no attempt systematize the Church's position on war. For example, to learn of Augustine's attitude toward the just war, one must read a dozen or more scattered passages in his letters and books, as will be seen shortly.

During the Middle Ages, however, the Church's needs and attitude changed. A unique relationship developed between the Church of Rome and the multitude of feudal principalities into which Christendom was divided, which created conditions that soon stimulated a renewed interest in systematizing the just-war criteria. For, during this period, the Church maintained enormous moral authority but had little interest in usurping the temporal power of the feudal barons. It was, as a result, an influential but a relatively disinterested observer of the innumerable wars that these petty princes waged. Being influential, the Church's endorsement of one side or the other in a war was of considerable political and psychological value. Being relatively disinterested, feudal barons felt safe in asking the Church to endorse their side and condemn the other. Conse-quently, Church authorities received a constant stream of requests from both sides for judgments as to which belligerent possessed justice on his side. As the heirs of ancient Roman administrative and legal practices and with the knowledge that the Romans had once possessed the *jus fetiale,* the natural response of the canon lawyers was to begin systematizing an explicit set of criteria with which they could organize their briefs and by which bishops and popes could render a decision.

At first, the criteria grew like topsy, multiplying seemingly uncontrollably to cover all aspects of war. Then, as noted above, Aquinas reduced the list to three essential *ad bellum* criteria, thereby simplifying, clarifying, and generalizing the criteria. In the 17th century, Hugo Grotius, relying largely upon the writings of Alberico Gentili, secularized the criteria and incorporated them into international law. In the 20th century, after further secularization and elaboration, the criteria provided the intellectual foundations for a series of conventions negotiated in the Hague and at Geneva. In this manner, the moral foundation of the just-war criteria— the strong presumption against war—became one of the foundations upon which the laws of war and international humanitarian law were built.

More recently, during the great antinuclear protests of the 1980s, the just-war criteria entered secular politics in a most remarkable manner. Drawing upon the Church's traditional just-war doctrines, first, the Catholic bishops in 1983 and, then, the United Methodist bishops in 1986 published long and thoughtful pastoral letters concerning America's nuclear policy. The Catholic bishops concluded on the basis of a just-war analysis that a "nuclear war" would be immoral and unacceptable, but found that a policy of "nuclear deterrence" was "conditionally" acceptable. The United Methodist bishops, however, went a step further and found that even "nuclear deterrence" was immoral and unacceptable on just-war and other grounds.

In response to the Catholic bishops' religion-based just-war challenges, Secretary of Defense Caspar Weinberger and Secretary of State George Shultz prepared thoughtful responses. Secretary Weinberger responded in a 28 November 1984 speech before the National Press Club and in his annual report to the Congress, while Secretary Shultz responded in a 9 December 1984 address at Yeshiva University. Both side-stepped the conclusions of the Catholic bishops concerning nuclear policy, with which they strongly disagreed, but both agreed that the just-war criteria were a necessary and valuable guide to decision making. They then went on to list the five criteria that they felt should guide policymakers before committing American combat forces to action. These included the three *jus ad bellum* criteria of just cause—reinterpreted as "national interests"—probability of success, and last resort and the two *jus in bello* criteria of proportionality of means and discrimination of means.

In this manner, the traditional just-war criteria were revived from within the Christian Churches, injected into the ongoing secular political debate, and stimulated prominent political leaders to secularize and formally introduce them into the highest policy-making levels. Secularization was achieved, in part, by listing only the most pragmatic of criteria but, more so, by redefining "just cause" as "national interest." Deciding for or against war on the basis of perceived "national interests" not only removes all religion from the debate, but, many would argue, all morality as well. Be that as it may, a fully secularized, slimmed down version of the traditional Christian just-war criteria is now firmly established at policy-making level in the Departments of Defense and State, as was seen during the Persian Gulf War.

B. Defining a "Just" Cause

But explicit systematization and secularization are not the only or, indeed, the most important distinguishing characteristics of the European just-war criteria. More important is the contentious issue of the value that defines a "just" cause. Needless to say, opinions differ. Indeed, even within the European tradition, different values are proposed. Some hold that self-defense is the defining value, while others insist that only justice can define a "just" cause. But, before addressing this division within the European tradition, a brief survey of other cultures will be useful.

1. Harmony in China

As already noted, the role of war in China is, not to punish aggressors, but to "chastise transgressors," those who have betrayed the benevolence of the emperor by disrupting the harmony of empire. The crucial question, therefore, is not the justice or injustice of the transgressors' demands, but rather the state of the emperor's benevolence. Having framed the moral issue in this way, two possibilities exist: If the temple council finds the emperor's benevolence inadequate, then he, and not the rebels, must be chastised. If, however, the temple council finds the emperor's benevolence adequate, then the dogs of war should be loosed, the transgressors chastised, and harmony restored to the empire. Debating the adequacy of the emperor's benevolence is, need-less to say, an exceedingly delicate task, not only politically, but logically as well, for, the mere existence of rebellious transgressors demonstrates a deficiency in the emperor's benevolence. This inconvenient conclusion generates a perplexing dilemma: A truly benevolent emperor never needs to war, while a warring emperor is not truly benevolent. However, the temple council might resolve this dilemma, the value that defines a "just" cause is not so much an European concern with either self-defense or justice as an East Asian concern with harmony.

2. Duty in India

In India, the defining value is not harmony, but duty, seen as the submission to the inexorable working of darma and karma. The primary problem, therefore, is learning how these forces have determined the world. Ideally, one learns of one's duty through enlightenment, as happens in the *Bhagavad Gita*. The *Gita* is a story of a dialogue in which Lord Krishna enlightens a skeptical Prince Arjuna on the karmic and darmic forces that determine his duty, which is to fight and win a great battle fated for the morrow. In general, the need for enlightenment arises out of the workings of the principle of double effect, "Whatever austerities you undergo, / Kunti's son, do as an offering to me. / Thus you will be released / From the bonds of action, its fair and evil fruits, ..." (9, 27–28). More particularly, the need arises out of a strong presumption against war: Why, Arjuna asks insistently, should he fight and shed the blood of his kinsmen? The crucial moment comes in the eleventh chapter when Lord Krishna gives the Prince "the eye of a god. / [To b]hold my mystery as the lord" (11, 8), in order that he may achieve enlightenment.

Having seen Krishna's myriad forms, but not yet understanding their meaning, Prince Arjuna asks again, "Tell me, you of awful form, who are you? / ... / I wish to know you, who have been from the beginning, / For I do not know what you have set out to do" (11, 31). To which Lord Krishna responds, "I am time, destroyer of worlds, grown old / Setting out to gather in worlds. / These warriors drawn up, facing the arrows, / Even without you, they shall cease to be. / Therefore, stand up. Seize honor. / Conquer your foes. Enjoy the rich kingdom. / They were killed by me long ago. / Be but the means, left-handed archer (11, 32–33).

Neither the justice or injustice of each side's demands nor the need to restore harmony is the primary value under discussion. Instead, it is the need to do one's duty so that one can conform to one's fate, to the workings of darma and his karma. The practical problem with valuing duty over justice, of course, is that Krishna seldom provides the required enlightenment. Gandhi, a close student of the *Gita*, resolved this problem by arguing that knowledge of one's fate resulted from "austerities": One did one's duty, suffered the consequences, and, from that suffering, truth emerged; one learned, *post facto*, how darma and karma had shaped his fate. Life, therefore, was *satyagraha*, a "struggle for truth." For, just as it was Prince Arjuna's duty to fight and "Enjoy the rich kingdom," it was equally the duty of his kinsmen to fight and "cease to be." No one but Lord Krishna knew this before the battle; all knew it after.

To be sure, Gandhi and others do not advocate blindly doing one's duty. Every effort should be made at enlightenment. One must analyze the circumstances as best as one can. The comparative justice of each side's cause, the probability of success, and so on, must be debated and judged. Yet, in the final analysis, the workings of darma and karma are seen but darkly. The only certainty is that one has a duty to suffer one's fate, especially when one is fated to "cease to be."

3. Religion and Justice in Islam

Islam distinguishes two types of war: *harb* and *jihad*. *Jihad* is war in defense of Islam. *Harb* is every other type of war. Lacking a religious motivation, *harb* (literally, war) is incapable of being "truly" just. Its nonreligious, purely political, purposes render it suspect, even when otherwise just. *Jihad* (both the personal and political struggle to overcome evil) promises more than simple political gain. It promises a just and equitable polity built upon Islamic values. Peaceful missionary activities are of course preferred in the creation of an Islamic polity, but, under certain conditions, war may be a necessary adjunct.

By the 9th century, Sunni jurists had developed criteria to define these circumstances: A *jihad* must meet *ad bellum* criteria of a just cause, right intention, competent authority, probability of success, aim for peace, and, before the combat begins, an invitation to accept Islamic rule must be issued. The *jihad* must also be conducted in accordance with Islamic values, which means the *in bello* criteria of discrimination in the use of military forces and preserving noncombatant immunity. The Shiite jurists generally accepted these same criteria, disputing with the Sunni jurists only the identity of the authority competent to declare *jihad* (Kelsay, 1993, 35–36).

The formal similarity with the European criteria is remarkable. However, the Islamic criteria always remained religious at heart. They were never secularized to the same degree as the European criteria. Thus, the invitation to accept Islamic rule is not the same as the European last resort criterion, and the just cause is often a simple refusal to accept the invitation to accept Islamic rule. Nor would "national interests" ever be acceptable as just cause. Still, the Islamic values that *jihad* is supposed to defend and extend are, "... the values associated with pure monotheism; to command good, forbid evil, and bring about justice in the earth" (*ibid.*, 1993, 42). Thus, it would appear that, should the Islamic criteria ever undergo secularization, the values that define a "just" cause in Islam are not far distant from those that define a "just" cause in the secularized European tradition.

4. Unresolved Values in Europe

As already noted, the values that define a "just" cause in the European tradition are not settled. The mainstream holds that self-defense constitutes a "just" cause. A countercurrent denies this and insists that justice alone can constitute a "just" cause. The countercurrent traces its origins from Roman law as filtered through Cicero to Augustine to parts of Aquinas (*Summa* IIa–IIae, q69, 4). The mainstream draws upon the natural law tradition and stretches from Aristotle to other parts of Aquinas (*Summa* IIa–IIae, q64, 7) to Thomas Hobbes to Grotius from whence it entered international law.

This last is what makes it the mainstream. Without an assertion of a right to self-defense, both international law and the modern nation-state system as we know them would be impossible. Indeed, the inviolable sovereignty that defines both modern nation-states and international law is meaningless unless nation-states also possess a right of self-defense. Consequently, this right is enshrined in innumerable documents, such as Article 51 of the United Nations Charter, "Nothing in the present Charter shall impair the inherent right of individual or collective self-defense...."

a. Self-Defense

Although denying a right of self-defense violates all of our intuitions, asserting such a right is not without problems. To begin with, the international law right is based upon an analogous individual right: Since each individual possesses a right of self-defense, then, by analogy, so do nation-states. But drawing analogies from individual persons to nation-states is extremely treacherous; nation-states are not simply large families.

More problematic is the fact that the assertion of a personal right of self-defense is based upon an instinct, the instinct for self-preservation. But can an instinct form the grounds for a right? Do we possess a right to free speech because we have an instinct to gossip? or because participation in politics is impossible unless each participant is able to speak his mind freely? Besides being an instinctive reaction to danger, what other grounds are there upon which to base a right of self-defense?

However one might answer, the consequences of the assertion are also problematic. Diplomatically, the assertion of a right of self-defense shunts debate into a discussion of "aggression." For, if the exercise of this right justifies a resort to war, it can be activated only by an act of "aggression." Unfortunately though, "aggression" cannot be defined mechanically as "The first use of armed force by a State …" as the 1974 United Nations Resolution 3314 (XXIX) on defining aggression notes. In the absence of a mechanical definition, "… whether an act of aggression has been committed must be considered in the light of all the circumstances of each particular case … ," as the preamble of the United Nations Resolution continues. In other words, whenever "all of the circumstances of a particular case" lead the Security Council to believe that the side that strikes first in a war was justified in striking first, then the "aggressor" is not an "aggressor." Hence, it is the comparative justice of each side, and not "aggression" *per se,* that really determines the case.

Legally, the assertion of a right to self-defense creates an extremely ambiguous situation. For, as soon as one nation exercises this right by responding to an attack, the attacking nation is no longer an aggressor, since she is now exercising her own right of self-defense against attack. To avoid this dilemma, criminal law has long since held that "There can be no self-defense against self-defense." The point, of course, is that the party exercising their right of self-defense also claims that the other party was unjustified in attacking in the first place. Again, it is comparative justice, not an instinct for self-preservation, that is really at issue.

Morally, the assertion of a right to self-defense largely annuls the proportionality and discrimination criteria. The point of calling for discrimination of means and due proportionality of both ends and means is to constrain the destruction of a war. In minor wars in which the existence of the state is not in question, no one objects to such constraint. However, all constraint is lost in what Michael Walzer in his very influential 1977 book, *Just and Unjust Wars,* calls "supreme emergencies," when the very existence of the state itself is in jeopardy. Walzer and others argue the consequences of the destruction of the state are so enormous that a right of self-defense overrides all constraints. In "supreme emergencies," the end of preserving the state justifies whatever means are available.

Opponents of this consequentialist perspective propose instead a deontological perspective. First, they deny that the continued existence of the nation-state is of absolute value. History demonstrates that they come and go too frequently to sustain such a claim. The French, for example, are on their fifth republic. Second, they point out that, if the survival of nation-state *does* represent an absolute value such that a "supreme emergency" frees the state from all moral constraints in a war, then what is the point of the criteria? In sum, the deontological perspective argues that Walzer and the consequentialists cannot have it both ways. They cannot argue for the constraining influence of the just-war criteria in minor wars, but deny that same influence in "supreme emergencies."

b. Justice

Interestingly, the problems just cited do not loom large in the traditional arguments for defining a "just" cause in terms of justice only. Cicero, for example, was dogmatic about the matter. Making a four-part argument, he asserted, first, that peace and justice were the only justification for war; second, that, "… justice, above all, [is] the basis of which alone men are called 'good', … [and] no one can be just who fears death or pain or exile or poverty, or who values their opposites above equity" (*De Officiis* II, x, 38); moreover, third, "… that if anything is morally right, it is expedient, and if anything is not morally right, it is not expedient" (*ibid.* III, iii, 11); from which he concluded, fourth, that ". . . there are some acts either so repulsive or so wicked, that a wise man would not commit them, even to save his country" (*ibid.* I, xlv, 159).

Aquinas was less dogmatic, but more ambiguous and more discriminating. He was ambiguous because he allowed that, "… the controlled use of counter-violence constitutes legitimate self-defense" (*Summa* IIa–IIae, q64, 7). He was more discriminating because he understood that the crucial case is not that of "counter-violence" but the imposition of the death penalty. Self-defense is usually argued by asking, "What would you do if a gunman attacked you or your family?" To which the usual response is "I would defend myself and my family." This case is a clear example of the instinct for self-preservation, from which it is then assumed that a person must possess a right of self-defense. But a direct attack, which must be presumed to be also an unjust attack, is not the crucial case. The decisive case is the imposition of the death penalty by a lawful authority.

When Aquinas takes this case up, he, first, acknowledges the instinctual basis of a right of self-defense, "A person condemned to death would seem to be entitled to defend himself, if he has a chance to do so. For whatever is prompted by nature would seem to be legitimate, as being in accordance with the natural law." He, then, replies that, "A man is condemned to death in two ways. First, justly. And in such a case he is not entitled to defend himself, ... A man may, however, also be condemned unjustly. Sentence in such a case is like the violence of brigands, ... It follows that one is in such a case entitled to resist evil sovereigns in the same way as one is entitled to resist brigands, ... " (*Summa* IIa–IIae, q69, 4). Once again, the justice of one's cause determines one's right of self-defense, not the simple instinct for self-preservation.

Unlike Aquinas, Augustine was unambiguous. He denied any right of self-defense, "In regards to killing men so as not to be killed by them, this view does not please me, ... (*Espistula XLVII, ad Publicolam;* cp. *De libero arbitro* I, 5). Augustine of course recognized a natural instinct for self-preservation, "That he [any man] loves his body and wishes to have it safe and whole is equally obvious" (*De doctrina christiana* I, 25). But that was precisely the problem. To defend oneself was only to demonstrate concupiscence, an inordinate desire for the things of this world, in general, and an inordinate love of self, in particular. Instead of this instinctual egotism, one should look to higher things, "... you should love yourself not on your own account but on account of Him who is most justly the object of your love, ... " (*ibid.* I, 22). Augustine, however, was not so other worldly that he counseled turning the other cheek whenever attacked. Justice, not self-defense, was his principle, "War and conquest are a sad necessity in the eyes of men of principle, yet it would be still more unfortunate if wrong doers should dominate just men" (*City of God*, IV, 15).

But, if "wrong doers" should not be allowed to dominate "just men," then there is little practical difference between defining "just" cause in terms of self-defense or in terms of justice. In most cases, the decision will be the same, because the attacker will also be a "wrong doer." Yet, in a small number of the cases, the attacker will not be a "wrong doer," and the decision will be different. In these few case, in these "supreme emergencies," by valuing justice over the survival of the nation-state, one would act like Cicero's "wise man," who would do no injustice even to save his country, and not like the Nazi SS, who would do any injustice to save their country, believing as they did that "*Unsere Ehre Heisst Treue*," "Our Honor Is Named Loyalty."

It would appear, therefore, that, while serviceable, the international-law principle of self-defense is not the most solid value with which to define "just" cause.

Defining "just" cause in terms of justice would appear more solid. However, justice is not without its difficulties, too. For, in any war, both sides will loudly proclaim the justice of their cause. More perplexing, in most wars, both claims will sound persuasive. Were this not the case, there would never be an occasion for war.

Inasmuch as both sides persuade themselves that *their* cause is "just," valuing justice over self-defense solves few problems. Indeed, it creates a situation that appears identical to the working of darma and karma: In defense of justice, both sides possess a duty to suffer their fates, to wage the war and, thereby, to learn the truth *post facto*. The difference between the Hindu and the countercurrent in the European tradition is that the Hindu speak of enlightenment and a "struggle for truth," while the Europeans speak, as the Athenian ambassadors did at Melos, of might making right (Thucycdides V, 89).

In summary then, while the systematized and secularized just-war criteria of today had their roots in ancient Greece and Rome and flourished and developed in the medieval Christian church before being taken over by modern-day international law and policy makers, these European criteria, nonetheless, have parallels in other cultures. All cultures possess a strong presumption against war, and all cultures acknowledge the operation of the principle of double effect. As a result, all cultures possess a more or less formal and systematic way to debate and decide whether a war is "just," namely, whether circumstances are such as to override the presumption against war and its many unintended evil effects. Where the cultures part ways is in their degree of systematization and secularization, on the one hand, and in the value that the "just" cause should embody, on the other hand. In China, the debate is conducted in terms of restoring harmony; in India, in terms of accomplishing one's duty; in Islam, in terms of fostering religion; in modern international law, in terms of self-defense and preserving the sovereignty of the nation-state, while in Augustinian Christianity, the debate is conducted in terms of justice.

Also See the Following Articles

GUERRILLA WARFARE • JUSTIFICATIONS FOR VIOLENCE • MILITARISM • TERRORISM • WAR CRIMES • WORLD WAR II

Bibliography

Johnson, J. T. (1981). *Just war tradition and the restraint of war: A moral and historical inquiry.* Princeton, NJ: Princeton University Press.
Kelsay, J. (1993). *Islam and war: A study in comparative ethics.* Louisville, KY: Westminster/John Knox Press.

Miller, R. (Ed.). (1991). *Interpretations of conflict: Ethics, pacifism, and the just-war tradition.* Chicago, IL: University of Chicago Press.

Nardin, T. (Ed.). (1996). *The ethics of war and peace.* Princeton, NJ: Princeton University Press.

Novak, D. (1992). Non-Jews in a Jewish polity: Subject or sovereign? In *Jewish social ethics.* New York: Oxford University Press.

Potter, R. B., Jr. (1970). The moral logic of war. *McCormick Quarterly, 23,* 203–233. Reprinted in C. R. Beitz & T. Herman (eds.). (1973). *Peace and war.* San Francisco, CA: W. H. Freeman.

Johnson, J. T., & Kelsay, J. (eds.). (1990). *Cross, crescent, and sword: The justification and limitation of war in Western and Islamic tradition.* New York: Greenwood Press.

Sun Tzu. (1963). *The art of war.* Samuel B. Griffith (Trans.). Oxford at the Clarendon Press.

The United States Catholic Conference. (1993, December 9). The Harvest of Justice Is Sown in Peace. *Origins, 23* (26).

United Methodist Council of Bishops. (1986). *In defense of creation: The nuclear Crisis and a just peace.* Nashville, TN: Graded Press.

Walzer, M. (1977). *Just and unjust wars: A moral argument with historical illustrations.* New York: Basic Books.

Juvenile Crime

Simon I. Singer

University at Buffalo

GLOSSARY

Delinquent A juvenile who commits an offense that would be considered a crime if committed by an adult is considered a delinquent. An adult who commits an offense for which he or she can be convicted in criminal court has committed an act of crime. A juvenile who similarly commits an offense for which he or she can be convicted in juvenile court has committed an act of delinquency.

Juvenile Court A legal setting in which juveniles may be adjudicated delinquent. The age of juveniles and the type of offenses that can be considered in the juvenile court are determined by state law.

Juvenile Crime Any act committed by adolescents in violation of the legal norms of society. It is broadly defined to be inclusive of a wide range of offenses as measured by self-report and official sources of criminological data.

Juvenile Offender A juvenile who commits an offense for which he or she is criminally responsible. This may occur through the juvenile's transfer from the juvenile court to the criminal court. In some states, juveniles are considered criminally responsible for certain types of offenses.

Status Offender A juvenile who commits an act that is considered illegal because of the juvenile's age. A juvenile who is repeatedly truant has committed a status offense. Adults are not required to go to school and therefore cannot be arrested for acts of truancy.

THE OFFICIAL DEFINITION OF JUVENILE CRIME is rooted in legal rules for classifying juveniles as delinquents, status or juvenile offenders. Criminology has long recognized the variability of such definitions and their attempt to identify the unique characteristics of juveniles as delinquents or as offenders. There are numerous textbooks on juvenile delinquency and juvenile justice that attempt to locate the nature and extent of juvenile crime. The textbook summary definition of delinquency is related to the legal definition of the delinquent.

The legal definition of the delinquent varies from state to state. In some American states, the general age of criminal responsibility is as low as 16 and as high as 21. In England and Wales, the upper age in which juveniles are eligible for youth court is 17. Juvenile courts and youth courts are just one legal avenue in the juvenile justice process. They determine whether or not a juvenile committed a juvenile crime. Criminal courts also may determine if juveniles are criminally responsible for certain types of offences.

Juvenile justice and its system of juvenile courts reflect the modern-day social extension of childhood. Prior to industrialization, juveniles past the age of pu-

Copyright © 1999 by Academic Press.
All rights of reproduction in any form reserved.

berty were more often treated like adults. This is the familiar history of juvenile justice. It is one that is coupled with other developments in society in which the definitional status of adolescence changed. For example, in the realm of education more juveniles were seen in need of formal compulsory public school training to meet the more technical demands of industrialization. Related to juvenile crime was the newly emerging category of delinquency for age-related deviance such as truancy which developed as a result of compulsory education.

The definition of juvenile crime can be inclusive of a wide range of behavior that is not normally considered illegal if committed by adults. These are acts that at one time might have been considered juvenile forms of crime and are increasingly viewed in a separate legal category. In some states, juveniles charged with a variety of status offenses, such as truancy, face the legal designation of Person in Need of Supervision (PINS). Although such labels might be considered quite distinct from juvenile crime, they reflect an emerging trend in modern-day societies to classify and label juveniles with a diverse set of legal categories.

But the definition of juvenile crime as crime that is committed by juveniles is not uniform. Juvenile crimes are at times redefined as adult crimes. This redefinition is a consequence of legal reforms that have lowered the age of criminal responsibility. It requires officials to bypass the juvenile justice system and to move youth directly into the criminal justice system. As is the case with status offenders, the definition of who is a juvenile offender is subject to variation in time and place.

I. CORRELATES

Our knowledge of the correlates of juvenile crime stems from official and unofficial sources from delinquency and crime data. Self-report data are obtained from random samples of the juvenile population who are asked in surveys to report the incidence and prevalence of their involvement in various acts of delinquency and crime. These surveys are generally specific to particular times and places. When they are administered over time to a large sample of the population, such as through the National Youth Surveys, they can inform us of national rates of delinquency and trends over time.

Another way of knowing about juvenile crime is through official sources of data. These may include arrest, court, and residential placement data. Each set of data has its own set of advantages and disadvantages for telling us about the correlates of juvenile crime.

One major disadvantage is that official sources of information about juvenile crime is selective. It is not based on the entire population of juveniles who commit acts of delinquency or crime, but only those juveniles who come to the attention of legal officials. Official sources of data tell us about the characteristics of juveniles processed in the juvenile justice system through arrest, adjudication, and disposition.

Case-processing decisions are related to how offense and offender characteristics are viewed by officials. Some offenses and offenders are viewed as more serious than others, warranting official intervention by means of arrest, adjudication, and disposition. The selective population of delinquents who are arrested constitute what officials might consider as the more serious population of delinquents.

There are several rules for interpreting or applying crime statistics to our understanding of juvenile crime. First, it is important to bear in mind that official statistics represent decision making on juveniles at varying points in the juvenile justice process. But some official statistics are better than others for telling us about the total amount of juvenile crime. Police arrest data provide a better indication of the total amount of delinquents than court or custody data. The official delinquent population based on juvenile court charges only includes the number of juveniles who were charged in the juvenile court, not the entire population of arrested juveniles.

Another criminological rule of official statistics is to consider the type and severity of the offense. The more serious the offense the more likely a juvenile crime will come to the attention of officials and lead to a juvenile's arrest. Similarly, the more serious the arrest, the more likely juvenile justice officials are to charge juveniles in juvenile court. Offense seriousness not only drives citizen reporting of juvenile crime, but also official processing decisions. In other words, juvenile crime is not crime unless it is serious enough to be observed, reported, and recorded as a crime or act of delinquency. But this does not mean that there are no other factors that lead to the recording of an offense as a crime. The reasons for arrest may be related to factors that are correlated with arrest, such as age, gender, and race, independent of offense seriousness characteristics.

The most often cited official measure of juvenile crime is that of the Federal Bureau of Investigation's Uniform Crime Report (UCR). The UCR program is based on police recorded incidents of crime for juveniles as well as for adults. The reports provide an indication of the amount of juvenile crime based on offenses cleared by arrest. They divide a diverse set of offenses into index and nonindex categories. Index offenses are technically more serious based on the level of violence and property offenses. Index offenses include murder, rape, robbery, serious assault, burglary, larceny, auto theft, and arson. Nonindex offenses include all other offenses and status offenses, such as running away and curfew violations.

The UCR arrest data also indicate that some crimes are more prevalent among juveniles than other crimes. Juveniles are involved in a higher proportion of property than violent offenses. The percent of persons arrested under age 18 is greatest for auto theft and arson among the index offenses. Among nonindex offenses, a large proportion of juveniles are arrested for vandalism and liquor law violations. As expected, 100% of all arrests for running away and curfew and loitering law violations are for juveniles.

Over time it appears that both index and nonindex juvenile crime is increasing at a faster rate than adult crime. Between 1988 and 1994, the percent of total arrests for juveniles increased by 42%, compared to 23% for adults. For index offenses the percent of juveniles arrested increased by 33%, compared to 17% for adults. From the UCR data it would appear that more persons under 18 are being arrested for more serious offenses.

Several personal characteristics are commonly correlated with juvenile crime. Gender is strongly correlated with serious forms of delinquency. The prevalence of delinquency is generally much greater among boys than it is among girls. Boys are generally arrested three to four times more often than girls. However, for less serious offense categories the difference between the rate of arrest is substantially less. Girls are generally more often arrested for running away and for prostitution than are boys.

Race is correlated with index and nonindex crime. For some index offenses Black juveniles are substantially overrepresented in contrast to their distribution in the population. Robbery for UCR reported arrests are more often committed by Black juveniles. For vandalism and arson the representation of White juveniles is closer to their distribution in the population.

Survey data based on the National Crime Surveys of victimization and self-report National Youth Surveys tend to confirm the official rates of delinquency and crime. They show that there are gender and racial differences in the rate of serious juvenile crime. Less serious forms of delinquency, however, are not as strongly correlated with race and gender. Self-report data tend to show that for minor offenses there are few differences

by gender and race in the incidence and prevalence of juvenile crime.

II. EXPLANATIONS

As noted the correlates of juvenile crime are directly linked to age. The UCR data and other research tracking the delinquent or arrest behavior of populations of juveniles over time show that young people commit a disproportionate amount of crime. Rising and declining rates of involvement in crime can be attributed to both social structure and process. Another way to think about structure and process is in terms of macro- and microlevel effects in the generation of delinquent and nondelinquent behaviors.

Structural theories suggest that the location of delinquents and juvenile crime are patterned by conditions in society independent of individual behaviors. According to a structural perspective, it makes a difference whether a person resides in a tightly knit community where neighbors are neighborly and where there are extended family relationships to support and to control the raising of youth. In the sociological image of a well-organized community, informal forms of social control are more likely to dominate with less of a need for juvenile justice. In a community with fewer calls to the police, there are fewer identifiable incidents of delinquency, and consequently fewer delinquents.

The macrolevel focus of structural theories of juvenile crime is different than a microlevel focus in which the juvenile and the process in which juveniles adapt to crime are considered. Biography becomes important in a microlevel analysis. The juvenile's personal biography, his or her biological, psychological, and social development, present a particular set of attributes that are considered important in distinguishing juveniles who commit crime from those who do not.

Early theories of juvenile crime stress biological and personality differences. They fall into the biological school of thought in which delinquents arise like criminals from an inherited predisposition to commit crime. Some scholars have posited a genetic link that produce a personality resistant to authority. Body type is further related in some studies, which, not surprisingly, find that delinquents are more muscular than nondelinquents.

It is difficult to separate the biological from the social. No studies of identical twins show a 100% concordance in criminal behavior, suggesting that genetic structure is not the sole cause of crime. But genetic structure can be expected to interact with social processes, such as the kind of frustration that a learning-disabled child experiences in school. That frustration reflects personal as well as social difficulties. It involves an educational tracking system that segregates and classifies juveniles into learning disabled or slower tracks of students.

Psychological assessments of a juvenile's well-being also reflect a modern-day image of what characterizes a normal juvenile. It involves a system of classifying and a vision of what is normal in terms of the juvenile population. Psychologists and others in the helping professions are in the business of normalizing the delinquent population. Standards are maintained as to where juveniles should be, not only educationally but also emotionally.

The diverse ways in which juveniles can be classified as delinquents or offenders in modern-day societies reflect more than heredity or personality disturbances. Juvenile crime in the sociological view of causation is a product of social interaction. At a structural level this interaction is patterned by variables, such as neighborhood and class, that go beyond particular personal characteristics. The social organization of class and neighborhood structures the social interaction of juveniles as well as adults.

An ecological approach to explaining juvenile crime stresses its geographical distribution. The pattern of social and physical space in a city is considered a good predictor of juvenile crime. In some neighborhoods, there is a greater sense of disorder and danger. These are areas that tend to be of low rent and physically deteriorated. Impoverished juveniles residing in such areas tend to have high rates of delinquency.

The term social disorganization has been used to describe the lack of informal sources of control that exist in impoverished areas of cities. There is a sense of disorder in such communities as exemplified by high rates of juvenile crime. But it is misleading to assume that because of high rates of juvenile crime, there is no social order. There is a social order that is differentially organized with the consequence of producing behavior that sometimes is in violation of legal norms.

The differential social organization of juvenile crime is captured in the sociological vision of learning delinquency through Edwin Sutherland's (1924) differential association theory. Sutherland's theory is sensitive to the social context in which the learning of delinquency takes place. He proposed that within intimate social groups definitions favorable to violation of the law are learned. Definitions favorable to violating the law exceed those that are unfavorable through the intensity, frequency, and duration of the learning process within intimate primary groups. Moreover, the learning of techniques and rationalizations for committing acts of juvenile crime are the same as the learning of noncriminal behavior.

Sutherland's theory ignored the initial motivation to commit an act of delinquency. It is assumed to be there and transmitted from one generation to the next. The initial source of juvenile delinquency is social disorganization or conflict between values and norms that are favorable to the law and those that are unfavorable. These differential definitions are rooted in cultures and the conflict that often emerges when varying cultures come into contact with each other.

Theories of culture and subculture are more specific to the conflicting characteristics of juvenile crime. Modern-day societies are not homogenous ones. There is a division that divides the young from the old, the employer from the employee, and the Black from the White. This division makes it possible for a variety of cultures or subcultures to coexist in ways that allow for unique ways of behaving to develop. Much of the social grouping that takes place may be a reaction to other groups within society.

There are several ways to interpret the meaning of the cultures and the subcultures that are related to juvenile crime. One perspective that comes from a structured view of norms and values relates delinquency to a delinquent subculture. In such a subculture, a normative order emerges that dictates the conditions for delinquency and crime. The normative order might be a reaction to middle-class values as lower class juveniles might first experience them in school. The status frustration that lower class boys may experience in school provides the impetus to gravitate to others through delinquent forms of behavior as a reaction to a common problem.

Albert Cohen's (1955) theory of delinquent boys is just the first of several subcultural perspectives on delinquency and juvenile crime. The delinquent subcultural view differs from that which sees youth culture as a part of a subculture of delinquency. In a subculture of delinquency as opposed to a delinquent subculture, according to David Matza (1964), the impetus for delinquent activities is the same as it is for dominant cultural activities. There are acts that are common to adolescents, but it is more appropriate to think about a subculture of adolescence as one that is conducive toward delinquent conduct.

In a subculture of adolescence, adult values are turned around to justify certain adolescent forms of behavior. What kind of values? First there is the value placed on drinking and having a good time in adult society that persists in adolescent youth cultures. It is difficult for youth in a subculture of adolescence to understand why drinking is illegal for them when it is not for adults. The social extension of childhood late into adolescence stresses that teenagers are different from adults, producing a normative order that does not always match natural biological rhythms.

There are other values besides that involving status offense behavior that becomes important in the subculture of delinquency view of juvenile crime. The stress on deviant values and norms suggests that risk-taking behavior is confined to delinquents. It ignores the fact that competition is an important part of contemporary Western economies. The competitive nature of sports and business encourages risk-taking activity as a dominant cultural value. It becomes misplaced when it is seen as a part of the ethos of impoverished delinquent youth. For Matza the convergence of adolescent and adult cultures in contemporary society creates conditions of deviance that Matza has described as a consequence of "subterranean convergence." Youth are linked to "the past through local legacies and to the wider social structure by a range of support" (Matza, 1964, 63). The sources of juvenile crime then reside not just in the individual delinquent, but are alive in the broader adult social world.

In contrast to the normative and subterranean view of subcultures, juvenile crime can be explained as a consequence of the changing consequences of families. The structure of single-parent households produces one less adult to watch over the behavior of adolescents. But the social control of juveniles is not just confined to direct physical supervision by parents. There is also a psychological element in the attachments to and involvements with adults that children are believed to need. Popular discussions of the modern-day breakdown of the family is another way of relating the absence of traditional, familial forms of control.

One important integrative approach to thinking about delinquency is presented in the work of John Hagan in his combination of macro- and microlevel indicators of delinquent behavior and official decisionmaking. John Hagan and associates suggest that power as a macrolevel variable is reproduced to produce microlevel effects in the form of social control that is not evenly distributed between girls and boys. The uneven distribution is attributed to conditions of class and patriarchy. Essentially, the theory states that conditions of dominance and control in the household organize delinquent conduct by gender. But unlike more traditional formulations of criminological theory that rely either on a macro- or microlevel analysis, power-control theory integrates social structure and social process. Class categories are critical to explaining parental control and the suppression of delinquent behavior. However, these class categories are based on the relative parental positions of dominance in the work place rather than measures of social prestige and status. Furthermore, the authority parents have in their positions of work is assumed to translate into conditions of dominance and control over children in the household.

In traditional patriarchal households where husbands are employed in positions of authority and wives are without employment, husbands are more likely to exercise control over their wives. The greater control that husbands enjoy over their wives is socially reproduced because of the differential involvement of mothers and fathers with their children. The critical link between class and social control within the family is the parental reproduction of their own power relationships through the control of their children.

Power-control theory further postulates an "instrument-object relationship" in which mothers and fathers are the instruments of control in the family, and sons and daughters are the objects of control. In patriarchal households, mothers are more often the instrument for maintaining control, because they are largely responsible for the day-to-day care of their children. However, in such households mothers are more able to control their daughters than their sons, because mothers keep their daughters closer to home. Hagan argues that mothers in traditional households reproduce daughters who are more focused around domestic labor and consumption in contrast to sons who are prepared for work outside the household.

Thus, power-control theory asserts that daughters are subject to more control than are sons, and sons are freer to deviate in households where fathers are in positions of authority and mothers are without authority. Traditional households produce boys who are freer than girls to deviate because they are subject to fewer controls. However, control is also linked to another major component of the power-control thesis—risk taking. In anticipation that they will hold positions of authority in the workplace, sons in traditional households are socialized to take risks while daughters are more often taught to avoid risks. This acceptance of risk-taking is reproduced among sons in the form of such risky behavior as delinquency.

A power-control perspective to delinquency is one way to explain gender differences. There are other perspectives that relate more specifically to gender differences in the socialization of girls and boys. But those gender differences are not confined to the manner in which children are raised. Moreover, a significant part of adolescent involvement or socialization takes place in schools. It is the formal structure of compulsory school education in modern-day societies that needs to be taken into account in a full explanation of juvenile crime. That structure is not based on a single school-house image of education, but rather on a complex one that marginalizes large segments of juveniles through the tracking that occurs in the modern world of education with its honor, academic, general, vocational, learning disabled, and mentally retarded categories.

So too is the legal as well as the criminological interpretation of juvenile crime a product of a diverse set of labels. In the world of law, there are the official PINS (persons in need of supervision), delinquent, restrictive delinquent, juvenile offender, and youthful offender categories. In the world of criminological terms, there are the common delinquent, the one-time, recidivist, chronic offenders, and super-predatory juveniles. All these terms are used to make the case about the varying levels in which juvenile crime is perceived in its public and official forms of seriousness.

III. REACTIONS

Few juveniles who commit serious acts of juvenile crime have not had some prior contact with the juvenile justice system. The consequences of that contact vary considerably. It may begin with a status offense, continue with a trivial act of delinquency, and then graduate to a more serious act of violence. The response of officials is usually in a sequence of avoidance and diversion until the juvenile commits an act that is serious enough to warrant last resort penalties, such as out-of-home residential placement or what might be referred to in less euphemistic terms as incarceration. Part of the justification that delinquents themselves draw on in relating the risks of punishment are the official reactions to their past behaviors. Moreover, future offenses may be justified by past offenses. The probability that a juvenile was not caught for the past offense improves the odds of not being caught for the next offense.

The official reactions to juvenile crime creates opportunities for sensing legal injustice as well. For a segment of delinquents injustice can be reproduced in the form of new justifications and rationales for more serious acts of juvenile crime. The sense of legal injustice assumes that delinquents have a sense of justice. That sense emerges early on by the mere fact that juveniles are not segregated from the wider norms of society. They not only encounter a sense of justice from their routine experiences, but also from their early experiences in the legal process.

The fact that a proportion of delinquents go on past their first arrest to repeat their delinquent behavior cannot be attributed solely to experiences outside the legal process. The legal process becomes part of the delinquent's socialization, particularly for those who are placed in court ordered residential settings. If the placement is for a status or nonserious offense, then it may be particularly difficult for the juvenile to accept the justice of the stated treatment.

A significant part of juvenile justice relies on the contemporary juvenile court. Today's juvenile court differs from a more traditional one that first emerged in the United States at the turn of the century and emphasized a nonadversarial, treatment oriented setting. Instead, the contemporary U.S. juvenile court is a criminalized juvenile court with a much more diverse, complex set of legal avenues. Diversion from and to the contemporary American juvenile court has created unique ways in which juvenile crime is identified. For serious incidents of juvenile crime, diversion to criminal court emerges through waiver. Waiver has always been a last resort policy, the capital form of punishment to exist in juvenile court for dealing with juvenile crime. But it has taken on a new form in the shape of juvenile justice policies that emphasize direct waiver through the exclusion of certain offense categories from the jurisdiction of the juvenile court.

The more complex development of juvenile justice in dealing with juvenile crime is illustrated by UCR data on the outcome of juvenile arrests. In 1971 fewer than 1% of all arrests produced a disposition in the adult criminal court compared to 5% in 1995. Police station house adjustments declined from 45% of all arrests in 1971 to less than 30% in 1995. The juvenile justice process for a significant proportion of juveniles has become more formal leading to dispositions that reflect a more bureaucratic setting in which to classify juveniles as either a status offender, delinquent or juvenile offender.

There is not just temporal variation in how juvenile crime is interrupted by the police and other officials. There is also significant cross-cultural variation in the manner in which juveniles are officially identified as delinquents. For example, in England the proportion of juveniles warned by the police has actually increased dramatically over the last several decades. This is because a cautioning policy in the early 1980s was put in place, encouraging police officials to deal with arrested delinquents within their stationhouse setting. For males between ages 14 and 16 the percentage of juveniles cautioned increased from 24% in 1970 to 63% in 1993. Figure 1 plots the percentage of juvenile arrests warned

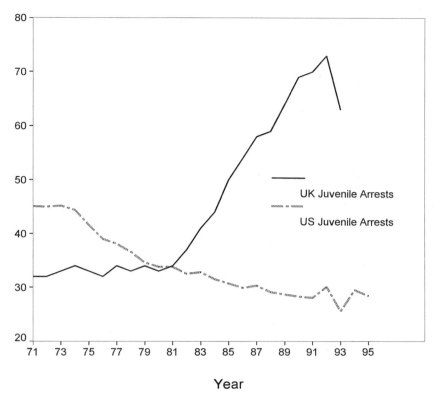

FIGURE 1 Percentage of juveniles warned by the police in the U.S. and England.

or cautioned by the police in the United States and in England. The plot shows a dramatic rise in juveniles warned or cautioned in England compared to the decrease in police warnings within the United States.

The reasons for a more bureaucratic system of juvenile justice with its diverse legal avenues are as complex as the system itself. They relate to the diverse political and organizational concerns and interests that have led to the public and official identification of juvenile crime. Part of the reason for juvenile justice is, of course, to prevent and to reduce the incidence of juvenile crime. But another part of its reason to exist is to maintain the legitimacy of a diverse set of legal avenues for dealing with juvenile crime, both within and outside systems of juvenile justice.

Although it is difficult to obtain life-course data that relate the experiences of delinquents to their sense of legal justice, there is considerable evidence that case-processing decisions are not based exclusively on offense or offender characteristics. It is how offense and offender characteristics are seen in the context of a set of other cases that appears to account for a substantial amount of juvenile justice decision making. The social context of legal decision making becomes a significant variable in accounting for juvenile crime based on its geographical and temporal characteristics.

There is considerable evidence that systems of juvenile justice do not operate in a fair or equitable manner. For instance, Singer found that Black juveniles were more often arrested as juvenile offenders for less serious violent offenses than were White juveniles. Moreover, Black juveniles were more often convicted in criminal court and given sentences of incarceration than were White juveniles, controlling for offense severity and prior offenses. The differences between Black and White juveniles may be related to how race is typified and associated with a wide range of personal problems that may be attributed to Black juveniles.

Singer further related disparities in the processing of juvenile crime based on time and place. There is a temporal dimension to juvenile justice that causes officials to be more or less severe in their adjudication and disposition based on a diverse set of political and organizational concerns and interests. Similarly, the geography of juvenile justice makes some courts of jurisdiction more severe in their treatment of juvenile crime than are other courts with their working group of officials. Despite the fact that a considerable amount of justice is regulated by state law, substantial variation exists within a single state with its diverse sets of officials and sets of cases.

The consequences of juvenile justice disparities on the actions of juveniles is difficult to determine. But it is apparent that the diverse set of legal avenues are increasingly complex, making it more difficult for officials and the public to track case processing decisions. This has led to calls for a more tightly focused system of justice to deal with juvenile crime. Such a system is seen as eliminating the social welfare objectives of the juvenile court, and replacing it with a more legalistic criminal court. In criminal court, Barry Feld suggests the types of dispositions that are applied to juveniles could involve a youth discount that takes into account the age-specific characteristics of juveniles and the best interests of the state in making treatment as the main disposition.

How the inevitable conflict between formal legal principles of justice and substantive concerns with the particular administration of legal decision making relates to prior and future definitions of juvenile crime is critical to understanding the future direction of juvenile justice. The official labeling of violent juvenile offenders as requiring the extralegal intervention of a criminal juvenile system is rooted in the belief that a continued division in types of juveniles is appropriate given the severity of their offending behavior.

IV. CONCLUSION

There are serious and nonserious categories of juvenile crime. Too often a minor act of delinquency progresses into behavior that is serious. The actions of juveniles and the reactions of adults, parents and school and juvenile justice officials, reproduce another set of actions that may further perpetuate conflict within households, schools, neighborhoods, and the broader society. How societies raise their youth to take on broader adult responsibilities without committing acts of juvenile crime has always been of utmost public concern.

What is different today is how juveniles are increasingly classified with a diverse set of social and legal labels to normalize their deviance and diverse forms of adolescent and adult behaviors. Acts of violence committed by juveniles are no longer considered in the category of delinquency as they once were with the emerging strength and all-encompassing power of the juvenile court. Editorial writers, politicians, and other legal officials along with general public opinion have redefined the delinquent as a juvenile offender as another way to confront juvenile violence.

But it is important to bear in mind that the legal process is not the only way that juvenile crime is being confronted. There are other avenues that have developed in our increasing complex systems of juvenile and criminal justice. These include extending the network of governmental programs of control into the families and schools so that parents and teachers act as better parents and teachers. Parent effectiveness training and teacher in-service training for preventing and controlling violence is now part of the continuing effort to reduce juvenile crime. It requires not only intimate knowledge of the personal histories of participants but also an awareness of the broader structures involved in the actions and reactions producing juvenile crime.

Also See the Following Articles

CRIMINAL BEHAVIOR, THEORIES OF • FAMILY STUCTURES, VIOLENCE AND NONVIOLENCE • GANGS • MINORITIES AS PERPETRATORS AND VICTIMS OF CRIME • PUNISHMENT OF CRIMINALS • SOCIAL CONTROL AND VIOLENCE

Bibliography

Bottoms, A., Haines, K., & O'Mahony, D. (1996). *Youth justice in England and Wales*. Cambridge: Institute of Criminology.

Cohen, A. (1955). *Delinquent boys*. New York: Free Press of Glencoe.

Emerson, R. M. (1969). *Judging delinquents*. Chicago: Aldine Publishing Company.

Feld, B. C. (1984). Criminalizing juvenile justice: Rules of procedure for the juvenile court. *Minnesota Law Review*, 69, 141–276.

Hagan, J. (1989). *Structural criminology*. New Brunswick, NJ: Rutgers University Press.

Hirschi, T. (1969). *Causes of delinquency*. Berkeley: University of California Press.

Frazier, C. E. & Bishop, D. M. (1995). Reflections on race effects in juvenile justice. In L. K. Kempf, C. E. Pope, & W. H. Feyerherm (Eds.), *Minorities in juvenile justice*. Thousand Oaks, CA: Sage.

Matza, D. (1964). *Delinquency and drift*. New York: John Wiley.

Singer, S. I. (1996). *Recriminalizing Delinquency: Violent juvenile crime and juvenile justice reform*. Cambridge: Cambridge University Press.

Sutherland, E. (1924). *Criminology*. Philadelphia: Lippincott.

Language of War and Peace, The

William C. Gay

University of North Carolina at Charlotte

I. Language, Perception, and Behavior
II. Language, Violence, and Nonviolence
III. The Language of War
IV. The Language of Peace

GLOSSARY

Linguistic Alienation A situation in which individuals cannot understand a discourse in their own language because of the use of highly technical vocabularies.
Linguistic Violence A situation in which individuals are hurt or harmed by words.
Negative Peace The temporary absence of active war or the lull between wars.
Positive Peace The negation of war and the presence of justice.
Warist Discourse Language that takes for granted that wars are inevitable, justifiable, and winnable.

LANGUAGE plays an important role in relation to war and peace. Language, which is rarely neutral, shapes perception and behavior. Language can be used to demean differences and inflict violence or to affirm diversity and achieve recognition. The language of war usually functions to mask the reality of the violence that is occurring. Official discourse about war makes extensive use of euphemisms and misrepresentation. By imposing

itself as legitimate, it coopts efforts by critics of war. The language of peace, like the condition of peace, can be negative or positive. A language of negative peace perpetuates injustice by only establishing a verbal declaration of an end to war and hostilities. A language of positive peace fosters open and inclusive communication that affirms diversity.

I. LANGUAGE, PERCEPTION, AND BEHAVIOR

Various uses of language precede and support the pursuit of war and the quest for peace. Military preparations for war and political negotiations for peace involve fairly obvious institutional structures. Discourse about war and peace also involves institutional structures, since language itself is a social institution. Whether we know the official language of the nation in which we live or a dialect relegated to low social esteem, whether we know only one or many languages, in whatever language we speak and write, we are faced with its lexicon and grammatical structure, which have embedded within them a wide range of terms that express not only arbitrary systems of classification but also actual relations of power. If knowledge is power, language too is power; those who control the language of war and peace exercise an enormous influence on how we perceive war and peace and what behaviors we accept in relation to war and peace.

Copyright © 1999 by Academic Press.
All rights of reproduction in any form reserved.

A. The Institutional Character of War and Discourse about War

Individuals who serve as warriors and soldiers have social roles that are structured by the military institutions of societies. The overt violent acts committed by these individuals when they act as a social group following official orders are sanctioned by the state as legitimate, even though the acts committed by these individuals are similar to types of physical violence that are prohibited by the state and for which individuals who commit them are subject to punishment. In order to mark the institutional character of military behavior, most societies use distinctive words to designate the violent acts of warriors and soldiers. The act that is designated as "murder" when performed by an individual may be redesignated "justified use of force" when carried out by law enforcement or military personnel. This power of redesignation, which allows for legitimation or condemnation of various actions, manifests how political uses of language precede and support the pursuit of war; the same is true for the political uses of language in the quest for peace.

From primitive war among archaic societies to the world wars of the 20th century, political and military leaders have introduced and reinforced linguistic usages that give legitimacy to the social roles and military actions of warriors and soldiers. Since the rise of the modern nation-state, almost all societies have coupled the aim of maintaining national sovereignty with the capacity to wage war. Not surprisingly, then, discourse about war is much more deeply ensconced in the languages of the world than is discourse about peace. "Warist discourse" refers to the resulting language that takes for granted that wars are inevitable, justifiable, and winnable. One of the most elaborate justifications for war arose during the medieval period and continues to this day, namely, the theory of just war that was given classic articulation by St. Augustine and St. Thomas Aquinas.

B. How the Institution of Language Shapes Perception and Behavior

To better understand the effects of the ways we talk and write about war and peace, one needs to recognize that language, as Ferdinand de Saussure established, is one of the most conservative social institutions. As such, language shapes both perception and behavior, influencing our thought and action in three important ways.

First, at any given time the words in the lexicon of a language limit one another. Every lexicon is finite, and every lexicon changes over time. Linguists have shown that the meaning of individual words is a function of the differences among them during each phase in the history of the lexicon. Terms designating ethnicity, race, gender, and sexual orientation are especially revealing in this regard. Consider the difference in the meaning within the United States of using the term "Negro" in the 1950s, 1970s, and 1990s to designate the race of one component of the population. After Martin Luther King, Jr. and others succeeded in having "Negro" accepted as the polite form of address, the term took on a different meaning in the 1970s, by which time the addition of "Black" was firmly established in the lexicon as the preferred designation and use of "Negro" became a signal of conformity to an earlier social norm. The term "Negro" took on an even more telling connotation once "African American" came into general usage in the 1990s and now one of the few remaining socially acceptable uses of the term "Negro" is its satirical employment by African American comedians such as Eddie Murphy. Languages vary in the number of terms available to communicate about a specific topic, and the available terms vary in how positively and negatively charged they are. While the English language currently includes "fag," "homosexual," and "gay" as terms which designate the sexual orientation of some men, these terms are on a continuum of rather negative, to more neutral, to fairly positive. For this reason, when analyzing discourse about war and peace, the words selected and the words not selected from the lexicon are rather important. Think, for example, of the difference between referring to armed troops as "freedom fighters" and as "guerrilla terrorists."

Second, because the vocabulary of a language provides charged terms, it serves as a means of interpretation. Individuals think about their world in the terms provided by their language. As a result of socialization individuals have a predisposition to select those terms which coincide with the existing values in their societies. For example, throughout the Cold War, many Americans regarded their government as the "champion of freedom" and the Soviet government as "an evil empire." Since the lexicon of a language also makes available further terminological options, individuals are also able to intentionally select words that are relatively more or less offensive. Hence, while the lexicon of a people has built into it a perspective on the world, it facilitates not only the official perspective but also alternative ones. These alternatives can include the potential for the positive renaming of a disenfranchised social group and the negative redescription of governmental accounts of military campaigns. Although many people refer to individuals who use a wheelchair as "handicapped," these individuals may prefer to refer to themselves and to have others refer to them also as "physically challenged." While the government may refer to a military campaign as a "just war," citizens can counter that it is "just another war."

Third, behavior is shaped by the linguistic perspective of an individual's thought. In other words, language gives a structure to consciousness, which guides action. Since changed behavior is so closely connected with the way language shapes consciousness, the "right of bestowing names," as Friedrich Nietzsche saw, is a fundamental expression of political power. In the 20th century, French sociologist Pierre Bourdieu has elaborated theoretically and empirically on the extent of the symbolic power that language can provide. Some social groups accrue enormous linguistic capital, which they generally use to advance their interests to the detriment of the social masses. Almost all of us are familiar with physicians and lawyers who rely on their technical vocabularies and seek to have their patients and clients simply defer to their authority. Similarly, many governmental and military officials use forms of strategic discourse that most citizens do not understand and to which they acquiesce, thereby enabling those with a monopoly of the instruments of force to go unchallenged in their explanations for their actions.

II. LANGUAGE, VIOLENCE, AND NONVIOLENCE

Debate continues about whether all terms in a language are ideologically charged or whether some terms avoid bias. Even if some uses of language are neutral, many are charged. Whenever more than one term is available, a difference in connotation is generally present even when the denotation is the same. Is the individual working in a field a "wetback," an "illegal immigrant," or a "migratory laborer"? In principle, individuals can select any among the available terms. However, linguistic freedom and linguistic creativity can be used to impose restrictions on social groups and distort their perceptions, just as much as it can be used to empower social groups and enrich their understanding. In practice, word choices are largely shaped by customary social usage. Beyond establishing an official language, most nations reinforce politically preferred choices through institutions of socialization such as schools and the

media. What makes some nations "rogue states" and some leaders "dangerous villains"? At this point, the prospect for linguistic violence arises and takes on a clearly institutional character. "Linguistic violence" is the situation in which individuals are hurt or harmed by words.

A. Linguistic Violence

Negatively, language can be used to demean differences among social groups and to inflict violence against them. Frequently, we think more about the ways one individual insults another than about how the lexicon itself reflects institutional structuring of social roles. As noted earlier, a distinction is made between personal overt violence, such as murder, and institutional overt violence, such as war. Likewise, as Newton Garver has noted, a distinction can be made between personal covert violence, such as a verbal insult, and institutional covert violence, such as the socially sanctioned use of demeaning terms to refer to specific social groups. Personal covert violence occurs when we try to dismiss opponents by calling them "morons." Institutional covert violence is practiced when members of the middle or upper class dismiss the poor by calling them "lazy." Not only do governments refer to their adversaries as a "peril," but also within the society demean the politically less powerful. (Those less powerful in society are not always less numerous, as is typically the case with women.)

Within moral philosophy Joel Feinberg has distinguished hurt and harm, and this distinction has been applied to language by Stephanie Ross and others. Sometimes, when we are conscious of the negative effects of terms, words hurt us. Such hurt is equally real in individual verbal insults and institutionally sanctioned demeaning terminology. It usually hurts a child when someone yells "You're ugly!" And it often hurts women when they are called "chicks," "babes," or "foxes." Language that hurts us is termed "offensive." On other occasions, when we are not conscious of the negative effects, words can still harm us. Such harm also occurs on both individual and institutional levels. We may not see the harm when someone calls adult females "girls," rather than "women," unless we hear them refer to adult males of the same age as "men" and not "boys." Inhabitants of Africa may accept their nations as "underdeveloped" and "less civilized" until they learn about the imposition of colonial rule and Eurocentric values. Language that harms us is termed "oppressive." This distinction between offensive and oppressive language is found on all levels of the continuum of linguistic violence that includes subtle, abusive, and grievous forms.

Subtle forms range from children's jokes to official languages. Even in the innocent manifestations of a child's attempt to make fun of adult authority figures, children's jokes involve issues of power. At other times, the linguistic violence of children's jokes is hardly subtle and contributes to prejudicial attitudes that subsequently can be directed against an "enemy." Various questions and answers can be altered in order to make fun of almost any racial, ethnic, religious, or national group. For example, a child may ask, "How do you break a ____'s neck?" The answer, regardless of the group cited, is, "Shut the toilet seat." Such humor contributes to acceptance later of physical violence against these types of persons. Within a particular country, the linguistic violence of an official language is generally more subtle to those who have mastered it than to those who have not. Internationally, official languages are another unfortunate legacy of colonialism, namely, alien languages, along with alien governments, were imposed onto indigenous peoples. The pains of colonization and the subsequent strife associated with independence are reflected in such classic works as Tunisian Albert Memmi's *The Colonizer and the Colonized* and Algerian Frantz Fanon's *The Wretched of the Earth* and in numerous lesser-known literary works such as Nigerian Kole Omotoso's *Just Before Dawn*.

Abusive forms are especially conspicuous in racist, sexist, heterosexist, and classist discourse. Abusive forms rely on offensive terms and frequently aim to hurt the individuals to whom they are directed. Both the practitioners and victims are more likely to be aware of the degrading intent of these forms of communication. Generally, when a heterosexual man calls a lesbian a "dyke" both individuals know that the man aims to hurt the woman's feelings. Moreover, many of these abusive terms recur within warist discourse in demeaning references to the enemy or even members of one's own military who are judged negatively. Vietnamese have been referred to as "gooks." Soldiers exhibiting fear are often called "sissies" or "girls." Of course, just as many speakers of an official language do not see how it is oppressive, many individuals who employ and some who hear and read racist, sexist, and heterosexist language are unaware of its oppressive nature. With the distinction between oppressive and offensive, one can demonstrate how a form of discourse may be oppressive, even though not all individuals experience it as offensive.

Grievous forms are found in many expressions of warist discourse, including nuclear discourse, totalitar-ian language, and genocidal language. In nuclear discourse, "collateral damage" refers to the thousands or even millions of civilians who would be the victims of nuclear strikes against military targets. Nazis used "special treatment" instead of "execution," while in Bosnia "ethnic cleansing" referred to genocidal practices. Grievous forms often have the intent to silence or even eliminate an entire social group. Unfortunately, warist discourse represents one of the most globally intractable practices of linguistic violence. Warist discourse in its multifarious and nefarious manifestations leads to the killing of large numbers of people by organized groups, such as the state, subnational political organizations, and religious, racial, and ethnic groups.

B. Linguistic Nonviolence

Alternatively, whether we are conscious of their effects, terms can comfort and advantage us. Positively, language can comfort us when used to affirm diversity and achieve recognition. During the civil rights struggle, the phrase "Black is beautiful" expressed a growing sense of pride and self-affirmation by African-Americans. Some feminists responded to the infrequent citation of the accomplishments of women in our history textbooks by seeking to write "herstory." Positive terms can advantage a social group even if its members do not always recognize that such terms function in this manner. As should be obvious, "linguistic nonviolence" is the antonym to "linguistic violence" as "peace" is the antonym to "war."

Many times the first step in reducing linguistic violence is to simply refrain from the use of offensive and oppressive terms. However, linguistic nonviolence requires the availability of terms that affirm diversity. Moreover, these terms need to be ones that are understood by most citizens. A nuclear war could kill millions or even billions of people. However, critics of nuclear war can make their message rather obscure when they refer to "omnicide" (the killing of all sentient life). "Linguistic alienation," as Ferruccio Rossi-Landi has shown, refers to the situation in which individuals cannot understand a discourse in their own language because of the use of highly technical terms.

Those seeking to change official designations run up against the danger that they will establish themselves as a specially trained elite who can lead the people. Vanguard parties can create linguistic alienation between themselves and the movements they are seeking to direct. For this reason, the practice of linguistic nonviolence requires the development of a broadly understood language of inclusion.

III. THE LANGUAGE OF WAR

The language of war, which frequently has truth as its first casualty, is an example of linguistic violence that functions to mask the reality of the violence that is occurring. Whenever truth is masked or distorted, communication is being used for manipulation. Such linguistic manipulation is episodic in many areas of social life, but it is constitutive of warist discourse. In *The Art of War*, written in China over 2000 years ago and perhaps the oldest text on war, Sun Tzu says "All warfare is based on deception." In the 20th century, the title of Phillip Knightley's book on war correspondents, *The First Casualty*, is based on U.S. Senator Hiram Johnson's 1917 statement, "The first casualty when war comes is truth."

A. The Use of Euphemisms for War

Linguistic manipulation, like physical coercion, does violence. Nevertheless, most people who are subjected to physical coercion are conscious of the violence being done to them. In the case of linguistic manipulation, the harm done can escape those subjected to it unless they can find an independent basis for exposing the distortions to which they have been subjected. Often, persons who learn that they have been the victims of linguistic manipulation feel a sense of violation. They feel that someone has deceived them into adopting false beliefs. On the basis of these false beliefs, these victims typically have communicated and acted in ways that they subsequently regret.

Some of linguistic manipulation in warist discourse is unintentional and involves self-deception on the part of the governmental and military officials. As occurs in many fields where individuals have to order or perform very unpleasant tasks, the use of euphemisms is prevalent. Official discourse about war makes extensive use of euphemisms. A linguistic alternative to the horrors of war is created in order to think, speak, and write about these events in an abstract or indirect way, since it would otherwise be difficult to visualize graphically or justify logically what is actually taking place. Likewise, when the public hears and reads these euphemisms, they often do not realize what is really occurring.

Warist discourse, in an important dimension of its linguistic manipulation, actually presents itself as a language of peace. "*Pax Romana*" ("Peace of Rome") stood for the military suppression of armed conflict throughout the Roman empire. The medieval "Truce of God" (1041) limited warfare to specific times. The term "Peacekeeper" refers to the MX missile, a nuclear weapon designed to contribute to a first-strike capability. The phrase "peace through strength" really promotes a military build up. While the totalitarian government in *1984* uses the slogan "Peace is War," modern nations prefer to omit reference to war whenever possible. Then, when war occurs, the claim is sometimes made that it is "the war to end all wars." So far, each such claim has turned out to be false.

Not surprisingly, the rhetoric about war is divided between not only the former East–West Cold War but also the continuing North–South conflict. While the North defended its "right" to "protect" its colonies, the colonized responded with arguments for the legitimacy of "wars of liberation." Whether wars of liberation bring about an end to war, and there is scant evidence that they do, they are still wars and involve small-scale to large-scale violence. Nevertheless, some supporters of wars of liberation prefer to forge an alternative language that refuses to designate their movements as violent since they are in response to practices of oppression. In his classic *Pedagogy of the Oppressed*, Brazilian Paulo Freire contends violence has never been initiated by the oppressed and designates as "a gesture of love" the admittedly violent response of rebellion by the oppressed against the initial violence of oppressors.

Such reversals in language are not confined to the distinction between colonial oppression and wars of liberation; it also occurs within both types. Even within the latter, as Norwegian feminist Birgit Brock-Utne has shown, the language used to recruit women into wars of liberation is different from the reality of the roles assigned to these women, as is illustrated in studies on such conflicts in Lebanon, Cuba, Zimbabwe, and the Philippines.

Scholars who have analyzed discourse about war, such as Aldous Huxley, George Orwell, and Haig Bosmajian, contend that language is corrupted in ways that make the cruelty, inhumanity, and horror of war seem justifiable. Language becomes a tool employed by political and military officials to make people accept what ordinarily they would repudiate if the true character were known. The language of war hinders civilians from recognizing that human beings are being mutilated, tortured, forcibly removed from their villages and hamlets, wounded, and killed.

An aggressive attack by a squadron of airplanes that ordinarily would be called an "air raid" is euphemistically referred to as a "routine limited duration protective reaction." Defoliation of an entire forest is spoken of as a "resource control program." "Pacification" is used to label actions that involve entering a village, machine-gunning domesticated animals, setting huts on fire, rounding up all the men and shooting those who resist, and prodding and otherwise harming the elderly, women, and children. The human face of war is thus replaced by benign abstractions.

At other times, the level of abstraction is so high that citizens do not even understand what officials are saying. In these cases, they suffer a type of linguistic alienation. What do officials mean when they refer to "the counterforce first-strike capability of a MIRVed ICBM facilitated by its low CEP"? Just as many people simply accept the advice of medical and legal professionals when they do not understand the technical jargon employed, even so many citizens are unable to challenge the military policies of leaders who rely on the technical vocabulary of modern warfare with its high incidence of acronyms and euphemisms.

B. The Use of Propaganda in War

Linguistic misrepresentation is not always unintentional. Propaganda and brain-washing seek to manipulate the minds and behaviors of the citizenry. In times of war, each of the nations involved presents its adversary as an evil enemy and itself as the embodiment of good. All parties employ linguistic misrepresentations of themselves and their adversaries. Nevertheless, an ally in one war may be the enemy in the next, while the enemy in one war may become an economic partner in the post-war global market. For this reason, in *The Republic*, Plato cautioned over 2000 years ago that we should be careful about calling another people an "enemy," since wars do not last forever and eventually they may again become our friends. Failure to recognize that the designation of a nation as one's "enemy" is transitory leads to the need for a kind of Orwellian "doublethink" that allows one to "forget" that current allies were former enemies and vice versa.

Orwell has observed that political speech and writing often intentionally defend the indefensible. In order to defend British rule in India, Soviet purges, and the United States's atomic bombing of Hiroshima and Nagasaki, officials resorted to bizarre arguments that contradicted the purported aims and values of their governments. These intentional uses of euphemisms, question-begging terminology, vagueness, and outright falsity demonstrate that when Orwell presented Newspeak in his novel *1984*, he was not referring to a merely fictive possibility.

In some cases, linguistic misrepresentation stretches all the way to the "figurative lie." This term, coined by Berel Lang, refers to descriptions of war that actually contradict the realities of war, as occurs in the extremes

of genocidal and nuclear discourse. The Nazis used syntax, grammar, and literary figures of speech as instruments for political ends, namely, genocide. This instrumental approach to language detaches language from history and moral judgment, converting it to a mere technique in the assertion of political power. *Endlösung* ("Final Solution") both disguises and reveals (at least to the people in the know) the plan of murder. The term reveals that there is a problem that must be solved and in a conclusive manner. *Endlösung* conceals that the action denoted will be the annihilation of all Jews and other "culture destroyers," including homosexuals and Gypsies, rather than actions like their deportation or resettlement.

While it is possible to speak of a concrete event as the "final solution" to a problem, it is contradictory and duplicitous to designate the concrete action of murdering millions of individuals abstractly as a "final solution." The language of genocide simultaneously promulgates and hides the intentional willing of evil. Thus, the language of genocide functions as an instrument of domination and as a mechanism of deceit: the language of genocide facilitates large-scale killing, yet denies the social reality of its intent and consequence.

Nuclear discourse, by personifying weapons while dehumanizing people, provides another illustration of the figurative lie. The names given to the first nuclear bombs, "Little Boy" and "Fat Man," convey that these vehicles of destruction are living persons and males. In fact, before the first atomic device was detonated in the Trinity test at Alamogordo, New Mexico, its inventors said they hoped the "baby" would be a boy. By implication, as Carol Cohn has observed, if the bomb had been a dud it would have been termed a "girl." Later, the expression "losing her virginity" was used to refer to India's entry into the nuclear club, while "being deflowered" is used to refer to any country that enters this elite club. Such warist discourse banters in public a figurative lie which simultaneously substitutes birth for death and degrades women.

C. Imposition of Warist Discourse as Legitimate

Finally, governmental and military officials are able to impose their form of discourse as the legitimate one and, thereby, coopt efforts by critics of war. Nations typically cultivate among citizens a belief in their legitimacy. In times of "national emergency," open opposition to the "official version" of events is often forbidden and may be severely punished. Citizens who question the "official version" are labeled "traitors" and "fellow travelers" with the enemy of the state.

At the extreme, officials use warist discourse as an authoritarian instrument. When Quincy Wright referred to the totalitarianization of war in the 20th century, he was thinking more about how most sectors of civil society, along with military units, are recruited into supporting military efforts. The 20th century made equally clear how governments and subnational groups have turned to "totalitarian language" as well in their efforts to "win" the hearts and minds of the masses in support of their political agendas. In these endeavors, they have relied extensively on the instruments of mass communication, as well as research in psychology, to increase significantly the degree of control that can be exercised over the mind by verbal means. Nevertheless, as John Wesley Young has shown, the language of totalitarianism practiced in the 20th century has had only limited success in achieving the goal of thought control. This failure of the attempt at linguistic control by totalitarian regimes provides significant evidence that the quest for linguistic emancipation, including a language of peace that gives expression to the deepest desires of humanity, is not quixotic.

Endeavors to establish a legitimate discourse about war, to propound an acceptable theory of war, have been ongoing in global civilizations. From Sun Tzu's *The Art of War* in ancient China to Carl von Klausewitz's *On War* in 19th-century Europe, the policy debate has not been on whether war is moral or whether it should be waged, but how to wage war effectively. Since the advent of nuclear weapons strategists have pulled back from the concept of "total war" in favor of the concept of "limited war," but they have not yet called for an "end to war."

The Hague Conferences, the Geneva Conventions, the League of Nations, and now the United Nations put forth principles that seek, though often ineffectively, to limit war and to put moral constraints on the conduct of war. However, official attempts at the abolition of war, such as the Kellog-Briand Pact, have allowed for some exceptions, such as in response to "wars of aggression" or to intervene in "certain regions of the world, the welfare and integrity of which constitute a special and vital interest for our peace and safety."

IV. THE LANGUAGE OF PEACE

The language of peace is an important component in the pursuit of peace and justice. The language of peace can be an example of linguistic nonviolence and can contribute to forging an understood language of inclusion. However, just because the language of war is not being used, a genuine language of peace is not necessarily present. The language of peace, like the condition of peace, can be negative or positive. "Negative peace" refers to the temporary absence of actual war or the lull between wars, while "positive peace" refers to the negation of war and the presence of justice.

A. The Language of Negative Peace

The language of negative peace can actually perpetuate injustice. A government and its media may cease referring to a particular nation as "the enemy" or "the devil," but public and private attitudes may continue to foster the same, though now unspoken, prejudice. When prejudices remain unspoken, at least in public forums, their detection and eradication are made even more difficult. Of course, just as legal or social sanctions against hate speech may be needed to stop linguistic attacks in the public arena, even so, in order to stop current armed conflict, there may be a need not only for an official peace treaty but also a cessation in hostile name-calling directed against an adversary of the state. However, even if a language of negative peace is necessary, it is not sufficient. Arms may have been laid down, but they can readily be taken up again when the next military stage in a struggle begins. Likewise, those who bite their tongues to comply with the demands of political correctness are often ready to lash out vitriolic epithets when these constraints are removed. Thus, in the language of negative peace, the absence of verbal assaults about "the enemy" merely marks a lull in reliance on warist discourse.

Immanuel Kant had a similar distinction in mind when he contrasted a "treaty of peace" from a "league of peace." Kant was concerned with the conditions that make peace possible. He did not want genuine peace to be confused with a mere "suspension of hostilities." The latter is the pseudo-peace of a "treaty of peace" (*pactum pacis*), which merely ends a particular war and not the state of war. Genuine peace, for Kant, must be founded and is impossible if war can be waged without the consent of citizens. Kant presumed that, for this end, republican states are preferred. He termed a genuine peace, one that negates war, a "league of peace" (*foedus pacificum*). Even if genuine peace is unlikely, Kant stresses the importance of its possibility; otherwise, if we knew we absolutely could not achieve it, any duty to try to advance genuine peace would be eliminated.

From the perspective of Mohandas Gandhi, much discourse about peace, as well as the rhetoric supporting wars of liberation, places a primacy on ends over means. When the end is primary, nonviolence may be practiced only so long as it is effective. For Gandhi and the satyagrahi (someone committed to the pursuit of truth and the practice of nonviolence), the primary commitment is to the means. The commitment to nonviolence requires that the achievement of political goals is secondary. These goals must be foregone or at least postponed when they cannot be achieved nonviolently. The nature of the language of negative peace becomes especially clear when, within social movements facing frustration in the pursuit of their political goals, a division occurs between those ready to abandon nonviolence and those resolute in their commitment to it. The resolute commitment to nonviolence was clear in the teachings and practices of Martin Luther King, Jr. and his followers and in the recent courageous behavior of other practitioners of nonviolent civil disobedience, including Vaclav Havel in eastern Europe, Mubarak Awad in the Middle East, Nelson Mandela in South Africa, and thousands of ordinary citizens in the Baltic republics, China, Czechoslovakia, Poland, the West Bank, and the Ukraine.

B. The Language of Positive Peace

The language of positive peace facilitates and reflects the move from a lull in the occurrence of violence to its negation. The establishment of a language of positive peace requires a transformation of cultures oriented to war. The discourse of positive peace, to be successful, must include a genuine affirmation of diversity both domestically and internationally. The effort to establish the language of positive peace requires the creation of a critical vernacular, a language of empowerment that is inclusive of and understood by the vast array of citizens.

The effort to eliminate linguistic alienation and linguistic violence is part of a larger struggle to reduce what Norwegian Johan Galtung calls "cultural violence." The critique of the language of war and the promotion of the language of positive peace are simultaneously contributions to the quest for societies in which human emancipation, dignity, and respect are not restricted on the basis of irrelevant factors like gender, race, or sexual orientation. Why is it that in some regional newspapers in which we still sometimes find references to a "black gunman" or a "black rapist" we do not find references to a "Caucasian gunman" or a "white rapist"? Why do we, however, sometimes hear about a "lady doctor" or a "female pilot"? And why is the union of same-sex partners often termed a "gay marriage" or a "lesbian commitment ceremony"? We can begin to see the harm being done when we reflect on the fact that, in relation to use of adjectives, reference to a person being "white" is sometimes omitted, while reference to a person being "female" or "gay" is sometimes included. Regardless of race, a rapist is a rapist; regardless of gender, a physician is a physician. Despite continuing legal and official restrictions based on orientation, a marriage is a marriage. Similarly, as long as nation states persist in legitimating some forms of military combat, we will continue, in these cases, to hear a military campaign referred to as a "just war," but regardless of any rationales, a war is a war. Legally and officially, social discrimination based on race and gender is prohibited, and a similar shift is beginning to occur in relation to sexual orientation. But a ban on the use of military force is a long way off. Regardless of the stage of social progress on these issues, there is an on-going need to expose all forms of discriminatory language that legitimates harm.

Various activities promote the pursuit of respect, cooperation, and understanding needed for positive peace. These activities go beyond the mere removal from discourse of adjectives that convey biases based on race, gender, and sexual orientation. Beyond meetings among political leaders of various nations, these activities include cultural and educational exchanges, trade agreements, and travel exchanges. We can come to regard races, sexes, and cultures as making up the harmonies and melodies that together create the song of humanity. Just as creative and appreciated cooks use a wide variety of herbs and spices to keep their dishes from being bland, so too can we move from an image of a culture with diverse components as a melting pot to one of a stew which is well seasoned with a variety of herbs and spices. Or, to employ another nonviolent metaphor, the garden of humanity will best flourish when composed of multiple plots with the varieties of life comingling and co-inhabiting.

Despite the primacy of the history of warfare in textbook histories of civilizations, the desire for peace and even elaborate discourses on plans for peace have been made persistently and eloquently throughout human history. In his study of primitive war, Harry Turney-High found that from a psychological perspective peace is the normal situation even among war-like peoples. In his study of the idea of peace in classical antiquity, Gerardo Zampaglione found that from the Pre-Socratic philosophers through Roman and Hellenistic writers to medieval Christian theologians, the quest for peace has been at the center of many artistic and literary movements. Of course, this influence had very little "policy sway" in the decision-making of those who exercise political power.

Some interesting recent developments in peace activism, including contributions to the language of positive peace, have occurred in Asia, Latin America, and elsewhere. Since 1963 the "engaged Buddhism" of Thich Quang Duc has spawned socially and politically engaged versions of Buddhism in India, Sri Lanka, Thailand, Tibet, Taiwan, Vietnam, and Japan. Central figures and movements include Thich Nhat Hanh in Vietnam, Buddhadasa Bhikkhu and Sulak Sivaraksa in Thailand, A. T. Ariyaratne and the Sarvodaya Shramadana movement in Sri Lanka, and Daisaku Ikeda and the Soka Gakkai movement in Japan. These movements also include two Nobel Peace laureates, Tenzin Gyatso in 1989 (the 14th Dali Lama) and Aung San Suu Kyi in 1991 (the Burmese opposition leader). As Christopher Queen and Sallie King have noted, these movements have reinterpreted or augmented traditional Buddhist discourse in order to emphasize their common practice of nonviolence and quest for global peace.

Likewise, though not as nonviolent in principle or in practice, liberation theology has had a major impact in Latin America, spawning socially and politically engaged movements among Roman Catholics. Beginning in 1973 with Gustavo Gutierrea, a Peruvian Roman Catholic priest, the leading exponents of this movement include Leonardo Boff in Brazil and Juan Luis Segundo in Uruguay. More recently, Emmanuel Martey has applied some of these principles to African theology. Further examples can be found in the ways other religious and philosophical traditions in many parts of the world have also reinterpreted or augmented their traditional forms of discourse in order to emphasize pursuing in this world goals of peace and justice.

Several attempts have even been made to spread the use of nonviolent discourse throughout the culture. The Quakers' "Alternatives to Violence" project teaches linguistic tactics that facilitate the nonviolent resolution of conflict. Following initial endeavors at teaching these skills to prisoners, this project has been extended to other areas. Related practices are found in peer mediation and approaches to therapy that instruct participants in nonviolent conflict strategies. Within educational institutions, increased attention is being given to Gandhism in order to convey nonviolent tactics as an alternative to reliance on the language and techniques of the military and to multiculturalism as a means of promoting an appreciation of diversity that diminishes the language and practice of bigotry and ethnocentrism. At an international level, UNESCO's "Culture of Peace"

project seeks to compile information on peaceful cultures. Even though most of these cultures are preindustrial, their practices illustrate conditions that promote peaceful conflict resolution. This project, which initially assisted war-torn countries in the effort to rebuild (or build) a civic culture, can now be applied even more broadly.

The diversity of movements for positive peace that have forged new styles of nonviolent communication and sociopolitical engagement is so great, in fact, that some system of classification is needed. Zampaglione divides the movements he surveys in the ancient world into four forms of pacifism: mystical (Leo Tolstoy, Romain Rolland), philosophical (St. Augustine, Abbé de Saint-Pierre, Kant, Bertrand Russell, and John Dewey), sociological (Auguste Comte, Henri Saint-Simon, and Charles Fourier), and political (Bohemian King George of Podebrad, Maximilien de Béthume duc de Sully). Duane Cady distinguishes deontological pacifism that is based on a commitment to principles, such as the rejection of violence, from consequentialist pacifism that is based on an assessment of the results of actions, such as the destruction of war. Deontological pacifism ranges from the absolute form, in which individuals refuse to resort to any use of violence, to cases in which nonlethal force and even lethal violence may be used by individuals who accept personal responsibility for their actions. Consequentialist pacifism ranges from cases in which our knowledge is simply too limited to judge whether resorting to arms is justified to cases based on our knowledge that the technology of war makes the results too grim and on the simple pragmatic conclusion that wars generally do more harm than good.

On some occasions, those seeking a language of positive peace fall silent at least briefly, especially after the occurrence of war. Kant suggests that after any war a day of atonement is appropriate in which the "victors" ask for forgiveness for the "great sin" of the human race, namely, the failure to establish a genuine and lasting peace. Immediately following the atomic bombing of Hiroshima, Albert Camus advised that this event called for much reflection and "a good deal of silence." At other times, advocates of positive peace are compelled to break the silence in order to respond to injustice. While adhering to principles of nonviolence, as Gene Sharp has noted, various levels of protest, noncooperation, and even intervention can be pursued. In these ways, the language of positive peace has a variety of correlative nonviolent actions by means of which to continue politics by the same means—by more intensive means of diplomacy rather than turning to war, which von Klausewitz defined as the pursuit of "politics by other means."

The language of positive peace is democratic rather than authoritarian, dialogical rather than monological, receptive rather than aggressive, meditative rather than calculative. The language of positive peace is not passive in the sense of avoiding engagement; it is pacific in the sense of seeking to actively build lasting peace and justice. The language of positive peace, a genuinely pacific discourse, provides a way of perceiving and communicating that frees us to the diversity and open-endedness of life rather than the sameness and finality of death. The language of positive peace can provide the communicative means to overcome linguistic violence and linguistic alienation. Pacific discourse, in providing an alternative to the language of war and even to the language of negative peace, is a voice of hope and empowerment.

Also See the Following Articles

JUST-WAR CRITERIA • PEACE CULTURE • PEACE, DEFINITIONS OF • REASON AND VIOLENCE

Bibliography

Bolinger, D. (1980). *Language—The loaded weapon: The use and abuse of language today.* New York: Longman.
Bosmajian, H. A. (1983). *The language of oppression.* Lanham, MD: University Press of American.
Bourdieu, P. (1991). *Language and symbolic power* (John B. Thompson, Ed., Gino Raymond & Matthew Adamson, translators). Cambridge, MA: Harvard University Press.

Cady, D. L. (1989). *From warism to pacifism: A moral continuum.* Philadelphia: Temple University Press.
Chilton, P. (Ed.) (1985). *Language and the nuclear arms race: Nukespeak today.* Dover, NH: Francis Pinter.
Cohn, C. (1989). Sex and death in the rational world of defense intellectuals. In D. Russell (Ed.), *Exposing nuclear phallacies* (pp. 127–159). New York: Pergamon.
Eriksen, T. H. (1992). Linguistic hegemony and minority resistance. *Journal of Peace Research, 3*(3), 313–332.
Gates, H. L., et al. (1994). *Speaking of race, speaking of sex: Hate speech, civil rights, and civil liberties.* New York University Press.
Gay, W. C. (1987). Nuclear discourse and linguistic alienation. *Journal of Social Philosophy, 18*(2), 42–49.
Gay, W. C. (1991). Star Wars and the language of defense. In D. L. Cady & R. Werner (Eds.), *Just War, nonviolence and nuclear deterrence: Philosophers on war and peace.* Wakefield, NH: Longwood Academic.
Gay, W. C. (1997). Nonsexist public discourse and negative peace: The injustice of merely formal transformation. *The Acorn: Journal of the Gandhi–King Society, 9*(1), 45–53.
Gay, W. C. (1998). Exposing and overcoming linguistic alienation and linguistic violence. *Philosophy and Social Criticism, 24* (2–3), 137–156.
Gay, W. C. (1999). The practice of linguistic nonviolence. *Peace Review, 10* (4), 545–547.
Kant, I. (1983). *Perpetual peace and other essays* (Ted Humphrey, translator). Indianapolis, IN: Hackett.
Lang, B. (1988). Language and genocide. In A. Rosenberg & G. E. Myers (Eds.), *Echoes from the Holocaust: Philosophical reflections on a dark time.* (pp. 341–361). Philadelphia: Temple University Press.
Queen, C. S., & King, S. B. (Eds.) (1996). *Engaged Buddhism: Buddhist liberation movements in Asia.* Albany, NY: State University of New York Press.
Tzu, S. (1963). *The art of war* (Samuel B. Griffith, translator). London: Oxford University Press.
Young, J. W. (1991). *Totalitarian language: Orwell's Newspeak and its Nazi and Communist antecedents.* Charlottesville: University Press of Virginia.
Zampaglione, G. (1973). *The idea of peace in antiquity* (Richard Dunn, translator). University of Notre Dame Press.

Law and Violence

G. David Curry
University of Missouri—St. Louis

GLOSSARY

Law A formal system of rules for behavior and governance that sustains a particular social order. As the concept of law is used here, it refers primarily to legal systems that follow the Eurocentric model, in the language of Max Weber, grounded on rational and traditional authority.

Violence The exertion of force by an individual, group, or organized aggregate to injure or abuse other individuals or groups.

I. VIOLENCE AND THE EMERGENCE AND DEVELOPMENT OF COMMUNITIES, STATES, AND LAW

A. Violence and Social Identity and Forms

Ritualistic intergroup strife plays a role in the emergence and development of social organization in societies where there is comparatively limited social struc-ture. Organized violence comparable to total intergroup warfare has been recorded by Jane Goodall in her studies of chimpanzee behavior. Anthropologists have suggested that violence between communities in nonliterate societies played a role in establishing collective identity and group boundaries. Sociologists from Durkheim to Erickson have emphasized how the ritualistic punishment of deviants (often violent in nature) strengthens social solidarity and collective conscience.

A more contemporary example underscores the link between loosely organized social structures and violence. Research on delinquent youth gangs has emphasized the role that violence plays in shaping the social organization and identity of such gangs and their members. In his research on Chicago gangs at the beginning of the 20th century, Frederic Thrasher described gangs as developing through increasing levels of conflict with other groups and authority figures outside the gang. Leadership, status, and order within the gang was likewise established through conflict, frequently violent. Near the end of the same century, Scott H. Decker described gang life in St. Louis as being characterized by violence. Members were initiated into groups through violent "beating in" rituals. Gangs protected criminal activity and geographic territory through violence, and one avenue to status in the gang was through toughness and willingness to perpetrate violence.

B. Law and Violence from the Classical Period to the Middle Ages

Legal traditions in the West and in Western civilization in general are not hesitant to claim the democratic

---

Copyright © 1999 by Academic Press.
All rights of reproduction in any form reserved.

legacy of the Greek city-states. It is no irony that the beginning of Greek history and literature is the *Iliad,* an account of war. Bernard Knox, in his introduction to that work, observed that from their appearance as organized communities until the loss of their political independence, the Greek city-states were "uninterruptedly" at war. Knox quotes from Homer and Plato to illustrate the point. In Homer's words, the Greeks are "the men whom Zeus decrees, from youth to old age, must wind down our brutal wars to the bitter end until we drop and die, down to the last man." From Plato's *Laws,* "Peace is just a name. The truth is that every city state is, by natural law, engaged in a perpetual undeclared war with every other city state." It is important to remember that the fate of the citizen of Athens is most often associated with logic and reason. The trial of Socrates was formal and dignified, but the aging philosopher was put to death at its end. The concluding centuries of the classical Mediterranean world were similarly marked by the bond between law and violence. Roman legions and Praetorian guards played an essential role in producing the order that was Roman law.

The collapse of Roman law brought the comparative chaos of the Dark Ages. Philosophically the medieval social order was based on loyalty to the blood of royal families or the symbolic blood of Jesus in the two major divisions of the Christian Church. Medieval lords ruled by force and in turn the Church maintained its institutional integrity by manipulating the loyalties and of these lords and the levels of violence committed by them. The royal families that provided the symbolic imagery from which modern states emerged accentuated blood as their source of legitimacy. In the social orders created by them, jurisprudence and governance was marked by bloody demonstrations of state power.

C. Violence Producing Law: The Case of Revolutions

The revolutions in law that brought law closer to a system based on equality and consistency came into being through a series of organized violent confrontations between ruler and ruled. The separation of the 13 North American colonies from the British Empire was marked by the second-longest war in U.S. history. From Lexington to Yorktown, confrontations between the new nation's armed forces and militias were sufficiently fierce to produce 4,435 battlefield deaths for the insurgents. The 1789 revolution in France moved from a relatively nonviolent transition in governmental structure to the period between April 1793 to July 1794 that bears the designation of the "Reign of Terror." The

increase in violence was facilitated by external pressure in the form of military action from the antirevolutionary regimes in Britain, Austria, and Spain. During the Reign of Terror, 2,639 persons were guillotined in Paris. In all, over 40,000 deaths of civilians were attributed to the revolutionary legal processes in operation during the Reign of Terror. Out of the violence associated with the American and French Revolutions grew the ideal of the citizen soldier in which the franchise for full legal participation was associated with military service. The traditions of national birth through revolution have become sanctified in the Western-style republics.

D. Law and Violence in the Preservation of Stability

In the case of revolutions, violence serves as a tool of legal change. The more conventional and frequent role of violence is in the preservation of an existing social order. According to Morris Janowitz, there are two processes at work to insure social control in Western industrial states—mass persuasion and social coercion. For social coercion to operate, an apparatus capable of bringing violence to bear on individual citizens must exist. The most obvious manifestation of such an institutional apparatus is the criminal justice system. The concept of deterrence as a means of diminishing the likelihood of criminal behavior requires that ultimately institutions capable of utilizing legitimize violence be maintained by the state at its various levels of organization. Cases in which applications of violence have been used to maintain aspects of the social order from which legitimacy is subsequently drawn illustrate well the dilemma of violence as applied by law. Here three such cases are examined.

1. Race and Law in U.S. History

Legal structures associated with race characterized North American contact between European settlers and indigenous peoples well before the first delivery of African slaves to the Jamestown colony in 1619. Spanish explorers took violent measures to extract wealth from the lands that they conquered in the Carribean and Latin America. The enslavement and ritualized robbery of native peoples were carried out with the full might of law and superior weaponry as their foundation. Kirkpatrick Sales described how Tainos were physically mutilated when they failed to provide the taxes of gold levied on them as the successors to Columbus' crews imposed their legal order on the island of Hispaniola. The 5 centuries that have followed have brought a lessening of the intensity of the brutality, but not in the ultimate life outcomes for the native peoples of what became the United States. As late as the first half of the 19th century, Eastern tribes such as the Cherokee were forcibly relocated from ancestral lands by the evolving institutions of democratic government. Those remaining in the states of original settlement were required to serve a period of indentured servitude to white masters from birth until adulthood. The last of the native nations to hold on to some level of independence in the West were ultimately forced to surrender any semblance of that independence as their traditional law was made subordinate to the expanding influences of U.S. federal and state laws. Every effort of organized resistance was met with greater levels of violent force from these "more modern" legal orders. The slaughter (1890) and resistance (1973) at Wounded Knee are among the best known examples. Less well known is the more formal mass hanging of 38 Santee Sioux in Mankato, Minnesota in 1862. Originally 303 Sioux had been sentenced to hang, but President Lincoln commuted the sentences of all but the 38. Still, this violent application of the law marked the largest mass execution in U.S. history.

Just as U.S. law from its first emergence has incorporated differential treatment of Native Americans based on race, so has the status of natives of Africa been a formalized legal issue throughout U.S. history. When the first slaves brought to an English colony in North America were sold by Dutch merchants on the docks at Jamestown, they were initially treated similarly to European indentured servants. By 1670, colonial laws that established the continuation of slave status throughout the life term and the inheritance of slave status by the children of slaves had transformed African slavery into the "peculiar institution" that was to endure until the American Civil War or "War between the States." It is estimated that 600,000 to 650,000 Africans were forcibly and brutally transported to the English colonies in North America. Slavery as a legal institution was legally reified in the U.S. Constitution in 1980, and 8 of the first 12 presidents of the United States owned slaves.

In the Northern states, the abolition of slavery was a peaceful legislative process that began in the revolutionary period and was complete by 1830. In the South, abolitionary efforts were for the most part illegal. The flight of slaves and the activities of abolitionists in the Southern states were violently repressed by the institutions of social coercion established by the individual states. One of the most highly publicized efforts to effect a violent end to slavery was John Brown's raid on the federal arsenal at Harper's Ferry in 1859. This illegal violent attempt to insight a slave rebellion was repressed by legal violent action by U.S. Marines. Taken alive, Brown was tried and executed. Ultimately, the abolition of slavery would come about through a presidential proclamation in 1863, a proclamation that was enforced by the federal government in the most costly, in terms of human life, violent legal action in U.S. history. Approximately 180,000 African-American soldiers served in the federal army during the American Civil War.

The end of the slavery was by no means the end of illegal and legal violence against Americans of African ancestry. The Fourteenth Amendment to the Constitution granted political rights to all male citizens including African Americans. The former states of the Confederacy were required to ratify this amendment before they were readmitted to the Union. Still, the newly won freedom of African Americans in the Southern states suffered dramatic setbacks. Chief among the illegal acts of violence against African-American were riots and lynching. Bloody riots against African Americans erupted in Louisiana and Memphis in 1866. In 1876 and 1877, similar organized mass killings of African American citizens occurred in South Carolina. Race riots were not just a Southern phenomenon. One occurred in Springfield, Illinois, in 1908, and one in Chicago in 1919. In the public mind, lynching generally connotes hanging, but lynchings of African Americans has involved a wide range of public, illegal executions that have included mutilations and burning alive as well as hanging. Between 1884 and 1900, white mobs lynched over 2,000 African Americans in the South. Another figure of over 10,000 lynchings between 1865 and 1900 was offered by Ida B. Wells, a major antilynching activist. Between 1900 and 1920, white mobs lynched another 2,000. As late as the turn of the century, a U.S. Senator from South Carolina described lynching of African Americans by outraged whites as an inevitable occurrence and a kind of natural law.

With the end of Southern reconstruction, legislation recapitulated the illegal violence inflicted on African Americans. In 1888, Mississippi enacted laws formalizing the practice of segregation that would endure until the Civil Rights movements of the 1950s and 1960s. The government of the state of Mississippi went a step further in 1890, ratifying a new state constitution that stripped African American citizens of the state of the rights guaranteed them by the Fourteenth Amendment. By 1918, Alabama, Georgia, North Carolina, Oklahoma, and Virginia had followed suit. In the economic sector, share-cropping became the replacement to slavery. Involuntary labor enforced through the incarceration of troublesome or uncooperative African Americans provided an incentive to strengthen the institutions charged with social coercion at the local and state levels. Among statistics that emphasize the discriminatory application of legal violence against African Americans, one example is the fact that of 455 men executed for rape between 1930 and 1967, 405 of them were of African ancestry.

Just as the disenfranchisement of African Americans after end of the Civil War featured both illegal and legal components, so did the movement to gain the full rights of citizenship. The illegal (in Southern states) element was represented by the great mass movement that involved nonviolent protests, boycotts, and sit-ins. At the same time that African American men and women were struggling in the streets, action was also taking place in the legal system, principally in the Supreme Court. Some of the legal successes came comparatively early in the 20th century. *Guinn vs the U.S.* (1915) declared unconstitutional "grandfather clauses" that allowed illiterate whites to vote while denying that right to illiterate blacks. *Buchanan vs Warley* (1917) declared unconstitutional laws requiring African Americans and whites to live in specific sections of cities. Finally, the successes of *Brown vs Board of Education* (1954), which outlawed legal segregation of schools, and *Gayle vs Browder*, which overturned the principle of "separate but equal," paved the way for the passage of the Civil Rights Act of 1964 and the Voting Rights Act of 1965.

2. Gender and Law in U.S. History

In the same year, 1619, and on the same docks (at Jamestown) from which the first African slaves were auctioned, 90 women were distributed to male colonists willing to pay the price of their passage plus a respectable profit to the Virginia Company. Historians now confirm that most of these women had been tricked or outright kidnapped. Others were shipped directly from prison. Marriage in that time was not totally unlike slavery. Women who struck their husbands in any way were sentenced to public beatings or time in the pillories. Men who killed their wives were subject at most (but unusually) to hanging. For a woman to kill her husband, however, was equivalent to killing a king, a crime against the deity. Several of the American colonies followed the English law that mandated that a woman convicted of killing her husband was to be burned at the stake. At the nation's founding, the separate states denied women the right to own property and the right to vote.

The women's rights movement in the United States had early roots in the movement to abolish slavery. Women were very active in the movement. According to Angela Davis, women's participation in the abolitionist movement stemmed from a belief that their ultimate freedom was contingent on freedom for African Americans. Just prior to the Civil War, a majority of the members of abolitionist groups were women. In 1848, approximately 200 women convened the Seneca Falls Convention in New York. Elizabeth Cady Stanton, Lucretia Mott, and other women leaders attending Seneca Falls produced a Declaration of Sentiments that proclaimed the equality of women with men. Like the quest for rights for African Americans, the struggle for women's suffrage was a long protracted struggle involving illegal and legal efforts. In 1872, Susan B. Anthony was arrested for illegally casting a ballot in the presidential election. Unlike the public illegal violent response to the African-American civil rights struggle, the violent response to women seeking their rights was a more private affair sustained by the general legal disregard for domestic violence and rape. It was not until 1920 that the Nineteenth amendment guaranteed women the right to vote. Still, an effort to pass an Equal Rights Amendment making discrimination against women illegal failed to gain legal passage by the required number of states in 1982.

3. Law and Social Class in U.S. History

Though deemphasized in the legitimating documentation of U.S. government, class differences have been a source of legal conflict since colonial times. In the 17th century, the distinction between social classes was especially distinct as a result of reliance on indentured servitude as a major source of labor in the colonies. In the Southern states, indentured servants made up a majority of the population. With the establishment of the republic, many of the states limited the right to vote to white males over the age of 21 who owned property or paid annual taxes that exceeded a specifically set limit. While most such property barriers to voting had disappeared for white males by the end of the Civil War, conflict between social classes was most clearly evidenced in the efforts of labor to organize.

Strikes by bakers in New York and shoe makers in Philadelphia occurred in colonial times, but development of a more widespread labor movement required the development of advanced industrialism. The mining industry was the setting of some of the most violent clashes between labor and management with available legal institutions of social coercion inevitably siding with the latter. During and just after the Civil War, a secret organization of Irish-American coal miners began to grow in strength in Pennsylvania. Known as the Molly MacGuires, the miners were as adept at sabotage and other forms of violence as they were at organizing strikes. Infiltrated by a Pinkerton detective agency agent-provocateur, major leaders of the organization were arrested in 1876, tried, and executed. In 1912, an extended strike of miners in Paint Creek and Cabin Creek, West Virginia, resulted in a year-long series of violent incidents. As a result, martial law was declared and scores of miners were imprisoned. By 1920, the United Mine Workers of America had grown to approximately 50,000 members, and West Virginia was once again the site of a bloody confrontation between workers and government. The center of the strike was Mingo County, also called "Bloody Mingo." Martial law was declared. Not all legal institutions were committed against the miners. The constable and the mayor of the town of Matewan in Mingo County chose to give their support to the miners who had elected them. Eventually both were gunned down. In August of 1921, thousands of coal miners from neighboring towns and states attempted to march to join the Mingo miners. The federal government committed over 3,000 armed troops to fortify Blair Mountain in Logan County, West Virginia, in order to block the advance of the miners. The battle, which extended for days, saw the federal forces use such weaponry as machine guns and bomber planes against the miners. Experiencing heavy casualties, the miners were thoroughly crushed. Court action against leaders and the union made the victory for the mine owners and the government complete.

The mines were not the only settings for violent confrontations between workers and the law. Federal army soldiers were used to suppress a strike by Pullman car workers in 1894. International Workers of the World (Wobblies), attempting to organize workers in Everett, Washington, were fired upon by county law enforcement resulting in several dead and approximately 50 wounded. In 1919, a strike by Boston police officers was suppressed by a major commitment of state troops. A confrontation across class lines that did not directly involve labor occurred in 1932 when 20,000 World War I veterans marched on Washington to demand a bonus promised them at the end of the war. When 400 of the veterans refused to depart from Washington, President Hoover ordered federal troops under the command of General Douglas MacArthur to attack the so-called "Bonus Army." With a combined use of tanks, calvary, and infantry and the use of tear gas, the troops were able to route the bonus marchers.

II. DIALECTICAL NATURE OF LAW AS A MANIFESTATION AND ANTITHESIS OF VIOLENCE

Recorded history has often overemphasized the role of organized violence in social change. Still, violence and the development and maintenance of law are fundamentally intertwined as social phenomena. A major function of law is the control or elimination of violence. At numerous points in history, law has reduced violence between individuals and even between societies. It is also true, however, that law has been established, maintained, and changed through violence.

In order to understand what on the surface appears to be contradictory conditions of phenomena, a dialectical approach is useful. An essential element of a dialectical approach is using seemingly contradictory propositions to produce an understanding of an underlying reality. Intellectually such an approach can be traced directly to Fredrich Hegel and indirectly to Plato. Incidentally both of these thinkers wrote about the nature and development of law. The dialectical approach had been implemented by scholars as distinctive as Georg Simmel to explain in idealistic terms the relationship between the individual and society and Karl Marx to explain the contradiction between material production and the reduction of human freedom. The relationship between law and violence is one that especially lends itself to a dialectical interpretation. A driving motivation (at least in terms of hindsight) for the emergence and support of law is a desire for a social order free from violence. A major mechanism for achieving and maintaining a system of law is violence. This dialectical relationship between law and violence has its historical basis in Eurocentric systems of law and selected non-Eurocentric social systems.

A. Law as Peacekeeping

The tradition of the legal system as a mechanism for dispute resolution is exemplified by the all-powerful (sometimes all-wise). The Biblical Solomon was prototypical. When the conflicting parties did not share a consensus with the ruler, the ruler's supreme power facilitated a resumption of the smooth operating of the social order. In ancient Greece, the collectivity or *polis* assumed the role of all-knowing, all-powerful mechanism of dispute resolution. In contemporary society, peaceful dispute resolution constitutes the bulk of legal activity. Courts at numerous levels resolve disputes between individuals, corporate actors, and units of government. Only rarely are the individuals and corporate entities involved in such resolutions made aware of the institutions of social coercion that ensure the peaceful surface appearances.

In exceptional situations, though, the law steps into a violent dispute as a neutral third party that must make its access to greater violence clear to both parties. At the microlevel, police officers and security guards break up fights between individuals. In Appalachian history, external forces stepped in to resolve the feud between the Hatfields and McCoys. (The neutral intervention model for this example is weakened by revisionist historians who stress the rising hegemony of coal and railroad interests as being intolerant of the semi-feudal conflicts of the region's inhabitants.) Perhaps, a better instance of this kind of neutral intercession was in the gang wars of prohibition. Since the opposing forces were both in violation of the law and a threat to the safety of those innocently exposed to the line of fire, the government could display a dispassionate ruthlessness in its application of violence and legal statute to bring the conflict to an end. A similar ruthless response to contemporary youth gang violence has been advocated by a number of policy-makers.

B. War as Lawkeeping

The perspective of law as a peacekeeping enterprise is only one step away from the quite antithetical conception of war as a means of establishing or preserving law. Or, more ironically, the perception of war as a mechanism for achieving peaceful legal consensus. From such a perspective, the American Revolution and the War of 1812 were institutional mechanisms for effecting agreement between the United States and England on issues of the limits of taxation and the legal boundaries of sovereignty. The Civil War could likewise be interpreted as the method by which a universal understanding could be reached between the states about the appropriate balance of powers needed to make a collective, collaborative legal system possible in the centuries to follow. Given these kinds of interpretations of historical conflicts, perhaps it is not surprising that since the end of World War II, U.S. armed forces have been almost routinely committed to resolve conflicts in international sessions. The success of the Korean War and the Vietnam War are still the subject of contention between left and right ideologues, but the Desert Storm incursion into Kuwait and southern Iraq, the humanitarian mission to Somalia, and the efforts to restabilize the former political components of Yugoslavia are less subject to widespread doubt.

C. The Violence of Punishment and Corrections

The transition of correctional institutions in Western societies from public demonstrations of individual pain and suffering to institutionally private processes of transformation was documented by Michel Foucault. Foucault began his *Discipline and Punish* by comparing two pieces of evidence. In the first, the public torture-execution of a perpetrator of regicide was recounted in startlingly gruesome detail. The second was simply a schedule of activities for an inmate of a facility for delinquent juveniles. The execution described a very precise ritual for reshaping and destroying the physical body of the offender. The tightly restricted schedule of the juvenile facility was a mechanism for reshaping and destroying the personality and self of the offender. As Foucault noted, the nature of punishment passed from touching the body to touching the soul.

Research on prisons has repeatedly demonstrated that the pains of imprisonment for prisoners manifests a far greater psychological impact than a physical one. At the maximum security level, this control reflects what Jeremy Bentham labeled a panopticon. A panopticon is a physically and socially constructed space designed to maximize the surveillance of its subjects. At the maximum security level, the role of violence in maintaining this system of surveillance and control is extremely visible in gun towers, barbed wire, and armed guards. As the prison system passes through the stages between maximum security and minimum security, the evidence of physical force becomes less and less visible, but for inmates of minimum security facilities and even parolees and probationers, the threat of forced movement into the next higher level of security is continuous condition of existence.

D. The Special Case of the Death Penalty

The ultimate manifestation of the violent dimension of the U.S. legal system is the death penalty. Legalized killing as it is carried out under the contemporary form of the death penalty is a methodical, systematic process carried out against an individual who has already been incapacitated by the correctional system. With an exception in the 1960s, public opinion polls since the 1930s have indicated that a majority of Americans favor the death penalty for at least some crimes. Throughout this time, substantial proportions of the populace have opposed the death penalty in all instances. In 1972, the U.S. Supreme Court ruled in *Furman vs Georgia* that the death penalty as it had hitherto been practiced in all of the states utilizing the penalty was arbitrary and discriminatory. The death penalty was, therefore, unconstitutional by being in violation of the Eight Amendment's restriction against "cruel and unusual punishment." The absence of the death penalty was short-lived with a majority of the justices in 1976 approving revised death penalty statutes that used "guided discretion" for juries in judges. Since 1977, the number of persons awaiting execution has steadily risen, passing the 2000-mark in 1990. In the late 1990s, the number of people on death row is at its highest in U.S. history.

III. SELECTED DEVELOPMENTS IN LAW AS A RESPONSE TO VIOLENCE

A. Hate Crime Reduction through Law

Hate crimes are defined as actions that are intended to harm or intimidate a person because of her or his race, sexual orientation, religion, or other group identification. In hate crimes, individual victims of an offense are not the only victims of that offense. All members of their groups are indirectly victims of the act. As a result of the unusually unrestrained violence of many hate crimes, there has been a concerted effort in recent decades to develop effective legal responses to hate crime. In 1989, the U.S. Congress passed the Hate Crime Statistics Act. By 1992, 27 states and the District of Columbia had passed laws designed to provide enhanced punishments for hate crimes. Under the Hate Crime Statistics Act, the FBI produced a report in 1991 tabulating 4558 hate crimes nationwide. There have been two definitional problems identified with hate crime legislation. The first is the difficulty in establishing motive. That is, is it possible for a crime to fit the functional definition of a hate crime and not involve "hate" by the perpetrator? The second problem is that it is similarly possible for a hate offense technically to not be a crime. This is the case of with some hate graffiti, shouted epithets, and the wearing of "hate" symbols such as swastikas. The ambiguity of hate crime definition has led the FBI to use the term "bias" crimes in some of its publications. A national study conducted in 1994 found that only six state statistical agencies were maintaining the kinds of statistics required by the Hate Crime Statistics Act. The study found such widespread differences in definition, statutes, and reporting procedures as to make available tabulations of hate crime statistics at the state level uninformative and misleading.

B. Gun Control

The Second Amendment to the Constitution guarantees the right to bear arms. Polls have indicated that 49% of U.S. households own firearms for an estimated total of 200 million guns. At the same time, the United States leads all industrial nations in homicides and other violent crime rates. Of homicides, 60% involve the use of firearms. A National Institute of Justice study conducted in 1995 revealed that one in five juvenile arrestees reported carrying a handgun all or most of the time. Half of the male juvenile arrestees related that they had been shot at at least once. Legal efforts to control the availability of firearms have included licensing, purchasing restrictions, and sentence enhancements for crimes committed with a firearm. Research on the effectiveness of gun control laws at reducing violent crime have produced conflicting findings.

Political forces constitute the greatest barriers to gun control laws. Opposition has pursued two strategies. The more straightforward approach is very simple. The Second Amendment renders any effort to limit the availability of firearms unconstitutional. The second approach is based on logical constructions that *a priori* expose alleged internal contradictions of any gun control law. Among such arguments is the suggestion that the possession of firearms by law-biding citizens serves as a deterrent to criminal activity. Any gun control law that reduces the level of such ownership would thereby increase criminal behavior. Such political opposition makes any effective legal solution to the gun and violence dilemma in the near future unlikely.

C. Domestic Violence and the Law

The magnitude of the problem of domestic violence in the U.S. is unknown. In recent decades compilations of statistics based on phone calls to police and social service agencies and complaints in family courts have indicated that the problem of abuse of female partners is widespread, with estimates of the number of victims in the hundreds of thousands. The most prevalent reaction to the problem has been the shelter movement. In most instances, shelters have been community based and organized by women themselves. As shelters have become more established, their staffs have discovered that cooperation and assistance from local law enforcement greatly facilitates their effectiveness.

Until recently police officers have been reluctant to intervene in domestic violence issues. When intervention was attempted, strategies were left up to the discretion of the officer resulting in an inconsistent diversity of techniques. In a classic experiment, the Police Foundation and the Minneapolis Police Department attempted in a systematic fashion to examine the impact of three different strategies for domestic violence intervention—arrest, separaration, and verbal advice. Outcome was measured through in-depth follow-up interviews with victims. The conclusion of this study was that arrest was the most effective of the three strategies. Attempts to replicate the findings of the Minneapolis study in other cities were, however, disappointing. In one such experiment in Omaha, the researchers found that arrests was no more likely to reduce abuse than other strategies.

A very different kind of legal response to domestic violence has been the use of the "battered wife defense" in instances where wives have killed abusive husbands. The battered wife defense is based on traditional self-defense law and argues that the offender would have herself eventually suffered serious harm or death had she not killed her assailant. Several successful applications of the defense have received national attention over the past 2 decades. While some have hailed the battered wife defense as a valuable innovation in protecting women from domestic abuse, others have minimized its significance. A major problem is the deviation from basic principles of self-defense. Self-defense laws were developed to protect offenders whose killings were absolutely unavoidable. In most cases in which the battered wife defense is raised, a case can be made by the prosecution that the danger to the offender was imminent but not immediate. Some contemporary research has suggested that domestic abuse and battered wives' violent response to it are decreasing as a result of liberalized divorce laws.

D. Legal Responses to Gang Violence

In the last decade, the public and policy-makers have become increasingly concerned with a perceived rising tide of gang-related violence. From an almost complete absence of interest in gangs in the early 1980s, the end of that decade witnessed what has been called an explosion of gang activity. In 1995, the National Youth Gang Center (NYGC) reported 664,904 gang members in 23,338 gangs in almost 1,500 jurisdictions. A comparison of NYGC data with previous findings suggested that between 1994 and 1995, gang problems were newly emerging in cities with populations between 25,000 and 150,000 at the rate of three per week.

Strategic responses to gangs have been classified into four major categories: suppression, social intervention, community mobilization, and opportunities provision.

A 1988 study of gang programs across the nation conducted by Irving A. Spergel found that while suppression was the most commonly applied strategy in communities, program staff members believed that community mobilization and opportunities provision were the strategies that were most effective. The Office of Juvenile Justice and Delinquency Prevention supported Spergel in developing the Comprehensive Community Response to Gangs Program. This comprehensive response is more commonly called the Spergel model. Currently the Spergel model is being applied in five cities nationwide with an evaluation design in place to measure each application's effectiveness.

From the earliest studies on gangs, researchers have suggested that the emergence and development of gang problems are as much influenced by community responses as the obverse. Researchers in Ohio and Milwaukee noted that the official denial of gang problems can result in hastily conceived and overly punitive responses when the denial strategy inevitably fails. Incarceration can actually strengthen gangs by allowing gangs to develop greater cohesion in correctional settings. Even certain kinds of counseling programs have been found to bolster gang cohesion. By 1993, a national study revealed that 13 states had developed state laws in response to gang problems. Other such laws were under development. The laws range from enhanced sentences for participation in gang-related crime to state-mandated "days of prayer against gang violence." To date, there is no research to substantiate the effectiveness of any of these legal efforts to reduce gang violence.

IV. THE POSSIBILITY OF A FUTURE FOR LAW WITHOUT VIOLENCE

The relationship between law and violence is a long and tightly interwoven one. Violence has played fundamental and symbolic functions in the development of contemporary law. Violence has been employed to establish new laws and social orders as well as preserve existing laws and social orders. All governmental units based on laws maintain some level of official apparatus for applying social coercion. None of a list of contemporary efforts to eliminate or reduce specific kinds of violence can be regarded as especially successful.

Given these conditions, can there be any hope of developing a social order in which violence does not play a major role in defining the social fabric? Morris Janowitz identified mechanisms for maintaining social control at the macrosocial level—mass persuasion and social coercion. There may indeed be some tendency for a greater role to be played by mass persuasion with a corresponding decrease in the role of social coercion. A third kind of social control identified by Janowitz may offer greater promise for law without violence. That is self-control as the major mechanism for social control. For self-control to become the only building block required for maintaining a nonviolent and functioning social order, individuals must be integrated into a pattern of what Robert Bursik has labeled systemic social control. This requires an integration of individuals into strong communities and the integration of strong communities into more encompassing collectivities. This also necessitates informed, empowered citizens with a concern for the collective good and the opportunities to actualize their own human potential.

Also See the Following Articles

CRIME AND PUNISHMENT, CHANGING ATTITUDES TOWARD • DEATH PENALTY, OVERVIEW • GANGS • LEGAL THEORIES AND REMEDIES • PUNISHMENT OF CRIMINALS • SOCIAL CONTROL AND VIOLENCE • SOCIAL EQUALITY AND INEQUALITY

Bibliography

Costanzo, M., & Oskamp, S. (1994). *Violence and the law.* Thousand Oaks, CA: Sage.

Davis, A. Y. (1981). *Women, race, & class.* New York: Random House.

Foucault, M. (1979). *Discipline and punish: The birth of the prison.* New York: Vintage.

Janowitz, M. (1978). *The last half-century: Societal change and politics in America.* Chicago, IL: University of Chicago Press.

Legal Theories and Remedies

Peter Weiss

Center for Constitutional Rights, International Association of Lawyers Against Nuclear Arms,
and the Lawyers Committee on Nuclear Policy

GLOSSARY

ius ad bellum Literally, law to war; the legal basis for commencing a war; i.e., the justification for fighting.

ius in bellum Literally, law in war; the legal basis for conducting a war; i.e., the acceptable methods of fighting.

Necessity The principle that actions against an enemy should not exceed what is reasonably considered necessary to gain victory in the conflict; e.g., it is a matter of debate whether the nuclear bombing of Hiroshima and Nagasaki violated the principle of necessity.

Proportionality The principle that reprisals against an enemy should be in proportion to the original offense; e.g., to execute 100 prisoners of war because one prisoner had killed a guard would violate the principle of proportionality.

Total War Warfare conducted with the aim of large-scale destruction of the enemy civilization rather than simply effecting the surrender of the opposing armed forces.

THERE ARE MANY SIMILARITIES between the legal approaches to violence in civil society and in war: In both, aggression is condemned, self-defense is condoned; force proportionate to a legitimate objective is permitted, excessive force is not; the lawful use of force is authorized, "taking the law into one's own hands" is frowned upon.

The main difference between the law of interpersonal violence and the law of armed conflict is that, while there are rules governing both, the former, by and large, is enforceable through domestic courts, while machinery for the enforcement of the latter is imperfect, allowing violators to escape punishment more often than not.

This is not to say, however, that the laws governing the use of force in armed conflict serve no purpose. Nuremberg, the trial of Lieutenant Calley for the My Lai massacre during the Vietnam War, and the International Tribunals for Rwanda and the former Yugoslavia are evidence to the contrary. This article will not deal with domestic crime, but will be limited to a discussion of that branch of international law known as "the laws of war."

Copyright © 1999 by Academic Press.
All rights of reproduction in any form reserved.

I. EARLY HISTORY OF THE LAWS OF WAR

Efforts to regulate both the lawfulness of commencing hostilities (*ius ad bellum*) and the manner in which war, once commenced, could be fought (*ius in bello,* or humanitarian law) are as old as war itself. Leon Friedman reports that "as early as the Egyptian and Sumerian wars of the second millennium B.C., there were rules defining the circumstances under which war might be initiated" and that "among the Hittites of the fourteenth century B.C., a formal exchange of letters and demands generally preceded hostilities" (Friedman, p. 3). As to the actual conduct of hostilities, Sun Tzu, in *The Art of War,* wrote in the 4th century B.C. that it was forbidden to injure an enemy already wounded and that "all soldiers taken must be cared for with magnanimity and sincerity so that they may be used by us" (Friedman, p. 3). This is one of the earliest examples of a rule of warfare based on pragmatism as much as on morality, a recurrent theme in the history of warfare.

Similar limitations and principles of moderation in warfare are found among the ancient Hindus, Babylonians, Greeks, Romans, Christian Church Fathers, and scholastics (Friedman, pp. 3–5). They deal with prohibitions against using concealed or poisoned weapons; protecting the wounded, neutrals, the unarmed, and prisoners; and respecting religious sites. Keegan tells us that the purpose of weapons among the Aztecs was not to kill, but only to wound. The purpose of war, according to St. Augustine, was to lead those whom Christian soldiers attacked "back to the advantages of peace" (Friedman, p. 7). Neither total war aimed at the destruction rather than the conquest of or defense against an enemy nor no-holds-barred warfare were sanctioned in principle during these millennia of armed conflict. The practice, of course, was often quite different, as is still the case today.

II. THE MODERN LAWS OF WAR

Until the 17th century, the rules governing the inception and conduct of war were rarely based on treaties or conventions creating mutually binding obligations between political communities. This is not surprising if one considers that the modern system of sovereign states traces its origin to a series of treaties enacted in 1648, putting an end to the Thirty Years' War and known collectively as the Treaty of Westphalia. However, these ancient regulations did make up a body of what international lawyers now call customary law, consisting as they did of internal edicts; the practice of states or the fiefdoms that preceded them; and the writings of theologians, philosophers, and jurists. The most famous and influential of these was *De jure belli ac pacis* (*The Law of War and Peace*),[1] published in 1624 by the Dutch diplomat and jurist Hugo Grotius, now generally regarded as the father of the modern law of war and, indeed, of modern international law.

A. Ius ad Bellum

Until modern times, the law concerning the inception of war consisted mainly of various rules concerning the formalities of declaring war and of the theory, developed by the Romans and elaborated on by subsequent Christian theologians, which held that "just wars" were permitted and "unjust wars" prohibited. Just wars were not only those waged in defense against an aggressor, but also those waged aggressively in accordance with natural or divine law. Needless to say, those intent on waging aggressive war were usually adept at squeezing their baser motives into a legal framework.

1. The Kellogg–Briand Pact

The brutality of the First World War led to the creation of the League of Nations and, for the first time, to a general condemnation of aggressive war. The document that formalized this principle was the General Treaty for the Renunciation of War, known popularly as the Kellogg–Briand Pact of 1928, which stated:

> 1. The High Contracting Parties solemnly declare in the names of their respective peoples that they condemn recourse to war for the solution of international controversies, and renounce it as an instrument of national policy in their relations with one another.
> 2. The High Contracting Parties agree that the settlement or solution of disputes or conflicts of whatever origin they may be, which shall arise among them, shall never be sought except by pacific means.

Today, hundreds of wars later, the Kellogg–Briand Pact is still in force for the vast majority of states that were in existence in 1928, including the United States.

---

[1] The original text was reproduced by the Carnegie Institution of Washington in 1913 followed by the publication a three-volume translation by the Carenegie Endowment in 1925.

2. Article 2(4) of the United Nations Charter

The United Nations Charter, enacted for the purpose of saving "succeeding generations from the scourge of war, which twice in our life-time has brought untold sorrow to mankind" retraces the first article of the Kellogg–Briand Pact in its Article 2(4), which provides that:

> All Members shall refrain in their international relations from the threat and use of force against the territorial integrity or political independence of any state, or in any other manner inconsistent with the Purposes of the United Nations.

It also retraces the second article of the Kellogg–Briand Pact in its Article 2(3), which reads:

> All Members shall settle their international disputes by peaceful means in such a manner that international peace and security, and justice, are not endangered.

3. The Gaping Loophole of Article 51

Why, then, has the world witnessed another 150 or so wars in the half-century following the signing of the Charter in San Francisco in 1945? One could give a cynical answer to this question in the words of Dean Swift: "Laws are like cobwebs, which may catch small flies, but let hornets and wasps through." The mechanisms by which the hornets and wasps of this world have escaped the prohibition of the use of force, i.e., the making of war, in Article 2(4) of the Charter are to be found in Article 51, which has turned out to be a gaping loophole. In its terms, the Article is quite straightforward and extremely restrictive:

> Nothing in the present Charter shall impair the inherent right of individual or collective self-defense if an armed attack occurs against a member of the United Nations, until the Security Council has taken measures necessary to maintain international peace and security.

But in practice, those capable of taking their countries to war have overridden the narrowness of the self-defense exception. They have either ignored Article 2(4) altogether, as in Senator Moynihan's pithy phrase, "in the annals of forgetfulness there is nothing quite to compare with the fading from the American mind of the idea of the law of nations." Or they have performed intellectual acrobatics on the concepts of "self-defense," particularly "collective self-defense," and "armed attack."[2] The somewhat tortured legal justifications for U.S. military interventions in Vietnam, Panama, and Grenada are cases in point.

4. Other Theories of Intervention

The world community's concern with human rights has led to a minority view among international lawyers justifying the use of force against regimes engaged in gross violations of the human rights of their own citizens. D'Amato and other proponents of this theory argue, *inter alia,* that since the promotion of human rights is a fundamental objective of the Charter, humanitarian intervention is not "inconsistent with the Purposes of the United Nations," in terms of Article 2(4). Other theories of intervention are based on the alleged rights of one country to protect its citizens in another country, to restore the legitimacy of overthrown governments, and to assist other governments in domestic conflicts by invitation. All of these have been invoked at one time or another, but they have not gained acceptance from a majority of the international law community. Nor should they, despite the moral and realistic factors which support them to some extent, for to accept them would undermine the basic purpose of Article 2(4), which is to outlaw the use of force by one state against another except in the clearest and most limited circumstance of genuine self-defense.[3]

It should be noted, however, that, under Chapter VII of the Charter, the Security Council, having determined the existence "of any threat to the peace, breach of the peace, or act of aggression" (Article 39), a definition clearly going beyond the confines of Article 2(4), and having found that measures short of the use of force, including sanctions, would be or have proved to be inadequate to remedy the situation, "may take such action by air, sea, or land forces as may be necessary to maintain or restore international peace and security." This provision has been invoked in situations like the Gulf War and Bosnia, in which all the permanent members of the Security Council supported military action

---

[2] For a stimulating debate on the relevance of Article 2(4) in international relations, see Thomas Franck, "Who Killed Article 2(4)?," *64, American Journal of International Law* (1970), p. 804; and Louis Henkin, "The Reports of the Death of Article 2(4) Are Greatly Exaggerated," *65, American Journal of International Law* (1971), p. 544.

[3] For a discussion of various theories of intervention, see Lori Fisler Damrosch and David J. Scheffer (Eds.), *Law and Force in the New International Order* (1991).

under the UN umbrella.[4] By the same token, any permanent member is in a position to veto such action. For this reason, Chapter VII has been criticized as providing a cover for the use of force by "the Big Five", while leaving the rest of the world at risk from the same Big Five.

B. Ius in Bello

The modern law of war governing the conduct—as distinguished from the commencement—of hostilities may be said to have begun with the Declaration Respecting Maritime Law signed in Paris in 1856 at the conclusion of the Crimean War. It provided, *inter alia,* that "privateering is, and remains, abolished" and laid down the important principle that "blockades, in order to be binding, must be effective, that is to say, maintained by a force sufficient really to prevent access to the coast of the enemy."

The first detailed, comprehensive codification of the laws of war was issued by President Lincoln in 1863, in the midst of the Civil War. Entitled *Instructions for the Government of Armies of the United States in the Field,* it was principally the work of Francis Lieber, a German-American historian and philosopher. The *Lieber Code,* as it came to be known, was the source and inspiration for most of the important subsequent enactments relating to the laws of war, both domestic and international.[5] The very opposite of the old Roman saw *inter armas silent leges* (in war laws are silent), its 157 articles cover almost everything contained in subsequent codifications and treaties, down to this day. Some examples:

> Military necessity does not admit of cruelty . . . of maiming or wounding except in fight, nor of torture to extort confessions. It does not admit of the use of poison . . . nor of the wanton devastation of a district. . . . [It] does not include any act of hostility which makes the return to peace unnecessarily difficult (Art. XVI).
>
> Commanders, whenever admissible, inform the enemy of their intention to bombard a place, so that the noncombatants, and especially the women and children, may be removed before the bombardment commences (Art. XIX).
>
> . . . [A]s civilization has advanced . . . so has

> . . . the distinction between the private individual belonging to a hostile country and the hostile country itself, with its men in arms. . . . [T]he unarmed citizen is to be spared in person, property and honor as much as the exigencies of war will permit (Art. XXII).
>
> Retaliation will . . . never be resorted to as a measure of mere revenge, but only as a means of protective retribution . . . cautiously and unavoidably (Art. XVIII).
>
> The United States acknowledge and protect, in hostile countries occupied by them, religion and morality; strict private property; the person of the inhabitants, especially those of women; and the sacredness of domestic relations. Offenses to the contrary shall be rigorously punished (Art. XXXVII).
>
> . . . Unnecessary or revengeful destruction of life is not lawful (Art. LXVIII).

And, in a curious anticipation of General Powell's doctrine of brief wars won by overwhelming force,

> . . . The ultimate object of all modern war is a renewed state of peace. The more vigorously wars are pursued, the better it is for humanity. Sharp wars are brief (Art. XXIX).

Ever since the enactment of the Lieber Code, military lawyers have advised U.S. field commanders on the legality of their actual or proposed actions under national and international law, but their advice has not always been heeded. Members of the U.S. armed forces have been prosecuted for violations of humanitarian law, as in the famous trial of Lieutenant Calley for the massacre of more than a hundred civilians in the Vietnamese village of My Lai in 1968.

In 1868, 5 years after the adoption of the Lieber Code, 16 European nations and Persia signed the *Declaration of St. Petersburg.* It was "to reconcile the necessities of war with the laws of humanity" and declared that "the progress of civilization should have the effect of alleviating, as much as possible, the calamities of war" (Friedman, p. 192). It was also the first instrument in modern times to prohibit a specific weapon, i.e. "any projectile of less weight than four hundred grammes, which is explosive, or is charged with fulminating or inflammable substances" on the grounds that the employment of such a weapon would uselessly "aggravate the suffering of disabled men" and would therefore be "contrary to the laws of humanity" (Schindler & Toman, p. 101). It is noteworthy that although the proscribed

---

[4] For a complete list of United Nations peacekeeping operations to date, consult the website of the UN Department of Peacekeeping Operations at http://www.un.org/Depts/dpko.

[5] Reprinted in Friedman, p. 158.

weapon, a bullet exploding on impact with the human body, had been developed by Russia, it was the Russian government who initiated the Declaration of St. Petersburg so that no state, including Russia itself, would be allowed to use it.

Still on the initiative of Czar Nicholas II of Russia, the First Hague Peace Conference was convened in 1899 "with the object of seeking the most effective means of ensuring to all peoples the benefits of a real and lasting peace and, above all, of limiting the progressive development of existing armaments" (Schindler & Toman, p. 49). This primary goal was not achieved, but the conference did produce the seminal set of documents on the modern law of warfare; the grandmother of all subsequent documents of this type. It comprised the following: A Convention for the Peaceful Adjustment of International Differences, a Convention Regarding the Laws and Customs of War on Land, a similar convention for maritime warfare and three Declarations prohibiting, respectively, "the launching of projectiles and explosives from balloons or by other similar methods" (Schindler & Toman, p. 201), the use of projectiles intended to diffuse asphyxiating or deleterious gases and the use of expanding (commonly known as "dumdum") bullets.

The two warfare conventions raised to the international level many of the detailed prescriptions contained in the Lieber Code. The section on "Hostilities" of the land warfare convention begins with an all-important article that confronts the conventional wisdom that "the laws of war" is an oxymoron, since "all's fair in love and war." Article XXII reads: *The right of belligerents to adopt means of injuring the enemy is not unlimited"* and Article XXIII puts flesh on the bones of this all-important principle by providing that "it is especially prohibited "to employ poison or poisoned arms, to kill or wound treacherously individuals belonging to the hostile nation or army, to kill or wound an enemy who . . . has surrendered, to declare that no quarter will be given, and to employ arms, projectiles, or material of a nature to cause superfluous injury" (Schindler & Toman, p. 82).

Another memorable and extremely significant contribution to the law of war made by the first Hague Peace Conference was the so-called *Martens Clause,* named after its author Frederic de Martens, then the legal advisor to the Russian Department of Foreign Affairs. By the time they adjourned, the representatives of the 26 participating governments—including the United States—were well aware that, while they had reached agreement on a substantial portion of the body of humanitarian law, it had not been possible "to agree

forthwith on provisions embracing all the circumstances which occur in practice." They therefore inserted the following language, drafted by de Martens, in the preamble to the land warfare convention:

> Until a more complete code of the laws of war is issued, the High Contracting Parties think it right to declare that in cases not included in the Regulations adopted by them, populations and belligerents remain under the protection and empire of the principles of international law, as they result from the usages established between civilized nations, from the laws of humanity, and the requirements of the public conscience.

Despite the touching and somewhat naive faith that de Martens exhibited in the possibility of future agreement on the precise content of "the laws of humanity and the requirements of the public conscience," his vision has played a major role in debates concerning the legality of weapons and tactics not covered by specific regulations throughout the ensuing century, as for instance with respect to the legality of nuclear weapons. Vague though it may be, the Martens Clause continues to be recognized—at least in principle—by military commanders throughout the world and their legal advisers continue to struggle with it in assessing the legality or illegality of new weapons and tactics. A recent example of recourse to the Martens Clause is the fact that, in connection with the nuclear weapons case decided by the International Court of Justice in 1996, nongovernmental organizations filed with the Court a "Declaration of Conscience" bearing hundreds of thousands of signatures from around the world, objecting to nuclear weapons as inhuman and in violation of the requirements of the public conscience.

An attempt to fill in the gaps left by the First Hague Conference was made by the Second Hague Peace Conference in 1907. It confirmed, with slight modifications, the texts adopted in 1899 and added a great deal more, including conventions on the opening of hostilities, the rights and duties of neutrals, the status of enemy merchant ships, the laying of submarine mines, and bombardment by naval forces. A Third Hague Conference was planned for 1915, but World War I intervened. As of this writing, both a rather low-key governmental conference and a major nongovernmental conference, The Hague Appeal for Peace 1999, are scheduled to take place in The Hague on the centenary of the first conference.[6]

_____

[6] See http://www.haguepeace.org.

Following the general revulsion against the use of poison gas in World War I, the *Geneva Gas Protocol,* precursor of the Chemical Weapons Convention, was enacted in 1925. It prohibited "the use in war of asphyxiating, poisonous or other gases, and of all analogous liquids, materials and devices."

During World War II, as is only too well known, the laws of war were more honored in the breach than in the observance. The aftermath of the war produced two documents of transcending importance. The *Nuremberg Charter* (1945) created the International Military Tribunal with jurisdiction over crimes against peace, war crimes, and crimes against humanity. It confirmed the principle of individual responsibility for these crimes,even if they were committed by heads of state or on the basis of superior orders. The *Geneva Conventions of 1949,* produced by a conference organized by the International Committee of the Red Cross (ICRC),[7] reaffirmed and expanded two earlier Geneva Conventions (1929) dealing with the treatment of prisoners and the sick, wounded, and shipwrecked and, in response to the enormous loss of civilian life during World War II, added, for the first time, a detailed "Convention Relative to the Protection of Civilian Persons in Time of War."

The *Genocide Convention* (1948), largely the work of one determined Holocaust survivor, Professor Raphael Lemke, criminalized the following acts "committed with intent to destroy, in whole or in part, a national, ethnical, or religious group": "(a) Killing members of the group; (b) Causing serious bodily or mental harm to members of the group; (c) Deliberately inflicting on the group conditions of life calculated to bring about its physical destruction in whole or in part; (d) Imposing measures intended to prevent births within the group; (e) Forcibly transferring children of the group to another group." Often invoked, but rarely applied, the Genocide Convention remains one of the surpassing legal creations of the postwar period, but one incapable, so far, of preventing the horrors of a Bosnia or a Rwanda.

Another conference was convened by the International Committee of the Red Cross in Geneva in 1977. It produced two protocols to the 1949 conventions. Protocol I, in essence, reaffirms and partially expands the provisions of the previous Hague and Geneva conventions concerning the protection of victims of international armed conflicts. More importantly, Protocol II, in recognition of the upsurge in civil wars and other internal armed conflicts, lays down, for the first time, rules "Relating to the Protection of Victims of Non-International Armed Conflicts."

There have been no treaties or conventions relating to the general conduct of warfare—as distinguished from the prohibition of specific weapons—since the 1977 Geneva Protocols. Space does not permit the listing of the many declarations and resolutions of a nonbinding character which have been adopted during the past 150 years by such bodies as the International Committee of the Red Cross, the United Nations, or the International Law Association. All of these, however, add to the body of humanitarian law in the form of customary law.[8]

3. The Principles of Humanitarian Law

From the foregoing account of the development of humanitarian law in modern times, it is possible to distill the following generally recognized and legally binding principles:

Moderation: The means of injuring the enemy are not unlimited.

Humanity: It is prohibited to use weapons or tactics which inflict unnecessary suffering or shock "the public conscience." Prisoners, the sick, and wounded must be treated in a humane manner.

Discrimination: It is prohibited to use weapons or tactics that fail to discriminate between civilians and combatants.

Neutrality: Belligerents are obliged to respect the territorial integrity of neutral states and the health and welfare of their inhabitants.

These principles are clear enough. Unfortunately, they tend to be obscured by two other principles of doubtful legal or moral value. One is the principle of proportionality, according to which reprisals must be proportionate to their antecedents. But what does this mean? Surely no one would argue that if country A starts beheading the prisoners it has taken from country B, then country B can do the same to the prisoners from country A. The other is the principle of necessity, which holds that belligerents may not use weapons or tactics greater than those required to achieve a legitimate military objective. This is the usual justification

---

[7] ICRC, an "independent humanitarian organization" whose task it is to promote and impement humanitarian law, was founded in Geneva in 1863, the same year in which the Lieber Code was promulgated in the United States.

[8] Virtually all of the treaties, conventions and declarations dealing with humanitarian law can be found on the excellent website of the Internaional Committee of the Red Cross, http://www.icrc.org/unicc/ihl.

for "collateral civilian damage." But this begs the question of what is a legitimate objective and how quickly it may legitimately be achieved. The United States, in World War II, was anxious to defeat Germany and Japan as quickly as possible with a minimum loss of American lives. Did this justify either the firebombing of Dresden or the nuclear devastation of Hiroshima and Nagasaki? Most military men would say "yes," most international lawyers "no."

It should also be mentioned that the emerging international law of the environment, while not traditionally part of humanitarian law, is increasingly coming to be seen as a restraining force on military activities.

C. Prohibition of Specific Weapons

1. Weapons of Mass Destruction

The desire to rid the world of weapons of mass destruction—biological, chemical, and nuclear—is part of the common moral/political vocabulary of the world community. Biological weapons have been outlawed by a convention in force since 1975, chemical weapons by a convention in force since April, 1997. There is no convention outlawing nuclear weapons, the most destructive of all, and no indication as of this writing that the nuclear weapon states have any intention of negotiating such a convention. Yet Article VI of the Nuclear Nonproliferation Treaty obliges all parties to it, including all the declared nuclear weapon states (United States, United Kingdom, France, Russia, and China) "to pursue negotiations in good faith on effective measures relating to . . . nuclear disarmament." Furthermore, the International Court of Justice, in an Advisory Opinion rendered on July 8, 1976 at the request of the General Assembly of the United Nations, held that "the threat or use of nuclear weapons would generally be contrary to the rules of international law applicable in armed conflict, and in particular the principles and rules of humanitarian law" and that "there exists an obligation to pursue in good faith *and bring to a conclusion* negotiations leading to nuclear disarmament *in all its aspects* under strict and effective international control."[9] A draft of a nuclear weapons convention, prepared by an international group of lawyers, scientists, and diplomats under the auspices of the New York-based Lawyers Committee on Nuclear Policy, was introduced by Costa Rica into the record of the 52nd United Nations General Assembly.[10]

2. Conventional Weapons

While weapons of mass destruction, particularly nuclear weapons, have the potential to wreak horrendous destruction, in fact a great many more people have been killed in this century by so-called conventional weapons, which might more appropriately be called killing weapons. Few weapons of this type have been banned by international agreement. Dum-dum bullets, as we have seen, were outlawed as early as 1899 and poison gas, which falls somewhere between conventional and mass destruction weapons, as early as 1925. More recently a number of states, but not very many,[11] have ratified a little-known and lengthily titled *Convention on Prohibitions or Restrictions on the Use of Certain Conventional Weapons Which May Be Deemed to Be Excessively Injurious or to Have Indiscriminate Effects*. The Convention has four protocols of rather limited scope dealing, respectively, with weapons that produce fragments not detectable by X-rays in the human body, land mines and booby traps, incendiary weapons, and blinding laser weapons. The first three are in force for certain countries, the fourth not yet, as of November, 1997. Because of the small number of ratifications, this treaty is more important for its reaffirmation of the basic principles of Hague and Geneva as of its date, October 10, 1980, than for its practical effects. For in the preamble, the High Contracting Parties recall the principle of moderation (the right to choose methods or means of warfare is not unlimited), humanity (superfluous injury and unnecessary suffering are to be avoided), and discrimination (the civilian population is to be protected). The preamble also restates the Martens Clause and picks up from Geneva Protocol I (Art. 55) the then novel proposition that "it is prohibited to employ methods or means of warfare which are intended, or may be expected, to cause widespread, long-term and severe damage to the natural environment."

A major step forward was taken in Ottawa in December, 1997, when 124 countries signed the *Convention on the Prohibition of the Use, Stockpiling, Production and Transfer of Anti-Personnel Mines and on their Destruction*. As of April 24, 1998, nine countries had ratified this

[9] UN Document A/51/218; also available at http://www.ddh.nl/org/ialana and at www.law.cornell.edu/icj. For an excellent analysis of the opinion, see John Burroughs, The (Il)legality of Threat or Use of Nuclear Weapons: A Guide to the Historic Opinion of the International Court of Justice (1997), available from the Lawyers Committee on Nuclear Policy (LCNP), 211 E. 43d St., New York, NY 10023; lcnp@aol.com.

[10] For the text of the draft convention, see http://www.dhl.nl/org/ialana/modelin.html. Also available from LCNP (see previous footnote).

[11] Seventy-one as of November 1, 1997.

Convention, which was largely the product of organizing and lobbying by civil society.

III. REMEDIES

A. The International Court of Justice

The International Court of Justice (ICJ) in The Hague is, under Art. 92 of the UN Charter, "the principal judicial organ of the United Nations." As such, it is the highest tribunal in the world dealing with questions of international law. It sits on disputes between states and renders advisory opinions to certain international organizations. Of the few cases involving the laws of war that have come before it and its predecessor, the Permanent Court of International Justice, the following stand out:

> In the *Corfu Channel* case (1949), the Court held Albania responsible for laying mines in the channel separating it from Greece without adequate notice to international shipping, resulting in severe damage to two British warships and attendant loss of life.
> In the *Nicaragua* case (1986), the Court held, *inter alia,* that the United States had violated customary international law by using force against Nicaragua.
> In 1994, *Bosnia Herzegovina* filed a complaint in the ICJ accusing Yugoslavia of genocide and of violating various provisions of the Hague and Geneva Conventions. The case is still pending as of this writing.

As noted above, the Court rendered an advisory opinion in 1996 on the legality under international law of the threat and use of *nuclear weapons.* The opinion, and the separate statements of the various judges, contain extensive discussions of the contemporary state of the laws of war.

These cases show that the doors of the International Court of Justice are open to the adjudication of claims of violation of the laws of war, both *ius ad bellum* and *ius in bello.*

B. Ad Hoc Tribunals

The best known international tribunal dealing with war crimes is, of course, the Nuremberg tribunal. This was followed by the International Military Tribunal for the Far East established in 1946 and by the International Tribunal for the Former Yugoslavia and Rwanda established in 1993. The Nuremberg and Tokyo tribunals were accused, rather unfairly, of representing victors' justice, since the judges went out of their way to make clear that they were operating under existing principles of international law and not newly created principles. The current Bosnia and Rwanda tribunals are accused, again unfairly, of being ineffective because they have managed to acquire jurisdiction over only a few of the "little fish" and none of the "big ones."[12] This is not their fault but that of the NATO military commanders and their superiors.

C. The International Criminal Court

As a result of the problems with the previous tribunals, there is now a worldwide movement for the establishment of an International Criminal Court with "teeth."[13] On July 17, 1998, the Statute of such a court was adopted in Rome at a diplomatic conference convened by the United Nations. The vote was 120 in favor and 7 against, including the United States. Initially, the court will have jurisdiction over genocide, war crimes, crimes against humanity, and aggression. It will be some time before the 60 ratifications required for the court to function are collected, but there is no doubt that the adoption of the Statute and the process of ratification now in progress constitute a major move toward the recognition and prosecution of universal crimes.

D. Domestic Tribunals

War crimes and other war-related human rights violations are cognizable not only by international tribunals, but also by domestic ones. Such trials may not only be directed at members of enemy armed forces or governments, but also against one's own citizens.

An example of the former is the court-martial of Captain Henry Wirz, commandant of the infamous Confederate Andersonville prison camp, by a military commission in Washington in 1865. Captain Wirz was convicted of causing the deaths of a large number of Union prisoners, "in violation of the laws and customs of war," (Friedman, p. 783) and sentenced to be hanged.

A prime example of the latter type of trial is the

---

[12] As of February 1998, 25 persons were in the custody of each of the two tribunals, being tried or awaiting trial.

[13] For the website of the Coalition for an International Criminal Court see http://www.igc.org/icc.

court-martial of Lieutenant William Calley for the My Lai massacre during the Vietnam war.

Such trials, however, are rare. States are not in the habit of prosecuting their own citizens for violations of humanitarian law, unless for an offense of great magnitude which has aroused considerable media attention.

IV. THE OBLIGATION TO RESOLVE DISPUTES PEACEFULLY

The obligation to settle disputes by peaceful means, in Article 2(3) of the UN Charter, is now generally accepted, as well as frequently disregarded. All kinds of mediation and arbitration procedures are available from the United Nations and other international and regional institutions, as well as from third-party countries and "eminent persons," like former Presidents Jimmy Carter and Oscar Arias. Sometimes they work, sometimes they do not. Whenever they do not, and hostilities break out, the Charter has been violated, but no one, since Nuremberg, has been convicted of launching a war of aggression.

The United Nations can and should do a great deal more than it has hitherto done in the areas of conflict prevention, peacemaking and peacekeeping. But it cannot do so as long as a number of countries, and particularly the United States, "the world's only remaining superpower," fail to pay their full share of UN dues and arrogate to themselves the right of unilateral diplomatic and military intervention in various conflicts, depending on their assessment of the impact of these conflicts on their "national interest."

V. CONCLUSION

The legal machinery, both practical and theoretical, for the prevention of conflicts, and for keeping conflicts within humane bounds when they do occur, is in place. The political will to use it, the ability to shed the caveman mentality after millennia of reaching for the sun, is still largely lacking. The vision of a world without war, which inspired the first and second Hague Peace Conferences, and the founding of the League of Nations and the United Nations, has dimmed considerably in presidential offices and chanceries throughout the world. At the same time, the role of civil society, which

is largely on the side of peace, has gained in importance. Perhaps the next century will see the abolitionists—of nuclear weapons, of inhumane tactics, of war itself—succeed in knocking together the heads of the "hard-headed realists" in government, who need to be reminded that war and the way wars are fought are not only immoral and impractical, but also illegal under the very precepts that they and their predecessors in government have written into law.

Also See the Following Articles

CHEMICAL AND BIOLOGICAL WARFARE • JUST-WAR CRITERIA • LAW AND VIOLENCE • NUCLEAR WEAPONS • WAR CRIMES • WARFARE, TRENDS IN • WEAPONRY, EVOLUTION OF

Bibliography

Boyle, F. A. (1985). *World politics and international law.* Durham, NC: Duke University Press.

Brownlie, I. (1963). *International law and the use of force by states.* Oxford: Clarendon Press.

Burroughs, J. (1997). *The (il)legality of threat or use of nuclear weapons: A guide to the historic opinion of the international court of justice.* Münster: Lit Verlag.

Damrosch, L. F., & Scheffer, D. J. (Eds.) (1991). *Law and force in the new international order.* Boulder-San Francisco-Oxford: Westview Press.

Falk, R. A. (1968). *Legal order in a violent world.* Princeton, NJ: Princeton University Press.

Friedman, L. (1972). *The law of war—A documentary history.* New York: Random House.

Grotius, H. (1925). *De jure belli ac pacis.* Carnegie Endowment for International Peace, Washington.

Hammer, R. (1971). *The court-martial of Lt. Calley.*

Keegan, J. (1993). *A history of warfare.* New York: Knopf.

Lachs, M. (1945). *The unwritten laws of warfare. Tulane Law Review, 20,* 10.

Meyrowitz, E. L. (1989). *Prohibition of nuclear weapons—The relevance of international law.* Dobbs Ferry: Transnational Publishers.

Moynihan, P. (1990). *On the law of nations.* Cambridge, MA: Harvard University Press.

Pictet, J. (1951). *The new Geneva Conventions for the protection of war victims. American Journal of International Law, 45,* 45.

Schindler, D., & Toman, J. (1988). *The laws of armed conflict—A collection of conventions, resolutions and other documents.* Dortrecht: Martinus Nijhoff.

Schwarzenberger, G. (1968). *From the laws of war to the laws of armed conflict. Journal of Public Law, 17,* 17.

Walzer, M. (1977). *Just and unjust wars.* New York: Basic Books.

Weiss, P. (Ed.). University of Iowa College of Law (1977). *Symposium: Nuclear Weapons, the World Court and Global Security. Transnational Law & Contemporary Problems, 7,*(2), p. 313.

Linguistic Constructions of Violence, Peace, and Conflict

C. David Mortensen

University of Wisconsin

GLOSSARY

Communication A process in which people interact with symbols and signs as mechanisms of mutual influence. Successful communication occurs insofar as one person is able to interpret the intended meanings of another person's actions.

Complex Language A system of communication, gestural, vocal, or written, based on an open and generative lexicon of several hundred signs amenable to meaningful combination and substitution.

Human Interaction Reality-testing activities where elaborated forms of language use are subject to an uneven mix of facilitative and subversive influences. Face-to-face interactions have the greatest impact when the vocabulary of one person can be readily translated into the vocabulary of any other person.

Public Conflict Struggle and strife over the distribution of scarce resources—material, economic, and symbol—in the human world.

Symbolic Violence The symbolic anticipation or re- construction of violent acts are intrinsic features of the violent actions themselves. Acts of physical violence emerge from acts of symbolic violence and vice versa.

HUMAN INTERACTIONS are constructed out of the real-world conditions that surround them. The use of complex language enables human beings to transform the cultural inheritance and fulfill basic tasks associated with the need for individual security and collective well-being. Tension, strife, and strain are decisive factors in shaping the larger potential for violence, peace, or conflict to be altered or changed at various levels of social and cultural organization. At issue is the dynamic interplay between violent acts and the linguistic or communicative atmosphere that surround them. In effect, the routine misuse or abuse of language contributes greatly to the question of how well or badly human beings treat one another on a larger scale. Consequently, conditions of violence, peace, and conflict are fully manifest both as distinctive social achievements and as abstract objectives or universal aims. One implication is clear. If we want to make the world a better place, we must be prepared to *construct* less violent means of cohabitation and communication. A central task is to trace shared effort and collective movement away from the radical disaffection implicit in acts of physical violence and toward their most plausible symbolic counterparts.

Copyright © 1999 by Academic Press.
All rights of reproduction in any form reserved.

I. THE LINGUISTIC INHERITANCE

On a small scale, human interactions have unintended consequences and social influences with global implications. On a larger scale, humans, unlike other animals, have well-developed capacities and abilities to transmit information, not just laterally, within generations, but vertically across generations. Intergenerational conflict is widespread and pervasive throughout the animal kingdom. Human conflict, it turns out, is simply the most complicated, obdurate, and potentially liberating source of conflict in the entire ecosystem. What stands out about so much small-scale human conflict is the sheer magnitude of what is possible.

Struggle and strife permeate human interactions in distinctive ways that are quite peculiar to the species. It is apparent, therefore, that human beings are fully capable of anticipating, maintaining, and resolving a wider range of conflicts than is any other species on earth. In terms of the sheer magnitude of what is possible, human beings have an enormous competitive edge that gathers momentum over time. Evolution, after all, is a process in time in which possibility and potentiality are important factors in establishing the conditions necessary for future elaboration. What acquires momentum are the unique effects and outcomes that make the greatest difference as a consequence of their total individual and collective use.

Ironically, the notion of humans having a "competitive edge" over other species linguistically points to the very problem that all humans share. We have the power to preserve or destroy one another, and other living creatures, in large part because of the enormous power of language that, historically speaking, is quite a recent arrival on the human scene. Such a sweeping capacity to solve problems on a global scale cannot be separated from an equally great potential to wreak havoc and (re)produce some of the most horrendous problems on earth. Against a global backdrop of threat and insecurity, the power of ordinary language can be seen as both curse and cure.

Questions of sustenance, security, and well-being go together, after all, because the human world is a material world and human beings are physical beings who have devised complex modes of language use, in some measure, as an expressive and communicative mechanism to facilitate individual reproduction and to enhance the perpetuation of the human race. As a consequence, public conflicts may be viewed as linguistic struggle and strife over the distribution of scarce resources—material, economic, and symbolic—in the human world. Personal conflicts are designed to facilitate the redistribution or reapportionment of whatever it is that humans may lack but nonetheless value. From a global standpoint, human knowledge is envisioned as transmitted largely through local and regional languages that remain somewhat obscure or incomprehensible to proximate neighbors or across cultural boundaries. Historical, regional, local, contextual, and situational differences are obviously significant, therefore, in shaping the selective and strategic nature of the speaking environment.

Shared activities are observed for the effects they produce on others and are repeated thereafter for the sake of those effects. By these standards, human interactions are sustained in a global network of reality-testing ceremonies where elaborated forms of language use are subject to an uneven mix of *facilitative* and *subversive* influences. All acts of observation are taken to be intrinsic aspects of the definition of the total situation. Individual actions are subject to a wide range of (re)interpretation from a constantly changing or shifting array of reference points. The question of *what* gets presented by one party is relative to *how* it is to be represented by any other. In effect, language and culture act as twin filters to regulate and monitor emergent conceptions of individuality, separation, and the degree of relatedness of individuals to each other.

II. SELECTIVE ADVANTAGES OF COMPLEX LANGUAGE

Complex language gives prior and implicit conditions an explicit form of mutual expression. Matters of definition, classification, and explanation involve a dynamic and systemic process where each expressive action is embedded within a larger sequence that tends to establish new possibilities for further explication. Evolutionary change thereby promotes the use of activities outside the body for functions previously performed by the body itself. The larger process favors the gradual transformation of individually sustained activities into those shared with many others. In critical situations the selection of those who speak is largely at the expense of nonspeakers. What matters most is not simply the long-term survival of the most articulate but the slow disappearance of the most inarticulate members of society. Moreover, those who speak well acquire or derive a host of secondary advantages over those who speak less well. At stake is the total magnitude of what is lost or gained at each step of the way.

Skillful use of complex language is highly advantageous. Differential sensitivity to slight variations in ordinary language use constitutes a basic human resource in matters to facilitate (a) constructive thinking; (b) adaptation to changing, unforeseen, adverse, or unwelcome circumstances; (c) cognitive growth; (d) the quality of life; and (e) the odds of survival. Conversely, the systemic misuse, abuse, or neglect of something at once so powerful and mysterious can be quite hazardous to one's health and well-being. Complex language allows the highly skilled to sustain day-to-day interactions in ways that affect considerations of individual well-being in the short run and collective survival in the long run. This is the case not only for matters of nourishment and sustenance but also for those affecting questions of social status and mate selection, two major determinants of the ability of a speaker to reproduce at relational and collective levels of existence.

In general, the wider the latitude of linguistic conditions that individuals are able to bring under a greater measure of volitional control, the more each party is placed in an enhanced position to maintain close and enduring ties with other people. Burling notes that when dealing with people, not material objects, we call upon our deepest and richest expressive and communicative resources. In matters involving personal cooperation, negotiation, competition, manipulation, and scheming to get our own way, subtle and intricate aspects of language become quite involving and highly salient. When disputes grow dangerous, we need language as an alternative to violent forms of retribution and reprisal. Burling concludes that language is both a *collective* resource to enrich the quality of life and a widely acknowledged *personal* resource to facilitate increasingly refined relations and vastly more complex organization of human society. By implication, anything that can be a resource for one person may be viewed as a liability by any other.

The potential for language use to prevail over violent actions is largely mediated through the preservation and cultivation of life-affirming rituals. In this equation, humans realize the greater potential for physical violence to erupt and strive, therefore, to civilize, appease, or tame the larger destructive threat through the daily (re)invocation of a litany of life-affirming customs, practices, and projects. Rituals of conversation, in particular, provide a margin of open-ended and low-risk opportunity to reveal or explore a rapid succession of aggressive urges and affectionate needs simultaneously. In this way, gradual and evolutionary change greatly expands the human capacity to love or hate in relation to who is identified as friend or foe or seen as located close or far away. Under favorable conditions, the threat of murder and sacrifice may be slowly displaced or

otherwise deflected by a greater measure of collective participation in shared actions designed to transform high-risk violent urges into low-risk symbolic substitutes. In this way, the progressively refined use of language and communication is able to take some of the sting out of the greater potential for outbreaks of violence. Conversely, daily rituals, projects, and routines may reverse, sometimes in a regressive way, the slant or tone of the larger enterprise. The misuse and abuse of abstract concepts and categories, for example, may transgress and violate human sensibilities to the point of great injury and harm.

III. COMMUNICATION AS SENSE-MAKING PRACTICE

Human beings are ordinarily quite sensitive to the larger issue of what transpires when things go quite well or turn out badly. Each individual has well-developed and deeply ingrained cognitive mechanisms to identify and categorize what sorts of things fit well together and what types do not. A succession of high-order achievements generally facilitates a greater measure of appreciation of the distinctive communicative value of what takes place. Favorable conditions are known to confer a broad range of secondary benefits. These include, among other things, greater personal sensitivity in the expenditure of scarce resources, willingness to contribute good ideas, faith in the pursuit of personal goals as worth the cost, and especially enhanced communication skills.

By these standards, unfavorable conditions include any harsh, unsafe, degraded, unhealthy, or otherwise unsuitable environments for human language to multiply and flourish. Discursive practices, after all, do not spring out of thin air. A rich confluence of behavioral and environmental factors must surely come together in order to secure a state of harmony and accord for all who are concerned. Diminished resolve to tolerate a given tradition of dispute or discord may weaken the wider search for common ground. Moreover, severe distortions in thought and feeling may become deeply ingrained in protracted episodes of badly misinterpreted or misaligned forms of social action. An upsurge of unwanted internal interference and external distraction add further to the overall level of bias, static, and noise in the larger system.

Favorable circumstances are shown to benefit core matters affecting the critical evaluation of personal performance in various public contexts. The distinction between *effective* and *faulty* interaction is quite decisive. An effective way of life is associated with the all-inclusive ability to adapt to changing or unforeseen circumstance. Matters of efficacy in self-expression require the ability to construct reasonably clear definitions of what transpires and an inclusive sense of direction from one moment to the next. In sharp contrast are those shared actions with unclear definition (aimlessness, lack of focus) or direction (indecision). In comparative terms, a refined sense of personal clarity is useful in maintaining close ties with others. Likewise, the absence of these same qualities is conducive to the formation of weaker ties with others. Personal fluency registers in the ability to (a) express oneself clearly and (b) interpret others accurately.

Faulty or ineffective courses of action imply a marked discrepancy between an individual's capacity for self-expression and subsequent evaluations of the performance in question by observers. A poor quality or low-level performance may be taken as weak, inarticulate, or misaligned or misapplied by one observer or another. In contrast, a good or efficacious performance may be viewed as strong, explicit, articulate, well aligned, or closely in synch (by some standard). At issue is what diverse types of personal actions are to be construed by others as well functioning, whole, and integrated, or else dismissed as fragmented, divided, and split. In sharp contrast, acts of successful communication occur whenever one person is able to understand the intended meanings of another person's actions. In effect, the force of face-to-face interactions have the greatest value when the vocabulary of any one person can be readily translated into the vocabulary of any other person in the surrounding community. In the wider search for alternatives to violence, it is a matter of great consequence to be able to communicate effectively.

IV. MISCOMMUNICATION

Nonetheless, there is a growing recognition that language use and communicative practice is pervasively and even intrinsically flawed, partial, and problematic. In human matters, no one is infallible. The margin of difference between success and failure is a matter of "more or less" rather than "all or nothing." In the moment-by-moment sequences of translation and interpretation, Grace shows why it becomes virtually impossible to discuss subject matter with anyone who has not previously been aware of the existence of that subject (qua subject). Since the rules of conventional language use are not identical from one speaker to another, each language has a unique potential for reality con-

struction—each subtends a different set of potential realities.

Skilled speakers are best prepared to engage in acts of mutual influence where the ground rules of situated knowledge are clearly specified or well known in advance. Routine interactions take place insofar as the parties in question are able to rely on a stable tradition of prior interactions for tacit guidance and direction in deciding what to do now or next. However, when dealing with highly unusual or uncertain circumstances, there may be a greater measure of difficulty in coping with rapidly increased levels of complexity, complication, and loss of control (long-term). Specific problems may pile up, one after another, without an equal number of solutions in sight.

Problematic interactions produce complicated or unsettled questions. A problematic issue registers as an archriding concern that does not lend itself to any apparent or self-evident means of articulation, course of action, or mode of resolution. The specific value of a problematic issue corresponds roughly with the total magnitude of what is at issue or construed as outstanding, unresolved, unsettled, or unknown. It is, in other words, a matter of the collective capacity to attend to the accumulation of unfinished discursive business. At no point is there any assurance that communication will be certain or relatively trouble free. By comparison, critical or urgent situations can be quite vexing to figure out when they operate at the outer limits of personal volition and conscious awareness. Invasive actions such as rape, natural disasters, death of family member, or serious illness threaten prior beliefs and entrenched behavioral patterns. In addition, severe trauma causes people to reconstruct belief systems and design alternative explanations for life-altering events that are not easy to comprehend, much less explain to anyone else.

Chronic exposure to densely crowded living conditions is also likely to foster problematic circumstance, disrupt support networks, and cause residents to cope, in part, by withdrawing from one another. Exposure to long-term chronic stress has insidious effects on basic levels of accessible social support. Terminal physical illness, recurring mental illness, and personal bereavement are chronic stressors that often lead to the withdrawal of affection and support from ailing individuals—due simply to the sheer magnitude of debt and threat of overwhelming obligation. Likewise, outbreaks of conflict and violence, by nature, cause intense forms of cognitive disorientation in how the respective victims view themselves in the context of the emotional aftermath. Social networks of violent offenders may be disorganized and chaotic, sometimes almost as a way of life. Those who observe violent actions may react from a stance of emotional distance that does not permit full appreciation of the magnitude of the total burden. It can be extremely difficult for victims of misuse and abuse to make clear and coherent sense of terrifying events in ordinary terms that others can readily grasp and comprehend. Disturbances in social and personal relations affect the well-being of individuals and disrupt the preservation and conservation of communal ties. Coping skills function best when there is a clear sense that stressful or extreme events are somewhat controllable when dealt with directly as against those viewed as mainly uncontrollable and avoided.

Problematic actions provide a rough measure of what goes wrong or may be valued but sorely lacking or missing. Sources of misinformation multiply where multiple efforts to communicate in a public sphere are left unfulfilled in more than one sense or another. A succession of poor-quality encounters accounts for an enormous amount of public discontent and ill will. Insofar as human conflict is linguistically constructed, repetitive acts of misinterpretation and misunderstanding figure heavily in matters of conflict escalation at all levels of social and cultural organization.

Basic linguistic miscalculations may interfere with the possibility of achieving a working consensus among the respective parties. In times of confusion and commotion, there is a tendency to repeat the same types of "interactive mistakes" over and over again. Matters of confused argument construction further distort the meanings of personal viewpoints and shifting frames of reference. People get stuck in a litany of poor performances with no way out and no better way to alter the larger parameters of the failing system. A tradition of faulty or ineffectual performances may be slowly transformed but only at the deepest levels of personal skill and collective resource. Nothing is set in stone. Some measure of risk necessarily blends in with an unspecified margin of opportunity.

V. SYMBOLIC VIOLENCE

Words and gestures may be used as aggressive weapons or basic means of self-defense. Notions of *sheer physical violence* are a misnomer here. Personal injuries are never merely physical in definition or consequence. Acts of physical brutality reveal a deeper, hidden truth, namely that acts of physical violence emerge from acts of symbolic violence and vice versa. In this way, acts of murder and suicide draw tacit inspiration from the surrounding communicative milieu. Unlike the overt outcomes associated with acts of physical violence, the hurtful and injurious effects of symbolic violence are often hidden from sight—as invisible damage or invisible wounds. Cultural violence occurs when exchange relations, whether in the sphere of religion, ideology, language, or empirical science, are used to justify acts of physical violence. In effect, the symbolic constructions of violent acts are intrinsic features of the violent actions themselves. Likewise, violence destroys the symbolic burdens that come with it.

Violent actions are permeated with symbolic implications and ritualistic overtones. The main themes are quite striking. Girard contends that violence is primordial. It is intrinsic to the larger scheme of things. The contaminating power of violence gives rise to the need for purifying ceremonies. Hence, there is hardly any form of violence that cannot be described in terms of sacrifice. All social rituals involve elements of mystery and sacrifice. A certain degree of mythos and mystery is required to cover up or hide the horrific nature of violence. In this way, the threat of physical force can be covered up, and slowly replaced, with substitutional or deflective actions where more of the weight can be born vicariously or symbolically. All concepts of impurity stem from communal fears of a perpetual cycle of violence arising in its midst. Likewise, sacrifice is primarily an act of violence without risk of vengeance; vengeance professes to be an act of reprisal, and every reprisal calls for another reprisal. While the possibility of violence is not to be denied, the larger threat may be diverted to another object. Hence, the sacrificial process fosters a certain degree of mutual misunderstanding. People can dispense with violence easier somehow if they view the process as a sheer necessity, an utter imposition from the outside world. In this way acts of sacrificial violence can serve as agents of purification—a single victim can be substituted for all potential victims. Everyone is intent on diagnosing the illness in order to find a cure; but in fact the illness is the other—the false diagnoses and poisonous prescriptions. The problem is always the same. Violence is both the disease (inside) and the cure (outside).

Symbolic violence may be viewed in terms of sacrifice and scapegoating. Burke describes the human condition as one of imperfect and muddled communication. We must solve our problems in society as best we can through recalcitrant and mystifying symbols that cause the problems we must yet solve if we are to act together at all. Thus, symbols are both a blessing and a cure—a blessing if we turn our study of their use into a method for acquiring better knowledge about the mechanisms of social control, a curse if we let their power overwhelm us until we accept symbolic mystification as reality. The fundamental temptation, cast in the manner of a misguided search for a false cure, arises with the ability to hand over one's ills to a scapegoat, thereby getting purification from dissociation. Burke describes scapegoating as symptomatic of overwhelming, powerful, and unrelenting stress that is collectively directed toward and projected upon an object, person, or institution that is consensually deemed worthy of sacrifice. The key tactics are seen as a means of expiating collective guilt and acquiring purification by disassociation with the medium in order to restore or promote social cohesion. In scapegoating one may expect to find some variation of killing in the work. In other words, we who victimize and are victimized by one another may disown or repudiate unwanted features of our self-images by projecting our personal weaknesses and inadequacies onto another and with the resultant discharge of collective hostility and antagonism, enhance our internal sense of integrity.

Acts of symbolic violence are not randomly distributed but are rather strategically located in the social fabric. Sagan claims that all societies assert, implicitly or explicitly, that certain groups of human beings are not human and are, therefore, legitimate objects of aggression—such societies divide the human world into those who are human (we) and those who are subhuman—the list of "them" is a catalogue of the oppressed, dominated, and exploited peoples of the history of the world. Mutual displays of affection and aggression sometimes become so intermixed in sacrifice that it is hard even to distinguish the two strands. Only if a means is found to satisfy aggressive needs symbolically is it possible to give up aggressive practices—all satisfaction of aggression outward is an act of self-destruction. To kill another human being, one must first recast the other into the status as an object. To continue to kill that person, even after the other is dead, is to continue to deny his reality, to prolong his status as object. Because war is inevitable only in the psyches of those who make it so, one must not dare talk of courage or nerve separated from love, because without eros courage ends up the power to kill.

Bourdieu equates symbolic violence with the power to impose meanings and also insist on their legitimacy while effectively concealing the underlying dynamic of power relations at work. Those who are subjected to symbolic-laden implications of inferiority are placed in a difficult position. They must struggle against the massive imposition of arbitrary cultural forces by arbitrary agents of power in heavily weighted situations where talk and conversation all too quickly become instruments of instruction and incubation. Symbolic violence registers in all instructions to treat a given system of assigned meanings as *exclusively* worthy of inclusion. All other possibilities are ruled out in advance. Assigned meanings reproduce and thereby legitimate dominant and subordinate relations into a domain of inflated but unspoken quest for privilege, status, and rank. Communication regulated by heavily imposed instruction reproduces a system of arbitrary subject matter that can never be seen in its full truth. The historical combination of the instruments of symbolic violence cannot be isolated from the instruments of concealment. Mythos and mystery regulate oppressive systems where there are few viable alternatives and no easy way out. One-sided claims of legitimacy reflect the relative strength of the relations between those whose material, economic, and symbolic interests they express. Misrecognition adds further to the legitimacy of the imposition. There is, in other words, considerable room for distortion and misrecognition of the truth on all sides.

Acts of physical violence acquire a great deal of communicative significance in the emotional aftermath. The public atmosphere that surrounds highly publicized acts of political violence is quite striking as a case in point. Mass media coverage of political violence strains the social fabric by disrupting traditional assumptions about what it means to be a member of a society. Public deliberations lead to a rapid succession of short-term changes in how ordinary citizens view themselves, their relations with others, and society at large. The clash of divergent sentiment has been found to produce an initial sense of public crisis followed by the emergence of a series of creative and innovative social mechanisms to represent and redistribute elements of threat and danger throughout the fabric of society. Basic structures of conflicting public sentiment, therefore, resemble, mimic, or imitate salient features of the act of political violence itself. Attacks on public officials reveal prevailing public/cultural biases toward displays of hostility, aggression, conflict, violence, and murder, and thereby bring to the surface explicit acknowledgment of whatever undercurrent of murderous urges already exist in public opinion of governmental authority.

Political displays of hostility and animus invoke the use of ritualized, agonistic codes involving considerable cognitive anticipation and reenactment of death wishes ("symbolic killing") directed toward and displaced upon another or others viewed as one would a rival, obstacle, or enemy. The possibility of killing or the thought of murder is not to be outstripped. In the work of Ibsen the notion of "soul murder" is defined in terms of the making use of, or exploitation, of another person. The killing does not have to be actual. It can occur symbolically, as for example in the withdrawal of love or in the desertion of a person. It can also be partial instead of total—a slow murder, as it were, through constant tormenting. The incremental destruction of human spirit qualifies for what Otto Rank terms "slow murder" between intimates, lovers, and kin.

Death wishes crystallize in symbols of killing—a curious effort in symbolizing for the purpose of destroying someone else's method of symbolizing. One may envision the murder of a person or the more limited destruction of what the presence of the person in question may evoke, express, or make manifest. Symbolic killing may assume any number of forms ranging anywhere from active annihilation to passive indifference. The urge to kill off what other people express or reveal constitutes a form of linguistically mediated violence that replaces a tangible physical force with an intangible symbolic force. The urgency of the death wish is sustained and nurtured through cognitive reenactment and anticipation of the murder itself.

A mood or atmosphere of linguistic militancy occurs where words and gestures function as "weapons" in ritualized clashes of conflicting public opinion that signify a communal desire for purification, atonement, and psychic protection of the observers from threatening aspects of societal events that unfold beyond their own personal control. Public dialogue may be viewed, then, as a vast reality-testing ceremony, one that measures the cumulative strength of human loyalties and the bond of political affiliations. Political controversy produces massive, redressive societal mechanisms that reaffirm, test, challenge, alter, or replace traditional values through expressive activity that provides a muted symbolic display with dramatic responses that change attitudes and values without major and unlimited conflict, and without the necessity for total involvement on the part of all members of society.

The notion of symbolic killing calls attention to the destructive consequences of abusive, neglectful, or misapplied forms of shared action. A collective representation of central tendencies: (a) early developmental damage and prolonged separation from love objects and care-takers; (b) generational poverty, deprivation, and collective devaluation; (c) unresolved hatred over atrocities against one's own kin; (d) abuse or neglect with no end in sight; (e) lack of access to scarce resources; and (f) legacy of largely unfulfilled possibilities—a sense of worthlessness and despair.

VI. ETHNIC CONFLICT

Ethnicity provides a strategic measure of personal identity and strength of communal affiliation. In severe ethnic conflicts, a host of self-serving devices may be used to diminish greater appreciation for the standards, values, beliefs, and customs of what takes place with other people, as in the use of foreign currency or exposure to alien territory. Linguistic tensions tend to cluster around periods of undue or prolonged exposure to information or situations that have been very troubling or unsettling in the past. When the language systems of competing ethnic groups are pitted against one another, three broad types of cognitive distortion are at issue.

Ideological bias occurs whenever a particular way of looking at the world is closed to further inspection from the outside world. A personal ideology can be used to create public justification for the privileges and perks of certain groups or institutions in prevailing social arrangements. Inflated or justificational use of language, whether designed to expand the scope of privilege and preogrative, or to strengthen collective resolve to obtain a greater share of resources, protects the vested interest and hidden agenda of those in charge of established norms and rules. Moreover, personal ideology can be used as a vision to be imposed on others as a matter of whim. The massive imposition is coercive and defensive in aspiration. It fosters a heavily slanted and stylized version that tolerates existing inequities and remains indifferent to the deprivation and suffering of others.

Ethnocentric bias arises with the inclination to see one's own group, kin, or tribe to be the center of everything in relation to the wider scheme of things. At issue is a wider tendency to be unaware of the biases due to one's own make-up and to judge and interact with others on the basis of those unspoken premises. The matter may be viewed in terms of the sheer magnitude of exaggeration in matters of deference (praise) toward insiders and suspicion (blame) toward outsiders. Double standards abound. Therefore, the fine line between "us" and "them" is subject to the force of self-monitored bias up and down the line. Distortion results from biased forms of misclassification and false or mythical categorization of competing reference groups.

Egocentric bias becomes a factor when one person makes assumptions, or forms expectations, associated with self-enhancing estimates of the degree to which others think, feel, or act as oneself. Alternative possibilities are easier to discount or rule out. Those who are threatened by difficult life conditions are particularly susceptible to exposure to abusive language based on concerted efforts at devaluation. It is difficult to account for all the harm and damage that occurs from the massive imposition of diverse and divergent ways of thinking about the world.

Ethnic conflict registers in the labels, categories, classifications, and stereotypes used to establish or deny access across social and cultural boundaries. Abusive language figures prominently in collective efforts to express, reinforce, undermine, or redress rank orders along prevailing ethnic lines. Nicknames used as epithets constrain those who use them. Name calling provides a blank check for characterizing out-groups as worthy or deserving of a constant outpouring of verbal abuse as a means to neutralize their efforts to gain status or acquire influence. For those in control, name-calling justifies inequality and prejudice and tolerates invidious ethnic comparisons in public settings. Minority protests against oppressive labels becomes stylized and highly rhetorical whenever counterlabels are used to neutralize or subvert the prevailing vocabulary of a local community. Ethnic slurs, particularly in jokes and humor, have one main goal—to neutralize and thwart outsiders. As language contact between competing groups become more prominent, multifaceted, sustained, or troubled, the magnitude of verbal abuse intensifies and more varied derogatory terminology is coined and used.

Hostile interactions among identity groups may become chronic or protracted, based on deep-seated hatred, long-standing grievance, or denial of basic needs. As Fisher indicates, standard or routine approaches deal with surface issues but are quite powerless to address nonnegotiable issues "in part because of a host of social-psychological processes, including cognitive rigidities and distortions, self-fulfilling prophecies, and irrational commitment mechanisms" with interlocking conditions where no one issue can be resolved in itself but is part of a larger sequence where "the process itself becomes a major source of contriving conflict" (p. 248). One objective is to marshal small-scale support and large-scale resources to enable especially disadvantaged groups to preserve and solidify the necessary linguistic skills to revitalize local cultural identities and neutralize political oppression. Here peace is measured as collective tolerance of small-scale disorder.

VII. THIRD-PARTY INTERVENTION

Faulty interaction is not always self-correcting. Severe linguistic difficulties may become intractable or impenetrable over time. The sheer perpetuation of poor quality performance raises the possibility or need for third-party intervention. The initial goal of mediation or arbitration is to improve the quality of interaction by reducing the severity of discord or dispute. This is not always possible, particularly if the adversaries have reached a hurting stalemate. The use of tough tactics—an unwillingness to compromise—may sabotage the possibility for *any* type of resolution. If each party insists on holding out, an impasse can be expected. Mediators may attempt to strike a power balance, expand the agenda, explore agreements that yield high benefits to both sides, determine what points are negotiable, reframe the dispute, exert pressure on second and third parties, and fine-tune strategies and tactics that work out well. On a larger scale, international mediators are required to facilitate communication, formulate strategies, and manipulate the course of decision making.

Flexibility is crucial. Rigid and tough bargaining strategies operate in hostile climates with a wide convergence of different interests and distinct personal concerns. Individual flexibility requires the willingness to forfeit gains in order to avoid further losses or a deadlock. Coercive tactics may be used to move one party off a position, onto a new position, or help to save face. However, successful settlements are difficult to broker when one or both parties have few resources or weak linguistic skills. Resource scarcity and power imbalance tend to reduce the total range of options. Also resistant to change is discord and dispute over principles and nondivisible issues. Low levels of verbal interaction generally makes matters worse.

The ability to compromise is also decisive. In an analysis of bargaining experiments reported over a 25-year period, Druckman found the strongest effect sizes were obtained for the mediator's own orientation, prior experience, time pressures, and initial distance between positions. Most resistant to change are social conditions where (a) the participants do not expect future interaction; (b) few issues are contested and a deadline exists; (c) competitive orientations are longstanding or where face-saving pressures are strong; (d) *differences between positions* on important issues are derived from long-held attitudes or linked to *contrasting ideologies*; and (e) when faced with *tough* or *explotive* opponents whose intentions are easy to discern. In effect, the entire sweep of conflict and dispute must be taken into account during the initial review of what is possible or ruled out.

Conflict and criticism are closely associated. Destructive forms of verbal criticism are known to promote anger, tension, and further resolve to handle future disputes with methods of resistance and avoidance rather than collaboration and compromise. Harsh or recriminating forms of verbal criticism gradually lower expectations of performance and self-efficacy. Poor criticism, in effect, promotes an atmosphere of conflict and confusion on all sides. Main targets are severely deficient or frequently misused aspects of personality with disproportionate blame and guilt induction over what goes wrong. The clash of discordant verbal sentiment—a heavy stockpile of claim weighted against counterclaim—may exhibit a constant recycling of stress and strain with heavy reliance on the same kinds of moves and tactics in successive turns of spirited talk during heated conversation. Mutual regulation of escalative tendencies by recycled maneuvers helps to even out, dilute, and attenuate the duration or severity of the verbal conflict at hand.

It is useful to think of the intensity of personal disputes in relation to the magnitude of what is at stake. Potential issues cluster around whatever humans value but find lacking, scarce, or uneven in matters of production, access, or supply. Grimshaw organizes personal issues around several basic considerations. Attention is focused on substantive "issues" seen as *causes* for participants' motivations. Conflict talk involves (restricted or elaborated) negotiation over personal identities, that is, what kinds of persons and what states of relations should come into play. At issue is the precise alignment of argumentative skills, complex negotiation of multiple identities, and muted instruction about the normative properties of talk. Much depends on the total stakes at work in an evolving context of mixed motives. What is crucial is whether the respective parties see themselves as speaking for themselves or for others. Verbal controversy has the potential to *expand* in focus, or *spread* along preexisting boundaries of classes, categories, groups, friendships, and institutional affiliation.

VIII. ALTERNATIVES TO VIOLENCE

Acts of nonviolence provide plausible linguistic substitutes for the threat of violent actions themselves. The symbolic resources that humans employ to threaten, injure, or thwart others may be altered, either by design or application, to neutralize, deflect, or dissipate the risk of violent action. Peace-making efforts involve a double substitution. At one level is the shared effort to find alternatives to the use of physical coercion or force. At another is the common struggle to devise the means and the methods of improved communication as a goal without inflicting further harm and injury. An underlying presumption is the possibility of mutual engagement in constructive change.

Fatalism is the enemy of constructive change. Static or faulty conditions may be reproduced in the manner of a bad habit or poorly executed routine. In matters of acquired deficiency or trained incompetence, the focal points of subject matter may change rapidly while the basic misconstructive processes remain much the same. Fatalism implies bargaining in bad faith, as when people get stuck in a long succession of poor performances with no way out and no (better) way to alter (the failing system). As a corrective, there must be some measure of faith in the larger possibility of changing the patterns of interaction that interfere with the gradual acquisition of more favorable or productive aspirations. The measure of required change may involve an incremental or stepwise gain or else it may assume a more sweeping and inclusive form—affecting the character, conditions and context of interaction.

What qualifies as questionable or problematic does not have to be taken as absolute or inherent in the greater scheme of things but is dependent rather on the particular mix of circumstance and behavior. It is useful to think of the requirements for movement away from the threat of violence or intractable conflict in terms of a series of small-scale changes in personal outlook and responsiveness to others. A measure of persistence refers to small-scale change (one state to another) within the same basic level or type of shared activity. Transformation, in contrast, refers to a far more dramatic or sudden shift, a jump, out of a faulty system (all-or-nothing).

Tolerance of change acquires definition from the point of greatest resistance. The lower threshold is a state of sheer intolerance toward any type of change in the trajectory of a course of action. One may decide to cling to a set of *static conditions*, whether taken as mainly harmonious, contentious, or volatile. A point of small departure is manifest in the willingness to tolerate an *incremental* or momentary change (one thing or another) but only for a specified period of time. Willingness to settle for a succession of slight or modest improvements may well leave the larger picture in tact. Slight change may be only begrudgingly accepted. *Episodic* change is due to a series of minor adjustments and accommodations to the forces of risk and change at work. *Generalized* change registers as a major shift in the definition or state of human relations during (a) some critical, urgent, or decisive period or else in (b) one's way of dealing with other people in general. More highly visible is a state of extensive change where the total impact of events is so dramatic and elaborated, a total break from the past. It may be even possible to envision a *radical* change in some salient mode of public conduct. A vision of *transformational* change enables someone to behave in a whole new way, as in a quest for a new way of life.

Mutual resolution of unfinished business opens up a larger array of possibilities. After all, a litany of global, regional, and local conceptions of peace, conflict, and violence are manifest as quite visible and highly distinctive conditions in the human world. We may speak of a peaceful, conflicted, or violent way of life almost any place on earth. Therefore, each major type of human activity fully qualifies as a linguistic construction of significant achievement. At issue are basic relations between language users, specific instances of language use, and matters affecting issues of individual security and collective well-being. Of greatest concern is whether the unforeseen consequences of all the stress and strain serves to undermine the prospect of future interaction. What hangs in the balance is a legacy of threat and support with only limited potential for movement on all sides. Short-term effects and long-term outcomes are subject to (micro) management and (macro) maintenance of shared circumstance.

Ordinary language is a basic mechanism of repair in human relations. Acts of compensation and appeasement (face-saving) may enable or allow old wounds to heal and prevent new ones from occurring. Certain types of violent action may be deflected or diverted into less intense forms of symbolic struggle. The rhetorical principles of imitation, substitution, conversion, or partial replication may be designed to direct or deflect public attention elsewhere. In this way the efficacious use of complex language invokes a spirit of accommodation, renewal, or rebirth.

From a third-party perspective, optimum conditions represent high-order linguistic achievements. They involve at minimum the courage to resist whatever would hold a person back from shared participation in communal efforts to fulfill the potentiality of shared moments rather than let them be misused, abused, or merely wasted. Successful communication is shown to be an individual and collective achievement, accomplished through compromise and mutual accommodation, rather than merely taken for granted as an entitlement of possibility. In such an intricate and fragile domain, favorable conditions revolve around the compatibility of individual interests with communal involvements in sustained and systematic sequences of interaction in which the effective use of personal resources leads to the maximum fulfillment of mutual possibilities.

Obtainable standards are reached each time that human beings are shown to be capable and willing to deal with intractable or problematic concerns in a manner that takes into account (1) the safety and security of each member; (2) the intrinsic worth of mutual exploration; (3) the stance of receptivity toward future interaction; (4) the courage to say and do whatever is required while there is still a margin of opportunity; and (5) a willingness to promote a more inclusive spirit of world openness. Most decisive is whether the activity in question is sufficiently open to inspection to enable each party to call into question the physical and material well-being of one another. At issue is any sense of deprivation that leaves certain individuals feeling unsafe and insecure in their respective dealings with one another.

Perhaps there should be greater provision in the communal landscape for skilled and well-trained linguists who act mainly on behalf of those who cannot or are not in a good position to speak out on their own behalf. Favorable conditions provide alternative methods to translate the implicit, unspoken urges of self and others into a salient and contemporary idiom. In other words, those who are most fluent and articulate give expression to the issues and concerns of those who lack the ability or resolve to represent their own strivings and concerns in the best possible light. A secure sense of collective achievement implies that no one is solely at the mercy of his or her own linguistic devices. Individual members are in a position to speak to, with, against, and through unfinished, urgent, or compelling business. Such displays of supportive communication have the potential to become a vital human resource. Hence, individuals must be able to maintain direct access to a wide circle of second and third parties for care and assistance in dealing with stressful demands and difficult or questionable behaviors. Routine exchange is predicated on the presumption of mutual helpfulness to sustain someone in a goal or cause in the context of personal appraisals of the use (or misuse) of collective resources. Support is on the side of a greater measure of human resources to be reproduced on a regular basis. A central goal is to preserve and protect the material, economic, and symbolic resources that people already value.

Linguistic support can be a major source of social stability through changing times. Affordable circumstance include: benefits derived from secure connections, satisfaction that is moderately stable, ability to maintain cross-situational consistency in the average level of success during daily contacts with others, and mutual tolerance of difficulties when those close connections are lacking, ambiguous, or insecure. Complex forms of social comfort are associated with (a) a greater degree of involvement with distressed others and their difficulties; (b) neutral forms of personal evaluation; (c) awareness and sensitivity to stressful feelings; (d) acceptance and validation of the other's distress; and (e) explanations for the urgency of another's condition. Supportive persons provide valuable but intangible resources—warmth, reassurance, help, assistance, and aid for troubled times. The degree of success increases the willingness to deal with signs of distress in more complexity and greater detail.

Global conceptions of support help shape one's sense of being worthy of help and assistance from others. Availability of support includes a general sense of nourishment plus specific orientations about significant others as caregivers. There is growing recognition that supportive actions are powerful forces in solving problems, forming amicable and productive work relations, sustaining close and enduring relations, promoting a healthy form of family life, and serving as global measures of competence. At stake is the willingness to understand the full range of adaptations and methods for circumventing limits. Progressive movement involves a journey to reawaken individual vision and collective resolve.

Also See the Following Articles

COMMUNICATION STUDIES, OVERVIEW • CONFLICT TRANSFORMATION • ENEMY, CONCEPT AND IDENTITY OF • ETHNIC CONFLICTS AND COOPERATION • INTERPERSONAL CONFLICT, HISTORY OF • LANGUAGE OF WAR AND PEACE • MASS MEDIA, GENERAL VIEW • RITUAL AND SYMBOLIC BEHAVIOR

Bibliography

Allen, I. L. (1983). *The language of ethnic conflict.* New York: Columbia University Press.

Bourdieu, P., & Passeron, J. C. (1977). *Reproduction in education, society and culture.* (R. Nice, Trans). Beverly Hills, CA: Sage.

Burleson, B. R., Albrecht, T. J., & Sarason, L. G. (1994). *Communication of social support: Messages, interactions, relationships, and community.* Thousand Oaks, CA: Sage.

Burling, R, (1986). The selective advantage of complex language. *Ethology and Sociobiology, 7,* 1–16.

Burnstein, E., Crandall, C. & Kitayama, S. (1994). Some neo-darwinian decision rules for altruism: Weighing cues for inclusive fitness as a function of the biological importance of the decision. *Journal of Personality and Social Psychology, 67,* 773–789.

Chernus, I. (1993). Order and disorder in the definition of peace. *Peace and Change, 18,* 99–125.

Druckman, D. (1994). Determinants of compromising behavior in negotiation. *Journal of Conflict Resolution, 37,* 236–276.

Ericsson, K. A., & Smith, J. (Eds.). (1991). *Toward a general theory of expertise: Prospects and limits.* Cambridge, England: Cambridge University Press.

Eriksen, T. H. (1992). Linguistic hegemony and minority resistance. *Journal of Peace Research, 29,* 313–332.

Fisher, R. J. (1993). The potential for peacebuilding: Forging a bridge from peacekeeping to peacemaking. *Peace and Change, 18,* 247–266.

Galtung, J. (1990). Cultural violence. *Journal of Peace Research, 27,* 291–305.

Girard, R. (1977). *Violence and the sacred.* (P. Gregory, Trans.). Baltimore: John Hopkins University Press.

Grimshaw, A. D. (1990). Research on conflict talk: Antecedents, resources, findings, directions. In A. D. Graimshaw (Ed.), *Conflict talk: Sociolinguistic investigations of arguments in conversations* (pp. 280–324). Cambridge: Cambridge University Press.

Grace, G. W. (1987). *The linguistic construction of reality.* London: Croom Helms.

Helgeson, V. S. (1994). Relation of agency and communion to well-being: Evidence and potential explanations. *Psychological Bulletin, 116,* 412–428.

Janoff-Bulman, R. (1992). *Shattered assumptions: Toward a new psychology of trauma.* New York: Free Press.

Lepore, S. J., Evans, G. W., & Schneider, M. L. (1991). Dynamic role of social support in the link between chronic stress and psychological distress. *Journal of Personality and social psychology, 61,* 899–909.

Mortensen, C. D. (1987). *Violence and communication: Public reactions to an attempted presidential assassination.* Landover MD: University Press of America.

Mortensen, C. D. (1991). Communication, conflict, and culture. *Communication Theory, 1,* 273–291.

Mortensen, C. D. (1994). *Problematic communication: The construction of invisible walls.* Westport, CN: Praeger.

Mortensen, C. D. (1997). *Miscommunication.* Thousand Oaks, CA: Sage.

Parks, C. D., & Vu, A. D. (1994). Social dilemma behavior of individuals from highly individualist and collectivist cultures. *Journal of Conflict Resolution, 38,* 708–718.

Perdue, W. D. (1995). Civilization. *Peace Review, 7:3/4,* 409–417.

Sagan, E. (1979). *The Lust to annihilate.* New York: The Psychohistory Press.

Valentine, D. P., Holahan, C. J., & Moos, R. H. (1994). Social support, appraisals of event controllability, and coping: An integrative model. *Journal of Personality and Social Psychology, 66,* 1094–1102.

Wall, J. A., & Lynn, A. (1993). Mediation: A current review. *Journal of Conflict Revolution, 37,* 160–194.

Long-Term Effects of War on Children

James Garbarino and Joseph A. Vorrasi

Cornell University

I. INTRODUCTION: BEYOND THE BODY COUNT

A recent volume on the mental health issues of children in war is entitled *Minefields in Their Hearts* (Apfel and Simon, 1996). The image of war as an emotional minefield captures the essence of the psychological challenges that war presents to children. In contrast, conventional thinking about warfare tends to focus on quantitative measures, most notably casualty rates: the number of people wounded or killed. In their efforts to subdue the rebels in Afghanistan, an effort resembling the role the United States played in Vietnam, Soviet forces lost 15,000 of their own troops dead, and through their bombing, they obliterated more than half of Afghanistan's 30,000 villages. All in all, about 1.3 million were killed—most of them women and children. This is war as children experienced it in Afghanistan:

> At first, it was just a morbid whistling overhead, the sound of an antipersonnel rocket in the dying moments of flight. Then it exploded in a shattering burst of smoke and dust. A group of children had been playing a noisy game of tag near their mud-walled homes. Now, as the smoke cleared on this bright December afternoon, there was only moaning. Near the crater dug by the rocket lay two children, a boy of 17 and his 6-year-old sister, shattered by shards of twisted steel. Around them nearly a dozen other children were strewn about, many of them grievously wounded. It took 20 minutes for any help to appear. By then, another youngster, a 4-year-old girl, had died. By dusk, three more children were dead (Burns, 1990).

Each war zone yields its own special story.

- *The Middle East:* A 10-year-old Palestinian girl is on her way to buy milk for her mother. While passing through the town square she is hit in the stomach by a bullet fired by a soldier shooting at a group of rock-throwing youths. A little Israeli girl on her way home to her West Bank settlement from a family gathering is critically injured when a rock thrown by a demonstrator smashes the window of her parents' car. A Palestinian boy is sitting in his yard with his family eating supper when a grenade explodes. He is blinded and loses both his legs and one of his arms.
- *Mozambique:* The bandits had attacked at 4:00 in the morning, while families were still sleeping. One 12-year-old boy had both his legs cut off by the

Copyright © 1999 by Academic Press.
All rights of reproduction in any form reserved.

bandits. A 6-year-old had a piece of his head hacked away with a machete and part of his brain came out. The hospital ran out of gauze, and these wounds were wrapped in rags or left uncovered. Basic necessities such as gauze, food, and drinking water could not get through to the hospital because the armed bandits would attack the supply trucks on the road, killing the drivers and stealing the supplies. The bandits had placed an explosive device between the engine of a train and the passenger cars. When the explosion occurred, people jumped off the train and began to run. The bandits shot them as they ran. Sixty-six people were killed. Some of the women and older children were not killed. They were to be porters, carrying things the bandits stole from the trains. The older boys would be trained to kill. The bandits told the very young children to run away. One 3-year-old child who would not leave his mother was riddled with bullets.

Children have been involved directly in the prosecution of war in extraordinary and increasing numbers throughout the 20th century. UNICEF estimates that whereas in 1900 the ratio of civilian to military casualties was about 1:9; in recent decades this pattern has reversed, and now stands at approximately 8:1 (civilians to solders). Children constitute a significant proportion of these civilian casualties. In fact, more than half of all victims of worldwide armed conflict are children.

This shift reflects the changing nature of war. The technology of modern warmaking puts an increased emphasis on antipersonnel weapons that do not target specific individuals, and on indiscriminate bombing and shelling. Also contributing to this change is the fact that the strategy of modern war more and more emphasizes attacks on civilian infrastructure (whether it be in the saturation bombing of "conventional war" or the struggle for the "hearts and minds" of the population characteristic of guerrilla wars—i.e., insurgency-counterinsurgency operations).

Like every other aspect of our understanding of the impact of war on children, the actual physical injuries to children must be understood in context. Casualty data that focus only on deaths provide an imprecise indicator of the overall problem, for behind each death may stand many nonlethal assaults. This ratio between assault and death varies as a function of both medical trauma technology (which can prevent an assault from becoming a homicide) and weapons technology (which can affect the lethality of an assault).

Military medicine documents this phenomenon. Over time, the ratio between deaths and casualties in conventional military operations has changed as improved medical trauma technology and transport of frontline casualties has improved. A civilian example shows parallel trends. Chicago's homicide rate in 1973 and in 1993 was approximately the same, and yet the rate of serious assault had increased approximately 400% during that period. Thus, the ratio of assaults to homicides increased substantially—from 100:1 in 1973 to 400:1 in 1993.

Each number in the body count of war represents a hole in the life of a child somewhere—a mother, father, brother, sister, aunt, uncle, or cousin ripped away. This is what "the body count" means to a child whose most cherished loved ones become statistics. Are these children not themselves casualties of war? This article deals with the long-term effects of war on children. It introduces the concepts of acute and chronic trauma as a basis for understanding the psychological impact of war, and it also considers the indirect impact of war on children via disrupted relationships and community infrastructure. It accesses data and concepts drawn from the international scene to provide a framework for understanding the developmental issues faced by children exposed to war.

An understanding of the impact of war on children and young people is practically important in a large number of societies around the world, including countries that do not have overt war within their borders but do accept numerous refugees coming directly from foreign war zones. In addition, some countries, such as the United States, have chronic community violence in the "urban war zones" that affects the development of children and youth.

In this article, the goal is to focus on the processes and conditions that transform the "developmental challenge" of growing up in a war zone into developmental harm in some children and enhanced development in others. Several themes ground this discussion in an ecological framework for understanding child and youth development. These include:

1. an accumulation of risk model;
2. the concept of "social maps";
3. the concept of trauma.

This conceptual foundation provides an intellectual context in which to better understand the impact of war on children. Therefore, we will initially consider these core concepts before detailing the specific forces working on the child that have long term implications.

II. ACCUMULATION OF RISK MODEL

Risk accumulates; opportunity ameliorates. This is one of the conclusions we draw from research dealing with childhood coping. As negative ("pathogenic") influences increase, the child may exceed his or her breaking point. Conversely, as positive ("salutogenic") influences increase, the probability of recovery and enhanced development increases—even in the presence of risk factors such as war exposure. We can term these pathogenic and salutogenic influences risk and opportunity.

Although most of the children of war in the latter part of the 20th century are found outside the First World, much of the available research dealing with risk and opportunity comes from North American and Europe. The human catastrophe of the recent wars in the former Yugoslavia has been a macabre gold mine for research since it has allowed the testing of trauma and stress models in a European war context, without some of the uncertain assumptions that must be made when trying to make this application across radical cultural boundaries outside of a "Western" framework—for example, in Cambodia. Similarly, the various war experiences of Israeli and Palestinian children and youth have been a focal point for research and clinical development as a result of being one of the few settings in the late-20th century in which highly sophisticated populations have both been exposed to war and accessible to Western-style research.

One such application of developmental research concerns models developed in the United States for understanding the impact of stressful life events on the development of competence in childhood. This research offers the hypothesis that most children are capable of coping with low levels of risk, but that once the accumulation moves beyond this low level there must be a major concentration of opportunity factors to prevent the precipitation of harm. A study by Sameroff and his colleagues illustrates this point.

Sameroff explored the impact of risk accumulation on intellectual development—itself a major salutogenic factor for children facing developmental challenges. Using a pool of eight risk factors that included indicators of maternal dysfunction (e.g., mental illness, substance abuse, low educational attainment), family structure (e.g., absent father, large number of siblings) and social status (e.g., low income), Sameroff and his colleagues found that one or two major risk factors in the lives of the children studied produced little damage (i.e., IQ scores remained within, even above the normal range). But when risk accumulated—the addition of a third

and fourth risk factor—there was a precipitation of developmental damage, and IQ scores dropped significantly below average.

Dunst and his colleagues augmented Sameroff's approach by including in the developmental equations counterpart measures of opportunity (e.g., a present and highly involved father as the "opportunity" counterpart to the risk factor of "absent father" and a "flexible and highly supportive" parent as the counterpart to a "rigid and punitive" parent). Such a simultaneous assessment of both risk and opportunity is essential to understand the total picture in assessing the long-term effects of early developmental experience, because it more accurately captures the realities of the child's experiences (i.e., the fact that in the real world of children, risk factors usually do not exist without some compensatory impulse in the social environment of family, school, neighborhood, and society). Indeed, one of the worst features of living in a war zone from the perspective of the child's development may be the dismantling of the compensatory, salutagenic infrastructure of the child's world.

This approach is made even more relevant by the work of Perry and others that documents the impact of early trauma (particularly neglect and abuse) on brain development. Put simply, this research documents the risk that such trauma can produce deficient development of the brain's cortex (the site of higher faculties such as abstract reasoning, moral development, and impulse control). The processes involved in the link between war and brain development appear to be both direct (by stimulating a stress-related hormone—cortisol—that impedes brain growth) and indirect (by disrupting normal care giving, with the result being neglect and abuse). As we will discuss, these issues are highly relevant to children living in war zones.

III. THE CONCEPT OF SOCIAL MAPS

Certainly one of the most important features of child development is the child's emerging capacity to form and maintain "social maps." These representations of the world reflect the simple cognitive competence of the child (knowing the world in the scientific sense of objective, empirical fact), to be sure. But they also indicate the child's moral and affective inclination, not just where the child has been, but how the child views pathways to the future.

In considering children who face war we are concerned with the conclusions about the world contained in the child's social maps. Which will it be? "Adults are powerless and unreliable," versus "Adults are to be trusted because they know what they are doing," "You can never be too careful in dealing with people," versus "People will generally treat you well and meet your needs." The forces shaping these maps are the child's social experiences in counterpoint with the child's inner life—both cognitive competence and the working of unconscious forces.

Young children must contend with dangers that derive from two sources not so relevant to adults. First, their physical immaturity increases vulnerability by placing them at risk for being injured by trauma that would not hurt adults as badly because they are larger and more powerful. For example, exposure to landmines is a far more detrimental experience for a child than it is for an adult. The nature of these weapons of destruction is to maim and incapacitate adult-sized bodies by shredding the lower limbs of soldiers and sometimes civilians who encounter them. The shrapnel is concentrated below the waist of the average adult frame and in most cases, does not cause death. Unfortunately, this is not the case with children as their entire body is within the target range of weapon's destructive force. This increases the likelihood of being blinded and suffering other head damage, as well as the likelihood of death.

Second, young children tend to believe in the reality of threats from what most adults would define as "the fantasy" world. This increases their vulnerability to perceiving themselves as being "in danger." These dangers include monsters under the bed, wolves in the basement, and invisible creatures that lurk in the dark corners of bedrooms. But there is a salutogenic opportunity present in this characteristic as well. Children are more likely than are adults to believe in ghosts, angels, and other supernatural beings who can serve in supportive roles during times of crisis. Their social maps may contain psychologically relevant features that are not present in the maps of most adults. Silverman and Worden offer documentation of this in a study of children whose parent had died. Some 57% reported speaking to the dead parent; 43% of those children felt they received an answer; 81% believed their dead parents were watching them. In contrast, Kalish and Reynolds found that 12% of adults reported such direct contact with the dead.

Security is vitally important for a child's well-being, and thus his or her social map. When children feel safe, they relax. When they relax they start to explore the environment. This is clear with both infants and very young children. When a parent or other familiar person is around, a child treats the adult as a secure base from which to explore the nearby space. If frightened—

perhaps by a loud sound or by the approach of a stranger—the child will quickly retreat to the familiar person. As can be seen, it is this sense of security that facilitates a child's exploration and subsequent understanding of the world.

This pattern is an integral part of "normal" child development. It is so common that it is used to assess the quality of children's attachment relations. Children who do not use their parents this way—showing anxiety when separated and relief when reunited—are thought to have a less than adequate attachment relationship (they are "insecure" or "ambivalent" or "avoidant"). Thus, for very young children, the question of security is relatively simple, and usually hinges upon access to competent and psychologically robust mothers. Thus, mental health surveys often report that when mothers in war zones (or more likely refugee camps) become depressed, they become psychologically unavailable to the their children and this may lead to disruptions in the process of attachment formation. Osofsky reports that in an urban war zone, half the mothers of young children are severely depressed, and more than half of their children evidenced inadequate attachment relationships at 12 months. A survey of mothers in a Khmer refugee camp reported similar rates of maternal depression, but did not assess infant attachment.

Of course as children grow older, their security needs are transformed, and their social maps change accordingly. Soon they are getting on school buses and visiting friends' houses by themselves. Eventually they are on the streets at night on their own. But security remains a constant theme for them. "Am I safe here? Will I be safe if I go there? Would I be safe then?" The social environment largely determines whether or not the child will make this transition smoothly.

Whether it is real life or television imagery, it does not take much violence and terror to set a tone of threat in a child's social map. Even in the worst war zones—Sarajevo, for example—shooting and killing is intermittent. In high-crime neighborhoods, it only takes a few shots fired per month and only an occasional homicide to create and maintain a year-round climate of danger and to establish insecurity as the dominant psychological reality. Memory of the emotions of trauma usually does not decay; it remains frighteningly fresh. The attention of traumatized children is easily captured by stimuli that remind them of the previously experienced trauma. These repetitive and often intrusive recollections can present a child with an overwhelming amount of fear and anxiety. Once this feeling of danger takes hold, it requires very little new threat to sustain it. Children are little anthropologists as they watch and listen to what goes on around them.

War can make children prime candidates for involvement in social groups that augment or replace families, and offer a sense of affiliation and security (and perhaps revenge). This may mean gangs. The violent and illicit economy that often exists in a war zone offers a sense of belonging and solidarity as well as cash income for kids who have few prosocial alternatives for either. The peer alliances offer some sense of security in an otherwise completely hostile world. If these children do not develop a sense of confidence that adults are committed to providing a safe zone, their willingness and ability to take advantage of developmental opportunities will decrease, whereby their future is adversely effected.

One important process that translates war into directly pathogenic experiences for children is the *social disruption* of families that often accompanies it. This disruption may be the explicit tactical and strategic goal of combatants. One evidence of the fact that war disrupts families it to be found in the fact that globally, one of the major consequences of modern war is the creation of refugees and other displaced persons—the majority of whom are mothers and children. We call this consequence of war *compensatory realignment* and will elaborate on it more fully in the discussion of our ecological model.

To recapitulate, how does the process of war affect children? Consider refugee camps as contexts for parenting and child development. This analysis derives from site visits to such camps in Thailand, Hong Kong, Sudan, the former Yugoslavia, and the Middle East conducted during the period between 1985 and 1994 by the senior author.

- The Arms Race: There is a proliferation of violence—a kind of "arms race"—that exacerbates the effects of conflict. It is common for young males to be heavily involved in the this violence, and even to be engaged in armed attacks and reprisals. Substantial numbers of "bystander" injuries are observed.
- Gangs: Representatives of "mainstream" society have only partial control over what happens. International relief workers leave the camps at the end of the working day, and as a result, semi-formal groups assume effective control. These gangs often employ violence—including sexual violence—as part of their control strategy.
- The role of mothers: Women—particularly mothers—are in a desperate situation. They are under enormous stress, often are the target of domestic violence, and have few economic and educational resources or prospects. Men often play a marginal role in the enduring life of families—having lost access to economically productive roles, and being absent for reasons that include participating in the fighting, fleeing to escape enemies, being injured or killed. Largely as a result, there is a major problem of maternal depression. As previously noted, 50% of the women are severely depressed.

IV. THE CONCEPT OF TRAUMA

Trauma arises when the child cannot give meaning to dangerous experiences. This orientation is contained in the American Psychiatric Association's definition of posttraumatic stress disorder, which refers to threatening experiences outside the realm of normal experience. Trauma has two principal components: overwhelming negative arousal and overwhelming negative cognition. The former component is especially relevant to young children who have not developed fully functioning systems to modulate arousal (e.g., brain stem maturation that is not complete until age eight). Trauma involves an inability to handle effectively the physiological responses of stress in situations of threat.

The second component of trauma—overwhelming negative cognition—is captured in Herman's formulation that to experience trauma is "to come face to face with human vulnerability in the natural world and with the capacity for evil in human nature." This is the human core of the term "overwhelming negative cognition" and it illuminates the traumatic nature of living in a war zone for children. In the war in Mozambique, children were forced to watch (and sometimes even participate in) the execution of their parents.

Experiences that are cognitively overwhelming may stimulate conditions in which the process required to "understand" these experiences itself has pathogenic side effects. That is, in coping with traumatic events, the child may be forced into patterns of behavior, thought, and affect that are themselves "abnormal" when contrasted with that of the untraumatized child. Children—particularly elementary school-age children who are too old to profit from the parental buffering that can insulate young children—may be particularly vulnerable to the trauma caused by threat and fear. So it is that one study of *non*war trauma reported that those exposed to trauma before age 10 were three times more likely to exhibit PTSD than those exposed after age 12.

Children and youth exposed to acute danger may require processing over a period of several months. Some children in war zones experience the psychological symptoms of posttraumatic stress disorder, symptoms that include sleep disturbances, day dreaming, recreating trauma in play, extreme startle responses, emotional numbing, diminished expectations for the future, and even biochemical changes in their brains that impair social and academic behavior. This trauma can produce significant psychological problems that interfere with learning and appropriate social behavior in school and that interfere with normal parent–child relationships.

If the traumatic stress is intense enough, it may leave some permanent "psychic scars." This is particularly the case for children made vulnerable because of disruptions in their primary relationships (most notably with parents). These effects include excessive sensitivity to stimuli associated with the trauma and diminished expectations for the future. But by and large, most children will return to normal functioning in the posttraumatic period.

This is acute traumatic danger, but the more common variety in war zones and the specific focus of this chapter is chronic danger. Chronic traumatic danger imposes a requirement for *developmental* adjustment. In the terminology of developmental psychology coined by Jean Piaget these developmental adjustments result from the inability of the child to *assimilate* these experiences into existing conceptual frameworks or schemata. Rather, these experiences require the child to alter existing concepts to permit the new experiential information to be known, and this involves what Piaget termed *accommodation*. In the case of chronic danger, the child must accommodate his psychic reality so that it allows for the processing of life's atrocities. Put simply, the child must adopt a negative view of his world.

What are these accommodations? They are likely to include persistent posttraumatic stress syndrome, alterations of personality, and major changes in patterns of behavior or articulation of ideological interpretations of the world that provide a framework for making sense of ongoing danger. Chronic traumatic danger rewrites the child's story, redraws the child's social map, and redirects behavior. This is particularly true when that danger comes from violent overthrow of day-to-day social reality, when communities are substantially altered, when displacement occurs, or when children lose important members of their families and social networks. As noted earlier, in the case of children exposed to the chronic horrors of Pol Pot's Khmer Rouge regime in Cambodia in the 1970s, 50% of the kids exhibited

persistent symptoms of PTSD 8 years after exposure. According to Van der Kolk, explosive outbursts of anger, flashbacks, nightmares, hypervigilance, psychic numbing, constriction of affect, impaired social functioning, and the loss of control over one's life are all characteristic of the traumatized child.

V. PREDICTING WAR'S LONG-TERM EFFECTS ON CHILDREN

No single variable can be isolated as the leading cause of the developmental damage that is so common among children living amidst or in the wake of war. Rather, it is the interplay of several social and developmental variables that dictates the course and severity of the child's maladaption. There are a number of factors that lead some children in war zones to thrive and others to deteriorate. It is our assertion that there are five primary variables mediating the relationship between living in a war zone and long-term negative consequence (see Figure 1).

The first of these determinants is the overall resilience and competence of the child. Those children best equipped to successfully cope with their war experience stand the greatest chance of physically and mentally surviving the conflict. The second determinant of maladaption is the child's degree of exposure to war atrocity, where the children most directly exposed to and threatened by the war are put at the greatest risk. The third determinant is demographic information that predicts the developmental outcomes for children living in war zones, although the relationship is less direct. The

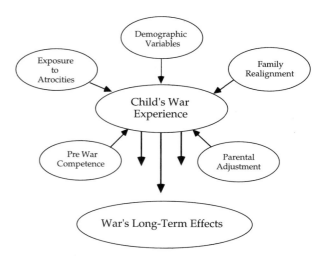

FIGURE 1 The determinants of war's long-term effects on children.

fourth determinant of maladaption is the breakdown or restructuring of the family unit as an institution of stability and security in response to the war condition. And finally, the variable that is most predictive of a child's response to the challenges faced while growing up in a war zone is the adjustment of their parents. During and in the aftermath of a traumatic event, children look to familiar adults when assessing the severity of the situation. Those children who have the opportunity to view actively coping adult figures suffer least developmentally and psychologically as they have adaptive coping responses to model and internalize.

A. Competence and Resilient Coping

An article concerning the long-term effects of war on children would be incomplete if it failed to point out the tremendous variance in the developmental outcomes of the children. A large portion of this variation can readily be explained by the child's prewar competence and use of resilient coping skills. Just as children *leave* the war arena with varying degrees of consequence, they *enter* the experience with similar disparity and inequity. While many are traumatized and developmentally impaired, others grow up to lead healthy, productive, and otherwise "normal" adult lives.

This developmental model predicts that the children most at risk for falling victim to the long-term negative consequences associated with war are those who already live in the context of accumulated risk. These vulnerable children are the socially marginal, those with fractured families, and those with mentally impaired or substance addicted caregivers. In contrast, children who approach their war experiences from a position of strength—that is, with the salutogenic resources of social support, intact and functional families, and parents who model social competence—can accept better the developmental challenges posed by the war experiences and deal with them more positively.

Cognitive ability has been found to be positively correlated with successfully coping with a childhood war experience. The ability to selectively implement planful and pro-social behavior is also a protective factor for postwar adaptation. Based on their review of the literature, Apfel and Simon posit several factors that collectively contribute to the successful childhood coping and well-adapted adult functioning that is commonly observed among war's most resilient children.

- *Resourcefulness*. The hallmark of this attribute is the ability to seek out and take advantage of the lim-

ited emotional resources available in an impoverished social environment such as the war zone. With diminished social support, particularly parental support, the resilient child will cling to any warmth and affirmation that is attainable. This requires children to be perceptive and sensitive to subtle changes in their environment because war is a time when parental attention and availability are limited. The failure to seize these scarce opportunities is costly to the child living in a war zone. Also, resourceful children are more likely to solicit necessary care and approval from adults other than their parents. This allows these children to meet their developmental and social needs by a number of means that are unavailable to more vulnerable children.

- *Curiosity and the ability to conceptualize.* Together, these factors of resilience afford the child living in a war zone the knowledge and perspective that are necessary to frame the war experience most adaptively. The curious child is one who actively pursues a deep understanding of life events. As active agents in their environment, children explore their ideas and collect information about the crisis through whatever resources are available. The ameliorating impact of this knowledge allows children to accurately and adaptively conceptualize the adversity in their lives and to process the war experience as a community and often as a national epidemic instead of as one that is targeted exclusively at any particular child. This insight combats the possibility of children feeling isolated and alone as they are more likely to be aware of the war's effects on other people.

- *Altruism and helping others.* Children who help others are aware of their ability to affect situations around them. This process of giving and helping often precedes the witnessing of a corresponding situational change and protects children (at least partially) from overwhelming feelings of helplessness. As actions are seen as having power and influence, coping becomes self-initiated and deliberate.

- *Commitment to survival and goals to life.* The commitment to survive often coexists with a sense of purposefulness and meaning. Children who regard their lives as serving a higher purpose will be more apt to psychically persevere in the face of trauma and have a greater insight into their vulnerabilities. Children with goals (either long-term, short-term, internally generated, or externally imposed) are likely to have this sense of internal purpose even if one did not exist prior to being assigned the new responsibility. This is not a function of self-esteem. Being told to look after the family residence or to accompany a sibling to a combat-free territory can supply a child with the psychic energy and sense of purpose to endure the atrocity and trauma that lies ahead.

• *Command of affect and ability to remember positive images.* A resilient child will be able to "compartmentalize" pain and anxiety and delay the expression of affect for the better good of survival. There are many instances in which the overt expression of emotion is dysfunctional. For example, Bosnian children often had to postpone grieving until after evacuation was complete and there was a safe environment in which to express their sadness to avoid becoming incapacitated. The same is true for victims of torture, who must await either a change of regime or resettlement in a safer country before beginning full processing of the traumatic experience. The point is not suppression or repression of appropriate affect, but rather *postponement* of affect until the child is in a safer context to appropriately express inner turmoil. In addition to the importance of suspending present psychic reality, it is equally important that children be able to recall their past and more positive psychic reality. The ability to remember the former strengths of a now diminished social map is crucial to resiliency. This process of "glorified recall" protects the child from overinternalizing the aspects of his present situation by allowing him to conceptualize and interpret adversity as temporary and specific rather than stable and global.

Experts agree that under adverse circumstances about 80% of children will "bounce back" from developmental challenges, particularly if they received adequate care during their first two years of life. If the majority of children are able to overcome what otherwise seems to be devastating threat, can the high rates of recovery be explained by only personal and internal strengths? Factors that lead to prosocial behavior and healthy adaptability in the face of stressful early experience also include a series of ameliorating factors that are the direct byproducts of the child's social map and social environment. As thorough as Apfel and Simon are in considering the protective factors in the lives of war-exposed children, their categories fail to focus enough on social factors of resilience. Losel, Bliesener, and Koferl augment the categories of resilience presented by Apfel and Simon in a way that places increased emphasis on social and familial components:

• actively trying to cope with stress (rather than just reacting);
• cognitive competence (at least an average level of intelligence);
• experiences of self-efficacy and a corresponding self-confidence and positive self-esteem;
• temperamental characteristics that favor active coping attempts and positive relationships with others (e.g., activity, goal orientation, sociability) rather than passive withdrawal;
• stable emotional relationships with at least one parent or other reference person;
• an open, supportive educational climate and parental model of behavior that encourages constructive coping with problems;
• social support from persons outside the family.

These factors have been identified as important when the stresses involved are in the "normal" range found in the mainstream of modern industrial societies—for example, poverty, family conflict, childhood physical disability, and parental involvement in substance abuse. Nonetheless, they provide insight for efforts to understand the special character of coping in the stressful circumstances of war where the risk of socially maladaptive coping is high. However, under conditions of extreme risk accumulation, resilience may be diminished drastically. For example, the research of Kinzie and colleagues on Khmer children exposed to the transcendent horrors of the Pol Pot war against Cambodian society revealed that most were experiencing long-term psychological disruption (in the form of posttraumatic stress disorder) many years after their departure from the war zone.

The magnitude of risk accumulation as a pathogenic influence and the corresponding limits of resilience are illustrated by research conducted by Tolan and his colleagues. While not conducted in a war zone per se, this research is relevant to understanding the long-term effects of war on children because it is drawn from a "urban war zone" in which there is a high level of community violence (some of it semistructured, and much of it involving gunfire). Tolan points out that in some environments virtually all children demonstrate negative effects of highly stressful and threatening environments. In his Chicago data, for example, *none* of the ethnic-minority males facing the combination of highly dangerous, low-income neighborhoods coupled with low resource/high-stress families was resilient at age 15 when measured by either by being more than one grade level behind in school or by scoring in the "clinical range" on the Achenbach Child Behavior Checklist for a period of 2 years. The concept of resilience is useful, but should not be taken as an absolute. Like all concepts of human development, resilience is contextual.

This finding parallels work done on the impact of chronic combat experience on adults. Studies from World War II and other conflicts indicate that if soldiers are exposed to chronic combat conditions for 60 days, 98% of them eventually end up as "psychiatric casualties." Only those classified as having "psychopathic" personalities are able to function without becoming symptomatic. Why? Grossman and Siddle conclude chillingly that psychopaths are so stress resistant because they did not have the same issues of arousal in the face of threat and did not face the stress of violating moral prohibitions about killing human beings by virtue of being "cold blooded." Psychopaths are antipathetic, emotionally impoverished, and detached, and have no real appreciation of others or societal norms.

The possible implications of this finding for child development in the urban war zone are equally chilling, that is, that the children best able to survive *functionally* are those who have the least to lose morally and psychologically. In James Gilligan's terms they are already dead and thus experience no fear or inhibition. They view the world as having neither emotional barriers nor moral terrain. Our interviews of youth incarcerated for murder or other acts of severe violence expand this view in the sense that we chronicle some of the most violent youths in the process of constructing elaborate defense mechanisms against anxiety, fear, and abandonment, defense mechanisms that culminate in the persona of the cold blooded "gangster."

B. Exposure to Atrocity

It is firmly established that war is not experienced the same way by different children. In fact, there is significant variance from one child to another. Many scholars have postulated that the degree to which a child is exposed directly to war dictates the severity and course of maladaption. These experiences can include separation from caregiver, bereavement, displacement, witnessing violent acts, or being malnourished, wounded, or killed. We offer two recent and well-controlled studies that validate the relationship between the direct exposure to war and developmental damage.

The first study was conducted by Youssef Al-Eissa, who surveyed 106 Kuwaiti children and their families who were displaced to Saudi Arabia after the Iraqi invasion of their homeland and compared them to 120 Saudi children who served as controls. The mothers or other close relatives of the children were asked to report the degree to which the child had been exposed to trauma (victimization, destruction of property, witness to assault, kidnapping, detention, or death of a close family member) and were also administered an objective measure of symptomatology (e.g., fear, anxiety, and maladaptive social behaviors).

The Kuwaiti children, when compared to the Saudi controls, were found to have been twice as likely to be anorexic, destructive, hostile, over-dependent, or withdrawn; more than three times as likely to be easily distracted or suspicious; more than four times as likely to have nightmares; more than five times as likely to have difficulty sleeping or concentrating; and almost nine times more likely to be generally unhappy.

Within the Kuwaiti group itself, it was suggested that the relationship between living in a war zone and subsequent somatic, affective, or behavioral symptoms is mediated by the child's personal experience with aggression. Kuwaiti children who were either personally assaulted or had a parent or sibling assaulted seemed to be at the greatest risk for maladaption. These children were twice as likely to have been suspicious, withdrawn, hostile, or easily distracted as their cohorts without a personal experience with aggression.

The second study investigated the behavioral manifestations of a sample of 200 Lebanese children, half of whom had been exposed to heavy shelling and half of whom had not been exposed. Behavior problems included bed wetting, excessive thumb sucking, stealing, frequent crying, nightmares, temper tantrums, refusal to sleep alone, and a general over-dependence on parents. The exposed group displayed twice as many problem behaviors as their "non-exposed" counterparts. The intensity of the behavior problems were also more severe for the exposed group than for the nonexposed.

These data, taken together, provide strong evidence for isolating the direct exposure to combat as *one of many* variables fueling the notable discrepancy among children on behavioral and psychological outcome measures. The frequency with which children are exposed to war's violence and aggression and the degree to which war affects and intrudes upon their day-to-day lives appears to at least partially influence whether or not the child will be developmentally impeded or enhanced. War is a time of great uncertainty and fear. Children's lives are often structurally disrupted (kept from going to school), socially disrupted (father and brothers leave home to fight), and emotionally disrupted (mother is less available and responsive). All this considered, it is plausible to expect that the exposure to violence and the witnessing of actual combat might be all that it takes to throw the child over their threshold of natural coping capacity. Regardless of the justification, we can be certain that children who witness war directly are put at a greater psychological, emotional, and developmental risk than those who live in relatively combat-free areas.

C. Demographics of War

There is little systematic evidence about the demography and sociology of children in war zones (e.g., the social class correlates of exposure to war trauma). Nonetheless, most observers note that the prewar social class system continues to operate in most war zones, most of the time. In general, the families at the bottom of the social ladder are most likely to be affected directly.

Before we get into the more controversial issue of social class, we begin this section by addressing the two demographic variables that have a clear and undeniable impact on the child's war experience—age and gender. Boys and younger children are put at the greatest developmental risk. War puts similar restrictions on both genders, but boys and girls have different developmental needs, and thus are affected differently by the war experience. Girls abstract resilience from a sense of independence in the absence of parental overprotection. Boys, on the other hand, draw resilience very differently. Boys thrive under conditions of rules, structure, and parental supervision—all of which are compromised during a time of war. The breakdown in child protection and lessened parental supervision may even benefit girls, however harmful it is for boys. We believe that this phenomenon largely explains the gender differences observed in postwar outcome measures of boys' and girls' levels of functioning—that is, girls fare better than boys.

If war trauma involves a combination of overwhelming arousal and cognitions, it seems logical that younger children would be at the greatest risk. Generally speaking, younger children have fewer neurological resources for combating intense arousal and fewer effective cognitive strategies for combating stress than do older children. Older children are better prepared to cope with the war experience largely because of their cognitive expertise. Older children can seek refuge and gather resources from areas outside of the family residence and they can benefit from nontraditional surrogate role models while younger child cannot. What is more, younger children have fewer life experiences from which to draw resilience. The reservoir of resilience in older children will be much deeper and as a result, facilitate adaptive coping.

Returning now to social class, consider a study conducted by Macksoud and Aber (1996). Among a sample of war-exposed children in Lebanon, they found that demographic variables do play a role in mediating the relationship between exposure to war trauma and developmental outcome, but in a counter intuitive fashion. Below is an abridged summary of their results and their explanations in the context of the war in Lebanon.

- *Children of higher SES were more likely to be exposed to direct shelling.* This finding could *not* be attributed to the region in which the family lived, because shelling was distributed equally throughout all the targeted areas of interest. It is suggested that this trend is potentially the result of the less-restrictive and liberal parenting styles that are characteristic of well educated mothers. These children are frequently afforded a more independent and less intruded upon childhood experience, and therefore, their chances of witnessing a direct attack or infrastructural damage is increased.
- *Children of higher SES were more likely to be direct victims of violent acts.* This finding could be partially explained if we apply the same logic as in the previous finding. Higher SES mothers supervise their children less, whereby they are put at greater risk than those who are kept under lock and key. However, Macksoud and Aber suggest that this is attributable to the increased likelihood for a wealthy child to be kidnapped for a ransom. The prevalence of kidnapping in Lebanon was not discussed in the report so we cannot confirm this.
- *Children of higher SES were more likely to be separated from their families.* In addition to the "kidnapping hypothesis," it is known that wealthier families are more likely to have the resources, namely social contacts and money, to send their children to safer regions of the country or world. This is not a panacea, however. As we will see, these separated children are at increased risk for a depression that is partially attributed to the ensuing feelings of helplessness.
- *Children of higher SES were more likely to have their entire family relocated.* This is largely attributable to the fact that well-educated mothers are believed to be better equipped to handle the demands put on the family unit by a new and foreign culture. In addition to cultural "know-how," these families also have greater access to the financial resources needed to uplift and collectively relocate a family unit.

• *Children of lower SES were more prone to maladaption.* Regardless of the frequency or type of war traumas experienced, higher status children are more likely to exhibit planful and pro-social behaviors. This finding is crucial if we are to develop an understanding the role played by SES in the developmental outcomes of children exposed to war.

Do some of these seemingly counterintuitive results actually suggest that children from higher social classes are at greatest risk during times of war? How can this be the case if Macksoud and Aber found the higher status children to be the most well-adapted group? It appears that war has a more immediate effect on children from the higher social classes in the same environments, but a more lasting impact on children in the lower social classes. That is, higher status children have a much higher threshold and resilience with respect to the war experience despite their increased exposure. Higher SES children with better educated parents may be encouraged to actively cope with the war experience. They may also have a greater degree of parental expectation and thus they may be asked to play a functional role in the collective coping of the family unit by providing a service that gives their plight meaning (e.g., caring for younger siblings, preparing family meals, or simply maintaining their present role as student). This sense of purpose may provide higher status children with an incentive and determination to psychologically persevere. Unfortunately, these conclusions are speculative in nature and as Macksoud and Aber point out, the generalizability of their results is limited based on the fact that there are no similar studies to which these can be compared. We strongly urge continued systematic and scholarly investigation into this rather underreported area of psychological literature.

D. Compensatory and Reactionary Realignment of Family Structure: A Case Study

The Hassim family had enjoyed years of stability as Palestinian residents of Kuwait. With a booming economy and an intense labor shortage, Kareem Hassim found steady work as a manager with a construction company. He spent time with his three children after work and on weekends. His wife, Safia, spent most of her time as a full-time mother and homemaker in the family's apartment in Kuwait City. Sixteen-year-old Nabil attended high school, as did his 13-year-old sister, Cairo. Seven-year-old Fatah was the baby of the family, doted on by everyone.

Life changed dramatically for the Hassim family in the wake of the Iraqi invasion of Kuwait in August 1991. Kareem followed the lead of his best friend, Assad, and joined the Kuwait armed resistance fighters. With Kareem gone from the home, Safia had to assume full responsibility for the family's finances, and she began to work full-time in a friend's store in the market. Nabil shouldered the burden of becoming the "man of the house" and found a job working for a neighbor who sold vegetables. He began to get in trouble with the authorities for vandalism and assault. Soon thereafter, he dropped out of school. Cairo also quit school so she could take care of little Fatah full time while her mother and older brother were working. This continued for nearly 2 months before Kareem sent word that his cousin was leaving the country and could take Fatah with him to stay with her grandparents in Jordan. Safia agonized over this possibility but when a child in the neighborhood was killed by an Iraqi soldier who was shooting at a resistance fighter she decided the child was better off living outside the country. Three days later Fatah was spirited out of the country and was separated from the rest of the family for nearly a year. Kareem was captured by the Iraqis and severely tortured, but ultimately released. Months later, he was still suffering the traumatic effects of his ordeal—he was depressed and prone to fits of rage.

"Wartime is a period in which the family is required to cope with vastly increased stresses" (Al-Eissa, 1995: 1033). Long before many children have any knowledge of the true nature of war, let alone real life exposure, their world is greatly altered. Foster care placements, loss of caregivers and authority figures, and the premature assumption of adult roles are all common challenges that a child faces when a father leaves for combat. The role that the father is forced to abandon has to be filled, and it is the ensuing realignment of the family dynamic that is so devastating to the child. The family must restructure to compensate for the loss of a key contributor—hence our term, *compensatory realignment.*

Schwab and colleagues illustrate the impact that family realignment plays in adding to both the immediate and long-term consequences of war on the child. As was the case with the Hassim family, it is common for women and adolescent boys to enter the workforce as soon as their husbands and fathers leave for combat. Doing so requires the mother to ignore many of her prewar responsibilities in an attempt to compensate for her absent husband; most commonly sacrificed are her roles as caregiver and authority figure. The eldest daughters are frequently expected to carry out the responsibilities of their mothers by caring for their younger siblings and elderly relatives. Like their brothers who often drop out of school to earn money for the family, many girls drop out to become full-time nurturers. While wage-earner and caregiver duties are regularly reassigned, the role of authority figure too often is grossly neglected. It is this lack of supervision that contributes to the high levels of delinquency, parental neglect, and displacement that is so prominent in the lives of children in war zones. The family now has more roles to fill than contributing members and thus, it breaks down.

1. Delinquency

Breakdown in parental supervision is a large contributor to the excessive levels of delinquency in war affected children. War is a time when even married mothers often consider themselves single parents. Even if the decreased supervision associated with war is eliminated as a catalyst, youth violence and delinquency are problems for any country involved in an armed conflict. The patriotism and dehumanization of the enemy decrease the normal forces inhibiting aggressive outbursts against others such as morality and human compassion. This is particularly true of young adolescent males. Based on these observations, it is easy to see how families with diminished parental availability and supervision would be at an even greater risk for having a juvenile delinquent in the home. Therefore, compensatory realignment may partially explain why Jamal, Shaya, and Armenian found problematically high levels of aggression, hyperactivity, and poor school performance among their sample of combat-exposed Lebanese children.

What is more, the effects of this breakdown in parental authority structure can be long lasting, depending on the developmental age of the child. John Coie and his colleagues at Duke University have linked the chronicity of antisocial behavior to the age at which it begins. Individuals who these authors refer to as "early starters" are the most predisposed to life-long delinquency. American research on conduct disorder presents a similar finding: early family trauma leads to a pattern of aggressive, antisocial behaviors that crystallize at around age 10. Based on these findings, the duration and course of the delinquency resulting from compensatory realignment will likely depend on the age at which the realignment occurred, where the youngest children are at greatest risk for chronic delinquency and adult criminality.

2. Displacement

Recall the youngest Hassim daughter who is relocated to a safer country. Initially it may have seemed like a good idea, but while familial intentions were to protect the vulnerable child from the evils of living in a war zone, childhood displacement is a separate and distinct risk factor in and of itself. These relocated children are at increased risk for the subsequent development of depressive symptomatology. This is especially true for girls and younger children.

It is important that we point out that realignment is not only at work on families originally headed by a soldier. Families living in highly combatant areas where both parents remain in the home often send their daughters and younger children to live elsewhere in response to the war condition—what we call reactionary realignment. This is particularly the case if the family is of higher social status because they are more likely to have the resources and social contacts to send a child a safer region or country.

Paradoxically, even children who are sent to safety are put at developmental risk, but for different reasons. As previously stated, children separated from parental figures are prone to depression. As with compensatory realignment, this reactionary realignment also involves the depletion of parental roles; and again they are caregiving and authority figure roles. However, with this type of realignment, both roles are usually filled by an age-appropriate surrogate parent whereby the child is protected from many of the risks associated with realignment. Despite the diathesis for depression, we conclude that these displaced children are not affected as negatively as those who remain in the war zone based on the finding that children manifest fewer psychological symptoms if they are evacuated from the site of conflict.

3. Foreclosure of a Role Called "Child"

"Childhood" is a cultural creation with important developmental payoffs. Childhood offers a protected context in which young humans can focus on developing competence through play. Many developmentalists see the social creation of "a long childhood" as being a key to human cultural evolution—one of the keys to enhanced civilization. However, neither this process nor context is automatic. When adult economic, sexual, and political forces preempt childhood, children lose the opportunity to fully experience the role of child. Unfortunately, this loss is a frequent casualty of war and yet is never included in the body count.

Family realignment is largely to blame for the loss of this critical period of development. The two older children in the Hassim family are forced to abandon their natural roles as "children" for adult roles left vacant by one or both of their parents. As unfortunate as this may seem, this is the common reality for many children living amidst war or community violence. War disrupts activities that are normally viewed as crucial components of child development. These "normal" activities include attending school, frequent contact with friends and family, playing outside, and sleeping in their own beds. As was the case with the older Hassim children, war often forces children to become nurturers and wage earners long before their time.

4. Other Long-Term Effects of Family Realignment

Resistance and conflict are not the only problems that likely persist once the war is over. After the Vietnam War, many of the surviving American troops returned with PTSD. As a result of the veteran's symptomatology, it was common for his children to feel unloved and rejected by him. It is this emotional distancing and outward displays of rejection and hostility that partially contributed to the prevalence of *married* mothers who considered themselves single parents even though their husbands had long since returned from the war.

Elder, Nguyen, and Caspi also documented this phenomenon in economically distressed American families who survived the Great Depression. Although not likely to have been traumatized, fathers during the depression, treated their children basically the same way in which the veterans of Vietnam did—they rejected them and became emotionally unavailable and unstable. Although these men were not tallied in an official body count, war (or in some cases, extreme societal stress and pressure) symbolically killed them, and their children lost the fathers that they once knew and loved. Despite the fact that he was still around in presence, these fathers were dead—a soul ripped away by war.

E. Parental Adjustment

In times of disaster, the strongest predictor of maladaption in children facing disaster is the reaction and level of functioning of their parents. This is made strikingly evident by research highlighting the power of parents and teachers to buffer very young children from traumatic encounters. Consider, for example, this observation from London during World War II at the height of the German bombing: Children measure the danger that threatens them chiefly by the reactions of those around them, especially trusted parents and teachers.

Another example comes from the Gulf War in Kuwait, where parents reported that they could often reassure young children by literally defining reality for them, but were largely unable to do this for older children. For example, parents were able to draw young children into fantasy play in which they felt safe and secure because of parental actions—"let's play the escape game"—as they prepared to escape from occupied Kuwait. Older children saw through this ruse and into the actual nature of the dangers they were facing in their attempt to evade detection while fleeing over the border into Saudi Arabia and could not benefit from the same reassurance.

Similarly, Green and associates found that younger children are less likely than older children to show symptoms of PTSD 2 years after experiencing a traumatic event. It is unclear whether or not this is attributable to levels of fantasy play, but nonetheless, their findings demonstrated the important role played by parental functioning in mediating whether or not children process an experience as traumatic. They found the presence of parental psychopathology to predict PTSD symptomatology and coping capacity in children exposed to natural disaster.

In a study of Southeast Asian refugee children, Harding and Looney reported that the children who were living amidst family support were far more adapted to their new lives than were those who were either separated from their families or placed in foster care. "Hence, if parents can sustain a strong attachment to their children and have access to the basic needs of shelter, food, and medical care, then children will continue to successfully cope with new environments" (Al-Eissa, 1995: pg. 1036). It is common for war-affected mothers to have their ability to meet their child's needs impeded as a result of the stressful and debilitating nature of war. Unfortunately, these mothers often report that they are fully aware that they are not meeting their child's needs and in most cases, they have no solution.

The task of dealing with the effects of war as a developmental challenge falls into the laps of the people who teach children in that particular society—their parents, relatives, teachers, and counselors. Adults are crucial resources for children attempting to cope with the chronic danger and stress of living in a war zone. Generations of studies focusing on the experience of children living in war zones testify to the importance of adult responses to danger as mediators of psychological responses in children exposed to war. As long as adults take charge of themselves and present children with a role model of calm and positive determination, most children can cope with a great deal of acute war-related violence. They may indeed be traumatized by their experiences, but the adults around them will be able to serve as a resource and will support the child in rehabilitative efforts to cope with the long-term consequences and perhaps even stimulate salutagenic experiences.

However, once adults begin to deteriorate, to decompensate, to panic, children suffer in the short term (and perhaps in the long run as well). This is not surprising, given the importance of the images of adults contained in the child's social maps. Traumatized children need help to recover from their experiences. Emotionally disabled or immobilized adults are unlikely to offer the children what they need. Such adults are inclined to engage in denial, to be emotionally inaccessible, and are prone to misinterpret the child's signals. Messages of safety are particularly important in establishing adults as sources of protection and authority for children living in conditions of threat and violence. But these adults take on this task facing enormous challenges of their own. After all, human service professionals and educators working in war zones are themselves commonly traumatized by their exposure to the violence.

In the long run—that is, in the process of accommodating to the war experience—children depend on adults as teachers. Thus, we must understand the teaching process as it relates to trauma. This leads us to the interactional model of development proposed by Lev Vygotsky. In this approach, child development is fundamentally social; cognitive development proceeds at its best through the process of interactive teaching. He focuses on the *zone of proximal development*: the difference between what the child can accomplish alone versus what the child can accomplish with the guidance of a teacher. How, one might ask, is this relevant to the child's ability to cope with war trauma?

In the case of isolated acute trauma in a setting of peace (a single horrible incident that violates the normal reality of the child's world), the child needs help believing that "things are back to normal." This therapy of simple reassurance is a relatively easy teaching task. But the child who lives with chronic trauma (e.g., the war zone) needs something more. This child needs to be taught how to redefine the world in moral and structural terms. Reservoirs of optimism, hope, and morality have been depleted as a result of the chronic exposure to atrocity. These children know very little about what it means to live in an orderly, compassionate, and moral world—a knowledge that must be explicitly taught or modeled if these values are ever to be learned.

VI. CONCLUSION

We must stop thinking about war in terms of sheer numbers. Casualty rates and spreadsheets grossly underestimate the true costs of war, for they fail to consider the psychological costs absorbed by children. The developmental challenge of growing up in a war zone is neither universally experienced nor universally harmful. In fact, there is significant variation in outcome across children that can be explained in terms of risk and opportunity. The goal of this article has been to explore the variables putting the children in war-afflicted areas at risk for long-term maladaption and to explain the mechanisms operating to impede or enhance the development of these children. Identifying these risk and opportunity factors allows us to better predict who will be most adversely affected by war, so our global society can focus rehabilitative efforts where they are needed most (i.e., intervention) and promote resiliency even prior to the onset of war (i.e., prevention).

One focus of international initiatives (such as the UN Convention on the Rights of the Child) is to create "zones of peace" for children—that is, to encourage combatants to institute and respect protected areas for children. Underlying all such efforts is an attempt to communicate a message of safety to children, to stimulate a redrawing of their social maps. We might go further to suggest that these zones of peace also include the freedom to engage in free play and in moral teaching in Vygotsky's zone of proximal development so that the long-term process of accommodation fosters salutagenic influences for children and youth, rather than pathogenic influences.

Also See the Following Articles

EFFECTS OF WAR AND POLITICAL VIOLENCE ON HEALTH SERVICES • HEALTH CONSEQUENCES OF WAR AND POLITICAL VIOLENCE • PSYCHOLOGICAL EFFECTS OF COMBAT • WARFARE, MODERN

Bibliography

Al-Eissa, Youssef, (1995). The impact of the Gulf armed conflict on the health and behaviour of Kuwaiti children. *Social Science and Medicine,* 41(7), 1033–1037.

Apfel, R., & Simon, B. (Eds.). (1996). *Minefields in their hearts: the mental health of children in war and communal violence.* New Haven, CT: Yale University Press.

Bell, C. (1991). Traumatic stress and children in danger. *Journal of Health Care for the Poor and Underserved, 2,* 175–188.

Coie, J., Terry, R., Lenox, K., Lochman, J., & and Hyman, C. (1995). Childhood peer rejection and aggression as predictors of stable patterns of adolescent disorder. *Development and Psychopathology,* 7, 697–713.

Coles, R. (1990). *The spiritual life of children.* Boston: Houghton Mifflin.

Dodge, K., Pettit, G., & Bates, J. (1997). How the experience of early physical abuse leads children to become clinically aggressive. In D. Cicchetti and S. Toth (Eds.), *Rochester's symposium on developmental psychopathology: Developmental perspectives on trauma,* 163–188. Rochester, NY: University of Rochester Press.

Dunst, C., & Trivette, C. (1992). *Risk and opportunity factors influence parent and child functioning.* Paper presented at the Ninth Annual Smoky Mountain Winter Institute, Ashville, North Carolina.

Ellison, C. Gay, D., & Glass, T. (1989). Does religious commitment contribute to individual life satisfaction? *Social forces, 86.* 100–123.

Frankl, V. (1963). *Man's search for meaning: An introduction to logotherapy.* New York: Washington Square Press.

Garbarino, J. (1995). *Raising children in a socially toxic environment.* San Francisco: Jossey-Bass.

Garbarino, J., Dubrow, N., Kostelny, K., & Pardo, C. (1992). *Children in danger: coping with the consequences.* San Francisco: Jossey-Bass.

Garbarino, J., Kostelny, K., & Dubrow, N. (1991). *No place to be a child: growing up in a war zone.* Lexington, MA: Lexington Books.

Garbarino, J., Guttmann, E., & Seeley, J. (1986). *The psychologically battered child.* San Francisco: Jossey-Bass.

Garmezy, N., and Masten. A. (1986) Stress, competence, and resilience: common frontiers for therapist and psychpatherapist. *Behavior therapy, 17,* 500–607.

Gilligan, J. (1996). *Violence.* New York: Putnam.

Groves, B. Zuckerman, Marans, S., & Cohen, D. (1993). Silent victims: children who witness violence. *Journal of the American Medical Association, 269,* 262–264.

Herman, J. (1992). *Trauma and recovery.* New York: Basic Books.

Janoff-Bulman, R. (1992). *Shattered assumptions: Towards a new psychology of trauma.* New York: The Free Press.

Jung, C. (1933). *Modern man in search of a soul.* New York: Harcourt, Brace and Co.

Kinzie, J., Sack, W., Angell, R., Manson, S., & Rath, B. (1986). The psychiatric effects of massive trauma on Cambodian children. *Journal of the American Academy of Child Psychiatry, 25,* 370–376.

Kurdahi-Zahr, Lina (1996). Effects of war on the behavior of Lebanese preschool children: Influence of home environment and family functioning. *American Journal of Orthopsychiatry, 66* (3), 401–408.

Losel, F., & Bliesener, T. (1990). Resilience in adolescence: A study on the generalizability of protective factors. In (Hurrelmann, K & Losel, F., Eds.), *Health hazards in adolescence.* New York: Walter de Gruyter.

Macksoud, M. S., & Aber, J. L. (1996) The war experience and psychosocial development of children in Lebanon. *Child Development 67,* 70–88.

Osofsky, J. (1995). The effects of exposure to violence on young children. *American Psychologist. 50,* 782–788.

Pargament, K., Olsen, H., Reilly, B., Falgout, K., Ensing, D., & Van Haitsma, K. (1992). God Help Me (II): The relationship of religious orientations to religious coping with negative life events. *Journal for the Scientific Study of Religion, 31,* 504–513.

Pynoos, R., & Nader, K. (1988). Psychological first aid and treatment approach to children exposed to community violence: research implications. *Journal of Traumatic Stress, 1,* 445–473.

Richters, J., & Martinez, P. (1993). The NIMH community violence project: Vol., 1. Children as victims of and as witnesses to violence. *Psychiatry, 56,* 7–21.

Sameroff, A., Seifer, R. Barocas, R. Zax, M., & Greenspan, S. (1987). Intelligence quotient scores of 4-year-old children: Socio-environmental risk factors. *Pediatrics, 79,* 343–350.

Schacter, D. L. (1996). *Emotional memories: When the past persists.* New York: Basic Books.

Terr, L. (1990). *Too scared to cry.* New York: Harper and Row.

Mass Conflict and the Participants, Attitudes toward

Sheldon G. Levy

Wayne State University

GLOSSARY

Chain of Command The hierarchy in any organization in which some individuals have authority over others. In the military these levels are typically identified as soldier, officer, and general. In other forms of conflict, two levels are distinguishable, the direct actors and the planners or leaders. A planner in a chain of command must be one who is involved in giving directions to those directly involved in the attack.

Combatant A person directly engaged in actions or direct military support in an armed conflict. Included are those who are a part of the organizational apparatus designed to conduct the conflict such as administrative personnel in the military, medical personnel in uniform, and reserve troops. Those directly involved in the action or planning of mass conflict events outside of formal military organizations, such as riots, terrorism, and ethnic conflict, are also combatants.

Conflict Antagonistic or incompatible behavior that defines one end of the behavioral cooperation–conflict dimension. The behavior may be verbal or physical.

Democide Mass killing of almost all forms except direct military engagement between two armies. The category includes killing by governments, ethnic conflict, riots, and massacres of civilians.

Mass Conflict Conflict involving large groups of people. The most common forms are armed conflicts such as war, ethnic conflict, and terrorism. However, the category also includes acts by governments or other authorities against citizens or other large groups of people.

Noncombatant Any person who is not a combatant. Civilians working in factories or in hospitals are noncombatants as are bystanders in any armed conflict. Citizens subjected to governmental repression are noncombatants.

Norms The general or typical view of the moral belief (oughtness) governing conduct. A law, therefore, is not necessarily a norm. Normative behavior is that which is typical.

WHILE THE TECHNOLOGICAL TRANSITIONS in weaponry are clearly identifiable, there has been no such continuous development in views of war. Depending on the historical era, the geographical region, and the nature of the group—nomadic, agricultural or urban, large or small, tribal or political state—beliefs

Copyright © 1999 by Academic Press.
All rights of reproduction in any form reserved.

and attitudes about conflict and the participants have differed. These differences have been dependent upon the goals sought, the status of the enemy, the degree of provocation, and the norms considered appropriate for conflictual engagements. In some regions and during some periods of history, there has been greater adherence to the contemporary rules of war than at present. Nevertheless, the overall human record is one of vast destruction of both noncombatants and combatants. The toll for both categories is in the hundreds of millions with the large majority having been noncombatants. Such destruction can only be accounted for by the realization that large portions of humanity, civilian and military, have been considered expendable, either by their own state or by others.

I. ORGANIZATION OF ARTICLE

This article deals with perceptions and individual views toward conflict and its participants rather than philosophical beliefs or those about the causes of war. Included in the general domain to be discussed are a variety of conflict categories. The greatest emphasis is on war and intergroup conflict. However, other examples include terrorism and governmental repression, particularly when the deaths of large numbers of people have occurred such as in the gulags under Soviet rule and the massacres in Cambodia by the Khmer Rouge.

Views of conflict must be gleaned from the historical record for all but the most recent periods. The first sections that follow examine a number of incidents across space and time both to allow some reasonable assessment of perceptions and motives and also to illustrate the variety of views that have existed. The discussion then examines formal attempts by political states to restrain armed conflict through international agreements governing treatment of combatants and noncombatants. Attempts to employ quantitative social science to examine views of individuals toward conflict and the participants is a recent phenomenon and some of these results will be discussed. Finally, implications for the future as well as important research problems are briefly examined.

II. OVERVIEW OF WAR

The historical record identifies that war has been conducted to achieve a number of nonmutually exclusive goals. These goals have also been associated with different degrees of violence, particularly against noncomba-

tants. Conflict as competition may at times be more similar to a game such as football or hockey than to a war. The most severe injury, death, may occur more often than in most games but still infrequently. In its least lethal forms, conflict is more symbolic than actual. In one variation, it may be between one representative from each of two conflicting groups, with the possibility of one or both being killed. This "symbolic" form of battle was practiced in disparate cultures that included some indigenous tribes of North America and the Samurai in Japan during the Middle Ages, although there were also major wars in Japan during this period.

In more serious forms of competition, as illustrated by battles among some ancient Greek city-states, the goal was to win the battlefield. Although the contest resulted in many deaths, retreating soldiers, once they had left the battlefield, were not pursued and massacred and their cities were not sacked. However, plunder, revenge, and control were also evident during this period. The sacking of Troy was not a token event.

The control of territory led to wars that varied greatly in mortality depending upon the circumstances. Among the factors likely to lead to massive rather than controlled destruction were the motive of revenge, the strategy of inducing terror, and the prevailing normative standards. Of course, these constituents are likely to be combined in any specific instance. Revenge, for deaths inflicted on one's military forces or civilians, or for some offense to the leader, was often a basis for complete destruction of an enemy. Moreover, resistance frequently resulted in much greater destruction than did rapid capitulation, as in wars in China during the first millennium of the common era as well as during the exploits of Genghis Khan.

On the other hand, some armies as well as populations were destroyed as a military tactic, the induction of terror. Since a major goal in armed conflict is to destroy the coherence of the enemy as a fighting force, terror was considered an important vehicle through which to demoralize the enemy. It has been advocated by military strategists for at least 3 millennia and is an important reason for organized loud sounds, from drums to trumpets to the shouts of the fighting men prior to battle. (These also functioned to mobilize one's own fighting force.) Destruction of people by an invading army accomplished, in a less benign manner, the goal of terror, particularly if it was reported to other regions yet to be invaded. Of course, such tactics may also result in a perceived necessity for greater resistance. Thus, devastation coupled with a feared reputation, such as that garnered by Alexander the Great, disposed future enemies in the intended direction.

Normative standards are important in determining the level of destruction in armed conflict. The behavior of the Mongols was both brutal and consistent with the norms that existed in warfare in Central Asia at that time.

Ideology is an important source for the most destructive forms of conflict especially when coupled with views of the enemy as not human or as not equally human. In the Roman empire, acceptance of the State religion was required as a sign of loyalty to the regime but adherence to more than one religion was tolerated. However, the religious basis for conflict appears much greater when a religion believes that it possesses the only "true" set of beliefs. In this case, wars of conversion or of destruction are more likely. Singular belief in the truth leads inevitably by definition, and almost inevitably psychologically, to a perception of the nonbeliever as holding an inferior belief. The inferiority in belief is only a short step from the perception of inferior status as a human being. Assessing the religious factor, or any other single influence, from the historical record is always difficult. While religious differences may exist, war also may be for control over resources or the political machinery. In addition, the participants are frequently motivated by greed.

Ideological resistance to a singular-truth religion exposes the resisters to genocidal attacks, particularly if the nonbelievers are viewed as deniers of the belief system rather than mere outsiders. The Jews of Europe are an example. The Holocaust of the Second World War was a culmination of lesser, but often large, massacres that occurred during the prior 1500 years of European history. Christian–Muslim and Muslim–Hindu conflicts, each having persisted for hundreds of years, are additional examples involving mass destruction in which ideology appears to have been a major factor. Christian–Christian wars of great devastation also occurred, suggesting perhaps that, particularly in religion, even relatively small differences in viewpoint are often interpreted as denial.

Singular truth is not always religious. The Khmer Rouge demonstrated this in Cambodia. The motivation for the Cold War, which lasted through the whole of the 20th century (China is still communist and antipathy by the West to the Communist revolution in Russia arose early in the century), was based on more than mutual threat. The belief systems were incompatible in religion, politics, and economics. The long-awaited war between the Soviet Union and the United States in the second half of the 20th century may have been postponed because, at least at the level of ideological incompatibility, some semblance of sanity may have been induced by MADness (Mutually Assured Destructiveness).

Of course, there are other bases for perceived inferiority, such as racial differences or a belief that the target is less civilized, which may be more likely when there are physical differences. Wanton destruction is generally coupled with another goal such as the "living space" ideology in Germany during the regime of Hitler, the less malevolent "manifest destiny" of the United States during the 19th century, and the greed of the Spaniards in the Americas, particularly during, but not limited to, the 16th and 17th centuries.

Perceptions of racial inferiority do not always lead to mass destruction but they inevitably provide a predisposition in that direction. Among a portion of the United States population, genocide of the indigenous peoples was justified on the grounds they were not at the same level of humanity. While this belief was also endemic among a large portion of the population toward Black slaves, their economic contribution tempered the level of destructiveness so that they were more the object of cruelty than of genocide.

The perception of the enemy as a threat to the integrity or continuance of the group is also an important factor and is related to those already discussed. Danger from enemies has always been an important motive for war. Since the enslaved tend to resent their enslavement, conquered peoples are always a threat. When it is advantageous to form alliances for economic and/or military benefits, conquered peoples are allowed to survive. When all that is desired are the spoils, survival is more problematic. The bounty that is sought varies greatly. In addition to economic wealth, it may include slavery and/or victims for religious sacrifice or sexual advantage.

III. HISTORICAL EXAMPLES

Historical incidents reflect the variability in views of conflict and its participants that have existed across time and space.

A. Value-Based Decision-Making—Views of Combatants

As early as 2600 years ago, values of fairness existed in China at an almost profound level. The following chronicle is from Creel (*The Birth of China*, p. 156). An army of the C'hu invaded the state of Sung in the 11th month of 638 B.C.E. greatly outnumbering the Duke Hsiang's forces. His advisors suggested attacking as the C'hu crossed the Hung river but he refused. He was then advised to attack after they crossed but before they regrouped; he again refused. The subsequent battle resulted in the predictable defeat of Duke Hsiang, who was thoroughly criticized by his citizens. He explained: "The superior man does not inflict a second wound, or take the grey-haired prisoner. When the ancients had their armies in the field, they would not attack an enemy when he was in a defile. Though I am but the unworthy remnant of a fallen dynasty I would not sound my drums to attack an unprepared enemy."

Such chivalrous action is doubted as having been universal since during this period of history there were surprise raiding parties conducted at night to capture prisoners (generally about 10–20) for enslavement or sacrifice. However, norms or principles have never been universally endorsed and, even when generally supported, there has been widespread violation in actual conflict. Duke Hsiang of Sung expressed his views 2500 years before European nations began to formalize the conduct of war through international protocols (and even then never at this level of restraint).

B. Ingroup Views of Noncombatants

1. Protection

The manner in which one's own people are treated in the attempt to defeat an enemy has varied throughout history. When Alexander the Great invaded Persia it was clear that his army's lines of supply would be stretched. Memnon, who commanded the Persians, supported a scorched earth policy so that Alexander's army could not live off the land. However, among Persian noblemen of the time there was a strong set of values governing one's duty. Arsites, Satrap of Hellespontine Phrygia, probably as commander-in-chief since operations were taking place in his territory, spoke for his fellow noblemen when he said, "For my part, I will not voluntarily see one house burnt of the people who have been placed under my charge." (Burn, pp. 90–91.) The subsequent conquest by Alexander resulted in a general amnesty although the Persian oligarchy were lynched and those Persian forces considered to have been traitors to Macedonia were enslaved.

In general in this region of the world at this time, the view toward enemy combatants was not benign and the fleeing enemy were often pursued and slain.

2. Sacrifice

The views of Arsites were not those of the Soviets when the Germans invaded during the Second World War. A scorched-earth policy in which large numbers of Soviets died was instituted. This did not necessarily represent a different level of morality. The racial views of the Germans about Slavs, the fear of the enemy, and the consequences of defeat for the individual and the ingroup as well as the strength of the ingroup identification were additional factors.

3. Civilian Sacrifice for Political Control

The organized starvation of millions of Ukrainians in the 1930s by Stalin is a clearer example of the view of the expendability of noncombatants to obtain political control. The Soviet gulags and Khmer Rouge massacres in Cambodia were similar in goal but differed in tactics.

C. The Factor of Revenge

In addition to the norms or values that exist at a particular time, situational factors are important determinants of the outcome for the defeated. For example, when the Macedonians attacked Tyre under Alexander (332 B.C.E.), a 7-month siege ensued. In addition to incurring the wrath of the Macedonians by their extended and vigorous defense, the Tyrians killed some of the Macedonian prisoners that had been captured earlier at Sidon in full view of the prisoners' friends. When Tyre was finally overcome, large numbers of the defenders were killed and even larger numbers sold to slave dealers.

Other factors, such as hardships endured by soldiers in campaigns or cruel treatment by their own officers, may lead to a displacement onto the victims. The harsh treatment of the Japanese soldiers by their officers, which had developed prior to the Second World War, may have been a partial factor, but only partial, in their repeatedly cruel treatment of the Chinese as illustrated by incidents such as the rape of Nanking.

D. Functional Factors

1. Control and Terrorization

Although many peoples from antiquity to the present have engaged in massacres, the leaders were frequently functionally motivated. One objective was to gain control. Massacres induced terrorization of future opponents who might be more willing to capitulate than risk a similar fate. Another objective was to provide rewards for service to soldiers through spoils. The Mongols of the 1200s destroyed large numbers of people and enslaved large numbers of women and children to gain control and induce terror. These tactics were consistent with norms for the conduct of war in those regions. The ancient Assyrians also were highly destructive. The destructiveness may be viewed as excessive from the view of the outsider, but the degree of terror required to achieve an objective is in the eyes of the actor, and these eyes are narrowed by historical precedent as well as individual perspective. Among these peoples or the ancient Romans, even during their cruelest period, racial differences do not appear to have been a factor.

2. Spoils

The abandonment of moral restraints against noncombatants may be a reward to soldiers for service that frequently requires extreme hardship. Greed is fundamental and is readily available for manipulation to achieve goals of leaders, although in many instances no manipulation is necessary.

Thai pirates who attacked the Vietnamese (boat people) fleeing Vietnam in the late 1960s and early 1970s were interested in robbery and rape.

During the Spanish conquest of the Americas, similar motives existed and were the basis for wholesale slaughter and enslavement. The North Americans, who viewed the indigenous population as inferior, would, if opportunity arose, capture Indians and sell them to Spanish in southern California. The Indian women were forced to work in the camps and to become "camp wives."

However, booty alone cannot explain such treatment of noncombatants since social organization almost always involves differential wealth. Therefore, while greed may be a motivating factor, other conditions must exist to account for wholesale mistreatment and devastation.

E. The Factor of Ideology

Ideology (and race) are major reasons for wholesale destruction of both combatants and noncombatants. The army of the First Crusade reached Jerusalem in 1099 with 12,000 of the original 30,000 remaining. Jerusalem was overcome, the 70,000 Muslims were put to death, and the Jews of the city were placed in a synagogue and burned. The Muslims and Jews were not given the choice of forced conversion but were simply eliminated. Such ideological elimination also could be wreaked upon fellow Christians. For example, the Albigensian heresy in the South of France led to their annihilation by the invading North French in the early 13th century. When the crusaders overwhelmed the city of Béziers, 20,000 people were massacred including Catholics, heretics, men, women, clerics, and children.

The role of ideology is difficult to establish since frequently there are inducements for both leaders and soldiers to engage in the attack. The attack on the Albi-

gensians was finally persuaded by a promise of their lands to the victorious armies by Pope Innocent III. Further, particularly at this time, religious beliefs were also central to the control of the State by the Church. Thus it was possible at times for more vigorous action to be taken by the Church against heretical Christians than against the separate Jewish and Muslim communities who did not threaten its control. Although religion was also a factor leading to conflict in ancient times; in Rome, for example, religious adherence was required primarily to maintain the legitimacy of state authority rather than to convert the world to a singular ideology.

The Inquisition, which lasted for almost 1000 years during the second millennium of the common era was wreaked upon Christians as well as those outside of Christianity. The purposes were to maintain theological homogeneity, political control, and the associated physical accoutrements and privileges of the clergy. The suffering of Christians at the hands of the Inquisition of its own church was far greater than it had been under the early Roman persecution of the new religion.

The Inquisition, although resulting in the deaths of many thousands of people, achieved its rule over a wide span of geography and time because relatively small amounts of terror induce great fear. Criminal organizations such as the Mafia have utilized terror similarly.

F. The Factor of Inferiority

The concept of other peoples as biologically inferior has provided the most important setting for mass destruction.

While the Nazi employment of such ideas (notably against the Jews) is well documented, other comparable judgments have arisen. Although these are frequently mingled with motives of greed, they do appear to have an independent contribution to the treatment of enemies, particularly noncombatants. While the property of the inferiors is always seized (and never distributed among the most needy of the victorious side), there is, when inferiority is a factor, destruction that goes beyond that which can be accounted for by greed.

The Holocaust was visited upon an enemy who, it was believed, could racially pollute the blood. The pollution was a biological and social plague against which protection required the complete destruction of the carriers. Although the views toward indigenous peoples in the Americas never reached such widespread perversity, it was believed by many that they were savages, incapable of attaining a level of "civilization." The inevitability of their extermination was accepted even among those who held more moderate beliefs.

Thus in North America there are accounts of California miners who slaughtered whole Indian villages, including mothers with infants at their breasts. The skulls of the infants were smashed for no apparent reason. Subsequently, a victory dance would be held during which bodies would be burned, even those of children who might still be alive. Those who escaped were enslaved, worked mercilessly, and were then butchered (Billington, pp. 131–132).

These events were sometimes publicly supported in the Western press. Chivington massacred Indians at Sand Creek, Colorado, a large portion of whom were civilians, after duping them into an indefensible position. A Western newspaper reported the massacre as a wholesome act that should be repeated once or twice a year. Custer's military loss in the Battle of Big Horn was described in the press as an act of Indian savagery that should not go unpunished.

The actual number of indigenous North Americans who were directly killed does not rank as extremely large across the full range of history. Nevertheless, it is a clear example of the consequences of the sentiment that others are lesser humans, a view that expressed itself in one of the major historical devastations, that of the indigenous peoples in Central and South America.

The atomic bombing of Hiroshima and Nagasaki was a result of several factors, revenge, terror, threat (from the anticipated casualties from an invasion), and the persuasion that the Japanese were less human. Revenge and terror were also factors in the firebombing of German cities such as Dresden, but in spite of the inhuman treatment by the Germans of many of the peoples that they conquered, the Allies perceived Germans to be equivalent in human status to their own.

G. Benign War

The immensely destructive conflict that is known to modern man and recorded in most of history has not been universal.

Among those whose views of conflict differed were the Walbiri Aborigines of Australia, the Bushmen of South Africa, and some of the indigenous peoples of the Americas. These groups were characterized by small bands, large amounts of territory and, frequently, non-hierarchical social organizations. War occurred but it contained large elements of a ritual or a serious game. As a result, killing was limited.

The characteristics of these groups has led to hypotheses that the "cause" of large-scale warfare is "civilization" or "urbanization" or the early equivalent, which was sedentary agriculture. The thesis is that these conditions led to the development of taking from others for self-serving purposes.

The explanation seems inadequate. Even in small groups the motive to dominate others and extend that domination to the known world might have arisen, as it did in Alexander the Great, Caesar, Genghis Khan, Napoleon, and Hitler. It does not require urbanization or any of the other presumed "causes" for the emergence of the inclination to confiscate food from a band that has already completed the hunt, or to enslave them for the performance of some mundane tasks, or to rape the women or capture them as additional wives.

It is possible that structural factors limited the practicality of certain types of spoils. For example, it might have been difficult to control slaves if they were obligated to hunt, but they could be employed as laborers for tasks such as the carrying of goods during periods of migration—and family might be held as hostages. It might also be expensive to conduct warfare over large regions since the time–distance factor between home and group to be plundered might have been great. Since the early peoples were nomadic, this should not have been a significant factor.

The above problems do not appear determinative and a full understanding of the conflict behavior of early peoples as well as of some contemporary groups must include their beliefs about the group, their social position within it, their major goals in life, the role definitions that existed, and their view of the value of the life of others outside the group.

In addition, the reasons for war lend themselves to explanations other than the structural. Most of the peoples were not isolated. Once a band of warriors inflicted damage, it became very costly to fail to defend oneself against the next attack. The result may have been a change in attitudes about conflict. This view may have become almost universal even though there were a limited number of independent incidents. Peace, or relative peace, or benign or symbolic or ritualistic war does not create the necessity for further peace. However, war does create the necessity for defense. Thus, even if the initiation of large scale warfare occurred randomly and infrequently, it would be expected ultimately to induce others to adopt comparable stances in self-defense. A good offense may be understood as one effective means of self-defense.

The structural factors as explanations possess severe limitations. They are associated with the development of large scale warfare but they do not explain how the motives of domination, greed, and slaughter came to displace those of cooperation, ingroup solidarity, live-

and-let-live, noncompetitiveness, and nonhierarchical roles in social organization.

H. The Military Organization and Internal Views of Combatants

1. The Leader as Example

The actions of participants in battle are frequently a direct result of the example set by the leader. If Alexander the Great exhibited cruelty, then one would expect to observe the soldiers imitating this behavior—likewise if restraint was displayed. The behavior is influenced by more than the factor of obedience or of threat for nonconforming behavior.

2. The Military Organization

The attitudes of the combatants themselves are shaped by the internal norms of the military organization as well as by more general standards. Thus, the loss of hundreds of thousands of soldiers from both sides at the battle of Verdun during the First World War was more a function of the accepted role of the soldier than of external threat or military strategy. The field of battle changed hands over 30 times. There is little doubt that it displayed to the two sides the futility of the war and one might guess that the soldiers could have decided that long before the officers and politicians came to the realization. Yet they fought as soldiers are supposed to fight. Axelrod, in *The Evolution of Cooperation*, states that a tit-for-tat strategy existed in which the soldiers from both sides arrived at an implicit agreement to not fire unless fired upon. If so, this would have led to a more rational approach on the part of the soldiers. The officers, realizing that this was the case, instituted measures to prevent this from happening, basically through increased supervision and coercion through severe penalties for the faiure to fight.

During the Crimean War (against Russia, 1853–1856) the British soldiers faced similar circumstances, although in all cases it must be realized that failure to obey might lead to imprisonment or death at the hands of one's officers. Thousands of British soldiers froze to death during the winter after the loss of supplies on ships during a storm. Many officers returned to England to avoid the cold winter. The armed soldiers, conceivably, could have revolted by forming a coalition against the officers, but they didn't.

Although the Crimean War antedated the first international agreements governing conflict, both sides did agree at times to short truces during which the wounded might be removed from the battlefield. The principle of removal of wounded under safe conditions was later incorporated into the international protocols.

Views of combatants within the military organization, and the acceptance by the soldier of the appropriate role beyond that achieved by coercion, were different for the Soviet soldiers who defended Stalingrad during the Second World War. Although there were desperate conditions during the winter and great loss of life, much of which was not a direct result of battle, they were in a struggle to achieve a common goal: the defeat of the German army and the protection of the motherland. The long Vietnamese war against Western domination may be a comparable instance as well as the militant pacifism of Mohandas Gandhi and his followers against British rule in India.

Understanding the beliefs of soldiers about their role is also informed by the Japanese in World War II. Surrender was dishonorable. Coupled with the role of the ruler as both secular and religious leader, great sacrifice by the Japanese was displayed. The Kamikaze pilots were only one example. In the defense of Iwo Jima, only 1000 of the 22,000 Japanese defenders were captured; the remainder died in battle.

I. Research on the Views of the Military

World War II occurred at a point in history at which more objective research methods had developed in the social sciences. The U.S. military and government utilized, to the fullest extent possible, these advancements to aid the war effort. The single most important reference that exists about attitudes of military personnel, *The American Soldier*, emerged. Over 170 military samples were studied during and after the war and a total of more that 500,000 respondents were included at various ranks in both the army and air corps. Questions examined all phases of army life including views of comrades, officers, the enemy, civilians, combat, and other facets related to the war and military service.

Among a very large number of findings were: American soldiers believed that the war was fought for survival rather than to serve the interests of big business (although the big business reason was agreed to by over 20% of the cross-section of 6000 White soldiers in August, 1942), a far greater percentage endorsed the sentiment that the whole Japanese nation should be wiped out compared to that expressed for Germany, and Black soldiers preceived the war differently than White soldiers.

There were also studies by Americans of German soldiers. One goal was to identify factors associated with surrender among the Wehrmacht. A major conclusion was that the primary group (such as a platoon of about 20 soldiers), rather than a more distant ideology, was the major influence. When the primary group disintegrated, surrender was more likely. The conclusion was reached that propaganda, including information about the strategic poisition of the unit, should not be aimed at political attitudes but at those factors that would facilitate the surrender decision should the primary group begin to disintegrate.

More recently, Benjamin Shalit, a psychologist serving in the Israeli army, has examined the psychology of combat. He found that Israeli verterans listed as a most frightening aspect of battle letting their comrades down (among enlisted men) and letting those serving under them down (among officers). As might be imagined, death and injury were large factors, but to a much greater extent among the enlisted than among the officers. Among Swedish UN soldiers, who had not seen battle, the results were similar for the infantry units studied.

Shalit also provided data on the degree of hatred among Israeli soldiers toward the enemy. Syria was the most hated and Jordan the least (with Egypt in the middle) Furthur, support troops provided evidence of significantly greater hatred than did the combat troops toward each of the enemies.

Since each war has many unique components, a great deal of research for a large number of events with some standardization of materials will be required before legitimate generalizations may be developed. Nevertheless, important research among soldiers has been accomplished.

J. Symbolic Rehearsal

A person only interacts directly with those elements of the social environment that influence behavior a portion of the time. The intensity of action, specifically the mass killing of people who pose no direct physical threat, is also influenced by prior thoughts that are rehearsed privately over a long period of time. Such thoughts can be induced by a society through the images that it presents of potential enemies and through the rules by which the individual is expected to abide. There are also individual differences in the extent to which such images or icons are repeated. If it were not for these individual differences, the concept of symbolic rehearsal would be superfluous. However, given essentially the same socialization experience and similar immediate environments, there are large differences among people in the degree to which they hate and are willing to engage in destructive behavior. Some reasonable inter-

nal process that consists of the frequency and nature of thoughts and associated feelings, in this case of the relationship of the potential actor to the intended target, seems relevant to understanding the behavior. In other areas of life such processes are readily accepted, for example, planning one's career or vacation or thinking repeatedly about winning the state lottery (and then placing a bet). Since such activity is not publicly available, it is difficult to develop tools for measuring its effects. Nevertheless, symbolic rehearsal appears to be a potent force in facilitating action, specifically, the massacre of innocents. If the motor that drives the thoughts is the societal characterization of the target, then the engine of restraint must be fueled by counterimages that engender different rehearsal patterns.

K. Overall Social Structure

The overall organization of a society affects its conception of the role of combatants. The roles of the leader and of the citizen vary greatly. For most of human history, the leadership was all powerful and much of the time it was endowed with religious sanction. The leader was a representative of the heavens or at least tried to convince the followers of this. Nonreligious totalitarianism is much more common in recent history. It is also true that individual rights within a society and severe limitations on those that govern, as represented by democracies, are also a more recent phenomenon. One would expect that these civil changes would affect views of combatants, noncombatants, and the conditions under which conflict is legitimate. This appears to be so, yet wanton destruction of humans is not a contemporary stranger.

Governments have, however, attempted to incorporate restraints in conflict through international agreements.

IV. FORMAL AGREEMENTS GOVERNING WARFARE

The formalization of principles governing armed conflict among political states is contained in a number of international agreements that are usually dated from the St. Petersburg Convention of 1868. These were modified and extended after the First World War in the Hague Convention and after the Second World War in the Geneva and other conventions. There have been subsequent declarations by the United Nations that cover human rights, the rights of women, and genocide. Many of these principles are extensions of those already developed for inter-state war but are applied instead to internal affairs and to ethnic entities not recognized as political units. These additional declarations do recognize the illegitimacy of the spoils, such as slavery, rape, and robbery, that underlie many historical conflicts. Soldiers, however, are not explicitly covered within their military organizations by these conventions. Thus nations are free to engage in military conscription without violating involuntary servitude prohibitions and once in the military, rights of personnel are severely limited (although individual countries vary in the civil rights that are afforded).

A. Civilians (Noncombatants)

The international Red Cross Committee's Declaration states that when military options are equally advantageous, the choice should be the one that involves the least danger to the civilian population. Even more restrictive is the obligation to refrain from the attack if the civilian loss is not proportionate to the expected military gain.

The Fourth Geneva Convention of 1949 obligates an occupying power to provide food and medical supplies to the population to as great a degree as possible, while the 1977 Geneva Convention outlaws starvation of civilians and attacks upon objects indispensable for the survival of the civilian population such as food, livestock, crops, drinking water, dams, dikes, and electrical generation. An exception exists if the facilities provide regular, significant, and direct support to the military provided that attack is the only way to terminate such support. Nevertheless, even these attacks are outlawed if they subject the civilian population to starvation and disease. The 1923 Hague Rules of Aerial Warfare require that the military concentration be sufficient to justify the bombardment when the danger to civilians is also taken into account. Hospitals are not legitimate targets nor are places of worship if there is any doubt about their use for military purposes. Finally, the 1971 Zagreb Resolution provides for United Nations liability for damage caused by its forces in violation of humanitarian rules of armed conflict.

B. Military Restrictions

The principle of proportionality is applied to both the grievance or provocation and to the engagement throughout the protocols. Excessive force for limited military advantage is outlawed. Also outlawed is the use of incendiary weapons of any form as well as chemical and biological weapons.

The U.S. Navy Department's *Handbook on the Law of Naval Operations* states that "Only the degree and kind of force, not otherwise prohibited by the law of armed conflict, required for the partial or complete submission of the enemy with a minimum expenditure of time, life, and physical resources may be applied." Applications of force inconsistent with this principle are prohibited.

The 1949 Geneva Convention requires that after an engagement there be opportunity to search and collect all wounded for treatment, that the wounded and dead be as fully identified as possible and that the information be transmitted to each person's government.

The Red Cross Diplomatic Conference on the Reaffirmation and Development of International Humanitarian Law Applicable in Armed Conflicts of 1977 summarizes a number of the principles. The choice of methods and means of armed conflict is not unlimited; orders for no survivors or threats to that effect are prohibited, and attacks involving excessive damage are considered as "indiscriminate."

C. Contemporary Views

1. Research Rationale

In spite of the general awareness of the destructiveness of war to both soldiers and civilians, the actual levels are probably underestimated by most. Rummel estimates about 200 million deaths occurred during the period 1900–1987 with 80% of the casualties outside of the military battlefield losses.

A large proportion of the deaths in battle and almost all civilian deaths have resulted from violations of a moral code which, in the abstract, all parties might endorse. It is evident that many of the aggressive actions violate either international agreements among nations (or domestic law) governing the treatment of soldiers and civilians during conflict.

It seems clear from the historical record that norms of conflict are important in influencing the image of both combatants and noncombatants and of the subsequent conduct of the hostilities. Of course, the motives and views of the direct attackers and of the observers are of interest but these are not independent of those of the larger society. Ancient Rome provides a direct illustration. Election as a Roman senator in Caesar's time required public support. Such support was forthcoming based on conquest that brought spoils back to the citizens. Success was evidenced by the return of 5000 enemy heads to Rome.

Research, therefore, is important to establish the norms that currently exist. There are many basic questions to be addressed. For example, are the norms different cross-culturally, are they different in the military compared to the general citizenry, is there an underlying psychology upon which judgements are based?

There have been a few attempts to obtain quantitative information about such views. First there are the investigations of Suedfeld and Epstein and Kelman and Hamilton after the My Lai massacre in Vietnam by U.S. military. An elaborate effort to provide more general information was the research of Brunk, Secrest, and Tamhiro. Their efforts will be reviewed briefly before some preliminary results are reported from an ongoing cross-cultural research project by the author to assess normative values. These results represent a very limited but important contribution to the objective study of the problem.

2. Understanding Attitudes toward War

The Brunk et al, research represents a comprehensive attempt to examine current beliefs about war. Questions were developed representing views that have been expressed over a long historical period. These were classified into a set of 10 categories. One, the Golden Rule cluster, examines beliefs in symmetry; for example, if the U.S. wishes other countries to keep treaties (or not to spy on it), then it should keep its treaties (and not spy on them). The Just War category identifies a number of restrictions that include the circumstances under which war can be declared by legal authority, self-defense as the only basis for war, and the goals that are legitimate (protection of civilians, proportional damage). Other categories include: Legalism, Moral Crusade, Moral Perfectionism, Nuclear Pacifism, Pacifism, Reason of State, Retaliatory Ethic, and Supreme Emergency.

The data were obtained through mail surveys from elite groups in the United States: retired military officers, diplomats, journalists, members of congress, and Roman Catholic clergy (priests and higher levels).

There was generally high support for statements in the Golden Rule and Just War categories, although a large difference occurred among the Just War restrictions between the clergy, who were most supportive, and the military, who were least. There was little support for the Pacifism category or for war as a Moral Crusade. The clergy were noticeably more committed to war that strictly adhered to moral standards and significantly more in favor of Nuclear Pacifism.

The inquiry has some limitations. While 60% of the military sample returned completed questionnaires the percentages for the others were much lower, generally 20–30%. Although this limits the ability to generalize to the total elite group, the investigations are significant because they provide insights into the values of a diverse array of elites. There are also some other caveats. Sixty percent of the items contain the word "moral" or "morality." There may have been variation among the groups in the extent to which they focused on that concept. The consistency in wording may have also led to some patterned responses based on an anticipation that the next item would also ask about "morality." Some of the statements were general while others referred to behavior by the United States. The data do not present information about any distinction between views about obligations of the ingroup compared to the outgroup. Nevertheless, the Brunk et al. study remains a significant contribution to the quantitative investigation of attitudes about conflict.

3. Cross-Cultural Investigations of Normative Views of Conflict

Several differences from the Brunk et al. study were incorporated into the following research. Although the samples that were selected were not from elite groups, they were obtained from four countries and differed substantially from each other. Further, principles were derived directly from international agreements covering armed conflict. A questionnaire format was employed but because a principle may be interpreted differently depending on the circumstances, two versions of the instrument were developed. In one, the key actor was the respondent's home country; in the other, it was an enemy. This allowed differences in judgments between ingroup and outgroup to be evaluated. In addition, a number of items were revised and incorporated based on the studies of Brunk et al.

Information was collected from six samples during late 1996 to early 1998. Four were university groups: one in the United States contained 446 students, one in England, 131 (obtained through the efforts of co-investigator Peter Jones at Reading University), and two in Russia (128, 141) obtained through the efforts of co-investigator Alexander Voronov at the Russian State University for the Humanities. A third sample (344 cases) consisted of the military personnel at a US naval training facility (through an invitation from the Captain of the base, Michael Riordan). The fourth was a random sample of 811 adults in the Beijing urban area (supervised by Shen Mingming, director of the Research Center for Contemporary China at Beijing University). Although the two nonuniversity samples differed from the others in age and education, analyses indicated that these were not important factors in the results.

a. Overview of the Data

The statements may be divided into three major groups, those primarily concerned with conflict, those that specify noncombatants, and those that refer to combatants. Table 1 presents the wording of the main set of items.

b. Summary of Results

Overall levels of restraint were not very high although there was substantial variation across items and samples. There was greater agreement among the groups about the appropriate restraint for an enemy than for the home country. Average enemy ratings were equivalent to slightly greater than "somewhat agree." However,

the restraint for the home country averaged in the somewhat agree to neutral point. The Reading, UK and Russian samples expressed somewhat higher degrees of restraint with relatively small differences between home and enemy ratings. The U.S. military and Chinese samples provided the largest difference between home and enemy versions and the least restraint for home actions.

The following comments apply to all samples except the Chinese because the Chinese questionnaire only included 12 items that overlapped any of the others. Greatest restraint was endorsed for symmetry (keeping treaties, not spying) and for what appears to be gratuitous use of force (that is, beyond that dictated by mili-

TABLE I
Value Items—Home Country (USA) Version

A president of the United States should be prohibited from starting a war.

US civilians who contribute to their country's war effort, for example, by working in factories, should be considered the same as military personnel.

If the United States wants treaty promises to it to be kept, then it should keep its treaty promises to other countries

Torture of enemy prisoners of war by the US military to obtain military information should be prohibited.

The US army should be required to allow the enemy army the opportunity to remove their wounded so that they may receive medical help.

US soldiers at war who kill enemy soldiers after they signal the desire to surrender should be penalized.

Suppose the US army captures enemy territory. International agreements should require that it provide food and medical supplies to the civilian population of that territory to the best of its abilities.

A US soldier who knowingly shoots innocent enemy civilians is guilty of a war crime even if he is under battlefield stress.

In a war, the United States should be allowed to inflict as much damage as it can on the enemy country even if the enemy has a limited ability to inflict damage on it.

During a war, the US army should be required to provide medical aid and food to enemy soldiers who surrender.

During a war, the US military should be prohibited from using unlimited force against the enemy to prevent injury and death to any of its own soldiers.

It is better for the United States to accept defeat than participate in a nuclear war.

The conduct of war by the United States should be subject to international restraints.

During war, the US military should be prohibited from forcing captured enemy prisoners of war to engage in propaganda against their own country.

If the United States spies on other countries then it should expect other countries to spy on it.

If the US army is at war it should be prohibited by international agreements from waging campaigns in which the goal is to kill all of the enemy soldiers.

If a superior orders a US soldier to kill enemy civilians that the solider knows are innocent, the soldier should obey the order.

The United States is only justified in conducting a war if it is for the purpose of self-defense.

US citizens should follow the laws of their country when they conflict with the individual's personal moral beliefs.

If the only way for the United States to avoid defeat in war is to commit war crimes, it should commit them.

It should be acceptable military practice for the US army at war to use tactical nuclear weapons against the enemy army.

During a war, it should be an acceptable strategy for US military forces to destroy civilian electricity and water supplies in enemy cities if the enemy military receives some benefits from those facilities.

During a war, the use by the US military of napalm or other incendiary weapons against enemy soldiers should be outlawed.

The United States is justified in threatening the use of nuclear weapons against the cities of an enemy country as a way of preventing nuclear attacks against its own cities.

Revenge against enemy civilians is justified if US civilians have been attacked.

If the United States thinks that another country is planning to attack it, it should have the right to attack that country first to destroy its ability to engage in the war.

If the United States launches an unprovoked attack, an unrestrained military response by the target nation is justified.

The United States is justified in attacking an enemy first to prevent that nation from becoming strong enough to defeat it.

tary conditions or which involved great suffering). These include the killing of surrendering soldiers, their torture, or forcing them to engage in propaganda against their own country. Comparable items for civilians are also at this level. There was, however, much less restraint expressed in the use of napalm. Although restraint in the use of tactical nuclear weapons was relatively high, most samples assigned a fairly large difference between its legitimacy by the home country compared to the enemy.

Least restraint was shown for those items that involved threat to the nation or retaliation when provoked. Responses were endorsed that were far greater than the provocations. Two examples were: (1) an unrestrained response to an unprovoked attack and (2) the commission of war crimes if that were necessary to avoid defeat in war. For the first of these, lack of restraint was similar for both the enemy and the home country. The level of restraint for war crimes was higher, but there were larger differences between home compared to enemy country.

Although there were differences in degree of restraint expressed by the different samples and the groups also differed in the extent to which they distinguished between home and enemy actions, there was fairly high agreement across all of the samples about which aspects of conflict are deserving of greatest restraint and which least. The results identified some domains, specifically, treatment of soldiers and wanton destruction of civilians, for which some general agreement has been reached. This leads to some optimism that the belief systems may be extended to cover other important domains. Expansion of beliefs is very important because the results show relatively little support for restraint when there is provocation. Since most conflict involves a belief by the participants that they are fighting a just cause, restraints supported in the abstract may easily be set aside. Such disinhibition is suggested by large ingroup–outgroup differences in the data. These investigations are obviously only a beginning.

c. General Conclusions

While there was some support for restraint in conflict for both combatants and noncombatants, there were a number of important principles for which significant support was lacking. Further, there were sometimes large differences between judged obligations of an enemy compared to the home country. The greatest ingroup–outgroup discrepancies occurred among the United States military and the Chinese samples, while the English and Russian students provided the least discrepancy and also the greatest support for restraint

in armed conflict. However, despite the considerable differences in the nature of the samples and cultural background, there was a large amount of intergroup agreement.

VI. FUTURE RESEARCH AND REDUCING THE INTENSITY OF ARMED CONFLICT

A. Quantifying Events

Scientific understanding requires quantification at least at the level of categorization. Humans, however, have achieved far more sophisticated means of identifying their behavior. Thus, in the 20th century there have been attempts not only to continue to discourse about human conflict but to identify and measure specific events including their intensity. However, such quantification is often only a rough approximation of the reality. In some instances, even for the contemporary 20th century, estimates differ by magnitudes of 10 or more. For example, the United States has tallied precisely the number of soldiers killed in battle from enemy fire during the Gulf War. That number is under 200. Estimates of Iraqi deaths, however, range from the untenably low figure of 8,000 to as many as 300,000.

Two additional examples will demonstrate that numbers killed based on historical descriptions are frequently open to question. The Ukrainian famine of 1932–1933 is discussed by Chalk and Johnasson with estimates that 7 million died during the famine and 14.5 million between 1930 and 1937, even though the 1939 census provides a figure that is 3 million below that in 1926. There is no estimate for emigration and census figures outside the famine region are not reported. (During the middle of the 19th century, the Irish potato famine resulted in over a million deaths from starvation but an even greater number emigrated.) Many millions of people are added to the figures based on an assumption of a 2% per year natural increase, but during famine fertility decreases substantially and, in addition, many women die before giving birth. Rummel lists 5 million deaths for the Ukrainian famine. The Gulf War and Ukrainian famine examples indicate that even numbers obtained from relatively recent historical records are difficult to accept at face value. They are even more questionable from earlier eras.

Rummel's work is the most exacting attempt to measure mass deaths from democide, a much broader category than war. His quantitative data are for the period 1900–1987. Almost one-half of the deaths due to democide are attributed to the Stalin reign (over 40 million) and to Chinese communist rule under Mao Tse-Tung (over 30 million). Revisions in these numbers would have a large impact on interpretations.

The imprecision of historical records is further demonstrated in the discussion of democide prior to the 20th century. He reports a total of decreases in population in China during the various dynasties of over 175 million. The total of the decreases is 96 million to the Song Dynasty (960–1270 C.E.) and an additional 86 million in the last reported transition (14 million at the beginning of the Qing Dynasty in 1655). Yet Rummel estimates that during the 21 centuries of Chinese history prior to the 20th, the total due to democide was 34 million. Further, the numbers are obviously inconsistent since the decrease to 7 million in the transition to the Three Kingdom period (222–589 C.E.) is then replaced at the beginning of the Sui Dynasty, which occurred immediately after, by the number 50 million.

Rummel's investigations and quantification represent the most complete effort to obtain information on democide. He explicitly identifies the imprecision of the historical record. The above discussion merely indicates, as Rummel states, that only levels of magnitude can be adduced from the information.

B. The Ingroup–Outgroup Problem

It is clear that the level of conflictual destruction among humans has been great throughout its history. Because of the absence of quantitative data of psychological evaluations, there has been little ability to scientifically determine the relationship of such views to the occurrence or intensity of the events. Therefore, an important basis upon which to develop social engineering that might reduce the levels of conflict is unavailable.

However, even in that absence, sufficient research has been conducted in a number of disciplines to at least partially understand the bases for human destruction. If there is a single key, it is that of ingroup–outgroup distinctions coupled with competition which heightens the psychological distance between groups and increases the likelihood of hostility. The cross-cultural research that has been reported suggests that judgments of home and enemy country obligations are similar with respect to treaties and spying. Levels of conflict might be substantially reduced if attitudes toward treatment of civilians and noncombatants in the ingroup and the outgroup were also similar. Since the historical record demonstrates the difficulty of such achievement, reducing ingroup–outgroup distinctions and socializing large numbers of people to principles of restraint would require social advances beyond those in technology for attaining human travel in space.

Also See the Following Articles

ANTHROPOLOGY OF VIOLENCE AND CONFLICT • COMBAT • COOPERATION, COMPETITION, AND CONFLICT • ENEMY, CONCEPT AND IDENTITY OF • GENOCIDE AND DEMOCIDE • MILITARY CULTURE • WARFARE, TRENDS IN

Bibliography

Axelrod, R. (1984). *The evolution of cooperation.* New York: Basic Books.

Billington, R. A. (1981). *Land of savagery; land of promise.* London: W. W. Norton.

Brunk, G. G., Secrest, D., & Tamashiro, H. (1996). *Understanding attitudes about war: Modeling moral judgments.* Pittsburgh, PA: University of Pittsburgh Press.

Burn, A. R. (1947). *Alexander the Great and the Hellenistic empire.* London: Hodder and Stoughton.

Chalk, F., & Johansson, K. (1990). *The history and sociology of genocide: Analyses and case studies.* New Haven, CT: Yale University Press.

Levy, S. G. (1995). Attitudes toward the conduct of war. *Conflict and Peace: The Journal of Peace Psychology,* 2(2), 179–197.

Roberts, A., & Guelff, R. (Eds.). (1989). *Documents on the laws of war.* Oxford, UK: Clarendon.

Rummel, R. J. (1994). *Death by government.* New Brunswick, NJ: Transaction.

Shalit, B. (1988). *The psychology of conflict and combat.* New York: Praeger.

Shils, E. A., & Janowitz, M. (1948). Cohesion and disintegration in the Wehrmact in World War II. *Public Opinion Quarterly,* 12(2), 280–313.

Stouffer, S. A., Lumsdaine, A. A., Lumsdaine, M. H., Willimas, R. M., Jr., Smith, M. B., Janis, I. L., Star, S. A., & Cottrell, L. S., Jr. (1948). *The American soldier: Combat and its aftermath* (Vol. II). Princeton, NJ: Princeton University Press.

Stouffer, S. A., Suchman, E. A. , DeVinney, L. C., Star, S. A. & Williams, R. M., Jr. (1948). *The American soldier: Adjustment during army life* (Vol. 1). Princeton, NJ: Princeton University Press.

Mass Media and Dissent

George Gerbner

Temple University

Dissent is the life-blood of the democratic process. It is the mark of a plurality of perspectives and a diversity of competing (and sometimes conflicting) interests.

At the same time, however, the right to dissent—although shielded by the First Amendment to the U.S. Constitution—is not unlimited and is always contested. Laws of libel, slander, defamation, and the protections extended to intellectual property are among obvious constraints on expression, including dissent.

But perhaps the principal limitation on political dissent is financial. It has been observed that the current cash-driven electoral system has a chilling effect on the nature and caliber of dissent. Furthermore, the market-driven and highly concentrated and conglomeratized media system has little room for ideological pluralty—and thus dissent. There are no socialist, communist, or religious fundamentalist parties in the American mainstream. And even though the airways belong to the public, they have been largely given away to the same market forces that marginalize dissent in politics.

This marginalization of fundamental dissent in the cultural/political mainstream contributes to the low voter turnout and narrow range of debate where substantive issues are ignored and personalities (not to mention private personal affairs) often dominate.

It is one thing to assure individuals the right to dissent without fear of government regulation or worse. Anyone can find a street corner on which to pontificate. It is another thing to say that any individual has the right to establish a free press to disseminate dissent to a broader audience than could be reached by the spoken word. Moreover, those who own the media are in a position to determine who is empowered to disseminate which dissenting views to the mass public.

The basic argument about political dissent, then, is whether the First Amendment protects the rights of media owners to suppress fundamental dissent regardless of the implications for democracy. The alternative is to view the First Amendment's protection of a free press as a social right to a diverse and uncensored press with ample room for dissent. In this view the right of dissent to be heard is a right enjoyed by all citizens, not just by owners of media. Otherwise there is no more need for its inclusion in the First Amendment than it would be to guarantee individuals the right to establish a baking business or a shoe repair service. As Alexander Meiklejohn points out, those commercial rights are explicitly covered in the Fifth Amendment to the U.S. Constitution.

Modern advertising emerged in the past century and is conducted disproportionately by the largest corporations. This corporate media system has none of the intrinsic interest in politics or journalism that existed in the press of earlier times. If anything, it tends to promote depoliticization. Fundamental political positions are closely linked to elites. Dissent may exist on the margins, but the commercial system assures that these voices have no hope of reaching a mass audience.

There are two solutions to the crisis for democracy generated by a corporate-dominated media system. The most radical is to create a large nonprofit, noncommercial media system accountable to the public. In earlier

Copyright © 1999 by Academic Press.
All rights of reproduction in any form reserved.

times John Dewey and the Hutchins Commission both proposed that newspapers be established as nonprofit and noncommercial enterprises, supported by endowments and universities, and managed through direct public election (or election by the media workers) of their officers.

The less radical solution is to tax the media giants or use public monies to establish a viable nonprofit and noncommercial media system that can serve the needs of citizens who are unable to own media corporations.

Of course, proposals such as these have met with significant corporate opposition and concerns that they would let the government control the media to an unacceptable extent, no matter how the nonprofit media system might be structured. From the Progressive Era to the present day, the corporate media giants have fanned the flames of this sentiment, using their immense resources to popularize the notion that a gulag-style, darkness at noon media system was the only possible alternative to the corporate, commercial status quo. Hence any challenge to their power was a challenge to democracy.

Broadcasting offers the best hope for those who wish to see the public airways committed to democratic media and reasonable opportunities for dissent. All Supreme Court decisions have affirmed the right of the government to regulate broadcasting in a manner that would be judged unconstitutional with the print media.

In the last 1920s and early 1930s, however, the government turned over the best parts of the broadcast spectrum to a handful of private commercial operators. There was no public or congressional debate on the matter. In the 1930s the ACLU was so alarmed by the explicit and implicit censorship in corporate and advertiser control of radio—especially against labor and the left—that it argued that the very system of commercial broadcasting was a violation of the First Amendment. For most of the 1930s the ACLU worked to have the government establish a nonprofit and noncommercial radio system that would foster more coverage of social issues and public affairs and greater opportunities for dissent. The ACLU backed off from this position when it became clear that the corporate power was entrenched and unchallengeable. After abandoning its commitment to structural reform, the ACLU went from being a proponent of regulation of commercial broadcasters in the public interest to being a defender of the commercial system without government interference. Finally, in the 1970s, the courts began to include corporate activities under the First Amendment, thereby eliminating or further weakening government regulation on behalf of an even playing field in the public airways.

Even political advertising is lame and devoid of fundamental dissent. It is commercialized political speech, indistinguishable from product advertising. Hence the content of political advertising generates apathy, cynicism, and mistrust, thereby reinforcing the depoliticizing aspects of the broader political culture.

It would be comforting to think that we could depend on the Supreme Court to reverse this situation. But members of the Court were placed in office by the politicians who benefit from the status quo. The task for advocates of the right and value of vigorous dissent is to make it a key component of a social movement that links electoral reform with media reform. One such movement is the Cultural Environment Movement, founded in 1996, and dedicated to diversity in media ownership, employment, and representation.

Mass Media, General View

Edward Donnerstein and Daniel G. Linz

University of California at Santa Barbara

GLOSSARY

Arousal Effects Emotional reactions, often accompanied by measurable physiological responses.

Critical Viewing Skills Curricula designed to teach individuals to recognize certain types of negative portrayals of social behavior in the media and to provide them with alternative ways of interpreting these portrayals.

Desensitization Effects Reductions in physiological and emotional arousal in the face of violence.

Fear Effects Learning about violence in the news and in fictional programming may lead to the belief that the world is generally a scary and dangerous place.

Mass Communication A process in which professional communicators use media to disseminate messages widely, rapidly, and continuously to arouse intended meanings in large and diverse audiences in attempts to influence them in a variety of ways.

Media Effect How an audience is changed or influenced by the mass media.

Media Violence Any overt depiction of a credible threat of physical force or the actual use of such force intended to physically harm an animate being or group of beings. Violence also includes certain depictions of physically harmful consequences against an animate being or group that occur as a result of unseen violent means.

Intended Media Effects Deliberate attempts on the part of the communicator to influence the recipient in some way.

Unintended Media Effects Media presentations which were designed for purposes other than to exert social influence, usually to entertain.

THE MAJOR SOCIAL FUNCTION of the mass media is to influence viewers' or listeners' cognitions, attitudes, or behaviors in some desired direction. Our world is most often comprised of these intended effects—deliberate attempts on the part of the communicator to influence the recipient in some way. The most

Copyright © 1999 by Academic Press.
All rights of reproduction in any form reserved.

obvious of these attempts at exerting social influence through the mass media is commercial advertising and adjunct activities such as political campaign messages and public service announcements. Other media presentations are designed not to persuade or convince but for other purposes, usually to entertain. Often, however, there are unintended effects from this entertainment. The one which has received the most attention is the media's influence on violent behavior. This article will present a general overview of the mass media and its effects, with a particular emphasis on violence.

I. WHAT WE THINK ABOUT THE MASS MEDIA?

American culture, particularly its mass media, is a useful and powerful resource. Although certain aspects are unattractive to some, American popular culture, embodied in products and communication, has widespread appeal. This is especially true in the field of mass media, where the acceleration of communication technology has led to declining costs in global markets. According to past studies by the United Nations Educational, Scientific, and Cultural Organization, the U.S. has been exporting about seven times as many television shows as the next largest exporter (Britain) and has had the only global network for film distribution. Although American films account for only 6 to 7% of all films made, they occupy about 50% of world screen time and a total distribution of approximately 80% of the world's films. In dominating the popular channels of communication, the United States has had more opportunities to get its messages across and to effect the preferences of others.

As satellite television brings films and programs into the homes of millions around the world, there will continue to be the concern noted by James Ferman, Director of the British Board of Film Classification: "There will always be some who feel that the values of their own regional culture are under threat from works which represent not the best but the worst which other cultures have to offer".

The concern raised by many in these countries is violence (the topic of this encyclopedia), its predominance in American mass media (particularly in film and television), and its potential impact on viewers. For instance, the Swedish Film Board recently refused a certificate for the motion picture "Casino" unless a certain scene containing extensive graphic violence was heavily censored. The British Film Board also has a long history of censoring violence in motion pictures that

it feels is excessively graphic, sadistic, or brutalizing. Furthermore cross-national research on public perceptions of media violence conducted in the U.S. and Great Britain has revealed that although public opinion regarding media violence is extremely complex, significant sections of both populations expressed concern about violent depictions that were considered very cruel or brutal.

A recent international survey of adult viewers in seven countries (see Table I) indicated that foreign viewers of American media are highly concerned about violent as opposed to sexual content. Public opinion data suggests that the adult Americans are likewise very concerned about the amount of violence on television and in the movies and are convinced that media violence can lead to negative effects. When asked if media violence is harmful to society, 80% believed that it was, with 47% labeling media violence as "very harmful"— double the percentage of the late 1980s. Likewise, while in the late 1970s 53% of those polled believed that media violence "desensitizes" people to actual violence, by 1993 this figure has grown to 78%. In a poll for Time/CNN, respondents were asked to speculate on the effects of depictions of violence in movies, television shows, and popular music. Seventy-six percent of the American public said that these depictions numb people to violence to the point that they are insensitive to it. Seventy-five percent said that the depiction of violence inspires young people to violence and 71% said that at the very least these depictions tell people that violence is fun and acceptable.

At least with respect to American society, media violence is not equally unacceptable to all viewers, however. A 1995 Times Mirror poll showed a pronounced generation gap in tolerance for violence. Violence is much more popular among young adults. Those under 30 are far more likely to be heavy consumers of violent

TABLE I

Percentage of Adults Objecting to US Films and TV

Country	Too much sex	Too much violence
Canada	16	45
France	8	49
Germany	19	58
Italy	15	47
Mexico	46	45
Spain	11	51
Britain	12	38

programming and movies. Seventy-four percent of those under 30 reported heavy consumption of violence, and 50% of the 30- to 49-year-olds fell into that category. Younger adults also report being far less bothered by violence on television and are less likely to feel that violence is harmful to society than are older Americans. Adolescents are also less prone to believe that televised violence is itself a cause of real-life violence.

This debate about the impact of the mass media on viewers is not new. For decades, there has been a genuine concern about the antisocial effects that can occur from exposure to the mass media, in particular to violence. In the next section we examine what we mean by mass communication and the general view of what types of effects are possible from exposure.

II. WHAT IS MASS COMMUNICATION?

DeFleur and Dennis offer a useful definition: "Mass communication is a process in which professional communicators use media to disseminate messages widely, rapidly, and continuously to arouse intended meanings in large and diverse audiences in attempts to influence them in a variety of ways".

DeFleur and Dennis consider mass communication to be an ongoing process with five distinct stages. In the first stage, professional communicators first create various types of *messages* for presentation to assorted individuals for diverse purposes. These messages are disseminated in the second stage in a *quick and continuous* manner through some form of mechanical media (e.g., film or television). In stage 3, this message eventually reaches a *vast* and diverse (i.e., mass) audience. In the fourth stage the audience somehow *interprets* these messages and gives them a meaning. This response from the audience is considered to be the *communication* part of the definition, since it implies some form of reciprocity between sender and receiver. Last, as a result of all the above, the audience is *influenced* or *changed* in some manner. In other words, there is a mass media effect.

How an audience is changed or influenced by the mass media, the fifth of the above stages, has been the focus of research for decades and is the major interest of this article. In fact, most research on mass communication has been the study of effects. This is not to say that researchers and others have not been interested in other aspects of the mass media, such as studying the characteristics of the vast and diverse audiences attracted to mass media or the cognitive and emotional

processes that may influence how we interpret mass media messages and give them a meaning. It is the process giving rise to effects, however, that is central to our discussion.

III. HOW ARE WE INFLUENCED BY THE MASS MEDIA?

In thinking of mass media effects, we should be cognizant of what have been termed *intended and unintended influences*. According to McGuire, the major social function of the mass media is to influence the receiver's cognitions, attitudes, or behaviors in some desired direction. Most often the world of mass media is comprised of intended effects, deliberate attempts on the part of the communicator to influence the recipient in some way. While there are many potential types of intended effects, six have been most frequently studied by mass communication scholars.

The two most widely acknowledged are commercial advertising and political campaigns. In addition there are public service announcements and multimedia campaigns to change lifestyles, such as in the areas of AIDS awareness, smoking, drug use, and other socially relevant issues. A fifth intended effect has been termed massive, monolithic, indoctrination effects on ideology. It is possible for some totalitarian governments to control nearly all aspects of the mass media. Government officials believe that by controlling the media the government can ensure loyalty of its people to the government ideology. Last, there has been the study of mass-mediated rituals in social control. Such mass media events as the World Series, the SuperBowl, and the Olympics are said to have particular affects on a region because of the community's symbolic participation in a ritualistic event. The large street demonstrations, parades, friendly drinking with strangers, and other festivities accompanying these sports media extravaganzas would imply some form of media influence. Likewise, media events like the showing of the film "Schindler's List" have been considered by media scholars as a means of unified viewing of certain mass media presentations, which can affect viewers' attitudes and perceptions.

There are often media events that are not planned by broadcasters, like an assassination of a major governmental official, or natural disasters, which result in mass viewer reactions. These unexpected viewer reactions represent the second kind of media effect discussed by McGuire. When we consider unintended media effects we are referring to what McGuire defines as media presentations that were designed for purposes other than to exert social influence, usually to entertain. While the eventual reaction from the audience may be one approaching antisocial behavior, the original creator of the media presentation never intended viewers to react in that fashion. There are a number of research areas that are central to our discussion that are part to these *unintended* media influences.

The first is televised violence and viewers' aggression. Perhaps no other area has received as much research attention as the effects of televised violence. As we noted earlier, media scholars, concerned citizens, congressional panels, and others have debated whether exposure to violence in the media leads to later aggressive behavior on the part of the viewers. A second major area has been misrepresentation effects on viewer stereotypes. Certain minority groups are often portrayed as perpetrators of violence, reinforcing negative stereotypes among viewers. Likewise, consistently showing women as being victimized by strangers outside the home leaves one with a false impression of the true realities of violence against women.

Another area of considerable research has been the effects of erotica and pornography on sexual thoughts, feelings, and behaviors. Can the viewing of sexually explicit movies and magazines, particularly those fused with violence, lead to rape and other forms of sexual violence? As with the subject of televised violence and its possible effects, researchers and policy-makers have been concerned with the potential effects of viewing sexually explicit materials for many years, particularly today with the increasing access to Internet images.

Finally there is the effect of new forms of mass media on thought processes and behaviors. For some of us, it might be hard to visualize a community without television. But such communities do exist. Tannis Williams, along with other researchers in Canada, found such a community and were able to examine what changes occurred to individuals and their community as a whole *after* the introduction of television. To what degree did the introduction of television change behaviors, cognitive development, and leisure activities in the community? Two years after the introduction of television, children who previously had no access to this type of mass media showed reductions in cognitive skills like reading and creativity, as well as reduced leisure activities with the family. Furthermore, there was evidence for an increase in aggressive behaviors.

While in years past the concerns were with television and film, today they are with newer technologies like video games, virtual reality, and the Internet. Nevertheless, intended or unintended, there is a general agreement among media researchers that the media do have an influence on its viewers. However, these effects undoubtedly differ from person to person. Just as importantly, effects can differ within each individual.

For some reason when we think about how the media influence people, we tend to do so most often in terms of observable behavior. For many, and in particular policy-makers, behavioral markers are thought of as the most powerful of media effects. After all, if we are concerned about televised violence shouldn't our concern be with changes in actual aggressive behavior? However, there are other avenues by which the media can impart its influence. The changing or reinforcing of one's attitude to violence is also a mass media influence. Likewise we can think of cognitive effects. Learning a fact from the mass media is the most straightforward type of cognitive effect. Obviously, television programs devoted to informing and educating viewers to the harmful effects of violence, such as a public service announcement, provide us with new facts we never would have known had we not tuned in. And of course, there are emotional reactions, often accompanied by some physiological reaction, which are also media effects. Some effects (like crying during a sad scene) we are readily aware of, but others (like an increase in blood pressure) might not be accessible at a conscious level. For some mass media theorists, excitement and its accompanying physiological arousal are indispensable components in explaining the relationship between media exposure and behavior.

IV. ISSUES TO CONSIDER ABOUT MEDIA EFFECTS

There remain several important questions that we need to raise in order to refine our understanding of mass media effects. These are questions that have often puzzled policy-makers, academics, and students of mass media effects for decades. First, how long does it take for the mass media to have an effect? For some effects, like physiological or emotional changes in a viewer or listener after exposure to a mass media depiction, we might expect almost immediate results. For other media influences the time interval will increase from minutes, to days, to months and even years. Are we concerned about a particular violent film or is cumulative viewing of violence over many years the issue?

Another temporal question that arises frequently concerns the duration of the effect. How long does physiological arousal last after exposure to a frightening or sexual film? Do most effects wax and wane over time and are they in constant need of a new infusion of new media exposure? For physiological arousal, the answer would be that the effect may last for only a few minutes and additional media exposure would be required to keep arousal high. For behaviors like aggression, however, the effect can last a lifetime. We should keep in mind that although it might appear that a particular media effect has vanished, or is short lived, it can appear sometime in the future. Media messages can be stored in memory for long periods of time and are reactivated later when conditions are suitable.

A second issue often raised is what type of content, shown in which context, produces effects? The content of most mass media messages is complex. All types of violent materials do not facilitate aggressive behavior. Violent content that is gratuitous, arousing, or sexual in nature is more likely to affect the viewer than other types of violent content. The context in which the message is received is important also. There are several contextual variables that may alter mass media exposure outcomes. One such context variable concerns the number of times people are exposed to a given message. For example we may ask of many study outcomes: Does the effect occur after a single exposure or does the effect depend on multiple exposures?

Third, there is the issue of exactly *who* is affected by the mass media. We can conceive of influences ranging from individuals to whole societies. Just as individuals will react differently to the mass media, as noted above, various subgroups within the population will also vary (e.g., children, elderly, the well educated). There has been a tradition in mass media research to emphasize the "micro" level or an individual unit of analysis. Yet, as students of the mass media we are well aware of the more "macro" level in which the media can have its influence on various groups in our society. This might entail not only the study of how small groups of people are influenced by the mass media but how entire communities and societies are affected.

Finally, we need to note that the mass media may facilitate two types of changes in attitudes and behaviors and feelings—*small changes in a large number of individuals* (such as a slight inclination for many viewers to be more accepting of violence against women after exposure to violent pornography) or *larger, more profound changes in a very small group of people* (actually raping a woman after exposure to a sexually violent film). In the latter example, only a small subgroup of the population are actually affected by the mass media but in a powerful way. In the former, many people are affected and in this sense the effect is powerful because

many people are involved but most people are affected in a small, limited, subtle way.

Changing people is not an easy thing to do. For example, it is unlikely that most people who have been socialized to have nonviolent values will be altered by exposure to violent pornography that portrays the myth that women enjoy sexual assault. However, for a small number of people the effect may be dramatic. It must be kept in mind that even if 1 or 2% of the people who view, listen, or read a certain message are affected by it in a strong way, this could translate into a very large effect for society. Any one message may have millions of viewers and listeners. A fraction of 1% of the viewing audience may include thousands of people. Thousands of children behaving more aggressively on the school playground because of exposure to a violent program on television the night before may have a dramatically negative effect on our society.

Policy-makers and government officials are concerned about both types of effects although they are most often alarmed by a dramatic effect limited to a few individuals. The effects that occur from viewing violence in the mass media are powerful but limited. The research shows that mass media is but one of many causes of aggression and that not everyone is affected in the same manner.

Rather than a "magic bullet" we must realize that under appropriate conditions televised violence could be a powerful contributor to violent behavior, but if conditions were not right few effects would occur. For complex behaviors such as crime to occur message factors, situational factors, and the characteristics of the individual must all interact to produce an effect. The probability that all of these factors will come together is relatively small. But even if the probability of such message, situation, and person combinations is 1 in a 1000 the outcome may be startling. Millions of people are exposed to mass media violence; as a result we might expect literally hundreds of additional violent crimes including rape and murder as a result of exposure to violence.

V. VIOLENCE: THE MAJOR CONCERN OF EXPOSURE TO THE MASS MEDIA

As we have noted a number of times, the influence of the mass media on aggressive behavior has been the predominate concern of individuals for decades. In this section we briefly examine this influence. However, first we need to define what we mean by aggression.

A. Defining Violence in the Media

In the late 1970s a leading researcher in the field of interpersonal aggression, Robert Baron, offered a relatively simple definition of that activity that is still acceptable to most social scientists and implicit in most research on the effects of media violence we discuss. Baron defines aggression as any form of behavior directed toward the goal of harming or injuring another living being who is motivated to avoid such treatment. This definition includes the notion that to be objectively defined, aggression, in the media or in any form of social interaction, must be some sort of goal-directed or purposeful behavior. It assumes that people are motivated to avoid it on the individual level or to devise sanctions at the group level to prohibit it. Intentionality is critical in order to exclude many harmful behaviors that are not reasonably considered violent. Without the vital concept of intention to harm, all accidental harms would be included as violence, including actions of surgeons or dentists. Accepting Baron's definition with its emphasis on intention to harm as a core feature and incorporating other features offered by mass media scholars, a recent definition of media violence has been suggested which is as follows: Any overt depiction of a credible threat of physical force or the actual use of such force intended to physically harm an animate being or group of beings. Violence also includes certain depictions of physically harmful consequences against an animate being or group that occur as a result of unseen violent means. Thus, there are three primary types of violent depictions: credible threats, behavioral acts, and harmful consequences.

There are several features of this definition that merit attention. First, it takes account of the fact that potential perpetrators of violence often try to harm but are unsuccessful. It is important to not exclude acts that attempt to cause harm but that prove unsuccessful. Such acts are clearly aggressive. Second, the definition recognizes that the consequences of violence are often present without the perpetrator or behavior actually being shown and this should be considered as violence. This would include violent actions that are not portrayed overtly but can be inferred clearly from the depiction of the harmful consequences (e.g., the police respond to the scene of a shooting and find a victim bleeding to death). Third, this definition specifies that animate beings must be the perpetrators or targets of violence. Harm can be caused to individuals by many forces other than those of living beings, such as acts of nature like a tornado or a lightning bolt. Consistent with the previ-

ous point that intention to harm is a fundamental aspect of the definition of violence, these authors have emphasized that at least one animate being capable of possessing intentions must be involved as a perpetrator in order to have an instance of violence. Similarly, an animate being must be a target in order to meet this definition of violence. Fourth, the definition takes note of the fact that the television world is inhabited by a wide range of creatures not all of whom occur naturally on earth. These include everything from "Smurfs" to "Teenage Mutant Ninja Turtles" to "Biker Mice from Mars," to name a few children's program characters, to beings from other planets such as "Superman" or "Alf." All are anthropomorphized beings that may perpetrate violence although these types of characters influence on the audience is not always equivalent to a more traditional human form.

Most of the effects of exposure to media violence are accounted for in this definition. These effects can be broken down to increased aggressive behaviors, fearfulness, or desensitization to violence. Each of the components of the definition make sense in light of these effects. For example, it is important to not exclude acts that attempt to cause harm but that prove unsuccessful; these credible threats of physical harm must be considered violent because, just as with a harmful act, they too will generally contribute to a fear response in the audience as well as to increased priming of aggressive thoughts that contribute to violent behavior. Violent actions that are not portrayed overtly but can be clearly inferred from harmful consequences should also be considered because of their likelihood of contributing to antisocial effects such as fear and desensitization.

Even the definition's specification that animate beings must be the perpetrators or targets of violence is both logically consistent with the focus on intentions and with the research literature on the effects of exposure to violence. Harm can be caused to individuals by many forces other than those of living beings. Although these actions might contribute to fear on the part of some viewers, in particular in young children, they would not raise concerns in terms of socialization or modeling of aggression. Similarly, an animate being must be a target in order to meet this definition of violence. Individuals often hit or kick inanimate objects in an aggressive fashion; sometimes this reflects spontaneous anger and other times a premeditated intention to damage a target's possession. The research evidence documenting antisocial effects of violence against living beings is compelling, while no comparable evidence exists regarding the impacts of violence against inanimate objects.

The definition does limit violence to physical acts. This is because physical harm or the threat thereof is at the root of all conceptions of violence and most of the operationalizations of the concept in past research. One might reasonably assert that verbal assaults that intimidate or physical acts that are meant to cause psychological or emotional harm should be considered as violence. Certainly such actions are aggressive and may in some cases be associated with antisocial impacts on the audience. However, the research is much less clear on this matter.

VI. WHAT TYPES OF VIOLENCE EXIST IN THE MASS MEDIA?

Surveys indicate that nearly 98% of American households have a television and many have more than one set. Within these homes, 2- to 11-year-olds have the TV set on for approximately 28 h a week and 13- to 19-year-olds for roughly 23 h a week. These patterns have been found consistently over many years of research. It is now widely known that television viewing occupies more time than any other nonschool activity. Furthermore, among children, it accounts for more than half of all their leisure activities. In addition, Black and Latino children have been found to view more television independent of their level of social economic status and many of the poorest and potentially most vulnerable groups in society are the heaviest viewers of television.

If children watch an average 2 to 4 h of television per day, how much violence are they being exposed to? Research indicates that by the time a child leaves elementary school, he/she will have seen approximately 8,000 murders and more than 100,000 other acts of violence. Near the end of their teenage years, they will have witnessed over 200,000 violent acts on television. These figures will be significantly higher if the child has access to cable programming or to violent films he/she can rent and watch on a VCR.

Numerous content analyses have assessed the amount and types of violent portrayals that are featured on television programming. For example, one study indicates that there are approximately 5 to 6 violent acts per hour on prime-time television and 20 to 25 acts on Saturday morning children's fare. Within the United States, this accounts for approximately 188 h of violent programming per week or about 15% of program

time. In addition to broadcast television, cable TV adds to the level of violence through new, more violent programs, and by recycling older violent broadcasts. One survey identified 1,846 violent scenes on broadcast and cable between 6 A.M. and midnight across 1 day of programming. The most violent periods were between 6 A.M. and 9 A.M. (i.e., 497 violent scenes identified) and between 2 P.M. and 5 P.M. (i.e., 609 violent scenes identified). Clearly, most of the violence was aired when children were most likely to be in the viewing audience. In addition to frequency, this study also assessed the different types of violence that were portrayed. Serious assaults accounted for 20% of the violence and 18% was accounted for by gunplay.

Now that television content has expanded to include R-rated movies, another related concern surrounds the types of characters that are being victimized by violence. A content analysis has revealed that in popular R-rated "horror" films, women are killed at a ratio of almost 3 to 1 compared to prime-time television and 2 to 1 compared to other R-rated films. In addition, there is an association in these films of sexual content with the victimization of females. The analyses showed that 33% of occurrences of sex were connected to violence (male or female). Fourteen percent of all sex incidents were linked to a death of a female. Further, nearly 22% of all innocent female protagonists were killed during or following a sexual display or act. These findings are important to note given the presence of cable and satellite TV, which has allowed even young children to view R-rated films on television.

Perhaps surprisingly, the level of violence on *broadcast* television has remained relatively constant since the late 1970s. The rates for cable television, however, have not yet been systematically studied. In 1994 the National Cable Television Association agreed to monitor violence on both cable and broadcast networks for 3 consecutive years. The results of the first 2 years of this study have been released, covering the television environment from 1994 to 1996. This study examined cable and broadcast television in a manner different from all other content analyses of television violence. The investigation had two primary goals: (1) to identify the contextual features associated with violent depictions that most significantly increase the risk of a harmful effect on the audience and (2) to analyze the television environment in depth in order to report on the nature and extent of violent depictions, focusing in particular on the relative presence of the most problematic portrayals.

In this study, violence was defined as an overt depiction of physical force, or the credible threat of such force, intended to physically harm an animate being or group of beings. Violence also included certain depictions of physically harmful consequences against an animate being or group of beings that occur as a result of unseen violent means. This was the definition provided earlier in this article. The study analyzed content at three distinct levels: a violent interaction, a violent scene, and the overall program. At each level, specific contextual measures were assessed.

The researchers randomly selected programs from 23 broadcast and cable television channels over a 20-week period of time ranging from October of 1994 to June of 1996 within the United States. Thus, a composite week of television content was compiled for each programming source for each of 2 years. Programs were selected between the hours of 6:00 A.M. and 11:00 P.M. across all 7 days of the week, yielding a sum of approximately 119 h per channel. In total then, this project examined approximately 5000 h of television programming. This is the largest and most representative sample of television content ever assembled and assessed in the history of social science research.

The results from this study indicated that a majority of the programs analyzed contained violence (57%). Premium cable was more likely to contain violence, whereas the broadcast networks and particularly public broadcasting were less likely. The majority of perpetrators and targets of violence were adult, white, and male. In 25% of all violent interactions, guns were used. Violence was rarely punished in the immediate or following scene. When it was punished, however, it was usually directed toward "bad" characters at the end of the program. In terms of the consequences of violence, it was found that: (1) roughly half of all violent interactions on television feature no observable harm or pain to the victim, (2) children's series contain the highest percentages of interactions involving unrealistic levels of harm, and (3) only 16% of all violent programs depict the long-term negative consequences of violence.

As we have seen, a majority of television programs in America are filled with images of violence and aggression. This has been documented across several different content analyses of both broadcast and cable programming. As we know, many of these programs reach viewers in many countries around the world. Studies have also shown that violence and sex are often presented concurrently in horror or "slasher" films featured on cable programming. One cannot help but inquire, "What types of effects do such portrayals have on children, adolescents, and adults?" The answer to this question is the focus of the next sections.

VII. CURRENT SOCIAL SCIENTIFIC VIEWS ON MEDIA VIOLENCE AND AGGRESSIVE BEHAVIOR

In our discussion of definitions of violence above we alluded to several effects. These effects can be more formally grouped into three major classes of outcomes stemming from exposure to media violence: (1) increases in aggressive behavior, (2) increases in fear, and (3) desensitization.

When most of us think about how the media influence us, and others, it is often in terms of some observable behavior. Your younger brother sees a character on a television cartoon show throw a chair at another character and immediately imitates the act, throwing a chair at the cat. For many, in particular policy-makers, behavioral markers are thought of as the most powerful of media effects. Indications of behavioral effects from mass media exposure to violence have been researched and often it is these findings that have the most important policy implications. Yet, direct behavioral reactions to media events, particularly antisocial reactions, may be relatively infrequent responses. It is often a person's exposure to mass media in combination with some other important characteristic of the individual or the situation that leads to a behavioral response. Relatively few people will become aggressive following exposure to violence unless the conditions are right. However, there are other avenues by which the media can impart its influence on behavior. Generally, behavioral reactions are mediated through mental structures such as attitudes about violence.

A. Attitudes and Behavior

The relationship between attitudes about violence and aggressive behavior can be illustrated by the following example. In the long-running daytime soap opera "General Hospital", one of the male characters, Luke, raped his girlfriend, Laura. A few weeks later Laura was shown responding favorably to Luke and eventually the two married in the series. Until recently, this was an all-too-typical portrayal of rape in the mass media—the victim is shown to have a positive reaction to sexual assault. This type of portrayal has been studied by media researchers such as Neil Malamuth who have hypothesized that viewing such "positive outcome" sexual assault scenes could influence viewers' attitudes about rape.

Malamuth did not predict that the viewing positive outcome rape scenes would directly cause someone to *behave* in a sexually aggressive manner—he realized that for a sexually violent behavior to be enacted many factors about the message and person viewing it would have to be just right. Instead, he predicted that viewing such materials may lead most men to be more accepting of a certain attitude about women, namely more accepting of myths about rape, such as the myth that women are secretly turned on by force and desire or enjoy being victims of sexual violence.

These are mass media effects about which many people are concerned. They are just not behavioral effects. These effects are important in their own right because no one would argue that increases in a man's belief that women want to be raped is trivial—this belief may lead to any number of effects short of violence, such as greater tolerance for rape in our society or the communication of an insensitive attitude toward rape to younger, more impressionable males who might be likely to engage in sexual assault.

The attitudinal effect is also important because attitudes such as greater acceptance of rape myths are often the precursors to behavioral effects for some people. Malamuth has been able to show that a person who possesses this attitude in conjunction with certain others is more likely to have engaged in aggression against women than men who do not have these attitudes. This same principal also holds for other attitudes and behaviors.

B. Media Violence and Crime

One significant debate in the area of media violence and aggressive behavior is whether such exposure can influence "real-world" aggression rather than behaviors observed in the laboratory. In order to adequately examine such a relationship investigators must rely on non-experimental field methods such as longitudinal studies, comparative national studies, or attempts to compare the cooccurrence of media broadcasts with the onset of violence. Three research projects employing these techniques have been undertaken. Taken together, these studies strongly suggest that exposure to media violence is a causal factor in antisocial behavior.

1. South African, Canadian, U.S. Comparison Study

Centerwall notes that South Africans have lived in a fully modern state for decades with one exception—they had no television until 1975. Tensions between Afrikaner- and English-speaking communities concerning programming content stalled the introduction of TV for years. In fact, for 25 years approximately 2

million White South Africans were excluded from exposure to television. The medium was introduced in the United States 25 years earlier. Television was introduced to Canada a few years after the U.S.

In order to test whether exposure to television is a cause of violence Centerwall compared homicide rates in South Africa, Canada, and the United States. Since Blacks in South Africa live under different conditions than Blacks in the United States, he limited his comparisons to White homicide rates in both these countries and the total homicide rate in Canada (which was 97% White in 1951). The homicide rate was chosen as a measure of violence because homicide statistics are extremely accurate. From 1945 to 1974, the White homicide rate in the United States increased 93%. In Canada, the homicide rate increased 92%. In South Africa, where television was banned, the White homicide rate declined by 7%.

Centerwall examined several other factors that could possibly explain the fact that violence increased in the U.S. and Canada but not in South Africa. Many of the more obvious explanations could be ruled out. He argues that economic growth cannot account for the murder rate growth. All three countries experienced significant economic growth between 1946 and 1974 (Canada, 124%; U.S., 75%; South Africa, 86%). Civil unrest such as antiwar and civil rights activity cannot be an explanation because the homicide rate in Canada also doubled without similar civil unrest. Other possible explanations include changes in age distribution, urbanization, alcohol consumption, capital punishment, and the availability of firearms. None of these provides a viable explanation for the observed homicide trends. The only appreciable difference among the three countries was the absence of television in South Africa.

Centerwall found a 10- to 15-year lag between the introduction of television and the subsequent increase in homicide rates in the United States and Canada. He attributes this time lag to the fact that television exerts its behavior-modifying effects primarily on children. Since homicide is primarily an adult activity, the lag represents the time needed for the "television generation" to come of age.

The relationship between television and the homicide rate holds within the United States as well. Different regions of the U.S. acquired television at different times. The regions that acquired television first were also first to see higher homicide rates. Urban areas acquired television before rural areas. As expected, urban areas saw increased homicide rates several years before the occurrence of a parallel increase in rural areas. White households in the U.S. acquired television sets approximately 5 years before minority households. The White homicide rate began increasing in 1958, 4 years before a parallel increase in the minority homicide rate.

The epidemiological approach used by Centerwall can be criticized. He can only measure the onset of television as a whole in the societies he studies. He has no measure of exposure to television content, specifically violent content. His research can only suggest that with television comes violent crime. There is no theory of media and behavior that would predict that merely owning a television will lead to violent behavior. Most theories, as we note below, emphasize exposure to violent programming as a causal factor in the development of violent habits. It could be argued that TV programming contains many violent depictions and that those who later engaged in violence must have been exposed to this content over the years. Centerwall has no evidence that this is the case, however. To be more convincing, Centerwall must either develop a theoretical explanation for why television itself, independent of content causes violence, or, more reliably, establish the link between those who have committed murder and the type of TV content they have been exposed to.

Finally, a critical test of Centerwall's thesis would be increases in White homicide rates in South Africa in the 1990s. If Centerwall's ideas are correct we should observe a doubling in homicide rates by that time. Unfortunately, the recent political changes in South African society may preclude us from ever knowing the answer to this question. However, Centerwall has found that as of 1983 the White South African homicide rate had reached 3.9 homicide deaths per 100,000—an annual rate greater than any observed in the pretelevision years, 1945–1974, the last year before television was introduced. In contrast, Canadian and American homicide rates did not increase between 1974 and 1983.

2. Publicized Media Events and Real-World Violence

Another approach to understanding TV violence and crime is to compare the rates of criminal violence with the onset of the TV events. Research by Phillips and his associates provides some initial evidence for a stable empirical relationship between highly publicized media events and the facilitation of real-world violence.

Phillips examined the patterns of over 140,000 U.S. homicides from 1973 to 1979 before and after publicity about prizefights, murder acquittals, life sentences, and executions. Regression analyses were used to measure the change in homicides while controlling for fluctuations due to day of week, month, and year and the effects of holidays. The researchers found that the number of homicides showed a significant increase several days after the fight—a finding replicated in other research. They also found evidence of an inhibition effect. The number of homicides taking place after publicized stories about death sentences, life sentences, and executions was lower several days following these events.

One of the more compelling features of the Phillip's research is the match between the content of the media events and the patterns of violence observed later. Studies of mass media imitative effects in the laboratory have shown that a violent media portrayal is most likely to be imitated if the violence is real, exciting, rewarded, justified, and intended to injure and if the perpetrator identifies with the character who uses aggression successfully in the media event. Thus, findings that the number of homicides taking place after death sentences and life sentences decreased while the rates remained unchanged following acquittals can be predicted from knowledge of the content of the publicized event. Similarly, Phillips found that the number of homicide victims increased in the population of the race of the defeated prizefighter.

3. The 22-Year New York State Studies

Both the Centerwall study and the Phillips studies are archival studies. These inquiries have detected relationships between two sets of events, television ownership and crime and the media depictions and criminal activity. The first longitudinal study to examine the long-term effects of television violence on aggressive and criminal behavior in individuals was a 22-year study of youths in Columbia County, New York. This study, when begun in 1960, was intended primarily to assess the prevalence of aggression in the general population. Originally, the researchers were interested in aggression as a form of psychopathology and how it related to other child, family, and environmental variables. The television viewing habits of the children were studied somewhat as an afterthought.

The researchers examined the entire third grade population of Columbia County, New York (public and private schools) in 1960—875 children. Children were first questioned and tested in classrooms. Their mothers and fathers were also interviewed. Ten years later in 1970 the investigators located 735 of the original subjects and interviewed 427 of them. Twenty-two years later in 1982 the investigators reinterviewed 409 of the original subjects again and collected criminal justice data on 632 of the original subjects.

In the first wave the investigators found that 8-year-old boys' aggression as determined from peer-nominations was very significantly correlated with the violence ratings of their favorite TV shows that they watched most often as reported by their mothers. However, there was no relationship between girls' aggression and preference for violent television shows. In the second wave of the study, 10 years later, the researchers did not find any evidence of a relation between an 18-year-old's television viewing habits and aggressive behavior either for girls or boys. However, the investigators did find that boys' preferences for more violent shows assessed 10 years earlier when they had been in 3rd grade were predictive of how aggressively they behaved now that they were 18. The investigators conducted an extensive set of longitudinal regression and structural equation modeling analyses that led them to conclude that it was likely that early exposure to television violence was stimulating the later aggression. Their analysis showed that aggressive habits are moderately stable over time while television viewing habits are not.

In the third wave of data, collected when the subjects were on average 30 years old, the investigators also found no relation between these males' current television viewing habits and any current aggressive or antisocial behavior. However, the researchers again found evidence of a longitudinal effect, this time one that spanned the 22 years from age 8 to age 30. For boys, early television violence viewing correlated with self-reported aggression at age 30 (especially aggression under the influence of alcohol) and added a significant increment to the prediction of seriousness of criminal arrests accumulated by age 30 (as recorded by New York State). These effects occurred independent of social class, intellectual functioning, and parenting variables. These researchers have concluded that early exposure to television violence stimulates aggression over several years, and early aggression is a statistical precursor of later criminal behavior leading to the longitudinal relation from habitual childhood exposure to television violence to adult crime. Their analyses suggest that approximately 10% of the variability in later criminal behavior can be attributed to television violence.

VIII. FEAR: THE MEDIA AND BELIEFS ABOUT A SCARY WORLD

We turn on the news tonight and hear about a gang-related shooting in our community. We have just learned a fact about our community—someone has been shot. Learning a fact from the mass media is a straightforward cognitive effect. Fear may result from these learning experiences. One of the most important

mass media effects might be audience conceptions of the social reality. The media are able to determine what we think about when we think about our social world. It communicates the facts, norms, and values of our society through selective presentations of social events. For many people television is the main source of information about critical aspects of their social environments. Learning about violence in the news and in fictional programming may lead to the belief that the world is generally a scary and dangerous place.

For children the effect may not be so general—that is, they may not believe that the world, overall, is dangerous, but their reactions may be more specific and urgent. Fright reactions to monsters and violent creatures can be immediate and dramatic. The child may scream or hide her face in her hands. Later, nightmares and recurring thoughts may keep both children and parents awake at night.

IX. AROUSAL AND DESENSITIZATION

How often have you nearly jumped out of your seat, startled by the sudden appearance of the killer in a horror film? These emotional reactions, often accompanied by a measurable physiological response, are among the most important media effects. Some effects, like crying during a sad scene we are readily aware of, but others, like an increase in blood pressure, might not be accessible at a conscious level. For some mass media theorists, excitement and its accompanying physiological arousal is an indispensable component in explaining the relationship between media exposure and behavior. Zillmann believes that people are drawn to some forms of mass media entertainment such as depictions of blood and gore primarily because of the excitement it generates in us.

Researchers have also examined desensitization effects—reductions in physiological and emotional arousal in the face of violence. Research has shown that repeated exposure to mass media violence leads to a diminished emotional (physiological) response. This callousness may "spill over" to evaluations of victims of real violence.

X. MITIGATING THE IMPACT OF VIOLENT MASS MEDIA

The American public, as well as many other people worldwide, appear to be stuck with violence in the media, at least for the time being. Lawmakers who have concluded that media violence is causally related to real-life aggression admit that the best way to protect the media industry from the heavy hand of government is to exercise self-restraint.

Despite the proliferation of bills to limit violence in the media in the United States Congress, the American public, perhaps surprisingly, is also not convinced that censorship is the best policy despite the majority opinion that media violence is potentially harmful. When Americans are asked how much responsibility should various groups have in reducing the amount of sex and violence in entertainment, most responsibility is assigned to consumers who buy, watch, or listen to this entertainment.

Rather than advocating censorship some educators and social scientists have urged that the effects of viewing violence in the media can be mitigated through the teaching of "critical viewing skills" by parents and in schools so that children learn to better interpret what they see on television. For example, one group of researchers attempted to motivate children not to encode and later enact aggressive behaviors they observed on television. They designed their intervention to take advantage of ideas from counterattitudinal advocacy research found effective in producing enduring behavioral changes in other domains. Specifically, the intervention was predicated on a notion contained in both dissonance and attribution theories—when a person finds himself or herself advocating a point of view that is either unfamiliar or even counter to an original belief he or she is motivated to shift attitudes into line with what is being advocated. Children in the Huesmann et al. experimental group were first credited with the antiviolence attitudes that the experimenters wished them to adopt and then asked to make videotapes for other children who had been "fooled" by television and "got into trouble by imitating it", even though they themselves knew better. The children composed persuasive essays explaining how television is not like real life and why it would be harmful for other children to watch too much television and imitate the violent characters. A videotape of each child reading his/her essay was then played before the entire group. This gave the child an opportunity to see himself advocate an antiviolence position and also made the child's position public. The intervention was successful both in changing children's attitudes about television violence and in modifying aggressive behavior. Four months after the intervention there was a significant decline in peer-nominated aggression and attitudes about the acceptability of television violence for the experimental group.

A number of programs have been designed to build "critical viewing skills" that may ameliorate the impact of televised violence on children. Curricula are designed to teach students to recognize certain types of negative portrayals of social behavior and to provide them with alternative ways of interpreting these portrayals. Others have speculated that the effects of exposure to certain mass communications could be modified if a viewer has the ability to devalue the source of information, assess motivations for presenting information, and to perceive the degree of reality intended. Dorr and her colleagues have identified five critical television evaluation skills: explicit and spontaneous reasoning, readiness to compare television content to outside information sources, readiness to use knowledge about the television industry in reasoning about television content, tendency to find television more fabricated or inaccurate, and less positive evaluation of television content.

Some of the techniques based on the cognitive consistency approach discussed above have been applied to interventions designed to mitigate the impact of exposure to mass media sexual violence As one example we tested the effectiveness of an intervention designed to modify reactions to sexually violent films, decrease rape myth acceptance, and sensitize viewers to the plight of a rape victim presented in a videotaped legal trial.

Male college students were brought into the laboratory and shown a documentary on the psychological impact of sexually violent films (an ABC "20/20" presentation in which the first author, film producers, and adolescents discussed the impact of such films on viewers and society). They then watched the two rape education films. After viewing, subjects were assigned to one of three experimental conditions: a "cognitive consistency" condition in which the men wrote assays about myths of sexual violence, videotaped these essays, and watched a videotape playback of themselves and others advocating their antirape position; a no-playback condition in which the men wrote the same essays and read them to the camera but exchanged their essays with others instead of seeing themselves advocate their position; or a "traditional persuasion" condition in which they wrote neutral essays about media use and watched a playback of these. Two additional control conditions, one in which men watched a film documentary on television news rather than the rape and sexually violent film documentaries and a no-intervention condition in which the men participated in the final phase of the research only were also included in the design. A few weeks later the men were contacted and asked to participate in a film viewing study in which they watched clips from sexually violent films and a videotaped reenactment of a rape trial and then evaluated both.

The results indicated that levels of rape myth acceptance were lowest for those men who had participated in either the cognitive consistency or the no-playback conditions. Subjects in these groups reported being more depressed in response to the violent films, were more sympathetic to the victim portrayed in the rape trial, and were more likely to perceive the victim as less responsible for her own rape than were subjects in other conditions.

We believe, as do other researchers, that educational interventions are effective to the extent that they are formed and administered on the basis of systematic research. We also believe that they are a viable means to mitigate the influence of mass media violence.

XI. CONCLUSIONS

In this article, we asked "What are mass media and its effects?" The mass media can be thought of as a process that includes program conception, production, transmission, and reception by the audience. It is this last step, mass media effects, that we are most interested in. Mass media messages may be divided into those intended to influence viewers and listeners, as in the case of commercial advertising, or they may be unintentional, such as increases in aggression following the broadcast of a violent television program. The mass media may influence our behaviors, attitudes, cognitions, or our physiological arousal. It is possible for the mass media to form new attitudes, beliefs, or behaviors; reinforce already existing ones; or change those attitudes and behaviors which we already possess.

It would be safe to conclude from our article that the mass media are contributors to a number of antisocial behaviors and problems, particularly violence in adolescents. We must keep in mind, however, that the mass media are but one of a multitude of factors which contribute and in many cases not the most significant. Other agents of socialization, like parents, schools, and peers, interact with the mass media to produce effects. Nevertheless, they are factors that can be mitigated by proper interventions, and further, factors that can be controlled with reasonable insight. In this article we have discussed a number of these techniques. There are a number of other suggestions that might also be effective. In his review of media's contribution to adolescent health Strasburger offered the following to improve the quality of television:

- An annual tax of television sets (as done in Britain) to help pay for public television. Countries like Japan and England with high levels of funding for public television tend to have more educational programming for children.
- Creation of a children's television network that would be commercial free.
- More responsible portrayals of sexuality, including the advertising of birth control products.
- A reduction in gratuitous violence and more of a willingness on the part of the industry to deal with controversial subjects, in particular those related to health.
- A ban on alcohol advertising in broadcast media and a total ban on tobacco products in all media.

From the perspective of those in the area of violence, peace, and conflict, these seem to be suggestions which can be implemented and which would have an impact on reducing antisocial behavior and related problems.

Also See the Following Articles

CHILDREN, IMPACT OF TELEVISION ON • PORNOGRAPHY • TELEVISION PROGRAMMING AND VIOLENCE

Bibliography

Baron, R. A. (1977). *Human aggression.* New York: Plenum.

Centerwall, B. S. (1989). Exposure to television as a risk factor. *American Journal of Epidemiology, 129,* 643–652.

Comstock, G., & Paik, H. (1991). *Television and the American child.* San Diego, CA: Academic Press.

DeFleur, D., & Dennis, E. (1988). *Understanding mass communication.* New York: McGraw–Hill.

Donnerstein, E., & Linz, D. (1994). Sexual violence in the mass media: Assessing the viability of legal solutions and recommendations for social policy. In M. Costanzo and S. Oskamp (Eds.), *Violence and the law.* Newburg Park, CA: Sage.

Donnerstein, E., Slaby, R., & Eron, L. (1994). The mass media and youth violence. In L. Eron and J. Gentry (Eds), *Youth and violence: Psychology's response,* Vol 2. Washington, DC: American Psychological Association.

Dorr, A., Graves, S. B., & Phelps, E. (1980). Television literacy for young children. *Journal of Communication, 30,* 71–83.

Federman, J. (1996). *Film and television ratings: An international assessment.* Studio City, CA: Mediascope.

Ferman, J. (1995). *British Board of Film Classification: Annual Report 1995–1996.* London: BBFC

Gerbner, G., Gross, L., Morgan, M., & Signorielli, N. (1994). Growing up with television: The cultivation perspective. In J. Bryant and D. Zillman (Eds.), *Media effects.* Hillsdale, NJ: Erlbaum.

Gunter, B. (1994). The question of media violence. In J. Bryant and D. Zillmann (Eds.), *Media effects.* Hillsdale, NJ: Erlbaum.

Harris, R. J. (1994). *A cognitive psychology of mass communication.* Hillsdale, NJ: Erlbaum.

Huesmann, L. R., Eron, L. D., Klein, R., Brice, P., & Fischer, P.

(1983). Mitigating the imitation of aggressive behaviors by changing children's attitudes about media violence. *Journal of Personality and Social Psychology, 44,* 899–910.

Huesmann, L. R., Eron, L. D., Lefkowitz, M. M., & Walder, L. O. (1984). The stability of aggression over time and generations. *Developmental Psychology, 20,* 1120–1134.

Huston, A. C., Donnerstein, E., Fairchild, H., Feshbach, N. D., Katz, P. A., Murray, J. P., Rubinstein, E. A., Wilcox, B. L., & Zuckerman, D. (1992). *Big world, small screen: The role of television in American society.* Lincoln, NE: University of Nebraska Press.

Kunkel, D., Wilson, B., Donnerstein, E., Linz, D., Smith, S. Gray, T., Blumenthal, E., Potter, W. J. (1995). Measuring television violence: The importance of context. *Journal of Broadcasting and Electronic Media, 39,* 284–291.

Linz, D., & Donnerstein, E. (1994). Sex and violence in slasher films: A reinterpretation. *Journal of Electronic Broadcasting and Media, 38,* 243–246.

Linz, D. G., Donnerstein, E., & Penrod, G. (1988). Effects of long-term exposure to violent and sexually degrading depictions of women. *Journal of Personality and Social Psychology, 55,* 758–768.

Malamuth, N. (1989). Sexually violent media, thought patterns, and antisocial behavior. *Public Communication and Behavior, 2,* 159–204.

McGuire, W. J. (1986). The myth of mass media impact. In G. Comstock (Ed.), *Public communication and behavior,* Vol. 1. New York: Academic Press.

Phillips, D. P., & Hensley, J. E. (1984). When violence is rewarded or punished: The impact of mass media stories on homicide. *Journal of Communication, 34,* 101–111.

Strasburger, V. C. (1993). Children, adolescents, and the media: Five crucial issues. *Adolescent Medicine State of the Art Reviews, 4,* 479–493.

Williams, T. M. (Ed.) (1986). *Impact of Television: A natural experiment in three countries.* New York: Academic Press.

Wilson, B. J., & Cantor, J. (1985). Developmental differences in empathy with a television protagonis's fear. *Journal of Experimental Child Psychology, 39,* 284–299.

Zillmann, D. (1979). *Hostility and aggression.* Hillsdale, NJ: Erlbaum.

National television violence study, Volume 2. (1998). Thousand Oaks, CA: Sage.

Means and Ends

Tamayo Okamoto

Hiroshima Prefectural College of Health and Welfare

GLOSSARY

Causal Efficacy The power in an agency to produce effect.

Justification The act of making something right on the basis of an acknowledged principle; the issue here concerns whether means can be justified by ends.

Kingdom of Ends Immanuel Kant's reference to a moral community where rational agents treat one another as ends in themselves, namely, for their own worth, instead of their serviceability only to one another.

Principle of Double Effect When a beneficial result is accompanied by a harmful side effect and when the harm was not intended but merely foreseen, then the act is considered morally more acceptable than when it was intended.

Value Intangible price or worth attached to a thing that we esteem or care for.

THE CONCEPT OF MEANS AND ENDS has two components that are reciprocally or circularly connected with each other. Means is a measure by which one attempts to carry out an intended end. The term *end* is synonymous with an aim, goal, purpose, or objective of an action, while *means* is synonymous with a way, method, or measure for the realization of a projected end. This article presents a multidisciplinary approach in discussing various aspects of the relationship between means and ends, focusing on the issue of the justification of means by ends, or more specifically, of the question whether violence as a means can be justified by a worthy social cause such as the realization of peace and justice. The discussion is given under four headings, namely, valuation, causation, justification, and alternatives.

Valuation concerns the two components in the concept of means and ends with respect to the matter of establishing their respective values. A value is an intangible price or worth attached to things that we esteem or care for. A thing is valuable when we esteem it as something good either for its own sake or for something else. Causation here concerns a necessary connection between means and ends. We discuss a claim that violence can lead to an outcome that involves harm to the party concerned. Justification is the act of making the means-ends connection on the strength of an ethical, religious, or political authority. We note that when harm shows up in a form of foreseen but unintended side effect, justification is hard to obtain.

Copyright © 1999 by Academic Press.
All rights of reproduction in any form reserved.

Our final topic is the importance of the search for alternative means for a project that can produce unconsented harm.

I. VALUATION

Both end-setting and means-conceiving are intentional, purposive activities that take place in our everyday life as well as in more complex social or scientific activities that require moral assessment. Morality presupposes that we are social beings in need of a certain (written or unwritten) code of behavior in various social relationships, which tells what is right or wrong in our dealing with others. We do not call actions moral or ethical when they concern only the interests of the actors, personal or collective. Other-regarding activities have been assessed in the past for their moral worth by standards set by the principles and rules of each society, with its different moral or ethical requirements. We are now looking for something that is universally applicable for all humanity and its environment as society becomes increasingly globalized. Here and elsewhere the terms morality and ethics are used interchangeably.

One of the often discussed issues of the means-ends relationship in the consideration of ethics or morality concerns whether violence can be justified as a means to attain social values such as peace and justice. Aldous Huxley, Mahatma Gandhi, and Martin Luther King are the foremost champions of nonviolence as a means for attaining a worthy social goal. They all emphasize that the end does not justify the means, that is, even if the projected end is worthwhile and desirable, violence will only generate violence, thereby reproducing the violent nature of the oppressive rule or practice that they want to counteract. We need to evaluate the claim that the end does not justify the means so that only a nonviolent strategy should be responsible for the success of a worthy social cause. We also should address the opposite argument: that the use of violent means is necessary for the breakdown of an oppressive government, rule, or practice that is basically violent in nature.

These considerations call for an analysis of the terms involved. Let us then break up the dichotomy, namely, the paired concepts of means and ends, give a conceptual and causal analysis, and give ethical valuation to the above claims. In our discussion we accept Johan Galtung's distinctions of direct and structural violence, and of positive and negative peace. For our purpose it suffices to mention that Galtung defines violence as something that hinders the realization of potentialities of the person at whom the violent action is directed, and that the realization of potentialities is taken here as something for which human beings are born to live for or something that is simply desirable and worthwhile for one to pursue. The potentialities may refer to our exercise of "species-specific" functioning, decision-making power, or hidden individual talent. This characterization of the purpose of our life and its realization in this way serves our discussion of means and ends first in terms of values.

Since end-setting and means-conceiving are purposive activities, both ends and means represent some sort of value. A distinction is often made for two kinds of values, namely, the concept of intrinsic value usually assigned to something that serves as an end of our undertaking, and the concept of instrumental value that is attached to means conceived to be useful for the realization of the end. This distinction is made in a temporarily static framework of the end–means relationship where they do not exchange their respective roles. In a series of events, it often happens that an end achieved could become a means to a further end. Here, however, we deal with a more or less limited field of the relationship.

Most of the usual discussions of the issue of justification of means by ends are based on such a distinction, except perhaps for an empiricist such as John Dewey, who refuses to assign a fixed or static nature to the concept of ends, claiming that the concept of ends expands as things develop. And this claim can be validated, because people's needs and desires do fluctuate in the course of time. On the other hand, we could also claim that there can be things that are relatively constant in our value system. These are valued and remain goals of human action over time. There is another distinction to be made, namely, between a projected end and the actual consequence of the action taken for the end. Dewey prefers to call this an end-in-view instead of just the end, which usually means a final point of a process.

Unlike a natural process, human elements play a determining role in actions that aim to bring about a certain consequence of an individual action as well as in a process of collective, social programs. It is not always the case that the same or similar means employed in the same or similar circumstances for a certain projected end can lead to the same result or consequence. On the other hand, if an unexpected consequence can satisfy those involved, then the process can be concluded. The nature of the actual consequence would matter regardless of its prior expectations. This, however, becomes more relevant to the discussion of the topic of justification.

Something with intrinsic value has a claim to being good in itself and worthy of pursuit, thereby rejecting scrutiny or examination from outsiders. Things that have intrinsic value in the actor's eyes often play a role of ends in her actions even though consequence-minded people may want to deny it.

There are also values in our daily life that are not assessed in terms of ends or means. We often enjoy things in our environment such as natural or art objects, and we exchange small kindnesses and experiences of heart-warming episodes. They provide us with immediate pleasure and often they are much more important than the pursuit of abstract social ideals such as peace and justice. Advocates of these so-called intermediate values between ends and means, however, are primarily concerned with the importance of the value of living a local communal life and they propose what is termed communitarian ethics. They have a tendency to concentrate on local values and they refuse to see problems such as world hunger, the nuclear threat, and global warming. But perhaps a more balanced person would not close her mind to the problems that, however remote they look, may threaten our life someday. This person realizes that it is obligatory for us to be receptive to or fight against those global issues and problems.

In our time we see an increase in views calling for a review of culturally closed values as the goal of activity in a closed traditional society when they might violate human rights such as claims for bodily integrity and privacy. There is a serious conflict between relativists who claim closed cultural autonomy on the one hand and universalists whose emphasis is on the universal nature of human affairs on the other.

The end of the 20th century has seen a lot of bloodshed motivated by racial, cultural, and religious self-interests. We need to recognize that a crude pursuit of political or religious self-interest can no longer have automatic self-justificatory power. These are being increasingly brought to broad awareness as the result of the development of a worldwide communication and information system and the formation of various international organizations. In this sense the development of the means of interaction enables the setting up and the realization of certain ends, including the discouraging of pursuits of local self-interests even though the present situation is still not very encouraging.

In our common value system we tend to place conditional or unconditional positive values on concepts such as life, birth, nature, survival, youth, growth, healing, creativity, talent, beauty, knowledge, education, progress, utility, efficiency, development, prosperity, unity, independence, harmony, community, reciprocity,

peace, health, pleasure, happiness, justice, equality, freedom, human rights, personhood, integrity, self-identity, self-realization, beneficence, co-existence, dialogue, friendship, and democracy. There are comparable virtues in the actors to these values such as love, compassion, trust, openness, understanding, and the like. Virtues are good characters or attitudes that recognize and work for the realization of these positive values. Life and peace may be a set of umbrella or overarching concepts over other items in the category especially when life is not empty and peace means what Galtung calls positive peace in contrast to negative peace, which denotes absence of violence, direct or structural. Without these two core values, other values in this category will not be fully realized.

By contrast, we tend to desire to rectify a situation in which some of the following or similar disvalues are prevalent: unnatural death, pain, suffering, disease, physical and mental disability, poverty, hunger, unemployment, homelessness, debilitation, ignorance, illiteracy, regress, disintegration, accident, antagonism, belligerency, dispute, conflict, violence, oppression, slavery, discrimination, harming, killing, genocide, terrorism, despotism, and warfare. Here unnatural death and violence can represent all other items in the category. Attitudes that are related to these include hatred, deception, manipulation, misunderstanding and the like.

These lists are by no means exhaustive or systematic. Some items may be more morally important than others. Also, many could be empty without adequate definition and factual specification. Many of the items in the latter category are the deficient form of those of the first category, while others may be items that are simply undesirable, bad, or morally and therefore unjustifiably wrong. We have an intuitive or rational objection to a plan to accommodate the items in the second category as ends of personal or collective endeavor. They cannot justifiably be ends or objectives of an action or a social plan. On the contrary the elimination of some or all of these as social evils can be objectives of a worthy social effort. So the realization of items from the first list and the elimination of the items from the second list should have positive values and can be worthy ends of human undertakings.

When we posit an end we also make a projection of a means to attain the goal. We can roughly say that the end thus posited has some positive value to realize or to satisfy one's own interest and/or to enhance the pleasure and happiness of other people. Although none in the first category can claim an absolute status and each item needs some qualification, all are said to have an intrinsic value, prized for its own sake rather than an instrumental value that is assessed for its usefulness for something else. In the past there has been a tendency to place intrinsic values in a hierarchical order.

You can see from the list that there are items such as human rights that only modernity has come to recognize fully. The ancient Greek civilization was made possible by the labor of slaves who were termed by Aristole as only "instruments." Other major civilizations were also based on a similar triangular social structure, with a huge population at the bottom that was exploited to serve the purposes of the minority at the top. Even though major ancient religious leaders such as Jesus Christ and Gautama Buddha taught the equality of all human beings, equal human rights were never socially recognized until the dawn of modern times when thinkers such as Jean-Jacque Rousseau and Immanuel Kant wrote about the worth and rights of all human beings.

As to the consideration of a possible hierarchy of ends or for that matter an existence of final ends, we must agree with Galtung's characterization of violence as an assault on the effort to realize the potentialities of each human person. Death marks the final point of our life process, and we are often characterized as beings who are moving toward death. But death cannot be the final end or purpose of our life. It is not proper to say that we live in order to have a good death, although a peaceful death should be an ideal and we all should be entitled to it. Likewise life is not an end per se, but a good life can be. The event of our own birth is not a matter that we can control, although the birth of others could be partly our own doing. As existentialist philosophers argue for the value of a person's existing or becoming over the value of having the static essence of a human being, we can say that we are thrown into this world and we cannot do anything about it, but that after a certain process of adequate education and training we can somehow achieve independence and project our own life plans, including perhaps how to die well in the end.

We say that these categories of values are represented by a worthy life and an unnatural death, respectively, or by positive peace and violence, respectively, but with qualifications. Although we cannot have consensus about the ultimate purpose of life, we can safely say that one of the plausible reasons for our life on this earth should be to fully develop our given potentialities and that no living person, even those bedridden or in confinement, is devoid of some kind of potentiality to develop.

Both common and theoretical morality tell us that we are interdependent and reciprocal to each other in the development of these potentialities. So whatever harms the common scheme should be termed bad. Wars, oppressive rules, starvation, epidemics, and natural disasters are often responsible for many untimely deaths and suffering that hinder the development of these potentialities as a plausible end of human life. These are causes for which most victims are not responsible. To identify and liberate people from such evil forces has been the end or objective of many past social movements and it will remain so as long as these social evils persist on the earth. The valuation of the items affects the choice of ends and means in our social life. They are all abstract concepts, but many of those in the first category and the elimination of the phenomena in the second category can provide motives for social actions.

Now we turn to the issue of assessment of a social action involved in the realization of a social ideal with reference to some representative modern theories of ethics. Kantianism, based on the thought of the 18th-century German philosopher, Immanuel Kant, on the one hand, and consequentialism, on the other, including John Stuart Mill's utilitarianism and John Dewey's instrumentalism, have contrasting approaches to the assessment of an action that is carried out with a notion of ends and means.

The former places emphasis on the intrinsic, therefore static, goodness of the end in itself. An action is assessed in terms of the motive of the agent to bring about the intended end. The motive in the Kantian sense should comply with the dictates of moral laws that can be obtained in the rational search within human reason that each person is born with. One of the moral requirements of obligation dictates that our acts have to comply with the principle of universalizability, namely, applicability regardless of time and place of the acts. This approach is often called deontologist, meaning obligation-centered. Acts of beneficence, namely, doing good to others, are assessed in terms of whether each act is carried out from the motive of obligation set by the moral, categorical, or unconditional imperatives or injunctions, or simply from a piece of humane compassion. In a strict sense, only the former has a moral value. Beneficence, self-realization, social justice, and liberation of the oppressed are all good ends to be aimed at, but they have to be done because they are obligatory objectives for a rational person to pursue. In a Kantian system even if the expected ends are not reached, the noble motive for the intended end would not diminish its worth. There is also another aspect of this theory, which states that the motive-end relationship excludes elements of doing harm to others.

Kant's motive mainly expresses goodwill to benefit other human beings.

The typical consequentialist, on the other hand, only notices the other end of the action process and seems only interested in the success of an action or policy in terms of its consequence, to the extent of disregarding the nature of the motives and the means used to attain a goal. The action is evaluated on the basis of the calculation of something that its actual outcome has brought about. Some of the consequentialists are utilitarians who pay attention to the utility of the action and the amount of overall happiness that it has produced for the maximum number of the people concerned. They do not usually question the quality of the means that was employed. This approach gives an impression that anything goes as a means as long as an intended result obtains, and it is close to the stance that stresses that the end justifies the means. The end refers to the actual result, because if one stresses the nature of the end-in-view, then one is inclined to make a commitment to the motive even to the point of disregarding the end result of the action or policy, which, however, the consequentialist would not want to accept. Dewey, on the other hand, stresses the importance of assessing the instrumental value of means to realize the end-in-view, which is conceived when the actor recognizes problems in the environment. For Dewey the assessment of the instrumental value of means is just as important as the recognition of the problem-solving needs.

Dewey takes issue with Kant's tendency to downgrade means as inferior to or at least separate from a projected end. For Dewey an end is an expression of desires and interests of the actor. The means are not inferior to the end since means and end are closely related to each other. It may indeed be the case that an idealist tends to believe that mere means is inferior to the end that has positive, intrinsic value. Following the tradition of dualism begun by Plato, Kant presupposes the world of noumena beyond the world of phenomena, the former giving meanings and values if not causal explanation to the latter. The projected ends that originate in the former sphere include activities of art, knowledge of the essence of things, and moral imperatives that call for dutiful actions. However, Kant's contribution to our moral thinking was something truly decisive in providing us with a proper perspective to look at a moral relationship in the present world.

Kant includes among his categorical imperatives or absolute commandments the moral treatment of other persons as members of the community of ends and not as means only. The Kantian ends thus formulated have intrinsic values that cannot be used as a means to other things. They are good in their own right and thus have a right to be treated with respect. The qualification for membership in this realm includes autonomy or self-governance in decision making about one's own affairs. A strict imposition of the qualification may make it difficult for all of us to join the community, but this institution should be inclusive as the realm theoretically aims to invite everybody who has long been denied access to such a community. The moral requirement and the tradition of treating others adequately and with respect began this way in the idealist philosophy of Kant. Following Kant's model, modern social reformers have set up ends of their movement such as freedom, justice, equality, friendship, and a well-ordered society that is fully recognized only in the kingdom of ends.

Kant's conception of persons as ends-in-themselves in the kingdom of ends had an enormous, decisive impact on the way we are supposed to treat each other if we are to take our moral relationship seriously. Today, implication increases its significance more than ever because war efforts, business efforts, developmental efforts, and the like expand the scope of global limits. Too often and too clearly we see that the powerless are subjected as mere means to the objectives of those engaged in efforts that extend beyond national boundaries. The Kantian conception has made undeniably clear the illegitimacy of treating others as means only.

Seen from this perspective, the production of human clones is ethically impermissible. The idea of having someone with exactly the same genetic structure as an existing person violates the idea of human diversity and uniqueness. In addition, the idea of having a human clone that serves the original person simply means that the clone is being used as an instrument or a means only; this is repugnant and morally unacceptible. Aristotle could be condoned for his remarks to the effect that slaves were instruments, simply because of his historical limitations. Instruments are replaceable and duplicable, but the idea of the instrument's someday replacing the host agent is self-defeating. A kingdom of means does not make sense. As for the mass production of cloned animals, we need a different kind of consideration because we do not usually apply the concept of a human person to nonhuman animals although of course we need to avoid creating unnecessary suffering for them. A possible motive of such an endeavor may be the researcher's boundless desire to meddle with the life process. Even if the mass production of animal clones profits some quarter of society, the rest of the world has to look at those entrepreneurs with fear and trembling as their desire to meddle with natural process seems to expand without limit.

If we regard ends and means separately as independent values we can affirm the superiority of some ends such as a peaceful, healthy, and just life over the means that should not be ends. We should avoid making an end of something that only has instrumental value such as money and weapons. We evaluate the goodness of ends as well as that of means. The instrumental value of means should be assessed in terms of the ethically unproblematic nature and not just because it is the most effective or shortest way to a goal. Violence, deception, or behind-the-scene dealings are undesirable means.

We have seen that both means and ends are values that are objects of valuing. Now we turn to the relationship between means and ends in the context of causation, that is, cause and effect, of an action in our discussion of the justification of means by ends.

II. CAUSATION

When we think of human intentional activities and alternatives to means in relation to a certain end, we do not think that everything is allowed, and we usually assume that there is a certain causal relationship between means and ends or more exactly between the means and the consequence (regardless of its satisfying the intended aim) that the action leads to. This section concerns the claim of the justifiability of means by ends in terms of causal efficacy or causal necessity.

Nonviolence advocates insist that nonviolence is necessary for the liberation of the oppressed. By contrast advocates of violent means to attain a social goal, such as Frantz Fanon and Malcolm X, seem to claim the necessity of the use of violence to achieve their intended goal. These belong to the claims for causal efficacy or causal necessity of means that are responsible for producing a desired consequence. Here we do not distinguish efficacy and necessity as different matters, although the former refers to power in an agency to produce an intended result while the latter refers to the process which is determined by the former.

The question whether there is a moral value in violence as a means to attain a valuable social end should be addressed. In normal circumstances violence is avoided because of the possibility of inflicting harm on an innocent party. What justifies violence may depend on a quick calculation of a possible benefit by means of violence over a harm done during nonviolent resistance or passivity. Although it is difficult to establish empirically a necessary connection between a violent intervention and an innocuous consequence and that between nonviolence and a harmful result, it looks more likely that violence leads to other violence. Nonviolence is not likely to produce much harm, if any.

Perhaps we should first examine the famous claim of the British empiricist philosopher David Hume, who maintains that there is no necessary connection between a seeming cause and an actual effect of a thing. For Hume causation is established by a habit of mind after observing similar beginnings and end results repeatedly. Hume's criticism is directed to a theory of a physical or natural causation in the Aristotelian sense that something has power to produce a certain effect, which explains the change in the affected thing. Hume also denies purposiveness in the causal relationship that the Aristotelian system affirms. There is a certain truth in his thesis that points out the element of indeterminacy in a natural process. We cannot rest assured on seeming lawfulness in nature and future natural events with a firm conviction that the expected result will obtain with absolute certainty. It is certainly difficult to identify a necessary connection between a certain causal event or behavior and an apparent end phenomenon. Even in this age of advanced technology, there are no absolutely fool-proof ways to determine brain death, to identify exact causes or cures for cancer, or to predict the exact course of a hurricane. The best we can do may be an approximation to what seems to be actually taking place. Science progresses day by day and probability may approach certainty, but never to the point of absolute certainty. It is safe to say that we are still living in an age of uncertainty and that we cannot make the necessary connection between cause and effect. David Hume did a great job of shattering the dogmatism and false generalizations that we tend to fall into. We always need to be reminded of the possibility of committing mistakes or meeting unexpected obstacles even when our action plans are carefully prepared in advance.

On the other hand we want to say that things cannot be that indeterminate. Indeed, as a popular proverb says, where there is smoke, there is fire. A certain cause can effect a certain result. There seems to be a lawlike regularity in nature that makes scientific prediction possible to a great extent. Even in the relationship between means and ends in which human elements are involved, there seems to exist an understanding of the most effective means to produce the most favorable results.

Dewey says that in conceiving means we rely on our past experiences to be able to make a prediction that the measure to be taken can possibly or probably produce a desired result in the most efficient way. He uses terms of interest and desires that motivate people to conceive an end-in-view and the most effective means. Thus he says that desires and interests are causal conditions for a consequence of an action. He also emphasizes the actor's intentional choice of a particular means out of many alternatives. Dewey once criticized the Russian Marxist Leon Trotsky's thesis that ends justify means by saying that Trotsky had only one means to attain his goal of the liberation of humanity. Although Dewey concurred with him about that ideal, Trotsky's logical move was problematic because for him the only possible means was the class struggle; this conclusion was deductively derived from his idea of historical materialism. For Dewey there should be many ways to bring about one such ideal. He could not accept a deterministic thesis such as Trotsky's.

Despite his problematic statement in which he termed slaves instruments, Aristotle provides us with a theory of causation that can be useful in our discussion. He deals with four causes of all beings, namely efficient, material, formal, and final causes. Although secular or scientific discussion often regards Aristotelian causation as obsolete or irrelevant, it can still be instructive in the humanities and social sciences. For example, when an artist creates an artwork, the end product as the final cause expresses the artist as the efficient cause of the product, while the material cause denotes the material without which the artist could not produce the work. The piece of work is the expression of the idea formed in the artist's mind as the formal cause that gives form to the material. The final cause may seem to come in the end chronologically, but the projected end product can be regarded as chronologically preceding the process of actual production, so it does relate to the end of a voluntary action toward which means (including the choice of materials and instruments) can be conceived. Aristotle seems to state the causal necessity to the effect that with these four causes the end product necessarily obtains. In another context Aristotle discusses the distinction between potency and actuality. This also refers to the fixed nature of a thing that has capacity ingrained in it that leads to a certain end product.

What we can get from the Aristotelian causation thesis is that it seems to explain the role of the agent who conceives an image of what she wants to attain and chooses the material as a necessary means to realize the conceived end image. Or, it may be the case that the means that are available determine the nature of the ends to be attained. The elements of intentionality and choice exist from the beginning. There may be involved in the course of action an element of letting nature take its course, but in human action intentionality determines its course by the act of making a choice. The intent to use physical force or weapons to harm others does harm the other party even if the latter can somehow escape the assault, because the actor knows what harm it can produce. The actual harm may be only psychological, but the psychological harm can be just as devastating as a physical harm. Human intentionality is ingrained in the Aristotelian causation. All four causes have to do with an act of choice, intention, and motives. This, however, does not validate a claim that harm done unintentionally should be free from the actor's responsibility.

Mahatma Gandhi sees the necessary causation between a violent social movement and violent nature of the social system that ensues it. He likens the connection between the violent means and the violent end to the relationship between a seed and a tree. According to him and other nonviolence advocates, a just and peaceful order has to be gained through nonviolent means. Although we cannot statistically endorse a statement that violence necessarily begets violence or that nonviolence leads to a peaceful social order, there is at least logical and factual contradiction in a remark that violence can produce a peaceful order.

A Kantian would say that harming others by using deception cannot be universalized; therefore, it cannot meet the condition of categorical imperative and must be prohibited. Consequentialists would say lies would produce lies and the effect will be unlikely to produce the greatest happiness of the greatest number of people. Gandhi refers to historical facts that even if a violent means attains a certain objective it will impose harm on the people concerned. Violence harms, and the negative effect can persist unless there is an appropriate expression of apology, or compensation takes place.

Thus it may not be just a wishful statement to say that violence is contagious, just as acts of love are. In this sense there can exist a causal relationship between violent acts and a violent outcome. And there can be no justification for the acts that involve violence, whether they be national, collective, or individual, whether the violence be verbal, physical, military, or structural. Violence harms.

On the other hand, nonviolence can be both a means and an end. It has a positive value. While the use of violence could have the same result easier and more quickly, the objective achieved by a nonviolent measure would give the achiever great satisfaction that the user of violence, such as stealing, robbing, deceiving, and the like, would never experience. Direct, indirect, and structural violence is a manipulation over others, as are deception and secrecy. The result of visible violence can well be violence and alternatives to avoid violence, even if it takes longer to achieve than does violence. This would be much more satisfying. As far as nonviolent action gives the sense of satisfaction, it can also be the legitimate objective of one's effort.

Although Dewey does not mention whether violence can lead to the liberation of humanity, he seems to be opposed to the idea of choosing violence as a necessary means to the intended goal since he insists on the choice of the most appropriate means from available alternatives and he does not have reason to choose violence over other means.

There are alternatives to harmful ends and means. Even when there are no alternatives, non-action is still an alternative, so the process of human action has a different starting point than a purely physical phenomenon. Yet there is a sort of causal necessity working in the means-ends relationship. The agent has to bear a certain responsibility because of individual or collective voluntary decision making at different stages of the process that determines the course of action.

III. JUSTIFICATION

Deontological and consequentialist arguments are based on certain established principles of ethics. As we have seen, a deontologist notices motives while a consequentialist pays attention to the consequence as to whether it maximizes the overall happiness of those concerned. The former tends to emphasize the worth and dignity of individuals while the latter gives priority to the overall welfare of society, to the extent of disregarding the interests and desires of its minority members. Sometimes consequentialists are at great pains to justify a hypothetical case of a release of pain for the great majority of people that is only possible through one person's sacrificial death. Conflicts between consequentialists and deontologists do exist but there could also be a middle road attained through democratic argument because both camps seem ready to accommodate a dialogic approach to difficult cases. After all, most people would be willing to suffer a minor headache rather than tolerating the death of a person for the sake of the relief of their minor pain. One innocent person's untimely death cannot be justified by any principle worth abiding by.

Now we turn to a discussion of the justification needed for actions that begin with good intentions to benefit others and end with some unintended but fore-

seen side effect that harms them. Some nonconsequentialists advocate a case-by-case approach, believing that harmful consequences in somes cases can be justified by what is called the principle of double effect. This refers to the means–ends relationship in which an intended consequence of a measure taken with good intention to benefit the concerned obtains but at the same time an unintended side effect that might affect them harmfully takes place. Medical examples are instructive: Medication to kill certain viruses often also destroys beneficial bacteria in the body. Another medical example concerns a painkiller such as morphine that is administered to a terminal patient and shortens her life. Likewise, a social action that is done through good will to satisfy many people may impose suffering on others, but this should be tolerated because of the original good-willed intention. Building dams and nuclear power plants for the procurement of water or the generation of electricity can destroy traditional villages and habitats but nonconsequentialists believe that their good intention should justify negligible side effects. Yet, an unintended but foreseeable accident at a nuclear power plant will be simply disastrous.

According to the principle of double effect that was first proposed by medieval Catholic theologians to determine the justifiability of actions without having a recourse to a religious or ethical mandate, it is said that the agents are responsible only for the intended consequence but not for the unintended, although foreseeable, side effect of the action taken. Four conditions have to be met for the justification: (1) the action is either morally good or neutral; (2) the actor aims at a good consequence; (3) the bad consequence is not a means for the goodness of the end; and (4) there is a balance between good and bad consequences.

As we have seen, a consequentialist looks at the quality of the consequence, while a deontologist, namely the advocate of good motives, questions the motivation or intention of the actor. Both approaches can be served by the conditions of double effect, as the end-in-view in each case is good and can be fulfilled if the harmful side effect can be ignored.

One would wonder what Dewey would say about the case of a patient who is relieved from pain but is killed by an overdose of the painkiller. Dewey would perhaps not regard the success of painkilling and the death caused by the overuse of a drug as two different things, because he would not distinguish between intending and foreseeing. Foreseeing means that there is a certain foreknowledge of the causal process. The actor cannot excuse herself from the accountability for her action, especially when the consequence is an avoidable death. There has to be a different justification, which, however, may not be available.

These conditions for justification are tenuous to say the least because they depend on the actor's report of a good intention. The principle is questionable all the more when it seems that the wishes and desires of the person at issue are neglected. If the person's wishes are unknown, this case should be one of paternalistic justification. If the person is actually competent, but his wishes are not known, there can be no justification for any intervention that is not requested by the person. Recent Western ethics has spelled out three conditions for justifying paternalism. These are: (1) when the person is temporarily incompetent but likely to acknowledge the benefit of intervention later; (2) the actor knows the childlike person well; and (3) the actor is motivated to benefit the person.

Justification is the act of making something right for rationally explainable reasons. As we have seen, justification or reason-giving in the past was based on different cultural traditions, philosophical systems, religious institutions, social-political ideologies, and so on. But today the source of legitimate justification is often considered to reside in people's consent, approval, or choice to be made on the basis of the necessary, sufficient, and adequate knowledge and information that one has access to. The principle of double effect relies on the actor's unilateral good will to benefit the person and disregards the need of paying attention to the wishes and desires of those subjected to the actor's action. Thus, this principle itself is in need of justification as in the case of a paternalistic approach in which the core justification lies in the beneficiary's incompetence. It is morally inadmissible to ignore the wishes and desires of the competent person even if the actor's intention to bring about the well-being or a good, peaceful death for the patient is good.

This observation can apply to other cases in which the principle is used overtly or covertly as a justification. Take the case of war efforts that result in a number of casualties of not only combatants but also noncombatants, including children, elderly, and foreigners. If a war objective is attained and the number of casualties is significantly small, then a utilitarian calculation would morally approve the overall consequence and therefore justify the war effort. A just-war theory may rely on this kind of logic that is not basically different from the principle of double effect. Noncombatant casualties were foreseen but not intended, and the intended war objective was well served; therefore the noncombatant casualties should be justified. The fallacy of this unac-

ceptible conclusion lies in the first premise, which distinguishes foreknowledge and intention.

Nuclear bombings over Hiroshima and Nagasaki in the final period of World War II were later given justification by American veterans as an effective means of preventing the deaths of many American soldiers as well as Japanese civilians. This paternalistic, presumptive justification is not persuasive in the face of the enormous number (more than 300,000) of actual deaths of mostly innocent civilians in the bombed cities. In addition, the alleged direct benefit in this case can never be convincingly proved.

The principle stating that a bad foreseen consequence can be tolerated or justified simply because the badness was not the result of the actor's intention does not treat the person adequately as an end in herself if it does not treat her as the means only. So a Kantian would not approve this principle and neither would a Deweyite for the reason stated above. The conclusion of this discussion then would be that we should avoid an effort to bring about a situation in which the principle of double effect can be applied. In the cited medical case of the use of painkillers we should look for alternatives other than just another sort of medication with life-threatening side effects. After all, consequences that involve harming or killing need far greater justification than the one offered so far.

If the actors in the process of conceiving means for certain ends knew that there were alternatives available, then the issue of accountability would arise. This is important for public policymakers whose responsibility lies in the possession of the best available knowledge, and in their readiness to share the knowledge, its application, and an explanation of the possible consequences with the general public, who should be the ultimate judges assessing the adequacy of means and ends in public policy. And this general public also refers to the world citizens of tomorrow.

The 20th century experienced two world wars, it saw omnicidal nuclear weapons, international trade friction, racial conflict, the large-scale destruction of nature, as well as remarkable technological advancement in the natural sciences, especially in medicine. Issues and problems have gained global importance and impact, so we cannot do without putting many things in a global perspective. Morality can no longer be confined to a narrow locality. The universalizability thesis addressed by Immanuel Kant seems to apply to all human affairs. Kantian respect for rational, autonomous persons as ends in themselves seems to have a universal application in this discussion. Justification should be the matter of rational argumentation among all human beings on earth. Questions as to whether violence can ever be justified as a means to attain a good social end can also be on the agenda of democratic argumentation.

The discussion of the rule of double effect makes it clear that we should try to avoid the foreseen inevitable harm even if the intended objective is attained. We have to think seriously of alternative means that can avoid inevitable harm.

IV. ALTERNATIVES

The concept of alternative means was perhaps first recognized when the assessment of the causation of actions, plans, and policies with effects that caused harm to living beings and the ecosystem led the assessors to review the plan. They then used a different approach that promised a safer, gentler end result with no foreseen harms. The term "alternative" has two meanings, one being things you can choose from and the other being something less harmful or more peaceful than the original choice. An alternative used in the latter connotation means ways of dealing with other people, animals, and the environment in a gentler and more caring manner, which might require a change of lifestyle to one based on values of symbiosis or living together cooperatively.

It may not be the case that a nonviolent and peaceful means will necessarily produce a comparable consequence, but we empirically know at least from the history of the events of this century that the vicious cycle of violence has to stop, and we need to be determined not to choose ends and means that can harm ourselves and our ecosystem. It is possible to follow Gandhi's example and commit ourselves to education, conscientious objection to war, and alternative means of energy production, instead of violence.

We also need to change our thinking to recognize that values can be consensual. There should be more openness in politics so that there would be no need for coups d'etat, terrorism, and violent countermeasures. The pursuit of social justice as the end of revolutionary effort has as its desired end the removal of inequality, social injustice, hierarchical structure. We have some historical record of nonviolent revolutions as means that have brought better results than those in which violence was employed. In place of revolutions that inevitably involve violence, gradual reforms in which democratic decision making is respected can be better options.

The realization of national or regional interests is believed to serve as the end of war efforts. If the U.S.

was aware of Japan's imperialism by the early 1940s because of the events of the past decade, and yet did not take adequate steps to prevent or curtail this, then the U.S. government was no less responsible for the Pacific War of 1941–45. In a war effort such as that of Japan and the United States, the pressure brought by the weapon industry was instrumental. The slogan "national prosperity with jobs for all people" served a justifiable ends for the popular mobilization of compliance and enthusiasm for war efforts. So strict legal measures are needed to ensure peace and justice in society. As a step for stable peace, Article Nine of Japan's so-called Peace Constitution enacted in 1946 renounces "war as a sovereign right of the nation and the threat or use of force as means of settling international disputes." This has served well for the prevention of a recurrence of militarisim and imperialism in a country that has a tendency toward insular nationalism. The illegality of the production and use of nuclear weapons to solve international disputes had to be determined by an international agreement; this was established by judges in the International Court of Justice in 1996. When efforts toward warfare cannot be blocked, policies to allow conscientious objectors to enter medical or welfare services should be universally regarded as legitimate alternatives to the participation in warfare.

Health or recovery of health is often termed as having an intrinsic value. But life cannot be prized unconditionally. The prolonging of life without attention to its quality is found to have little intrinsic value. It seems that this is a matter that all humanity should decide on once and for all. In bioethics there was a certain positive progress in resolving clinical conflicts and dilemmas with the introduction of the concept of informed consent in 1957 in the hitherto paternalistic physician–patient relationship. There are still problems in patient care in big hospitals but a committee approach in the form of hospital ethics committees and institutional review boards helps to resolve many serious dilemmas. Also in terminal care, the hospice's palliative approach is a reasonable alternative to euthanasia, which is brought about intentionally or unintentionally with or without the use of the principle of double effect. If the administration of fatal medication is requested by the patient then it could be a case of physician-assisted suicide which is morally more easily justifiable than the case in which the rule of double effect is applied and frees the physician from responsibility.

More apparent means-ends problems in medical practice and research concern human experimentation in which medical researchers tend to regard patients as a means to their medical findings. An unfortunate consequence of the Tuskegee Incident, in which many poor Black syphilis patients were used by federal government researchers as objects of experimentation and observation without receiving medical care, so that future patients might be helped, is a deep mistrust toward the medical profession among Black AIDS patients who refuse to participate in the AIDS care program. The grave immorality of medical researchers who, however, insist that medical progress has to compromise if a full-disclosure condition is necessary has been noted. A sensible bioethics thinker, however, would want to remind the researchers that human life is not endless and that there should be limits to the pursuit of medical technology that tends to use human and nonhuman subjects only as a means to their research objectives.

Nuclear energy is used as a relatively easy means to maintain the standard of life that modern technology has enabled us to enjoy. Yet there is a serious doubt as to its alleged peaceful use. It cannot be as harmless as nuclear scientists claim. We have good reasons to be cautious about it after we have seen the terrible harm done by the Chernobyl accident in which there seem to be more victims than in the atomic bombings of Hiroshima and Nagasaki. If a foreseen harm is inevitable, then the actual harm, even when it is unintended, is impermissible. The logical answer to this problem is the further development of alternative energy sources such as solar and wind power. At the same time we must reduce the daily consumption of energy, including the use of fossil fuels, that seems to be the main cause of the global warming crisis.

V. CONCLUSION

We have examined the implication of the consideration of means and ends in terms of values, causation, justification, and alternatives. Our main concern was the issue of the justification of violent means if the end produced is a morally desirable social action program. We have examined deontologist and consequentialist views of this issue, which emphasize one or the other of the dichotomous set of concepts. In our consideration of causation we saw that motives for an action plan are as important as the actual consequence. There seems

to be interdependence or some causal relationship between the two and there is a strong possibility that violence begets violence in social action. Therefore, in order for us to be serious about a peaceful world order we have to look for nonviolent means to attain it.

While we cannot ignore the importance of good motives and intentions, the gravity of consequence should be reemphasized. The saying, when the end result is good, everything is good, is often used to console those affected by the unexpected and unforeseen ups and downs of the process that does bring some satisfaction after all. But when a problematic means is employed, the satisfaction one gets from the consequence is less than when both desirable ends and means are employed.

In the planning of a public policy to remove problems from society and to promote positive peace, it is an ethical imperative to be careful about setting up an end that should reflect the general consensus and a nonviolent means that is considered best to bring about the most satisfying consequence. When the expected end result can involve irreparable harm to any persons, a pursuit for alternative means should be in order.

Also See the Following Articles

JUSTIFICATIONS FOR VIOLENCE • JUST-WAR CRITERIA • MORAL JUDGMENTS AND VALUES • PEACE, DEFINITIONS AND CONCEPTS OF

BIBLIOGRAPHY

Beauchamp, T. L., et al. (1994). Principles of biomedical ethics. New York: Oxford University Press.
Daniels, N., et al. (1996). Is justice enough? Ends and means in bioethics. Hastings Center Report, 26 (6), 9–15.
Galtung, J. (1996). Peace by peaceful means. London: Sage Productions.
Herman, B. (1993). The practice of moral judgment. Cambridge, MA: Harvard University.
Overby, C. M. (1997). A call for peace: The implications of Japan's war-renouncing constitution. New York: Kodansha America.
Schmidtz, D. (1994). Choosing ends. Ethics. 104 (2), 226–251.
Singer, P. (ed.). (1993). A companion to ethics. Cambridge, MA: Blackwell.
Weston, A. (1992). Between means and ends. The Monist, 75 (2), 236–249.
Whitlock, G. (1996). Reexamining Dr. King and Malcolm X on violence. Philosophical Forum, 27 (4), 289–320.

Mediation and Negotiation Techniques

Jacob Bercovitch

University of Canterbury

GLOSSARY

Conflict The presence of divergent interests or incompatible perceptions between people or groups, and the desire to pursue behavior commensurate with these perceptions.

Conflict Management Methods and activities designed to influence the course or outcome of a conflict. These may range from verbal retorts to coercive measures.

Mediation A type of conflict management whereby an outsider or third party intervenes in a conflict, in a voluntary, noncoercive manner, in order to arrest its destructive tendencies.

Negotiation A process of conflict management in which only the parties involved attempt to discuss, directly or indirectly, the issues that separate them, and how best to reach a joint decision on these issues.

Strategy An overall plan or a broad conception parties in conflict have in order to deal with or manage their conflict.

MEDIATION AND NEGOTIATION are the most important methods for dealing with conflict between individuals, groups, organizations, and nations. The main advantage of mediation and negotiation is their voluntary and noncoercive nature in which ultimate decision-making power is in the hands of the parties involved. Mediation and negotiation comprise a complex system of relationships, activities, and moves. Students of mediation and negotiation seek to study the conditions under which these social processes take place, the various moves and phases involved, and the strategies that may assist the parties in conflict to achieve a satisfactory outcome. As conflicts become more brutal, the search for more effective mediation and negotiation should figure prominently in our future research agenda.

I. INTRODUCTION

Conflicts and disputes are found everywhere. They are present in all societies and all human relationships regardless of their geographical location or time. Conflicts exist between and among individuals, groups, organizations, and even states. Some of these conflicts manifest themselves as contests, challenges, debates, or lawsuits; others escalate from mere controversies to combat, violence, and even war. Conflicts can be productive and creative; they can also have high costs and harmful consequences. It is precisely because conflicts can be unproductive and destructive that we need to search for better ways of dealing with, or managing, conflict.

Copyright © 1999 by Academic Press.
All rights of reproduction in any form reserved.

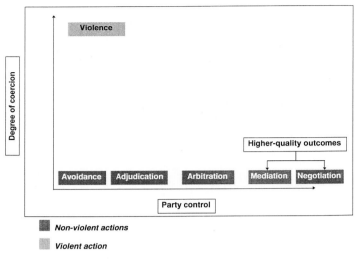

FIGURE 1 Approaches to conflict management.

Conflict management is learning about how to make conflicts more productive and less costly.

Traditionally, conflict has been seen as an overt struggle (the term itself is derived from Latin words which mean to strike together), and the best means of dealing with it was that of fighting or coercion. This, with its connotation of victor and vanquished, is only one, and by no means the most desired, approach to conflict. Conflict may be avoided (flight rather than fight), or it may be ignored. It may be resolved by a third party empowered to make a binding decision on the basis of the legal systems. Or, as is more commonly the case, conflict may be resolved through direct negotiations between the parties involved, or by having an impartial mediator to assist with the parties' own conflict management and negotiation. In mediation, the parties do not relinquish responsibility for their conflict, nor are they likely to experience high levels of coercion (on the relationship between approaches to conflict, degree of coercion and party control, see Figure 1). Our concern here is with the procedures of mediation and negotiation as the most important voluntary approaches to conflict between individuals, groups or nations.

II. MEDIATION

For a long time the study of mediation has been characterized by a startling lack of information. Practitioners of mediation, whether formal or informal, whether in the interpersonal or international context, were keen to sustain its perception as a mysterious practice taking place behind closed doors. Scholars of mediation, for their part, did not think that such behavior was susceptible to systematic analysis. Neither did they seem to believe that broad patterns could be discerned, or that any valid generalizations about the process could be made. The dominant agnosticism toward systematic approaches, and the desire to maintain the intuitive mystique or mediation resulted in a proliferation of descriptive cases of mediation in which the techniques used and the outcome achieved were invariably the product of a unique set of personal attributes of the mediator.

Over the past two decades, it has become widely accepted that mediation, like other serial phenomena, is a process that can be analyzed systematically, and that theoretical insights can be blended with practical experience to produce a general understanding of the process, and an awareness of what the process is like and how it might be improved. This is the road I propose to take here.

A. Definition

As there is rarely any consistency in the usage of the term mediation, confusion inevitably abounds. This is unsatisfactory and should be remedied. And yet mediation is not easy to define. Many of the difficulties stem from the very flexibility of mediation, its voluntary and ad-hoc character, and the fact that it is practiced in a wide diversity of settings. The term is also used in different ways by different people, some of whom may work as "private mediators," while others may operate within an institutionalized framework.

Definitions of mediation can be either prescriptive—that is, define the process as it ideally should be like (e.g., identify all issues, create new options, consider alternatives, etc.), or descriptive—that is, define the process very much in terms of what actually happens in practice (e.g., deadlines, power imbalances, etc.). Whether prescriptive or descriptive, definitions of mediation purport to capture the gist of what mediators do or hope to achieve, distinguish between mediation and related processes of conflict management, and emphasize mediators' attributes. Most definitions of the first category emphasize the mediators' primary objective of facilitating a termination of a conflict and helping the parties reach a mutually acceptable agreement. Definitions of the second category highlight the voluntary and nonbinding nature of mediation as compared, for instance, with arbitration. Finally, there are definitions that stress the importance of mediators' attributes such as impartiality, neutrality and lack of bias.

To quibble over definitions may seem to some as a futile exercise in semantics. It is most decidedly not so. Definitions are significant in that they may limit the concept, justify what mediators may or may not do, and take us beyond the exclusive claims and definitions of different professional groups. The reality of mediation is that of a complex, changing, and dynamic interaction between an outsider or third party, with an interest in the conflict or its outcome, and the protagonists or their representatives. Mediation is a decision-making process in which mediators may change their role or identity, issues may alter, and even those involved may change. A comprehensive definition is a primary requisite for understanding the reality of mediation. Mediation is defined here as "a process of conflict management, related to but distinct from the parties' own efforts, where the disputing parties or their representatives seek the assistance, or accept an offer of help, from an individual, group, state or organization to change, affect or influence the parties' perceptions or behavior, without resorting to physical force or invoking the authority of the law" (Bercovitch, 1992: 7). This is a broad definition indeed, but one that can be widely acceptable.

What, then, are the features and characteristics of mediation? These are derived from the definition of mediation and include the following:

1. Mediation is a decision-making and conflict management process.

2. It is activated when a conflict can not be resolved by the parties only, and it involves an extension and continuation of the parties' own conflict management efforts.

3. Mediation involves the intervention in a conflict of an acceptable third party—the mediator—who is there to assist the disputants with their decision making. Mediation is essentially negotiations with the involvement of an additional actor.

4. Mediation is a noncoercive, nonviolent, and ultimately nonbinding form of reaching decisions. Mediators have no authority to force the parties to resolve their differences.

5. Mediators enter a conflict in order to resolve it, affect, change, modify, or influence it.

6. Mediators bring with the, consciously or otherwise, ideas, knowledge, resources, and interests of their own.

7. Mediators operate on a temporary basis only. There is no permanent machinery for mediation; it is activated and terminated when required.

B. Motives for Mediation

As a form of conflict management and diplomacy, mediation has become as common as conflict itself. It is carried on by such different actors as private individuals, government officials, religious leaders, experienced lawyers, and representatives of regional or international organizations. Each of these mediators bring his/her own interests, perceptions and resources, and each adopts a mediation role that is commensurate with these interests and resources. Mediators' roles may range from fairly passive (e.g., chairing sessions) to quite active (e.g., developing settlement proposals). The form and character of mediation in a particular conflict will be determined by the interaction of four factors: (a) the context of the conflict; (b) the issues at stake; (c) the nature of the parties involved in conflict; and (d) the identity and resources of a mediator. Mediation is a truly reciprocal process; it both affects and reflects the original conflict.

A central issue in conflict management concerns finding the most appropriate way of resolution for each conflict. When is mediation the appropriate response to conflict; when, in other words, should it be used to increase the chances of a settlement? Broadly speaking, mediation should be used when:

1. A conflict is long, drawn out, and complex, and shows no signs of being resolved.

2. The parties' own negotiation and conflict management have reached an impasse.

3. Neither party is prepared to countenance further costs or loss of life.

4. Both parties are prepared to cooperate, tacitly or openly, to break their stalemate.

5. The cost of alternative approaches, such as arbitration or ertigation, are known to be prohibitively high.

There can be little precision in specifying the conflicts that should be mediated. Judgments on the appropriateness of mediation must be made by the parties concerned and the third party. However, in most conflicts mediation is likely to be an appropriate response in situations in which, there is a relative power balance between the parties, a likelihood of a continuing relationship between them, and the conflict between the parties is not severe or existential, mediation is likely to be an appropriate response to conflict.

Once initiated, the mediation process can therefore be used to simply identify issues and problems in a conflict, negotiate contracts, redefine a relationship; or actually resolve a conflict. As such, mediation can be an appropriate method of dealing with labor–management issues, conflicts between ethnic groups, or nations. It can be applied to landlord–tenant conflicts, used in the private sector, be part of a community-based approach, practiced in schools and other educational institutions, and in corporate and commercial arenas. Mediation can be used extensively in almost every area of public policy. But what of the rationale of mediation? Why would a mediator wish to intervene in other people's conflict, and why, come to that, would parties to a conflict accept a mediator?

Usually we assume that parties to a conflict and a mediator have one overriding reason for initiating the process; namely, the mutual desire to reduce or resolve the conflict. To this end considerable involvement of time, personnel, and resources is made by all concerned. This shared humanitarian interest may indeed be the reason in some cases of mediation, but normally even this joint interest intertwines with political and other less altruistic interests.

From the perspective of a mediator, mediation may be initiated because (a) a mediator may desire to be instrumental in changing the pattern of a long-standing conflict; (b) a mediator may wish to spread his or her ideas on conflict management and enhance his or her personal standing and professional status; (c) a mediator may want to do something about a conflict whose continuance could adversely affects its own interests; or (d) a mediator may see mediation as a way of extending and enhancing his or her influence. Mediators are actors in the political arena; they mediate because they are mandated to do so, or because they may gain something from it (be it prestige, influence, recognition, or gratitude).

What then, of parties in conflict, why would they seek or accept the intervention of an outsider? Parties too have a number of reasons for initiating and engaging in mediation. They may (a) genuinely believe that this low-risk and flexible form of conflict management will reduce their conflict risks; (b) welcome mediation in the expectation that the mediator might nudge, or put some pressure on, the other party; (c) wish to have someone be the scapegoat, should mediation fail; or (d) desire mediation in the hope that a mediator could be used to verify and monitor the agreement. One way or another, both conflicting parties and a mediator have pretty compelling reasons and a strong rationale for engaging in mediation.

III. THE MEDIATION PROCESS

Mediators can have many different types of relationships with conflict parties. This means that the goals and tasks of mediation, as well as its stages or phases, are sometimes difficult to identify, and often vary from context to context. Notwithstanding such difficulties, the relationship between a mediator and parties in conflict does not unfold as one undifferentiated continuum, but rather as a series of fairly distinct phases. These phases, and the behavior associated with each, constitute the mediation process. It may be useful to think of a mediation process in terms of three sequential phases: (a) preparation for mediation; (b) mediation meetings; and (c) postmediation activities. Let us examine each of these stages in turn.

A. Preparation for Mediation

Mediation is initiated as a result of request by a mediator or the parties themselves, or more commonly, referral by other parties (e.g., a judge, a board, a council, an organization). The way mediation is initiated and prepared is frequently a determining factor in the outcome and effectiveness of the mediation. A joint request by both parties for mediation represents a commitment to the process that may well be important in securing a subsequent agreement. A request for mediation by a single party, on the other hand, may be indicative of some reluctance to engage in mediation, a reluctance which may well produce an impasse.

Once mediation is introduced as the option for conflict management, the gathering and exchange of information on all matters relating to the conflict become important activities. At this stage a mediator may assess what data and information are needed, what can be disclosed, and which documents should be exchanged.

On many occasions, and regardless of how mediation was initiated, a mediator may wish to meet separately with one or both parties. Among other things such preparatory meetings may help mediators (a) assess the parameters of the conflict; (b) build their personal and institutional credibility; (c) educate participants about the mediation process; (d) gain a commitment for the mediation process; and (e) make the necessary organizational arrangements. By now a mediator has a fairly clear idea of what the conflict is all about, and what plan of mediation should be adopted.

B. The Mediation Meeting

This phase generally involves four distinct interactions, the first of which is the formal opening of negotiation, in which the parties will greet each other and begin to exchange information. After a short preparatory statement from the mediator (introduction, description of mediation process and logistics), the parties are invited to make and formal and uninterrupted presentation. From here on the parties become an active part of communication and the mediation process. Following these presentations mediators may ask questions and seek clarifications. Often mediators may summarize each party's presentation.

Opening statements and mediators' summaries are designed to outline the substantive issues in conflict, establish conflict management procedures, and build a rapport with the other side. The most critical feature of this stage is the attempt to establish an accurate exchange of information. The second major stage consists of mediators' attempts to identify areas of agreement (on substantive or procedural matters) and provide a productive basis for the subsequent efforts. This stage concludes with the mediator and the parties focusing on issues for discussions and the setting of an agenda. An agenda that can contribute to a productive dialogue is one that frames values in conflict into interest conflicts, where issues on which the parties are likely to reach an agreement are dealt with early in the negotiation, and where issues may be combined, traded, or packaged. A mediator may circumvent many of the problems associated with ineffective conflict management by facilitating or structuring a productive agenda.

Once an agenda is agreed upon, negotiations between the parties begin in earnest. Information and feeling are exchanged about the issues themselves, or past events leading up to the conflict. A mediator will at this stage encourage the parties to explore a wide range of options. A mediator can be instrumental in developing new options by establishing a climate of trust and confidence within which brainstorming and open discussion sessions may take place.

In the third stage of mediation, the parties assess their interests, review their options, and determine the best option or alternative they can live with. Here a mediator invites the parties to think in terms of the consequences and feasibility of each option. The parties may now assess options in separate meetings (caucus) that give parties the opportunity to express their own emotions, as well as test how realistic the options on offer are. During this stage a mediator intervenes quite often to keep the process going and to ensure that each party understands the other's perspective. Final details may now be settled, so that a decision making on an agreement may be precipitated.

The fourth and final stage of the mediation proper is taken with producing a formal agreement or settlement. This is usually embodied in a document that outlines the parties' intentions, decisions, and future behavior. The mediator will now ensure that the document drafted reflects accurately what has transpired in the negotiations. With the signing of the document, and the mediator's closing words, the formal process of mediation is brought to an end. The whole process is depicted diagrammatically in Figure 2.

C. Postmediation Activities

Once an agreement between the parties is formalized, the parties will try and put into practice what they agreed to verbally. Mediated agreements are rarely clear and totally unequivocal, as numerous problems regarding the agreement may arise. At this stage a mediator may now be required to help with the criteria used to measure successful compliance with and implementation of the agreement. This stage takes place outside the mediation setting, and may require a mediator to work out specific operational details, or identify people or organizations that can help to implement the agreement. Mediators must make themselves available to review problems during the immediate implementation phase.

In some instances mediators may also assume the responsibility of monitoring the agreement (e.g., UN mediation is often followed by UN peacekeeping mis-

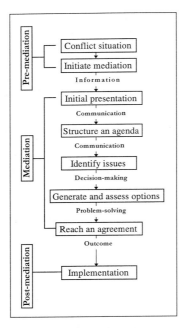

FIGURE 2 The mediation process.

sions). Mediator monitoring is intended to prevent non-compliance with the agreement and encourage the participants to stick with their plan as time goes on. Follow-up activities by a mediator at monthly or other regular intervals may ensure that the agreement is executed faithfully and loyally.

IV. MEDIATION STRATEGIES AND TACTICS

How do mediators, without the power to make formally binding decisions, move the process of mediation forward and create the conditions for more effective decision making? Which strategies and tactics may be used by a mediator? With so many actors capable of initiating and conducting mediation, it is not easy to make sense of the bewildering range of mediation behavior. This is why we often think of the broad categories of mediation roles, mediation strategies, and mediation tactics.

Mediators' roles refer to a generalized and predictable pattern of behavior in mediation. Mediators' roles may be characterized in a number of ways. We may talk of formal versus informal roles, advisory versus directive roles, or invited versus noninvited roles. Mediators' roles may be fisted more specifically as catalyst, educa-

tor, agent of reality, and scapegoat. Each of these categories is useful in drawing attention to aspects of mediation behavior. Unfortunately it is unwise to assume that mediators carry out only one role throughout their mediation. The reality of mediation is that of a dynamic situation where mediators may enact a number of roles in the course of their mediation.

This is why the notion of strategy offers a more useful approach to question of identifying mediator behavior and tactics. A strategy is a broad or overall approach to conflict. A strategy may entail one or more roles and various types of behavior. There are various ways of thinking about mediation strategies. Mediators may adopt incremental (i.e., segmenting a conflict into smaller issues) or comprehensive (i.e., dealing with all aspects of a conflict) strategies. They may use strategies of integration (i.e., searching for common grounds), pressing (i.e., getting parties to focus on one alternative), or compensation (i.e., increasing the attractiveness of a particular alternative). Another approach to describing mediator strategies distinguishes between reflexive strategies (i.e., facilitating better interactions), nondirective strategies (i.e., producing a favorite climate for mediation), and directive strategies (i.e., promoting a specific outcome).

Touval and Zartman's threefold classification of strategies is the most apposite for the scholar or practitioner of mediation. They identify three basic strategies that mediators use to induce the parties to reach a peaceful and satisfactory outcome. These are communication-facilitation, formulation, and directive strategies. The use of any of these strategies is designed to change, affect, or modify aspects of a conflict, or the nature of interaction between the parties. Different mediators may use different strategies. These will depend on mediator's identity, attributes, and resources. Clearly, some individual mediators may not use directive strategies extensively; a major superpower, on the other hand, will not rely on communication-facilitation strategies only.

Mediators pursue their objective of conflict resolution by entering a conflict and adopting a particular strategy (which may change later). Each strategy is effected through a series of specific tactics. It is worth noting the tactics associated with each strategy.

1. Communication-facilitation strategies:
   • Make contact with parties;
   • gain the trust and confidence of the parties;
   • arrange for interactions between the parties;
   • identify issues and interests;
   • help to reframe issues;

- clarify situation and define issues;
- provide confidence and reassurance;
- avoid taking sides;
- guide communications;
- develop a rapport with parties;
- supply missing information;
- facilitate disclosure of information;
- develop a framework for understanding;
- listen actively;
- encourage meaningful communication;
- offer positive evaluations;
- summarize positions and interests;
- allow the interests of all parties to be discussed.

2. Formulation strategies:
   - Choose site for meetings;
   - decide which parties should be involved;
   - control pace and formality of meetings;
   - control physical environment including seating;
   - establish protocol;
   - suggest procedures for speaking, intermissions, and caucusing;
   - highlight common interests;
   - reduce tensions;
   - control timing;
   - deal with simple issues first;
   - structure agenda;
   - keep parties at the table;
   - help parties save face;
   - keep process focused on issues.

3. Directive strategies:
   - Change parties' expectations;
   - take responsibility for concessions;
   - identify settlement range;
   - make substantive suggestions and proposals;
   - make parties aware of the costs of non-agreement;
   - impose deadlines;
   - supply and filter information;
   - suggest concessions parties can make;
   - help negotiators to undo a commitment or "save face";
   - help to construct settlement formulae;
   - reward party concessions;
   - help devise a framework for acceptable outcome;
   - change expectations;
   - press the parties to show flexibility;
   - promise resources or threaten withdrawal.

This is what mediators actually do and these are the tactics they use when they intervene in conflict.

The choice of an appropriate strategy and its related tactics can be effective in achieving one of the central objectives of mediation; namely, (a) changing the physical environment of the conflict (e.g., by maintaining secrecy, or imposing time limits, as President Carter did at Camp David); (b) changing the perception of what is at stake (e.g., by structuring an agenda, identifying and packaging new issues); and (c) changing the parties' motivation to reach a peaceful outcome (e.g., using subtle pressure). To be effective, however, mediation strategies must reflect the reality of the conflict, the nature of the parties involved, and the resources of the mediator. To that extent mediation is a truly reciprocal activity.

The strategies and tactics of numerous mediators are so very different, not merely because mediators are different, but because the nature and context of a conflict, and the characteristics of the parties involved are different too. To be effective mediation strategy and behavior must match and reflect these conditions. The process of mediation and the context of a conflict are closely interrelated.

V. NEGOTIATION

Negotiation is by far the most common process of resolving conflict. It shares many characteristics with mediation. In many aspects negotiation may be seen as "unassisted mediation." Negotiation is a joint decision-making or conflict resolution process that involves two distinct parties (rather than three) who have a conflict of interest over one or more issues. Like mediation, negotiation is a voluntary, dynamic, and evolving relationship, where the parties involved have a strong incentive to cooperate, but also a strong desire to push for their own interests. The tension between cooperative and competitive tendencies defines the nature of negotiation. When this tension becomes too disruptive, a mediator may be called in to help put the negotiations back on track.

Broadly speaking, we can identify two types of negotiating situations: distributive (or competitive) negotiations and integrative (or cooperative) negotiations. In distributive negotiations (often referred to as "zero-sum negotiations") the issues to be negotiated, or total payoff, are fixed, and each party attempts to secure a larger slice of a fixed resource. The basic structure of distributive negotiations consists of:

1. The party's target point (what one hopes to achieve);
2. the party's resistance point (the point at which one will rather break off negotiations); and
3. the bargaining range (all possible outcomes between target point and resistance point).

Integrative negotiations are often described as "win-win" negotiations. Such negotiations emphasize joint efforts directed at maximizing options and finding solutions that can increase the total value or payoff for *both* parties. Integrative negotiations are about recognizing common interests and creating mutually beneficial solutions. The basic structure of integrative negotiations consist of:

1. Identifying both parties' needs and interests;
2. generating alternative solutions; and
3. choosing solution that provides maximum joint benefit.

Integrative negotiations are obviously very different from distributive negotiations. In order for integrative negotiations to take place, the parties must have a common goal, trust one another, respect each other's needs and interests, and share a commitment to working together. This may happen in some but not all conflict situations.

Clearly distributive and integrative negotiations are very different forms of joint decision making and conflict resolution. The form negotiation takes is dependent, just like mediation, on the nature of the issues, the characteristics of the parties, and the context of the conflict. Each negotiation entails different strategies and different tactical tasks. In distributive negotiations the bargaining is usually over a single issue, and the fundamental strategy each party uses is that of social influence. Each party attempts to influence the other to change his or her subjective utilities and to accept terms that are more favorable to oneself. Distributive negotiation is thus usually accompanied by threats, commitments, bluffs, and other expressions of power. The main strategy used by parties who find themselves in a distributive negotiation is a tough or aggressive strategy. The following tactical moves exemplify an aggressive strategy:

- Issue mild threats;
- ignore opponent's interests;
- set deadlines;
- express readiness to escalate;

- begin negotiations with an extreme offer;
- do not reciprocate concessions;
- use commitments extensively;
- indulge in personal attacks;
- refuse to disclose intentions or goals;
- withhold information;
- demand opponents make first offers;
- break communications;
- mislead the other party about your intentions;
- hint at use of coercion;
- boycott negotiation sessions.

Tactical moves in distributive negotiations are designated to learn as much as possible about the other party, and to influence its perceptions and position, particularly in regard to its own resistance points. The outcome of such negotiations is usually a short-term win for one party, at the expense of their long-term relationship.

Distributive negotiations are quite competitive and adversarial. The goals appear to be irreconcilable, and each party is anxious to have more of what it believes is only a "fixed pie." Integrative negotiations, on the other hand, while acknowledging the different interests of the parties, attempt to go beyond compromise and promote a genuine problem-solving approach. The salient features of integrative negotiations are that they are predicated on the attempt to go beyond initial positions, and understand each other's real needs and interests, they emphasize commonalities between the parties, and they help to create the conditions for a free flow of information and an open dialogue.

Integrative negotiation is for most people a more desirable and efficient form of dealing with a conflict, but it does require a number of preconditions. Among these are the parties' willingness to share information, and to do so honestly and reliably, a belief in the validity of the other party's interests and needs, and a commitment, and motivation, to collaborate rather than compete.

There are three major strategies in integrative negotiations. They are problem identification, generating solutions and creative options, and choosing the best alternative. The specific tactics that implement these strategies are set out below:

- Define issues in conflict in a mutually acceptable way;
- separate the people from the issues involved;
- do not blame or judge other party;
- display trust in the other party;
- acknowledge other party's feelings;

- focus on real interests, not expressed positions;
- build friendships with other party;
- make goals, interests and tactics plain to the other party;
- consider a wide range of options;
- use brainstorming or outsiders to generate new options;
- use role reversal and question-and-answer sessions;
- maintain open communication channels;
- evaluate options in terms of objective criteria;
- choose the option around which there is a clear consensus;
- take time out to cool off when negotiations become emotional;
- minimize formality and record-keeping;
- avoid threats or any coercive tactics.

The essential differences between the two kinds of negotiations are depicted in Figure 3.

Choosing between distributive and integrative negotiations for the purpose of managing a conflict requires each party to assess the issues in conflict, the nature of the parties involved, and the context in which negotiations occur. If the issues in conflict involve the distribution of a scarce resource, if the parties are unfamiliar with each other and not likely to have a relationship beyond the present negotiations, and if the conflict occurs within a structure that lacks effective norms or traditions, we will expect distributive negotiations to be used. Negotiating successfully means matching strategies to conflict situations.

VI. CONCLUSION

Coping with conflict remains one of the most important tasks that individuals, groups and nations face in the 1990s and beyond. The problem of how to cope with conflict resolves itself into the question of how much control the parties in conflict wish to have over the outcome. At one end of the spectrum we have procedures for dealing with conflict that place severe constraints on the parties' behavior (e.g., adjudication). At the other end, we have procedures such as mediation and negotiation that leave most, if not all, major decisions in the hands of the parties. From this perspective alone the incentives to engage in mediation or negotiation are quite overwhelming.

Distinguishing between conflict management processes, and gaining an understanding of the essential features of each process and how it unfolds in the real world is the first step toward affecting the quality of outcomes associated with each process. If we could offer some definitions of quality that emphasize party satisfaction and autonomy, legitimacy, and empowerment, we would find a close correspondence between mediation, negotiations and these outcome qualities. Mediations and negotiations may not be ideal for all conflict situations, but in most cases they represent the most effective way to manage conflicts. An understanding of mediation and negotiations may contribute, in a small way, to a better future.

Also See the Following Articles

CONFLICT MANAGEMENT AND RESOLUTION • CONFLICT TRANSFORMATION • COOPERATION, COMPETITION, AND CONFLICT • DIPLOMACY

Bibliography

Bercovitch, J. (1992). The structure and diversity of mediation in international relations. In J. Bercovitch and Jeffrey Z. Rubin (Eds.), *Mediation in international relations*. London: Macmillan.

Bercovitch, J., & J. Z. Rubin (Eds.). (1992). *Mediation in international relations*. London: Macmillan.

Bercovitch, J. (Ed.). (1996). *Resolving international conflicts*. Boulder, CO: Lynne Rienner.

Bowl, L. (1996). *Mediation: Principles, process, practice*. Sydney: Butterworth.

Hall, L. (Ed.). (1993). *Negotiation: Strategies for mutual gain*. Newbury Park: Sage.

Halpern, A. (1992). *Negotiating skills*. London: Blackstone Press.

Kleiboer, M. (1997). *Success and failure of international mediation*. Boulder, CO: Lynne Rienner.

Dimensions	Distributive negotiation	Integrative negotiations
1. Objective	Increase one's gain	Increase joint gain
2. Information	Restricted, unreliable	Open, reliable
3. Focus of negotiations	Winning at all costs	Future relationship
4. Relationship	Formal, adversarial	Informal, trusting
5. Trust	Low	High
6. Process	Focus on positions, demands and influence	Focus on interests and areas of agreement
7. Tactics	Contentious	Collaborative
8. Outcome	Short-term compromise	Long-term resolution of conflict
9. Openness and creativity	Minimal	Maximal
10. Wider benefits	Decreased conflict	Longer lasting solutions, improved conflict resolution skills

FIGURE 3 Patterns of distributive v. integrative negotiations.

Kovach, K. K. (1995). *Mediation: Principles and practice.* St. Paul, MN: West Publishing Co.

Lebow, R. N. (1996). *The art of bargaining.* Baltimore: Johns Hopkins University Press.

Moore, C. W. (1996). *The mediation process: Practical strategies for resolving conflicts. (2nd Ed.). San Francisco: Jossey Bass.*

Rubin, J. Z., Pruitt, D. G., & Kim, S. H. (1994). *Social conflict: Escalation, stalemate and settlement.* New York: McGraw Hill.

Princen, T. (1992). *Intermediaries in international conflict.* Princeton, NJ: Princeton University Press.

Pruitt, D. G., & Carnevale, P. (1993). *Negotiation in social conflict.* Pacific Groves, CA: Brooks/Cole Publishing.

Rupesinghe, K. (Ed.). (1995). *Conflict transformation.* London: Macmillan.

Slaikeau, K. A. (1996). *When push comes to shove: A practical guide to mediating disputes.* San Francisco: Jossey Bass.

Touval, S., & Zartman, I. W. (Eds.). (1985). *International mediation in theory and practice.* Boulder, CO: Westview Press.

Zartman, I. W. (Ed.). (1995). *Elusive Peace: Negotiating and end to civil wars.* Washington, DC: Brookings Institution.

Mental Illness: Assessment and Management of Violent Patients

Kenneth Tardiff — Cornell University Medical College

I. Types of Mental Illness Associated with Increased Violence Potential
II. Short-Term Violence Potential
III. Emergency Management of Violence
IV. Long-Term Treatment
V. Conclusion

GLOSSARY

Emergency Management Interventions to diminish or control violence by patients that is occurring or is imminent such as verbal intervention, psychotropic medication, physical restraint, and/or seclusion.

Mental Illness A clinically significant behavioral or psychological syndrome that is associated with a person's distress, disability, or important loss of freedom as defined in the Diagnostic and Statistical Manual—Fourth Revision (DSM-IV) of the American Psychiatric Association.

Long-Term Treatment Interventions to decrease future episodes of violence by a patient such as psychotropic medication, psychotherapy, and behavioral therapy.

Violence Physical aggression directed toward another person with the intent of causing injury and/or pain.

Violence Potential The likelihood of violence by a patient in the next few days or over a longer time such as a year or more.

THIS ARTICLE focuses on physical violence by persons who have mental illnesses that cause or contribute to their violence. It describes how patterns of violence are related to various types of mental disorders. Factors that increase the potential for violence are described since clinicians often are called upon to made decisions on the risk of violence, particularly in the short-term for the purpose of planning treatment, for example, hospitalization. The emergency management of violence by patients and the long-term treatment of violent psychiatric patients is discussed.

In the treatment of violent psychiatric patients, there are important principals that must be emphasized. First, the modalities used for the control of violence, at times administered on an involuntary basis, apply to the treatment of psychiatric *patients;* that is, persons who are diagnosed as having a mental disorder contained in the DSM-IV. The use of means of control for other types of violence, for example, that stemming from political or economic sources, is beyond the realm of psychiatry.

I. TYPES OF MENTAL ILLNESSES WITH INCREASED VIOLENCE POTENTIAL

Some mental disorders have an increased potential for violence during the patient's lifetime. There are varying patterns of violence that reflect the unique underlying pathologies of various mental disorders. One should keep in mind, however, that environmental factors interact with the pathology of a particular mental disorder

Copyright © 1999 by Academic Press. All rights of reproduction in any form reserved.

so as to alter the frequency, severity, and characteristics of violence by a specific patient at a specific time.

A. Schizophrenia

In paranoid schizophrenia, there is delusional thinking usually in terms of persecution. Patients may believe that people are trying to harm them; for example, that the police are spying on them or that some unknown mechanism is controlling their minds. Paranoid schizophrenics may react to these persecutory delusions by retaliating against the presumed source of this persecution. Other types of schizophrenics may attempt to kill others because of some form of psychotic identification with the victim, usually a well-known entertainer or a political figure. Hallucinations associated with schizophrenia, particularly command hallucinations (e.g., the patient is commanded by a voice to kill someone), have been known to result in violent behavior. In addition, hallucinations in which people are cursing or insulting the patient may result in retaliation against a supposed source of these insults.

Some schizophrenics are violent because of a generalized disorganization of thought and a lack of impulse control, with purposeless, excited psychomotor activity resulting in violence. Schizophrenic patients may be violent because of the side-effect of restlessness caused in some cases by antipsychotic medication. With this agitation and restlessness, they may bump into other patients and start a fight. Other disease processes superimposed on the schizophrenic disorder may be responsible for the violence rather than delusions per se. These include brain damage secondary to heavy drug or alcohol use, head trauma, and other numerous neurologic or systemic diseases discussed later in this article. Other psychiatric disorders such as mental retardation or personality disorders may be responsible for violence by schizophrenic patients. Last, schizophrenic patients may be violent to attain what they want, to express anger, or to deliberately hurt others. It is very important to determine the cause of violence by a schizophrenic patient and not to assume it is due to psychosis and respond with an increase or change of antipsychotic medication.

B. Delusional Disorder

Although delusional disorder is uncommon, it can often be associated with violence. Delusional disorder, unlike schizophrenia, has only a core delusion as the abnormality and no other psychopathology. The persistent delusions possessed by these patients may be of the persecutory type in which patients feel they are being conspired against, cheated, spied on, poisoned, or otherwise harmed. In addition to resorting to legal action and appealing to governmental agencies, patients with this disorder often become resentful and angry and may become violent against those they believe are harming them. Delusional disorders of the jealous type involve the persistent belief that the patient's spouse or lover is being unfaithful. These patients may attempt to follow the spouse. They may resort to physical attacks on the spouse or the person identified as the spouse's sexual partner.

C. Mood Disorders

Most violence by manic patients is not premeditated. With manic patients impulses are put into action. If some of these impulses are violent, then they become violent actions. The typical situation where manic patients erupt with violence is when they feel contained and not free to do what they want to do. This may be physical, as being contained in a small examining room in the emergency room, or interpersonal, as when a nurse insists that the manic patient take medication. Other patients with mood disorders are rarely violent. An infrequent exception is the psychotic depressed patient. In this type of patient, extreme hopelessness, feelings that life is not worth living, or delusional feelings of profound guilt may result in violence, usually involving murder followed by suicide.

D. Personality Disorders

The DSM-IV describes personality disorders as follows: "Personality traits are enduring patterns of perceiving, relating to and thinking about the environment and oneself that are exhibited in a wide range of social and personal contexts. Only when personality traits are inflexible and maladaptive and cause significant functional impairment or subjective distress do they constitute personality disorders." There are four personality disorders where there is an increased potential for violence and one where violence is often threatened but infrequently committed.

1. Intermittent Explosive Personality Disorder

The intermittent explosive personality disorder in DSM-IV is subsumed under the diagnosis of organic personality syndrome. A key characteristic of this syndrome is the episodic recurrent outbursts of aggression and violence that are grossly out of proportion to any precipitating psychosocial stressor. There is often remorse following this violent episode with pleas from the perpetrator that the victim forgive him or her and that "it won't happen again." There is little evidence of other behavioral problems between these violent episodes, which is in distinction to four other personality disorders associated with violence: the borderline personality, the antisocial personality, the paranoid personality, and the narcissistic personality.

2. Borderline Personality

In the case of the borderline personality disorder, in addition to exhibiting frequent displays of anger and recurrent physical violence toward others, the patient manifests other behavioral problems between the violent episodes. There is often a wide range of impulsive behaviors, including suicidal or self-mutilating behaviors, excessive spending, indiscreet sexual behavior, drug abuse, shoplifting, and reckless driving. In addition, there is a marked and persistent identity problem manifested by uncertainty about self-image, sexual orientation, career goals, and other values. There are often manipulative attempts to obtain caring from others. Violence is characteristically in response to feelings of or rejection by someone from whom the patient wants love, caring, or merely attention. Violence is accompanied by intense emotional displays and emotional instability.

3. Antisocial Personality

Violence manifested by persons with the antisocial personality disorder is just one of many antisocial behaviors. These patients repeatedly get into physical fights and violence involving their spouses, children, and individuals outside of the family. A number of other antisocial behaviors include destroying property, harassing others, stealing, engaging in illegal occupations, driving in a reckless or intoxicated manner, and being involved in promiscuous relationships. The patient often lies, does not honor financial obligations, and is unable to sustain consistent employment. Alcohol and substance abuse are often a problem. The violence toward others and other aspects of antisocial behavior are not accompanied by remorse or guilt. Violence is often accompanied by little display of emotion and seems cold blooded. Issues of self-esteem and/or revenge frequently underlie the violence.

4. Paranoid Personality

The patient with the paranoid personality is suspicious and believes that people conspire against him or her, whether they are in government, in other organizations, or are members of a certain race or class. They may be racist or sexist and perceive others to be so. They may belong to militaristic organizations or be preoccupied with militaristic themes. They tend to be preoccupied and possess firearms. Episodic violence is not frequent in their past; however, threats of violence against others are frequent (for example, against people at work after being discharged from a job). Most patients with a paranoid personality will not be physically violent but when violence does occur, it is often lethal (for example, the "disgruntled employee" who appears at work and shoots fellow employees).

5. Narcissistic Personality

The patient with a narcissistic personality feels he or she has a right to control others and to be the focus of their attention and admiration. The patient is exploitative in relations with others and has little or no remorse in doing so. Unlike the borderline patient there is a lack of chaotic disruption of interpersonal relationships and unlike the antisocial patient, there is little flagrant criminal activity with the exception of professional killers who have narcissistic personality. More often the violence is due to frustration and anger that the other person has not given them what they think they deserve.

E. Psychoactive Substances

1. Alcohol

The ingestion of alcohol often may be associated with aggression and violence as a result of disinhibition, particularly in the initial phase of intoxication. Intoxication is accompanied by emotional lability and impaired judgment. The patient may appear to have slurred speech, incoordination, unsteady gait, and a flushed face. Violent behavior can also be found in persons who drink small amounts of alcohol insufficient to cause intoxication in most people. This is known as the alcohol idiosyncratic intoxication. Violence may be associated with alcohol withdrawal after cessation of prolonged, heavy ingestion of alcohol for 2 or 3 days.

2. Cocaine

Cocaine initially produces a feeling of well-being and euphoria. With continued use, particularly when used intravenously or when smoked in the form of crack, euphoria turns to grandiosity, psychomotor agitation, suspiciousness, and, frequently, violence. With continued use, suspiciousness becomes paranoid ideation and, subsequently, paranoid delusional thinking. Thus violence results from delusional thinking as well as from the effect of cocaine of overall stimulation.

3. Amphetamines

With intense or prolonged amphetamine use, a feeling of well-being and confidence turns to confusion, rambling, incoherence, paranoid ideation, and delusional thinking. With this there are agitation, fighting, and other forms of aggression and impaired social judgment.

4. Hallucinogens

Hallucinogens such as lysergic acid diethylamide (LSD), dimethyltryptamine (DMT), and mescaline may result in impaired judgment and paranoid ideation in addition to other perceptual changes, including depersonalization, derealization, illusions, synesthesias, and hallucinations. Violence may occur during intoxication with the above-mentioned hallucinogens, but it is not as common as in phencyclidine (PCP) intoxication. Within 1 h of oral use (within 5 min if smoked or taken intravenously), PCP often produces marked violence, impulsivity, unpredictability, and grossly impaired judgment. There may be delusional thinking or delirium.

5. Inhalants

Inhalants are hydrocarbons found in substances such as gasoline, glue, paint, and paint thinners. These are often used by young children and early adolescents to produce intoxication, which may be characterized by belligerence and violence as well as impaired judgment.

6. Prescription Drugs

Prescription drugs may cause violence either by excessive doses or through side-effects. Examples of this are anticholinergic medications and steroids. In addition, restlessness from antipsychotic medications may be interpreted as intended violence or aggression.

F. Organic Disorders

Organic disorders involve damage to the brain caused by gross diseases of the brain or by medical disorders that affect the brain. As a result of impaired thinking and perceptual disturbances, violence in organic mental disorders and syndromes may be the result of decreased control over aggressive and other impulses and poor social judgment as well as the result of paranoid thoughts or even delusions in these patients who feel threatened by their cognitive impairment. In delirium, there may be increased psychomotor activity with violence accompanied by disordered thinking, fluctuating level of consciousness, perceptual disturbances, disorientation, and memory impairment. In dementia, patients are more alert but can be irritable, hostile, and violent as a result of their frustration with impaired memory and higher cortical functions. In addition, suspicious, irritable personalities may be intensified with dementia.

In organic delusional syndrome, there are prominent delusions that may lead to retaliation and violence against others if of a paranoid nature. In organic hallucinosis, a prominent symptom is that of hallucinations that may lead to violence against others if threatening or derogatory. In organic mood syndrome, a manic state with hyperactivity and disorganization may lead to violence toward others.

1. Primary Diseases of the Brain Associated with Violence

A number of primary diseases of the brain can be associated with violent behavior. Violence in temporal lobe epilepsy is not frequent. When it occurs, it may occur during the ictal period; if so, it is often purposeless. Violence has been found in between seizures among patients with temporal lobe epilepsy. Following generalized seizures, violence has been found with encephalopathy. Infections of the brain, including viral encephalitis, acquired immune deficiency syndrome (AIDS), tuberculosis, fungal meningitis, syphilis, and herpes simplex can be associated with violent behavior. Other primary diseases of the brain associated with violence include head trauma, normal-pressure hydrocephalus, cerebrovascular diseases, tumors, Huntington's chorea, multiple sclerosis, Alzheimer's disease, Pick's disease, multi-infarct dementia, Parkinson's disease, Wilson's disease, and postanoxic or posthypoglycemic states with brain damage.

G. Systemic Medical Disorders Associated with Violence

There are a number of systemic disorders associated with violence. Unlike the primary diseases of the brain, many of these are treatable and reversible. Thus, recognition is important, and appropriate medical care is necessary. These disorders include hypoxia; electrolyte imbalances; hepatic disease; renal disease; vitamin deficiencies such as of B12 folate or thiamine; systemic infections; hypoglycemia; Cushing's disease; hyperthyroidism; hypothyroidism; systemic lupus erythematosus; poisoning by heavy metals, insecticides, and other substances; and porphyria.

H. Mental Retardation

Although most patients with mental retardation are not violent, when violence does occur it is often difficult to treat. Violence due to poor intellectual ability is associated with anger and frustration at not being able to obtain what is desired or at not being able to verbalize concerns and feelings. This is accompanied by poor impulse control and then violence toward others or the self. Some of the causes of mental retardation can be subsumed under organic mental disorders (e.g., head trauma during birth or as an adult, hypoxia, and lead poisoning in childhood).

II. SHORT-TERM VIOLENCE POTENTIAL

In distinction to recognizing that the preceding mental disorders have an increased potential for violence during a patient's lifetime one must assess the short-term potential for violence by a specific patient. The following includes information that the clinician should collect so as to make a decision about a patient's potential for violence in the near future, i.e., within the next few days or a week at the most. This is the time frame during which decisions about changes of treatment or protecting potential victims must be made. Furthermore, beyond a week, there is the opportunity for intervening factors to change the state of the patient and the environment that existed at the evaluation of violence potential. These intervening factors may include noncompliance with medication, resumption of drinking or substance use, threats of divorce by a spouse, and other stressors.

A. Sources of Information

Information is collected from the interview with the patient, but other sources of information must be sought. These include past records from hospitalizations and other treatment, police records, and other records. It is essential that the clinician speak or attempt to speak to the family, therapists, and others who may have knowledge of the patient. Some patients, such as those with paranoid delusions, may be reluctant to divulge thoughts of violence, so the clinicians must listen carefully and follow-up on any hints of violence that may surface during the interview. If there are thoughts of violence or even threats, the degree of formulation of the ideas or plan of violence should be assessed.

B. Degree of Formulation

A well-formulated or detailed plan should make the clinician concerned about the risk of violence that a patient poses. This includes details about where and when and how the patient will attack the victim as well as knowledge about the potential victim's personal life such as daily schedules and address. For example, vague thoughts of "getting even" are not as serious, all other things being equal, as specific plans on attacking the victims.

C. Intent

If a patient has thoughts of harming someone, it is important to assess his or her intent to harm the person. Just because thoughts of violence occur in a patient's mind may not be sufficient to warrant action by the clinician.

D. Availability of Victim

Availability of a potential victim is important. This refers to access to the victim as well as geographic distance. For example, a potential victim living in an apartment with a doorman who can be informed of the potential for violence is generally safer than a potential victim living in a house in the suburbs. Geography plays a part in assessment of risk of violence to a potential victim. For example, a schizophrenic patient who threatens his father and who lives thousands of miles away poses less of a danger than a schizophrenic patient who is threatening his parents with whom he lives.

E. Weapons

Availability of a weapon is relevant as to the lethality of the violence. Patients should be asked if there is a concern about violence as well as suicide, if there is a gun in the household, whether they have other access to guns, or as to how they would go about buying a gun.

F. History of Violence and Other Impulsive Behaviors

A history of violence or other impulsive behaviors by the patient is a major factor in the prediction of violence. Past violence predicts future violence. Episodes of past violence, for example, the most recent episode, must be dissected in a detailed, concrete manner by the clinician. This includes details of the time and place of the violence, who was present, who said what to whom, what did the patient see, what does the patient remember, what do family members or staff remember, why was the patient violent (e.g., delusions versus anger), and what could have been done to avoid the violent confrontation? Often there is a pattern of escalation of violence; for example, a couple interacting in domestic violence or the schizophrenic patient on the inpatient unit escalating as interactions with other patients become too intense.

The "past history" of violence includes the information about date of onset, frequency, targets, and severity. Severity is measured by the degree of injury to the victim(s) from pushing; to punching; to causing injuries such as bruises; to causing injuries such as broken bones, lacerations, internal injuries; or to even death. Last, past history of violence should include prior evaluations (for example, psychological testing or imaging) and treatment (for example, hospitalization, medications, and response to treatment).

G. Psychosis

The presence of psychosis in a patient expressing thoughts of violence or threatening violence increases the risk of violent behavior. The most frequent type of patient who is psychotic and violent is the schizophrenic patient, but other sources of psychosis (for example, from mood disorders or substance abuse) have been associated with violence. These patients are violent because they believe others are attempting to or have harmed them and they regard violence as justified in self defense or as retaliation. Hallucinations, particularly auditory hallucinations, can be associated with violence by schizophrenic patients. These may be command auditory hallucinations telling the patient to kill others or to harm him- or herself.

H. Personality Disorders

The presence of a personality disorder, particularly the antisocial or borderline types, increases the risk of violence for patients who have violent ideas or who are making threats of violence.

I. Alcohol and Substance Use

Alcohol and drug use should be assessed. Substances that increase the risk of violent behavior include alcohol, cocaine, amphetamines, phencyclidine (PCP) and other hallucinogens, anticholinergics, and steroids as well as inhalants such as glue. Alcohol withdrawal has been associated with violence.

J. Organicity

Organicity increases the risk of violence. Central nervous system disorders and systemic disorders that produce violence through delirium or dementia have been discussed above.

K. Background of the Patient

The sociocultural background of the patient must be taken into consideration as one tries to determine whether a patient poses a risk of violence. Violence is an accepted way of expressing oneself in some segments of society usually characterized by poverty and lack of education.

L. Compliance with Treatment

Compliance with treatment is a factor in determining a patient's risk of violence. This involves regular attendance for treatment sessions and compliance with medication and other treatments. Blood levels of medications assist the clinician in monitoring compliance with medication. Contact with the patient's family also helps in monitoring compliance with medication. Schizophrenic patients with a history of violence related to psychosis are best managed with injectable long-acting haloperidol or fluphenazine so as to assure compliance with medication.

III. EMERGENCY MANAGEMENT OF VIOLENCE

A. Safety

Violence by psychiatric patients can erupt unexpectedly in any clinical setting: in the emergency room, in the inpatient unit, or even in the outpatient setting. The foremost thought in the clinician's mind at that point should be safety. The clinician must feel safe with the patient or it will interfere with the evaluation or may result in physical injury to the clinician. In talking to the patient, a wide range of options should be considered, from being alone with the patient in an office with the door closed, to being alone with the door open, to being alone with aides outside of the room, to being alone with aides inside of the room, to the most extreme option, interviewing the patient while the patient is in physical restraints. In addition to relying on one's feelings concerning safety, one should take into consideration the possibility of inappropriate reactions, such as denial or overreaction, that will interfere with the effective management of a particular patient.

B. Verbal Intervention

Verbal means of intervention and even prevention should receive serious consideration. The staff should talk to patients in a calm, nonprovocative manner and also listen to patients. As tension increases before violence occurs, even the most psychotic schizophrenic patient may respond to nonprovocative interpersonal contact and expression of concern and caring.

C. Seclusion and Restraint

In 1982 the United States Supreme Court ruled in the case of Youngberg v. Romeo that Mr. Romeo, a violent, profoundly mentally retarded man who was institutionalized, could be deprived of his liberty in terms of being restrained if it could be justified on the grounds of protecting others or himself and, most important, if the decision was based on the clinical judgment of a professional that is not a substantial departure from professional standards. At the time the court decision was rendered, this author was chairing a Task Force of the American Psychiatric Association to develop guidelines for the psychiatric uses of seclusion and restraint. The guidelines have been approved by the Association and have set reasonable, minimal clinical standards for management of violence using seclusion and restraint in the context of verbal intervention, involuntary medication, and other factors in the treatment environment. The guidelines are expanded upon in a book by members of the Task Force.

Indications for emergency use of seclusion and restraint are as follows:

1. To prevent imminent harm to others, namely staff and other patients, if other means are not effective and appropriate.
2. To prevent imminent harm to the patient if other means of control are not effective or appropriate.
3. To prevent serious disruption of the treatment program or significant damage to the environment.

These indications for the emergency use of seclusion and restraint state that violence need not actually occur but that the staff may use these measures for imminent violence, as in the case where a patient's past pattern of escalation to violence is known or if it is apparent that a patient is on the verge of exploding. The decision as to whether seclusion, restraint, or involuntary medication is used is a clinical one and should be based on the individual needs and status of the patient. For example, restraint probably would be preferable if the

patient is delirious and the etiology of the delirium is unknown. In this case, one would prefer to keep the patient free of drugs, certainly antipsychotics, until the underlying etiology is determined, and seclusion would not be appropriate since the sensory deprivation may worsen the patient's delirium. Restraint might also be preferred if close medical monitoring is necessary. On the other hand, seclusion may be the method of choice in the case of a manic person who needs a decrease of stimulation. Involuntary medication may be the preferred method of control, perhaps with seclusion or restraint, for the paranoid schizophrenic patient who has stopped taking medications and has become violent or is imminently so.

D. Use of Emergency Medication

Emergency medication is useful for psychotic violent patients who are violent. Emergency medication is indicated for nonpsychotic, violent patients when verbal intervention is not appropriate or effective. It may be used instead of seclusion or restraint. On the other hand, it may be used with seclusion or restraint when severe agitation or violence is present to minimize detrimental effects that violence may have on patients even though they are secluded or restrained.

1. Antipsychotics

Antipsychotic medication should be used primarily for the management of violent patients who manifest psychotic symptomatology. Occasionally it may be indicated for patients who are not psychotic but who are violent, as in the case of elderly patients with dementia or other organic brain dysfunction where anxiolytic agents or sedatives may exacerbate the clinical picture. Respiradone is recommended in such cases because of this low frequency of anticholinergic side-effects. It may be offered by mouth, with the clear stipulation that if the patient does not take the medication, the medication will be given intramuscularly to manage violence that is a danger to others or to the patient.

2. Anxiolytics

The benzodiazepines, particularly lorazepam, can be used very effectively in emergency situations where violence is in the process of occurring or where it is imminent. Lorazepam may be used with the antipsychotic medications for schizophrenics, manics, and patients in other psychotic states. Lorazepam may be used alone for the management of nonpsychotic patients. For patients who appear to have some degree of control, it may be offered as oral medication. However, in most emergency situations, lorazepam is used intramuscularly.

IV. LONG-TERM TREATMENT

A. Medication

There is no one drug for treatment of violence because the underlying etiology for violence differs among patients. Before one embarks on the use of a drug on a long-term basis, there must be an established baseline for the violence manifested by the patient. A good measure of the frequency, severity, and target of the violent behavior is the Yudofsky Overt Aggression Scale. Since the build-up, maintenance, and withdrawal phases in the use of medications, particularly propranolol, lithium, and the anticonvulsants, will be long, there must be a quantitative measurement of response after months of treatment and comparison to the baseline before the medication was started.

1. Antipsychotics

Antipsychotic medications are used for schizophrenia and mania and in some organic disorders for delusional thinking or control of violence. For paranoid schizophrenics who have manifested violent behavior or made threats of violence, compliance with medication is bad. Thus clinicians should consider the use of the long-acting injectable forms of antipsychotic medications haloperidol or fluphenazine.

Clozapine and respiradone have been found to be effective in the treatment of violent psychotic patients who do not respond to other antipsychotic medication. Clozapine and respiradone may have antiaggressive effects separate from their antipsychotic effects.

2. Anxiolytic Drugs and Sedatives

The use of anxiolytic drugs and sedatives for the control of violence over a long period of time is generally not recommended. This stems from a concern that long-term use of these medications will result in drug abuse, dependency, and tolerance. In addition, they can produce sedation, confusion, and depression. Buspirone has been shown to be effective in managing anxiety yet it appears to lack the abuse potential of other antianxiety agents.

3. Carbamazepine and Other Anticonvulsants

There have been a number of case studies and open drug trials that have indicated that carbamazepine is effective for the management of aggression in a number of different types of psychiatric patients. Carbamazepine may be effective in terms of managing aggression and irritability in patients with overt seizures, both complex partial seizures and generalized seizures; in schizophrenic patients with and without electroencephalogical abnormalities; and with other types of patients with episodic violence without gross brain damage or mental retardation. Valproate has been found to be effective for violent patients who cannot be treated with carbamazepine. Low doses of clonazepam may be effective for episodic violence.

4. Propranolol and Other Beta-Blockers

Review of a number of control studies, open trials, and case reports shows the effectiveness of propranolol in the management of aggressive behavior. Most of the patients studied and responding to propranolol were those with organic brain disease, often with gross impairment. Nearly all the patients in these studies were refractory to other medications, including antipsychotics, anxiolytic agents, anticonvulsants, and lithium. In a number of cases, concurrent antipsychotic medication was used. Before using propranolol, there should be a thorough medical evaluation of the patient. Patients with the following diseases should be excluded from treatment with propranolol: bronchial asthma, chronic obstructive pulmonary disease, insulin-dependent diabetes, cardiac diseases including angina or congestive heart failure, diabetes mellitus, significant peripheral vascular disease, severe renal disease, and hyperthyroidism.

There are a number of other case studies using beta-blockers other than propranolol. These include the use of nadolol in the treatment of aggressive patients with chronic paranoid schizophrenia. Pindolol has been reported to be effective in the treatment of aggression in patients with organic brain syndrome. Metoprolol has been reported effective with two patients: one with intermittent explosive disorder related to meningitis and alcohol abuse and the other with a penetrating brain trauma with temporal lobe epilepsy.

5. Lithium

The use of lithium for disorders other than bipolar disorders for the management of aggression has shown promise. In a double-blind trial testing the effectiveness of lithium in the treatment of aggression in adult mentally retarded patients, patients showed a reduction in aggression during treatment. Although there have been other reports of the use of lithium in other disorders, there is a sparsity of double-blind controlled studies. These disorders include patients with organic brain syndrome or head injury; aggressive schizophrenics; non-psychotic, aggressive prisoners; and delinquents and children with conduct or attention-deficit hyperactivity disorders.

6. Psychostimulants

The use of amphetamines is accepted in controlling aggressive behavior associated with attention-deficit hyperactivity disorder. There have been some reports of the successful use of amphetamines to control aggression in adults with a history of this disorder as well. Further studies are indicated. The clinician should proceed with caution in prescribing amphetamines because there is great potential for addiction, abuse, and the production of violent behavior through hyperactivity, emotional lability, or delusional thinking as a result of abuse of psychostimulants.

7. Serotonergic Drugs

The development of selective serotonin reuptake inhibitors has made it possible to test the theory that serotonin is responsible for impulsive violent behaviors. Fluoxitene has been used successfully to treat impulsive violent patients with personality disorders without depression and violence by patients with depression. With the introduction of sertraline, paroxetine and other such drugs, more research on the use of serotonergic drugs for the treatment of violent patients is anticipated.

B. Other Long-Term Treatment

As with many problems in psychiatry, treatment of violent patients must adhere to the biopsychosocial model. Not all violent patients need medication, but it should be considered in the formulation of the treatment plan. Psychological intervention may be in the form of psychotherapy or behavioral therapy. The impact of the patient's violence on various levels of the social order, from the family to society, must be addressed in treatment, as should the role of social factors in causation of the patient's violence.

1. Long-Term Psychotherapy

Although psychotherapy of the violent patient may be on an individual basis, often therapists involve the spouse or family in treatment. This is advisable because of the role of the family in the dynamics of violence. However, if the safety of the spouse or other family outside sessions cannot be guaranteed, then their involvement is not advised. Some therapists prefer group therapy for violent patients because it is less threatening to the patient than a one-to-one relationship

and allows the patient to appreciate that other people have problems with violence. The group is often supportive yet, at the same time, the group can confront a patient rather than having the therapist do so.

The best candidates for long-term psychotherapy are nonpsychotic patients without antisocial personality disorder. The goals of psychotherapy are first to evaluate the motivation of the patient and the reason for psychotherapy. An inappropriate reason to enter psychotherapy is an attempt to impress the court prior to a trial for some violent crime. A more appropriate reason would be to avoid divorce or loss of a job and/or because the patient feels guilty about his or her behavior. The second goal of psychotherapy is to develop a sense of self-control of emotions and behavior. At first the patient relies on the strength and self-control of the therapist. The therapist and the patient must be aware that following this honeymoon period in psychotherapy, subsequent violent episodes can occur and they must be prepared to analyze them without feelings of disappointment.

Third, verbal communication should be facilitated. The patient should be encouraged to talk rather than act and to express concerns and weaknesses without fear of retaliation or humiliation, which has often been the case when such concerns have been shared with the spouse, family, or friends in the past.

The fourth goal of psychotherapy, tied to increased verbal ability, is the appreciation of the consequences of violent behavior. For example, the patient should be encouraged to think about what it would be like to be in jail or what it would be like to be divorced if spousal abuse continues.

The last goal of psychotherapy is increased insight about the dynamics of violence and early warning signs; for example, flushing of the face, rapid heart beat, sweating, and a feeling of tension. The patient should be taught how to avoid a violent situation. The patient must develop insight so as to be able to deal with the psychological causes of violence, which often involve poor self-esteem.

2. Behavioral Therapy

Lieberman and his colleagues have succinctly described the use of behavioral analysis and therapy in the management of violent behavior. They caution that such a program of treatment should be planned and conducted only by clinicians skilled in behavioral analysis and therapy and that there should be standardized policies and review processes to prevent abuse of patients. Programs of behavioral management of violent behavior should definitely not be ad hoc attempts on inadequately staffed and trained general inpatient units.

V. CONCLUSION

There has been progress in the delineation of violence by patients in regard to types of mental disorders. Guidelines have been developed for the emergency management of violence by patients with a concern for safety of clinicians and patients. Violence can be controlled in the emergency situation through the use of verbal intervention, physical restraint, seclusion, and medication. The long-term management of violence involves the treatment of the disorder causing violence with medication and psychological and social interventions. Studies of anticonvulsants, beta-blockers, lithium, and serotonin-specific reuptake inhibitors have shown these drugs may have antiviolence effects separate from the treatment of the primary disorder such as schizophrenia, mania, or depression. Future study of these drugs for the treatment of violence should strive to be more rigorous methodologically through the use of controls and more precise in the measurement of violence as an outcome variable.

Also See the Following Articles

AGGRESSION, PSYCHOLOGY OF • BEHAVIORAL PSYCHOLOGY • BIOCHEMICAL FACTORS • DRUGS AND VIOLENCE • PUBLIC HEALTH MODELS OF VIOLENCE AND VIOLENCE PREVENTION

Bibliography

American Psychiatric Association (1994). *Diagnostic and statistical manual of mental disorders,* 4th revision. Washington, DC: American Psychiatric Association.

Bowie, V. (1989). *Coping with violence: A guide for the human services.* Sydney, Australia: Karibuni Press.

Eichelman, BS, & Hartwig, A.C. (Eds.) (1995). *Patient violence and the clinician.* Washington, DC: American Psychiatric Press.

Hillbrand, M., & Pallone, N.J. (Eds.) (1994). *The psychobiology of aggression.* New York: Haworth Press.

Levine, F.J., & Rosich, K.J. (1996). *Social causes of violence: Crafting a science agenda.* Washington, DC: American Sociological Association.

Reiss, A.J., & Roth, J.A. (Eds.) (1993). *Understanding and preventing violence.* Washington, DC: National Academy Press.

Sensky, T. (1996). Assessment and clinical management of risk of harm to other people, Council Report CRS3, Royal College of Psychiatrists, London.

Stoff, D.M., Breiling, J., & Maser, J.D. (Eds.) (1997). *Handbook of antisocial behavior.* New York: Wiley.

Tardiff, K. (1996). *Assessment and management of violent patients,* 2nd ed. Washington, DC: American Psychiatric Press.

Tardiff, K. (Ed.) (1984). *The psychiatric uses of seclusion and restraint.* Washington, DC: American Psychiatric Press.

Tardiff, K. (Ed.). *Medical management of the violent patient: Clinical assessment and therapy.* New York: Marcel Dekker, 1999.

Thackrey, M. (1987). *Therapeutics for aggression.* New York: Human Sciences Press.

Toch, H. (1992). *Violent men: An inquiry into the psychology of violence.* Washington, DC: American Psychological Association.

Volavka, J. (1995). *Neurobiology of violence.* Washington, DC: American Psychiatric Press.

Wilson, J.P., & Raphael, B. (1993). *International handbook of traumatic stress syndromes.* New York: Plenum.

Militarism

Arden Bucholz

State University of New York, Brockport

GLOSSARY

Militarism An inversion of political end and military means in human politics; the dominance of military men, decisions, methods, and goals over civilian; an imbalance in the civil-military relationship in favor of the military.

I. BACKGROUND AND PHILOSOPHY

Confusion of end and means is a classic problem in human affairs. The Greek philosophers, the Chinese, Indian philosophy, and, more recently, writers such as Machiavelli and Clausewitz, dealt with this problem. The specific contexts in which this confusion occurs are many. War is one of the most common and most important. The reason is simple and profound: unlike most human social activities, war deals with death, usually on a large scale.

Death undergirds and animates the organizations that pursue it, known as armies, and the individuals who engage in it, called soldiers. Armies are large public organizations, created and maintained primarily to compete against each other on future battlefields. At the uttermost bounds of this competition, one or both of the organizations will suffer some degree of death. Because armies serve as instruments of death, a point that cannot be overemphasized, and because of their size and the extent and manner in which they command the loyalties of their societies, armies are unique among the organizations of human society. Because soldiers deal, sooner or later, in their mind or in practical experience, with large-scale death, their occupation is different from all others in society.

Militarism in all its guises arises from the confusion these relationships enforce. Organizations and individuals, when confronted with the anxieties, real or imagined, caused by the possibility and threat of death, fall into confusions and mental disturbances. To avoid death, they sometimes succumb. Any means becomes a legitimate escape. Often invisibly, insidiously, the means become the end. During the era of modern war, roughly between 1796 and 1989, this juxtaposition again and again threatened. It is no accident that the definition and usage of the term "militarism" accompanied these events.

But perhaps this is too simple. If we examine the term from Machiavelli's point of view, we see an inver-

Copyright © 1999 by Academic Press.
All rights of reproduction in any form reserved.

sion: the sheer terror at the start of war that ends in the exuberance of victory or the despair of defeat and the political order or anarchy that results. Again it is a question of degree. In the shift from the agricultural elite armies of the 18th century to the industrial mass armies of the late 19th and the entire 20th century, the possibility of military victory over an opponent changed from the terrible double carnage of Frederick the Great's wars—40% casualties on both sides so that neither could really do anything after fighting—to the lightning victories of Napoleon and Moltke with their ensuing political transformations, the terrible stalemates of the "Great War" (1914–1918), the mobile battles of the "Good War" (1939–1945), and four decades of Cold War with its Koreas, Vietnams, and Afghanistans. Each of these war and peace scenarios resulted in rhetorical storms and civil-military inversions.

Most of those who have written about this problem—beginning with their response to the French Revolutionary armies of Napoleon—have responded viscerally to what they perceived to be a monstrosity of the modern age. Nothing could be further from the truth. Among human animals, the problems caused by the inversion of end and means within the specific context of war and death begins virtually at the beginning.

And from the time of Auguste Comte and Herbert Spencer, there has been a consistent intellectual response. Societies in which armies played an important part were criticized as morally inferior to modern industrial society. Societies in which the military performed important political, economic, and social roles were regarded as cruder, more "barbaric" forms, destined to be replaced as "civilization" progressed to more liberal and more rational structures.

As one reads the literature of "militarism," mainly from the 20th century, one senses immediately that industrial mass war has given the term its fundamental meaning. For example, take Alfred Vagts' 1937 classic, *A History of Militarism,* which was on the *New York Times* best-seller list and got its author a stint on the Harvard faculty. Vagts—writing from his own experiences in World War I, and the postwar Weimar years in Berlin—wrote that every war and every army has both a military and a militaristic way. The military way is characterized by primary attention of men and material on political victory with the least casualties. It is, Vagts says, limited, confined, and scientific: in other words, rational. Militarism, in contrast, is a vast array of customs, interests, prestige, caste, cult and belief: it is an irrational sham. But death, the central foundational concept undergirding war, is an irrational event that humans cannot describe for themselves. Its looming

threat often forces inversions that overwhelm the rational mind.

Therein lies the problem that Vagts in 1937 did not see. It is the mind/body dualism, the one part rational, thinking, the other part emotional, visceral, feeling. Confronting death, which is what war and armies are about, attacks the human animal in both places. But in worst case scenarios, it is the visceral, feeling, irrational that often overwhelms. In death agony and fear of it, mental control slips beneath physical necessity.

Under normal conditions, these relationships are not absolutes, but they can become so. They often play themselves out and develop like yin/yang. As the Taoist argues, there is a tendency for every existing object or arrangement to continue to be what it is. Interfere with its existence and it resists, as a stone resists crushing. If it is a living creature, it resists actively, as a wasp being crushed will sting. But the kind of resistance offered by a living creature is unique. It grows stronger as the interference grows stronger up to the point where the creatures' capacity for resistance is destroyed. Somewhere along this continuum the rational always threatens to give way to the irrational in all but the strongest individuals and nation-states.

II. ANCIENT WARFARE

For this process history is full of examples. At Cannae in 216 B.C. Hannibal was attacked by 16 Roman legions. He absorbed the initial attack, turned both wings into the Roman formations, surrounding thousands. Then, with the battle won, he took hours slaughtering the encircled and defeated opponents. Nearly 30,000 Romans may have been killed. Just prior to the battle, the terrified Romans had appointed Quintus Fabius Maximus dictator. This reminds us of the Germans in Russia after 1941,where both sides devolved to the level of true barbarism: the Russians lost 25 million in that war. The German army was reduced, transmogrified, and demodernized, killing almost everything in its wake as it was being frozen and slaughtered itself during the final days of Hitler in the war that solidified the Stalinist dictatorship. Both situations inverted the balance.

When the Romans invaded Gaul in 58 B.C., they initiated a revolt among the Germanic tribes that went on for 10 years. Caesar may have plotted rationally and mathematically at first, but at the end it was a vicious and irrational war that killed women and children. In the next decade Caesar became absolute dictator. We note the jubilation of military victory which so overwhelms civilians that soldiers are sometimes raised to extraordinary heights. Witness what happened to Norman Schwartzkopf after the Gulf War of 1991.

As Machiavelli wrote, men and iron could always find bread and money. Soldiers and politicians are fond of reminding us that armies guarantee the existence of everything else. But the extremes of this inversion were hidden until the 20th century. They never went very far prior to the French Revolution and the armies of Napoleon. The term "militarism," after all, originated in the memoirs of an early 19th century critic of Napoleon, Madame de Chastenay.

III. THE ERA OF MODERN WAR, 1796–1989

Modern war begins with Napoleon's Italian campaign of 1796, reinforced by his wars against Austria, Russia, and Prussia, which aimed at destroying his opponents militarily, politically, and economically, while mobilizing French resources to these ends. Unlimited war aims and huge popular armies were reciprocally interdependent: they created a new civil-military chemistry. Although Frederick the Great could think about destroying his opponents, only Napoleon could do it. His armies were 10 times the size of Frederick's and, if casualties were high, he could always replenish them because, unlike the small professional and impressed armies of the 18th century, Napoleon's soldiers believed they had a stake in the political outcome of the war. Men of the *levee en mass* believed they would participate in the political fruits of military success.

Modern war then, the main object of the militarism debate, is different in size, space, and time from previous war: everything gets bigger and more intense. And the definition of war changes terminologically, chronologically, and cosmologically. For example, by the term "avant garde" Napoleon understood a force that invades unknown territory, exposes itself to the dangers of sudden, shocking encounters, and conquers land as yet unoccupied. With such a term, we are no longer in the classical 18th-century world of limited war, formal sieges, and honorable surrenders. A new time consciousness begins. Napoleon was the first general to issue time-specific orders. Later during the 19th century, with electricity and standardization of zones, time becomes altered, reduced, and conquered. Industrial mass war brings mobility, acceleration, and discontinuity. The new time consciousness enters philosophy through the work of Henry Bergson for whom reality was the continual process of change itself, *la durée*.

With modern war comes an increasing reliance on future expectations. Armies are the most future-oriented of all modern organizations. They spend their time mainly preparing for future wars, not fighting them. The more a particular time is experienced as new, modern, and different, the more demands are made on the future: expectations increase. In periods of rapid change, such as the French or Russian revolutionary periods, there is an acceleration of these processes.

All of these factors reinforce the possibility that political ends will be overwhelmed by military means. War captured popular imaginations. Its winners, Napoleon, U. S. Grant, Mao Zedong, were often catapulted into politicial prominence.

Some of this is recognizable in the memoirs of Madame de Chastenay, credited with inventing the term "militarism" in 1816. Recognizing that civil government was somehow under novel threat, her theme was picked up in 1861 by Pierre Proudhon, who began a systematic critique. Separating political and constitutional from social and economic aspects, he wrote that this novel autocratic relationship reflected one phase in the progressive development of society toward the abolition of armies altogether. These themes were continued 20 years later by Herbert Spencer, who described the military and the industrial as polar opposites. In the former the individual was owned by the state and success in war was the highest glory, whereas the latter defended the citizen's individuality instead of sacrificing it to the state: it was geared toward industrial production and economic interchange.

Even while these thoughts were being written, a new chapter in civil-military relations was being created. Reacting to Napoleonic victories, the Prussians invented a whole new format: the first industrial mass organization devoted to war. The Prussian army, wrote Peter Drucker, was the amazing organization of the world of the 1870s just as Henry Ford's assembly line was for the world of the 1920s. Their invention, developed and perfected during the 19th century, institutionalized the possibilities of end-means inversion, which had plagued humanity from the Greek and Roman wars. It was no longer a matter of single commanders such as Hannibal, Caesar, or Napoleon whose overwhelming victories unbalanced the delicate relationship. As army sizes swelled toward the 12 million soldiers mobilized in August 1914, these huge forces were directed by a professional general staff, supported by a formal educational system that created technical experts, guided by world-class cartography, and prepared by war gaming and war planning processes that looked ahead and planned in 5- and 10-year increments. The scientific and bureaucratic consistency these new methods gave to armies enhanced the possibility that, in a worst-case scenario, the military means might replace the political end. Western European armies became one of the most modern organizations in world society. Death anxieties had become institutionalized. All this had near fatal outcomes for humankind in the 20th century.

Three other factors conditioned the debate over "militarism" in the pre-1914 world. One was the beginning of the military-industrial complex. Essentially what happened after about 1880 was the creation of a unique system of counteractive forces. A series of technological innovations revolutionized the weapons, transportation, and communication of armies. The process began in Germany, France, and England. Soon, counteractive defense spending began its escalation as each great power tried to catch up and keep up with the leaders. The escalating arms race resulted in two competing alliance systems, the Triple Entente and the Triple Alliance. The members of these systems targeted each other with counteractive war plans. All of this could not but provoke commentary and it did. But whether this in fact constituted the domination of the military over the civilian, as it appeared at least in Germany, Austria-Hungary, and Russia, or whether it was the normal infighting of domestic politics—the first German Naval Bill of 1897, after all, was a carefully balanced political deal between East Prussian land owners and West Prussian industrialists in which each got something they wanted—is arguable. One of the most careful observers of these matters in Germany, Hans Delbrück, the first modern military historian and editor of the leading journal of German political commentary, in a famous exchange with Lord Esher in the 1909 *Contemporary Review* over the question, "Why does Germany build warships?" replied that its purpose was to protect her commerce. But, for Germany as well as for France, England, Russia, and Austria-Hungary, this was only half the story. The other half was that it spurred domestic industry.

All of this provided a visible and valid target for criticism of the evolving military-industrial complex and its influence in the culture. Ludwig Quidde objected to the largest part of the male population being drafted. Military values, he said, infiltrated civilian life. Officers, especially naval and artillery officers, were sometimes closely intertwined with big business such as Krupp, Schneider-Creusot, Vickers, and Armstrong. Big business in turn hired tens of thousands of former soldiers, considering military service the best factory work credentials. All of this invisibly began to turn the means into the end even before war began.

Second, spurred on by their declining position in society as a whole, officers helped write a new mythology of war. As they lost position overall, they maintained and strengthened it, so maintained Alfred Vagts, within 19th-century armies. Central to this was a reassertion of elite and noble values, especially the concept of honor. As the heritage of feudalism was swept away by religious reformation, high finance, and large-scale manufacturing, standing armies became the citadel and last bastion of feudalism. Leadership in these armies often was dominated by the nobility, for whom soldiering remained one of the few legitimate and honorable jobs in the emerging industrial society. Thus they emphasized protocol, birth, and prestige, rather than technical knowledge, work efficiency, and industriousness. Honor and its adjunct, the duel, became the litmus paper of the military officer. War ideology placed less emphasis on technology and efficiency, more emphasis on the bayonet charge, courage in the face of death, and the ideals of duty and patriotism as the dominant forces on the battlefield. In reality the most feudal element of armies was not honor, it was death, which did not go away with the advent of modernity.

Thus was created a powerful war mythology in the decades just prior to 1914. All European armies adopted the *offensive à outrance,* which, rejecting the reality of superior weapons technology, advocated sheer will power as the decisive force on the battlefield. Few at that time recognized this mythology for what it became: an ideology legitimizing the death of large numbers of men at the hands of novel technology, with which no one understood how to fight.

A third factor of late 19th-century European armies was their export of modern warfighting processes abroad. In the early 19th century French methods were popular in Russia, the Ottoman Empire, and even Japan. But from about 1880 through 1945, Prussian-German methods prevailed. As noted above, the European country that invented 20th-century war-fighting methods was Imperial Germany.

The most successful product of this exporting was Japan. During the Meji Restoration a revolution from above enabled Japan to avoid Western domination while industrializing and joining the ranks of the world's great powers. How was this accomplished? For one thing a military ruling class, the samurai, had become a elite officialdom independent of land owning and separated from agricultural society. The great merchant families, such as Mitsui and Mitsubishi, accepted their subordination to the samurai bureaucrats and looked to the state for industrial leadership and top-down modernization. By 1873 Japan had established a universal conscript army and a new tax system, and land reform had made government finance secure and predictable. The army and the bureaucracy became the dominant institutions.

Introducing a national and imperial ideology into the country required years of primary school; peasants universally enrolled in the army were exposed to modern life. Housed in barracks equipped with beds, stoves, and electric lights, they ate rice, fish, and meat on a regular basis, and received a monthly salary. None of these experiences were typical of peasant life at the time. Military uniforms were the earliest articles of Western-style dress to be adopted on a large scale, styles and designs that later became everyday features of Japanese life. Through conscription, the army gave generations of peasant boys their first glimpse of the modern world. These forms of modernity were seductive.

All of this had a great impact on economic development. Factories established to meet the material requirements of the new army formed the leading edge in the industrialization processes. Modern cotton textiles, metallurgy, and engineering came about in order to meet military demand. Manufactures and exports to pay for the purchase of arms abroad became central. Through semiofficial companies such as the South Manchurian Railway the government, the military, and the private sector cooperated. From 1895 through 1935 Japanese defense expenditures accounted for 40% of the national budget.

Within the army as a whole a technical-specialist educational system was built, following the Prussian-German model, including a War College (1883) and General Staff College. The general staff system, brought in after 1878, soon resulted in a transformation of the whole top management of the country. From these schools came the new bureaucratic and political elite of Japan: it became the principal talent pool for modern Japan. In the late 19th century, half of the prime ministers had been officers, and for the period as a whole up to 1945, about 28% of all civilian ministries were headed by military men.

All of this was enshrined in the Constitution of 1889 in which the emperor was the supreme commander of the army and navy, exactly the same position as Emperor Wilhelm II in Germany. The Japanese went on to separate the military sphere from the rest of the political system. Both halves were united, but only in the person of the emperor, again very similar to the German model. All of this was then mythologized in the concept of "bushido," the code of militarism. In fact it was the old ethos of the samurai. This reminds us of the mythology of honor and death in Germany, France,

Austria-Hungary, England, and Russia on the eve of the Great War.

A huge polemic described these events and further defined the term militarism. Among these commentators a few stand out. One was Eckart Kehr. His shattering book, *Battleship Building and Party Politics, 1894–1902,* which effectively banned its author from German academic life after its publication, demonstrated that the great German fleet was built on the basis of a comprehensive interest group arrangement between the navy, big business, and big agriculture. Traditional military values had permeated modern society.

For Japan the critics were less outspoken but equally trenchant: for example, Eitaro Noro and Moritaro Yamada. Two roads lead to modernity, they said, the Prussian and the Anglo-American. Whereas the Anglo-American road led to the erosion of the power positions of traditional preindustrial elites, the Prussian way secured their survival and, at the same time, blocked the way to parliamentary government. Japanese developments were not seen as products of monopolistic capitalism, but as a result of underdevelopment. The Japanese accepted the military as dominant over the civilian: the arrangement was needed, they said, in order for Japan to catch up in the race to modernize, exactly the same sentiments as had been used in Germany several decades earlier.

Other criticism came from the European socialists. All presocialist, "class societies" were, of course, "militaristic." Armies were portrayed as instruments of social class. Rosa Luxemburg, for example, argued in her 1913 book, *The Accumulation of Capital,* that militarism created new opportunities for highly profitable investment when the monies concentrated in government treasuries by taxation were used to purchase armaments. Foreshadowing the world systems approach of the 1990s, she noted that armies were important in the acquisition stage of capitalism; they aided in colonization and the subordination of imperial colonies to the economic interests of the mother country. Militarism was a key component of imperialism abroad. At home it enhanced economic concentration—the military-industrial complex. From the start the socialists placed the problem of military influence in politics and society into a utopian and developmental model: they asked at what point does this pernicious influence begin and at what point will it end?

As for mainstream political commentators discussing the possibilities of civil-military imbalance, two stand out in the pre-World War I era. One is the Polish banker Ivan Bloch, the other is the German military historian Delbrück. Writing in 1899 Bloch argued that modern weapons technology and mass conscription would result in a war so terrible that the misery inflicted would be all out of proportion to the anticipated goal: a classic inversion model. Battles were no longer feasible because this technology would destroy everything in its path. The old needle gun of l866 was effective at 800 yards, contemporary rifles killed at more than twice that. The grenade of 1870 burst into 30 pieces, those of 1900 exploded into 340. Rapid-fire smokeless cartridges produced much more severe wounds. Nineteenth century wars were fought with 3% of the population, but Bloch speculated that the next wars would engage not hundreds of thousands but millions. These wars, he implied, would militarize political power.

Delbrück, in a celebrated essay during the height of the second Moroccan crisis in 1911, reminded his countrymen that the sufferings of a Europe-wide war would be horrible: economic life would come to a standstill, factories would become rusty, and weapons would destroy what generations had built; tenants would pay no more rent, believers no more alms, corporations no more dividends, and the state would receive no more taxes. Later that same year he wrote that a general war in Europe would be a disaster of the first order: it would make the Russo-Japanese war of 1905 look like a limited colonial skirmish. But until October 1918, he publicly defended his country against charges of militarism. Only in the closing weeks of World War I did he admit that German policy decisions had been dictated by military men. Citing unrestricted submarine war—the decision which in his opinion sealed Germany's fate in the Great War—he admitted that civilian politicians had been subordinated to military leadership. If this is militarism, Delbrück concluded—when such decisions were made only or mainly from the military point of view—then the charge of Germany's wartime opponents that Germany was ruled by militarism, was correct.

But overall the debate over "militarism" cooled in the last year before the Great War and that again demonstrates the end/means inversions basic to the definition. In 1913 the largest antiwar rally was held in Berlin with over 250,000 participants. The next year the peace movement collapsed. In the July crisis of 1914, 20 German cities were under siege from pro-war and antiwar demonstrations. But when the final vote on war credits came, the socialist parties in Europe voted in favor with scarcely a dissent.

Thus one might say that all of the rhetoric prepared and formulated in the decades prior to 1914 became useful only after 1918 and again after 1945, when it was used to explain what had happened during the catastrophes which dominated virtually the entire 20th century. These catastrophes fall under a single name, industrial mass total war: cold at first (1894–1914), then very hot (1914–1918), then cold (1918–1939), then hottest (1939–1945) then cold (1947–1989). The 20th century may be summed up by saying that in World War I, the whole civilization nearly died and its participants soon plunged into a second utter catastrophe, World War II, from which it has not fully recovered after half a century.

IV. THE IMPACT OF INDUSTRIAL MASS TOTAL WAR, 1914–1945

The bad dreams of Bloch and Delbrück became reality from 1914 to 1945. Here again the classical relationship was inverted, but this time on a scale undreamed of by critics and prophets. What had happened?

As we have seen, in two key countries, Germany in the west and Japan in the east, the military had become the most modern elements in rapidly changing ("modernizing") societies.

Second, the possession of a very good modern army—linked to hyper-rapid industrialization, a mood of Social Darwinism, and aggressive and mindless political leadership—was one factor that encouraged these countries to become involved in a series of wars: Japan against China (1894, 1937–1945), Russia (1904–1905), and finally the United States (1941–1945). Germany fought twice against a coalition dominated by France-England-Russia-United States. Having plunged in, both Germany and Japan found the water unexpectedly frigid. World War II was an alien and overwhelming experience that, in spite of some enormous successes at the start—if one can call the very brutal conquest of large parts of Europe and Asia successes— ultimately resulted in a shattering and total defeat. Their homelands were bombed and occupied, their national honor stained and their political, economic, and military power destroyed. During the last phase of this 75-year run, after 1945, neither Germany nor Japan recreated an armed force of major power proportions to accompany their world-class industrial position—at first by international fiat, later by their own choice.

The 20th-century inversion was caused mainly by the creation of the first deep future-oriented, knowledge-based war planning process in the kingdom of Prussia and then by its adoption by the European great powers and by Japan. By 1914 these processes had created technical, professional, and modern bureaucracies. The war planning bureaucracies had made the jump to industrial mass warfare, but they existed within agricultural elite governments, traditional antiques of the 19th century world in terms of decision making, threat perception, and international diplomacy. The leadership in these governments had decided that the state could not be simultaneously strong and technologically backward; they had decided to modernize their military. Having done so guaranteed speed, volume, regularity, and dependability in one aspect of government, war fighting.

But it also created a strange rift, since the political components had fallen behind their military bureaucracies. There was an imbalance, a cultural lag, a reverse salient. The means of warfighting—weapons, transportation, communications, and planning processes—had jumped ahead whereas the political and social systems in which these warfighting means were embedded operated in a 19th-century cabinet atmosphere where the whim of the monarch or prime minister called the tune.

This odd creation, the modern military, had unique appeal. The meticulousness and specificity of bureaucratic planning—goal oriented and rational—combined with the appeal to the senses, the emotional and psychological force of the ancient and traditional drive for power. Because its ultimate goal entailed some degree of death, these war-planning organizations were one of those industrial organizations that not only possessed the attributes of organization, power and technical perfection, but also generated spiritual impulses, social models, and cultural ideals. The organizations described here were industrial. In the two world wars they broke down the traditional boundary between civilian and military. The result was a merger and a new creation. By preparing for war using comprehensive national management techniques, the traditional boundaries between elites, the masses, and the national institutions was melted and fused. As a result these armies and especially their directors, the general staffs, became part of the national mythology. In rapidly changing societies, suffering from both identity and security crises, they became a symbol of both patrimonial and rational values. Some critics called this "militarism." We can recognize it today as a new form of the ancient imbalance between civilian and military.

The First World War brought into being much of what had been prophesied before 1914. When it ended, the debate was tinged with political rhetoric, especially among the losers. In Germany, for example, paramilitarism became popular. Both leftist and rightist parties created paramilitary units, drawing upon their wartime experience and reacting sharply to the Versailles Treaty war guilt and reparations clauses. Ernst Juenger, a dec-orated combat veteran, fused militarized nationalism and modern industrial technology. Juenger wrote in celebration of the bonds that war fused between citizens. Warriors and workers were both engaged in battles, the one in factories, the other on battlefields. Both used their tools skillfully. Both called for sacrifices. Juenger was anti-Western, looking to Prussia to lead a new race of soldier-workers, and his ideas blended with the romanticism of reactive nationalism.

Twentieth century commentators had a field day with all of this turning of civilians into military. Alfred Vagts described this militarization of the civilians, caused, he argued, because modern armies spent more time preparing for war than fighting it. Herald Lasswell introduced the garrison state concept, with its socialization of danger as a permanent fixture of modern nation states. In other words, mobilization of mass populations on the basis of external threats, an ancient tradition here aided by law, technology, and the media, was thereby enabled to reach hitherto unparalleled levels. Civil life was penetrated and compromised by death anxieties, natural in the situation but enhanced, magnified, and distorted by the mass media.

V. CIVIL-MILITARY RELATIONS IN THE THIRD WORLD, 1945–1997

Between 1914 and 1945, Europe and America had created the first industrial mass armies and then used them in the only two world wars. This not only meant that industrial mass total war has dominated virtually the entire 20th century, it fundamentally weakened the old imperial powers. In this sense the world wars were also European civil wars, forcing the imperial powers to begin the process of releasing colonial bondages. As empires fell and new states emerged and tried to modernize, armies caught their attention. In the period of decolonization following 1945, one way to modernity apparently lay through the military. That elusive mythology was called "military modernization" by some, "militarism" by others. The Cold War, 1947–1989, spurred on this process.

The theoretical literature that accompanied this grew from several centers. One was the Committee on the Comparative Study of the New Nations at the University of Chicago. Another was the New York-based Social Science Research Council's Committee on Comparative Politics. The Council on Foreign Relations, New York, and the Rand Corporation in California also contributed to these ideas. During the 1960s, military modernization became academically fashionable.

After 1945, so the arguments went, the new nations had two problems: identity and security. The problem of identity was that many of these states had been colonies, with the imperial or national identity of their captivity superimposed over their precolonial, traditional ethos. Yet their new elites had been educated and trained primarily in their empires' home universities and bureaucracies. Their languages, bureaucratic styles, and even cultures were affected. As newly independent states, they no longer wanted to be colonies, but they were neither the traditional states they had once been nor the modern ones they hoped to become. In this transition modern armies filled a need: they seemed easier to create than other modern institutions.

Armies are simultaneously modern and traditional organizations. They are modern because they must look abroad for their major threats, thus keeping up with the newest technologies. They are modern in that they are future-oriented. They are traditional in that death and fear of death underlines everything they do, from small unit training to operations, strategy, and major weapons acquisition. Death dangers had now become institutionalized and exportable: they had become part of the socialization process and a technology of power essential to national identity.

A second problem of the developing nations was security against both domestic and foreign enemies. Security has to do with how a state is ordered and determines its boundaries, both physical and psychological. It is related to state formation and the problems involved in holding new nations together.

New nations are fragile constructions fraught with political, ethnic, religious, and social conflict. As old empires dissolved, the new nations created within them often struggled mightily with identity and with security. In these struggles armies were often able to address effectively both issues. As for security, a strong modern army is considered the sine quo non for new state's existence. Law and order had to precede economic and social modernization. As for identity, the good soldier is also to some degree a modern person. Breaking the bonds of traditional civilian life and adjusting to the more impersonal military is akin to the process of moving out from a particularistic, traditional lifestyle to the more universal relationships of modern industrial society.

Some armies trained their soldiers in literacy, the rudiments of science and health care as well as in more narrowly focused military work. This acculturation took place within an organization that gave its members a high degree of psychological security. It trained soldiers to identify with the larger political state in place of local and regional allegiances. In other words it provided some form of citizenship training. Finally armies ideally promoted by merit not birth. Characteristic of modernity is achievement: to recognize a definite and predictable relationship between effort and reward in contrast to the ascribed, inherited positions of traditional society.

Obviously, there is a controversy over whether these armies were modernizers, whatever that term means, whether they were enemies of liberal political and social values, as many commentators maintained, and whether in this process there was a natural, often inescapable, inversion of end and means. Perhaps armies were all three. They often built modern educational systems, roads, health care facilities, communications networks, and social overhead capital: especially transportation and communication. In some ways they contributed to nation building and decolonization, if often ending up working for dictators and despots.

Major criticism of these developments came from several sides. Morris Janowitz, another Chicago school writer, asked why military officers in the new nations were more influential in politics, in comparison to Western industrialized societies. And why does their capacity differ from country to country? To the first question he replied that it was the social structure of their countries that predisposed the officers in this direction. To the second he concluded it was due to the characteristics of the military profession. Samuel Huntington added that armies in modernizing states served as gatekeepers in the expansion of political participation, letting in the middle class but blocking the lower classes. Huntington adopted a consciously antirevolutionary position. He was criticized by those who saw no postrevolutionary progress in the militarized regimes.

But what of the alternatives available to the young revolutionaries, modest and egalitarian in spirit, when they had become middle aged and enjoyed the fruits of office, the symbols of status, and the benefits of power? In Latin America, for example, many of the 20 republics were governed by their armies throughout much of their independent existences. In Burma, Thailand, and Indonesia, representative of the post-1945, newly independent states of Southeast Asia, the military was a modernizing and Westernizing force, so wrote John Johnson in 1962. But later they turned in a very different direction. For example, in Turkey and Egypt, the army has played a dominant and very similar role. At the same time, armies that were very important from the 1920s through the 1980s have in several venues receded.

In placing the role of armies into the transition from rural to urban, agricultural to industrial, it was noted that, although they have certain characteristics of "modern" societies, they are, as we have emphasized repeatedly, also fundamentally traditional in their basic raison d'être both in terms of goals and methods. In concluding, we can note that many armies in Third World countries have had a relatively easy time seizing power but a rather more difficult time actually governing.

VI. THE MILITARY-INDUSTRIAL COMPLEX

The proper origin of the military-industrial complex is in the pre-1914 cold war world of Germany and Japan. Both attained world power status by simultaneously modernizing their military and their industrial base. Both created novel systems or combinations of organizations and instutitions that cooperated instead of competing: big business, universities, government bureaucracies, and the military. The relationship between these agencies was galvanized by the two world wars but it did not reappear in either country after 1945 primarily because, as defeated nations, their armies were initially closed down by the victors, and then proscribed or strictly limited by the ensuing civilian governments. It is ironic that after 1945 their major antagonists, the United States and Soviet Russia, in a sense took up where Germany and Japan had left off and continued and strengthened these relationships during the Cold War. When Dwight Eisenhower took office in 1953, for example, 70% of American federal spending went to the military.

Although in 1953 Dwight Eisenhower sought "maximum security at minimum cost and without danger to free institutions" by reorganizing the U.S. defense establishment, by 1961 he had again returned to the classic theme with which this article began. About to retire from office, he spoke of the dangers of the military-industrial complex. He cautioned that Americans must guard against the acquisition of unwarranted military influence, whether sought or unsought, because the potential for a disastrous rise of misplaced power existed and it would persist. Later a historian noted that America was a country in which institutions and men who possessed military, economic, and political power had become so intertwined that they had merged.

Key features here include sophisticated weapons that are continually becoming obsolete and constantly replaced by the next generation, an elaborate publicity system, a burgeoning federal defense budget, military contractors in the private sector, and the flow of retired officers from active duty to defense contractors, lobbyist groups, and congressional committees. In both the Korean and Vietnam wars, defense budgets again rose past the half-way mark for American expenditures. However, except for communist ideologues, few labeled the United States militaristic, perhaps because Truman fired MacArthur and Lyndon Johnson fired himself when these wars began to verge out of control. Yet any realistic examination of the American budget, the defense contractors, and other institutions of life such as the disastrous McCarthy affair, the civil defense organizations, or the extragovernmental agencies, might conclude that American culture was clearly in danger of domination by military goals and methods, technology and expenditure, and ideals and models. Some might believe that this is limited to high-technology industrial countries engaged in a modern cold war. But it is not. Developing states also frequently follow this path.

In 1972 Soviet physicist Andrei Sakharov described the Soviet military-industrial complex, which he said occupied an analogous role to that of the United States. Soviet Russia possessed a large military, an extensive armaments industries, a research and development establishment, and a firmly entrenched bureaucracy to keep everything moving together. The current debate over Cold War origins and development encompasses many of these same points, and the pressures and tensions that caused and fueled it have spilled over into our world. Although it is doubtful if they can be described as militaristic, as their domestic problems lie in an entirely different direction, today several former provinces of the Soviet system, now independent states, are active in the defense markets of the world as both sellers and buyers. As in the period between 1850 and 1914, in the postmodern world of 1998 international arms traffic is a major force in the world economy.

VII. CONCLUSION

It is not surprising that the term "militarism" rose to prominence in the era of modern war—from Napoleon's Italian campaign of 1796, through World Wars I and II and the Cold War, to the downfall of the Berlin Wall and the Soviet Union and the retargeting of ICBMs by Presidents Bush and Gorbachev in 1989. In the era of postmodern war in which we now find ourselves—a period of low-intensity wars or even police actions without much political involvement and a period in which several prominent former communist governments, notably those of Russia and China, are turning to capitalism, the once-strident rhetoric about militarism and imperialism has subsided.

Not that its fundamental meaning—an inversion of end and means—will disappear. It is alive and well even in our own contemporary world of relative great power détente. Whereas at one time states did not need a war plan until after formal war declaration, since 1914 and certainly in 1998 major powers without war plans risk extinction should action be initiated by those using deep-future oriented planning processes and weapons of mass destruction. In a competitive world, preparation is destiny. To do this requires some "give-ups"—social and economic involvement at a very complex level—and always risks other give-ups with more serious consequences, such as the loss of political control to the military.

Specialization of labor and knowledge depend on the extent of the market, as Adam Smith wrote in 1776. Today the market for war-planning processes is global. Its high-technology software and equipment require a degree of specialization of knowledge undreamed of a century ago. Also, a century ago there were no dentists. If one had a toothache, one went to the family doctor, but even he was not very scientific. People often pulled teeth out themselves and in many cases, suffered and sometimes died. Today we no longer "d.i.y" our teeth, but instead go to those with medical education and knowledge. The same may be said about war. In worst-case scenarios, political leaders are dependent on expert military knowledge. Only the strongest of leaders, caught in a worst-case war scenario, can resist the blandishments of the military technican. In this situation all risk inversion to militarism. The institutionalization of death and the socialization of danger on a world scale only enhance this possibility.

The threat and possibility of inversion remains a reality but the description of this reality continues to be in the eye of the beholder. One of the most famous 19th-century European generals, Prussian Field Marshall Count Helmuth von Moltke, was described in 1955 by the most celebrated post-World War II American writer on German history as "driven by ideological passions to wars of annihilation." In 1998 it is clear that Moltke was neither an evil genius nor, as others described him, a philosopher king. Instead he was closer to the modern dentist who just fills the tooth without paying much attention to the state of health of the body as whole. But a bad toothache, just like a war, can take over a whole body, both in theory and in practice.

Also See the Following Articles

COLD WAR • COLONIALISM AND IMPERIALISM • MILITARY CULTURE • MILITARY-INDUSTRIAL COMPLEX, CONTEMPORARY SIGNIFICANCE • MILITARY-INDUSTRIAL COMPLEX, ORGANIZATION AND HISTORY • WARFARE, MODERN • WARFARE, TRENDS IN • WARRIORS, ANTHROPOLOGY OF • WEAPONRY, EVOLUTION OF • WORLD WAR I • WORLD WAR II

Bibliography

Bartlett. (1938). *Familiar quotations* (11th ed.). Boston: Little Brown.
Berghahn,V. (1981). *Militarism: The history of an international debate, 1861–1979.* Cambridge: Cambridge University Press.
Bartov, O. (1992). *Hitler's army.* New York: Oxford University Press.
Bucholz, A. (1994). Armies, railroads and communications: The birth of industrial mass war. In J. Summerton (Ed.), *Changing large technical systems.* Boulder: Westview Press.
Bucholz, A. (1991). *Moltke, Schlieffen and Prussian war planning.* Oxford: Berg Publishers.
Bucholz, A. (1997). *Delbrück's modern military history.* Lincoln and London: University of Nebraska Press.
Conze, W. (1978). Militarismus. In *Geschichtliche Grundbegriffe: historisches Lexikon zur politisch-sozialen Spraches* in *Deutschland, IV, 1–47.* Stuttgart: Klett.
de Chastenay, Madame, ([1816] 1987). *Memoirs: la revolution et l'Empire.* Paris: Librairie Academique Perrin.
Drucker, P. (1995). *Managing in a time of great change.* New York: Dutton.
Geyer, M. (1986). German strategy in the machine age. In P. Paret, *Makers of modern strategy.* Princeton: Princeton University Press.
Johnson, J. J. (1962). *The role of the military in under-developed countries.* Princeton: Princeton University Press.
Kehr, E. (1977). *Economic interest, militarism and foreign policy: Essays on German history.* Edited and introduced by G. A. Craig, translated by Grete Heinz. Berkeley: University of California Press.
McNeill, W. H. (1982). *The pursuit of power: Technology, armed force and society since* A.D. *1000.* Chicago: University of Chicago Press.
McNeill, W. H. (Ed.). (1969). *Classical China. Readings in world history, Vol. 5.* Chicago: University of Chicago Press.
Paret, P. (1986). *Makers of modern strategy from Machiavelli to the nuclear age.* Princeton: Princeton University Press.
Ralston, D. B. (1990). *Importing the European army: The introduction of European military techniques and institutions into the extra-European world, 1600–1914.* Chicago: University of Chicago Press.
Vagts, A. ([1937] 1959). *A history of militarism.* rev. ed. New York, Free Press.
Ward, R. E., & Rustow, D. (1964). *Political modernization in Japan and Turkey.* Princeton: Princeton University Press.

Militarism and Development in Underdeveloped Societies

Peter B. Mayer

University of Adelaide

I. Historical Origins
II. Extent of Military Rule in Developing Countries
III. Explanations: Why the Military Intervenes in Politics
IV. The Military in Power: The Role of the Armed Forces in Modernization and Development
V. Impact of Military Spending on Development
VI. Disengagement: The Transition from Military Rule to Democracy

GLOSSARY

Caudillo (Sp.) A military–political leader.
Coup d'État Overthrow of an existing government by force.
Disappearance Secret, extra-judicial murder. In Spanish the victims are termed *desaparecidos*.
Human Capital The stock of productive human capabilities, including education, training, health and nutrition.
Militarism Domination of government and society by the armed forces of a country.
Personalist Regime Government centered on a single individual.
Rent-Seeking Use of government control of the economy for personal benefit.

MILITARISM is a word to which many different meanings are attached. The archetypal image of militarism is the equestrian figure of a ruler dressed in military costume, the Man on Horseback, the heroic, martial savior of the nation. Most commonly, militarism refers to predominance—political, economic, or social—of the military in government or society. Thus Prussia in the 19th century and Japan in the late 19th and first half of the 20th centuries—both societies in which military ideas and ideology were predominant, the military class was extremely influential, and conscription was widespread—are often characterized by the term "militarism." In developing countries, militarism describes the many new nations which have experienced control of government and direct rule by the military.

I. HISTORICAL ORIGINS

Soldiers have been involved in politics for almost as long as there have been states. In Imperial Rome, for example, the Praetorian Guard created by Augustus as his bodyguard were soon involved in making and unmaking Emperors.

II. EXTENT OF MILITARY RULE IN DEVELOPING COUNTRIES

Contrary to the expectations of some scholars in the 1950s and 1960s, rule by the military has proved to be one of the most common and significant forms of government among developing countries. The hopes that post-World War II Latin America had made a permanent transition to democratic governments or that Africa would not follow the path of Latin America in the 19th century were rudely flattened by the unprecedented intervention of the military in the politics of the developing nations. In the post-World War II period nearly one in five changes of government leadership occurred as the direct result of military intervention and in that period military personnel formed part of the political executive in 4 out of 10 of the world's governments. In the late 1980s nearly 60 of the world's nations had military governments. Although the military have intervened or participated in governments in all regions, the significance of rule by the military is especially evident in the histories of Latin America and Africa.

A. Latin America

In no part of the developing world has the influence of the military been more profound than in Latin America. There, more than anywhere else, political intervention and rule by the military have been almost the norm and not the regrettable exception. Following their liberation from Spain and Portugal virtually every South and Central American state experienced repeated incidents of violent overthrow of the government and rule by populist and nationalist military officers called *caudillos*. In 19th century Bolivia, for example, six presidents were assassinated and 60 revolts took place. Before the end of the century, Venezuela had experienced 50 revolutions. At the eve of World War I, governments in Latin America had been changed by force over 100 times. Generals ruled some Latin American states for extended periods. General Pofirio Diaz dominated Mexico from 1876 to 1910. General José Santos Zelaya ruled Nicaragua from 1893 to 1909. The dictator General Juan Vicente Gómez ruled Venezuela virtually as a personal estate between 1908 and 1935.

In Latin America as a whole, the period immediately following World War I was characterized by a return to elected civilian governments. On the eve of the Depression, only six countries, whose populations made up only 15% of the total of the continent, had military rulers. The onset of economic hardship after 1929 was followed by an increase in rule by the military. By 1936 there were "presidents in uniform" in half the nations of Latin America.

Between 1935 and 1964 force had been used to overthrow governments on 56 occasions. In that period there were on average between one and three successful coups each year. Military rulers had ruled El Salvador for 48 years when they stepped down in 1979; Nicara-

gua had been dominated by the military for 43 years when they too relinquished power to civilians in 1979; and General Alfredo Stroessner had ruled Paraguay for 35 years when free elections held in 1989 after his overthrow brought his protegé General Andres Rodriquez to power. Many of the coups that brought the military to power were directed against left-wing movements that ranged from constitutional trade union struggles to revolutionary guerilla movements following extreme forms of communism.

In the third quarter of the 20th century, the military intervened in the political life of all Latin American countries except Costa Rica and Mexico. Argentina, for example, experienced eight coups d'état and attempted coups between 1950 and 1963. The coup of March, 1976 ushered in an era of military government in Argentina of unprecedented brutality. All independent political institutions, such as courts, parliament, political parties, and mass media were either closed or brought under direct military control. Institutions of civil society, such as universities and trade unions were closed or banned. A systematic campaign began against "subversives," a term that could include anyone who dared express opposition to the military regime—or indeed many with no discernible political connections at all. During this "dirty war" abduction and torture followed by deliberate secret execution became widespread. These abductions and murders came to be known as "disappearances" and the victims as *desaparecidos*. At the height of the repression in 1976 and 1977 between 8,000 and 20,000 blue-collar workers, students, teachers, priests, nuns, journalists, agricultural laborers, men, women—10% of whom were pregnant—and even children and the elderly were seized by agents of the state and "disappeared." Even following the return of civilian government after the defeat of General Galtieri's government in the Falklands/Malvinas War in 1982 and the holding of a commission of enquiry into the disappearances, the Argeninian military continued to exert great political influence, to the extent that those accused of torture and extra-judicial killing were granted amnesties.

Brazil experienced three periods of military rule between 1945 and 1984. Even after the restoration of civilian rule in 1984, military officers remained in the cabinet and the constitution promulgated in 1988 guaranteed a legitimate political role for the military in government. In elections in 1989 and 1994 the armed forces directly expressed their opposition to candidates of the Workers' Party.

During the 21 years that the Brazilian military were in power (between 1964 and 1985), they fostered a developmental model that relied heavily upon foreign investment. It was during this period in Brazil that vast areas of the Amazonian forests were destroyed. To encourage development of the Amazon investors in the region were given generous tax breaks as well as matching grants from the government. Cattle ranching, sometimes on a gigantic scale, was encouraged which promoted wholesale deforestation. Because these developments were promoted by a military government, protests over the impact of logging and clearing on indigenous peoples, endangered species, or small holding farmers were interpreted as unacceptable foreign interference in domestic affairs or the actions of communist agitators. Hence military force was used with little restraint against any protests made against the impact of development in the Amazon basin.

The 1980s and more especially the half decade following the collapse of the Soviet Union witnessed a remarkable reversal of regimes in Latin America. Since 1979 many Latin American nations have returned to civilian rule; civilians were ruling in nearly 20 nations that had formerly been controlled by generals. Between 1985 and 1991 there were only four coups, three of the four occurred in Haiti.

B. Africa

Most African states became independent in the late 1950s and early 1960s. By the mid-1960s there had already been nine coups d'état, four of which had been successful in toppling the existing government; in the following 2 years alone, eight more coups occurred. Few sub-Saharan African states had not experienced a period of rule by the military in their first 30 years of independence. In one African state or another, the military had been in power 1 year in every 3 during that period and in the states that had experienced military rule, the military had held power for half of the period since independence was secured. In nearly 30 countries several hundred coups had been attempted without success and over 70 leaders had been displaced by the military. The coup d'état had become the most common means of changing regime in sub-Saharan Africa.

Nigeria, for example, experienced its first coup when the republic was overthrown in January, 1966 during which military officers assassinated the Prime Minister Sir Abubakar Tafawa Balewa and the premiers of the Western and Northern regions. Most of the officers involved in the coup were Ibos from the relatively advanced Eastern region, and the coup was quickly perceived by Northern Nigerians in regionalist and tribalist

terms. By the middle of that year the new regime's attempts to create a unitary state led to an attack on Ibo officers and a "counter-coup" which installed Lieutenant Colonel Gowon of the lower Northern region into power. In the ensuing months there were pogroms of Ibos in various parts of the country which in their wake produced a separatist movement in "Biafra" and precipitated a prolonged and bloody civil war that lasted for $2\frac{1}{2}$ years and which claimed more than a million lives.

Gowon ruled for 5 years following the surrender of the Biafran separatists in 1970; he was overthrown by an internal coup in 1975 after he had promised a return to civilian rule in the following year. The new military leadership that replaced Gowon was itself overturned 6 months later. The new regime, in a manner that was surprising given its origins, set about preparing for the transition to civilian rule. This included the drafting of a new constitution, the creation of a Constituent Assembly, the legalization of political parties, and the holding of elections in 1979.

The elected civilian government lasted only until the begining of 1983 when it was overthrown by military officers. Like the earlier government of Gowon, the new Buhari government was dominated at both federal and state levels by military and security personnel. After barely 20 months in office, during which time his government had become widely unpopular, Buhari was removed by Major General Babangida. Though the new regime promised a return to civilian rule by 1990, that was revised to 1992 and then to 1993. When it became evident that Chief Mashood Abiola would win the presidential election in 1993, the military refused to relinquish power. Another internal coup later in 1993 led to the emergence of General Sani Abacha, who had led an authoritarian and harsh regime for more than 5 years.

Like many other military governments, the Nigerian military over the years has been responsible for many human rights violations, with shootings of students, peasants, and the arbitrary detention of many of its critics, including Chief Abiola. The Abacha regime became the focus of worldwide protest in 1995 over its execution of author and environmental activist Ken Saro-Wiwa. Saro-Wiwa led protests by the Ogoni people over oil spills, water and soil contamination, and air pollution caused by Shell Petroleum Development Company operations in the Niger delta since 1958. The military responded to widespread protests by the Ogoni by arresting and sometimes shooting protesters. The regime arrested Saro-Wiwa on charges of murder in April, 1994 and after a trial condemned by outside observers for substantial irregularities, he was sentenced to death in October, 1995. Despite international outcry, Ken Saro-Wiwa was hanged on November 10, 1995.

Another aspect that has characterized successive military regimes is the growth and spread of corruption by its rulers. Fueled by Nigeria's oil wealth, corruption has become pervasive, endemic, and predatory. Transparency International has ranked Nigeria as one of the world's most corrupt governments. There seems little doubt that the institutionalization of militarism in Nigeria's postindependence history has played a major part in the conversion of the state apparatus into a vehicle for personal enrichment. The unexpected death of General Abacha in June 1998 and the equally surprising death of Chief Abiola—on the eve of being released from prison—a month later, appeared to have placed Nigeria on the path leading back to civilian rule. Action to recover vast sums of money, allegedly stolen by Abacha, his family, and associates was one of the first acts of the transitional regime.

Many of Africa's difficulties stemmed from the arbitrary patchwork of national borders and peoples which were the legacy of colonialism. Extensive periods of military rule were an indication of chronic instability and the failure to develop strong civilian political institutions. Periods of ineffective civilian rule were punctuated by the increasingly intensive use of force including military and paramilitary power against the state's own citizens. Rwanda, for example, experienced repeated episodes of communal murder between Tutsis and Hutus, culminating in the holocaust of 1994 in which up to a million people, mostly Tutsis, were killed by paramilitary forces and government-sponsored civilian militias. During the Cold War Africa became a cockpit for proxy wars fought out between the United States and the Soviet Union. Persistent, bloody internal wars were fought in Angola and Ethiopia in which protagonists were supported by one or other of the superpowers. South Africa played a similar role in sustaining the civil war in Mozambique in the 1980s.

III. EXPLANATIONS: WHY THE MILITARY INTERVENES IN POLITICS

The unmistakable evidence of widespread military intervention in the politics of the newly independent countries of the Third World led scholars to explore many aspects of the military in power. Among the principal topics on which investigations have concentrated are the immediate mechanisms of the seizure of power, the deeper forces that lead to military intervention, the nature and effects of rule by military governments, and

the forces that lead military governments to turn power over to civilian regimes and return to their barracks. As might be expected, there is considerable diversity of opinion surrounding each of these aspects.

A. Different Forms of Military Coup

The military intervenes in national politics for a variety of reasons. A number of different typologies of these reasons have been offered by scholars. Huntington, for example, distinguishes between four categories of coups which reflect different stages of political development. In the initial stages of modernization there are "palace revolutions" in which one member of the ruling oligarchy uses force to supplant another. The second sort of coup, the "reform coup," typically occurs following the emergence of middle-class officers in the military; these middle-ranking officers overthrow the old order so as to implement social and economic reforms. The "Free Officers" who overthrew the government of King Farouk in Egypt in 1952 were an example of such a coup. As modernization proceeds and the lower classes become increasingly involved in politics, the military tend to execute "veto coups" that seek to maintain the exclusion of the masses from political participation. Acting as "guardians" of the middle-class order that they have helped establish, the military act to "forestall" the election of an unacceptable candidate or overthrow a newly elected government.

Janowitz distinguishes between "reactive militarism," in which the military is drawn to intervene in politics by the weakness of civil institutions and public pressure, and "designed militarism," in which the military have a developed reform agenda that they seek to implement once in power. Pinkney has distinguished between the "South American model" of military intervention on the one hand, in which a highly professionalized military takes power to defend its own interests and those of a social and economic elite, and the "tropical African model" in which weak political institutions collapse in the first confrontation with the military.

B. Defence of the Nation

In many countries, the military see themselves as custodians or guardians of the nation or of the constitution. Where the military conceive themselves in these terms, they justify their interventions as necessary to restore order or a balance that they perceive has been lost and that threatens the nation. Thus when Pakistani general Ayub Khan overthrew the government just a decade after the nation had received independence and a short time before general elections were due to be held in 1958, he claimed that military rule was necessary to prevent the nation from descending into chaos.

C. Deeper Causes: Economic Transition from Traditional, Agrarian Societies to Industrialised Societies

It has long been evident from the experiences of Europe and North America that the transition from an agrarian society to an industrialized one is profoundly upsetting for a country. Not only are there large-scale physical movements of populations out of once-stable rural communities to burgeoning urban areas, but there are profound psychological and social adjustments that are imposed. This period of transition is one in which social order is placed under the greatest strain. In developing countries the strains are even greater because popular political participation is better established than it was in 19th-century Europe, but there is as well the visible example of living standards in already-industrialized societies. These conditions have led theorists to propose the existence of a "revolution of rising expectations".

One influential analysis of why the military play such a significant role in developing societies is that offered by Samuel P. Huntington. Huntington, like many analysts, emphasizes the socially disruptive nature of modernization. Nation states, political parties, and modern communications all act to undermine older forms of village and local authority. The fracturing of older institutions and loyalties unavoidably leads to increased conflict and violence in society. In effect, Huntington suggests, between the relative stabilities of traditional societies on the one hand and mature modernized societies on the other, there is a dangerous domain of modernizing transition that is characterized by political disorder and insurrection. There are two principal paths that traverse the zone of transition. There is a path of "civic politics" where political institutions are relatively well developed. The alternative path, where institutionalism is weak, is that of "praetorianism." Military intervention in politics is particularly common in praetorian societies. The political position of the military changes as society modernizes: "In the world of oligarchy, the soldier is a radical; in the middle-class world he is a participant and arbiter; as the mass society looms on the horizon he becomes the conservtive guardian of the existing order" (Huntington, 1968, p. 221). In an earlier study Huntington argued that as societies become industrialized, their militaries will become increasingly professionalized and will consequently absorb and support the liberal democratic view that the military should serve and not dominate society. Though this view is widely cited, it is not clear that it helps explain a great deal about the behavior of military groups in developing countries. In Latin America in the 1970s, for instance, highly professional armies in Argentina and Chile overthrew democratically elected governments. In South Asia, the army created in British India was divided between India and Pakistan; while the Pakistani military over the past 50 years has overthrown several elected governments and retains a preponderant position in national politics, the Indian military has remained strictly subordinate to civilian authority.

D. Coups as a Reaction to Economic Deterioration, "Rent-Seeking" Behaviour

It has been widely observed that military intervention in politics appears to be associated with economic crisis and stagnation of growth. Needler, in a study of intervention in politics by the military in Latin America, suggested that governments were more likely to be overthrown by force when economic conditions deteriorated; when conditions were improving, the military was unlikely to intervene in politics. More recently Dix has argued that when military regimes are associated with acute economic deterioration they tend in turn to lose their principal claim to legitimacy.

The state-centered development model followed by many Latin American and most African nations has been seen as a principal reason for the great frequency of military intervention in postindependence regimes. The concentration of economic activities in the hands of state economic agencies, parastatals, state-owned trading corporations, and the like have given enormous powers of patronage to whatever group or party secures control of the government. This has required most entrepreneurs to cultivate relations with those in political power to secure permits, licenses, access to foreign exchange, and other economic assets. In many African states the military have emerged as the most successful of these entrepreneurial groups. Seizures of power have been the most effective way to channel the resources of the state to the military and to their supporters.

E. Military as Agents of Class Domination

An alternative view of the relationship between the military and other forces in society is provided by scholars working within the neomarxist tradition. One particularly influential formulation was provided by Hamza Alavi. Drawing particularly upon the postcolonial experiences of Pakistan and Bangladesh, Alavi argued that the newly independent states that succeeded colonialism were "overdeveloped" with relatively powerful bureaucracies and armies that had been the instruments of colonial domination. Weak political parties, such as Pakistan's Muslim League, were forced to rely on the army and bureaucracy to govern and became dependent on powerful landlords for electoral support. State patronage, in turn, is critical for the development of the emerging business class. In these circumstances, according to Alavi, irrespective of whether there is civilian rule, the military–bureaucratic oligarchy are in effective control of the state.

IV. THE MILITARY IN POWER: THE ROLE OF THE ARMED FORCES IN MODERNIZATION AND DEVELOPMENT

Finer has identified three major classes of military regimes. The first of these rules indirectly, through a nominally civilian executive. Finer discerns two forms of indirect rule, one which he terms "limited" or "intermittent," the other is "continuous." The second kind, which he terms a "dual" regime, combines both direct military involvement in government and a form of civilian political party or organization. The regime of General Juan Domingo Perón in Argentina is a prime example of a dual regime; both the army and the Partido Justicialista with its working class support base were the twin pillars of Perón's populist regime. The third type of military regime identified by Finer is one he terms "direct rule," which, as the terms suggests, refers to a military government that exercises power in its own right. Here again there are two important varieties of direct rule; one is the unvarnished rule by generals; the other is a civilianized form in which the colonels and generals reinvent themselves as civilian presidents, as did Colonel Nasser of Egypt in 1956.

A. Personalism

Seizure of power for personal aggrandizement is one of the most common motives for a coup d'état. One of the most notorious examples of a personalist regime is that of General Idi Amin, who seized power from the corrupt civilian regime of Milton Obote in 1971. Some have suggested that Amin's motives in moving against Obote while the latter was overseas, were essentially personal and stemmed from fears that Obote intended to dismiss Amin. Once in power, Amin sought to enhance personal loyalty by recruiting extensively from his own ethnic group and from the West Nile Province. During his 8 years in power, the hallmark of Amin's rule was personal and group self-interest, a reign of terror against much of the population including the expulsion of all of Ugandan citizens of Asian origin, and the devastation of the Ugandan economy. Other predatory military regimes in contemporary Africa have been those of General Mobutu of Zaire and of Jean-Bedel Bokassa, the notorious self-styled King of the Central African Empire.

Corruption by personalized military governments in Latin America is also well documented. A succession of Venezuelan dictators in the 1930s through the 1950s absconded with hundreds of millions of dollars. Juan Perón of Argentina is alleged to have looted $700 million from his country. More recently, military dictators like Panama's General Manuel Noriega added profits from drug running to the more traditional robbery of the state.

B. Ideological Orientation of Military Governments

The common stereotype of military regimes is that they are almost uniformly conservative in ideological outlook. Although many military regimes are indeed defenders of the status quo, it is by no means true that all or even most military regimes are either reactionary or conservative. A survey of 56 countries that have experienced one or more periods of rule by the military since 1960 indicates that approximately one-third have been left-leaning, one-third have been centrist, and one-third have been of a right-wing orientation.

1. Military as Apolitical, Conservative, and Unable to Be Modernizers

The conventional perception of the military in power is one of authoritarian and conservative political actors. Characteristic of the military as a conservative political force is the use of armed power to suppress dissent, ban political opponents and organizations such as trade unions, and end expressions of political dissent. In their conservative form they are *par excellence* defenders of the established economic and social order in society.

2. Military Prime Force for Modernization in Society

A second view of the military as a prime driving force for modernization in society was put forward by Lucien W. Pye. Pye argued that in many developing countries the military is often a uniquely modern, rational institution. Military structures reflect industrial models of specialization. Military recruitment and training serve in a way that is both rapid and psychologically reassuring to induct soldiers from traditional backgrounds into the attitudes, behaviors, and skills that are essential for building a modernized society.

3. Fiscal Impact of Military

Countries differ greatly in the degree to which spending on the military dominates the economy. As Table I indicates, military spending as a percentage of a country's Gross Domestic Product ranges from as high as 16% in Oman to as low as 0.7% in Costa Rica. In general, the high-income oil-producing countries of West Asia and countries facing direct military threat spend the greatest proportion of their wealth on the military.

The proportion of national income spent on defence in developing countries taken as a whole declined between 1985 and 1994 from 5.5 to 3.6%. In the least developed countries spending fell from 4.0% of GDP to 2.9%. In West Asia and North Africa spending declined between 1985 and 1996 from an average of 12.3 to 6.8%. In the Carribean and Latin America, military spending fell from 3.0 to 1.8%. In South Asia, spending in Pakistan and India fell by an average of .65%; it rose by 2.6% in Sri Lanka and Myanmar. Spending remained nearly constant in sub-Saharan Africa at 3.0% of GDP.

Only a handful of developing countries manufacture a significant portion of their own equipment, especially sophisticated armaments such as fighter aircraft and tanks. They therefore constitute a significant market for arms manufactured in industrialized countries and their reliance on overseas sources is frequently used as a measure of economic dependence. The largest share of the arms export market is held by the United States, which in 1996 made 42.6% of global arms deliveries. It was followed by the UK (22.1%), France (14.1%), Russia (8.6%), and Germany (1.6%).

The most significant regional markets for armaments were West Asia and North Africa, which purchased 39.5% of world arms exports. The next most important developing country markets were East Asia (23.0%), Latin America (4.1%), South Asia (3.6%), and sub-Saharan Africa (1.9%).

Another measure of the impact of militarization on a society is the military participation ratio—the proportion of the population which bears arms. Once again we find that there is a considerable spread between nations, ranging from a high of 34 per 1000 people in the population of the United Arab Emirates to Costa

TABLE I

Military Spending as a Percentage of Gross Domestic Product (1994)

High	Medium-high	Medium-low	Low
Oman, 15.9	Sri Lanka, 4.7	India, 2.8	Fiji, 1.5
Iraq, 14.6	Morocco, 4.3	Cuba, 2.7	Cameroon, 1.4
Kuwait, 12.2	Malaysia, 3.9	Algeria, 2.7	Bolivia, 1.4
Saudi Arabia, 11.2	Iran, 3.8	Ethiopia, 2.6	Guyana, 1.4
Angola, 8.7	Libya, 3.7	Thailand, 2.6	Indonesia, 1.4
Syrian Arab Rep., 8.6	South Korea, 3.6	Liberia, 2.5	Philippines, 1.4
Rwanda, 7.7	Sudan, 3.5	Uruguay, 2.5	Paraguay, 1.4
Mozambique, 7.1	Tanzania, 3.5	Uganda, 2.4	Tunesia, 1.4
Jordan, 7.1	Zimbabwe, 3.5	Colombia, 2.3	Honduras, 1.3
Pakistan, 6.9	Chile, 3.5	Kenya, 2.2	Malawi, 1.1
Egypt, 5.9	South Africa, 3.3	Nicaragua, 2	Nepal, 1.1
United Arab Emirates, 5.7	Turkey, 3.2	Zaire (Republic of Congo), 1.9	Guatemala, 1.1
China, 5.6	Ecuador, 3.2	Bangladesh, 1.8	Dominican Republic, 1.1
Bahrain, 5.5	Nigeria, 3.1	Peru, 1.8	Zambia, 1
Cyprus, 5.4	Myanmar (Burma), 3.1	Argentina, 1.7	Ghana, 0.9
		Brazil, 1.6	Jamaica, 0.9
		Venezuela, 1.6	Côte d'Ivoire, 0.8
			Mexico, 0.7
			Costa Rica, 0.7

Source: Adapted from UNDP Human Development Report (1996).

TABLE II

Military Participation Rate: Total Armed Personnel per 1000 Population

Very high	High	Medium-high	Medium-low	Low
United Arab Emirates, 34.2	Cuba, 9.7	Fiji, 4.9	Zambia, 2.7	Haiti, 1.1
Syrian Arab Rep., 29.8	Saudi Arabia, 9.2	Bolivia, 4.7	Uganda, 2.5	Bangladesh, 1.0
Oman, 21.5	Turkey, 8.5	Algeria, 4.6	China, 2.4	Malawi, 0.99
Qatar, 20.2	Uruguay, 8.3	Sudan, 4.4	Ethiopia, 2.3	Papua New Guinea, 0.9
Jordan, 20.1	Iran, 7.99	Thailand, 4.4	Brazil, 2.2	Kenya, 0.9
Iraq, 19.6	Angola, 7.96	Pakistan, 4.4	Argentina, 2.1	Nigeria, 0.7
Singapore, 19.3	Morocco, 7.5	Zimbabwe, 4.4	South Africa, 1.98	Zaire (Republic of Congo), 0.7
Bahrain, 16.2	Egypt, 7.3	Colombia, 4.3	Mexico, 1.9	Rwanda, 0.7
Brunei, 14.7	Sri Lanka, 7.0	Tunisia, 4.1	Tanzania, 1.8	Côte d'Ivoire, 0.6
South Korea, 14.4	Chile, 6.7	Venezuela, 3.8	Nepal, 1.7	Niger, 0.6
Cyprus, 14.3	Myanmar (Burma), 6.4	Nicaragua, 3.7	Philippines, 1.6	Burkina Faso, 0.6
Libya, 14	Malaysia, 5.96	Paraguay, 3.5	Guinea, 1.53	Ghana, 0.4
	El Salvador, 5.6	Dominican Republic, 3.3	Indonesia, 1.4	Panama, 0.3
	Peru, 5.0	Honduras, 3.2	India, 1.4	Mozambique, 0.01
				Costa Rica, 0.0

Source: Adapted from UNDP Human Development Report (1996).

Rica which—because it has a police force but no formal armed forces—is shown as having a zero ratio. Oil-rich states make up a large proportion of those with very high participation ratios. Kick *et al.* have suggested that militarization characterized by high participation ratios appears to have beneficial effects on economic growth and infant mortality (Table II).

V. IMPACT OF MILITARY SPENDING ON DEVELOPMENT

Spending on the military is a significant item of national expenditure in many developing countries. Developing country expenditure on the military has risen from about 7% of world expenditure in the 1960s to around 20% in the mid-1980s. Developing countries now spend an average of 20% of their national budgets on the military, about the same proportion as in more developed countries. Developing countries now constitute the most important market for armaments.

Differing assessments have been made of the impact of military spending on economic development. Some scholars have pointed to the developmental effects of military governments. Others have argued that military spending competes with developmental efforts.

A. Guns vs Butter? Guns for Butter?

Benoit analyzed the relationship between national expenditure on defence and rates of increase in civilian Gross Domestic Product in 44 developing countries. He found that the two are related and concluded that this arises because of the modernizing role of the the military and because of the stable economic environment promoted by military rule. Others have concluded that military spending stimulates demand and thus has a "multiplier effect" on economic development.

These findings reinforced those offered earlier by Janowitz. Janowitz emphasized the importance of the military as a training ground for administrative and technical skills, what economists refer to as "human capital investment." Armies do not merely take recruits from rural backgrounds and inculcate values such as discipline. Soldiers must be taught the use, maintenance and repair of machinery, vehicles, and communications equipment as well as construction techniques and so forth. In many cases they may be taught reading and mathematics as well as given instruction in principles of health and sanitation. Because military bases are often located in remote areas and because staff are regularly posted to different areas, militaries also provide for the education of the children of officers and other ranks. Many have extensive education and training establishments.

In addition, armies are significant economic enterprises. In many countries the military control significant manufacturing enterprises whose scope spreads far beyond the production of armaments; some have widespread retail distribution networks. Firms owned by the military in Ecuador, for example, manufacture a number of civilian and military vehicles and produce a wide range of building products from metal sheets to plumbing equipment. They also mine gold, export agricultural products, own a bank, an airline, and a shipping company.

In addition, militaries frequently are the driving force behind national investment in communications infrastructure. In order to defend the nation, they create roads and airports and establish telecommunications networks. Because they represent an "economy within an economy," the military frequently plays a special role in responding to natural disasters.

The military is also seen to be a significant agent in promoting social change. In many cases the military draws its recruits from a diverse range of cultural and ethnic backgrounds and seeks self-consciously to inculcate a sense of national identity and citizenship. Many contemporary militaries are relatively unique in their societies in offering meritocratic promotion and thus opportunity for poor but able young people to rise to positions of influence in society.

Military governments commonly claim that they have taken power to impose order. The resultant stability when it occurs is also argued to be a factor which contributes to economic development.

Subsequent studies have come to differing conclusions, finding on the whole that there is no simple, unambiguous relationship between military spending and increased national wealth.

B. Guns or Butter?

1. Impact of Military Spending on Social Welfare

The impact of military spending on trends in infant mortality, a particularly sensitive marker of national development and well-being, has been studied by a number of scholars. Woolhandler and Himmelstein showed that higher levels of military spending, because they result in poorer development of health services and infrastructure such as access to clean water, are closely correlated with elevated infant mortality rates. Kick *et al.* found that the relationship between military regime and infant health is a complex one. Health infrastructure—access to medical attention and to clean wa-

ter—has the most direct impact. Spending on health is affected by a wide range of factors including levels of national income; it is adversely affected by spending on armaments and by the existence of military regimes. Paradoxically, both democratic participation and a relatively large military establishment were found to promote infant well-being, the former through its emphasis on direct welfare expenditure, the latter through its promotion of human capital and infrastructure for defense purposes.

Table III presents data on a selected group of nations and compares the ratios of their military spending to education and health spending with their ranking on the United Nations Development Programme's Human Development Index, their achievements in female literacy, life expectancy at birth, and infant mortality rates. Although it is evident that those spending relatively large amounts on the military relative to education and health are either West Asian oil-producing countries or nations facing severe security threats, the relationship between spending on armaments and levels of human development is at best complex.

The findings of a study by Bullock and Firebaugh offer an explanation for the contradictory interpretations of the impact of military spending on economic and social well-being. The study examines the impact of two different components of military expenditure: expenditure on equipment and services on the one hand and spending on military personnel on the other. While there is little discernible impact, either positive or negative, from spending on goods and services, "social militarization" is associated with higher levels of per capita income, nutritional levels, literacy and with reduced infant mortality. The effects associated with spending on people rather than things appears to be the result of the increased levels of skill, that is, of human capital, which result from this aspect of military spending.

VI. DISENGAGEMENT: THE TRANSITION FROM MILITARY RULE TO DEMOCRACY

During the 1980s, but especially following the collapse of the Soviet Union, militarization in the world has been in retreat. This trend began in Latin America in the mid-1970s, became evident in East Asia a decade later, and in Africa from 1990 onward. It is yet to have much impact on West Asia. Pinkney has identified five major explanations that have been offered for why military regimes step down. These are: changes in civilian

TABLE III

Military Spending and Human Development

	Military expenditure as a % of spending on education & health	UNDP Human Development Index	Life expectancy at birth	Female literacy (%)	Infant mortality rate
High					
Syrian Arab Rep.	373	0.69	67.3	53	39
Oman	293	0.716	69.8	46.0	29
Iraq	271	0.599	66.1	42.3	58
Myanmar (Burma)	222	0.451	57.8	76.6	82
Angola	208	0.283	46.8	28	123
Ethiopia	190	0.237	47.8	2.5	118
Saudi Arabia	151	0.771	69.9	47.6	28
Jordan	138	0.741	68.1	79.4	35
Singapore	129	0.881	74.9	85	6
Pakistan	125	0.442	61.8	23	89
Cuba	125	0.726	75.4	94.6	12
Brunei	125	0.872	74.3	81.6	8
Mozambique	121	0.261	46.4	21.4	147
China	114	0.609	68.6	70.9	44
Sri Lanka	107	0.698	72	86.2	17
Nicaragua	97	0.568	6.1	65.9	50
Honduras	92	0.576	67.9	71.2	42
Kuwait	88	0.836	75	73.6	18
Turkey	87	0.711	66.7	70.9	64
Medium-high					
Tanzania	77	0.364	52.1	53.9	85
Chad	74	0.291	47.7	32.4	121
Morocco	72	0.534	63.6	28.8	67
Zaire (Republic of Congo)	71	0.371	52	64.9	92
Libya	71	0.792	63.4	59.3	67
Thailand	71	0.832	69.2	91.4	36
Chile	68	0.882	73.9	94.5	15
Zimbabwe	66	0.534	53.4	78.6	67
El Salvador	66	0.576	66.8	68.5	44
India	65	0.436	60.7	36	81
Zambia	63	0.411	48.6	68	103
South Korea	60	0.886	71.3	96.1	11
Bolivia	57	0.584	59.7	73.9	74
Colombia	57	0.84	69.4	90.6	37
Mali	53	0.223	46.2	20.8	158
Egypt	52	0.611	63.9	37	66
Gabon	51	0.557	53.7	53.3	93
Argentina	51	0.885	72.2	95.9	24
Indonesia	49	0.641	63	76.9	56
Cameroon	48	0.481	56.3	49	62
Liberia	47	0.311	55.6	29	124
Medium-low					
Sudan	44	0.359	53.2	32	77
United Arab Emirates	44	0.864	73.9	78.2	18
Paraguay	42	0.704	70.1	89.9	38

continues

continued

	Military expenditure as a % of spending on education & health	UNDP Human Development Index	Life expectancy at birth	Female literacy (%)	Infant mortality rate
Bangladesh	41	0.365	55.9	25	106
Papua New Guinea	41	0.504	56	60.6	68
South Africa	41	0.649	63.2	80.8	52
Philippines	41	0.665	66.5	93.9	43
Bahrain	41	0.866	71.7	77.6	18
Togo	39	0.385	55.2	34.3	85
Peru	39	0.694	66.3	81.6	64
Iran	38	0.754	67.7	56.4	34
Malaysia	38	0.826	70.9	76.3	13
Uruguay	38	0.883	72.6	97.4	20
Guinea	37	0.297	44.7	20.1	133
Madagascar	37	0.349	56.8	41.8	91
Congo (Brazaville)	37	0.517	51.2	67.7	84
Fiji	37	0.853	71.6	88.1	23
Nepal	35	0.332	53.8	13	98
Panama	34	0.859	72.9	89.5	25
Senegal	33	0.331	49.5	21.5	67
Central African Republic	33	0.355	49.5	47.9	101
Nigeria	33	0.4	50.6	43.8	84
Venezuela	33	0.859	71.8	89.9	23
Guatemala	33	0.58	65.1	47.6	48
Tunesia	31	0.727	68	51.6	43
Burkina Faso	30	0.225	47.5	8.4	129
Haiti	30	0.359	56.8	40.5	85
Suriname	27	0.737	70.5	91.0	27
Ecuador	26	0.764	69	87.5	49
Low					
Rwanda	25	0.332	47.2	45.0	110
Malawi	24	0.321	45.5	39.8	142
Kenya	24	0.473	55.5	66.8	69
Namibia	23	0.573	59.1	74.0	59
Brazil	23	0.796	66.5	82	57
Dominican Republic	22	0.701	69.7	81.2	41
Botswana	22	0.741	65.2	5.8	42
Guyana	21	0.633	65.4	97	47
Uganda	18	0.326	44.7	47.7	115
Cyprus	17	0.909	77.1	91.0	8
Côte d'Ivoire	14	0.357	50.9	27.4	91
Ghana	12	0.467	56.2	50.5	80
Niger	11	0.204	46.7	6.1	123
Gambia	11	0.292	45.2	23.1	131
Algeria	11	0.746	67.3	45.8	54
Trinidad & Tobago	9	0.872	71.7	96.6	17
Jamaica	8	0.702	73.7	88.3	14
Mexico	5	0.845	71	86.4	35
Costa Rica	5	0.884	76.4	94.6	13
Barbados	5	0.906	75.7	96.4	9
Mauritius	4	0.825	70.4	77.2	18

Source: Adapted from UNDP Human Development Report (1993, 1996, 1998).

attitudes, development of political structures and institutions, alterations in the objectives of the military rulers, and changes in political culture and socioeconomic development.

Popular disenchantment with the results of military rule has led to pressures in a number of countries for the reintroduction of party politics. In a number of cases such as South Korea, Argentina, and Pakistan the military has responded by permitting a circumscribed set of moderate parties to engage in political work and eventually to contest elections.

The existence of viable political institutions that can sustain civilian rule is an important factor in the success of a political transition. In Pakistan, for example, the emergence of a relatively stable two-party system based on the Pakistan Peoples Party under Benazir Bhutto and the Pakistan Muslim League led by Nawaz Sharif has facilitated the withdrawal of the military from direct intervention in Pakistani politics.

In a number of cases, changed political conditions, such as a reduction in internal or external threats or the failure of a military government to achieve major political or economic objectives may lead to internal tensions and generate internal pressures within the military for a return to the barracks.

Another aspect that fosters a return to civilian rule is the nature of the national political culture. Where, as in Turkey, there is widespread consensus both within and outside the military that government should be restored to civilian authorities once order and stability have been restored, it is relatively easy for the military to withdraw from politics. Where these attitudes are relatively weak, as in Nigeria, the attractions of power and patronage are likely to prevail.

Dix has suggested the international climate toward military rule is much less favorable, following the end of the Cold War. As a consequence, would-be architects of military coups must take into consideration the condemnation and economic penalities they are likely to face. The wide-spread reduction in levels of military spending and in government (above all military) ownership of productive enterprises seem to have reduced the likelihood of future military intervention in politics. This is because economic reforms make the business class less dependent upon government patronage and less threatened by the actions of populist regimes.

One of the most consistent findings to emerge from several decades of scholarly study of militarism is its association with low to middle levels of economic development. One of the first to report this assocation was S. E. Finer, who noted that between 1958 and 1973, 57% of states in the lowest category of per capita income had experienced coups; of those in the second income band 29% had had coups; in the third band, 16% had had coups, while only 6% had in the highest band (Finer 1988). One of the implications of such findings is that social and economic development within societies are likely to generate forces for the military to withdraw from political involvement.

Huntington has argued that there is an economic "coup-attempt ceiling" and a "coup-success ceiling." Countries with per capita GNPs of under $500 are those in which successful coups take place. Attempts to mount coups in countries with per capita incomes between $1000 and $3000 are unsuccessful; they are above the "coup-success ceiling." Attempts by the military to seize power do not occur in countries whose per capita income levels are over $3000, the "coup-attempt ceiling." Huntington suggests the widespread movement toward democracy seen from the 1970s to the present reflects the widespread achievement of economic growth and the movement of states above the different "coup ceilings" (Huntington 1996).

Many observers of economic development in East Asia have noted that the emergence of a sizable middle class has given rise to powerful demands for democracy. In Taiwan, South Korea, and Thailand military elites have given way to democratically elected governments. Pinkney's judgement well summarizes the general position: "socioeconomic development does not guarantee military disengagement, but lack of development ensures that any military withdrawal will be only partial or temporary" (Pinkney, 1990).

Also See the Following Articles

ARMS PRODUCTION, ECONOMICS OF • ECONOMIC CONVERSION • ECONOMIC CAUSES OF WAR AND PEACE • MILITARISM • MILITARY-INDUSTRIAL COMPLEX, CONTEMPORARY SIGNIFICANCE • MILITARY-INDUSTRIAL COMPLEX, ORGANIZATION AND HISTORY

Bibliography

Argentine National Commission on Disappeared People (1986). *Nunca mas (never again): A report by Argentina's National Commission on Disappeared People.* London: Faber and Faber.

Alavi, H. (1973). The state in postcolonial societies: Pakistan and Bangladesh. In K. Gough and H. P. Sharma, (Eds.), *Imperialism and revolution in South Asia.* New York: Monthly Review Press.

Benoit, E. (1978). Growth and defense in developing countries. *Economic Development and Cultural Change* **26**, 271–280.

Bullock, B. Firebaugh, G. (1990). Guns *and* butter? The effect of militarization on economic and social development in the third world. *Journal of Political and Military Sociology,* **18**, 231–266.

Dix, R. H. (1994). Military coups and military rule in Latin America. *Armed Forces and Society, 20*, 439–456.

Finer, S. E. (1988). *The man on horseback: The role of the military in politics.* Boulder, CO: Westview Press.

Goodman, L. W. (1996). Military roles past and present. In (L. Diamond and M. F. Plattner, Eds.), *Civil-Military Relations and Democracy.* Baltimore: The Johns Hopkins University Press.

Hanneman, R. A., & Steinback, R. L. (1990). Military involvement and political instability: An event history analysis 1940–1980. *Journal of Political and Military Sociology, 18*, 1–23.

Harbeson, J. W. (1987). Military rulers in African politics. In (J. W. Harbeson, Ed.) *The military in African politics.* New York: Praeger.

Huntington, S. H. (1957). *The soldier and the state: The theory and politics of civil–military relations.* Cambridge: Harvard University Press.

Huntington, S. P. (1968). *Political order in changing societies.* New Haven: Yale University Press.

Huntington, S. P. (1996). Reforming civil–military relations. In (L. Diamond and M. F. Plattner, Eds.), *Civil–military relations and democracy* Baltimore: The Johns Hopkins University Press.

International Institute for Strategic Studies (1997). *The military balance 1997/98.* London: Oxford University Press.

Janowitz, M. (1964). *The military in the political development of new nations: An essay in comparative analysis.* Chicago: University of Chicago Press/Phoenix Books.

Johnson, J. J. (1964). *The military and society in Latin America.* Stanford: Stanford University Press.

Kick, E. L., Nasser, R., Davis, B. L., & Bean, L. (1990). Militarization and infant mortality in the third world. *Journal of Political and Military Sociology, 19*, 285–305.

Lieuwen, E. (1962). Militarism and Politics in Latin America. In (J. J. Johnson, Ed.), *The role of the military in underdeveloped countries.* Princeton, NJ: Princeton University Press.

Luttwak, E. (1969). *Coup d'etat: A practical handbook.* Harmondsworth: Penguin Books.

Martin, P. M., & O'Meara, P. (Eds.) (1986). *Africa.* Bloomington: Indiana University Press.

Mbaku, J. M. (1994). Military coups as rent-seeking behavior. *Journal of Political and Military Sociology, 22*, 241–284.

Needler, M. C. (1966). Political development and military intervention in Latin America. *American Political Science Review, LX*, 616–626.

Pinkney, R. (1990). *Right-wing military government.* London: Pinter.

Pye, L. W. (1962). Armies in the process of political modernization. In (J. J. Johnson, Ed.), *The role of the military in underdeveloped countries.* Princeton, NJ: Princeton University Press.

Rippy, J. F. (1958). *Latin America: A modern history.* Ann Arbor: The University of Michigan Press.

United Nations Development Programme (1996). *Human development report 1996.* New York: Oxford University Press.

Woolhander, S., & Himmelsteins, D. (1985). An international analysis of arms spending and infant death rates. *The Lancet* (June 15), 1375–1378.

Military Culture

James Burk
Texas A&M University

GLOSSARY

Ceremonies The rituals of collective action that mark (and often celebrate) certain events or passages to new rank or status within the life of the military unit.

Cohesion The emotional bond of shared identity and camaraderie among soldiers within their local military unit; in sociological terms, horizontal or primary group integration.

Esprit de Corps The commitment and pride soldiers take in their military establishment and its effectiveness; in sociological terms, vertical or secondary group integration.

Etiquette Normative prescriptions that guide or control interpersonal behavior especially between those of different rank or military status.

Military Discipline Behavior of military personnel—as individuals or in group formations, in battle or in garrison—in conformity with previously prescribed rule, usually in response to command and the result of instruction and drill.

Professional Ethos Normative understandings that define the corporate identity, code of conduct, and social worth of the officer corps.

THE STUDY OF MILITARY CULTURE combines institutional and cultural analysis. It does not encompass every cultural contribution (or response) to the preparation for or conduct of war, but is limited rather to the study of those particular beliefs, values, and other symbolic productions that organize and sustain military organization. It does include the reception of these by the larger society to which the military belongs.

Even with these restrictions, the subject matter is vast. A complete treatment would include detailed comparisons of military cultures from ancient times to the present and include societies from around the globe. Of particular interest would be comparisons based on the different approaches to war that characterize military culture in Europe, India, and China. Historically, the so-called Western way of war has, with few exceptions, emphasized the importance and glory of war, aiming at a decisive victory over one's enemy through battles of annihilation; and it elevated the warrior to a position of high status, second only to the political leader, who was often a warrior-king and the highest ranking member of society. The strategic culture was quite different in India, where following the Vedic age and over a long period of transition, the Brahman priestly caste established its dominance over the (still elite) Kshatriyas warrior caste. Particular Brahmans sometimes ruled by military means, but that was not typical and not the basis of their power. More generally, the Brahman were committed to the principle of nonviolence and thought violent acts degraded the ritual purity on which their high status depended. Similarly,

Copyright © 1999 by Academic Press.
All rights of reproduction in any form reserved.

in China, much has been made of the rule of Confucian scholars over military warriors and of the Confucian strategic culture, which downplays the use of force. Rather than engage in all-out wars of attrition, Chinese rulers favored the use of stratagems or minimum force. As may be expected, however, such broad contrasts are sometimes more misleading than helpful. In an important recent study of China during the Ming dynasty, Alastair Iain Johnston provides clear evidence that in addition to the better-known Confucian culture there was another "parabellum" culture. The parabellum culture more closely resembled Western notions of "strategic realism" than the Confucian ethos and it was the primary guide to Chinese military practice.

To avoid problems of misleading generalization, my treatment of military culture will be confined to the experience of Western armed forces in the modern era broadly conceived. This focus is due also to the ready availability of sources. And it may be justified on substantive grounds by the relative predominance of Western military organization over the last four centuries. Employing a historical and comparative perspective, I cover three themes: (a) the elements of military culture; (b) the sources of continuity and change in military culture; and (c) the relation between military culture and the larger society.

I. ELEMENTS OF MILITARY CULTURE

Modern military institutions are organized and supported by states to wage war and to enforce domestic order. The precise balance between these two tasks has varied by state and historical circumstance. At any one time, armies are usually engaged in one task or the other. So the European armies that fought in the Napoleonic Wars early in the nineteenth century spent much of their time over the next 30 years suppressing internal rebellions. And the army of the United States occupied by preparing for and fighting wars in the 20th century spent the 30 years following the Civil War enforcing Reconstruction in the South, opening the frontier against the resistance of native Americans, and quelling labor disputes. Sometimes, however, armies perform both tasks simultaneously. The British army, for instance, from the 1970s until the end of the Cold War, maintained order in Northern Ireland and deployed in Germany to help deter war with the Soviet Union. Only on rare occasions have states—such as Costa Rica and, to a lesser extent and for quite different reasons, Japan—maintained armed forces only for domestic and limited defensive purposes.

Before the age of nation-states, however, one could not so clearly distinguish between these tasks. Preparing for and fighting war was the military's central mission and arguably its only mission. Despite the proliferation of humanitarian and peacekeeping assignments which armed forces have taken on since the Cold War, war fighting still determines the central beliefs, values and complex symbolic formations that define military culture.

Military culture is no more homogeneous than war itself. It is composed of at least four distinct elements: discipline, professional ethos, ceremonies and etiquette, and esprit de corps and cohesion. In general, however, one finds in each element an attempt to deal with (and, if possible, to overcome) the uncertainty of war, to impose some pattern on war, to control war's outcome, and to invest war with meaning or significance.

That is not to assert a simple functional theory of culture, in which the elements of culture operate together as mechanisms to adapt armed forces to war's turbulent environment. It is especially not to assert that these cultural elements are instrumentally rational, "fitting" armed forces to the task of fighting wars. Historically, there is abundant evidence to show that they may or may not be functional or instrumentally rational for military organization and that they may or may not operate cooperatively. Nor is it to conceive of military culture as simply derivative from the experience of war, as if war was an external stimulus evoking military culture in response. Rather, military culture is an elaborate social construction, an exercise of creative intelligence, through which we come to imagine war in a particular way and to embrace certain rationalizations about how war should be conducted and for what purposes. While it is a response to war, one effect of military culture (perhaps its most important effect) is to influence the likelihood and form of war itself.

A. Discipline

Military discipline refers to the orderly conduct of military personnel—whether individually or in formation, in battle, or in garrison—most often as prescribed by their officers in command. A high level of discipline begins with instruction and is perfected through repetitive drill that makes the desired action a matter of habit. (This may explain why many believe that the military is an institution that requires uncritical and instant obedience to orders. The belief is exaggerated.) An obvious aim of discipline is to minimize the confusion and disintegrative consequences of battle by imposing order on it. Discipline provides military personnel with a repertoire of patterned actions that they may use on their own initiative or in coordination with others quickly to adapt to and (hopefully) to prevail in battle. Another aim, perhaps less obvious, is to ritualize the violence of war, to set it apart from ordinary life. Following the discipline reassures soldiers, defining when and how they (and not others) are "authorized" to violate the usual taboos against killing and destruction.

What kind of discipline the military requires and how it is achieved varies historically. At least two patterns can be discerned. One is ancient and has to do with the relative importance of individuals versus military units in waging combat. The other is modern and has to do with changing methods for enforcing discipline.

1. Individual versus Group Discipline

Historically, it is common for military organizations to be little more than a charismatic band of individual warriors each fighting for his own reputation and honor. Occasionally, but characteristically in our time, military organization entails a high level of coordination with fighting carried out by well-drilled units in formation. War as combat among individual "warrior heroes" is not without discipline or ritual, as readers of Homer's *Iliad* will know. Fighting of this kind is frequently governed by complex conventions and rituals. In any case, it requires extraordinary personal discipline to overcome the fear of close combat, to endure the physical strain of battle, and to express oneself through skill in wielding weapons. Such warfare was not confined to primitive infantry. It characterized war dominated by cavalry from the ancient charioteers to the ritualized feudal warfare of European knights or the raids of Cossacks swooping across the steppes of Central Asia. Air combat among fighter pilots continues the tradition in the midst of modern war. In these cases, military discipline is a personal attainment achieved, if at all, through individual competence and exertion.

In sharp contrast is warfare based on the group discipline of well-drilled infantry. Whether we look at the hoplites of ancient Greece, Swiss pikemen fighting feudal knights, the armies of Maurice of Nassau and Gustavus Adolphus harnessing the power of gunpowder, or the conduct of joint force operations as prescribed by contemporary air-land battle doctrine, fighting with these forces envisions the coordinated and simultaneous movement of soldiers as a group in response to their leaders' commands. This is only possible to do after countless hours of instruction and much practice in the arts of close-order drill. In these armies, individual will is subordinate to the group. The results of group discipline have often been astonishing, enabling well-disciplined troops to deliver an enormous shock when on the attack and to remain intact while bearing the brunt of enemy fire. But the results were gained at a cost. Because group discipline requires continuous drill in preparation for war, whenever it gained influence, it encouraged formation of either a military class, as in ancient Sparta and in Japan under the Samurai, or a professional standing army, as it has done in Europe since the 17th century.

Neither the looser discipline of individual warriors nor the stricter discipline of well-drilled infantry guaranteed victory or survival in battle. Historically, the dominance of one kind of discipline or the other depended largely on what kind of weapons were used, a matter to which we will return. For now, it is enough to observe that modern military cultures assume a high (perhaps even an increasing) level of group discipline as part of their operational strategy, and have done so, with some exceptions, since the 17th century.

2. From Punitive to Positive Social Control

Discipline, of course, is a means of social control. It may be defined by customary beliefs about how to wage war, but it is enforced by authority. When we confine attention to modern militaries, we observe an important shift in the methods authorities use to enforce their discipline away from harsh corporeal punishment to a more positive leadership by persuasion, manipulation, and example. It is no exaggeration to say that group discipline in the new militaries formed in the 17th century was enforced by the lash and continued to be so through the 19th century. British soldiers serving during Queen Victoria's reign could expect to receive 150 lashes for failing to answer roll call, more for stealing a pig, more still for failing properly to perform one's duty as a sentinel, and many more for stealing money from a comrade. Major crimes were punished by death. Yet these 19th-century punishments were more moderate than those meted out before—King George III limited (to 1000) the maximum number of lashes that could be inflicted for a serious breach of discipline— and they became more moderate still. Flogging was abolished before the end of the 19th century. In the early 20th century, British officers punished soldiers by confinement to barracks or, for more serious offenses, by turning the case over for adjudication by court-martial. Following World War I, the use of court-martial to impose death penalties was restricted. This moderation did not mean an end to discipline but marked a different perception of how discipline should be achieved.

Morris Janowitz noted a similar trend in his classic study of the American military, *The Professional Soldier* (1960). In his terms, discipline based on domination declined in effectiveness as war industrialized. With industrialization, military organization became more complex and its discipline required coordination of technological specialists stretching from the front lines to the home front. For such an organization, authoritarian discipline was no longer effective. Leaders had rather to influence behavior by emphasizing the importance of achieving group goals, to gain the benefits of discipline by building consensus. No doubt, Janowitz is right to emphasize the importance of industrialization and the growing complexity of military organization as a cause of this change in the means of enforcing discipline. Not less important, however, was the preindustrial rise of the mass armed force whose power was demonstrated by the French Revolutionary Armies led by Napoleon. Before the French Revolution, enlisted personnel were typically outcasts, misfits, or worse who were impressed from the lower reaches of society and forced to serve. While the 18th-century officer corps were careful not to waste scarce military assets, they did not strongly identify with these men or regard them as people entitled to respect. The power of the mass army, harnessed to nationalist democratic social movements, changed the social composition of military forces in the 19th and 20th centuries. As the officers of World War I learned through bloody trial and error, a mass army, representative of the population, could not be led to fight by authoritarian means; it had to be convinced of the technical competence of its leaders and of the reasonableness of the goals it was asked to achieve. Military discipline is not absolute, but must conform to the expectations of the society it represents.

B. Professional Ethos

Depending on how one defines "military professional," it is anachronistic to speak of a professional military before the 17th century or even later. To be sure there are earlier examples of warrior castes or groups (like the Roman legions) for whom war fighting was the chief means of employment. And one may say, at least in terms of ideal culture, that the warrior knights of feudal Europe conceived of themselves as engaged in a calling, not very different from a religious vocation. A professional officer corps, however, entails more than this. It possesses a corporate identity based on expert knowledge of and control over the means of violence, with that knowledge and control deployed in the service of the state and rendered in accordance with a relatively explicit normative code of conduct. Not until the 17th century do we begin to discern development of such a corps. Its beginnings are due largely to requirements of the "military revolution" in discipline and organization. The newly forming standing armies of the (then) absolutist nation-states needed a relatively large number of officers serving full-time to instruct, drill, and command soldiers in the new techniques of close formation fire, to use scientific, engineering, and tactical knowledge for inventing new guns, cannon, or other weaponry, and to manage the increasingly heavy logistical demands these new armies imposed. While still important, traditional hereditary qualifications and part-time service, central to feudal military organization, were not sufficient to accomplish these tasks. Over time, they lost importance.

A key element distinguishing the emergent modern officer corps was its professional ethos. Its ethos, a set of normative understandings, defined its corporate identity, its code of conduct, and (for the officers at least) its social worth. It expressed the ideal commitments of the modern military officer. It was and still is a complex amalgam of (a) the heroic traditions of knighthood inherited from the feudal past; (b) the technological traditions associated with modern weaponry's design and use; and (c) the managerial traditions of modern bureaucracies that emphasize skilled leadership and coordination of human effort to achieve group goals by rationally efficient means.

The knightly heroic traditions emphasize bravery in combat and loyalty to one's comrades and liege. They retain power today, as shown in the symbols used in advertisements for military recruiting and more importantly in the high prestige accorded those who have faced combat. Modern officers are normatively proscribed from turning down a combat command and are always supposed to deplore "desk jobs" as a distraction from their "true" calling. This is so even in the late 20th century when combat arms represent only a small proportion of the total military establishment. Preparing for and facing battle remains the central commitment. It is a shared commitment that presumes personal willingness to kill and to accept the risk of being killed, for oneself and for those one commands—not indiscriminately, of course, but in defense of the state and in the context of war. This commitment underlies the professional soldier's corporate identity, as the pursuit of truth underlies the corporate identity of scholars.

Fulfilling the commitment, however, requires more than a knight's bravery. Over time, it required increasingly specific theoretical and technical knowledge that could not be obtained without formal study. Once recognized, early in the 19th century, it led states throughout Europe and North America to establish military academies to train junior officers and staff colleges and other advanced schools to train field-grade and senior officers. First in Germany, then elsewhere, formal training was put to use under the direction of a general staff of senior officers who engaged in formal planning for the waging of possible future wars. This imposition of formal education had normative overtones. The virtue of professional officers rested and rests still on their ability successfully to accomplish their mission. Though offering no guarantees, formal training was necessary for officers to be competent in the use of modern weapons and tactics.

Encompassing both bravery and technical competence, the professional ethos rests also on beliefs about effective leadership. Willingness and skill at facing combat are not enough. To be effective in combat, soldiers must believe that they are being asked to risk their lives for some higher good, now typically that they are waging war not for its own sake but for the sake of their country. They must also believe that their leaders hold their well-being in high regard. These beliefs are earned, if at all, by the officer's managerial competence to discern and provide for the needs of those he (or she) commands. Meeting these needs demands bureaucratic skill to organize and supply basic provisions of food, shelter, clothes, medical care, and the means to fight. But moral competence is required as much as bureaucratic skill: to know when battle serves a purpose; to calculate that battle has some fair chance of success, consistent with the risks being run; and to possess the rudimentary decency and integrity to refrain from useless slaughter.

In short, the professional ethos of the officer corps sets a high standard. The ideal of heroic, technically and morally competent combat leaders is rarely, perhaps never completely, realized. Its importance, however, for us and for those in the military, lies in what it imagines professional officers to be. Its defines their virtue and worth in terms of their preparation to fight war.

Since the end of World War II, the foundations of this professional ethos have been subject to erosion. Professional officers may wish still to define themselves in its light. But the ethos is rooted in assumptions about the inevitability and in some sense the positive value (or justice) of interstate war. The changing nature of war over the last 50 years, perhaps longer, challenges the relevance of both assumptions. If nothing else, the threat of nuclear war has caused militaries to prepare more for deterring than for fighting war. Following the logic of deterrence, preparations for war are successful when no war actually occurs. This stands in sharp contrast to the logic of war fighting that judges success at war preparations by victory in battle. The shift in outlook has meant the military spends much time engaged in what Martin van Creveld has called "make-believe" war—in the simulation of combat to demonstrate both to oneself and to potential adversaries that any real war would be self-defeating. Under these circumstances, the traditional ethos of professional soldiers based on combat seems no longer appropriate. Yet no suitable alternative has developed to take its place. Meanwhile, departure from tradition risks turning the professional soldier's vocation into an ordinary career; rather than a special calling, it is just another job. Justifying its importance, which is necessary to gain funding and other social resources, becomes a more difficult task. Increasingly, justifications are based on the performance of new military tasks such as peacekeeping and humanitarian relief. But, however similar these are to war, they are not war; and the ethos of the professional peacekeeper, unlike the ethos of the professional warrior, has yet to be defined.

C. Ceremony and Etiquette

Outside of war, perhaps, the ceremonial displays and etiquette that pervade military life are the most readily observable elements of modern military culture. These displays are connected to the business of war. Bright-colored uniforms and unfurled flags were an aid to commanders and soldiers in early modern warfare, if only because they helped to distinguish friendly from enemy forces. Similarly, the drum rolls and bugle calls that punctuated a day in garrison helped maintain a system of communication to direct force movements. Foot parades and the more contemporary air shows by military aviators exhibit excellence in close-order movement and maneuver on which well-drilled militaries depend for success in battle. But the connection of military ceremonies and etiquette to war is looser and more subtle than these illustrations suggest. Today's battlefields call for camouflaged dress, electronic communication, and dispersed movement in motor vehicles, but military uniforms for dress occasions remain brightly colored and drummed cadences still pace military parades.

Military ceremonies and etiquette make up an elaborate ritual and play the role that ritual typically plays in society: to control or mask our anxieties and ignorance; to affirm our solidarity with one another; and to celebrate our being, usually in connection with some larger universe.

No matter how fought or when, war presents harsh realities of death, disease, and destruction, realities that have not grown less harsh over time. These are difficult to experience and, once experienced, difficult to contemplate, much less to comprehend. They can only be approached at a distance, through the filters of social forms. Some few, like the British poet Wilfred Owen, use their art to help with the task. Most in the military (and elsewhere) are not so creative and rely instead on already constructed rituals to guide their conduct and to preserve a semblance of order and meaning in a situation that threatens to overwhelm both. The effectiveness of military rituals to control anxiety about facing war arises from their familiarity, acquired by use in garrison, long before battle is joined. Ceremonies of induction and promotion or change of command, for military weddings, retirements, and funerals—these mark the life cycle of soldiers as formations at dawn and dusk, ceremonies for changing the guard, marching in review, and periodic inspections mark the passing of the soldier's working day. No doubt, in peace time, they also occupy and make up part of a boring, seemingly endless routine; and they may degenerate, in peace or war, into burdens soldiers rightly call "chickenshit." Yet, when tragedies occur—a plane crash killing a company of peacekeepers on their way home for Christmas, a terrorist bomb ripping a barracks, or death in battle—they provide a ready framework for survivors to mourn and commemorate the dead and to uphold albeit fragilely the structure of a world where (in their lives) chaos took root.

Apart from tragedy, military ceremonies and etiquette are rituals that mark collective identity and group affiliation. They take a variety of forms but are usually highly visible and officially sanctioned. Almost universal among militaries is the practice of saluting as a sign of deference and the wearing of distinctive uniforms that bear emblems of one's unit, one's rank, and one's achievements. They may be illustrated best perhaps by the traditions surrounding the British regimental system. Some dating back to the 17th century, these regiments often wear the colors and crest of the royal who led them. They have a flag of their own, traditions of dining, reunions with former members, and annual celebrations of the day they won their major battle honor. Such practices forge a common identity and symbolize a common fate. And, while the strength of the regimental system today is not what it once was, similar practices in the military establishments of other nations suggest that they are unlikely to disappear. One can point for instance to the Canadian military's attempt in recent times to institute a common uniform to be worn by members of the air force, army and navy. Probably cheaper and certainly emphasizing the importance of joint operations in the present age, the attempt at uniformity was nevertheless enormously unpopular and finally abandoned. A common military identity bears the marks of its various services, branches, and units, and of the history associated with each one. They are not easily abandoned. They are totems around which one's military identity and purpose are formed.

It would be a mistake to assume that this ceremonialism is an anachronistic persistence of tradition into modern times. Not the least important role they play is to celebrate or honor unique achievements by those who have served. The practice is as old as the laurel crowns given heroes in ancient Greece and probably older. Membership in honorary orders, like the Order of St. John of Jerusalem or the Order of the Garter, began in the Middle Ages as a means of recognizing extraordinary service by particular knights. But the institution of decorations and medals for gallantry in combat or other kinds of service only began in the 19th century. The French Legion of Honor and the German Iron Cross were first awarded during the Napoleonic Wars, the British Victoria Cross in 1857 to veterans of the Crimean War, and the U.S. Congressional Medal of Honor in the Civil War. The French Croix de Guerre was not introduced until 1915. The importance of these awards to the honor of military personnel was illustrated tragically in the United States recently when its Chief of Naval Operations committed suicide in part because of accusations that he wore a badge for valor that he had not earned. Even more recently, a federal judge assigned the stiffest possible penalty to two men convicted of making and selling unauthorized tokens of the Congressional Medal of Honor.

An important purpose of these awards and other public military ceremonies is to connect the burdens of military service with the larger society the military serves. The connection is largely symbolic, of course, but weighted with meaning. Sometimes the ceremonies are grave as they are when heads of state lay wreaths on the tombs of unknown soldiers. Sometimes the ceremonies are joyful, as are commemorations of the Queen's Birthday in Britain, of Bastille Day in France, or Independence Day in the United States. Grave or joyful, they hope to convey the full meaning of military service, to show how central military service is to the life and well-being of the country. Precisely because this is their aim, they can also arouse controversy. So, for instance, President Reagan's decision to lay a wreath in a German cemetery in Bitburg horrified some Americans (including veterans of World War II) who thought his act might seem to honor Nazi war dead buried there. And so it was a powerful symbol when some Vietnam War veterans returned medals they had earned in protest against policies continuing the war.

D. Cohesion and Esprit de Corps

Less visible than ceremonies or displays of etiquette, but hardly less important to military effectiveness, is the morale of military personnel, whether high or low. Morale is a product of cohesion and esprit de corps; and these are intangible, highly changeable elements of military culture. Military cohesion refers to the feelings of identity and comradeship that soldiers hold for those in their immediate military unit; it is an outgrowth of face-to-face or primary group relations or, in formal terms, of horizontal integration. Esprit de corps, in contrast, refers to the commitment and pride soldiers take in the larger military establishment to which their immediate unit belongs; it is an outgrowth of secondary group relations or, again formally, of vertical integration. Both result to an important degree from structural factors of military organization, but they are primarily matters of belief and emotional attachments. They refer in particular to beliefs and attachments that shape the willingness of military personnel actually to perform their mission. They refer, in short, to the soldiers' willingness to fight.

Appreciation of the importance of cohesion and esprit de corps as aspects of military culture has grown over time. The reasons for this are twofold. The French Revolution introduced the idea of the military as a "nation in arms." Those in the military were not a class separate from society. They were drawn from and representative of the society as a whole, preparing or mobilized for war. But they were not professionals. The rank and file were civilians conscripted into service, in peace for a short term of training and in war, particularly the world wars, for the duration of the conflict. How they would respond to military discipline and to the stress of combat was open to doubt. At the same time, industrialization of war—which introduced long-range artillery, smokeless gunpowder, and machine gunfire—required troops to be widely dispersed over extended battle lines, a requirement that unfortunately took some time to grasp. No longer in close physical proximity with one another, soldiers had to exercise initiative in

carrying out their orders and they had to be confident that their comrades would do the same.

Initially it was thought that the beliefs that underlay high levels of cohesion and esprit de corps derived from the love of country and attachment to ideological commitments of the state. Many writers at the turn to the 20th century dwelt on the importance of state-sponsored efforts to inculcate patriotic sentiments in youth in schools and to provide opportunities to enact these sentiments through paramilitary clubs and other military training programs, voluntary or compulsory. These ideas intensified during World War I. The British Army, for example, instituted an extensive program of political education in response to worries of senior officers that their men did not understand what they were fighting for and so might not fight at all. During World War II, American soldiers (and civilians) were shown short movies of high quality, directed by Frank Capra, and other leading Hollywood directors, to explain and justify "why we fight." In both wars, countries on all sides printed posters relying on simple slogans and graphic images to convey ideas (often ideas for action) the government wanted people to believe. These programs may have had some positive effect on esprit de corps, providing a vague sense of the justice of one's cause and the basic goodness of the society for which one fought. But a long stream of social science research has shown that other factors than ideology are more important in forming military cohesion.

Cohesion among soldiers, especially in war, rests on concrete and primary experiences. The historian William McNeill has recently suggested that cohesion results from military drill, that there is a kind of "muscular bonding" arising from the practice of marching together in time, not very different from the bonding that occurs among those engaged in a collective dance or enacting a common religious ritual. There may be something to this claim. But there is more to cohesion than "muscular bonding." In their classic essay studying cohesion and disintegration of the Wehrmacht during the last months of World War II, Edward Shils and Morris Janowitz directly challenged the argument that German soldiers continued to fight from commitment to Nazi ideology. More important, they argued, was the capacity of the soldiers' immediate unit, their company and platoon, to meet their basic needs for food and shelter, and for affection and esteem. These were more important because war posed a genuine threat to their sense of security and to the recognition of their worth as human beings. So long as these needs were met, soldiers believed themselves part of a powerful group and felt responsible, even empowered, to fight for their group's well-being. When these needs were not being met, soldiers felt alone and unable to protect themselves; the unit disintegrated and fighting stopped.

Esprit de corps is an important factor affecting small-unit cohesion. Small units, to be effective, must be tied to a larger group. Their capacity to operate depends on links with larger units (the battalion, the regiment, the division, etc.), which provide their supplies, maintain symbols of the homeland, and regulate their exposure to war's danger through the exercise of command. Clearly, more is involved than material organization. Small-unit nesting within a hierarchical organization constructs a situation-specific context within which unit operations gain or lose meaning and become objects of pride or disgrace. The defense of Bastogne during the Battle of the Bulge illustrates the point. The American general commanding the defense of the city, encircled by Germans, was confident when refusing German terms of surrender. He knew that holding the city was critical to Allied war plans and that relief was on the way from Patton's Third Army. His confidence and commitment, communicated to the rank and file, reinforced their cohesion, strengthened their pride in their division, and increased their willingness to fight despite being surrounded by the enemy and perilously short on supplies. In the same way, members of Patton's army drove hard through foul weather and overcame stiff German resistance to relieve the besieged city. They did so knowing that their local sacrifice was meaningful: to rescue one's countrymen from an enemy and to stop the Germans from advancing into France. Without the sense that sacrifice is worthwhile, esprit de corps declines, threatening military discipline, effectiveness, and cohesion. This was true, for instance, for U.S. forces in Vietnam during the last years of American involvement in that war. The relationship between esprit de corps and cohesion, however, is more complex than these examples suggest. While esprit de corps cannot be high when cohesion is low, the reverse is not necessarily true. French soldiers who survived Verdun and the Somme in 1916 mutinied after another failed and bloody offensive in April of 1917. But their mutiny did not signal the disintegration of small units. On the contrary, cohesion remained high. It was their esprit de corps, their pride and dedication to the larger military command, that unraveled. What they refused to do was fight for generals who would lead them into another offensive slaughter. Their obedience was regained and discipline restored, but only after a change in command and an agreement to deploy troops defensively.

E. A Cautionary Note

A cautionary note is in order. Those concerned with the effectiveness of military institutions may wish to conclude that while military culture is heterogeneous, its elements are reinforcing. If discipline is strong, professional ethos is well-developed, military ceremonies and etiquette are fully observed and esprit de corps and cohesion are high, then military institutions presumably operate at their best. Yet it is unwise to argue this way for at least two reasons. First, this list of elements of military culture is not exhaustive. I do not think any description of military culture could ignore the elements included here. They are necessary. But they may not be sufficient. Social historians in particular may wish to pay attention (say) to soldiers' songs and religious beliefs or to the moral life of military encampments; philosophers and legal scholars may wish to pay attention to the laws and conventions regulating the justice and just conduct of war; and students of language may wish to examine how military terminology (often euphemisms) clarify or obscure our reasoning about war. In any case, military culture does not live in isolation. It breathes—influences and is influenced by—the air of the larger culture of the society the military serves. The full effects of military culture on military performance are determined in this larger context. Second, it is not at all clear that these various cultural elements are mutually reinforcing or that they enhance military effectiveness. The cohesion of French mutineers is only an obvious case in point. Consider another. Close observance of ceremonies and etiquette handed down from the past may reinforce a corporate identity on which professional ethos rests. But the ceremonialism and etiquette that reinforced the professional ethos of mounted cavalry officers hindered their military effectiveness in World War I, as it hindered the Mamelukes who faced Napoleon more than 100 years before. Examples could be multiplied. Certainly future studies should examine how cultural elements are related and trace the effects of these relationships on military organization and performance. We may find some reasons for the persistence of dysfunctional military cultures, say, in the all-too-human habit to repeat in the future ways of acting that worked in the past or else in the practice of many modern militaries to rotate leaders from one job to another, thus limiting their ability to undertake long-term or fundamental reforms. But it is idle to expect a general theory of military culture that precisely prescribes cultural relationships that invariably enhance that performance.

II. SOURCES OF CULTURAL CONTINUITY AND CHANGE

Like all cultures, military culture varies in form and substance, and for many of the same reasons. Military culture is handed down across generations. Some, of course, are attached to the status quo, whether critically or not, and they try to reproduce in the future what they inherited from the past. The strength of this attachment no doubt is stronger for victorious than defeated militaries. Yet even with victorious militaries, passing on a military culture is difficult to do. Successful transmission is selective at best. Many factors push military culture to change. It changes from within when basic patterns of military action change, usually in response to new technologies, from stirrups and gunpowder to jet planes and nuclear bombs. It changes as military innovators such as Maurice of Nassau or Gerhard von Scharnhorst reflect on the experience of war and devise new practices or promote new beliefs that they hope will, if adopted, increase the likelihood of wartime success. And it changes in response to influences from the larger society, as memories of war shape beliefs about what the military can or ought to be like and as other social and political trends alter the context within which judgments are made about the quality of military life.

A. Technology and the Experience of War

That technology affects culture is an old and well-documented belief. In the case of military culture the rationale for it is often simple and direct. Technology, particularly weapons technology, profoundly affects the experience of war and the military culture that is in large part a response to that experience.

To illustrate the point, consider first the effects of industrialization on war and military culture, effects that have already been mentioned in passing. Industrial development of the means of communication (e.g., telegraph, radio, radar, computer, and satellite) and transportation (e.g., steamships and railroads, trucks and tanks, airplanes and rockets) radically reshaped the ability to move, supply, and control the power of armed forces at war. For the first time, militaries were deployable largely without regard to the seasons, which is to say without remission. Application of industrial technology to the weapons of war (from rifled projectiles and machine guns to nuclear weapons of mass destruction) radically increased the lethality of military firepower and the geographical theater of battle. The force of these developments were first shown in the American Civil War but were not fully felt until the world wars of the 20th century. The effects on military culture were profound. Horse-mounted cavalry and the bayonet charge, with their associated culture of brave warriors seeking glory in war, were abandoned as suicidal in the face of long-range and rapid-fire weapons. For similar reasons, traditional bright-colored battle attire, and the spectacle that went along with it, gave way to camouflage and the search for cover in trenches and foxholes. Not less important was the transformation of the ethos of the professional officer corps. Industrial war required military leaders who were more than heroic characters. Indeed, senior officers who planned campaigns might not see the battlefield at all. What counted was their ability to mobilize and command the new technologies of destruction and their ability to organize and manage the huge logistical demands of an industrial army at war. Most radical, industrialization increased the destructive power of weapons to such a degree that serious military thinkers now believe that the use of modern weapons, without restraint, would be self-defeating. The idea challenges the previously taken-for-granted belief that war is an inevitable (if lamentable) feature of social life.

Consider also organizational differences and the still intense rivalry among army, navy, and air forces. The bases for these differences can be explained in part by the self-interested competition for scarce resources; money spent building stealth bombers means less money for building aircraft carriers or tanks. Yet more is at work than competitive self-interest. Each service fights in a unique environment to gain effective control over the land, sea, or air. The unique features of these environments affect weapons technology, the way force is organized and controlled and, as a result, fundamental beliefs about the nature of war and the qualities of effective leaders. In *Command, Control, and the Common Defense*, Kenneth Allard has examined how these differences molded the doctrine and professional ethos of U.S. army and navy officers.

For the army, success in battle depends on the application of mass force at the decisive point of the battle line, which requires a division of authority organized and coordinated hierarchically. This belief rests on the army's need in land battles to maintain flexible control over the movements of large numbers of soldiers through subordinate commands. Successfully acting on this belief depends on communication technologies (whether messengers, flags, drum rolls, bugle calls or, now, computers and radio) that enable the commander to instruct subordinates on how to deploy. For the navy, in contrast, success in battle depends on the exercise of the undivided and unchallenged authority of the ship's captain. Historically, this belief rested on the small number of ships most navies could afford, which were typically deployed alone or in small squadrons. And it rested, before the age of radio, on the technical impossibility of exercising central control over a squadron once battles began. Commanders could not readily extend their influence beyond their own ship.

Not surprisingly, navies developed a unique service culture that cherishes decentralized organization and distrusts concentrated authority, while the army culture cherishes centralized organization and distrusts authority that operates outside a chain of accountability and policy control. The navy cultivates a professional ethos that rewards a field commander's willingness to act independently. The army cultivates a professional ethos that rewards a field commander's willingness to act interdependently.

We would nevertheless be mistaken to believe that the technology of war determines military culture. In fact, the relationship is a complex one of mutual influence. The prevailing military culture affects whether or how new military technologies are received or rejected. Samurai warriors in 16th-century Japan, for instance, were quick to adopt and soon to manufacture firearms once they were introduced on the island. But the social leveling effects of firearms in battle seriously threatened the military and political dominance of the warrior knights (and indeed of the existing social order). Early in the 17th century the ruling Tokugawa lord moved effectively to ban firearms from Japanese warfare. He established an effective monopoly over the manufacture, purchase, and use of firearms and, over the course of the 17th century, restrictions on the use of firearms multiplied and their manufacture decreased virtually to nothing (despite Japan's relatively advanced technological capacities). In this case, the military potential of the new technology was recognized, but after a trial its adoption was rejected in order to preserve the samurai's rule and to support what samurais thought was a superior military culture. Their rejection of firearms succeeded for 200 years.

In other cases, the military potential of an invention may lay unrecognized for long periods of time. Though invented centuries earlier in China, the military value of the stirrup was not realized until the 8th century, when the stirrup arrived in Frankish realms and was adopted by Charles Martel and his sons to permit a new and devastating mounted shock combat. The effect (as we know thanks to Lynn White, historian of this event) was to establish feudalism as a new type of warfare, dominated by knights, and with it a new social and cultural order in Europe, elements of which persist to this day.

Most often, a new technology will be received, but how it is deployed or developed reflects the military culture of the particular armed force. Many differences in the design of "rugged" Russian versus "sophisticated" American fighter jets, for example, owe more to differences in their respective beliefs about the nature of air combat than to differences in their technological capacities.

B. Military Education and Training

Before the 19th century, formal military education was rare, and state-sponsored institutions to promote the education of the officer corps were rarer still. Military education, such as it was, consisted largely of military drill and hands-on weapons training. In some cases, officers were sent to observe when others fought in war. Technical schools were founded in the 17th century to promote the application of science to artillery; but this was an exception, not a model. Only in the 19th century were schools established for advanced officer education and, even then, it was 100 years before the practice of relying on noble but (relatively) untrained officers died out completely.

Three reasons can be suggested to explain why schools for advanced officer education were established at this time. First, Enlightenment thought emphasized the capacity of reason and the applicability of scientific thought in particular to explain and regulate all human affairs. The general influence of Enlightenment ideas made it possible to think that war was more than a practical art; that it was also a subject governed by scientific laws that might be discovered through a positivist, empirical study. The greatest product of this belief is Karl von Clausewitz's still influential work *On War*. A second reason was the shock of defeat in war. Military defeat had the effect of discrediting the competence of the officer corps and encouraging a search for new methods to organize and fight war. It is not surprising therefore that the first important school for advanced military education was the Prussian *Allgemeine Kriegsschule* founded in 1810 under the leadership of Gerhard von Scharnhorst in reaction to Napoleon's defeat of Prussia at Jena in 1806. This school set a standard for excellence in training an elite corps of officers in the operational art of war, training that was thought so effective that the Treaty of Versailles formally abolished it, along with the German General Staff, following

World War I. (In fact, of course, the school was continued in disguise and openly resurrected under Hitler.) The French and British also established schools for advanced instruction in the wake of defeats. The first French school was established in 1818 after Napoleon's downfall, but it was notably ineffective. In 1876, after the Franco-Prussian War, a more effective institution replaced it, more effective in large part because it more closely copied the German example. Emphasis on schooling was weakest in Britain. Yet even there, in 1856, owing to dissatisfaction with the conduct of the Crimean War, the Camberley Staff College gained an independent existence from the Royal Military College (founded in 1799). It did not become an important institution for advanced officer education, however, until the Haldane reforms of 1906 were instituted in response to the Boer War. Finally, schools were needed to train officers in the military uses of the new industrial powers. Officers serving on the general staff had to plan for the movement, arming, protection, and supply of large militaries in the field. This meant having to master the military uses of new industrial means for transportation and communication and to harness new industrial production techniques as they applied to the manufacture and invention of new weapons of war, from machine guns to battleships.

These schools had both conservative and innovative effects on military culture. They were innovative most notably in defining service in the officer corps as a profession through which one advanced by education. They helped (albeit slowly) to dissolve the inherited feudal belief that only aristocrats were suited to lead men into battle. They were innovative also insofar as the practice of industrial war forced them to reexamine inherited beliefs about the tactics and scale of war. They were conservative in a narrow sense because they encouraged systematic study of military theory and history. They became literal bearers of military tradition, explicitly preserving, codifying, and passing down knowledge about previous beliefs and practices that influenced the conduct of war. More broadly, to the extent of their own prestige, which varied by nation, they also elevated the status of the military profession, indirectly promoting respect for military values in the larger society.

C. Collective Memory

A diffuse, but still important, influence on military culture is the collective memory or imagination of past war that is widely shared among members of the military and is frequently relied on as a normative guide for behavior in the present. In our century, memories of World War I and the Vietnam War for the American military have been especially powerful in shaping the professional ethos of the officer corps.

For both France and Britain, the experience of World War I quickly crystallized into a narrative about the stupid slaughter of high-minded but innocent men misled by general officers who seemed incapable of adjusting their tactics to the realities of trench warfare or to minimize the cost in lives of the men they sent into battle. Perhaps lower ranking soldiers and civilians were more prepared to accept this narrative than the officers who conducted the war and who might prefer a more qualified and generous account of their endeavor. But, collective memories are not histories, characterized by concern for detail and accuracy; they are symbolic constructions condensing events to communicate their essential meaning simply and powerfully. Ironically, one cause of this (for the officers) unflattering memory and the tragic circumstances on which it was based was the stubborn persistence of an earlier collective memory that extolled the efficacy of the bayonet and infantry charge. That memory was accurate enough before war's weapons were industrialized. It held only woe for those who relied on it to guide their conduct in 1914. Certainly after 1918, if not sooner, French and British officers gave up this earlier vision and were guided instead by the cautionary tale of World War I. They were more careful with the lives of their men in World War II.

For the American military, the experience of loss in Vietnam was equally profound. Unlike World War I, there was no one narrative widely shared (if differently valued) to summarize the American experience in Vietnam. Yet for the officers who fought there and remained in the military, the experience nevertheless forged a common memory of "lessons learned" that have not been forgotten. Four lessons, in particular, have become articulated as a political doctrine on the use of force: (1) do not go to war without public support; (2) clearly specify the military objective to be achieved; (3) send overwhelming force to ensure (so far as possible) the mission's success; and (4) do not micromanage commanders in the field. These may seem rudimentary lessons, part of the taken-for-granted discipline with respect to the use of force. But, in memory at least, all four lessons were followed with success in World War II and violated in Vietnam to the detriment of military cohesion, discipline, and effectiveness. On reflection, it is clear that these lessons are directed as much to civilian political leaders and as they are to military leaders. They shape the military professionals self-understanding of how to act responsibly. But they also shape the culture of civil–military relations in a democratic regime. Up to now, there has been no serious disagreement between presidents and the military elite over whether these lessons should be applied. The potential for conflict, however, raises questions about how to manage civil–military relations when there is a clash between military and political cultures.

D. Political and Social Trends

Military culture is not and cannot be hermetically sealed from the rest of society. As our discussion of industrialization has already shown, societal trends may exert tremendous influence on the content of military culture. (How military culture affects the culture of the larger society is discussed in the concluding section.) Here, two other trends merit attention. One trend is toward reduced confidence in the power of central governments, manifest in demands to end government regulation of (and intervention in) economic markets, to lower individual and corporate taxes, and to abandon conscription of soldiers in favor of professional all-volunteer forces. The other, more recent, trend is toward expanding the circle of citizenship, to devalue exclusionary practices based on race, religion, or gender, and to institutionalize practices of equal opportunity throughout the public sphere.

Confidence in the power of central governments has fallen steadily over the last generation and led to contraction of state power to gain or control social resources by coercive means. For our purposes, the most relevant symptom of this decline has been the end of conscription for military service. This end came first in the English-speaking nations, all of which abandoned conscription by 1973. With the end of the Cold War, other Western European states are moving quickly in this direction. At the moment there are comparatively few national (and fewer comprehensive comparative) studies that examine the causes and consequences of this event. Based on British and American experience, however, we can say that transition from a conscript to a volunteer force has had enormous effects on military culture. Some are quite predictable. For instance, because they rely on volunteers, the militaries of both countries have been freer than they were to separate from the ranks soldiers who for whatever reason are unable to conform to the rigors of military life. This practice encourages stricter discipline. Perhaps more important, freedom to select who should join and stay in the military narrows the range and diversity of values represented in the force. Self-selection and anticipatory socialization reinforce the narrowing.

At the same time, ironically, some new value conflicts have developed, particularly with respect to the priority of military over family life. Unlike the conscript forces, in which relatively few enlisted persons were married, volunteer forces have seen a steady rise in the number of military personnel who are married with children. The result tests traditional military solidarity manifest through esprit de corps and cohesion. The bonds of loyalty on which esprit de corps and cohesion depend are bonds among a community of warriors. They entail a commitment to self-sacrifice that places the well-being of the outfit above all else, including the responsibilities of family life. In practice, these bonds can be sustained only if the military provides practical social and material support for its members' families, to limit worries about family well-being while on the job. (Someone had to care for the children of single-parent soldiers sent to the Gulf War.) Nonetheless, when the military uses scarce resources to support military families in hopes of maintaining esprit and cohesion, it often provides a perverse incentive encouraging young military personnel to marry. The average age at first marriage of British army enlisted personnel is far below that of the society at large. (The same is true in the United States. A century ago, it would have been much higher, as lower ranking enlisted personnel were prohibited from marrying.) This only increases demand for the resources, compounding the problem, all the more so because younger married couples are less mature and less wealthy and so are more likely to require assistance.

The second trend—expanding the circle of citizenship, encouraging inclusionary policies that are blind to distinctions based on race, religion, and gender—has had enormous consequences for military culture as well. Excluding citizens because of race or religion from the enlisted or officer ranks and reserving the most prestigious positions for members of the dominant group are both practices that have declined over the course of the century. In the United States, in particular, the military over the last 50 years has become a model institution for racial integration. This is not to say prejudice and discrimination are absent. But in the face of social and legal pressures to include minority groups, and worried about the effects on cohesion, the military over time developed a relatively strict policy of intolerance toward discrimination and made advancement through a military career depend on effective leadership in sustaining good intergroup relations.

It has proved more challenging to integrate women into military service. The problems here are subtle and defy brief description. Traditionally, military culture has been thoroughly masculine; military service was often said "to make a man" of those who served. Emphasis on male military culture was reinforced in the larger society. Women were defined in terms quite opposite those of a warrior, by their capacity for nurturance and by their need for male protection. Of course, the truth was more complex. (Against aggressive acting out of male strength as a warrior one must juxtapose the—usually sublimated—homoerotic elements of love for one's comrades.) In this context, integration of women into the armed forces has been incomplete. In Britain and in the United States the number of women serving in the military increased with the need for recruits in all-volunteer forces. Once serving, women were entitled to legal protections against sexual harassment or sex discrimination. Yet women have been barred from holding most combat jobs; they were assigned instead to branches in combat support and combat service support. Military culture, however, is still rooted in the culture of combat. Failure to have combat experience or to hold combat positions limits one's ability to rise in the profession. Dealing with this is made more difficult owing to legal and social pressures that value equal opportunity. Increasing promotion opportunities for women with limited exposure to combat or training for combat erodes the central value on which military culture depends. Failure to do so reproduces gender inequality. Increasing women's exposure to combat assignments is a possibility, of course; and some have proposed using gender blind tests of physical abilities and assigning jobs without regard to gender. Yet, despite broad support to include women in the military service and to ensure that they receive fair and decent treatment, there is only limited support to require women to kill or be killed in combat on the same basis as men. In any case, it is unknown how complete gender equality (or a gender-blind policy) would affect cohesion and esprit de corps, especially in time of war.

III. RELATION OF MILITARY CULTURE TO THE LARGER SOCIETY

Military culture spreads by various means beyond the boundaries of military organization. With what effects is a matter of some controversy. In the 18th and 19th centuries, from the writings of Immanuel Kant to those of Herbert Spencer, hope was expressed that the influence of military culture and the culture of war was waning; that the cultures of democracy, sweet commerce, and industry (not to mention reason) were leading modern society to the possibility (in Kant's words)

of "perpetual peace." It was a hope that made military affairs and culture seem retrograde. Complete confidence in this thesis was shaken, as the need for it was intensified, by the 20th century's experience of world war. There is no wonder why. Yet, the earlier hope, if not yet realized, was not baseless. The political organization of Western nation-states emerging from the Middle Ages did rest on a historical differentiation of civilian political and military elites and the subordination of military to political power. If wars in the 20th century have been all too many and too intense, it is still true that Western states have spent fewer years at war than in previous centuries. There is also much evidence, carefully combed in recent years, to support the hypothesis that modern democratic states have been less likely to use force against one another, however likely they have been to war against others. It is in the context of these larger trends that we consider who carries military culture into civilian society and what reception awaits it there.

A. Bearers of Military Culture in Civilian Society

Relatively few people in contemporary society actually serve in the military and fewer still see combat. Yet representations of military culture and the experience of war are not foreign to everyday life. They are conveyed by a variety of means, ranging from the use of camouflage patterns in high-fashion clothing to public ceremonies remembering past sacrifices in war and current news reports carrying home images of the effects of armed conflict (say) in Bosnia or Northern Ireland, in the Middle East or Rwanda. The wide range of means by which military culture is carried into society makes an adequate discussion of the topic more difficult. What is possible here is to identity the key groups that are bearers of military culture in civilian society and to indicate what forms their representations of military culture may take.

The principle creators and bearers of military culture are those that belong to and lead the military. Military life is not entirely isolated from civilian life. Service members directly carry military culture with them into the civilian society. They make an impression on civilian society when they are on parade, wear their uniform to travel home on leave or on recruiting trips to schools, or when they give public lectures or testify before congressional or parliamentary committees. Here are direct embodiments of the military ceremony and etiquette and intimations of the kind of discipline and ethos that military service entails. The strength of this influence depends in part on the size of the military or on the military's presence within the civilian population. It is naturally greater in towns and in state capitals where the military are garrisoned.

More pervasive perhaps are representations of military culture carried in newspapers and magazines, in novels and movies, and on television. These are the creation of journalists and artists, who are sometimes remarkably schooled in military affairs. Their creations are not always independently done. They often depend for information and support and, under some circumstances, even the approval of the military to produce their work. (That is especially true for the production of motion pictures that may require military cooperation for props and staging.) Through them, the military exerts an indirect yet substantial influence on how military culture and war are represented to civilian society. But the point should not be exaggerated. Like all organizations, the military is concerned to manipulate its public image. During wartime, given the need to maintain public support for the war effort, presenting a positive view of military culture will seem essential to the government and its supporters. To accomplish this, censorship can be exercised. But symbols often carry more meaning than censors can control. A World War II poster urging Germans to hold Frankfurt nevertheless shows Frankfurt in rubble and in flames and suggests that Frankfurt's defense depends on the efforts of women, old men, and children. And sometimes symbols censors approve carry little or no persuasive power as (one may guess) was true of an early World War II exhortation from the British government that "Your Courage, Your Cheerfulness, Your Resolution will Bring Us Victory." In any case, in war or peace, the productions of artists are hard to rein in, whether the works are paintings by Goya and Dix, sculptures by Luytens and Kollwitz, movies by Gance and Kubrick, poems by Owen and Jarrell, or novels by Graves and Vonnegut. Perhaps to a lesser degree, the same is true of journalists reports, television documentaries, and scholarly writing.

Not to be overlooked as culture bearers are veterans. Recruiters for today's volunteer forces are well aware that veterans among family and friends greatly influence the attitudes of young people toward enlisting in the service. Once discharged, some veterans have been sufficiently affected by the experience of military service to join veterans' associations. These associations typically provide opportunities for socializing in clubs with people who have shared experiences similar to one's own. But they are also engaged in local community service or vaguely patriotic civic education projects. And they are integrated into larger national networks that keep them appraised of military affairs and lobby for veterans' benefits. On occasion, veterans' associations can form an important national social movement as they did, for instance, in France after World War I, to win pensions, to seek relief for disabled men, and to promote a conservative yet still democratic politics that would steer clear of war. Nor was theirs the only activist movement. In 1932, in the US, 25,000 unemployed veterans—some with their families—marched on and encamped for months in Washington demanding that Congress relieve their economic misery by paying immediately a $500 bonus the government had promised in 1924, but not intended to pay until 1945. In the end, they were forcibly decamped by federal soldiers under the command of Douglas MacArthur. Veterans' representation of military culture is as various as the culture itself and is sometimes so various that veterans are divided against themselves. That was so in the United States during the 1970s when veterans disagreed about whether to support the Vietnam War and veterans from previous wars were reluctant to recognize the claims of Vietnam veterans who were described us suffering from exposure to Agent Orange or from PostTraumatic Stress Disorder. To be effective at all, the claims of veterans in these organizations must clearly convey to their civilian audience something of the experience, the worth, and the culture of military life.

B. Civilian Reception of Military Culture

Civilian response to military culture depends on the context within which it is represented and the form it assumes. On ceremonial occasions or days that celebrate important events in the nation's history, it is not unusual to see a military presence. Few are offended by it and many take pride or pleasure (say) at watching the Horse Guards on parade to and from Buckingham Palace. Yet generalizations are always hazardous. Britain is not a society haunted by memories of recent defeat in war nor a society accused of harboring a militarist past. In contrast, in Germany in the 1960s, the military had to beware of conducting simple evening exercises (or tattoos) for fear of stirring protests and controversy. And while Muscovites might have taken pride in the Soviet Union's May Day military parades, civilians elsewhere seeing highlights of the event may have had a more fearful response. Another key difference between these events is that the German and the Soviet displays, however different in scale, are displays of ready forces. The Horse Guards parade in a ceremonial dress that no military deployed for war would wear today; the fangs of yesterday are no threat today.

In our century of total war, when weapons of war have been used against civilians as well as soldiers, reactions to military culture have been understandably extreme, both pacifist and militarist, either wholly rejecting or wholly accepting (even celebrating) military beliefs, values, and symbols. These extreme reactions were strikingly evident after World War I. In the 1920s, an international peace movement flourished whose numbers far exceeded those who belonged to traditional pacifist religious groups. Its members believed that the horrid experience of trench warfare had proved beyond doubt that modern war on such a scale could not be waged again. In Britain, France, and the United States, they launched a campaign to outlaw war. They wrote antiwar plays and songs for school children to perform and lobbied heads of state on the need to outlaw war. In 1928, they achieved what seemed a victory when these three powers, joined by Japan and others, signed the Kellogg-Briand Pact renouncing war as an instrument of national policy. Unfortunately, the pact had less capacity than the League of Nations to bring about this happy result. And the movement that led to its signing was animated in part by the knowledge that other forces loose in the world pushed in the opposite direction. Germans showed another way of responding to the experience of war. Offended by the harsh peace and persuaded (wrongly) that the military had been "stabbed in the back" by its civilian leaders, many believed that Germany's future would be determined by its military strength. This belief was supported by government policy that sought to avoid complying with the Versailles Treaty and it supported in turn large paramilitary movements in the 1920s, with parades and marches and field exercises held in remote forests. These movements had roots in the old Prussian militarism but were not simply reactionary. Trench warfare imposed a regimented and egalitarian experience, literally a primitive nationalist socialism, that some Germans wished to use as a model for building a new Germany. Reactionary or not, it was an embodiment of militarism, celebrating military values above all other social goods. And it found partners in Italy and Japan where similar social currents had strength. Where that partnership led is too well known.

Since World War II, civilian reaction to military culture has been less extreme, but remains divided. One may point to the hysteria for building bomb shelters, to fantasies of redemption by Star-Wars weapons systems, and to the episodic protests against nuclear weapons, the draft, and the Vietnam War. The advanced industrial societies of the West confront a "moral defense dilemma." The difficulty is to manage social movements that would either so enhance military organization for the sake of national security as to undermine liberal democracy or so enhance liberal democracy as to neglect the requirements of military organization and undermine national security. The difficulty of managing this dilemma was obvious during the Cold War when major powers adopted the logic of deterrence, the validity of which relied on the grim promise of mutually assured destruction. The difficulties have not disappeared with the end of the Cold War. They may have been added to. Armed forces must still prepare for—in hope of deterring—general war. They must also engage in peacekeeping, intervening in conflicts where possible to contain them, using armed force to hold the lid on war until diplomatic solutions can be worked out. How to ensure that military culture promotes a democratic peace remains our dilemma to resolve.

Also See the Following Articles

COMBAT • CONFORMITY AND OBEDIENCE • MASS CONFLICT AND THE PARTICIPANTS, ATTITUDES TOWARD • MILITARISM • PROFESSIONAL VERSUS CITIZEN SOLDIERY • WARFARE, STRATEGIES AND TACTICS OF • WARFARE, TRENDS IN • WARRIORS, ANTHROPOLOGY OF •WEAPONRY, EVOLUTION OF

Bibliography

Allard, K. (1990). *Command, control, and the common defense.* New Haven: Yale University Press.

Beevor, A. (1991). *Inside the British army.* London: Corgi Books.

Berghahn, V. R. (1982). *Militarism.* New York: St. Martin's Press.

Burk, J. (1996, Spring). Recent trends in civil-military relations. *Tocqueville Review,* 17, 83–106.

Dunivin, K. (1994, Summer). Military culture: Change and continuity. *Armed Forces & Society,* 20, 531–547.

Farwell, B. (1987). *Mr. Kipling's army.* New York: Norton.

Howard, M. (1991). *Lessons of history.* New Haven: Yale University Press.

Hynes, S. (1990). *A war imagined.* New York: Atheneum.

Johnston, A. I. (1995). *Cultural realism.* Princeton: Princeton University Press.

Janowitz, M. (1960). *The professional soldier.* New York: Free Press.

Keegan, J. (1993). *A history of warfare.* New York: Knopf.

Manning, Frederick J. (1991). Morale, cohesion, and esprit de corps. In R. Gal, & A. D. Mangelsdorf (Eds.), pp. 451–470. *Handbook of military psychology.* New York: John Wiley & Sons.

McNeill, W. H. (1995). *Keeping together in time.* Cambridge, MA: Harvard University Press.

Milner, M., Jr. (1993). *Status and sacredness.* New York: Oxford University Press.

Moskos, C. C., & Butler, J. S. (1996). *All that we can be.* New York: Basic Books.

Paret, P., Lewis, B. I., & Paret. P. (Eds.). (1992). *Persuasive images:*

Posters of war and revolution. Princeton: Princeton University Press.

Prost, A. (1992). *In the wake of war*. Providence, RI: Berg.

Nath, R. (1990). *Military leadership in India*. New Delhi: Lancers Books.

Segal, D. (1996, Spring). The social construction of peacekeeping by US soldiers. *Tocqueville Review, 17,* 7–21.

Shils, E., & Janowitz, M. (1948, Summer). The cohesion and disintegration of the wehrmacht. *Public Opinion Quarterly, 12,* 280–315.

van Creveld, M. (1990). *The training of officers*. New York: Free Press.

White, L. (1962). *Medieval technology and social change*. Oxford: Oxford University Press.

Winter, J. (1996). *Sites of memory, sites of mourning*. Cambridge: Cambridge University Press.

Military Deterrence
and Statecraft

Paul K. Huth

University of Michigan

GLOSSARY

Credible Threat The belief of a potential attacker that a defender state possesses the military capabilities and will to inflict heavy military losses on it in the event of a military confrontation.
Deterrence A policy that seeks to prevent the leaders of a country from resorting to the use of military force by threatening military retaliation.
Deterrence Success The decision by state leaders to refrain from initiating international crises and wars due to the threat of military retaliation by a defender state.
Extended Deterrence A policy that seeks to prevent military threats and attacks against another country.
Rational Choice An approach to making decisions in which political leaders compare the expected utility of alternative policy options and select the option that they believe will produce the most favorable outcome.

A POLICY OF DETERRENCE seeks to prevent armed conflict between states by threatening military retalia-

tion against the leaders of a country considering an attack. In this article I address the question of when do military threats succeed in deterring armed conflict. I first discuss deterrence theory and then I summarize findings from a number of empirical studies of deterrence.

I. CONCEPT OF DETERRENCE

A. Definition of Deterrence

In general terms the concept of deterrence can be defined as the use of threats to persuade an individual to not initiate some course of action. A threat will act as a deterrent if it convinces the individual that they will suffer harm if they proceed with their intended actions. In international politics a policy of deterrence is commonly understood to refer to the use of military threats of retaliation to prevent the leaders of a country from initiating military actions. A comprehensive analysis of deterrence in international politics would include both military and nonmilitary threats that are intended to prevent both military and nonmilitary actions. In this article, however, I restrict my analysis of deterrence to the use of *military threats* by states to prevent national leaders from resorting to the use or threat of *military force* in support of foreign policy goals.

While a policy of deterrence relies on the use of military threats as a means to prevent armed conflict between states, there are alternative policy options available to state leaders that do not include the use of

Copyright © 1999 by Academic Press.
All rights of reproduction in any form reserved.

military threats. It is important to recognize, then, that deterrence is but one type of policy to be pursued by foreign policy leaders who seek to prevent the outbreak of crises and wars in the international system. Alternatives to deterrence include a range of diplomatic policies such as third-party mediation efforts, legal adjudication by international bodies such as the International Court of Justice, and peacekeeping operations by the United Nations. Throughout history states involved in international disputes have employed a variety of such policies in an attempt to prevent armed conflict.

My objective in this article is to evaluate when policies of deterrence have been successful in preventing armed conflict. State leaders have turned to deterrent threats often in an attempt to ensure their country's security and therefore it is important to know when such efforts are likely to succeed or fail. While my analysis of deterrence requires a focus on military threats, I do address the question of whether the effectiveness of such threats is enhanced when they are coupled with diplomatic initiatives such as the offering of limited rewards and positive inducements.

B. Different Cases of Deterrence

A policy of deterrence can be directed at preventing an armed attack against a country's own territory (direct deterrence), or that of another country (extended deterrence). In addition, deterrent threats may be issued in response to a pressing or short-term threat of attack (immediate deterrence), or a deterrent policy may seek to prevent a crisis or militarized conflict from arising (general deterrence). If we combine these two dimensions of deterrence policies, as in Fig. 1, we have four situations in which deterrence can be pursued by states: (a) direct-immediate deterrence; (b) direct-general deterrence; (c) extended-immediate deterrence; and (d) extended-general deterrence. In each of these four situations of deterrence, state leaders may threaten the use of conventional military forces or nuclear weapons. While it is common to equate deterrence with the threat of nuclear weapons, the fact is that conventional military forces are the primary means of deterrence for most states. Only for a small number of countries since 1945 have nuclear weapons played a deterrent role in military doctrine and foreign policy.

A few examples will illustrate each type of deterrence situation. Since the end of the Korean War the United States has maintained an alliance with and military presence in South Korea as part of a policy of extended-general deterrence against North Korea (cell 4, Fig. 1). The United States has practiced extended-immediate deterrence in the Persian Gulf in the aftermath of the Gulf War when Iraqi troops have been concentrated and moved into positions close to the Kuwaiti border (cell 3, Fig. 1). In response to such threatening Iraqi military actions, the United States moved naval forces into positions off the coastline of Iraq and placed its air and ground forces in Saudi Arabia on heightened alert. Following the Six Day War of 1967 the Israeli

Threat Posed by Attacker

		Actual	Potential
Target of Attack	*Defender*	2 Direct-Immediate Deterrence (Outbreak of Arab-Israeli War in 1973)	1 Direct-General Deterrence (Israeli-Syrian border dispute in Golan Heights since 1967)
	Ally of Defender	3 Extended-Immediate Deterrence (U.S.-Iraqi crises over Kuwait since 1991)	4 Extended-General Deterrence (U.S. forces stationed in South Korea since 1953)

FIGURE 1   A Typology of Cases of Deterrence

military presence in the Golan Heights and its declaratory policy of intent to defend its control of the Golan Heights has acted as a direct-general deterrent against Syria (cell 1, Fig. 1). Finally, in October 1973 Israel's policy of direct-immediate deterrence failed when Egypt and Syria launched attacks despite Israeli threats and the prior mobilization of its military forces for war (cell 2, Fig. 1).

Deterrent policies have often been attempted in the context of territorial disputes between countries. This reflects the fact that, historically, territorial disputes have been a primary cause of crises and wars between states. Deterrence then is often directed against state leaders who have specific territorial goals that they seek to attain by either the seizure of disputed territory in a limited military attack, or by the occupation of disputed territory following the decisive defeat of an adversary's armed forces. In either case, the strategic orientation of potential attackers is generally short-term and driven by concerns about military costs. Thus, they prefer to utilize military force quickly to achieve military-territorial goals without suffering heavy attrition of manpower and weapons.

C. Deterrence Success and Failure

A successful policy of deterrence has both a political and a military dimension. In military terms, general deterrence success refers to preventing state leaders from issuing military threats and actions that escalate a situation of peacetime diplomatic and military competition into a crisis or militarized confrontation that threatens war. Immediate deterrence success is defined then as preventing state leaders already within a crisis or militarized confrontation from resorting to the large-scale use of military force. To establish that a policy of deterrence has prevented crises and wars requires a careful analysis of available evidence regarding the military actions and policy goals of attacker states. Given that national leaders seldom acknowledge that they have been deterred by an opponent, scholars studying deterrence must often look for indirect evidence of deterrence operating. Not surprisingly, scholars have disagreed about what evidence should be collected to assess the utility of deterrent policies and what conclusions can be drawn from the historical record about the impact of deterrent threats.

The prevention of crises or wars, however, is not the only goal of deterrence. Just as importantly, defenders must be able to avoid crises and wars without capitulating to the political and military demands of a potential attacker. Put differently, armed conflict cannot be avoided at the price of diplomatic concessions to the primary demands of the potential attacker under the threat of war. Deterrence failure includes then the initiation of crises or militarized disputes (general deterrence failure), their escalation to war (immediate deterrence failure), or the avoidance of crises and war by defender states that make far-reaching concessions to the potential attacker (both general and immediate deterrence failures).

It is important to recognize that deterrence success should not necessarily be equated with successful conflict resolution. The avoidance of crises and wars between states due to deterrence may not be accompanied by a settlement of the underlying issues in dispute between adversaries. Whether, in the absence of armed conflict, two disputing parties can settle their differences is largely a question of diplomatic bargaining and the ability of state leaders to devise agreements they can accept and believe will be upheld by their adversary. Deterrent policies may contribute to conflict resolution indirectly by persuading states that there is not a viable military solution to a dispute, but it is also possible that deterrent threats may complicate diplomatic efforts by making it more difficult to make concessions to an opponent. I will not attempt to answer here the larger question of whether successful deterrence promotes conflict resolution. I restrict my focus to the issue of under what conditions do deterrent policies prevent crises and war between states.

II. THEORIES OF DETERRENCE

A. Rational Choice Approach

Scholars who have developed theories of deterrence have relied generally on a rational choice approach to analyzing foreign policy decision making. Examples would include the early efforts of Thomas Schelling and Glenn Snyder as well as more recent work by Robert Powell and James Fearon. In a rational choice approach foreign policy leaders who are considering the use of military force compare the expected utilities of using force versus refraining from a military challenge to the status quo, and they select the option with greater expected utility. Expected utility is composed of two elements: (1) the value attached to an outcome and (2) the likelihood of attaining that outcome. In the context of deterrence, a potential attacker considers the possible gains to be secured by the use of military force as well as how likely it is that force can be used successfully. This estimate of the expected utility for conflict is then compared to the anticipated gains (or losses) associated with not using force and an estimate of how probable those gains/losses would be.

The basic logic of deterrence theory focuses on how military threats can be used to reduce the attacker's expected utility for using force by persuading the attacker that the outcome of a military confrontation will be costly and unsuccessful. In addition, some deterrence theorists have also given attention to how defender policies can increase the expected utility of not using force for attackers. Thus, scholars such as Thomas Schelling and Robert Powell have analyzed the issue of whether deterrent threats can lead to preemptive strikes by an attacker who fears that a defender's deterrent threats are actually a prelude to offensive attack. Scholars have also argued that positive inducements can be utilized to make the diplomatic and political status quo in the absence of a military confrontation more attractive to potential attackers. For example, Paul Huth has proposed that by offering contingent and limited political concessions defenders make it more likely that attackers will back away from threats of force. Richard Ned Lebow and Janice Gross Stein have argued that carefully designed unilateral concessions can help to reassure attackers that defenders do not seek to threaten their vital security interests.

In theoretical terms the most effective deterrent policy is one that simultaneously decreases the expected utility of using force while increasing the expected utility of not using force for a potential attacker. The problem for defenders is how to strike a balance between policies that credibly threaten war while also making continued peace acceptable to the attacker. The challenge for a defender is to include enough positive inducements to make the expected utility of not using force acceptable, while not sacrificing vital security interests or undermining the credibility of the threat to use force.

B. Critics of Rational Choice Deterrence Theory

The rational choice approach to deterrence theory has been criticized by scholars, however. These critiques can be categorized broadly into one of two types: (1) cognitive psychological biases in decision making by individual leaders, and (2) problems of command and control in the implementation of deterrent policies by military organizations. Leading critics who draw on insights from cognitive science include Robert Jervis, Richard Ned Lebow, and Janice Gross Stein. One prominent argument advanced is that misperceptions caused by emotional stress lead to biased estimates of the resolve and military capabilities of defender states. The result is that attackers can greatly underestimate the risks of challenging the status quo with military force. More recently, scholars drawing on a theory of risk taking from cognitive psychology termed prospect theory have argued that leaders are especially prone to taking risky courses of action when they believe it is necessary to act in order to avoid a deterioration in the status quo. The implication is that it will be difficult to deter state leaders who believe that the use of military force can redress existing and expected losses to the political and military status quo.

Critics who focus on problems of command and control, such as Scott Sagan, Bruce Blair, and Barry Posen, shift the analysis from patterns of individual decision making to the larger organizational setting in which deterrent policies are implemented by the military. These critics consider issues such as: (1) political and military leaders may lose tight central control over the movement and operation of military forces in the field; (2) the vulnerability of command and control systems to military attack could provide incentives to both attackers and defenders to strike quickly, fearing a first strike from the other; and (3) breakdowns and errors in early warning systems could lead to mistaken conclusions about the hostile intentions of an adversary and how imminent the threat of attack is. The implications for deterrence then is that crisis stability can be undermined, that political leaders will not be able to coordinate as desired military actions with diplomacy to settle conflicts short of armed conflict, and that military conflict will be initiated on the false belief that an attack is about to or has already been launched.

C. Credibility of Conventional Threats

Deterrence theorists have consistently argued that deterrence success is more likely if a defender's deterrent threat is credible to an attacker. A credible threat is defined as the defender possessing the military capabilities to inflict substantial costs on an attacker in an armed conflict as well as the attacker's belief that the defender is resolved to use its available military forces. Exactly what capabilities and actions by a defender create a credible threat is a matter of debate among scholars, however. In conflicts involving conventional military forces there is general agreement, as represented in the work of Alexander George and Richard Smoke, John Mearsheimer, and Paul Huth, that a defender needs to have flexible military forces that can respond quickly and in strength to a range of military contingencies and thus is able to deny the attacker its military objectives at the outset to early stages of an armed conflict.

There is a scholarly debate as to when attackers are likely to believe that a defender is resolved to use force. On the one hand, some scholars argue that concrete military actions such as the movement and positioning of forces in a crisis can communicate a commitment to respond with force, as would a past record of utilizing force to protect security interests when challenged. On the other hand, other scholars caution that commitment signals are not always credible because even weak and irresolute defenders have strategic incentives to bluff and act tough. Furthermore, some scholars argue that attackers will look beyond the short-term bargaining tactics of a defender in current or past conflicts and ask what are the interests at stake for the defender that would justify the risks of a military conflict.

D. Credibility of Nuclear Threats

When nuclear weapons are employed as a deterrent, scholars such as Thomas Schelling, Robert Jervis, Frank Zagare, and Robert Powell offer differing assessments of whether such threats can be credible. For example, in situations where both defender and attacker possess the ability to retaliate with nuclear weapons, there is debate whether a defender's threat to use nuclear weapons can be credible since any nuclear response will risk a very damaging counterattack. In situations where a nuclear defender confronts a nonnuclear attacker analysts have argued that normative and political constraints limit the credibility of a nuclear strike in all but the most extreme situation where the nuclear defender is confronted with a large-scale defeat on the conventional battlefield. The counterargument made by some scholars is that given the unprecedented destructive power of nuclear weapons, even the slightest chance of nuclear retaliation by a defender can act as a powerful deterrent.

Scholars also disagree if credibility depends on whether nuclear threats are directed at military or civilian targets. Some scholars propose that nuclear threats operate in much the same way as conventional threats and therefore the most credible threat is one in which the defender can employ nuclear weapons against military targets in order to achieve specific military objectives. Other scholars argue that the counterforce capabilities of nuclear weapons are not as important as the threat that nuclear weapons will destroy cities and kill large numbers of civilians in a retaliatory strike.

III. EMPIRICAL STUDIES OF DETERRENCE

There is no single and fully agreed upon set of hypotheses even among rational choice theorists about the conditions that lead to deterrence success. Furthermore, critics of rational deterrence theory argue that cognitive biases and organizational problems can make it difficult for the leaders of both attacker and defender states to act in ways consistent with the theory. Given this theoretical debate, it is especially important to take a close look at empirical studies of deterrence to see what conclusions can be drawn about when a policy of deterrence is likely to be effective.

A. Conventional Deterrence

1. The Balance of Military Forces

A number of empirical studies have presented consistent findings that the balance of military power is an important but not overriding determinant of deterrence success and failure. The findings from scholars such as John Mearsheimer, Jonathan Shimshoni, Eli Liberman, and Paul Huth indicate that when defenders have the military capabilities to repulse a large-scale attack from the very outset of a military conflict, the prospects of immediate deterrence success increase significantly. As noted earlier, attackers seek to utilize military force in relatively quick and decisive military operations. If defenders possess the military capabilities to counter an attack from the outset, then attackers are reluctant to initiate a military conflict that risks a quick defeat or could become a prolonged war of attrition.

The strategic perspective of attackers poses a difficult challenge then for defenders attempting extended-immediate deterrence. While major powers have historically been the states to practice immediate deterrence in most situations, their ability to project military forces beyond their own national borders quickly and in large numbers is a very demanding military task. In most cases, such states over a longer period of time can mobilize and transport substantial forces, but extended-immediate deterrence success places a premium on the rapid movement of forces into position to repulse an attack. Thus, major powers may fail in their attempts at extended-immediate deterrence even though they are able to bring to bear decisive force in a lengthy military conflict. Furthermore, the need for the timely projection of military power to bolster extended-immediate deterrence can be undercut by domestic political constraints that preclude extensive military preparations early on in a crisis when they can be most critical. The broader implication is that while scholars have identified many of the military conditions conducive to immediate deterrence success, it is important to recognize that defenders can be hampered by military and political constraints that prevent leaders from carrying out an effective deterrent policy.

When we examine general deterrence situations we find that the balance of military strength has weaker effects on deterrence outcomes. Defenders find it more difficult to deter low-level military probes and threats of force since attackers avoid committing large numbers of forces and can pull back if the defender responds quickly with a buildup of powerful forces. Alexander George and Richard Smoke, in their study of American deterrence policy, found that attackers often devised ways to test and probe the strength of U.S. deterrent forces by the calculated use of limited force. Similarly, studies of Israeli attempts to deter its Arab neighbors found that small-scale border raids and skirmishes were frequent and more difficult to deter than large-scale attacks. Finally, the research of Paul Huth has indicated that while the conventional balance of military forces had a consistent and appreciable impact on immediate deterrence outcomes, it had a much smaller effect on preventing challenges to general deterrence.

2. Crisis Bargaining

Studies of crisis bargaining behavior indicate that the military and diplomatic actions of defenders can have strong effects on whether immediate deterrence succeeds or fails. One intuitive finding that emerges from case studies is that clarity and consistency in communicating a deterrent threat can be very important in reducing misperceptions about the defender's resolve. By clearly communicating a threat the defender can help to establish what are the important issues at stake for it in the conflict and that there exists firm domestic and international political support behind a deterrent policy. In addition to the clarity of threats, other studies have found that particular patterns of threat and response in bargaining are related to deterrence success. Russell Leng, Paul Huth, and Chris Gelpi have found that measured policies of reciprocating the military actions of attackers is the best way to deter the escalation of crises to wars. In contrast, alternative policies of being very cautious or aggressive in the level of military response were more likely to lead to crisis escalation and deterrence failure. It is important to recognize that such tit-for-tat policies of military response did not often produce spirals of escalation culminating in pre-

emptive strikes. For example, over the past 2 centuries the outbreak of war has very rarely been triggered by preemptive attacks by states. The reasons as to why attempts at immediate deterrence rarely result in conflict spirals may be twofold: (1) Defenders worry that spiral dynamics may occur and thus avoid overly escalatory military policies, and (2) attackers weigh the political value of not being viewed as the aggressor who strikes first versus the military benefits of preemption and attackers do not consistently give greater weight to military over political advantages.

Another important finding relating to crisis bargaining and immediate deterrence is that diplomatic policies that include elements of accommodation and positive inducements can significantly increase the likelihood of deterrence success. In particular, diplomatic policies that combine a refusal to concede on vital security issues with flexibility and a willingness to compromise and negotiate on secondary issues increases the likelihood of deterrence success. These firm-but-flexible diplomatic strategies can help leaders from attacker states retreat from their threats by reducing the domestic or international political costs of backing away from a military confrontation. Leaders can claim that defender concessions on certain issues were a major gain, or that a defender's willingness to hold negotiations was a new and promising diplomatic development. In either case, foreign policy leaders can use the accommodative diplomatic actions of the defender to fend off domestic or foreign political adversaries who will claim that the government retreated under pressure.

Russell Leng also presents evidence that the combination of threats and limited positive inducements is more effective in preventing crisis escalation than is simply relying on deterrent threats. The deterrent value of this carrot-and-stick approach reflects the fact that such a policy seeks to alter both aspects of an attacker's expected utility calculation. The use of the stick can persuade the attacker that a military conflict will be costly and risky, while the carrot provides some favorable, even if limited, political changes that can convince leaders that in the absence of a military conflict there exists an acceptable status quo.

Once again, however, the ability or willingness of defenders to execute firm-but-flexible or carrot-and-stick approaches may be limited by domestic as well as international political conditions. For example, offering even limited concessions may be politically risky when the attacker is a long-term rival. Consider the case of the Cuban Missile Crisis in which the Kennedy administration was willing to offer in private to the Soviets a pledge to not invade Cuba and to remove missiles from Turkey, but warned that if the Soviet's made these concessions public, they would disavow them. The Arab-Israeli conflict is another example where political leaders on both sides of the dispute have found it very difficult to make concessions knowing that domestic political opponents of the regime would be sure to denounce the government. Indeed, fears of domestic political repercussions have historically been a critical factor limiting the willingness of defenders to pursue what scholars have identified as effective deterrent policies.

3. Reputations and Past Behavior

Do defender states develop reputations based on their past behavior in crises and deterrence situations? While it is intuitive to argue that the past behavior of a defender should shape an attacker's assessments of what defenders will do in current confrontations, the existing empirical literature provides, at best, only partial support for such a relationship. Conclusions about past behavior and reputations, however, should be treated as quite tentative given that there are only a limited number of empirical studies on the subject. The available evidence indicates, however, that attackers are most likely to impute reputations to a defender state if the two states have a history of direct bilateral confrontations and previous deterrence encounters. In contrast, attackers are less likely to draw strong reputational inferences from the past behavior of the defender in conflicts with other states.

For example, Paul Huth reports that extended-immediate deterrence is more likely to fail if defenders had either backed down or had forced the attacker to back down in previous confrontations between the same two states, but that the defender's behavior in disputes with other states had no clear impact on attacker decisions. Ted Hopf, in his study of Soviet reactions to U.S. foreign policy successes and defeats in the Third World, argues that U.S. behavior in the Third World had little impact on Soviet assessments of U.S. security commitments in Europe and Asia. Finally, Eli Liberman and Jonathan Shimshoni argue that the leaders of Arab countries did learn lessons about Israeli military capabilities and resolve from past military defeats on the battlefield with Israel. Liberman and Shimshoni, however, also note that these reputational inferences were not necessarily long-lived and that changing military technologies and new military planning could render past lessons less relevant. Janice Gross Stein, in her analysis of the Arab-Israeli conflict, is even more doubtful about the longev-

ity and impact of reputations on deterrence outcomes. A possible conclusion to be drawn then from these various studies is that when reputations do form they may have important effects on attacker calculations but only for a relatively short period of time. The importance of reputations may well fade then as the international strategic environment changes over time and as new leaders assume positions of power within defender and attacker states.

4. Military Alliance Ties

An important policy option available to state leaders who seek to bolster extended deterrence is the formation of military alliances and cooperative military ties with states that might be threatened with attack. The deterrent value of alliances, however, is not confirmed by the results of studies on extended-immediate deterrence. Paul Huth, for example, has found that alliances between a defender and ally are clearly not related to a higher likelihood of extended-immediate deterrence success, and if there is any pattern at all, it is that extended-immediate deterrence failures are more likely when alliances are present.

While this finding may seem surprising at first, there are two very good explanations for it. As James Fearon argues, it may be that attackers believe that defenders will honor their alliance commitments if their ally is attacked. Thus, if we observe a crisis in which an attacker threatens a state with alliance ties, the implication is that the attacker must be highly resolved to use force since it knows that the defender will most likely support its ally if attacked. Highly resolved attackers in turn should be more likely to challenge immediate deterrence and thus the presence of alliances would be correlated with the failure of extended-immediate deterrence. A different explanation would be that attackers believe that the credibility of alliance commitments varies substantially and therefore attackers only threaten states with alliance ties when they believe that the defender is not a reliable alliance partner. As a result, the attacker is more likely to risk a war by threatening the allied state based on the expectation that the defender is unlikely to come the military aid of its ally.

The fact that alliance ties fail to promote extended-immediate deterrence, however, does not necessarily imply that they are also ineffective as an extended-general deterrent. Indeed, the very logic of the two arguments just presented suggests that some military alliances should act as powerful deterrents and prevent attackers from challenging general deterrence. There are, however, no existing studies that directly and carefully test for the extended-general deterrent value of alliances. A suggestive answer would be that alliances that include the actual peacetime deployment of defender forces on the territory of the ally are likely to be much more powerful deterrents than alliances in which defender states must project their forces overseas in a crisis in order to offer direct military support to allies. Nevertheless, it may even be the case that alliances supported by overseas deployments of defender forces will not be highly effective as a general deterrent. The reason is that, as already argued above, low-level military probes and actions are quite difficult to deter and foreign troops are often deployed abroad for purposes of fighting a large-scale war and not to deter limited border clashes. In conclusion, given the limited empirical evidence available on alliances, it is not possible to make strong arguments about their utility as extended deterrents. What evidence does exist suggests that their deterrent value in situations of immediate deterrence is limited. However, alliances serve purposes other than just deterrence and numerous studies have found that allies play critical roles in enabling states to win wars that they become engulfed in after deterrence fails.

5. Misperceptions and Miscalculations

The final set of findings to consider centers on the limits to rational decision making and their adverse consequences for deterrence. While critics and proponents of deterrence theory do disagree about how frequently irrational processes of decision making account for failures of deterrence, there is more of a consensus regarding how the limits to rationality can impair the effectiveness of deterrence policies.

Scholars argue that a common feature of many deterrence situations is that policymakers are uncertain about the military capabilities and resolve of defender states. A variety of factors can account for these uncertainties with the result being that political and military leaders can find it difficult to know with high confidence the size and quality of opposing forces, the likely outcome of battlefield engagements, how domestic politics may effect the military policies of adversaries, or what are the interests of third parties in a dispute. In situations of extended deterrence, in particular, uncertainties are more likely to arise concerning the defender's power projection capabilities and its political will to use force. If these uncertainties lead attackers to underestimate the capabilities and resolve of defenders, then deterrence is more likely to fail since the credibility of the defender's deterrent threat will be weakened. In

retrospect, then, we may claim that the attacker's beliefs about the credibility of the defender were based on misperceptions that, in turn, caused the attacker to miscalculate the costs and risks of a military conflict. In this line of argument even rational attackers can mispercieve and miscalculate given the difficulties of accurately judging the capabilities and resolve of adversaries.

One example would be the decision by the President Truman and his advisors to cross the thirty-eighth parallel and invade North Korea in September 1950 despite warnings by China that it would intervene in support of North Korea. U.S. policymakers discounted both the resolve of China to intervene as well as the military strength of its ground forces. The result was that Truman and his advisors believed that the risks of a larger conflict with China were not that great while the prospects of a quick defeat of a weakened North Korean army seemed very favorable. More generally, from existing research it seems that two types of misperceptions can be identified that have contributed to the failure of deterrence: (a) Attackers can be overconfident of their ability to translate short-term military advantages into quick and favorable diplomatic and political settlements, or (b) that short-term military advantages will result in a very quick and decisive military victory. The problem seems to be that attackers either underestimate the likelihood of military intervention by defenders when their allies have suffered heavy initial military losses, or they underestimate the military and political capacity of large states to withstand initial military setbacks and continue fighting. The immediate origins of World War II can be traced back to these types of misperceptions by Japanese and German leaders.

Critics of rational deterrence such as Richard Ned Lebow and Janice Gross Stein argue, however, that problems of decision making and misperception can be even more fundamental. These scholars argue that even when the uncertainties of assessing capabilities and intentions are not that large, attackers may still mispercieve and miscalculate because motivated biases distort their analyses of risks and costs. They argue that deterrence failures often stem from the biased calculations of attackers who convince themselves that adversaries lack the military strength and resolve to resist a military and diplomatic challenge to the status quo because they want to believe that a diplomatic or military victory is possible. The need for a foreign policy victory, in turn, is linked to the attacker's concern about adverse domestic political developments, or a declining international strategic position for their country. Leaders within the attacker state believe then that a confrontational foreign policy can help resolve either these domestic or international problems. Thus, according to Lebow and Stein misperceptions are not caused solely by the limits and quality of available information about defenders, but also because leaders distort their reading of available information in order to support their preferred foreign policy goals.

Both supporters and critics of deterrence generally agree that an unfavorable assessment of the domestic or international status quo by leaders can undermine or severely test deterrence. The debate then centers not on whether a declining status quo position can lead to deterrence failure, but more specifically what is the causal process by which leader's concerns about the status quo lead to challenges to deterrence. In a rational choice approach a low expected utility for not using force due to a declining status quo position makes deterrence failure more likely since the alternative option of using force becomes relatively more attractive. Rational deterrence theorists have argued then that the risks of a crisis or war can be acceptable to decision makers when the alternative is the loss of political power, or the belief that their country's international security position will be clearly weakened. Conversely, psychological theories of motivated misperceptions or risk-taking in prospect theory question this type of expected utility explanation and provide different interpretations of leader decisions.

The scholarly debate about the role of misperceptions and risk taking in failures of deterrence then is not easily resolved. Difficult questions must be answered about how much information was available to leaders at the time decisions were made, what were reasonable inferences to draw from the information, how did decision makers define the status quo position of their country domestically and internationally, and how risky was it for decision makers to have initiated a crisis or large-scale attack. Clear-cut answers may not be possible to such questions in all historical cases, but the debate over evidence and interpretation should not obscure the larger area of agreement between critics and rational deterrence analysts, which is that deterrence is much more likely to fail if leaders believe that there are substantial political and/or military costs to be paid for failing to pursue a more aggressive foreign policy.

B. Nuclear Deterrence

The first point to make is that nuclear weapons may serve a deterrent role in one of two situations: (1) against an attacker who also possess nuclear weapons, and (2) against an attacker who enjoys an advantage in conventional military forces. Nuclear weapons are recognized by most state leaders to be very different from other military capabilities and therefore the first recourse for leaders is to turn to conventional forces in order to meet security threats. Only when leaders believe that their country's conventional forces are not adequate would we expect them to turn possibly to nuclear weapons as a supplement to conventional forces. Thus, when a defender possesses strong conventional forces nuclear weapons are unlikely to play a deterrent role in peacetime military planning or crises. Instead, conventional forces will be relied on to try and deter adversaries.

The second point to make is that the empirical basis for drawing conclusions about nuclear deterrence is much more limited than is the case with conventional deterrence. Fortunately, we do not have a number of cases of nuclear wars to study in order to analyze why deterrence of nuclear war can fail. In addition, states that possess nuclear weapons do not frequently resort to nuclear threats either verbally or by the movement and alerting of nuclear-capable forces. As a result, there are only a limited number of conflicts and crises since 1945 in which states have even indirectly turned to nuclear weapons as a deterrent. However, even if nuclear threats are seldom explicitly issued by states, it is possible to argue that the possession of nuclear weapons can act as a deterrent. Thus, I will consider the deterrent value of nuclear weapons for purposes of general and immediate deterrence based on either explicit threats or the latent threat implied by possession of nuclear weapons.

1. Superpower Crisis Behavior During the Cold War

What can we say then about the deterrent value of nuclear weapons? One useful source of data for answering this question comes from the various diplomatic and military crises between the two superpowers from 1945 until the end of the Cold War. Richard Betts examined 12 cases between 1948 and 1980 where nuclear threats at least indirectly were used by leaders, and Richard Ned Lebow and Janice Gross Stein have analyzed two of those cases—the Cuban Missile Crisis of 1962 and the Arab-Israeli War of 1973—in greater detail. In addition, Frank Harvey has studied 28 crises between the superpowers between 1948 and 1984 to see what impact nuclear weapons had on crisis outcomes.

Three conclusions can be drawn from these various

studies. First, political and military leaders were often cautious and sought to avoid military actions involving nuclear-capable forces, which clearly heightened the risk of a direct U.S.-Soviet military encounter, or to take military actions with nuclear-capable forces which ensured that they would be involved in an armed conflict from the very outset. Put differently, U.S. and Soviet leaders did not frequently engage in the type of commitment tactics that Thomas Schelling argued could be used by leaders to make deterrent and nuclear threats, in particular, more credible. Instead of leaders seeking to limit their military options in a crisis, they preferred to hold in reserve the option of moving conventional and nuclear forces into positions of close proximity to the other superpower's forces. Second, the evidence would seem to indicate that precise or nuanced calculations about the relative nuclear balance did not play an important role in decisions. It would seem that Soviet and U.S. leaders in crises generally did not think about how nuclear weapons could be used to achieve military advantages that could then be used to exert political leverage. Instead, the limited evidence available indicates that the threat of even a limited nuclear attack was of primary concern to leaders. In contrast, the logic supporting declaratory policy and operational planning that called for the ability to carry out limited nuclear attacks with counterforce weapons to ensure a credible deterrent was not evident in the arguments and statements of leaders. In the context of scholarly debates about nuclear doctrine, leaders seemed to think much more in terms of minimal deterrence than countervailing strategies of damage limitation and military advantage. Third, nuclear weapons seemed to have a deterrent effect on both parties in the dispute generally inducing the challenger to be more wary of escalating the crisis to a direct military confrontation at the conventional level, while defenders avoided pressing for one-sided diplomatic settlements and were willing to offer concessions if necessary.

2. The Larger Historical Record

This final point about the deterrent effect of nuclear weapons in superpower conflicts can be further developed when a broader range of empirical work and international rivalries are considered: (1) findings from more general studies of major power initiation of crises and their escalation to war; (2) Sino-Soviet crisis behavior during the 1969 border clashes and during the 1979 Sino-Vietnamese War; and (3) Indo-Pakistani conflicts over the disputed Kashmir border. When one pieces together findings from theses various studies and other interstate conflicts, one conclusion that can be reached

is that nuclear weapons are probably a much stronger deterrent in situations of immediate deterrence than in cases of general deterrence. The threat of nuclear retaliation most likely does little to deter low-level conventional military probes and challenges, but it may very well induce greater caution about the risks of a large-scale conventional military conflict. One way of summarizing the findings and arguments in the scholarly literature is that the deterrent value of nuclear weapons for a defender can vary from relatively high to very low levels. One possible ordering would be as follows:

1. Deterrence of a nuclear attack on homeland territory.
2. Deterrence of a large-scale conventional attack on homeland territory.
3. Deterrence of a nuclear attack against an ally.
4. Deterrence of a large-scale conventional attack or threat against an ally.
5. Deterrence of a low-level conventional attack or threat against homeland territory.
6. Deterrence of a low-level conventional attack or threat against an ally.

As we look at the rank ordering of these six deterrence situations, we see that the credibility of nuclear threats varies with whether homeland or ally territory is at risk as well as whether the military threat is a large-scale or low-level conventional attack. Thus, case one has a relatively high deterrent utility while in case six nuclear deterrent effects are probably absent altogether.

IV. CONCLUSION

With the end of the Cold War the threat of conventional and nuclear confrontations between the United States and Russia seems quite remote. Issues of conventional and nuclear deterrence, however, remain pressing security problems for a number of states in the post-Cold War international system. Territorial disputes that could escalate to higher levels of international conflict persist in regions such as Europe, the Middle East, South Asia, and the Far East. The proliferation of nuclear weapons in many of these same regions is quite possible as well. Finally, the breakdown of domestic political order within states can prompt outside threats of, and actual military intervention by states. Wars and international crises, then, will continue to occur and state leaders will attempt to maintain their country's security against external military threats by a range of diplomatic and military policies. Leaders in many states then will view deterrent policies as a necessary component of their country's overall foreign policy.

The continuing relevance of deterrence underscores the need for further research on the causes of deterrence success and failure. While research on deterrence has advanced considerably over the past decade, there are still important limits to our knowledge and depth of understanding. An agenda for research then would include the following:

1. Much further theoretical work is required to identify when reputations should form and what impact they should have on deterrence. In addition, careful empirical work is required to test arguments about reputation formation and its causal impact. Policymakers often justify policies of immediate deterrence as necessary to avoid damage to their country's international reputation, but the fact is that our understanding of the importance of reputations to deterrence is quite rudimentary.

2. The domestic political sources of defender and attacker policy choices in situations of deterrence is a very promising area for research. Recent work has found strong evidence that domestic conditions can: (a) be causes of initial challenges to general deterrence; (b) constrain and shape the deterrent response of defenders to attacker threats; and (c) influence the attacker's decision to escalate an immediate deterrence confrontation to a war. In each of these areas scholarly debates exist about how and to what degree domestic factors shape state behavior. Progress in resolving theses debates should lead to major contributions in our understanding of deterrence.

3. More research should be directed toward analyzing the conditions under which threats and rewards can be combined into a coherent and effective deterrent policy. Recent research suggests that reciprocating as well as carrot-and-stick bargaining strategies enhance the prospects of deterrence success, but much greater refinements can be made in identifying effective strategies and under what conditions they are most effective. This type of research would encourage analysts of deterrence to think more rigorously and broadly about the fact that deterrent policies are but one component of a country's security policy and that the strengths and limits of deterrence are more apparent when placed in the context of the full range of diplomatic and military options available to states.

4. Situations of general deterrence require much more extensive empirical analysis. States devote large amounts of diplomatic and financial resources as well as manpower to support general deterrence but there are few empirical studies of the subject. There exists then a rich historical record for scholars to examine and the results of such research should significantly advance our understanding of how conflicts first emerge and what compels leaders to risk military confrontations.

Also See the Following Articles

COLLECTIVE SECURITY SYSTEMS • CONFLICT MANAGEMENT AND RESOLUTION • DECISION THEORY AND GAME THEORY • MEDIATION AND NEGOTIATION TECHNIQUES • NUCLEAR WEAPONS POLICIES • SECURITY STUDIES • TERRITORIAL DISPUTES • WARFARE, MODERN

Bibliography

Betts, R. (1987). *Nuclear blackmail and nuclear balance.* Washington, DC: Brookings.

Blair, B. (1993). *The logic of accidental nuclear war.* Washington, DC: Brookings.

Fearon, J. (1994). Signaling versus the balance of power and interests. *Journal of Conflict Resolution, 38*(2), 236–69.

Gelpi, C. (1997). Crime and punishment. *American Political Science Review, 91*(2), 339–360.

George, A., & Smoke, R. (1974). *Deterrence in American foreign policy.* New York: Columbia University Press.

Glaser, C. (1990). *Analyzing strategic nuclear policy.* Princeton: Princeton University Press.

Harvey, F. (1997). *The future's back.* Montreal: McGill-Queens University Press.

Hopf, T. (1994). *Peripheral visions.* Ann Arbor: University of Michigan Press.

Huth, P. (1988). *Extended deterrence and the prevention of war.* New Haven: Yale University Press.

Huth, P., Gelpi, G., & Bennett, D. S. (1993). The escalation of great power militarized disputes. *American Political Science Review, 87*(3), 609–623.

Jervis, R. (1984). *The illogic of American nuclear Strategy.* Ithaca: Cornell University Press.

Lebow, R. N. (1981). *Between peace and war.* Baltimore: Johns Hopkins University Press.

Lebow, R. N., & Stein, J. G. (1994). *We All Lost the Cold War.* Princeton: Princeton University Press.

Leng, R. (1993). *Interstate crisis bargaining behavior, 1816–1980.* Cambridge: Cambridge University Press.

Liberman, E. (1994). The rational deterrence theory debate. *Security Studies, 3*(3), 384–427.

Mearsheimer, J. (1983). *Conventional deterrence.* Ithaca: Cornell University Press.

Mercer, J. (1996). *Reputation and international politics.* Ithaca: Cornell University Press.

Posen, B. (1991). *Inadvertent escalation*. Ithaca: Cornell University Press.

Powell, R. (1990). *Nuclear deterrence theory*. Cambridge: Cambridge University Press.

Sagan, S. (1993). *The limits of safety*. Princeton: Princeton University Press.

Schelling, T. (1966). *Arms and influence*. New Haven: Yale University Press.

Shimshoni, J. (1988). *Israel and conventional deterrence*. Ithaca: Cornell University Press.

Snyder, G. (1961). *Deterrence and defense* Princeton: Princeton University Press.

Stein, J. G. (1996). Deterrence and learning in an enduring rivalry. *Security Studies, 6*(1) 104–152.

Zagare, F. (1987). *The dynamics of deterrence*. Chicago: University of Chicago Press.

Military–Industrial Complex, Contemporary Significance

Gregory McLauchlan

University of Oregon

GLOSSARY

Cold War The global struggle between the United States and the Soviet Union for international political, economic, and military dominance between 1947 and 1989.

Economic Conversion The idea, put forward by scholars as well as policy analysts, that significant amounts of the capital, technology, and labor force of defense industries can be redirected toward civilian production in post-war periods.

Military–Industrial Complex (MIC) The network of military agencies and industrial corporations involved in the development and production of armaments. Some authors refer to the "scientific–military–industrial complex" to denote the increasing role of science and technology research institutions (including universities) in an era of high technology armaments.

Peace Dividend The expectation that the end of the Cold War would be accompanied by significant eco-nomic conversion by the U.S. and other states, where economic and other resources would be redirected from military to civilian investments.

Revolution in Military Affairs (RMA) A U.S. military doctrine developed after the Cold War that claims battlefield effectiveness of a given number of troops can be dramatically increased by combining numerous innovations in high-technology weapon systems with major changes in how military forces are deployed.

Superpower A term denoting the historical combination of political, military, and economic power achieved by a few states that exercise global influence. During the Cold War, the U.S. and Soviet Union were the two superpowers, in large part because of the unequalled size of their nuclear arsenals, which allowed them to create two opposing blocs of political–military alliances and to control in significant respects the nature and scope of international conflicts.

I. CRISIS TENDENCIES IN THE MILITARY–INDUSTRIAL COMPLEX [1]

It is necessary to take a view spanning several decades to understand the contemporary significance of the mil-

---

[1] Parts of sections I–IV,A are excerpted from McLauchlan, G., & Hooks, G. (1995). Last of the Dinosaurs? Big Science, Big Weapons, and the American State from Hiroshima to the End of the Cold War. *The Sociological Quarterly*, 36, 749–776.

Copyright © 1999 by Academic Press.
All rights of reproduction in any form reserved.

itary–industrial complex (MIC). The following sections examine the relationship of the MIC to the economic crises of the two superpowers, the role of peace movements and critiques of the technology of the arms race in delegitimizing the MIC in the 1980s, the collapse of the Soviet Union and its MIC, and the changing nature of the MIC in the United States in the aftermath of the 1990–1991 Persian Gulf War. A brief overview of the (significantly smaller) role of the MIC in other societies is presented, and these cases are compared to the Cold War experience with the U.S. and the Soviet Union MICs.

The MIC reached its peak in the United States and Soviet Union in the decades of the 1950s through the early 1970s. The MIC enjoyed widespread prestige; it commanded the most sophisticated science and technology resources of the two societies, supervised the rise of new industries such as aerospace and microelectronics, and developed the technologies that enabled men to walk on the moon in 1969. But the period from the mid-1970s to the present has been one of significant institutional crisis for the military–industrial complex.

The big science- and technology-intensive weapon systems—especially nuclear ones—produced by the MIC experienced attacks from political opponents and peace movements, while major technological failures, increasing fiscal pressures, and new international challenges in the form of conflicts that are not easily fought by traditional military–industrial means have raised questions about the future of the MIC. Viewed as a whole, the second half of the Cold War era (from the early 1970s to 1989) and its aftermath in the 1990s are a period of partial decomposition and restructuring of the MIC, though with dramatically different outcomes in the United States and the states comprising the former Soviet Union.

The period climaxed with the unexpectedly rapid collapse of the Soviet Union—the world's biggest state (in terms of capital resources under state control) and second "superpower." Both superpowers had been defeated in major wars (the U.S. in Vietnam and the Soviet Union in Afghanistan), where their high-technology weaponry was no match for highly motivated and innovative Third World opponents and where nuclear arsenals were of little value. In the 1980s, even as it "won" the Cold War and undertook the largest peacetime military build-up in its history, the United States went from being the world's largest creditor nation to the world's largest debtor, financing its military build-up using government debt that exceeded $1.5 trillion for the decade. In the same period Germany became the world's largest

exporter and Japan became a manufacturing and financial superpower, challenging the idea that global influence rested primarily on military power.

Many perceptive analyses of the world-historic changes since the 1960s have tried to understand these, in part, as the result of the role and contradictions of military power and institutions in modern society and the world system.

II. THE MILITARY-INDUSTRIAL COMPLEX AND ECONOMIC CRISIS

A. Modernizing or Parasitic Institutions?

In the 1970s and 1980s critics such as Kaldor, Kennedy, Melman and others began to argue that the U.S.–Soviet arms race and their attendant military–industrial complexes were undermining the economic health and world position of the superpowers. During this period the U.S. lost significant world share in important markets, including high-technology sectors, mainly to rising economic competitors such as Germany, Japan, and newly industrializing East Asian countries. In the same period U.S. productivity growth stagnated, recessions became more frequent and more severe, and U.S. financial hegemony disappeared with the end of the gold standard and the beginning of sustained balance of payments and trade deficits. The most modernizing countries in the economic arena were increasingly those that were not so heavily invested in military spending, and it was pointed out that states such as Germany and Japan devoted a far larger proportion of their national research and development spending to civilian, versus military, objectives than did either the U.S. or the Soviet Union.

From a longer-term view, Kaldor pointed out that the route by which much of the economic and technological stimuli that did "spin off" from the MIC to the civilian economy in the first decades of the Cold War had become inverted to the point where the MIC excised a sustained drain on the economy's scientific, technological, and fiscal resources. From the 1940s to the 1960s, for example, military R&D programs to build long-range bombers had significant applications to civilian jetliners, which shared airframes and other characteristics. Military-funded research for atomic propulsion of ships overlapped significantly with atomic power R&D programs; indeed in the U.S. there likely would have been no significant private nuclear power industry without massive Cold War R&D subsidies.

An underlying reason for the spin-offs in this period

was that much military R&D, in the new nuclear and space ages, was directed toward making advances in what might be termed "foundational" technologies. Thus, the military needed operational nuclear reactors, integrated circuits, microprocessors, fast computers, space rocket boosters, and satellites. It was assumed that once developed these would lay the foundations for new growth industries, and this is what happened in a number of cases. But in the 1970s and after military R&D increasingly was devoted to esoteric aims with comparatively few civilian applications. Weapon platforms such as stealth bombers had no fundamental civilian characteristics, and military R&D increasingly focused on ways to make existing weapon systems more sophisticated, including the ability to operate under conditions of nuclear attack, rather than to develop fundamentally new technologies. Thus evolved what Kaldor termed the "baroque arsenal," produced by an MIC that was parasitic on the larger economy.

Analysts also pointed to organizational and cultural characteristics of military industry and R&D that contributed to economic crisis tendencies. Because of its devotion to baroque weapons, military research and development was geared to the singular, hi-tech product rather than to the process innovations that, for example, the Japanese so successfully carried out in manufacturing industries in the period. Moreover, the U.S. had virtually no coherent industrial policy to systematically shepherd the science and technology advances from military R&D that did have civilian uses into commercial or social applications. Finally, the devotion to baroque products and a cost-plus procurement system (i.e., where R&D costs, plus a profit, are virtually guaranteed) led to a military-industrial structure that was exceedingly management heavy and to the creation of a "wall of separation" between huge, military-oriented firms, which could not survive in competitive markets, and the rest of the civilian economy. As Markusen and Yudken argued, this made the challenge of post-Cold War economic conversion of the MIC a daunting one.

The prescience of the earlier critics of the social and economic costs of the MIC was evident in the embrace of many of their critiques in mainstream proposals for post-Cold War economic conversion; for example, those put forward by the Carnegie Commission in 1992 and U.S. Office of Technology Assessment in 1993. But due to political opposition, significant economic conversion efforts were never undertaken.

The economic crisis associated with a burgeoning MIC was far worse in the Soviet Union. Both superpowers feared falling behind in an MIC-driven nuclear arms race, thus the investments of both societies in military industry and weapon systems were similar in kind and in scale. But as the size of the Soviet economy was approximately half that of the U.S., it devoted proportionally probably twice the resources to military R&D and production, such that the MIC accounted for between 10 and 15% of Soviet GNP in the 1980s. This burden was compounded by the gulf between the relatively modern military sector and the underdeveloped civilian sector, a gulf maintained by a planning system where the budgets of the MIC came first and all other economic sectors got what was left over.

The military's command of qualitative resources, coupled with a Soviet autarky that insulated the civilian economy from international competition—and comparison—led the Soviet Union to fall further behind world standards in civilian technology and production, especially as there were no market forces to test the civilian economy and reveal its problems. The relative success of Soviet military, versus economic, competition with the West favored reinvestment in the MIC rather than in civilian industry. By the late 1970s the Soviet Union had become the world's largest arms exporter, earning the bulk of its foreign exchange from arms exports.

Yet this served merely to reinforce the longer-term economic crisis tendencies associated with the Cold War MIC. Since the 1950s the rate of Soviet growth in GNP had been in decline: from an average near 6% in the decade of 1950–1960 to about 4% in 1970–1975 to under 3% in the 1980s. And while the Soviet Union made impressive investments in science and engineering—surpassing the U.S. with 873,500 versus 534,500 scientists and engineers by 1975—this talent was concentrated in the military sector.

As in the U.S. case, Soviet support for wars in the Third World had serious economic consequences. While an important political and symbolic victory, the costs of the North Vietnamese and Viet Cong defeat of the U.S. and South Vietnamese regime were immense and were borne largely by the Soviet Union. In the 1970s a series of Soviet-supported revolutions in the Third World—in Ethiopia, Angola, Mozambique, Guinea Bissau, and Nicaragua—were net economic burdens to the Soviet Union as these were extremely poor societies facing large costs of reconstruction. Finally, the 1979 invasion of Afghanistan turned into a costly, unwinnable war—the Soviet Union's Vietnam.

B. Resurgent Cold War and Soviet Crisis

In the late 1970s and continuing into the 1980s both the U.S. and Soviet Union sought to displace these crisis tendencies by reasserting their military and political "superpower" status as leaders of the respective Cold War blocs. Both significantly accelerated military spending and emphasized qualitative advances in weapons technology, including a new generation of highly accurate nuclear weapon systems—leading to what many analysts referred to as the "Second Cold War."

The U.S. was able to mask and delay the economic costs of this resurgent militarism through borrowing on the international financial markets that often exceeded more than $200 billion of new debt per year in the 1980s. In effect, the U.S. was able to take out a 30-year mortgage to pay for the major military expansion of that decade. In marked contrast, without access to international capital the Soviet Union was forced to finance its military program and the cost of the Afghan war out of deficits in the current budget, producing growing inflation, shortages of industrial materials, and stagnation in the consumer sector.

These developments combined with other trends to create among many Soviet political leaders a sense of imminent crisis. The Chernobyl nuclear disaster in this period was the costliest industrial accident in history and produced serious doubts about the status of Soviet technology, while the costs of high-technology military competition with the West, highlighted by President Reagan's announcement of a Strategic Defense Initiative (or "Star Wars") program in 1983, were increasingly evident.

Of even greater significance in Soviet perceptions was the overall trend in the world-economy. The economies of the Western allies, and especially those of the newly industrializing East Asian allies of the U.S., expanded dramatically in the 1970s and 1980s, far greater than the Eastern bloc economies. In short, the long-held Soviet belief of the impending crisis and ultimate collapse of the capitalist world was simply not being borne out by reality. The result was a profound crisis in ideology, cutting to the very core of a Soviet-inspired communist identity that had existed since the 1930s.

Mikhail Gorbachev's rise to power in 1985 represented the ascendance of elites seeking to reverse these trends. Gorbachev's program of "new thinking" was an explicit effort to stop the nuclear arms race, reduce the MIC and shift Soviet efforts to civilian goals, and end the Cold War. A major source of opposition to his programs of *perestroika* ("restructuring") and *glasnost* ("openness") was the MIC. To counter this, Gorbachev launched a historic Soviet "peace offensive" that involved major concessions in Soviet positions in arms control negotiations in an effort to force the U.S. to come to agreement to radically limit the nuclear arms race, a development that would also undermine the domestic power of the Soviet MIC.

III. PEACE MOVEMENTS AND THE CRITIQUE OF THE NUCLEAR ARMS RACE

Gorbachev's efforts were aided by the emergence in the 1980s of a massive peace movement in Western Europe and the U.S., which opposed a new generation of highly accurate, so-called "first strike" nuclear weapons that were being introduced by the MICs of both superpowers, as well as new strategic doctrines that claimed nuclear wars could be fought and "won." In generating some of the largest political demonstrations of the post-WWII period in the West, the peace movements of the 1980s created an unprecedented crisis of legitimacy for the MIC by calling into question its claim to be the provider of stability and security through nuclear deterrence based on increasingly "modernized" nuclear weapon systems.

The peace movement developed sophisticated critiques of both the technology and the politics of the nuclear arms race. Widely read works by Thompson and others opposed the technological momentum of the arms race and sought to radically democratize nuclear politics, in part by exposing the gulf that separated the awesome destructive capacities of nuclear technologies or "hardware" from the comparatively infantile "science" of deterrence and nuclear strategy that was based on unproven assumptions about human behavior and decision-making.

Many peace movement leaders were women, including Helen Caldicott of Physicians for Social Responsibility and Randall Forsberg, author of a "nuclear freeze" proposal that was passed by voters in many states in the U.S. In this period a "gender gap" opened in U.S. voting patterns, with significantly fewer women than men voting for candidates who supported the renewed arms race and MIC. Authors such as Enloe and Cohn subjected the masculine character and gender consequences of the MIC and nuclear weapons laboratories to important feminist critiques. Additionally, a number of prominent scientists and military officers, including Freeman Dyson and Lord Zuckerman, "defected" from the MIC and published widely read critiques of the new nuclear weapon systems and doctrines.

The first Reagan administration responded to this crisis with the announcement of a Strategic Defense

Initiative (SDI) or "Star Wars" program in 1983. While the rhetorical shift from "offensive," horribly destructive nuclear weapons to a "defensive" system attracted a certain degree of public support, the SDI effort in turn became the subject of bitter controversy, especially in the scientific and technical communities. Critics of SDI pointed to its unprecedented costs and dangers. Many pointed out that such a system would have great offensive capabilities, and would violate the U.S.–Soviet Anti-Ballistic Missile Treaty. Others saw it as a way for nuclear weapons labs and the MIC to develop new projects, as the prospects of anything new in offensive weapons were running out. "Star Wars" represented an increasingly parasitic arms race, where now offensive and defensive weapon systems could race each other in a never-ending spiral. Many military officers and strategists were also wary, as SDI technology developed by an adversary would threaten the very foundation of U.S. nuclear deterrence.

Finally, critics such as Zuckerman pointed to the technological arrogance: the most complex weapon system ever proposed, with command and control relying on execution of trillions of lines of software code and much of its hardware deployed in space—a system and software that could never be operationally tested in advance—would have to perform flawlessly on its first use to defend against nuclear attack. Despite a 15-year, $50 billion research and prototype development effort from 1983 to the late 1990s, the SDI failed to inaugurate a second long wave of MIC-led expansion comparable to the earlier nuclear arms race.

Instead, the legitimation crisis of the 1980s revealed a Cold War technological era coming to an end. The nuclear arms race had become exhausted, both technologically and in its scientific-ideological legitimations, i.e., theories of nuclear strategy that tried to justify departures from basic nuclear deterrence. The deconstruction of the scientific and technical aura of the nuclear arms race by the peace movement was a central development here. The peace movement undermined what had previously been a central political and social function of the MIC: to unite publics and blocs behind a symbolic sense of military-provided security and to claim to be the leading edge of scientific-technological, and hence economic, modernity.

By the end of the decade the U.S. and Soviet Union had concluded or were negotiating a series of historic nuclear arms control treaties, and the Soviet Union had relinquished its military and political claims over the Warsaw Pact nations of Eastern Europe, paving the way for a series of relatively peaceful transitions in those societies. In 1989, with the fall of the Berlin Wall, the Cold War was over. What was left were large military–industrial complexes, with their huge nuclear arsenals, without a purpose.

In the Soviet case, the end of the Cold War and diminution of the arms race represented a systemic crisis; what continued justification was there for a national structure dominated by the MIC in light of the end of the Cold War and deepening economic crisis? Within a few years the Soviet Union had disintegrated into 13 independent republics and its MIC, inherited mostly by Russia, was a hollowed-out shell of its Cold War peak.

In the case of the United States, the end of the Cold War was accompanied by public discussion of the possibility of a historic "peace dividend," entailing a major demobilization of military forces (as in the aftermath of previous wars) and reorientation of economic and scientific resources to civilian ends. But a full-scale re-evaluation of the MIC dominance of U.S. governmental priorities and resources was diverted by the first major international crisis of the 1990s: the 1990–1991 Persian Gulf War.

IV. THE MILITARY–INDUSTRIAL COMPLEX AT THE END OF THE 20TH CENTURY

As changing social dimensions of war and military technology figured prominently in the evolution of the MIC from WWII through the Cold War, the character of war and the political sociology of the U.S.'s global role in the post-Cold War era are shaping the contemporary MIC.

A. The Persian Gulf War: Defining a New Era

The 1990–1991 Persian Gulf War submerged talk of a peace dividend as the U.S. led one of the largest and certainly most technology-intensive military operations since WWII to repel Iraqi military forces from Kuwait and punish the Iraqi regime. A number of observers pointed to the Gulf War as marking the ascendence of a new U.S. military doctrine of "mid-intensity conflict" that requires the U.S. to maintain technological superiority over emerging regional powers in the global arena.

Analyses such as Hiro's cited domestic and international political factors to explain the Bush administration's determination to carry out a decisive military conclusion to the 1990–1991 Gulf crisis, a determination that involved systematic rejection of several opportunities for a negotiated settlement or the longer-term strategy of United Nations imposed economic sanctions. These factors included the precipitous decline of President Bush's political ratings in the months before the war due to mounting domestic political and economic problems, the strategic and economic importance of Middle East oil, and the role of the U.S. as the sole global superpower in an era when Germany and Japan (two oil-dependent states) were increasing their economic and political influence dramatically. Overlaying these motives was the opportunity to revive the political capital of the MIC by demonstrating the awesome power of the conventional high-technology weapons which had been deployed in an "imaginary war" with the Soviet Union, but which might now also be strategically critical for use against new enemies.

In the first 2 weeks of the 42-day Gulf War the U.S.-led allied air attack dropped more explosives than in the entire Second World War. A single U.S. armored division of 350 M1 tanks used more fuel oil in the Gulf War than did the U.S. 3rd Army during its invasion of Germany in 1944–1945. In short, as Hiro and Kellner have shown, the Gulf War involved a massive quantitative deployment of military force, and a historically unprecedented concentration of aerial bombing, even as it was politically and socially constructed in media accounts as largely a high-technology military campaign that relied on qualitative technological superiority to achieve a rapid and devastating Allied victory.

For example, Hiro showed that the widely touted "smart" bombs with precision guidance used by the U.S. Air Force accounted for only 7% of munitions; most of the bombing was carried out with conventional "dumb" bombs with an accuracy of less than 25%. A March 1991 United Nations survey of civilian bombing damage in Iraq called it "near apocalyptic," and this and subsequent reports by international investigators documented widespread destruction of Iraq's civilian infrastructure. Similarly, military pronouncements and media coverage of the role of the U.S. Patriot antimissile system against Iraqi Scud missiles claimed it an "unqualified success," though a subsequent analysis by Postol revealed that the large majority of Patriots failed to intercept their targets and that they did not reduce ground damage in Israel—and may have increased it in some cases. It is clear weapons such as cruise missiles, antitank missiles, night-fighting technology, and sophisticated electronic jamming used against Iraqi defenses contributed to the immense devastation wrought by Allied forces. But many of the claims for, and public perception of success of, the hi-tech weapons of the Gulf War were the products of military public relations and uncritical media coverage.

Kellner persuasively argues the Gulf War was socially constructed as an advertisement for the continuing dominance of the U.S. MIC and its high-technology weapons. An arena of increasing importance to the MIC was the ability to shape public perception of the effects and success of its weapons systems. Having learned the dangers of unfavorable media coverage in Vietnam, the military exercised unprecedented control over media reporters, controlling what sources would be available for interviews, where reporters were allowed to travel (always under military escort), and requiring all press reports to go through military censors for clearance. This gave the military extraordinary influence in determining how military operations and the use of weapons would be portrayed. Much of the television footage of U.S. weapon systems in the war was provided directly by the military or came from videos provided to the networks and their affiliates by major defense contractors. *Fortune* magazine exemplified this media trend in a February 25, 1991 cover story on "The Future of Arms:" "We speak proudly of AWACS, Tomahawks, Hellfires and Slams—above all, of the Patriot, the knight who parried the evil Scud right there in our family room . . . . And thanks to missile-mounted cameras, you and I—like Slim Pickens in 'Dr. Strangelove'—can mount a bomb and ride it to its devastating detonation."

The Gulf War was significant in recalibrating the military R&D agenda for the post-Cold War era and in blocking a substantial redirection of resources away from the MIC to civilian pursuits anticipated by a "peace dividend." In the months after the war defense industry publications and the business press were filled with articles speculating on a Gulf "war dividend" for the defense industries and military laboratories. A common theme in these analyses was how impressive U.S. hi-tech weapons were in the war, especially in comparison with those of other states, including the Soviet Union and France. Many financial analysts expected the Gulf War legacy would lead to a boom in U.S. exports of sophisticated arms, helping to offset its declining competitiveness in other hi-tech industries. Indeed, in the early 1990s the U.S. became by a significant margin the world's leading arms exporter.

Additionally, during the Gulf War military planners stressed the threat to the U.S. and its allies from states such as Iraq that may be developing a significant chemical, nuclear, or biological weapons capability (weapons of mass destruction or "WMDs" in military jargon). Following a series of high-level Defense Department reports documenting this threat—more than 20 nations were claimed to be developing or already have nuclear, chemical, or biological weapons—the Pentagon initiated what was called by some the "defense initiative of the 1990s," a multiagency effort involving developing technologies to detect the development or deployment of WMDs and to destroy them. Ironically, the collapse of the former Soviet Union and the impressive military technologies developed by the superpowers in the Cold War, as well as the rapidly expanding biotechnology industry (inherently difficult to regulate or monitor), are major sources of the new threat. Hundreds of former Soviet experts in WMDs were unemployed and living in poverty and possibly willing to sell their services to other states, while the vast stocks of Cold War military science, technology, and weapons materials are difficult to control in an era of globalized communications and markets. In short, much of the proliferation of weapons technology is the product of the Cold War-era U.S. and Soviet MICs.

The 1991 Gulf War marked the periodization between two eras—the end of big weapons that dominated the nuclear arms race, but the consolidation of a new era where, even with declining procurement budgets, the MIC will continue its dominance of the state's high-technology research and development agenda. Mann speculated we are at the beginning of the era of "spectator-sport militarism," where the vast majority of citizens are removed from direct participation in military forces or industry, the latter being increasingly monopolized by professional warriors and specialists in science- and technology-intensive weapons.

B. Reorganization in the Military–Industrial Complex

In the decade following the end of the Cold War and the 1990–1991 Persian Gulf War the U.S. MIC has been downsized and restructured, but it remains in a class by itself as the world's largest institutional concentration of scientific and industrial resources for the pursuit of military ends. U.S. yearly military spending in the late 1990s of about $270 billion per year represents about 80% of peak Cold War military commitments, and military spending accounts for about 50% of U.S. discretionary spending (i.e., the budget financed by general tax revenues). U.S. plans call for more than $1.6 trillion (1997 U.S. dollars) in military spending between 1997 and 2002, at a time when the U.S. has no major military rivals. In the late 1990s the U.S. military budget exceeded the spending of the next 10 largest military powers combined.

The decline in U.S. military spending has been re-

flected mainly in reduced procurement (i.e., fewer of a given weapon purchased) rather than the cancellation of weapon systems. The attenuation of the nuclear arms race has contributed to this trend, and by the late 1990s procurement spending was less than half of its Cold War peak, falling from $97 billion in 1985 to $44 billion in 1997.

Yet analysts describe a post-Cold War MIC that still commands significant power in domestic politics and Congressional budgetary decisions. As Gottlieb has shown, many Cold War-era weapon systems such as the Seawolf nuclear attack submarine and B-2 stealth bomber have been continued even as there is no strategic justification for these with the collapse of the Soviet Union. In many cases, Congress has insisted on continuing major military contracts at the behest of powerful senators or representatives who have large defense industries in their states or districts and who want to preserve the jobs and economic benefits concomitant with large military contracts.

Political support for the MIC also remains strong because the Pentagon and military contractors perfected the system of "political engineering" in the 1970s and 1980s, where subcontracts on major weapon systems, sometimes totalling billions of dollars, were deliberately spread out to smaller industries across numerous states and congressional districts, guaranteeing a widespread base of support. Additionally, as the world's largest arms supplier, averaging between $12 and $16 billion of weapons exports per year in the 1990s, many U.S. firms in the MIC earn a substantial share of their income from foreign sales. To insure continued support and government subsidies for arms exports (subsidies were about $7.5 billion yearly in the mid-1990s), the 25 largest weapons-exporting firms contributed a record $10.8 million to Congressional political campaigns in the 1995–1996 election year.

The post-Cold War downsizing has produced a new organizational structure within the MIC industries. In response to reduced demand for its products a wave of mergers and consolidation has swept the MIC, with larger contractors swallowing scores of smaller firms, and some formerly huge corporations such as General Dynamics have shed tens of thousands of workers to focus on a reduced level of defense contracts rather than try to expand into civilian markets in which they had little experience or expertise. Where in the 1980s there were perhaps 50 large military contractors, by the late 1990s there were only about 5, including Lockheed Martin, Boeing, Raytheon, Northrop, and United Technologies. Many of these firms, especially those in aerospace, have expanded their commercial ventures and rely on the Pentagon for a declining share of their revenue. Moreover, as the MIC consolidated and laid off workers, the stock value of many of the largest firms increased, reflecting the increased market power and hence profitability of a handful of large corporations who face little to no competition in their contracts with the Pentagon.

The Pentagon responded to this shift in power by joining the Justice Department in an antitrust lawsuit to block the merger planned in 1998 of two of the largest military contractors, Lockheed Martin and Northrop. Military planners argued that additional mergers would effectively end the competitive incentives for weapons innovation that existed when there was more than one possible supplier (a dynamic that helped fuel the arms race in the Cold War), and would further drive up the costs of weapons as the remaining firms would be monopolies. The claim is that over time the U.S. could lose much of its lead in military technology vis-à-vis the rest of the world. While the final outlines of this historic consolidation of the MIC remain to be seen, it is perhaps ironic that industries such as aerospace, whose very existence was largely a product of Pentagon-financed research and development, have evolved to where they are dominated by giant corporations who are now the equals of their former master.

The overarching reason for the continuation of a Cold War-scale MIC is the stated U.S. commitment to play a dominant global military role. This official posture has been elaborated on in numerous forums and in post-Cold War military interventions and commitments, including the 1991 Persian Gulf War, Bosnia, Haiti, Yugoslavia, the Korean peninsula, the Taiwan straits, and in additional Middle East conflicts. This policy was affirmed in the 1997 Quadrennial Defense Review, which called for the U.S. to continue the forward deployment of 100,000 troops and equipment in both Europe and Asia and to maintain the capability to fight two major, nearly simultaneous regional wars. In addition, it is U.S. policy to aggressively promote the "Revolution in Military Affairs" (RMA), a Pentagon strategy that calls for technological advances in numerous weapons systems combined with radical changes in doctrine and force structures to produce a military with significantly greater power, though not necessarily more troops, in the coming decades. An even more science-and-technology-intensive MIC is the centerpiece of this strategy.

C. Comparative and Long-Term Views

Originally coined by President Eisenhower in his 1961 farewell address to describe a powerful concentration of military, industrial, and scientific resources in the United States (and extended by analysts to describe developments in the other nuclear superpower, the Soviet Union), the term "military–industrial complex" is nevertheless often used to indicate similar institutional combinations in other states. If it is the case, as a number of prominent social theorists have argued in recent years, that the formation of modern nation-states has been in large part the result of the melding of nationalist ideologies with the war-making capacities afforded by the combination of military and industrial institutions, then the concept of the MIC would seem to have widespread significance.

But it is necessary to recognize differences in scale and additional qualitative dimensions between the MICs of the two superpowers and those in other states. First, in the years during and after the Cold War other industrial states typically spent less than 15% (most less than 10%) yearly of what either superpower devoted to armaments and military R&D. Second, other states (including the declared nuclear powers) have not made the commitment to rapid modernization and expansion of nuclear arsenals such as what took place during the U.S.–Soviet nuclear arms race. Third, other states have not sought to develop the extensive power projection capabilities, involving the naval and airlift capacity to deploy forces and equipment globally, that the superpowers did, nor have the large majority of these states in recent decades intervened militarily outside their borders, except in United Nations-sponsored operations, in contrast to the practices of the Soviet Union and especially the U.S.

Finally, because the MICs in other industrial states do not control the same scale of resources nor possess the same claim of strategic importance, the political power wielded by these MICs has been correspondingly less. For example, the western European social democracies typically spent a significantly larger share of their budget on social programs such as health care, education, job training, unemployment benefits, and civilian R&D than did the U.S. And the government ministries that directed these programs and their domestic constituencies had comparatively greater political influence than their parallels in the U.S.

This is not to say that the MIC is insignificant in other nations; it is, but it is a matter of degree and of historical trajectory. Moving beyond the nuclear superpowers, we can usefully distinguish several types, or stages of development, of the MIC in the contemporary world. First are the MICs of the industrial states of western and eastern Europe, particularly those states that are partners in the NATO alliance and the former states of the Warsaw Pact. All of these states have significant domestic arms industries, some are major arms exporters, and the MICs in these societies are more developed than most others because of their history as junior partners in the military blocs established by the superpowers during the Cold War.

In particular, the United Kingdom, Germany, and France have substantial arms industries and military R&D efforts and are major weapons exporters, with the UK challenging Russia in the 1990s for position as the world's second leading exporter of arms. Additionally, France and Britain's status as nuclear weapons powers have committed them to major investments in military high-technology sectors, such as satellite-based command, control, and communications systems.

Yet, as Sivard indicates in recent decades, the share of GNP devoted to military spending has declined by almost half in these three states from a 1960 average of 5.3% to one of 2.8% in 1994, indicating that contemporary MICs can persist even as the larger economy becomes less militarized. Shaw has pointed to this trend as one component of the emergence of "post-military" society in the west, where a more insular military establishment claims less social space and economic resources, even as it maintains impressive military capacities. In this view the population as a whole is increasingly pacific, evident, for example, in the politically popular decline of conscription.

In east Asia other major industrial states show a similar trend. Work by Klare and others indicates that in recent decades China, Japan, South Korea, and Taiwan (and to a lesser extent Indonesia, Singapore, Malaysia, and Thailand) have devoted significant efforts to expanding domestic arms industries under the aegis of an MIC reminiscent of the pattern established by the superpowers in the Cold War. These states have put in place models of government military–industrial planning aiming to expand military capabilities, develop military export industries (except Japan), and foster dual-use military and civilian high-technology sectors of the economy. As in Europe, arms spending by the four largest military powers here had also declined significantly by the mid-1990s as a share of GNP (to between about 4% for Taiwan and 1% for Japan). But it must be borne in mind that the vast expansion of the industrial economies of these states means that potent military–industrial capabilities can be purchased for these investments. For example, by the mid-1990s Japan had become the world's second or third largest military spender, even as it devoted only about 1% of its GNP to this effort.

The emerging arms races guided by east Asia's MICs

are fueled by historical rivalries, economic competition, nationalist pride, and the desire of some states to step out from dependence on the military protection of one or another superpower. Yet there are also historical and political influences tempering the growth of the MIC in what are by far the two largest economies of the region: China and Japan. China has maintained comparatively modest military investments for a nation its size, with the political leadership favoring investment in commercial sectors and expansion of export-led capital accumulation. China has relied on a modest nuclear deterrent for its strategic security. Japan's MIC, largely destroyed in World War II and then rebuilt with U.S. aid in the Cold War, was for several decades held in check by political and constitutional limits (for example, bans on weapons exports, deployment of troops overseas, and the development of nuclear weapons), but as many analysts point out the trend since the 1980s has been to relax these under increasing political pressure by conservative supporters of greater Japanese military power and a corresponding MIC.

The situation in other states reveals a more complex picture, indicating that the size or sophistication of a state's MIC does not bear any simple relationship to a state's level of economic development or political ideology. For example, Israel has a sophisticated MIC producing many of its own weapons, is a major arms exporter, and has possessed for probably more than 2 decades an undeclared nuclear weapons capability. Oil-producing states such as Iraq, Saudi Arabia, Kuwait, and Iran have used their wealth to build substantial military establishments. However, the large majority of the weapon systems possessed by such states are imported, and military R&D efforts have in some cases focused on cheaper (and less detectable) substitutes for expensive conventional weapons, including efforts to develop chemical, biological, and nuclear weapons.

The less developed countries in the South typically show a different pattern. While many of these states have invested heavily in armaments or have been ruled in recent decades by military-backed regimes, the large majority do not possess sophisticated domestic arms industries or an MIC in the sense previously described. These states import their advanced and heavy weapons, often at great cost, and international arms exporters from the MICs of the industrial states maintain a high-level international sales effort, offering both the latest models and often Cold War-era surplus weapons at bargain prices. As Sivard indicates, in the first half of the 1990s developing states imported an average of about $20 billion in arms yearly, accounting for more than two-thirds of all international arms purchases. Societies do not require an MIC to be highly militarized.

Nor is it the case that only rich countries with large scientific establishments can afford to develop nuclear weapons. China had already broken this mold in the 1960s, but the May, 1998 multiple nuclear weapons tests by India and Pakistan shattered the idea that the world would remain indefinitely divided between the five declared nuclear powers (the U.S., Russia, Britain, France, and China) and the rest. India and Pakistan, ranking 130th and 120th in the world respectively in per capita GNP, demonstrated that even comparatively poor societies are able to deploy the military, industrial, and scientific resources necessary to develop nuclear weapons and their delivery systems.

Moreover, the Indian and Pakistani nuclear tests were met with waves of nationalist approval in the two countries, even as critics noted the large economic sacrifices that would have to be made to further develop and deploy nuclear arsenals. In these countries, with more than several hundred million living in extreme poverty, the trade-offs between growing nuclear MICs and desperately needed social spending would be far more stark than had been the case in the economically developed nuclear states. But proponents of Indian and Pakistani nuclear status argued that the bomb would bring a new kind of respect to their states, as well as the potent, if risky, security bought by nuclear deterrence. For some the bomb was the "poor persons alternative" to a costly and sophisticated conventional military arsenal.

Thus, at the end of the 20th century the status, and future, of the MIC was in crucial ways still bound up with the legacy of its quintessential mid-20th century product: the nuclear bomb.

Taking a longer view, analysts such as van Creveld and Shaw suggest that the changing nature of warfare, technological developments, and additional social and global trends may in the near future make the MICs developed since the end of WWII anachronistic, though perhaps not obsolete. In part, the MIC may fall victim to its own successes: having concentrated immense military power under centralized direction by powerful nation states, the modern MIC has made it clear that total war on the scale of WWII would be unmitigated disaster. If there were any doubt of this, the nuclear revolution brought about by the MICs of the great powers has settled the debate. Thus, in the west as well as in many other societies the expectation by the majority of the population is that large-scale warfare with the aim of a major transformation of geopolitical relationships is a thing of the past.

At the same time new forms of conflict have emerged in response to the concentrated power of the MICs of the industrial states. Guerilla warfare, low-intensity conflict, and the use of terror for political objectives are strategies developed by states and political movements that cannot match the concentrated power of the MICs of the industrial states. Such strategies, which can be highly effective, do not require an MIC and indeed represent its obverse. The technology is low-tech, combatants often are indistinguishable from the civilian population, and military force is not amassed for decisive victories but is dispersed and relies on surprise and cunning for success. The fact that civilian deaths represented about 5% of casualties in warfare at the beginning of the century and more than 90% in its last decade is testimony to the changing strategy and ethics of war. If these trends continue, the baroque weapons of industrial MICs may be nearly useless in such conflicts.

Finally, trends in economic globalization and environmental crisis at the turn of the century place the MICs that originated mid-century and their modes of global conflict management in a different historical perspective. In the contemporary world a major financial crisis, such as the east Asian economic collapse of 1997–1998, can represent a greater threat to the economic security of the west than could any military action by a medium-level regional power. Similarly, the effects, and costs, of transnational and global environmental crises, including acid rain, species extinction, and global warming, are being increasingly viewed as threats to security and social stability. In the face of these challenges MICs are virtually helpless.

We might also anticipate that peace movements will once again resurface to decisively shift the course of history, as they did in helping to end the Cold War in the 1980s. An element of globalization is the emergence of a transnational civic culture emphasizing human rights, the need for economic security, and environmental justice. The Internet is fostering unprecedented levels of global communication among peace activists and nongovernmental organizations from different countries and cultures. It would be one of the 21st century's ironies if a technology originally developed by the U.S. MIC for pursuit of the Cold War arms race played a major role in its subsequent demise.

Also See the Following Articles

ARMS PRODUCTION, ECONOMICS OF • ARMS TRADE, ECONOMICS OF • CHEMICAL AND BIOLOGICAL WARFARE • COLD WAR • ECONOMIC CONVERSION • ECONOMICS OF

WAR AND PEACE, OVERVIEW • MILITARY DETERRENCE AND STATECRAFT • MILITARY-INDUSTRIAL COMPLEX, ORGANIZATION AND HISTORY • WARFARE, MODERN

Bibliography

Carnegie Commission on Science, Technology, and Government (1993). *Science, technology, and government for a changing world.* New York: Carnegie Commission.

Cohn, C. (1987). Sex and death in the rational world of defense intellectuals. *Signs, 12,* 687–718.

van Creveld, M. (1991). *The transformation of war.* New York: The Free Press.

Enloe, C. (1983). *Does khaki become you? The militarization of women's lives.* Boston: South End Press.

Gottlieb, S. (1997). *Defense addiction.* Boulder, CO: Westview Press.

Hiro, D. (1992). *Desert Shield to Desert Storm: The second gulf war.* New York: Routledge.

Hooks, G., & McLauchlan, G. (1992). The institutional foundation of warmaking: Three eras of U.S. warmaking, 1939–1989. *Theory and Society, 21,* 757–788.

Kaldor, M. (1981). *The baroque arsenal.* New York: Hill and Wang.

Kellner, D. (1992). *The Persian Gulf TV War.* Boulder, CO: Westview Press.

Kennedy, P. (1987). *The rise and fall of the Great Powers: Economic change and military conflict from 1500 to 2000.* New York: Random House.

Klare, M. (1991). The Pentagon's new paradigm. In M. L. Sifry & C. Cerf (Eds.), *The Gulf War reader* (pp. 466–476). New York: Random House.

Klare, M. (Ed.) (1997). East Asia's arms races. *Bulletin of the Atomic Scientists, 53*(1), 18–61.

Mann, M. (1988). *States, war, and capitalism.* New York: Basil Blackwell.

Markusen, A., & Yudken, J. (1992). *Dismantling the Cold War economy.* New York: Basic.

Melman, S. (1974). *The permanent war economy: American capitalism in decline.* New York: Simon and Schuster.

Shaw, M. (1991). *Post-military society.* Philadelphia: Temple University Press.

Sivard, R. L. (1996). *World military and social expenditures.* Washington, DC: World Priorities.

Thompson, E. P. (Ed.) (1982). *Exterminism and Cold War.* London: Verso.

U.S. Office of Technology Assessment (1993). *Defense Conversion: Redirecting R&D.* Washington, DC: Government Printing Office.

Walker, G. B., Bella, D. A., & Sprecher, S. J. (Eds.) (1992). *The military–industrial complex: Eisenhower's warning three decades later.* New York: Peter Lang.

Zuckerman, L. (1987). *Star Wars in a nuclear world.* New York: Vintage.

Military-Industrial Complex, Organization and History

Gregory Hooks

Washington State University

GLOSSARY

Industrialism The systematic production of goods, typically involving the mechanization of production in factory settings.

Logistics Transportation and supply of military forces.

Militarism The maintenance of armed forces, emphasis on weapons development and production, and threatening armed aggression.

Military-Industrial Complex The network of military agencies and production firms (including private and public concerns) involved in the development and production of armaments. When a military-industrial complex is large and well-established, selected legislators, communities, unions, businesses, and scientists depend on the MIC and actively support it.

Strategy Planning and implementation the large-scale and long-term aspects of a military campaign.

Tactics Planning the immediate and short-term aspects of a military effort.

THE MILITARY-INDUSTRIAL COMPLEX has never been a neutral term. Dwight Eisenhower coined the term "military-industrial complex" (hereafter, MIC) in 1961 during his farewell address to warn the nation of a looming danger. The threat to democracy has been a recurrent theme in the many studies of the MIC since Eisenhower's warning, including works by Gordon Adams, Sydney Lens, Ann Markusen and Joel Yudken, and Seymour Melman. At a descriptive level, the MIC refers to military agencies and firms that produce military goods. In addition a number of political and economic actors are also dependent on the defense program and are included in the MIC, including legislators, workers, and businesses that serve and depend upon the military market. Although the term was coined with specific reference to the United States, it has been extended to identify industrialized military establishments in other times and places. This essay will describe the firms, agencies and institutions that comprise the MIC and will consider the dangers posed by this concentration of economic and military power.

When warning the nation of the threat posed by the MIC, Dwight Eisenhower stressed the unprecedented concentration of economic and military resources:

Our military organization today bears little relation to that known by any of my predecessors in peacetime, or indeed by the fighting men of World War II and Korea.... Until the latest of our world conflicts, the United States had no armaments industry. American makers of plowshares could,

Copyright © 1999 by Academic Press.
All rights of reproduction in any form reserved.

with time and as required, make swords as well. But now we can no longer risk emergency improvisation of national defense; we have been compelled to create a permanent armaments industry of vast proportions.... We annually spend on military security more than net income of all United States corporations.... The conjunction of an immense Military Establishment and large arms industry is new in the American experience. The total influence—economic, political, even spiritual—is felt in every city, every statehouse, every office of the Federal Government.

In the councils of government we must guard against the acquisition of unwarranted influence whether sought or unsought, by the military-industrial complex. The potential for the disastrous rise of misplaced power exists and will persist. We must never let the weight of this combination endanger our liberties or democratic processes. We should take nothing for granted. Only an alert and knowledgeable citizenry can compel the proper meshing of the huge industrial and military machinery of defense with our peaceful methods and goals so that security and liberty may prosper together (Eisenhower [1961] 1992, p. 364).

In the broadest sense, the military-industrial complex describes a wide variety of military establishments in the industrial and postindustrial eras. The fusion of militarism and industrial production was evident shortly after the Industrial Revolution made possible the mass production of weapons and military transport. This article stresses a more precise and narrow use of the term and examines a small handful of instances in which the MIC was prominent. The following cases shall be highlighted: the pre-World War I arms race between Germany and the United Kingdom, on a temporary basis the industrialized belligerents of World War I and World War II, interwar Germany and Japan, and the postwar United States and Union of the Soviet Socialist Republic. The global wars of the 20th century and the postwar US-USSR arms race provide the clearest and most developed MICs. In the decades since Eisenhower's 1961 speech, the MIC in both nations has declined dramatically. The Soviet Union has disintegrated—in large part because its economy could not sustain such an enormous MIC. In the United States, the reliance on nuclear weapons from the 1970s onward and the investment in technologically advanced weaponry has decreased the industrial content of the U.S. military. Even as the United States has maintained

global military leadership, the military has shifted away from a mass industrialized military and toward a postindustrial and information-intensive military organization.

I. THE FUSION OF MILITARISM AND INDUSTRIALISM, 1830–1914

William McNeill dates the fusion of militarism and industrialism to 1840, shortly after the Industrial Revolution transformed economic activity. The Industrial Revolution was neither set in motion, nor did military leaders control it. However, as industrialization gained momentum in Europe and North America, military leaders quickly recognized the threats and exploited the opportunities. At the dawn of the industrial era (ca. 1830), the differences between civilian and military transport were quite modest. On the land, the military traveled on foot, by horseback, or by horse-drawn carriage. On the sea, civilians and sailors relied on wooden boats propelled by the wind. Other than optical telegraphy (flags, etc.) there was little in the way of a distinctly militaristic means of communication. The sharpest distinction between military and civilian sectors was in the area of weapons and ammunition. However, the metallurgy and chemical processing required to produce the soldiers' firearms and ammunition differed only modestly from practices employed to produce civilian goods.

The Industrial Revolution induced two important changes in military strategy. During the Napoleonic era, the largest military forces were less than a million troops, and battlefields extended over several kilometers at most. Military leaders harnessed new sources of energy to facilitate transportation (i.e., steam-powered trains and ships) and new means of communication (i.e., the telegraph). These improvements enabled military leaders to deploy millions of troops across battle lines many kilometers in width. These improvements in logistics did not require a distinctly militarized industrial sector, only the military's ability to commandeer commercial goods to feed, clothe, and transport significantly larger military forces. Martin van Creveld makes the case that industrialism also gave rise to the invention of uniquely military end-items and the emergence of large industrial concerns (including defense firms and state-owned armories and shipyards) to produce them.

The U.S. Civil War was one of the first conflicts to reflect the industrialization of warmaking. The North and even the less industrialized South sent millions of troops to frontlines that spanned nearly half of the

North American continent and kept these large armies supplied with food and fiber for many months. On the sea, the North and South deployed (in small numbers) "ironclad" warships that could only be used for war. These steam-powered ships were wrapped in iron and quite compromised for transport. However, as warships, they could not be harmed by existing cannons and could attack wooden sailing ships with impunity. On the land, the North and South supplied troops with arms of unprecedented quality and abundant ammunition. The consequence was a sustained slaughter for several years and a casualty rate that surpassed all previous wars. When compared to the horrors of the mass industrial wars of the 20th century it is easy to lose sight of the bloodiness of this Civil War. For contemporaries, the Civil War was surprisingly destructive and violent, its dynamics unprecedented.

While the Civil War was the most prolonged and bloody, the Crimean War (1854–1856) and the Prussian success against Austria (1866) and France (1870–1871) provided compelling evidence to the European powers that industrialism had transformed war. While the artillery, rifles, and ammunition employed in the Crimean War displayed modest improvements attributable to industrialization, the major innovations occurred in logistics. France and Britain took advantage of improved water-borne transportation to supply its forces in the Black Sea. However, due to the underdevelopment of the Russian overland transportation system (i.e., bad roads and few railroads), Russian troops on the northern shore of the Black Sea lacked munitions to fend off the British and French. As a consequence, a small expeditionary force defeated Russian troops fighting on their home soil. The Prussian military was quick to adapt its military strategy to accommodate industrial innovation. In its Austrian campaign (1866), Prussia used trains to facilitate its advance and strung telegraph wire to maintain communication with its advancing forces. While the communications infrastructure was neither robust nor secure, the Prussian high command retained an unprecedented control over a large and dispersed force during this campaign. Several years later, in the Franco-Prussian War, both nations harnessed telegraph and railroads to improve supply. But the victorious Prussian army had also adapted its use of weapons, force training, and battlefield tactics to overwhelm its enemy.

European nations had colonized and subjugated the peoples of America, Asia, and Africa in the centuries preceding the Industrial Revolution. In 1776, Adam Smith recognized the threat posed to less-developed nations by the accumulating economic advantages of the European powers. "In modern war the great expense of firearms gives an evident advantage to the nation which can best afford that expense; and consequently to an opulent and civilized over a poor and barbarous nation. In ancient times the opulent and civilized found it difficult to defend themselves against poor and barbarous nations. In modern times the poor and barbarous nations find it difficult to defend themselves against the opulent and civilized" (Smith, in Milward, 1977: 55). As Smith anticipated, the leap in logistics and firepower made possible by industrialism accelerated imperial conquest in the 19th century.

Thus, from the 1840s onward, far more dramatically than in any earlier age, Europeans' near monopoly of strategic communication and transportation, together with rapidly evolving weaponry that remained always far in advance of anything local fighting men could lay hands on, made imperial expansion cheap—so cheap that the famous phrase to the effect that Britain acquired its empire in a fit of absence of mind is a caricature rather than a falsehood (McNeill, 1982: 258).

A similar dynamic was at work in the U.S. case. The editors of *Fortune* (in Mills 1956: 177n) pointed out that between 1776 and 1935, the U.S. "filched more square miles of the earth by sheer military conquest than any army in the world, except only that of Great Britain. And as between Great Britain and the U.S. it has been a close race, Britain having conquered something over 3,500,000 square miles since that date, and the U.S. (if one includes wresting the Louisiana Purchase from the Indians) something over 3,100,000." But the United States did not create a military-industrial complex to conquer North America. In fact, the United States retained a surprisingly small professional army and spent relatively little on national security. Rather, settlers and loosely organized militias led the conquest of the American frontier. The "technical and numerical superiority of the American frontiersman who confronted the American Indian made it unnecessary for a true warrior stratum and a large, disciplined administration of violence to emerge" (Mills, 1956: 178).

Japan recognized the strategic danger posed by economic backwardness and responded with a state-led (in large measure military-led) and top-down industrialization program. The modern Japanese state was born on January 3, 1868, when the Meiji Restoration was proclaimed. The Japanese state played a direct and prominent role in amassing and allocating capital to infrastructural projects and industrial activity. The Japanese state extracted heavy taxes from peasants, suppressed consumption in rural areas, and promoted the investment of capital that landlords amassed through rents. Large-scale industrial projects were created with government capital and imported technology. Nineteenth century Russia provides another example of a nation that undertook a top-down industrialization program in an effort to compete with industrialized European nations. Despite the military's heavy involvement in Japan and Russia, neither nation created an MIC in the strict sense of the word. Rather, Russia and Japan spurred the development of basic heavy industries (e.g., mining, steel and iron, etc.). While a relatively large share was consumed by the military, these efforts concentrated on building the infrastructure and commercial industries needed to sustain and transport modern military forces. Only after a sufficiently large industrial base had been created (Japan and Germany in the 1930s and the USSR after World War II, see below) would these nations maintain a MIC in the strict sense of the word.

One of the legacies of industrialization for warmaking has been the emergence of arms races. The first arms race occurred during the decades immediately preceding World War I and pitted the United Kingdom against Germany. In the course of this arms race, Germany and the United Kingdom created the first military-industrial complexes. The newly united Germany challenged the reigning (if declining) international leader in industrial production and world diplomacy. Closer to home, the United Kingdom and Germany shared the North Sea and directly threatened the naval security of one another. This competition took the form of a naval arms race in which these nations competed to make battleships that were larger, protected by more effective armor, and equipped with more formidable weapons. This arms race foreshadowed many of the dynamics that would characterize the post-World War II competition between the United States and the Soviet Union. An unprecedented portion of each nation's national product was diverted to the development and deployment of spectacular weapons, the profits and employment provided by the arms race politicized military procurement, and glamorous and technologically innovative firms grew dramatically by virtue of this arms race (Krupp in Germany and Vickers and Elswick in the United Kingdom). The economic and political repercussions are not the only dimensions of the post-World War II arms race that the U.K.-German competition foreshadowed. When all systems worked, these ships were quite formidable. However, because they integrated a number of emerging technologies, they frequently did not work and maintenance costs were high in the best of circumstances. Worse still, neither nation could afford to lose the visible symbols of naval strength—a risk that grew dramatically with the development of torpedoes, submarines, and mines. As such, these warships spent much time in port and diverted key resources to their protection when they were on the open sea. Thus, as Mary Kaldor has observed, the industrial era ushered in a unique irrationality: baroque weapons consumed enormous resources for little gain, but neither nation could resist the competition.

II. MASS INDUSTRIAL WARFARE, 1914–1945

During World Wars I and II, the industrial capacity of leading economic powers was harnessed to perpetrate an unprecedented slaughter of soldiers and civilians. This industrialization of warfare transformed the battlefield and military organization. Equally important was the social organization—bureaucracy, social control and infrastructure development—that was characteristic of industrialized societies and concentrated on waging war. In dramatic fashion, these mass industrial wars transformed the risks, the role, and casualty rates among civilians. Nation states conscripted millions of soldiers and regimented civilian life to focus the entire nation's efforts to wage war.

A. World War I

The character of World War I was stamped by the means of transportation and communication. The development and density of railroads and telegraph in Europe enabled belligerent nations to amass, equip, and coordinate enormous armies along a front that extended over hundreds of kilometers. However, from the nearest railhead to the front lines, horse-drawn wagons transported the necessary goods. The inflexibility of rail transportation and delays in building new track made it difficult to supply troops once they had broken through the enemy's lines. In contrast, it was relatively easy to supply stationary troops, and retreating armies could destroy the rail lines needed to supply the advancing enemy army. Trenches could be reinforced and stationary troops were supplied with a seemingly endless supply of ammunition. The extraordinarily bloody trench warfare that marked World War I was in large measure the result of the industrial character of the war and the limitations of currently available transportation technologies.

Society's role was redefined in this protracted mass war. Belligerent nations hurled a large portion of the national product across the no-man's land that stood between the mass armies. Some World War I battlefields are still sterile 8 decades later due to the trauma of war and toxicity of the weapons employed. Nations unable to sustain this continued diversion of industrial output could not compete. The Russian army's effectiveness declined precipitously in 1915 and 1916 due to its inability to supply a mass industrialized military force—months before the Bolshevik leaders formally withdrew from the war. For Germany, the entry of the United States into the war spelled disaster. More important than its introduction of fresh troops along the western front, the United States was the world's leading producer of many of the most important industrial products and could readily supply Allied forces with the means of war.

B. The Interwar Years

Given the centrality of industrial products and technological development, it should come as no surprise that this era of mass industrial wars spawned military-industrial complexes, that is, interwar Japan and Germany. By virtually any measure, Nazi Germany was more militarized than its neighbors. The impression that Nazi Germany was consumed by the preparation for war "was strengthened by the outward appearance of the state, monolithic, militaristic, nationalistic, bellicose, and apparently, highly efficient" (Milward, 1977: 24). Despite the strength of this impression and the very real military buildup, the Nazi regime undertook a large and diverse public investment program, including roads, infrastructure, and so on. Until 1938, civilian investments exceeded the military efforts in Nazi Germany. (Milward discusses the difficulty of reliably distinguishing between military and civilian given the commitment to total industrialized war. For example, building roads did not merely assist the civilian infrastructure, it facilitated the transport of troops and munitions. Milward's assertion that civilian investments exceeded military investments until 1938 is based upon the definition of military spending employed in the United Kingdom and the United States.) As would be the case with military spending in the postwar United States, Nazi Germany's large public spending program (military and civilian) stimulated the economy and reduced unemployment.

In a narrow sense, Blitzkrieg refers to a highly mobile and mechanized attack designed to overwhelm the enemy in a short period of time. This battlefield strategy

was developed to compensate for Germany's acute economic and industrial disadvantages. The decisive victories promised by Blitzkrieg offered an avenue for Germany to defeat its many enemies despite its compromised access to raw materials and limited ability to produce industrial goods. To succeed, Blitzkrieg required ample ammunition and weaponry for a brief and violent campaign, but did not need to sustain a large force for a prolonged campaign. Nazi Germany built a military-industrial complex to supply the weapons, ammunition, and transportation equipment to wage Blitzkrieg-style warfare. From the mid-1930s on, defense-oriented firms received large orders and worked steadily to supply the German military. After Blitzkrieg stalled on the outskirts of Moscow in 1942, Germany was obliged to fight a war of industrial attrition. By 1944, the military effort consumed more than half of the national product and 40% of all industrial output was consumed.

While it was possible to exaggerate the militarization of the German economy, this error is less likely for interwar Japan. During the 1920s and 1930s, Japanese military leaders grew increasingly hostile to civilian control of the government and economy. These sentiments within the military, particularly among junior officers, were so strong that radical militarists committed a number of antiestablishment acts, including the assassination in 1932 of a finance minister, the chairman of the board of the Mitsui Holding Company, and a prime minister. The apex of direct military control was reached in 1941 and 1942, during the same period that Japanese imperialist expansion appeared to be succeeding. Japan tried to compensate for limited access to raw materials and its relatively small industrial base by regimenting the entire economy in pursuit of war production. Because the Japanese economy was relatively small and its commitment to militarism was resolute, military production played a disproportionate role in the Japanese economy. In 1932, military spending accounted for approximately 7% of the Japanese GNP. This share of the GNP had doubled by 1937 and surpassed 17% in 1938. Moreover the military consumed over half of all state spending after 1938. The Japanese military-industrial complex permeated every aspect of Japanese life and every political and social institution—including the large and diversified holding companies (i.e., zaibatsu) that dominated the economy.

C. World War II

World War I imposed significant hardships on civilians and greatly expanded the risk of conscription, injury, and death. Whereas reliance on rail transportation kept World War I battlefields stagnant and contained, the wide use of internal combustion vehicles during World War II enabled troops to travel on and off roads throughout expansive war zones. As such, millions of civilians were displaced or caught in a deadly crossfire. Improvements in aircraft magnified these risks. Because World War II was a war of total industrial mobilization, industrial targets in densely populated areas became prominent targets. Large portions of London and several Soviet cities (most notably Leningrad) were decimated by German attacks. As the tide turned in the favor of the Allies, German and Japanese cities were exposed to the dangers of the air war. Dresden and Tokyo were consumed in firestorms and Berlin was reduced to rubble. The war ended with the deployment of nuclear weapons that destroyed two Japanese cities. Martin Shaw points out that the risks to civilians were also expanded by the refinement of social organization. Improved record keeping and social control allowed states to identify, transport, incarcerate, and in some cases slaughter millions of civilians (with the Holocaust being the most spectacular example).

After World War II, the victorious allies were determined to eliminate the military threat posed by Germany and Japan. Much of the German industrial infrastructure had been destroyed in the course of the war, with the destruction of military production facilities being a high priority. After the war, Nazi politicians and high-ranking military officers were driven from public life (if not tried and executed for war crimes). In postwar Germany, rearmament and military production were sharply constrained by occupying powers, and the German military-industrial complex was dismantled. In Japan, the United States purged thousands of military officers and abolished the Imperial Army and Navy. But the United States did not dismantle the antidemocratic civilian agencies that had guided the war effort. In part, the insulation of the economic planning agencies was the result of last minute reorganization. "Bureaucrats were aware that their presurrender cooperation with militarists and zaibatsu interests constituted a threat to their continued hegemony. In the weeks before the occupation began officially, personnel records were destroyed, wholesale shifts of higher officials were made, and initial steps were taken to divorce administration from some of the most obvious features of aggressive imperialism" (SCAP in Johnson, 1982: 172–173). The postwar Ministry of International Trade and Industry (MITI) was a direct descendant of the wartime Munitions Ministry (in mission, personnel, and policies) and developed a statist (but not militarist) economic policy

during and after the occupation. In an effort to stabilize postwar Japan, the United States actively encouraged the economic planning undertaken by MITI in the late 1940s and early 1950.

III. THE APEX OF THE MILITARY-INDUSTRIAL COMPLEX, 1945–1989

The big victors—the United States and the USSR—systematically dismantled the military-industrial complexes maintained by Germany and Japan. They also built and maintained a large and diverse manufacturing complex devoted to the development and deployment of state-of-the-art weaponry. In competition around the globe and on a number of fronts, the United States and the Soviet Union harnessed the industrial capacity of their respective nations to build and maintain unprecedented military organizations. It was the sustained fusion of industrialism and militarism in the postwar United States that Dwight Eisenhower attempted to govern as President and about which he warned the American public as he left office.

A. The MIC in the Union of Soviet Socialist Republics

Despite its enormous size, the USSR's economy lagged behind its leading rivals. The authoritarian, often totalitarian, domestic policies are consistent with the pattern of coercive militarism in which a state relying on a smaller economy resorts to coercion to pursue geopolitical objectives. The Soviet Union diverted such a high level of resources to the military to be only nation to keep pace with Nazi Germany in the mid-1930s and was the only rival for the United States in the postwar years. Because the Soviet economy was smaller and less developed than its competitors, this commitment to military spending sharply curtailed the production of civilian goods, ensured a scarcity of physical and human capital in commercial sectors, and distorted the functioning of the entire political-economy.

Although Germany failed to conquer the USSR, it captured much of the European portion of the nation and destroyed much of the industrial infrastructure. Soviet planners moved essential industrial facilities to the east, protected from German attack by vast distances and a mountainous barrier. Throughout the war, central planners controlled the allocation of capital goods and raw materials. The hardships placed on the Soviet people were severe. When comparing 1944 to 1940, total national income was down, total industrial production had recovered to prewar levels, and agricultural production had been reduced by 50%. However, weapons production—that is, the output of the MIC—more than doubled.

Mary Kaldor observes that military organizations tend to be structured around a great historical watershed. The Great Patriotic War was the watershed that constrained decision making throughout the remaining years of the USSR. In the immediate postwar years, the Soviet Union was much weaker than the United States in virtually every economic and military measure. By overinvesting in the military, the Soviet Union closed (but did not overcome) this gap in the 1960s and 1970s. One of the most enduring and debilitating legacies of World War II was the underinvestment in commercial sectors and overreliance on centralized direction of economic decisions. The entrenched, powerful, and pervasive MIC repeatedly stymied Soviet economic reforms. In the early 1960s, Nikita Khrushchev complained: "I know from experience that the leaders of the armed forces can be very persistent in claiming their shares when it comes time to allocate funds. . . . I'm not denying that these men have a huge responsibility but the fact remains that the living standard of the country suffers when the budget is overloaded with allocations to unproductive branches of consumption. And today as yesterday, the most unproductive expenditures of all are made by the armed forces" (Khrushchev in Kaldor, 1981: 117). Throughout the Cold War—and across a wide array of indicators—the Soviet Union committed a disproportionate share of its limited resources to the military. In 1980, the military consumed: over 10% of the gross national product, 30 to 40% of the labor force, 15 to 25% of industrial output, 50% of durable goods, and one-third of all machine tools. Moreover, the Soviet MIC consumed the best human and physical capital, thereby depriving civilian sectors of essential prerequisites. Scholars accounting for the collapse of the USSR, for example Randall Collins and Clifford Gaddy, contend that the strain placed upon the Soviet state and economy by this overinvestment in military production played a direct role.

B. The MIC in the United States

Prior to World War II, U.S. national security was premised on isolationism and oriented toward protecting the nation's borders. While the Monroe Doctrine had long defined U.S. interests to extend throughout the Western Hemisphere, this had not required the United States to be concerned with the balance of power in Europe and Asia, nor did it necessitate ongoing military preparedness. By the end of the 1940s, the United States asserted that its national security was impacted by developments throughout the world, even when U.S. sovereignty was in no way threatened. The United States took a keen interest in the industrial and technological prowess of its potential enemies. The Axis powers and the Soviet Union posed a threat because they set out to build economies that could match the U.S.'s ability to produce munitions and deny the United States access to raw materials. Within months of Germany's surrender, President Truman expressed his concern that the westward expansion of the Soviet Union's control would leave the United States "isolated from our sources of supply and detached from our friends" (in Leffler, 1992: 13). The military-industrial complex was forged during the mobilization for World War II. The U.S. spent relatively little on the military in the 1930s compared to other nations, and the defense industries were relatively small in the prewar economy. From 1939 to 1941, even as the United States stayed out of the European war, political and military leaders concluded that the United States had no choice but to build up a mass industrial army. This required: an armada of vehicles to transport troops and wage war on the air, sea, and ground; a dramatic expansion in the production of ordnance goods; and the development of bureaucracies to coordinate armed force waging war on several continents. During World War II, the state extracted industrial products from an economy of unparalleled size. Defense spending represented more than 35% of the gross national product from 1943 to 1945 and more than 80% of federal discretionary spending. The all-out mobilization for World War II pushed the U.S. state beyond the mere extraction of resources. The federal government controlled the flow of strategic commodities, invested in a staggering portfolio of capital equipment and factories, and actively guided the production process. But this was not an omnipotent state coercing firms to participate. Rather, as Aaron Friedberg has documented, business leaders helped manage important state agencies and in that capacity ensured that leading firms were generously rewarded for their participation.

The 1950–1970 period marks the high point of the MIC in the United States. During this period, the industrial base of the military remained paramount and the United States committed very large outlays to maintain world supremacy. In large measure, the MIC was an enclave in the large U.S. economy. Defense firms and defense-oriented subsidiaries of diversified firms specialized in defense contracting, while civilian sectors of the economy were not directly impacted by the ongoing Cold War mobilization. In the MIC, cost plus contracting and an emphasis on performance over cost considerations and reliability were sustained by the unique institutions and business practices that prevailed in the defense sector.

Ann Markusen and Joel Yudken provide evidence that over time, a "wall of separation" grew between the defense and civilian sectors of the economy. Because the MIC in the United States constituted a smaller share of the economy than its Soviet counterpart, the MIC was less corrosive in the United States. Nevertheless, as Eisenhower had warned, the MIC did distort technological development and diverted scarce human and physical resources, especially in technologically demanding fields. A very large literature has documented the costs and the threats to democracy that are attributable to the MIC in the postwar United States; a sampling of this literature would include works by Gordon Adams, Sydney Lens, Ann Markusen and Joel Yudken, and Seymour Melman. Even as the large investments in the military proved costly at the national level, the MIC played a decisive role in the growth of new technologies, firms, and regions. The MIC is synonymous with the rapidly growing and lucrative aircraft sector and played a major role in the early growth of semiconductors and integrated circuits. Defense-oriented firms and diversified corporations that garnered defense contracts were among the fastest growing firms over this period—displacing civilian-oriented firms among the nation's largest corporations. In turn, the regions housing military bases and munitions factories grew rapidly.

IV. MILITARISM WITHOUT THE INDUSTRIAL COMPLEX

World War I and II were wars of industrial attrition that entailed total mobilizations, the diversion of enormous economic resources to war, and state-led economic planning on an unprecedented scale. No previous war entailed such a total mobilization—nor is it likely that the Great Powers will again mobilize in this fashion. Contemporary weapons of mass destruction such as nuclear weapons are extraordinarily destructive, but their production and use consume only a small share of the gross national product.

In both the United States and the Soviet Union, the MIC declined after 1970. For the Soviet Union, the overinvestment in the military (see above) was exacer-

bated by the war in Afghanistan and costly military and diplomatic commitments around the globe. The chronic fiscal strains on the state and the centrifugal tendencies among the republics contributed to the collapse of the Soviet Union—and with this collapse a dramatic reduction in the size and the scope of the military-industrial complex in successor states.

Even during the 1970s and the 1980s, the industrial content of warmaking was in decline for both of the superpowers. The weapons, tactics, and strategies placed less emphasis on industrial inputs while emphasizing science, capital, and information-intensive weapon systems. It is not the case that U.S. military spending has declined steadily since the early 1970s. In fact, the Reagan Administration secured an unprecedented peacetime increase in defense spending. However, this Reagan-era defense buildup was directed toward science-intensive initiatives such as the Strategic Defense Initiative and nuclear weapons production. This investment accelerated a shift away from a mass industrialized armed force and toward a highly science and capital-intensive military. Whereas a mass-industrial war requires the mobilization of millions of troops and the mass production of munitions to sustain these troops, postindustrial warfare requires much smaller force structures and far less industrial input. The irony and the danger of nuclear weapons is that they require a small portion of the gross national product to produce, are controlled by a small bureaucracy of professional soldiers, but could destroy enemies and the entire planet in a few hours. In contrast, mass industrial troops waging war over a number of years could not do comparable damage.

In the wake of the Vietnam War, U.S. military leaders confronted the delegitimation of the military, active resistance to conscription, and budget cuts throughout the 1970s. The United States responded by relying on a smaller all-volunteer military and greater reliance on nuclear weapons. Despite a shrinking total defense budget, the United States increased production of nuclear weapons at an exponential rate, developed customized explosives to alter the yield of radiation, and perfected new means to deliver weapons (especially cruise missiles). The military's shift toward a post-industrial force structure was well underway before the Soviet Union's collapse. With the end of the Cold War, U.S. troop strength and defense spending have declined significantly. Thus, the shrinking U.S. military of the late 1980s and 1990s is not merely a reaction to the end of the Cold War—it is part of a long-term trend toward a smaller, more science-intensive, and more lethal force structure.

In addition to nuclear weapons, chemical and biological weapons are also produced through sophisticated scientific processes and are therefore less dependent on an industrial complex in the traditional sense of the word. The new sensing, computing, and communication devices that are being assembled to create an electronic battlefield are transforming even the nominally conventional forces. In all of these endeavors, science-intensive weaponry is becoming more important while the number of troops and mass produced industrial goods play a declining role. The efforts to militarize space—for example, the Strategic Defense Initiative—constitute another dimension of this movement toward a more science and capital-intensive military force. If satellites capable of destroying moving missiles or stationary targets were deployed, highly automated weapons far removed from Earth would be at the center of the war and would pose the greatest threat to human life.

V. CONCLUSION

For most of the postwar era, critics of the military-industrial complex (including President Eisenhower) looked to the day in which it would shrink in size. For these critics the expansive MIC corroded democratic institutions and the civilian economy. Arguably, as the United States enters the post-Cold War era, the contraction of the MIC has begun. Although the United States spends far more on the military than any other nation and is the world's leading arms trader, military spending has declined since the Soviet Union's collapse. As of 1996, military spending (as a share of the nation's economy) was at a lower level than at any time since World War II, military bases were being closed, and a smaller share of the economy was devoted to producing weapons. The decline of the MIC must not be confused with a declining commitment to military dominance. At the dawn of the 21st century, military power no longer depends on mass-industrialized armies. Whereas earlier critics of the MIC equated its decline with a turn away from war, the shrinkage of the MIC has been accompanied by technological accomplishments that have made warfare still more lethal.

In the current context, few citizens are directly involved in war and (provided their nation is not attacked) few citizens make sacrifices when the nation goes to war. However, the elites who command the military are constantly preparing for short and (relatively) painless conventional wars (e.g., the Persian Gulf War) with lesser powers while managing an arsenal of weapons of mass destruction, including nuclear arms. Michael Mann refers to this bifurcation between the pacific experiences of the majority of citizens and the constant vigilance of the military bureaucracies as "spectator sport militarism." Although citizens have little direct experience with war, they watch televised reports of military engagements in which state-of-the-art weapon systems receive a great deal of attention. This is not the first time that Western nations have engaged in spectator sport militarism. In the 19th century, the European colonial conquests, and U.S. Indian Wars were in large measure spectator events. For the victorious nations, these wars posed little danger and imposed few costs on the vast majority of the population. But these wars were well publicized. Whereas industrialism provided the United States and European nations with a decisive advantage during the 19th century spectator sport wars, the deployment of science-intensive weaponry currently provides the United States and other leading military powers with a decisive military advantage.

Dwight Eisenhower worried that the MIC would permeate and corrode the social, political, and economic fabric of the United States. The shrinking MIC of the late 1980s and early 1990s has reduced this threat. The vast majority of the citizenry are mere spectators—not soldiers, while a small (relative to the size of the population) and volunteer force wages war. In similar fashion, a small number of defense-oriented corporations (and specialized subdivisions of diversified firms) produce complex weapon systems. While several of the defense firms are large, the overall size of the defense sector is modest, and a wall of separation insulates the military and civilian sectors. The threat posed by the current form of militarism is not the pervasive influence of an ever-expanding MIC—it is the callousness of being removed from war by a science-intensive military force. Citizens forced to make sacrifices, serve in mass industrial armies, and experience directly the horror of war often question the necessity of fighting. It is far more likely that citizens will cheer on technological marvels as they kill thousands of people and destroy cities and less likely that the citizenry will empathize with the suffering caused by this highly scientific and distant form of slaughter. In his warning, Eisenhower pointed out that "only an alert and knowledgeable citizenry" could check the undue influence of the military during an era of mass industrial warfare. In the current period, an alert and vigilant citizenry is confronted with a new challenge—to evaluate the moral foundations of war when citizens feel insulated from the horrors of war and waging war can be conducted as a spectator sport.

Also See the Following Articles

ARMS PRODUCTION, ECONOMICS OF • COLD WAR • MILITARISM • MILITARY DETERRENCE AND STATECRAFT • MILITARY-INDUSTRIAL COMPLEX, CONTEMPORARY SIGNIFICANCE • NUCLEAR WARFARE • WARFARE, STRATEGIES AND TACTICS OF • WARFARE, TRENDS IN • WEAPONRY, EVOLUTION OF • WORLD WAR I • WORLD WAR II

Bibliography

Adams, G. (1981). *The iron triangle.* New York: The Council on Economic Priorities.

Collins, R. (1995). Prediction in macrosociology: The case of the Soviet collapse. *American Journal of Sociology, 100,* 1552–1593.

Eisenhower, D. ([1961] 1992). President Eisenhower's farewell address to the nation. In G. Walker, D. Bella, and S. Sprecher (Eds.), *The military-industrial complex: Eisenhower's warning three decades later,* pp. 361–368. New York: Peter Lang.

Friedberg, A. (1992). Why didn't the United States become a garrison state? *International Security, 16,* 109–142.

Gaddy, C. G. (1996). *The price of the past: Russia's struggle with the legacy of a militarized economy.* Washington, DC: Brookings Institution.

Hooks, G. (1991). *Forging the military-industrial complex: World War II's battle of the potomac.* Chicago: University of Illinois Press.

Hooks, G., & McLauchlan, G. (1992). The institutional foundation of warmaking: three Eras of U.S. warmaking, 1939–1989. *Theory and Society, 21,* 757–788.

Johnson, C. A. (1982). *MITI and the Japanese miracle.* Stanford: Stanford University Press.

Kaldor, M. (1981). *The baroque arsenal.* New York: Hill and Wang.

Kennedy, P. (1987). *The rise and fall of great powers: Economic change and military conflict from 1500 to 2000.* New York: Random House.

Kolko, G. (1994). *Century of war: Politics, conflicts, and society since 1914.* New York: The New Press.

Leffler, M. (1992). *A preponderance of power: National security, the Truman Administration, and the Cold War.* Stanford, CA: Stanford University Press.

Lens, S. (1970). *The military-industrial complex.* Philadelphia: Pilgrim Press.

Mann, M. (1988). *States, war, and capitalism.* New York: Basil Blackwell.

Markusen, A., & Yudken, J. (1992). *Dismantling the Cold War economy.* New York: Basic Books.

McNeill, W. (1982). *The pursuit of power: Technology, armed forces, and society since A.D. 1000.* Chicago: University of Chicago Press.

Melman, S. (1970). *Pentagon capitalism: The political economy of war.* New York: McGraw Hill.

Melman, S. (1985). *The permanent war economy: American capitalism in decline.* New York: Simon & Schuster.

Mills, C. W. (1956). *The power elite.* New York: Oxford University Press.

Milward, A. (1977). *War, economy and society, 1939–1945.* Berkeley: University of California Press.

Shaw, M. (1988). *The dialectics of war.* London: Pluto.

Skocpol, T. (1979). *States and social revolutions.* New York: Cambridge University Press.

Tilly, C. (1990). *Coercion, capital and European states.* AD 990–1990. New York: Basil Blackwell.

van Creveld, M. (1989). *Technology and war: From 2000 BC to the present.* New York: Free Press.

Minorities as Perpetrators and Victims of Crime

Marvin D. Free, Jr.

University of Wisconsin—Whitewater

GLOSSARY

Bias Crimes (or Hate Crimes) Defined by the U.S. government as crimes that are motivated by prejudicial attitudes related to one's race, religion, sexual preference, or ethnicity. Recently, disability has been added to this list.

Minority Group Any group whose members are singled out by the dominant group(s) for unequal treatment. In this article the term minority group is restricted to racial and ethnic groups.

National Crime Victimization Survey (NCVS) An annual survey by the Bureau of Justice Statistics that examines the victimization of a representative sample of individuals 12 years and over living in the United States.

Part I Crimes (or Index Crimes) Refers to eight crimes analyzed in the Uniform Crime Reports. The crimes are: murder and nonnegligent manslaughter, forcible rape, robbery, aggravated assault, burglary, larceny-theft, motor vehicle theft, and arson.

Part II Crimes The remaining 21 offenses contained in the Uniform Crime Reports.

Self-Reported Crimes Refers to offenses that respondents of surveys (questionnaires, interviews, or both) admit to having committed. Includes crimes not known to the police.

Uniform Crime Reports (UCR) Published by the FBI annually, this government publication contains data on selected crimes known by the police as well as persons arrested for those same crimes.

THIS ARTICLE examines the involvement of minorities in criminal activities in the United States. It further analyzes the disproportionate number of minorities in jails, prisons, and on death row. To better understand this relationship, both traditional and nontraditional views on race and crime are presented. There is also a discussion of minorities as victims of crime.

I. MINORITIES, CRIME, AND PUNISHMENT IN THE UNITED STATES

Any discussion of crime and minorities must proceed with caution as commonly used terms such as "crime" and "race" can have different meanings depending on

Copyright © 1999 by Academic Press.
All rights of reproduction in any form reserved.

the source of the information. For instance, the types of illegal behavior typically examined in self-report surveys are not necessarily comparable to the legal categories of crime employed by the FBI in its compilation of statistics for the Uniform Crime Reports. Moreover, the racial category "Black" is not used consistently in the research. Sometimes this term includes Black Hispanics; at other times, it is reserved for Blacks who are not of Hispanic origin. At all times it should be regarded as a *social* construct since a majority of African Americans have at least one White ancestor. With these caveats in place, let us now turn to self-reported data to see what relationship minority status has to criminal behavior.

A. Involvement in Crime According to Self-Reported Data

Self-report measures of crime typically suggest relatively few differences in the offending patterns of Whites and African Americans. (Whites are usually compared to Blacks [or non-Whites] because the number of other minority group members is commonly so small that it precludes any meaningful analysis of group differences.) According to a national survey of high school seniors in 1995, White youths were generally less likely than their African American counterparts to have engaged in delinquent activities during the previous year, though the differences were not especially large. For example, 86.4% of the White seniors had not "gotten into a serious fight in school or at work." The comparable figure for African American seniors was 82%. There were also few racial differences to the question asking if they had "used a knife or gun or some other thing (like a club) to get something from a person." Almost 98% of the White respondents answered "not at all" to this question compared to approximately 93% of the African American respondents.

Slight racial differences also emerge when examining property offenses. When asked if they had "taken something not belonging to you worth over $50," 91.6% of the White and 87.6% of the African American seniors responded with "not at all." Another item on the survey inquired about school vandalism. Whereas 85.7% of the White respondents indicated they had not "damaged school property on purpose," 87% of the African American respondents replied that they had not engaged in such activity.

Another self-report survey based on interviews with persons age 12 and over in randomly selected households reveals modest group differences in drug use in 1994. Some selected results of that survey appear in Table I. The table discloses that Whites are more likely than African Americans and Hispanics to have ever used alcohol, marijuana, and cocaine. However, African Americans are more likely than Whites and Hispanics to have reported using crack cocaine and heroin. Hispanics, on the other hand, are less likely than Whites to have ever used alcohol, marijuana, and cocaine, but only somewhat more likely than Whites to have ever used crack cocaine and heroin. Given the disproportionate number of minorities (particularly African Americans) arrested for drug offenses, the relatively minor differences in illicit drug use reported in this survey are largely unexpected.

B. Involvement in Crime According to Victimization Data

It is also possible to deduce the extent of minority involvement in crime through the use of victimization

TABLE I

Self-Reported Drug Use by Race and Ethnicity for 1994*

Race/ ethnicity	Alcohol		Marijuana		Cocaine (includes crack)		Crack cocaine		Heroin	
	Ever used	Used within last 30 days	Ever used	Used within last 30 days	Ever used	Used within last 30 days	Ever used	Used within last 30 days	Ever used	Used within past year
White	87.6%	56.7%	33.5%	4.8%	11.3%	0.5%	1.8%	0.2%	0.9%	0.1%
Black	73.9%	43.8%	27.5%	5.9%	7.8%	1.3%	3.3%	0.7%	1.5%	0.5%
Hispanic	76.2%	47.7%	21.6%	4.1%	8.1%	1.1%	1.9%	0.4%	1.1%	0.3%

* Based on interviews with persons age 12 and over in randomly selected households in the United States ($n = 17,809$).

Source: Tables 3.73, 3.74, and 3.77 in *Sourcebook of Criminal Justice Statistics—1995* (Kathleen Maguire and Ann L. Pastore [eds.], Washington, DC: U.S. Government Printing Office [1996]).

surveys that ask victims about the characteristics of their perpetrators. The National Crime Victimization Survey (NCVS), which analyzes a representative sample of American households, is the best known of these instruments. An analysis of the 1993 NCVS reveals some interesting results (see Table II).

An examination of crimes involving single offenders discloses that a majority of the crimes of violence included in the NCVS are committed by Whites. African Americans, by contrast, constitute only about one-fourth of the violent offenders, while "other" races (mainly Asian Pacific Islanders, and American Indian, Aleut, and Eskimo) comprise 8.4% of the violent offenders. To ascertain the meaning of these figures, however,

requires a comparison of these percentages with figures on the racial composition of the United States population. When this comparison is made it becomes apparent that since Whites constitute approximately 83% of the total population, the fact that 64.4% of all violent single offenders are White means that Whites are actually *under*represented in the data on violent offenders. Moreover, despite comprising 25.5% of all violent single offenders, African Americans are *over*represented as violent offenders given that they are only 12.5% of the total American population. Also disproportionately involved in violent crimes are "other" races (4.3% of the general U.S. population but 8.4% of the single violent offenders identified in the NCVS).

TABLE II

Perceived Race of Offenders for Violent Crimes Based on 1993 National Crime Victimization Survey

		Single-offender victimizations				
			Percent of single-offender victimizations			
	Number of victimizations			Perceived race of offender		
Type of crime		Total	White	Black	Other	Not known
Crimes of violence	8,175,570	100%	64.4%	25.5%	8.4%	1.8%
Completed violence	2,219,870	100%	59.0%	29.1%	9.7%	2.2%
Attempted/threatened violence	5,955,690	100%	66.4%	24.1%	7.9%	1.6%
Rape/sexual assault*	429,790	100%	69.2%	17.4%	9.1%	4.3%**
Robbery	641,100	100%	35.0%	49.3%	12.0%	3.8%**
Assault	7,104,670	100%	66.7%	23.8%	8.0%	1.4%
Aggravated assault	1,768,590	100%	59.8%	29.4%	8.5%	2.2%
Simple assault	5,336,080	100%	69.0%	22.0%	7.8%	1.2%

		Multiple-offender victimizations				
			Percent of multiple-offender victimizations			
	Number of victimizations			Perceived race of offenders		
Type of crime		Total	All White	All Black	All other	Mixed races	Not known
Crimes of violence	2,437,620	100%	40.3%	33.4%	12.0%	11.5%	2.8%
Completed violence	900,860	100%	31.2%	40.8%	14.1%	10.9%	2.9%**
Attempted/threatened violence	1,536,750	100%	45.7%	29.0%	10.8%	11.8%	2.7%
Rape/sexual assault*	50,790	100%	44.5%**	15.6%**	13.4%**	26.5%**	0.0%**
Robbery	619,270	100%	20.4%	54.0%	12.9%	10.7%	2.0%**
Assault	1,767,550	100%	47.2%	26.6%	11.7%	11.3%	3.2%
Aggravated assault	697,940	100%	43.6%	27.5%	13.7%	11.2%	4.0%
Simple assault	1,069,600	100%	49.6%	26.1%	10.3%	11.4%	2.6%

* Includes verbal threats of rape and threats of sexual assault.

** Estimate is based on about 10 or fewer sample cases.

Source: Tables 40 and 46 in *Criminal Victimization in the United States, 1993* (Craig A. Perkins, Patsy A. Klaus, Lisa D. Bastian, and Robyn L. Cohen, Washington, DC: U.S. Government Printing Office [1996]).

When examining the single-offender data by racial category some differences between Whites and African Americans emerge. Whites, for instance, are least likely to be involved in robbery and most likely to be involved in rape/sexual assault and simple assault. The results are reversed in the case of African Americans: rape/sexual assault and simple assault are the least common crime categories while robbery is the most common crime category for crimes involving a single offender.

Some additional findings appear when investigating violent crimes involving multiple offenders of the same race. First, proportionally more African Americans are offenders in violent crimes with multiple offenders (33.4%) than violent crimes with single offenders (25.5%). Further, while Whites (40.3%) are still more likely than their African American counterparts (33.4%) to be offenders in violent crimes with multiple offenders, the White/Black difference observed in violent crimes with single offenders is considerably diminished. Finally, "other" races are proportionally more likely to be offenders in violent crimes with multiple offenders (12%) than in violent crimes with single offenders (8.4%).

According to the NCVS, all-White multiple offenders are most commonly involved in simple assaults and least involved in robbery. For all-African-American multiple offenders the most and least common violent crimes are robbery and rape/sexual assault, respectively. Hence, the patterns reflected in violent crimes involving multiple offenders are similar to those observed in violent crimes involving single offenders.

C. Involvement in Crime According to the Uniform Crime Reports

The Uniform Crime Reports (UCR) represent a third way of obtaining data on minority crime. Published annually by the Federal Bureau of Investigation, these statistics rely on information provided by police departments across the United States. Typically, about 98% of all police departments furnish data on crime. The data are dichotomized into Part I (or index) offenses and Part II offenses. Part I offenses (murder and nonnegligent manslaughter, forcible rape, robbery, aggravated assault, burglary, larceny-theft, motor vehicle theft, and arson) are emphasized in the annual publication and are therefore discussed first in this article.

1. Arrest Statistics of Index Crimes

As depicted in Table III, Whites and African Americans are the racial groups most likely to be arrested for the eight index crimes. American Indian or Alaskan Native and Asian or Pacific Islander categories account for no more than 2% of all arrests for any of the offenses listed in the table. As a result, discussions of index crimes tend to focus on arrests of Whites and African Americans. When the analysis is restricted to these groups, the data show that African Americans are more likely than Whites to be arrested for murder and nonnegligent manslaughter and robbery, whereas Whites are more likely than African Americans to be arrested for forcible rape, aggravated assault, burglary, larceny-theft, motor vehicle theft, and arson.

TABLE III
Total Arrests for Index Crimes in 1995

Offense charged	Percent distribution			
	White	Black	American Indian or Alaskan Native	Asian or Pacific Islander
Murder/nonnegligent manslaughter	43.4	54.4	.8	1.4
Forcible rape	55.6	42.4	1.0	1.1
Robbery	38.7	59.5	.5	1.3
Aggravated assault	59.6	38.4	.9	1.1
Burglary	67.0	31.0	.9	1.1
Larceny-theft	64.8	32.4	1.1	1.6
Motor vehicle theft	58.5	38.3	1.2	2.0
Arson	74.2	23.7	1.0	1.0

Source: Table 43 in *Crime in the United States, 1995* (Federal Bureau of Investigation, Washington, DC: U.S. Government Printing Office [1996]).

Another way of approaching this data is to determine if Whites and African Americans are under- or overrepresented in the arrest statistics. Examined in this light one discovers that Whites are *under*represented for all crimes since no arrest figures are comparable to the distribution of Whites in the United States population (although arson at 74.2% comes close to the 83% figure for the White population). The antithesis is true for African Americans: African Americans are *over*represented in every crime category.

Disaggregating the data by racial group reveals that the type of offense one is arrested for varies along racial lines. Generally, Whites are more likely than African Americans to be arrested for property crimes, while African Americans are more likely than Whites to be arrested for crimes of violence. Whites, for example, are most likely to be arrested for arson, followed by burglary, larceny-theft, aggravated assault, motor vehicle theft, forcible rape, murder and nonnegligent manslaughter, and robbery. Thus, four of the five most common crime categories are property crimes. By comparison, in descending order, African Americans are likely to be arrested for robbery, murder and nonnegligent manslaughter, forcible rape, aggravated assault, motor vehicle theft, larceny-theft, burglary, and arson. A glance at this list discloses that the top four categories are all violent crimes.

2. Patterns of Criminality According to the Uniform Crime Reports

The data up to this point seem to indicate different offending patterns for Whites and African Americans and if one goes no further than an analysis of the index crimes it is tempting to conclude that Whites and African Americans do indeed engage in different criminal acts. However, this analysis is flawed in that the arrests for index crimes in 1995 represented only about *one-fifth* of all arrests for that year. Consequently, to obtain a more accurate measure of criminal activity one should examine arrest data for all 29 offenses reported in the UCR.

As displayed in Table IV, the 10 most common and 10 least common crimes based on arrests reveal considerable *similarity* in the offending patterns of Whites and African Americans. Although the rankings vary somewhat, 9 of the 10 most common crimes appear on the lists of both groups. The only apparent differences lie in the fact that liquor law violations are among the most common crimes for Whites but not among the most common crimes for African Americans, while robbery is one of the most common crimes for African Americans but not for Whites. When the least common

crimes based on arrests are examined, a similar picture emerges. Again, 9 of the 10 crime categories are shared by the two groups. Robbery, nonetheless, appears only on the list for Whites and curfew and loitering law violations appears only on the list for African Americans. Apart from these differences, the offending patterns are more similar than dissimilar.

Not addressed by the above analysis, though, is the possibility that racial differences in offending exist between White and African American juveniles. To evaluate this hypothesis the data are now limited to arrests of persons under the age of 18 (see Table V).

Comparisons between White and African American youth under the age of 18 reveal a continuation of the similarity in crime patterns noted earlier with a few exceptions. For the most common crimes based on arrests, the table shows that vandalism and liquor law violations are common only for White juveniles. Conversely, African American juveniles are more frequently arrested and charged with robbery and aggravated assault than their White counterparts.

Focusing on the 10 least common crimes based on arrests discloses even greater similarity between White and African American juveniles than found in the preceding analysis. Nine of the crime categories appear on both lists. The only discrepancies are that White juveniles are less likely than African American juveniles to be arrested for forcible rape, while African American juveniles are less likely than White juveniles to be arrested for driving under the influence.

What can one conclude from the UCR data? It appears that approaching the data from the standpoint of *overall* arrests demonstrates a greater similarity of offending patterns for Whites and African Americans than is typically observed when the analysis is restricted to index crimes. Yet, despite these similarities some differences do exist. Based on arrests, robbery continues to be a more significant crime for African Americans than for Whites, and African American juveniles are more likely than are White juveniles to be charged with aggravated assault. Hence, while the Black/White differences detected in index crime arrests are not corroborated by overall arrest statistics, the tendency toward somewhat greater involvement in violent crimes by African Americans receives some support.

D. Shortcomings of the Various Measures of Criminal Behavior

Few conclusive remarks can be made regarding the issue of minority involvement in crime because each of these three major measures of crime suffers from

TABLE IV

Most and Least Common Crimes for Whites and African Americans Based on Arrest Statistics for 1995

	10 most common crimes		
Offense charged	White arrests	Black arrests	Offense charged
1. Driving under the influence	880,635	421,346	1. Drug abuse violations
2. Larceny-theft*	753,868	377,143	2. Larceny-theft*
3. Drug abuse violations	709,704	338,038	3. Other assaults
4. Other assaults	613,098	196,919	4. Disorderly conduct
5. Drunkenness	425,514	167,857	5. Aggravated assault*
6. Disorderly conduct	352,965	110,920	6. Fraud
7. Liquor laws	345,127	110,839	7. Driving under the influence
8. Aggravated assault*	260,778	90,421	8. Burglary*
9. Fraud	204,473	86,608	9. Drunkenness
10. Burglary*	195,486	81,957	10. Robbery*

	10 least common crimes (excluding category "all other offenses [except traffic]")		
Offense charged	White arrests	Black arrests	Offense charged
1. Suspicion	4,697	3,543	1. Arson*
2. Murder/nonnegligent manslaughter*	7,245	3,840	2. Embezzlement
3. Embezzlement	7,529	4,302	3. Suspicion
4. Gambling	8,360	6,468	4. Gambling
5. Vagrancy	10,749	9,074	5. Murder/nonnegligent manslaughter*
6. Arson*	11,083	9,225	6. Vagrancy
7. Forcible rape*	14,739	11,234	7. Forcible rape*
8. Prostitution/commercialized vice	49,334	16,342	8. Sex offenses (except forcible rape and prostitution)
9. Robbery*	53,370	24,445	9. Curfew/loitering law violations
10. Sex offenses (except forcible rape and prostitution)	54,141	29,866	10. Prostitution/commercialized vice

* Indicates an index crime.

Source: Compiled from data in Table 43 in *Crime in the United States, 1995* (Federal Bureau of Investigation, Washington, DC: U.S. Government Printing Office [1996]).

various limitations. Criminologists generally agree, however, that UCR data tend to vastly underreport actual crime and that minorities tend to be disproportionately arrested for index crimes. There is also a consensus that UCR data exaggerate minority crime, although the extent to which this occurs is in dispute. Self-report surveys and victimization surveys are not without their faults either, and therefore have limited utility. To better understand this dilemma a brief discussion of the criticisms of the three methods is necessary.

Self-report surveys facilitate an understanding of criminal behavior as they include crimes unknown by the police. Yet, self-report surveys have their detractors, too. Until recently, an absence of national samples and an overemphasis on trivial offenses were major complaints. While there are still few national samples and the less serious offenses remain dominant in these surveys, some ameliorative action has been taken. Self-report surveys are also admonished for their preoccupation with youth crime since most self-report surveys have been administered to minors. Others point out that the crime categories used in the surveys do not correspond to legal categories of crime, making comparisons between self-reported crime and official measures of crime unwise. And finally, some criminologists argue that African American youth have a tendency to underreport their delinquent offenses, particularly the more serious ones. This issue takes on special importance to the researcher investigating minority offending.

Victimization surveys, like self-report surveys, disclose a considerable amount of undetected crime. Despite their usefulness as an alternative measure of crime, they too have several shortcomings. There is, for instance, the potential problem of selective recall when respondents are asked if they have been the victims of any crimes. Even if this problem is not evident, there is potential distortion when respondents choose not to answer truthfully. (This might occur if the respondent had been victimized while engaging in an illegal activity.) Further, some victims may not be cognizant of their victimization (e.g., in cases involving fraud and embezzlement). Critics also note the absence of some

major crimes, such as murder and kidnapping, where the victim is (for obvious reasons) not able to be questioned.

Perhaps of greatest concern is the representativeness of the sample: a nonrepresentative sample will yield biased results. The NCVS attempts to include people from diverse backgrounds, yet the people most at risk for criminal victimization (e.g., runaways, the homeless, etc.) tend to be underrepresented in these surveys. Thus, little is known about minorities found in these at risk groups.

The most severe criticisms, however, are usually reserved for the UCR. While the data from the UCR are used by many researchers and are extensively disseminated by the news media, the accuracy of these statistics

TABLE V

Most and Least Common Crimes for Whites and African Americans Under 18 Years of Age
Based on Arrest Statistics for 1995

	10 most common crimes		
Offense charged	White arrests	Black arrests	Offense charged
1. Larceny-theft*	271,234	102,854	1. Larceny-theft*
2. Runaways	145,904	57,389	2. Other assaults
3. Other assaults	100,988	50,952	3. Drug abuse violations
4. Drug abuse violations	93,721	45,093	4. Disorderly conduct
5. Curfew/loitering law violations	86,902	35,977	5. Runaways
6. Vandalism	83,238	26,799	6. Robbery*
7. Disorderly conduct	82,962	26,765	7. Aggravated assault*
8. Liquor laws	79,339	25,068	8. Burglary*
9. Burglary*	74,694	24,445	9. Curfew/loitering law violations
10. Motor vehicle theft*	36,238	23,864	10. Motor vehicle theft*

	10 least common crimes		
Offense charged	White arrests	Black arrests	Offense charged
1. Gambling	274	296	1. Suspicion
2. Embezzlement	616	310	2. Embezzlement
3. Prostitution/commercialized vice	664	349	3. Prostitution/commercialized vice
4. Murder/nonnegligent man-slaughter*	1,009	660	4. Driving under the influence
5. Suspicion	1,218	958	5. Vagrancy
6. Vagrancy	1,784	1,001	6. Gambling
7. Forcible rape*	2,250	1,252	7. Forgery and counterfeiting
8. Offenses against family and children	3,539	1,297	8. Offenses against family and children
9. Forgery and counterfeiting	5,208	1,429	9. Arson*
10. Arson*	6,216	1,477	10. Murder/nonnegligent manslaughter*

* Indicates an index crime.

Source: Compiled from data in Table 43 in *Crime in the United States, 1995* (Federal Bureau of Investigation, Washington, DC: U.S. Government Printing Office [1996]).

has been called into question by criminologists. Of relevance to minority crime are a number of issues. A frequent complaint concerns the types of crimes *excluded* from the Part I and Part II offenses. Most white-collar, corporate, and political crimes are ignored by the UCR. Because these are crimes in which the perpetrators are disproportionately White, their absence serves to overstate the relative involvement of African Americans in crime.

Another issue focuses on the differential clearance rates of property and violent crimes. There are considerably higher clearance rates for violent crimes (for which African Americans are more likely to be arrested) than for property crimes (for which Whites are more likely to be arrested). In 1995, 45% of the violent index crimes, but only 18% of the property index crimes, were cleared. Since a crime is typically cleared through an arrest, the disproportionately high arrest rates for African Americans reflect in part their somewhat greater involvement in crimes that are likely to receive the attention of the police.

Political pressure can additionally affect the accuracy of arrest statistics. To the extent that political pressure comes to bear on the police to enforce laws that differentially impact minorities, the statistics can distort the relative incidents of White and minority crime. This was especially evident in the mid-1980s when the War on Drugs focused on crack cocaine use and distribution, a topic to be discussed in a subsequent section of this article.

Citizen nonreporting further introduces bias into the UCR statistics. The case of rape is illustrative of this bias. It is estimated that perhaps 75% of all *completed rapes* in the United States go unreported. Additionally, White females of a completed rape are *less* likely than their African American counterparts to report the rape to the police. Since rape is typically an *intra*racial event (i.e., White perpetrators and White victims, African American perpetrators and African American victims), the underreporting of White completed rapes leads to the underreporting of White rapists.

At least two other issues are worthy of mention. First, it should be noted that African Americans and other minorities are disproportionately found in areas most closely patrolled by the police thereby increasing their likelihood of detection and arrest. A more troubling concern, though, is the frequent finding that African Americans are more likely than Whites to be arrested without sufficient evidence to support criminal charges. These two issues raise serious questions about the use of arrest data as a measure of minority criminality.

E. Disproportionate Incarceration of Minorities in the United States

The prison population has substantially expanded since 1980. An estimate of the 1994 total correctional population (including persons on probation or parole) by the Bureau of Justice Statistics places this figure at over 5 million. Of this number, approximately one million were in prison and almost half a million were in jail. The period from 1980 to 1994 witnessed a 178.7% increase in the estimated total correctional population, with the prison population growing by 210.3% and the jail population expanding by 165.4%. What these figures do not reveal, however, is the impact these incarceration trends have had on minorities, a topic covered in the following section.

1. Trends in Incarceration of Offenders

The relative impact of the incarceration explosion on minorities can be seen by disaggregating the figures by race and ethnicity. As of year-end 1994, the federal and state prison population was estimated to be 1,054,774. Of this number, 464,167 (44%) were classified as White, 501,672 (47.6%) were classified as Black, 9283 (.9%) were classified as American Indian or Alaskan Native, and 6005 (.6%) were classified as Asian or Pacific Islander. The race of 73,647 inmates (7%) was unknown. When ethnicity is considered, it is found that 14.9% of all state and federal prisoners are Hispanic (Hispanics account for 10% of the total U.S. population). Given the small percentage of American Indian/Alaskan Native and Asian/Pacific Islander inmates, these groups are not examined further.

An analysis of data from 1980 forward discloses a change in the racial and ethnic structure of the prison population. While African Americans in 1980 comprised 41.1% of the new court commitments to state and federal prisons, by 1988 virtually half (49.8%) of the new court commitments were Black. The following year saw this figure climb to 52.3% where it continues to hover today (52.5% of the new court commitments in 1993 were African American). Hispanics experienced increases during the same period as well. They represented 7.7% of the state and federal prison population in 1980; 10.9% in 1985, 13.3% in 1990 and, as mentioned earlier, 14.9% in 1994.

It can thus be concluded that the prison population commencing in the 1980s began to not only grow larger but also to change in other ways. African Americans became a majority of new admissions to state and federal penitentiaries. Moreover, Hispanic prisoners increased from 25,200 of the 1980 prison population to 156,908 of the 1994 prison population. Consequently, by 1994 approximately one of every seven state and federal inmates was Hispanic.

2. The Impact of the War on Drugs on the Minority Community

Escalation of the War on Drugs in the mid-1980s had a profound impact on minorities, especially on African Americans living in the inner city where much of the drug enforcement was concentrated. Because a national campaign to reduce the availability of crack cocaine (a cheaper form of cocaine that was more frequently used by African Americans than by Whites) focused on lower level street dealers and crack users who were more visible and consequently more easily arrested, the "typical" Black prisoner changed dramatically in a short period of time. As depicted in Table VI, the percentage of African Americans in state prisons in 1986 charged with drug offenses was virtually the same as their White counterparts (7% versus 8%). Within 5 years, however, African Americans were slightly over twice as likely as Whites to be incarcerated in state prisons on drug charges. And despite the concern of many Americans with what was perceived to be increasing violence, as a segment of the total African American state prison population, violent offenders declined by 12 percent during this 5-year period.

While the strict enforcement of drug laws has swelled the prison population of African Americans *and* Whites, the impact of drug enforcement continues to be disproportionately felt by minorities. An examination of new court commitments to state prisons in 1992 discloses

TABLE VI

Inmates in State Prisons for 1986 and 1991 by Race and Most Serious Offense

| | Percent of inmates | | | |
| | White | | African American | |
Most serious offense	1986	1991	1986	1991
Violent	50%	49%	59%	47%
Property	36%	30%	29%	22%
Drug	8%	12%	7%	25%
Public-order	6%	8%	4%	5%
Number	177,181	248,705	202,872	321,217

Source: Figure 4 in *Survey of State Prison Inmates, 1991* (U.S. Department of Justice, Washington, DC: Bureau of Justice Statistics [1993]).

that, although 30.4% of *all* new court commitments to state prisons were for drug offenses, the likelihood of incarceration on drug charges varied by race, with 21.6% of all Whites, 36.3% of all African Americans, and 15.3% of "other" races (i.e., American Indians, Alaska Natives, Asians, and Pacific Islanders) committed to state prisons on drug charges. Thus, African Americans are more likely than any other racial group to be incarcerated for drug offenses.

Ethnicity is also an important determinate of incarceration for drug law violations. Hispanics, a category that includes persons of all races, are disproportionately imprisoned for drug possession and/or trafficking. Of all Hispanics committed to state prisons in 1992, 41.3% were charged with drug offenses.

F. Capital Sentencing and American Minorities

In 1972 the U.S. Supreme Court temporarily invalidated capital punishment statutes in *Furman v. Georgia*. By 1976, however, the death penalty was reinstated in *Gregg v. Georgia*. Since the mid-1980s, there have been erratic increases in the numbers of persons executed under civil authority in the United States. Although from 1977 to 1983 only 11 prisoners had been executed, in 1984 alone there were 21 executions. In 1985 and 1986 the annual number of executions dropped to 18, but then rose to 25 in 1987. Since that time the number has fluctuated between 11 and 74, the latter figure reflecting the number of executions in 1997, the latest figure available as of the writing of this article. Nonetheless, despite these impressive numbers the death penalty is infrequently imposed. In 1991 only .5% of all White inmates in state prisons and .3% of all African American inmates in state prisons were sentenced to die.

As of year-end 1996, there are 3219 prisoners under sentence of death. Of that number 1820 (56.5%) are White, 1349 (41.9%) are African American, and 50 (1.6%) are other racial groups. There are 259 Hispanic inmates (8.8% of the inmates whose ethnicity is known) on Death Row. Of the 48 female inmates under sentence of death, 32 (two-thirds) are White and 16 (one-third) are African American. Thus, relative to their numbers in the general U.S. population, both male and female African Americans are overrepresented among prisoners awaiting execution in the United States.

African Americans are also disproportionately found among the persons executed under civil authority. From 1930 to 1995, 4172 persons were executed in the United States. Disaggregation of the data reveals that 1940 (46.5%) were White, 2187 (52.4%) were African American, and 45 (1.1%) were other races. African

Americans constituted approximately 40% of those executed in 1995.

Historically, the death penalty has been differentially applied to African American and White offenders. In the 1830s in Virginia, for instance, 70 offenses for Black slaves carried the death penalty compared to only 5 offenses for Whites. Moreover, African American victims have not been typically accorded the same protection as White victims. Investigating almost 16,000 executions in the United States since the 18th century, Radelet (1989) detected only 30 instances where a White offender was executed for a crime involving a Black victim.

One source of racial disparity in capital punishment was eliminated in 1977. In *Coker v. Georgia* the U.S. Supreme Court declared the death penalty for cases involving a nonlethal rape of an adult to be in violation of the Eighth Amendment. The significance of this decision can be seen by examining executions for rape: from 1930 to the early 1970s, almost 90% of those executed for rape were non-White.

An analysis of the literature on race and capital punishment suggests at least two conclusions. First, racial disparity in capital cases has been reduced through such Supreme Court decisions as *Furman*, *Gregg*, and *Coker*, although (a) White victims continue to receive greater protection under the law than their African American counterparts and (b) African Americans who victimize Whites are still more likely to receive death sentences than other offender-victim combinations. Second, despite the presence of racial disparity in capital cases, legally relevant variables (e.g., seriousness of the crime, prior record, etc.) are major determinants of decisions involving the death penalty.

II. ARRESTS AND INCARCERATION OF MINORITIES IN OTHER COUNTRIES

The overrepresentation of minorities in arrest statistics and inmate populations is not confined to the United States. While a paucity of reliable statistics makes comparisons among societies problematic, an analysis of data from selected countries reveals racial and ethnic disparities. In Britain 5.5% of the population is composed of minority groups, yet in 1995 in England and Wales minorities constituted 18% of the prison population. Afro Caribbeans (i.e., Blacks) made up the single largest minority group. While approximately 1.5% of Britain's population is Black, this minority group represented 12% of the inmates. Moreover, black females were more likely than black males to be incarcerated

(20% of the female inmates compared to 11% of the male inmates were Black). The "Chinese and other" category was also overrepresented among the prisoners. This group, although comprising 3% of all inmates, is only about 1% of the population of Britain. In contrast, South Asians (i.e., those of Indian, Pakistani, or Bangladeshi origin) are not overrepresented in the inmate population.

What accounts for the disproportionate number of Blacks in British prisons? A partial explanation is that many are foreign Black women who are incarcerated for the importation of illegal drugs and are serving long sentences. This explanation is incomplete nonetheless as racial disparity remains even after excluding foreign nationals. While only 1% of all British nationals between the ages of 15 to 64 are Black, Blacks make up 9% of the British national male prisoners and 12% of their female counterparts.

Despite the overrepresentation of Blacks in the criminal justice statistics in Britain, Blacks are not necessarily more likely than Whites to commit crime. A Home Office survey of self-reported crime published in 1995 found that (a) the rate of offending for Whites and Blacks ages 14 to 25 years of age was similar and (b) Black youths were less likely than were their White counterparts to use illegal drugs.

Various studies of Blacks in Britain suggest race is also a factor in other areas of criminal justice. Even when controlling for legally relevant variables research suggests that (a) young Afro Caribbean males are more likely than are White males to be stopped by the police; (b) young Afro Caribbeans are more likely than are comparable White offenders to be prosecuted; and (c) Afro Caribbean defendants are more likely than are their White counterparts to be remanded in custody.

Statistics from the Australian Institute of Criminology demonstrate the disproportionate involvement of minorities in the criminal justice system of that country. Aboriginal youths from 10 to 17 years of age in 1993 were 24.2 times more likely than their non-Aboriginal counterparts to be in custody. For Aboriginals 18 to 21 years of age the difference was 9.6 times greater. Further, in 1992 indigenous Australians were more likely than nonindigenous Australians to be incarcerated. The disparity ranged from approximately 4 times greater for indigenous Australians in Tasmania to more than 20 times greater for indigenous Australians in Western and South Australia. Moreover, the type of offense with which one is charged influences the disparity. Based on the most serious offense for those in prison, Aboriginals were 30 times more likely than non-Aboriginal people to be in prison for assaults, 16 times more likely to be incarcerated for breaking and entering, and 12 times more likely to be incarcerated for homicide.

Another country with disproportionate representation of minorities in the criminal justice system is Canada. Although only about 2% of the Canadian population is Native Indian and Inuit, this segment is overrepresented among identified and incarcerated offenders. Blacks are additionally disproportionately incarcerated in Canada. A 1995 report by the Commission on Systemic Racism in the Ontario Criminal Justice System noted that Black adults in that province were more than five times more likely than were White adults to be incarcerated. Further, Black Canadians were more likely than were White Canadians to be detained prior to trial and to receive a prison sentence if convicted of a drug offense. Black/White differences were especially pronounced in the latter as Blacks were almost twice as likely as Whites to be incarcerated if convicted of a crime involving illegal drugs.

As is evident from the nonrandom sample of countries analyzed in this section, minority populations are frequently overrepresented in official crime data. What is less clear, though, is the extent to which these disparities reflect bias in the criminal justice system processing of minorities versus actual differences in the offending patterns of minority and nonminority populations.

III. EXPLAINING THE RELATIONSHIP BETWEEN RACE AND CRIME

The disproportionate number of arrested and incarcerated African Americans has led to the development of theories to explain the relationship between race and crime. Although a complete analysis of these theories is impossible in an article of this length, some discussion of the theories is desirable. Following a succinct review of the more common explanations for this relationship is an overview of some alternative explanations that have been proposed.

A. Traditional Views on Race and Crime

1. Subculture of Violence Theory

One of the most popular interpretations of Black violence borrows from the subculture of violence thesis. Developed by Marvin Wolfgang and Franco Ferracuti in the 1960s, the theory argues that in certain segments of society (e.g., the inner city where many minorities reside) a subculture has emerged that is generally more supportive of the use of physical force in everyday social interactions than is the larger society. Although members of this subculture share some of the larger society's values, their greater reliance on physical force in their daily lives increases the likelihood of a violent confrontation. Moreover, according to the theory, rejection by the peer group can ensue if one chooses to ignore this mandate.

2. Strain Theories

Strain theories, such as Robert Merton's anomie theory, focus on the social structure as a determinant of deviant behavior. They note that strain can result from not having the adequate means to successfully attain the goals of one's society. Therefore, those segments of society (e.g., the lower class and minorities) having limited resources for reaching the goals of society (in particular, material wealth) are more likely to experience strain and to use illegitimate means to accomplish their objectives.

3. Other Theoretical Interpretations

Some theories have emphasized the role of deviant peers in the learning of delinquent and criminal behavior. Edwin Sutherland's differential association theory, for instance, attempts to explain the process through which individuals acquire the values and definitions necessary to engage in such activities. According to the theory, delinquent and criminal behavior is predominantly learned through interaction within intimate personal groups. It is in this arena that individuals acquire the skills, techniques, and rationalizations necessary to engage in the illegal behavior. Thus, since minorities are more likely than nonminorities to live in areas with higher concentrations of known delinquents and criminals, they should have more interaction with individuals subscribing to deviant value systems. The end result is an increase in involvement in illegal activities.

Another theory sometimes applied to minority crime is Travis Hirschi's social control theory. Unlike the earlier perspectives that aim to explain deviant behavior, social control theory attempts to explain why people *conform* to society's norms. The theory examines the effectiveness of social control mechanisms in inducing conformity. Generally, the weaker an individual's bond to conventional society, the freer that individual is to engage in criminal behavior when the opportunity arises. According to Flowers (1990):

> Under control theory, the high rate of minority crime can be attributed to a weaker attachment to social institutions such as schools or jobs, economic opportunity (as related to their dispropor-

tionate representation in the lower classes), and family (there is some indication that minorities have higher rates of broken homes and illegitimacy than whites) (p. 69).

Despite their widespread acceptance in criminology, traditional theories do have their detractors. Critics have alluded to the fact that these theories ignore the possibility that the laws themselves may be racially biased. The previous discussion of the War on Drug's focus on crack cocaine offenses offers an illustration of this potential problem. Another question not addressed by the traditional theories is the extent to which arrest statistics for minorities are a product of selective law enforcement by the police. It has been argued that the physical appearance of many minority youths corresponds to police officers' perceptions of a "typical" juvenile delinquent thereby increasing the likelihood of police intervention. Others contend that the assertive behavior of many young, male African Americans is misinterpreted by the police, thus contributing to the higher arrest rates of Black males.

Two additional criticisms warrant mention. The first of these focuses on the failure of traditional theories to acknowledge the potential for discrepancy in minority/White offending rates resulting from differential patrolling by the police. Because many minorities are lower class and thereby relegated to the areas of the city where police surveillance is greatest, any transgression of the legal code is more likely to come to the attention of the police than a similar incident occurring in other parts of the city or in suburban or rural areas. A final criticism of the theories comes from Coramae Richey Mann (1993, p. 103) who observes the irony "that so many of the explanations of minority crime focus on minority violence when American history is filled with violence, particularly as directed against its minority citizens."

To provide a somewhat different perspective on minority crime the next section examines nontraditional theories. While these theoretical perspectives are more commonly espoused by minorities, the following discussion will not be restricted to minority theorists.

B. Nontraditional Views on Race and Crime

1. W.E.B. DuBois's Early Explanation of African American Crime

Two of the earliest investigations of the relationship between crime and race were conducted by W.E.B. DuBois, the first African American to receive a doctorate at Harvard University. Two of his works (*The Philadelphia Negro: A Social Study* [1899] and *Notes on Negro Crime, Particularly in Georgia* [1904]) examine sociological factors affecting the Black crime rate. In particular, DuBois notes the impact of slavery and economic deprivation on Black criminality. His views represent a departure from the prevailing theories of that time, which focused on the presumed biological deficiencies of people of African descent.

2. Alvin Poussaint's Psychological-Political Perspective

This theory attempts to account for the high rate of reported Black-on-Black homicide through an examination of the political and psychological processes influencing such behavior. Taking the view that years of political oppression have led to psychological scarring in many impoverished African Americans, Poussaint contends that institutional racism, through its teachings of Blackness as a negative attribute, produces "despair, low self-esteem, self-hatred, and rage" (Poussaint, 1983: 165). This, in turn, spawns a lack of respect for the criminal justice system. It is this mixture that encourages a high homicide rate among African Americans. Poussaint, an African American psychiatrist, thus suggests a nexus between the political system and the psychological well being of African Americans.

3. Conflict Perspectives on Race and Crime

The conflict perspective assumes that society is characterized by conflict caused by the competition among various groups in society for the scarce and desirable commodities of their society. At least two of the alternative explanations employ this theoretical viewpoint.

a. Power-Threat Hypothesis

Hubert Blalock proposes a theory of social control that has implications for studies of minority crime. According to the hypothesis, the amount of social control is curvilinear to the visibility of the minority group. Hence, social control increases as the size of the minority group increases until that group reaches a numerical dominance, after which social control begins a descent. Applying this theory to the overrepresentation of minorities in crime data, one could argue that at least some of the disproportionality results from the increased surveillance of minorities as their numbers begin to pose a threat to the dominant group.

b. Internal Colonial Model

This model views African Americans and other minorities as being victims of social, economic, and political oppression. As a result minorities are likely to develop a sense of alienation that can manifest itself in several forms, including alienation from an individual's own group. Feelings of alienation, in turn, lead to three possible adaptive forms of behavior, one of which involves delinquency and crime. This theory thus tries to explain minority criminality by shifting the analysis from the individual who has committed the crime to the exploitative structural system in which the individual resides.

4. Other Nontraditional Explanations for Minority Crime

The last theories to be discussed use as a point of departure the subcultural theory of Wolfgang and Ferracuti. According to William Harvey's (1986) subculture of exasperation explanation the subculture of violence thesis as applied to Black homicide is inappropriate since violence is not the cause of the high homicide rates, but only symptomatic of the larger social-structural pattern of pathology. He contends that the combination of systemic factors (high unemployment, low status, and substandard living conditions) and emotional factors (frustration, anger, and powerlessness) increases the likelihood that violence will occur in the African American community. Institutionalized racism, consumption-oriented values, high unemployment, and the inability to vent hostility on those in power encourage many young African American males to express their aggression through illegal activities and exhibitions of "toughness." Because American society tends to be segregated along class and racial lines, young African American males come into frequent contact with others of similar status; hence, homicide is most likely to involve African Americans from the same social class.

Lynn Curtis argues for a contracultural explanation of Black violence. In his 1975 book, *Violence, Race, and Culture*, Curtis posits that two exogenous structural variables—structural economic constraints and structural racial constraints—are related to violent behavior. A third exogenous variable consists of violent stimuli from the dominant culture. The theory suggests that the contracultural system is maintained through the learning process involving experiences primarily within the Black urban ghetto.

Contemporary influences from the dominant culture (e.g., television and the accessibility of firearms) help to perpetuate violence among poor African American youth living in the inner city. This explanation of Black violence thus proposes that individuals can be simultaneously influenced by multiple cultural systems (the dominant culture, the violent contraculture, and the Black poverty subculture).

As with traditional explanations of race and crime, nontraditional explanations also have their shortcomings. A common problem is their inability to precisely measure concepts such as institutional racism and oppression thereby hindering any rigorous testing of the proposed relationships. Another limitation of many nontraditional theories stems from their assumption that these concepts are "causes" of criminal behavior. If these variables are in fact a primary reason for criminal behavior, then why aren't even more minorities involved in criminal lifestyles? It is very easy to forget that the vast majority of minority group members are law abiding citizens. Moreover, conflict perspectives tend to overemphasize those laws that differentially apply to minorities without acknowledging the benefits accruing to minorities from those same laws. For example, while the focus on crack cocaine has had a disproportionate impact on African American arrests and incarceration, it has also had the desirable outcome in some communities of reducing the amount of illegal drug trade and violence that may accompany drug trafficking.

IV. MINORITIES AS VICTIMS OF CRIME IN THE UNITED STATES

A. A Brief History of the Victimization of Minorities in the United States

Minority victimization is perhaps most clearly understood by examining the African American experience in the United States. Although the first Blacks to arrive in what is presently the United States were probably indentured servants (since English law contained no precedents for slavery), by the mid-1600s some colonies were acknowledging differences between White and Black servants. Eventually the status of the Black changed to that of slave.

The slave codes of the Southern states served to clarify the lowly status of the slave. Slave marriages were not legally sanctioned in the South, although the slaves themselves recognized marriage. Consequently, it was possible for a slave owner to break up slave marriages since they were not officially recognized by law. Also indicative of their low status was the prohibition against testifying against Whites in court. Because slaves could not testify against Whites, there were few legal remedies open to them. To better protect slaves from harsh treatment by their masters, South Carolina permitted the use of a slave's body or corpse as *circumstantial* evidence of the abuse. Despite this provision, a master had virtual immunity from conviction since the law further stipulated the honoring of a master's oath of innocence. The legal distinction drawn between slaves and nonslaves is further revealed by the fact that the murder of a slave did not become a felony until 1821. Moreover, during the antebellum period the crime of rape did not apply to Black women.

After emancipation lynching became a common means of controlling the recently released slaves. Rapidly the state prison system replaced slavery in the South. It is estimated that shortly after the Civil War more than 95% of the Southern state prison population was Black. The convict lease system enabled the financially frail Southern governments to benefit monetarily from this incarceration.

Violence against African Americans continued into the 20th century. In 1917 in East Saint Louis, Illinois, 125 African Americans were massacred and burned by a mob of angry Whites. The summer of 1919 is referred to as the Red Summer due to extensive racial violence. From June to September a total of 25 race riots occurred. In Chicago alone 23 of the 38 persons killed were African American.

Disregard for the lives of African Americans is readily apparent in the Tuskegee Syphilis Study sponsored by the United States Public Heath Service (PHS). Beginning in 1932 almost 400 African American men with syphilis in impoverished Macon County, Alabama, were monitored to determine the progressive effects of untreated syphilis. The subjects were never informed that they had the disease (they were told that they had "bad blood") and even when penicillin was discovered, adequate treatment was denied. Only after a PHS investigator in San Francisco disclosed this ongoing project in 1972 did the unfavorable publicity lead to the termination of the project.

In 1991 the videotaped beating of African American motorist Rodney King exposed many Americans to the use of excessive force by the police, a "fact" long accepted as true by African Americans but dismissed as atypical by many White Americans. Later, the O. J. Simpson trial provided further documentation of police prejudice toward minorities when the racist remarks of Los Angeles Police Detective Mark Fuhrman became known.

Do the police single out African American suspects for differential treatment? While some research supports the view that African Americans are more likely than Whites to be arrested even after controlling for relevant variables, the evidence is inconclusive. In contrast, investigations of police use of force tend to show racial disparities in police shootings of civilians. The meaning of this disparity is somewhat unclear though as some investigators have argued that the disparity results from the greater involvement of African Americans in serious crime.

Although the focus of this section is on the victimization of African Americans, it would be erroneous to conclude that this is the only minority group receiving unequal treatment. For instance, the U.S. Supreme Court in *Johnson v. McIntosh* (1823) upheld the land claims of Whites who had "discovered" land on which Native Americans resided. Thirty-one years later the California Supreme Court ruled in favor of an earlier decision that prevented the Chinese from testifying in a court of law. The relocation of Japanese living in the western portion of the country during World War II serves as an additional reminder that other minorities have been singled out for differential treatment.

B. Minorities as Victims of Violence

Tables VII and VIII depict the rate of personal victimization for the year 1994. As Table VII demonstrates, African Americans are more likely than either Whites or other races to be victimized by violent crimes. When ethnicity is examined, the table discloses that Hispanics are more likely than non-Hispanics to become victims of crimes of violence.

An examination of victimization by type of violent crime reveals that, compared to the other racial categories, African Americans have the greatest probability of becoming victims of sexual assault, robbery, and aggravated assault, whereas Whites have the greatest likelihood of becoming victims of simple assault. When the data are disaggregated by ethnicity, ethnic differences emerge. Hispanics, like their African American counterparts, are more likely than non-Hispanics to be victims of sexual assault, robbery, and aggravated assault. The rate of victimization for simple assault is virtually the same for Hispanics and non-Hispanics.

Table VIII depicts the rate of personal victimization for Whites and African Americans dichotomized by gender. This breakdown enables us to see the interactive effect of race and gender on victimization rates. A perusal of this table suggests two conclusions. First, gender is an important determinant of victimization. The overall victimization rates for violent crime for White and African American females are *lower* than the rates for White and African American males. Second, despite the significance of gender, race is a substantial predictor of violent crime victimization. Although the overall violent crime victimization rates were lower for females

TABLE VII

Estimated Rate of Personal Victimization by Race and Ethnicity for 1994 (per 1000 persons age 12 and over)

		Type of crime						
		Crimes of violence						
Victim characteristics	All crime	All crimes of violence	Rape/ sexual assault	Robbery	Assault			Personal theft
					Total	Aggravated	Simple	
Race								
White	51.5	49.4	1.9	4.8	42.7	10.9	31.8	2.1
Black	65.4	61.8	2.7	14.0	45.0	16.6	28.4	3.6
Other	49.1	47.6	2.5*	9.0	36.1	11.9	24.2	1.6*
Ethnicity								
Hispanic	63.3	59.8	2.6	9.8	47.4	16.2	31.2	3.5
Non-Hispanic	51.9	49.8	2.0	5.6	42.1	11.1	31.0	2.1

* Estimate is based on about 10 or fewer sample cases.

Source: Table 3.2 in *Sourcebook of Criminal Justice Statistics—1995* (Kathleen Maguire and Ann L. Pastore [eds.], Washington, DC: U.S. Government Printing Office [1996]).

TABLE VIII

Estimated Rate of Personal Victimization by Race and Gender for 1994 (per 1000 persons age 12 and older)

| | Male | | Female | |
Type of crime	White	Black	White	Black
All personal crimes	60.4	71.7	43.1	60.1
Crimes of violence	58.6	68.5	40.7	56.2
Completed violence	14.2	29.3	13.0	20.7
Attempted/threatened violence	44.4	39.2	27.6	35.4
Rape/sexual assault*	0.2**	0.5**	3.5	4.5
Robbery	6.5	18.4	3.2	10.3
Assault	51.8	49.5	34.0	41.3
Aggravated	14.6	20.5	7.4	13.3
With injury	3.3	7.9	2.3	3.8
Threatened with weapon	11.2	12.6	5.1	9.6
Simple	37.2	29.0	26.6	27.9
With minor injury	7.5	6.2	6.5	6.5
Without injury	29.7	22.8	20.1	21.4
Purse snatching/pocket picking	1.8	3.2	2.4	3.9

* Includes verbal threats of rape and threats of sexual assault.

** Estimate is based on about 10 or fewer sample cases.

Source: Table 3.8 in *Sourcebook of Criminal Justice Statistics—1995* (Kathleen Maguire and Ann L. Pastore [eds.], Washington, DC: U.S. Government Printing Office [1996]).

than for males, *African American females* have almost as great a chance of becoming victims of violent crime as *White males* (56.2 per 1000 African American females versus 58.6 per 1000 White males). An analysis of individual violent crimes reveals the African American males are about twice as likely as White males to be victims of completed violence, almost three times as likely as White males to be victims of robbery, and over two times as likely as their White counterparts to be victims of aggravated assault involving injury. Similar racial differences are detected when analyzing African American and White females. In every violent crime category, except simple assault with minor injury where the rates are identical, African American females are at greater risk of victimization than are White females.

So far it is apparent that African Americans are generally more likely than Whites to be the victims of violence. But do the high victimization rates for African Americans reflect the higher rates of Black crime suggested in an earlier analysis, or do these rates indicate that African Americans are especially vulnerable to victimization by other groups? While some of the victimization is the result of bias crime (or hate crime), much of it appears to be the effect of living in areas where crime rates tend to be high and the perpetrators are frequently other African Americans.

Examining recent data on victim-offender characteristics reveals the intraracial nature of much violent crime. The National Crime Victimization Survey discussed earlier in this article provides an illuminating analysis of the race of the victim and the perceived race of the offender for single-offender victimizations. When crimes of violence are aggregated one finds that 73.8% of the White victims identified their perpetrators as White and 81.1% of the African American victims identified their perpetrators as African American. Further dividing the victimizations by type of violent crime discloses similar figures with the lone exception of robbery. While 87.7% of the African American victims were robbed by African Americans, only 44% of the White victims were robbed by Whites. Because the NCVS is unable to examine victims of murder, figures for this crime must be obtained from the Uniform Crime Reports. In 1994, according to the UCR, 94% of Black murder victims and 84% of White murder victims were killed by a single offender of the same race. These findings seem to corroborate the notion that much violent crime is Black on Black or White on White.

C. Minorities as Victims of Property Crimes

Returning to Table VII discloses, once again, the significance of race and ethnicity in criminal victimization. African Americans are more than 50% more likely than Whites to be victims of personal theft (3.6 per 1000 African Americans versus 2.1 per 1000 Whites). The difference between Hispanics and non-Hispanics is virtually the same (3.5 per 1000 Hispanics compared to 2.1 per 1000 non-Hispanics). Although the earlier disparity noted for violent crimes continues when property crimes are analyzed, the risk of personal theft is considerably less than the risk for violent crimes in general for all racial and ethnic categories appearing in the table.

Table VIII examines purse snatching/pocket picking by race and gender. When a comparison is made between African Americans and Whites while controlling for gender, the earlier racial difference resurfaces: African American males are more likely than White males to be victimized and African American females are more likely than their White counterparts to be victimized. When males and females are compared, however, an interesting finding appears: White males are the *least* likely of the four categories to be victims of this type of crime.

If the unit of analysis changes to households instead of individuals, racial and ethnic differences remain. NCVS data show substantial differences in victimization rates for property crimes based on the race of the head of the household. Whereas there was a rate of 314.8 property crimes per 1000 White households in 1993, the rate for Black households was 368.8. Racial dispari-

ties were particularly evident in the categories of household burglary (85.6 per 1000 Black households versus 56.6 per 1000 White households) and motor vehicle theft (33.7 per 1000 Black households versus 17.2 per 1000 White households). Although African American households were somewhat more likely than their White counterparts to be victimized by theft (249.6 compared to 241.0), the difference was not pronounced.

Ethnic differences are also found in the 1993 NCVS data. Overall, the property crime victimization rate for Hispanic households was 442.2 per 1000, compared to 313.2 per 1000 for non-Hispanic households. The Hispanic victimization rate for household burglary was about 50% larger than that for non-Hispanic households (87.1 per 1000 Hispanic households versus 57.9 per 1000 non-Hispanic households). For motor vehicle theft the magnitude of the difference was even greater: Hispanic households were twice as likely as non-Hispanic households to be victimized (36.8 per 1000 Hispanic households versus 18.4 per 1000 non-Hispanic households). Theft, numerically the most common of the property crimes analyzed in the survey, also exhibited ethnic disparity. Whereas 236.9 of every 1000 non-Hispanic households experienced a theft in 1993, 318.4 of every 1000 Hispanic households reported a theft.

D. Bias Crimes and Minorities

1. The Hate Crime Statistics Act of 1990

Bias crimes (also commonly referred to as ethnoviolence, ethnic intimidation, and hate crimes) have been present since earliest recorded history. Consider, for instance, the persecution of the Christians by the Romans or, more recently, the "ethnic cleansing" in Bosnia. The accumulation of data on such offenses, though, is of recent origin. In 1990 the Hate Crime Statistics Act was passed by Congress authorizing the collection of data on offenses that "manifest evidence of prejudice based upon race, religion, sexual orientation, or ethnicity." The crimes included in the Act are murder, nonnegligent manslaughter; forcible rape; aggravated and simple assault; intimidation; arson; and destruction, damage, or vandalism of property. Despite the attention given to the Hate Crime Statistics Act, the federal government was not the first to acknowledge the importance of bias crimes. Oregon in 1981 became the first state to pass bias crime statutes. Today only Nebraska and Wyoming lack such legislation.

The national collection of bias crime statistics has been hampered by the lack of a single accepted definition. As recently as 1993 the Federal definition of a bias crime had been adopted by less than a majority of the states. Further complicating the accumulation of national data is the problem of nonreporting by the states. In 1996 bias crime data was still not reported by five states. Additional problems include nonreporting by victims and the subjective assessment of motivation in crimes known to the police.

2. What Do the Data Tell Us about Bias Crimes?

The most frequent motive for bias crime is the race or ethnicity of the victim, with African Americans being the most common targets of bias crimes. According to recent FBI statistics, approximately 60% of bias crime incidents are motivated by racial bias and an additional 10% are the result of bias based on ethnicity or national origin. Religious bias and bias against sexual orientation account for 18 and 12%, respectively. Nonetheless, the percentage of hate crimes involving African American victims varies considerably from jurisdiction to jurisdiction. Phyllis Gerstenfeld (1994, p. 6) found, for instance, that the percentage of bias crimes involving Black victims varied from 22.8% to 53.1%. African Americans are also perpetrators of bias crimes. An examination of homicides by Klanwatch, a project of the Southern Poverty Law Center, revealed that from 1991 to 1993 African Americans accounted for 46% of the racially motivated homicides involving White, Asian, or Hispanic victims. In Gerstenfeld's previously mentioned study, which was not limited to homicide, the percentage of bias crime offenders who were Black ranged from 14.9 to 33.8%, depending on the jurisdiction.

Contrary to popular belief, organized hate groups, such as the Ku Klux Klan, Aryan Nations, and the Silent Brotherhood, do not account for the bulk of bias crimes. Actually, juveniles and young people are disproportionately likely to be perpetrators of bias crimes. Supportive evidence can be found in a 1990 Louis Harris poll of high school students. That survey showed that a majority of the respondents had observed a racial confrontation either "very often" or "once in a while."

Compared to nonbias crimes, hate crimes are more likely to involve physical assault and injuries. Another defining characteristic of bias crimes is the offender-victim relationship. Whereas many other offenses are committed by someone whom the victim knows, bias crimes are typically committed by strangers. An investigation of bias crimes in Boston, Massachusetts, for example, found that 85% of the bias crimes known to the police involved perpetrators who were strangers to their victims.

Despite the accumulation of data, it is still impossible to determine if bias crime is increasing or decreasing.

The data amassed by the FBI's Hate Crime Data Collection Program reveal that bias crime incidents increased from 1991 to 1993, decreased in 1994, and increased again in 1995 and 1996. What this means is unclear as the FBI bias crime figures contain data only on crimes known to the police and recorded as bias crimes. Moreover, as the number of participating law enforcement agencies reporting hate crime data increases, some growth in hate crime incidents is inevitable.

Typically, there has been a large gap between the data supplied by the police and that provided by various nongovernmental organizations. In 1994, for example, the Anti-Defamation League reported 2066 incidents of anti-Semitic bias crime while the FBI acknowledged only 908 anti-Semitic incidents for the year. The FBI in 1991 reported 209 bias crime incidents against Asian and Pacific Islanders. By contrast, the National Asian Pacific American Legal Consortium counted 452 incidents of bias crimes involving violence for the same year.

V. MINORITIES AS PERPETRATORS AND VICTIMS OF CRIME: WHAT DOES THE FUTURE HOLD?

While some disparity between minorities and nonminorities is undoubtedly the result of racial and ethnic discrimination in the juvenile and criminal justice systems, the actual impact is unknown. It is thus impossible to accurately predict whether the level of discrimination will increase, decrease, or stay the same over the foreseeable future. This factor notwithstanding, demographic data suggest that high official rates of minority criminal activity and victimization will likely continue.

One such statistic—place of residence—is particularly revealing. Living in the inner city contributes to official criminality in two ways: (1) it increases one's exposure to criminal activities and (2) it increases one's chance of being caught if one engages in any of these activities as a result of the greater police presence in the inner city. Yet, African Americans have been largely unable to escape this area of the city. Data from the U.S. Census Bureau disclose virtually no change in residency for African Americans. In 1980, 55.5% of all African Americans lived inside central cities; the 1994 figure was 56.1%. (The comparable figure for non-Hispanic Whites in 1994 was 22.5%.)

Age is another demographic variable correlated with delinquency and crime. Arrest data show that the typical offender is young. And minority populations in the

United States are generally younger than their White counterparts. Furthermore, Census Bureau forecasts reveal that these populations will remain younger than the White population. The Census Bureau estimates that the median age of the White population on July 1, 2010, will be 38.9 years. While the White population will be approaching its 40th birthday, African Americans will have a median age of 30.7 years and American Indians/Alaskan Natives will have a median age of 28.5 years. Moreover, Hispanics (who may be of any race) are projected to be the youngest of all (27.7 years old). Thus, the projections indicate that Whites will continue to age beyond the crime-prone years while minorities will remain comparatively young and therefore more likely to be involved in criminal activities.

Social class represents another variable that is closely associated with official crime. In part this is a function of the criminal justice system itself, which actively pursues crimes that are more likely to have been committed by members of the lower social classes. Consequently, white-collar crimes, which are more common among members from higher social classes, tend to go unacted upon. (It should additionally be noted that many white-collar crimes are *not* violations of the criminal code and thus fall under the jurisdiction of other enforcement agencies.) Whether or not the lower classes are actually more involved in crime than other classes remains a controversial subject; what cannot be debated is the fact that members of the lower classes are disproportionately arrested and incarcerated.

An examination of economic data reveals a continuing high level of African American poverty. In 1974, 26.9% of all African American families lived in poverty. By 1993, the percentage had climbed somewhat to 31.3%. Whites, however, had rates of 6.8 and 9.4%, respectively. Further evidence of stagnation in this area can be gleaned from an investigation of Black to White median household income for 1969 and 1993. This ratio has remained virtually unchanged (in 1969 the ratio was 0.60; in 1993 the ratio was 0.59).

Hispanics and American Indians are also disproportionately poor. In 1995, 27% of all Hispanic families were below the official poverty line established by the U.S. government. Even more disadvantaged are American Indian families where approximately half are officially impoverished.

Unemployment, an obvious barrier to upward mobility, is considerably higher for minorities than for non-minorities. The seasonally adjusted unemployment rate for the civilian labor force for June 1997 discloses that Hispanics and African Americans are more likely than Whites to be unemployed. For persons 16 years and older the unemployment rate is 4.2% for Whites, 7.6% for Hispanics, and 10.4% for African Americans. When the analysis is restricted to 16 to 19-year-olds and a comparison is made between Whites and Blacks, one finds that Black unemployment is more than twice that of Whites (32.7% for Blacks versus 14.5% for Whites). As long as these differences remain, one should expect to find crime more attractive to African American youth than to White youth. And since these racial disparities in unemployment rates have long been documented, there is little reason to anticipate a change in the near future.

Also relevant is the enforcement of drug legislation. As noted earlier, crack cocaine, which is more likely to be used by African Americans than by Whites, has been singled out for stringent enforcement. Federal drug laws have more severely sanctioned possessors of crack cocaine than powder cocaine. The 1986 Anti-Drug Abuse Act established different minimum sentences for crack and powder cocaine. To receive the same sentence as a crack cocaine user, the powder cocaine user would need to possess an amount 100 times greater than the user of crack cocaine. Moreover, the passage of the 1988 Omnibus Anti-Drug Abuse Act resulted in a mandatory minimum sentence of 5 years in federal prison for the *first-time* possession of 5 grams of crack cocaine (about the equivalent of a weekend supply for a serious crack user). Racial disparity in arrests and incarceration due to violations of these laws was the eventual outcome. When the Sentencing Commission recently investigated this disparity it recommended a modification of the existing legislation differentiating the two types of cocaine. However, since that time no changes have been forthcoming and opposition to a lessening of the severity of the sanctions has developed.

In conclusion, the political climate and demographic factors suggest no appreciable change in the conditions influencing disparity in official crime statistics. Given the intraracial nature of much crime, the higher levels of minority victimization are also likely to continue into the near future.

Also See the Following Articles

DEATH PENALTY • DRUG CONTROL POLICIES • HATE CRIMES • JUVENILE CRIME • POLICING AND SOCIETY • PUNISHMENT OF CRIMINALS

Bibliography

Bureau of Justice Assistance. (1997). *A policymaker's guide to hate crimes*. Washington, DC: U.S. Department of Justice.

Curtis, L. A. (1975). *Violence, race, and culture.* Lexington, MA: Lexington Books.

DuBois, W. E. B. (1899). *The Philadelphia Negro: A social study.* New York: Benjamin Blom.

DuBois, W. E. B. (Ed.). (1904). *Notes on Negro crime, particularly in Georgia.* Atlanta: Atlanta University.

DuBois, W. E. B. (1971 [1935]). *Black reconstruction in America.* New York: Atheneum.

Flowers, R. B. (1990). *Minorities and criminality.* Westport, CT: Praeger.

Free, M. D., Jr. (1996). *African Americans and the criminal justice system.* New York: Garland.

French, L. (1994). *The winds of injustice: American Indians and the U.S. government.* New York: Garland.

Georges-Abeyie, D. (Ed.). (1984). *The criminal justice system and Blacks.* New York: Clark Boardman.

Gerstenfeld, P. B. (1994). *Race and allegations of hate crime offenses: What the statistics can tell us.* Paper presented at the Annual Meeting of the Academy of Criminal Justice Sciences, Chicago, IL.

Hamm, M. S. (1994). *American skinheads: The criminology and control of hate crime.* Westport, CT: Praeger.

Harvey, W. B. (1986). Homicide among young black adults: Life in the subculture of exasperation. In D. F. Hawkins (Ed.), *Homicide among Black Americans,* p. 153. Lanham, MD: University Press of America.

Hawkins, D. F. (Ed.). (1995). *Ethnicity, race, and crime: Perspectives across time and place.* Albany, NY: SUNY Press.

Leonard, K. K., Pope, C. E., & Feyerherm, W. H. (Eds.). (1995). *Minorities in juvenile justice.* Thousand Oaks, CA: Sage.

Levin, J., & McDevitt, J. (1993). *Hate crimes: The rising tide of bigotry and bloodshed.* New York: Plenum.

Lynch, M. J., & Patterson, E. B. (Ed.). (1997). *Justice with prejudice: Race and criminal justice in America.* Albany, NY: Harrow and Heston.

Mann, C. R. (1993). *Unequal justice: A question of color.* Bloomington, IN: Indiana University Press.

National Association for the Advancement of Colored People. (1995). *Beyond the Rodney King story: An investigation of police conduct in minority communities.* Boston: Northeastern University Press.

Poussaint, A. F. (1983). Black-on-black homicide: A psychological-political perspective. *Victimology, 8,* 161.

Radelet, M. L. (1989). Executions of whites for crimes against blacks: Exceptions to the rule? *Sociological Quarterly, 30,* 529.

Walker, S., Spohn, C., & DeLone, M. (1996). *The color of justice: Race, ethnicity, and crime in America.* Belmont, CA: Wadsworth.

Moral Judgments and Values

Sidney Axinn

Temple University
University of South Florida

GLOSSARY

Categorical Imperative The fundamental command of morality (according to Kant), "Act only on a principle that you could intend to operate as a universal law."

Cognitive Knowable by experiment.

Fanaticism The view that there is just one inherent value, and everything and everyone must serve that value.

Hedonism Taking pleasure as the goal of life.

Inherent Value A value desired for itself alone, not as a means to anything else.

Instrumental Value An efficient means to a goal

lex talionis The so-called law of retaliation, that it is legitimate to respond to a pain by inflicting an equal pain.

Monism There is a single principle or basis for making moral judgments.

Moral Judgment A classification of an act as either right or wrong, or either good or bad.

Nihilism There is no such thing as moral truth.

Pluralism There is no single basis for deciding moral judgments; the basis changes for different cultures, times, places, and persons.

Skepticism While there are moral beliefs, there is no basis for their justification.

Utilitarianism The morality of an act depends on its results.

Values Entities for which one is willing to sacrifice.

A JUDGMENT is a statement that classifies an act as falling under a particular category. A moral judgment classifies an act as right or wrong, or as having some degree of rightness or wrongness. A more detailed formulation will be presented below. What makes an act right or wrong has been variously understood by different people, different cultures, and at different times. This article will present many of these alternatives. Individuals who apparently cannot distinguish between right and wrong have been described medically as suffering from pathomania. As well as the right/wrong terms, moral judgments are also taken to be pronouncements on the good or evil of an act.

The word value has a number of senses. In connection with moral judgments, it refers to the desirability of something or someone. To have instrumental value is to be useful in reaching some desired goal, to be an efficient means. To have inherent value is to be desirable

Copyright © 1999 by Academic Press.
All rights of reproduction in any form reserved.

for itself alone, to be a desirable end independent of its efficiency in achieving anything else. Fundamental problems have involved the matters of the source of inherent values, of choosing between them when they conflict, and of sorting them into hierarchies. Another kind of problem arises in judging the relationship between means and ends, between instrumental values and the inherent values they are used to reach. The means to reach an end can sometimes be inconsistent with that end. The source of inherent values will be considered below.

I. EXAMPLES OF MORAL JUDGMENTS AND VALUES

Is it better to suffer evil than to cause evil? An argument in Plato concludes (in the dialogue, *Gorgias*) that suffering evil is preferred. While certain Christian martyrs agree with Plato, a large part of the human species apparently takes the other view. Whichever side of the matter one chooses, that choice is a moral judgment. In the *Analects* of Confucius we find, "The Duke of Sheh told Confucius, 'In my country there is an upright man named Kung. When his father stole a sheep, he bore witness against him.' Confucius said, 'The upright men in my community are different from this. The father conceals the misconduct of the son and the son conceals the misconduct of the father. Uprightness is to be found in this.'" Both the Duke of Sheh and Confucius have made moral judgments, obviously different. Their different foundations will be considered below.

Classical name-dropping is hardly necessary to find moral judgments, and opposed judgments. If I decide to buy myself a new car instead of sending the money to feed starving people, and my neighbor decides to continue with his or her old car and send the saved money to help those unfortunate people; we have each made a choice that can be understood as a moral judgment.

Some pairs of different moral judgments can be considered merely different personal styles, and the individuals involved may each tolerate the other. However, the world is well-stocked with conflicting moral judgments that do not sit consistently together. These are cases in which the person or the community must choose one or the other alternative. Should the nuclear powers eliminate such weapons or not? During the Vietnam War or any war, should people drafted for the military avoid service or should they serve? During a war, should the war be shortened and lives saved even if that requires committing war crimes (for example, torturing prisoners to get information)? In the final section of this article we shall return to specific moral judgments.

II. ALTERNATIVE WAYS OF DECIDING MORAL JUDGMENTS

One of the basic questions in the history of thought about moral judgments turns on the issue of whether there is a single principle or basis by which to solve such questions. Absolutism or monism is the view that there is such a principle or source for decision: relativism or pluralism is the alternative, the position that insists that there is no fixed basis that holds independent of culture, time, person, and place.

Under the monist assumption that there is one basis for all morally right decisions, we find most of the history of moral theory and moral judgments. The urgent question arises, How can conflicts between opposed moral judgments be resolved? A number of articles in this encyclopedia are directed to that problem, as their titles make clear.

III. THE FRAMEWORK OF A MORAL JUDGMENT

A complete moral judgment may be thought of as a sentence with four variables, each highly contested, and an equally contested term expressing moral obligation. The pattern is:

Based on method W, X should (by rule R) perform Y, for the benefit of Z.

Example: Based on (W) the duty of citizens, (X) all draft-age persons should (Y) accept military service, for the benefit of (Z) the nation.

Example: Based on (W) the sacredness of human life, (X) everyone should (Y) refuse military service, for the benefit of (Z) the human race.

This is the framework for a complete moral judgment, but the common expression of such a judgment is ordinarily limited to the sentence between the commas, the moral assertion, "X should perform Y." The first and final phrases are usually left unmentioned, and the speaker may be unaware of them. Sometimes the term, *judgment,* is used to refer merely to the moral rule.

The variables, and the moral rule, have been specified in many ways, all significant in the history of the matter. The following lists outline many of the alternatives for each variable. The letters, W, X, Y, Z, and R refer to the positions in the framework sentence above.

W, the method for choosing the moral rule may be:

1. Cognitive (subject to empirical experiment).
2. Noncognitive (intuition, conscience, moral sense, and others).

X, the agent, can be:

1. An individual.
2. A group (class).
3. An institution?

according to R, Where R stands for:

1. Rules taken to be moral, traditional, rational, or based on social pressure. Golden Rule, categorical imperative, etc.
2. Principles, systems of moral thought, law.

Y, the act:

1. Act of commission.
2. Act of omission.

Z, the beneficiary:

1. All humans. 2. Some humans. 3. Not some humans. 4. No humans.

We shall consider some of the details involved in the several different positions, following the letters over the lists, above,

A. (W). Various Methods for Choosing a Moral Judgment

1. Cognitive methods are those that require observations or logical operations. They aim at finding truth or falsity in proposed moral judgments. Examples might be counting votes to determine a group's preference, or presenting a logical argument to show that a proposed action is or is not consistent with a certain assumed principle.

2. The noncognitive methods include consulting one's conscience, and using intuition. By intuition is meant the notion that sometimes one simply knows something without being aware of using any reasoning or empirical process. Those who take this position hold that some truths are "immediately" known without the need for any formal methodology.

B. (X). Possible Subjects, Actors, in Moral Judgments

1. Individuals who can reason and understand principles are the subjects of moral judgments. Children too young to understand principles are exempt, as are those who are senile or suffering from mental illness. Those under duress are usually exempt. The question of how much animals reason is contested, but they are not taken to be subject to moral judgments.

2. A group of individuals such as a family, an army patrol, or the members of a religious congregation may also be the agents in a moral judgment. There may be a collective intention to follow or to disregard a moral rule.

3. For some authors, an institution may be considered to have goals and intentions, and to either follow or flout moral or legal rules. For example, a corporation may desire a certain piece of property and act either properly or not in trying to get it. For an example of corporations that have knowingly chosen profit over human health one could point to the tobacco companies.

This role for institutions is contested. Many authors deny that a legal or social entity (an abstract entity) can have its own reasoning powers, apart from those of its members, and therefore refuse to have moral judgments apply to institutions themselves. The correlative issue is whether institutions have rights that are distinct from those of their members. By well-developed law, corporations have the right to own property and carry on various operations: legal judgments certainly apply to them, but moral judgments apparently do not. In parallel, nations own and operate military forces: for most authors, nations are subject to legal judgments but not moral judgments. For example, the decisions of the World Court at the Hague are legal judgments. For some authors there is "a court of world opinion" that makes moral judgments: the American Declaration of Independence was stated to be required out of "a decent respect to the opinions of mankind." To repeat, for most authors corporations are legal fictions that may own and operate a vast concentration of power, but moral issues involving them must be addressed to individual officers of the corporation, or boards or groups of such persons. (To use a certain religious vocabulary, nations and other corporations have no souls and can not be threatened with problems in an afterlife.)

C. (R). The Moral Term, ''Should''

Different judgments have been based on material taken from the entire world history of moral theory, Eastern and Western. What follows below is merely a small sample of the ways that the moral term in a judgment has been specified. No inference on moral strength is intended by the order of items to follow.

1. An Obvious Source of Moral Pressure Is Social

The community in which one lives has patterns and expectations that specify what one "should" do, is expected to do. Whether it is the tradition of the group, an institution, or the majority viewpoint, the force is quite palpable.

a. One Ought to Obey One's Parents

This is a clear imperative in Confucian thought, in a Hebrew commandment (phrased as the command to "honor" parents), and it resonates throughout many of the world's cultures. In the modern period we find the question, Is there a point at which one should not continue to obey one's parents?

b. Soldiers Are Expected to Protect and Defend the Constitution, as Sworn at Induction

This statement includes a phrase that is in the induction oath for the United States military, but the idea is not limited to that culture. In the Japanese army during World War II, when soldiers surrendered, their families were subject to considerable neighborhood opprobrium: siblings might be chased from school, and the family may have had to move to avoid other consequences of the disgrace of surrender when the duty was to fight for the Emperor.

c. "Members of the Armed Forces Are Bound to Obey Only Lawful Orders"

This famous phrasing of a point in the Uniform Code of Military Justice, Art. 92, makes clear that if charged with a war crime, a soldier cannot claim that he or she was forced to act by superior orders. Under the Geneva and Hague Conventions, all military personnel are supposed to be taught the nature of war crimes, and that orders to carry out actions that would be such crimes are illegal orders. In knowing what are illegal orders, they are not to obey them. (It may be added that military education on this matter is difficult and not always successful).

For example, Two individuals under the command of Lt. Caley at My Lai did not shoot and kill civilians: they were not court-martialed (or otherwise punished) for disobedience.

The idea of a moral basis for disobeying orders has a small but notable precedent. There is a biblical report of disobedience of an immoral command of God . . . in Saul's war against the Amelekites (in 1 Samuel 15), the king refuses the Divine command to slaughter the enemy, man, woman, and child.

d. *lex talionis*, the Law of Retaliation

This is the principle that insists that it is legitimate to respond to a pain caused by someone by inflicting an equal pain on that individual. This is used, sometimes, to justify the judgment of capital punishment, as well as the response to lesser crimes. For example, an eye for an eye.

It is also invoked by some "terrorists" to explain their judgment that violence is acceptable as a response to certain situations. For example, "never again without a rifle." This example was the judgment offered by a group called the Italian Red Brigade, in the 1960s. Their argument was that the police had treated them by extremely violent means, and therefore using rifles was justified.

e. Thou Shalt Not Kill

This one of the Ten Commandments, from the King James Version, would seem to require strict pacifism, and there are those who understand it that way as well as those who offer permissive qualifications. For Christian pacifists, a guiding example is Jesus's "resist not evil." It should be noted that the same commandment is translated as, "Thou shalt not murder," in the English version used by Jews in America. The term, "murder," keeps open the permissibility of killing under circumstances that are not murder. For example, legitimate military engagements are not taken to be murder, even when they result in killing.

Each of the Ten Commandments is a moral judgment. The specification of each variable is obvious. For *A*, the methodology, Moses claimed to have received the commandments from the absolute ruler, God. *B*, the agents, were to be all the Israelites (all humans?). The moral rules were the ten specific commandments. The actions were sometimes in need of interpretation by clergy. The beneficiaries were all members of society, including the agents themselves.

2. Principles

In this section we have principles that are more general than specific rules, but the line between the two is arbitrary. The history of morality is largely a history of systems based on the monist idea that there is one and only one proper rule or principle for deciding all interpersonal conflicts. There is also nihilism, holding that there is no such thing as moral truth; and skepticism, holding that we have moral beliefs but there is no basis for their justification. The alternatives to these are divided into absolutism (or monism), insisting that there is a single universal answer; and relativism (or pluralism), holding that moral positions are relative to different persons, cultures, histories, and so on. (Again, no inference on moral strength is to be drawn from the order of theories to follow.)

a. The Categorical Imperative

"Act only on that principle whereby you can will that it should become a universal law." Immanuel Kant, the author of this rule, has given other formulations as well, but our object here is not a history of moral theory but a consideration of the use of moral rules in judgments. An imperative is an order, and a categorical imperative is an order that is to be obeyed without consideration of any other goal. It is not an instrument for reaching any end: it is simply an absolute command. Kant took it that this command is the basic requirement of rationality: to be rational is to have a mind that can intend only a consistent universe. Inconsistency cannot be understood. Therefore, a rational being can only intend a consistent collection of rules: a universal principle must be consistent. If the principle on which we act is one that can be universalized, it must apply to everyone in the same situation. For Kant, the categorical imperative is the foundation of moral behavior; it is the one and only moral law.

To be moral, Kant held that it is not enough that an action conform to the moral law, the categorical imperative: it must be done purely out of respect for the moral law. This is clear "intention morality," the measure of the morality of an act is found in the intentions of the actor (see "utilitarianism" below, for a consequent morality). Self-interest may often be consistent with moral behavior, but such a combined intention earns no moral credit: only action done purely for the sake of the law can be considered moral. This is the common person's idea of morality, according to Kant, although here dressed in formal clothes.

For example, may I lie to avoid a personal problem? Universalizing the rule of this act would mean that everyone could lie when convenient. In such a world, no one would trust any statement. Under those conditions lies would not be possible, since a lie requires that an audience believe the statement to be true. Because universalizing the rule permitting lying would be self-contradictory, it is wrong to lie. The foundation of the categorical imperative is in the conception of reason: rationality determines morality.

b. The Golden Rule

Do to others as we would have them do to us. This demand for symmetry has obvious attractions, and many people take this rule to be the essence of morality. Impressive as it is, this pattern has some problems. It focuses on behavior rather than on rules or principles. For example, if one is physically robust, a willingness to box might satisfy the requirement of symmetry but might not satisfy fairness to a weaker opponent.

c. Moderation in All Things

This principle is just one of the many contributions that Aristotle has made to the subject. He qualifies the assertion by adding that there are activities that should not be carried out in moderation: crimes that are forbidden are not to be indulged in at all; and virtues that are demanded, such as integrity, are not to be followed in a merely partial way. Otherwise, the extremes of too much and too little are equally to be avoided.

Of course the idea of "extremes" is contextual; Aristotle quickly noted that a minimum meal for a child and for a huge wrestler are not the same. The idea is not merely Western: there is also a Buddhist rule, "neither too much nor too little."

d. The Tao Is All

This principle and the meaning of the Tao has varied considerably in the history of Chinese philosophy. No brief remark is adequate. One dominant sense of the Taoist school was that following Tao (or Nature) means leading a life of simplicity, spontaneity, tranquility, and letting Nature take its own course. This short paragraph is hardly adequate to explain a rich tradition that has developed and varied through centuries.

e. Utilitarianism

The morality of an act depends on its consequences. Utilitarians are consequent moralists: not the intention of the actor, but the product of the act is the measure of morality. This group is divided into those for whom the specific act is the subject of their concern (act utilitarians), and those for whom a rule under which the specific act falls is the matter to be considered (rule utilitarians).

For the formulators of the position (Jeremy Bentham, John Stuart Mill, Henry Sidgwick), maximizing pleasure (hedonism) is the object of life. Should pleasure be maximized for the majority or for one's self? Utilitarianism is usually a position that benefits the majority: it holds that the greatest good for the greatest number is the fundamental assumption. There can also be an individualistic variety of the view that pleasurable consequences are the goal of morality. For an egoistic utilitarianism, efficiency in maximizing personal pleasure is the basic principle.

This utilitarian's view of the basis for the key part of a moral judgment has certain advantages and disadvantages. In its favor, it is cognitive; consequences can be tested. One can expect to observe and learn what does and does not produce pleasure. There remain ambiguities, however; is it long-run or short-run pleasure? Are there higher and lower pleasures, as Mill thought?

f. Hedonism

This is the viewpoint found in many positions, that pleasure is the goal of life. It was cleanly phrased in Ancient Greek philosophy. Epicurus was so troubled by the risks of directly pursuing pleasure and having pain as a result (the hangover effect) that he advocated pursuing "negative pleasures," (the removal of pains), and seeking those pleasures that may be prolonged such as peace of mind and the pleasures of friendship. Because they were more dependable, less likely to lead to pain, he advised that one seek the pleasures of the mind rather than the body. Another group of hedonists, the Cyrenaics (4th and 3rd centuries, B.C.) took it that the immediate, intense pleasures are the best. Therefore, far from the caution of Epicurus, their principle was: Eat, drink, and be merry for tomorrow we may die.

g. Holy War

It is right to fight for one's religion, even at the cost of one's life. In ancient Judaism, in Christianity, in Shintoism, and Islam the concept of a holy war has been significant. The call for a holy war (a jihad) remains a current feature for some in Islam, where a jihad is still called for.

Islam is much more ambivalent on the status of jihad than outsiders may think. The Koran has passages in which oppression of the weak is condemned, and sections in which believers are to fight only in self-defense. However, there are also passages that provide justification for war to defeat unbelievers. Current debate exists over who can properly authorize a jihad.

D. (*Y*). The Action

1. An Act of Commission

This refers to an obvious behavior pattern. Intention moralists do not require actual behavior to judge moral-

ity, but consequent moralists do. A difficulty is that an action can be classified in more than one way. Punching someone may be (a) self-defense; (b) assault and battery; (c) a friendly boxing match. For example, President Roosevelt called the day of the Japanese attack on Pearl Harbor a day that would live in infamy. The Japanese saw it as a day of honor, a different report.

What is to be called violence is not always clear. Robert Paul Wolff has presented the case of the owner of the diner who might prefer some physical violence (a beating behind his diner) to the peaceful sit-in that had the potential to drive him into bankruptcy. White-collar actions (denying bank loans, refusing employment to capable people, taxing the poor more heavily than other groups, etc.) are not judged by the agent to be violence, although they may destroy lives even more completely than a physical attack.

2. An Act of Omission

To avoid a certain behavior may sometimes be judged right or wrong. As above, there are ambiguities in describing just what it is that is not being done. If one does not contribute to charity, is that stinginess or an effort to encourage sturdy independence on the part of the poor?

A classical position, that of the Stoics, held that one should have no interest in matters that are not under personal control. One's body, property, reputation, and office depend on external matters, and so should be considered of no importance. One's own thoughts were taken to be personal decisions and so were of moral significance. For example, Be indifferent to anything not under one's control.

E. (*Z*). The Beneficiary of a Moral Judgment

The part of a moral judgment that we have just considered, the act, will ordinarily have a beneficiary, or moral object. The beneficiary is the person, persons, or entity for whose benefit the act is undertaken, or who benefits from it. Therefore, the moral principle used in the judgment usually indicates the target, goal, or beneficiary of the act. To whose advantage is that particular choice of principle?

The square of opposition of traditional logic (presented in introductory logic texts) can give us a complete assortment of possible beneficiaries:

1. *All* Members of Mankind Are the Moral Object

This is also called universal fairness. When the categorical imperative is the moral principle, all rational beings are the beneficiaries. That includes essentially all humans. Does this view of the moral object allow for capital punishment and warfare? In the section on *lex talionis,* above, we found a basis for capital punishment. In the so-called theory of the "just war" there is an effort at a defense of warfare under certain conditions. But, taking all humans to be equal moral beneficiaries makes it clear that the judgment that a war is just faces a great hurdle. In a war, some people risk and lose their lives for the benefit of others. If all humans are equally valuable moral objects, why must some die for the benefit of others? In fact, there are those who volunteer to sacrifice themselves for others: more will be said about this later.

Parallel arguments can be made for a judgment that calls for capital punishment. Under the principle that takes all humans to be equal moral objects, killing by any agency, including a government, must be immoral. To be a moral object is to have inherent value, not to be a means for an external goal. Both the objectives of a nation and the concern to warn others about undesirable behavior are social but not personal goals. If individuals have inherent value, they must not be used in support of goals that are external to their own desires. As already mentioned, the *lex talionis* principle is regularly used to oppose this view of the immorality of capital punishment.

It is a special hallmark of Buddhism to have universal compassion. This means respect for all forms of life, taking all forms of life as moral objects, not merely humans.

2. *Some* Members of Mankind Are to Be the Moral Object

This is the social utility position. Where the major variety of utilitarianism is the moral principle, a certain social group will often be the moral object. If the greatest good for the greatest number is the moral principle, it is a proper judgment to hold that when killing a few is the only way to save the many, such killing is proper. For utilitarians, the sacrifice of the few for the many is exactly the proper moral judgment. The might of the majority does make for right.

On this view, minorities deserve no "bill of rights." Whatever is to the benefit of the majority is judged to be right. There is occasionally the embarrassing question of just what is to the benefit, the ultimate benefit, of the majority. Decision by voting may or may not be an accurate measure of that. For example: Some should be drafted into the military to risk their lives for the majority. Or, can we say that it is proper to commit a war crime for the sake of saving lives by shortening a war?

3. Some Humans Are Not to Be Moral Beneficiaries

Individualism is obtained by taking an elongated variety of this position. Let "some" mean that all but one human is excluded; just one person is the proper moral object. Individualism is also called selfishness by its opponents. Should I mug an old women carrying a pocketbook? The judgment on this basis depends only on whether or not the act is estimated to help or harm the individual agent.

Individualism need not produce a chaos of arson, rape, and murder: these results are often not in the interest of the individual agent. The sympathetic argument for individualism notes that a slave lives for someone else, a free person lives for him- or herself. On this view, it is a proper judgment to insist that I should live my life for my benefit. Self-reliance is the virtue of this basis for judgments. For example, If desertion under fire is an individual's preference, it is justified.

4. No Human Is the Moral Object

Religious foundations for moral judgments hold that something outside of human beings is the proper moral object. One obvious version of this presents God or a group of gods as the beneficiary of moral judgments. In another version, a nation is taken to be more important than the citizens of that nation. Therefore, sacrificing the citizens for the welfare of the nation is judged to be moral. In these terms, complete patriotism is a variety of religion. In another version of this fourth position, a principle may take the place of the ultimate moral object.

When something greater than, more important than, human interests is the moral beneficiary, we still need to know just what is the desire and need of that beneficiary. When God is the beneficiary, the source of information about God's desires might be direct revelation, a sacred writing, or religious officials. The question arises: Does a God need anything from mere humans? For philosophers such as Spinoza and Kant, the answer is, no. For some conventional religions there is the idea that sacrifice in this world will bring a reward in another world. A believer in the ultimate importance of a principle, a God, or a nation may be willing to do anything, however violent, on behalf of that ultimate. On this basis we can understand the judgments that have led individuals:

(a) To become Kamikaze pilots, and die for the Emperor;
(b) To become terrorists and die for "the cause" (whatever it be);

(c) To say with Martin Luther, "the hand that wields the sword is not really man's but God's."

IV. VALUES

A. The Source of Inherent Value: Sacrifice

The beneficiaries of moral judgments are the values of the agents. In addition to the classification of beneficiaries or moral objects given above, more detail must be added on the nature of values. In the first section of this article the concept of a value was classified in two ways. The distinction was noted between instrumental and inherent values. Instrumental values are easy to understand, they are sorted by their efficiency as a means to reach some desired end. The concept of inherent value was left a bit mysterious, as it usually is. There is the general understanding that instrumental values are not enough for decision making. Without at least one inherent value there is no reason for instrumental values. Without a goal or an end, why care about means?

We can hope to answer a question about which of two or more means is the most efficient in reaching a certain goal. This is often a matter of measurement: Which road is the shorter? Which path takes less time? Which item is cheaper, or more complete? When we face the matter of choosing inherent values, however, no measure of efficiency is relevant. For some authors, the source is simply a feeling or intuition that presents us with such absolute values. There is, nonetheless, a behavioral test that indicates how we create such values.

Our values are displayed by our sacrifices and willingness to sacrifice. The classical literary example of the behavioral test is the Biblical story of God's test of Abraham's devotion. Would he sacrifice his only son if commanded to do so? Presumably, Abraham showed the value he placed in God by his preparations to do exactly that, to sacrifice his son. Some commentators (Kant) have taken the story to show the immorality that an absolute religious commitment can produce: to kill an innocent child is criminal! However, the point here is that one shows one's values by the willingness to sacrifice, and by the degree of sacrifice.

A significant relationship exists between the donor and the recipient of a sacrifice. Let us understand a sacrifice to be a case of giving a gift without any expectation of repayment. As Aristotle pointed out, the donor of a sacrifice thinks more highly of the recipient than the recipient thinks of the donor. By making a sacrifice,

the donor has created a value for him- or herself. The recipient may be happy to have the gift, but for the recipient, the donor has just instrumental value—the value of a means to a gift.

As an example; a Gold Star Mother, someone who has sacrificed a child to the nation, may well be quite patriotic and defensive of that nation. The nation means more to her, has more value, than it does to one who has not sacrificed and who has no intention of sacrificing for it. The national government, however, may simply think of this mother as useful for its objectives, but not of inherent value. The parent–child relationship has many variations besides this one, but Aristotle's observation does cover significant examples. To generalize, inherent values are created by the sacrifices that individuals make.

B. Male and Female: Different Values?

In a much-discussed book that appeared in 1982, Carole Gilligan offered examples of the different judgments that girls and boys came to upon hearing the same story. This has led to a considerable literature exploring the differences between taking "care" as a prime value, and taking "conflict" as the prime and natural value. For some authors, these two different value systems are matters of gender; females naturally take care to be the obvious main value, males take conflict and aggression to be the natural response to a wide variety of problems. For other authors, there may well be two or more different voices or basic values, but they can not be classified by gender. Nature does not fix these matters. For these authors, the different genders are not determined by nature.

For some, war has a male gender. As one writer has put it, "the female gender ethos may be the most truly international value system on the planet. The needs of nurturance are universal; they transcend political boundaries and offer an opportunity for unity despite human conflicts. The female gender ethos, therefore, can provide the grounds for a new international understanding and, possibly, the first true commitment to global peace in the history of the world" (S. L. Kitch, in collection edited by A. E. Hunter).

A number of old myths involving relations between women and men have come under attack in recent philosophic literature. In the words of one author (V. Held), "The picture often presented in popular myths is that men use violence against each other to protect women and children from harm. Violence is then seen as a necessary evil for the sake of peace and for the sake of women. But this is probably a false picture. It seems likely that in societies where a lot of violence is used against other men, a lot of violence is used against women *also*."

While the preponderance of feminist literature is antiwar, there has been some ambivalence. As another author puts it (Elshtain, in a collection edited by Nardin), feminism has not quite known whether to fight men or to join them; whether to lament sex differences and deny their importance or to acknowledge and even celebrate such differences; whether to condemn all wars outright or to extol women's contributions to war efforts. For some authors, the ethics of care can yield an antiwar feminism situated uneasily between pacifist and just-war convictions.

C. Fanaticism

To have just one inherent value is to be a most incomplete person. One dictionary defines a fanatic as a person affected by excessive enthusiasm, unreasoning zeal. A person with just one inherent value judges everything in terms of its efficiency in reaching that one goal, or heaven. Anything that stands in the way of approaching the one value must be overcome, of course. If there is only one inherent value, no reason could exist in favor of any other cause.

In the ordinary person of good mental health, there is always some interest in alternative values, always more than one inherent value. Therefore, moral judgments can be at least imagined that are directed to alternative values. The healthy person is at least a dualist, if not a pluralist. Even while placing enormous value on his or her own life, such an individual can understand, and may at times consider, suicide. For the fanatic, only a single inherent value exists and anything competing may need to be dealt with violently.

For example, The rational soldier knows that the enemy of today may be the ally tomorrow: the fanatical soldier can not imagine this, cannot stand the thought. Of course the fanatic makes a ferocious soldier, but military leadership must be more rational, to be a dependable agent for a democratic nation.

V. CRUCIAL JUDGMENTS ABOUT NUCLEAR WEAPONS AND WORLD PEACE

Moral judgments are made constantly, about matters small and large. On the individual level we choose to justify or criticize in terms of a judgment about which

moral principle to apply. Of course, humans are capable of rationalizing almost anything embarrassing, and regularly choose their own interests above alternatives. Still, selfishness is not the only pattern; we do sacrifice or else we would have no values. Beyond the personal and small group decisions that make up daily life, there are a number of matters of international significance. This section deals with two such judgments.

A. The Use of Nuclear Weapons

Our confidence in moral judgments and values is pressed to the extreme when we consider nuclear warfare. Are nuclear weapons acceptable in warfare or would their use be a war crime? Consider the features of each of these two judgments.

1. Nuclear Weapons Are Acceptable in Wartime

This judgment, as all judgments, must be chosen by some methodology, has an agent, a moral principle, an action, and a moral beneficiary. The methodology, what we know about the use of the weapon, points to what has been called omnicide (everyone is killed), not warfare. The historic idea behind the term warfare was that one side would emerge victorious. Turning to the moral principle, it was phrased in the 1960s as "better dead than red." The assumption was that either we must be willing to use nuclear weapons and risk the end of civilized life or we would live under the rule of communism. Against this assumption, it is now argued that nuclear weapons can be used without producing omnicide, and that the bombing of Hiroshima and Nagasaki shows that the destruction can be limited to one city or less. While those bombs were atomic, not nuclear, the world now has both larger multiple nuclear missals and much smaller "battlefield" nuclear warheads, and varieties of bombs with limited capacities.

The beneficiary, presumably, is the nation that uses these weapons. However, we now have a world in which a fairly large number of nations are known to have nuclear weapons, and some small nations also have projects to produce or acquire them. The examples of the one-sided benefit in Hiroshima and Nagasaki may have no predictive force since so many nations now have these weapons.

Let's consider the alternative judgment.

2. Nuclear Weapons Are Not Acceptable in Wartime

Since the object of war is to win, to be intact enough to gain the fruits of victory, (and because they violate the moral demands of the War Conventions) certain weapons have been banned by treaty. Nuclear weapons, following poison gas and biological weapons, violate the Hague and Geneva Conventions and one expects that they will also be forbidden.

If an enemy uses nuclear weapons in a first strike and almost completely destroys the population of one's country, is it a moral retaliation to respond in kind and destroy the enemy population? It should be noted that as of this writing the United States of America has renounced the first-strike use of both gas and biological weapons, but has retained the right to retaliate with gas weapons against their use. The government has renounced the use of biological weapons, even in retaliation. One formal or "text" reason for renouncing these weapons is found in the United States Department of the Army's Field Manual, *The Law of Land Warfare* (FM 27-10). The Manual explains that one of the purposes of the law of war is "protecting both combatants and noncombatants from unnecessary suffering." Given that basis for the decision on biologicals, since the use of nuclear weapons in retaliation is also an obvious producer of "unnecessary suffering," one would expect that the use of nuclear weapons will also be renounced. It must be added that at the present the nuclear powers show no sign of doing this.

Another judgment on this subject was sometimes heard during the recent Cold War with the Soviet Union. If our nation has been destroyed, but we have nuclear weapons on submarines, the commanders should have orders to completely destroy the remaining human life in the Soviet Union and elsewhere. The moral principle here would follow the Roman slogan, *aut Caesar aut nihil*, either Caesar or nothing. Either we win or the civilized world will end. Presumably the basis for this revenge would be the principle of *lex talionis*, the principle that one may retaliate against an injury by returning an equal injury. This seems to reduce the principle to absurdity. It must be emphasized that all human principles have limits. To take one rule or principle as absolute is to be fanatical (see above).

B. Nationalism vs. Internationalism

The remark is sometimes made that only a strong world government can keep the peace and avoid wars between nations. This comment is often followed by saying that the world is not yet ready for a single world government. These are each speculations about the future, about a balance of risks, and it is a subject on which no one is expert. There are moral judgments that stand behind each of these positions, and demand attention. Here is one phrasing of the issues between what can be called nationalism and internationalism.

1. For Nationalism

Patriotism is a basic value. One's nation is the natural, obvious, and necessary beneficiary of one's sacrifices. To have no such loyalty is to be missing the foundation of moral judgment. Socrates gave a classic explanation of the moral basis for loyalty to the laws of his city. In the dialogue *Crito*, he explained the need, the moral need, for him to remain in prison and suffer the punishment of death, even though he could have escaped. The laws of the city had formed him, educated him, protected him; and he had the correlative moral obligation of a citizen to obey those laws and protect that city. Historically, this position holds that fundamental human attachments require that one defend one's family, friends, king, and social structure. Not to do so is to risk the contempt that the French King Henry IV expressed in a letter to one of his lieutenants, "Hang yourself, Brave Crillon! We fought at Arqués, and you were not there."

2. For Internationalism

This position argues that the nation-state is obsolete. No king or government can protect its citizens in a world of nuclear, chemical, and biological weapons. Therefore, safety must be found by some other political mechanism.

The way to end warfare in an area (the classic theory of Thomas Hobbes) is to have everyone in that area turn over all their weapons to one individual. That individual, the king, then has the power to keep everyone else in fear of him. His commands are law, and peace is the situation in which people are in more fear of the king than of each other. War is the alternative in which people depend on themselves for their own protection; they are sovereign. Peace means that a strong central power defends everyone. This also applies to nations: a sovereign nation depends on itself for protection, and is therefore at war, hot or cold, with all other nations. Therefore, nations break treaties whenever it is to their advantage.

One obvious solution to the present situation, international anarchy (as Kant called it), is a single world government. Such a government would have the only major military power; individual nations would be limited to police forces restricted to their own borders. The United Nations, after considerable changes, could develop into a dependable world government. After the establishment of a single world government, there might be civil wars, but not international wars.

Loyalty to individual nations would be replaced by loyalty to the world government. Separate cultures, religions, languages, pose no threats to world peace, if their governments do not have the power or legal right to cross borders. Refusal to go beyond national sovereignty can be called cultural lag, holding on to parts of a culture that are simply inefficient or outgrown in the present world. When even the weakest nation has the strength to destroy the strongest, all nations are essentially in equal danger. The solution to the problem of international peace, just as domestic peace, is the rule of law administered by a power capable of enforcing the law.

3. Judgments on the Issues between Nationalism and Internationalism

The antinomy between patriotic nationalism and a commitment to a single world government is argued on many levels; economic, political, cultural, and moral. On one side there is the example of the United States of America, whose constitution has provided a mechanism for the relations between states and the federal government. On the other, it is held that without a common language and culture, the American example is not relevant. To this there is the retort that English has become the second language of the world, certainly the economic world; and the example of the European Common Market is offered. And so the debate, when it is conscious, continues.

What are the moral judgments and values on each side? The national patriot values his or her nation and its citizens as the highest beneficiaries. The world government advocate values the end of warfare, international peace, and all humans as still higher beneficiaries worthy of sacrifice. One suspects that the decision between these two basically different positions will be decided, not by moral judgments, but by fears about the increasingly dangerous world. The risk of the use of weapons against which no nation can be secured, weapons that are conventional, nuclear, chemical, or biological, may push an unwilling world into the next step in civilization, a serious and strong world government.

VI. CONCLUSION

A. Judgments

As noted earlier, a judgment is an assertion that a particular act does or does not stand under a certain rule or principle. The problems involve a related pair of decisions: (1) choosing which rule is relevant to a certain situation; and (2) deciding that the act in question falls under that rule. In a moral judgment, the rule is a moral rule. As the material in this article has shown, there is a wide choice of rules to be used. In addition to that choice, it takes what has been called "insight" to realize that a particular act is an example or case of a certain rule. In the literal sense of the word "understand," the decision must be made that the act does stand under, or is an instance of a certain rule. The ability to understand, in this sense, is said to be the mark of human intelligence.

One of the greatest modern philosophers (Kant), after a thorough study of the matter, concluded that "judgment is a peculiar talent which can be practiced only, and cannot be taught. It is the quality of so-called mother-wit; and its lack no school can make good . . . [there are] no rules for judgment. Deficiency in judgment is just what is ordinarily called stupidity, and for such a failing there is no remedy." Of course, there is a range of intelligence within every society.

Insulting those whose judgments or values vary from ours is hardly productive. Often it turns out that people differ on means but not on their ultimate values. The basic necessities of human life—food, clothing, and shelter for oneself and one's family—are values in every human society. Moral codes that appear different may have more agreements than differences. Honesty and its opposite are understood and appreciated across many (all?) cultural divides. That we now live in one economic world is obvious to all. Moral judgments and other evaluations are similar enough to have led almost every nation on earth agree to the Geneva Conventions on the conduct of warfare. The optimistic prediction is that there is enough agreement on ultimate moral rules and inherent values for us to expect a single world government to come into existence in the not distant future, and to succeed in maintaining world peace. As suggested above, the force to produce a single world government is more likely to come from fear of the present international anarchy than to come from abstract moral judgments.

B. Moral Pessimism and Optimism

The choice of moral judgments shows an enormous range. For almost anything that one wishes to do, a rationalization can be found, a justification can be offered. Occasions for violence as well as bold steps toward peace can each be defended by pointing to one or another personal moral loyalty. This article has specified many of the alternatives produced by the history of thought. However, there is another viewpoint that has not been included in this contribution. Consider matters from the standpoint of the human species rather than the individual members of the species.

The history of the human species, as a group, shows an impressive march toward larger and larger loyalties. Optimism about the future of a peaceful civilization can be found if we look, not at matters of individual morality, but at the larger and larger groups in which social and cultural obligations have developed.

Historically, humans have moved from attachment to small groups, to cities, to many-sized kingdoms, to nations, and now to regional associations of nations and to a United Nations organization. As loyalties widen, justifications for conflict diminish. Individuals may prefer to remain within the old and smaller boundaries, but history goes the other way. Fortunately, moral progress can take place in the group whether or not it does in individuals. In many nations, slavery has largely ended, great progress has been made toward equal rights for women, children, different sexual orientations, and foreigners—without noticeable improvement in personal morality for individuals. Probably we are no more or less honest than our grandparents, to consider just one area. Personal honesty and public honesty are different matters, as are personal morality and public morality. The very clash of individuals seems to lead to social if not personal progress. People and nations fight, and this sometimes leads to arrangements to keep the peace. On the record, we can hardly be more than pessimistic about individual moral progress: individuals continue to selfishly rationalize their moral judgments. But when we turn to mankind as a whole, the historical marks show the moral progress of humans considered as a social group. Taking mankind as the moral actor, there is a basis for optimism.

Also See the Following Articles

CRITIQUES OF VIOLENCE • ETHICAL AND RELIGIOUS TRADITIONS, EASTERN • ETHICAL AND RELIGIOUS TRADITIONS, WESTERN • ETHICAL STUDIES, OVERVIEW • HUMAN NATURE, VIEWS OF • MEANS AND ENDS • RELIGIOUS TRADITIONS, VIOLENCE AND NONVIOLENCE

Bibliography

Aristotle, *Nichomachean ethics*.

Gilligan, C. (1982). *In a different voice: Psychological theory and women's development*. Cambridge, MA: Harvard University Press.

Held, V. (1993). *Feminist morality, transforming culture, society, and politics*. Chicago: The University of Chicago Press.

Hunter, A. E. (Ed.). (1991). *On peace, war, and gender: A challenge to genetic explanations*. New York: The Feminist Press at The City University of New York.

Kant, I. (1987). *Critique of judgment*. (W. S. Pluhar, Trans.). Indianapolis: Hackett Publishing Co. (Original work published 1790).

Kant, I. (1965). *Critique of pure reason*. (N. K. Smith, Trans.). New York: St Martin's Press. (Original work published 1781).

Kant, I. (1795). Perpetual peace. In L. W. Beck (Trans. and Ed.), *On history*. Indianapolis: Bobbs Merrill Co.

Kant, I. (1784). Idea for a universal history from a cosmopolitan point of view. In L. W. Beck (Trans. and Ed.), *On history*. Indianapolis: Bobbs Merrill Co.

MacIntyre, A. (1988). *Whose justice? Which rationality?* Notre Dame, IN: University of Notre Dame Press.

Nardin, T. (Ed.). (1996). *The ethics of war and peace: Religious and secular perspectives*. Princeton, NJ: Princeton University Press.

Wells, D.A. (Ed.) (1996). *An encyclopedia of war and ethics*. Westport, CT: Greenwood Press.

Wing-Tsit Chan (Trans. and Ed.). (1963). *A source book in Chinese philosophy*. Princeton, NJ: Princeton University Press.

Wolff, R. P. (1969). On violence. *Journal of Philosophy, 66*, 601–616.

Neuropsychology and Mythology of Motivation for Group Aggression

Jordan B. Peterson

Harvard University

A. B___v has told how executions were carried out at Adak—a camp on the Pechora River. They would take the opposition members "with their things" out of the camp compound on a prisoner transport at night. And outside the compound stood the small house of the Third Section. The condemned men were taken into a room one at a time, and there the camp guards sprang on them. Their mouths were stuffed with something soft and their arms were bound with cords behind their backs. Then they were led out into the courtyard, where harnessed carts were waiting. The bound prisoners were piled on the carts, from five to seven at a time, and driven off to the "Gorka"—the camp cemetery. On arrival they were tipped into big pits that had already been prepared and *buried alive*. Not out of brutality, no. It had been ascertained that when dragging and lifting them, it was much easier to cope with living people than with corpses. The work went on for many nights at Adak. And that is how the moral–political unity of our Party was achieved.

(A. I. Solzhenitsyn, *The Gulag Archipelago,* p. 39)

GLOSSARY

Behaviorism A movement or school in psychology based on the premise that only observable physical actions can be employed as the grounds for conclusions and principles, and that therefore mental phenomena such as ideas and emotions are to be disregarded.

Defensive Behavior Any of an array of non-aggressive actions by an animal to avoid falling prey to a predator; e.g., flight, concealment, camouflage, immobility.

Habituation The lessening or disappearance of the response to a stimulus due to repeated or continuous exposure to the stimulus; in general, the process of becoming acclimated to a novel environment or circumstance.

Territory A distinct space occupied on an ongoing or recurring basis by an individual or group, having recognized boundaries and, in many species, defended against intrusion by others outside the group.

Theriomorphized Literally, in the shape of a beast; having the body form of an animal; used especially to describe a deity that has animal form.

The individual is fundamentally territorial—and, furthermore, is a creature capable of endless abstraction. Deep understanding of these two characteristics immensely furthers comprehension of the human capacity for the commission of atrocity in the service of belief. Territoriality and higher-order symbolic intelligence unite in the production of "abstract territories" of vast expanse. These abstract territories—belief systems or ideologies—promise deliverance of behavioral stability in otherwise potentially chaotic and dangerous social groupings of individuals, motivated by their own particular and idiosyncratic concerns. Proper analysis of the nature of essential human affect helps make the

Copyright © 1999 by Academic Press.
All rights of reproduction in any form reserved.

attraction and overwhelming power of this ideological promise understandable.

Psychology is littered with unconscious presuppositions. Sometimes these exist as theoretical foundation blocks: behaviorists, for example, presume the existence of the reflex arc—a convenient fiction, whose adoption allows for the "atheoretical stance" of behaviorism (Miller, Galanter, & Pribram, 1960). Psychoanalytic thinkers, existentialists, and humanists alike all believe that emotional stability depends on intrapsychic stability—that a happy, productive person is such because he or she is possessed of an integrated, conflict-free psyche, or an ego adapted to reality, or an actualized self. Western psychology is embedded inextricably in the western philosophical tradition. The idea of the autonomous and self-governing individual is so much a part of that tradition that it forms an "invisible" axiom of all theories of psychological health. But it is possibly the case that our vaunted psychological stability depends as much—or more—on the continued predictability of the "external" environment as on the properly integrated state of hypothetical intrapsychic systems. Consider Hebb's words (Hebb & Thompson, 1985):

> One usually thinks of education, in the broad sense, as producing a resourceful, emotionally stable adult, without respect to the environment in which these traits are to appear. To some extent this may be true. But education can be seen as being also the means of establishing a protective social environment in which emotional stability is possible.

Hebb points out that education alters the cognitive and emotional structure of the individual—thus "stabilitizing" him or her—but also produces "a uniformity of appearance and behavior" in the social context, which helps remove the impetus for dangerous and unpredictable affective outbursts. He continues:

> On this view, the susceptibility to emotional disturbance may not be decreased. It may in fact be increased. The protective cocoon of uniformity, in personal appearance, manners, and social activity generally, will make small deviations from custom appear increasingly strange and thus (if the general thesis is sound) increasingly intolerable. The inevitable small deviations from custom will bulk increasingly large, and the members of the society, finding themselves tolerating trivial deviations well, will continue to think of themselves as socially adaptable.

What does the healthy and socially adapted individual do when the custom he holds dear is challenged? He demonizes the enemy, as prime threat to his "identity," and goes to war. And when he is in barbarian lands, outside the rule of law and the harbor of tradition and restraint, he is a terrible, resentment-ridden predator, whose capacity for unconscionable behavior can hardly be overstated.

Carl Rogers, the eminent humanist, adopted what is arguably the most extreme position, equating intrapsychic integration with emotional regulation, following Rousseau's dictum: "With what simplicity I should have demonstrated that man is by nature good, and that only our institutions have made him bad!" (Morley, 1923). Rogers/Rousseau believed that the human being was innately good—would develop, of his or her own accord, into a healthy and complete person, in the absence of (detrimental) social pressure. There are at least two substantive problems with this hypothesis. It is clear, first, that the idea of what constitutes "good" varies substantially from society to society. This fact does not necessary preclude the possibility that some form of "goodness" is innate—but it certainly puts the onus on those who posit that such is the case to account simultaneously for the variance in ethical behavior that characterizes different times and places. Second, the "arbitrary social pressure = individual psychopathology" hypothesis suffers from insufficient recognition of the benefits of tradition and communitarianism. Social order is a terrible force, clearly—crushing individuality, forcing conformity—but is also the structure that makes communication and cooperation between individuals possible. It is unreasonable to presume that the individual could be social in the absence of socialization.

Intrapsychic integration—a primary consequence of individual development—accounts primarily for psychological stability: questionable axiom number one. Social harmony is by contrast an unquestionable precondition for individual health and well-being. It is impossible for an individual to be free of severe emotional and motivational conflict in the conditions prevailing, for example, in the Somalian state prior to the recent UN occupation, or in the Rwandan civil war, or in Stalinist Russia. When the actions of others have become entirely unpredictable, when every person is a potential enemy or traitor, when theft and homicide are daily occurrences—individual psychological health, practically speaking, becomes impossible: it is "not healthy" to be emotionally stable under such circumstances. Unbridled fear, hostility, suspicion, and aggression will manifest themselves inevitably when social order has vanished. As the poet Leonard Cohen has it—"there is no decent place to stand, in a massacre." It is for this reason—to take an example from mythology—that Gautama Buddha gave up the Nirvana he was capable of achieving personally (as an archetypally "intrapsychically integrated" individual) to work for the salvation of the rest of the world. The Buddha realized that his complete redemption was impossible in the midst of the constant suffering of less-enlightened others. This central Eastern myth stresses the necessity of social harmony as a precondition for complete individuation (stresses the responsibility of each individual to work for that state, as well as to further personal development).

Questionable axiom number two: *anxiety or fear is a learned state.* In its most elementary formal incarnation, this idea is predicated on the notion of "primary" and "secondary" reinforcers (Dollard & Miller, 1950). Painful stimuli are primary. Previously neutral stimuli, paired with primary stimuli that produce pain, become "secondary" reinforcers, whose presence signals imminent punishment, and then produce anxiety. This basic notion is based on an even more fundamental and "unconscious" presupposition, however—that of the "normative" somnolence and emotional stability of organisms. Lab animals—such as rats—can clearly be taught fear, in the classic manner. A rat in a cage will learn to associate a light with a shock if the two are paired together consistently within a relatively short intervening time. Two considerations are of particular interest, however, with respect to this apparently self-evident phenomenon.

First: fear-conditioning experiments are almost inevitably conducted on animals who have already "habituated" to the environment in which the experiment takes place. The fact of this preexperimental "habituation" in fact constitutes one of the implicit theories of the experimental manipulation (that implicit theory being—*habituated* rats comprise appropriate subjects for the derivation of conclusions about fear acquisition). In actuality, it is the behavior of the rat placed in a novel cage or open field that is of primary interest and relevance for the comprehension of fear or anxiety. When a rat is removed from his familiar ground and placed in new circumstances, he first freezes (he is, to speak anthropomorphically, shocked into immobility: imagine being dropped naked into a jungle at night). The rat is paralyzed in consequence of the infinite number of potential horrors that await him in this unexplored environment (not that the rat consciously apprehends these horrors. He is, rather, biologically prepared to respond behaviorally, *a priori,* with "caution" when he

does not know where he is). Anxiety—manifested in behavioral inhibition—is the prepotent response to novel territory. While the rat is frozen, he engages in preliminary exploratory behavior, motivated by the incentive–reward properties of the novel circumstance (as a new thing or situation also beckons with promise, as potentially fruitful or useful territory). If his initial tentative exploratory maneuvers (sniffing, visual mapping) do not produce actual negative consequences, the rat gradually becomes less behaviorally inhibited and starts to explore motorically—starts to move around and to "map" the new domain. Once this mapping is complete—that is, once the rat has moved through the new locale and interacted in its rat manner with all the objects in that locale—"habituation" occurs. The rat is now calm. It is this "calm" rat—who went to a lot of trouble to attain his theoretically baseline "calm" state—who can now be "taught" fear. In truth, he was initially terrified, when he was not on home ground. Then he regulated his own emotional upheaval in consequence of active exploration. Then, because of a radical and unpredictable environmental transformation—in this case, the introduction of the light–shock procedure into previously familiar territory—the rat became afraid, once again.

Second: even self-evidently "neutral" stimuli—that is, stimuli to which no "association" has been made—are clearly not neutral, at least upon initial contact. Recent investigations into the phenomena of *latent inhibition* make this absolutely clear. Take two groups of rats, or two groups of human beings, for that matter. Show one group a light, repeatedly. Do not pair the light (theoretically neutral) with any reinforcer. Then take both subject groups and present them with the light, paired with a shock. The "preexposed" group—that is, the group that saw the light repeatedly, in the absence of "reinforcement"—will be much delayed in learning the light–shock relationship. This is because the members of that group learned the "irrelevancy" of the light by exploring its manifestation numerous times and attaching to that (potentially and *a priori* meaningful) manifestation a valence of zero. The importance of the latent inhibition experiments cannot be overstated: *the irrelevancy of "meaningless" stimuli is learned, not given.* The novel phenomenon, whatever it might be (that is, whatever its intrinsic properties) is not neutral in the absence of learning. The novel phenomenon has *a priori* meaning, which must be eliminated, prior to its classification as "something safely ignored" (something like the chair you are sitting on, for example, or the ceiling above your head).

The question then becomes: what is the *a priori*

significance of the unclassified or unexplored (or novel) thing or situation? The answer to this question can be derived from two completely separate domains of inquiry. First, let us turn to Mircea Eliade, the historian of religion, for two observations. Eliade (1959/1987) states:

> One of the outstanding characteristics of traditional societies is the opposition that they assume between their inhabited world and the unknown and indeterminate space that surrounds it. The former is the world (more precisely, our world), the cosmos; everything outside it is no longer a cosmos but a sort of "other world," a foreign, chaotic space, peopled by ghosts, demons, "foreigners" (who are assimilated to [undistinguished from, more accurately] the demons and the souls of the dead).

More specifically, "everything outside" occupies the same categorical space as chaos and disorder itself—often given the theriomorphized form of a terrible reptile (perhaps because snakes/reptiles are easily feared and may therefore be productively used as "root metaphors" for the "place of fear itself") (Sarbin, 1986). The ancient Egyptians regarded the Hyksos, "barbarians," as equivalent to Apophis, the serpent who nightly devoured the sun, according to Egyptian mythology; the early Indo-Europeans equated the destruction of enemies in battle to the slaying of Vṛtra (the precosmogonic "dragon of chaos") by Indra (the world-creating hero); and the archaic Iranians (Zoroastrians) equated the mythic struggle of King Faridun (a culture-creating hero, analogous to Romulus or Remus, the mythic founders of Rome) against a foreign usurper—the dragon Azdahak—with the cosmogonic fight of the hero Thraetona against Azi Dahaka, the primordial serpent of chaos (Eliade, 1978).[1,2] The enemies of the Old Testament Hebrews suffer the same fate: they are regarded as equivalent to Rahab, or Leviathan, the serpent Yahweh overcame in his battle to establish the world

["Speak, and say, Thus saith the Lord GOD; Behold, I am against thee, Pharaoh king of Egypt, the great dragon that lieth in the midst of his rivers, which hath said, My river is mine own, and I have made it for myself." (Ezekiel 29:3); also, "Nebuchadrezzar the king of Babylon hath devoured me, he hath crushed me, he hath made me an empty vessel, he hath swallowed me up like a dragon, he hath filled his belly with my delicates, he hath cast me out." (Jeremiah 51:34)]. It is of great interest, in this regard to consider the behavior of rats in their natural habitat toward a stranger. Rats are highly social animals, perfectly capable of living with their familiar compatriots in peace. They do not like members of other kin groups, however, and will hunt them down and kill them. Accidental or purposeful intruders are dealt with in the same manner. Rats identify one another by smell. If an experimenter removes a well-loved rat from its familial surroundings, scrubs it down, provides it with a new odor, and returns it to its peers—it will be promptly dispatched by those who once loved it. The "new" rat constitutes "unexplored territory;" his presence is regarded as a threat (not unreasonably) to everything currently secure. Chimpanzees—perfectly capable of killing "foreign devils" (even those who were once familiar)—act in much the same manner (Goodall, 1990).

Eliade (1987) continues, commenting on the nature of rituals for "consecrating" or "taking possession" of unfamiliar territory (that is, the territory characterized by demons, ghosts, dragons, and barbarians—and, to speak psychologically, the place of *a priori* uncertainty, terror, and aggression:)

> At first sight this cleavage in space appears to be due to the opposition between an inhabited and organized—hence cosmicized—territory and the unknown space that extends beyond its frontiers; on one side there is a cosmos, on the other a chaos. But we shall see that if every inhabited territory is a cosmos, this is precisely because it was first consecrated, because, in one way or another, it is the work of the gods or is in communication with the world of the gods.... An unknown, foreign and unoccupied territory (which often means "unoccupied by our people") still shares in the fluid and larval modality of chaos.

He points out that the occupation and settling of "unknown land" transforms it by repeating the "cosmogony"—that is, by "acting out" or embodying the creative processes, undertaken by the gods, that originally sepa-

---

[1] "Indra's combat served as model for the battles that the Aryans had to sustain against the Dasyus (also termed *vrtani*): 'he who triumphs in a battle, he truly kills Vṛtra.' (Maitrayana-Samhita 2.1.3)."

[2] Eliade also points out that the name Faridun is derived from Thraetona (Thraetona = Freton = Faridun) and states, "in Iran as elsewhere, the process of historicization of mythical themes and personages is counterbalanced by a contrary process: the real adversaries of the nation or the empire are imagined as monsters, and especially as dragons."

rated the "domain of order" from the original chaos, at the beginning of time:

> For in the view of archaic societies everything that is not "our world" is not yet a world. A territory can only be made ours by creating it anew, that is, by consecrating it. This religious behavior in respect to unknown lands continued, even in the West, down to the dawn of modern times [and was reflected recently in the "planting of the flag" on the moon by the American astronauts.] The Spanish and Portuguese conquistadors, discovering and conquering territories, took possession of them in the name of Jesus Christ [the world-creating *logos*].

This is a great and interesting notion. The "unexplored" world is equivalent to chaos (something that might be considered akin to "latent information," in more modern parlance). The establishment of order in that chaos—that is, the subjection of the unknown to exploration, law and tradition—is equivalent, mythologically speaking, to the heroic "creation of the world." That makes every inhabitant of extracultural space an emissary of chaos (easily assimilated to the devil, the "strange son of chaos," in Goethe's terminology)—and every conqueror an incarnation of the world-engendering God.

To complete our understanding of the unknown, we turn from religious phenomenology to experimental psychology. Jeffrey Gray has been at pains to establish the *a priori* affective valence of the novel phenomenon. He notes that something novel can be regarded, from the perspective of functional neuropsychopharmacology, as a threat and as an incentive reward—simultaneously. What precisely does this signify? Well, the classic view is that stimuli unpaired with primary reinforcers have no motivational valence. This is clearly incorrect, as we have seen. But what valence could something unexplored possibly possess, given that the unexplored thing or situation is by definition unknown and not yet subject to the sort of categorization that would allow for intelligent attribution of value? The answer to this lies in consideration of possibility. The unknown can reasonably be considered a domain of punishment, in potential, as well as reward (as the Lord giveth, so to speak, and taketh away). Cues of punishment are threats, technically speaking, and produce anxiety (which is behavioral and emotional response to threat). Cues of (consummatory) reward, by contrast, are "promises"—have incentive properties, technically speaking, and produce positive affect of various forms (curiosity, hope, and excitement). The unknown there-

fore produces two conflicting states of affect/motivation "simultaneously"—anxiety/behavioral inhibition and excitement–hope–curiosity/behavioral activation. This state of affairs is much reminiscent of Dollard and Miller's approach–avoidance conflict—so, it might be said that the unfamiliar or unknown produces approach–avoidance conflict like nothing else (see Fig. 1). And is this so hard to believe? We are powerfully attracted—and powerfully repelled—by things we do not understand (this is why we must "boldly go where no one has gone before"). Whether attraction to or repulsion by the unknown dominates might depend on context (and, perhaps, on character).

Gray's model of information-processing looks something like this (although he is not entirely to be blamed for the following discussion, which is predicated more fundamentally on cybernetic theory). Animals engage in goal-directed activity—which is to say, try to get from someplace to someplace else or try to get from one state of being to another. For an animal—and, not infrequently, for a human—territorial location and internal state are closely linked. Food tends to be "elsewhere" for a currently hungry rat. Otherwise he would just eat and would not be hungry. Anyway—things

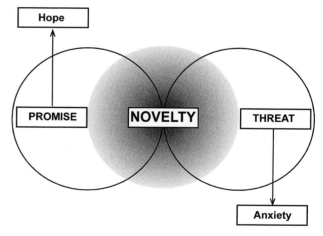

FIGURE 1 Schematic portrayal of the ambivalent valence of "novelty"—considered as the class of all things that have not yet been categorized. Novel phenomena (that is, events, processes, or situations that occur contrary to desire in the pursuit of a particular goal) are both threatening and promising (considered as "stimuli"). The threat exists because what you cannot control might kill you; the promise exists because new things offer new information. Threat produces anxiety and behavioral inhibition; "promise" constitutes incentive reward and produces joy, hope, and curiosity. Anxious responses to novelty appear prepotent (as the unknown should be approached cautiously). Once anxiety recedes (assuming sufficient nonpunishing exposure), curiosity moves to the forefront and drives (or accompanies) exploratory behavior.

encountered in the course of goal-directed activity, currently irrelevant to that activity, accrue a motivational label of zero (are regarded as meaningless, given the present state of affairs). Things encountered which impede progress are regarded as negative (frustrating, anxiety-provoking). Things encountered which facilitate progress are regarded as positive (hope-inspiring, exciting). Unexpected or unknown things encountered are both—frustrating and threatening and hope-inspiring/exciting. However, as Dollard and Miller pointed out, proximal novelties produce anxiety, preferentially. The appropriate response to something new is caution, in the short term. The appropriate response in the long run, however, is exploration. Animals therefore freeze to something new—then, cautiously explore. The response of rats unexpectedly confronted with a cat, on once-familiar ground, is instructive. Modern experimental psychologists have begun to examine the response of animals to natural sources of mystery and threat. They allow the animals to set up their own environments, realistic environments, and then expose them to the kinds of surprising circumstances they might encounter in "real life." The appearance of a predator, in previously "safe" space (space previously explored, that is, and mapped as useful or irrelevant) constitutes one type of realistic surprise. Blanchard and colleagues (1989, 1991) describe the naturalistic behavior of rats under such conditions:

> When a cat is presented to established mixed-sex groups of laboratory rats living in a visible burrow system, the behaviors of the subjects change dramatically, in many cases for 24 hours or more. The initial active defensive behavior, flight to the tunnel/chamber system, is followed by a period of immobility during which the rats make 22 kHz ultrasonic vocalizations, which apparently serve as alarm cries, at a high rate. As freezing breaks up, proxemic avoidance of the open area gradually gives way to a pattern of "risk assessment" of the area where the cat was encountered. Subjects poke their heads out of the tunnel openings to scan the open area where the cat was presented, for minutes or hours before emerging, and when they do emerge, their locomotory patterns are characterized by [behaviors that theoretically reduce their visibility and vulnerability to predators] and [by] very short "corner runs" into and out of the open area.

These "risk assessment activities" help the (unsettled and terrified) rats gather new information about the possible danger source (Pinel & Mana, 1989). The marshalling of such information appears to provide the basis for a gradual return to "nondefensive" behaviors, (Blanchard, Blanchard, & Hori, 1989). This is clearly not mere habituation. The rats are reconstructing their world—integrating the anomalous occurrence with what they "understood" previously—while engaged in fear-regulated incentive–reward-mediated exploratory behavior. Such behavior is

> ... not seen during early post-cat exposure, when freezing and avoidance of the open area are the dominant behaviors, but rises to a peak about 7–10 hours later, and then gradually declines. Nondefensive behaviors such as eating, drinking and sexual and aggressive activity tend to be reduced over the same period (Blanchard, Veniegas, Elloran, & Blanchard, 1993).

The unexpected appearance of a predator, *where nothing but defined territory previously existed,* terrifies the rats—badly enough so that they "scream" about it, persistently, for a long period of time. Once this initial terror abates—which only occurs if nothing else horrible or punishing happens—curiosity is disinhibited, and the rats return to the scene of the crime. The space "renovelized" by the fact of the cat has to be transformed once again into explored territory—*as a consequence of active modification of behavior (and representational schema), not by passive desensitization to the unexpected.* The rats run across the territory "contaminated" by the presence of the cat, to find out if anything dangerous (to running rats) still lurks there. If the answer is "no," then the space is defined, once again, as home territory (which is that place where commonplace behaviors produce desired ends). The rats transform the dangerous unknown into familiar territory, as a consequence of voluntary exploration. In the absence of such exploration, terror reigns unchecked.

Gray drew on the work of the pioneering Russian neuropsychologist Sokolov (1969) who began work on the "reflex basis" of attention in the 1950s. By the early 1960s this work had advanced to the point where he could formulate the following key propositions—*first:*

> One possible approach to analyzing the process of reflection is to consider the nervous system as a mechanism which models the external world by specific changes that occur in its internal structure. In this sense a distinct set of changes in the nervous system is isomorphic with the external

agent that it reflects and resembles. As an internal model that develops in the nervous system in response to the effect of agents in the environment, the image performs the vital function of modifying the nature of behavior, allowing the organism to predict events and actively adjust to its environment.

and *second*:

My first encounter with phenomena which indicated that the higher divisions of the central nervous system form models of external agents involved the study of reactions to "novel" [stimulus features. I characterized these reactions as] orienting reflexes. The peculiar feature of the orienting reflex is that after several applications of the same stimulus (generally five to fifteen) the response disappears (or, as the general expression goes, "is extinguished"). However, the slightest possible change in the stimulus is sufficient to awaken the response.... Research on the orienting reflex indicates that it does not occur as a direct result of incoming excitation; rather, it is produced by signals of discrepancy which develop when afferent [incoming] signals are compared with the trace formed in the nervous system by an earlier signal.

Sokolov was concerned primarily with the modeling of the events in the objective external world—assuming, essentially, that when we model, we model facts. Most of the scholars who have followed his lead have adopted this central assumption, at least implicitly (including Gray). This position requires some modification. We do model facts, but we concern ourselves with valence or value. It is therefore the case that our maps of the world contain what might be regarded as two distinct types of information—sensory and affective. It is not enough to know that something *is*. It is equally necessary to know what it signifies. It might even be argued that animals—and human beings—are primarily concerned with the affective or emotional significance of the environment.

Along with our animal cousins, we devote ourselves to fundamentals: will this (new) thing eat me? Can I eat it? Will it chase me? Should I chase it? Can I make love to it? Will it make love to me? We model facts—there is no doubt about that. But we model facts to keep track of meaning. We may model facts, and it is no doubt useful to do so. We must model meanings, however, in order to survive. Our most fundamental

maps of experience—maps which, I would argue, have a narrative structure—portray *the motivational value of our current state*, conceived of *in contrast to a hypothetical ideal*, accompanied *by plans of action*, which are our pragmatic notions about how to get what we want (see Fig. 2). Description of these three elements—current state, future state, and means of mediation—constitute the necessary and sufficient preconditions for the weaving of the most simple *story*, which I would argue is a means for describing the valence of a given environment in reference to a temporally and spatially bounded set of action patterns. Getting to point B presupposes that you are at point A—you can't plan movement in the absence of an initial position. The fact that point B constitutes the end-goal means that it is valenced more highly than point A—that it is a place more desirable when considered against the necessary contrast of the current position. It is the perceived improvement of point B that makes the whole map meaningful—that is, affect-laden; it is the capacity to contrast hypothetical or abstract end points, such as B, that makes human beings capable of using their cognitive systems to modulate their affective reactions. Descriptions of such maps—whether acted, orally transmitted, or written—are intrinsically interesting, as they capture our emotional systems and engage us, abstractly, in a simulated world.

George Kelly predicated his personality theory on the notion that human beings were very motivated to be right. He believed that we act as natural scientists, formulating theories about the unfolding of the world and arranging those theories to maximize their predictive utility. He thought, furthermore, that we were constantly engaged in the process of extending the application of our predictive notions and that we were very likely to manifest hostility to any thing (or any one) whose existence or conceptions upset our theoretical apple-cart. Kelly's work has been criticized for its lack of attention to motivation. Indeed, he does say that to be wrong is tantamount to encountering chaos—but he does not say why chaos is so problematic. The marriage of Kelly's thinking to cybernetic theory and Gray/Sokolov's affective model pretty much solves that problem. Chaos—the unknown—has *a priori* motivational significance, which is negative, upon initial encounter. Avoidance of the unknown phenomena ensures that its labeling as negative remains intact; cautious voluntary exploration, by contrast, may transform it into something positive (but is a procedure not without mortal risk). One more piece of theorizing is necessary, however, to make of this discussion something truly applicable to human behavior.

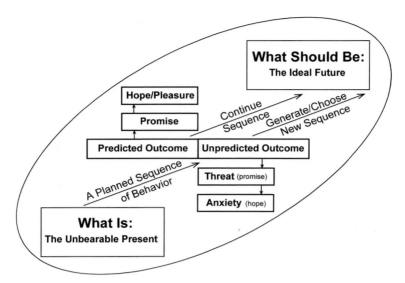

FIGURE 2 Schematically represents the emergence of "normal" or "bounded" novelty. An unexpected event may only be sufficiently unexpected to necessitate the transformation of means. This transformation is accompanied by the "release" of a bounded quantity of emotion (so to speak). The end remains clearly in sight; only the means have to be changed. It might be suggested that novelty emerging at this level might even be interesting a priori (rather than threatening)—assuming that the "recipient" has the time and will to explore.

Rats can engage in goal-directed behavior, but they cannot abstract (or if they can abstract, they can only do so in a nonverbal manner). Human beings, by contrast, have an apparently endless capacity for abstraction—can make hierarchies of abstractions: a number, for example, which is in and of itself a symbol for a thing (or many things) can be abstracted into the algebraic *x*, which becomes a symbol for any number. Carver and Scheier, working on a variant of cybernetic theory, have constructed a theory of "hierarchical goals." They state—quite reasonably—that "a hierarchically organized system by definition has both superordinate goals and subordinate goals. Attainment of the latter are requisite to—and intimately involved in—attainment of the former" (p. 112). That is, the attainment of "big goals" is dependent upon the attainment of a multitude of "little goals." Becoming a doctor means going to medical school means getting good grades means studying hard means bringing many books home from the library. The converse of Carver and Scheier's statement is also true, however: the validity of subordinate goals (that is, their manifestation as stably positively valenced phenomena) is dependent on the continued integrity of higher-order goals. This means that "bringing many books home from the library" is only considered a satisfying and incentive-rewarding sequence of action when the higher-order goal of "becoming a doctor" is still considered a reasonable, likely, and desirable possibil-

ity. This means that anything that disrupts higher-order goals throws the affective valence of lower-order, subsidiary plans and goals into question. Speaking metaphorically: the disruption of superordinate goals transforms subsidiary actions and concepts into a state of chaos. Chaos is possessed of ambivalent affective status, *a priori* (is indicative of potential punishment and potential reward)—but the threatening aspect dominates on initial contact. This means that anything deemed capable of disrupting higher-order plans is reasonably viewed as a threat to the stable affective "labeling" (or phenomenological presentation) of all things subordinate to that plan. This is a deadly serious problem, because the actions and contingent beliefs that actually compose an individual life are played out at levels subordinate to, for example, maintenance of the stable culture, polity, and economy (and, more importantly, to maintenance of their perceived mythological/metaphysical *legitimacy*).

Let us now consider how goals—stories—might be hierarchically constructed in a typical social circumstance (since individuals have to pursue their individual goals in a social structure that consists of "higher-order" arrangements allowing such pursuit, in the relative absence of conflict). Imagine a father and husband, middle-class businessman, capitalistic in philosophy, wedded to the "American Way," liberal in political philosophy, Judeo-Christian in (unconscious) ethics (see Fig. 3). His activities as a father, which he values, are predicated on the economic security guaranteed by his business. His business exists as a valid and valued enterprise in the social value-schema constituting a capitalist society. Capitalistic endeavor is viewed, more generally—by our exemplary citizen and by vast numbers of his compatriots—as unequivocally "positively-valenced," as an article of faith: it is one aspect of the good life, the pursuit of happiness, recognized as an intrinsic "right of man" by the founders of the American state (hence identification with the "American Way").

The complete embedding of the entire subsystem in the traditional Judeo-Christian ethic is evident in acceptance of the (mythological/metaphysical) notion of "intrinsic right" (We hold these Truths to be self-evident, that all Men are created equal, that they are endowed, by their Creator, with certain unalienable Rights...).

At each level of analysis, "unknown" territory exists—and is easily regarded as suspect. For the individual in his role as father and husband, the radical feminist might be considered contaminated by chaos, as she is "naturally" seen as a threat to the family he holds dear

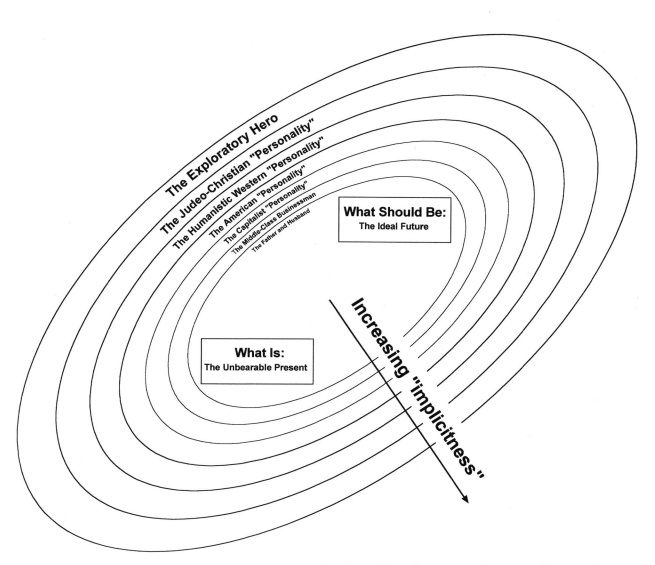

FIGURE 3 Schematically represents an exemplary individual psyche as a hierarchically arranged structure of "stories" of the form presented in Figure 2. Stability of the outermost stories constitutes a precondition for maintenance of the validity of innermost stories. A given individual is more likely to identify with those whose story-hierarchies most closely match his or her own. Those who only share "superordinate" identity but who differ "closer to home" are increasingly likely to be viewed as "emissaries of chaos."

(and whose existence lends positive meaning and predictability to his life). His competitors might be regarded as "enemies" (agents of the unknown, sources of frustration, bearers of uncertainty and anxiety) from his perspective as businessman—but these same "enemies" would surely unite behind him in his denunciation of socialism as a philosophy and those left-wingers whose ideas and actions border on incarnation of the communist ideal. Still more terrifying (more reptilian?) might be the radical Islamic fundamentalist/fascist—against whose potential unthinkable hegemony both the left-wing feminist and our exemplary pillar of society might be willing to rail. It might not even be so unreasonable to presuppose that "all things unknown" constitute a valid and relatively basic affective category—so, in the mind of the Christian capitalist American businessman husband and father *radical feminists, Islamic fundamentalists, economic competitors,* and *things that go bump in the night* may fail to be distinguished from one another, and easily acquire "characteristics" of one another (as "enemies" of the current, stable, predictable, and reinforcing social state of affairs).

It is easy to see, from this example, how social order might be regarded as more fundamental than intrapsychic integration with regard to affective regulation. The individual can only strive to be ideal as father, businessman, capitalist, and so on. The utility of this striving (which would certainly be considered an indication of optimal psychological health, if genuinely pursued) nonetheless remains dependent on the existence of a social order which (1) attributes value to those pursuits and (2) allows such pursuits to garner reinforcement in a predictable manner on a predictable schedule. It can be seen, as well—from consideration of such a hierarchy—how individual identity shades imperceptibly into social identity (as there are many more individuals joined into "unity" at each step up the hierarchical ladder—more businessmen than father/husband/businessmen, more capitalists than businessmen, more Americans than capitalists, more Christians than Americans)—and why, at least under certain conditions (when the threat is believable and proximate), that challenge to social identity is sufficiently motivating to produce aggressive behavior in defense of the entire "system" (which includes individual identity as a subordinate part).

Elkhonen Goldberg has posited that the human brain is divided into two subsystems, one of which deals with novelty and one of which deals with familiarity. These subsystems are lateralized: in the right-handed individual, the right hemisphere (whose frontal operations

Richard Davidson has associated with negative affect) preferentially deals with the unknown, while the left hemisphere (whose frontal operations Davidson has associated with positive affect) deals with the previously categorized and explored. There are apparently good reasons for such a division: Grossberg has noted that artificial categorization "machines" tend to break down when confronted by novel information unless they are composed of separate systems for maintenance of categories and update of those categories. It strikes me as reasonable, however, to suppose that "novelty" is too abstract an entity to account for something as fundamental as hemispheric division. Perhaps it is more likely that the "novelty" subsystem is really specialized for operation in unfamiliar territory, while its partner is specialized for operation where things are explored/understood. This would mean that as territory becomes "abstracted"—that is, representable in image and word—the "unfamiliar territory hemisphere" would increasingly begin to operate in the presence of unfamiliar concepts (and that unfamiliar concepts would easily come to be categorized with the other denizens of the unknown). This would imply a fundamental identity between the strange occurrence, the strange person, and the strange idea—all threatening (although useful with sufficient exploration), all "foreign," all easily demonized—and all easily transformed into valid targets for aggression (Peterson, 1999).

George Kelly's theory is once again valid in this regard. He believed that human beings were apt to repress or otherwise restrict the appearance of "data" that invalidated their conceptual models. These data might include the ideas of other human beings—or the individuals who embodied those ideas themselves. He entitled this tendency "hostility" and regarded it as "extortion of confirmation"—a particularly apt phrase, reminiscent of the (incomprehensible) insistence by Stalinist Soviet officials that their inevitably-to-be-punished-anyway victims "confess" before being jailed or killed. Kelly (1969) states:

> . . . a major revision of one's construct system can threaten [one] with immediate change, or chaos, or anxiety. Thus it often seems better to extort confirmation of one's opinion—and therefore of the system that produced them—rather than to risk the utter confusion of those moments of transition.

Kellyan "hostility" is clearly a category that could be extended to include Freudian mechanisms of defense, Adlerian living the life-lie, Jungian failure to identify with the hero, or even with existentialist or Rogerian inauthenticity (to give Rogers his due). The inability to confront evidence of systemic error is clearly central to our notions of individual psychopathology. Perhaps we should extend that notion to the social realm and begin to speak of "social psychopathology"—that is, the tendency to demonize evidence of social/personal conceptual insufficiency or the bearers of that evidence—and then to "morally" attempt to eliminate them for existence.

From a certain perspective, this is a depressing theory. Human beings "naturally" divide the world up into chaos and order, darkness and light, nature and culture, fear and security, stranger and kinsman. The meta-category of fear/stranger/darkness/chaos leaps perhaps as naturally to mind. It is reasonable, furthermore, to fear the unknown: it is after all the place where death and destruction truly lurk. Does this mean that there is an irrevocable human tendency to demonize the foreigner and to strive for the shedding of his blood? We might look to mythology—and to neuropsychology—one final time for a more optimistic conclusion. It is "moral," from the mythological standpoint, to exist as the embodiment of social order—to follow the ten commandments, to take a traditional example, and to make of social propriety the highest good. There are two detrimental aspects to this morality, however. The blind worship of tradition makes positive change impossible—first, as *what is* is regarded as *what should be,* from the socially identified standpoint (and no higher good is thus deemed possible) and, second, as the bearer of change is inevitably regarded as evil (as no good could possibly come from transformation of the status quo). This makes the strange, the stranger, and the strange idea all sworn enemies of those who preferentially value social identity. Mythology pushes forward another ideal, however, which supersedes social identity as moral pinnacle: that of identity with the *logos*—the creative Word, the process that makes order out of chaos (without being the order itself).

The message from this mythological perspective (which underlies hero mythology in its multitude of guises) is straightforward: identity with the process that generates social order (presuming mastery of that order) is preferable to identity with social order itself. Thus, participation in the process that bestows acceptable emotional valence on heretofore unknown phenomena is to be regarded as more appropriate than adherence to traditional modes of apprehension, no matter how valuable these proved to be in the past—particularly in the circumstance where the two moral positions (exploration/update vs maintenance of group

identity) produce conflicting messages for action (Peterson, 1999). Kelly states:

> The acknowledgement of defeat or tragedy is not a destructive step for man to take. It characterizes, instead, the negative outcome of any crucial test of our way of life, and it is, therefore, an essential feature of human progress toward more positive outcomes. Hostility does not, for this very reason, contribute to human achievement. Primarily because it denies failure it leads, instead, to the abatement of human enterprise, and substitutes for nobler undertakings a mask of complacency.

It is clear from the neuropsychopharmacological perspective that participation in this process—conceptualized as the constant voluntary encounter with the unknown and its exploration-guided categorization—is intrinsically rewarding (since the unknown in its positive guise has potent incentive reward properties). This intrinsic reward likely accounts for the positive value frequently attributed to exploration, creativity, and discovery.

The logic which associates the *other* with the Devil (or which fails to initially distinguish between the two) only applies for those who think that morality means nothing but obedience and belief—identification with a set of static facts—and not incarnation of the creative process in behavior. The existence of the anomalous fact, properly considered—the fact, embodied in the stranger or rendered abstract in the form of differing philosophy—is by contrast a *call to moral action and not an evil.* It is the motivated inertial proclivity to cling to undeserved security, despite evidence of error, that in fact underlies the human tendency to evil—and that produces a truly Satanic perspective:

> Farewell happy Fields
> Where Joy for ever dwells: Hail horrors, hail
> Infernal world, and thou profoundest Hell
> Receive thy new Possessor: One who brings
> A mind not to be chang'd by Place or Time.
>
> (*Milton, Paradise Lost,* 1667)

Frye (1990) links the mindset associated with this perspective explicitly with "Luciferian" presumption—in the sense that Milton attempted to render, if not explicit, at least dramatic. He points out that:

> A demonic fall, as Milton presents it, involves defiance and rivalry with God rather than simple disobedience, and hence the demonic society is

a sustained and systematic parody of the divine one, associated with devils or fallen angels because it seems far beyond normal human capacities in its powers. We read of ascending and descending angels on Jacob's and Plato's ladders, and similarly there seem to be demonic reinforcements in heathen life that account for the almost superhuman grandeur of the heathen empires, especially just before they fall.

Frye describes the "mythological representation" of the "spirit of such empires" in the Judeo-Christian tradition:

> Two particularly notable passages in the Old Testament prophets linked to this theme are the denunciation of Babylon in Isaiah 14 and of Tyre in Ezekiel 28. Bablyon is associated with Lucifer the morning star, who said to himself: "I will be like the Most High"; Tyre is identified with a "Covering Cherub," a splendid creature living in the garden of Eden "till the day that iniquity was found in thee." In the New Testament (Luke 10:18) Jesus speaks of Satan as falling from heaven, hence Satan's traditional identification with Isaiah's Lucifer and his growth in Legend into the great adversary of God, once the prince of the angels, and, before being displaced, the firstborn son of God. The superhuman demonic force behind the heathen kingdoms is called in Christianity the Antichrist, the earthly ruler demanding divine honors.

Stable tradition conjoined with the capacity for flexible change means security without tyranny. Sacrifice of the capacity for necessary change, however, means destruction of the capacity to turn chaos into order. Without that capacity, chaos eventually overwhelms order—no matter how solidly constructed by the heroes of the past. When chaos rules, all hell breaks loose, and individual desire for revenge—in any form—becomes paramount. Thus, the archetypal evil that characterizes every individual surfaces and works to destroy suffering life:

> The spirit I, that endlessly denies.
> And rightly, too; for all that comes to birth
> Is fit for overthrow, as nothing worth;
> wherefore the world were better sterilized;
> Thus all that's here as Evil recognized
> Is gain to me, and downfall, ruin, sin
> The very element I prosper in.
>
> *(Goethe, Faust)*

Two concrete historical events—otherwise very difficult to comprehend—might reasonably be considered from the theoretical standpoint outlined so far.

First: the Nazis, having begun World War II were no doubt very motivated to win it. However, they persisted in acting in at least one peculiar way that certainly limited their war-time capacity. In theory, the Jews were to provide (valuable) labor in the camps before they were killed—labor necessary to further the war effort. In practice, however—as Daniel Jonah Goldhagen has been at pains to establish—Jewish camp "work" was merely nonproductive torture as a prelude to inevitable death. It must be understood: the "nonproductive" aspect of the work was part of what made it torture. After all, an enslaved bricklayer might still extract some satisfaction (no matter how trivial) from a wall well laid, even if he is compelled against his will to build it. Carrying sacks of wet salt back and forth, by contrast—a familiar task in Buchenwald—clearly constitutes a pathological mimicry of work, demanded only to increase the sum total of misery in the world. So Goldhagen (1996) states:

> The phenomenon of Jewish "work" was such a triumph of politics and ideology over economic self-interest not only because the Germans killed irreplaceable workers, but also in the more profound sense that even when they were not killing them, Germans, owing to the character of their racial antipathy, had great difficulties employing Jews rationally in the economy. The words and deeds of Heydrich, Himmler, and countless others reveal the real relationship between Jewish "work" and Jewish death in Germany. Work put into motion beings whom the Germans themselves had already condemned to death, socially dead beings with a temporary lease on socially dead life. In its essence, Jewish "work" was not work in any ordinary sense of "work"—but a suspended form of death—in other words, it was death itself.

It is an indication of possession by a true aesthetic of evil to become sufficiently preoccupied with the torturing of a victim to sacrifice even self-interest to that end—or, more to the point, to acquiesce willingly to one's own (eventual) misery, as long as one was first allowed the pleasure of ensuring the misery of others.

Second: in the final stages of World War II, when the Germans had clearly lost, when the German state was collapsing, and when Himmler had explicitly ordered those guarding Jews in concentration camps to desist from their killing—the destructive and still-geno-cidal phenomenon of the " death march" nonetheless "spontaneously" emerged (and in a number of different locales). Essentially what happened was this: various camps were emptied of prisoners, marching under the supervision of their jailers, bereft of direction—or apparent rationale. Goldhagen (1996) states:

> Viewing the maps of some. . .death march routes should be sufficient to convince anyone that the meanderings could have had no end other than to keep the prisoners marching. And the effects were calculable—and calculating. The Germans in charge of the marches, who, cut off from their headquarters, were almost always on their own while under way, were under no compulsion to trek aimlessly; they could have chosen to remain in one place, feed their prisoners, and deliver them to the Allies, who, no matter what, were bound to reach them in a few days or weeks. As far as is known, this never occurred. The death marches were not means of transport; the marching transports were means of death.

Explaining a phenomenon of the first sort (that is, the wastage of work useful to the Nazi wartime effort) is beyond the capacity of a theory that relies solely on protection of group identity as source of motivation—as the Germans were clearly engaging in a destructive enterprise with regard to the Jews that worked at cross-purposes to their own survival. Explaining a phenomenon of the second sort—which is voluntary engagement in torture and destruction, bereft of supervision (even undertaken in defiance of previous authority)—is beyond the capacity of group-identity theories and of explanations relying on the phenomenon of "obedience to authority," like those of Milgram (1974). Neither can these occurrences—or others like them—be explained through recourse to standard economic or political theories of motivation, positing "rational self-interest" as the directing force underlying human behavior and belief. An alternative is needed, of the following sort (which extends the "maintenance of affective-regulation/group-identity theory," laid out initially).

Individuals work to maintain and extend the boundaries of the stories that regulate their social existence, their individual goals, and their emotions—that is, work to maintain and extend the boundaries of stories they embody and represent abstractly. Sources of anomalous information—which threaten the structure of those stories—can be confronted and mined for significance. This means voluntary tolerance of an interim period of anxiety followed by reestablishment of (enhanced) stability (see Fig. 4). This pattern of voluntary "simple story" transformation has been conceptualized, simply, as steady state, breach, crisis, redress (and is central to complex narrative—mythology—itself). The same pattern underlies archaic rites of initiation, processes of theoretical transformation, and more abstract religious systems of thought, such as Christianity or Buddhism. Our great rituals, dramas, and religions—our most profound narratives and protonarratives—are erected upon the (meta)story of paradise, encounter with chaos, fall, and redemption.

Alternatively, anomalous information can be avoided—not precisely repressed, but *not explored* (or, if extant in the guise of another, actively and violently suppressed or eliminated). This means (voluntary) failure to update the story guiding ongoing action in consequence of desire to avoid (intermediary) chaos. Such failure means existence in an ever-more narrow frame—and increasing "distance" of that frame from the world it purports to explain. The "avoidance or suppression" of novel or unexpected experience, which is the abstract equivalent of running away, transforms it perforce into threat (casts it into the terrible "reptilian" domain). This is refusal of the left-frontal-hemisphere-dominated cortical systems that underlie the "ego," so to speak, to communicate with the right, which always bears bad news—and the consequent dissociation and disintegration of the intrapsychic universe. The domain of unprocessed novelty, defined prima facie by inaction and avoidance as "threat too intolerable to face", expands inevitably with time when the past is held as absolute. More and more experience is therefore rendered intolerable, inexplicable, and chaotic, as the cumulative effects of using the lie as a mode of adaptation inexorably manifest themselves. The lie transforms culture into tyranny, change into horror, while sickening and restricting the development and flexibility of adaptive ability itself (see Fig. 5). Reliance on the lie ensures—as fears grows—heightened, pathologized identification with the past (manifested as fascism and in personal and political intolerance) or decadent degeneration (manifested as nihilism and in personal and social deterioration). Use of the lie as a mode of adaptation makes a trap of the past and pandemonium of the present. Identification with the spirit of denial eventually makes life unbearable, as everything new—and, therefore, everything defining hope—is merely regarded as punishment and threat. The attendant and unavoidable suffering experienced as in consequence generates the desire for—and motivates actions predicated on the attainment of—absolute annihilation as compensation

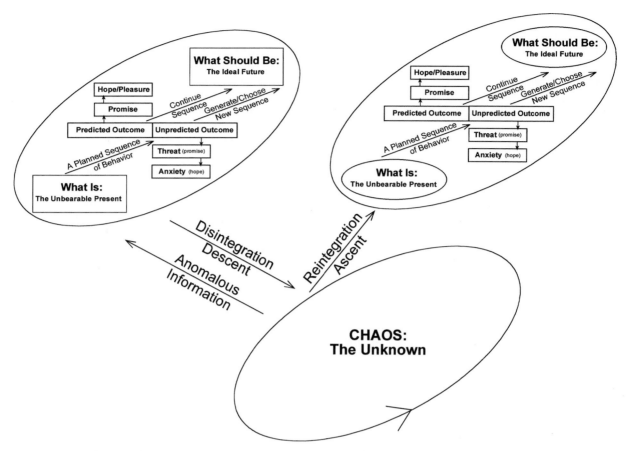

FIGURE 4 Schematically portrays the dissolution and regeneration of a stable story. Sufficiently anomalous information can undermine not only the means to an end, but the end itself. Such disruption produces emotional dysregulation, as the stable meaning attributed to events in the course of normal goal-directed behavior disappears and is replaced by more global and negative emotion (consequent to the "renovelization" of previously categorized experience). The reemergent story—which will only emerge as a consequence of voluntary exploratory behavior—should be more "complete" than the story it replaces, as it "consists" of the constituent elements of the previous story "integrated" with the information exploration of the anomalous occurrence generated. The reemergent story should be more stable—that is, less easily disrupted by ongoing events (since it now accounts for an additional possibility: that is, the previously destructive anomaly). The reestablishment of a new story might be considered another "stage" in cognitive development.

and revenge for sterility, absence of meaning, anxiety, hatred, and pain:

> The Marabout draws a large circle in the dirt, which represents the world. He places a scorpion, symbolic of man, inside the circle. The scorpion, believing it has achieved freedom, starts to run around the circle—but never attempts to go outside. After the scorpion has raced several times around the inside edge of the circle, the Marabout lowers his stick and divides the circle in half. The scorpion stops for a few seconds, then begins to run faster and faster, apparently looking for a way out, but never finding it. Strangely enough, the scorpion does not dare to cross over the line. After a few minutes, the Marabout divides the half circle. The scorpion becomes frantic. Soon the Marabout makes a space no bigger than the scorpion's body. This is "the moment of truth." The scorpion, dazed and bewildered, finds itself unable to move one way or another. Raising its venomous tail, the scorpion turns rapidly 'round and 'round in a veritable frenzy. Whirling, whirling, whirling until all of its spirit and energy are spent. In utter hopelessness the scorpion stops, lowers the poisonous point of its tail, and

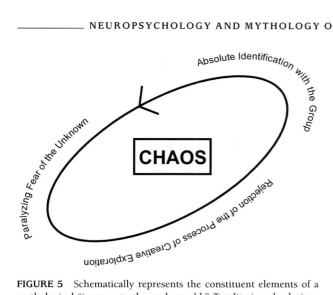

FIGURE 5 Schematically represents the constituent elements of a mythological "journey to the underworld." Totalitarian absolutism, rejection of the process of creative exploration, and consequent paralyzing fear of the unknown are viewed here as interacting parts of a process that inevitably produces dysregulation of individual emotion and increasing meaningless suffering. This cycle produces an individual "inhabitant of chaos," who is easily led to acts of resentment-motivated hatred. The "adversary" is here conceptualized as the "archetypal" and omnipresent enemy of courageous and creative thinking.

stings itself to death. Its torment is ended (Edwardes & Masters, 1963).

The individual who lives by the lie continually and inevitably shrinks his domain of competence—his "explored and familiar territory" and his "capacity for independent creative exploration." This means, as well, that he surrounds himself with an ever-growing "domain of unexplored chaos"—intrinsically terrifying, at first encounter, magnified in its unacceptability by the implicity "categorical" act of constantly running away. When this chaos eventually engulfs the deceitful authoritarian (which it certainly will, as the "environment" moves inexorably farther away from his "conceptualization") and presents him with a problem that his ever-more-rigid group identity just will not solve—he will also be unable to rely on himself. He will find his personality deceitful, shrunken, and cowardly as a consequence of too much obedience and his pattern of habitual avoidance. He will be left, under such circumstances, in the grip of resentment, hatred, and fear, in consequence of his existence in a world that he has voluntarily rendered "beyond his capacity for successful adaptation." The chaos he rejected, in search of security, will thereby attain its inevitable victory—as another "sold soul," so to speak, finds its ultimate resting place.

The "vicious circle" created by the obedient/avoidant individual spirals down inevitably to the underworld, which waits to engulf him:

> Him the Almighty Power
> Hurled headlong flaming from the ethereal Sky
> With hideous ruin and combustion down
> To bottomless perdition, there to dwell
> In Adamantine Chains and penal Fire.
>
> *(Milton, Paradise lost,* 1667)

This miserable existence fills him with hate—hate that he expresses in identity with archetypal evil, in active revenge against existence:

> —for whence
> But from the author of all ill could spring
> So deep a malice, to confound the race
> Of mankind in one root, and Earth with Hell
> To mingle and involve, done all to spite
> The great Creator?
>
> *(Milton, Paradise Lost,* 1667)

So the human desire to "be right, above all"—to presume personal omniscience—produces a state of being antithetically opposed to the process of anomaly-incorporation, and characterized by increasing environmental maladaptation. This process has been represented mythologically as the heavenly insurrection of Lucifer, motivated by the desire to be placed above God in the "spiritual hierarchy." Such maladaptation produces increased suffering of an increasingly meaningless sort; that suffering in turn breeds resentment and the desire for revenge. Vengeful desire and resentment broods, patiently, waiting for a forum of risk-free manifestation. When patriotism calls for brutality—during the "call to war," for example—the individual is well-prepared. He can torment the "enemies of the state," hide behind a mask of admirable social conformity—even bravery—and fulfill his darkest fantasies:

> With cohesion, construction, grit and repression
> Wring the neck of this gang run riot!
>
> *(Mayakovsky in Solzhenitsyn, 1973)*

Thus the existential cowardice of the individual pathologically increases the danger of the intrinsic and necessary territoriality of the species—and atrocities committed "in the name of the state" continue to threaten both human self-regard and the likelihood of long-term human survival.

Also See the Following Articles

AGGRESSION AND ALTRUISM • AGGRESSION, PSYCHOLOGY OF • ANIMAL BEHAVIOR STUDIES • BEHAVIORAL PSYCHOLOGY • ENEMY, CONCEPT AND IDENTITY OF • ETHNIC CONFLICTS AND COOPERATION • TERRITORIAL DISPUTES

Bibliography

Blanchard, D. J., & Blanchard, D. C. (1989). Antipredator defensive behaviors in a visible burrow system. *Journal of Comparative Psychology, 103,* 70–82.

Blanchard, R. J., Blanchard, D. C., & Hori, K. (1989). Ethoexperimental approach to the study of defensive behavior. In R. J. Blanchard, P. F. Brain, D. C. Blanchard, & S. Parmigiani (Eds.), *Ethoexperimental approaches to the study of behavior* (pp. 114–136). Boston: Kluwer–Nijhoff.

Blanchard, D. C., Blanchard, R. J., & Rodgers, R. J. (1991). Risk assessment and animal models of anxiety. In B. Olivier, J. Mos, & J. L. Slangen (Eds.), *Animal models in psychopharmacology* (pp. 117–134). Boston: Birkhauser-Verlag.

Blanchard, D. C., Veniegas, R., Elloran, I., & Blanchard, R. J. (1993). *Journal of Studies on Alcohol, 11,* 9–19.

Bruner, J. (1986). *Actual minds, possible worlds.* Cambridge, MA: Harvard University Press.

Campbell, J. (1968). *The hero with a thousand faces.* Princeton, NJ: Princeton University Press.

Carver, C. S., & Scheier, M. F. (1982). Control theory: A useful conceptual framework for personality-social, clinical and health psychology. *Psychological Bulletin, 92,* 111–135.

Chang, I. (1997). *The rape of Nanking: The forgotten holocaust of World War II.* New York: Basic Books.

Cohen, L. (1984). The captain. *Various positions.* CBS Recordings.

Davidson, R. J. (1984a). Affect, cognition and hemispheric specialization. In C. E. Izard, J. Kagan, & R. Zajonc (Eds.), *Emotion, cognition and behavior* (pp. 320–365). New York: Cambridge University Press.

Davidson, R. J. (1984b). Hemispheric asymmetry and emotion. In K. Scherer & P. Ekman (Eds.), *Approaches to emotion* (pp. 39–57). Hillsdale, NJ: Erlbaum.

Davidson, R. J. (1992). Anterior cerebral asymmetry and the nature of emotion. *Brain and Cognition, 20,* 125–151.

Dollard, J., & Miller, N. E. (1950). *Personality and psychotherapy: An analysis in terms of learning, thinking and culture.* New York: McGraw–Hill.

Edwardes, A., & Masters, R. E. L. (1963). *The cradle of erotica.* New York: Julian Press.

Eliade, M. (1958). *Rites and symbols of initiation: The mysteries of birth and rebirth.* New York: Harper–Colophon.

Eliade, M. (1959/1987). *The sacred and the profane: The nature of religion.* New York: Harcourt Brace.

Eliade, M. (1978). *A history of religious ideas (Vols. 1–3).* Chicago: University of Chicago Press.

Freud, S. (1965). Lecture XXXI: The dissection of the psychical personality. In J. Strachey (Ed.), *The standard edition of the complete works of Sigmund Freud: New introductory lectures on psychoanalysis* (pp. 51–71). New York: Norton.

Frye, N. (1990). *Words with power: Being a second study of the Bible and literature.* New York: Viking.

Fukuyama, F. (1993). *The end of history and the last man.* New York: Avon Books.

Goethe, J. W. (1979). *Faust, part one and two.* (translated by P. Wayne). New York: Penguin.

Goldberg, E., & Costa, L. D. (1981). Hemisphere differences in the acquisition and use of descriptive systems. *Brain and Language, 14,* 144–173.

Goldberg, E., Podell, K., & Lovell, M. (1994). Lateralization of frontal lobe functions and cognitive novelty. *Journal of Neuropsychiatry and Clinical Neuroscience, 6,* 371–378.

Goldhagen, D. J. (1996). *Hitler's willing executioners: Ordinary germans and the Holocaust.* New York: Alfred Knopf.

Goodall, J. (1990). *Through a window.* Boston: Houghton–Mifflin.

Gray, J. A. (1982). *The neuropsychology of anxiety: An enquiry into the function of the septal–hippocampal system.* Oxford: Oxford University Press.

Gray, J. A., & McNaughton, N. (1996). The neuropsychology of anxiety: Reprise. *Nebraska Symposium on Motivation, 43,* 61–134.

Gray, J. A., Feldon, J., Rawlins, J. N. P., Hemsley, D. R., & Smith, A. D. (1991). The neuropsychology of schizophrenia. *Behavioral and Brain Sciences, 14,* 1–84.

Hebb, D. O., & Thompson, W. R. (1985). The social significance of animal studies. In G. Lindzey & E. Aronson (Eds.), *The handbook of social psychology* (pp. 729–774). New York: Random House.

Jung, C. G. (1960). *Two essays on analytical psychology.* Princeton, NJ: Princeton University Press.

Jung, C. G. (1967). *Symbols of transformation: An analysis of the prelude to a case of schizophrenia* (translated by R. F. C. Hull). Princeton, NJ: Princeton University Press.

Jung, C. G. (1969). *Psychology and Religion: West and East.* (Volume 13, Collected Works). Translated by R.F.C. Hull. Princeton, NJ: Princeton University Press.

Jung, C. G. (1980). *Psychology and alchemy.* Princeton, NJ: Princeton University Press.

Kelly, G. (1955). *The psychology of personal constructs.* New York: W. W. Norton and Co.

Kelly, G. (1969). The threat of aggression. In B. Maher (Ed.), *Clinical psychology and personality: The selected papers of George Kelly* (pp. 281–288). New York: Wiley.

Kuhn, T. (1970). *The structure of scientific revolutions.* Chicago: University of Chicago Press.

Lorenz, K. (1974). *On aggression* New York: Harcourt Brace Jovanovitch.

Lubow, R. E. (1989). *Latent inhibition and conditioned attention theory.* Cambridge: Cambridge University Press.

Maslow, A. H. (1954). *Motivation and Personality.* New York: Harper & Row.

Milgram, S. (1974). *Obedience to authority: An experimental view.* New York: Harper & Row.

Miller, G. E., Galanter, E., & Pribram, K. H. (1960). *Plans and the structure of behavior.* New York: Henry Holt and Co.

Milton, J. (1667/1961). *Paradise lost (and other poems)* (annotated by E. LeComte). New York: New American Library.

Morley, J. (1923). *Rousseau and his era: Volume 1.* New York: Harper and Brothers.

Neumann, E. (1954). *The origins and history of consciousness.* Princeton, NJ: Princeton University Press.

Oatley, K. (1994). A taxonomy of the emotions of literary response and a theory of identification in fictional narrative. *Poetics, 23,* 53–74.

Peterson, J. B. (1999). *Maps of meaning: The architecture of belief.* New York: Routledge.

Pinel, J. P. J., & Mana, M. J. (1989). Adaptive interactions of rats with dangerous inanimate objects: Support for a cognitive theory of defensive behavior. In R. J. Blanchard, P.F. Brain, D.C. Blanchard, & S. Parmigiani. (Eds.), *Ethoexperimental approaches to the study of behavior* (pp. 137–155). Boston: Kluwer–Nijhoff.

Rogers, C. R. (1951). *Client-centered therapy.* Boston: Houghton–Mifflin.

Sarbin, T. R. (1986). The narrative as a root metaphor for psychology. In T. R. Sarbin (Ed.), *Narrative psychology: The storied nature of human conduct* (pp. 3–21). New York: Praeger.

Sokolov, E. N. (1969). The modeling properties of the nervous system. In I. Maltzman, & K. Coles (Eds.), *Handbook of contemporary soviet psychology* (pp. 670–704). New York: Basic Books.

Solzhenitsyn, A. I. (1975). *The gulag archipelago* (Vol. 2). New York: Harper & Row.

Tolstoy, L. (1983). *Confessions* (translated by D. Patterson). New York: W. W. Norton and Co.

Wiener, N. (1948). *Cybernetics: Or, control and communication in the animal and the machine.* Cambridge, MA: Technology Press.

Nongovernmental Actors in International Politics

Janet Welsh Brown

World Resources Institute

GLOSSARY

Biological Diversity (or Biodiversity) The full variety of organisms, including plants and animals, genetic variation within species, and diversity of ecosystems.

Civil Society The term used to denote a whole array of organized voluntary or community efforts, sometimes used interchangeably with nongovernmental organizations or efforts.

Global Warming The trend of increasing temperatures on the earth's surface and in the lower atmosphere, caused by the entrapment of heat due to the accumulation of certain gases, mainly carbon dioxide.

Ozone Layer A protective concentration of ozone in the stratosphere, between 9.3 and 31 miles above the earth, depending on the season and other factors.

I. INTRODUCTION—THE VARIETY OF ISSUES AND ORGANIZATIONS

One of the most astonishing current developments in world affairs is the growing effectiveness of nonstate actors in international politics. Only national governments can be parties to treaties, of course, but nonstate entities play a role at many other levels. They come in different forms. There are international organizations such as the World Bank and regional interstate organizations like NATO, the European Union, and the Organization of American States, which take part in security, trade, and peace negotiations as participating entities, even while individual member governments pursue their own particular agendas. Substates—that is, provinces, states, and even municipalities—may pursue their own foreign policies declaring nuclear-free zones and offering development assistance, commerce, and cultural exchanges with sister cities. Some individual states—such as California, whose economy is bigger than that of all but a handful of the United States' major trading partners—have sufficient leverage to foster their own trade deals. Cities from many parts of the world have organized together for the purpose of making an impact on major negotiations or UN Conferences on Habitat, or the Environment and Development.

Business and industry, which in past generations, have pursued their international interests solely through their governments, now come to negotiations as independent players—to represent their company's

Copyright © 1999 by Academic Press.
All rights of reproduction in any form reserved.

interests or as expert consultants to international bodies. They may organize for that purpose. Indeed, there are two different groups of energy corporations representing support for any opposition to stronger environmental measures at recent Climate Convention conferences of the parties, where important treaty amendments are negotiated. In these times of the multinational corporation, business interests do not always wait on their governments to represent their interests, which are not necessarily identical with those of their governments.

But it is the nongovernmental organization (NGO)—defined here as a private, nonprofit organization that is not beholden to either a government or profit-making company—that we are concerned with here, for it is this category of nonstate players that has experienced phenomenal growth in the past decade and has become a major new force in international politics. Nongovernmental organizations active in international politics come in great variety, but they are all issue oriented and advocacy organizations to some degree. They may be professional, commercial, or scientific societies, human rights, population, or women's organizations. They may represent sectoral interests: farmers or fishing interests or foresters. They may have rural, urban, or coastal development interests or be ethnic or religious groups. They may be trade organizations representing the arms industry, pulp and paper, or textile manufacturers.

Nongovernmental organizations are also organized at different levels; they may be national policy organizations or international organizations, such as Friends of the Earth International (FOEI), with more than 60 independent national affiliates. They may be *ad hoc* coalitions that come together around an issue or occasion, as the U.S. environmental groups and labor unions have done over the North American Free Trade Agreement and the General Agreement on Tariff and Trade, or permanently linked organizations, such as the international family-planning, emergency relief, and human rights organizations that have stayed with an issue over time, and deal with problems all over the world.

For purposes of illustrating in greater detail the history and influence of NGOs on international politics, we will use here as an example the work of environmental and development organizations whose overall objective is sustainable development, that is, economic development that meets the needs of the present generation without compromising the ability of future generations to meet their own needs.

II. THE GROWTH AND INFLUENCE OF ENVIRONMENTAL AND DEVELOPMENT NONGOVERNMENTAL ORGANIZATIONS

A. Nongovernmental Organizations in the Northern Countries

Even with this category—environmental and development NGOs—the variety seems uncountable. Among Northern environmental organizations that are active in international issues, for instance, there are the long-established international conservation organizations such as the World Wildlife Fund International, with chapters in many countries, that are effective players at wildlife conservation treaty negotiations and funders of wildlife protection programs. There are more activist international organizations, such as Friends of the Earth International and Greenpeace, with affiliates from the South and North who democratically determine their annual policy priorities for international campaigns to save the ozone layer or to stop trade in hazardous waste. There are powerful U.S. national organizations, such as the Environmental Defense Fund and the Natural Resources Defense Council, who pioneered economic analyses of environmental costs and benefits and take that well-developed expertise to all the international negotiations on climate change, arguing for such innovations as tradeable permits. There are policy research institutes such as the World Resources Institute in Washington, DC and the International Institute of Environment and Development in London and Buenos Aires that research and then promote with policy-makers alternative policies to protect the environment.

Increasingly the policies proposed by NGOs affect economic development as well as the environment, and so one finds established development policy organizations such as the Overseas Development Council and the Development Gap in the United States and the International Development Research Council of Canada collaborating with environmentalists. Active in the development coalitions are population and church groups—the Catholics, Lutherans, and Friends, among others—who are some of the most persistent advocates for poor people before the U.S. Congress and who also run development programs of their own overseas. All of these groups have become more professional, more expert, and more sophisticated in their strategies since the early 1980s. Their flexibility and ability to move quickly are assets in fast-breaking developments.

These organizations have very different styles, tactics, and political orientations. Some seek policy change through the courts or legislation in their own countries, some through big demonstrations and grassroots organizing—and often through a combination of these strategies. Some are low profile, like The Nature Conservancy, which protects biological diversity by purchasing key habitat areas, but seldom joins with other organizations in advocacy. Some have a high profile, like Greenpeace's daring challenges to nuclear and whaling vessels. Some, like the Environmental Defense Fund, are willing to cooperate with business, while others continue to hold the for-profit corporations responsible for most environmental damage. A few organizations, e.g., Sierra Club, have their own political action committees that evaluate legislators' voting records and campaign and raise money for candidates who champion environmental causes. (U.S. NGOs themselves are forbidden by law from participating in electoral politics.)

There is also variety in the venues in which environmental NGOs are active. They are regularly present at the meetings of some of the most powerful institutions in the world. They have been active in treaty negotiations and meetings of the Whaling Commission starting in the 1960s and on the Convention in International Trade in Endangered Species since its drafting in 1973. Since the mid-1980s they have operated effectively at the annual meetings of the World Bank and the International Monetary Fund, some demonstrating in the streets or scaling buildings to hang gigantic accusatory banners and others running parallel meetings on policy alternatives.

Major international organizations whose interests coincide with UN objectives have the right to seek on-going (permanent) observer status with the United Nations. The Quakers, the Bahai community, and the United Nations Association have long played that role. During official sessions accredited NGOs are allowed to attend most meetings, distribute information, and talk informally with delegates and the press that follows such events. In the preparatory conference for the 1992 United Nations Conference on Environment and Development, NGO representatives—well respected by the conference leadership for their expertise and support—were given the right to speak in some committee meetings and in plenary sessions. This precedent was followed, though not without objection, at the subsequent UN conferences on population, economic and social issues, women, and habitat—and at the follow-up conferences on those issues.

Starting in 1990 at Houston, environmental and development NGOs have been at the annual G-7 economic summit meetings to publicize the need for G-7 environmental cooperation or to attack the damaging effects on poverty and the environment of G-7 activity. For several years now, they must be credited for keeping environmental concerns on the G-7 agenda. And when the environmental organizations finally focused on trade issues in the early 1990s, they appeared at negotiating sessions and raised environmental and social issues. Their attention forced the U.S. negotiators to produce a formal review of the environmental impact of the proposed North American Free Trade Agreement (with Canada and Mexico) and finally to negotiate side agreements to the main treaty on environmental and labor considerations. Although most of the activities were initiated by Northern NGOs who have enjoyed larger resources and more frequent support from their political leaders, NGOs of developing nations have joined in these efforts more fully in the ensuing years.

B. Nongovernmental Organizations of Developing Nations

The variety of NGOs in developing countries is just as rich as the mix in Northern states. Some are founded and run by well-educated urbanized professionals, quite similar to those in Northern national organizations. Some are development support groups, organized around development environmental, and women's issues from the 1970s onward. Of these, some have been able to get government or foreign aid funds to run their projects. Some are peasant or urban community groups that have coalesced around a particular need—to get a community well dug or a road built—or to fight a government undertaking, such as mandatory relocation to make way for dam construction. In recent years there have also been a number of policy research institutions created in the developing countries.

Many environmental and development NGOs coexist cooperatively with government authorities and even play an intermediary role, a kind of buffer between government and the local community. Others are fiercely opposed to government policies, and environmental leaders have been jailed, even killed, for their efforts to protect tropical forests, indigenous peoples, or agricultural land in countries as different from one another as Malaysia, Brazil, and Nigeria. Traditional societies—water-users' groups, kinship organizations, mothers' clubs, street vendors, or foresters—have often evolved into development organizations. And often they are concerned about environmental problems such as soil loss, sanitation and health, or depletion of firewood sources. Perhaps the first of these to achieve popular recognition in the industrialized countries of the North was the Chipko movement in India, where peasant women sought to protect the forests from logging companies by "hugging" the trees.

To some extent, all of these organizations involve empowerment of citizens. No matter what the issue, they are likely to be putting pressure on their local, provincial, or national governments and indirectly making democratic demands for more responsible and responsive government. They are, therefore, agents of social change demanding social justice. In the 1980s, as citizens in many countries became disillusioned with their governments' ability to deliver development and related services, these elements of the civil society more and more took matters into their own hands and sought their own solutions.

Some NGOs faded away when the issue receded; some collapsed when their leaders burned out or the treasurer misspent government grant money. But many groups that have come together for a single purpose simply apply their experience and resources to another issue or join with others to work at a different level. Thus, in many countries, there are national confederations of NGOs with similar interests—such as the Kenya Environmental Non-Government Organization, which has some 70 members and ties with NGOs in a score of other African countries, and the Brazilian NGO Forum, which had 1000 members at the time of the 1992 Earth Summit in Rio.

There are probably hundreds of thousands of these organizations in the developing world. In most of them, there is no sharp distinction between environmental and development aims. The environmental issues developing country NGOs deal with are usually manifest locally rather than globally—that is, they are concerned with the health effects of traffic-polluted air rather than with global warming, with soil erosion and resulting crop loss rather than downstream pollution of coastal waters, though there are exceptions. Chilean and Argentinian NGOs, for instance, being so close to the South Pole, where the ozone layer is thinning, are active in ozone politics. But on the whole, the priorities of developing country NGOs tend to be more local and immediate than those of their counterparts in the highly industrialized countries of the North. Nor do they always have the kind of national paid memberships that provide some North American organizations with a constituency and political clout. Some are conceived as a threat not only by the sector they criticize, but also by their governments. It is those governments, usually, that have tried to block the expansion of NGO access and participation in the UN and other international forums.

Two and one-half years' preparation for the 1992 United Nations Conference on Environment and Development (UNCED) stimulated NGO growth worldwide. Assisted by improved and relatively inexpensive communications technology—telephones, faxes, and especially e-mail—NGOs were able to cooperate across borders as never before. The UNCED set the stage for a new level of NGO participation in international policymaking, first on environmental and development issues and subsequently on human rights, population, and women's issues.

C. The Earth Summit on the Environment

It was at the United Nations Conference on Environment and Development, dubbed the Earth Summit, held in Rio de Janeiro in 1992, that the nongovernmental organizations really came into their own and established themselves as a permanent factor in international negotiations. They were present in Rio in very large numbers, encouraged in part by the conference's Secretary-General, Maurice Strong, who saw them as allies and used them as resources to provide background information and position papers. The Secretariat even established an NGO liaison office to facilitate their operations. During the 2 weeks of the conference, there were 20,000 NGO participants, representing 9,000 organizations from 171 countries. Primarily environmental and development organizations, they included also women's organizations, indigenous peoples, population organizations, and religious groups. They scheduled 350 formal meetings and sponsored at least 1,000 additional substantive meetings. Their booths and tent meetings were more colorful and interesting than much of the official deliberations and so drew maximum attention from the 9,000 journalists and 450,000 other visitors at UNCED.

During the preparation for UNCED, including the four official preparatory conferences called PrepComs, NGO activity steadily increased. To the dismay of some delegations, NGOs gained access to meetings of working groups and permission to speak (albeit, last and often very late in the day) at the PrepCom plenary sessions. They distributed fact sheets and position papers. They befriended like-minded delegations, especially those from smaller countries who had few resources of their own and sometimes heavily used the materials provided by NGOs. Some delegations, including the U.S., had NGO representatives officially on their delegations, which did not noticeably change a nation's stance on the issues, but did provide yet another source of information for the NGO community on the latest developments.

There was periodic tension among the NGOs at Rio, and usually the differences broke out along North–South lines. The Northern NGOs, better staffed with more resources behind them and often more experienced in international meetings, were sometimes resented by developing country NGOs as domineering and insensitive, even ignorant, of developing country conditions. Even though most of the Southern NGOs were critical of their own governments' environmental and development policies, when thrown together with Northern counterparts at the meetings, they often criticized Northern colleagues for reflecting the same attitudes as the Northern governments, who sometimes seemed to blame developing countries for problems for which they themselves were the primary cause. What happened during the PrepCom and Conference meetings was a mutual education of Northern and Southern NGO representatives and the building of an invaluable network that lasted well beyond the Conference itself. Networks also included women's groups, human rights, and population organizations that deliberately used the Environment and Development Conference to build forward to the subsequent UN Conferences on Human Rights (Vienna, 1993). Population and Development (Cairo, 1994), and the Women's Conference (Beijing, 1995). Indeed, at the Beijing Conference, it was the women's NGOs, building on their participation at the Earth Summit in Rio, who helped to inject onto the Agenda the special impact on women of environmental and development issues (as well as human rights and social justice) and women's roles in resource management. The Chinese hosts, though amply warned, were totally unprepared for the variety, intensity, and effectiveness of the NGO women, who overcame all obstacles hurled at them by the weather and the Chinese government.

The participation of these and other organizations throughout the UNCED process had a clear effect on the outcome, stretching its agenda more broadly than the General Assembly ever intended when it set up the Conference. At NGO insistence, the delegates were forced to include population and consumption and trade issues in the Conference agenda and recommendations. The official documents from Rio, a *Declaration of Principles* and *Agenda 21*, witness NGO influence. More than 170 governments signed on to some revolutionary ideas: broad citizen participation in decision-making, access to information and the states' obligation to educate citizens (women included), to promote public awareness of environmental problems, and to provide citizens access to redress and remedies.

In *Agenda 21*, a detailed, 280-page blueprint of direc-

tions to achieve sustainable development, 10 of the 40 chapters are devoted to NGO constituencies—women, children and youth, indigenous peoples, local authorities, workers, business, the scientific community, and farmers—and to the continuing role of NGOs in "policy design, decision-making, implementation, and evaluation" of efforts to achieve sustainable development. Both governments and international organizations were told to "promote and allow" NGOs' participation and access to information to that end. The text refers in complimentary tone to the NGOs' "established and diverse experience, expertise and capacity" and their importance to the implementation and review of sustainable development. In every one of these chapters, references to the need for poverty alleviation and the particular roles of women were testimony to the influence of the NGOs. In *Agenda 21*'s final sections on institutions and financing, the delegates called for financial support for the participation of developing country NGOs, a prospect most developing-country governments were not enthusiastic about. At subsequent meetings of the UN Commission on Sustainable Development (the body subsequently created by the General Assembly to monitor and coordinate implementation of *Agenda 21*) and all other UN development agencies, the multilateral banks, and the World Trade Organization, the NGOs' struggle for access (to which meetings, by which organizations, with what privileges?) and information (which documents and with what timing?) has continued, but the principle of NGO participation has been firmly rooted.

III. THE FUNCTIONS OF ENVIRONMENTAL NGOs

Environmental NGOs contribute to international cooperation in significant ways through the process of treaty-making and implementation. Indeed, they have been on the front line in developing international agreements to protect the ozone layer, curb global warming, slow biological diversity loss, and halt international transport of hazardous wastes. In doing so, they perform a variety of functions. They may be important agents in identifying and defining an issue, either through contributing to the science or in publicizing and translating technical information to the public and political leaders. In the actual negotiation of a treaty, NGOs may help formulate protective measures through partnership with friendly official delegations or they may even present the first draft of a treaty, as the International Union for the Conservation of Nature did in 1972 for a treaty protecting World Culture and Natural Heritage, which was based on a draft written by the NGO. Most NGOs do not have the resources to draft such a long, complicated document, but they will often draft the sections they are most interested in.

Nongovernmental organizations have often been the most interested parties working to strengthen a treaty once the initial agreement has been signed. For instance, in the United States they have applied constant pressure to achieve and maintain a ban on the use of methyl bromide (a pesticide used to fumigate soils for fruits and vegetables), which is destructive of ozone and is an especially persistent contributor to global warming. They are often the ones to come up with new ideas, such as the possibility of trading permits under the Climate Treaty. In Europe, the NGOs have promoted totally different substitutes for the refrigerants that destroy the ozone layer than have the active official delegations. NGOs are often in a better position than governments to promote new or different technologies because they are not beholden to important industries that do not want to lose market share or are worried that job loss will contribute to disaffection at election time.

Another function that NGOs play in the treaty process is to help achieve signing and ratification in their own countries. Thus, in 1993, right after president Clinton's inauguration, U.S. NGOs and selected pharmaceutical companies called on him and persuaded him to sign the Biodiversity Treaty, which President Bush had declined to do.

Nongovernmental organizations often play an important role in monitoring and compliance with a treaty once it has come into operation. Environmental treaties are, by necessity, self-enforcing: states meet their commitments because of a perceived benefit for their citizenry and the planet. When they slip behind in their commitments, public disclosure and embarrassment are important means of leveraging compliance. Because there is never sufficient funding for monitoring treaty compliance, the most interested parties to a treaty or NGOs supplement official watchdog activities. They gather facts and publicize egregious violations of treaties. For instance, Greenpeace investigated and publicized instances of hazardous waste shipments from rich countries to poor, in both the country of origin and the receiving country, and published documentation of the 1000 worst cases. Thus, in the 2 years between meetings of the parties to the Basel treaty to control trade in wastes, Greenpeace helped to bring about a worldwide climate of moral outrage that led in 1994 to a ban on hazardous wastes from OECD (Organization for Economic Cooperation and Development) to non-OECD countries.

In rare circumstances NGOs have contributed to an electoral change when a particular treaty was a factor in victory or defeat. In 1989, negotiations over the future of Antarctica were torn between proposals to permit mineral exploration and proposals to create an international nature reserve off-limits to all commercial activity. Elections in Australia brought to power a government that had pledged, under pressure from NGOs, support for the latter choice, and the balance in negotiations tipped, permanently, in favor of the park.

Nongovernmental organizations—initially U.S. environmental and development NGOs—have also led the battle for reform of important multinational financial institutions that affect the use and abuse of natural resources and pollution levels. They have been remarkably effective in the case of the World Bank. In 1983, alarmed by the environmental degradation that appeared as a side-effect of large dam construction, road building, relocation schemes, and huge coal-fired electricity-generating plants funded by the World Bank (and the regional banks as well), environmental NGOs in the United States teamed up with key Congresspersons who were looking for ways to cut U.S. annual financial contributions to the Bank. They got language written into the appropriation legislation requiring U.S. Executive Directors of the Bank to work for environmental reform—to hire adequate environmental expertise, consult indigenous NGOs, and finance environmentally beneficial projects. As the largest shareholder in the World Bank, in which voting is weighted according to a country's contribution, the U.S. Director held 17% of the votes on the Executive Board. As the NGOs acquainted the U.S. Director with the environmental effects of Bank-funded projects, the Director questioned loan proposals more carefully. The environmentalists teamed up with other development, religious, and human rights NGOs and built a very effective coalition that formed the Bank Information Center to monitor the multilateral development banks. They publicized bad projects and in 1987 succeeded in stopping, through veto by the U.S. Director, road construction on the Polonoroeste rainforest colonization project in Brazil. That was followed by other successes, as the Banks withdrew their support for the Narmada dams in India and the Three Gorges dam in China.

But the NGOs did not just oppose projects; they also fought for a series of institutional changes that would force all proposed loans (and eventually sectoral loans as well) to go through an environmental impact review. They successfully pressed for large increases in the environmental staff and for implementation of tough new policies (1992–1993) that made *sustainable* development the objective of all Bank work on energy, water, agriculture, and so on. Five years later, those policies and staff had made some modest changes in the kind of lending the Bank does, and the NGOs were still on the case. Two other policy changes demanded by the NGOs have made possible participation of NGOs in Bank deliberations—including NGOs from developing countries—and transparency of proceedings and public access to documents before funding decisions have been made.

This long struggle, begun in the United States but joined by NGO pressure from European and developing countries, continues at the World Bank. The changes are very unpopular with many governments of developing countries and former Soviet-bloc countries that have not yet internalized the principles of sustainable development. These kinds of changes are possible because an NGO coalition with real expertise and staying power organized in countries that, because of their large donor status, have financial leverage in the Bank.

Good science lies at the basis of good environmental policy and workable treaties, and NGOs have contributed in several ways. They have helped identify issues requiring international action. In the United States and Germany, for instance, scientists from environmental organizations and their colleagues at universities contributed to making the cross-boundary transportation of acid rain an issue. By challenging the conventional scientific wisdom on other matters, especially through detailed reviews of scientific justification for a particular strategy, NGOs have often helped chart a new course and helped clarify legitimate differences among scientists. Even among scientists who agree on the facts, some are more willing than others to take risks or to find certain trade-offs acceptable. There have been, for instance, legitimate differences on ocean dumping between those in the "dilute and disperse" school (who argue that ocean disposal of some hazardous substances is preferable to disposal on land) and those in the precautionary principle school (who advocate prevention or alternative treatments even when the exact dimension of risk is not known). Environmentalists are more likely to push the latter, and in more and more issues they are winning increasing acceptance for the precautionary approach.

Nongovernmental organization scientists, including economists, have also contributed to the work of official scientific bodies created by certain conventions. The science committee of the International Whaling Commission (1946) was for many years the captive of industry scientists until challenged by NGO technical staff and their university colleagues. The International Panel

on Climate Change, considered by many to be a model for evaluating changing scientific conditions important to an environmental treaty, has invited analyses from NGO experts among others.

The NGOs are often more willing to oppose a given technology or to support a new one than are official government delegations because they have no constituency that has a stake in staying with the established technology. The U.S. NGOs, for instance, are unlike certain Congressional representatives, who feel pressure from growers or manufacturers of the pesticide methyl bromide—constituents who want Congress to postpone the proposed ban on its use.

And finally, NGO scientists help the delegations of small developing nations, whose own diplomatic and technical resources have been stretched thin by the demands of multiple environmental negotiations and simultaneous meetings of working groups and subcommittees. In return, those delegates become the eloquent political spokespersons for the environmental NGOs. This has happened in the Climate Treaty negotiations where the representatives of small island states in the Caribbean, South Pacific, and Indian Ocean, fearful of innundation by sea-level rise induced by global warming, have become vigorous participants in the on-going debates.

The role of the environmental NGOs in educating policy-makers and the general public has been very important. Especially in the United States and other industrialized countries, NGOs are the suppliers of a steady stream of readable and increasingly professional publications. Some of these also receive wide distribution in developing countries and are used in schools and universities worldwide. Many find their way to legislators' desks, and in the United States, NGO professionals and, less often, grassroots organization leaders testify before Congressional committees and produce extensive background material and policy alternatives on pending legislation for friendly Senators and Representatives. Every incoming administration is deluged by policy proposals from NGOs. The NGOs have also become adroit in using the news media, often by timing their pronouncements to coincide with some other newsworthy event—the G-7 economic summits, the World Bank/International Monetary Fund annual meetings that bring the world's finance ministers together, or the visit of some important dignitary. Or the NGO may create its own drama, as Greenpeace has done in its confrontations of nuclear testing in international waters. Sometimes national organizations have linked up with communities taking local action as a way of bringing remote global issues, such as damage to the ozone layer, closer to home by running campaigns against the use of Styrofoam fast-food packaging and other ozone-depleting materials. Such local actions are often effective educational tools because, by creating a controversial political issue, they achieve on-going news coverage in the community.

Environmental NGOs have built some valuable alliances with peace organizations, human rights groups, and labor unions. In the 1980s, during the Contra war in Nicaragua and the prolonged civil strife in El Salvador and Guatemala, environmental organizations joined human rights and peace groups in protesting U.S. involvement. Among other things they proposed creation of international nature preserves, dubbed "peace parks," along borders to make a buffer zone between warring armies. Also in the 1980s, U.S. rainforest protection groups partnered with indigenous rubber tappers from the Amazon. Assassination of one of their leaders awakened Northern NGOs for the first time to the mutual interests of environmentalists, workers, and human rights advocates. And in Nigeria a decade later, after the government's execution of a leading environmentalist and journalist opposed to the corruption and environmental damage of the military and oil companies, human rights and environmental organizations in Africa, Europe, and America came together again. In a similar way, labor organizations have teamed up with environmentalists to oppose a North American Free Trade Agreement that ignored environmental and workers' concerns and have worked together across the U.S.–Mexican border through the Coalition Against Pesticide Abuse, trying to protect workers and nature from pesticide poisoning. And the Nobel Prize-winning international campaign to ban land mines, though correctly understood primarily as a humanitarian and anti-military issue, is also directed at the most long-standing connection between security and environmental issues, that is, the physical effects of war on the environment.

In conclusion, it must be said that the proven ability of NGOs—environmental and others—to fulfill several important functions on the international stage assures them of a permanent, albeit, still-evolving role. Their ability to advance an agenda of international cooperation around some of the most difficult on-going issues

facing the world at the millennium—human rights (including women's rights), equity, refugees, civil strife, health and environmental destruction—will make them increasingly valuable in circumstances where military action and economic sanctions no longer provide security. It is true that NGOs have been much more successful on some issues than on others: it is certainly clear that the environmentalists have been more effective in this decade than the opponents of international arms trade. But it is also true that one group learns from another the strategies and tactics and modifies them for their own issues. And there are lessons that apply across issues: NGOs have their greatest effect when the timing is right and they are able to frame an issue so that it appeals to the interests ready to move on it. They do their best work when they have access to and leverage with pivotal decision-makers at home or in the appropriate international setting or institution. Those who are well grounded in their subject and obvious in their expertise do best. And building effective coalitions across issues and national boundaries, especially across North–South divisions, is essential.

Also See the Following Articles

ENVIRONMENTAL ISSUES AND POLITICS • HUMAN RIGHTS

Bibliography

Clough, M. (1994). Grass-roots policymaking: Say good-bye to the "Wise Men." *Foreign Affairs*, January/February, 2–7.

Fisher, J. (1993). *The road from Rio, sustainable development and the nongovernmental movement in the third world*. Westport, CT/ London: Praeger.

United Nations Non-Governmental Liaison Services (1997). Implementing Agenda 21, NGO Experiences from Around the World, Geneva.

Kakabadse, N., Yolande, with S. Burns (1994). *Movers and shakers: NGOs in international affairs*. Washington, DC: World Resources Institute.

Porter, G., & Brown, J. W. (1995). *Global Environmental Politics* (2nd ed., pp. 50–59). Boulder, CO: Westview Press.

Stairs, K., & Taylor, P. (1992). Non-governmental organizations and the legal protection of the oceans: A case study. In A. Hurrell & B. Kingsbury (Eds.), *International politics of the environment, actors, interests and institutions*. Oxford: Clarendon.

Nonviolence Theory and Practice

Bryan Teixeira

Camosun College

I. Theory
II. Practice
III. Conclusions

GLOSSARY

Aggression Behavior that is intended to harm or destroy.

Noncooperation Some degree, either partial or total, of not engaging in activities that further the goals or interests of a particular social group.

Nonviolence An evolving, holistic theory and practice of personal and social empowerment that rejects aggression and violence as means of achieving goals or resolving conflicts.

Persuasion The process of getting others to change their attitudes and/or to agree with an advocated position or message.

Violence An extreme form of aggression involving significant physical or psychological force.

WE LIVE IN A WORLD that is increasingly caught in ethnocultural rivalries and even all-out torture and war. Violence based in sexism and homophobia, for example, seems to be escalating in direct proportion to a growing recognition of the human rights of women and of sexual minorities. Scarce resources clumped in wealthier na-tions are exacerbating the social inequalities of our world and providing some of the most fertile ground for violence. And urbanization continues to spawn forms of individualism that make it a lot easier to see one's neighbor as a stranger, resulting in violence against strangers being a lot easier to rationalize or ignore.

At its most functional, the use of force to achieve conflict resolution in situations such as the above is increasingly seen as an emergency and short-term solution. However, such force is a two-edged sword. It can create a context in which conflicted parties may find the breathing space to make a new start at resolving their disagreements. But it can also complicate the relationship and worsen the tensions between opponents and thereby heighten the conflict.

We live in a conflicted world. Nevertheless, at macrocultural levels, we are witnessing a slow but growing recognition of the limits of the use of force—whether it be the force of law, or the police or the military—to resolve conflict. And, as environmental, peace and social justice activists become increasingly influenced by nonviolence, we are witnessing the creation of new microcultures of nonviolence. This is the context that drives a growing interest in nonviolence theory and practice.

The following is a broad overview of nonviolence theory and practice. It addresses conflict and its nonviolent resolution within a context of human diversity. It offers a holistic approach to human beings, acknowledging the physical, intellectual, emotional, and spiritual components of human experience. It also summa-

Copyright © 1999 by Academic Press.
All rights of reproduction in any form reserved.

rizes and explores a range of nonviolent preventive and confrontative approaches to conflict.

I. THEORY

Nonviolence is the alternative to violence and aggression. It is therefore important to have some insight into the latter in order to fully appreciate the significance and mechanisms of the former.

Aggression can be seen as any behavior that expresses a harmful intent. Violence is an extreme form of harm, usually regulated by criminal law: it involves significant physical and/or psychological force. The harm can result simply from uncontrolled *hostility*, associated primarily with anger, as seems to be the case with most homicides. It can also be *instrumental*, as a means associated with achieving a supposedly justifiable or useful end, for example, for peacekeeping, using violence to confine or suppress a greater violence, to defend a vulnerable person, or to punish a wrongdoer in order to sway him/her away from some offensive behaviors. Without harmful intent, however, there is no aggression. Someone may do an action that results in harm as a side effect, for example, poverty in Manchester as a result of Gandhi's movement to achieve Indian self-government and economic self-sufficiency. But if the harmful effect was not intended, it would be inappropriate to consider the original action as aggressive. It is possible, nevertheless, that the original action may be found to be violent in terms of the law.

Furthermore, aggression can be seen not only as behaviour involving harmful intent, but also behavior done not only to humans but to any living beings that would prefer to avoid such treatment. This definition includes aggression not only to fellow humans, but also to the ecosystem with which we are inextricably connected, for example, how we treat animals. It also addresses the possibility of choosing some level of harm in order to achieve a more valued goal, for example, the athlete accepting degrees of pain inflicted in order to achieve greater self-discipline and skill, or sexual partners involved in certain forms of highly charged sexual play.

Nonviolence assumes the rejection of harmful intent and therefore of both hostile and instrumental forms of aggression. While it does not deny the emotion of anger, it requires that people learn ways of channeling that anger when they come to interact interpersonally for the purpose of conflict resolution. It requires that means and ends be congruent: an instrumentally aggressive act cannot be justified by a seemingly socially bene-

ficial outcome. And, increasingly, it is being applied to our relationship with the nonhuman world and in discussions about whether or not vegetarianism is a central or an optional aspect of the nonviolent lifestyle.

The key strands of this emerging general theory of nonviolence can be grouped as follows: (1) nonviolence is a *global* phenomenon—it is found around the world, and throughout human history; (2) nonviolence is *holistic*—it is not just about the pragmatics of strategizing for social change, it is also about personal transformation on all levels of human experience and behaviour; (3) nonviolence is *sociocritical*—it draws on value-based understandings of human persons and societies; and (4) nonviolence is *practical*—it effectively responds to social violence.

A. Global

The evolution of any species requires the development of intraspecies nonviolence at least in terms of nonkilling. Animals of the same species develop rituals of dominance and submission that usually allow for the termination of aggression and conflict short of death. Similarly, from an evolutionary perspective, nonviolent conflict resolution among fellow humans can be seen as a more preferable strategy than is violence. It is no surprise, then, to find more or less organized examples of and approaches to nonviolence spanning human history and cultures. Nonviolence is neither a recent nor an ethnospecific phenomenon. It is a global and possibly evolutionary endeavor.

Our earliest traditions of human health and wholeness live on in aboriginal and shamanic cultures. Fundamental to these traditions is a sense of the interrelatedness of all beings: we are all related, not only human to human, but also human to all living beings. Whether we have two or four legs, whether we fly in the air or swim in the sea, all living beings are relatives. The more peace loving of these societies—such as the Pygmies of Africa or the Inuit of Northern Canada–tend to enjoy life's pleasures, lack a warrior class, make little distinction between masculine and feminine traits, and not idealize aggression or have aggressive deities. This aboriginal experience and sensitivity to our familial relationship provide key theoretical and practical bases for a comprehensive and global approach to nonviolence.

Specific to the West, many examples of nonviolent struggle have been identified, from the plebian resistance of ancient Rome to Martin Luther King in modern-day Montgomery, Alabama. Josephus, one of the earliest historians, described the nonviolent resistance of ancient Israelites in Jerusalem to the Roman colonizers.

"Peace churches" that emerged centuries ago, such as the Mennonites and Quakers, continue today, living and teaching nonviolence. And in the East, nonviolence remains the very first and most basic step toward yogic accomplishment, and is the heart of Buddhist compassion.

While nonviolence is a fundamental human aspiration that can be observed across human evolution and around the planet, it is also true that Mahatma Gandhi has been significant in developing the first comprehensive theory and practice of nonviolence. Gandhi's thought is truly global, including influences from the Hinduism and Jainism of his Indian homeland, Christian socialism and social anarchism of England and Russia, and American political philosophy. Although Gandhi's work continues as a benchmark, other approaches to nonviolence continue to emerge and adapt to our changing cultures and world, globally.

B. Holistic

In the West, nonviolence is well recognized for its tactical, strategic, or political aspects. It is seen as a powerful tool for redressing social inequality. This approach says more about the instrumental and behaviorist emphasis of Western thought and practice than it does about the full potential of nonviolence.

In fact, nonviolence has other dimensions besides external social change. As a truly human phenomenon, nonviolence can also be seen from an holistic perspective. Yes, it is about change and about justice. But, it is also—and perhaps more fundamentally—about transformation on all levels of human experience (thought, affect, and activity) and all dimensions of relationship and communication (intrapersonal, interpersonal, and transpersonal). People from collectivistic cultures that stress harmony and interdependence—rather than autonomy and independence, as in the industrialized West—may find it easier to grasp the value of such holism. Figure 1 presents an especially clear illustration of this worldview in the Medicine Wheel used by many North American aboriginal peoples. The Medicine Wheel demonstrates the interconnectedness of many aspects of the microcosmic individual as well as the macrocosmic world: the four colours of the peoples of the planet, essential elements of life,

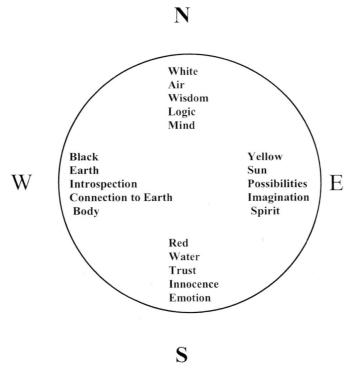

FIGURE 1   The Medicine Wheel of North American aboriginal peoples demonstrates the interconnectedness of the individual and the larger world. Such holistic perspectives are essential to the development of nonviolence theory as a social science of "total revolution."

key psychological attitudes, and elements of human personality.

Intrapersonally, nonviolence simultaneously produces and enhances a stable sense of high self esteem. Refraining from violence because of fear or cowardice can result in less violence. But such action emerges from helplessness and denial. It expresses weakness rather than strength, avoidance and passivity rather than power. As such, it would not be classified as active nonviolence. Undergirding nonviolence is the philosophical awareness that each human being, including oneself, is significant, valuable, and powerful. No one is a second-class person. Nonviolence is based in the courage of standing up for what one believes, for professing and adhering to one's own truth.

This profound respect for oneself extends to others and is crucial to understanding nonviolence interpersonally. No one is indispensible, including one's opponent. Violence can then be seen as a profound disruption of this ethos. Since interpersonal contact at its simplest as well as its more complex levels will always involve differing perceptions of reality, conflict is unavoidable. What nonviolence places before us is the challenge of addressing conflict humanely. Peace is then not the absence of conflict—which would be an impossibility—but rather a context in which conflict is addressed with as much mutual respect as possible. A key is how the opponents perceive themselves and each other: Do I see myself and my group as peace loving and respectful of others, or do I see myself and my group as tough and aggressive?

Nonviolence therefore includes not only a "physics" addressing how to deal with the material world. It also includes a "metaphysics" addressing fundamental ways of perceiving and thinking about oneself and the world. It assumes an interconnectedness that is transpersonal or spiritual. This was clearly the case for Gandhi and for Martin Luther King, two of the most recent exemplars of this tradition. For Gandhi, nonviolence involved the recognition that although we were many bodies, we were actually one soul. This way of talking about nonviolence clearly emerged from Hindu metaphors and the concept of Brahman. Martin Luther King used a different metaphor to express the same insight, that of being "caught in an inescapable network of mutuality". The strength of awareness of this transpersonal dimension is, furthermore, directly related to the nonviolent practitioner being prepared to suffer rather than harm anyone, including the opponent. Since we are all interconnected, to harm anyone is ultimately to harm oneself. As a result, there can be no justification for using nonviolent means with an intent of harming another: such intent denotes aggression and violence, regardless of the means used. It is a contradiction of our unity.

Nonviolence is then more than a technique or a praxis. Such technique without accompanying personal change might seem to work in the short term but would not be sufficient to produce enduring social change. Nonviolence therefore also includes an evolving body of holistic knowledge and skill, a veritable social science of "total revolution."

C. Sociocritical

Nonviolence involves an analysis and critique of society, especially of social power, inequality, and change. Clearly, one of the major reasons for social unrest and violence is inequality, for example, men treating women as less competent or valued human beings, one ethnocultural group stigmatizing another as inferior, the majority attempting to impose its behavioral norms on the minority.

As noted above, nonviolence includes a strong respect for the worth of the breadth of individual experiences, the value of human relationships, and the diversity of both. The social goal of nonviolence is therefore the development and support of a pluralistic society: multiethnic, multicultural, and multifaith. Specific to India, Gandhi made it clear that his goal was the creation of a political state where Hindus, Muslims, and others could all live together. He insisted that the idea of one state, one culture, one religion was illusion: it had never been the case, and never would be. The only realistic and at the same time most effective option was to recognize and celebrate variety. A similar attitude is exemplified today in South Africa's new constitution, a document that was certainly influenced by Mandela's well-known commitment to nonviolence. Relative to the creation of political states, it is the first constitution in world history to ban discrimination based, among other things, on sexual orientation. Human society—like life itself—is grounded in diversity. Rejecting such diversity is violence. Accepting and building on such diversity is "truth," the power behind nonviolence.

Nonviolence is also a potent resource in minority group struggles for self-rule and self-sufficiency, both crucial prerequisites for a strong and enduring nonviolent society. Effective minority struggles require clarity of social critique, consistent and persistent social action, and respected and respectful leadership. In this regard, one of the groups that is turning to nonviolence as a guide in its struggles for "self-government" is aboriginal people. Ovide Mercredi, the then-Grand Chief of the Assembly of First Nations in Canada, had long been personally committed to nonviolence. In the summer of 1996, he hosted a national Conference in Vancouver on the use of nonviolence theory and practice to address his people's claims against the government of Canada. Aboriginal leaders, people, and a strong youth contingent from across the country reflected for three days on their own traditional sources for nonviolence, both at the political and the domestic levels. Among the most special invited guests were two prominent Gandhians from India.

Nonviolence theory also recognizes the centralization and urbanization of power and money, so common to modern society, as harmful and socially violent. Both traditional capitalist and Marxist approaches to society see such centralization in a positive light. However, this centralization leads to neglect, and to the false perception of the nonurban world primarily as hinterland and garbage dump. These and other related effects were well documented by the World Commission on Environment and Development (1987) in its report: *Our Common Future*. A vital respect for the ecological interdependence of our world is easily lost, leading to major social and environmental disruptions. In addition, fast-paced urbanization encourages the growth of individualism, and with it, a measurable decrease in caring and helping behavior and an increase in violence.

Social life will always include degrees of conformity and obedience. Knowing when not to conform and when to disobey is crucial to an effective nonviolence. Ultimately, nonviolence theory envisions a society based primarily on freely associating individuals and groups. In this latter regard, as a coherent theory continues to evolve, the philosophical bases of nonviolence can be seen as sharing many characteristics with anarchist (as distinct from communist) socialism. Nonviolence theory presents a value-based and planned approach to radical societal transformation.

D. Practical

Nonviolence is a pragmatic theory: it is about achieving a more human world, and about the process of individual and social change in order to achieve that end. This process will be discussed later, both in terms of preventing as well as confronting violence and aggression. However, its pragmatism can also be seen in a theoretical approach to the value of anger, and to the significance of the the outcast.

Hostile aggression is based in anger. The individual exhibiting such behavior has been carried away by his/her anger. However, there is a positive role for anger as one of our human emotions. Anger is the warning

signal that we experience some attack: we are in fear of losing something we believe important, and we respond to that fear with anger which motivates a fight response. Without some anger and discontent, we would not be motivated to change. How one then subsequently negotiates the change process, how one fights, is extremely relevant. Nonviolence is not about denying anger. It is rather about validating anger while limiting its legitimate role to that of a wake-up call and initial motivator. Ulitmately, it is about channeling the energy behind anger into powerful and yet respectful preventive and confrontative change strategies.

Specific to the significance of the outcast, Gandhi assumed addressing violence and aggression required using not only "truth power," the *satyagraha* that includes civil disobedience when necessary. He believed that nonviolence simultaneously requires specific involvement with the uplift of "untouchables" or most outcast individuals and groups, what he called *sarvodaya*. Basic social responsibility requires that we address the specific concerns of those in need, including and especially the most neglected sectors of the society. In addition, however, nonviolent theory recognizes the *strategic* importance of socially outcast groups as levers for change in the wider society. Outcast groups are foci of a society's distorted beliefs, fears, and prejudices. They are therefore excluded. Such exclusion serves to further reinforce a society's exaggerated views of the difference between itself and its outcasts. Including an outcast group would therefore require a society to review and revise its beliefs and attitudes, and the discriminatory way it treats that outgroup. Such a review and revision would certainly be transformative, benefiting an outcast group as well as a society as a whole. Furthermore, the more outcast the group initially, the more transformative the process of including them. A nonviolent social change process would then tend to emphasize an inclusive approach to the experience, needs, norms, and beliefs of outcasts. The organization of outcast groups, especially the most excluded, into self-aware resistance movements is therefore an important feature of overall nonviolent change.

E. Summary

Nonviolence theory is neither a justification of passivity nor of cowardice. It includes ideas and insights gathered over the stretch of human history, from various parts of the world. It certainly is a change theory focused on coming to grips with and responding to social violence: it has a strong pragmatic orientation. However, it is also an holistic theory of personal and societal transfor-

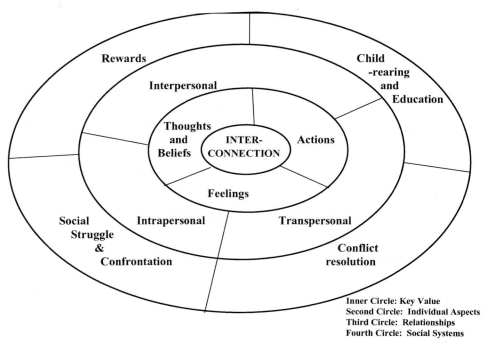

Inner Circle: Key Value
Second Circle: Individual Aspects
Third Circle: Relationships
Fourth Circle: Social Systems

FIGURE 2 Nonviolence theory requires a holistic perspective on personal and societal transformation. It speaks not only to the physical, but also to the mental, emotional, and metaphysical or spiritual dimensions of human experience and behavior.

mation, addressing itself to the full range of human experience and behavior. It speaks not only to the physical, but also to the mental, emotional and metaphysical or spiritual dimensions of humanity (see Fig. 2).

II. PRACTICE

The practice of nonviolence can be divided into preventive (with a strong emphasis on empowerment of the outcast, or Gandhi's *sarvodaya*) and confrontative (resisting injustice, or Gandhi's *satyagraha*) strategies. Both approaches seem to be necessary, all the time.

A. Prevention

1. Rewarding Nonviolence

Many societies tend to reward violence and aggression more than nonviolence. This is certainly true among modern, industrialized societies, where "aggressivity" is seen as a positive quality of the popular sports figure or the successful businessperson. A significant amount of the news and entertainment provided by the print and electronic communications media either overtly or covertly glorifies aggression and provides a certain fame to socially and even sexually aggressive individuals. The

home and the school often unwittingly support these trends, especially in the way young males are socialized. Resistance to these influences will involve efforts to deglorify violence, reward nonviolence, and emphasize cues and symbols of nonviolence.

Campaigning against the glorification of violence has already begun. For example, parents in many countries around the world are organizing to address "entertainment" violence in television and the music industry. The rationalizations that such violence on television merely mirrors existing social violence and that it is a catharsis for our pent-up aggression are increasingly rejected. In general, we are likely to be exposed to far more of such violence on television than we are ever likely to witness in daily life. And the exposure to such violence, rather than decreasing our attraction for aggression, seems rather to enhance it.

In addition to addressing media violence, classroom curricula are being developed and implemented to teach about inclusion and diversity, and the effectiveness of nonviolence. Children are being taught to respect and celebrate difference, rather than to stigmatize it. They are being exposed to nonviolent heroes, and trained to use nonviolent forms of conflict resolution. And slowly, at a global level, from childhood through to adulthood, traditional gender roles are being revised. There is an emerging respect for and inclusion of women's experience. And, perhaps more significantly for nonviolence theory and practice, there is a recognition that a future without aggression requires a new approach to the socialization of male children and adolescents.

2. Education of Children and Adolescents

A significant amount of how we think, feel and act in the world depends on what we learn from our parents. Children who are raised in authoritarian, threatening, and/or punishing contexts tend to be highly aggressive. Children who are raised in rewarding contexts, based in praise, where reasoning is used to address issues and conflicts, and are taught problem-solving and conflict resolution skills are rarely aggressive. A key strategy in creating a more nonviolent world would therefore necessarily emphasize the appropriate education of parents in nonviolent child rearing practices, for example seeing punishment and threats as ineffective learning tools, engaging children in creative discussions and problem solving about issues, and using praise as a reward to reinforce desired behaviors.

A growing competitor to the influence of the early parental context is television. Television, whether in the form of news or entertainment, exposes children to a great amount of violence. Whether this exposure leads to increased aggression as children grow into adults may have a lot to do with whether the parental context already encourages violence or nonviolence. For a child who is already in an aggressive context, much current television programming is likely to reinforce preexisting aggression. For a child raised in a more positive context, such exposure is likely to have a lesser impact. Nevertheless, given the amount of exposure to television that some children have, and given the current extent of glorification and positive modeling of aggression, especially relative to males, television may still be seen as a major threat to a nonviolent future in terms of its potential influence on all children.

Specific to violence against women, a key educational focus is the gender socialization and sensitivity especially of adolescent males. There is evidence that this age group is becoming the primary consumer of sexually explicit pornographic movies. These movies instill a distorted perception of sexuality and women. As a result, this age group is becoming more accepting of sexual violence. Sexuality education that challenges sexist and heterosexist gender role rigidity, and leads to an skilled appreciation of intimate, interpersonal relationships would need to be a crucial ingredient in the education of children and youth, especially males, toward a more nonviolent world.

3. Conflict Resolution Training

There are many approaches to conflict resolution. However, two sets of skills are particularly important: *communication skills,* for example, listening, dialogue, and problem solving, and *practice in intervening in and addressing social conflict.*

Our greatest tool for achieving conflict resolution is communication. Yet, while practically all of us learn to speak our native language, a lot fewer of us become effective communicators within our various cultural contexts. Effective communicators have high self-esteem and are not particularly threatened by being open to other people's beliefs, attitudes, feelings, or behaviors. In a conflict situation, they can demonstrate sensitivity to nonverbal cues, empathetic listening in order to appreciate someone else's experience, clear and non-judgmental feedback of one's own experience, joint setting of concrete goals, and detailed problem solving. All these skills have to be learned.

There is a significant amount of evidence about the "bystander effect" and the diffusion of social responsibility, that is, the more people there are witnessing an emergency, the less likely it is that someone will intervene to help. This suggests that conflict resolution, especially in social contexts, may require the ability to take leadership in intervening. However, a key emphasis in human socialization is on conforming and obeying social norms. While this aids social identity, it is also a recipe for inaction when faced with heated conflicts or sudden emergencies. Encouraging conformity does not prepare us to intervene effectively in such situations. What is required is being able to take on leadership, to stand out from the group, to not conform, and even to break certain existing norms in order to help someone in need or to achieve resolution in a conflict. People require training if they are to be able to both accept the importance of group norms as well as the necessity of breaking those same norms at times in order to effectively address social needs or conflicts. Like competent communication, the ability to take social responsibility nonviolently, especially when others do not, requires a high degree of self-awareness, confidence, and courage.

4. Social Justice Activism

A significant amount of violence is a by-product of a society's inequities and injustices. Such systemic discrimination against various minorities is the preexisting violence that has become effectively invisible because it is so pervasive. Preventing the more visible resulting violence in the foreground therefore requires addressing the hidden and often more oppressive background violence: the exclusion of the needs and rights of minorities, especially the most vulnerable.

Each society has its outcasts, its untouchables. By example and by preaching and teaching, each generation is taught by their parents, religious leaders, teachers, and other socializing agents to look down on some other group of people. This socialization usually includes a pecking order among outcasts: some outcasts are more so than others. In Gandhi's time and relative to India's intricate caste system, the bottom rung of that pecking order was reserved for the "untouchables." At the bottom of that pecking order in many contemporary societies, it is not uncommon to find victims of homophobia (gay and lesbian people), and victims of racism (people with skin colors that differ from that of the historically dominant group).

A nonviolent future requires addressing the background oppression within societies: unmasking prejudice, dismantling discrimination, and replacing them both with a celebration of human diversity. Minority movements are an essential component in enabling this more just and therefore less violent world. They manifest a society's blindspots and injustices. These movements are particularly vital when they are organized and led by members of the minority themselves. However, if these movements are not to simply return violence for violence and impose new forms of exclusion, a firm commitment to and training in nonviolence is essential. This is especially so, since while they are likely to achieve some degree of social transformation through dialogue and reasoned persuasion, it is too often the case that many issues will only be addressed through escalating levels of nonviolent confrontation.

B. Confrontation

Nonviolent confrontation is a way of fighting, a practice of actively engaging social conflicts. It involves a series of steps, escalating from persuasion to increasing forms of noncooperation. What is unique about this method of conflict resolution is that it is based in respect for the opponent, and in using only those means that are likely to enable an enduring and workable relationship among opponents after the conflict. This clearly excludes intentional harm and violence towards the opponent. However, this also excludes any imposition of a solution by a third or outside party, for example, the legal/court system or an arbitrator.

1. Persuasion and Negotiation

In this early phase of nonviolent confrontation, the goal is to use consistent reasoning and communication skills in order to arrive at a mutually acceptable solution. This process is usually initiated by the party that feels violated. The offended party clearly identifies the perceived offense; demonstrates negative impacts of the offence on his/her need fulfillment, feelings, opinions, and other consequences; enters into dialogue with the opponent, including exploring the opponent's experience of the conflict; and commits to joint problem-solving intended to be mutually beneficial to both parties. This process may be engaged by the parties face-to-face, or through their representative negotiators. It may also be engaged with the assistance of a third party process facilitator, counselor, or mediator who enables the parties to arrive at their own solution.

Persuasive methods themselves allow for some escalation. Initially, persuasion may occur privately, among the parties involved. However, if this fails, it may be necessary to go more public, drawing on highly credible supporters, public communications media, mass protests and demonstrations, and so on. This gives social visibility to the conflict and begins to involve others in the conflict resolution. Such an escalation has its positive and negative sides. On the positive side, it opens the confrontation to other perceptions and other helpful ways of addressing and resolving the issues. On the negative side, it can introduce nonrational or peripheral pressures to come to agreement that may not arise from a commitment to nonviolence, for example, using strategies that are aimed at a quick political fix rather than enabling an enduring solution.

Each escalation includes risks and challenges. The level of personal maturity, as well as commitment to and skill in nonviolence, required to proceed effectively increases with each escalation. In turn, the opponent's resistance is also likely to increase, requiring further personal and organizational strength on the part of the activist to withstand added pressure while maintaining a commitment to nonviolence. Therefore, personal and group discipline, including coping with a certain amount of suffering, needs to increase. It was this realization of the need for nonviolent training and discipline that encouraged Gandhi to be concerned not only with his own personal readiness and self-control, but also about the selection and formation of his *satyagrahis*. At times, this concern had led him to withdraw from particular struggles either because he doubted his own or his followers' readiness, or to prepare himself and ensure that he was ready for the next level of confrontation. He eventually proposed an ongoing peace army of trained nonviolent "soldiers" that continues today in India as the Shanti Sena (Peace Army).

With the help of some Indian Gandhians, a similar international organization called Peace Brigades International was started in Canada in 1981. This grassroots organization is committed to exploring and implementing nonviolent approaches to peacekeeping and support for basic human rights. The first peace brigade was sent to Guatemala in 1983, and since then teams have worked in other conflict-torn areas, including Sri Lanka, North America, Colombia, Haiti, and the Balkans. Gene Sharp's proposal (1985) of civilian-based deterrence and defense as a way of making Europe unconquerable is another way of recognizing the need for and value of such nonviolent training.

2. Noncooperation

If persuasion fails, then the confrontation may escalate to forms of nonconforming behaviour, e.g., breaking social norms, boycotts, strikes, civil disobedience or illegal actions, and even the creation of alternative social systems (see Fig. 3). Such nonconformity and noncooperation demonstrate at least a temporary breakdown in dialogue. The nonviolent activist is unable to reach and/or convince the opponent. From this point on, nonviolence resorts to actions that graphically demonstrate the gulf between those in power and those who feel victimized by that power.

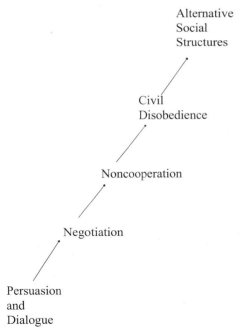

FIGURE 3 Nonviolent confrontation begins with persuasion and dialogue. If this fails, confrontation may then escalate, step by step, to higher degress of nonconforming behavior.

Gandhi believed confrontation should be carried out in a way that shows unswerving commitment to the struggle and the needs of the minority, without disrespecting the person of the opponent. His goal was to eventually convince the opponent of the rightness of the outcast group's cause. He was unwilling to participate in actions that compromised the purity of his nonviolent ideals. Other nonviolent activists, including Martin Luther King, however, accept that confrontative noncooperation could be a way of pressuring the opponent to act even against his/her own better judgment to comply with the requests of the minority without necessarily being convinced of the value of their request. Perhaps because of his Protestant background or some influence from Marxist socialism, King was quite willing to settle for justice, as he saw it, where he could not achieve love or empathy.

Justice might come about, for example, because the courage, moral integrity or consistent argumentation of the minority eventually won over a significant enough segment of the wider society and/or international community. This increased support brought pressure to bear on the opponent and strengthened the power base of the minority, giving it a new status from which to reopen dialogue with the opponent. The dismantling of South African apartheid involved many of these elements. Such tactics, however, can arguably be seen as a form of coercion, that is, pressuring someone to act in ways he or she really does not choose. As a result, there is debate. Some agree that there is a place for "nonviolent coercion," coercion that stops short of *intentional* physical or psychological harm. Others see nonviolence as contrary to any coercion.

Consistency and clarity are key elements in the success of any minority attempt to confront and change social attitudes and behavior. If the nonviolent activist can sustain such noncooperation, despite the possibility of failure and the very likely increased suffering from the opponent's reprisals, history and social science research demonstrate that success is possible.

III. CONCLUSIONS

Nonviolence is more than a social change strategy that stops short of direct physical or psychological harm to the opponent. Such nonharming of one's opponent may, for example, coexist with strong hateful attitudes toward the opponent and it may be a result of one's weakness or even cowardice, arising from lack of weaponry or confidence. Nonviolence, however, is a theory and a practice of empowerment. It includes a strong commitment to social justice, equity, and pluralism.

Nonviolence has a value base, including an interconnected perception of self and others (see Fig. 4). It recognizes the need for organized and disciplined group action in the process of conflict resolution. It teaches norms about fighting that commit the activist to not intentionally returning harm with harm, while as directly and respectfully as possible confronting the opponent about beliefs, attitudes, or activities that are experienced as harmful. However, for many activists, it allows for some circumscribed moral and psychological pressure to achieve compliance where other more reasoned forms of persuasion have proved ineffective.

Nonviolence is an evolving global phenomenon. It is not the product of one culture. It is based in a recognition of the interconnectedness of all life, and therefore an unwillingness to use harm to redress harm. Within many animal species, rituals of conflict and power rebalancing have evolved to minimize intraspecies violence and further that species' survival. It may be that the emergence of nonviolence especially over the last 2 millenia signals a huge progression in the evolution of human rituals to cope with our aggression and facilitate our survival.

Groups and cultures tend to define themselves by excluding certain other people. In addition, new outcasts and "untouchables," as well as pecking orders

FROM	TO
Alienation	Inter-connectedness
Individualism	Community
Low self-worth	High self-worth
Inhumane conflict	Humane conflict
Inequity	Equity
Exclusivity	Inclusivity
Centralization	Decentralization
Aggression	Assertion
Rigid gender roles	Flexible gender roles
Male dominance	Gender equality
Passivity	Power

FIGURE 4 Nonviolence is a theory and practice of empowerment: it has a value base. It includes a strong commitment to social justice, equity, and pluralism.

among them, continue to be generated as groups and cultures change. As a maturing and applied philosophy and psychology of social change, nonviolence would therefore seem to have an enduring place in our world.

There are still, however, certain outstanding questions about nonviolence that deserve study, including the following.

Will nonviolence work in all situations? Gandhi assumed that active nonviolence could have worked in Nazi Germany. However, social psychology has well documented a fundamental error in our tendency to overestimate the significance of personality, values and attitudes in human endeavors and underestimate the power of each situation or context. In simpler interpersonal relations, there seems to be a place for a range of conflict styles. Assertive and win-win styles, for example, may be ineffective in a context where the opponent is not willing to respond in kind. It is debateable, therefore, whether or not a consistent and unswerving nonviolence, which may be personally satisfying in terms of one's inner congruence, is always the most effective conflict resolution strategy. This all begs the further question of the effectiveness of nonviolence in contexts where opponents share significantly different value bases.

Will nonviolence work where there is no simultaneous alternative threat of a violent resolution? It has been argued that, in social change contexts, nonviolence works best where it coexists with the threat of violence. In other words, nonviolent strategies have a better chance of being successful when an opponent realizes that the alternative is violence. Without in a sense being coerced by that alternative, opponents would be less likely to entertain dialogue or respond positively to nonviolent confrontation. Violence and nonviolence therefore need each other: they are in a kind of symbiotic relationship. Would Gandhi have been successful if the British were not simultaneously facing the alternative of ongoing social violence? Would the relatively nonviolent liberation of the Philippines from the Marcos regime have occurred without the existence of violent revolutionaries? Would South Africa's nonviolent campaigns have been as effective without growing violence in the townships and cities?

Is psychological or moral coercion really compatible with nonviolence? Many theorists and practitioners of nonviolence accept the necessity of what has come to be called nonviolent coercion. Gandhi, while respected as a significant figure in the tradition, is seen as ultimately being more committed to his spiritual path—the pursuit of *moksha* or liberation through *karma yoga*, the path of service—than to societal change. His inner conflict between the mystic and the change agent in him is mirrored after his assassination in the subsequent conflict among his followers between his chosen successor, Vinoba Bhave, and the Marxist, Jayaprakash Narayan. For nonviolence to thrive as a style of conflict resolution and social change, some argue that it is therefore wiser to take a more pragmatic stance. It may be acceptable in certain situations to pressure or force someone to change his or her ways, whether they really want to or not, if it can be justified that this is not intended as harm but rather is in the best interests of everyone. Whether or not this constitutes a major inconsistency in nonviolence theory and practice—a significant conflict between means and ends—continues as an open question.

Also See the Following Articles

AGGRESSION AND ALTRUISM • AGGRESSION, PSYCHOLOGY OF • CONFLICT MANAGEMENT AND RESOLUTION • CONFLICT TRANSFORMATION • HUMAN RIGHTS • MEDIATION AND NEGOTIATION TECHNIQUES • PEACE EDUCATION • PEACEFUL SOCIETIES • WARRIORS, ANTHROPOLOGY OF

Bibliography

Bush, R. A., (1994). *The promise of mediation: Responding to conflict through empowerment and recognition.* San Francisco: Jossey-Bass.

Chapple, C. (1993). *Nonviolence to animals, earth and self in Asian traditions.* Albany: State University of New York Press.

Coakley, J. (Ed.). (1993). *The territorial management of ethnic conflict.* Portland: Frank Cass.

Eagley, A., & Chaiken, S. (1993). *The psychology of attitudes.* San Diego: Harcourt Brace Jovanovich.

Fisher, R., Ury, W., & Patton, B. (1991). *Getting to yes: Negotiating agreement without giving in* (2nd ed.). New York: Penguin.

Folger, J. P., Poole, M. S., & Stutman, R. K. (1993). *Working through conflict* (2nd ed.). Glenview, IL: Scott, Foresman.

Gandhi, M. K. (1927). *Young India: 1924–1926.* New York: Viking.

Hocker, J. L., & Wilmont, W. W. (1994). *Interpersonal conflict.* Madison, WI: Brown & Benchmark.

Kimmel, P. R. (1997). Cultural perspectives on international negotiations. In L.A. Peplau & S. E. Taylor (Eds.), *Sociocultural perspectives in social psychology.* Upper Saddle River, NJ: Prentice Hall.

King, M. L., Jr. (1963). *Why we can't wait.* New York: Harper & Row.

Lore, R. K., & Schultz, L. A. (1993). Control of human aggression. *American Psychologist, 48,* 16–25.

Morse, P. S. (1996). *Face to face: Communication and conflict resolution in the schools.* Thousand Oaks, CA: Corwin Press.

Olson, J. M., & Zanna, M. P. (1993). Attitude and attitude change. *Annual Review of Psychology, 44,* 117–154.

Pedersen, P. (1993). Mediating multicultural conflict by separating behaviours from expectations in a cultural grid. *International Journal of Intercultural Relations, 17,* 343–353.

Powers, R. S., & Vogele, W. B., Eds. (1997). *Protest, power, and change.* New York: Garland.

Sharp, G. (1985). *Making Europe unconquerable: The potential of civilian-based deterrence and defense.* Cambridge, MA: Ballinger.

Teixeira, B. (1992). *A Gandhian futurology: A futurology of nonviolence.* Madurai: The Valliammal Institution.

Wehn P., Burgess, H, & Burgess, G. (1994). *Justice without violence.* Boulder, CO: Lynne Rienner.

World Commission on Environment and Development. (1987). *Our common future.* Oxford: Oxford University Press.

Nonviolent Action

Gene Sharp
Albert Einstein Institution

GLOSSARY

Civilian-Based Defense A national defense policy to deter and defeat aggression, both internal (i.e., coups d'état) and external (i.e., invasions) by preparing the population and institutions for massive nonviolent resistance and defiance.

Mechanism A particular process by which various factors interact to produce a specific outcome. In nonviolent action the mechanisms are conversion, accommodation, nonviolent coercion, and disintegration.

Method Specific forms of action within the technique of nonviolent action. They are grouped into three broad classes of nonviolent protest and persuasion, noncooperation, and nonviolent intervention.

Noncooperation Acts that deliberately restrict, withhold, or discontinue social, economic, or political cooperation with an institution, policy, or government. A general class of methods of nonviolent action.

Nonviolent Action A technique of action in conflicts in which participants conduct the struggle by doing—or refusing to do—certain acts without using physical violence. It may also be called nonviolent struggle.

Political Power The totality of influences and pressures available for use, especially by the institutions of government, by the state, or in opposition to them, to determine and implement policies for the society. Such power may be directly applied, or may be a reserve capacity.

Strategy The conception of how most effectively to apply one's resources to achieve one's objectives in a conflict.

Violence The infliction on people of physical injury or death, or the threat to do so.

NONVIOLENT ACTION is a technique of socio-political action for applying power in a conflict. Nonviolent action consists of many specific methods of psychological, social, economic, and political action without the use of physical violence.

Nonviolent action conducts protest, resistance, and intervention without physical violence by: (a) acts of omission—that is, the participants refuse to perform acts which they usually perform, are expected by custom to perform, or are required by law or regulation to perform; or (b) acts of commission—that is, the participants perform acts that they usually do not perform, are not expected by custom to perform, or are forbidden by law or regulation from performing; or (c) a combination of both.

Copyright © 1999 by Academic Press.
All rights of reproduction in any form reserved.

This type of struggle includes a multitude of specific methods that are grouped into three main classes: nonviolent protest and persuasion, noncooperation, and nonviolent intervention. These are described below.

Nonviolent action is a way to wield power and to confront the power of opponents. It is a technique of waging active conflict and as a sanction to achieve certain objectives in a conflict, where in its absence submission or violence would likely have occurred.

Nonviolent struggle is used when milder types of action—such as negotiations, conciliation, arbitration, persuasion, and the like—are not available, are not expected to be effective, or have failed to resolve the conflict satisfactorily in the users' opinion. When the nonviolent group determines that the time for open struggle has arrived, it may choose whether to use forms of violent conflict or nonviolent conflict. In its stronger forms of noncooperation and intervention, nonviolent action is therefore the counterpart of violent action, an alternative means of last resort.

As a means of last resort and of conducting direct conflict, nonviolent action resembles military action, except that nonviolent action excludes violence and uses instead psychological, social, economic, and political pressures. One of the seminal studies in the 1930s of Gandhi's use of nonviolent action and its similarities to war was titled *War Without Violence* by Krishnalal Shridharani. Several other analysts have also pointed to the similarities between nonviolent and military action.

This broad phenomenon of nonviolent action has variously been referred to by such terms as nonviolent resistance, *satyagraha*, passive resistance, positive action, nonviolent direct action, and civilian resistance. A preferred term is nonviolent struggle. The simple term nonviolence is best avoided because of its ambiguity and confusion with various types of principled nonviolence.

Nonviolent action is commonly chosen to be used in a conflict because it is believed to be the most likely in the circumstances to achieve the objectives. The users of the technique often do not have the resources to wage strong violent struggle, especially as their opponent is commonly a regime with vast military capacity. Or, the resisters may see that the nonviolent technique will likely avoid much of the negative consequences of the use of violence. In some situations, the pragmatic grounds for the choice of nonviolent means have been mixed with a relative moral or religious preference for nonviolent means. In a small number of cases, the conflict has been waged by groups that reject violence completely on grounds of principle.

I. WHAT IS NONVIOLENT ACTION?

A. The Methods of Nonviolent Action

Nearly 200 specific methods of this technique have been identified, but clearly there exist many more and new ones are continually being invented. All of these specific methods can be classified under three broad classes.

The mildest of these is nonviolent protest and persuasion. This class contains symbolic acts, and not simply words, that are intended to communicate protest against some action, policy, or condition. These include such methods as distribution of leaflets, holding vigils, conducting a march, and maintaining silence. These are the weaker methods of the technique but, depending on the situation and on how they are implemented, they can make a major impact in the conflict.

The second, more powerful, class is noncooperation. The methods of noncooperation wield greater power by withdrawing or withholding, usually temporarily, certain forms of cooperation that enabled the social, economic, or political relationships to function as they did previously. This halt to cooperation potentially makes a much greater impact on the conflict than do purely symbolic acts. The slowing or halting of the previous cooperation can be disruptive or even paralyzing for the opponents.

This class contains three subclasses. Social noncooperation includes cecessation of cooperation on the social level, by applying such forms as social boycotts and boycotts of social occasions and functions. The impact of social boycotts is primarily psychological, especially on those boycotted. The impact may also be symbolic, as in refusing to attend ceremonies and occasions sponsored by the opponents in a conflict. Economic noncooperation includes both economic boycotts and labor strikes. There are many forms of both of these types of economic noncooperation. Their impact depends on such factors as the number of people participating, their previous economic roles in the society, and the relation of those roles to the opponents. Political noncooperation includes many methods by which groups, or individuals, refuse to initiate or to continue any of many forms of cooperation in political matters with an opponent group, usually a government. The many specific methods of action included here vary widely, and they include boycott of rigged elections, walking out of government bodies, civil disobedience, and a work stoppage by civil servants. Again, as with economic noncooperation, the impact will largely depend on the number of people, groups and individuals, withholding their cooperation. On a small scale the action may be primarily symbolic but on a large scale such action may paralyze a political system.

The third broad class is nonviolent intervention. These are methods that actively disrupt the normal workings of the system. The intervention may take psychological, physical, social, economic, and political forms. The strength of these methods depends in large degree on the scale on which they are practiced and the discipline and persistence of the practitioners. The widely diverse types of action include hunger strikes, sit-ins, creating new social, economic, or political institutions, establishing new forms of social behavior, and parallel government. Some of these methods of action, such as sit-ins, may at times make possible a strong impact by a relatively small number of people. Other methods, such as forming new institutions and a parallel government, require the backing of large numbers of participants.

It should be noted, however, that because of the nature of their challenge to the system these methods often are met with sharp repression. Highly disciplined behavior is often required, especially in the use of the methods that are especially disruptive and that may be conducted by relatively small numbers of resisters.

The impact of those methods of intervention that involve the establishment and operation of new institutions (social, economic, and political) will be to a large degree determined by the extent and duration of their operations.

In revolutionary situations the formation of a parallel government as a rival to the current one is a dramatic challenge. When a regime has been targeted for replacement, a parallel government may be organized during or following a large-scale noncooperation campaign. This can occur when the aim of the resisting group is to replace the old oppressive regime with a democratic government. When this is attempted, a difficult transition period should be expected. The dangers come not only from the remnants of the old regime, but also from other sources. During the time of uncertainty and the shift of authority, serious efforts are required to prevent a new clique from conducting a coup d'état to impose a new oppressive regime.

The boundaries of the technique of nonviolent action are thus measured by this range of methods. The technique is defined by what it is and does, and not by the simple rejection of violence. The simple absence of violent action can indicate passive submission, cowardice, and acceptance of the status quo. All of those are incompatible with the use of nonviolent action, and must not be confused with it.

B. Mobilizing and Undermining Power

This technique can operate effectively against otherwise powerful opponents and established regimes because of its ability to mobilize power of previously dominated populations and to undermine the power of oppressive systems and governments. It empowers people by providing them with a technique of group action that they can use as an alternative to military capacity. This mobilized strength can then be targeted to undermine the power of the opponents. This targeting is possible because this technique can affect the sources of the opponents' power.

The sources of power of all governments include authority, or legitimacy. Authority is perhaps the most important single source of power, since belief in the regime's right to rule helps to provide other important sources of power. There are five additional sources.

Human resources means the number of persons and institutions that obey, cooperate with, and assist the regime. The skills and knowledge provided by these persons and institutions are also very important. They fuel the regime. Intangible factors involve the population's habits and attitudes toward obedience and submission. Material resources include natural and financial resources, the economic system, communication, and transportation. The regime inflicts sanctions (punishments) by police and military action to enforce obedience. If the regime receives a plentiful supply of these six sources of power it remains strong.

However, nonviolent action can be targeted to undermine the supply of each of these sources of power. The regime is weakened when the supply of these is sharply restricted. When the supply is severed, the regime is paralyzed or falls apart.

If the regime does not receive sufficient acceptance of its right to rule, if the needed skills and knowledge are not available, if the needed support of institutions and the civil service is not forthcoming, if the regime does not retain control of economic resources (including finances, communications and transportation), if the population does not submit even in face of repression, if the police and troops do not obey orders efficiently or even mutiny, then the regime's power is gone.

The ability of the population to conduct nonviolent struggle and to weaken or remove the sources of power will be highly influenced by the existence, strength, or absence of nonstate social groups and institutions in the society. These may be called loci of power (places where power is located and can be wielded). These may be families, social classes, religious groups, cultural and nationality groups, occupational groups, villages, towns, cities, provinces and regions, smaller governmental bodies, voluntary organizations, and political parties. Most often these are traditional, established, formal social groups and institutions, but sometimes they may be less formal and even recently created or revitalized in the course of resistance.

These loci of power can make resistance a group or corporate activity, as distinct from acts by individuals. For example, a labor strike led by a strong trade union is more powerful than the refusal of an individual to continue work. In other times, in the absence of resistance, these loci of power may supply needed sources of power to the established order. They may then be called pillars of support. Examples in the political order may include the civil servants and bureaucracy, religious bodies, controllers of the economy, the police and military forces, political parties, and others. When these same groups and institutions shift allegiance and become opposed to the status quo, they can restrict or sever the supply of particular sources of power. This action thereby can become potentially highly coercive or even cause the collapse of a given regime.

C. Mechanisms of Change

Nonviolent action may thus be not only coercive—that is, that it forces the regime to accept changes it does not wish to make. Nonviolent action can also disintegrate a once highly repressive regime even if its top officials remain determined to stay in control. Nonviolent coercion and disintegration are the most powerful mechanisms of change by nonviolent struggle. In some situations this technique also may operate with one of two milder mechanisms. The technique may induce the opponents to compromise. This is called accommodation, with both sides gaining part of their objectives. Accommodation often occurs in labor strikes for economic grievances and claims, for example. Very rarely, the emotions or minds of the key persons in the opponent group may be strongly moved by the tenacity and nonviolent suffering of the resisting group. Or, members of the opponent group may change their opinions about the merits of the issues, and agree to accept the claims of the nonviolent group. This is called conversion. It does not occur easily or frequently.

Of course, not all cases of nonviolent struggle are successful. If the requirements for effectiveness are absent, if the resistance collapses in face of repression or the population resorts to violence, if the potential resisters are too weak or frightened to act strongly, if a poor strategy has been selected or there was none, and if various other unfavorable conditions are present,

then success cannot be expected until those conditions are changed.

D. Correcting Misunderstandings

Two points of misunderstanding need to be corrected at this point. The use of these nonviolent methods does not require the presence of moral or religious injunctions against use of violence. Nonviolent action is a technique of conflict and is not to be confused with creeds of moral, ethical, or religious nonviolence. Believers in such principles may or may not use this technique. However, the technique can be—and overwhelmingly has been—used by people who do not share such beliefs and may have used or considered using violence in the past. These nonviolent responses to conflict do not require the practitioners to achieve a higher level of moral development. Indeed, for the most part these forms of resistance owe more to the human capacity for stubbornness than to religious injunctions to love one's enemy or to practice *ahimsa* (noninjury and nonkilling in Hindu and Buddhist beliefs).

The other point is that the use of this technique does not require a charismatic leader. In the popular mind the use of nonviolent action is often associated with Mohandas K. Gandhi, often known as "Mahatma Gandhi." It is often thought that a leader with supposedly saintly or charismatic qualities is needed to inspire and guide a large-scale nonviolent struggle. Whether that characterization of Gandhi is justified or not is not the point here. The point, instead, is that in very many powerful cases of nonviolent action, including successful ones, the leader or leaders had no such attributes. At times it was difficult or impossible to identify a specific leader or group of leaders guiding a mass movement. At other times, it can be argued, the attribution of extraordinary qualities to a leader in nonviolent action has even had a negative impact on the effectiveness of the struggle. Clearly, as the knowledge of the needed skills and behavior required in applying this technique competently and its strategic principles are diffused, there will be reduced need for strong leaders whether charismatic or not.

II. THE PRACTICE OF NONVIOLENT ACTION

A. Origins of Nonviolent Action

The technique of nonviolent action is not a recent invention. It did not begin with Mohandas K. Gandhi, for example. Quite to the contrary, the use of these methods is very old, minimally a few centuries and probably millennia. Although most of that early history is doubtless lost forever, it does appear to be the case that the technique has undergone significant refinement at least from the final decades of the 18th century and particularly in the 20th century.

For centuries, symbolic protests, withholding of cooperation, and disruptive activities—all without physical violence—have occurred widely in conflict situations. These are basically simple and understandable responses to specific conflicts. No great intellectual sophistication was required to develop such methods of resistance.

B. Widespread Occurrence

Nonviolent action has occurred in widely differing cultures, periods of history, and political conditions, prominently including those of extreme oppression and repression. Nonviolent struggle has occurred in "the West" and in "the East," and on all populated continents. Nonviolent action has happened in industrialized countries and nonindustrialized countries. It has been practiced under conditions of constitutional democracy and under empires, foreign occupations, and dictatorial systems. Nonviolent struggle has been waged on behalf of a myriad of causes and groups, and even for objectives that many people would reject. It has also been used to prevent, as well as to promote, change.

The technique of nonviolent action has been applied in quite diverse conflicts. These include social and economic conflicts that have little or nothing to do with the government. Cases include efforts to impose or resist pressures for social conformity and labor-management conflicts. Nonviolent action has also been used in religious conflicts. There are also other types of conflict situations, such as between students and university administrations. However, conflicts between the civil population and controllers of the state apparatus have also occurred very widely and at times have been very important. Examples offered here are often of the civil population versus the state variety.

From the late-18th century through the 20th century, the technique of nonviolent action was widely used in highly diverse conflicts: colonial rebellions, international political and economic conflicts, religious conflicts, and antislavery resistance. This technique has been aimed to secure workers' right to organize, women's rights, universal manhood suffrage, and woman suffrage. This type of struggle has been used to gain national independence, to bring about economic gains, to resist genocide, to undermine dictatorships, to gain civil rights, to end segregation, and to resist foreign occupations and *coups d'état*. In more advanced applications of nonviolent action, leaders have planned the activities with attention to the vulnerabilities of the opponent group and to its dependence on the group with grievances.

Cases of the use of this technique early in the 20th century included major aspects of the Russian 1905 Revolution. Also, in various countries the growing trade unions widely used the strike and the economic boycott. Chinese boycotts of Japanese products occurred in 1908, 1915, and 1919. Germans used nonviolent action against the Kapp *Putsch* in 1920 and against the French and Belgian occupation of the Ruhr in 1923. In the 1920s and 1930s, especially, Indian nationalists used nonviolent action under the leadership of Mohandas K. Gandhi in their struggles against British rule.

From 1940 to 1945 democrats in various European countries resisted Nazi occupation and rule by nonviolent struggle, especially in Norway, Denmark, the Netherlands, and Bulgaria. Nonviolent action was used to save Jews from the Holocaust in Berlin, Bulgaria, Denmark, and elsewhere. The military dictators of El Salvador and Guatemala were ousted in short nonviolent struggles in the spring of 1944. The American civil rights nonviolent struggles against racial segregation changed laws and long-established policies in the U.S. South, especially in the 1950s and 1960s.

In 1968 and 1969, following the Warsaw Pact invasion, Czechs and Slovaks held off full Soviet control for 8 months with improvised nonviolent struggle and refusal of collaboration. From 1953 to 1990 democrats in communist-ruled countries in Eastern Europe, especially in East Germany, Poland, Hungary, and the Baltic countries, repeatedly used nonviolent struggles for greater freedom, which was eventually achieved. The sophisticated Solidarity struggle in Poland began in 1980 with strikes undertaken to support the demand for a legal free trade union and concluded in 1989 with the end of the communist system. The attempted hardline coup d'état in Moscow in 1991 was defeated by noncooperation and defiance. Nonviolent protests and mass resistance were highly important in undermining the apartheid policies and European domination in South Africa, especially between 1950 and 1990. The Marcos dictatorship in the Philippines was destroyed by a nonviolent uprising in 1986.

In July and August 1988 Burmese democrats protested the actions of the military dictatorship with marches and defiance, brought down three governments, and finally succumbed to a new military coup d'état and mass slaughters. In 1989 Chinese students and others in approximately 60 cities, including in Tiananmen Square, Beijing, conducted symbolic protests against government corruption and oppression, which finally collapsed following massive military killings. In Kosovo the Albanian population has conducted a noncooperation campaign against repressive Serbian rule, followed by guerrilla warfare. Starting in November 1996 Serbs conducted daily parades and protest in Belgrade and other cities against the autocratic governance of President Milosovic and secured correction of electoral fraud in mid-January 1997.

In some of these cases nonviolent action served as a tool of empowering populations in conflicts with oppressive and powerful governments. In some cases, nonviolent struggle helped to achieve democratic control over rulers who did not wish to be controlled. This technique therefore has significant implications for democratic theory and practice.

In some of these cases violence has occurred along side the predominant application of nonviolent struggle. A prominent example is the Russian 1905 Revolution. Such violence has often been practiced to the detriment of the effectiveness of the nonviolent action; indeed the opponents have often deliberately sought to provoke such violence in order to help to defeat a strong nonviolent movement. Leaders of these movements have often gone to considerable lengths to prevent such violence because it was recognized as being counterproductive.

These cases are only a few from a much larger list of cases that occurred during those decades. They illustrate, however, the widespread practice of the technique. It appears that the use of this technique has expanded in political significance and prominence during the 20th century.

Generally, nonviolent action is used only in conflicts that are felt by the users to be extremely serious. The major exception to this is that the symbolic methods of nonviolent protest and persuasion may be much more widely used. Many of those methods, such as distribution of leaflets and marches, for example, are widely used in constitutional democracies, and the right to use them is regarded as an important civil liberty. Sometimes, however, particular methods, such as sit-ins, that are by nature fairly strong methods may come to be regarded by some groups as a standard mode of expression and become used so frequently that some of their impact is lost. In more acute conflicts, as against a dictatorial regime or a foreign occupation, much greater power and therefore effectiveness can be and has been wielded by the stronger methods, especially those of noncooperation.

III. THE FUTURE OF NONVIOLENT ACTION

A. New Scholarly and Strategic Attention

The 20th century brought new intellectual efforts to understand this phenomenon, mostly from social scientists, and at times from advocates of this technique. Among such studies, beginning in 1913 and going to 1994 are these (listed chronologically): Harry Laidler, *Boycotts and the Labor Struggle* (1913); Clarence Marsh Case, *Non-violent Coercion* (1923); E. T. Hiller, *The Strike* (1928); Wilfred H. Crook, *The General Strike* (1931); Karl Ehrlich, Niels Lindberg and Gammelgaard Jacobsen, *Kamp Uden Vaaben* (1937); Bart. de Ligt, *The Conquest of Violence* (1938); Krishnalal Shridharani, *War Without Violence* (1938); Joan V. Bondurant, *Conquest of Violence* (1958); Theodor Ebert, *Gewaltfrier Aufstand* (1968); Gene Sharp, *The Politics of Nonviolent Action* (1973), and Peter Ackerman and Christopher Kruegler, *Strategic Nonviolent Conflict* (1994). Of these, Laidler, Hiller, and Crook draw heavily on the labor movement in Europe and North America. Case, Ehrlich and colleagues, and de Ligt include examinations of diverse historical cases. Shridharani and Bondurant base their studies heavily on the movements led by Gandhi. Ebert, Sharp, and Ackerman and Kruegler also use various historical cases and represent a significant advance in their analyses of the technique.

The combination of the growing practice of nonviolent struggle and such intellectual efforts to learn about this technique mean that greater knowledge is now available than previously to groups that wish to use nonviolent action.

Efforts have also recently been made to enhance the effectiveness of future nonviolent action by study of strategic principles. The most important single contribution to this is Peter Ackerman's and Christopher Kruegler's, *Strategic Nonviolent Conflict*.

B. Efforts at Planned Adoption

Past uses of the technique of nonviolent action have mostly been improvised to meet a specific immediate need and were not the result of long-term planning and preparations. However, the planned and prepared substitution of nonviolent action for violent means has been recommended for consideration in certain types of acute conflicts. These include the following purposes:

- Conducting severe *interethnic conflicts* with "no compromise" issues;
- Producing fundamental social change to correct oppressive social, economic, or political conditions;
- Resisting a *dictatorship* or attempting to disintegrate it;
- Deterring and resisting coups d'état;
- Deterring and resisting external aggression; and
- Deterring and resisting attempts at genocide.

There exist unplanned, improvised, cases of the application of nonviolent struggle for all these purposes. It has been claimed, and recent studies suggest, that advance analysis, planning, and preparations can increase the capacity of this technique to be effective even under the extreme conditions mentioned above. In the struggles against dictatorships, oppressive systems, genocide, coups d'état, and foreign occupations the appropriate strategies all involve efforts to restrict and sever the sources of power of the hostile forces. Application of nonviolent struggle in all of these acute conflict situations involves resistance in face of extreme repression.

The planned and prepared application of this type of struggle against internal or external aggression is known as civilian-based defense.

In assessing the viability of nonviolent struggle in extreme circumstances, it is also important to examine critically the adequacy and problems of applying violent means, rather than assuming axiomatically its superior effectiveness.

Expanded knowledge gained through scholarly studies and strategic analyses and its spread in popularized forms is likely to contribute to increased substitutions of nonviolent struggle for violent action. Some policy studies have already been initiated for dealing with coups d'état, defense, and other national security issues.

C. Nonviolent Action for "Wrong" Objectives

Concerns have been voiced that nonviolent action could be used by certain groups for "wrong" objectives, for purposes that many would not endorse. For example, in the 19th century, Scottish, English, and U.S. factory owners combating trade union activities sometimes shut down operations in a lock-out, Nazis organized economic boycotts of Jewish businesses in the 1930s, and Southern segregationists in the United States used social and economic boycotts of civil rights activists in the 1960s. Comparable cases are likely to occur in the future.

The response to this situation of some specialists on nonviolent struggle is that the use of nonviolent action for those purposes is preferable to those groups continuing to apply violence for the same purposes. Suffering from the results of an economic boycott is preferable to being lynched, for example.

In acute conflicts the contending groups are unlikely to abandon or even compromise their beliefs and objectives. However, there sometimes *is* a possibility that such a group might shift to other means of conducting the conflict. It is argued that the real question is not, therefore, whether one would prefer them to change their beliefs and goals (since that is almost certainly not going to happen), but whether one prefers them to struggle for those same goals by violent or by nonviolent means. The target group of those applications of nonviolent action would need to decide how to resist the "wrong" objectives, whether by violent repression, educational efforts, or counter-nonviolent action.

D. Needed Future Explorations

The technique of nonviolent action has been disproportionately neglected by academics, policymakers, and exponents of major social and political change. As the practice of this type of struggle grows and scholarly studies of it increase, it is becoming ever clearer that nonviolent action merits increased attention in several fields. Significant efforts are still required to correct the long-standing neglect of this phenomenon.

Studies of nonviolent action and the dynamics of this technique are likely to cross disciplinary boundaries, but certain disciplines have been identified as particularly relevant. Nonviolent action is of major significance for the social sciences, especially for the study of social conflict, social movements, historical sociology, and political sociology. Social psychologists can shed light on the shifts in attitudes, emotions, opinions, and group action during the course of a nonviolent conflict.

Some historians have identified the need to examine understudied developments of the past to correct the historical record that has usually given priority attention to violent action rather than nonviolent struggle. Recent studies that focus on nonviolent struggles are: Walter H. Conser, Jr., Ronald M. McCarthy, David J. Toscano, and Gene Sharp, Eds., *Resistance, Politics, and the American Struggle for Independence, 1765–1775*, and

Nathan Stoltzfus, *Resistance of the Heart: Intermarriage and the Rosenstrasse Protest in Nazi Germany*.

Recent studies of the practice of nonviolent action provide grounds for political and social theorists to reexamine basic concepts such as power, authority, sanctions, political obligation, and the presumed necessity of violence. Additionally, it has been suggested that some important problems in political ethics and moral theology related to the use of violence require reexamination in light of the growing practice of nonviolent struggle and the scholarly studies of the phenomenon.

IV. CONCLUSION

Nonviolent action is an important technique for conducting social, economic, and political conflicts without the use of physical violence. Nonviolent action is an old technique that in recent decades appears to be coming into increasingly significant use in conflicts in various parts of the world.

The phenomenon has been attracting scholarly attention in recent decades and also efforts to refine its strategic application. Expanded knowledge of nonviolent action, its operation, and potential is likely to have a significant impact on its future consideration in conflicts and the quality of its application. New efforts have been initiated to make the technique more effective in dealing with the hard cases, such as foreign occupations, coups d'état, and ruthless dictatorships. Steps are being taken to disseminate the increasing knowledge of the technique through popularizations for the general public.

Although knowledge of the technique has expanded, nonviolent struggle still merits additional careful attention by scholars in various disciplines and policy analysts and also policy makers dealing with internal and international conflicts.

Also See the Following Articles

CRITIQUES OF VIOLENCE • CONFLICT TRANSFORMATION • ETHICAL STUDIES, OVERVIEW • INSTITUTIONALIZATION OF NONVIOLENCE • PEACE CULTURE • PEACE EDUCATION • PEACEFUL SOCIETIES • SPIRITUALITY AND PEACEMAKING

Bibliography

Ackerman, P., & Kruegler, C. (1994). *Strategic nonviolent conflict: The dynamics of people power in the twentieth century.* Westport, CT: Praeger Publishers.

Bondurant, J. V. (1958). *Conquest of violence: The Gandhian philosophy of conflict.* Princeton: Princeton University Press.

Case, C. M. (1923). *Non-violent coercion: A study in methods of social pressure.* New York: Century Co.

Conser, W., McCarthy, R. Toscano, T., & Sharp, G. (Eds.). (1986). *Resistance, politics, and the American struggle for independence, 1765–1775.* Boulder: CO: Lynne Rienner.

Crook, W. H. (1931). *The general strike: A study of labor's tragic weapon in theory and practice.* Chapel Hill, NC: University of North Carolina Press.

Ebert, T. (1968). *Gewaltfrier Aufstand: Alternative zum Bürgerkrieg.* Freiburg: Verlag Rombach.

Karl E., Lindberg, N., & Jacobsen, G. (1937). *Kamp uden vaaben: Ikkevold som kampmiddel mod krig og undertrykkelse.* Copenhagen: Levin & Munksgaard, Ejnar Munksgaard.

Hiller, E. T. (1928). *The strike: A study in collective action.* Chicago: University of Chicago Press.

Laidler, H. (1913). *Boycotts and the labor struggle: Economic and legal aspects.* New York: John Lane.

de Ligt, B. (1938). *The conquest of violence: An essay on war and revolution.* New York: E. P. Dutton.

McCarthy, R., & Sharp, G., with Bennett, B. (1997). *Nonviolent action: A research guide.* New York and London: Garland Publishing.

Powers, R. S., & Vogele, W. B. (Eds.) and Kruegler, C., & McCarthy, R. M. (Assoc. Eds.). (1997). *Protest, power, and change: An encyclopedia of nonviolent action from ACT-UP to women's suffrage,* New York and London: Garland Publishing.

Roberts, A. (Ed.). (1968, 1969). *Civilian resistance as a national defense.* Harrisburg, PA: Stackpole Books; Baltimore: Penguin Books.

Sharp, G. (1973). *The politics of nonviolent action.* Boston: Porter Sargent.

Sharp, G., with Jenkins, B. (1990). *Civilian-based defense: A post-military weapons system.* Princeton: Princeton University Press.

Shridharani, K. (1939). *War without violence: A study of Gandhi's method and its accomplishments.* New York: Harcourt, Brace and Co.

Stoltzfus, N. (1996). *Resistance of the heart: Intermarriage and the Rosenstrasse protest in Nazi Germany.* New York: W.W. Norton & Co.

Nuclear Warfare

Dean A. Wilkening

Center for International Security and Cooperation, Stanford University

GLOSSARY

Fission A nuclear reaction in which the nucleus splits apart after absorbing a neutron, releasing substantial amounts of energy and several additional neutrons in the process.

Chain Reaction A process wherein the neutrons released from a single fission reaction cause fission in several nearby nuclei, the neutrons from which subsequently cause fission in several other nearby nuclei and so on, assuming a critical amount of material is present to capture these subsequent neutrons, leading ultimately to an exponentially growing series of fission reactions until the fissionable material is consumed.

Fusion A nuclear reaction in which two light nuclei stick together to form a heavier nucleus, thereby releasing substantial amounts of energy and an extra neutron.

Deterrence A strategy aimed at dissuading another party from taking some proscribed action out of fear that the expected consequences associated with the threatened retribution will outweigh the expected gains associated with taking the action, relative to maintaining the status quo.

Central Deterrence The strategy wherein a nuclear-armed state dissuades an opponent from attacking its homeland by threatening nuclear retaliation.

Extended Deterrence The strategy wherein a nuclear-armed state dissuades an opponent from attacking its allies by threatening nuclear retaliation.

Counterforce An attack aimed at destroying an opponent's nuclear forces in a preemptive strike.

Countervalue An attack aimed at destroying that which an opponent values most, usually thought to be the opponent's cities.

Secure Second Strike The ability to retaliate with nuclear weapons after absorbing a counterforce first strike; i.e., nuclear command and control systems and sufficient nuclear forces can survive, penetrate the opponent's defenses, and inflict unacceptable damage even in the presence of passive defenses to act as an effective deterrent.

TECHNOLOGY has always had a profound influence on the character of war. In the past century alone the industrial revolution, culminating in the development of modern aircraft, tanks, artillery, and naval vessels increased the lethality of war manyfold. However, the advent of nuclear weapons in 1945 represented a quan-

Copyright © 1999 by Academic Press.
All rights of reproduction in any form reserved.

tum jump in the lethality of war. Looking ahead, one wonders how emerging information technologies and bio-technologies might revolutionize warfare in the future.

The history of the Cold War can be attributed to the confluence of two factors: the development of nuclear weapons and the rise of the former Soviet Union and the United States as the two dominant military powers after World War II. It may seem paradoxical that the development of the most destructive form of warfare, nuclear warfare, led to a period of relative peace, the Cold War. In fact, nuclear weapons have been used only twice in war—the U.S. bombings of Hiroshima on August 6, 1945 and Nagasaki on August 9, 1945. This is not to say that wars on the periphery of U.S. and Soviet interests did not occur, but simply that war between the major powers was absent. This article discusses the development of nuclear weapons, their effects, and the impact they have had on the character of war and military strategy. The ascendance of deterrence as the central strategic concept for nuclear warfare helps explain the apparent paradox mentioned above.

I. WHAT ARE NUCLEAR WEAPONS?

A. Fission Bombs

The 1930s witnessed rapid developments in our understanding of the atomic nucleus—the small positively charged core that contains most of the mass of all atoms and around which a cloud of electrons swirl. The nuclear force, which holds the nucleus together, is approximately one million times stronger than the electromagnetic force that binds the electrons to the nucleus. For our story, one discovery was particularly important. In 1938, Otto Hahn and Fritz Strassman, two Germans, discovered that the uranium nucleus splits apart, i.e., undergoes fission, when bombarded with neutrons, liberating considerable amounts of energy. Within a year, several research teams discovered that extra neutrons were also emitted, a fact of considerable significance, as Leo Szilard recognized years before, because it meant that large amounts of energy could be released in a chain reaction.

The reaction that Hahn and Strassman discovered is,

$$n + U^{235} \rightarrow \text{fission fragments} + 2\text{--}3\ n + \text{energy},$$

where n represents a neutron, the fission fragments are nuclei (usually highly radioactive) with a mass roughly half that of U^{235}, and the energy is released as kinetic en-

ergy of the fission fragments and neutrons. However, this reaction occurs only with one isotope of uranium, U^{235}, at least for relatively low-energy bombarding neutrons. Natural uranium consists of 99.3% U^{238} and only 0.7% U^{235}. Somewhat later a similar reaction was discovered in an isotope of plutonium, Pu^{239}. Several isotopes of other nuclei also undergo fission but, for technical reasons, none are as well suited for making nuclear weapons.

The key to extracting large amounts of energy from a macroscopic amount of fissile material, e.g., in nuclear bombs or nuclear power reactors, is to create a chain reaction, as depicted in Fig. 1. In a chain reaction the neutrons released from an initial fission reaction are absorbed by neighboring U^{235} nuclei, which subsequently undergo fission. This process keeps multiplying until nearly all the U^{235} (or Pu^{239}) is consumed. Of course, some neutrons will escape without hitting another U^{235} nucleus. If too many neutrons escape, the chain reaction will not proceed very far. Therefore the shape and amount of U^{235} present influences the amount of energy released. The amount of material needed for a self-sustaining chain reaction is called the critical mass, which is the amount required for a simple fission bomb. The critical mass for U^{235} is approximately 30 lbs. and for Pu^{239} is approximately 10 lbs.

The acquisition of fissile material (i.e., U^{235} or Pu^{239}) is the principal technical challenge in developing nuclear fission bombs. Since U^{235} is only 0.7% of natural uranium, it must be separated from the more common isotope, U^{238}. This is a challenging proposition because these isotopes have nearly identical chemical properties. Gaseous diffusion (originally used by the United States in the Manhattan Project), gaseous centrifuge techniques, electromagnetic separation (the method used by Iraq in the late 1980s), and laser isotope separation are among the techniques used. For efficient bomb designs, uranium enriched to more than 90% U^{235} is re-

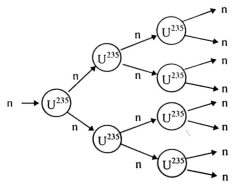

FIGURE 1 Fission chain reaction.

quired, although one can fashion a crude fission bomb with uranium enriched to only 20% U^{235}.

Plutonium, on the other hand, does not occur in nature because all of its isotopes decay in a relatively short period of time (Pu^{239} has a half-life of approximately 20,000 years). However, Pu^{239} can be manufactured in a nuclear power reactor by bombarding U^{238} with neutrons and then chemically separating the Pu^{239} from the radioactive waste in a reprocessing facility.

The crux of the nuclear proliferation problem, as with all proliferation problems involving dual-use technologies (i.e., ones with civilian and military applications), is to devise arms control regimes that allow states to develop nuclear power while at the same time restrict the development of nuclear weapons. This is the central challenge of the nuclear Non-Proliferation Treaty, the Nuclear Suppliers Group that coordinates export controls on sensitive nuclear materials and facilities, and the International Atomic Energy Agency, which monitors the nuclear nonproliferation regime.

Once sufficient fissile material is obtained, two designs can be used to make a bomb. The first is the "gun-type" design where a subcritical mass of U^{235} is shot into another subcritical mass, thereby creating a super-critical mass for a brief time. A neutron source injects a few neutrons to start the chain reaction at the proper moment. For technical reasons, this relatively simple assembly technique works only with U^{235}. A bomb of this design was dropped on Hiroshima on August 6, 1945, exploding with a force of 12,500 tons (12.5 kilotons) of TNT, killing approximately 70,000 people and wounding another 80,000. Because of its simplicity, this bomb design was not tested before it was used—which makes it of interest to states that wish to develop fission bombs covertly because nuclear tests are not essential. South Africa took this approach to build an arsenal of six gun-type U^{235} bombs in the 1980s.

The second fission bomb design creates a critical mass by crushing a sphere of fissile material, thereby creating very high densities. This implosion design is more challenging technically, but is more efficient with respect to the use of fissile material. Moreover, it works with both U^{235} and Pu^{239}. A bomb of this design was tested at Alamogordo, NM on July 16, 1945 and a second bomb of this design was dropped on Nagasaki on August 9, 1945 exploding with a force of nearly 20 kilotons (kT) of TNT. It missed the center of the city and, hence, killed only approximately 40,000 people and wounded another 20,000.

The major technical hurdle to developing implosion bombs, besides acquiring the fissile material, is to perfect the implosion mechanism, i.e., to develope explo-sive lenses that can crush a sphere of fissile material in a perfectly symmetric manner to create a supercritical mass. Small deviations from spherical symmetry cause the bomb to fail. Hence, implosion designs are usually tested. The former Soviet Union was the next country to test an implosion device in August, 1949. Great Britain followed suit in 1952, France in 1961, and China in 1964. India tested a "peaceful nuclear device" probably of this design, in 1974, and again in May 1998. Pakistan followed suit later that same month, although it is not clear whether their tests involved implosion or gun-type uranium devices. Israel is also thought to have developed implosion bombs, however, the evidence for an Israeli test is equivocal.

In general, first generation fission bombs of the sort described above weigh between 1,000 lbs. and 10,000 lbs, and detonate with an explosive force between 5 kT and 20 kT.

B. Fusion Bombs

Nuclear energy also is released when two light nuclei fuse together. Nuclear fusion describes the process by which two light nuclei, usually isotopes of hydrogen, fuse together to produce heavier elements. The standard reaction is,

$$D + T \rightarrow He^4 + n + energy,$$

where D stands for deuterium (an isotope of hydrogen with one proton and one neutron in the nucleus), T stands for tritium (an isotope of hydrogen with one proton and two neutrons in the nucleus), He stands for a nucleus of helium, and n is a neutron. More energy is released in this reaction than in a fission reaction. In fact, fusion reactions are the source of energy within stars. The critical problem in designing weapons based on nuclear fusion is to heat the deuterium and tritium to temperatures high enough to overcome the electrostatic repulsion between these two positively charged nuclei. This is done by detonating a fission bomb next to the fusion fuel (usually Li^6D, which creates D and T when bombarded with neutrons). Acquiring Li^6D is less difficult than U^{235} or Pu^{239}. Finally, the neutron emitted from the fusion reaction is of sufficient energy that it can actually cause U^{238} to undergo fission. Therefore, if the fusion bomb is surrounded by a U^{238} jacket (or tamper), a fission-fusion-fission reaction results. Although a relatively small fraction of a fusion bomb's yield comes from the fission trigger (e.g., several kilotons), fission within the U^{238} tamper can contribute a significant amount to the total weapon yield (e.g., several hundred kilotons for a megaton-size fusion bomb).

Very large fusion bombs (also called hydrogen bombs or thermonuclear bombs) can be made by increasing the amount of fusion fuel. Typically, fusion bombs are 100 to 1000 times more powerful than fission bombs. The first U.S. test of a fusion bomb occurred in November, 1952. The Soviet Union was quick to follow in August 1953. The largest fusion bomb ever tested was one of Soviet design which detonated with an explosive force equivalent to 60 megatons (MT) of TNT.

Most nuclear weapons in the arsenals of the five declared nuclear powers (i.e., the United States, Russia, France, Great Britain, and China) are fusion bombs with yields ranging between a few kilotons to 1000 kT or more. The smaller yields are usually associated with tactical nuclear weapons—intended for threatening an opponents conventional forces on the battlefield—and the larger yields are associated with strategic nuclear weapons—intended for threats against an opponents homeland using long-range delivery vehicles.

Modern nuclear weapon designs are much smaller and lighter than the original U.S. and Soviet fission bombs, ranging in size from that of a bread box to a refrigerator and in weight from around 100 lbs. to 2000 lbs. The fact that they are small and light means they can be delivered in a variety of ways (e.g., ballistic missiles, aircraft, cruise missiles, artillery shells, and torpedoes, to name a few). Moreover, the fact that they are relative cheap implies that large arsenals can be built. The initial investment cost to produce fission weapons is around $2 to $10 billion for indigenous programs; however, the marginal cost thereafter can be as low as $1 to $2 million per nuclear bomb for large programs of the sort that existed in the United States and the former Soviet Union. Note that if nuclear weapons were so large that the only practical means for delivering them was by cargo ship and if they cost a sizable fraction of a country's GDP to build, the history of the nuclear age would be very different. But they are not and this has made all the difference.

C. The Effects of Nuclear Weapons

Despite the fact that several nuclear weapon designs exist, the effects of nuclear explosions are essentially the same for all types. In particular, the intensity of nuclear weapon effects depends almost entirely on the bomb's yield. However, the effects vary depending on the environment in which the explosion occurs (outer space, the atmosphere, under water, or under ground). Most discussions of nuclear weapon effects refer to weapons detonated within the atmosphere because, if nuclear war ever did occur, this would be the most common type of explosion.

When a nuclear weapon explodes, the kinetic energy from the fission fragments, neutrons, and helium (for fusion reactions) heat the weapon debris to approximately 20 million degrees centigrade (the temperature of the sun) within a few microseconds. This hot core radiates energy like the coals in one's fireplace. However, because the temperature is so high the radiation is in the X-ray portion of the electromagnetic spectrum. As the hot core expands, it begins to cool. The result is a huge sphere of very hot air or fireball (around 1 mile in diameter for a 1-megaton explosion). This fireball begins to rise, eventually creating the mushroom cloud so often associated with nuclear explosions.

Ultimately, the energy from a nuclear explosion appears as five weapon effects: blast, thermal radiation, prompt nuclear radiation, fallout, and an electromagnetic pulse. There are two aspects to blast; the shock wave and winds. The shock wave (so called peak overpressure) is a wall of compressed air traveling outward from the explosion at speeds above the speed of sound, dissipating as it goes. It crushes objects in its path. The wind (so called dynamic overpressure) follows behind the shock wave, blowing over objects in its path. Houses can withstand peak overpressures of approximately 5 pounds per square inch (psi) whereas hardened military structures can withstand peak overpressures over 1000 psi. Blast waves are lethal to humans primarily because the wind picks up objects that become lethal projectiles. The lethal range for winds against humans is roughly equivalent to the range of the 5 psi shock wave. Table I shows the distance out to which various blast effects extend for 20-kT and 1-MT explosions. For atmospheric bursts, blast carries away approximately 50% of the energy of a nuclear explosion. Moreover, blast is the principal cause of damage, accounting for between 55% and 75% of the casualties at Hiroshima.

As the fireball cools, the radiated energy shifts in wavelength until most of it occurs in the visible and infrared portions of the electromagnetic spectrum. This heat flash occurs within a fraction of a second after the explosion and, depending on its intensity, can melt objects, start fires, burn flesh, or cause blindness. The intensity of this radiation drops off faster than the square of the distance from the explosion and is affected by the weather and the presence of clouds, smoke, or haze. Thermal radiation comprises about 35% of the

TABLE I

Approximate Magnitude of Nuclear Weapon Effects

Distance (mi)	Peak overpressure (psi)		Dynamic overpressure (mph)		Thermal radiation		Prompt nuclear radiation (rads)	
	20 kT	1 MT	20 kT	1 MT	20 kT	1 MT	20 kT	1 MT
1/4	50	1500	900	>2000	Melts metal		>100,000	>1,000,000
1	5	50	160	900	Ignites wood, 3rd degree burns	Melts metal	~350	~34,000
4	0.9	5	50	160	1st–2nd degree burns, blindness	Ignites wood, 3rd degree burns	<1	<1
8	0.5	2	30	70		1st–2nd degree burns, blindness		

energy released in an atmospheric nuclear explosion. Approximately 20–30% of the casualties at Hiroshima have been attributed to thermal radiation.

Firestorms are a related effect. They occur when several fires coalesce in an urban area, regardless of whether the fires start from the thermal pulse or the blast (e.g., creating electrical fires). Winds up to 100 mph are created as the hot air at the center of the firestorm rises above the city. Firestorms tend to destroy everything within their periphery. However, they also tend to self-limiting because the in-rushing winds limit their outward expansion. Moreover, firestorms are not unique to nuclear explosions. During World War II, firestorms from incendiary bombs occurred in Hamburg, Dresden, and Tokyo. A firestorm was produced by the nuclear bomb dropped on Hiroshima, but not on Nagasaki.

Prompt nuclear radiation is the third nuclear weapon effect. It consists of an intense burst of gamma rays and neutrons coming from the nuclear explosion. This effect is unique to nuclear weapons. If sufficiently intense, prompt nuclear radiation can kill or incapacitate humans or other living organisms, and destroy or upset electronic circuitry. The lethal dose for humans is approximately 500 rads. Prompt nuclear radiation accounts for about 5% of the energy released in a nuclear explosion and its intensity falls off quickly with distance. Hence, it is not a principal cause of damage, especially for high-yield nuclear weapons (>20 kT) although it can be significant for lower-yield weapons (<20 kT). The neutron bomb is a low-yield weapon with enhanced neutron output—thereby making prompt nuclear radiation the principal lethal effect against humans while reducing the blast and thermal

effects. They originally were developed as tactical nuclear weapons for use in Europe, but the United States never deployed them.

Fallout is radioactive material (mostly fission fragments) that attaches itself to small pieces of dust or dirt entrained in the mushroom cloud of a nuclear explosion. Approximately 10% of the energy from a nuclear explosion is contained in these fission fragments. Fallout is a serious problem only when the explosion occurs so close to the ground that the fireball touches the surface of the earth and, hence, entrains a large amount of material in the mushroom cloud. The radioactive dust then settles back to Earth over a period of hours to months depending on the particle size. The lethal effects are the same as for prompt nuclear radiation although they can occur much further from the site of the explosion depending on the wind speed and weather (e.g., tens to hundreds of miles). Finally, fission fragments have relatively short radioactive half-lives so the radiation intensity from fallout decays rapidly with time. For example, after 2 weeks the radiation intensity is 1 one-thousandth that at 1 hour after the explosion.

The fifth nuclear weapon effect is the electromagnetic pulse (EMP). The EMP is a strong electromagnetic wave generated by intense electric currents that can be created by a nuclear explosion. It is analogous to the much less intense electromagnetic wave caused by lightening that most people have experienced interfering with AM radio reception. The EMP is most intense for nuclear explosions in the upper atmosphere (around 50 km in altitude). Only a minute fraction of the energy from an explosion ends up as EMP. However, it can wreak havoc with electronic equipment. Although it does not affect humans, it may cause electric power grids to fail and disrupt or destroy civilian and military communications equipment, radars, computers, etc. The EMP is of concern largely because of the need to communicate with military forces during a nuclear conflict.

The above description of nuclear weapon effects is for a single nuclear explosion. However, nuclear Armageddon results not from a single explosion, devastating as that might be, but from the effects of hundreds or thousands of explosions. A single nuclear bomb can certainly destroy a large military facility or a small city; however, it can take up to tens of nuclear bombs to destroy a large city, around 500 300-KT nuclear weapons to promptly kill half the U.S. urban population, and more to destroy the military facilities within a large country like the United States or Russia.

Other effects must be considered if a large number of explosions occur. Global fallout and "nuclear winter"—the hypothesis that dust carried aloft by hundreds or thousands of mushroom clouds will cause temperatures to drop by up to 15°C over large portions of the northern hemisphere for several months or more—are probably not more serious than the direct effects of a large number of nuclear explosions. However, widespread social and economic collapse may cause severe problems. Medical support, food, and energy supplies may disappear because the transportation infrastructure could be severely disrupted, and political and financial institutions may collapse. This could lead to widespread starvation, epidemics, and political instability or civil war. Obviously, the magnitude of such effects is difficult to determine and will depend on the size and scope of a large-scale nuclear war.

II. HOW HAVE NUCLEAR WEAPONS AFFECTED MILITARY STRATEGY?

A. Nuclear Weapons and the Character of War

Nuclear weapons have done more than simply raise the level of violence possible in war. They also give an unprecedented advantage to the offense over the defense and they have increased the emphasis on inflicting pain in war as opposed to defeating the opponent's military forces. In short, they have increased the salience of deterrence in military strategy.

Throughout the history of warfare offensive and defensive weapons have vied for dominance on the battlefield (e.g., crossbows gave an edge to the offense over

body armor, while machine guns made attacks against fortified positions very costly). Nuclear weapons tend to favor the offense for three general reasons: (1) nuclear weapons are very destructive, (2) they are relatively inexpensive, and (3) they are light in weight.

The fact that nuclear weapons are very destructive and inexpensive implies that defenses must be very good to have much effect because large numbers can be built. For example, if 1000 nuclear weapons are launched at a defense that can shoot down 90% of the attacking warheads, 100 nuclear weapons would leak through the defense—enough to cause immense damage to cities. Moreover, by historical standards a 90% effective defense is unprecedented. For example, the monthly average attrition rate inflicted by German air defenses during World War II varied between 2 to 9% for U.S. bombers, although the attrition rate for individual raids was as high as 26% for U.S. bombers and 56% for British bombers. In short, when dealing with large numbers of nuclear weapons, defenses must be near perfect to protect the defender's cities. Less perfect defenses could complicate offensive planning and, hence, have some value, but they cannot significantly limit the damage from a large-scale nuclear attack. The problem with near-perfect defenses is that they are technically very difficult to build. Moreover, they tend to cost more than the offense must spend to overcome them, implying that an offense–defense arms race would be a losing proposition for the defense.

The fact that nuclear weapons are small and light suggests that they can be delivered in multiple ways, thereby complicating the job of the defense. For example, ballistic missiles can deliver nuclear warheads over intercontinental ranges at very high speeds—giving rise to our image of nuclear war as one large spasm of war that could be over in a matter of hours. Bombers and cruise missiles take longer but can incorporate stealth design or fly at low altitudes, making detection difficult. Covert delivery by boat or truck involves entirely different defenses, in particular, ones that require effective intelligence to intercept the covert operation before it succeeds. Again, nuclear war—in particular, the ability to defend against nuclear attack—would be very different if nuclear weapons were so expensive and large that only a few could be built and they had to be delivered by large ships.

The second major change brought about by nuclear weapons has been the relative emphasis on threatening to inflict pain in war as opposed to defeating the opponents military forces. Conventional war mostly involves defeating opposing military forces. Inflicting pain has been a part of conventional war, e.g., the conventional bombing of German and Japanese cities in World War II, but has received less attention in military strategy because it is uglier and less heroic. The fact that the offense is dominant with respect to nuclear weapons implies that a state can inflict tremendous pain on an adversary by attacking its homeland well before its military forces are defeated. This power to hurt gives a nuclear-armed state bargaining power or, as Thomas Schelling put it, nuclear weapons give rise to the diplomacy of violence. Of the coercive threats that nuclear weapons make possible, threatening to retaliate with nuclear weapons if an opponent attacks a state's vital interests, i.e., deterrence, is the most common.

B. The Ascendance of Deterrence

At the dawn of the nuclear age Bernard Brodie stated that the sole purpose of military establishments had become to avert wars not to win them. The recognition that the offense was dominant and that the power to inflict pain was one of the principal attributes of the nuclear age implied to many that the most sensible role for nuclear weapons was to threaten their use to deter attacks on a state's vital interests. Alfred Nobel—after whom the Nobel Prize is named—would have appreciated this point since he invented TNT in an attempt to find a weapon so horrible that it would make war unthinkable. Nuclear weapons are Nobel's dream come true. Thus, deterrence came to dominate U.S. nuclear strategy, as well as that of the other nuclear powers. As Winston Churchill put it, peace in the nuclear age had become the sturdy twin of terror. Deterrence, of course, was not the sole strategy for dealing with conflict because wars still occurred below the nuclear threshold, e.g., the U.S. involvement in wars in Korea, Vietnam, and Kuwait and the Soviet involvement in wars in Africa and Afghanistan. Nuclear weapons were thought to be largely irrelevant to these conflicts.

Deterrence can be defined as an attempt to dissuade a state or individual from taking some action by threatening to impose some cost or sanction that outweighs the benefits of acting. As such, it is part of the larger class of strategic choice which involves inducements (i.e., carrots) and sanctions (i.e., sticks) as instruments to influence the decisions of another party.

At its core, deterrence theory relies on a rational model of state behavior. That is, states (or their leaders) are supposed to accurately assess the expected outcomes (i.e., the likelihood times the consequences) associated with different actions and to act so as to maximize the value associated with these outcomes. The assumptions underlying deterrence theory have been the subject of much debate. For example, decisions are often made by leadership groups, not individuals, and it can be shown that a group's decisions may not be rational (e.g., the group's preferences may not be transitive) even if the individual members of the group act rationally. Cognitive limitations and cognitive biases also give rise to misperceptions and misunderstandings that often distort a decision maker's perception of costs, benefits, and their likelihood. "Bounded" rationality is probably a better way to describe the behavior of states and their leaders. Despite these critiques, deterrence theory still provides a useful framework for thinking about nuclear strategy. After all, how rational does one have to be to understand the costs associated with nuclear war?

C. The Strategy of Deterrence

The conceptual underpinnings of deterrence theory are not the main problem but rather attempts to put deterrence into practice, i.e., the strategy of deterrence. To put deterrence into practice one must understand the opponent's preferences to determine what to threaten. What does the opposing leadership value such that the threat to destroy this will deter him/her (e.g., their economy, the leadership's lives, their military forces, etc.)? To what extent does a state's history, culture, or the personality of the leadership make a difference, and if it does, can one discern the important elements to tailor deterrent threats? For example, threatening a dictator's population may not have as much deterrent value as threatening his instruments of political control (e.g., the secret police, special military units designed to maintain internal order, etc.). Would the same threats deter an American President and Saddam Hussein or would different threats be required?

Once one determines what to threaten, there is the question of how much to threaten to deter specific actions (one city, half the population, two-thirds of the economic potential of a state, half of their conventional military forces, etc.). In other words, what is the criterion for sufficiency? This depends on the opponent's risk-taking propensity which, among other things, depends on whether the leadership is acting for gain or is trying to avert some impending loss in status or power (in which case leaders will likely take greater risks). For example, would deterring the United States during prosperous times be easier than deterring North Korea on the brink of political and economic collapse? Suffice it to say that no unambiguous criterion exists for determining how many nuclear weapons are enough because deterrence exists in the mind of the beholder.

This creates endless opportunities to debate the appropriate size of a state's nuclear force.

The second important aspect of deterrence strategy is making threats credible. If the opponent does not believe the threat, then it has little deterrent value. There are two parts to credibility. The first is the opponent's perception of the deterrer's resolve. Will the deterrer carry out the threats made? Resolve, in turn, is measured by the interests at stake, the deterrer's reputation, the perceived legitimacy of the threat, and the potential costs inflicted upon the deterrer for carrying out the retaliation. The size of the threat may also affect its credibility because, if the threat is too large, the deterrer may not have the resolve to carry it out because it will be perceived as disproportionate to the act being deterred. Obviously, nuclear threats would not be credible for resolving trade disputes. On the other hand, nuclear threats may be quite credible for deterring large attacks against one's homeland. The second component to credibility is capability, i.e., can the deterrer carry out the threats made? If either the perception of resolve or capability are wanting, the opponent may not be deterred. Capability is measured relative to the sufficiency criterion.

Communicating the threat is also an important element of deterrence. If the opponent never receives the threat, or does not understand the threat, then deterrence is apt to fail. Similarly, if the proscribed action is not made sufficiently clear, deterrence may fail because the opponent does not understand what action will provoke a response. When Iraq attacked Kuwait in August, 1989, did Saddam Hussein understand that this action would precipitate a U.S. response or was Ambassador Gilespie's statement that the United States would not get involved in inter-Arab disputes ambiguous, despite her comment that the United States was against the use of military force to resolve such disputes?

Note that, despite the need for clear communication, leaders often opt for some degree of ambiguity with respect to what actions will trigger a response and what that response might be to make deterrence effective over a wider range of behavior and to avoid tying their hands. When asked about whether the United States would use nuclear weapons to deter the use of chemical or biological weapons by Iraq in the 1991 Gulf War, President Bush said he would use whatever means necessary. Did this include the use of nuclear weapons? It is not clear, although most observers believe it did. On the other hand, credibility can be undercut if a gap exists between what one says one will do (declaratory policy) and the forces one acquires—not to mention that declaratory policy itself may seem inconsistent because it is designed to address several audiences. Finally, tacit communication is also an important part of deterrence. During the Cold War, the United States and the Soviet Union developed tacit understandings that governed their behavior, e.g., not placing their military forces into the same conflict unless vital interests were involved so as to avoid unnecessary escalation.

In summary, the efficacy of deterrence as an instrument of policy depends on numerous factors. The burden is on the deterrer to understand how much of what to threaten to deter specific acts within a specific political/military context. If the threat is too little, deterrence may fail because the costs don't outweigh the benefits of acting. On the other hand, if the threat is too large, it may appear incredible. It is difficult to determine a priori the effectiveness of deterrent threats. Moreover, this description of deterrence glosses over some political/diplomatic nuances that can have an impact on the effectiveness of deterrence, e.g., the existence of alliances, individual personalities, etc. Ultimately deterrence relies on the rationality of one's adversary. For core security interests like the survival of the nation, it is uncomfortable to have one's fate depend on the rationality of another. Nevertheless, it is precisely because defenses against large nuclear attacks are so difficult to build that U.S. and Soviet survival rested on deterrence throughout the Cold War. There was no real alternative, regardless of what one thinks about the conceptual foundations of deterrence theory or the efficacy of deterrence strategy.

D. Nuclear Targeting

The question of what one should target to deter an adversary has been at the center of deterrence debates from the beginning. By specifying not only what should be targeted but how many targets of each type should be destroyed, nuclear targeting addresses the question: "How much is enough?" Two general schools of thought have emerged on nuclear targeting, "countervalue" and "countermilitary" targeting. These schools are discussed here as ideal types. Actual targeting strategies are a mix of both.

The countervalue school maintains that nuclear weapons should be used to threaten the opponent's civil society, under the assumption that this is what leader's value most. Typical targets are the opponent's urban population, industrial facilities, and perhaps the political leadership. In general, countervalue targeting doctrines require smaller nuclear arsenals because the targets are fewer in number and quite vulnerable to nuclear weapon effects. The classic formulation of the countervalue school was former Secretary of Defense Robert McNamara's "assured destruction" criterion which specified that U.S. nuclear forces should be able to destroy approximately one-third of the Soviet urban population and one-half to two-thirds of the Soviet industrial base—although it is not clear whether McNamara intended this criterion as an instrument for budget battles within the Pentagon or as a guide to U.S. nuclear targeting policy. Meeting this criterion required a nuclear arsenal containing approximately 1000 survivable and deliverable 50-kT weapons. "Limited" deterrence and "minimal" deterrence also describe countervalue targeting strategies, the idea being that the forces required to support this targeting doctrine are relatively limited or minimal compared to those required for a countermilitary doctrine.

The countermilitary school focuses on threats against the opponent's military forces. According to this school nuclear weapons should be targeted against the opponent's conventional forces, nuclear forces, the logistics infrastructure, command and control elements, and the opponent's war supporting industry. Targeting an opponent's nuclear forces, in particular, may help limit damage in the event deterrence fails. Because threatening the opponent's nuclear forces occupies such an important role in nuclear strategy, it is called counterforce targeting. One could argue that the countermilitary school focuses on threats to the opponent's military forces because this is what their leaders value most. While this formulation has merit, it blurs the distinction between countervalue targeting, which emphasizes threats to inflict pain by targeting that which the opponent values most, and countermilitary targeting, which emphasizes threats to deny the opponent's war aims by destroying its military forces. In general, countermilitary targeting requires larger nuclear arsenals because of the sizable military infrastructure within large states and because many military targets are hardened against nuclear weapon effects.

The U.S. and Soviet nuclear targeting doctrines have been a mix of these two approaches throughout the Cold War, with different emphases at different times. In general, countermilitary targeting received greater emphasis in both countries. This is reflected in the large strategic nuclear arsenals each side deployed during the Cold War, numbers far in excess of the requirements for a pure countervalue strategy. Moreover, the existence of tens of thousands of tactical nuclear weapons, whose only purpose was to threaten the opponent's military forces on the battlefield, suggests that countermilitary targeting dominated U.S. and Soviet strategy. For example, the U.S. doctrine of Massive Retaliation announced by John

Foster Dulles during the Eisenhower Administration was thought by many to embody a countervalue targeting doctrine when, in fact, it had more of a countermilitary flavor. The McNamara "assured destruction" criterion mentioned above also suggests a countervalue targeting doctrine, although actual U.S. war plans during this period emphasized countermilitary targeting. Finally, the "countervailing" strategy announced by the Carter Administration and still in effect today largely embodies countermilitary targeting.

Future U.S. and Russian targeting doctrines are less clear. If the START II Treaty is ratified by the Russian Duma, it will place a ceiling of 3500 weapons on the U.S. and Russian strategic nuclear arsenals. At such levels, both sides could still maintain countermilitary targeting doctrines. However, if in the future strategic force levels go below 1000 nuclear weapons and similar constraints are placed on tactical nuclear weapons, then U.S. and Russian targeting doctrines will be driven more toward countervalue targeting.

The nuclear targeting doctrines of France, Great Britain, and China largely appear to be countervalue in nature. During the Cold War France and Great Britain explicitly sized their forces to threaten major urban areas within the former Soviet Union. China continues to adhere to a policy of limited deterrence, although recent Chinese writings suggest an interest in limited counter military threats. Countervalue targeting is also consistent with the size of each state's strategic nuclear arsenal, which contain approximately 200–400 weapons. Despite the dominance of countervalue targeting, each of these countries have deployed some tactical or "prestrategic" nuclear weapons for use on the battlefield. However, their purpose appears to be less to defeat opposing conventional forces and more to signal a final warning before escalation to the strategic (i.e., countervalue) level of warfare.

III. THE TWO U.S. STRATEGIC PROBLEMS OF THE COLD WAR

The two main problems facing U.S. strategists during the Cold War were how to deter a nuclear attack on the homeland (central deterrence) and how to deter a conventional or nuclear attack on U.S. allies in Europe and Northeast Asia (extended deterrence). Extended deterrence is extended in two senses, extended to less vital U.S. interests (i.e., protecting allies) and extended to cover nonnuclear attacks against these interests (i.e., conventional, chemical, or biological attack). Developing plausible strategies for each type of deterrence and resolving tensions between the requirements for each preoccupied American strategic thinkers throughout the Cold War.

A. Central Deterrence

Central deterrence arose as a serious concern after the Soviet Union detonated its first fission bomb in 1949. Referring to the elements of deterrence strategy discussed above, U.S. retaliatory threats for central deterrence were clearly communicated in its declaratory policy (i.e., attacks upon the United States would be met with swift retaliation), U.S. threats were credible because the United States certainly had the resolve to defend its most vital interest—protecting the U.S. homeland—and the United States had the capability to make good on its threat because in the 1950s nuclear-capable bombers and short-range ballistic missiles were deployed around the Soviet periphery. As for what to threaten and by how much, the requirements for central deterrence were always thought to be less demanding than for extended deterrence. Specifically, countervalue threats alone were thought to be sufficient for central deterrence because the resolve to carry out such retaliation is very high if the United States is attacked with nuclear weapons first.

The main problem with central deterrence arises because nuclear weapons may have the capability to destroy the opponent's nuclear forces. Counterforce attacks, if they are highly effective, are one of the few rational reasons for initiating nuclear war—for if one side can destroy the bulk of the opponent's nuclear forces by striking first, that side significantly improves its chance for survival in the ensuing conflict. Moreover, if counterforce first strikes can be successful, then, by definition, the opponent will have difficulty deterring these attacks. If both sides have effective counterforce capabilities, the situation becomes quite unstable because whoever strikes first wins the war, leaving the other side largely disarmed and vulnerable to further coercion. Since surprise attack is common in conventional war (for similar reasons), early nuclear strategists wrestled with the problem that surprise counterforce attacks, whether premeditated or preemptive, posed for central deterrence. The mutual fear of surprise attack was a key concern in the U.S.–Soviet nuclear standoff, giving rise to fear that, in a crisis, each side might feel pressured to attack preemptively in the belief that the other side was preparing to strike first. This fear is pronounced if both sides are believed to have effective counterforce

capabilities and diminishes as either side's counterforce capability becomes less effective. This concern with "crisis instability" preoccupies nuclear debates to the present day. For example, the rationale for banning intercontinental ballistic missiles (ICBMs) with multiple independently-targeted reentry vehicles (MIRVs) in the START II Treaty derives from this concern.

The solution to this instability, according to the early theorists, was to provide a "secure second-strike" capability, i.e., to ensure the ability to retaliate after absorbing a massive counterforce attack. This requires that the forces survive the attack in sufficient number so they can inflict unacceptable damage on the nation that attacked first, even in the presence of defenses. In other words, the size of one's nuclear arsenal was not an indication of the quality of one's deterrent, only the size of the secure second strike capability. Although it seems commonplace today, in the 1950s it was surprising to realize that the existence of nuclear weapons did not equate to stable deterrence. In thinking about nuclear proliferation, one wonders whether emerging nuclear powers understand this point.

By the 1960s, the concept of a secure second strike had become a central tenet in U.S. thinking regarding stable central deterrence. However, arguments persisted about the character of Soviet strategy. Their interest in air and civil defenses as well as preemptive counterforce doctrines indicated to some that Soviet leaders paid less attention to the concept of crisis stability, although one should note that U.S. targeting doctrine also incorporated counterforce elements.

The requirements for a secure second strike led the United States and the Soviet Union to deploy ICBMs in underground concrete silos that could withstand peak overpressures greater than 1000 psi, mobile ICBMs that were difficult to locate, submarine-launched ballistic missiles (SLBMs) that could hide beneath the ocean's surface (submarines are difficult to locate once submerged), and bombers that were placed on high states of alert so they could escape from their bases upon warning of an incoming attack. For reasons of strategic culture and bureaucratic politics, the United States emphasized SLBMs and bombers, while the Soviet Union emphasized silo-based and mobile ICBMs. In fact, ensuring the survival of their strategic nuclear forces has been one of the principal rationales for U.S. and Soviet strategic nuclear force modernization throughout the Cold War.

An effective secure second strike also requires survivable nuclear command and control systems so that, in the event of an attack, the orders to retaliate can be properly communicated to forces that may be dispersed worldwide. Ensuring the survival of the national command authority (the top U.S. leaders with responsibility for authorizing a nuclear retaliatory strike) and the communication links to the nuclear forces was one of the more challenging problems of the Cold War. Using redundant command and control nodes, mobile command posts, and facilities located deep underground the United States and the Soviet Union were probably able to ensure survivable command and control over their strategic nuclear forces, although this was hotly debated several times during the Cold War.

Finally, a secure second strike capability requires that surviving forces penetrate any defenses that might stand in their way in sufficient numbers to inflict unacceptable damage. That is, arriving warheads as opposed to surviving warheads deter. Since the offense has the advantage in the nuclear age, this usually is not too difficult. Nevertheless, one of the most intense arms competitions during the Cold War was the competition between Soviet strategic air defenses and the penetration capabilities of the U.S. strategic bomber force. On the U.S. side, this competition spurred the development of low-altitude bomber penetration tactics in the late 1950s, defense suppression attacks in the 1960s to destroy selected Soviet air defense facilities before the bombers arrive, strategic cruise missiles in the early 1970s to saturate Soviet air defenses, electronic countermeasures to foil Soviet radars, and stealth aircraft in the 1980s and 1990s (i.e., the B2 bomber).

During the late 1960s, and again in the 1980s, there was an intense debate within the United States regarding the feasibility and wisdom of deploying ballistic missile defenses, a debate that has resurfaced today. Aside from the question of whether such defenses are technically feasible, one of the strategic concerns is that such defenses would provoke an offense–defense arms race of the sort described above for U.S. bomber penetration and Soviet air defenses. Chances are that it would if U.S.–Russian relations once again become adversarial and if Russia remains wedded to a deterrent strategy based on nuclear retaliation. On the other hand, if cooperative relations continue to grow between these two countries, an offense–defense arms race may not be axiomatic.

A secure second-strike capability also requires that the arriving weapons inflict unacceptable damage even in the presence of civil defenses. The debates regarding civil defense were relatively minor during the Cold War. However, there were concerns that the large Soviet civil defense program undermined the U.S. secure second-strike capability, particularly for countervalue threats

against the Soviet political leadership because of evidence that they would be relocated to deeply buried bunkers in the event of war, bunkers that presumably were very hard to destroy with nuclear weapons. Though the United States had a civil defense program in the early 1960s, it atrophied by the late 1960s because of the belief that it would be ineffective and because of the logic that societal vulnerability was important for stable central deterrence.

There is nothing illogical about attempts to acquire a secure second-strike capability while denying it to one's adversary. However, it was argued that states should avoid damage-limiting capabilitie's, i.e., counterforce capabilities, attacks aimed at the opponent's strategic command and control network, and national defenses (i.e., air, ballistic missile, and civil defenses) because they are destabilizing, i.e., opponents tend to interpret them as a sign of hostile intent, they may spur an arms race as the other side attempts to reestablish the effectiveness of its deterrent, and, if modest counterforce capabilities are achieved, they may destabilize crises.

Although the requirements for a secure second strike seem reasonable, they are quite paradoxical when viewed from the point of view of conventional military strategy. First, the threat to inflict tremendous damage to the opponent's civil society, at least for the countervalue school of deterrence, is quite inimical to traditional military thinking and to the ethical tradition of just wars. Militaries plan and train to defeat opposing military forces, not the civilian population. Noncombatant immunity is central to most theories of just war, yet the countervalue school explicitly threatens noncombatants. The countermilitary school also encounters ethical problems because, even though the intent is not to kill civilians, the collateral damage to civilian populations would be enormous in any nuclear attack.

Second, it seems odd not to threaten those weapons that pose the greatest danger to one's survival—the opponent's nuclear weapons. Counterforce attacks are a staple of conventional military strategy, yet they are anathema to stable central deterrence. Moreover, in conventional war one attempts to maximize surprise, not minimize it.

Perhaps more bizarre is the notion that one should leave one's country vulnerable to nuclear attack by one's mortal enemy. Yet this mutual hostage situation is required for stable central deterrence. To the extent stable central deterrence calls for defenses, it is to protect the survival of one's retaliatory forces not one's society. It is not surprising that the acronym that came to describe this situation was MAD, for "mutual assured destruction," although this acronym is more a description of the condition of mutual vulnerability in the nuclear age as opposed to a preferred strategy. One doesn't leave one's society vulnerable as a favor to the adversary, but rather out of recognition that attempts to reduce the level of damage one might suffer to acceptable levels will likely prove futile because the opponent will counter whatever damage-limiting capability is developed. In this sense, the above aspects of central deterrence appear paradoxical only if one commits the "fallacy of the last move," i.e., assumes that the deployment of damage-limiting capabilities would be the final move in the game. If one understands deterrence as a strategic interaction involving a reactive opponent, then effective damage limitation may not be achievable and eschewing such capabilities no longer appears paradoxical.

There is also a tension within central deterrence regarding what one should do to maximize deterrence versus what one should do in the event deterrence fails. Would it actually be wise to carry out the threats one made in the name of deterrence if deterrence failed? If one answers this question in the negative then, obviously, one must keep this secret from one's adversary, otherwise the deterrent value of these threats is undermined. The Catholic bishops, in a famous 1983 letter, gave conditional approval to nuclear threats for the purpose of deterrence (i.e., avoiding war), but were quite clear that carrying out such threats would be immoral if deterrence ever failed. When one begins to think about the unthinkable and contemplates the failure of deterrence, one naturally gravitates toward damage-limiting options. Thus, a policy that makes sense for stable central deterrence makes less sense if deterrence fails. On the other hand, if one places too much emphasis on damage-limiting options, one may precipitate the failure of deterrence. About all one can say is that stable deterrence should take higher priority because limiting damage only becomes important if deterrence fails. Pursuing damage-limiting options to such an extent that deterrence becomes more fragile would be putting the cart before the horse.

B. Extended Deterrence

Extended deterrence refers to the use of nuclear retaliatory threats to deter attacks on one's allies, both conventional and nuclear. This strategic problem arose after World War II because the United States demobilized its military forces rapidly, whereas the Soviet Union maintained sizable conventional military forces in Eastern Europe. The asymmetry in the conventional military balance in Europe was not redressed until possibly the late 1970s or 1980s because the United States and her West European allies did not want to pay the price (political and financial) for large standing armies in Europe. Nuclear weapons were viewed as defense on the cheap, or "more bang for the buck" as the Eisenhower Administration put it. Consequently, the United States relied on the threat to use nuclear weapons first if its allies were ever attacked with superior conventional forces. In addition, U.S. extended deterrence alleviated the need for other European states, notably Germany, to develop nuclear weapons of their own since their security was provided by the U.S. "nuclear umbrella"— although France and Great Britain developed independent nuclear arsenals.

The main difficulty with extended deterrence is to make retaliatory threats credible because leaders may question the U.S. resolve to defend its allies, especially after the Soviet Union acquired intercontinental-range nuclear weapons, because U.S. nuclear first use could precipitate a nuclear attack on the U.S. homeland. Defending U.S. allies at the risk of the survival of the United States appeared to many to be irrational. Or, as President Charles de Gaulle put it, would the United States risk New York to save Paris? As a result, numerous attempts were made to communicate the U.S. commitment to Europe. Most importantly, U.S. troops were stationed on European soil so the United States would become involved if a conflict ever occurred. United States declaratory policy was also a vehicle for communicating U.S. resolve, starting with John Foster Dulles's announcement of the doctrine of "massive retaliation" whereby the United States would respond to Soviet aggression "instantly, by means and at places of our choosing" and leading up to present day NATO doctrine, which still reserves the right to use nuclear weapons first, although they now are considered to be "weapons of last resort."

The U.S. strategy for extended deterrence during the Cold War was called "flexible response." Flexible response posits that conventional attacks against U.S. allies would be met first with conventional forces. If conventional defenses failed to hold, then the United States was willing to escalate to the first use of nuclear weapons, starting most likely with battlefield use. If tactical nuclear weapons were unsuccessful at halting the attack, the United States would consider escalating to higher rungs of the "escalation ladder." This could have involved attacks using U.S. nuclear forces deployed in Europe (or Asia) against a broad array of military targets within the theater and, at higher rungs of the ladder, attacks using strategic nuclear forces based in the U.S. homeland against military targets in theater as well as military targets in the former Soviet

Union. The initial attacks against the Soviet homeland could have been limited in size, though they could also have been massive strikes against a broad array of Soviet civilian and military targets. Obviously, flexible response was largely a countermilitary doctrine.

The rationale for this escalation ladder was to tailor the response so it was proportional to the threat and to exercise restraint so that attacks against the U.S. homeland might be avoided, thereby increasing the credibility of U.S. first-use threats. In fact, an explicit "no cities" doctrine was espoused in the early 1960s, only to be abandoned later. Escalating directly to attacks against the adversary's homeland, especially against his cities, was thought to be incredible for extended deterrence because, in a world of mutual assured destruction, the United States would not attack Soviet cities to defend Europe, only to have its own cities destroyed in return. Limited attacks against military targets made more sense.

Initially, the United States believed it would have "escalation dominance" whereby it could escalate to a level of nuclear war that the Soviet Union could not match. Not surprisingly, the Soviet Union always took steps to match U.S. escalation options, making escalation dominance a chimera. Later the interpretation of flexible response came to be that, although the United States could not dominate the escalation process, the Soviet Union could not dismiss the possibility that the United States might cross the nuclear threshold first in the event of a large conventional war. Once this occurred further escalation could not be ruled out, potentially leading to massive attacks against the Soviet homeland. The important question for flexible response was whether escalation could be controlled. Some thought it could not be, others believed it might be. In fact, one interpretation of flexible response was a "threat that left something to chance." While not entirely satisfactory, it is hard to argue that it didn't have some deterrent effect.

Flexible response rejected all-out countervalue targeting as being incredible except at the highest rung of the escalation ladder. Instead the emphasis was placed on countermilitary targeting, both with tactical and strategic nuclear weapons. Consequently, thousands of tactical nuclear weapons were deployed to provide the initial and intermediate escalation options against Warsaw Pact military targets. U.S. strategic nuclear forces were also sized for comprehensive countermilitary strikes against East European and Soviet targets, thereby providing the capability for escalation options at the high end of the escalation ladder.

West Europeans were often of two minds about flex-

ible response. They welcomed U.S. nuclear guarantees for extended deterrence but were often fearful that nuclear escalation would leave their homelands a smoking irradiated ruin, while the United States and the Soviet Union would stop short of attacks against each other's homelands. To manage this concern West Europeans argued in favor of deploying U.S. Pershing II intermediate-range ballistic missiles and ground-launched cruise missiles to Europe in the late 1970s. These intermediate-range nuclear forces had the capability to strike the Soviet homeland from European soil. If the Soviet homeland was attacked by U.S. intermediate-range forces stationed in Europe, the Soviet Union would retaliate against the U.S. homeland, or so the argument went. Therefore, these forces "coupled" the vulnerability of Europe to the vulnerability of the superpower homelands, thereby ensuring that nuclear war would not remain confined to Europe.

In addition, the requirements for extended deterrence make strategies that limit damage to the United States (i.e., either counterforce targeting or active defenses) look more attractive. If the United States is relatively invulnerable to attacks against its homeland at the high end of the escalation ladder, then it is more plausible that the United States would begin the escalation process at the low end of the ladder. While this makes sense for extended deterrence, it is in direct conflict with the requirements for stable central deterrence. Herein lies one of the main tensions in U.S. nuclear strategy throughout the Cold War—a tension that fueled many nuclear debates over the past 50 years.

By the end of the Cold War no resolution of the tensions within central deterrence or between central and extended deterrence had occurred. Counterforce targeting was pursued, but without the conviction that it could lead to meaningful damage limitation. As for defenses, one still hears arguments that they are either good or bad for deterrence, with little recognition that different types of deterrence are being discussed. With respect to flexible response, no successful answer was ever reached about whether escalation could be controlled.

IV. THE ROLE OF ARMS CONTROL

Early attempts at arms control were aimed at the elimination of all nuclear weapons (e.g., the Baruch Plan in 1946). By the late 1950s most arms control efforts were directed at managing the U.S.–Soviet nuclear relationship at the margins (e.g., the limited Test Ban Treaty; treaties banning the deployment of nuclear weapons in outer space, on seabeds, and in the Antarctic; and the nuclear Non-Proliferation Treaty). During this period, arms control had three main objectives: to reduce the likelihood of war, to reduce the consequences of war if it occurred, and to reduce the costs associated with maintaining one's security. Obviously a fundamental tension exists between reducing the likelihood of war and reducing the consequences of war because nuclear deterrence relies on the prospect of unacceptable damage.

Arguing that defenses upset stable central deterrence and recognizing the technical and economic difficulties in building an effective defense, the United States agreed to ban the deployment of effective national ballistic missile defenses in the 1972 Anti-Ballistic Missile Treaty—one of the most prominent arms control treaties of the Cold War—although the Soviet Union may have signed the ABM Treaty less out of a concern for stability and more to halt what they believed was an American lead in ballistic missile defense technology. Attempts to limit U.S. and Soviet offensive nuclear forces were slow to start. For example, the SALT I Treaty, ratified in 1972, essentially placed a freeze on the number of launchers then in existence or under construction. The SALT II Treaty, signed in 1979 but never ratified, placed a limit of 2,400 on the allowed number of strategic nuclear delivery vehicles and banned certain force modernization options, but did little to restrict the number of nuclear weapons each side could deploy. As a result, the U.S. and Soviet strategic nuclear arsenals continued to grow above 10,000 strategic nuclear weapons in the 1980s, in addition to approximately 10,000 tactical nuclear weapons deployed by each side.

The end of the Cold War created the possibility for much more radical steps in arms control. The INF Treaty, signed in 1987 and ratified in 1988, banned all intermediate-range ballistic and cruise missiles (i.e., missiles with a range between 500 and 5500 kilometers); the START I Treaty, signed in 1991 and ratified in 1993, limited the number of accountable strategic nuclear weapons to 6000 (approximately 6500 to 8500 actual weapons); and the START II Treaty, signed in 1993 but yet to be ratified by the Russian Duma, limits the actual number of strategic nuclear weapons to 3500—a 70% reduction from the Cold War peak. A possible followup START III Treaty may limit the number of U.S. and Russian strategic nuclear weapons to between 2000 and 2500. None of these treaties place limits on the number of French, British, or Chinese nuclear weapons. Finally, the end of the Cold War also made the Comprehensive Test Ban Treaty possible,

which bans all nuclear tests by any party to the treaty (it has yet to enter into force).

V. WHERE ARE WE TODAY?

Today, the likelihood of premeditated nuclear attacks between the major nuclear powers is greatly diminished. The dominant concerns are with the possibility of unintentional attacks, i.e., accidental or unauthorized Russian ballistic missile launches due to the deteriorating state of their nuclear infrastructure, and with the proliferation of nuclear, biological, and chemical weapons to a small number of states (e.g., Iran, Iraq, Libya, Syria, Israel, Pakistan, India, and North Korea).

Nuclear deterrence is still an element of the nuclear powers' security strategies, though one that seems to be receding—with the possible exception of Russian strategy where nuclear weapons are viewed increasingly as a means to compensate for inadequate conventional forces much like U.S. nuclear strategy in the 1950s. Little has changed with respect to the fundamentals of deterrence. The major debates today, at least at government levels, are about how much and how fast to reduce the role of nuclear weapons. Specifically, debates revolve around the role of nuclear weapons for deterring biological and chemical attacks; whether reductions below START III should be pursued and when; whether tactical nuclear weapons should be included in arms control agreements; whether warheads as well as fissile materials can be included in treaties; and when the arsenals of France, Great Britain, and China, not to mention the arsenals of the three virtual nuclear states (Israel, India, and Pakistan) should be included in the arms control process. Most of these debates do not question the central premise that nuclear weapons, at some level, are important for maintaining peace.

A debate has also emerged about nuclear abolition, i.e., that nuclear weapons, or at least operational nuclear forces, should be eliminated entirely. Abolitionists challenge the very notion that deterrence is an appropriate role for these weapons and that stable deterrence is possible—although one might wonder about the attractiveness of zero as an endpoint given that concerns regarding breakout surely will arise because the knowledge and materials for reconstituting large nuclear arsenals will still exist. Moreover, we know that deterrence can break down with small asymmetric nuclear arsenals (witness Hiroshima and Nagasaki). The nuclear abolition debate occupies one end of the spectrum, while the main stream arguments concern how far and how fast to reduce the role of nuclear weapons. At the other extreme, advocates for effective damage-limiting options, especially ballistic missile defense, also seem less interested in deterrence because, for them, the threats of the future cannot be deterred (i.e., accidental or unauthorized attacks and the proliferation of nuclear, biological, and chemical weapons to "rogue" states).

Notwithstanding these debates, it is perhaps surprising that the public today doesn't seem to care much about nuclear weapons, the circumstances under which they might be used, or the arcane subject of nuclear arms control. While moving nuclear matters into the background of relations between the major powers seems appropriate today, ignoring them altogether could lead to disaster.

Also See the Following Articles

ARMS CONTROL • CHEMICAL AND BIOLOGICAL WARFARE • COLD WAR • ECONOMIC CAUSES OF WAR AND PEACE • MILITARY DETERRENCE AND STATECRAFT • NUCLEAR WEAPONS POLICIES • WARFARE, MODERN

Bibliography

Ball, D. & Richelson, J. (Eds.) (1986). *Strategic nuclear targeting.* New York: Cornell University Press.

Blair, B. (1985). *Strategic command and control: Redefining the nuclear threat.* Washington, D.C.: The Brookings Institution.

Bobbitt, P., Freedman, L., & Treverton, G. (Eds.) (1989). *U.S. nuclear strategy: A reader.* New York: New York University Press.

Brodie, B. (1959). *Strategy in the missile age,* Princeton, NJ: Princeton University Press.

Carter, A., Steinbruner, J., & Zraket, C. (Eds.) (1987). *Managing nuclear operations.* Washington, D.C.: The Brookings Institution.

Freedman, L. (1989). *The evolution of nuclear strategy,* 2nd ed. New York: St. Martin's Press.

Friedberg, A. (1980). A history of the U.S. strategic doctrine, 1945–1980. *Journal of Strategic Studies.* 3, No. 3, 37–71.

George, A. & Smoke, R. (1974). *Deterrence in American foreign policy: Theory and practice.* New York: Columbia University Press.

Glasstone, S. & Dolan, P. (1977). *The effects of nuclear weapons,* 3rd ed. Washington, DC: U.S. Government Printing Office.

Holloway, D. (1994). *Stalin and the bomb,* New Haven, CT: Yale University Press.

Hopkins, J. & Hu, W. (1995). *Strategic views from the second tier.* New Brunswick, NJ: Transaction.

Jervis, R. (1989). *The meaning of the nuclear revolution.* New York: Cornell University Press.

Kahn, H. (1978). *On thermonuclear War,* 2nd ed. Westport, CT: Greenwood Press.

Kaplan, F. (1983). *Wizards of Armageddon.* New York: Simon and Schuster.

National Academy of Sciences (1997). *The future of U.S. nuclear weapons policy.* Washington, DC: National Academy Press.

Office of Technology Assessment (1979). *The effects of nuclear war.* Washington, DC: Government Printing Office.

Rhodes, R. (1986). *The making of the atomic bomb.* Touchstone Books: New York, NY.

Schelling, T. (1966). *Arms and influence.* New Haven, CT: Yale University Press.

Schelling, T. (1980). *The strategy of conflict.* Cambridge, MA: Harvard University Press.

Schelling, T. & Halperin, M. (1985). *Strategy and arms control.* New York. Pergamon–Brassey.

Snyder, G. (1961). *Deterrence and defense.* Princeton, NJ: Princeton University Press.

Stern, P., Axelrod, R., Jervis, R., & Radner, R. (Eds.) (1989). *Perspectives on deterrence.* Oxford University Press.

Wholstetter, A. (1959). The Delicate Balance of Terror. *Foreign Affairs,* 37, No. 2 211–234.

Nuclear Weapons Policies

Stephen J. Cimbala

Pennsylvania State University

GLOSSARY

Arms Control A process that accepts the inevitability of military deployments and seeks to reduce their numbers and to make their exercise and training less susceptible to accidental or inadvertent outbreak of war. Arms control is not disarmament, which aims at the prevention of war by elimination of all means for waging war.

Deterrence A psychological process of influence exerted by one party on another by manipulating the latter's perception of threat, costs, and benefits. Deterrence can be accomplished by denial (of the opponent's capacity to attack successfully) or by punishment (after the fact of attack, which the opponent is incapable of preventing).

Proliferation The spread of weapons of mass destruction from states having those weapons in their possession to other states or nonstate actors. The prevention of proliferation is "nonproliferation," as in the Nuclear Non-Proliferation Treaty.

Revolution in Military Affairs (RMA) A concurrence of advancements in precision guidance, automated decision and command systems, and aerospace re-connaissance making possible more effective, long-range conventional weapons.

Weapons of Mass Destruction A collective term including nuclear, biological, and chemical weapons in the arsenals of major state and nonstate actors.

NUCLEAR WEAPONS brought about a revolution in strategy, but the exact character of that revolution and its impact on military planning and operations were indeterminate. The end of the Cold War is not the end of the nuclear age. Nuclear weapons have emerged from the Cold War with a status of declared international pariahs. Extension of the Nuclear Nonproliferation Treaty (NPT) in 1995 and the opening for signature of the Comprehensive Test Ban Treaty (CTB) in 1996 showed the desire of many states to cap the growth of existing nuclear arsenals and to limit the number of international actors holding weapons of mass destruction. On the other hand, the know-how for weapons fabrication and the delivery systems for using nuclear weapons are already trickling from the nuclear "haves" to the "have nots," including in the latter group some very dissatisfied states and regimes.

The present study is not a bibliographical essay, nor a survey of the literature on nuclear strategy. Instead, I review nuclear policy issues of the past that retain some relevance for present and future nuclear policy debates. First, I consider the development of thought about whether nuclear weapons could ever be used to advantage in war, or whether they had abolished actual

Copyright © 1999 by Academic Press.
All rights of reproduction in any form reserved.

war fighting in favor of deterrence. Second, I discuss the role played by nuclear weapons and nuclear arms control in the Cold War. Third, I ask what we have learned from experience about the role of nuclear weapons in crisis management. Fourth, and last, the issues of nuclear proliferation and, more broadly, the role of nuclear weapons in the "new world order," receive specific attention.

I. THE DEVELOPMENT OF NUCLEAR STRATEGY

The "social contract" on which nuclear deterrence rests is based on the exchange of hostages. It is a relationship between states which is based on terror as a medium of exchange. The lives of innocents, and on an unprecedented scale, are placed at immediate risk should either side stray over the boundary between peace and war. If this is what makes nuclear deterrence as one form of military persuasion seem so horrible, it is also what makes nuclear weapons credible as instruments of coercion. There are other ways to discourage potential attackers: none of them involves an advance commitment to destroy promptly the society of the attacker, and perhaps also that of the defender, as a consequence of either having broken the peace. It would seem to follow that nuclear weapons have severed the connection between war and politics. The end of Cold War and the rebirth of Russia cast further doubt on the political utility of nuclear force, and perhaps, on the threat of force. Without a global opponent and favoring regionally oriented military strategies, U.S. military planners are left in great uncertainty about the relevancy of nuclear weapons except as weapons of last resort.

Nuclear weapons appeared to reverse the traditional relationship between offensive and defensive military strategies, in which the making of attacks was thought to be more risk laden and problematical of success than the conduct of a successful defense. On the other hand, the speed and lethality of nuclear weapons made offensive technology look more imposing, but not necessarily an offensive *strategy*. Weapons that could be protected from a first strike could be used to execute a retaliation of unprecedented destructiveness against the attacker. Unless the attacker could obtain preclusive protection against retaliation from the victim, the difference between the attacker's and the defender's postwar worlds might be politically and militarily insignificant.

The paradoxical implications of nuclear weapons for military strategy, as noted above, led to military planning solutions that followed one of two paths. First,

planners could put all their eggs in one basket, emphasizing the certainty of a massive retaliatory response for almost any aggression, including attacks using conventional forces only and those attacks launched against allies protected by a U.S. or Soviet nuclear umbrella. Second, and opposed to the first, planners could emphasize the use of nuclear retaliation in selective doses, including strikes by tactical and theater nuclear forces stationed outside their home territories and by specially tasked strategic nuclear forces aimed at targets in a particular theater of operations.

It turned out that massive retaliation and flexible nuclear response became sequentially preferred attempts by U.S. policymakers and planners to square the nuclear circle. Massive retaliation as a one variant strategy made less and less sense as the U.S. nuclear monopoly, and later relative superiority, were overturned by the Soviet attainment of nuclear parity. Massive retaliation faded from declaratory policy by the end of the 1950s and was eventually supplanted in the 1960s by the less hubristic "assured destruction" in declaratory, but not in operational, policy. Massive retaliation and flexible response also had the vices of their virtues: inflexibility that might freeze leaders into inaction for all but the gravest provocations, in the first case; and seduction into what was expected to be a small war but turned out to be a larger one, in the second case. Accordingly, the Eisenhower administration by its second term had begun to recognize the virtues and vices of both massive and flexible nuclear retaliation, although it produced no actual war plans that placed serious constraints on the geographical scope or societal destructiveness of U.S. retaliatory attacks.

Despite a considerable U.S. superiority in numbers of delivery vehicles and warheads during the latter 1950s and early 1960s, U.S. leaders expressed little confidence in the stability of nuclear deterrence and approached the idea of nuclear brinkmanship gingerly. During the Cuban missile crisis and despite a favorable ratio of approximately 17 to 1 in deliverable nuclear weapons, President Kennedy pulled back from invasion of Cuba or the bombing of Soviet missile sites in Cuba, disregarding strong urgings from military and other advisors. Concerned about the danger of escalation that might get out of control during the crisis, Kennedy and his advisors held back their conventional military sword in favor of coercive diplomacy. Instead of seeking military victory below the nuclear threshold that the Soviets were powerless to prevent, Kennedy sought to give Khrushchev a face-saving exit from a preestablished path of mutual confrontation. U.S. nuclear options and war plans were relevant to management of the Cuban missile crisis not because they promised to provide victory at an acceptable cost, but because they created a zone of uncertainty through which Khrushchev and Kennedy were determined not to move.

Although the Kennedy administration would subsequently begin a process of refining U.S. nuclear war plans with the objective of creating a larger spectrum of military options, neither Kennedy nor his successors could escape the limits placed on strategy by the upper end of the ladder of escalation. Successors to Eisenhower were able to discard the rhetoric of massive retaliation, but not the reality that any feasible plan for U.S.-Soviet nuclear war would of necessity involve massive nuclear responses and unacceptable collateral damage for both sides. Additional refinements to those SIOPs (*Single, Integrated Operational Plans* for nuclear war) subsequent to those of the Kennedy administration did not change this condition of nuclear rigidity. Accordingly, critics of U.S. nuclear strategy and of NATO nuclear dependency for the deterrence of war in Europe fought a rearguard action to establish credible options short of massive nuclear response, from the 1950s through the 1980s.

The U.S. strategy of massive retaliation invited dissatisfied analysts and policymakers to borrow from prenuclear thinking and from disciplines other than military history and political science. During the "golden age" of U.S. strategic nuclear theorizing (from the latter 1940s through the middle 1960s) operations researchers, social psychologists, and economists contributed important new insights to the field of U.S. military strategy. Although these insights revolutionized the way in which the field was conceptualized in academic studies, they provided no consolation to policymakers and planners who sought to overcome obstinate nuclear technology that stood in the way of proportionality and discriminate uses of force. Not only technology stood in the way of nuclear proportionality as a pathway to the reestablishment of the connection between war and politics. Politics were even more important; ends became as controversial as means became unyielding. NATO members other than the Americans were never completely sold on the advantages of nuclear flexibility, and in Paris leaders opted for nuclear unilateralism as a guarantee that French national interests would not be hostage to graduated deterrence.

It soon became apparent that the case for flexible nuclear response would be politically controversial in the U.S. policy debate and among NATO allies. Once former Secretary of Defense Robert S. McNamara had abandoned counterforce and damage-limiting strategies in favor of a declaratory emphasis on assured destruc-

tion, traditional military strategy seemed to have been sold out in favor of nuclear stalemate. McNamara argued that assured destruction described a condition as much as it summarized a preferred policy, although assured destruction was also appealing to him as a metric for establishing minimum force sizes against the more ambitious demands of military services. A classical strategy, for the credible use of nuclear offenses and antinuclear defenses for victory, was judged by McNamara as both unattainable and undesirable.

Growth in U.S. and Soviet strategic nuclear forces during the 1960s, and McNamara's persistent advocacy in U.S. and alliance policy debates, drove out of the realm of political feasibility a damage limiting strategy based on offensive force modernization combined with ballistic missile defenses. By the early 1970s, as the conclusion of the SALT I treaty demonstrated, the Soviet leadership as well as the American had accepted the anticlassical logic that mutual deterrence could be based on offensive retaliation combined with limited defenses incapable of nationwide protection. The acceptance by both nuclear superpowers of this condition increased the difficulty of U.S. officials in selling nuclear flexibility to a justifiably skeptical European audience.

If SALT codified the death of any feasible search for classical strategy by means of defenses and offenses combined, there was still the possibility that additional military feasibility could be introduced into nuclear strategy by tinkering with offenses alone. The policy innovations from 1974 through the present in U.S. doctrinal guidance for strategic target planning were based on this search for an exit from the apolitical strategic impasse of assured retaliation, judged by the standards of classical strategy. Advocates of flexible nuclear response, from the 1950s through the 1980s, argued from basic premises that constituted modified versions of prenuclear thinking applied to nuclear strategy. The term "neoclassical" is more appropriate for these modifications of classical strategy for victory because they acknowledged the futility of traditional war-winning strategies applied to a situation of mutual deterrence. Instead, the neoclassicists attempted to modify assured destruction at the edges by adapting offensive forces to the exigencies of bargaining and coercive diplomacy. Neoclassical reasoning combined psychological arguments about the influence of perceptions on deterrence or escalation control with traditional aspirations for military superiority or favorable outcomes in war. (Table I summarizes the variations of neoclassicism described below.)

The neoclassical arguments for nuclear flexibility had two principal variations. The first variation was

TABLE I

Varieties of U.S. Nuclear Strategy

I. Assured destruction/Assured retaliation
II. Neoclassicism (nuclear flexibility)
   A. Perceptions of Russian strategy
   B. Intrawar deterrence
      1. Escalation dominance
      2. Manipulation of risk

that, while U.S. officials actually recognized that nuclear war was politically pointless and that nuclear flexibility was of little or no value, for deterrence to work Soviet leaders must also believe those things. It was argued that the Soviet leadership did not share these convictions about the absurdity of nuclear war or about the disvalue of selective nuclear options. Therefore, it followed that the ability to deter a massive Soviet attack against North America did not necessarily deter a lesser provocation, such as an attack on Europe or selective strikes against U.S. territory. Psychologist Steven Kull has referred to arguments of this type as "greater fool" arguments: U.S. officials acknowledged the futility of nuclear flexibility, but suggested that the possibility of Soviet belief in nuclear flexibility required equivalent U.S. preparedness for similar options.

The second version of neoclassical nuclear flexibility called for the U.S. to improve its offensive forces in order to deter escalation to advantage by the opponent, that is, for intrawar deterrence. Although unprecedented societal destruction could not be avoided in nuclear war, there were, in this view, meaningful distinctions among postwar outcomes, including postwar states of affairs that could be characterized as victory or defeat. The second version of nuclear flexibility sought counterforce capabilities, but not in numbers or in quality sufficient to make possible a credible first strike against Soviet forces. Counterforce capabilities were useful as part of a strategy of bargaining and coercion during war. Two rationales were advanced for improved counterforce, on behalf of intrawar deterrence, in this variant of neoclassicism: escalation dominance and risk manipulation.

Escalation dominance means that one side can establish through favorable exchange ratios, in one or more components of postattack nuclear forces, a position so superior that the other side is forced to yield to its demands. Escalation dominance is a form of limited nuclear retaliation or warfare. The ability to prevail in a nuclear endurance contest below the level of all-out war is a necessary condition for influencing the wartime behavior of the opponent. In contrast, the manipulation of risk approach does not depend on the ability to prevail at any level of actual nuclear exchange. Manipulation of risk gets both contestants into a competition in brinkmanship and nerve. The purpose of higher levels of destruction is not to impress the opponent with the damage already done, but with the possibility of unlimited and uncontrollable escalation which might follow.

Whereas escalation dominance was more relevant in the case of a war that was begun by means of deliberate attack, the other variation was more appropriate for nuclear wars that resulted from accidents or from inadvertent escalation. The escalation dominance approach presupposed that rational actors would continue their utility-maximizing calculations after nuclear war had already begun. Manipulation of risk approaches were based on a more skeptical appreciation of rationality in the actual conduct of nuclear war. Manipulation of risk actually depended upon a "threat that leaves something to chance," as Thomas Schelling explained it. A process of nuclear brinkmanship or a two-way competition in risk taking left open the possibility that both sides would lose control over events, thereby suffering greater than expected or greater than acceptable losses. The possibility of losing control over events was the element that created the shared interest in restraining the level of violence and in moderating political objectives.

Arguments for flexible nuclear response were stigmatized by their use in the U.S. policy process as ingredients in force-building rationales. In addition, the Soviets showed little apparent interest in flexible nuclear response as a means of bargaining, especially in the case of strategic nuclear weapons exploded on Soviet territory. Nevertheless, the construction of a Soviet adversary determined to exploit any relative counterforce imbalance was all too often perceived by policymakers as a necessary part of the case for counterforce and nuclear flexibility. While Soviet military doctrine in its politico-military aspects (grand strategy) remained essentially defensive and potentially open to the concept of limitation in war, the military-technical level of Soviet military doctrine offered little in the way of encouragement to those U.S. scholars who sought to find Politburo or General Staff interest in limited nuclear war or controlled nuclear exchanges.

II. NUCLEAR WEAPONS AND THE COLD WAR

The Cold War is now seen by many, combining hindsight with nostalgia, as a period of political peace and military tranquility. The relationship between nuclear weapons and the long peace from 1945 to 1990 was a peculiar one. Nuclear weapons were not incorporated into a traditional military strategy for attaining victory at an acceptable cost. Instead, they were part of an experiment in applied psychology in which the leaders of states, the designers of weapons and the operators of forces and command systems played roles knowingly and unknowingly. The experiment did not really work as intended, but war was avoided anyway. The avoidance of war was overdetermined by other forces between 1945 and 1990, so that nuclear deterrence, dangerous as it was, left the relationship between the United States and the Soviet Union more or less as it would have been without those weapons.

Subsequent to the Cuban missile crisis of October, 1962, U.S. and Soviet leaders perceived a mutual interest in strategic arms limitation, in the avoidance of accidental or inadvertent nuclear war, and in preventing the spread of nuclear weapons. Agreements concluded during the 1960s included the Nuclear Test Ban Treaty of 1963 and the "Hot Line" (Direct Communications Link) for emergency discussions between heads of state. Discussions between Moscow and Washington about strategic arms limitation got under way during the latter years of the Johnson administration, continued under Nixon, and culminated in the SALT I (Strategic Arms Limitation Talks) agreement of 1972. SALT I provided for: (1) a treaty of indefinite duration limiting each side's antiballistic missile defense systems (the ABM Treaty); and, (2) a 5-year interim agreement placing ceilings on the numbers of land- and sea-based missile launchers (ICBMs and SLBMs respectively) of the two sides. SALT I was a significant diplomatic as well as military milestone. It codified military-strategic parity between the Soviet Union and the United States and it supported Soviet diplomatic efforts to obtain U.S. and allied NATO acceptance of the political status quo in Europe. Washington and Moscow also concluded in 1971 two agreements on the prevention of accidental/ inadvertent war and the avoidance of unnecessary fears of surprise attack.

The interim agreement on offensive arms limitation embodied in SALT I was superseded by SALT II, signed in 1979 and carried forward (although never formally ratified by the U.S.) until it was transformed into START (Strategic Arms Reduction Talks) during the Reagan administration. The ABM Treaty remained as the cornerstone of U.S-Soviet strategic arms limitation until the end of the Cold War. As amended by a 1974 protocol signed at Vladivostok, it limited both sides' national missile defense systems to one site of no more than 100

defensive interceptors. The U.S. chose to deploy its ABMs at Grand Forks, N.D., and the Soviets around Moscow. (The U.S. system was eventually closed down by Congress in the mid-1970s). The ABM Treaty became a powerful symbol of affinity for the advocates of mutual deterrence based on offensive retaliation. When the Reagan administration proposed its Strategic Defense Initiative (SDI) in 1983, opponents of the deployment argued that it would overturn the ABM Treaty of 1972 and reopen the race in offensive weapons hitherto capped by the SALT/START process. Even after the Cold War, the U.S. and Russian efforts to arrive at an agreed definition of acceptable theshold between permitted "theater" ballistic missile defenses for overseas forces and allies, versus impermissible "strategic" ballistic missile defenses of their respective state territories, were based on awareness of the diplomatic fallout of any attempt to circumvent the ABM Treaty.

Even more shock resistant than the ABM Treaty was the Nuclear Non-Proliferation Treaty (NPT) ratified in 1970 and supported by both the United States and the Soviet Union. The agreement was intended to prevent the spread of nuclear weapons or weapons-related technology from the nuclear "haves" to the "have nots." Non-nuclear states were offered the promise of support for verifiably peaceful uses of nuclear energy, under an inspection regime conducted by the IAEA (International Atomic Energy Agency, an affiliate of the UN). The ABM Treaty surprised its parents by living to the end of the Cold War (after which its political, if not military, relevancy came into question). The NPT not only outlasted the Cold War but has become even more relevant since. NPT was extended indefinitely in 1995 by near unanimity, with the important demurrals of India, Pakistan, and Israel. The favorable climate established by NPT extension carried forward into the 1996 multilateral agreement on a comprehensive test ban (CTB) on nuclear weapons testing, extending and deepening the impact of the original Test Ban Treaty and the subsequent Threshold Test Ban and Peaceful Nuclear Explosions (TBT and PNE, respectively) treaties.

Not all U.S. or Soviet governments gave equal emphasis to arms control, but despite fluctuations in attention span, enduring benefits matured. First, continuing arms control negotiations educated both sides during the Cold War about each other's strategic and defense cultures. Second, the strategic arms limitation agreements of the 1970s and 1980s (SALT-START) did provide a framework that allowed both sides to avoid expensive deployments of systems that would have been militarily superfluous, or eventually obsolete in the face of improved technology. Third, cooperation between

Washington and Moscow to limit the spread of nuclear weapons technology helped to limit the number of nuclear aspiring states during the Cold War and set a useful precedent for multilateral cooperation against proliferation after Cold War. This U.S.-Russian post-Cold War cooperation against nuclear weapons spread included the Cooperative Threat Reduction (CTR) authorized by the U.S. Congress in 1991 to encourage denuclearization and demilitarization within the states of the former Soviet Union, especially within the four successor states (Russia, Belarus, Kazakhstan, and Ukraine) that inherited the former Soviet nuclear arsenal.

Efforts to limit the significance of nuclear weapons during the Cold War were complicated by the role of nuclear weapons in U.S. and allied NATO strategy for the prevention of war in Europe and for the establishment of a credible defense plan if deterrence failed. Some U.S. and European analysts and policymakers doubted that conventional deterrence was feasible; others feared that it might be. Those who doubted that conventional deterrence was feasible tended to see a viable Soviet threat of invasion, absent NATO military overinsurance. Those who feared that conventional defense was feasible noted that a conventional war in Europe would involve very different sacrifices for Americans and Europeans. A conventional deterrent for NATO might not be as convincing as a conventional defense, backed by nuclear deterrence. Lawrence Freedman explained the painful dilemma with which NATO policy makers were faced, even if they were inclined to credit conventional defenses with more credibility than official NATO doctrine acknowledged:

> Whereas the threat of nuclear war would make the risks of war too great, if the threat was only of conventional war the risks might be tolerable. Thus the problem with a nuclear strategy was that it was hard to demonstrate why the U.S., as the only power which could implement such a strategy, should be willing to risk nuclear war in the event of a conventional invasion of Europe: the problem with a conventional strategy was that it was hard to demonstrate why the Russians would be deterred.

The Soviet Union might easily have been deterred by the prospect that even victory in a short conventional war in Europe, however victory might have been defined in Moscow, could not have been sustained. In a protracted nonnuclear conflict between East and West, the likelihood for most of the Cold War was that the United States and its allies would have defeated the Soviet Union and its allies. The United States and its allies in Europe and Japan marshaled economic and industrial power far superior to that of the Soviet Union and its probable wartime allies. Stalin, whose brutal terror industrialized the Soviet Union between the world wars, knew as well as anyone the significance of comparative industrial and technological power. In addition, in a protracted war the maritime superiority of the United States and its NATO allies would have forced upon the Soviet Union a Hobson's Peace in Western Europe, even assuming the most favorable wartime cooperation of the Soviet Union's East European "allies."

NATO's willingness to settle for an active duty deployment in Western Europe of about 30 ground forces divisions was not forced by the economics of defense, as some politicians contended. NATO could have created conventional forces capable of credible deterrence against massive and protracted, as well as limited and short, Soviet conventional probes. The point was proved to reluctant Europeans by McNamara's "whiz kids" when the latter recalculated the relative strength of Soviet and U.S. (plus allied NATO) divisions in the 1960s. Taking into account the different organizations of the U.S. and Soviet forces, Pentagon analysts recalculated the relationship between Soviet and NATO force sizes, firepower indices, and other attributes related to probable performance in war. By 1965, McNamara's staff felt they had convincing evidence that a Soviet division force cost about a third of the cost of a U.S. division force, that the Soviet force had about one-third as many personnel, and that the Soviet force was about one-third as effective as the U.S. division force (U.S. division forces were larger and in the early 1960s included a great deal of division force combat power outside the division itself, compared to Soviet forces). As Adam Ulam has argued, NATO's psychology of conventional inferiority was based on the circumstances of its origin in 1949:

> There was no reason why the assumption of NATO's conventional arms inferiority, reasonable in 1949, should still have persisted in 1965. It was then fully within the capabilities of America's European allies more than to match the Warsaw Pact's forces; yet they continued to profess (though ever less confidently) their reliance on the U.S.'s now increasingly porous nuclear umbrella to save them both from the Russians and from having to spend more on defense.

These calculations did not prove that NATO's then-available conventional forces were adequate deterrents against truly desperate Soviets, nor were they insurmountable conventional defenses against all of NATO's political and military vulnerabilities. The calculations did show that NATO's deployed forces were sufficient to deny the Soviets victory in a short war without running an unacceptable risk of protracted military stalemate, or nuclear escalation. Nuclear weapons added a component of uncertainty and risk to Soviet calculations, but they were as much a curse as a blessing for any NATO approximation of rational strategy. As the numbers of nuclear weapons deployed with tactical air and ground forces multiplied, the problem of command and control, including NATO nuclear release, became more intimidating. NATO's apparently hodgepodge theater nuclear force structure was not entirely coincidental: it was not designed to fight efficiently a substrategic war in Europe prior to, or in lieu of, a larger war including attacks on American and Soviet homelands. Instead, NATO's nuclear command system was *intended*, and made quite obvious to the Soviets, as a waltz toward Armageddon:

> The NATO strategy of relying on nuclear weapons is politically and militarily credible because the governing command structure is so unstable and accident-prone that national leaders would exercise little practical control over it in wartime. What other command mechanism could possibly be built to invoke a nuclear conflict that, for all practical purposes, is tantamount to a regional doomsday machine?

Professor Bracken may be charged with overstatement in a good cause: the alliance nuclear command and control system was not *intended* to fall apart on the night. But pessimism about its resilience in the face of all but token nuclear strikes was prudent, and the situation was not strategically foreordained. A nuclear dependency was not forced on NATO by its inability to spend money for ground divisions or tactical air wings compared to the Warsaw Pact. NATO was unwilling, not unable, to do so.

The second argument for NATO's nuclear dependency pivoted on the exposed position of West Germany, and especially of West Berlin, as a symbol of Western anticommunist resistance to Soviet communism. The United States and its NATO allies arguably could not have defended West Germany, and definitely not West Berlin, with conventional forces under any set of assumptions. Berlin could not be defended by conventional forces, but Soviet pressure against Berlin might be mitigated by nuclear coercion. And the Germans' insistence that NATO corps be deployed close to the inter-German border in a "forward defense" posture meant that any Soviet penetration of about 100 kilometers or more into the Federal Republic would have unhinged NATO's short war conventional defense plan. Germans rejected a rearward-leaning instead of a forward-leaning strategy for political reasons, and the French left NATO's military command structure in 1966 for their own political reasons. The result of German forwardism and French abstinence was that neither the head nor the tail of NATO's conventional defenses could be fitted into a plan for victory in a short war without nuclear escalation.

In sum, the Cold War experience with nuclear weapons taught that, at least with regard to conflicts among major powers, nuclear weapons were unlikely to redeem a failed or implausible defense strategy. Fortunately for posterity, the Soviet Union from 1945 to 1990 had no plausible attack strategy against Western Europe at an acceptable cost to Moscow's political or military leadership. If nuclear weapons could not serve as war winners or war stoppers, could they perhaps be war preventers?

III. Crisis Management and Nuclear Weapons

Crisis management prior to the nuclear age was less important to planners and to policymakers than was military preparedness for actual war fighting. It was assumed that preparedness for actual combat was the best deterrent. Admittedly this assumption was not always correct: some historians thought that the July crisis of 1914 had ended in a war because the war preparations of the various sides stimulated countervailing preparations by their enemies. A conflict spiral of increasing tensions and suspicions had resulted in an August 1914 outbreak of war that none of the sides really wanted, according to his argument. Whether World War I is an exception to the general rule, or whether historians have misread it as an example of failed crisis management, it remains the case that before nuclear weapons crisis management was less important because the costs of war were not obviously catastrophic for all concerned. Nuclear weapons changed that calculus, and changed it forever. Now even small military exchanges by forces holding these powerful weapons could inflict historically unprecedented damage on their enemies, and nuclear weapons made it obvious to even the most obtuse leaders that this was so.

The choices facing crisis ridden political leaders and

military planners are usually an array of bad and worse options. The point of no return may not have been passed and the crisis may still be resolved short of war. A crisis resolved short of war is going to be resolved in favor of one side or the other, so the outcome from a political standpoint is not one that distributes postcrisis rewards and punishments equally. For example, the Cuban missile crisis of 1962 was resolved because Soviet Premier Khrushchev realized that his Cuba missile ploy had overextended his strategic reach. He backed off after having been reassured against further U.S. escalation of the crisis once Kennedy had received a guarantee that Soviet missiles would be removed from Cuban soil.

Because the outcomes of crises can distribute benefits unequally, it follows that leaders may prefer a larger risk of war, by means of continued crisis, to a peaceful settlement. Leaders can always persuade themselves that one additional demarche or a little more arm twisting can bring the opponent around without actually stepping over the brink that separates coercion from violence. Leaders might mistakenly infer, for example, that the other side, lacking in military power compared to its opponent, would not dare to start a war. Therefore, it must back down. During the Cold War as well as prior to it, there were important examples of states without nuclear forces that were willing to attack a nuclear-armed state or to threaten the vital interests of the latter. Egyptian leader Anwar Sadat, as a case in point, launched his attack against Israel in 1973 despite the near certainty that Israel already had nuclear weapons and the certainty that Egypt and its allies did not.

An article of faith by some policymakers during the Cold War, for example, the influential U.S. former Secretary of Defense Robert S. McNamara, was that strategic nuclear weapons served only to deter one nuclear armed state from attacking another. They served no other useful purpose: in other words, they were irrelevant to the deterrence of conventional war. McNamara meant to say that the threat of escalation from conventional to nuclear war could not be manipulated *deliberately* by the Soviet Union against the United States, or vice versa, because either side could absorb a first strike and still deliver an unacceptable retaliatory strike against the other. But the danger of Cold War confrontation was not only deliberate, but also *inadvertent,* escalation. Both sides might get into a process of bargaining in which the stakes were not entirely clear. One or both sides might not fully understand the military operational details of nuclear alerts, thereby sending signals not intended and generating a process of escalation over

which they ultimately lost control. Political leaders and some theorists dismissed this possibility of inadvertent war during the nuclear age because they thought of war as *outcome* and not as a *process*. An outcome is something concrete that has a clear "before" and "after": a process is a continuous sliding scale that allows for a mountain climber to gradually fall down a cliff, only recognizing his peril when he hits bottom.

The pernicious interaction of mobilization systems that contributed to the outbreak of World War I was not intended by the leaders of that time. But the crisis management of the Cold War years probably depended, and subsequent nuclear crisis management might very well depend, on leaders' expectations that a deliberately created risk of loss of control over escalation would save the peace. The logic of deliberately created loss of control is thought by strategists to work by frightening one or both sides into some bargain as an outcome preferred to uncontrolled escalation. If uncontrolled escalation is uppermost in the minds of national leaders at a time of crisis, it may turn out that the avoidance of uncontrolled escalation is a priority of such magnitude that further coercion of the other side is forestalled. However, there is nothing to guarantee that forbearance will appeal to leaders because nothing guarantees that fear of uncontrolled escalation will be sufficiently daunting to them.

If leaders in a crisis between nuclear armed states fear uncontrolled escalation more than they desire expected values that can be obtained through additional nuclear blackmail, then they have stronger incentives to end the crisis than to continue it. On the other hand, if continued use of nuclear blackmail seems to be paying dividends and is expected to cause the opponent to yield, then the priority attached to the avoidance of uncontrolled escalation is diminished. Further, nuclear blackmail comes in more than one variety. There is a nuclear blackmail that is intended by the blackmailer, and a nuclear blackmail that grows out of the crisis bargaining between two sides. Even if neither side makes explicit threats of nuclear first use or of nuclear escalation, the presence of nuclear weapons in their arsenals creates an existential risk of wider and more destructive conflict. Both the existential and the deliberate forms of nuclear blackmail were present in the Cuban missile crisis, and both were recognized by Soviet and American leaderships for what they were.

In October, 1962, Khrushchev, for example, was able to distinguish between the risk of deploying nuclear weapons covertly and without their having been discovered by the Americans before they were launch ready, versus the discovery of those same weapons in the midst of assembly and preparation. Faced unexpectedly with U.S. premature discovery of his missile ploy, the Soviet leader about-faced and declared that he and President Kennedy should not "tie the knot of war" too tightly lest it become impossible for them to disentangle. Khrushchev was able to communicate this concern to Kennedy, and it was shared by the U.S. President and his advisors. They discovered during the crisis that some of their expectations about how military forces were operated during crisis were mismatched with the actual conditions of those operations. It is not that U.S. military commanders were insubordinate during the crisis: they were not. It is the unavoidable fact that military commanders and policymakers are looking at a crisis from different perspectives and with competing priorities. Policymakers want to avoid inadvertent escalation or war without sacrificing important national values. Military commanders know that they will be held accountable for a surprise strike that catches their forces unprepared, or for failure to carry out efficiently authorized presidential commands.

Khrushchev and Kennedy were able to distinguish in 1962 between controllable and uncontrollable risks because they were aided by advisors trained in the operation of mature command and control systems, and because in neither country was the legitimacy of the ruling political order at risk. Relax either condition, either the maturity of the command and control system or the undoubted legitimacy of the political order, and a crisis, especially a crisis between nuclear powers, becomes much more dangerous. In fact, during the Cuban missile crisis, the transmission of two letters from Khrushchev with conflicting terms for settlement of the crisis almost caused some members of Kennedy's ExComm (Executive Committee of the National Security Council, the President's key crisis advisory group) to conclude that Khrushchev had in fact been the victim of a coup.

For example, in a future crisis between Pakistan and India, or between Israel and a nuclear-armed Arab state, neither the stability of the existing political order nor the maturity of its nuclear command and control system could be taken for granted. This is *not* a statement that Third World states are in any fundamental sense less mature politically, socially, or culturally than U.S. and Soviet Cold War states were. The comparison is more specific. The Americans and Soviets learned through trial and error how to build into nuclear warning and intelligence systems checks and balances against prompt launch based on mistaken indicators. They also learned how to compensate for the interaction of the two sides' warning and intelligence systems with each other during a crisis. For example, during the Cuban missile crisis the Soviets may have deliberately avoided placing their strategic nuclear forces at higher than normal states of launch readiness. They also avoided dangerous confrontation tactics at sea of the kind that American and Soviet captains frequently engaged in during peacetime maneuvers. Finally, Kennedy and Khrushchev engaged in reciprocal exchanges of reassurance, from head of state to head of state, about the intention of each to resolve the crisis short of war. Had the same crisis happened between the Americans and the Soviets during the early 1950s with their comparatively primitive command and control systems in place, and with leaders probably less insistent upon reassurance than upon brinkmanship, a different outcome might have resulted.

Gordon Craig and Alexander George note that, for coercive diplomacy to succeed, certain conditions must be met. Three conditions are of special significance: the coercer must create a sense of urgency about compliance with its demand in the mind of its opponent; second, the threatener must be perceived by the threatened or coerced party as being more highly motivated to fulfill its goals; and, third, in the mind of the coerced or threatened party a fear of "unacceptable escalation" must exist. The point about unacceptable escalation might seem to support the argument that nuclear weapons are ideal for coercion, and some policymakers, including Khrushchev from the onset of his first Berlin ultimatum until the Cuban missile crisis of 1962, acted as if nuclears were coercive trumps. However, as George has emphasized, coercive diplomacy is essentially a defensive, not an offensive strategy for crisis management. Coercive diplomacy has one of three objects: (1) to persuade an opponent to *stop* an encroachment already begun; (2) to convince an opponent to *undo* an action previously taken or under way; and, (3) to obtain a change in the opponent's *government or regime* favorable to a desired change in his behavior.

Barry M. Blechman and Stephen S. Kaplan studied the U.S. use of military force to support political objectives from 1946 through 1975. The deployment of many U.S. nuclear weapons with general purpose forces makes it possible that any movement of forces possessing nuclear weapons might send an inadvertent nuclear message. A stricter criterion for isolating cases of intended nuclear signal, adopted by Blechman and Kaplan, was to select cases in which a force that had a designed role in U.S. strategic nuclear war plans was employed to send a political signal. They tabulated 19 incidents that met this standard, as listed in Table II. Several conclusions follow from this table. Nuclear

TABLE II

Involvement of U.S. Strategic Nuclear Forces in Conveying
Political Signals, 1946–1975

Incident	Date
U.S. aircraft shot down by Yugoslavia	November 1946
Inauguration of president in Uruguay	February 1947
Security of Berlin	January 1948
Security of Berlin	April 1948
Security of Berlin	June 1948
Korean War: security of Europe	July 1950
Security of Japan/South Korea	August 1953
Guatemala accepts Soviet bloc support	May 1954
China-Taiwan conflict: Tachen Islands	August 1954
Suez crisis	October 1956
Political crisis in Lebanon	July 1958
Political crisis in Jordan	July 1958
China-Taiwan conflict: Quemoy and Matsu	July 1958
Security of Berlin	May 1959
Security of Berlin	June 1961
Soviet placement of missiles in Cuba	October 1962
Withdrawal of U.S. missiles, Turkey	April 1963
Pueblo seized by North Korea	January 1968
Arab-Israeli war	October 1973

Source: Barry M. Blechman and Stephen S. Kaplan, *Force without War: U.S. Armed Forces as a Political Instrument* (Washington, DC: Brookings Institution, 1976), p. 48.

threats were used sparingly, and their use was much more common during the early Cold War when U.S. nuclear superiority or relative advantage over the Soviet Union was assumed by policymakers. About one-half of the incidents took place during the first third, or 10 years, of the period from 1946 through 1975; three-fourths of the episodes occurred during the first half, or 15 years, covered. These cases refer only to discrete movement of forces that are included in strategic nuclear war plans: other kinds of support provided by presence, military aid, or other means were not tabulated in the study. Nevertheless, the Blechman-Kaplan data demonstrate that the apparent U.S. appetite for nuclear coercion diminished, instead of intensifying, as the Cold War lengthened. After the Cuban missile crisis of 1962 was resolved without war, incidents virtually fall off the chart (two incidents in the last 10 years from 1965 through 1975).

Deterrence theory is basically a theory of opportunity: states jump through windows of opportunity to gain some territorial or other prize at the expense of an adversary whose commitment or resolve to defend that commitment seemed weak. It may be equally useful to assume that initiators of crises are motivated by perceived domestic policy needs or strategic vulnerabilities. As Richard Ned Lebow and Janice Gross Stein have argued, when leaders become desperate "they may resort to force even though the military balance is unfavourable and there are no grounds for doubting adversarial resolve." The possibility that leaders may be moved by fear and perceived vulnerability as much as they are moved by perceived opportunity adds an entire dimension to the analysis of deterrence, especially deterrence based on the threat of nuclear escalation.

Leaders driven by need toward objectives that may involve them in war against other states may rationalize away a military imbalance unfavorable to them and favorable to their opponents. This ability of need-driven leaders to rationalize away unfavorable military balances is all the more likely with nuclear weapons, since so few weapons convey so much striking power. The perceived vulnerability of a state's crisis predicament can also be made more acute by nuclear than by conventional threats, motivating the defender to engage in preemption. The problem with nuclear crisis bargaining is not only that the effects of nuclear weapons defy meaningful limitation, but also that the implications of firmness or irresolution for the bargaining process and its outcomes are not entirely clear to the participants.

IV. NUCLEAR PROLIFERATION

The Cold War nuclear powers saw themselves as members of an exclusive club. The Big Five acknowledged nuclear powers (U.S., Soviet Union, Britain, France, and China) sought to keep club membership small on the grounds that nuclear weapons spread was certain to increase international instability. However, what was to be denied to the ganders was still appropriate for the geese: there was no serious thought to nuclear disarmament among the "haves." The end of Cold War increased the pressure on the nuclear weapons states to limit their own arsenals in the interest, not only of détente, but also of nonproliferation. The U.S. arms control community was gratified by indefinite extension of the NPT in 1995 and by the approval of a text and release for signature of CTB in 1996. In January, 1993 Presidents Bush and Yeltsin signed the START II strategic arms reduction agreement. If fully implemented as scheduled by 2003, it would reduce U.S. and Russian force sizes to between 3000 and 3500 warheads each. (U.S. and Soviet/Russian reductions in strategic nuclear forces from the end of the Cold War to current (end 1996) levels are summarized in Table III).

Despite this good news, nuclear and other mass destruction weapons were still out there, weapons expertise was widely available, and ballistic and cruise missiles were hot market items as delivery systems. (See Table IV).

Briefers of new nuclear powers may be able to persuade their leaders, especially leaders intent upon the coercion of a non-nuclear state, that there are winnable and fightable nuclear wars. Regional antagonists who no longer fear American or Russian intervention in theater war might square off until one side reaches for nuclear trumps. Even if actual nuclear use is avoided, another danger is the use of nuclear threats to intimidate the leaders of states lacking a nuclear arsenal: a few nuclear weapons will look formidable to a non-nuclear state, even if the latter has sufficient forces to prevail in a conventional war. For example, one study of nuclear proliferation concluded that Iran's leadership had made a decision to develop nuclear weapons. According to the study, this decision by Iran will put pressure on Syria, Iraq, and Saudi Arabia to create their own nuclear forces: otherwise, those states "would be in a profoundly disadvantageous position in a confrontation with a nuclear armed Iran." Even among new nuclear states thought to have secure second strike capabilities, deterrence is not necessarily stable: misperception of enemy willingness to carry out retaliatory threats, or of enemy capability to do so, has many historical precedents. As Louis Rene Beres warns:

> Even if all of the new nuclear powers were actually able to maintain secure nuclear retaliatory forces, prospective aggressors might, through errors of information, still perceive insecurity. Here, nuclear deterrence could fail in spite of the fact that each nuclear power had "succeeded" in protecting its nuclear retaliatory forces.

The evidence is abundant that even leaders of mature democratic states react to crisis by selecting among a few broad policy options that leave open many important details. The perceived threat of an actual attack would not permit more than hastily assembled advisors, broadly packaged options and preliminary data analysis even in the case of the highly developed U.S. apparatus for crisis management. How much less likely is it that

TABLE III

U.S. and Soviet/Russian Strategic Nuclear Forces, 1989–1996

Year	ICBM launchers	ICBM warheads	SLBM launchers	SLBM warheads	Air launchers	Air warheads	Total launchers	Total warheads
			United States					
1989	1,000	2,440	592	5,152	311	5,158	1,903	12,780
1990	1,000	2,440	608	5,216	267	4,648	1,875	12,304
1991	550	2,000	480	3,456	209	3,844	1,239	9,300
1992	550	2,000	488	3,456	158	2,824	1,196	8,280
1993	550	2,000	336	2,688	159	2,840	1,045	7,528
1994	580	2,090	360	2,880	157	2,808	1,097	7,778
1995	575	2,075	384	3,072	122	2,176	1,081	7,323
1996	575	2,075	408	3,264	102	1,808	1,085	7,147
			Soviet Union/Russia					
1989	1,378	7,030	949	2,938	161	1,572	2,488	11,540
1990	1,378	6,938	908	2,900	128	1,414	2,414	11,252
1991	1,006	6,106	832	2,792	100	1,266	1,938	10,164
1992	950	5,725	628	2,492	112	1,392	1,690	9,609
1993	898	5,156	520	2,384	113	1,398	1,531	8,938
1994	818	4,314	456	2,320	113	1,398	1,387	8,032
1995	771	3,709	440	2,272	113	1,398	1,324	7,379
1996	755	3,589	440	2,272	113	1,398	1,308	7,259

Source: Natural Resources Defense Council, *NRDC Online,* 1997.

TABLE IV

Third World Ballistic Missiles and Weapons of Mass
Destruction: Countries Equipped or Attempting to Acquire

Country	Ballistic missiles	Nuclear weapons	Chemical weapons	Biological weapons
Afghanistan	yes			
Algeria	yes			
Argentina	yes	possible	possible	
Brazil	yes	possible		
Burma			likely	
Cuba	yes		possible	
Egypt	yes		likely	
Ethiopia			likely	
India	yes	yes	likely	
Indonesia	planned		possible	
Iran	yes	possible	likely	
Iraq	yes	possible*	yes	likely
Israel	yes	yes	likely	
Korea (North)	yes	possible**	likely	likely
Korea (South)	yes		likely	
Kuwait	yes			
Libya	yes	possible	likely	
Pakistan	yes	yes	likely	
Saudi Arabia	yes		possible	
South Africa	yes	no	possible	
Syria	yes		likely	likely
Taiwan	yes		likely	likely
Thailand	possible		possible	
Vietnam	possible		likely	
Yemen	yes			

* Iraq's nuclear capability diminished by Gulf War of 1991 and subsequent UN inspections.

** North Korean nuclear program limited by Framework Agreement of 1994.

Table from Steve Fetter, "Ballistic Missiles and Weapons of Mass Destruction," *International Security,* No. 1 (Summer, 1991), p. 14. Revised by author to take into account more recent developments in some cells.

a politically unaccountable regime with an untested command and control system could distinguish reliably between valid and false crisis warning, or between deterrence and reassurance signalling offered by the opposing side? As Alexander L. George has noted, at the onset of a crisis a number of complex standing orders come into effect throughout the military chain of command. Lacking detailed knowledge of these standing orders and of the rationales for them, political leaders may "fail to coordinate some critically important standing orders with their overall crisis management strategy." An historical example is provided by the efforts of Rus-

sian Foreign Minister Sazanov in the July crisis of 1914 to improvise a plan for partial mobilization only against Austria, as opposed to total mobilization against both Austria and Germany. The Russian General Staff regarded any planning for partial mobilization only as disruptive of the efficiency of general mobilization, and, therefore, no serious planning for partial mobilization had taken place.

There are at least two different issues here, relative to the crisis management potential of immature nuclear control systems: political accountability and operational flexibility. The two issues are closely related: the capability for operational flexibility is indispensable for policy makers who hope to control their crisis time forces. Political accountability is necessary in order to prevent military usurpation of civil authority in favor of preventive war or preemptive attack. Against proliferation pessimists, Kenneth Waltz argues that the current nuclear powers have solved these problems. Therefore, there is no reason to assume that newer nuclear states will not do as well:

> All nuclear countries live through a time when their forces are crudely designed. All countries have so far been able to control them. Relations between the United States and the Soviet Union, and later among the United States, Soviet Union, and China, were at their bitterest just when their nuclear forces were in the early stages of development and were unbalanced, crude and presumably hard to control.

In addition to the political fragility of regimes and the disorderly character of newly acquired nuclear command and control systems, a third problem for immature nuclear forces is the potential vulnerability of the forces themselves. Some of the aspiring nuclear states outside of Europe are unlikely to be able to field nuclear forces based on diverse launch vehicles or on survivable platforms. First strike forces will certainly precede second strike forces in most nuclear aspiring states. These early generation, nonsurvivable forces offer a temptation to prospective attackers. If those forces can be struck preemptively and disarmed, the attacker can dictate terms to the victim. Vulnerable *nuclear* forces are even more attractive than conventional forces, which are thought to be susceptible to surprise attack. Nuclear preemption removes nuclear deterrence from the equation, limiting the victim to conventional deterrence and war fighting that depend almost exclusively on battlefield prowess, not on skill in coercive bargaining. According to U.S. Air War College analysts William C. Martel and William T. Pendley:

> ... the existence of an Iranian nuclear deterrent invites preemptive attacks. For the states that view Iranian nuclear weapons as an inherently destabilizing development, sooner or later there will be an attempt to destroy those facilities, despite the political and military problems associated with preemptive attacks.

Related to the preceding point, some first generation nuclear forces, once they have been verified by observation and targeted by enemy planners, may be vulnerable to preemption by an attacker using only conventional weapons. Conventional preemption of a nuclear retaliatory force would be an inviting move for an attacker that could claim to occupy the moral high ground of a disarming antinuclear strike, even though its purposes were aggressive and designed to challenge a legal status quo. Menachem Begin's attack against the Iraqi Osirak nuclear complex was widely applauded, although sometimes in sotto voce, by states outside the region, which feared the development by Iraq of a usable nuclear arsenal. The Israeli attack was made despite the fact that, at that time, Iraq was in apparent compliance with the Nuclear Nonproliferation Treaty and subject to regular IAEA inspections. We subsequently learned, of course, that the inspections were not foolproof, and this adds retrospective justification in the minds of some observers for Begin's action.

If small states and nonstate actors have learned anything from the Cold War, it is that nuclear weapons, whether useful in war or not, carry prestige that opens the door to outside intervention for conflict termination. Thus, another incentive for small power acquisition of nuclear arsenals will be to neutralize the anticipated propensity of nuclear powers for power projection of their conventional forces, backed by their nuclear weapons. British power projection against Argentina in 1982 was undoubtedly made possible by the backdrop of British nuclear weapons, which the Argentines knew could be used against them should Britain suffer conventional military defeat. Guerrillas have little use for nuclear weapons in their tool kits, but the state actors that back those guerrillas in unconventional wars against foreign enemies might feel less vulnerable to nuclear coercion if they had their own nuclear forces to call upon.

In the case of conventional weapons employed by combatants of roughly equivalent technology and strategic competency, numbers do count. In the case of nuclear weapons, numbers are almost irrelevant once more than "none" have been acquired. This is obviously not true for a state planning large-scale nuclear first strikes against a responsively protected nuclear adversary. But for small states with nuclear miniforces, the deterrence of the strong by the weak is quite feasible. It is not necessary to threaten the entire destruction of an opponent's society in order to deter him, according to this logic. It is only necessary to threaten the plausible loss of social value or military objectives commensurate with the potential gains of an attacker. Nuclear weapons make the defender's job easy, and the attacker's, difficult, because so very few weapons can cause so much unprecedented, and unacceptable, damage.

The future holds, therefore, the potential for a lethal combination of conventional and unconventional military conflicts with the proliferation of weapons of mass destruction. Some of these weapons may be owned by unaccountable movements with no particular address. Others will be acquired by nationalist or religious separatists who seek a kingdom on earth instead of a territorial state. Other weapons of mass destruction may be found in the hands of formerly celibate Germans and Japanese who feel threatened by neighbors or insufficiently respected by their global and regional peers. Still others will be sought by aspiring regional hegemons, such as Saddam Hussein or Muammar Quaddafi, as weapons of checkmate against U.S. or United Nations coercive diplomacy. What many of these new nuclear owners will have in common is unaccountable authority and immature command and control systems, mated to weapons of extreme lethality.

There is another issue besides the probable acquisition of weapons of mass destruction and delivery systems by state and nonstate actors who are opposed to the international status quo. In addition, dissatisfied actors may not behave according to the expectations of rational or sensible deterrence theory. Rational leaders insist on a logical relationship between ends and means and have at least a crude cost-benefit calculus for making policy choices. Sensible leaders also take into account "common sense" factors, including situational variables that may affect a decision. Both rationality and sensibility are culturally derived. The "generically sensible foe" posited in much of Western deterrence theory during the Cold War is now passe: in its place are a multitude of possible threats of unknown or indeterminate origin, based in cultures unfamiliar to the United States and its allies. As Keith B. Payne has noted:

> Unfortunately, our expectations of opponents' behavior frequently are unmet, not because our op-

ponents necessarily are irrational but because we do not understand them—their individual values, goals, determination, and commitments—in the context of the engagement, and therefore we are surprised when their "unreasonable" behavior differs from our expectations.

Against these trends, those favoring the status quo and nonproliferation may have to choose among several unpleasant alternatives once cases of proliferation move from gestation to fruition: talk them out, by diplomacy; squeeze them out, by coercion; or shoot them out, by destruction. A widely held prognosis, popular after the Gulf War of 1991, was that new high technology conventional warfare strategies would curb states' lust for nuclear forces and for the kinds of terror which can be derived from them. A "Revolution in Military Affairs" based on information age weapons could, in this optimistic view, supersede nuclear weapons and deterrence based on weapons of mass destruction. Military planners were especially interested in precision-guided weapons, automated command/control systems, and real-time reconnaissance/surveillance that might make possible improved future Desert Storms. The impact of information technology on warfare is expected to go beyond the improved collection of information. Military experts foresee an emerging competition for "dominant battlespace awareness" based on newer generations of decision aids and models that permit the unprecedented exploitation of knowledge as applied to battle:

> A DBK (dominant battlespace knowledge), defined not as data (the transparent battlefield) but as knowledge (a significant exploitable asymmetry) offers powerful implications for the organization of warfare. DBK provides synoptic integrative knowledge, not just data on discrete objects and events. DBK lets its possessors pierce the fog of war and thus master the unfolding progression of circumstance, decisions and actions in the battlespace; it puts commanders in real-time command.

Information warfare or any other emerging war form does not necessarily diminish the significance of nuclear weapons in the new world order. To the contrary, as "third wave" militaries like that of the United States and other dominant information powers become more competent at conventional warfare, weapons of mass destruction could increase in their appeal to weaker states opposing the international status quo. "Weapons of mass destruction" include not only the chemical and biological weapons arsenals available to malefactors, but the distribution of ballistic missiles and other delivery vehicles of medium and longer ranges. In addition, there is no reason for complacency in the game of information warfare. The price of entry or sustained competition in strategic information warfare is not necessarily steep for those well acqainted with the vulnerabilities of their adversaries. A final caveat against the assumption that the revolution in military affairs will make nuclear weapons passe is the possibility that precision guidance will allow for miniaturization of nuclear charges down to the "micro" level, at which users are less reluctant to strike on account of reduced fear of collateral damage. That would be an especially imprudent and dangerous form of dialectical materialism: combining a nuclear "thesis" with nonnuclear "antithesis" in order to erode the salience of the nuclear threshold.

V. CONCLUSION

A considerable literature and U.S. and other government practice established during the Cold War that nuclear weapons, however useful they might be as deterrents, were not usable as traditional military counters on the chessboard of diplomacy, nor as instruments of classical combat. All of this theory and experience left open the future of nuclear weapons after the demise of the Soviet Union and the end of Cold War. Nuclear weapons, justified as the saviors of the West against communist hordes, were now liabilities that could spread to dissatisfied state and nonstate actors outside of the control of the existing nuclear powers. The revolution in military affairs, especially in precision weapons and automated control systems, has as yet unknown implications for the role of nuclear weapons in military strategy. Since few states can as yet play in the league of postnuclear, high technology powers, nuclear weapons may appeal to the comparatively weak as one means of jiujitsu against the conventional superiority of the strong. The staying power of nuclear weapons is underscored by the fact that some theorists still argue, mistakenly in my view, that the spread of nuclear weapons is not necessarily destabilizing or threatening to world peace.

Also See the Following Articles

Bibliography

Allison, G. T. (1971). *Essence of decision: Explaining the Cuban missile crisis*. Boston: Little, Brown.

Ball, D., & Richelson, J. (Eds.). (1986). *Strategic nuclear targeting*. Ithaca, NY: Cornell University Press.

Betts, R. K. (1987). *Nuclear blackmail and nuclear balance*. Washington, DC: Brookings Institution.

Blair, B. G. (1993). *The logic of accidental nuclear war*. Washington, DC: Brookings Institution.

Blight, J. G., & Welch, D. A. (1989). *On the brink: Americans and Soviets examine the Cuban missile crisis*. New York: Hill and Wang.

Bracken, P. (1983). *The command and control of nuclear forces*. New Haven, CN: Yale University Press.

Brodie, B. (1959). *Strategy in the missile age*. Princeton, NJ: Princeton University Press.

Bundy, M. (1988). *Danger and survival: Choices about the bomb in the first fifty years*. New York: Random House.

Carter, A. B., Steinbruner, J. D., & Zraket, C. A. (Eds.). (1987). *Managing nuclear operations*. Washington, DC: Brookings Institution.

Craig, G. A., & George, A. L. (1983). *Force and statecraft: Diplomatic problems of our time*. New York: Oxford University Press.

Dunn, L. A. (1982). *Controlling the bomb: Nuclear proliferation in the 1980s*. New Haven, CN: Yale University Press.

Enthoven, A. C., & Smith, K. W. (1971). *How much is enough? Shaping the defense program, 1961–1969*. New York: Harper and Row.

Feaver, P. D. (1992). *Guarding the guardians: Civilian control of nuclear weapons in the United States*. Ithaca, NY: Cornell University Press.

Freedman, L. (1981). *The evolution of nuclear strategy*. New York: St. Martin's Press.

Garthoff, R. L. (1990). *Deterrence and the revolution in Soviet military doctrine*. Washington, DC: The Brookings Institution.

Garthoff, R. L. (1989). *Reflections on the Cuban missile crisis* (Revised Ed.). Washington, DC: Brookings Institution.

George, A. L. (1991). The tension between "military logic" and requirements of diplomacy in crisis management. In George (Ed.), *Avoiding War: Problems of Crisis Management* (pp. 13–21). Boulder, CO: Westview Press.

George, A. L., & Simons, W. E. (Eds.). (1994). *The limits of coercive diplomacy* (2nd Ed.). Boulder, CO: Westview Press.

Gray, C. S. (1986). *Nuclear strategy and national style*. Lanham, MD: Hamilton Press.

Gray, C. S. (1982). *Strategic studies and public policy: The American experience*. Lexington, KY: University of Kentucky Press.

Holloway, D. (1983). *The Soviet Union and the arms race*. New Haven, CN: Yale University Press.

Holsti, O. R. (1989). Crisis decision making. In P. E. Tetlock, J. L. Husbands, R. Jervis, P. C. Stern & C. Tilly (Eds.), *Behavior society and nuclear war* (Vol. I, pp. 8–84). New York: Oxford University Press.

Jervis, R. (1984). *The illogic of American nuclear strategy*. Ithaca, NY: Cornell University Press.

Jervis, R. (1989). *The meaning of the nuclear revolution: Statecraft and the prospect of Armageddon*. Ithaca, NY: Cornell University Press.

Kaufmann, W. W. (1964). *The McNamara strategy*. New York: Harper and Row.

Kissinger, H. A. (1957). *Nuclear weapons and foreign policy*. New York: Houghton Mifflin.

Kull, S. (1988). *Minds at war: Nuclear reality and the inner conflicts of defense policymakers*. New York: Basic Books.

Lebow, R. N. (1987). *Nuclear crisis management: A dangerous illusion*. Ithaca, NY: Cornell University Press.

Lebow, R. N., & Janice, J. G. (1994). *We all lost the Cold War*. Princeton, NJ: Princeton University Press.

Mandelbaum, M. (1981). *The nuclear revolution: International politics before and after Hiroshima*. Cambridge: Cambridge University Press.

Morgan, P. M. (1977). *Deterrence: A conceptual analysis*. Beverly Hills, CA: Sage Publications.

Payne, K. B. (1996). *Deterrence in the second nuclear age*. Lexington, KY: University Press of Kentucky.

Powell, R. (1990). *Nuclear deterrence theory: The search for credibility*. Cambridge: Cambridge University Press.

Quester, G. H. (1986). *Deterrence before Hiroshima: The Airpower Background of Modern Strategy* (2nd Ed.). New Brunswick, NJ: Transaction Books.

Reiss, M. (1995). *Bridled ambition: Why countries constrain their nuclear capabilities*. Baltimore, MD: Johns Hopkins University Press.

Rosenberg, D. A. (1986). U.S. nuclear war planning, 1945–1960. In D. Ball & J. Richelson (Eds.), *Strategic nuclear targeting* (pp. 35–56). Ithaca, NY: Cornell University Press.

Sagan, S. D., & Waltz, K. N. (1995). *The spread of nuclear weapons: A debate*. New York: W. W. Norton.

Sagan, S. D. (1989). *Moving targets: Nuclear strategy and national security*. Princeton: Princeton University Press.

Schelling, T. C. (1966). *Arms and Influence*. New Haven, CN: Yale University Press.

Slessor, Sir John. (1954). *Strategy for the West*. London: Cassell.

Slocombe, W. (1984). The countervailing strategy. In S. E. Miller (Ed.), *Strategy and nuclear deterrence*. (pp. 245–254). Princeton, NJ: Princeton Univiersity Press.

Spector, L. S., & Foran, V. (1992, October). *Preventing weapons proliferation: Should the regimes be combined?* Warrenton, VA: Stanley Foundation.

Organized Crime

H. F. (Rika) Snyman

Police practice: Technikon SA
Florida, South Africa

ORGANIZED CRIME has historically been regarded as a law-and-order problem restricted to specific groups or areas, but since the late 1980s the nature of organized crime has changed globally. Not only has organized crime expanded its areas of interest to become a transnational phenomenon, it has also changed the nature of its operations. Comparative evidence suggests that organized crime grows more quickly in periods of political transition and violence when state resources are concentrated in certain areas and gaps emerge in which crime syndicates may operate. The most notable example is the former Soviet Union where the collapse of communist rule allowed the emergence of literally thousands of criminal organizations involving current and former members of the establishment. Organized crime is not random or episodic, but a patterned and structured activity that finds and exploits opportunities for illicit gain and operates across time regardless of individual changes in leadership in a country.

I. CLARIFICATION OF THE CONCEPT OF ORGANIZED CRIME

In part because of its highly diversified nature, it is impossible to precisely define what organized crime is. Organized crime means different things to different people such that views of its seriousness and prevalence vary. Organized crime is not a specific type of crime, but is a collective term and is based on the context within which the crime(s) is committed rather than on the type of crime.

Albanese (1995) states that "... there seems to be as many descriptions of organized crimes as there are authors." Passas (1995) defines organized crime as "the unlawful activities of the members of a highly organized, disciplined association engaged in supplying illegal goods and services including, but not limited to, gambling, prostitution, loan sharking, murder, and the smuggling of goods." This is a practical definition used by international law enforcement agencies to develop action programs to counter organized crime.

Early sociologists used the term organized crime to describe "professional" criminals in contrast to "amateur" criminals, and theorists like Sutherland and Cressey view organized crime as "the association of

Copyright © 1999 by Academic Press.
All rights of reproduction in any form reserved.

a small group of criminals for the execution of a certain type of crime". Recently the term organized crime is used more narrowly and there are two major approaches to defining it, namely the law enforcement perspective and the social/economic perspective. From a law enforcement perspective, organized crime is seen as an organization of thousands of criminals that operate in a complex structure that has rules that are strictly enforced. The main goals are power and money, and legitimate and illegitimate businesses are infiltrated. If viewed from a social/economic perspective, organized crime can be regarded as an integrated part of a nation's existence where it is regarded as one of the major social ills like racism and poverty. It is similar to any other economic enterprise that provides services and goods to persons who cannot obtain them otherwise, like illegal drugs and the products of endangered species.

II. CHARACTERISTICS OF ORGANIZED CRIME

The question arises as to why organized crime exists and why it is so difficult to prevent and control. Organized crime involves supplying a desired commodity or service that is otherwise not legally available in a community. As long as there is a market for the goods, someone will offer to provide it and violate the laws of the country to fulfill the need. In this process considerable profits are generated because the degree of risk and the unavailability or price of the goods on the open market push the prices up. The trade in drugs and the products of endangered species are good illustrations of the need for illicit goods and the high profits generated by providing them. Weak spots in the laws and regulations of a country facilitate the work or organized crime. Lax control at points of entry and the ineffective monitoring of imported/exported goods furthermore make the smuggling of drugs and other products in and out of a country very easy. The corruption of politicians, law enforcement officers, and business people is a critical factor in organized crime. Violence is often used to gain control of a specific market and to monopolize it.

Myers & Sullivan identifies the following characteristics of organized crime that distinguish it from ordinary gangs, terrorist groups, and guerilla organizations. Organized crime does not include terrorists dedicated to political change, although organized criminals and terrorists have some characteristics in common, including violent acts being committed and its hierarchical structure.

1. *Organized hierarchy.* Each organized crime group has a single leader or tribunal that sets priorities and guidelines for the group, and a series of subordinate structures that carry out the orders.

2. *Organizational continuity over time.* Organized crime groups are very flexible in their structure and activities as they must be able to continue their activities if their leader(s) are imprisoned or if the opportunities for crime change due to new legislation or increased policing.

3. *Willingness to threaten or use force.* Power and control stand central in organized crime and are therefore prevalent in the control of its own members, as well as of other groups and victims. Loyalty to the group, intimidation of rival groups, and the silencing of possible witnesses are ensured through violent acts like assault, murder, and rape.

4. *Restrictive membership.* The restriction of membership is based on factors like ethnicity (for example the Triads), special skills (for example motor theft syndicates), or common background (for example the Russian Mafia). There is very often an elaborate initiation ceremony, like in the case of the Chinese Triads, that is based on traditional customs, or a specific crime that needs to be committed to allow entry into the organization.

5. *Legitimate business involvement.* Front organizations like shops, restaurants, and legal firms are used to cover up the activities of the group or launder the money from the sale of goods.

6. *Use of specialists.* Although much of the criminal activity is carried out by members of that group, specialists like pilots, chemists, doctors, and lawyers are contracted to assist the group with sophisticated tasks.

The most important factor in the growth of organized crime has been the development of a global network for illegal drug trafficking that produces multibillion-dollar profits. Other developments like the growth of capitalism in China, the break-up of the former Soviet Union, and the democratization of South Africa brought added momentum and growth potential to formerly less-exploited areas.

The world's most powerful intelligence weapon against the escalation of organized crime is the hi-tech database at Interpol's headquarters in Lyons, France. With a staff of over 800 police officials from 45 countries and some 240 civilians, Interpol operates in every one of its 177 member states through the National Central Bureau staffed by local police seconded to the organization. It is the second largest international body after the UN and the only criminal organization spanning the entire world with over 150 member states linked by computer. Up to 70% of Interpol's time is spent fighting international organized crime. Drug cartels are actively subverting economies and stifling rising democracies and the amounts of money involved are overwhelming. The UN's central European Headquarters in Vienna has estimated that the world's major crime syndicates' income in 1997 exceeded $100 trillion.

III. THEORETICAL FRAMEWORK FOR THE EXPLANATION OF ORGANIZED CRIME

Criminological phenomena are "understood" through an intertwined grid of definitions, research, and theoretical explanations. In the case of organized crime, it is not as straightforward as it would be for a phenomenon like murder or fraud, for example. It is not the specific crimes that are the key to the understanding organized crime, but rather the criminal activity that is carried out as part of a particular process, which is known as an organized crime process. The explanation of organized crime must therefore be viewed from two perspectives, namely why organized crime exists and why individuals become involved with organized crime activities. Therefore it is not only the crimes, but also the groups and individuals involved in organized crime activities that differ in terms of their motivation, sophistication, and commitment to crime.

There are various theoretical frameworks that can be adopted to explain organized crime. Because definitions of organized crime tend to focus on the criminal activity as a distinct type of "crime," it has been assumed that one or two theories can be uniformly applied across all of the groups involved in organized crime. But if the perspective is adopted that organized crime is a process, it becomes clear that different groups have completely different reasons as to why they involve themselves in organized crime activities. A holistic perspective is therefore needed to provide a theoretical framework for the explanation of organized crime.

A. Rational Choice Perspective

The rational choice perspective assumes the point of view that a definite rational decision is made by the individual based on the benefits and consequences of the crime he/she is about to commit. A process of decision-making is followed through which the individual feels that the act is justified to achieve the desired end result. In the case of organized crime, this end result may be the status gained by following an instruction from some one higher up in the hierarchy, exercising power over a lesser member of the group, achieving a specific goal by eliminating a competitor, or for financial gain.

Individuals are differently motivated, depending on various factors within their personal make-up, the social structure within which they find themselves, and/or the social processes within which they function. These three factors are used within the context of the rational choice perspective, to explain why a specific individual commits crime.

- Biopsychological theories suggest that there exists a link between certain personality deficiencies like certain genetical traits such as the XYY chromosome syndrome and anxiety and conduct disorders that make people susceptible to violence and psychopathy. There is great controversy as to whether crime and biopsychological factors are linked, as the same traits have been found in people that have never committed crime. Recent research demonstrates that biological and psychological factors play some role in the etiology of violence but as with social risk factors, they do not cause crime, but can increase the chance of involvement with crime.

- The social structure within which an individual finds him-/herself can play a direct role in the individual committing a crime. Various theories exist that explain how, and the extent to which, social conditions prevalent in neighborhoods, the socioeconomic stratification, or the class structure within the society contribute toward a person's criminal career. One example of such a theory is that of relative deprivation which links social and economic deprivation to the high rate of crime in inner cities. This ecological approach suggests that the inequality within communities where wealth is flaunted and access to it is denied to a large group creates feelings of anger, hostility, and social injustice.

- The social processes within which an individual functions impact directly on his/her chance to get involved with crime. The theories that use this explanation stress the attitudes, ability, values, and behaviors needed to maintain a criminal career. Poverty and social class are regarded as not enough to explain a person's propensity for criminal activity. This point is well illustrated through Sutherland's differential association theory, which states that criminal behavior is learned as a result of association with others, and the chance of committing crime depends on the strength of these associations. Differential association is viewed as a product of socialization in which criminals are guided by the same principles that guide law-abiding people not to commit crime. He identified nine principles of differential association that guides criminals to pursue their goals through unlawful means.

B. Organized Crime as a Community Social Institution

Because organized crime consists of various criminal acts committed by various criminals, the question arises as to why crime is committed within an organized context rather than in an individual context. The production–distribution–consumption function can be taken as the key point of departure in explaining organized crime's existence. Organized crime activities move in where gaps exist in the legitimate markets and many similarities can be found between legitimate and illegitimate businesses. Thus organized crime is a result of the dynamics of the production–distribution–consumption factor of the community in which these activities are found.

• Organized crime groups align with legitimate business to front their activities because they seek profitable and safe investments. Various needs of organized crime activities are addressed through this alignment, as it offers concealment opportunities, a chance to launder the proceeds of the criminal activity and give it a "legitimate" source of income, and participation with members of the legitimate business community.

• Some organized crime activities are beneficial to legitimate businesses and are used to further their competitiveness in the market. Racketeering services, for example, are potent weapons for harassing competitors or securing favorable employment contracts. This symbiotic relationship benefits organized crime as well as legitimate business. The beneficial relationship is often extended to investment opportunities or start-up money for new businesses.

• Especially in economically depressed or deprived areas, organized crime activities provide valuable income and job opportunities for the community. Gambling, prostitution, and money-laundering activities are a source of income for individuals who otherwise would have to turn to other types of crime for survival. In a bizarre way, organized crime may serve to reduce threats of more conventional criminality. Although these particular communities may not agree with the ethical and moral bases of their sources of income, the organized crime activities are tolerated as they are viewed as the lesser of two evils. The investment of the proceeds of crime through money-laundering furthermore leads to legitimate businesses being set-up that would otherwise not have existed. A spin-off of this is legitimate employment opportunities and legal methods of spending money.

• The socialization function helps explain why organized crime is tolerated and often not regarded as evil or wrong. Organized crime offers avenues for social mobility especially in communities where legitimate paths are either blocked or difficult to achieve. This explains the phenomenon of ethnic-organized crime activities all over the world. Immigrants often get established in legitimate businesses or professional jobs through the profits and contracts made in their involvements in organized crime. In addition to the value of legitimate success routes, some communities have specific conditions that make innovation more likely to result in criminal outcomes as it shapes modes of adaptation to social conditions. These people who have succeeded through innovation, influence other members of that community to follow the same route.

• Collusion with law enforcement and political groups within the community is a well-known characteristic of organized crime and ensures continuity in the activities of organized crime groups. This collusion is more than just corruption and involves a subtle interplay among community forces. This not only permits accommodations with the criminal justice system, but also allows organized crime to be used as a means of resolving contradictions inherent in the enforcement of pertinent laws. For example, it is inevitable that certain laws prohibiting illicit services and goods will be selectively enforced because those involved in illegal transactions will not regard themselves as victims and will not report the illegal transaction to the authorities. And when the law is enforced, its selective nature serves organized crime groups at the expense of individual entrepreneurs. Stronger organization by a group decreases the risk of prosecution, especially as organized crime groups employ specialists like lawyers to avoid prosecution. Another consideration is that the criminal justice system is faced with the enforcement of morality legislation on which differential consensus levels exist. For example, community elite involved in organized crime, seeking an expansion of their base of support, often support community members who are offended by activities like gambling, drug dealing, and prostitution. This results in legal proscription against this behavior. Therefore, relationships between organized crime groups and individuals within the criminal justice system represent the ultimate example of the social organization of crime in the community. The role of organized crime activities in providing assistance to the community in its major functions while taking advantage of opportunities provided by the community makes it a functional community institution.

Organized crime occupies a key role in a community's production–distribution–consumption function, which is the rationale for the existence of organized crime. Because organized crime activities complement functions of formal social control agencies and have an important position in a community's socialization functions, they provide a socially acceptable means for social participation to persons otherwise excluded from community functions. Thus, organized crime often uses opportunities and gaps left by legislation and legitimate businesses to provide goods and services that the community in which it functions requires.

IV. THE NATURE AND STRUCTURE OF ORGANIZED CRIME SYNDICATES

In order to understand the organizational structure of organized crime syndicates, it is necessary to obtain an overview of prominent criminal organizations whose influence stretches all over the world. The Colombian, Cuban, Asian, European, Russian and African organized crime syndicates well illustrate how the characteristics or organized crime are operationalized.

A. Colombian Organized Crime

Colombian organized crime plays a major role in the global crime scene in the 1990s. It is responsible for various crimes associated with drug trafficking and is known for the violent manner in which competition is eliminated, members are protected, and government interference is avoided. For almost 2 decades, these crime groups have become so sophisticated that they handle all the phases of drug trafficking themselves—from the manufacturing of drugs to the distribution in foreign countries. This obviously necessitates the active

involvement of specialists like chemists, pilots, and security personnel. Most of the Colombian organized crime groups have a hierarchal structure with the oldest member taking the authority position. It is estimated by the Drug Enforcement Agency in the United States that the Colombian drug trade brings in $5 billion in total revenues annually and that an estimated 22,000 Colombians are actively employed in the USA–South American drug trade alone.

Colombian organized crime is divided into cartels, with the Medellin and Cali cartels being the most prominent. All of the characteristics of organized crime are present in their structure and functioning. These cartels operate much like legitimate businesses as they are very flexible and pragmatic. This allows them to adapt their operational patterns to suit changing markets and to avoid increased law enforcement in certain areas. The specialists they employ enable them to avoid detection by authorities, and when this protection fails, to afford highly capable lawyers to defend their members. In the U.S. the Colombian cartels operate through cells in different states, which are self-contained and range in size. In 1990 16 cells were identified in the U.S. and in one seizure 20 tons of cocaine and $10 million in cash were confiscated. These cells seem to specialize in different aspects of the drug business such as the distribution and selling of drugs and the laundering of money.

B. Cuban Organized Crime

Between 1959, when the Batista regime in Cuba was overthrown, and 1980, a large number of Cuban people emigrated to the U.S. The last large group that emigrated in 1980, the Marielitos, organized themselves into criminal groups that involved themselves in the drug trade. Other organized crime groups often used them in crime-related activities and the Marielitos became notorious for their aggressiveness and violence. This reputation was gained from their many years of imprisonment in Cuban prisons, as well as their involvement in wars in countries like Angola and Central America. These immigrants never received any education and/or job-related training and their past connections with criminals and exposure to violence molded them into ideal candidates for organized crime groups. Their structure, however, is very loose and not hierarchal, which is atypical of organized crime syndicates.

C. Asian Organized Crime

Asian organized crime can be divided into different categories, with the Triads and the Yakuza being the most prominent organizations. There are also other groups, like the Sicilian-Coc alliance, the Shan United Army, and Vietnamese gangs that are active within Asia but who do not extend their activities globally.

D. The Triads

Triads can be defined as ancient secret societies which trace their roots to 17th century China. There are an estimated 80,000 members in 60 societies. "Triad" means a triangle of heaven, earth, and man. A core component of the Triads is the concept "Guanxi." Guanxi refers to the "brotherhood" and mutual support that the Chinese have among themselves. The Triads are among the toughest criminal organizations functioning internationally. Most of them are based in Hong Kong, Vietnam, and Taiwan. They are based on many separate and autonomous cells answering to no authority but the collective dictates of their own officials. Typical of the Triads is the initiation ceremony in which the members are bound together, known as "hanging the lantern." The initiation rituals are very elaborate with the idea of implanting a strong sense of secrecy and loyalty and requires 36 oaths of loyalty. Numerology and occultism influence the organization of a traditional Triad. The two highest ranks use the code numbers 489 and 438, and common member uses the number 47. The possible interpretations of the code numbers are so numerous that it is unlikely that their true significance will ever be ascertained. The only code number that has a straight-forward meaning is that of the ordinary member, number 49. When multiplied (4 × 9), it equal 36, the number of oaths a new member swears to obey when joining the society. The Triads are mainly involved internationally in the drug trade, gambling, and the smuggling of endangered species and products thereof.

E. The Yakuza

The Yakuza is regarded as the largest organized crime group in the world, as their membership is estimated at 110,000 belonging to 2,500 gangs. The Yakuza was originally formed during the 16th and 17th centuries by dissident Samurai warriors, who adapted to changing times and replaced their "Robin Hood" image with a ruthless violent one. Seven major groups have been identified within the Yakuza, with the Yamaguchi Gumi, with a membership of 10,000, as the largest. The hierarchy in the Yakuza is based on an author-

ity model, called the oyabun-kobun. This provides strength and cohesion, which ultimately translates into blind obedience to the boss. The value of membership does not rest within the specific group to which the member belongs, but in his willingness to pass on illicit revenues as an "earner" to the organization. Individual members therefore attempt to find new sources for illicit revenue and they exploit legitimate businesses for it. The main focus of the Yakuza is in the export of illegal goods to Japan, with a specific focus on firearms. The Yakuza has systematically established itself as a shareholder in major corporations internationally and real estate is frequently bought in major international cities, like Sydney, to gain a foothold in the specific area.

F. European Organized Crime

Organized crime groups have existed in Europe since before the Industrial Revolution, with the best known being the Italian Mafia. There are, however, few clearly defined organized crime groups in Europe, yet there is much activity in the organized crime field.

One of these few identifiable organized crime groups are the Italian Mafia. They originated during the 19th century in Sicily as a system to achieve justice under the then-oppressive government. The Mafia developed gradually into a criminal organization, particularly gaining momentum after the Second World War. Its structure consists of the family as its basic unit with each having a chief, the Capo famiglia, who is aided by a counselor, with deputies and sergeants completing the hierarchy. Above the families is the high command that controls three families, who answer to a provincial, a regional, and a central committee. The Sicilian Mafia is a unique organized crime group, as it operates almost like a state within a state. It imposes its own laws and levies its own taxes. Apart from the extortion of local businesses, the Italian Mafia is a player in the international drug trade.

Political, social, and economical changes in Eastern and Central Europe have produced dramatic developments on all levels of society which have in turn upset traditional systems and created much insecurity on various levels. This creates an ideal opportunity for organized crime groups to move in to fill the voids. Organized crime in Central and Eastern Europe is regarded more as a loose network of organizations that provide illegal goods and services to the public.

Europe has a strong organized shadow economy that, since not run by organized crime groups, exhibits elements of organized crime characteristics. This shadow economy consists of two sectors, namely the black market, which deals with illegal and smuggled goods like drugs, and the gray market, that provides legal goods and services, but in a price-war against the state-controlled market. This shadow economy centers around drug trafficking; corruption; theft of cultural artefacts and expensive cars, terrorism, and firearms.

G. Russian Organized Crime

Since the break-up of the Soviet Union, organized crime has increased dramatically and impacted severely on the economy and safety of the country. It is claimed that there are 174 Russian crime organizations that operate in 29 countries. Organized crime in Russia is not as organized as its classification denotes. Many actions that the Russian people dislike are labelled as "Mafia," without actually being part of organized criminal activities. The organized crime groups prefer to victimize the wealthy Russian citizens and foreign tourists. It is claimed that, on average, 80% of Russian business people pay protection money which is then used to control approximately 400 banks. These groups easily corrupt government officials and the police, as they generally earn very low wages and can gain great profits from collaborating with organized crime.

The structure of Russian organized crime groups is not very clear, but can be understood as that of a cell, with its purpose to minimize contact with other cells within the same organization that could lead to the identification of the whole organization. At the head of a group of four cells is a "pakhan," who exercises his control through an intermediary called a brigadier. Two people spy on this intermediary to protect his loyalty and power. The bottom of the structure is made up of other cells that all specialize in criminal activities and are not aware of the identity or decision-making processes higher up in the hierarchy.

H. African Organized Crime

Various organized crime groups operate from Africa, with groups in Sierra Leone, Ghana, Benin, Nigeria, and South Africa, being the most prominent. The Nigerian Scam is the group with the most far reaching tentacles internationally, as its operations are closely integrated with the legitimate economy in the country. They have expanded their activities from drug smuggling to credit card and bank fraud. They are also well known for the quality of their forged documents, which surface worldwide.

Currently in South Africa, no single group dominates the organized crime scene although there is some evidence that local operations have forged links with international crime groups. There is substantial evidence that sophisticated organized crime operations such as the Cosa Nostra of Sicily, the Russian Mafia, and the Chinese Triads have recruited local partners to secure markets. Such connections bring new players into the field. Several Nigerian and Turkish organizations that began simply as carriers for larger criminal operations have now begun to establish their own networks specializing in specific products in South Africa. But of increasing concern in South Africa is the degree to which organized crime syndicates have been able to penetrate the state.

Organized crime has traditionally been seen as a domestic problem affecting only a few states, like the U.S., Italy, and China. Various factors, like the rise of a global market for illicit drugs, the end of the Cold War, the breakdown of barriers between East and West, and the emergence of global financial and trading systems have changed the context in which criminal organizations operate. Mostly domestic groups in various countries have developed ties with international organizations or have grown into transnational criminal organizations themselves.

V. THE PREVENTION AND CONTROL OF ORGANIZED CRIME

In contrast to crimes that are not linked to organized crime groups, the prevention and control of organized crime requires a more sophisticated approach and should be more proactive than reactive in nature. To control and prevent organized crime, the system itself must improve and public support and help must be sought.

Because organized crime penetrates all levels of society, a new morality is needed to neutralize the power and control of crime syndicates. The prevention and control of organized crime can therefore not be left to policing alone; it demands that everyone—from private companies and state departments to the man on the street—resist the lucrative deals that crime syndicates offer and report corruption and blackmailing.

Organized crime is very difficult to prevent and control because inherent in crime syndicates are survival mechanisms that neutralize prevention efforts that would otherwise have worked. Barlow identifies three such mechanisms.

1. *Role imperatives.* Crime syndicates are highly organized and hierarchical in nature with specific individuals having definite roles and functions to fulfill. Two such positions, namely those of "buffer" and the "corrupter," ensure the loyalty of all members to the syndicate and forewarn on dissatisfaction that may lead to someone disrupting the functioning of the group. The task of the "buffer" is to be the eyes and the ears of the leader of the crime group. He facilitates internal communication by smoothing out conflict before it erupts and reporting on any member that may betray the group to the police. The "corrupter," on the other hand, works within government organizations and ensures through bribery, intimidation, and persuasion that members of the crime group maintain immunity from arrest, prosecution, and punishment.

2. *Legislation of morality.* Most of the activities of organized crime are aimed at providing goods and services that are not regularly available or are prohibited. Goods like ivory and rhinoceros horn and counterfeit products are smuggled because they are unavailable or too expensive in certain communities. Prostitution and drugs are so profitable because they are criminalized through legislation. This is called the "crime tariff" because communities protect their morality through legislation. Members of a community desire certain goods and services that others wish to prohibit, and organized crime groups step into this market to provide what is not legitimately available.

3. *Public attitudes and behavior.* Organized crime activities depend very much on demand for the goods and services that it can provide. The man in the street comes into contact with the crime syndicate when buying counterfeit goods or the drugs or sex that he/she cannot obtain legally and does not view the sellers of the goods and services as criminals but as people who are providing a necessary service and doing them a favor. The way in which the public views crime leads to perceptions and attitudes that do not regard organized crime as a big threat. The actions of organized crime groups are also regarded as individual actions and are not seen in perspective as part of a larger whole. For example, a stolen car is regarded as a crime committed by an individual that is motivated by greed and is not viewed as a crime committed by a the front man who supplies the car to the syndicate that smuggles it out of the country.

The United States is leading in its efforts to combat organized crime and illustrates the value of a holistic approach to the prevention and control thereof. Their success lies in their recognition of the need to approach the control and prevention of organized crime on a broad level by focusing not only on legislation and prosecution, but also on businesses and labor unions. The implementation of the recommendations for a national strategy from the President's Commission on organized crime in 1986, together with the Organized Crime Control Act of 1970, and specifically the Racketeer Influenced and Corrupt Organizations Statute (RICO) have led to a drastic clampdown on organized groups in that country.

The man-in-the-street's role in preventing and controlling organized crime should be regarded as abstinence from its products and service, and that of the criminal justice system as providing effective investigation, prosecution, and sentencing. Organized crime is a dynamic phenomenon that has a local as well as an international dimension. Because of the way in which organized crime syndicates function it is very often difficult to see organized crime for what it is. Increased public awareness of the nature and incidence of organized crime activities need to be increased as the need for the products and services that these syndicates offer gives it a reason to keep operating and even increase its activities. An equal raising in awareness levels are needed in the criminal justice system so as to prevent and control organized crime effectively.

Also See the Following Articles

CRIMINAL BEHAVIOR, THEORIES OF • CRIMINOLOGY, OVERVIEW • DRUGS AND VIOLENCE • GANGS • LAW AND VIOLENCE • POLICING AND SOCIETY

Bibliography

Albanese, J. (1989). *Organized crime in America*, 2nd ed. New York: Anderson.

Beare, M. (1996). *Criminal conspiracies. Organized crime in Canada.* Toronto, Canada: Nelson.

Block, A. A. (1991). *The Business of crime: A documentary study of organized crime in the American economy.* Oxford, UK: West View.

Fijnaut, C., and Jacobs, J. (Eds) (1996). *Organized crime and its containment. A transatlantic initiative.* Boston: Kluwer.

Freemantle, B. (1996). *The octopus.* Paris: Orion.

Kelly, R. J. (Ed.) (1986). *Organized crime: A global perspective.* Ottawa, Canada: Rowman & Littlefield.

Lyman, M. D., and Potter, G. W. (1997). *Organized crime.* New York: Prentice-Hall.

Myers, W. H., and Sullivan, B. R. (1996). Transnational Enterprise crime and US National Security: New Threats and New Responses. Paper delivered to the American Society of Criminology. November 1996. Chicago US.

Pace, D. F., and Styles, J. C. (1993). *Organized crime: Concepts and control,* 2nd ed. Englewood Cliffs, NJ: Prentice-Hall.

Passas, N. (Ed.) (1995). *Organized crime.* Brookfield: Dartmouth.

Ryan, P. J. (1995). *Organized crime: A reference handbook.* Santa Barbara, CA: ABC Clio.

Strobel, B. (1997). Interview, UNDP. Vienna, Austria.

Williams, P. (1996). *Grave new world: Transnational organized crime on the eve of the twenty-first century.* Pittsburgh, PA: Ridgway Center for International Security Studies.

Peace Agreements

Fen Osler Hampson
Carleton University

GLOSSARY

Demobilization The process of disarming and disbanding the armed forces and/or guerrilla armies of warring factions.

Governance The exercise of political, economic, and administrative authority to manage a country's affairs either at the national, provincial, or local levels.

Human Rights Commission An impartial body charged with the responsibility of investigating and collecting evidence (but not prosecuting) of human rights abuses.

Peacekeeping The deployment of international military personnel to verify and monitor a cease-fire. Other functions may include the use of military forces to assist with civilian tasks such as food distribution, transportation, and the restoration of basic services.

Ripeness A term or the point in a conflict at which the parties no longer believe that they can use military force in order to achieve their goals.

War Crimes Tribunal An international criminal forum before which individuals accused of human rights atrocities can be held legally accountable for their actions.

IT HAS LONG BEEN RECOGNIZED that peace agreements sometimes contain the seeds of their own destruction. Perhaps the most famous—though by no means only—example of this self-destructive tendency in the Versailles Peace Treaties that followed World War I. The harsh punitive terms of the settlement, which severed Prussia and demilitarized the Rhineland, helped pave the way for the rise of Adolph Hitler in the 1930s. However, even less exploitative settlements can also self-destruct as Kal Hosti argues in his monumental study, *Peace & War: Arms Conflicts and International Order*, because they fail to adequately anticipate new problems that may arise in the future.

However, there are many additional reasons why peace agreements can fail or unravel. The parties to a settlement may simply conclude after a period of time that it is no longer in their self-interest to abide by the agreements they have negotiated. Without proper monitoring and enforcement mechanisms, agreements negotiated in good faith can still self-destruct in an escalating spiral of alleged violations and counter-recrimination, or what some analysts call "the security dilemma." Ambiguities in the text of an agreement may also become major points of contention that cannot be resolved through legal or procedural means. Clearly, there are many reasons why peace treaties fail.

Copyright © 1999 by Academic Press.
All rights of reproduction in any form reserved.

The end of the Cold War has presented a new kind of challenge in international politics, namely, the problem of implementing peace agreements that have been negotiated to end civil or substate violence within the borders of a sovereign state. In recent years, much diplomatic energy and human and financial resources have been directed at helping countries negotiate an end to conflicts within their borders in order to prevent a continuation of violence and bloodshed. Some of the most prominent examples of negotiated settlements directed at ending civil conflict in recent years are in Bosnia, Guatemala, Nicaragua, El Salvador, Mozambique, Angola, the West Bank of Israel and Gaza, and Cambodia. There are also many instances where negotiations have failed to produce a settlement such as in Chechnya, Rwanda, Sri Lanka, Northern Ireland, Nagorno Karabakh, and Liberia, or where there have been major difficulties with implementation as in Bosnia and Cambodia.

The international community is just beginning to grapple with the implications of implementing peace settlements in situations where the military outcome on the battlefield may be, at best, inconclusive and where former combatants are having to resolve their disputes through political versus coercive means, often for the first time. This article discusses the challenges of implementing an agreement once a negotiated settlement to end a civil conflict has been reached and argues that outside third parties, notably the United Nations and other international actors, have a key role to play in assisting with the wide range of peacebuilding tasks that follow a negotiated political settlement.

I. THE COMPLEXITY OF INTERCOMMUNAL CONFLICT

Before turning to this problem, however, a number of caveats are in order. First, it is worth remembering that negotiated settlements to end civil wars are a rarity in international politics and a relatively recent phenomenon. Out of a total of 65 civil wars fought between 1900 and 1989, according to Stephen Stedman, only 11 were resolved through negotiation (and 6 of the 11 through mediation) (Stedman, 1988: 9). Negotiated settlements of civil conflicts are also more likely to collapse than those where one side is victorious on the battlefield. Since 1945, as Roy Licklider documents, only one-third of the negotiated settlements of so-called identity civil wars have resulted in a lasting peace (Licklider, 1995: 686).

Second, in reviewing contemporary conflicts in countries such as Bosnia, Liberia, and Sri Lanka, great care should be taken in applying the sweeping label "ethnic conflict." Reality has been shaped by many factors: the collapse of central institutions, the holding of ill-prepared elections, the emergence of opportunistic politicians who use ethnicity as a platform, the splintering of armies and the rise of warlords, the logic of preemptive military moves creating a chain reaction of violence, arms transfers, and the availability of natural and financial resources, legal and criminal, to fuel the descent into violence. There are relatively few cases of pure ethnic conflict in the sense of a spontaneous mass eruption of ethnic antagonisms within a state. A strong case can be that an apparently pure example such as Rwanda was an ersatz creation of ambitious, ethnic entrepreneurs. Perhaps the most obvious instances of immutable ethnic conflict are, in fact, nationalist rejections of alien, minority, or foreign rule, as happened in Afghanistan after the 1979 Soviet invasion; in the Dutch East Indies/Indonesia from 1945 to 1949; in South Africa from 1952 to 1994; in Namibia from 1966 to 1989; in Algeria from 1954 to 1962; in Rhodesia/Zimbabwe from 1965 to 1980; and in Vietnam from 1946 to 1975. But even in these cases, the struggles had complex histories, and their outcomes were influences by many local and external factors.

II. INGREDIENTS FOR A SUCCESSFUL SETTLEMENT

The definition of a successful settlement is also a matter of some debate. For some scholars, such as John Burton, the conflict termination process must produce some set of political arrangements that last for generations or withstand some other test of time. The problem with this definition is one of infinite regress; exactly when do we conclude definitively that a peace settlement has succeeded. Christopher Mitchell, on the other hand, argues that success is inherently relative and should be linked to different phases of the peace process: negotiation, settlement, implementation.

Mitchell's definition does not fully resolve the definitional problem, however. Do we define success in minimalist terms, as being associated, for example, with the onset of formal negotiations and the conclusion of an agreement? Or should we include more comprehensive criteria like the demobilization of forces, the laying down of arms, and the restoration of political order? The renunciation of violence by warring factions is clearly a necessary precondition for political order, but success in this sense is only partial. For a settlement to be durable, institutions and support structures must be in place so that the parties are actively discouraged from taking up arms again. Greater levels of success are therefore associated with the comprehensiveness and durability of the confidence-building measures that are put in place during the post-settlement or peace-building phase of an agreement.

Beyond keeping the peace itself, the list of tasks in bringing about a durable settlement includes: (1) reconstructing civil society at both the national and local level; (2) reintegrating displaced populations into society and economy; (3) redefining the role of the military and police forces in the maintenance of law and order; (4) building communities and allowing them to survive by bridging the gap between emergency assistance and development; (5) addressing the needs of particularly vulnerable sectors and groups in society such as women and children; (6) establishing the rule of law, "due process," and respect for human rights; and (7) restoring civil society and establishing participatory political institutions.

III. CULTIVATING "RIPENESS"

Given that negotiated settlements are difficult to achieve, and, as noted above, somewhat of a rarity, the question of what determines success in bringing about a restoration of domestic order and an end to civil violence is a critical one. The recent history of international relations is marked by some notable successes and some conspicuous failures in postconflict peace-building efforts directed at ending civil conflict. While some peace settlements have proven durable and have succeeded in bringing about an end to military hostilities and violence, others have failed to prevent a relapse into armed confrontation and violence, or, to transform a cease-fire into a genuine political settlement.

Some scholars argue a conflict has to reach a plateau, the level of a hurting stalemate, in order for a negotiated settlement to be successful. This occurs when the parties no longer think they can use force to gain a unilateral advantage and they become willing to consider other options. At this point, the conflict is, to use William Zartman's phrase, "ripe for resolution"; that is, the parties perceive the costs and prospects of continued confrontation to be more burdensome than the costs and prospects of a settlement (Zartman, 1985).

The ripeness thesis is problematic because the conditions associated with ripeness are difficult to find in most civil conflict situations. The concept suggests that at the point of a negotiated settlement a conflict has reached a stable equilibrium such that the parties are seriously committed to laying down their arms and embarking on a course that will lead to peace. In many low-intensity conflict situations, however, the possibility of unripening remains high even after a negotiated settlement is reached because demobilization of military forces usually only begins well after the formal agreement has been signed. The notion of ripeness wrongly implies that a conflict has reached a new, stable equilibrium at the point at which an agreement is signed. This is clearly not so. Parties may decide to negotiate an agreement as a delaying or regrouping tactic or because the agreement is forced upon them. Even if the situation is ripe, that is, it meets all of the above conditions and a new equilibrium in the conflict is reached, this new equilibrium itself may not be stable because the parties view their positions and interests differently following the signing of the agreement.

For these reasons, a successful peace process generally depends on a lot of outside help and assistance from third parties who are willing to assist with the implementation of the settlement in question. By being involved in the implementation of a peace settlement, third parties can help restore confidence, build trust, and change the perceptions and behavior of disputing parties. Third parties can facilitate conflict resolution by restructuring issues, identifying alternatives, modifying adversaries' perspectives, packaging and sequencing issues, building trust, offering side payments, or threatening penalties and sanctions. Through their intervention in the peace-making process, third parties can change disputants' perceptions of the costs, risks, and benefits associated with an agreement versus a "no agreement" situation. Third parties therefore serve as a crucial catalyst in developing a supportive relationship between adversaries and establishing the conditions that lead to not only conflict de-escalation, but also a redefinition of the conflict.

The intervention or engagement of the third party thus transforms a dyadic bargaining system into a three- or multicornered relationship in which the third party effectively becomes one of the active participants in the peace process. The tasks performed by the third party can cover a potentially wide range of functions, including meeting with stakeholders to assess their interests, helping choose spokespeople or team leaders, identifying missing groups or strategies for representing diffuse interests, drafting protocols and setting agendas, suggesting options, identifying and testing possible tradeoffs, writing and ratifying agreements, and monitoring and facilitating implementation of agreements.

Third parties can also help to restore confidence, build trust, and change the perceptions and behavior of disputing parties by assisting with technical activities such as peacekeeping and monitoring of cease-fires, which help to reduce the likelihood of armed confrontation and "accidental" encounters, and by assisting with the establishment of participatory political institutions, for example, supervising and monitoring elections, which channel the frustrations and aspirations of the politically mobilized elements of society, thus reducing the prospects of armed violence. As Brian Mandell notes, confidence-building measures are especially crucial in the early stages of a peace settlement because they can forestall a resort to the use of force by the disputants, generate additional confidence-building measures beyond those initially implemented, heighten the cost of returning to the status quo ante, and create additional incentives for collaboration (Mandell, 1990: 218). Mediation, conciliation, and arbitration by third parties can also help to resolve outstanding or unanticipated issues that emerge during the postconflict, peacebuilding phase and threaten to derail the peace process.

Who are these third parties? Typically, they include international organizations such as the UN and its associated relief and development agencies, regional organizations, great powers, regional powers, and even groupings of smaller states. By acting independently or together, in unison, these third parties can help to sustain the commitment and cooperation of the disputing parties in the overall peace-making/peace-building process. This has important implications for the long-term management and resolution of the conflict if such interventions are skillful and properly executed. The converse is also true. Clumsy and poorly timed or executed interventions can raise tensions and undermine the goals and objectives of the peace agreement and peacemaking process.

IV. INGREDIENTS OF SUCCESSFUL PEACEBUILDING

A useful first step in understanding the ingredients for successful peacebuilding is to draw a distinction between those activities that are likely to help consolidate the peace in the immediate aftermath of negotiated settlement and those activities that are likely to ensure that the peace lasts in the weeks, months, and years that follow. Some of these functions are tied to security considerations, others to social and economic concerns, and others still to governance and democratization processes and the restoration of political order and the rule of law.

A. Military and Security Challenges

It is now recognized that the military and security components of peacebuilding represent a critical and ongoing component of the peacemaking process. Peacekeeping—defined as the "use of international military personnel, either in units or as individual observers, as part of an agreed peace settlement or truce, generally to verify and monitor cease-fire lines" (McLean, 1996: 321)—continues to remain an essential element in international efforts to prevent the renewed outbreak of military hostilities and violence in a country. The early deployment of peacekeepers helps develop confidence in the peace process, but peacekeepers may also be required to stay on the job for a long time if the situation remains unstable long after the settlement is signed as we have seen with the continued deployment of peacekeeping forces in Bosnia-Herzegovina, which are there to defuse tensions and prevent the outbreak of violence among Croatian, Serbian, and Muslim communities in that country.

The actual forms and functions of peacekeeping have also varied widely over the years. Cyprus is generally viewed as the classic model of a peacekeeping operation. UNFICYP (United Nations Force in Cyprus) forces are deployed in a neutral buffer zone that separates the island's two communities. Maintenance of the buffer zone has been an important confidence-building measure and has served to prevent accidental confrontations from escalating to greater levels of conflict. Even so, UNFICYP has also been involved in a wide range of activities that go beyond military peacekeeping, including assistance with food distribution, transportation, and restoration of basic government services. Many of these functions are central components of what Adam Roberts calls the "third generation" peacekeeping operations (Roberts, 1996) or what others have called "multidimensional peacekeeping operations" that include a large nonmilitary component.

Many of these new peacekeeping operations go beyond traditional military peacekeeping to include assistance with postconflict political, economic, and social reconstruction. As William Durch notes, the mandates for these operations have been much more complex and may even include provisions to use force, if necessary, against parties who stand in the way of a settlement. The number of civilian components to these operations is also larger than the military.

Although monitoring cease-fire provisions is a key element in these new peacekeeping/peacebuilding operations, guarding polling stations, transporting refugees to resettlement areas, and assisting with the demobilization and disarmament of local forces are other key functions. The latter is especially crucial to the peace process and the implementation of a settlement. Demobilization is "the process by which the armed forces (government and/or opposition factional forces such as guerrilla armies) either downsize or completely disband" (World Bank, 1993: vi). A restructuring of the armed forces to include an "ethnically and/or politically balanced 'national army,'" may also accompany demobilization. Demobilization, disarmament, and restructuring of armed forces are politically sensitive and challenging tasks. When they are not undertaken, either because they are excluded from the negotiated settlement or because the job is done poorly, the peace process has a greater chance of breaking down than when they are.

Evidence suggests that generally successful peace settlements in recent years, such as those concluded in El Salvador, Mozambique, and Namibia, were achieved because the demobilization (in some instances only partial) of forces occurred and a major effort was made to reintegrate guerrilla factions into a reformed military and/or into society itself. Where settlements failed, as in the 1991 Bicesse accords in Angola, the suspension or collapse of demobilization plans was followed by the resumption of fighting as various parties opted out of the peace process.

The case of Cambodia illustrates both the difficulties and dilemmas of demobilization plans that go awry. Under the terms of the Paris Peace Accords for Cambodia, the United Nations was to demobilize and disarm 70% of the each of the four factional armies and supervise the activities of the remainder prior to elections for a new constituent assembly. To help with this task, UNTAC (United Nations Transitional Authority in Cambodia) deployed nearly 16,000 military personnel. However, the Khmer Rouge's refusal to participate in the peace process and its repeated delays in meeting cantonment, demobilization, and disarmament schedules led to the eventual suspension of the second phase of the demobilization program, leaving more than half a million Cambodians still armed. Although legitimate national elections were held in an atmosphere that was generally free of violence and political intimidation, the inability to complete the demobilization plan mandated in the Paris agreements has plagued the restoration of civilian rule in Cambodia ever since.

The absence of comprehensive demobilization and disarmament provisions in the 1995 Dayton Peace Accords in Bosnia, which allows for the continued existence of three armies in Bosnia-Herzegovina—one in the Serb Republic and two others in loose association in the Muslim-Croat federation—has had an adverse impact on the long-term future of peace process in that country. Although integration of the forces of all sides into a single, unified military structure is political unfeasible, the high levels of armaments poses a threat to stability if the political situation were to deteriorate and fighting resume.

Demobilization and reintegration are key peacebuilding objectives, but achieving them is highly political process and one that is ultimately linked to the terms of the political settlement itself and the commitment of previously warring parties to those terms. As a major study by the World Bank notes: "Because DRP [demobilization and reintegration of military personnel] is essentially a political process, particularly in countries emerging from civil strife, the first step in determining whether investment in reintegration programs is warranted would be to assess the strength of the political settlement preceding demobilization and the commitment of a key stakeholder, the military. Appropriate economic incentives (such as demobilization allowance and targeted reintegration programs) can *facilitate* the DRP process, but sufficient political incentives are key to determining whether demobilization will succeed" (World Bank, 1993: 95).

B. "Proxy Governance"

A second priority for peacebuilding lies in the area of what might be termed "proxy governance" undertakings. Most civil conflicts usually take a severe toll on the administrative and fiscal capacity of the state and its various institutions. Not only do such institutions lack political legitimacy in the form of trust and support from the people, but they often have difficulty performing basic administrative tasks and providing essential services to the people. Restoring the functional capacity of the state, specifically, getting an operational civil service, a workable judicial system, and a reformed police force, are key challenges of peacebuilding. By taking over some of the key administrative functions of the state until local authorities are able to perform them themselves, outside third parties (including nongovernmental organizations and various international agencies) can help with the administration and governance of the state, thus contributing to a more stable social, political, and economic order. Such activities, however, should not be confused with the much bigger task of nation-building about which most third parties are neither enthusiastic nor willing to commit resources and political capital. Jump-starting a state by assisting with various governance functions for a limited period of time is not the same as trying to drive it.

The term "proxy" describes these various governance functions, because third parties, typically the UN and other international actors, are temporary stand-ins for local authorities who may be unable or unwilling to perform these activities themselves. Certainly, it is desirable that within a relatively short span of time these responsibilities are turned over to local officials once the situation has stabilized and local authorities have the resources and personnel to provide these services themselves.

In Cambodia, the proxy governance functions undertaken by UNTAC were extensive. The elections for a new Cambodian government were organized by UN-TAC. UNTAC's civil administration unit also managed those government bodies or agencies perceived to be vulnerable to outside manipulation and, therefore, able to influence the election process including foreign affairs, national defense, finance, information, and public security. UNTAC relinquished its monitoring functions over these bodies once the new government had been formed. A similar devolution of control to third parties occurred in Mozambique where the UN for a time was also extensively engaged in a wide range of proxy governance undertakings during the implementation of the peace settlement.

In Namibia, the United Nations Special Representative also had extensive review powers over the activities of the local South African Administrator-General and helped draft electoral laws and plans for a Constituent Assembly. ONUSAL's (UN Observer Mission in El Salvador) involvement in helping with the reform of the judiciary, political institutions, armed forces, and police in El Salvador was quite extensive as well, going beyond its initial mandate. Various UN agencies such as UNDP (United Nations Development Programme), FAO (Food and Agricultural Organization), and UNHCR (UN High Commissioner for Refugees) also played key roles in helping El Salvador with its social, political, and economic reforms.

As the difficulties that were experienced by UNTAC's Civil Administration component in Cambodia indicate, however, proxy governance is a difficult undertaking and successful implementation can be hindered by a lack of resources and adequate numbers of personnel; delays in deployment; a third party's lack of familiarity with local conditions, culture, and forms of government; and the lack of a cease-fire, which can upset timetables and thwart cooperation among the parties at other levels. The situation in El Salvador, where the UN was criticized by some for overstaying its welcome, illustrates this risk. Furthermore, if outsiders become too intrusive, they may actually weaken local infrastructure and rehabilitation elements rather than strengthening them. It is important to set clear and realistic peacekeeping and peacebuilding mandates that are sensitive to local conditions, that do not compromise local sovereignty and autonomy unduly, and that limit intervention to functional areas where the need is compelling and mandates can be properly executed. Otherwise, outside efforts to develop local governance structures will be counterproductive and possibly self-defeating.

C. Establishing Democracy and the Rule of Law

The third major challenge of peacebuilding is in the area of democratic development and the establishment of the rule of law. This is perhaps the most problematic aspect of peacebuilding, not only because it raises delicate questions about state sovereignty and how far local actors are prepared to allow outsiders to shape domestic institutions and political practices, but also because the issue goes right to the core of the relationship between peace and democracy and whether a stable political order must also necessarily be a "just" one.

One of the major findings of social scientists who have examined the relationship between peace and democracy in recent years is that there is a strong, positive statistical correlation between peace and democratic political institutions: Democratic states are more likely to be internally stable and less likely to engage in wars with other democratic states. However, the relationship between peace and democratization is far more problematic. As Edward Mansfield and Jack Snyder note in a major new study, there is also a strong statistical correlation between states undergoing the transition to democracy and the outbreak of war: "[C]ountries do not become mature democracies overnight. More typically, they go through a rocky transitional period, where democratic control over foreign policy is partial, where mass politics mixes in a volatile way with authoritarian elite politics, and where democratization suffers reversals. In this transitional phase of democratization, countries become more aggressive and war-prone, not less, and they do fight wars with democratic states" (Mansfield and Snyder, 1995: 5). The reasons for this lie in the processes of competitive mass mobilization and elite appeals for political support that are typically based on a volatile mix of ideology and nationalism.

Mansfield and Snyder's findings have important implications for peacebuilding efforts that are aimed at promoting democracy via activities such as elections, the formation of political parties, and the creation of participatory governance structures. In the unstable social, economic and political environment of societies that are coming out of a civil war, a too-rapid shift to democracy may actually prove counterproductive if pressures for political participation cannot be accommodated by newly created political institutions. The result may be greater levels of political instability and with it the increased likelihood of intercommunal violence and war.

The decision about when to hold elections illustrates some these risks. In some circumstances, an election can become a deadline for an ethnic plebiscite. A poorly prepared and inadequately supervised election in Angola in 1992 was a major factor contributing to escalated warfare. Separate elections in the republics of Yugoslavia in 1990 empowered ethnic nationalists and paved the way for intercommunal warfare that led to the breakup of the federated union. In Rwanda, Hutu extremists used the excuse of upcoming elections mandated by the 1993 Arusha Accords to launch a brutal genocidal campaign against civilian Tutsis because they feared losing power to this minority.

Democratization efforts (either those sponsored externally or promoted indigenously) need not have calamitous results, however, if attention is paid to proper timing, that is, laying the groundwork, and to pairing elections with power-sharing formulas that are acceptable to all parties and that provide a safety net such that politics does not become a zero-sum game. Unless there is some form of compensation, those who lose at the ballot box will have a strong incentive to take up arms and resort to force to achieve their political objectives. The lack of a power-sharing arrangement is one reason why the 1991 Bicesse Accords in Angola fell apart. In contrast, the elections that followed the peace settlement in Cambodia resulted in a coalition government between the ruling Cambodian People's Party (CPP) and the United National Front for an Independent, Neutral, Peaceful, and Cooperative Cambodia (FUNCINPEC), which had won the popular vote. This was because the parties recognized early on that a coalition government was necessary to appease rival factions and advance the process of national reconciliation.

In arguing for the importance of looking to power-sharing arrangements to moderate the winner-take-all elements of the democratic political process, we must recognize that there is no single formula or preferred model that can be taken "off the shelf" and applied to a given country. Power-sharing arrangements have historically been marked by a wide range of practices and approaches, each arrived at indigenously. Arrangements which are imposed from the outside typically do not work as well as those which are developed internally and that are tailored to local conditions. The power-sharing formula devised by British, Greek, and Turkish authorities for Cyprus in the 1960 Zurich-London Accords, for example, resulted in a constitution that was too rigid to accommodate the conflicting demands of Greek majority rule and Turkish minority rights. Power-sharing also has a greater potential for laying the groundwork for democratic practices and institutions when it is embraced by moderate political leaders who are flexible and adaptable in addressing conflicts between contending communal interests as we have seen in Malaysia and most recently in post-apartheid South Africa.

Power-sharing is also a temporary political device and not a substitute for constitution writing. Power-sharing seldom lasts beyond the first election. For settlements to be durable, societies have to take longer range steps. The longer term problem is the rebuilding of a police force and the development and reform of the judiciary. Civil society cannot thrive without them.

Turning to the issue of human rights, it is a sad truism that one of the unfortunate characteristics of civil wars is that atrocities and violations of human rights are all too common. The security institutions of the state, that is, the armed forces and the police, are usually suspect because they are seen as instruments of coercion by the state against its people. Reform of these institutions is usually fundamental to the peace process and the consolidation of democratic reforms, but the dismantling and/or reform of these institutions can lead to an increase in anarchy and violence in a society that is unaccustomed to the rule of law and where elites feel threatened and vulnerable. Similar problems face reform of the judiciary and legal system, which are seen as instruments of repression and state-sponsored violence and whose overhaul is essential. Yet, if a new social order based on the rule of law and accepted principles of justice is to be fashioned, respect for human rights and due process must be nurtured.

The creation of international war crimes tribunals is one response to assigning responsibility for those who have committed human rights abuses in the past. This option requires instituting an impartial international criminal forum before which to hold individuals accused of atrocities legally accountable. The advantage of such an approach is that it may serve as a deterrent to future atrocities, provide closure for victims and/or their families and relatives, individualize guilt, create an historical record, and strengthen respect for human rights norms in the community-at-large. The principal disadvantage with this approach, however, is that international tribunals have not had the power to arrest or detain suspected war criminals. As the experience of the Yugoslav and Rwandan Tribunals illustrates, the international community is not yet prepared to enforce the decisions of international criminal tribunals, thus limiting their potential for success.

A second approach is to create international human rights commissions, which are impartial bodies that investigate wartime and postwar atrocities. These commissions are composed of experts from the international community and sometimes representatives from different local factions. The purpose of such commissions is to collect evidence and document human rights abuses in order to lay the basis for possible future legal action.

Finally, a third approach is to establish an impartial investigative forum, known as a truth commission, which is not empowered for criminal prosecution but through which individuals are granted legal amnesty if they fully disclose information concerning their involvement in wartime atrocities and other gross human rights violations. This is approach taken by the truth commission in South Africa. In other instances, a truth commission may collect this information and publicly disclose the names of perpetrators of human rights abuses without their consent as was case in El Salvador where the truth commission ignored government demands not to publish the names of individuals who had committed atrocities or violated human rights. Although the form of truth commissions varies, all truth commissions have historically shared a common set of objectives: to create an historical record of abuses in order to lay the foundation for national reconciliation without the potentially divisive ramification of criminal trials; and to individualize guilt for atrocities, thereby contributing to the potential for national reconciliation among the various groups who were parties to the conflict.

Early attention to human rights in the negotiation and implementation of a peace settlement can also advance the peace process. In El Salvador, the deployment of ONUSAL's human rights monitoring team before the fighting had ended and the final accords were signed helped instill a sense of confidence among Salvador's warring parties in the nascent peace process. ONUSAL investigated cases and situations involving human rights violations and followed up these investigations with relevant bodies in the government. It also developed regional and local contacts with the main political, judicial, and military authorities and maintained an ongoing contact with FMLN (Farabundo Marti Liberation Front) leaders inside the country. By working closely with local human rights organizations ONUSAL was also able to design a human rights program for the armed forces, a group responsible for some of the worst human rights abuses in the country. By putting parties on notice that certain actions and behaviors will not be tolerated and that human rights violators will be dealt with accordingly, third parties can help advance the cause of justice. The El Salvador experience illustrates that the early promotion of human rights can also serve as an important confidence-building measure before a formal negotiated settlement is reached.

In any peace settlement, however, there is a significant political tension between conflict resolution and the promotion of human rights, judicial reform, and the development of legal systems governed by due process. Peace and justice do not always work in tandem. The need to establish power-sharing structures that accommodate rival factions and interests may well clash with the desires of some to root out the perpetrators of human rights abuses. Similarly, the need to reform the security institutions of the state, including the police and military, may be at odds with the practical need to bring those groups who wield power and have a monopoly on the instruments of coercion in a society into the peace process. Without peace there can be no justice. Without justice, democratic institutions, and the development of the rule of law, the peace itself will not last. But the political requirements for reaching a peace settlement may well clash with the desire to lay the foundations for long-term democratic stability. Which model works best when and where: the power sharing, conflict managers model or the democratizers, political justice model? Evidence suggests that a concern for justice must be tempered by the realities of negotiation and the parties' interests in reaching a political settlement.

In Cambodia, for example, implementation of the human rights provisions in the Paris Peace Accords was weak not only because of the practical difficulties of implementation, but also because "more vigorous pursuit of human rights goals ran the risk of upsetting the delicate political balance that was necessary for election to take place." Moreover, in "a country with a history of human rights abuses that approached genocide, it was going to be an uphill task to educate the population, to develop indigenous human rights organizations, and most important, to develop mechanisms that would truly protect the peoples from human rights abuses" (Heininger, 1994: 39). That being said, by opting out of the elections, the Khmer Rouge, which was guilty of the worst human rights in Cambodia, isolated itself and weakened its own political position.

In contrast, in El Salvador there was great sensitivity to the need to address human rights problems at the outset of the peace process by all parties. The success of the peace process is largely attributable to the fact that political reform was linked to the promotion of human rights and the principle of accountability for those who were guilty of the worst human rights abuses. However, given the volatile conditions in El Salvador and the fact that the local efforts to investigate human rights abuses were unfeasible and not credible, the solution was to rely on international authorities to evaluate and assess the evidence assembled by local interests. The Truth Commission helped develop greater confidence in the peace process and efforts to reform the judicial system and the security institutions of the state, even though not all of its recommendations were implemented. The slow pace of judicial reform reflects the fact that there continue to remain significant obstacles to such reforms.

In the peace process in Namibia following externally supervised elections for a constituent assembly all parties recognized the need to develop strong democratic institutions based on the rule of law which simultaneously entrenched minority rights in the constitution. In El Salvador human rights problems were initially addressed via the formation of a truth commission that identified perpetrators of the most egregious human rights abuses. In Cambodia the question of accountability and how to prosecute those responsible for war crimes under the Pot Pot regime was a difficult and controversial one. It was not clear to Cambodia's leaders whether an attempt to put Khmer Rouge leaders on trial for war crimes, genocide, and crimes against humanity would advance the process of national reconciliation or further radicalize the Khmer Rouge and jeopardize political stability. Ultimately, the Cambodian government decided to grant amnesty to some senior members of the Khmer Rouge leadership, thus opting for a course that put political stability—some would say expediency—ahead of accountability for war crimes and genocide in the order of national priorities.

The problem in any settlement is not how to resolve the theoretical tension between human rights, democracy, and power sharing, but how to work with the parties themselves who may be reluctant to push the frontiers of the human rights envelope too far. The challenge for third parties is to advance the cause of human rights without undermining the settlement itself and to foster institutional mechanisms that will advance human rights and democratic development once the political situation has stabilized. Third parties can play a critical role in investigating human rights abuses and other war crimes and evaluating evidence assembled by local authorities before arrests are made. In the fragile political climate that exists following a settlement, the temptation for retribution and revenge are considerable. International commissions and tribunals bring the necessarily element of impartiality that is required to restore faith in the judicial process and the rule of law. It is both unwise and unreasonable to expect parties to be able to reestablish the rule of law and due process on their own. This is therefore one of the most important areas of peacebuilding a priority for outside, third party involvement in the peace process.

D. Social and Economic Challenges

Another main challenge of peacebuilders is to rebuild and reconstruct society for long-term peace and stability. There is a vital link between sturdy civic institutions, including the norms and networks of civic engagement, and the performance of representative government. Not only is civil society important to democracy, but it also has an important role to play in consolidating the peace process in societies making the transition from war to peace. International development agencies and nongovernmental organizations (NGOs) have a pivotal contribution to make to this particular aspect of postconflict peacebuilding.

Economic reconstruction involving major infrastructure projects takes months to plan, years to implement, and a level of resources that most NGOs are not in a position to provide. Hence the World Bank and the regional banks, like the Inter-American Development Bank, have a crucial role to play, providing loans and lines of credit and coordinating reconstruction aid. The coordination of donor efforts is increasingly recognized as a fundamental ingredient for success, even though it is difficult to achieve because of turf battles among competing agencies. Leadership is necessary to establish priorities in social and economic reconstruction efforts and to channel scarce resources. But donor-country and greater levels of NGO cooperation will accomplish little unless the security environment is conducive to reconstruction. Reconstruction and development require a threshold level of security and political order to take hold. While some projects can promote confidence-building and improve social relations at the community level, others may worsen social and political relations if certain groups are "privileged" because they are seen to be getting scarce resources at the expense of others. Development assistance programs have to be developed with great care and sensitivity to local conditions if they are to be effective in advancing the peace process.

There are various views about when and how donors should become involved in the peacebuilding process. Nicole Ball argues that "During the negotiation phase, a relatively modest amount of resources should be devoted to planning and to building collaborative relationships with the parties to the conflict. The speed with which events occur once peace agreements are signed argues very strongly in favor donor involvement at the earliest possible moment in the peace process" (Ball, 1996: 613). One of the principal reasons why Ball feels that donors should play a larger role in the negotiation process is that this allows economic issues to be dealt with in a "realistic manner" and helps to downgrade expectations by determining what levels of assistance will be available and forthcoming from potential donors. Ball also recognizes the importance of tying economic and development assistance and programs in war-torn societies to a *negotiated* peace settlement. This further underscores the point made above that peacebuilding activities cannot and should not be carried out in a political vacuum. The real test is whether the parties to the conflict themselves are willing to live up to the terms of a negotiated political settlement and to allow postconflict reconstruction efforts to move forward. If they are not, then all the outside assistance in the world is likely to achieve little in helping with the tasks of social and economic reconstruction.

V. CONCLUSION

This article has argued that constitutes a successful peace settlement in today's world is problematic, particularly in the context of a negotiated settlement that is directed at ending civil conflict or intercommunal violence. For some, the peacebuilding process must produce some set of arrangements that lasts for years (perhaps generations) or stands some other test of time, demonstrating robustness and permanence. The problem with this definition is one of infinite regress—that is, exactly when do we conclude definitively that a peace settlement has succeeded? We cannot because the prospect of failure may lie just around the corner. Success is inherently relative and it is perhaps more useful (certainly in operational terms) to link success to different phases or stages of the peace process. Because the renunciation of violence by warring factions is clearly a necessary precondition for the restoration of political order, the definition of success begins with the ending of civil violence and armed confrontation. But success, in this sense, is only partial. For a settlement to be durable, institutions and support structures must be put in place so that the parties are discouraged from taking up arms again. Greater levels of success are thus associated with the comprehensiveness and durability of confidence-building measures that are put in place during the postsettlement, that is, peacebuilding, phase.

The ultimate success of the peacebuilding process in situations of civil conflict is thus directly related to a society's ability to make the transition from a state of war to a state of peace marked by the restoration of civil order, the reemergence of civil society, and the establishment of participatory political institutions. However, we must recognize that this process takes many years and that the democratization process is fraught with risk. These risks are not insurmountable, but prudence is desirable. The fact that we now seem to be entering a period of diminished expectations about the prospects and possibilities of peacebuilding should not deter us from the challenges of rebuilding war-torn societies. Not only can outside third parties, both governmental and nongovernmental, to use the proverbial phrase "make a difference," but the demands for such assistance are likely to grow, not diminish, in the years ahead.

In those instances where a workable settlement was reached, such as El Salvador, Mozambique, or Namibia, third parties made a critical contribution to the peace process by helping not only with the negotiation but also the implementation of the agreement in question. On the other hand, in those instances where the peace process clearly failed, such as in Angola in 1992, failure was associated with a lack of adequate third party support and involvement during the peace process. If settlements aimed at ending civil conflict are to take root, third parties must entrench and institutionalize their role in the peacemaking/peace-building process. They must also have staying power and remain fully engaged in the negotiations which lead up to the settlement and the implementation of the agreement in question.

Also See the Following Articles

CIVIL WARS • CONFLICT MANAGEMENT AND RESOLUTION • ECONOMIC CONVERSION • HUMAN RIGHTS • MEDIATION, ARBITRATION, AND NEGOTIATION • PEACE AND DEMOCRACY • PEACEKEEPING • PEACEMAKING AND PEACEBUILDING • WAR CRIMES

Bibliography

Akhavan, P. (1996, May). The Yugoslav tribunal at a crossroads: The Dayton Peace Agreement and beyond. *Human Rights Quarterly, 18,* (2), 259–285.

Azar, E. E. (1990). *The management of protracted social conflict: Theory and cases.* Hampshire, UK: Dartmouth Publishing Ltd.

Bailey, S. D. (1969). *Peaceful settlement of international disputes.* New York: UNITAR, 1969.

Baker, P. H. (1996). Conflict resolution versus democratic governance: Divergent paths to peace. In C. A. Crocker and F. O. Hampson, *Managing global chaos: Sources of and responses to international conflict,* pp. 563–572. Washington, DC: United States Institute of Peace Press.

Ball, N. (1996). The challenge of rebuilding war-torn societies. In C. A. Crocker & F. O. Hampson (Eds.), *Managing global chaos: Sources of and responses to international conflict.* Washington, DC: United States Institute of Peace Press.

Bercovitch, J. (1985, Autumn). Third parties in conflict management: The structure and the conditions of effective mediation in international relations. *International Journal, 37,* (4), 736–752.

Bercovitch, J. (1984). *Social conflicts and third parties: Strategies of conflict resolution.* Boulder, CO: Westview.

Burton, J. (1990). *Conflict resolution and provention.* New York: St. Martin's.

Diehl, P. F. (1987, Winter). When peace-keeping does not lead to peace: Some notes on conflict resolution. *Bulletin of Peace Proposals, 18,* (1), 47–53.

Diehl, P. F. (1988, Autumn). Peace-keeping operations and the quest for peace. *Political Science Quarterly, 103,* (3), 485–507.

Doyle, M. (1996, December). Liberalism and world politics. *American Political Science Review, 80,* (4), 1151–1169.

Durch, W. J. (Ed.). (1993). *The evolution of U.N. peacekeeping.* New York: St. Martin's.

Durch, W. J., (Ed.). (1996). *UN peacekeeping, American policy, and the uncivil wars of the 1990s.* New York: St. Martin's.

Gurr, R. T. (1993). *Minorities at risk: A global view of ethnopolitical conflicts.* Washington, DC: United States Institute of Peace Press.

Haass, R. N. (1990). *Conflicts unending: The United States and regional disputes.* New Haven: Yale University Press.

Hampson, F. O. (1990, Spring). Building a stable peace: Opportunities and limits to security cooperation in Third World regional conflicts. *International Journal, 45* (2), 454–489.

Hampson, F. O. (1996a). *Nurturing peace: Why peace settlements succeed or fail.* Washington, DC: United States Institute of Peace Press.

Hampson, F. O. (1996b). The pursuit of human rights: The United Nations in El Salvador. In W. J. Durch (Ed.), *UN peacekeeping, American policy, and the uncivil wars of the 1990s,* pp. 69–102. New York: St. Martin's.

Hanning, Husch., (Ed.). (1985). *Peacekeeping and confidence-building measures in the Third World.* New York: International Peace Academy.

Heininger, J. (1994). *Peacekeeping in transition: The United Nations in Cambodia.* New York: The Twentieth Century Fund Press.

Holsti, K. J. (1991). *Peace and war: Armed conflicts and international order, 1648–1989.* Cambridge: Cambridge University Press.

James, A. (1969). *The politics of peacekeeping.* New York: Praeger.

Kamarotos, A. S. (1995, Winter). Building peace, democracy and human rights: International civilian missions at the end of the millenium. *International Peacekeeping, 4* (2), 483–509.

Kaufman, J. & Schrijver, N. (1990). *Changing global needs: Expanding roles for the United Nations system.* New Hampshire: Dartmouth College, The Academic Council of the United Nations System.

Keashly, L., & Fisher, R. J. (1990, Spring). Towards a contingency approach to third-party intervention in regional conflicts: A Cyprus illustration. *International Journal, 25,* (2) 424–453.

Kriesberg, L. (1989). Transforming conflicts in the Middle East and Central Europe. In L. Kriesberg, T. A. Northrup, S. J. Thorson, (Eds.), *Intractable conflicts and their transformation,* pp. 109–131. Syracuse: Syracuse University Press.

Kritz, N. J., (Ed.). (1995). *Transitional justice: How emerging democracies reckon with former regimes,* Vols. I, II, III. Washington, DC: United States Institute of Peace Press.

Lake, A. (Ed.). (1990). *After the wars.* New Brunswick: Transaction Books.

Licklider, R. (1995, September). The consequences of negotiated settlements in civil wars, 1945–1993. *American Political Science Review, 89,* (3), 685–687

Mack, T. D. (1995, Winter). The case against an international war crimes tribunal for former Yugoslavia. *International Peacekeeping, 4,* (2), 536–563.

Mandell, B. S. (1990, Spring) Anatomy of a confidence-building regime: Egyptian-Israeli security cooperation. *International Journal, 45,* (2).

Mandell, B. S. (1987). *The Sinai experience: Lessons in multimethod arms control, verification, and risk management.* Arms Control and Verification Studies No. 3. Ottawa: Arms Control and Disarmament Division: Department of External Affairs.

Mansfield, E. D., & Snyder, J. (1995, Summer). Democratization and the danger of war. *International Security, 20,* (1).

McLean, D. (1996). Peace operations and common sense. In C. A. Crocker & F. O. Hampson (Eds.), *Managing global chaos: Sources of and responses to international conflict.* Washington, DC: United States Institute of Peace Press.

Mitchell, C. R. (1989, August). Conflict resolution and civil war: Reflections on the Sudanese settlement of 1972. *Working Paper No. 3.* Center for Conflict Analysis and Resolution, George Mason University.

National Democratic Institute for International Affairs. (1990). *Nation building: The U.N. and Namibia.* Washington, DC: The National Democratic Institute for International Affairs.

Roberts, A. (1996). The crisis in UN peacekeeping. In C. A. Crocker & F. O. Hampson (Eds.), *Managing global chaos: Sources of and responses to international conflict,* pp. 297–320. Washington, DC: United States Institute of Peace Press.

Russett, B. (1993). *Grasping the democratic peace.* Princeton: Princeton University Press.

Russett, B. (1995, Spring). The democratic peace: "And Yet It Moves." *International Security, 19,* (4), 164–175.

Stedman, S. John. (1988). *Peacemaking in civil War: International Mediation in Zimbabwe, 1974–1980.* Boulder, CO: Lynne Reinner.

Sisk, T. D. (1996). *Power sharing and international mediation in ethnic conflicts.* Washington, DC: United States Institute of Peace Press.

The World Bank (1993). *Demobilization and reintegration of military personnel in Africa: The evidence from seven country case studies,* Report No. IDP-130. Washington, DC: The World Bank.

Third party intervention in regional conflict: A Cyprus illustration. *International Journal, 45,* (2) 424–453.

United Nations Institute for Disarmament Research. (1996b). *Managing arms in peace processes: Cambodia.* New York: United Nations.

United Nations Institute for Disarmament Research. (1996a). *Managing arms in peace processes: Mozambique.* New York: United Nations.

United States Institute of Peace. (1995, October). Accounting for war crimes in Cambodia. *Peace Watch, 1,* (6).

Wiseman, H. (1987). *Peacekeeping and the management of international conflict.* Ottawa: Canadian Institute for International Peace and Security.

Zartman, I. W. (1985). *Ripe for resolution: Conflict and intervention in Africa.* Oxford: Oxford University Press.

Peace and the Arts

Steven C. Dubin

Purchase College, State University of New York

When the cannons are heard, the muses are silent;
when the cannons are silent, the muses are heard.
Truman Capote, 1956

GLOSSARY

Art Creative expression in a wide range of forms, including painting and sculpture, music, dance, writing, film, and theater.
Battlefield Artists Individuals officially commissioned by their government to document combat, channel information, and boost morale.
Guernica A town in northen Spain bombed by German planes in 1937, whose casualties were immortalized in a painting by Pablo Picasso.
Oppositional Culture Anti-militaristic works of art, particularly in the 20th century.
Public Art Art designed for civic display and general audiences.

THROUGH THE CENTURIES, artists have habitually turned to *eros* and the human body for inspiration. Yet perhaps just as frequently, *thanatos*—death and destruction—have triggered their imaginations as well. These contradictory impulses buttress a significant proportion of human creative output with the subject of peace a point of mediation between the two.

The pioneering sociologist E. A. Ross declared in 1897, "In war stress the artist must be alchemist enough to turn lead into gold. Pain he must make sweet, disease comely, mutilations lovely, and death beautiful." But Ross forced artists into a creative stranglehold that only superficially reflects the variety of responses they have mobilized to violence, death, war, and peace. While Ross's description might be apt for government-sanctioned artists, it falls considerably short of capturing the complexity and scope of other artists' work.

Copyright © 1999 by Academic Press.
All rights of reproduction in any form reserved.

Artists have frequently lent support to their society's battles. But, as time has gone on, they have increasingly adopted an oppositional stance toward war and have redoubled their efforts to represent resistance and peace. There is, in other words, no singular response to these issues. In the following discussion, a preponderance of examples is drawn from the visual arts. However, "art" will be defined in the broadest manner to include other varieties of expression as well, such as music, dance, writing, film, and theater.

I. SYMBOLIC ALLEGIANCE AND RESISTANCE DURING AN AGE OF IDEOLOGY

From the Classical period until the mid-19th century, premodernist artists for the most part dutifully served their masters, be they lords of the manor or earthly agents of the Lord, those who wielded great power because of their material wealth or those whose authority derived from their state of grace. For most of recorded history, artists have typically served the needs of the community or of influential individuals; they extolled either the virtues of group life or celebrated the distinctive achievements of particular citizens. Seldom was there room for unique expression or for dissenting opinions. In other words, art in the past was largely enlisted as an ideological tool, symbolically shoring up the status quo. Consequently, battles are a familiar artistic theme.

The *Mah'bh'rata,* the naional epic of Hindu India (500–400 B.C.), pits two groups of cousins against one another in a battle of catastrophic proportions. *The Iliad,* Homer's epic poem chronicling the Greek siege of Troy, is another prime example. Similarly, the friezes on the Parthenon feature powerful bodies frozen in time with battle scenes paramount: the sacking of Troy, for instance, or Greeks fighting Amazons or Centaurs and gods combating giants. Furthermore, the majestic stone friezes that once adorned the walls of such powerful Assyrian cities as ancient Nineveh and Nimrud also depict successful military campaigns and the plundering of conquered neighboring peoples.

The mausoleum at Halicarnassus (359–351 B.C.) repeats the motifs of Greeks fighting Amazons and Lapiths battling Centaurs, and even some of the haunting remains of 1st century B.C. mosaics from Pompeii commemorate massive scenes of conflict. And to cite merely one more example from an enormous archaic archive, the *Column of Trajan* (erected 106–113 A.D.) is a monumental remnant of Imperial Rome, a 125-foot high column commemorating victory over the Dacians with reliefs spiraling around its entire height. It depicts the extensive preparation for battle as well as its enactment. In general, it is impossible for moderns to conjure up images of these times *without* envisioning war.

Leaping through history, the *Bayeux Tapestry* (ca. 1073–1083), is a 230-foot-long embroidered frieze of wool on linen composed of 72 compartments or scenes. It illustrates William the Conquerer's Norman invasion of England, culminating with the Battle of Hastings. It was probably assembled by the ladies of William's court and with the assistance of the conquered Saxons. A complex narrative interweaving fables, analogy, and reportage unfolds between the top and bottom borders and the main panels. The work culminates in a chaotic scene of English and French soldiers and their horses tumbling over one another, a slaughter that litters the lower border with bodies. In the last scene, the English turn in flight; peace is not depicted, although damage at the edges indicates that some additional scenes—presumably of the Norman triumph—may be missing.

Whether it be tribes of men at war, gods versus mortals, or even men clashing with mythological creatures, therefore, recording the fight has been the main event in so much art of the past. A slight counterbalance to these heroics is a genre depicting the wounded or dying warrior, the human story within the larger drama. But for the most part, the individual costs of war have been subsumed under considerations of the greater glory of the community.

Some notable exceptions exist. For example, the comedy *Lysistrata* by Aristophanes (41 B.C.) presents what may well be the first successful antiwar campaign. Women accomplish what men have been unable to do: broker peace between Athens, Sparta, and other enemy states. Their strategy is twofold. First, they pledge to withold sex as long as hostilities continue. And second, the women seize the Acropolis and arrange a peace conference. Female shrewdness trumps male prowess in this instance. Moreover, the *Ara Pacis Augustae* (the Altar of Peace, completed 9 B.C.) is a monumental altar built in Rome during the reign of Augustus, an era of peace and prosperity. It presents an imperial procession and offers mythological and allegorical images to connect the Emperor to the founding of Rome, thereby establishing divine origins. One panel displays a mother gently tending two infants, a figure that has sometimes been identified as Pax. A cow and a sheep rest contentedly at her feet, and an overturned water jug has been interpreted as the Augustan peace overflowing the land.

(This imagery has a contemporary analog: the Franklin D. Roosevelt memorial, dedicated in Washington, DC in May, 1997, has a section entitled "The Seeds of Peace," featuring a waterfall cascading into a series of pools). Similarly, the edicts of the great king A'oka (ca. 269–232 B.C.) are found throughout India, engraved upon pillars (or *lats*) crowned with animals, tablets, and other surfaces. Once a fierce warrior, A'oka counsels his subjects to practice nonviolence within these public Buddhist displays.

Ambrogio Lorenzetti's *Good and Bad Government* (1338–1340), a fresco series covering three walls of the Palazzo Pubblico in Siena, Italy, also depicts the advantages of peace. Lorenzetti's panorama presents a bustling, prosperous, and well-ordered city, complemented by a view of the outlying verdant vineyards and olive groves. This affluence and abundance is overseen by Pax, identified with the designation *Securitas* around her head. She holds a scroll indicating the blessings of

peace, while over her head a criminal swings from a gallows, indicating that peace means security, contingent upon the enforcement of laws. Pax is crucial to the stability that allows this burgeoning activity, a chamber-of-commerce view of what peace yields. And in another section, she lounges casually against a pillow, wearing a comfortably flowing gown. Soon after this cycle of paintings was completed, they were referred to as *War and Peace*.

A further conspicuous example is *The Peaceable Kingdom* by Edward Hicks (1780–1849), a Bucks County, Pennsylvania Quaker preacher who earned his living as a coach maker and a sign painter, but who also painted allegorical and historical themes (Fig. 1). More to the point, we should say Hicks provides notable *counterexamples*: he painted about 100 versions of an Edenic paradise with scores of species peacefully coexisting, a perfect world illustrating *Isaiah* 11: 6–8, commonly quoted as "The lion shall lie down with the

FIGURE 1 Pennsylvania Quaker preacher Edward Hicks painted one hundred versions of *The Peaceable Kingdom*, a 19th-century vision of harmony and brotherly love. (Courtesy of Philadelphia Museum of Art.)

lamb." Here the categories predator and prey are no longer apropos, embodying the Quaker doctrine of pacifism and affirming the tenet of brotherly love.

Hicks is an exception to the general rule in two regards: he was not producing for wealthy or powerful patrons and the strength of his particular religious beliefs set him somewhat apart from the mainstream. Nevertheless, artists in general have gradually taken a critical step backward from their own times in order to frankly depict the horrors of war.

Pieter Brueguel the Elder's 1567 engraving *Fight of the Money-bags and the Strong-boxes* makes explicit the connection between waging war and gathering plunder; war is not merely to defend ideals, but also to line some peoples' pockets. Jacques Callot's (1592/3–1635) magisterial *Les Grandes Misères de la Guerre* (1633) chronicles the enormous death and destruction wrought by Richelieu's invasion of Lorraine during the Thirty Years' War. Goya later used these etchings as a source for his own critique of war. And an anonymous 1635 etching *Peasant Uprising* (1635), commemorating a German rebellion 10 years earlier when over 100,000 peasants were murdered, shows clumps of bodies dangling from the three trees where they have been hanged, "strange fruit" to borrow the title of a 20th century book and song decrying the lynching of African-Americans.

But it is arguably the work of Francisco de Goya y Lucientes (1746–1828) that ushers in the modern critical sensibility toward war that is common today. His series of 82 etchings entitled *Los Desastres de la Guerra* (*The Disasters of War*, 1810–1820) expresses Goya's outrage at the barbarism displayed by the French invaders of Spain. His notation "Yo lo ví" ("This I saw") underneath one of the plates reveals Goya's unrefutable eyewitness status, as does the passion with which he records the relentless cruelty of the French soldiers— hanging, maiming, raping, and torturing their Spanish victims in an orgy of violence. And his extraordinary oil painting *May 3rd, 1808* presents a queue of eight French executioners with bayoneted rifles, a wall of methodically trained infantrymen acting in unison, staring down a group of Madrileños. The scene is dramatically lit by a lantern on the ground, spotlighting a white-shirted prisoner, wild-eyed with terror, with his arms spread aloft, echoing a crucifiction. The man at the center is obviously about to be shot, dead bodies already litter the foreground, and a column of others likely await the same fate.

This painting chillingly anticipates images of cold-blooded massacres that 20th century artists have repeatedly captured, as does Edouard Manet's (1832–1883) *Execution of Maximilian* (1867), which presents another scene of point-blank execution. And the prolific French satirist Honoré Daumier (1808–1879) explored similar territory, with lithographs such as *Rue Transnonain, April 15, 1834* [a man looks as though he might be sleeping off a drunken stupor, until you notice a dead child half-hidden beneath his nightshirt and other bodies scattered about, all victims of a violent police raid (1834)] and *Peace, an Idyl* [a skeleton surveys a devastated landscape, oddly bedecked with a bonnet, and gaily playing two horns (1871)]. Goya, Manet, and Daumier, along with many other contemporary artists, present their most forceful pleas for peace by exposing the horrors of war.

II. BATTLEFIELD ARTISTS AND THE MOBILIZATION OF POPULAR SENTIMENT

Rulers and government officials have frequently commissioned artists to record the battlefield experiences of their armies, in many instances removed in space and time from actual events. And although their media and equipment may have changed, numbers of artists have willingly shouldered this responsibility in different periods. It is in this role that artists come closest to fulfilling the mandate that E. A. Ross defined for them near the turn of the century. But he failed to foresee the range of contributions artists have made to the conduct of war, including (1) documentation of events; (2) boosting of morale; (3) facilitating recruitment; (4) circulating crucial information to civilians; and (5) designing camouflage for military positions. During those 20th-century conflicts for which there has been popular consensus, artists, too, have lent their support through drawing, painting, sculpture, posters, editorial cartoons, photography, literature, and film.

Writing in 1919, A. E. Gallatin noted that World War I (the "Great War") was the first instance where artists were mobilized *en masse*, just as citizens of all types contributed to this modern, "total war." Artists heeded the official call in England, France, Canada, Italy, and Australia. American artists joined in, too, but they were accorded formal status much later than their colleagues in these other countries, and the number of positions granted to them was extremely small. Gallatin observed that what these artists produced differed in two fundamental respects from preceding epochs. First, the instruments of war changed so dramatically due to industrialization that it was no longer as possible to capture the individual heroics of warriors locked in hand-to-hand combat, as in the Classical period. And second, the horrors of the trenches rendered absurd the sort of pageantry that marked battles in medieval times.

Artists during WWI were confronted with a scale and ferocity of destruction that exceeded previous conflagrations, creating a baptism by fire which spawned an extremely large creative output. Exhibits of such work included a display at the Arts Club of Washington, DC, April, 1919 of sketches made by the camouflage unit and the Allied War Salon in New York City, December, 1918, which contained over 800 items, including 200 drawings by the eight official American war artists working in France, work by homefront artists, French and British artists, and posters and sculpture as well. For observers such as Sir William Orpen, the war had a positive impact upon art. In *The Outline of Art* he noted that it weaned young artists from their dependence upon experimentation and the pursuit of the "isms" of countless art movements; it drew them out of themselves and thrust them into a public role: "Not only did the War restore to sanity many of the most promising of the younger artists," he remarked, "it also prepared the public to accept and understand their works."

The mobilization of creative individuals was even larger during World War II. In Great Britain, for example, over 300 artists were employed by the War Artists' Advisory Committee; an overview of what they produced was assembled for a 1941 exhibition at New York City's Museum of Modern Art. There a visitor could see a watercolor of the twisted remains of a salt factory in Birmingham destroyed by German bombs; view a drawing of a British crew in action with a six-inch gun; and examine photographs of mine-sweeping flotillas, portraits of fighter pilots, and pictures of civilians anxiously waiting out air raids in shelters and caves. (In the catalog there was also a poem," *Defense of the Islands*," penned by T. S. Eliot.)

In the United States, New York City-based artist Sidney Simon helped organize the War Art Unit of the Army in 1942, which dispatched artists to accompany fighting units and record what they witnessed. When Congress cut off funds to the unit, many of the artists were picked up by *Life* magazine, and they eventually produced more than 3000 oil paintings, watercolors, and drawings of war scenes. Abbott Laboratories was another private sponsor, underwriting the work that culminated in the collection *Men Without Guns*. The title refers to the United States Army Medical Department, and the artwork focused on the care of casualties, including work by such notables as John Steuart Curry

and Peter Blume. As DeWitt Mackenzie assured readers on the first page of his introduction to the book by the same title, "[W]hile the good news will far outweigh the bad in this chronicle, you will be told the truth as we know it."

In 1943, Artists for Victory, a nonprofit organization representing over 10,000 painters, sculptors, designers, and printmakers that expedited the use of artistic talent by government agencies and private industry engaged in defense work, sponsored an unprecedented "America in the War" exhibition: the same selection of prints opened simultaneously in 26 museums across the United States, highlighting such themes as "Heroes of the Fighting Front," "Heroes of the Home Front," "The Enemy," and "The Victory and Peace to Follow." And in 1945, the National Gallery of Art in Washington, DC sponsored a 215-piece show and book of *Soldier Art*, with a strong emphasis on off-duty scenes: the photograph *Tuck Edgerton—Flying Low,* for example, captures an African-American soldier performing an aerial split in front of a band.

In the main, the official war art from WWI and WWII stemmed from the belief that art was a significant adjunct to the mobilization for combat. Artists had their specific roles to play, just as did foot soldiers and "Rosie the Riveters"; the quantity as well as the quality of what they produced confirms that they fulfilled their duties eagerly. This *esprit de corps* even trickled down into the realm of popular culture, where cartoon favorites such as Donald Duck (jeering Hitler in *Der Fuhrer's Face*, paying increased income taxes in *The New Spirit*, or gathering metal in *Get in the Scrap*), Bugs Bunny (bearing arms against the Axis Powers in *Super Rabbit*), Superman (battling Japanese industrial spies), and the Seven Dwarfs (doffing public health hats to instruct soldiers how to avoid contracting malaria) distinctively pitched in.

The Disney Studios in particular retooled to create educational and propaganda material, most importantly producing *Victory Through Air Power* (1943), a combination animation and live-action feature highlighting the history of aviation. And Hollywood in general turned its attention to bolstering the war effort, from Frank Capra's seven-part orientation series *Why We Fight* (providing servicemen with background regarding how the democratic way of life was being threatened), to mass-market movies such as *Blockade* (the Spanish Civil War), *Mrs. Miniver* (the Battle of Britain), *The North Star* (Russia's struggle against the Nazi invasion), *Thirty Seconds Over Tokyo, Guadalcanal Diary, The Great Dictator, God Is My Co-Pilot,* and scores of others.

An interesting counterpoint to these sometimes jingoistic materials is a painting by self-taught African-American artist Horace Pippin (1888–1946) entitled *Mr. Prejudice* (1943). Pippin, directly descended from slaves, claimed that he began painting as therapy for an injury he sustained in WWI. *Mr. Prejudice* places the Statue of Liberty on the opposite side of a large "V for Victory" from a cloaked KKK member. Segregated groups of machinists and soldiers stand beneath, although an African-American sailor and a White pilot seek to bridge the gap by extending their hands toward one another. Mr. Prejudice, meanwhile, is driving a wedge through the nadir of the V, threatening to split it in two. Pippin's painting is a rare commentary on centrifugal social forces such as racial segregation that compromised the general sense of wartime solidarity.

It has, in fact, become a sociological truism that nothing unites people more effectively than a common enemy. That explains a good deal of the willingness of countless artists to contribute what they could to winning WWI and WWII, widely perceived to be "just wars." Once those hostilities ended, however, and in encountering wars of a much more ambiguous nature, artists have reacted quite differently. Combat artists worked in Vietnam, too, but on nothing approaching the scale of earlier 20th-century engagements. It was, after all, the war brought right into peoples' living rooms via television; it did not require filtering through an artist's eyes, as in preceding generations.

III. AFTER THE TRUCE: ARTISTIC RESPONSES TO MASS DESTRUCTION

Once the treaties are signed, once the smoke clears, once the dead are buried, it becomes the time for more sober and critical reflection. After hostilities cease, in other words, artists often grapple with the human costs of violence and armed conflict.

Winslow Homer was an eye witness to Civil War encampments and battles. Like other artists such as Edwin Forbes, some of their experiences contributed to sketches and wood engravings published in *Frank Leslie's Illustrated Newspaper* (Forbes) or in *Harper's Weekly*, such as Homer's *Our Watering-Places—The Empty Sleeve at Newport* (1865), which shows a woman driving a carriage, her male companion with the empty sleeve tucked into his jacket lapel, signaling a serious war injury. Homer's 1865 oil painting *The Veteran in a New Field* depicts a solitary figure in a lush field, cutting wheat with a scythe under the bright sun. His back is turned to the viewer, yet we can tell he is a recently

returned soldier: his uniform jacket and canteen rest in the lower right corner. This Everyman represents the legions discharged at battle's end, now making the transition from warrior to citizen. Several critics note that this veteran is a contemporary counterpart to the legendary Roman Cincinnatus, a warrior who forswears his weapons for the tools of a farmer. C. K. Wilson further observes that the "harvest of death" was a common theme throughout the Civil War, surfacing in countless poems, drawings, and as the caption for an 1863 battlefield photograph of the Gettysburg Battleground in Pennsylvania, itself a wheat field. The painting therefore points to an optimistic future where warfare is laid aside, mankind is once again united with nature, and where the sacrifices and waste of conflict are now supplanted by the possibility of redemption and future abundance.

Stephen Crane's *The Red Badge of Courage: An Episode of the American Civil War* (published 1895; film version, 1951) helped establish a popular genre of stories that has emerged after every major war since the mid-19th century where being heroic becomes ambiguous, unattainable, or even undesirable. Crane's main character, Henry Fleming, is usually referred to as "the youth," a universalizing device as with Homer's faceless veteran. This is a psychological study of a young man who is at first eager to plunge headlong into battle, then experiences a loss of nerve, but who ultimately triumphs by bearing his regiment's colors. It is an unsentimentalized version of heroism, where the protagonist's doubts and fears, combined with experience, ultimately season him into a quietly courageous man.

The German author Erich Maria Remarque's *All Quiet on the Western Front* (published 1928; film version, 1930) is the other most important benchmark for a skeptical view of war and heroism. Told in the first person, it describes how sensitive soldier Paul Baumer embarks on what has become an all-too familiar journey from idealism to disillusionment. Baumer survives being wounded, and he witnesses the deaths of enemies as well as friends. Then, just after a communiqué reports "all quiet on the Western front," the 19-year-old is killed by a stray bullet. An interesting historical footnote is that actor Lew Ayres, who played the role of Baumer in the film, was a conscientious objector during WWII. He was shunned in Hollywood as a result, and in some cases exhibitors would not show his movies. A courageous and moving performance that touched audiences' hearts during peacetime could not offset what many people defined as an act of cowardice during wartime.

The British war poets Wilfred Owen, Rupert Brooke, and Siegfried Sassoon similarly represent the disenchantment and embitterment of men of good will when the day-to-day realities of "the war to end all wars" set in. Owen's *"Anthem for Doomed Youth"* (1917), for example, asks "What passing-bells for these who die as cattle?/ Only the monstrous anger of the guns./ Only the stuttering rifles' rapid rattle/ Can patter out their hasty orisons." Furthermore, since Owen was killed in action in WWI and Brooke died of blood poisoning, their work became more elegiac, and the loss of their potential was keenly felt in the postwar years. Other writers of the WWI era such as e.e. cummings (serving in the Ambulance Corps provided the experiences for writing *The Enormous Room* [1922]) and Ernest Hemingway (*A Farewell to Arms* [published 1929; film versions, 1932, 1957]) simply reinforced strongly antiwar sentiments in peacetime.

Since the 1920s, numerous films and books have joined the chorus of dissent from war. King Vidor's *The Big Parade* (1925) demythologized WWI as senseless slaughter from the point of view of a young private. William Wyler's *The Best Years of Our Lives* (1946), with its strong undercurrent of discontent, depicted the difficult postwar readjustments of three men, representing three branches of the armed services and three social classes. Extra poignancy was achieved because Harold Russell, the actor playing the returning sailor who had lost both his hands in the war, was a man who had sustained just such an injury. Norman Mailer's *The Naked and the Dead* (1948; film version, 1958), Joseph Heller's *Catch-22* (1961; film version, 1970), whose black-humored version of the world has entered into everyday parlance), and Mitchell Goodman's *The End of It* (1961) are all examples of classic antiwar novels.

Throughout the 20th century, and particularly since the American experience in Vietnam, these types of works have become fictional staples. Dalton Trumbo's *Johnny Got His Gun,* a disturbing tale of a man who suffered catastrophic war injuries in 1918, was published in 1939 and then released as a film in 1971, nourished by the strong antiwar sentiments generated by the Vietnam War. Stanley Kubrick's absurdist fantasy about nuclear holocaust, *Dr. Strangelove, or, How I Learned to Stop Worrying and Love the Bomb* (1963) wryly examined the deep-seated anxieties generated by the dramatic conclusion to WWII (Robert Arneson's *General Nuke,* a 1986 lithograph of a heavily-decorated general with a phallic-looking missile for a nose also springs to mind). *M*A*S*H* (book, 1968, film version, 1970, and subsequent television series) was a rare depiction of the Korean Conflict, albeit also strongly flavored with anti-Vietnam War sentiment when it was presented on the screen. And Kurt Vonnegut's *Slaughter-house Five* (1968; film version, 1972) uses sci-fi, space/time distortions to attempt to grapple with the horrors of WWII; Billy Pilgrim's exploits in Dresden invite comparison with the Celestial City in John Bunyan's *Pilgrim's Progress*. While the styles of this material may change significantly, the tone remains deeply suspicious and critical of military exploits.

One of the more recent additions to an impressive array of antiwar stories—and one that is remarkably free of irony, sarcasm, or self-conscious literary tricks—is William Wharton's poetic *A Midnight Clear* (published 1982; film version, 1992). The setting: the Ardennes Forest near the French/German border, December, 1944. The end of the war feels imminent. When small squadrons of Yanks and Germans occupy the same area, each side seems reluctant to engage the other. The Nazis and the Americans meet face-to-face one moonlit night, and *mirabile visu* the Germans first offer a tree decorated for Christmas, then sausages—even a serenade of carols. The Americans reciprocate with bottles of wine and a hand grenade, with which the Germans decorate one tree branch. The encounter closes with the singing of traditional hymns of joy, each person chiming in in his own language. During this brief moment of grace—reenacting similar fabled liminal rendezvous across the no-man's-lands of WWI—these are merely men, not soldiers, their mutual enmity pushed aside. But soon thereafter, the prevailing rules of war shatter their "separate peace," and the eerily beautiful landscape is stupidly drenched in blood.

IV. DEFIANCE IN THE EYE OF THE STORM: ARTISTS AGAINST WAR

Artists may swim against the current; that is, they may orient themselves to a set of values from the past or in the future, and they may resist the tide of popular opinion. A number of German artists stand out particularly in this regard.

Käthe Kollwitz (1867–1945), the socially committed wife of a doctor who hung out his shingle as well as lived in the slums of Berlin, brought enormous empathy to the people she portrayed, be they peasants or the urban poor. Her choice of graphic media (primarily drawing, etching, woodcut, and lithography) was a carefully calculated populist gesture to guarantee that her work would be available to a large audience. Her first major print series to garner wide attention was *Weavers' Revolt* (1897), depicting a workers' uprising in Germany in 1844 (the art was a popular success, although the Kaiser halted the awarding of a gold medal to her at an 1898 exhibition in Berlin). From *The Peasant War Cycle, Outbreak* (1903) features a woman urging her comrades on to battle, her arms uplifted and her body swaying like a passionate orchestra conductor. And the ominous *Sharpening the Scythe* (1905) shows a woman scrupulously honing a large farm implement; her eyes closed to near slits, she is extremely concentrated on her work.

Kollwitz's artistic interest in these armed proletarian struggles was tempered after she lost a son in WWI, and later a grandson in WWII. Her work was suppressed at times, and the Nazis expelled her from her position at the Berlin Academy of Art in the 1930s. One of her most widely reproduced images, the 1924 lithograph *Nie Wieder Krieg! (Never Again War!)* presents an ardent youth, hand thrust into the air with two fingers extended, with the other hand placed over the heart. It appears to be a pledge held with such commitment that it cannot be compromised and reflects Kollwitz's own devotion to the cause of peace.

Such an intrepid image was overshadowed by Kollwitz's themes of grief, sorrow, resignation, pain, and death. For example, *The War Cycle* (1922–1925) reflected the despair many social idealists felt over WWI, bearing such titles as *The Sacrifice, The Widow I and II, The Mothers,* and *The People. The Parents* (1923), for instance, presents a couple whose bodies are enfolded into one another, their faces covered and the depth of their loss palpable. And in the 1942 lithograph *Seed for the Planting Must Not Be Ground,* a hypervigilant woman hovers protectively over three cowering children; for Kollwitz, the "harvest of death" must be stopped. Such unbearably sad and desperate victims and survivors of war, primarily women and children, dominate a large portion of her corpus of work.

John Heartfield (1891–1968) was born Helmut Herzfelde in Berlin but adopted his Anglicized pseudonym during WWI to protest the intense xenophobia he witnessed in his homeland. He is best known for 236 bitingly satirical anti-Fascist photomontages published between 1930 and 1938 in the leftist *Arbeiter Illustrierte Zeitung* (*AIZ* or *Worker's Illustrated Press,* changed to *Volks-Illustrierte* or *People's Illustrated* in 1936), over half of them gracing the front or back cover. Many of his originals were destroyed by the Nazis—Heartfield himself scrambled from Berlin to Prague to France to England during that era—but copies exist of his published work, and other work survived because it was shown outside Germany. His medium is subversive by nature, giving the artist "permission" to assemble fragments of disparate material at will, frequently into startling juxtapositions.

A photomontaged self-portrait from 1929 keenly captures his craft *and* his craftiness: *John Heartfield with Police Commissioner Zörgiebel* presents an earnest-looking Heartfield efficiently snipping off the bureaucrat's head, a one-man bloodless coup. A staunch communist and anti-Nazi, Heartfield entitled an exhibition that marked his escape to England "One Man's War Against Hitler." And Hitler, his henchmen, and his industrialist partisans came in for extensive skewering. *Adolf, the Superman: Swallows Gold and Spouts Junk* (1932) transplants Hitler's head onto a chest X-ray, the spinal column made up of a towering stack of coins that spill into his diaphragm. *The Meaning of the Hitler Salute* highlights an industrialist placing Deutschmarks into the Fuhrer's raised palm. And *Goering, The Executioner of the Third Reich* (1933) binds four bloody axes together to form the swastika.

One of his signature images is *The Meaning of Geneva* (1932), where the dove of peace hangs limp, impaled upon a bloody bayonet, set against the building housing the League of Nations. (In Christian symbolism, the dove represents the Holy Spirit or the human soul; in *Genesis* 8:11, the story of Noah's Ark, it becomes a peace symbol with an olive branch in its mouth; it also symbolizes purity, simplicity, and affection.) A swastika has replaced the Swiss flag; the force of world opinion is impotent to prevent this sacrifice of peace in the face of Hitler's expanding power. Heartfield also addressed the suppression of civil rights in Nazi Germany as well as the severe food shortages. One collage depicts a man being spread onto a piece of bread; the implication is that Germany can eat its Jews to satisfy its hunger, an uncanny foreshadowing of the mass executions to come.

And briefly, Hannah Höch's (1889–1978) most renowned photomontage, *A Slice with the Kitchen Knife Through the Beer-Belly of Weimar Culture* (1919), pitted the Dadaists (who counted Heartfield among their number) against Weimar politicians as the forces of darkness. She was banned by the Nazis. Otto Dix (1891–1969) populated many of his images in the 1920s with war cripples, championing an antiwar position. The same sentiments underlie his series of 50 etchings *The War* (1923–1924). Max Beckmann (1884–1950) pictured violence and atrocities in his postwar series of lithographs *Hell* (1919), including his noted *The Night.* And George Grosz (1893–1959), a close associate of Heartfield's, attacked German militarism during and after WWI. In the 1920s, he was prosecuted several times for blasphemy and obscenity for his bitingly satirical works.

These artists created bodies of work that are powerful and moving to the modern eye. It must be noted, however, that in the face of the political realities of their times, they were little more than spitting into the wind.

V. AN ENDURING SYMBOL: THE RECEPTIONS AND RECYCLING Of PICASSO'S *GUERNICA*

On April 26, 1937, German bombers flying on behalf of General Francisco Franco strafed Guernica, Spain. They pounded the central part of the Basque city relentlessly for three hours, and buildings remained in flames for several days. Scores of people were killed, and up to 70% of the town's buildings were destroyed, although military targets such as munitions factories and a strategic bridge were left intact. This deplorable episode in the Spanish Civil War presaged the saturation bombings and mass slaughter of civilians during WWII.

Pablo Picasso had already been commissioned by the Spanish republican government to create a mural for the Spanish Pavilion at the Paris World Fair. Within days of the events at Guernica, Picasso was in his studio creating what many people believe to be his most powerful and important work. In 6 feverish days he sketched out much of the design; little more than a month later, *Guernica* was completed and installed for public view (Fig. 2).

Visitors were confronted with an immense black, white, and grey tableau of suffering: a severed head screams; a fallen warrior clutches his broken sword; a woman keens to the heavens, her dead child cradled in her arms; another woman lifts her arms in despair in front of a burning building; and a horse and a bull are caught within the chaos and tangle of bodies. Art historian Herschel B. Chipp argues that Picasso was aroused by a particular, outrageous act of aggression, and then drew upon both cultural themes (e.g., the bullfight) and personal iconography (e.g., the minotaur, distinctive images of women) to produce an extraordinarily powerful depiction of suffering from the victim's point of view.

Guernica alludes to a real event, but it is universal because it is devoid of specific historical referents. That feature caused some critics on the political Left to criticize it for not being specific enough; it made those on the Right uneasy and defensive because the connection was so obvious. In the years since its creation, *Guernica* has become a rallying point for proponents of democracy and peace. Moreover, it has taken on new meanings and has been appropriated for different purposes, a development Picasso himself seemed to have antici-

FIGURE 2 Pablo Picasso's *Guernica* (1937), arguably the most important political artwork of the 20th century, memorializes a specific event yet resonates with universal significance. (Copyright 1999 Estate of Pablo Picasso/Artists Rights Society (ARS), New York; print courtesy of Giraudon/Art Resource, NY.)

pated: "[W]hen [a painting] is finished," he argued, "it goes on changing, according to the state of mind of whoever is looking at it. A picture lives a life like a living creature, undergoing the changes imposed on us by our life from day to day."

Picasso refused to allow the painting to ever appear in his native Spain until democracy was assured there. As a result, *Guernica* was in exile until 1981, displayed at New York's Museum of Modern Art (MOMA). It was transferred to Spanish officials 6 years after dictator Franco's death. In 1967, Rudolf Baranik copied and incorporated a section of the mural showing a fallen man into his design of a poster for Angry Arts Week, a week of cultural events opposing the Vietnam War sponsored by Artists and Writers Protest. Likewise, Carlos Irizarry included *Guernica* in his 1969 montage of antiwar images *Moratorium*. In 1970, members of the Guerrilla Art Action Group and the Art Workers' Coalition held a memorial service, and also a political demonstration, in front of the mural at MOMA. The memorial service included the laying of wreaths and a ceremony conducted by a clergyman; the rally demanded that posters showing the gruesome aftermath of an American massacre of Vietnamese civilians at Song My ("Q: And babies? A: And babies.") replace Picasso's work, or at least be hung in the same room until the Southeast Asian conflict ended. (Baranik's *Napalm Elegy*, a haunting series of paintings made in the late 1960s and early 1970s also derived from a news photograph of a Vietnamese child whose features have nearly melted away because of the caustic effects of napalm.) And in 1974, artist Tony Shafrazi painted "KILL ALL LIES" across the painting, although it sustained no permanent damage.

Guernica has also embellished dozens of record and book covers, particularly those addressing themes of peace and humanitarianism. To cite merely a few examples: *Chants de la Guerre d'Espagne* (1963), *Why Bosnia?* (1993), and *Worlds of Hurt: Reading the Literature of Trauma* (1995).

With the cessation of hostilities after Vietnam, however, the iconic nature of *Guernica* has also made it a target for artistic revision. Peter Saul reinterpreted it in a Pop Art idiom (*Saul's Guernica*, 1973), a Technicolor romp with self-conscious artworld references; Ron English's *Culture Wars* (1997) gives *Guernica* a postmodernist spin, replacing all the faces with cartoon characters like Mickey Mouse and Donald Duck. Moreover, it has entered the cultural archive of stock images and as such is now subject to be commodified, its original meaning perverted. To wit: in 1996, a large hotel chain proposed to renovate 100 guest suites in a Kansas City,

Missouri hotel using *Guernica* as a wall covering. To the decorators, it evoked "Midwestern warmth" (the tormented animals, perhaps?) and "European sophistication" (the aura of Picasso's genius?). Even after a lively and highly critical debate in the local newspaper, the corporation stuck by its plan.

This clearly trivializes Picasso's antiwar intent, an impulse which also surfaced in other of his works. *The Charnel House* (1945) depicts a jumble of bodies, *Guernica*-style, and *Massacre in Korea* (1951) pits a robotic-looking execution squad against a cluster of naked women and children. But each is rather static, and neither captures the anguish of his 1937 masterpiece. Picasso joined the Communist Party in 1944, a move that led officials in both Spain and the United States to compile dossiers on him. But it also motivated his participation in international peace conferences and inspired his 1949 *Dove of Peace* poster, which was widely reproduced. And his drawings for a mural *La Guerre et La Paix* (published in 1952) highlight the dividends of peace with children dancing and climbing a tree and a woman contentedly suckling her baby—after the war god is vanquished. In these politically informed works, Picasso was unabashedly partisan, transcending the emphasis on *eros* that dominated much of his work. In *Stonewall Jackson's House,* a 1997 play about multiculturalism and "political correctness" by Jonathan Reynolds, a character exclaims, "Art is supposed to take sides—should Picasso have given equal time to the other side to balance *Guernica*?" Picasso's defiant "no" is clearly contained within the work itself.

VI. PEACE ACROSS GENRES: HOW *ALL* THE ARTS ADDRESS THE ISSUE

In 1981, art critic Lucy Lippard wrote in the *Village Voice,* "[O]ppositional culture is rising like mushrooms after a hard rain." Clearly, such meteorological conditions have appeared at several historical junctures, nourishing repeated crops of peace-oriented artistic work. Perhaps this provides a new meaning for "global warming": as militarists rattle their sabers, artists take aim, too, with their pens, their greasepaint, or toe shoes.

For example, the antiwar ballet *The Green Table* was choreographed by Kurt Jooss in Germany in 1932. The Joffrey Ballet presented the first American production in 1967 during the Vietnam War; they revived it in 1991 to coincide with the Persian Gulf conflict. Among Jooss's influences were the medieval dance of death and post-WWI German pacifist writings. The cast of characters includes Mars, a resistance fighter, a smarmy war profiteer, and youthful victims of war, whose stories each unfold against the backdrop of old men parleying among themselves. Moreover, political dance groups proliferated in the United States in the 1930s, a reflection of the *zeitgeist* of radical politics and proletarian culture. In 1935, to cite one example, the Workers' Dance League presented such works as *Forces in Opposition* and *Anti-War Trilogy*. Mention must be made also of the dancer Anna Sokolow, and later on, venues such as New York's Judson Memorial Church, which nurtured progressive artists for years.

In the realm of theater, the Bread and Puppet Theater stands out. The group was founded by German-born sculptor Peter Schumann on the Lower East Side of Manhattan in 1961. One principal remains central: audiences are to be nourished by ideas as well as by communally sharing the home-baked bread the troupe distributes after its performances. It is recognized by its trademark larger-than-life-sized puppets of people (archetypal religious figures, politicians, and common folk of many lands) and creatures of various sorts (figures can tower as much as 40 feet high, and performers may strut on 20-foot stilts). It combines a spirit of play and pageantry with a broadly progressive, pacifist/anarchist viewpoint—something like a circus with a keen social conscience. During the 1960s, Bread and Puppet Theater was a ubiquitous presence at peace rallies, street demonstrations, and parades against the Vietnam War, in New York City, Washington, DC, and elsewhere. An ad Schumann placed for volunteer workers and performers in the *Village Voice* in 1968 captures the group's irrepressible spirit: "Papier Mache Against the War!!!!" the headline exclaimed.

Bread and Puppet Theater's activities provide a virtual checklist of the peace movement's activities during the 1960s: Schumann made the death mask worn in a street march as part of the Living Theatre's World Wide General Strike for Peace in 1962; the troupe marched *en masse,* masked and with giant puppets, in periodic Fifth Avenue Peace Parades, beginning in 1965; Schumann and his associates participated in a 1965 silent vigil at United Nations headquarters in memory of two antiwar protestors who immolated themselves and held a 1966 silent vigil in front of New York's St. Patrick's Cathedral dressed as Mary, Joseph, the shepherds, and the three kings, bearing a blood-stained doll representing the Christ child and a sign reading "I am Mary. My child was napalmed in Vietnam"; and their giant figures surfaced in front of the U.S. Capitol during a massive peace demonstration on April 24, 1971. Furthermore, in productions such *The Great Warrior; Fire; A Man*

Says Goodbye to His Mother; and *When Johnny Comes Marching Home,* Bread and Puppet Theater offered simple tales, often silently enacted, containing heart-rending lessons about life and death, war and peace, and ultimately, redemption.

Another group, the San Francisco Mime Troupe, first began performing in 1959, and its distinctive blend of *commedia dell'arte* and politics has engaged audiences—often in outdoor public spaces—ever since. In 1967 they adapted Carlo Goldoni's *L'Amant Militaire* as a trenchant anti-Vietnam War statement. *The Dragon Lady's Revenge* (1971) pursued a related theme, uncovering the connections between diplomats, politicians, secret operatives, and the drug trade in a Southeast Asian country. And in 1991, *Back to Normal,* a play critical of the Persian Gulf conflict, continued the decades-long tradition of this group's antiwar work.

Artists have protested bellicose government activities at other critical political moments. In 1984, for example, ARTISTS CALL Against U.S. Intervention in Central America rallied together cultural workers in 20 cities in the U.S. and Canada to protest U.S. policy in El Salvador, Nicaragua, Guatemala, and elsewhere in the region. In an unprecedented mobilization, over 1000 poets, visual artists, performance artists, dancers, filmmakers, musicians, and video artists donated time and works to raise money for exiled Latino artists, the National University of El Salvador, and a Salvadoran labor organization and to raise the consciousness of the American public about American support of right-wing forces in Central America. Highlights included a death-to-life Procession for Peace from the Battleship Intrepid anchored at a Hudson River pier to Washington Square in the heart of Greenwich Village.

And in the realm of music, too, examples abound of a creative engagement with the subject of peace. *Symphony No. 7 (Leningrad)* by Dmitri Shostakovich (1906–1975) was composed during the 1941 German siege of Leningrad. Shostakovich was a member of the local fire-fighting brigade and took his manuscript with him to a shelter during air raids. When the maestro and his family escaped the city, his composition was secreted out to the rest of the world and became an immediate sensation, an urgent manifesto for the preservation of humanist values. It has been described as a meditation on war and peace: the initial mood of tranquility is disrupted by blitzkrieglike passages signaling the growing presence of the Nazi invaders, this gradually crescendos into furious battle and eventually closes with the attenuation of the Nazi theme and an evocation of the ringing of the bells of victory. Significantly, a Vanguard recording of the symphony by the

Leningrad Symphony Orchestra, conducted by Eugene Mravinsky, features the painting *Echo of a Scream* (1937) by David Alfaro Siqueiros (1896–1974), a wrenching image of a child screaming, likely derived from a newsreel report on casualties of the Spanish Civil War.

Further, Benjamin Britten's (1913–1976) *War Requiem,* first performed in Coventry, England in 1962, incorporated the *Missa pro Defunctis* and the poems of Wilfred Owen to memorialize those lost in battle. As such, it joins over 1600 masses for the dead composed over the past 5 centuries. And Leonard Bernstein (1918–1990), who scandalized the Establishment by his "radical chic" flirtation with the Black Panthers during the 1960s, ruffled more feathers with his *Mass,* created to inaugurate the Opera House at the Kennedy Center for the Performing Arts in Washington, DC in 1971. Bernstein fused the traditional Catholic service with classical and folk music, rock, and blues and with a strong antiwar, antiauthoritarian message. J. Edgar Hoover, troubled because Bernstein had consulted with antiwar activist Daniel Berrigan on the composition, tipped off Attorney General John Mitchell; the message apparently reached the President's office because Nixon did not attend the premiere. It was battered by many music critics and condemned as blasphemous by many Catholics.

And popular music in the 1960s, of course, offers a multitude of examples of peace-oriented material. The 1965 British musical revue *Oh What a Lovely War* put an ironic spin on WWI, incorporating documents and newspapers from the time, as well as accounts by Churchill, Sassoon, Robert Graves, several generals, and others (*Journey's End* in 1928 also presented the war in an English music-hall context). The American rock musical *Hair* (1968; film version, 1979) is probably best remembered for extoling the hippie philosophy of "peace and love" and hearalding the dawning of the Age of Aquarius—perhaps the most widely supported popular culture of peace ever generated. But recall as well that one of its central plot elements is the imminent threat of the draft looming over the head of Claude Bukowski, and the song "Three–Five–Zero–Zero" ("a surrealistic anti-war song," according to the liner notes) immortalizes the obsessive body counts during the Vietnam War. (It was paired with the moving ballad "What a Piece of Work Is Man," the lyrics taken directly from Shakespeare's *Hamlet.*) Pete Seeger's "Where Have All the Flowers Gone?" and "Waist Deep in the Big Muddy," Arlo Guthrie's "Alice's Restaurant," Country Joe and the Fish's "I Feel Like I'm Fixin' to Die Rag" (be "the first on your block to have your boy come home in a box"), and Cat Stevens's "Peace Train" are merely a few examples of peace songs popular in the 1960s, representing a range of styles and moods.

Finally, the paintings of Leon Golub (1922–) recapitulate the history of artists addressing war and violence. During the 1950s, Golub harvested mythological themes from Classical times, such as syphinxes and warriors. As the Vietnam War intensified in the 1960s (and both he and his wife Nancy Spero were active with Artists and Writers Protest, the first such group to take a public stand against the war, and they also participated in Angry Arts Week in 1967), Golub began *Gigantomachy,* a series recalling Olympian battles between Giants and Gods. References to the Southeast Asian conflict gradually begin to creep in; works such as *Napalm I* (1969) and *Vietnam I* (1972) depict victims of this specific conflict. Since that time, drawing upon an archive of images he has assembled of conflict worldwide, Golub has captured the essence of violence and brutality, from riots to political repression. Creating such series as *Mercenaries, Interrogation,* and *White Squad,* work so large-scale and so raw that it is painful and exhausting to view, Golub has produced a searing indictment of violence, whatever its genesis.

VII. EXPERIENCE AND MEMORY: THE STRUGGLE TO REFLECT, REMEMBER, OR FORGET

Has art ever changed the course of world events? Ever stopped a war? Probably not, but it *can* help mobilize public sentiment at critical moments, it may soothe people when it is quoted in times of stress, and it might help to heal their wounds. On occasion, artists become the canary in the coal mine: they signal distress, but few may notice their chirp. Their gestures may be both inspired and frivolous at the same time, like the full-page notice placed in *The New York Times* (December 21, 1969): "War Is Over!/If You Want It/Happy Christmas from John and Yoko Lennon" (John Lennon also being the author, of course, of one of the anthems of the 1960s, "Give Peace a Chance").

Many artists opposed the Vietnam War and participated in the peace movement. In 1966, for example, sculptor Mark di Suvero erected *Peace Tower* on L.A.'s Sunset Strip, incorporating 400 individual panels designed by different artists worldwide. And on May 22, 1970, Art Strike was called in reaction to the U.S. bombing of Cambodia and the killling of students at Kent State and Jackson State. New York's Whitney Museum of American Art and the Jewish Museum closed, as did 50 private galleries. But except for people primarily oriented to affairs in the artworld, what impact could this have had? Was it merely preaching to the choir?

Since the Vietnam War's ambiguous end—and its legacy of cynicism, distrust of the government, and a less self-assured national character—a number of exhibitions have grappled with the meaning of Vietnam and in that respect have spurred an on-going dialogue about war, responsibility, and peace. "War and Memory: In the Aftermath of Vietnam," sponsored by the Washington (DC) Project for the Arts in 1987, focused primarily upon the photographic record of the era. "A Different War: Vietnam in Art" toured eight cities across the United State from 1989 until 1992. It contained more than 100 works by antiwar artists of the era, Vietnam veterans, and younger artists relating the war to their own times and lives. Among the more powerful images in the catalog are Michael Page's 1980 wood sculpture *Pieta* (a stunned G.I. holds a dead Vietnamese baby) and Cynthia Norton's 1985 painting *Madonna* (an obviously anxious G.I. gently cradles a baby in a classic Renaissance pose). And "As Seen by Both Sides" featured work by 20 Vietnamese artists and 20 Americans and began to tour the U.S. in 1991; it then traveled throughout Vietnam. Two museums, the San Jose Museum of Art and the Minnesota Museum of Art in St. Paul, pulled out after members of both the Vietnamese and veterans communities raised objections: in the first instance, expressing concern that only communist propaganda was included in the Vietnamese selections; in the second, feeling that only an antiwar position was being spotlighted. The debate was a microcosm of concerns swirling within a newly post-Cold War climate of opinion.

Furthermore, the National Vietnam Veterans Art Museum opened in Chicago in 1995, housing a collection of over 600 pieces of art assembled since 1981 by a nonprofit group of veteran artists. It had toured the country sporadically over the years. One vet describes his work as "closet art," created for intensely personal reasons and not necessarily intended for public display. There is no editing or curating of work; entry into the collection is automatic with veteran status. One piece was done "in country" with diluted C-ration coffee on paper; many incorporate an ironic or sarcastic sense (*We Know What's Good for You* and *Happy Birthday Captain*); while others poignantly capture tragedy and loss (*We Regret to Inform You* and *Blood Spots on a Rice Paddy*).

As public art, memorials have the potential to crystallize a community's emotions, positively or negatively.

Consider the experiences of sculptor George Segal (1924—). He has created two versions of the Biblical tale of the sacrifice of Isaac by Abraham, both of which have been derailed from being placed in their originally proposed settings because of intense controversy. In 1973, the Tel Aviv Foundation for Literature and Art commissioned Segal to cast a public sculpture. Their expectations and ideas collided when the artist presented Isaac on rocky terrain, dwarfed by Abraham towering overhead, clutching a knife in his hand. *The Sacrifice of Isaac* sparked a vigorous negative response, raising metaphorically, as it did, the sacrifice of youth by an older generation in defense of its values. The analogy cut too close to the bone in a society where war is an omnipresent possibility, and the sculpture was exiled to an inconspicuous spot in Tel Aviv's Mann Auditorium.

In Memory of May 4, 1970, Kent State: Abraham and Isaac was commissioned in 1978 by a private foundation, the Mildred Andrews Fund, to commemorate the killing of four antiwar demonstrators at Kent State University in Ohio. It was to be donated to the university, yet a controversy erupted there, too, and the sculpture was subsequently donated to Princeton University. The motif alludes not only to specific historical events, but also raises universal questions regarding the allegiance to abstract principles overriding love for your child. (And it bears mentioning that Judy Collins popularized Leonard Cohen's song "Story of Isaac" during the Vietnam War era, a story told from the potential victim's point of view, making it as much a story about blind faith as impending doom.)

The Ohio school also rejected *Kent State Doors* (1980) by Peter Gourfain, wood-framed, ceramic sculpted doors with 10 scenes reflecting the local tragedy (inspired by the famous *Gates of Paradise* by the Florentine Renaissance sculptor Lorenzo Ghiberti who, incidentally, is also well-known for another set of doors entitled *The Sacrifice of Isaac*). And in Santa Monica, California, a proposed new veterans memorial was stalled in 1991 after some veterans and politicians turned a thumbs down on the design: they deplored *Promises Kept,* a locked door encased in metal bars and a chain-link fence and instead desired something "uplifting." Of course, no memorial of this type has generated as much debate as Maya Lin's Vietnam Memorial, completed in Washington, DC in 1982. A V-shaped wall of polished black granite engraved with the names of all the U.S. soldiers and related personnel who died in Vietnam, the design was harshly dismissed at first, reviled as "a black gash of shame." Subsequently "balanced" by three larger-than-life sized bronze G.I.s sited nearby, it has become a place of pilgrimage, catharsis, and healing, one of the most revered spots in America's memorial landscape.

Such wrangling has become a commonplace feature of American culture near the millennium. In 1991, for example, the U.S. Congress officially changed the name of a remote, windswept site in southern Montana from the Custer Battlefield—a name that memorializes defeated White troops—to the Little Bighorn Battlefield National Monument. The promoters of an American Indian monument at the site suggested "peace through unity" as its slogan, but by 1997 all that had resulted was a "war of words" over "dueling monuments," pitting the 19th-century 12-foot high granite obelisk marking the mass grave of calvarymen against a proposed grass-covered berm or raised circular shoulder (in the designer's words, "a weeping wound" in the ground) that would commemorate the Indian warriors and families who also lost their lives there. A panel appointed by the National Park Service approved the plan, but critics argue it should not be placed too close to—nor interrupt the view of—the established marker. At this writing the design remains on the drawing board.

When artists have addressed issues of war and peace, their sympathies have clearly been on the side of peace for at least the past half century. England's Imperial War Museum and the Canadian War Memorials were each established as repositories for the artistic record of the Great War. The United States never followed suit. However, the Peace Museum, founded in Chicago in 1981, is the only art and history museum dedicated to this subject. The museum sponsors both on-site and traveling exhibitions, maintains an archive, and sponsors community education programs confronting issues of violence and peace on an interpersonal, national, and international scale. Among its presentations have been "Unforgettable Fire" (wrenching memory drawings by survivors of what they witnessed immediately after the atomic bombings of Japan), "Give Peace a Chance" (highlighting music), and "Martin Luther King, Jr.: Peacemaker." "Drive-By Peace," an annual exhibition of work by area 6th graders that emphasizes nonviolent conflict resolution skills, demonstrates how this institution expands the typical boundaries of a museum in order to have a direct impact upon its community.

Artist Nancy Burson practices photographic alchemy, using computer technology to fuse individual portraits into striking new amalgamations. For example, *Lion/Lamb* transported Edward Hicks's 19th-cen-

tury vision of harmony into the present by appealingly blending the great cat's features with the precious mien of the lamb. And in a fascinating series of portraits called *Warheads* done in the 1980s, Burson combined the features of major world leaders in proportion to the number of deployable nuclear warheads each one controlled. In *Warhead I* (1982), for example, Reagan's features represented about 55% of the composite, Brezhnev's accounted for about 45%, and Thatcher, Mitterand, and Deng contributed less than 1% to the outcome. Glaring faces replaced a largely unseen threat, as an artist once again lent tangibility—and a sense of responsibility—to pressing issues of war and peace.

Also See the Following Articles

COMMUNICATION STUDIES, OVERVIEW • LINGUISTIC CONSTRUCTIONS OF VIOLENCE, PEACE, AND CONFLICT • MASS MEDIA AND DISSENT • MASS MEDIA, GENERAL VIEW • POPULAR MUSIC

Bibliography

Bruckner, D. J. R., Chwast, S., & Heller, S. (1984). *Art against war.* New York: Abbeville Press.

Capote, T. (1956). *The muses are heard.* New York: Random House.

Chipp, H. B. (1988). *Picasso's Guernica: History, transformations, meanings.* Berkeley: University of California Press.

Cork, R. (1994). *A bitter truth: Avant-garde art and the great war.* New Haven, CT: Yale University Press.

Gallatin, A. E. (1919). *Art and the great war.* New York: E. P. Dutton & Co.

Japanese Broadcasting Corporation (1977). *Unforgettable fire: Pictures drawn by atomic bomb survivors.* New York: Pantheon Books.

Landau, E. G. (1983). *Artists for victory: An exhibition catalog.* Washington, DC: Library of Congress.

Lippard, L. R. (1990). *A different war: Vietnam in art.* Seattle, WA: The Real Comet Press.

McCormick, K., & Perry, H. D. (1990). *Images of war: The artist's vision of World War II.* New York: Orion.

Mackenzie, D. (1945). *Men without guns.* Philadelphia: The Blakiston Company.

Moeller, S. D. (1989). *Shooting war: Photography and the American experience of combat.* New York: Basic Books.

Orpen, W. (1923–1924). *The outline of art* (2 vols.). New York: Putnam.

Roeder, G. H., Jr. (1993). *The censored war: American visual experience during World War Two.* New Haven, CT: Yale University Press.

Ross, E. A. (1897). Social Control. *American Journal of Sociology, 3,* 64–78.

Shikes, R. E. (1969). *The indignant eye: The artist as social critic.* Boston: Beacon Press.

Wilson, C. K. (1985). Winslow Homer's *The Veteran in a New Field:* A study of the harvest metaphor and popular culture. *American Art Journal, 17,* 2–27.

Peace and Democracy*

Nils Petter Gleditsch

International Peace Research Institute, Oslo & Norwegian University of Science and Technology

I. The Goals of International Development
II. The Democratic Peace Phenomenon
III. The Limits of Democratic Peace

GLOSSARY

Democratic Peace The concept, or historical pattern, that modern democracies do not wage war on each other but pursue peaceful means of settling policy disputes or sharing scarce resources.

Liberal Theory In this context, the view that a democratic nation, other conditions aside, is inherently more likely by reason of its form of government to promote and pursue a policy of peace than is a non-democratic nation; contrasted with the realist theory.

Militarized Dispute A description of conflict between nations that falls short of actual combat on a significant scale, but that nevertheless involves some form of confrontation such as threat of military action or the deployment of forces, or even limited use of force.

Realist Theory In this context, the view that the conduct of nations is determined mainly or entirely by the power relations of the states involved, and that

the form of government of a nation therefore has no significant role in determining issues of war and peace; contrasted with the liberal theory.

DEMOCRACIES RARELY FIGHT ONE ANOTHER, although they participate as much in war as other countries, and the process of democratization may involve temporary instability and disorder. At the domestic level, stable democracy tends to eliminate major violence, while semidemocracies experience more civil war than do stable autocracies where all dissent is repressed before it can organize. Over a certain threshold of democratization, a more democratic world is likely to be more peaceful in terms of domestic as well as interstate relations. These are central tenets of democratic peace theory, which forms a core element in the revival of liberal international relations theory.

I. THE GOALS OF INTERNATIONAL DEVELOPMENT

Democracy and peace are two of the major goals of international development. Most countries, even many that are not themselves highly democratic or very peaceful, pay lip service to these ideals, as do the United Nations and other international organizations. The central question of this article is whether these two goals are compatible with each other, or even whether they mutually support each other.

* This article draws on earlier work published in Gleditsch (1992) and Gleditsch and Hegre (1997). Some material, including Fig. 1, is republished here with the permission of the editors and publishers of the journals in which these articles were published. The work was supported financially by the Norwegian Research Council.

Copyright © 1999 by Academic Press.
All rights of reproduction in any form reserved.

Realist theory, traditionally the leading mode of thought within the academic study of international relations, views national characteristics other than power, including the political system, as being of little relevance to relations between states. The international system is seen as near-anarchic, with little legal regulation, without a central powerful authority, and with little possibility of disciplining its powerful members for deviant behavior. Thus, the issues of war and peace would be decided mainly by the structure of power between states, as determined by national military capabilities, conditions for successful deterrence, and alliance patterns. Periods of peace were understood mainly as the successful practice of a balance of power between states.

The recent emergence of the concept of "the democratic peace" challenges the realist paradigm in claiming that there is a growing "zone of peace" between democracies, which on a permanent basis have abandoned war as a means of settling disputes among themselves. In line with this thinking, the continued spread of democracy is seen as promoting a more peaceful international community of states. If this holds true, the promotion of one important international value will provide a bonus in terms of the other.

II. THE DEMOCRATIC PEACE PHENOMENON

The relationship between international peace and democracy can be analyzed at three different levels. At the dyadic or pairwise level, a number of studies have found that *democracies rarely if ever fight one another*. At the nation level, most analyses have concluded that *democracies participate in war just as much as countries with other political systems*. Whether this means that they are no more peaceful in their overall behavior is a more controversial point. At the system level, the question is whether *a world with a higher share of democracies will also be more peaceful*. Most of those who have addressed this question have assumed that the answer can be inferred from findings at one of the other levels of analysis. To date, there is relatively little empirical analysis at the system level. Finally, since civil war and other domestic violence is now the dominant form of armed conflict, we should also ask whether *there is a democratic peace at the intrastate level*. The theory and evidence will be reviewed at each of these four levels, along with a discussion of objections to the theory of the democratic peace, and finally a few comments on possible policy implications.

A. Democracies Do Not Fight One Another

Many Enlightenment philosophers saw democratic government as encouraging a more peaceful interaction between states. As early as in 1795 Immanuel Kant described a "pacific federation" or "pacific union" created by liberal republics. At that time, there were few if any democracies in our sense of the word, and Kant's prescription for peace had little force as a description of the international system. As democratic government took hold in an increasing number of countries in the 19th century, the possibility arose that democracy might have a perceptible impact on international relations. The observation that democracies do not fight one another was noted at least as early as the late 1930s, and a first statistical study was published in the mid-1960s. However, it was not until the 1980s that the empirical study took off, giving rise to an enormous and sometimes heated debate.

The period after the Napoleonic wars and the Congress of Vienna is fairly well covered by statistical data on wars and the political characteristics of the independent states. Depending a little on the what thresholds are set for "democracy" and "war," there appear to be few if any cases of war between democracies during this period. Indeed, this regularity has been characterized by Jack Levy as being as close to a law as anything we have in international relations. Ignoring cases that result from quirks in the data (notably imprecise timing of regime changes), the three most problematic cases are the Spanish-American War in 1898, World War I, and the British declaration of war on Finland in World War II. In the first of these cases, the classification of the Spanish political system in 1898 is controversial. While Spain had an elected parliament, the monarchy retained considerable executive power. U.S. decision makers did not perceive Spain as a democracy. Regarding World War I, it has been argued that Germany was largely democratic in 1914 when war broke out against Britain, France, and other Western democracies. However, even more clearly than in the case of the Spanish king, the German emperor had special prerogatives, particularly in foreign and defense policy. This is one reason why systematic data score Germany as less democratic than its main opponents in the West, and below the level required for the democratic peace to work. Finally, in the case of World War II, the Finnish dispute was with the Soviet Union, not with the Western democracies. However, when Germany attacked the Soviet Union in 1941 and forced Stalin to change sides in the war, Finland found itself on the wrong side. Following pressure from Stalin, the United Kingdom declared war on Finland. Technically, Finland was at war for 3 years with the UK (and with several British Dominions, but not with the United States). However, there was no military action between them, and the Western democracies regarded Finland more as a victim than as an enemy. While one should be careful not to reclassify cases on an ad hoc basis, the empirical evidence points to a much lower probability of war between democracies than for other combinations of states, and the evidence is consistent with the idea of a near-perfect relationship.

War is usually defined as organized military action with annual battle deaths exceeding 1000. The peace between democracies appears to hold up if the threshold on violence is lowered to 100 deaths annually, and probably even lower. However, there have been a number of "militarized disputes" between democracies, that is, conflicts with threats of military action, force deployed, and even limited use of force. Many such disputes are conflicts over fishing rights ("cod wars"), where the use of force is generally between fishing vessels on the one hand and military or coast guard vessels on the other, with no direct forceful confrontations between the representatives of the two states. Indeed, such incidents may be illustrative of the reluctance of democracies to use force against each other, even in the case of sharp disputes. Other low-level conflicts are more serious, such as the repeated border incidents between Ecuador and Peru, some of which have taken place in periods where both countries were under democratic rule. They have claimed a limited number of lives, but much lower than the threshold usually set for war.

Although the debate about the democratic peace frequently assumes that countries can be neatly divided into democracies and nondemocracies, empirical studies face similar threshold problems as in defining war. In the previous century, few countries satisfied the requirements that most democrats today would specify for calling a country democratic, such as universal suffrage, full freedom of speech, and so on. Indeed, some studies of the democratic peace have used suffrage thresholds as low as 10%. However, if even such inclusive definitions of democracy yield no or very few wars between democracies, more restrictive definitions will not alter the relationship. They will, however, diminish the area of applicability of the democratic peace. In terms of Robert Dahl's classical two main dimensions of democracy (or "polyarchy"), *competition* and *participation*, the competition between political alternatives seems to be more decisive than the level of participation in promoting a democratic peace.

There is less agreement on *why* democracies do not fight each other than on the statistical regularity. The most common explanation is that democracies use nonviolent means to resolve domestic political conflicts. A competitive political system requires a second-order agreement that alternative views are legitimate, which takes precedence over the first-order disagreement between political parties. When the verdict is in from the ultimate arbiter of political disagreements, the people or its elected representatives, all parties generally accept the outcome. If they challenge it, they do so by other nonviolent means, such as verbal protest or legal procedures, but they do not resort to violence. When two parties to an international conflict are both democracies, they can transfer this nonviolent conflict behavior to the interstate level. Decision makers in one democracy know that the other country is a democracy, and they therefore expect nonviolent conflict behavior to be reciprocated. Each party has a stable expectation about the other. Conflictful issues, which in other contexts might be expected to lead to war, will stimulate the search for political compromises. Thus, democracy is, in Rudolph Rummel's words, "a general method of nonviolence." This is why competition for scarce resources, be they oil, water, or fish, do not result in armed conflict between democracies but rather in negotiations and agreements for shared use of the resources. In the event that the negotiations are protracted, both parties will adopt a cautious wait-and-see attitude in the interim period. Such caution is of course not unknown in mixed democratic/nondemocratic dyads. For instance, Norway and the Soviet Union started negotiations concerning the delimitation of the economic zone in the Barents Sea in the mid-1970s. When the Soviet Union was dissolved in 1991 the issue was still being negotiated, but neither side had made any dramatic move. But while such caution is common between countries with different political systems that have developed a stable relationship, it is virtually the rule between democracies.

A competing explanation for the democratic peace, formulated by, for example, Bruce Bueno de Mesquita and David Lalman is framed in terms of institutional constraints. The executive power is answerable directly to the people or to its representatives and is bound to seek their tacit or explicit consent before engaging in dramatic forms of conflict behavior. This will delay escalation in a crisis, and increase the probability of finding a diplomatic solution. A variant of this argument suggests that war is more costly to the general population than to the central decision makers. In a democratic political system the decision makers will eventually be called to account for whatever support they have given to policies that led to war. To forestall this, decision makers will be more cautious. It is sometimes seen as a weakness of the structural constraints explanation in that it does not seem to be able to explain why the overall participation in war is as high for democracies as for nondemocracies. However, a pattern where democracies more selectively chose to fight in low-cost wars (notably wars that they can win quickly) may be consistent with this empirical pattern of warfare. The reluctance of the public to support the war impedes the executive only in cases where a costly war is expected. A modified structural argument is that only certain types of democracies with a higher degree of restraint on the central decision makers, such as parliamentarian systems (as opposed to presidential ones) or consensus (as opposed to majoritarian) democracies, will be less warprone.

Attempts to test the two explanations against each other have been somewhat inconclusive. For one thing, it is difficult to measure the intervening variables, which are generally attitudinal, for all or most of the nation dyads in the statistical studies. If the democratic peace requires a stable set of mutual expectations, this is much more difficult to establish historically than is a particular institution pattern. Another problem is that upon closer examination, the analytical distinction between the normative and the structural explanations becomes less clear and they blend into each other.

A different kind of attempt to explain the democratic peace is one that looks for a common explanation for both, thus making the democratic peace spurious. For instance, Melvin Small and J. David Singer have suggested that democratic states are few and far apart. Since war primarily takes place between neighbors, a lack of democratic neighbors might account for the lack of war between democracies. In fact, democracies tend to cluster together rather than to be farther apart than the average pair of states. Thus, this factor can hardly account for the lack of war between democracies. Other attempts to find third variables that would render the relationship spurious have included wealth, alliance patterns, an international environment where democracies face a common enemy, or a shared preference for the status quo among democracies. No such factor on its own has been shown to account for the strong dyadic democratic peace. Indeed, given the very strong relationship between joint democracy and dyadic peace, it is intrinsically unlikely that any such factor will be found. Third factors may account for some of the statistical relationship. For instance, wealthy market economies tend to be democratic, and they also have a high degree of economic interdependence, which makes war

highly costly. However, the democratic peace cannot be completely reduced to a "capitalist peace," since poor democracies are also disproportionately peaceful toward each other and rich market economies have frequently fought each other, as in World War II.

While many have concluded that the relationship between shared democracy and the lack of war is one of the strongest empirical relationships found in international relations, the lack of democracy is by no means the most powerful explanation for international war. Multivariate studies of war indicate that more of the variation in interstate war since the Congress of Vienna is accounted for by factors such as geographical distance, wealth, and alliance patterns. The reason for this is that over most of this period democracy was relatively infrequent. Thus, while joint democracy is close to a *sufficient* condition for the absence of major armed conflict, it is far from a *necessary* condition. If the democratic peace continues to hold up in a post-Cold War world of many democracies, it will become an increasingly significant factor in explaining war and peace.

Some critics of the democratic peace have also suggested that because wars are relatively infrequent and because democracies initially were few and far between, the lack of war between democracies might be a statistical accident. A variant of this argument is that only during the Cold War do we find a fairly high number of democracies. The lack of war between these countries might be accounted for by the fact that most of them were allied with the United States, or by the peculiar stable bipolar pattern of mutual deterrence that prevailed during the Cold War, the so-called Long Peace. However, double democracy is associated with a lack of interstate armed conflict even before or after the Cold War. (Tests of the democratic peace by Bruce Russett, Spencer Weart, and others have extended all the way back to Ancient Greece.) And as time passes since the end of the Cold War without war breaking out between two democracies, the force of the argument that involves the stable bipolar pattern is weakened. Many observers had expected armed conflict to rise after the Cold War. As Peter Wallensteen and associates have shown, the immediate aftermath or the breakup of federal states like the Soviet Union and Yugoslavia was accompanied by violence, but this is now more than compensated for by the ending of a number the armed conflicts that were fueled by the Cold War, such as the conflicts in Central America and in Southern Africa.

Some sceptics have looked in detail at specific conflicts where war was narrowly avoided and have failed to find evidence of either structural constraints or non-violent norms of conflict behavior at work. Rather, they have found traditional realist factors such as power politics to have prevented full-scale war in the end, as when Layne (1994) examined four crises between the United States, Great Britain, France, and Germany in the period from 1861 through 1923. Others have examined these or other cases, reaching different conclusions. For instance, political factors have been found important in explaining how Scandinavia was transformed from a region ridden by domestic and interstate wars to a virtual zone of peace. The interpretation of single cases seems highly dependent both on the theoretical preferences of the researcher, as well as those of the historians whose work is synthesized. Most of the history of war and peace has been written in a realist mode. The theory of the democratic peace may indeed result in a reexamination of the historical description of interstate relations.

It has also been suggested by William Thompson and others that the democratic peace thesis may put the cart before the horse in that the resolution of regional conflicts frequently predates the development of democracy. Thus it may be peace that leads to democracy rather the other way around. On the other hand, democracies tend to win the wars they join and regimes which lose are frequently subject to regime change. In this sense, war can be seen as the midwife of democracy. The political transformation of Japan and Germany after World War II are classical cases.

Finally, an important statistical objection to many of the quantitative studies is that they treat each pair of nations as an independent unit of analysis, whereas it is more realistic to see long wars as a series of highly dependent events. The probability of continued war in a dyad already at war is likely to be higher than the probability of war in a new dyad. Bremer chose to deal with this problem is by limiting the analysis to the *outbreak* of war rather than its *incidence*. The dyadic democratic peace continues to be statistically significant using outbreak as the dependent variable. However, this method has another weakness in that major multi-country wars are reduced to one or just a few dyads. World War II, for instance, is reduced to the outbreak of war between Poland and Germany in 1939. A radically different approach is to model the interstate dyad as a continuous process, where the effect of previous war in the same dyad and war in neighboring dyads may also be taken into account. In such an analysis Raknerud & Håvard Hegre confirm the existence of a democratic peace, while at the same time emphasizing the recurrence and diffusion effects in interstate war.

B. Democracies Fight as Much as Other States

The persistence of the empirical finding that democracies do not fight wars against each other is matched by the lack of a relationship between the political system and war at the nation level. Most studies have found that democracies participate as much in war as do non-democracies, at least if one looks at the entire period since the Napoleonic wars. Some studies have found democracies to be less (or more) involved in war in smaller areas or for shorter time periods. For instance, democracies have been somewhat less involved in war during the Cold War and in the post-Cold War period. Many have nevertheless found the lack of war between democracies and the high participation of democracies in war to be a paradoxical combination, which raises questions about the "peacefulness" of democracies. Statistically, the two findings are perfectly compatible, and they imply that war is more frequent between democracies and non-democracies than between two non-democracies. In other words, the politically mixed dyads are the most warprone, and this is confirmed by empirical studies. These findings do not seem to depend much on the exact threshold set for democracy or for the level of violence.

One possible explanation for why democracies fight as frequently as others is that they might be attacked by nondemocracies, and that their own war participation is mostly reactive. By their very example, democracy may be seen as a subversive challenge, provoking attack from neighboring autocracies. Such a pattern would be consistent with a view of democracies as constrained in their foreign policies, as well as with the explanation of the democratic peace in terms of a nonviolent normative culture in democracies. To date, there are no statistical studies that show democracies to initiate war less frequently than do nondemocracies. However, war initiation is notoriously difficult to measure, as difficult perhaps as to determine which of two children started a fight at the dinner table. The question of the initiation of violence easily becomes mixed up with patterns of escalation and extension of the conflict. Thus, in the most commonly used dataset on international war, the Correlates of War data generated by Singer & Melvin Small, the United States is coded as the initiator of the Vietnam War in 1965. But this is a result of the start of U.S. bombing of North Vietnam, which in the eyes of the investigators tipped the balance of the war from a civil war to an interstate war. Vietnam was not at peace when the United States escalated the war. The question of preventive or preemptive war also complicates the link between war initiation and peacefulness. However, the six most violent wars since the Congress of Vienna (all of which occurred in this century), the two World Wars, the Sino-Japanese, the Korean war, the Vietnam war, and the Iran-Iraq war, were all initiated by nondemocracies, although other nondemocracies were most often the original targets. Generally, while democracies participate in war as frequently as do nondemocracies, they are less frequent participants in the outbreak of war. Democracies tend to join the war later, they may escalate the war, but they are less frequently present at its creation. This is not tantamount to saying that democracies are more peaceful. Such a statement would require a much more detailed analysis of patterns of escalation and consideration of colonial wars in addition to wars between independent states. To date, these "extrasystemic" wars have generally been ignored in studies to date of the democratic peace.

One clear reason for the high war participation of democracies is that they more frequently participate in military alliances among themselves and also with nondemocracies. Thus, in the great multicountry wars of this century (the two World Wars, the Korean War, and the Vietnam War) the number of participants allied with the democracies was much higher than the number of countries on the other side (and they included many nondemocracies). Frequently, democracies that are pulled into war through their alliances suffer relatively minor losses—the Netherlands, for instance, suffered but 100 casualties in the Korean War—and it can be argued that their war participation is more symbolic and political than a material contribution to the war effort. The data that show war participation to be as high for democracies as for nondemocracies do not distinguish between different levels of war participation.

Rudolph Rummel has taken this argument one step further to show that democratic countries suffer much smaller losses in war. While democratic countries suffered battle-related losses of .23% of their population per year in the first 80 years of this century, autocratic countries lost .35%, and totalitarian countries .56%. Democracies are known to show greater respect for human life in the sense that they generally do not engage in genocide of their own citizens or those of other countries, they rarely if ever permit scarcities of food to develop into mass starvation, and they have more frequently abolished the death penalty. It would be consistent with this to find that democracies tend to avoid fighting wars in a way that will sacrifice great numbers of people in meaningless confrontations. However, as Allan Stam has shown, democracies have usu-

ally overpowered their opponents in war and have tended to win the war eventually. Regardless of how the war started, a disproportionate share of the violence has eventually taken place on the territory of nondemocracies. Democracies are also generally more advanced technologically and can project force at greater distances. This is a plausible explanation for why democracies suffer fewer casualties and it does not necessarily imply that democracies are more peaceful. The lower casualty rate of democracies is even compatible with notions of democracies as arrogant and self-righteous, and anxious to fight their wars by proxy in the Third World where their violence will affect the democracies less. To properly relate the severity of war to the question of peacefulness would at least require more detailed data on *who* kills *whom*, and *where*, and such data have not yet been collected in systematic form.

Even if there is no clear tendency for established democracies to participate more or less in war, there is some evidence that the process of political change may destabilize countries and make them more prone to domestic as well as international violence. However, changes away from democracy are probably at least as dangerous as changes in the other direction. And the risks resulting from political change are eventually overcome as the system stabilizes at a high level of democracy.

C. More Democracy, More Peace?

During the last 150 years, there has been a process of increasing democratization at the national level. This process has not been monotonic; rather there have been "waves" of democratization, in Samuel Huntington's famous phrase, followed by periods of stagnation and setbacks. The current wave of democratization, which started well before the end of the Cold War, has sent the share of independent countries with a reasonably democratic political system well over 50% (see Fig. 1), and higher than ever before. However, human rights groups are concerned that civil and political rights have not kept pace with the increase in formally democratic procedures, and speculation abounds as to whether the third wave has already crested or will do so in the near future.

The most pressing question arising out of the debate about the democratic peace is at the system level: Should we expect a rising level of democracy to be accompanied by less war in the international system? Most of those who have commented on this question have assumed that the lack of war between democracies implies logi-

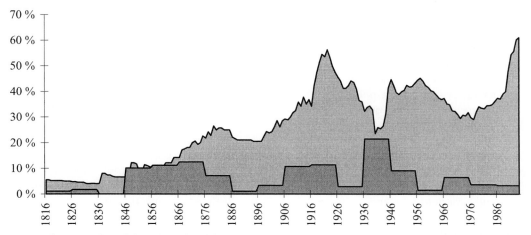

FIGURE 1 Relative number of democracies in the world, 1816–1994 (%). The data were taken from the Polity III dataset compiled by Jaggers & Gurr (1995), as corrected in 1996 and available on anonymous ftp from ⟨isere@colorado.edu⟩. Democracy is defined as 3 or higher on the difference between the indices for institutionalized democracy and autocracy indices. The war data are aggregated by 10-year periods and are taken from the Correlates of War project.

cally that an increase in the share of democracies (which also implies an increasing share of jointly democratic dyads) must lead to less war. However, the lack of a relationship between democracy and the overall participation of countries in war might lead us to expect no change in the frequency of war with increasing levels of democracy. This seems truly paradoxical, and both inferences cannot be true at the same time.

The reason for the apparent paradox is that at a low level of global democracy an increase in the number of democracies produces more double-democratic dyads (which are peaceful), but also more politically mixed dyads (which are the most warprone). In the early stages of a process of global democratization, adding one new democracy implies a much greater increase in mixed dyads than in double-democratic dyads. The first democracy introduces no joint democracies, the second, one, and so on, while the number of new mixed dyads is (n-1) (where n is the number of countries in the international system), (n-2), and so on. If the probability of war in the different kinds of dyads remains the same, it follows that the initial process of democratization must be accompanied by an *increasing* frequency of war in the system as a whole. Only when a certain threshold is passed will further democratization lead to a decreasing frequency of war in the system. Thus, the relationship between democracy and war at the system level assumes an A-shape (or inverted U-shape). Increased levels of democracy first produces more war, then less. Obviously, if democracies do not fight one another at all, war will be eliminated in a world where all countries are democratic.

Empirical studies of democracy and peace at the system level provide some tentative support for the curvilinear relationship between democracy and peace for the world as a whole. Since most wars take place between neighbors, a regional perspective may be relevant here. In Europe, the process of democratization is probably far enough along that increasing democratization will contribute to reducing the incidence of war (disregarding any temporary destabilization as a result of the process of political change). But this may be very different in other parts of the world. In some areas, the emergence of more democratic regimes may still be seen as a challenge to authoritarian rule and provoke new wars. "The clash of civilizations" predicted by Huntington cannot be prevented by the democratic peace alone, unless all of these civilizations tend toward democracy. However, the emergence of democracy as the hegemonic form of government worldwide makes it somewhat less likely that an authoritarian country can attack a democratic neighbor without retribution.

D. Democracies and Civil War

Since the end of World War II most wars have been civil wars, although the bloodiest wars are still mostly international ones. During the period from 1989 until 1996, Peter Wallensteen and his colleagues at Uppsala University have identified a total of 101 armed conflicts occurring in 68 different locations, most of them in the Third World and all but a handful of them domestic. For conflicts large enough to qualify as wars, international conflicts are also in a small minority. Does the democratic peace have any relevance to this type of conflict?

The idea of democracy as a "method of nonviolence" would indicate that democracies should solve their internal problems without using violence. The more democratic, the higher the regard for the political rights of minorities, which may one day become majorities or parts of ruling coalitions. From this perspective, one might expect a monotonic relationship: the more democratic a country, the less domestic violence.

On the other hand, the theory of resource mobilization argues that the more democratic a regime, the more conflict it will experience. Openness in a political system encourages political activity of all kinds, and all of this activity will probably not be expressed through political institutions. A certain degree of conflict may be a price that democracies have to pay for the individual freedom that they permit. Thus, the more democratic a regime, the more likely is it that various groups express political protest, nonviolent as well as violent. This is one reason that the democratic wave after the end of the Cold War has resulted in some new conflicts, because liberalization has permitted the open expression of old hostilities, which were previously repressed by autocratic forces. This might lead us to expect more domestic violence with increasing democracy.

Treating these two perspectives as complementary rather than competing, Edward Muller and Erich Weede concluded that domestic violence is likely to be low under very strict authoritarian rule, but also in highly democratic countries. In the former, there is *no opportunity* to form an opposition, and any rebellion is nipped in the bud before it develops into an organized force. In democracies there is *no motive* for rebellion, because conflicts are handled in nonviolent ways. In the in-between societies—the semidemocracies—the opposition is able to organize. But it is unable to get full recognition for the legitimacy of its demands, and the political bargaining process is skewed in favor of the executive authority. In this in-between area, then, armed rebellion may seem justified and may offer greater promise of change than to wait for the rulers to change their ways peacefully. Empirical studies clearly support this view, for civil wars as well as for minor domestic armed conflicts.

Some democratic countries have experienced severe cases of terrorism during and following the Cold War. Some of this terrorism has been supported politically and financially from nondemocratic neighboring states. But Jan Oscar Engene has linked the occurrence of terrorism to flaws in the practice of democracy and a relatively recent legacy of authoritarian rule, as in

Germany and Japan. Stable, well-established, and "inclusive" democracies are generally free of significant political terrorism.

III. THE LIMITS OF DEMOCRATIC PEACE

The democratic peace thesis is one of the most promising findings to come out of the quantitative study of war and peace. Indeed, the observation that democracies do not fight one another is so simple and obvious that it is a little surprising that it was not made earlier. Of course, the idea that a single factor (a common dedication to democracy) could virtually eliminate the possibility of war between two countries may seem to good to be true. The first systematic study was made by a criminologist, Dean Babst, and as an outsider he may have found it easier to spot the most obvious correlate of war, while the insiders were pursuing various more sophisticated but less productive leads.

There may also be political reasons for the initial reluctance of scholars in peace research and international relations to take the democratic peace thesis seriously. Virtually all systematic research on the causes of war was taking place in countries affected by the Cold War. Research attributing major importance to political democracy seemed propagandistic to many peace researchers and others who subscribed to a "third way" between East and West and disliked anything that smacked of propaganda for "the free world" (which included many nonfree countries). The debate on imperialism in the 1970s focused on the belligerent nature of some of the leading democracies (notably France and the U.S.) rather than on their peacefulness toward other democracies. On the other hand, the idea of a democratic peace seemed too "soft" for many realists, who felt more comfortable with the traditional ideas of bipolarity and deterrence. Of course, since the democratic peace offers no particular formula for peace between different regime types (short of converting the nondemocracies to democracy) realist ideas were more relevant to the main dividing lines in the Cold War world. The emergence of zones of peace based on shared democracy among traditional enemies, for instance in Western Europe, could be attributed to their common fear of the Soviet Union. The end of the Cold War ended not only the bipolar deterrence pattern, but also the hegemony of realist thought.

The emergence of the idea of a democratic peace is part of a broader revival of liberal theories of international relations. John Oneal, Bruce Russett, and others have revived interest in the old idea that war does not pay for economically highly interdependent countries and have found new evidence for it. Most wars have taken place between highly interdependent states, but that is now more commonly interpreted as an artifact of the relationship between contiguity and war, although relating economic interdependence to peace remains more controversial than the democratic peace. There is new optimism about the respect for international law and increased recognition of international organizations.

However, the idea of the democratic peace remains politically controversial to some extent and is attacked both from "the right" and "the left." A series of critical articles in the journal *International Security* in the mid-1990s may be interpreted as a realist counterattack, based mainly on the idea that the democratic peace is at best a temporary phenomenon arising during the Cold War and a spurious effect of the stable bipolar pattern of that period.

On the other hand, radical and liberal critics of the democratic peace thesis have focused on the use of covert action and overt military intervention against regimes that resisted the hegemonic world order. For instance, during the Cold War, the United States repeatedly tried to undermine radical regimes in Latin America. These types of confrontations do not reach the level of violence required to qualify as wars, but they do not exemplify a nonviolent system of conflict resolution either. The extensive colonialism practiced by democratic countries is also difficult to reconcile with the idea of the peacefulness of democracies. The response of the proponents of the democratic peace hypothesis has usually been that at least the more drastic forms of covert action and military intervention are morally impossible to justify for democracies when the opponent is fully democratic. Military interventions and covert action against regimes like Castro's Cuba or the Sandinistas in Nicaragua are brought within the realm of the politically feasible and morally quasi-defensible precisely by the lack of democratic practice in these regimes.

Those who agree that military intervention and covert action have primarily been directed against nondemocratic regimes, may nevertheless have reservations against a trend toward increased interventionism in the service of democracy. In the United States the Clinton administration has formulated a "strategy of enlargement" that aims to expand the world community of democracies. If this were to involve extensive use of military intervention, a peacebuilding strategy would require the use of unpeaceful means, with debatable net effects. Action on behalf of the international community will still effectively be carried out by the major powers, which may find it difficult to distinguish between global interests and their own. The question may also be raised whether democracy is likely to take hold if countries are forced to democratize. Germany and Japan after World War II are the prime examples that such a strategy may be successful, but at great cost. Attempts to export democracy to Third World countries—whether by peaceful or not so peaceful means—have not been equally successful. Moreover, during the Cold War many interventions by democratic countries led to the establishment or consolidation of authoritarian rather than democratic regimes, as in Iran in 1953 and in Guatemala in 1954. However, it is becoming increasingly rare for a major power to intervene without reference to the authority of an international organization.

The major means for promoting the expansion of democracy will remain economic and political rather than military. These means of influence are slower and less dramatic, but they may also have a lower probability of backfiring. At the end of the day, democratization is probably mostly a matter of internal forces, and the outside world may have limited influence over this process. Only then can a worldwide democratic peace be built on a solid foundation.

Also See the Following Articles

CIVIL WARS • CONFLICT MANAGEMENT AND RESOLUTION • DIPLOMACY • PEACE AGREEMENTS • PEACE, DEFINITIONS OF • PEACEMAKING AND PEACEBUILDING • PEACE STUDIES, OVERVIEW • WARFARE, TRENDS IN

Bibliography

The literature on the democratic peace is enormous and is increasing rapidly. The following list is by necessity selective. For reviews of the literature, see Gleditsch (1992), Gleditsch & Hegre (1997), Chan (1997), Ray (1995), Russett (1993), and Thompson & Tucker (1997), as well as special sections or entire issues of periodicals such as *European Journal of International Relations* (4/1995), *International Interactions* (3/1993), *International Security* (2/1994), *Journal of Conflict Resolution* (2/1991), and *Journal of Peace Research* (4/1992 and 4/1997).

Bremer, S. A. (1992). Dangerous dyads. Conditions affecting the likelihood of interstate war, 1816–1965. *Journal of Conflict Resolution, 36,* 309–341.

Bueno de Mesquita, B., & Lalman, D. (1992). *War and reason: Domestic and international imperatives.* New Haven, CT: Yale University Press.

Chan, S. (1997). In search of democratic peace: Problems and promise. *Mershon International Studies Review, 41,* 59–91.

Engene, J. O. (1994). *Europeisk Terrorisme. Vold, stat og legitimitet*

[European terrorism. Violence, the state, and legitimacy]. Oslo: TANO.

Gleditsch, N.P. (1992). Democracy and peace. *Journal of Peace Research, 29,* 369–376.

Gleditsch, N. P. (Ed.) (1997). *Conflict and the environment.* Dordrecht: Kluwer.

Gleditsch, N. P., & Hegre, H. (1997). Peace and democracy: Three levels of analysis. *Journal of Conflict Resolution, 41,* 283–310.

Huntington, S. P. (1991). *The third wave. Democratization in the late twentieth century.* Norman, OK, & London: University of Oklahoma Press. [Paperback edition, 1993.]

Jaggers, K., & Gurr, T.R. (1995). Tracking democracy's third wave with the polity III data. *Journal of Peace Research, 32,* 469–482.

Layne, C. (1994). Kant or cant. The myth of the democratic peace. *International Security, 19,* 5–49.

Levy, J. S. (1989). The causes of war: A review of theories and evidence. In P. E. Tetlock, J. L. Husbands, R. Jervis, P.C. Stern, & C. Tilly (Eds.), *Behavior, Society, and Nuclear War.* (pp. 209–313). New York: Oxford University Press (209–313).

Muller, E.N., & Weede, E. (1990). Cross national variation in political violence. A rational action approach. *Journal of Conflict Resolution, 34,* 624–651.

Oneal, J. R., Oneal, F. H., Maoz, Z., & Russett, B. (1996). The liberal peace: Interdependence, democracy, and international conflict, 1950–86. *Journal of Peace Research, 33,* 11–28.

Raknerud, A., & H. Hegre (1997). The hazard of war. *Journal of Peace Research, 34,* 385–404.

Ray, J. L. (1995). *Democracy and international conflict. An evaluation of the democratic peace proposition.* Columbia, SC: University of South Carolina Press.

Rummel, R. J. (1995). Democracy, power, genocide, and mass murder. *Journal of Conflict Resolution, 39,* 3–26.

Russett, B. (1993). *Grasping the democratic peace. Principles for a post-Cold War world.* Princeton, NJ: Princeton University Press.

Singer, J. D., & M. Small (1994). *Correlates of war project: International and Civil War data, 1816–1992 (ICPSR 9905).* Ann Arbor, MI: Inter-university Consortium for Political and Social Research.

Stam, A. (1996). *Win, lose, or draw: Domestic politics and the crucible of war.* Ann Arbor, MI: University of Michigan Press.

Thompson, W. R., and R. Tucker (1997). A tale of two democratic peace critiques. *Journal of Conflict Resolution, 41,* 428–454. [See also debate with H. Farber and J. Gowa & E. D. Mansfield and J. Snyder in the same issue.]

Wallensteen, P., & M. Sollenberg (1997). Armed conflicts, conflict termination and peace agreements, 1989–96. *Journal of Peace Research, 34,* 339–358.

Peace Culture

Elise Boulding
Dartmouth College

GLOSSARY

Ahimsa The principled practice of nonkilling, non-destruction of any living thing. An ideal taught by Gandhi but acknowledged by him as not always possible in practice.

Altruism Concern for the welfare of others even at the expense of one's own well-being.

Biophilia A concept developed by Edward Wilson to refer to a postulated biologically based emotional affiliation of human beings to other living organisms, subject to being mediated by social learning.

Civil Society Citizens interacting in community spaces on behalf of shared common interests. In character civil society is nongovernmental, nonmilitary, and—traditionally—also nonecclesiastical. NGOs (nongovernmental organizations) are often referred to as the backbone of civil society.

Conscientious Objectors Citizens who refuse military service either because of deeply held views on the sacredness of human life, or because of a secular, humanistic valuing of human life. Such citizens are committed to nonviolent alternatives to war.

Culture of Peace A cluster of relational and institutional chacteristics that ennable a society to respond peacefully and creatively to difference and conflict.

Nonviolence A practice of doing no harm, physical or mental, to others. When practiced in social change movements, nonviolence calls for a strategy of noncooperation. Nonviolent conflict resolution emphasizes cooperative problem solving that meets the needs of all parties.

Peace (1) Negative peace refers to the absence of war. (2) Positive peace refers to a condition in which social and economic justice and well-being are ensured for all. (3) Inner peace refers to a condition of inner harmony in the individual.

Power Power *over* is the ability to make others do something they do not want to do. Power *with*, or empowerment, enables others to carry out actions of social value that they have previously felt unnable to perform.

Sarvodaya A concept frequently used by Gandhi to refer to "the welfare of all."

Utopia The subject and title of a book by Thomas More (1516) meaning literally "no place"—an imagined place or society that has achieved a perfect social system.It also refers to intentional communities whose goal is to create an ideal miniature society.

Copyright © 1999 by Academic Press.
All rights of reproduction in any form reserved.

PEACE CULTURE refers to a cluster of attributes that enables peaceable behavior to take place in a society. This cluster can be thought of as a mosaic of identities, attitudes, values, beliefs, and institutional patterns that lead people to live nurturantly with one another and the earth itself without the aid of structured power differentials, to deal creatively with their differences, and share their resources. This article will review (I) conceptual dimensions of peace culture; (II) cultures of war and peace in the historical record; (III) utopianism; (IV) peace-war dualism in religious cultures; (V) the role of peace movements in peace culture; (VI) women's culture; and (VII) peace culture in everyday life.

I. CONCEPTUAL DIMENSIONS OF PEACE CULTURE

Peace cultures as separate entities exist but are not common. They can be identified in communities that adhere to religious teachings of nonviolence, and in relatively isolated indigenous communities that handle all conflicts with an easy but practiced nonviolence. More generally, peaceableness and aggression coexist as clusters of attitudes and behaviors present in varying proportions in most societies, reflecting the basic human need for bonding on the one hand, and the equally basic human need for autonomy, for personal space, on the other. Each society develops its own patterns of balancing these needs, and the pattern may be primarily nonviolent, or one of intermittent violence alternating with relative periods of peace. A peace culture cannot be said to be present simply in the absence of war. Rather, it is a continuous process of nonviolent problem solving and the creation of institutions that meet the needs of all its members. Peace culture is thus stronger in some societies, weaker in others. Many different blends of peaceable and "warrior culture" themes can be found, with the balance between them shifting from society to society and from historical moment to historical moment.

Peace culture is not synonomous with civil society, but is closely related to it, only with a stronger emphasis on the skills, processes and institutions that ennable nonviolent solutions in the face of serious differences, and on the attitudes and values that make peaceful behaviors possible.

UNESCO's Culture of Peace Program, initiated in 1995 to assist wartorn societies in the work of reconciliation and rebuilding, has six components that help to elucidate the goals and methods of intentional development of peace culture:

(1) Power is redefined not in terms of violence or force, but of active nonviolence. This component builds upon the experience of active nonviolence as a means of social change and its proven success during the 20th century. Using nonviolence as a means and strategy, social movements contribute to the establishment of new institutions consistent with the other components of a culture of peace.

(2) People are mobilized not in order to defeat an enemy but in order to build understanding, tolerance, and solidarity. This component, corresponding to the central tenets of nonviolence developed by Gandhi, King, and Mandela, emphasizes the need for liberating the oppressor as well as the oppressed, and places strategies for developing unity at the center of deliberation and action.

(3) The hierarchical, vertical authority that characterizes the culture of violence and war is replaced by a culture of peace, characterized by a democratic process, in which people participate on a continuing basis in making decisions that affect their lives. This approach represents both a tactical means and a strategic end, engaging people in decision making at all levels, involving them, and empowering them through the victories achieved.

(4) Secrecy and control of information by those in power is replaced by the free flow and sharing of information among everyone involved. The accessibility of information undermines authoritarianism and encourages social change. It is the necessary basis for real, participatory democracy, both in the process of social change and in the new institutions resulting from it.

(5) The male-dominated culture of violence and war is replaced by a culture based upon power sharing between men and women, especially the caring and nurturing capabilities traditionally associated with and developed by women. This strategy—and goal—places the engagement and empowerment of women at the center of the process of peacebuilding, as well as in the new institutions emerging from it.

(6) Finally, the exploitation that has characterized the culture of violence and war (slavery, colonialism, and economic exploitation) is replaced by cooperation and sustainable development for all. This component distinguishes the culture of peace from static conceptions of peace which perpetuate the violence of the status quo, and links it intrinsically with social justice and the changes necessary to attain and to preserve it.

II. CULTURES OF WAR AND PEACE IN THE HISTORICAL RECORD

For every society, regardless of how violent, bonding activity is central to the reproduction of that society. Daily life revolves around raising and feeding families and organizing the work of production and of meeting human needs, interspersed with times of feasting and celebration of human creativity in poetry, song, dance, and art. The historical record, however, is generally written as the story of the rise and fall of empires, a chronicle of reigns, wars, battles, and military and political revolutions. According to this view, well expressed by the historian W. H. McNeil, the story of the ingestion of weaker societies by stronger ones and of rivalries among the strong is the story of humankind. If we want to know why so few historians record the more complex interplay of human activities in various domains of life, we can look to the record explicitly left for posterity for the answer: monuments glorify achievements in battle. From ancient times, written records recount the triumphs of priest-kings and their gods in this world and the next.

The glorification of the warrior in history has a powerful effect on the human self-image. It leads to viewing the struggle for power as the basic theme of human existence. Current high levels of reported local and national interethnic and intercultural violence and high levels of military preparedness for interstate violence on every continent, confirms this view. Yet a closer inspection of the historical record, a new look at the biosphere of earth, and a new look at what Native Americans call "all our relations," suggests a different basic model of human relationship with life itself. The possibility of a nonviolent integration of bonding and autonomy needs for humans removes the specter of a continuous precarious balancing of warrior culture and peace culture, and opens the way for more robust conceptions of peace culture for the future. The seeds for this development already exist in many warrior traditions. Note for example the prayer recited on ceremonial occasions by the sailors of the British Navy: "Go forth into the world in peace; be of good courage; hold fast that which is good; render no man evil for evil; strengthen the fainthearted; support the weak; help the afflicted; honor all men."

Looking first at the activity within the scholarly community, it was in the 1920s and continuing through the 1950s, that a small group of interdisciplinary-minded scholars and activists began laying the foundations of a new social science discipline that would develop new perspectives on war, and focus on alternative methods of conflict resolution between states. Quincy Wright's pathbreaking Study of War Project represented a major conceptual breakthrough in questioning the inevitability of war in human history.

During this same period Sorokin analyzed the dynamics of historical change in culture systems from the 5th century BCE through the 1920s, and the relationship between culture types (ideational-idealistic or sensate/materialistic) and the frequency of warfare over time. Was warfare dyng out or increasing over time? The answer was, *neither*. There were only random fluctutations over the centuries, though war itself was becoming more lethal. The very fact of random fluctuations undermined the concept of war as unavoidable.

As historians continued to ask sharp new questions of history, in the 1960s a group of American scholars formed the Council on Peace Research in History, which soon linked with the comparable European Working Group on Peace Research in History. These historians have documented peace movements and peace processes through the centuries. Their task has been not only to change the image of human history as the record of war, by documenting the far more ubiquitous activities of everyday problem solving and conflict resolution at every level from local communities to interstate relations, but also to demonstrate how often such behavior created effective alternatives to military action.

Timetables of History, a project begun in Germany and subsequently translated into English by Bernard Grun, represents an important step in changing the image of history. *Timetables* tabulates events year by year from 501 C.E. (and by half centuries before that starting at 4000 B.C.E). The column entries for the year-by-year records include (a) History and Politics, (b) Literature, Theater, (c) Religion, Philosophy, Learning, (d) Visual Arts, (e) Music, (f) Science, Technology, Growth and (g) Daily Life. The (a) column, listing the battles and kingdoms won and lost, is the fullest, but the other columns get fuller over time, recording peaceful human activities in the civil society.

Voices from the natural science community have also contributed to this image-changing process. In 1984 Edward Wilson contributed the concept of *biophilia*, "an innate tendency to focus on life and lifelike processes," and asks that we "look to the very roots of (human) motivation and understand why, in what circumtances and on which occasions, we cherish and protect life." Proposing that biophilia is genetically based in humans, Wilson opens up a new way of thinking about the possibilities in human and social development, including a strong emphasis on the sociobiological importance of human altruism and helping behavior, and the role of nature in human emotional bonding. In recent decades primatologists have also been producing studies of social behavior of humankind's relatives, the apes, that underline their community-oriented behavior and strategies for containing disruptive behavior that would destroy group harmony.

Add to this the appearance in 1986 of the UNESCO-sponsored *Seville Statement on Violence,* which states that "It is scientifically incorrect to say we have inherited a tendency to make war from our animal ancestors" ; that "War is biologically possible, but it is not inevitable," and that "There are cultures which have not engaged in war for centuries, and there are cultures which have engaged in war frequently at some times and not at others." The Statement concludes, "Just as 'wars begin in the minds of men', peace also begins in our minds. The same species who invented war is capable of inventing peace. The responsibility lies with each of us." While not every scientist agrees with this statement, It has been signed by many scientific and scholarly associations, and suggests that a wider future development of peace culture is possible.

III. UTOPIAN THOUGHT AND EXPERIMENTATION AS EXPRESSIONS OF PEACE CULTURE

A. Historical Utopianism

The fact that all civilizational traditions have recorded imagery of the Other and Better, and that this Other is peaceful, in contrast to the (often) turbulent present, suggests a powerful human longing to live in peace. Not only do we have the classical visions of Elysian Fields, the Isles of the Blessed, Zion, Valhalla, and Paradise, but blessed isles are also part of the dream-world of tribal peoples. Utopian elements are also found in Taoism, Theravada Buddhism, Medieval Islam, and in Chinese, Japanese, and Indian stories about imaginary havens of delight.

Under the pressure of social upheaval, the archetypal vision is transformed into concrete imagery answering to specific social problems. Plato's *Republic* was a response to the Peloponnesian Wars. The millennialist movements that erupted by the hundreds in the Middle Ages were responses to plague, famine, and the gradual breakdown of the feudal order. Although utopian thinking is thought of as a flight from reality (Thomas More's pattern-setting *Utopia* meant "no place"), actually the

great utopians of history tended to be masterful critics of their own time.

Two contradictory themes of modern utopian thought are the passion for order and the longing for what is "natural." The reality of expansionist urban-based industrial states and an accompanying worldwide military forcing system has produced contrasting responses of alienation on the one hand, and of faith that humans are clever enough to design social and physical technologies that could solve all social problems, on the other. One school of utopians sees science and technology as offering the tools for creating a rational and peaceful order. Robert Boguslaw points out that automation systems are designed to reduce as far as possible the number of responses that humans can make (i.e., reduce human error) while increasing as far as possible the number of responses the (error-immune) machine makes. Behavioral modification is the psychological equivalent. Society as a perfectly functioning mechanism, however, is a concept that readily makes room for authoritarianism.

In tension with the passion for order is the longing for the spontaneous untidy abundance of nature. The second, organic approach sees nature as evolving in its own way, accepts that transformation is possible, and calls for a new human consciousness able to recognize and work with that transformation. On the whole, transformationists are peaceful, though the chiliastic uprisings of the Middle Ages could become bloody, and the recent violence of the Aum Cult in Japan and the mass suicide of the Gate of Heaven cult in the United States reveal a revisionist concept of spiritual peace. The feminist utopian tradition, seen in Gilman's classical *Herland*, is an example of a grounded utopianism that takes account of both nature and humanity.

Since utopia is always The Other, the changes implied by utopia are in effect revolutionary whether based on commitment to gradual evolutionary change or sudden restructuring. Thus revolutionary violence keeps appearing in many utopian efforts, even when the goal is equality, justice and peace, as in the case of the French Revolution. In this century, the macrolevel utopian experiments in the Soviet Union, Spain, Cuba and China, as well as in Tanzania, Mexico, and Iran, all ran into difficulties because of the problem of scale, quite apart from the issue of the viability of the design itself. Microlevel utopias do not suffer from that problem, and represent practical efforts to create peaceful and just communities within the larger society. They may be thought of as islands of peace culture.

B. Current Small-Scale Utopian Communities

Significant contemporary utopian community movements have originated in the Two-Thirds World. The *sarvodaya* movement builds on the *panchayat* tradition in India and incorporates Gandhi's concept of nonviolent village communities carrying out local development using local resources, with careful use of other technologies when appropriate. This is now an international movement with linkages to comparable groups on other continents. In Sri Lanka the counterpart institution is the *shramadama*, involving community work-sharing with a strong spiritual component.

The United States has had a strong tradition of utopian communities since its earliest days. Nordhoff's 1875 survey of "communistic" societies found 72 communes, the oldest 80 years old, the youngest 22. All religiously based, with various patterns of communal ownership and similar work ethic, high craft skill level, quality schooling for children, these communes were peaceable, with a high standard of morality, generosity, and sharing with the local poor. Members enjoyed their lives—though Nordhoff found them terribly dull! The religious communes, usually with experienced farmers, had long lifespans (some are still functioning in the 1990s). Socialist experiments, secular and humanistic, intended to be working models that could change the world, had the same generosity, peaceableness and highmindedness, but little skill in farming, and tended to be short-lived.

The Depression saw a whole new wave of utopian communities, born of economic necessity combined with strong idealism, demonstrating viable alternative lifeways in capitalist society. This was followed by a wave of communities founded by the generation of conscientious objectors from World War II, who came out of alternative service camps and prisons determined not to return to the same old world, but to translate their visions for the good society into experimental communities. Some were short-lived, but 27 of the communities founded in the Depression, war, and postwar years still exist, and are listed in the 1995 *Communities Directory*.

The 1960s and 1970s generated a new round of utopian experiments, often lumped together as "hippie" or "new age" communities. Some disintegrated rapidly, but 200 have continued to be operational to the present. Each of these communities has developed a viable work discipline and a critical mass of altruistic members with some vision of society for which they are willing to keep working. This vision includes the abolition not only of militarism, but of war itself, and of substantial changes in the character of the state. It includes a sense of social justice, a strong environmental ethic, and a discerning attitude toward science and technology. Many are rural, all have active rural-urban networks.

These utopian movements to create islands of peace continue. In the 1980s and 1990s, 268 additional communities have been founded, all with a strong ecological and earth-stewardship orientation, also strongly peace-activist and family centered, favoring homeschooling for their children. Many, but by no means all, have a spiritual base. The Danish co-housing movement, providing extended-family relationships for families and individuals who build contiguous housing in planned settlements, is now a growing phenomenon in the United States. A partial and incomplete list from the same 1995 *Directory* of 70 communities in 21 other countries in Europe, Latin America, the Asia Pacific, and Africa, suggests very similar community themes and activity patterns to those already described.

While utopian thought and experimentation has its dark side, a strong case can be made that intentional experimental communities directed toward an increase in human sharing, cooperation, gentleness, justice, and gaia-awareness, do in fact function as elements of peace culture for the larger societies in which they find themselves. They are not simply isolated islands of peace. These utopias are connected with the larger society through all kinds of people networks leading into the national and transnational world of nongovernmental organizations (NGOs), and serving as a leaven in the civil society of each country in which they are found.

IV. PEACE-WAR DUALISM IN RELIGIONS CULTURES

A. Historical Background

While each religious faith has generated utopian communities as discussed above, it is nevertheless true that religious cultures are not by definition peace cultures. Instead, each religion has two cultures, one based on a vision of a warrior god whose followers wage holy war against god's enemies, the other based on a vision of a loving creator who teaches that there is one family of humankind, that humans are to love and care for one another and for all living things. The male warrior culture headed by a patriarchal warrior god demands the subjection of women, children, and other aliens to men, the protopatriarchs. This image, found in the major world religions, has served as the template for the institution of patriarchy in the social order. The divine legitimation of violence provides a blessing to the household patriarch when he uses violence against the women and children of his household, much as it blesses the soldier who goes forth to war. This institutionalization of violence at the level of the family, where primary socialization takes place, has weakened the peace teachings of Christianity, Judaism, and Islam, as well as Buddhism and Hinduism.

Yet reminders that the nonviolent way is the higher way are frequent in sacred scripts of all faiths. Military service was a forbidden occupation for early Christians up to the conversion of Constantine in the 4th century. Even after the new Christian aristocracy embraced war, the peace traditions fostered by monasticism continued to generate inventive modifications of imperial warfare, such as the "Peace of God"—days of the week and times of the year when there would be no fighting, in the 9th and 10th centuries. There were large-scale peace movements all through the years of the Crusades.

One group of religious peace cultures has had a very long history. Anabaptists emerged in response to Joachim de Fiore's teachings about the post-bureaucratic Age of the Holy Spirit in 12th-century Europe. Men and women all over the continent, relating as equals, translated and taught from the Bible in the vernacular, set up communities where goods where held in common, and kept to a nonhierarchical, socially and spiritually open set of lifeways based on total nonviolence. The descendants of that tradition are today known as the historic peace churches: Quakers, Mennonites, and Brethren. They are by no means all social activists, but the cultural symbolism of the peace witness they represent has had a public influence out of all proportion to their numbers (see Section VI).

B. Contemporary Faith-Based Peace Groups

While the Anabaptists are the most easily identifiable peace culture today, there are many other faith-based peace groups, and the World Council of Churches has made strengthening the Christian peace witness of member churches a priority since its founding in 1948. Within the Catholic church, the Orthodox church, and various protestant denominations there are intentional peace communities on every continent. The Buddhist Peace Fellowship, the Muslim Peace Fellowship, and the Jewish Peace Fellowship are examples of other faith-based peace groups active locally and internationally. Many are affiliated with the international interfaith Fellowship of Reconciliation, which was founded in 1919 to work for a world order based on a culture of nonvio-

lence. It provides nonviolence training for members in Europe, the Americas, Africa, and Asia. Faith-based peace brigades modeled on the Gandhian *shanti sena* and supported by faith communities are currently working with their local counterparts in many countries to create zones of safety and peace. Efforts to strengthen the peace culture of every faith group gave rise in the 1970s to the NGO, the World Council on Religion and Peace, and more recently to the interfaith World Peace Council. The latter is to meet each year at one of the world's trouble spots to bring interfaith resources to bear on the task of peacemaking. While the holy war culture is still alive and well today, noteworthy energies are going into a process of recovering and rebuilding a peace culture that has never ceased to be part of the core spirituality of every community of faith.

V. SECULAR PEACE MOVEMENTS AND PEACE CULTURES

A. Historical Background

The gradual secularization of Western cultures in recent centuries has meant the rise of secular peace movements. Their contribution to peace culture lies less in building models of peaceful community, and more in confronting and seeking to change the structures that foster violence and war. In the broader sense, both secular and religious peace movements are peace-*building* movements. Peace building may be thought of as any activity directed toward the replacement of armed violence and physical coercion in situations of conflict by nonviolent justice-seeking behavior. Peace building creates new kinds of social space in society for new behaviors and new social relations, broadly conceived.

The systematic work to build peace structures that could enable peace cultures to flourish began with the establishment of the International Peace Bureau in 1892. By 1899 there were several thousand peace activists in more than 100 national peace organizations. Their activities contributed to the political climate in which the first Hague Peace Conference was held, and to the developments that followed it. Peace movement energies and public interest ran so high that states could not afford to ignore the Czar's invitation to the Hague, disinclined though political leaders were to take Czar Nicholas seriously. Writes historian Sandi Cooper, "A small army of indefatigable workers—men and women—travelled lecture circuits, published and catalogued libraries of books and brochures, raised money from governments and private donors, confronted politicians, challenged military budgets, criticized history curricula, combatted chauvinist and establishment media, lobbied diplomats, questioned candidates for office, telegraphed congress resolutions to foreign ministries, and held congresses nearly every year from 1889 to 1914 to thrash out common positions." The peace education movement in the schools of Europe, and the publication of large numbers of peace education textbooks, was another part of this movement aimed more directly at creating a peace culture for the next generation to grow up into.

If World War I saw the temporary collapse of these strategies for building a culture of peace, it also witnessed the birth of a remarkable peace culture in India as Gandhi and his disciples worked tirelessly to train masses of Indians to carry out nonviolent acts of public protest such as fasting, marching, or civil disobedience in an independance movement based on the concepts of *satyagraha,* truth force, and *ahimsa,* refusal to do harm. The network of ashrams in which leaders learned self-discipline, strategic analysis of the social settings in which action was to be carried out, and a spirit of deep concern for the well-being of the opposition, provided the institutional base for the movement, and for the emergent peace culture. As postindependence India moved away from Gandhi's *satyagraha,* communal violence increased and the peace culture shrank to the modest network of ashrams that still exist. Nevertheless Gandhi's teachings continue to inspire peace movements around the world; the *seeds* of that peace culture remain viable.

B. Contemporary Peace Movements

The postwar revitalization of peace movements was shadowed by splits between the one-issue antinuclear movements that were more concerned with political effectiveness than with a way of life, and the older organizations working for social transformation. Strikes, demonstrations and vigils, transcontinental peace walks, protest ships sailing in forbidden waters, all helped lead to the declaration of nuclear weapons-free zones in Latin America and the South Pacific, and a partial test-ban treaty, but weapons production, testing, and deployment by the major powers went steadily on.

As peace movements became more sophisticated in terms of political effectiveness, they became more specialized, and the links between peace movements and peaceful lifeways are harder to find, although the relevance of movement activities for peace culture continues. For example, the interdisciplinary peace research movement that began in the early 1960s soon expanded

its work beyond disarmament studies to economic conversion, alternative development, alternative defense, and ecological security, thus linking alternative security policy with grassroots alternative lifeways movements. Zone of Peace studies helped conceptualize specific social spaces for nonviolent lifeways.

Occupationally based peace organizations helped give specific content to general peace movement activity. The 1988–1989 *Peace Resource Book* listed 22 such organizations in the United States, at least half linked to transnational organizations with sections in a number of countries. The list includes associations for architects, business executives, computer professionals, educators, high-tech professionals, physicians, lawyers, media professonals, veterans, nurses, parliamentarians, performing artists, psychologists, social scientists, writers, and publishers. The fruits for peace culture include architects designing peace parks, educators designing conflict resolution curriculae for schools, physicians and nurses reconceptualizing health and illness, and artists offering drama, music, poetry, and art that express the peacemaking dimension of human experience.

Then there are the scientists' organizations addressing basic issues of the health of the planet and the hazards of nuclear and other weapons developments. They include such groups as the Pugwash Conferences on Science and World Affairs, founded in 1965 to focus the world scientific community on possibilities of disarmament; the Union of Concerned Scientists founded in 1969, and the Commission established by the International Council of Scientific Unions in the 1970s to investigate nuclear hazards. These communities have helped develop an international consensus on the need for nonviolent dispute settlement and more attention to the natural environment of an endangered planet—key elements for a macrolevel culture of peace. As powerful voices in the international community, listened to by national governments and the United Nations, they are laying the groundwork for current and future shifts in state security behavior.

Most, if not all of the 200 international peace organizations listed in the 1997 Housman's *Peace Diary* have consultative status at the United Nations and work with various United Nations bodies including Regional Disarmament Centers—there is one on each continent— and at times with special programs on regional conflicts, with the UN University based in Tokyo. Many of them will be working with UNESCO's new Culture of Peace Program, helping war victims regain personhood, helping former soldiers and guerillas—many of them children—learn new occupational skills, new habits of caring and cooperation, and community-building skills, as well as skills of rebuilding destroyed soils and forests. Other projects involve creating new school programs for war-traumatized children and new support systems for war-traumatized women, often rape victims. Like all the groups mentioned in this section, they are helping to lay the groundwork for an emerging culture of peace.

VI. WOMEN'S CULTURE AND PEACE CULTURE

A. The Concept of Women's Culture

The theme of women's family roles and women's culture as representing the ways of nurturance and peace in societies dominated by warmaking is an ancient theme in history. Identifiable women's cultures can be said to have emerged as a result of a shift from an earlier egalitarian hunting-and-gathering way of life to settled agriculture. A gradual subordination of women came about with the rise of cities, kingdoms, and empires and the patriarchal palace-temple power structures that confined women to the interiors, the *dedans*, of each society. From those hidden places, women were constantly at work in creative and inventive ways to provide nurture, healing, and the possibilities for growth and development of the men and children in their care. It often fell to women to rebuild what was destroyed in war, from tillable fields and irrigation canals to hospitals and places of refuge for war victims, and to keep alive the arts of music, dance, and poetry. From time to time individual women—queens, courtesans, artists, and philosophers—emerged from obscurity to a place in recorded history, but most of their work has been unrecorded. If the *dedans* was hidden, it was hardly protected, for the patriarch-head of each household had power of life and death over its members, and women could be victims of violence even as they wove the strands of peace culture that kept their society from extinction.

With industrialization and the rise of a new urban poverty class there also emerged the educated middle-class women who found ways to translate their sense of traditional responsibility for the well-being of their family to the community level. By the 1800s, as their concern with multiplying social problems pushed them into public spaces and political arenas, the *dehors*, they discovered that they had no civic or legal identity, no political rights, no economic power. Out of the sheer need to *act,* the suffrage movement was born, with its claims to equal rights for women and men. Slowly the link was made between the exclusion of women from public life, recurring wars, exploitation in factories, and the suffering of the poor. The new mobility for women made possible a rapid internationalization of the new women's movement . By 1915 there were 15 international women's organizations. By 1986 there were 189, 61 of them directly devoted to international understanding and peacebuilding. The remainder, organizations for women professionals, for training and development, and for religious communities, all have relevance to peacebuilding . At first Eurocentric, they have gradually shifted to a broader representation of continental perspectives around the world.

With the new critique of patriarchy as the source of the domination systems that lead to violence and war, the old *essentialist* view that women are inherently peaceable—and therefore by nature the guardians of peace culture—came to be questioned in the women's movement. As women discovered what they could do in public spaces, and entered into the whole range of hitherto male occupations and roles, they came to see differential socialization and occupational segregation as the primary causes of women's "specialization" in peacemaking. Others noted that it was precisely women's inventiveness in their new roles, their ability to imagine alternatives and to create new and effective organizational patterns and structures in many of the settings in which they worked, that demonstrated that women were "different." The debate continues. (To the extent that some fathers are beginning to share more fully in the nurturant work of parenting, it may be discovered that it is children who socialize adults into the skills of nurturance, and are a key source of basic elements of peace culture.) There are strong arguments for the position that women's knowledge and experience worlds have equipped them to function creatively as problem solvers and peacemaker in ways that men have not been equipped to function by *their* knowledge and experience worlds. More sharing of experience worlds between women and men would then be an important step in strengthening peace culture.

B. Conceptual Contributions to Peace Culture

At the intellectual level, women often mistrust their own capacity for analytic and systems thinking, essential for the kind of social restructuring required for a stronger peace culture. Yet this is precisely where women leaders have made outstanding contributions by linking the analytic and the intuitive; some examples follow.

Buddhist feminist general systems theorist and peace development activist Joanna Macy, is a leader in the *sar-*

vodaya shramadana community self-help movement originating in Asia, with strong links to the international environmental and peace movement. Macy writes,

> . . . interconnectedness with life and all other beings . . . is the living web out of which our individual, separate existences have risen, and in which we are interwoven. Our lives extend beyond our skins, in radical interdependence with the rest of the world . . . every system—be it cell, a tree or a mind—is like a transformer, changing the very stuff that flows through it.

Limits to Growth author Donella Meadows concentrates on making the theory and practice of modeling system dynamics more accurately reflect the reality of everyday life so that it can be used to understand what goes wrong with existing policy practice in the real world. Writing on the transformation of modeling she reminds us of how poorly policymakers have performed in relation to high death rates produced by starvation, leveling of forests, species extinctions, nuclear weapons accumulation. Her transformational modeling "is a release of possibilities and capablities already within the system" . It is not imported from outside. Meadows, an American, is also a sheep farmer who knows the rhythm of sowing and reaping, the rhythm of birthing and shearing. As a farmer-teacher-scholar-computer modeler who travels the world's airways and writes her own newspaper column on environmental issues, she practices systems transformation daily.

In Kenya, Wangari Maathai, professor of biology and political activist, realized that desertification in her country was part of a whole system of land deprivation, poverty and victimage of women. With other women she launched the Green Belt Movement, a community tree-planting project that is transforming deteriorating ecosysems across the country and revitalizing women's farming and community life.

In India, physicist Vandana Shiva is a practitioner of transformative systems modeling for the deteriorating ecosystems of that vast subcontinent. Responding to the traditional ecological wisdom of local peoples, she works with the Chipko (hug the trees) movement, based on village women's understanding of the role of forests in protecting the land and water and stability of mountain watersheds. She calls for a redefinition of science and rationality, of technological choice and economic development. and a reconceptualization of what is meant by the good life.

Swedish family sociologist and disarmament expert Alva Myrdal understood social systems "from the inside" as she struggled with the demanding triple task of rearing three children while partnering a world-reknowned economist and both researching and actually creating the kind of local institutions and services that a society would need to produce peaceful citizens in a humane world. Over time her systems analysis expanded in complexity from child, family, and nation to the international realm of diplomacy, first as Ambassador to India and then as Swedish Minister of Disarmament. She kept finding new entry points for social change even as the world continued to become more dangerous, maintaining that "Giving up is not worthy of a human being."

Clearly, the feminist capacities just illustrated for both analytic and intuitive thinking in terms of highly complex systems, related to a strong sense of the on-the-ground reality, are important for the double task of conceptualizing and developing peace culture . Now we will turn to some examples of actual peace movement inventions, that show the variety and range of approaches to creating a peace culture taken by different women's groups.

C. The Peace Education Movement

Contemporary peace education is to a signficant degree the product of the work of many different women's groups—teachers, social workers and peace activists, whose labors from the l840s on laid the foundation for the establishment of UNESCO 100 years later. Their goal was to develop the kind of education that would be needed for a world in which disputes would be settled peacefully. Their work included the study of child development from the perspective of how children can learn to be peaceful with one another—outstandingly exemplified in the innovative work of Maria Montessori. They also started international schools, and worked with training teachers and developing social visions of what a peaceful international community could be like. When the new field of peace research developed in the l960s, it was women peace educators who insisted that the research should not only deal with intergovernmental relations, but should conceptualize the interrelationships of peace, security, economic and social development, environmental issues, human rights, and the participation of women and minorites, as part of the central problematique of peace learning.

D. Peace Journeying

Women have walked, sailed, ridden horseback, and otherwise traveled in public spaces for peace since the beginning of the colonial era, but the peace walks and marches of the post-World War II era have had a special flavor and flair. A new level of activity was reached in 1961 with the Women's Strike for Peace Movement, which began in North America and quickly spread to Europe. The concept of the strike, of noncompliance with the basic duties of homemaking, as a way of protesting nuclear testing and preprations for war, immediately exploded into an active women's invasion of public spaces from court houses to parliaments. A *women's agenda*, based on women's understandings of the meanings of security, became a new force in politics. With humor, laughter, and flowers, as well as great seriousness, a new wave of women candidates for public office from local to national appeared in the public arena.

In this same decade, inspired by Ambassador Alva Myrdal, women's groups became visibly present at Disarmament Commission meetings in Geneva, insisting on audiences with ambassadors and heads of state. Women for Meaningful Summits has carried on this tradition, together with the more recently organized WEDO, Women's Environment and Development Organization. In short, women have become increasingly articulate and experienced in what it takes to affect Summit diplomacy.

A World War I generation women's peace organization, the Women's International League for Peace and Freedom, added to the drama of women's presence in places of high-level decision making when in 1985 its members undertook (with leadership from its Swedish Section) the Great Peace Journey. Over a 3-year period international delegations of women traveled first by bus to 25 countries in Europe, and then to countries of the Pacific, South and East Asia, the Americas, large parts of Africa, and the Middle East for a total of 90 states visited. In each country five questions were put to heads of states and senior officials in foreign ministries regarding national defense policy and willingness to use peaceful means of dispute settlement. The responses they received were reported to the Secretary General of the UN and to representatives of national missions to the UN. The grand finale was a 1988 global popular summit at the UN, giving new saliency to the UN as a place where the peoples of the world could face a general assembly of their governments seeking clearer explanations of dispute settlement practices.

E. Peace Colonies

In contrast to adventurous journeys across continents, women have also created encampments, guardian sites,

and zones of peace at munitions storage and testing sites. Living in tents right up against the barbed wire of a military base, the women of Greenham Common, England, for some years maintained a lively protest community. They lived simply, in harmony with nature and in peace with one another, practising the culture of peace they wished their country to adopt. Similar encampments were maintained at Seneca Falls, New York; Frauenfeld, Switzerland; Comiso, Sicily; Kita Fuji, Japan; Neve Shalom, Israel—and elsewhere.

F. Global Peace Services

Another idea that originated with Swedish women was the concept of a women's global peace service. The original plan was to train all-women teams to do the work that mixed peace teams such as Peace Brigades International do—interpositioning between parties in combat, protective accompaniment for endangered locals in high-violence situations, creating safe spaces for normal activities like farming, education, and care of children, help for refugees, and for humanitarian provision of health and food services in the midst of war. In fact, the group has expanded to include men, but it continues to have strong involvement of women.

G. Networking

The rapid expansion from the 19th century on of women's contacts across and between continents and the growth of women's international nongovernmental organizations through the 20th century has already been mentioned. A new phase in women's networking began with the 1975 International Women's Year world gathering of women in Mexico City. Succeeding world gatherings for women under the auspices of the United Nations in Copenhagen, Nairobi, and most recently in Beijing in 1995, have consistently maintained a triple focus on equality, development, and peace. The development of a new world sisterhood to prepare for global change was greatly assisted by the emergence of new, less formal nonhierarchical women-to-women contacts to supplement more formal nongovernmental organizations. Thirty new international contact groups came into being between 1974 and 1986, each devoted to one or more aspects of the trinity of equality, development, and peace.

In addition to the proliferation of new transcontinental contact groups, three major networks of networks developed during or after 1975: (1) ISIS, which prepared for the first Mexico City Women's Conference by holding an International Tribunal on Crimes Against

Women in Brussels in 1974; (2) the International Women's Tribune Center, which came into being to facilitate communication among NGOs during the Mexico City Conference; (3) GROOTS, which developed during the Nairobi Women's Conference, concentrating entirely on grassroots low-income rural and urban women. A strong sense of being involved in a process of social transformation permeates the interaction within and between all these networks. All are involved in creating the conditions for a peaceful and just society.

This overview of women and peace culture has considered the ways in which women have approached the challenge of creating significant strands of peace culture within the larger society—and world—in which they live. The fact that the social vision and abilities of women continue to be frustrated by male-dominated social structures, limiting the contributions women can make, accounts for the continuing emphasis in women's movements on gender equality as a condition for human development and peace.

VII. PEACE CULTURE IN EVERYDAY LIFE

A. Basic Social Bonding

What is already present in daily life that contributes to peace culture? There is a general human predisposition to be responsive to other humans. Hans Hass has undertaken a remarkable documentation of the universality of that predisposition. Traveling around the world with his camera, he has photographed a series of expressive human gestures of smiling, greeting with glad surprise (eyebrows raised), comforting another in grief by having the griever's head resting on the comforter's shoulder, a reaching-out gesture to protect a child in danger—in settings as far apart as Kenya, Samoa, and France. In cultures that practice disciplined control over such expressive gestures, one finds their fullest expression in children who have not yet learned the discipline.

Hass points out that children learn early what a smile can do. Why do humans smile so much? Because they are not, basically, unfriendly creatures. A smile is a means of eliciting contact readiness from others and of conveying accessibility to contact. A smile serves as a social bridge builder. This is only possible because humans have a certain awareness of "species identity," an awareness that exists in warrior societies as well as elsewhere. The wars of ancient China, for example, did not prevent the development of Confucian thought, in which heaven is described as father and earth as mother, and all in between as one body. "People are our brothers and we are united with all things."

This theme of being kin with all peoples is rooted in a basic experience of the social bonds of kinship and intergroup alliances, and the need for mutual aid systems in order to survive, whether in inner cities or on overstressed farmlands. Women's nurturant role in that mutual aid system is taken for granted. Less well understood is a complex interfacing role, stemming from the widespread practice of women moving to the male partner's community and being expected to serve as communication channels and mediators when differences between the communities arise.

The role of infants and young children in the gentling of the human species is often understated, and it is about more than smiling. Watching small children discover with delight the most ordinary and humdrum items of daily existence literally refreshes adults, as does seeing children at play, creating a wondrous imaginary world that has no purpose but itself.

Through most of human history people have lived in rural settings and in small-scale societies. Just as each familial household develops its own problem-solving behavior, so each social group has developed its own strategies of conflict resolution over time, uniquely rooted in local culture and passed on from generation to generation. Similarly, each society has its own fund of adaptability, built on knowledge of local environment and the historical memory of times of crisis and change. Such knowledge and experience are represented in the individual familial households that make up a community. The knowledge is woven into religious teachings, ceremonies and celebrations, in the world of work and the world of play, in environmental lore, in the sagas of times past. These are the hidden peace-building strengths of every society.

As societies become more complex, and elites become differentiated from "common people," center-periphery problems based on mutual ignorance develop. Elites not only cease to share locally based knowledge but cease literally to share a common language with locals. Traditional conflict resolution methods then break down, and new ones are slow to develop. This breakdown of communication and lack of common conflict management practices between ethnies and the larger states of which they are a part is a major problem in the contemporary world where "10,000 societies," each with its own signficant historical identity, are spread across 185 states. Current levels of intrastate as well as interstate violence are not surprising when thought of in those terms. Rediscovery of the hidden strengths of local cultures is one important aspect of peace building for this difficult transitional period in human history.

Given the diversity of negotiation and conflict-resolving behaviors that go on every day in every household and every community in those 185 states, illustrating everyday peace behavior is a challenge. The approach here will be to give one example from that small set of contemporary indigenous societies living in a preindustrial mode yet with some degree of contact with the larger world, societies that maintain a distinctive identity and set a high value on peaceableness. How they manage conflict, and how they train their children to such behaviors, will be examined. The second example will come from the Anabaptist-historic peace church culture, which consists of microsocieties that are more connected to the larger society than indigenous communities, yet remain distinctive. These examples will highlight the strategies and skill-based nature of peaceful behavior, and its dependence on an explicit set of values about nonaggression. That examination will be followed by an overview of how basic processes of socialization for peaceful behavior are at work in different aspects of daily life.

B. Selected Contemporary Societies

1. The Mbuti

The hunter-gatherer, rainforest-dwelling Mbuti in northeastern Zaire find their peacefulness in their relationship to the rainforest—their mother, father, teacher and metaphoric womb. The family hut is symbolically a womb. Mbuti is a listening culture. Children are taught to listen to the trees, learning to climb them early so they can sit high above the ground, listening and watching the life that unfolds in the treetops and the life that unfolds below. They learn to think of the whole forest as their extended family. Adults and children also sing and dance with the trees. *Ekima*, quietness, is a central value as opposed to *akami*, disturbance. While the preference for quietness and harmony is reinforced at every stage of life, it does not preclude children' rough-and-tumble play, and low-key squabbling among adults, which tends to be controlled by ridicule. Children learn interdependance and the skills of cooperation early. Adults enjoy horseplay and disputation. Semihumorous "sex wars" in which men and women line up for a tug of war between the sexes serve as tension dissipators—as the tugs of war break up with much laughter. Most groups have a "clown"—one person whose antics also help keep conflicts from getting out of hand.

The contrast between the forest as womb and the love of the silences of the forest on the one hand, and the frequency of arguing and the use of joking and ridicule to keep arguments under control, suggests an easy social equilibrium of listening quietness, singing, dancing, squabbling, and clowning. By not letting conflicts fester, disagreements do not get out of hand.

A modernizing government and current civil war are destroying the Mbutis' environment, but they are linking with other rain forest peoples in new transnational indigenous peoples' networks, doing their best to negotiate for the survival of their lifeways.

2. Anabaptists

The three major Anabaptist communities include the Brethren, Mennonites, and Quakers, plus smaller groups such as the Amish and the Hutterites. They define themselves as living "in the world but not of it," holding to testimonies of simplicity, gender and racial equality, and personal and social nonviolence, but challenged by increasing urbanization of formerly rural communities. Many of the Quaker communities have no "hireling shepherds" (pastors), and practice a special consensus method of decision making based on "the sense of the meeting", as members seek divine guidance on what is to be done in the face of diverse views of participating individuals. This method respects the presence of conflict and allows for full airing of differences. It also demands a disciplined spiritual maturity in seeking collective inward illumination, and skill in intellectual discernment and interpersonal communication.

Anabaptist culture is shaped in the home. Parenting is taken very seriously by both men and women; an important part of that parenting is the cultivation of the divine seed in each child. Family worship, reading, discussion, and times of quiet in the home are supplemented by explicit training in nonviolent responses to conflict, and alternative ways of dealing with conflict, so that children may be prepared for their responsiblities to work for peace and justice in the world. Conflict suppression, however, is not encouraged. Rather, children are enjoined to "work things out."

Local churches, or Meetings, actively participate in the education of their young, helping prepare them spiritually, intellectually, and in terms of social skills for peacemaking. Traditionally they have operated their own schools, from kindergarten to college, but today only a few communities maintain their own local schools. Boarding schools and colleges however continue to flourish and attract non-Anabaptist families who want their special type of education for their children. Community history, and the stories of Quaker, Mennonite, and Brethren heroes and heroines are an important part of this education. "Enemy" concepts are never used, or the language of fighting. There can be no enemies, only strangers with whom a relationship needs to be developed. Peacemaking is seen as building bridges across differences, finding solutions to the problems of each disputant in ways that injure none, and reframing disputes so that common interests can be discovered. All three communities have developed remarkable service organizations that carry out peace-building projects around the world. Many of their young people are trained to participate in these projects.

Quakers, Mennonites, and Brethren would be the first to say that they have difficulty living up to their own ideals as peacemakers. "The world" presses all around, with many distractions. A high value is placed on humor and the ability to laugh at shortcomings.

C. Everyday Peace Behavior

1. The Family

Today much of humanity lives in societies marked by various kinds of violence, yet underneath the layers of violence the peace behaviors survive—and one of the places it survives is in the familial household. This is the most adaptive of human institutions, expanding and contracting though history according to changing social conditions, from single-person or couple units to 200-person multifamily communes, the *frèrêche* or *zadruga* common in parts of medieval Europe, or the monastic household of monks or nuns. Patriarchal traditions of actual or potential violence should not obscure the reality that adult humans can become fond of one another—even fall in love—and that infants would not survive if they were not nurtured. Barring pathological conditions, domestic partnerships achieve a familiar comfort level, and parenting has many rewards as well as challenges. Gentle child-rearing produces gentle adults, and nonviolent practices tend to be reproduced in succeeding generations. (Unfortunately the reverse is also true—violence begets violence from generation to generation.)It is in the protected spaces of the familial household that children's earliest practice in bargaining and negotiating takes place, and in the household that adult skills in conflict resolution are developed and refined. Here is where sharing is learned, and a worldview developed as experiences in the outside world are brought home and processed. Also, it is the family that mediates the contact of individuals with the more impersonal institutions of the civil society.

2. Celebration and Ritual

Celebrations are the play life of a society. Feasting and gift giving emphasize sharing and reciprocity, a sense of the community as one family. The spontaneity and exuberance of gifting, singing, and dancing is a powerful reenforcement of peaceful community relations. These are times for letting go of grudges, times of reconciliation. Since celebration is usually patterned in ritual, it becomes a reconnection with creation itself, a reminder of the oneness of all living things. Celebrations mark the rites of passage from birthing to childhood to puberty to adulthood and marriage. They mark wounding and healing, and they mark dying, as well as great historical moments of the remembered past (and great traumas). Religious rituals, when they give primacy to a loving and forgiving creator, can be especially and deeply joyful. When celebrations lose their playfulness, when performances become competitive, then they lose their character of replenishing the human spirit, and are a poor resource for general peaceableness.

3. Trade and Exchange, and the Civil Society

More than 300 years ago Adam Smith set out to inquire how it was possible for humans to engage in just and orderly economic transactions, and what institutions would be required to sustain such transactions. He came to see that it is our own experience that enables us to imagine what goes on in the minds of others. This capacity for recognizing what others might be feeling lies at the heart not only of economic exchange, but also the many transactions involved when citizens come together to make decisions about community affairs. Civil, like civic, derives from the Latin *civitas,* or city. Each city is a company of strangers who are able to develop some level of workable strategies for communicating across the barriers of language and custom. The development of civil society can be thought of as part of the process of developing peace culture.

The institutional infrastructure that enables the civil society to flourish—as for example the courts of law that ensure the protection of human rights, legislative bodies freely elected by the people and the electoral process itself, and a free press, can also be thought of as part of peace culture. That infrastructure represents basic mechanisms of nonviolent conflict resolution, peaceable management of difference. When it is absent, difference is managed by the authoritarian exercise of force and violence.

The establishment of trade relations with neighboring and more distant social groups can also be thought of as part of peace development. Trade relations contribute to the mutual well-being of participants when each has something the other wants, even in the absence of other elaborating behaviors (as in the famous anthropological examples of silent trade). What is necessary is that each party see the exchange as fair and reasonable. The practice of trade is a desireable substitute for simply raiding one's neighbors—a habit that can easily lead to more or less continual warfare.

The line between the more impersonal behaviors of trading and voting , and a more spontaneous responsiveness to the other, is difficult to draw. Marketplaces often have an air of festivity about them even when all transactions are apparently commercial, and so do town meetings, and polling booths at election time (unless voting represents a bitter contest of opposing parties). What actually happens in many situations involving human exchanges whether of services, goods, or ideas, is that a reciprocity multiplier effect is at work. Each person throws in a little extra for "good measure," whether it is the extra quarter-ounce of meat on the butcher's scales, or a warm smile to the clerk at the checkout counter. The reciprocity multiplier effect ensures that economic, social, and political exchanges will further continuing good will among the parties involved, and helps people deal resourcefully with conflicts when they do arise.

4. Play of the Imagination

Celebrations and games can be thought of as society at play. But play by its very nature also performs a serious creative function for each community. Although taking place outside the realm of everyday life, play nevertheless creates rules and roles ("let's play house—you be the daddy and I'll be the mommy"). For children, play structures spaces within which they can create their own realities in fantasy. At a more sophisticated level, it does the same for adults. Play also involves learning. The lessons of nonviolence and self-control may be absorbed when play leads to injuries. However, as the historian Johan Huizinga points out, play is basically *for its own sake*, "for fun." This makes playing important for adults, who tend to get too serious about their other activities. Even in competitive sports the rudiments of the spontaneity of play survive. Many forms of play are not thought of as such: the mind at play in solving tricky problems, the "muse" at play in creating poetry, music, painting, sculpture; the body at play in song, dance, and drama. While it takes different forms in terms of style, language, and content in folk cultures as compared to elite culture, play is ubiquitous. It has to be noted that some art, and some sports, have become so violent that they have lost the spontaneity of play. The rediscovery of all the different forms of play, including artistic and scientific play, and releasing the dynamics of that play into shared celebrations in public spaces, will also be a recovery of peace culture.

5. Sanctuaries and Zones of Peace

The designation of certain spaces as sanctuaries, or safe spaces for anyone under threat, is an ancient human practice that survives into the present. Temples and holy places have traditionally served as sanctuaries, and marketplaces have usually been treated as zones of peace, where violent behavior is unacceptable. Since the beginning of the nuclear age, successful grassroots efforts to get the states of various regions to declare their regions as nuclear-weapon-free zones have had local counterparts in citizen initiatives to declare individual towns and cities as zones of peace.

Currently there are well over 5000 such peace zones and they can be thought of as zones of peace culture. Communities often begin with economic conversion of military plants, cleaning up toxic waste dumps and creating local-to-local international trade with a strong emphasis on human and social development. Projects include developing peace education and conflict resolution programs in schools, and in particularly embattled inner-city areas. Schools declare themselves as violence-free zones where no one is to fight (or to carry guns or knives) and so do the neighborhoods around them. Other projects include special peace collections in museums and libraries, creating peace parks and public peace sites, and generally creating a strong local awareness of the town or city as a peacemaking community. The Zone of Peace Foundation and the Global Land Authority for the Development of Peace Zones work at the grassroots level to expand these zones of peace. In some countries the peace zone strategy is used to help local groups caught in areas of civil war and guerilla violence negotiate with local fighters to honor designated areas as weapon-free zones of peace where processes of peace building can take place unhindered.

VIII. A REVIEW OF PERSPECTIVES

Peace culture has been examined from the perspectives of the utopian longing to live in peace, and through actual efforts to create micro-utopias. It has been considered in the context of religious faith, where holy war teachings coexist in tension wih teachings of holy peaceableness. It has been suggested that peace movements function as seedbeds for peace culture, with particular attention to the special characteristics of women's culture and the movements arising from it. In all these cases we have been looking at elements, fragments, strands, and islands of peace culture in societies that accept violence and war. It has been noted that there is a scarcity of coherent social entities beyond the commune level that handle conflict peaceably and that have systematic patterns for maintaining that peaceableness from generation to generation. Yet many examples of peaceful conflict management and violence avoidance are easily discovered in everyday social life, stemming from the twin human needs for bonding and autonomy. Proportions of violence-proneness and peace-proneness vary, and the activities of the utopians, and of religious and secular peace movements, are aimed at increasing the overall proportion of peace behavior, and the enabling structures for that behavior. These activities are carried on in the conviction that war is a cultural invention, one that can be replaced by another set of cultural inventions that will make it possible for humans to live in a condition of dynamic and adventurous peace with other humans and the earth.

Also See the Following Articles

ANTHROPOLOGY OF VIOLENCE AND CONFLICT • CIVIL SOCIETY • CONSCIENTIOUS OBJECTION, ETHICS OF • CONFLICT MANAGEMENT AND RESOLUTION • MILITARISM • NONVIOLENCE THEORY AND PRACTICE • PEACEMAKING AND PEACEBUILDING • PEACE MOVEMENTS • RELIGION AND PEACE, INNER-OUTER DIMENSIONS OF • WARRIORS, ANTHROPOLOGY OF

Bibliography

Adams, D., & True, M. (1997). UNESCO's culture of peace program: An introduction. *International Peace Research Newsletter, 35*(1), 15–18.

Bernstein, E., *et al.* (1986). *Peace resource book.* Cambridge, MA: Ballinger Publishing Company.

Bok, S. (1991). *Alva Myrdal: A daughter's memoir.* Reading, PA: Addison Wesley Publishing, Inc.

Bonta, B. (1993). *Peaceful peoples: An annotated bibliography.* Metuchen, NJ: Scarecrow Press.

Bondurant, J. (1971). *Conquest of violence.* Berkeley: University of California Press.

Boulding, E. (1992). *The underside of history: A view of women through time.* (Rev. Ed., 2 Vols.). Newbury Park, CA: Sage Publications.

Boulding, E. (1988). *Building a global civic culture.* Syracuse: Syracuse University Press.

Chatfield, C., & Van Den Dungen, P. (Eds.). (1988). *Peace movements and political cultures.* Knoxville, TN: University of Tennessee Press.

Communities Directory (1995). (2nd Ed.). Langley, VA: Fellowship for Intentional Community.

Cooper, S. (1991). *Patriotic pacifism: Waging war on war in Europe 1815–1914.* Oxford, UK: Oxford University Press.

De Waal, F. (1996). *Good natured: The origins of right and wrong in humans and other animals.* Cambridge, MA: Harvard University Press.

Grun, B. (1975). *The timetables of history* (based on W. Stein's *Kulturfahrplan*). New York: Simon and Schuster, Inc.

Hass, H. (1970). *The human animal: The mystery of man's behavior.* New York: G. P. Putnam's Sons.

Huizinga, J. (1955). *Homo ludens. A study of the play element in culture.* Boston: Beacon Press.

Jegen, M. E. (1993). *Global peace service.* Cincinnati: Sisters of Notre Dame.

Kellert, S., & Wilson, E. (1993). *The biophilia hypothesis.* Washington, DC: Island Press.

Macy, J. (1983). *Dharma and development.* Hartford, CT: Kumarian Press. Marx, L. (1964). *The machine in the garden.* New York: Oxford Press.

Meadows, D., with Robinson, J. M. (1985). *The electronic oracle.* Chichester: John Wiley and Sons.

Nordhoff, C. (1966). *Communistic societies of the United States* (reprint from 1875 ed.). New York: Dover Publications.

Shiva, V. (1990). *Staying alive: Women, ecology and development.* London: Zed Books.

UNESCO (1996). *From a culture of violence to a culture of peace.* Paris: UNESCO.

UNESCO (David Adams, Ed.). (1991). *Seville Statement on violence.* Paris: UNESCO.

Peace, Definitions and Concepts of

Anatol Rapoport

University of Toronto

I. THE DUAL FUNCTION OF DEFINITIONS

Definitions appear to serve two functions: (1) to facilitate communication by use of language and (2) to organize formulation of theories, induce formation of attitudes, or, generally speaking, influence thought or feeling. The first function is commonly performed by *descriptive* definitions, the second by *prescriptive* ones.

A. Descriptive Definitions

Definitions found in dictionaries (except technical terms) are, for the most part, *descriptive*. They call attention to how the words defined are actually used by members of a given language community in given situations (not how they should be used, which is the function of *prescriptive* definitions). Descriptive definitions are formulated either in terms of synonyms (or near-synonyms) or illustrated by contexts defined by examples of usage. As a rule, several such synonyms are listed or contexts illustrated related to a variety of experiences associated with the word defined.

For example, in the *Explanatory Phonographic Pronouncing Dictionary of the English Language* (1850) "peace" is defined as a list of synonyms (or near-synonyms):

> **Peace:** Respite from war. Quiet from suits or disorder. Rest from any commotion. Stillness from riots or tumult. Reconciliation of differences. A state not hostile. Rest, quiet, content; freedom from terror; heavenly rest; silence; suppression of the thoughts. That quiet order of tranquility which is guaranteed by the government. A word commanding silence.

It is, perhaps, noteworthy that the first four of these are "definitions by exclusion": "peace" is defined by the *absence* of "nonpeace." In contrast, the *Random House Dictionary* (1983) begins with a "positive" definition implied by the word "normal."

> **Peace:** The normal, non-warring condition of a nation, group of nations, or the world.

The several following definitions are accompanied by illustrations of usage.

> An agreement or treaty between warring or antagonistic nations, groups, etc. to end hostilities and abstain from further fighting or antagonism: *The Peace of Ryswick.*

Copyright © 1999 by Academic Press.
All rights of reproduction in any form reserved.

A state of mutual harmony between people or groups, esp. in personal relations: *Try to live in peace with your neighbours.*

The normal freedom from civil commotion and violence of a community, public order and serenity. *He was arrested for being drunk and breaking the peace.*

A state of tranquility or serenity. *May he rest in peace.*

It is important to note that descriptive definitions are not meant to adjudicate in arguments concerning the "true meaning" of a word. S. I. Hayakawa (1949) was particularly emphatic on this point:

The writing of a dictionary ... is not a task of setting up authoritative statements about the "true meanings" of words, but a task of *recording* ... what various words *have meant* to authors in the distant or immediate past.... Looking under a "hood" we should have ordinarily have found, five hundred years ago, a monk; today, we find a motorcar engine.

The range of definitions of a word makes descriptive definitions sources of information not only on what the word means or has meant at various times or places to people in general but at times even to particular compilers of dictionaries. This is particularly true of value-laden words like "war" and "peace."

For example, the illustrations, following definitions of "peace" in the *Century Dictionary* (1890) may be regarded as reflecting predominantly psychological, religious, or authoritative connotations of "peace."

(a) A state of quiet and tranquility, freedom from disturbance and agitation; calm, quietness, repose. Calm, quietness, repose.

... and after him Mango Chan, that was a gode Cristene man and baptised, and zaf Lettres of perpetuelle *pes* to alle Cristene men... Mandeville, *Travels*, p. 230.

(b) Freedom from agitation or disturbance by the passions.

Great *peace* have they which love Thy law. Ps. cxix. 165

(c) A state of reconciliation between parties at variance; concord.

St. Anselm and his *Peace* or composition with Henry the First.

(d) Public tranquility, that quiet order and security which are guaranteed by the laws ...

... the *king's peace,* the observance of which is due to the will of the lord and the breach of which is a personal offence against him. J. R. Green, *Conq. of Eng.*

A definition of "peace" in the context of *international relations* comes last:

(e) A compact or agreement made by contending parties to abstain from further hostilities ... as the *peace* of Ryswick.

Comparison of the most exhaustive definitions of "peace" and "war," namely those in the *Oxford Dictionary of the English Language* (1989) suggests a difference in the amount of attention devoted in our day to the two cardinal relations among states and other social collectives. Eight columns (about 7,000 words) are devoted to "peace," 16 (about 15,000 words) to war. It might be of interest to discover the sociopsychological or ideological sources, if any, of this difference.

B. Prescriptive Definitions

Definitions of terms used in scientific discourse are usually prescriptive. They *direct* the "correct" usage of a word with the view of making it available as a tool in the construction of a theory.

For example in mathematics, a "transcendental" number is defined as one that is not algebraic, an "algebraic" number is defined as one that can be a root of a polynomial with rational coefficients, and a "rational" number is be defined as one that can be expressed as a ratio of two integers. Since infinite regress is impossible, the process ends with terms assumed to be intuitively understood. These definitions *direct* participants in mathematical discourse to understand the term *only* in the way prescribed, for only in this way can they understand the theory in which the terms serve as building blocks. This means, for example, that the term "transcendental," as applied to a number has no relationship to "transcendental meditation" or "transcendental reality." Nor is "rational" in this context related in any way to "sane" or "logical."

In biology, definitions are often classificatory directions. Thus, Aristotle defined "man" as a "rational animal," that is, as an entity belonging to the class of animals and distinguished from other animals by being "rational." Classificatory definitions in biology are prescriptive because in that field one can speak of "correct" and "incorrect" classification, the former but not the latter being correctly informative of the evolutionary history of living things. Thus, a layman's classification of a spider as an insect is wrong. Having eight legs, a spider belongs to the class of *Arachnida* rather than six-legged *Insecta*. Biblical classifications, for example, those referring to running, flying, or crawling creatures or edible and inedible organisms are useless in biological science. There the prescribed classifications of animals and plants (taxa) refer to their relative distances from each other on the evolutionary tree.

An important variant of the prescriptive definition is the *operational definition*, which indicates what to do and what to observe in order to understand the word defined in the context of a theory. Thus "force" is defined in mechanics as the product of the mass of a body and its acceleration; moreover, both mass and acceleration are defined in terms of precisely described operations involved in measuring their magnitudes. No other meanings of "force" suggested by the everyday usage (e.g., "force" of effort or of convictions or as a means of enforcing peace) are permitted to intrude into statements involving "force" in the context of mechanics.

The *extensional definition*, another variant of prescriptive definition, is often useful because of its direct indication of observable referents. It can be applied if the referents of the term defined can be easily enumerated. For example, in legal documents we may find a definition by enumeration of "close relatives" as "parents, offspring, siblings having at least one common parent, spouses ..." implying that those and only those are to be understood by the term.

The question arises whether prescriptive definitions of "peace" can be recognized as such. In other words, does "peace" occur in some technical context, like "force" in physics or "transcendental" in mathematics? Perhaps international law can be regarded as such a context. Indeed, in international law we find what amounts to prescriptive definitions of "an act of war" (by enumeration), e.g., "invasion of the territory of one state by another, blockade, etc." These may be thought to induce a prescriptive definition of peace, namely, as a situation, in which acts of war, as defined above, do not occur.

It seems that in the case of a value-laden term like "peace," the concept of prescriptive definition can be extended beyond technical usage. Definitions (often tacit) that can be regarded as prescriptive are found in the course of proselytizing. It is thought that people's attitudes, commitments, prejudices can be established, changed, or controlled by inducing them to associate certain categories of persons, events, conditions, and

so on with particular qualities, attractive or abhorrent. Compare Karl von Clausewitz's famous definition of war as "the continuation of politics by other means" with one that might be offered by a pacifist or a peace activist: "massive, organized destruction of people, dwellings, means of production, and the like, usually instigated, organized, and directed by governments of sovereign states." Both definitions are informative. Each can serve as a foundation of a "theory of war" or of a complementary theory of peace. It stands to reason, however, that theories based on the two definitions as points of departure will be substantially different.

II. EXPANDED DEFINITIONS OF PEACE

A. Encyclopedia Entries

Entries in encyclopedias can be sometimes regarded as greatly expanded definitions. As has been said, the range of associations induced by a word may differ, sometimes drastically from one period to another and in different societies. As expected, these changes are even more conspicuous in encyclopedias. By way of example, the 11th (1911) edition of *Encyclopaedia Britannica* devotes 15 pages and 16 colored illustrations to "Robes" (clerical, judicial, academic, etc.), while this entry does not appear at all in the 15th (1993) edition. More relevant to entries related to war and peace is the observation that the 11th edition of the *Encyclopaedia Britannica* devotes 10 pages (about 10,000 words) to the entry "Uniforms," displaying several extensive tables in which colors of tunics, plumes, and even buttons of uniforms of several countries and of different units (hussars, lancers, fusiliers, etc.) are listed (in Britain by counties). The entry "Uniforms" does not appear in the 15th (1993) edition. The observation suggests something about a changed conception of war between the beginning and the end of our century.

Comparing the entries of "Peace" in various encyclopedias, we may infer something about the way concepts of peace differed or changed from one society or period to another. For example, the entry "Peace" in the 1911 *Encyclopaedia Britannica* begins with the following, a formal definition:

> **Peace** ... the contrary of war or turmoil, the condition that follows their cessation. Its sense in international law is not being at war...

The expository treatment begins with

Peace, until quite recently was merely the political condition that prevailed in the intervals between wars.... The very name of [Grotius] historic treatise, *De Jure Bellie et Pace* shows the subordination of peace to the main subject of war. In our time peace has attained a higher status. It is now customary among writers on international law to give peace at any rate a volume to itself.

This opening suggests that already almost a century ago, peace was an object of theory-generating contemplation, a concept underlying nascent theories. The conjecture is reinforced by the predominance of references to relations among states, which in the early 20th century were regarded as "civilized," essentially those subsumed in our time under the First (affluent) World.

Following a historical survey of the various manifestations of the peace concept (Amphytrionic Council, *Pax Romana*, the medieval Truce of God, various Utopias), much space is devoted in the 1911 *Encyclopaedia Britannica* to treaties between individual states, assumed at the time to be guarantors of peace. Over 100 of these treaties are listed under "Peace" along with the conclusion, namely that these treaties "[form] a network of international relations, which shows that at any rate, the wish for peace is universal among mankind."

An altogether a different approach underlies the entry "Peace" in the *Encyclopedia Americana* (1987). The entry "Peace" begins with the following observation.

Unfortunately, peace has received less attention than its counterpart war. The word itself has neither been acceptably defined, nor has there even been agreement on how to define peace.

Reference to "acceptability" of a definition of peace suggests that the definition is not going to be a descriptive one, since, as has been suggested, descriptive definitions only reflect how the word defined is actually used in various contexts or, perhaps, in various dialects of the language or among various social groups. In this sense, there can be no question of the "acceptability" or "unacceptability" of a definition. The same applies to "agreement." The listing of the variants of the definition reflects agreement on the meaning only within a given context, while agreement among groups that use the word in different senses is not expected. Clearly acceptability of and agreement on a definition are desiderata mainly when the word defined is to play a conceptual

role in the development of a theory. Indeed the remainder of the entry "peace" in the *Encyclopedia Americana* is offered as a theory.

Two conceptions are distinguished, one reflected in the attitudes or actions of "pacifists," the other in the activities of "peace advocates." The relevance of the distinction between them to a definition of peace becomes apparent when the envisaged goals of pacifism and peace advocacy are compared. "Goals" in this context refer not to the envisaged final state (absence of war, on-going cooperation, etc.) but to the state of affairs that makes the attainment of the final goal possible. Pacifism envisages this "penultimate" goal as the purging of the human psyche of aggressiveness, as rejection of violence by human individuals as means to whatever ends. It typically characterizes the mentality prevailing in certain religious sects (Quakers, Menonites, Dukhobors) or cults (Tolstoyans). Proselytizing activities of pacifists are typically directed at converting individuals to the ethos of nonviolence. Peace advocacy, on the other hand, emphasizes organized action assumed to promote conditions conducive to peace. These may range from massive demonstrations against threatened or on-going wars to advocacy of "strong defence" (*si vis pacem para bellum*) as reflected in theories of deterrence or in the slogan of the U.S. Air Force ("Peace is our profession").

B. Conceptions of Peace on the Personal–Political Axis

Extreme forms of pacifism have manifested themselves in some Eastern philosophies and religions. Jainism, an offshoot of Hinduism, is an example. Central to this religion is the view that all life is sacred and that even things which we regard as inanimate are in some sense alive. The ultimate virtue, according to this belief is refraining from doing any harm to life. Jainists are tolerant of all religions and do not proselytize.

The original form of Buddhism prescribes intense introspection as the way to what in Christian theology is conceived as "salvation." The blessed state, Nirvana, is freedom from desire.

It is noteworthy, however, that some outspokenly pacifist religions nurture activist programs. The Quakers, who have participated in a number of war-preventing and conflict-resolving activities are a notable example. Of the Eastern religious communities, the Baha'i (an offshoot of Islam) have been long engaged in extensive educational programs; the Soka Gakkai (an offshot of Buddhism) energetically opposed Japanese expansionism in the 1930s and actively opposes the pressures for the remilitarization of Japan through a major political party.

The personal–political axis also encompasses attitudes toward government. Leo Tolstoy, who in the last decades of his life was an ardent pacifist, was also a philosophical (that is, violence-rejecting) anarchist. In his letter to the American correspondent Crosby he wrote,

> .... present disturbances [the revolution of 1905–1906] are only the precursors of the great revolution [which he hopes] will begin at once everywhere and will consist in the annihilation of state power (Corcel, 1980, p. 304).

At the same time he categorically rejected the terrorist activities of anarchists, who, "do note recognize divine law ..." (Corcel, 1980, p. 304).

Another clear example of pacifist anarchism is the outlook of the New England Non-resistance Society founded by the American abolitionist–pacifist William Lloyd Garrison. In the manifesto of the Society we read,

> We cannot acknowledge allegiance to any human government. Christ is the only ruler and lawgiver, and we must obey Him and his laws rather than any earthly being or government... Our country is the world, our countrymen are all mankind.

The last sentence was on the masthead of Garrison's newspaper *The Liberator*.

At the other end of the axis is the modern world government movement. Like the philosophical anarchists, advocates of world government believe that the roots of large-scale organized violence are in the loyalties induced in people to their respective governments among which struggles for power are inevitable. Unlike the anarchists, however, they see the remedy not in abolishing governments but, on the contrary, of extending sovereignty to encompass the whole planet. Several drafts of a "World Constitution" have been proposed by activists in this movement.

Intermediate between anarchist pacifism, now largely defunct, and federalism (as the world government movement is sometimes called) is the conception of a "civil society" manifested in organized political action by constituencies outside governmental institutions, the so-called NGOs (nongovernmental organizations), which have attained official status in the structure of the United Nations.

C. Persuasive Expanded Definitions

We have examined three expanded definitions of peace: the predominantly legalistic definition exemplified in the 11th edition of the *Encyclopaedia Britannica,* the predominantly psychological (implied in "pacifism") definition, and the predominantly systemic or political (implied in "peace advocacy") definition under the entry "Peace" in the *Encyclopedia Americana.* We have suggested that these expanded definitions are implicitly prescriptive because they call attention to what are regarded by their proponents (e.g., students of international relations, pacifists, or peace advocates) as the principal conditions for the existence, the establishment, or the preservation of peace. In this form the definitions are, in a way, directions about how to think about peace with the view of constructing a theory of it or with a view of promoting it, the two goals being often interlocked. Still the "prescriptions" in these encyclopedias do not include specific comparative evaluations in the sense of recommending one conception in preference to another considered, say, as a rival.

In contrast, such a preference can be easily discerned in the treatment of "peace" in the *Great Soviet Encyclopedia* (published in English in 1983, that is, before the dissolution of the Soviet Union). As in the 15th edition of the *Encyclopaedia Britannica,* where "Peace" does not appear as an entry, except "Peace, disturbance of," only peace-related terms, such as "International Relations," "Peace Fund," "Peace Manifesto," "Peace of God," and so on appear in the 1983 edition of the *Great Soviet Encyclopedia.* By far the most extensive category, under which peace-related terms are subsumed is "Peace Movements." Three will suffice as extreme examples of attitude-inducing definitions.

> **Pacifism,** an antiwar movement whose adherents believe that the principal means of preventing war is to condemn its immoral character. Pacifists condemn all war, denying the legitimacy of wars of liberation. They believe that by means of persuasion it is possible to prevent wars without eliminating the socioeconomic and political conditions that give rise to them. Associated with bourgeois liberal ideology, pacifism draws fairly broad democratic circles under its influence ... V. I. Lenin regarded the pacifists' abstract preaching of peace—pronouncements without any relation to the anti-imperialist struggle—as "one of the means of duping the working class."
>
> **World Peace Council,** the supreme permanent body of the world wide movement of Partisans of

Peace ... formed in the Second World Congress of Partisans for Peace, held in Warsaw in November, 1950. It directs and coordinates the activity of the partisans in various countries, mobilizes them for the struggle against the threat of world war and against imperialist aggression ... supports the struggles of peoples for national independence....

Declaration of the Conference of the Representatives of the Communist and Workers' Parties (1960), defined the principal position of the international communist movements ... Developed the principal of mutual relations among the socialist countries ... Indicated the path of successful development of each socialist country ... Reconfirmed the conclusion of the Twentieth Congress of the Communist Party of the Soviet Union ... Indicated the necessity of combatting revisionism as the chief danger of our time ... The Leaders of the Chinese Communist Party attempted to force their own anti-Marxist ideas upon all fraternal parties. It was only because they were in danger of remaining in complete isolation that the delegates of the CPC signed the declaration. However, the leadership of the CPC soon renewed their schismatic activity in the international communist movement. This same position was also taken by the leadership of the Albanian Workers' Party. Their schismatic position evoked the condemnation of the overwhelming majority of the communist and workers' parties.

Note that although the word "peace" does not appear in this entry, it is nevertheless subsumed under the entry "Peace Movements."

D. The Scope of Peace-Related Definitions

A most comprehensive survey of classificatory definitions of "peace" appears in the *International Encyclopedia of the Social Sciences.*

Galtung offers a fourfold classification of relations between nations: "war" (organized group violence), "negative peace"—absence of violence but also of any other significant relation; "positive peace"—marked by absence of violence and occasional cooperation; and "unqualified peace"—absence of violence and a pattern of lasting cooperation.

In addition to this fourfold classification, Galtung offers a "typology of peace plans," a catalog of classificatory definitions. One axis of this typology is the level

of a social unit, for example, a human individual, a group, a nation, the international system of nations or an envisaged world state. The other dimension is the inter-intra axis. For example, one can focus on "intraindividual peace" (e.g., "peace of mind"), "intragroup," "intranation," "interindividual," or "international" peace. A discussion of all these approaches follows based on fundamental assumptions (psychological, sociological, political, etc.) underlying each.

III. CONCEPTIONS OF PEACE

So far, we have presented encyclopedia entries related to peace as expanded definitions. In passing to "plans for peace" Galtung in effect presents various conceptions of peace on which recommendations for attaining or preserving peace are based.

The following terms reflect conceptions of peace that imply ways of achieving it or moving toward it. Some refer to the role of power of states (its source or distribution) as a stimulant or inhibitor of wars; others to interrelationships among states.

A. Conditions Related to the Role of Power

1. Hegemony

This is concentration of power in one nation or system. The above mentioned terms, *Pax Romana* and *Pax Britannica,* reflect a conjecture that peace can be kept by making goals pursued by war unattainable, that is to say, by "deterrence." Following World War II, the United States was regarded by some as aspiring to similar hegemony (*Pax Americana*). The impression was reinforced following the end of the Cold War, when the status of "superpower" could be reasonably applied only to that country.

2. Balance of Power

This conception is an antithesis of hegemony. Instead of being concentrated, power on the international arena is envisaged as being equally distributed at least among the major nations. It is supposed that given this condition, no nation is capable of defeating any other. In a stronger version, this balance becomes "balance of terror." That is, a nation attacking another risks being totally destroyed. Occasionally *Pax Atomica* has been defined in this way. (See, however, Wohlstetter, 1959, where an inherent instability of this sort of "balance of power" is discussed.)

3. Decentralization of Power

Immanuel Kant argued that wars were caused by struggles for power among monarchs and hence would cease once European nations became republics. Curiously, at the time this essay was published the most severe and extensive series of wars since the Thirty Years' War was launched in Europe with republican France as a principle belligerent.

4. Disarmament

Much of so-called "peace research" is concerned with a search for "correlates of wars" on the basis of which hypotheses about their causes could be formulated. As expected, the conjectured causes turn out to be interlocked in a complex network of correlations, changing in the course of history. Thus, *sufficient* causes of wars are extremely difficult to identify. An easily identifiable *necessary* cause of wars, however, is apparent, namely weapons. Perhaps for this reason disarmament has become a most prominent goal of activist peace movements.

The earliest recorded reference to disarmament (specifically by conversion) is probably the prophesy of some 28 centuries ago: "And they shall beat their swords into ploughshares and their spears into pruning hooks ..." (Isaiah 2:4). However, it is likely that at the time disarmament was envisaged as the *result* of establishing universal peace rather than as a step toward it. Progressive disarmament as a controlled trend *toward* peace was proposed in the so-called Graduated Reciprocation of Tension Reduction program. The process is supposed to be driven by small *unilateral* tension-resolving steps, including small reductions of armaments. The measures were supposed "to put the arms race in reverse." Being insignificant in themselves, the disarmament steps could not be seriously counted on to threaten the security of the state making them. Yet by stimulating responses in kind in the course of a sort of "positive feedback," the process could turn an arms race into a disarmament race.

B. Conditions Related to Interrelationships among States

In another set of conceptions of peace, networks of interrelationships rather than distribution of power are at the focus of attention.

1. A Crisscross Network of Conflicts

Paradoxically, on the basis of this assumption, one could hypothesize that the more conflicts pervade the international system, the more stable is the overall "peace," provided the conflicts are short of overt violence and involve different pairs or groups so that adversaries with regard to some issues turn out to be allies on others. Note that "the more dangerous the safer" principle underlies also the hypothetical *Pax Atomica*.

2. A Crisscross Network of Loyalties

If loyalties of citizens of countries are divided (say between the country of which they are citizens and a country of their origin), it may be more difficult to mobilize support for a war than if every one is an avowed patriot.

3. Degree of Homology

The extent to which two nations (societies, cultures) are similar with regard to institutions, forms of government, customs, value systems, and so on. Curiously, arguments are offered to the effect that maximum homology is conducive to peace and also that minimum homology is likely to inhibit war. The first argument is based on the supposition that it is easier to identify with someone similar to oneself, which tends to inhibit aggression. The second argument is based on the supposition that widely dissimilar societies are less likely to compete for resources important to both, a common factor in the genesis of wars. There may be some support for the second argument in the case of clashing religions or ideologies. Often heretics have been more intensely vilified than pagans. In the 1920s and 1930s enmity between communists and Social Democrats in Europe was at times more intense that between either and the politically more distant. A tacit alliance between extremes against the middle is not seldom observed in politics.

4. Degree of Interdependence

A high degree of both interdependence and of independence among nations have been conjectured to favor peace for reasons similar to those mentioned in connection with homology and dissimilarity.

IV. PEACE AS A FOUNDATION OF A WORLD ORDER

Following the usual terminology in peace theory, we will collapse Galtung's three categories of peace into two, namely *negative peace* and *positive peace*. What Galtung calls negative peace (absence of war or of any other significant relationship between states) is not interesting, as is seen in Galtung's trivial example—the absence of war between Norway and Nepal. Of fundamental interest is absence of significant violence in a society characterized by sharp division between Topdogs and Underdogs (Galtung's terms), whereby the latter are practically powerless. Throughout history the instability of peace imposed by a monopoly of power has been dramatically demonstrated; in the past by violent revolutions, in recent decades by intertribal, interethnic, or interreligious massacres among the erstwhile underdogs following the break-up of empires, decolonization, or collapses of authoritarian states (Soviet Union, Yugoslavia). By positive peace we will understand what Galtung calls "unqualified peace"—absence of violence attained by on-going cooperation. It is this sort of peace that is envisaged by its advocates as a foundation of a world order that fulfills fundamental human needs.

A. Utopias

In descriptions of imaginary ideal societies (so called utopias) by European social philosophers, questions arising from relations with other societies are usually bypassed. Indeed, utopias (as their generic name, meaning "nowhere," implies) have been generally imagined to be totally isolated from other societies, so that problems that commonly underlie intersociety wars simply do not arise. Utopias are also depicted as free from internal strife. This internal peace, the hallmark of utopias, is depicted as a consequence of either complete monopoly of decision making as by "philosopher-kings," as in Plato's *Republic* (4th century B.C.), or in complete decentralization of power, as for example, in Tomasso Campanella's *Civitas solis* (1623), in which the executive is controlled by one man or a few men for only short periods of time. In either case, power struggles, apparently long regarded as obstacles to peace, are assumed to have been eliminated.

B. The Integration–Polarization Dialectic

Humankind has apparently reached a stage of development in which elimination of massive violence has become an imperative, the alternative being widely imagined to be impending extinction. Since isolation is a practical impossibility, the problem of developing a violence-free society has become global. The one political unit that has been to a degree successful, at least in some cases, in providing an environment relatively free from massive violence is the state. It is not surprising, therefore, that models of global organization of humanity by and large resemble a modern state with its constitution, centralized decision-making authority, and more-or-less extensive welfare dispensing apparatus.

Now scanning the evolution of social organization, we note that a principal stimulus to integrating smaller units into larger ones, thus extending the relatively conflict-free area, has been a perception of a common enemy. Thus, as interclan strife subsided, intertribe strife took its place, which in turn gave way to international, then to interalliance warfare, culminating in the confrontation between two superpowers in the second half of the 20th century. Ironically it was this integration process that gave rise to the gravest danger of demise of humanity as a consequence of a final spasm of mass violence. With the disappearance of a serious candidate for the role of a common enemy, integration could continue only if a comparably effective stimulus appeared. Perhaps the perception of the threat is taking root in sufficiently large sectors of societies to provide such a stimulus. Possibly a vision of a realizable positive peace on the global scale is beginning to play the role of such a stimulus. If so, the need arises for a prescriptive definition of such a peace.

C. Conditions of Positive Peace

As has been said, states more or less successful in providing certain satisfactions to its citizens come to mind as natural models for a global cooperative community. The most important of these satisfactions seems to be *security,* primarily assurance against acute deprivation of the necessities of life and against being assaulted or victimized. The latter need (security of person), in turn, is seen by some as including a need for *respect* either for the individual as a unique entity or for a "culture" with which the individual identifies. Thus, a necessary condition for security so understood appears to be an equitable distribution of access to the necessities of life and recognition that a primary purpose of the "rule of law" is protection of the weak from the strong. In sum, cooperation, assumed to be the principal mode of interaction under positive peace, presupposes both compliance with some authority and also limitation of authority in the interest of preserving individual and group autonomy.

D. Three Modes of Social Control

K. E. Boulding called attention to three modes of social control: *threat, trade,* and *integration.* Threat of punishment to insure compliance characterizes authoritarian rule; trade (exchange of resources, reciprocation of services, etc.) is the main mode of cooperation in market-dominated societies; integration insures cooperation by inducing identification of self with others. A. Etzioni called the same three types of social control *coercive, contractual,* and *normative.* Assessment of the relative importance and realizability of these three modes determines one's conception of a permanently peaceful society.

The social orders of both ancient Sparta and the antebellum South, based on chattel slavery maintained by threat, were conspicuously free from massive overt violence. Galtung calls this mode of control "structural violence." Note that the designation of the relation between topdogs and underdogs as "negative peace" is consistent with the definition of negative peace as the absence both of war, that is, of large-scale elaborately organized violence and of (voluntary) cooperation.

Social control based on trade is relatively free from internal violence, either overt or structural. It is frequently pointed out that "democratic countries" no longer make war on each other. "Democracy" is often implicitly identified with the primacy of a market economy, and the latter with growing prosperity, presumably an antidote to addiction to war. The inadequacy of the trade system as a foundation for positive peace is revealed in the same integration–polarization dialectic that has characterized the merging of political units. Unimpeded pervasion and growth of market economy, now called globalization, is accompanied by a conspicuously growing gap between the rich and the poor, particularly between the affluent ("First") and the destitute ("Third") worlds. Thus the planet may be heading toward a global negative peace with all the dangers that it entails.

There remains the integrative model of the world order as the foundation of positive peace. It is interesting to recall that "integration" replaced "love" in Boulding's trichotomy. Perhaps he felt that reference to "love" was not quite proper in scientific discourse. Whether it is or not, it is not quite proper in the present context. It implies integration but is not implied by it. We normally love our children. We nourish and protect them, not because they threaten with reprisals if we do not and not because they pay us for our services, but simply because they are our children. The term "love" fits in this context. In a fully cooperative society, every person's fundamental needs are provided for—safety, well-being, dignity, freedom—again neither in consideration of payment nor in response to threats, but simply because the person is a member of society; in the globally integrated cooperative society a member of the human race. However, "love," as this word is commonly understood is not a motivating factor. Indeed, it is possible

to love only a few persons. "Civility" describes more accurately the attitude of people toward each other (including total strangers) in a society where each person and each collective is regarded as a potential cooperator rather than a potential rival, competitor, or enemy. In economic terms, civility implies the widest possible access by every one in equal degree to public goods, that is, goods to which everyone is entitled regardless of power status or ability to pay. It is only in this respect that "civility" and "love" intersect.

E. Two Models of a Peaceful World

Among current conceptions of a peaceful world, two predominate, one based on a world government, the other on global governance. They differ in the degree of authority ascribed to a central decision-making center. A world government would presumably be an analog of a modern state. Intermediate corporate bodies, for example, former sovereign states, would lose much of their autonomy. Their range of authority would be fixed by a world constitution. Their supporting functions, such as securing individuals against deprivation and aggression might also be taken over by the central authority. In other words, individuals would become citizens of the superstate in the sense of identifying themselves with it and with what would eventually become a world culture.

Global governance, on the other hand, would preserve autonomy of smaller bodies, possibly to the extent of sovereignty except with regard to activities that threaten the global community, of which the most conspicuous are those of war-making institutions. General and complete disarmament is a prerequisite of both models of a permanently peaceful world. Other areas, where centralized final authority appears necessary are protection of the environment, in particular of the biosphere, protection of basic human rights, and assurance of equitable distribution of the basic resources of the planet.

This leaves open the problem of exercising the authority conferred upon the central governing body when compliance is imperative and cannot be insured except by physical coercion. It seems that the problem of eliminating violence in human affairs would be more severe in the case of establishing a world state, traditionally an organ of coercion, than in the case of an organized global governance in the context of voluntarily cooperating autonomous units. Another feature of confederation, as opposed to subordination of constituent units to a central authority is that it is consistent with the principle of "unity in diversity," believed to be a fertile soil of integration as a foundation of positive peace. In particular, the extent to which the contractual (rather than integrative) mode of social control would remain dominant in a given constituent society or culture would be determined by a historically shaped ideology or the value system of the particular autonomous society or culture rather than by the central authority. Finally, small, usually spatially compact units, would probably be better equipped than a central authority to satisfy material and spiritual needs of their people, who would effectively hold a dual citizenship: one in their country, the other in the world.

The author's apparent preference of global governance over world government as a model of positive peace demonstrates the inevitability of bias in definitions of value-laden terms of which "peace" is an outstanding example.

Also See the Following Articles

LANGUAGE OF WAR AND PEACE, THE • LINGUISTIC CONSTRUCTIONS OF VIOLENCE, PEACE, AND CONFLICT

Bibliography

Boulding, K. E. (1974). The relations of economic, political and social systems. In L. D. Singall (Ed.), *Collected papers* (Vol. 4, pp. 151–62). Boulder, CO: Associated University Press.

De Courcel, M. (1988). *Tolstoy, the ultimate reconciliation.* New York: Charles Scribner's Sons.

Etzioni, A. (1961). *A comparative analysis of complex organizations: On power, involvement, and their correlates.* New York: Free Press.

Galtung, J. (1964). A structural theory of aggression. *Journal of Peace Research, 2,* 95–119.

Galtung, J. (1968). Peace. In *International Encyclopedia of the Social Sciences.* New York: Macmillan and the Free Press.

Galtung, J. (1971). A structural theory of imperialism. *Journal of Peace Research, 1,* 81–117.

Kant, I. (1795/1903). *Perpetual peace: A philosophical essay.* London: Swan Sonnenschein & Co.

Osgood, C. E. (1962). *An alternative to war and surrender.* Urbana, IL: The University of Illinois Press.

Rapoport, A. (1997). The dual role of the nation state in the evolution of world citizenship. In *World citizenship: Allegiance to humanity.* London: Macmillan.

Wohlstetter, A. (1959). The delicate balance of terror. *Foreign Affairs, 37* (2), 211–234.

Peace Education: Colleges and Universities

Ian M. Harris

University of Wisconsin-Milwaukee

I. History
II. Courses and Programs
III. International Education
IV. Safety in Schools
V. Conflict Resolution
VI. Building a Peace Consciousness

GLOSSARY

Peacebuilding Averting violence by teaching about nonviolence.
Peacekeeping Stopping violence by using force or deterrence.
Peacemaking Resolving conflicts through communication.

PEACE EDUCATION attempts to draw out of people their natural desire to live in peace. It involves learning about different forms of violence as well as alternatives to violence. Traditionally, peace education in universities has been carried out through peace studies programs, usually housed in political science or international relations departments. Peace education, delivered in schools of education, has had as its focus international education or world studies, where it prepared teachers to understand the complex dynamics of international affairs. With the growth of violence in schools

and concern about domestic crime, professors in schools of education began in the 1990s to consider how to prepare teachers to address the problems of violence they will face. They have been offering courses that take three different directions—violence prevention that emphasizes peacekeeping strategies to make schools safe, conflict resolution programs that use peacemaking techniques to manage conflicts, and courses on nonviolence that build in students' minds a consciousness that desires peace. These pedagogical activities move students away from ways of thinking and acting that promote a warring world to ways of behaving that create a peaceful global order.

I. HISTORY

Education in the service of human betterment can be traced throughout history in attempts to socialize the young. One of the first to espouse education as a means to attain peace was Comenius, the Czech educator who in the 17th century argued for formal attempts to educate people about how to acheive peace. In spite of his efforts and the moral teachings of religious leaders like Christ, Buddha, and Mohammed—all of whom emphasized the value of nonviolence—colleges and universities have been slow to initiate courses and programs that provide young people with understandings of violence and an appreciation for peace.

In the 19th century, most of the impetus to establish courses and programs to teach peace on college and

Copyright © 1999 by Academic Press.
All rights of reproduction in any form reserved.

university campuses came from concern about the horrors of modern warfare. After the American Civil War—that introduced the machine gun, ironclad battleships, and sophisticated instruments of death—peace clubs sprang up on various college and university campuses throughout the West (North America and Europe). These clubs were often aligned with various peace societies that sponsored national speakers who would travel from campus to campus speaking about the evils of war, and promoting international organizations like the League of Nations that were designed to outlaw war. Many of them were associated with regional and national peace societies.

Nongovernmental organizations (NGOs), including peace movements, were early advocates for peace education. Peace societies came together in world peace conventions, the first of which took place in the Hague, Netherlands, on May 18, 1899, a day thereafter commemorated as peace day. A further Hague world conference in 1907 tried to place limits on war. After World War I, peace activists and educators promoted in many countries "education for international understanding," which focused on different cultures and political systems. In the latter half of the 19th century and the first half of the 20th century most of the peace-related activities on campuses in the United States revolved around student groups, visiting speakers, demonstrations, and programs. Peace education, as an academic program with courses and degrees, had not yet appeared on college campuses.

World War II created new interest in "education for world citizenship." Educational efforts for peace in this period focused on politics practiced by the dominant world powers, the United States and the Soviet Union. The United Nations Educational, Social, and Cultural Organization (UNESCO) with its famous statement, "Since wars begin in the minds of men, it is in the minds of men that the defenses of peace must be constructed," provided an important focus for peace education efforts around the world. In 1953 UNESCO sponsored an Associated School Project to study critical world issues in schools throughout the world. The six main objectives of this project are:

i. To improve the capacity of secondary school teachers to teach about world problems;

ii. To increase young people's awareness of world problems;

iii. To provide young people with skills which will eventually be useful in solving such problems;

iv. To develop more effective teaching methods and materials to improve teaching of three specific world problems (disarmament, the economic order, and human rights);

v. To shed new light on how these issues can effectively be studied in different countries;

vi. To understand better the complexity of world problems and facilitate finding solutions to them as a result of knowing other people's views and opinions regarding them.

As a result of these initiatives professors in schools of education throughout the world started slowly to express interest in what they could do to contribute to building a more peaceful world order.

In 1948 at Manchester College in North Manchester, Indiana, the first academic program in peace studies began at this small liberal arts college sponsored by the Brethren church. At the same time in India scholars and professors at universities were promoting Gandhian studies as a way to teach youth to value nonviolence. Peace research institutes were established in Europe in the 1960s, although many of these do not offer formal peace studies courses. As a response to the Vietnam War, Manhattan College, a private Catholic college in New York City, began its peace studies program in 1968, while Colgate University in upper New York state started a program in 1969. In England the first department of peace studies was founded at Bradford University in 1973. In the 1970s quite a few campuses offered courses relating to the war in Vietnam. On these campuses faculty organized courses around academic programs, mostly minors, that enabled students in a concentrated way to study the problems of war and peaceful resolution of conflicts. Many of the faculty who created these programs were responding to student demands to create courses of study that had relevance to their lives. In these early days of peace studies some of the coursework focused on new approaches to a world order.

In the 1980s peace studies saw a huge growth on college campuses as a result of growing alarm about the production and threatened use of nuclear weapons. Concern about the fate of the planet created a host of new courses and programs aimed toward promoting global survival. At the same time peace research became an important field of academic inquiry. By the middle of the 1980s peace studies courses in Western Europe and North America focused mostly on international conflict and the threat of nuclear destruction. Much of the impetus for these courses came from the grass roots, from citizens who were involved in peace movements that were concerned about the fate of the Earth.

With the end of the Cold War the emphasis of peace

studies courses on college campuses has shifted somewhat from international politics to the domestic scene to cover issues of structural, domestic, and civil violence. The breadth of peace studies courses and programs has been reflected in a broadening of the concept of security. Whereas "national security" once dominated the field, academics at the end of the 20th century started to recognize the relationship between national security and both international and individual security. In the post-Cold War period peace studies professors were teaching about collective security, common security, environmental security, and comprehensive security. This shift in emphasis in peace studies reflects an attempt by scholars to move from research and teaching about negative peace, the cessation of violence, to positive peace, the conditions that eliminate the causes of violence.

At the close of the 20th century peace studies courses and programs that address the effects of political and social violence, the causes of this violence, and what can be done to resolve conflicts peacefully appeared on many college campuses in North America. The rapid growth in interest in peace studies reflects alarm about growing levels of violence (the nuclear threat, low-intensity conflict, the cost of the arms race, environmental destruction, domestic violence, ethnic and regional conflicts, etc.) Those concerned about the threats of violence are turning to education as a means to heighten awareness about the problems of violence, to stimulate research into alternative forms of dispute resolution, to teach conflict resolution techniques, and to promote nonviolent alternatives. In order to eliminate the threats of war, violence, and environmental destruction, a new way of thinking will be required, a transformation of the human animal from a brute using violence to get one's way to a compassionate, cooperative being who understands how to manage conflicts without resorting to force. Professors of education at colleges and universities are starting to provide students with the knowledge and skills to promote that transformation.

II. COURSES AND PROGRAMS

A. Courses

Most peace education in schools of education occurs through infusing peace and justice concepts into existing curricula. As part of their preservice education teachers are required to take foundations courses that try to provide contemporary schooling with a global context, preparing students for an ever-shrinking world as global communications become more sophisticated and business more international. In their preparation to become teachers many college students are learning how to establish a peaceable classroom in their methods courses where they are introduced to cooperative education, peaceful pedagogy, and conflict resolution techniques.

The formal preparation of teachers in schools of education requires so many courses that perspective teachers do not have room in their course of study to take courses that emphasize the teaching of peace. Most courses dealing specifically with peace education content are offered at the graduate level for teachers acquiring inservice credits to renew their certification, accumulating courses to earn a higher salary, or earning a master's degree. Teachers who fit into these categories are attracted to offerings in peace education because they are confused about how to respond to the high levels of violence they experience in their classrooms and see in their students' lives. They are dealing on a daily basis in their classroom with student anger, depression, and hostility caused by violent incidences that can vary from domestic abuse, to gang rivalry, to drug and alcohol addiction, to competition, and to bullying. Many students give up on their work in school because they are depressed about violence around them, whether it be structural violence that denies them good job opportunities, or the threat of war that makes it hard for them to plan for a future.

A basic peace education course identifies the roots of violence, presents different strategies for responding to violence, and argues that peace education is an important way to avert violence. Students in these courses study power imbalances that cause inequities that result in both interpersonal conflicts, environmental degradation, and wars. They learn about types of conflict and they examine cultural, political, and social structural influences that contribute to the violence they experience in their lives. Such an introductory course tends to be holistic, looking at all the different forms of violence and arguing that teachers can contribute to making a more peaceful world by teaching students about alternatives to violence.

More specific peace education courses in schools of education teach conflict resolution techniques and strategies to create safe schools. They emphasize peacemaking methods. These courses empower students to deal constructively with interpersonal conflicts, cultural differences, and violence in daily society. In these courses teachers study intervention and prevention programs that help them handle violence in schools. Professors explain how education can be a force in reducing intergroup conflict. Many of these courses have a multicultural emphasis that prepares teachers to teach students from differing cultural backgrounds.

B. Programs

Specific programs that have a peace education focus demonstrate institutional support above and beyond the commitment of individual professors who infuse peace and justice concepts into their classes or teach specific courses with peace education themes. At the end of the millennium there are only three programs in schools of education that offer specific peace education programs. They are a certificate program at the University of Cincinnati, a graduate program that offers a Masters of Education in Curriculum and Instruction at Lesley College in Cambridge, Massachusetts, and graduate studies in conflict resolution at Teachers College at Columbia University in New York City.

Students at the School of Education at the University of Cincinnati who complete 10 courses receive a certificate in peace education. These courses are "Alternatives to Violence," "Introduction to Peace Education," "Liberation Theology," "Global Education: Issues and Problems," "Multicultural Education," "Theories of Conflict Resolution," "Peace Education and Popular Cinema," "Readings in War and Peace," "Peace Education Seminar," "Mediation for the Classroom Teacher," "Children's Creative Response to Conflict," and "Cooperative Discipline." Several of these courses are based on curricula that have been developed by community-based organizations such as Peace Grows in Akron, Ohio, which has published an extensive curriculum for teachers on alternatives to violence, and Children's Creative to Conflict in Nyack, New York, which has developed a curriculum called the "Peaceable Classroom" that is being used throughout the world. The program at Cincinnati has a strong emphasis on racism, sexism, colonialism, and other systematic forms of discrimination.

Graduate students at Lesley College learn conflict resolution skills and how to integrate social and emotional learning into educational settings. This program has strong ties with another NGO, the Resolving Conflict Creatively Program, in New York City, which promotes cultural competency. Courses in this program include "Alternatives to Violence in Education Settings," "Creating Just and Caring Communities in Classrooms and Schools," "Resolving Conflict, Valuing Diversity: Peacemaking in Educational Settings," "Peaceable Schools Internships," "Curriculum: Philoso-

phy, Theory and Development," "Computer Literacy for Educators," and "Educational Research and Evaluation." The program is geared toward working teachers with intensive weekend formats at off-campus sites.

The graduate program at Teachers College focuses on constructive conflict resolution skills for educational professionals and trainers in social service agencies, civic, business, and community groups. The courses consist of practicums offered through weekend workshops with titles such as "Collaborative Negotiation Skills," "Cross-Cultural Conflict Resolution Skills," and "Mediation Skills." A summer institute offers a practicum called "Fundamentals of Cooperation, Conflict Resolution and Mediation." Faculty are members of the Interdisciplinary International Center for Cooperation and Conflict Resolution. In addition, Betty Reardon runs a Peace Education Program at Teachers College that offers peace education courses to doctoral students.

These three programs provide prototypes for the study of peace education in schools of education. Violence is a complex topic that requires a wide variety of approaches. A single professor mentioning different aspects of violence during several lessons will not provide students with enough knowledge and skills so that they can teach others to be peacemakers. A more comprehensive approach hinted at by these programs provides teachers with a wide range of skills that will help them handle violence in their classrooms and develop in their students' minds a peaceful consciousness.

C. Support Networks

The field of peace education relies on a wide variety of support networks that link together peace activists, peace researchers, and peace educators. Foremost among these is the Peace Education commission (PEC) of the International Peace Research Association (IPRA), which has provided a biannual forum for peace educators to share ideas and research since 1970. Members of PEC have published proceedings, edited special editions of international journals, and produced books on different aspects of peace education. A former executive secretary of PEC, Ake Bjerstedt from Sweden, produced a journal, *Peace, Environment, and Education*, that allowed peace educators from around the world to share insights into this growing field.

The American Education Research Association has a peace education special interest group that meets during the annual meetings. In the United States the Consortium for Peace Education Research and Development (COPRED) has for the past 20 years provided a newsletter, a journal (*Peace and Change*), and an annual conference where peace educators, activists, and researchers can learn from each other about their efforts to promote peace. More recently, the Peace Studies Association has provided a forum for university-based peace educators in the United States and Canada to exchange research and insights from the growing field of peace studies. In the United States, Educators for Social Responsibility is a large NGO for teachers and professors of education that provides workshops for teachers and a newsletter about the latest developments in the field. In England a similar organization, Teachers for Peace, which was an outgrowth from the Campaign for Nuclear Disarmament, has promoted peace education throughout Great Britain. Another teacher organization that has grown rapidly in the United States is the National Association for Mediation in Education (NAME), which provides training for teachers using peer mediation techniques in their classrooms.

D. Electronic Links

Peace educators have come to the realization that telecommunications offers rich possibilities for advancing peace education in the new millennium. For example, the Internet links students and scholars in projects that promote global understanding and sensitivity. E-mail has allowed teachers to share ideas, concerns, and solutions to problems and to join in discussion groups with people all over the world in order to be informed about the latest developments in the fast-growing field of peace education. One project, "country focus," provides information about different countries as well as activities on Human Rights Day, International Women's Day, and World Health Day, among others.

An online discussion group for peace educators has been established at the University of Wisconsin-Milwaukee and can be accessed by contacting listserv@csd.uwm.edu and subscribing to "pec," an electronic discussion group established under the auspices of the peace education commission of the International Peace Research Association. This same association publishes an electronic peace through literature and culture magazine that can be accessed through IPRA's homepage at http://www.antioch.edu/;ti;peace/ipra/IPRA.html. "Peace Education Now" is a resource that provides multimedia activities for building a culture of peace at http://gnv.fdt.net/sblythe/peacednow. "Stopping the Cycle," a homepage about violence prevention for educators, can be found at http://www.smplanet.com/violence/violence.html. All these resources that help peace educators communicate throughout the world contribute to the formation of a global village. One of the goals of peace education is to break down national barriers and facilitate communicate between diverse peoples. These transnational dialogues in cyberspace are creating virtual communities that allow professors and students with common pursuits to join together, overcome physical distances, and create electronic villages that foster collaboration.

III. INTERNATIONAL EDUCATION

Peace studies and international security studies have the same goal of preventing war. Peace educators teach about different cultural traditions in order to promote a sense of solidarity between people. An important aspect of this is education about human rights and fundamental freedoms as spelled out in the United Nations charter. Peace educators provide students with an understanding of the world's problems and how different governments and international systems are mobilized to address such issues as food supply, raw materials, environmental degradation, increasing world population, development, and disarmament.

These educational efforts are carried out under different names in different countries and regions of the world. Teachers in countries of the South are mostly interested in development education promoting political and social reforms designed to raise people out of poverty. In many countries of the South hunger, illiteracy, malnutrition, inadequate health care, and poverty contribute to underdevelopment that causes structural violence and leads to suffering and misery. Peace educators in those countries seek to educate citizens about an alternative economic order that will help resolve some of problems created by imperialism, racism, and lack of human rights. In India, such an approach to peace education is closely allied with Gandhian studies with its emphasis upon "Satyagraha," or the search for truth. In Europe, peace educators promote disarmament studies, focusing on violence caused by the arms trade among poor countries. In South and Central America peace education focuses on development and leans on some of the traditions of liberation theology, providing literacy to poor people in base communities. In Japan peace education started out being promoted by teachers in Hiroshima and Nagasaki, where it was called "A-bomb" education. It has since expanded to include human rights education and disarmament studies. In all these different venues peace educators promote an understanding of the global dimensions of local problems and emphasize the quest for peace that has been an important human endeavor throughout history.

Peace educators focus on concepts of national and domestic security as they apply to the global, national, regional, local, and individual levels. The highly militarized world order does not meet the needs of most of the world's population. Nationalism and differing economic investments have caused wars and divided the world into armed camps. Nation-states and large multinational corporations compete for scarce resources with the protection of militarized national security apparatuses. The disparity between rich and poor nations is tremendous and contributes to an unjust economic order, where rich nations exploit poor nations, and such exploitation is undergirded by a militaristic international order. Peace educators help their students figure out what is the best way to provide security throughout this planet. With the end of the Cold War, peace educators encourage their students to create alternative world orders based on peaceful and just relations. They promote civic responsibility within a world community through such international organizations as the United Nations and the World Court. They foster track-two citizen exchanges between people from different lands to nurture citizen diplomacy apart from the formal channels of communication that dominate relations between nation-states. Educational programs within various NGOs have played an important role in cultural transformation for a world community. UNESCO has formed a culture of peace program aimed toward regions of the world scarred by ethnic conflict. Peace educators contribute to this global transformation away from militarized nation-states by fostering democratic values within their classrooms. These values promote a world climate of respect for the diverse cultures and people who inhabit planet Earth.

IV. SAFETY IN SCHOOLS

Violence increasingly is becoming a problem for young people. Suicides and gun-related homicides are at record high levels. Since the mid-1970s homicides by juveniles involving a firearm have increased nearly threefold in the United States. In the 1990s 1 in 20 youths in the United States indicated that he or she carried a gun to school. Studies show that violence is changing the behavior of teenagers. Six percent of adolescents are estimated to have been the victims of a violent crime. Nearly 3 million crimes take place in or near schools daily, 1 every 6 seconds in the schoolday. About half of 6th through 12th grade students in the United States personally witnessed bullying, robbery, or physical assault at school. About 1 of 8 students

reports being directly victimized in school. The specters of crime and violence are scaring America's young people into carrying weapons, cutting classes, and settling for lower grades. One of 4 primary or secondary students indicates that violence has lessened the quality of education in his or her school. Although this is a nationwide problem, the fears of violence exist more heavily in inner city, at-risk neighborhoods.

In addition to its traditional emphasis on global education, peace education is also used as a strategy to promote safety in schools. School boards concerned about increasing protection for students are appropriating funds for security expenses. College professors in schools of education are responding to rising incidences of violence both in school and society by teaching about different ways to create safe schools. The majority of these peacekeeping approaches to school violence rely on peace through strength strategies used to deter hostile students with such severe consequences that they will obey the law and not cause conflicts or bodily harm on school property.

In response to problems caused by violence in schools, educators are implementing violence prevention programs to create a safe climate at schools. Many schools have initiated weapons searches, expulsions, and metal detectors. Some schools have installed surveillance and warning devices to monitor students, ID badges, closed-circuit television, and walkie-talkies. Among other responses, some schools are adopting uniforms to avoid some of the thefts that occur when young people wear expensive clothing and valuable jewelry to school. These peacekeeping strategies are aimed toward chronic troublemakers and are designed to create a safe school environment.

Violence prevention programs also have an educational component that goes under a variety of different names—such as anger management, antiracism/antisexism, drug/alcohol education, gang awareness, domestic violence prevention, and handgun violence. These peace education programs provide youths with knowledge about the consequences of violent behavior in the hope that they will make wise decisions to avoid self-destructive activities in their own lives. The expectation is that when youths learn constructive ways to address what leads to violence, the incidence and intensity of violent confrontations will diminish.

Violence prevention programs are most often introduced in communities that experience high levels of violence. Each year approximately 25,000 people die from homicide and 31,000 die from suicide in the United States. Violence is the second leading cause of death for Americans between the ages of 15 and 24 years and is the leading cause for death of African Americans in this age group. Adolescents are disproportionately represented among victims and perpetrators of violence. Children in communities that experience high levels of violence can be traumatized in ways that make it hard for young people to participate positively in school. The trauma of violence interrupts and distorts the development process of children at every age. Educators in such communities are struggling to find ways to help children cope with violence. They do this in individual group counselling sessions in which young people voice their pain and confusion in artistic activities that provide creative ways to ventilate hostilities and fears, and through schoolwide recognition of the trauma experienced by youths exposed to gunfire, suicides, homicides, or assaults.

In order to deal with these high levels of violence, school officials are teaming with parents, law enforcement and juvenile justice officials, and community and business leaders to develop schoolwide plans to create safe, disciplined, gun- and drug-free schools. Part of this plan includes developing a site assessment and review related to students' rights and responsibilities, liability, and legal issues. School districts are creating committees to assess the administrative structure related to security incidents and appointing crisis intervention teams that help a school community respond to violent incidents such as suicide or attacks on teachers that create a climate of fear, anger, and grief within a school. Such a committee develops a school inventory and supplies both students and teachers with personal safety information. Members of this team develop an emergency plan to address possible crises with a checklist of procedures and responsibilities.

In 1994 the U.S. government passed a Gun-Free Schools Act that required local educational agencies to implement a policy requiring referral to the criminal justice or juvenile delinquency system of any student who brings firearms to school. This law requires local educational agencies to expel from school for not less than a year a student who is determined to have brought a weapon to school. School districts throughout the United States are creating alternative educational programs to deliver educational and other services to expelled students. Some school systems are modifying existing programs to accommodate the large numbers of students expelled for disruptive behaviors, while others are creating new programs, often in collaboration with social agencies and nonprofit service organizations.

School districts are seeking security coverage to maintain violence-free buildings. In the 1970s a new type of full-time professional specialist committed to designing and administering school security programs began to emerge in a variety of school systems across the United States. Sometimes these professionals come from police-community relations programs that use specially trained school-based officers to project a supportive presence in daily school life. Many police districts are training officers to run drug and crime resistance education programs in schools where teachers feel inadequately prepared to deal with these exigencies.

School systems also have hired large numbers of a new type of aide—security personnel who patrol the halls and playgrounds to provide a security presence in school buildings. There exists in school districts tensions between those who believe in a law enforcement orientation and those who desire a primarily educational approach to school violence. Hiring security aides in a climate of tax-payer resistance to paying for new programs means that there is less money available for human relations programs and other educational approaches to creating safe schools. Throwing expensive hardware or policing programs at these problems may provide a quick and necessary fix to stop the violence but it neither addresses the question of what can be done to stop the incidences of violence from breaking out in the first case, nor does it empower students to solve their own conflicts without authoritarian adult interventions.

Educators who only focus on punitive measures to deal with safety issues in schools ignore many of the crucial aspects of the violence problem. Deterrence policies do not provide students with a understanding of the problems of violence nor with strategies to avoid violence. Such approaches to conflict in school mirror punitive strategies used in the criminal justice system, which attempts to deal with juvenile crime by locking up youth. Removing violent offenders from schools will not make the problems associated with violence disappear. This practice promotes a negative peace that has as its goal the cessation of violence and the resolution of conflicts.

V. CONFLICT RESOLUTION

Conflict resolution in schools attempts to teach young people peacemaking skills. It grew out of a Quaker project introduced in New York City schools in 1972, the Children's Creative Response to Conflict. In the late 1970s, neighborhood justice centers established during the Carter administration become involved with school systems. Community Boards in San Francisco led this effort to incorporate peer mediation programs in schools to help students and teachers deal with school violence and neighborhood conflicts. In the 1980s Educators for Social Responsibility, a national organization, began to promote alternative dispute mechanisms in schools. By 1994, with the founding of the National Association for Mediation in Education, more than 1000 schools in the United States had some kind of conflict resolution program.

The growth of conflict resolution programs in schools has been accompanied by an interest in courses in schools of education that help prepare teachers to deal with violence in their classrooms. Violence is multifaceted. Teachers taking courses in conflict resolution at the university level learn about the sources of conflicts. These professionals find out about different ways of analyzing conflict, so that they can determine what different conflicts are about. They study different conflict styles and they learn communication skills that enhance conflict resolution processes. They investigate the relationship between culture and conflict. They explore alternative dispute resolution processes—negotiation, mediation, and consensus building. They analyze the differences between negotiation, conciliation, mediation, fact-finding, and arbitration. They explore the role of a third party, sometimes themselves, but most often peer mediators, in helping parties reach agreements. They learn to use these skills to maintain and improve relationships between those who disagree so that they can build peaceful communities within their schools and classrooms.

From the beginning proponents of conflict resolution programs in schools have been teaching young people better problem-solving strategies and decision-making skills to build a climate that more conducive to learning in school and to empower young people to solve their conflicts without using force. These efforts offer an alternative to the peacekeeping strategies mentioned above (expulsion, suspension, detention, or court intervention), and have in some schools reduced violence, discipline referrals, vandalism, and chronic school absences. Peace educators involved in conflict resolution programs promote a view of conflict as a positive force that can accompany personal growth and institutional change. They help young people and school personnel acquire a deeper understanding of themselves and others through improved communication. Students who learn about nonadversarial conflict resolution and its relationship to the legal system can acquire a heightened knowledge of peacemaking strategies at all levels of social institutions.

Conflict resolution programs in schools consist of several different components—a curriculum for learning about peace, peer mediation programs, staff development programs, and changes in policies and procedures to create a more cooperative school environment. Conflict resolution skills can be taught through traditional curriculum in social studies, language arts, or health education. It can also be reflected through pedagogical practices in a teacher's management style. Peace educators who value alternative dispute techniques set up democratic classes where students have some say in how the class is structured. They also teach cooperative lessons where students learn from each other, as opposed to teacher-centered classes where teachers play an authoritarian role, telling students what to do and when to do it. They encourage students to engage in problem-solving activities.

Peer mediation programs use trained students to guide their fellow students through a mediation process, where two conflicting sides get to state their disagreements and, with the help of a mediator, find a mutually acceptable compromise. The steps involved in mediation are to set the stage in a safe environment, to gather perspectives, to identify interests, create options, to evaluate choices, and to generate an agreement. These programs often take place in a separate place, a "mediation room," and are supervised by an adult, often a school psychologist, who oversees the mediations and trains the students. Peer mediation programs handle disputes involving rumors, misunderstandings, fights, jealousies, and personal property. Peer mediators do not take on problems involving drugs, weapons, or abuse.

A comprehensive approach to conflict resolution in schools has been referred to as the peaceable school that uses conflict resolution as a system for managing the school as well as the classroom. Conflict resolution principles and processes are learned and utilized by every member of the school community—teachers, counselors, administrators, students, and custodial staff. Peace educators use noncoercive school and classroom management practices. They do not rely on punishment and they adopt natural consequences as a method of providing discipline to students. This comprehensive approach to conflict resolution in schools implies a transformation of a school away from competitive to cooperative structures that promote a win-win climate that respects diversity. In peaceable schools educators promote peacemaking as a normative activity that contributes to individual, group, and institutional goals. The goal of a peaceable school is to create a schoolwide discipline program focused on empowering students to regulate and control their own behavior.

VI. BUILDING A PEACE CONSCIOUSNESS

Some professors of education are responding to increased concerns about the problems of violence by trying to build respect for peace in the minds of their students. Peace, a complex and inspiring topic, appeals to ideology in youths. Youths are surrounded by violent images in the broader culture, they experience corporal punishment at home, and they are being urged to be tough by their peers. This leaves little room for youths to pursue peaceful behavior. This approach to peace education teaches young people the power of peace and it attempts to alter patterns in students' minds based on the violent ways of behaving they see around them, replacing violent ways of responding to culture with a peace consciousness that values cooperation, kindness, honesty, compassion, tolerance, charity, and justice. A peacebuilding strategy provides a long-range approach to the problems of violence, filling children's heads with powerful images of peace that will inoculate them against the seductive attractiveness of violence. Whereas conflict resolution teaches skills, this approach to peace education motivates the will so that people use those skills when they are faced with conflict.

Building a peace consciousness focuses on the positive nature of nonviolent alternatives. The goal of nonviolence in education is not just to stop the violence and reduce conflict in schools but rather to create in young people's minds the conditions for positive peace. When young people watch the news, they see terrorism and acts of violence committed all around the world. When they study history, they learn about wars. To provide positive images of peace to counteract violent cultural images, teachers teach the power of nonviolence.

Nonviolence has a proud history. Teachers interested in sharing this history can teach the peace movements and nonviolent cultures that have existed in various human communities. Students can learn in school that violence is unacceptable and they can understand how nonviolent strategies have been used to address injustice. Teachers explain this to their students by telling the stories of peace heroes and heroines such as the winners of the Nobel Peace Prize. Through art they encourage students to express images of violence and their wishes for peace. Peace educators involve students in peace projects such as planting a tree or volunteering in a shelter. They provide resources—books, posters movies, and videos—that have peace themes. They connect students with community-based organizations that promote nonviolence—women's shelters, violence re-

duction programs for batterers, peace groups, and anger management support groups. Involvement in such projects motivates pupils to value peace.

Nonviolence does not seek to defeat an opponent but rather to win friendship. A nonviolent strategy is not about humiliation. Young people should understand that the goal of a nonviolent strategy is to defeat the problem, not the persons involved. It is directed against the forces of evil rather than the people who happen to be doing evil. A person or a group of people practicing nonviolent resistance accept blows from an opponent without striking back. Such a person avoids not only external physical violence but also internal violence of the spirit. Both Dr. King and Mahatma Gandhi provide excellent examples of how nonviolent strategies can resist injustice. Nonviolent resistance is based on the conviction that the universe is on the side of justice. Consequently, a student who has acquired a peace consciousness has a deep faith in the future and attempts to create a better future by building beloved communities.

Nonviolence in education is committed to democratic practices, because a democracy allows for all points of view to be heard in the promotion of the truth. Such an approach to education has been heralded in recent school reforms through the promotion of multicultural education. A multicultural approach to knowledge teaches that all cultures have important insights into the truth. A nonviolent approach to conflict resolution in a diverse world requires that all voices be respected and urged to create a dialogue that will build a consensus about how to create positive peace. In order to appreciate the diversity of life on this planet, students should be taught global awareness, where they learn to respect different cultures. Respect for different cultures develops a consciousness essential for living together in a "global village."

Students in classes where teachers promote nonviolence acquire both theoretical concepts about the dangers of violence and the possibilities of peace, as well as skills about how to live nonviolently. Peace educators teach the power of generative love, care, and justice to build the beloved community. Here, nonviolence extends to personal relationships and relationships with the broader environment. Do teachers help students find peace within themselves? Adults who listen to and show concern for the problems caused by violence in young people's lives can help heal some of the wounds that often lead to hostile, aggressive behavior.

Nonviolence in education requires more than a theoretical understanding of the problems of violence and knowledge of strategies for peace. Peace educators interested in nonviolence in education attempt to stimulate the human heart to be charitable, and they provide students with skills that demonstrate their feelings of compassion for all forms of life. A challenge provided by a commitment to nonviolence in education is to figure out how to increase students' abilities to love. Teachers instruct youths in alternatives to dysfunctional, violent behaviors. They also try to make students aware of their own biases, the ways they stereotype others by gender, their sexual preference, religious beliefs, or skin color. Children learn about racial differences and gender identity formation to help them avoid discriminatory behavior. This approach to peace education moves children beyond hate and enables them to become more loving.

Nonviolence in education does not just mean a quiet classroom. It suggests a learning environment in which students are acting on problems constructively, managing their conflicts creatively, and taking on challenging tasks. Educators committed to nonviolence in education urge their schools to play a proactive role in relation to the problems of violence that make education so difficult. Professors who promote nonviolence in education attempt to correct failure in schools that comes from the problematic nature of the modern world so deeply steeped in violence. Addressing the chaotic, frightening aspects of this world by teaching young people about the potential of nonviolence to prevent violence provides youths with hope that they might be able to resolve conflicts that distract them from school tasks. Students will have a hard time learning in school as long as they are worried about violence. Children who come from violent homes and communities often cannot focus on cognitive lessons until some relief is provided for the anxiety they feel about violence in their lives. This happens in affluent communities with dysfunctional homes, in crime-ridden inner city neighborhoods, and in war-torn areas. Children learn better when their teachers address directly the many forms of violence that make their worlds so frightening.

School personnel who address problems of violence in the postmodern world can give students an appreciation for the value of nonviolence by teaching values such as justice, truth, freedom, equality, and democracy. It is in the interest of the greater society that schools build a peace consciousness in students' minds by promoting the values of peace, justice, and truth, since so many children learn to value violence from the media and from watching it in their own lives where in families torn by domestic abuse, in gangs, in areas of ethnic conflict, and in crime-filled neighborhoods, might makes right. Such instruction helps youths find

alternates to the violent behavior they see all around them and it can build a foundation for creating a beloved community based on justice and freedom, as opposed to a garrison state based on might and force. Although educators cannot always guarantee the safety of their students, they can teach them a variety of alternatives to violence that might help them deal constructively with conflict in their lives.

Also See the Following Articles

CONFLICT MANAGEMENT AND RESOLUTION • NONVIOLENCE THEORY AND PRACTICE • PEACE EDUCATION: PEACE MUSEUMS • PEACE EDUCATION: YOUTH • PEACEMAKING AND PEACEBUILDING

Bibliography

Bey, T. M., & Turner, G. (1996). *Making schools a place of peace.* Thousand Oaks, CA: Corwin Press, Inc.

Bodine, R. J., Crawford, D., & Schrumpf, F. (1994). *Creating the peaceful school.* Champaign, IL: Research Press.

Boulding, E. (1988). *Building a global civic culture.* New York: Teachers College Press.

Brock-Utne, B. (1985). *Education for peace.* London: Pergamon Press.

Brock-Utne, B. (1989). *Feminist issues on peace and peace education.* London: Pergamon Press.

Burns, R. J., & Aspeslaugh, R. (1996). *Three decades of peace education around the world.* New York: Garland Publishing.

Crawford, D., & Bodine, R. (1996). *Conflict resolution education guide to implementing programs in school youth serving organizations, and community and juvenile justice settings.* Washington, DC: U.S. Department of Justice.

Girard, K., & Koch, S. J. (1996). *Conflict resolution in schools: A manual for educators.* San Francisco: Jossey-Bass Publishers.

Harris, I. (1988). *Peace education.* Jefferson, NC: McFarland & Co.

Harvard educational review: Education and the threat of nuclear war. (1984). Volume 54, Number 3.

Henderson, G. (Ed.). (1973). *Education for peace: Focus on mankind.* Alexander, VA: ASCD Press.

Hicks, D. (Ed.). (1988). *Education for peace: Issues, principles, and practice in the classroom.* New York: Routledge.

Hoffman, A. (Ed.). (1996). *Schools, violence and society.* Westport, CT: Praeger.

Johnson, D., & Johnson, R. (1995). *Reducing school violence through conflict resolution.* Fairfax, VA: Association for Supervision and Curriculum Department.

Kriedler, W. J. (1984). *Creative conflict resolution: More than 200 activities for keeping peace in the classroom.* Glenview, IL: Scott, Foresman and Co.

Lantieri, L., & Patti, J. (1996). *Waging peace in our schools.* Boston: Beacon Press.

Lasley, T. (1994). *Teaching peace: Toward cultural selflessness.* Boston: Bergin and Garvey.

Meltzer, M. (1985). *Ain't gonna study war no more.* New York: Harper & Row.

Merryfield, M., & Remy, R. (1995). *Teaching about international conflict and peace.* Albany, NY: State University at New York Press.

Montessorri, M. (1949). *Education and the peace*. Chicago: Regnery.

Nesbit, W. A. (1971). *Teaching about war and war prevention*. Washington, DC: Foreign Policy Association.

O'Hare, P. (1983). *Education for peace and justice*. New York: Harper and Row.

O'Reilly, M. R. (1993). *The peaceable classroom*. Portsmouth, NH: Boynton/Cook Publishers. *Peace and Change: The Pedagogy of Peace*. (1990). Volume 13, Number 3.

Peabody Journal of Education: Peace Education in a Postmodern World. (1996). Volume 71, No. 3.

Ray, D. (1988). *Peace education: Canadian and international perspectives*. London, Canada: Third Eye.

Read, H. (1955). *Education for peace*. New York: Harper Colophon.

Reardon, B. (1978). *Militarization, security and peace education*. Valley Forge, PA: United Ministries in Education.

Reardon, B. (1988). *Educating for Global Responsibility*. New York: Teachers College Press.

Reardon, B. (1989). *Comprehensive peace education*. New York: Teachers College Press.

Reardon, B., & Nordland, E. (1994). *Learning peace: The Promise of ecological and cooperative education*. Albany, NY: State University of New York Press.

Teachers College Record: Special Issue on Peace Education. (1982). Volume 84, Number 1.

Thomas, D. C., & Klare, M. T. (Eds.). (1989). *Peace and world order studies: A curriculum guide* (5th ed.) Boulder, CO: Westview Press.

Peace Education: Peace Museums

Peter van den Dungen

University of Bradford

PEACE MUSEUMS aim to inform the public about peace, using illustrations from the lives of individuals, the work of organizations, and historical events. This article presents an overview of existing peace museums throughout the world, showing the variety in their origins and content. It also discusses peace-related museums and reviews the prospects for the further development of the field.

I. THE FIRST PEACE MUSEUMS

The 20th century, and particularly the latter half, which inaugurated the nuclear age, has witnessed the realization of many proposals for promoting peace that earlier critics of war had formulated. For instance, in order to put an end to war in Europe, many schemes were put forward for a European parliament or union. Likewise, most plans for world peace stipulated the need for a global assembly or a league of nations. Both kinds of proposal are now a reality. Early proposals were not confined to the political realm, but also addressed the important educational tasks that lay ahead. "Peace education" may be a modern expression, but the idea itself is an old one. Erasmus attempted to persuade rulers, at a time when war was still regarded as "the sport of kings," that their duties, and the interests of their subjects, demanded that wars be avoided at all costs. In *The Education of a Christian Prince* (1516), Erasmus, the tutor of young princes and the counselor of kings and cardinals, wrote: "Our first and foremost concern must be for training the prince in the skills relevant to wise administration in time of peace, because with them he must strive to his utmost for this end: that the devices of war may never be needed."

With the growth of democracy, critics of war increasingly realized that the citizens needed to be enlightened on such vital questions as the causes and consequences of war as a precondition for its abolition. Military academies and war studies had long been established in many countries with the aim of prosecuting war successfully; a similar professionalization was required for peacemaking. In the 19th century, ideas emerged for establishing a scholarly discipline devoted to the elimination of warfare and the promotion of peace through scientific study and for the creation of peace research institutes and peace studies departments in universities. What was once held to be fanciful has become widely acceptable in modern times. The same evolution characterizes

Copyright © 1999 by Academic Press.
All rights of reproduction in any form reserved.

1. An office for butchering the human species.
2. A widow and orphan making office.
3. A broken bone making office.
4. A wooden leg making office.
5. An office for creating private and public vices.
6. An office for creating public debt.
7. An office for creating speculators, stock jobbers & bankrupts.
8. An office for creating famine.
9. An office for creating political diseases.
10. An office for creating poverty and the destruction of liberty & national happiness.

FIGURE 1 Benjamin Rush's indictment of the War Office.

another instrument of (popular) peace education: peace museums.

The first known proposal for establishing a peace museum was made 200 years ago. In 1798 Dr. Benjamin Rush, an eminent Philadelphian physician, proposed the appointment of a U.S. Secretary of Peace as well as the organization of exhibits that would assist him in his work of advancing the abolition of war. Rush had acquired first-hand experience of the reality of war when he served as an army surgeon in 1776. For him, war was a catastrophe that resulted in many evils; making people aware of the reality of war was tantamount to educating them for peace. Rush confronted the institution of war with his blunt suggestion that a sign be placed over the door of the War Office bearing the following inscription (Fig. 1).

Rush was not satisfied with this purely verbal indictment of war, evocative though it was. He imagined that in the lobby of the War Office there would be displayed "painted representations of all the common military instruments of death; also human skulls, broken bones, unburied and putrefying dead bodies, hospitals crowded with sick and wounded soldiers, villages on fire, mothers in besieged towns, eating the flesh of their children, ships sinking in the ocean, rivers dyed with blood, and extensive plains without tree or fence, or any other object but the ruins of deserted farm houses. Above all this group of woeful figures, let the following words be inserted in red characters, to represent human blood: NATIONAL GLORY."

By thus vividly depicting the unspeakable evils of war through permanent exhibits displayed at the heart of the machinery of government responsible for unleashing the Moloch, Rush seemed to imply that a powerful restraint would be placed on it. His provocative proposal was, no doubt, meant to be merely rhetorical, as no War Office could allow its work to be described in such devastating terms. His proposal anticipated the nature and function of the first peace museums when these emerged over a century later. They were antiwar museums whose prevailing theme was the destructive nature of war.

The International Museum of War and Peace, founded by the Polish–Russian entrepreneur Jean de Bloch (see Fig. 2) in Lucerne (Switzerland) in 1902, can be regarded as the first established museum conceived as an antiwar museum. Alarmed by the development of modern weaponry and the prospect that a future war between the great powers would be suicidal, Bloch conceived his museum in order to convince the society of his day that war had come to an end as a rational instrument of statecraft and that henceforth it could only be waged at an unacceptably high price (which involved not only mass slaughter but also the overthrow of the established social order). The exhibits, which largely consisted of all manner of weapons starting with the mid-15th century, documented the increasingly destructive nature of warfare.

The Great War of 1914–1918 proved Bloch correct (and all the military experts wrong) and it provided an abundance of raw material for the second peace museum, Ernst Friedrich's "First International Anti-War

FIGURE 2 Jean de Bloch, founder of the International Museum of War and Peace, Lucerne (1902–1918)

FIGURE 3 Ernst Friedrich's Anti-War Museum, Berlin (1925–1933).

Museum." Opened in Berlin in 1925 (Fig. 3), it aimed to keep the memory of the horrors of the war alive as a warning to future generations. Friedrich's museum constituted the perfect embodiment of Rush's indictment of war by displaying photographs, each more shocking than the other, of the horrors of the battlefield. Friedrich dramatically enhanced the impact of these photographs by means of a device already suggested by Rush. He systematically contrasted the official view of war, which proclaimed its glory and honor, with the reality of its pathos and squalor. Nazis destroyed his museum in 1933, and its founder, whose life was at risk, escaped abroad. His grandson, Tommy Spree, reestablished the museum in (West) Berlin in 1982.

II. MUSEUMS IN JAPAN

Just as the First World War provided both the emotional stimulus and the material content for Friedrich's museum, so did the Second World War lead to the creation of new peace and antiwar museums. That war culminated in the atomic bombings of Hiroshima and Nagasaki, which added a wholly new dimension to warfare. Ten years after the end of the war, both cities—by now almost miraculously risen from the ashes—inaugurated municipal museums (and public parks) dedicated to preserving the memory of the tragedy that had befallen them and decided to play an active role in the worldwide campaign for nuclear disarmament. That campaign first emerged as a mass protest movement in Japan following the 1954 U.S. hydrogen bomb test on Bikini Atoll in the Pacific Ocean. Its fall-out affected the Japanese fishing vessel *The Fifth Lucky Dragon*. Some 2 decades later, the vessel was restored by a group of private citizens in Tokyo and became the spectacular centerpiece of a third Japanese antinuclear museum (Fig. 4).

Particularly in the late 1980s and the early 1990s many other peace museums were opened, often as a result of decisions by prefectural or municipal authorities. These museums (such as those in Kawasaki and Saitama) are complemented by several peace museums initiated by private individuals (such as the Maruki and Sakima antiwar art galleries, or Grass Roots House Peace Museum) or by nongovernmental bodies such as the Kyoto Museum for World Peace at Ritsumeikan University. The number of museums involved, the diversity of their sponsors, and the continuing trend in creating such institutions all make Japan the only country where it is possible to speak of a "peace museum movement" (see Table I for details of 35 peace museums worldwide, one-third of which are in Japan). In 1994, the Hiroshima Peace Memorial Museum hosted the first national conference of peace museums, bringing together the seven

FIGURE 4 Display house of the *Fifth Lucky Dragon*, Tokyo.

TABLE I

Existing Peace Museums (with Dates of Opening or Foundation)[a]

1946	Geneva	League of Nations Museum
1955	Hiroshima	Hiroshima Peace Memorial Museum
1955	Nagasaki	Nagasaki Atomic Bomb Museum
1959	Castiglione	International Museum of the Red Cross
1959	Madurai	Gandhi Memorial Museum
1960	Amsterdam	Anne Frank House
1960	New Delhi	National Gandhi Museum and Library
1963	Ahmedabad	Gandhi Smarak Sangrahalaya
1963	Berlin (West)	Museum "Haus am Checkpoint Charlie"
1967	Saitama	Maruki Gallery for the Hiroshima Panels
1976	Tokyo	Display House of the Fifth Lucky Dragon
1980	Lindau	Peace Museum Lindau (Lake Constance)
1980	Remagen	Bridge at Remagen Peace Museum
1981	Chicago	The Peace Museum
1981	Sievershausen	Anti-War House Peace Centre
1982	Berlin (West)	Anti-War Museum
1982	Meeder	Peace Museum Meeder
1984	Berlin (East)	Peace Library and Anti-War Museum
1986	Detroit	Swords into Ploughshares Peace Center & Gallery
1986	Samarkand	International Museum of Peace and Solidarity
1988	Caen	Caen Memorial
1988	Geneva	International Red Cross & Red Crescent Museum
1989	Kochi	Grass Roots House Peace Museum
1989	Okinawa	Himeyuri Peace Museum
1989	Osaka	International Peace Centre
1990	Kochi	Kochi Liberty & People's Rights Museum
1991	Memphis	National Civil Rights Museum (at the Lorraine Motel)
1992	Kawasaki	Kawasaki Peace Museum
1992	Kyoto	Kyoto Museum for World Peace, Ritsumeikan University
1993	Saitama	Saitama Peace Museum
1993	St. Radegund	Franz Jägerstätter House
1993	Wolfsegg	First Austrian Peace Museum
1994	Okinawa	Sakima Art Gallery
1994	Verdun	The World Centre for Peace, Freedom & Human Rights
1995	The Hague	Yi Jun Peace Museum

[a] The full details for each museum, except for the last one listed, are in the UN publication *Peace Museums Worldwide*.

leading institutions. Annual conferences have been held since then.

The peace museum field in Japan is characterized not only by numerical expansion but also by qualitative change. Whereas the exhibits in the Hiroshima and Nagasaki museums traditionally confined themselves to the "victim" aspects of the bombings, newer museums such as those in Osaka and Kyoto have courageously widened their purposes and displays by also documenting the country's aggressive militarism during the so-called "Fifteen Years War" (1931–1945). In this manner they have initiated the painful process of public discussion of issues surrounded by guilt and shame, denial and taboo. Never before has the gruesome evidence of Japanese misdeeds been so fully and openly acknowledged as in these museums. Thus they are making a vital contribution to a more accurate and honest understanding of the country's wartime past on the part of its own citizens. At the same time these newer museums are helping to restore among the countries of the region trust and confidence in Japan. It can be truly said therefore that the efforts of these peace museums go beyond peace education and assume aspects of peace-making.

Peace museums in Japan, in which traditionally the

nuclear issue has prevailed, are increasingly also addressing other aspects of war and peace in the post-1945 world (such as the role of the United Nations and of international law in achieving world peace). In this way, the antinuclear and antiwar message of Japanese peace museums is being complemented by constructive, positive approaches to peace and nonviolent conflict resolution.

III. MUSEUMS IN GERMANY

Germany is the only other country where several peace museums have been established in recent times. The fact that six museums were founded during the early 1980s would seem to suggest that the stimulus for their creation was not so much the experience of World War II (which ended 35 years previously) as the fears generated by the onset of the "Second" Cold War (1979). They led to the emergence of large peace movements and demonstrations in several countries in western Europe, including (West) Germany. Apart from the political climate in which they appeared, these museums also have in common a modest scale and a traditional approach to presenting exhibits. Four owe their existence to strong support from church or religious bodies. They include the Peace Library and Anti-War Museum, established in (East) Berlin, which specializes in producing large photographic exhibitions with text panels that are also loaned to other peace museums. The Peace Museum Lindau documents the life and work of individuals who have worked for peace and reconciliation. The Bridge at Remagen Peace Museum is the only one that focuses on a famous episode during World War II. It is also the only one that has exploited the remnants of war (the Museum is housed in a massive pillar of the collapsed bridge over the river Rhine) in order to teach peace and engage in practical peace-building and reconciliation. The Museum organizes reunions of German and U.S. veterans and of German POWs who barely survived in camps near Remagen at the end of the war.

It is obvious that the location of a museum can be one of its main attractions because of the symbolism involved: no museums are better placed than those in Hiroshima and Nagasaki for educating visitors about the devastation caused by nuclear war. In fact, sites that preserve remnants of buildings convey the peace message more powerfully than any exhibit in a museum. This is the case, for instance, with the Hiroshima atom-bomb dome, which was formally included in UNESCO's register of World Heritage sites in 1996 (Fig. 5).

FIGURE 5   A-bomb dome, Hiroshima.

From this point of view it is interesting to note that the most popular and best-known peace museum in Germany is the "Haus am Checkpoint Charlie." Opened in (West) Berlin in 1963 during the height of the Cold War, the museum was located near the Wall (at the crossing point for entering East Berlin in the American sector of the city), the most visible and poignant evidence of the East–West divide. The museum displays a whole range of original vehicles and other ingenious devices that were used by individuals in their dramatic attempts to escape. The museum has, in addition, become a center for information about human rights violations and also documents the nonviolent struggles against them.

IV. MUSEUMS DEDICATED TO INDIVIDUALS

Location is also a significant factor for museums devoted to the life and work of individual peace-makers. Just as the places of birth, residence, and death of famous individuals often have museums established in them (such as composers or novelists) so, too, have museums been established for peace-makers. They serve the double purpose of being, on the one hand, a shrine and place of homage and commemoration and, on the other hand, a center for learning about and promoting the ideas and values associated with the person concerned. In the 1990s at least three such museums have been created for individuals who had died many years previously in tragic circumstances and whose ideas and significance have not been diminished by the intervening years.

This is evidently so in the case of Franz Jägerstätter, a brave and simple farmer in a small Austrian village who followed his conscience rather than Hitler's orders and who was beheaded in a Berlin prison in 1943 for his pacifist stance. His moving story, which is now also told in what used to be his home, continues to inspire and encourages all those who have difficulties in reconciling the demands of the state for army service with the dictates of their own conscience.

Very different but no less dramatic is the story of Yi Jun who died in 1907, the year of Jägerstätter's birth. He is a famous Korean educational reformer, diplomat, and patriot who was active in the struggle for Korean independence from Japan in the early years of the century. In 1907 the Korean emperor (under house arrest) secretly sent him to The Hague to plead there for Korea's participation in the Second Hague Peace Conference and for a condemnation of Japan's occupation. His mission created diplomatic embarrassment at the conference but proved unsuccessful. Yi Jun died in his hotel, reputedly through suicide. In 1995, on the 50th anniversary of Korea's independence, a museum dedicated to him and to the causes of Korean and world peace was inaugurated in the same building. Regarded today as a heroic father of the nation in both parts of his deeply divided country, Yi Jun is a figure around whom both Koreas can unite in order to start the process of overcoming hostility and division. In 1997, on the 90th anniversary of the 1907 Conference and Yi Jun's tragic death, the Museum organized an international peace conference on Korea.

While Yi Jun is hardly known outside his country, and Jägerstätter's reputation is only slowly spreading beyond his native Austria, Martin Luther King, Jr. is widely regarded as the most charismatic and successful exponent of nonviolent action since Gandhi. In 1991 a museum focusing on the history of the U.S. civil rights movement of the 1950s and 1960s was opened in the motel in Memphis where King was assassinated (1968). The exhibits in the National Civil Rights Museum include interactive scenarios that convey for the visitor a strong sense of participation in the various struggles represented. Some 10 years before the museum was opened, several blocks in Atlanta, including the house where King was born, the church where he prayed, and the crypt where he lies buried were declared by the U.S. Congress a national historic area (which was placed under the administration of the U.S. National Park Service). It has since become the third most popular site operated by the Service (exceeded only by the Statue of Liberty in Manhattan and the Liberty Bell in Philadelphia). In 1994 the King family announced plans for an ambitious M. L. King Interactive Museum at the site to complement the M. L. King Center for Nonviolent Change established there by the family in 1982.

In India, at least half a dozen museums are devoted to preserving and promoting Mohandas Gandhi's message; some of the most significant ones are mentioned in Table I. It is obvious that, given his preeminence in the philosophy and practice of nonviolence and given the number of people and movements that he has inspired, Gandhi is also presented in many peace museums around the world.

In the United States, museums have been dedicated to the life and work of individual presidents, and some of these museums can be regarded partly as peace museums to the extent that they document the efforts for peace of the president concerned. This is the case for the Woodrow Wilson House in Washington, DC, the last home of the American president who was the chief architect of the League of Nations and Nobel Peace Prize laureate in 1919. A later president who made significant contributions to international peace-making, also following his term of office, is Jimmy Carter. The Jimmy Carter Library and its museum in Atlanta (Georgia) features exhibits on the Carter presidency, including his efforts for peace. Museums are also devoted to other leading figures in American public life, for instance, the Jane Addams Hull House Museum in Chicago. Addams was a pioneer social worker who opened a settlement house in 1889 in one of the poorest districts of the city, mainly for the benefit of poor immigrants. She was also an ardent feminist and internationalist who received the Nobel Peace Prize in 1931, making her the leading woman in the nation.

Chicago is also the home of the first United States peace museum (Fig. 6). It was created in 1981 by a number of concerned individuals who recognized that the arts could powerfully express the horrors of war as well as the visions of peace. A similar view informs the work of the Swords into Plowshares Peace Center and Gallery in Detroit, founded in 1986.

Support The Peace Museum!

FIGURE 6 Poster for The Peace Museum in Chicago.

V. MUSEUMS DEDICATED TO INTERNATIONAL ORGANIZATIONS

The work of peace is complex and multifaceted and involves the efforts of individuals and groups as well as organizations and institutions. Indeed, peace thinkers and activists have traditionally placed hope for a world without war (the basic meaning of peace) in the development of institutions that would facilitate international cooperation, strengthen international solidarity, and promote the growth of international law and justice. This process started in earnest around the turn of the century and the two Hague Peace Conferences (1899 and 1907) may be interpreted as evidence of a growing recognition on the part of states of the desirability of the pacific settlement of disputes between them and of the concomitant need to develop the requisite international machinery.

Andrew Carnegie donated $1.5 million for the building of the Peace Palace in The Hague (Fig. 7) in order to provide a proper home for the Permanent Court of

Arbitration (PCA), whose creation was the main success of the 1899 conference. When a more substantial court, the Permanent Court of International Justice, was created after World War I, it also took its seat in the Peace Palace. Opened in 1913, the latter is a peace museum only in the sense that the building's ornate architecture and rich decorations are steeped in the symbolism of peace and justice and in the sense that for most of the 20th century it has been the preeminent venue for international jurisprudence on the vital issues of war and peace. The Peace Palace is thus only incidentally a peace museum; the several legal institutions that it houses (first and foremost the UN's International Court of Justice) play an increasingly significant role in the peaceful resolution of inter-state conflicts. Plans for a proper museum in or near the Peace Palace to illustrate the evolution and importance of international law for world peace have been intermittently suggested. They are likely to gain more support in the context of the 1990s "UN Decade of International Law," one of whose main aims is to raise public understanding of and support for international law. The forthcoming centenaries of the two Hague Peace Conferences will provide further opportunities for promoting the establishment of such a museum.

Like The Hague, Geneva is also a peace "Mecca," both from the historical and contemporary perspectives. Just as the Peace Palace was constructed to house the PCA, so the "Palais des Nations" was built for the League of Nations. After World War II and the demise of the League, the Palais became the headquarters of the European Office of the UN. It has also housed since then (1946) a Museum of the League of Nations and the History of International Organization. The Museum's displays have been drawn from the rich archives from the League itself as well as from the organized peace movement. In 1996, on the occasion of the 50th anniversary of the dissolution of the League, a large exhibition showing its history was mounted in the Museum.

Since 1988 Geneva has also been the home of the International Red Cross and Red Crescent Museum (Fig. 8), located very near the imposing building of the International Committee of the Red Cross. Through documents, objects, and films, the goals, ideals, and achievements of the movement are explained. Thirty years before (1959) the Italian Red Cross inaugurated an International Museum of the Red Cross in Castiglione. The occasion was the centenary of the battle of Solferino (1859), which inspired Henry Dunant to found an organization to help wounded soldiers on the field of battle. Since his days, the organization has become truly global and official national societies have

FIGURE 7 Peace Palace, The Hague.

been established in nearly all countries. Museums devoted to the activities of the national Red Cross society have been founded in several countries. Dunant was born and grew up in Geneva and several memorial plaques are a reminder of this. The hospital in Heiden (at the eastern end of Switzerland) where he lived during the last 18 years of his life and where he died in 1910, opened a one-room museum devoted to him in 1969.

The first international conference of the Red Cross, resulting in the first Geneva Convention of August, 1864, was held in a room (which later became known as the Alabama Room) in the Cantonal headquarters building in the city center. Eight years later, the same room was the venue for the international tribunal that arbitrated a serious dispute between the U.S. and Britain. This dispute was about the damages which the *Alabama* (a "pirate" vessel built in a British shipyard for the Confederate Navy) had inflicted on Union ships during the American Civil War. The Alabama meeting room displays many memorabilia concerning this historic case whose successful outcome considerably strengthened the belief that great powers were willing, when serious disputes threatened the peace between them, to abandon war in favor of arbitration.

Equally famous as the name "Alabama" but even more momentous for the student of international relations is "Westphalia." The Peace of Westphalia (1648) signified the end of the Thirty Years' War. It resulted

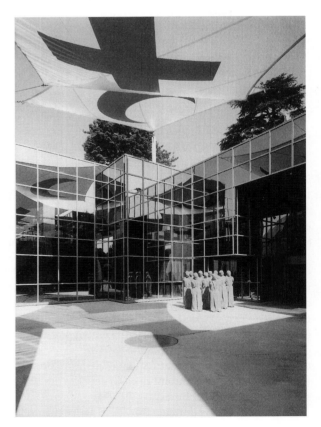

FIGURE 8 International Red Cross and Red Crescent Museum, Geneva.

not only in the formal recognition of the independence of the United Provinces and the Swiss Confederation but also, more generally, laid the foundations for a new legal international order consisting of sovereign states. Peace negotiations took place in the cities of Münster and Osnabrück during a period of 5 years and brought together some 230 diplomats with their retinues (totalling about 10,000 persons) from all over Europe. Many of the negotiations were held in the historic council chamber of Münster town hall, which since then has become known as the "Hall of Peace." It displays the portraits of the sovereigns and of the most important envoys as well as some other reminders of the peace negotiations successfully held in the Hall. Although not a museum as such, it is an important locale whose historic visual displays commemorate an important peace. The "Hall of Peace" is a building of the greatest significance in European history and one of the relatively few reminders of peace-making in comparison with those of Europe's war-making.

VI. WAR MUSEUMS AND MEMORIALS

The last observation about the prevalence of war in history, and the resulting wealth of war museums (including army, navy, and air force museums as well as battlefield sites), raises the question of whether such museums can also be regarded as belonging to the category of peace museums. To the extent that such museums are a celebration of weapons and of war, the answer seems clear (Fig. 9). Few countries have achieved or maintained their independence without war and sentiments of nationalism and patriotism have almost universally been identified closely with the "martial virtues." However, the 20th century has witnessed a steady decline in the glorification of warfare; the processes of its progressive delegitimization and increasing lethality seem to go together.

This evolution is also reflected in the ways in which wars are officially commemorated. The Veterans' Memorial in Washington DC or the Cornerstone of Peace memorial in Okinawa are above all simple yet moving reminders of the cost of war in human lives. The Okinawa memorial commemorates *all* the 230,000 people who lost their lives in the Battle of Okinawa—civilians as well as soldiers, both Japanese and American (and also a small number of Koreans and Taiwanese). Such material symbols are not only commemorating the victims of war but also expressing the desire to overcome

Imperial War Museum

Here, let us say, all war is sanitised –
the question of the *product* isn't raised.
It's like a factory where clean machines
hint at well-ordered past production lines.
The guns stand silent in their lovely paint
and it is innocent air at which they point.

There are no shells scream witchlike as they ride
or charred black corpses on the Basra road.
There's camouflage, and razor wire, and scrim –
but not the wounded or the dying scream.
War was imperial, even now it's royal.
Some bodies here would make it much more real!

Some glorious wounds, to frighten or amaze
(some mustard gas would not come much amiss),
some arms and legs, perhaps a severed head?
To reconstruct what History likes hid,
waxworks could re-create the grievous harms
that are not seen in television homes.

This is the War that time cannot corrode,
the Fly-Past and the Victory Parade.
Sadness and Pride, of course, are in the cast –
but no true indication of the cost.
Bring on the war-struck, dazed, the dim civilians!
They should be here, the mild maltreated millions.

GAVIN EWART

FIGURE 9 "Imperial War Museum" by Gavin Ewart.

old antagonisms and engage in reconciliation. The Okinawa memorial is explicitly conceived as a peace monument and will be complemented by a large peace museum which is currently (1998) under construction by the Okinawa Prefectural Government and will replace the Peace Memorial Museum established in 1975.

On the other hand, there are still strong forces at work today that display traditional attitudes to war and its commemoration. In the U.S., the Smithsonian Institution in Washington DC was unable to mark the 50th anniversary of the end of World War II—and of the bombing of Hiroshima—with an exhibition that would have offered different perspectives on that controversial event. Veterans' organizations and conservative members of Congress forced the cancellation of a major exhibition and also the dismissal of the director of the Smithsonian's National Air and Space Museum, who was responsible for organizing the exhibition. Its conservative critics were pleased to have the *Enola Gay* (the plane that dropped the bomb) restored and displayed as the centerpiece of the exhibition but hardly willing to show the devastation and suffering that the bomb caused (and still causes) or to air the debate concerning the reasons for the bombing.

This episode has its counterpart in Japan where for several years an influential conservative organization, that of the War-Bereaved Families, has wanted to establish in central Tokyo a Memorial Museum of the War Dead. Paid for by the Ministry of Social Welfare, the Museum will be dedicated to the Japanese victims of World War II and seems to ignore the countless victims of Japanese militarism in the region during the Fifteen Years' War. Japan's neighbors, not least China, regard the final outcome of this controversial project as a litmus test of Japan's transformation since 1945. Meanwhile, several war museums and war memorials have been established in China in recent years (sometimes taking the form of ossuaries), which are reminders of the atrocities committed by Japanese troops in the period leading up to (and including) World War II. Examples are the Museum for Recording Japanese Gas and Germ Warfare in China and the Chinese People's War Resistance against Japan Memorial Hall. To the extent that these memorials keep alive or strengthen anti-Japanese sentiment they can hardly be seen as constituting peace monuments or museums.

That there is a new spirit afoot, especially in that continent whose soil is drenched in blood spilled in war, is exemplified by a number of recently established museums in France. In Verdun, site of the longest and one of the bloodiest battles of World War I (which in 1916 cost the lives of more than half a million French and German soldiers), a former episcopal palace houses the World Centre for Peace, Freedom and Human Rights, which was opened in 1994. The location of a peace museum of a semiofficial character in the French city that was reduced to rubble and whose name has become synonymous with the slaughter of World War I can be seen as a symbol of the determination not to repeat the past. The Center actively promotes education contributing to global peace and to freedom and human rights which are its foundations. It is a peace museum of a modern kind that displays hardly any traditional artifacts but makes use of the full range of audiovisual and other modern communications media.

The other great killing fields of the "Great War" in France were in the valleys of the Somme. Some of the heaviest fighting of the Battle of the Somme took place near Péronne. The Historial of the Great War, a new kind of war museum, was opened here in 1992. The museum is not about weapons or uniforms but about the war experience of civilians and soldiers of both sides. The Historial is deliberately nonpartisan and attempts to present an unbiased appraisal of the war that

it interprets as a "European civil war." In the process it aims to depict what the English war poet Edmund Blunden later wrote of that fateful day, July 1, 1916, when 60,000 British troops were killed or wounded during the first day of the battle (without gaining a yard): "neither race had won, nor could win the War. The War had won and would go on winning."

Fully in the nonpartisan spirit of the museum, its contents and exhibits have been developed by a team of British, French, and German historians. This provides an interesting contrast with the *Enola Gay* debacle (when the views of U.S. veterans and conservative politicians prevailed over those of American and Japanese historians). It may well be that only the passage of time (and the death of veterans) will enable later generations to adopt a more detached and dispassionate approach toward such emotionally charged and symbolically laden events. Although the Historial does not describe itself as a peace museum, its message is clear and unambiguous.

In France, World War II produced no equivalents of Verdun or the Somme, and it was U.S., Canadian, and British armies who were involved in the Normandy landings in 1944. Heavy fighting took place around Caen and, in 1988, the rebuilt city inaugurated an impressive "Mémorial" which carries the description, " A museum for peace." It not only documents, in a frank manner, the history of France during the war, but also addresses contemporary issues regarding war and peace. A gallery of all the Nobel Peace Prize laureates is the main instrument used to display the variety of peace efforts and achievements of the present century. Such a gallery is ideally suited to illustrate the important theme that peace has its own heroes, no less than war. More generally, peace museums are able to demonstrate the truth of Milton's observation that "Peace hath her victories no less renowned than war."

In the west of Flanders in Belgium, the catastrophic battles at the western Front during the First World War have also left a legacy of many sites of memory and mourning, particularly in the form of war graves and memorials. The most notable memorial is the *IJzertoren*, a 50-meter high tower near Diksmuide, which was opened in 1930. It has become the center of the annual pilgrimage (under the motto: "Never Again War") to commemorate the soldiers who lost their lives in that war. This annual commemoration is also an expression of the Flemish struggle for emancipation in a Belgian state that has been traditionally dominated by a French-speaking minority. After the destruction of the *IJzertoren* in 1946, a new, 84-meter-high tower was opened in 1965. In the 1990s, following the federalization of the state, the Flemish parliament appropriated funds for a large-scale restoration of the tower. The related themes of war, pacifism, and the Flemish struggle for emancipation during the First World War will, by 2002, form a permanent exhibition on 24 floors.

Meanwhile, in 1998 a peace museum opened in nearby Ieper (Ypres) as a result of a private initiative. Taking its name from one of the best-known poems about the war, the museum *In Flanders Fields* is largely a reaction to the many war monuments (in an area where battlefield tourism is well developed) whose message is frequently held to be an ambiguous one. By contrast, the museum's initiators want *In Flanders Fields* to represent an impassioned cry for peace.

VII. PEACE-RELATED MUSEUMS

A comprehensive definition of the concept of peace involves a consideration of the relations not only between states but also within states and comprises a wide spectrum of human rights issues. However, in order to make the concept of a peace museum distinctive and practicable, and not all-encompassing, it is desirable to impose some limitations on what is meant by peace. First and foremost, it suggests ideas and efforts aimed at the reduction and elimination of war between states—an urgent and complex task in its own right. Second and more generally, peace involves the pursuit of freedom and justice by individuals and groups through nonviolent means. The museums introduced so far are classified as peace museums because they conform to this interpretation of peace. The museums referred to in this section deal more with human rights issues and therefore may be classified as "peace-related" museums rather than as peace museums per se.

The 20th century has witnessed many tyrannical regimes that have perpetrated acts of unspeakable atrocity against their own citizens (in the pursuit of ideological or ethnic purity). After the demise of such regimes, museums documenting their evils have often been created in order to remember and to mourn the victims and to warn new generations against repetition. Examples are the Cambodian Genocide Museum and the museums established recently in various parts of the former Soviet Union, which are a reminder of the Gulag. In the 1990s, civil war in countries such as Rwanda and the former Yugoslavia has been accompanied by genocidal policies that are documented in museums currently being developed in the countries concerned.

The extermination of 6 million Jews by Nazi Germany during World War II is commemorated in more than 100 museums and other memorial institutions worldwide, particularly in Israel, Europe, and the United States. The first memorial sites (which often were turned into museums) were places of destruction themselves, such as the concentration camps in Majdanek (near Lublin) and Auschwitz/Oswiecim (near Krakow), both in Poland, as well as in Germany (e.g., Dachau). The most elaborate complex of memorial institutions is Yad Vashem in Jerusalem—The Holocaust Martyrs' and Heroes' Remembrance Authority—Israel's national institution of Holocaust commemoration. A proposal for this had already been made during wartime, in 1942, well before the creation of the state of Israel. Several of the most important Holocaust museums have been established in the United States in the 1990s: the U.S. Holocaust Memorial Museum in Washington, DC (1993), the Museum of Tolerance of the Simon Wiesenthal Center in Los Angeles (1993), and the Museum of Jewish Heritage in New York (1997). The last decade of the century has also seen the initiation of important national Holocaust museums elsewhere, such as in London (at the Imperial War Museum) and Berlin. Apart from providing places of memory and mourning, these museums also have the function of conveying important lessons: about our capacity for evil, about the dangers of intolerance, about the need for democratic and rule-based systems of government. Holocaust and genocide museums are likely to evoke in their visitors a whole range of emotions, including pity and outrage, but hopefully also a determination to do one's utmost in ensuring that history will not be repeated.

The growing realization that western expansionism and colonialism of the past 500 years have been accompanied by policies verging on the genocidal—as exemplified by the fate of the Native Americans in both North and South America or of the aborigines in Australasia - has also resulted in a movement for remembrance and restitution. These forgotten or repressed chapters from the history of mankind's cruelty are increasingly being documented in museums. Likewise, the history of slavery and the slave trade (as well as the campaign for its abolition) are the subjects of a growing number of museums, particularly along the coast of West Africa (and also in such coastal cities in the United Kingdom as Liverpool and Hull).

In the wake of decolonization, many newly independent countries founded national museums detailing their struggle for independence (or national revolution). In South Africa the prison on Robben Island, the most prominent symbol of the oppressive apartheid system, has become the Robben Island Museum. It is meant to be a monument not only to hardship and suffering but also to the triumph of humanity's striving for freedom and dignity.

Another kind of peace-related museum focuses on the resistance of a country that has been subjected to attack or occupation during war. Such museums have been established in several countries in Europe as a result of World War II.

VIII. FUTURE PROSPECTS

The creation of many peace museums around the world in the last decades of the 20th century is an expression of the perceived effectiveness of these institutions in promoting peace education among a wide public. Significant sites, memorable exhibits, inspiring stories, and modern communications media combine to inform and instruct the visitor about the nature and possibilities of peace-making.

Several new museums are likely to be inaugurated in the near future (see Table II and Fig. 10). In addition, some museums of a general kind are in the process of adding the theme of peace to their existing displays. This is the case, for instance, at the Museum of Ethnology in Hamburg where a new, permanent display will focus on peace (and war) in European history. The National Museum of Australia in Canberra has been collecting artifacts to enable it to document the history of the country's peace movement.

In order to highlight the importance of developing cooperative rather than conflictive relationships (between states, communities, and individuals), UNESCO has launched a Culture of Peace program (UNESCO's dedication to peace is clearly expressed in its preamble—see Fig. 11). Museums are well-established and highly regarded vehicles for the preservation, transmis-

FIGURE 10 Schlaining Castle (European Peace Museum).

TABLE II

Planned Peace Museums

Bradford (UK)	National Peace Museum
Nairobi	Africa Peace Museum
Netherlands	Anti-War Museum
New York	Metropolitan Peace Museum
Nürnberg	Peace Museum
Oslo	Nobel Peace Prize Museum
Stadtschlaining (Austria)	European Peace Museum
York (Ontario)	Sharon Temple & Historic Site Peace Museum

"Since wars begin in the minds of men, it is in the minds of men that the defences of peace must be constructed."

Preamble of UNESCO

FIGURE 11 Logo and motto of the First Austrian Peace Museum, Wolfsegg.

sion, and development of knowledge and values, thus contributing significantly to the education of their numerous visitors. Peace museums, likewise, are potentially powerful instruments for the dissemination of a culture of peace.

Also See the Following Articles

PEACE AND THE ARTS • PEACE EDUCATION: COLLEGES AND UNIVERSITIES • PEACE EDUCATION: YOUTH • PEACEMAKING AND PEACEBUILDING • PEACE PRIZES

Bibliography

Bjerstedt, A. (Ed.). (1993). *Peace museums: For peace education?* Malmö, Sweden: School of Education.

Breon, R. (1996). Museums that commemorate peace instead of war. *The Chronicle of Higher Education, 6,* B5.

Buruma, I. (1994). *The wages of guilt: Memories of war in Germany and Japan.* London: J. Cape.

Duffy, T., et al. (1997). Peace museums: Keeping the peace. *Museums Journal, 97*(1), 19–23.

Strikland, S. (1994). Peacemaking sites as teaching tools. *OAH Magazine of History, 8,*(3), 89–90.

Tsuboi, C. (1992). Peace museums in Japan: Numbers, visitors and types. *Jinbungakkai Kiyo, 52,* 137–151.

United Nations Library at Geneva (1995). *Peace museums worldwide.* Geneva: United Nations.

van den Dungen, P. (1994). Peace museums: Recent developments. *Medicine and War, 10*(3), 218–229.

Yamane, K. (1996). A peace museum as a center for peace education. In R. Burns & R. Aspeslagh (Eds.), *Three decades of peace education around the world.* (pp. 307–319). New York: Garland.

Zolberg, V. (1996). Museums as contested sites of remembrance: The Enola Gay affair. In S. Macdonald & G. Fyfe (Eds.), *Theorizing museums.* (pp. 69–82). Cambridge, MA: Blackwell.

Peace Education: Youth

Janet Patti

Hunter College

Linda Lantieri

Educators for Social Responsibility

GLOSSARY

Creative Conflict Resolution The peaceful resolution of conflict based on the values of respect, fairness, and cooperation. It urges that we view conflicts not as contests of will, but as problems to be solved, collaboratively, by the parties involved. Conflict resolution programs in schools are often referred to as Peace Education.

Mediation The resolving of conflict between two or more parties; a neutral third-party skilled in conflict resolution techniques assists the parties involved to come up with win–win solutions to their problem.

Peer Mediation The process of resolving conflict between two or more students with student mediators, who have been extensively trained in mediation skills and assisting.

Violence Prevention The prevention of physical assaults and threats as well as verbal assaults and threats including name-calling or put-downs between students. Conflict resolution and peer mediation are methods of violence prevention being implemented in schools.

Social Emotional Learning The body of knowledge that imparts prosocial skills to young people to enhance their own social and emotional competencies.

I. INTRODUCTION

Roosevelt Middle School overlooks the mountains in Oceanside, California, fifty miles north of San Diego, just a few miles east of the Pacific Ocean. Roosevelt appeared to be a peaceful school compared to so many schools I had known throughout the years. The struggles of inner city schools seemed nonexistent here in this part-suburban, part-rural neighborhood. But, I (Janet) soon learned that no place was exempt from the violence that was ensuing in schools and communities.

The warning signs soon became evident. The Old English script on notebooks, certain clothing in designated colors of red or blue; hand gestures that only the kids identified; the growing number of gangs in the nearby community—all were in-

Copyright © 1999 by Academic Press.
All rights of reproduction in any form reserved.

creasingly more common. The usual daily skirmishes had become much more aggressive and intolerant of differences. Cliques, common to this age, separated young people by the color of their skin and the clothes they wore to school. We kept putting out the fires, thinking we could keep above it—until, that one hot, sunny day in May during 8th grade lunch recess.

In the midst of joyful, middle schoolers at play there was suddenly, an increase in activity and an apparent commotion over by the restrooms. I arrived in time to see Manny, the leader of the "wanna-be" Crips flashing his gang signs at Cesar, one of their "wanna-be" Vista Home Boys, who was returning these signs with his own and moving speedily towards Manny. Each of the boys were followed by about 15 other boys moving rhythmically behind their respective leaders, robot-like, gliding along as if they were the robot's connected parts.

I had once heard it said that in a time of crisis such as this the best thing to do was to divert attention away from the center of the conflict by becoming the visual myself. So, knowing no better strategy I ran towards the boys, waved my arms in the air and screamed at the top of my lungs, "No, not here! Not in this school! Not now! Not ever! "Much to my surprise the boys froze and stared at me. Just at that moment, fate intervened, and the bell rang! With this, all of the bystanders, who had gathered around to see a fight, headed towards their classes. As I regained my composure, I was relieved and thankful that we had been spared from violence but recognized that a lot needed to change to assure that this would never happen again.

That was the beginning of a long-term commitment of creating a safe haven for all students at Roosevelt. The road was long and winding with many mistakes along the way, but together adults and students were committed to creating a new Roosevelt, inclusive of all students. We began that next day by bringing the young people around the table, those that were willing to work with us, straight A students and at-risk students, Crips and Home Boys and representatives of all groups of our school community to explore solutions instead of creating or ignoring problems. And so it was through the lens of conflict resolution and intergroup relations that we began to intentionally and comprehensively address the varied social, emotional and ethical needs of the young people

at our school. (Roosevelt Middle School is a participating School in the Resolving Conflict Creatively Program.)

Events similar to those narrated above have become all too common in a variety of communities across the United States. The problem of youth violence is multifaceted and requires a concerted effort on the part of all citizens who care about creating a more peaceful world. The past decade has taught us a great deal about how to tackle the violence that has invaded our homes, schools, and communities. Perhaps the most encouraging fact is that we now know that youth violence is preventable, not inevitable. Young people can shift their habits of thinking about violence by learning skills and strategies that offer alternatives to violence. Fostering an appreciation of diversity and valuing the social and emotional well being of the child is paramount to educating today's youth for the 21st century.

It is possible to create a culture of nonviolence and an ethic of peace in schools. The task is arduous, particularly when indifference, prejudice, and hatred toward others are so pervasive. Yet, in order to assure a more peaceful world, it is imperative to begin with the children.

Schools have an essential role to play in preventing this senseless violence and mean spiritedness that is robbing young people of their childhood. Schools must take the responsibility to educate the heart along with the mind. To participate as citizens in today's pluralistic world, to really embrace the notion of world peace, young people need to learn about the diversity of its peoples and cultures—and they need to develop their thinking about how to approach conflict, handle emotions, and solve problems.

This article draws on real examples, recent theory, and on the many years of experience of school practitioners working with young people and adults. It describes several peace education initiatives highlighting the work of Educators for Social Responsibility (ESR), a nonprofit organization dedicated to the promotion of ethical and social responsibility among young people. It focuses extensively on the work of the Resolving Conflict Creatively, the largest program initiative of ESR, and shares strategies that have been found to be successful in creating peaceable schools and classrooms in rural, suburban, and inner city schools across the United States. It also shares some of the more recent work ESR has been doing in other countries who have looked to the United States to help them rethink their pedagogy about how to educate their youth.

II. THE CALL FOR SOCIAL AND EMOTIONAL LEARNING

For decades, many concerned adults in the fields of education, sociology, and psychology have been promoting the need for teaching young people social and emotional skills along with their cognitive skills. Efforts such as cooperative learning, affective education, and character education have drifted in and out of the national education agenda. These vital movements have expanded the notion of how young people learn and what they should learn. They have created forums for critical thinking and social competence development for children of diverse backgrounds who have a variety of learning styles and educational needs. Yet, despite the successes of these innovations, educational policies continue to devalue the teaching of social and emotional competencies that instill in young people the ability to manage their emotions, make sound decisions, empathetically listen to the needs of others and value the perspectives of others. The focus of American schools continues to be on academic achievement as an indicator of success. While academic achievement is imperative, young people's success in the 21st century will also depend on the development of much-needed social and emotional skills.

The ability to handle conflict is crucial to successful employment. According to a 1994 Census Bureau survey of hiring, training, and management practices in American business, the two qualities employers most value are attitude and communication skills. The survey shows an alarming failure on the part of most American schools to focus directly on the cultivation of these skills.

Daniel Goleman, in his groundbreaking book *Emotional Intelligence*, makes the case that how one fares in the workplace seems to be linked to one's emotional intelligence. He claims that skills such as empathy and managing difficult emotions and the ability to motivate oneself may be more important than scores on traditional cognitive tests in determining what happens in adult life.

While school systems grapple with which strategies are more powerful for learning—whole-language or phonics, traditional computational skills or hands-on, problem-solving approaches to mathematics—over 135,000 guns continue to enter our nation's schools daily. Although the 1994 and 1995 Uniform Crime Report indicated a decrease in homicide rates in the United States, homicide rates for teens and young adults are still on the rise.

The safety net that once existed for young people isn't there to protect them the way it protected many adults in their youth. Communities aren't functional villages anymore. Many young people today are surrounded by messages of loss, violence, and despair in their homes and communities. The adult models they so need to guide them often struggle themselves with how to deal with the conflict in their own lives, leaving little opportunity to help young people with the conflicts they confront.

Brandon, a former student at Roosevelt Middle School and now a senior in high school, describes what growing up in his Oceanside, CA neighborhood has been like for him.

> Just last week I went to the beach with my friends. I think of the beach as safe. My love is the ocean. One of my friends gave a hard look to a guy and all of a sudden a bunch of guys all came around us. I was able to break it up but was just amazed. I just see this violence all over. If we can learn violence, why can't we learn peace?

Calvin, a high school junior, heightens our awareness of how closely violence lurks in young people's lives.

> In my old neighborhood I knew a kid. His name was Robert. He was walking down the street one day and a guy stopped him who wanted to get initiated into a gang. He said to Robert, "Where are you from?" Meaning what gang are you from. Robert said, "I'm not from anywhere." And the other kid said, "Well what do you do if you don't gang bang." Robert said, " I stay home and play Sega." Which was the truth, and then the guy shot him and killed him. That was all about him trying to get in a gang. That could have been me. That could have been anyone of my friends. It's just hard living with that day to day. In a sense, we have to turn it off because it happens so often, so frequently.

More than ever before, the challenge exists to provide young people with a sense of belonging, an identity and a belief that the adults in their lives will be there to support them. When children and young adults receive the tools to be in control of their lives, they feel competent and are successful. Their sense of power motivates them to either take risks or not, accept responsibilities, and work hard to achieve success. In order for young people today to envision success, a sense of hope and self-efficacy needs to replace much of the hopelessness and loss they see around them.

Creating safe, peaceful learning communities in schools requires more than installing metal detectors, hiring additional security officers or purchasing a curriculum in conflict resolution. It requires a long-term commitment by adults and young people to educate the heart along with the mind. This means reexamining the theoretical underpinnings of the purpose of schools. Educators need to ask themselves, "Are we preparing today's youth for the times in which they are living and for the challenges they will be facing?" To develop emotional and social competence in youth, adults need to model the values and behaviors they would hope for their children and students. Responsible, caring schools strive to promote a culture reflective of a pedagogy, structure, and climate that holds the young person at the center of its vision of education.

III. ROOTS OF CONFLICT RESOLUTION: WORLD TRADITIONS

While conflict resolution programs as we know them today have primarily been developed by practitioners from Western traditions and cultures, many of the skills and principles of conflict resolution and nonviolence are derived from the wisdom of traditions that have existed over time in varying countries of the world. In Buddhist monasteries, practices have been in place for the last 2000 years to settle disputes with the help of a third party—in this case the entire community. Thich Nat Hanh, Zen master and author, describes the technique in his book *Being Peace.*

> In a convocation of the whole Sangha community, everyone sits together with the willingness to help. The two conflicting monks are present and sit face to face knowing that everyone expects them to make peace. People refrain from listening to stories outside the assembly. Everything must be said in public, in the community. Both monks try to remember the whole history of the conflict, every detail, as the whole assembly just sits patiently and listens. Everyone expects the two monks to try their best for reconciliation. The outcome is not important. The fact that each monk is trying his best to show his willingness for reconciliation is most important.

Buddhist monks and nuns have been practicing this form of mediation for thousands of years in India, China, Japan, Vietnam, Korea, and many other countries.

Throughout Africa we can find examples of dispute resolution being completely interwoven into the community. One method of mediation is a natural part of the regional culture among the Dogan people in Mali. In every village there are low platforms that serve as places to reconcile conflicts. When two people in a village have a dispute, the tribal elders bring them to the platform and they sit beneath it until the conflict is resolved. The platforms are built low so that disputants are not able to stand up and engage in physical fighting. The elders serve as mediators and apparently perform their task nonverbally. The spaces under the platforms resemble quiet, private mediation rooms—sacred places that hold a history of peaceful solutions in their very structure.

Native American conflict resolution practices have found their way into mediation circles everywhere. Indeed, they are probably at the root of many commonly used mediation processes in this country. Manu Aluli Meyer, in a paper to fulfill course requirements at the Harvard Graduate School of Education, explained that the native people of Hawaii have an ancient family problem-solving process called *ho'oponopono* which means "to set right." In this process, a *kapuna* (elder) or another respected person who is not involved in the issues at hand serves as *haku* (facilitator). The *haku* becomes a vital element in facilitation and in setting the tone of *aloha* or love and affection which is at the center of the *ho'oponopono.*

The *ho'oponopono* is a complicated process consisting of several phases. It moves from identification of the problem to the discussion phase; from expression of feelings to recognition of the resulting hurt and pain; to resolution or forgiveness, and in some cases, restitution to the wronged party.

More familiar to many are the examples and teachings of Mahatma Gandhi that have influenced social movements around the world. Gandhi believed in the goodness of all people. He believed that true and enduring peace could only be achieved through peaceful means, and that, love and truth were the vehicles to achieve peace. Gandhi spoke of the importance of respect, understanding, acceptance, and appreciation of differences. For Gandhi, strength was associated with "holding on to the truth." This is evidenced by Gandhi's use of the term Satyagraha, the doctrine that favored passive resistance and noncooperation in opposing British rule in India combines. As defined in Webster's Dictionary the two words *satya* (truth) and *graha* (grasping) imply firmness with love. In holding on to the truth, opposition can be defeated. Gandhi once said, "My optimism rests on my belief in the infinite possibilities of the individual to develop nonviolence. The more you develop it in your own being, the more infectious it becomes till it overwhelms your surroundings and by and by might oversweep the world."

In the 1960s Dr. Martin Luther King, Jr. put Gandhi's principles into practice. These principles are well remembered from the time of the Montgomery bus boycott in 1955 to the multitude of events that followed. Today, Kingian nonviolence continues to reach many children and adults as they work together for social change. Those who seek to follow the guidance of Kingian nonviolence know the importance of gathering information, educating oneself and making a personal commitment to work for justice. They learn and apply the techniques of artful negotiation and use direct action with moral force. Finally, they know that a true resolution, the place where healing can happen, only occurs with reconciliation. Dr. King believed that "unarmed truth and unconditional love will have the final word in the end."

IV. CONFLICT RESOLUTION IN EDUCATION

The field of conflict resolution emerged about 75 years ago as an approach to improving labor-management relations. During the 1920s Mary Parker Follett, a business consultant and one of the field's pioneers, began showing business managers how to better deal with conflict in the workplace in order to increase productivity. Follett had the insight that many conflicts could be solved in mutually satisfactory ways if the parties could avoid bickering over "positions" and could focus instead on finding creative ways to fulfill their underlying needs. Follett's insight, sometimes called the win–win solution, lies at the core of contemporary approaches to negotiation, popularized in books such as Roger Fisher and William Ury's 1981 bestseller *Getting to Yes: Negotiating Agreement without Giving In.*

Much of the philosophy upon which conflict resolution and peer mediation in schools is derived from the early work of Morton Deutsch, who in 1949 began the study of cooperation and competition on group processes. His work supported the theory that "the cooperative process leads to the defining of conflicting interests as a mutual problem to be solved by a collaborative effort" and "the competitive process stimulates the view that the solution of a conflict can only be one that is imposed by one side on the other." More recently

social theorists, Johnson and Johnson, Robert Slavin, and others have concentrated on the teaching of cooperative skills in classrooms. Research in this area supports the theory that when young people are taught cooperative skills and view adults and others around them working together cooperatively, they become more cooperative.

Theories and practices from the field of conflict resolution began to make their way into the educational arena in the late 1970s and early 1980s. In 1972, Priscilla Prutzman and the Children's Project for Friends, a Quaker educational project in New York City, first brought this work to schools. They worked with children in the inner city of New York using a variety of techniques and strategies to improve their skills in cooperation and conflict resolution. These beginning roots soon inspired others to investigate the effectiveness of developing these skills in children.

In the early 1980s, Educators for Social Responsibility began to provide training for educators and disseminate conflict resolution curriculums in classrooms. The Community Board Center for Policy and Training of San Francisco introduced a model of peer mediation programs in schools derived from their work in community mediation, which was soon replicated in schools. In 1984, the National Association of Mediation in Education was founded at the University of Massachusetts. In 1995, it merged into the National Institute for Dispute Resolution and became the Conflict Resolution Education Network. It is now a professional association of conflict resolution educators, teachers, students, parents, and youth serving organizations.

Today, conflict resolution programs are integral parts of many schools. Young people from kindergarten through high school learn how to express their feelings in ways that others can hear. They use their active listening skills while communicating with others. They think before making decisions. Young people recognize that conflict is a natural, normal part of life. They know that *how* they approach it can make all the difference in the outcome of a conflict situation. And, they are empowered by the skills they possess that prepare them to resolve their conflicts in productive, nonviolent ways.

V. THE ROLE OF CONFLICT RESOLUTION IN VIOLENCE PREVENTION

It has been almost a decade since Deborah Prothrow-Stith, Professor of Harvard's School of Public Health, in her informative book *Deadly Consequences*, helped to create a U.S. public agenda to begin to address this issue of youth violence. The work of Dr. Stith and others in the field of violence prevention expanded our thinking about violence by including prevention along with intervention. With the support of the field of public health, educators began to implement programs designed to turn around this epidemic of violence that young people are exposed to.

In the early 1990s conflict resolution was being looked to as an important element in violence prevention among young people. In 1994, Goal 6 of the Goals 2000: Educate America Act was adopted by Congress and signed into law by President Clinton. It said that "by the year 2000, every school in America will be free of drugs and violence and will offer a disciplined environment conducive to learning." In that same year, the National Association of State Boards of Education encouraged states to incorporate long-term strategies to prevent violence in schools.

A variety of school-based programs emerged to teach young people new ways of channeling their anger into constructive, nonviolent responses to conflict. Many of these programs centered around the delivery of curriculum to classroom teachers. Many educators and other trained practitioners used the *Violence Prevention Curriculum for Adolescents* developed by Dr. Deborah Prothrow-Stith as their guide. The curriculum utilizes 10 discussion/activity sessions for classroom use. The curriculum has had a positive impact in many schools in which it has been used; particularly it's treatment of the causes, effects, and strategies to prevent interpersonal violence.

National interest in conflict resolution and violence prevention continues to grow, as more and more educators look for solutions to the increasing violence and breakdown of civility among young people in their schools. In 1996, The U.S. Departments of Justice and Education collaborated to prepare a report that would advance the development of conflict resolution programs in schools, youth-servicing organizations, and community and juvenile justice settings. This guide provided schools with necessary information as to how to incorporate conflict resolution programs into their schools. It was made available to thousands of schools across the United States.

Studies over recent years have confirmed that when young people are taught prosocial skill development at an early age they are less likely to commit violent crimes as adults. A study by Hammond and Yung showed how referrals to juvenile courts were reduced by teaching young people how not to insult, how to praise others,

and how to accept feedback from others. G. D. Gottfredson reported that schools that aim at increasing resiliency in young people can reduce a young person's possibilities of becoming a juvenile offender by 40%. It appears that even if young people have a predisposition to aggression, with help they can change. Karen Bierman's work at Pennsylvania State University indicated that after 10 sessions in which aggressive boys were taught lessons in cooperation, how to ask questions and how to share, the boys became less aggressive.

Lanitra, is a young person who in the 6th grade at Roosevelt Middle School became a Young Ambassador, a leader for peace and justice. In the 7th grade she became a peer mediator. Now, as a senior in high school she shares her story of the changes that took place in her after her connection to this work.

> This group was trying to bring together positive and negative role models to work together to make the school a safer place. It was kind of hard to believe in the group so I wouldn't come to the meetings at first. I didn't tell anybody about anything that happened to me in my life or how I felt about anything until I came to this school and they were saying, "You need to tell people how you feel." I thought I didn't have to tell people what I was feeling. I thought I was big and bad. I went to the meetings because it made the teachers happy and I got out of class. But then it was like, "Well, I do have all this stuff inside and I want people to know about it and I do feel upset. I am hurt by a lot of things. I want to be able to tell my mother how I feel inside. And soon—I didn't even know that I was using "I" messages—I did tell people how I felt. I learned that I became a better person on the outside cause I was telling people how I feel.... I was letting my feelings out, not just making believe things weren't happening to me."

Lanitra was an at-risk student, but she found the safety within this leadership group to express her feelings and change her behavior. By the time she was in the 8th grade she had become a primary role model for many other young girls at Roosevelt. Additionally her grades improved. She became the Commissioner of Peace for her leadership group and was well respected by young people and adults.

Young people, when given the skills to change, opportunities to use their skills, and recognition for using these skills, develop protective factors and increase their resiliency. It is never too late to reach a child at risk.

Psychologist Daniel Goleman reminds us that the mark of truly educated people is the ability to identify feelings, manage emotions, empathize, and care about what others think and feel. He cites recent brain research that upholds the importance of the teaching of prosocial skills up through adolescence, the time when the emotional centers of the brain are truly formed. The teaching of social and emotional competencies should continue for all young people throughout their school lives.

Today, there are many successful schools implementing conflict resolution, violence prevention, peace education, and other related programs in schools. All of these programs strive to help young people become caring, responsible, and knowledgeable through the systematic teaching of social and emotional competencies. The goal of these efforts is that peaceful, nonviolent responses to conflict will become a way of life for young people. As Gandhi once said, "Nonviolence is not a garment to be put on and off at will. Its seat is in the heart, and it must be an inseparable part of our very being."

VI. EDUCATORS FOR SOCIAL RESPONSIBILITY: THE RESOLVING CONFLICT CREATIVELY PROGRAM

The mission of Educators for Social Responsibility is to help young people develop the skills and convictions to shape a safer, just, and sustainable world. In 1985, Linda Lantieri, then Curriculum Specialist for the New York City Board of Education, and Tom Roderick, Director of the ESR Metro Chapter, joined together with teachers and administrators in New York City to create what is now the nationally recognized Resolving Conflict Creatively Program (RCCP). It is a comprehensive school-based program that teaches social emotional learning in schools through the lens of conflict resolution and intergroup relations. It also provides a model for preventing violence and creating caring and peaceable communities of learning. Its goal is to help transform the cultures of participating schools so that they model the values and principles of creative nonviolent conflict resolution and respect for diversity.

The program's primary strategy is to reach young people through the adults who relate to them on a daily basis at home, in school, and in their communities. It works with school staff, parents, families, and the larger community to create more peaceful, just, and democratic learning environments.

In 1993, the national office of Educators for Social Responsibility opened the RCCP National Center to disseminate the RCCP model throughout the United States. A key aspect of the RCCP National Center's mission is its work in advocacy and informing school systems, policymakers, and the general public about the impact of such work in schools. The national office also provides technical assistance to participating school districts to assist them with attaining successful implementation.

The RCCP National Center contributes to the development of social and emotional learning of young people by showing them that they have choices other than passivity or aggression for dealing with conflict; giving them skills to make those choices real in their own lives; increasing their understanding and appreciation of their own and others' cultures; and empowering them to play a significant role in creating a more peaceful world.

The program differs from some conflict resolution programs in that it involves every member of the school community in the process of implementation. School systems embrace RCCP and commit themselves to a long-term process of school change. Over the 3 to 5 years of implementation the RCCP National Center works closely with school districts to assure institutionalization of the program.

In RCCP schools across the nation, young people and adults consciously work together to create school norms in which violence is not acceptable, nonviolent solutions to resolving conflict are encouraged, and efforts to increase intercultural understanding are widespread.

Both the content of RCCP trainings and curricula and the model of implementation that has been developed have been influenced and informed by many years of direct involvement in educating young people. In developing the model, three concerns were paramount. What would help young people handle their emotions better and think differently about conflict and diversity? What model would best assure that young people received the social and emotional skills along with their academic skills? Finally, what would it take to prepare the adults in young people's lives—parents, teachers and administrators—to do this?

The RCCP model includes the following components:

1. *A K-12 classroom curriculum* that focuses on the teaching of key skills: active listening, assertiveness (as opposed to aggressiveness or passivity), the expression of feeling in appropriate ways, empa-

thy and perspective-taking, cooperation, negotiation, the appreciation of diversity, and methods for countering bias. The program's lessons involve role-playing, interviewing, group discussion, brainstorming, "teachable moments," and other experiential and affective learning strategies.

2. *Professional training and ongoing support for teachers* that provides 24 h of introductory training on the RCCP curriculum as well as training in communication, conflict resolution, and "infusion" strategies for integrating these concepts and skills into social studies, language arts, and other academic subjects. A key to RCCP's success is follow-up support. Each teacher is assigned a staff developer, who visits the school between 6 and 10 times during the year to help with preparation, observe classes, give demonstration lessons, discuss concerns, and otherwise help sustain that teacher's efforts in the classroom.

3. *A student-led mediation program* that provides a strong peer model for nonviolence and the appreciation of diversity and reinforces students' emerging skills in working out their own problems. The mediation component can make a large contribution to a more peaceable school climate, but it is not a substitute for an effective disciplinary policy (if strictly enforced sanctions against fighting are not in place, students are unlikely to turn to mediators for help). The RCCP sees the peer mediation component as part of a larger effort in working with staff and students in the classroom first.

4. *Parent training* that reaches beyond the schoolyard both to increase family support for the program's efforts and to give parents the opportunity to learn about intergroup relations, family communication, and conflict resolution. Parents participate in a series of four 3-h workshops called "Peace in the Family." Parents come to the sessions hungry for support and eager to learn these new skills. At the workshops they are able to stop and think about how they act as parents—what works and what they would like to do differently. The RCCP provides concrete skills in active listening, I-messages, win–win negotiation, and many of the other strategies that are also taught to young people.

5. *Administrator training,* which introduces RCCP concepts and shows school administrators how they can use their leadership to encourage everyone within the school community to embrace and model humane, democratic, and creative approaches to dealing with conflict and diversity.

The RCCP begins by teaching the adults. Since the field of conflict resolution is a recent innovation in education, most adults need to be immersed in the concepts and skills of conflict resolution before they can even think about teaching this body of knowledge in their classrooms. The work with adults is a fine balance between skill building and introspection. They explore their own approaches to conflict and attitudes toward diversity before they bring the work to their classroom and schools.

Schools today talk a lot about restructuring and reforming. The major purpose of any reform is to create schools that are designed to best serve the students. In peaceable schools all members of the school community work together to transform schools such that the culture of the school is reflective of the beliefs and values inherent in RCCP. As school leaders across the country approach RCCP to begin the program they are encouraged to look within and ask themselves " where they are" and "where they would like to get to" with this work. Schools embracing the program know it isn't a quick-fix, but a long-time commitment to building a new school culture.

Currently, RCCP serves 5,000 teachers and 150,000 young people in 350 schools nationwide, including the New York City Public Schools and eleven other diverse school systems that are in various stages of implementation: the Anchorage School District in Alaska; the Atlanta Public Schools in Georgia; the Boston Public Schools in Massachusetts; the Lawrence Public Schools in New York; the New Orleans Public Schools in Louisiana; the Vista Unified School District in Southern California; the West Orange, South Orange-Maplewood School and Newark districts in New Jersey; the Lincoln County School District in Oregon; and the Roosevelt School District in Phoenix, Arizona. The RCCP is also being implemented in the 30 Freedom Schools of the Children's Defense Fund which are in undeserved communities throughout the country, reaching an additional 2,000 young people.

A. The Curriculum

The content of the training and curricula is based upon conflict resolution expert William Kreidler's peaceable classroom model and emphasizes six principles: cooperation, caring communication, expression of feelings, appreciation of diversity, responsible decision-making, and conflict resolution. Drawing upon these principles, young people and adults acquire skills and strategies they need to approach conflict situations nonviolently.

This kind of classroom supports critical thinking,

expression of feelings, open communication, perspective taking and positive group interactions. The following scenario provides a look at this kind of classroom.

Mrs. Frye sits for the moment at her desk, off to the side in the back of the classroom. Tammy, a fourth-grade student, approaches her to discuss a story she's writing. Off in the front right corner of the room, designated "the peace corner" by a student-made multicolored sign, several students are busily working. Two girls are seated on a couch, silently reading books together. Another student has donned a set of headphones and is listening to music while writing in his journal. Others work quietly with their groups at their tables. Suddenly Frank, a short boy at the table near the door, breaks the silence.

"Hey, give me back my pencil, Tom. I know you took it!"

"I don't have your stupid pencil," Tom responds in a shrill voice. This is mine." They continue to yell at each other until Sara, a student mediator, walks over and asks, "Why are you arguing with each other? Do you want a mediation? Would you like me to help?" For a brief moment the boys stop their bickering.

By this time, Mrs. Frye is standing behind the two angry boys. Placing her arm around Sara, she says, "Thank you, Sara." Turning to the boys, she says, "It does seem like there's a problem. I'd like you both to calm down and decide whether you'd like to discuss this with me or whether you'd like a mediation. You know the rules about fighting. I hope you'll think about them before making your decision."

The two boys, still angry, stalk off to different sides of the room. They both know the procedure. They will sit apart for a while and calm themselves down before they attempt to resolve the conflict they are having; they may ask either their teacher or a class mediator for help. Fighting is not acceptable; they know they will be suspended from school if they fight.

During the three or four minutes that this conflict interrupts the class, other students look on, but continue to work at their tables. It's clear that in this classroom this kind of behavior will not be tolerated or supported by either young people or adults.

In Mrs. Frye's class, while the rules are very clear, well defined, and understood, students also know that there are many means to address conflicts before they escalate and become physical. In this classroom—and others like it—kids know it's their job to express and control their anger appropriately. Mediation and negotiation are used by staff and students, and discipline is not just a matter of teacher-made edicts; the students have taken part in the rule making, know what happens if rules are broken, and have skills to resolve conflicts nonviolently. Adults evaluate their classroom management approaches and many begin to shift to more democratic classrooms versus traditional autocratic management in which the teacher had the final say in everything and the students simply followed their rules. The norms underlying the culture of the peaceable classroom are clear to all of its members. Not only does physically aggressive behavior have strong sanctions against it, but hurtful, painful words and "put-downs" are not tolerated either.

The children become the peacemakers. They encourage their peers to resolve conflicts nonviolently. Student mediators equipped with high-level conflict resolution skills ward off potential fights among friends. They may even prevent violence from occurring.

Mariana, a former classroom teacher who is now coordinator for RCCP in New York City, reported on her early experience with the program:

At the beginning of this school year there was a lot of tension in my classroom. The boys were using put-downs, doing a lot of "dissing" and "ranking" and this was intimidating the girls.... We had discussions and did exercises on dealing with anger and on cooperation and then I helped them process these experiences, talking about [both] the difficult and good parts of their efforts. By January, students began to mix more naturally in cooperative learning groups. Dissing, ranking, and put-downs virtually disappeared. The children began helping each other by taking time to talk through conflicts that occurred in their school life. The change in the climate of the classroom was palpable and very satisfying for me."

Like Mrs. Frye and her class, Mariana and her students felt an ease of learning in their classroom once they had established a culture of cooperation, caring, and respect. Many school reform efforts of today focus on maximizing students' academic learning. While there are many excellent models designed to reach this goal, its imperative to teach young people how to get along and how to resolve the conflicts in their lives so that they learn effectively.

Teachers teach a variety of skills and strategies to help young people address their anger in positive ways, not hurtful ways. Young children learn that they can use I-messages to communicate what they want or need and not put others down with painful, biting remarks. They learn early on that anger is a natural emotion but controlling it and releasing it in appropriate ways makes the difference for a conflict resolved, a friendship kept, and the absence of physical harm to others. They begin to listen to each other more. They learn that what others have to say matters and that by really listening to the other person they might be able to resolve a conflict so that both parties get what they want or need.

Win–win solutions are powerful concepts to young people. They begin to problem-solve alone and with others to find solutions to conflicts that arise. Expression of feelings is encouraged in peaceable classrooms. Young people need ways to develop a rich vocabulary of feelings that they can draw upon in conflict situations and help them express what they are feeling inside.

Problem-solving so needed for making decisions in today's world becomes part of the class culture. Young people learn how to brainstorm possible solutions and come to an agreement on something that will meet the needs of all parties involved. Negotiating and mediation are tools that are used throughout the classroom and school for helping students resolve their differences.

Finally, various activities provide a vehicle for expressing and exploring feelings about differences. The more young people learn about each other's cultures, the more they learn to respect their differences and release their prejudices. Teachers encourage young people to explore their own stereotypes and to see that they are based on misinformation. They provide students opportunities to ask questions about diversity and to receive knowledge and factual information about physical differences and cultural or historical events and traditions. Young people become actively engaged in the new learning and slowly begin to accept the perspectives of others.

The classroom curriculum along with the teacher's modeling of the core principles of the peaceable classroom creates a common language for the students. Beyond the classroom, the schoolwide focus of the program provides the students with a clear understanding of the norms and behaviors that are acceptable at their school.

B. Evaluation Results

Such national leaders as Children's Defense Fund President Marian Wright Edelman, U.S. Secretary of Educa-tion Richard Riley, and U.S. Attorney General Janet Reno have recognized RCCP. When RCCP began, efforts to bring conflict resolution into schools were so new that there was very little data indicative of long-term outcomes. Over the years, RCCP has worked steadfastly, both through formative and summative evaluation processes, to identify the aspects of the program that are working and to learn from areas that remain yet unclear.

An independent evaluation of RCCP-New York, released in May, 1990 by Metis Associates, found that teachers reported fewer fights, less verbal abuse, and more caring behavior on the part of their students. More than 90% of the teachers rated the overall implementation of RCCP as very good or excellent. Fully 87% of them said that RCCP was having a positive impact on their students. They reported the following changes: children spontaneously using conflict resolution skills, less violence in the classroom, increased self-esteem and sense of empowerment, increased awareness of feelings and verbalizing of those feelings, more caring behavior, and more acceptance of differences.

Metis Associates recently completed an evaluation of RCCP-Atlanta. In addition to finding positive results similar to those in the RCCP-New York study, they also noted significant improvements in course failure, dropout, student attendance, and in and out-of-school suspension rates. Suprisingly, teacher attendance rates at the pilot elementary schools also showed a dramatic improvement.

The RCCP Research Program is assessing the effectiveness of RCCP in New York City during the 1994–1995 and 1995–1996 school years. The study, funded by the federal Centers for Disease Control and Prevention and private foundations, has three components: a short-term longitudinal process and outcome study of the impact of RCCP on 9000 children in 15 elementary schools; a management information system tracking the implementation of the program; and in-depth interviews with teachers in a subset of participating schools. The principal investigator for the school impact study is Dr. J. Lawrence Aber, director of the national Center for Children in Poverty.

For the child impact component of the study, researchers put together age-appropriate surveys that were administered to children in their classrooms. These included measures of problem-solving strategies, aggressive fantasies, and hostile attributional biases. Previous research has shown that children's scores on these measures are correlated with their actual behavior.

The findings so far, based only on year-1 data, are that RCCP had a significant positive impact on children who received a substantial amount of instruction in the curricula from their teachers (on average, 25 lessons during the year). The final results of the study will be available in the spring of 1999.

VII. EDUCATING FOR PEACE, A GLOBAL CONCERN

In 1994, the Peace Education Commission of the International Peace Research Association met in Malta to explore issues and concerns. To sensitively and accurately educate the world's children regarding issues such as equity, social justice, and domestic as well as world peace is an international agenda.

In addition to efforts with RCCP and other efforts in U.S. schools and communities, Educator's for Social Responsibility works internationally to meet the needs of educators looking for programmatic answers to building bridges between divisive cultures and providing peaceful solutions to the resolution of conflict among young people.

In 1996, while visiting Johannesburg, South Africa, several colleagues and I visited a local nongovernmental organization, the Community Conflict Management and Resolution Center headed by Pat Mkhize. The Center specialized in community mediation as well as in school conflict resolution. There on the office wall, a T-shirt caught my eye—it was the same shirt worn by RCCP student mediators! Unknown to any of the visitors, the Center had received training in mediation techniques and strategies from a visiting New York City RCCP teacher trainer! In meetings with several key educators from the Department of Education and other agencies, conflict resolution skills were identified as much-needed tools for young and old alike.

In Capetown, the Center for Conflict Resolution conducts research, disseminates information, and provides training to schools and other organizations. South Africans are steadfastly working to bridge the long-standing divide between peoples who have been forced to shun and hate one another because of the atrocities of the Apartheid. They have gone to tremendous lengths to reform their governmental structures, to equalize power, and to promote justice. The efforts of the Truth and Reconciliation Hearings provide a model from which many of us can learn.

Many South African educators believe that true hope for systemic change lies in teaching the children skills that open communication and allow them to empathize with those who are different from them. Peaceable school projects are being experimented with in schools throughout the country. What is the human capacity for forgiveness and how can we truly heal the pain of the past? South Africa's determination to appeal to reconciliation as it claims justice provides a model for all who struggle with conflict personally as well as politically.

Two years ago, workshop leaders from Educators for Social Responsibility were called upon to work with Palestinian, Israeli Jewish, and Israeli Arab educators to help them explore ways to teach conflict resolution and intercultural understanding. The project is a collaborative effort of ESR and Givat Haviva, an Israeli based organization that has worked for more than 50 years on programs to create better understanding between Jews and Arabs. Meetings with teachers and students provided ESR staff with a sensitivity and knowledge of the difficulties involved in opening intercultural dialogue and awareness. They learned that within the school environment it has traditionally been prohibited to discuss political conflicts or differences. Subsequently, Palestinian and Israeli children have grown up, for the most part, not only segregated from one another, but also learning little or nothing about one other. In his book *Children's Social Consciousness and the Development of Social Responsibility*, Sheldon Berman tells us that empathy and self-discipline provide the foundation upon which moral behavior is constructed. While the challenge is great to achieve this goal in the Middle East, the commitment of educators to forge ahead toward nonviolent conflict resolution is noteworthy.

In October, 1997, a group of concerned citizens from Rio Grande do Sul, Brazil, including the state's First Lady and the Secretary of Education, came to New York to learn about the work in social emotional development. They visited RCCP schools and met extensively with ESR staff to plan ways to bring this work to Brazil. This December three ESR consultants visited Rio Grande do Sul to begin a pilot program in social emotional learning in the region. This new program will be implemented in the 4th, 5th, and 6th grades of 10 elementary schools. These forward thinking citizens of Rio Grande do Sul hope to provide both teachers and pupils the emotional skills needed to get along better with one another and create safe and nurturing homes, schools, and communities.

VIII. CONCLUSION

One day, Linda received a phone call from a woman who had seen the following interaction at a local playground in New York City after school hours. A group of students, probably in about 3rd or 4th grade, who were playing basketball, were being harassed by another group of slightly older kids who evidently wanted to play too. The older kids were clearly about to start a fight. The woman wanted to intervene but wasn't sure if or how she should. All of a sudden another group of young people who had been standing nearby surrounded the arguing kids in a circle and started to sing. "Peacemakers talk about it, they don't fight about it, they want to make up and be friends." The children who were starting the fight were so surprised by this behavior they quickly dispersed and the clash never took place. The woman, stunned and moved to tears by the actions of these children, asked them who they were and where they were from. It turns out that they were mediators from the school nearby and had learned the song during mediation training.

Mr. Muller's words serve as an inspiration to many educators creating peaceable classrooms and schools in the United States and throughout the world. Perhaps with these collaborative, concerted efforts we will be able to live up to his heartfelt dream for the next millennium.

I dream
That on 1 January 2000
The whole world will stand still
In prayer, awe and gratitude
For our beautiful, heavenly Earth
And for the miracle of human life.
I dream that young and old, rich and poor,
Black and white,
peoples from North and South,
From East and West,
From all beliefs and cultures
Will join their hands, minds and hearts
In an unprecedented, universal
Bimillennium Celebration of Life.
I dream
That the few remaining years
To the Bimillenium
Be devoted by all humans, nations and institutions
To unparalleled thinking, action,
Inspiration, elevation,
Determination and love
To solve our remaining problems
And to achieve
A peaceful united human family on Earth.

Robert Muller
Dialogues of Hope

Peace education needs to remain an integral part of the national agenda. More schools—elementary, secondary, and institutions of higher education—need to take responsibility for educating adults and young people in the ways of peace. The University of Peace in Costa Rica is one such institution that offers degrees in global peace studies. During a visit that Linda and I had with Robert Muller, former assistant to the Secretary General of the United Nations, he asked rhetorically, "Why do we continue to teach the history of war to our young? If we want to have world peace, we have to teach children about how to make peace."

Also See the Following Articles

CONFLICT MANAGEMENT AND RESOLUTION • CONFLICT TRANSFORMATION • GANGS • JUVENILE CRIME • NONVIOLENCE THEORY AND PRACTICE • PEACE EDUCATION: COLLEGES AND UNIVERSITIES • PEACE EDUCATION: PEACE MUSEUMS • PEACEFUL SOCIETIES

Bibliography

Bierman, K., & Goleman, D. (October, 1995) Early violence leaves its mark on the brain. *New York Times*.

Berman, S. (1997). *Children's social consciousness and the development of social responsibility*. Albany, NY: SUNY Press.

Crawford D., & Bodine, R. (1996). *Conflict resolution education: A guide to implementing programs in schools, youth-serving organizations and community and juvenile justice settings*. Washington, DC: U.S. Dept. of Justice and U.S. Dept. of Education.

Department of Justice, Federal Bureau of Investigation (1996). *Crime in the United States: 1995 uniform crime report*. Washington, DC: Government Printing Office.

Deutsch, M. (1982). *Conflict resolution: Theory and practice*. New York: Teachers College, Columbia University.

Fisher, R., & Ury, W. (1981). *Getting to yes: Negotiating agreement without giving in*. New York: Penguin Books.

Gottfredson, G. D. (1988). An evaluation of an organizational development approach to reducing school disorder. *Evaluation Review, 11*, 739–763.

Goleman, D. (1995). *Emotional intelligence*. New York: Bantam.

Hawkins, J. D., & Catalano, R. F. (1992). *Communities that care*. San Francisco: Jossey–Bass.

Hammond, R., & Yung, B. (1990). Preventing violence in at-risk African-American youth. *Journal of Health Care for the Poor and Underserved, 2*, 359–373.

Hanh, T. N. (1987). *Being peace*. Berkeley, CA: Parallax Press.

Johnson, J., & Immerwahr, J. (1993). *First things first: What Americans expect from the public schools*. New York: Public Agenda.

Kreidler, W. J. (1994). *Conflict resolution in the middle school*. Cambridge, MA: Educators for Social Responsibility.

Lantieri, L., & Patti, J. (1996). *Waging peace in our schools*. Cambridge, MA: Beacon Press.

Muller, R. (1990). *Dialogues of hope*. Ardsley-on-Hudson, New York: World Happiness and Cooperation.

Patti, J. (1996). *Perceptions of the peer mediation component of a school-wide conflict resolution program: Resolving conflict creatively.* Doctoral Dissertation, Northern Arizona University, UMI No. 9625767.

Prothrow-Stith, D. (1991). *Deadly consequences.* New York: HarperCollins.

Prothrow-Stith, D. (1987). *Violence Prevention Curriculum for Adolescents.* Education Development Center Inc., Newton, MA.

Slaby, R. (Fall, 1994) "What Violent Kids Think, "Safe and Drug Free Schools."

Resource Information

The Resolving Conflict Creatively National Center
40 Exchange Place, Suite 1111
New York, New York 10005
(212) 509-0022
email: ESRRCCP@aol.com

Educators for Social Responsibility
23 Garden Street
Cambridge, Ma. 02138
(617) 492-1764
email: Educators@esrnational.org

National Institute for Dispute Resolution
1726 M Street, NW, Suite 500
Washington, D.C. 20036-4502
(202) 466-4764
email: nidr@nidr.org

The King Center
449 Auburn Ave. N.E.
Atlanta, GA 30312

Centre for Conflict Resolution
UCT Private Bag
7700 Rondecosch
South Africa
Email: GGALANT@CCR.UCT.AC.ZA
Contact: Valerie J. Dovey, Youth Project Co-ordinator

Community Conflict Management and Resolution (CCMR)
14th Floor
Devonshire House
49 Jorissen Street
Braamfontein
Johannesburg RSA
2001
Tel: 011-465-5308
Director: Pat Mkhize

Peaceful Societies

Douglas P. Fry

Åbo Akademi University and University of Arizona

GLOSSARY

Aggression Acts that inflict physical, psychological, and/or social harm (pain/injury) on an individual or individuals. Aggression can stem from emotional arousal (e.g., anger, frustration, fear) and/or be instrumental (i.e., engaged in for a reward or to avoid punishment).

Becharaa' A dispute-resolving assembly used by the Semai people of Malaysia.

Belief System/Cosmology Conceptions that are held and shared by the members of a society, both implicitly and explicitly, about the nature of humans, the world, supernatural beings, and spirituality.

Conflict A perceived divergence of interests—where interests are broadly conceptualized to include values, needs, goals, and wishes—between two or more parties, often accompanied by feelings of anger and hostility.

Enculturation The processes through which culture is transmitted to new generations.

Peaceful Society A society with an extremely low level of physical aggression among its members as well as shared beliefs that devalue aggression and/or positively value harmonious interpersonal relationships. Consequently, conflicts in peaceful societies tend to be dealt with in ways that do not involve aggression.

Violence Severe acts of *physical* aggression generally resulting in some degree of injury or even death.

THE MEMBERS OF A PEACEFUL SOCIETY rarely if ever engage in physical aggression, and correspondingly, they share a system of beliefs that eschews aggression and instead promotes harmonious, nonviolent interpersonal relations. Section I of this chapter provides a brief overview of key comparative and analytical sources on peaceful societies. Section II presents two detailed case studies, one on the Semai of Malaysia and the other on the La Paz Zapotec of Mexico. Perhaps the Semai represent a pinnacle of human social tranquility; they demonstrate the human capacity to construct and live a nonviolent social existence. As part of the case study, a description of the Semai dispute resolution procedure, the *becharaa'*, is presented. The La Paz Zapotec demonstrate the importance of enculturation processes for the maintenance of peace. Psychocultural mechanisms thought to contribute to the peaceful lifestyle in La Paz are considered, with emphasis being given to how individuals internalize values, beliefs, and behavioral patterns that are incompatible with violence.

Copyright © 1999 by Academic Press.
All rights of reproduction in any form reserved.

Section III reviews several theoretical issues, including intracultural variation in peacefulness, within-group versus between-group peacefulness, changes in peacefulness of a society over time, and the multidimensional nature of aggression and conflict. Section IV draws on cross-cultural data to discuss common features observable in at least some peaceful societies. The presence of a belief system that promotes nonviolence and/or social harmony and therefore does not condone physical aggression is perhaps the most critical feature found in peaceful societies. Additionally, typical ways in which peaceful societies keep the peace include avoidance, internalization of self-restraints against expressing anger and aggression, and use of informal social controls such as ridicule, gossip, social pressure from kin, and so on. Humans are capable of creating peaceful societies. This statement is not utopian, because peaceful societies already exist.

I. OVERVIEW: THE EXISTENCE AND NATURE OF PEACEFUL SOCIETIES

Attitudinal research shows that neo-Hobbesian beliefs that human beings are naturally war-like or naturally violent continue to be widespread among Westerners today. For example, 64% of college student respondents viewed "war as an intrinsic part of human nature" and 40% agreed that "wars are inevitable because human beings are naturally aggressive creatures," findings reported by Douglas and Brooks Fry in 1997. A view of humanity as naturally aggressive is also suggested by the statement, "violence is always present in society" (Balandier, quoted by Sponsel, 1996a, p. 97), an assertion implying that nonviolent societies cannot exist. However, a cross-cultural perspective shows such a view to be incorrect. Nonviolent, peaceful societies do exist.

Peaceful societies—those with extremely low levels of physical aggressiveness—can be found in various parts of the world, although, as noted by Lawrence Keeley, they are not nearly as numerous as more violent societies. Peaceful societies include, for example, the Amish of North America, the Batek of the Malay Peninsula, the Buid of the Philippines, the Chewong of Malaysia, certain Canadian Inuit groups, the Hutterites of Canada and the United States, the Ifaluk of Micronesia, the !Kung of the Kalahari in Africa, the Mbuti of central Africa, the Piaroa of Amazonia, the Semai of Malaysia, the Siriono of Bolivia, the Tahitians of the central Pacific, the Tikopia of the western Pacific, the Toraja of Indonesia, the Veddahs of Sri Lanka, the Yames of Or-

chid Island off the coast of China, and certain Zapotec communities of Mexico, among others. Additionally, warfare is not engaged in by all societies, being absent in cultures such as the Andaman Islanders, Arunta, Arapesh, Birhor, Buid, Hadza, !Kung, Mission Indians, Punan, Semai, Semang, Todas, Yahgan, and so on. Clearly the existence of peaceful, nonviolent societies shows that violence and war are not inevitable features of human social life. As Carl O'Nell expresses "we appear *not* to arrive at birth biologically 'prepackaged' for violence" (in Howell & Willis, 1989, p. 117, emphasis added).

Leslie Sponsel, writing in the *Encyclopedia of Cultural Anthropology*, proposes some general tendencies of peaceful societies. They are likely to be small communities with egalitarian social structures—including relatively high gender equality—that emphasize cooperation, generalized sharing, and decision-making through group consensus. Additionally, Sponsel suggests that peaceful societies have world views, values, attitudes, enculturation practices, and conflict resolution procedures that emphasize nonviolence.

Marc Ross also lists some typical features of what he terms "low-conflict" societies. In parallel to Sponsel, Ross notes that norms in such societies emphasize nonviolence and cooperative approaches to dispute resolution among community members. After making the caveat that each society is different, Ross (1993, pp. 59–60) suggests that seven characteristics are important in "low-conflict" societies:

> Psychocultural practices which build security and trust; a strong linkage between individual and community interests and high identification with the community so that individuals and groups in conflict trust that its interests are their own; a preference for joint problem solving which leaves ultimate control over decisions in the hands of the disputants; available third parties (sometimes in the form of the entire community) to facilitate conflict management; an emphasis on the restoration of social harmony that is often at least as strong as the concern with the substantive issues in a dispute; the possibility of exit as a viable option; and strategies of conflict avoidance.

A number of descriptions and analyses of peaceful cultures are now available in the anthropological literature. In addition to a diverse set of articles and books that provide information on particular nonviolent societies, for example, Robert Dentan's *The Semai: A Nonviolent People of Malaya* published in 1968 or Douglas

Hollan's 1988 article "Staying 'Cool' in Toraja: Informal Strategies for the Management of Anger and Hostility in a Nonviolent Society," the following sources provide comparative analyses and/or collections of writing on peaceful societies. David Fabbro briefly summarizes information on seven peaceful societies, the Copper Eskimos, Hutterites, !Kung, Mbuti, Semai, Siriono, and Tristan da Cunha Islanders. In a volume edited by Ashley Montagu, *Learning Non-Aggression*, the contributors pay special attention to socialization and enculturation processes occurring in low-violence societies such as certain Canadian Inuit groups, the !Kung, the Mbuti, the Semai, Tahitians, and others. Additional descriptions of peaceful cultures, such as the Buid, Chewong, Piaroa, and La Paz Zapotec, are found in *Societies At Peace*, edited by Signe Howell and Roy Willis. Marc Ross briefly reviews published accounts on five "low-conflict" societies, namely, the Papago, Norwegians, Tikopians, Semai, and !Kung, in Chapter 3 of his book, *The Management of Conflict*. Contributors to Leslie Sponsel and Thomas Gregor's edited book, *The Anthropology of Peace and Nonviolence*, provide further data on the certain peaceful Inuit groups, the Semai, and the La Paz Zapotec, as well as on several other peaceful cultures. Sponsel's 1996b article provides a concise overview of certain issues and sources related to peaceful societies and nonviolence. Finally, Bruce Bonta focuses on conflict resolution and other salient aspects of peacefulness using information from 24 societies with low levels of violence.

II. CASE STUDIES: THE SEMAI AND THE LA PAZ ZAPOTEC

A. The Semai of Malaysia

1. Peaceful Lifestyles

Clayton Robarchek (1997, p. 51) characterizes the Semai as "one of the least violent societies known to anthropology," and Robert Dentan writes of this culture that "although their technology is so simple that there is no metalwork, weaving, tanning, or pottery, nevertheless they seem to have worked out ways of handling human violence which technologically more 'advanced' people might envy" (1968, p. 6).

The Semai live in small bands, seldom consisting of more than 100 persons, and sustain themselves through a combination of swidden gardening, hunting, fishing, and gathering. Semai social organization is extremely egalitarian. A headman (occasionally a headwoman) has some moral authority over the members of the band, but this leader lacks any institutionalized power.

Based on independent field studies, Robarchek and Dentan reach similar conclusions about the peaceful nature of Semai society. Dentan explains that the Semai people perceive themselves as a nonviolent culture and that Semai individuals hold conceptions of themselves as nonviolent persons. Furthermore, Dentan notes that violence seems to terrify the Semai. Adults do not strike each other and children are not physically punished, aside from the mildest pinching or patting on the hand.

Robarchek concurs with such assessments of Semai nonviolence, noting, for instance in a 1980 article, that aggression simply is not perceived as a behavioral possibility among the Semai. In another article, Clayton and Carole Robarchek (1996, p. 64) specify that "Husbands and wives do not assault one another, parents do not physically punish their children, neighbors do not fight with one another, and homicide is so rare as to be virtually nonexistent." It is necessary to point out that a calculation of the Semai homicide rate published by Bruce Knauft in 1987 is extremely inaccurate. As Robarchek and Robarchek (1998, p. 124, note 2) explain, this unfortunate error resulted in part from Knauft's use of a population figure for the Semai of 300 "rather than on the population of 15,000," thus producing a homicide rate that is at the minimum 50 times too high. Regrettably, this inflated homicide calculation continues to create confusion as it is perpetuated in the literature, as illustrated, for instance, when Keeley concludes on the basis of this erroneous calculation that the Semai "homicide rate was numerically significant" (1996, p. 31).

2. The Enculturation of Nonviolence

Both Dentan (in Montagu, 1978) and Robarchek have discussed the enculturation processes through which Semai children learn and adopt nonviolent attitudes and patterns of behavior in the natural course of growing up. Robarchek emphasizes the importance of the Semai social learning environment as one where children see very few instances of aggression. Children also learn the values, attitudes, and beliefs of their elders. For instance, Semai children, who themselves are not punished corporally, acquire the Semai belief that hitting a child may cause the youth to become ill and die. Robarchek (1980, p. 114) concludes that, "for developing children, the learning of aggressive behavior by observation and imitation is almost entirely precluded.... The image of the world, of human goals, and of the means of attaining them that is presented to Semai children simply does not include violence as a behavioral alternative."

3. Belief System

Robarchek explains that the Semai view the world as filled with dangers, most of which are beyond any human control. The Semai conceptualize human aspects of the world as split dichotomously between members of the band and all outsiders. The Semai also believe in both good and bad spirits. Security and nurturance are found within the band, while danger and death are found outside it. The good, protective spirits are called *gunik* and help to protect people from the malevolent spirits, called *mara'*, which attack band members causing injuries, illnesses, and deaths. However, Dentan notes that "*Gunik* and *mara'* are not merely opposites; *mara'* become *gunik* without ceasing to be *mara'*" (personal communication, May 5, 1998). Robarchek emphasizes that the community and its *gunik* are the only defense against the *mara'*. In a hostile world filled with malevolence and danger, a person's security and nurturance can be derived only from others in the community. Thus nurturance (expressed through both emotional and material support) and affiliation (maintaining harmonious interpersonal relationships within the band) are two primary values among the Semai. Robarchek (1997, p. 53) explains that "good and bad are defined primarily in terms of behaviors associated with these values, with goodness defined positively in terms of nurturance (helping, giving, sharing, feeding, and so on) and badness in terms of behaviors disruptive of affiliation (getting angry, quarreling, and fighting)." Thus in this culturally constructed Semai belief system, aggression runs directly counter to community values and the images persons hold of themselves as cooperative and nonviolent. (See Box.)

4. Perceptions of Conflict

Robarchek notes that not only do the Semai fear aggression and violence, but they also feel intensely threatened by any type of interpersonal conflict. Robarchek reports that when he orally administered a sentence-completion test to a sample of Semai, the finding clearly indicated the critical importance of maintaining harmony in interpersonal relations. In completing the sentence "more than anything else, he/she is afraid of …" the most commonly expressed fear was "a conflict," outnumbering the responses for "malevolent spirits," (*mara'*), "tigers," and "death" combined.

The fact that the Semai are nonviolent does not mean that conflicts never arise within the band. It does mean, however, that violence is not used as an approach to conflict. In daily life a certain number of conflicts inevitably occur, such as when spouses are unfaithful, goats invade another person's garden causing crop damage, someone becomes offended by the words of another, and so on. Such disputes are called *hal*, which is roughly equivalent to the term "affair" in English, except that *hal* carries an extremely negative connotation in Semai usage. The Semai "go to great lengths to avoid conflict and will usually tolerate annoyances and sacrifice personal interests rather than precipitate an open confrontation" (Robarchek 1997, p. 54). Much of the time persons manage to deny or suppress angry feelings as a way to avoid *hal*. This point is illustrated by Dentan's (1968, p. 55) observation that "the Semai do not say, 'Anger is bad.' They say, 'We do not get angry,' and an obviously angry man will flatly deny his anger."

Robarchek provides an illustration of how Semai attempt to avoid *hal*. When an owner of some fruit trees discovered that someone was coming in the night and taking his fruit, he went to build a temporary shelter in the forest so he could spend the night to protect his fruit from theft. As he was in the process of building the shelter, he talked a great deal about his plan to guard the trees so that everybody in the band became aware of his plan to camp-out near his fruit trees. He did not want to run any danger of actually surprising the thief. Robarchek (1979, p. 106) explains the strategy as one which avoided open confrontation while simultaneously protecting the resource: "He wished only to stop the theft, not to discover or catch the thief; for if he were to confront the thief, their relations would be disrupted, and *hal* would result."

5. Becharaa': A Dispute Resolution Assembly

With an egalitarian band type of social organization, the Semai lack superordinate mechanisms for resolving disputes. On occasions when *hal* cannot be avoided, the headman convenes a dispute resolution assembly called the *becharaa'*. The persons who are engaged in a dispute, their relatives, and any other members of the community who choose to attend, meet at the house of the headman, usually in the late afternoon. At first, the persons present discuss any number of topics, *except* the dispute that is the reason for the gathering. After some while, several elder members of the band each present lengthy monologues referring to the mutual interdependence of all members of the community. Everyone is reminded of their dependence on the other members of the band and that maintaining harmony and unity is of primary importance. Following these reiterations of community values and cosmology, one of the disputants eventually begins to discuss the *hal*.

Box 1

Anthropological Quotations on Peaceful Societies

"Anger is ignored as much as possible, as with angry children, but when it becomes too manifest, people physically remove themselves, just as they flee from outsiders.... Their mythology has no instances of human physical violence. I asked about murder. They insisted it never happened."—Signe Howell on the Chewong of Malaysia (in Howell & Willis, 1989, p. 55).

"Available statistics on crime and suicide, impressions of administrators, and my own observations during a period of more than two years in a rural village and a small enclave in urban Papeete indicate in comparison with Western experience and in comparison with reports of many other non-Western societies an extreme lack of angry, hostile, destructive behavior."—Robert Levy on the Tahitians (in Montagu, 1978, p. 224).

"They had no policemen, no jails, no external controls of any kind for outbreaks of aggression. Nevertheless, aggression did not break out [p. 71].... Perhaps the most important cultural factor in the valued peacekeeping practices of the Ju/wasi was the phenomenal self-control that was practiced by everyone but the smallest children [p. 75]."—Elizabeth Marshall Thomas on the Ju/wasi of Namibia (Thomas, 1994).

"In my view, the Buid may be fairly described as a society 'at peace' because of the extremely low *value* they attach to 'aggression' and the extremely high *value* they attach to 'tranquility.'"—Thomas Gibson on the Buid of the Philippines (in Howell & Willis, 1989, p. 60).

"The concept of good is tied to peacefulness. A villager's reputation and moral worth depend on being circumspect in behavior, avoiding confrontations, and rarely showing anger. These behaviors are regarded as 'harmonious' and aesthetically pleasing."—Thomas Gregor on the Mehinaku of Brazil (in Sponsel & Gregor, 1994, p. 246).

"I have been describing ways of avoiding conflictful confrontations by respecting the autonomy and privacy of others: being indirect, discreet, not putting oneself forward, not making claims on others, or attempting to influence them. Another way of avoiding confrontations was to deny that one was unhappy, angry, dissatisfied, resentful.... A very frequently used technique was to turn the situation into a joke; to laugh at it."—Jean Briggs on the Utkuhikhalingmiut and Qipisamiut Inuit of Canada (in Sponsel & Gregor, 1994, p. 165).

"Piaroaland is almost free of all forms of physical violence, a place where children, teenagers, and adults alike never express anger through physical means.... Since the Piaroa totally disallow physical violence, and children are never physically punished, the children have no model of such action."—Joanna Overing on the Piaroa of Venezuela (in Howell & Willis, 1989, pp. 79, 92).

[The Toraja devalue] "... anger and hostility and successfully control overtly aggressive behavior through a number of cultural practices [p. 54].... Anger (*sengke*) is one of the 'hot' emotional states most feared and avoided by the Toraja ... the conscious awareness of angry, 'hot' feelings is upsetting to people, even if such feelings are not openly expressed [p. 59]."—Douglas Hollan on the Toraja of Indonesia (Hollan, 1988).

Next the other disputant offers a portrayal of the dispute. Others join in, offering opinions and observations, or perhaps asking clarifying questions. The disputants do not confront each other or argue, but rather they calmly address the gathered assembly. The *becharaa'* continues without ceasing for hours or typically for several days and nights. The headman's household provides food, and people may nap from time to time on the floor as the discussion continues. Throughout the *becharaa'* meeting, anger and other emotions generally are not displayed.

Robarchek explains that during the *becharaa'*, all events related to the dispute are explored from "every conceivable perspective in a kind of marathon encounter group. Every possible explanation is offered, every imaginable motive introduced, every conceivable mitigating circumstance examined ... until finally a point is reached where there is simply nothing left to say" (1997, p. 55). The headman then lectures one or both of the parties, noting their guilt in the *hal*, instructing them in how they should have acted differently, and directing them not to repeat such behavior. The headman and other elders again offer monologues reaffirming the paramount necessity of maintaining the unity and harmony of the band. In his 1979 article, Robarchek emphasizes how, through the *becharaa'*, the Semai are able to deal nonviolently with serious conflicts—involving property ownership, infidelity, divorce, land claims, and so on—in such a way as to (1) dissipate angry emotions, (2) deal with the substantive issues of the dispute, (3) promote the reconciliation of the antagonists, and (4) reconfirm and reinforce the interdependence of all members of the band and the need for social harmony.

6. Summary

In summary, the following points can be highlighted about the belief system and behavior of the Semai. Nonviolence is a central aspect of the Semai belief system, making physical aggression unacceptable. Behaviors of individuals closely correspond with the nonviolent beliefs: physical aggression of any type is practically nonexistent.

Another aspect of the Semai belief system is that conflict (*hal*) is to be feared and avoided. Behaviorally, Semai relocate to avoid external threats to the band and respond to conflict within the band by denying and suppressing anger, tolerating others, and, when necessary, employing the *becharaa'* to resolve disputes.

Within the Semai belief system, the band and protective, good spirits provide nurturance and security, while the world beyond the band is the realm of malevolent spirits and potentially harmful foreigners and therefore extremely dangerous. Aggression and conflict endanger the core of Semai existence by threatening the nurturance and security obtainable only through life in the community. Behaviorally, the overriding tendency is for people to cooperate, share, avoid conflicts, and act nonviolently.

Through enculturation, children internalize the Semai perceptions of the world, the core values, and other aspects of the belief system. Children also learn to behave nonviolently, to avoid conflicts whenever possible, and to suppress any feelings of anger.

B. The La Paz Zapotec of Mexico

1. Respect

Benito Juárez was a Zapotec Indian from the Mexican state of Oaxaca who became the President of Mexico in the mid-1800s. Juárez wrote, "Respect for the rights of others is peace," a sentiment which is in accordance with the emphasis that at least some Zapotec communities place on *respect*. La Paz and San Andrés are pseu-

donyms for two adjacent Zapotec communities, with populations of about 2000 and 3000 respectively. Members of the communities are peasant farmers, subsisting on maize, beans, and squash. While the people in both communities regularly espouse the virtues of acting respectfully, the citizens of La Paz take their own words more seriously than do the people of San Andrés. Persons from San Andrés are more likely to abandon this ideal in daily life by arguing, insulting, lying, coming to blows, and damaging another's property than are the Zapotec of La Paz, who live in much closer correspondence with the ethic of respect. In terms of fistfights, wife beatings, jealous feuds, assaults, and murders, San Andrés has a substantially higher level of violence than La Paz.

The citizens of La Paz maintain a self-image of themselves as nonjealous, respectful, and nonviolent (*pacíficos*), while in San Andrés, by contrast, the community self-image includes aggression, as voiced in such sentiments that avenging a relative's murder may be honorable, that jealously killing a rival is understandable, and that fighting, especially among intoxicated persons, is simply to be expected. In other words, the people of San Andrés internalize an ambivalent belief system regarding aggression and do not hold a nonviolent image of their community analogous to the one held in La Paz.

2. Socialization for Peace

Data gathered by Douglas Fry in San Andrés and La Paz illustrate how socialization and enculturation patterns perpetuate peaceful social life. In the first part of this case study, methods of child discipline and children's behavior are compared between peaceful La Paz and more aggressive San Andrés. In the second part of the case study, the focus shifts to peaceful La Paz, and certain social mechanisms that appear to contribute to the social tranquility of the La Paz Zapotec are reviewed.

Observing that physical punishment of children is absent or very rare in some cultures with low levels of aggression, in a 1993 article Fry predicted that parents in La Paz would employ less physical punishment than parents from San Andrés and furthermore that La Paz parents would favor verbal means of disciplining their children. Both attitudinal and behavioral data were gathered.

The assessment of attitudes toward disciplining and raising children was addressed during tape-recorded structured interviews with samples of fathers from La Paz and San Andrés. One interview question asked what a father should do if his son let the farm animals under his care eat alfalfa belonging to another farmer. In San

Andrés, 65% of the fathers included punishment in their responses, while only 20% of the sample from La Paz suggested punishment, statistically a very significant difference.

Answers to other interview questions also showed that parents from San Andrés advocate the use of physical punishment very significantly more often than do respondents from La Paz. Typical San Andrés responses were: "hit him then so that he grows up with some discipline" and "hit her so she will have a little respect." By contrast, the most favored reaction to children's misbehavior among the La Paz parents is to talk, tell, show, correct, and educate the children—in other words, positive verbal responses. For instance, one La Paz father told how he would talk to a disobedient son, and in his speech, the core value of *respect* and adherence to proper father and son roles are emphasized: "Listen son, if you do not obey ... I am not able to assist you.... You, as my son, ought to [have] respect.... I am your father.... You ought to respect my words, because you know that your father and your mother are the ones that raise you." Other La Paz respondents also regularly mentioned respect, for example: "Teach them ... so that they have respect. Educate them." And La Pazian nonviolent thinking regarding child training is expressed by a father who explained that, "One must explain to the child with love, with patience ... so that he is educated more." Some La Paz respondents also mentioned the importance of setting a good example for their children through their own behavior.

Figure 1 graphically portrays the major differences in approaches to child discipline between parents in San Andrés and La Paz: in neither community do respondents advocate much use of negative verbal approaches, such as scolding or threatening children, but

San Andrés respondents clearly favor physical punishment, while La Paz respondents lean strongly toward positive verbal responses.

Ethnographic observations correspond with the attitudes and beliefs voiced by the fathers. Fry recounts how during fieldwork in the 1980s he saw 11 child beatings in San Andrés as well as other types of aggression directed at children, but never observed in La Paz a child receiving a beating nor any other type of physical aggression from an adult. On two occasions, La Paz parents were observed to threaten children with a beating, but they did not actually punish the children. Correspondingly, Carl O'Nell, who conducted fieldwork in La Paz during the 1960s, writes "the physical disciplining of a child might be undertaken with a *vara* (cane), reported to be so by fathers *but never observed*" (emphasis added, O'Nell, 1969, quoted in Fry's 1993 article). Thus, corporal punishment in La Paz is very rare.

The parents in San Andrés and La Paz also hold markedly different opinions as to the "nature of children," and this relates to their expectations about children's behavior. In San Andrés, a fair amount of disobedience is tolerated as *natural* among children. The people of San Andrés view children as mischievous and somewhat uncontrollable, and the children live up to these expectations. In comparison, the Zapotec of La Paz perceive children as basically well behaved. La Paz adults believe that children naturally will learn how to behave correctly, and La Paz children typically do obey adults.

3. Internalization of Peaceful Behavior

It would seem that the positive verbal approaches as well as the positive expectations that La Paz parents hold may help children develop their own *internal* controls against acting aggressively. La Paz parents explain the consequences of misdeeds to children and convey both in words and actions the ideals of respect and nonviolence. For example, one father said, "If my boy sees that I ... do not have respect for other persons, well ... he thus acquires the same sentiment. But if I have respect for others, well, he imitates me.... Above all, the father must make himself an example, by showing how to respect." On the other hand, the heavy reliance on physical punishment in San Andrés may not be conducive to the internalization of self-restraints against aggression. Physical punishment reflects an *external* locus of control, and thus San Andrés children may come to expect a controlling response from others rather than develop their own self-restraints. Additionally, as San Andrés adults model physical aggression during punishment episodes and at other times, the

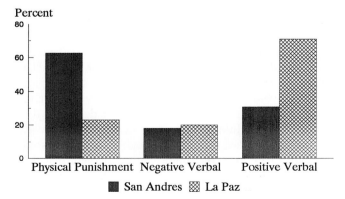

FIGURE 1 Disciplinary styles: San Andres and La Paz.

children are presented with messages that sometimes aggression is acceptable.

One line of evidence in support of this interpretation involves the behavior of young children in San Andrés and La Paz. As reported in a 1992 article, Fry conducted systematic behavior observations on samples of 3- to 8-year-old children from both communities in order to record data on fighting and play fighting behavior (such as beats, slaps, kicks, and so on). The samples of children were similar regarding sex composition, mean age, the age of their parents, number of siblings, and economic standing of their family within the community. Whenever the child who was being observed engaged in aggression or play aggression, the details of the interaction were recorded, including the identities of the interactants and any facial expressions or gestures.

Children from San Andrés participated in significantly more play aggression than the La Paz children (6.9 versus 3.7 episodes/hr). Likewise, the rate of aggression was significantly higher in San Andrés than in La Paz (.78 versus .39 episodes/hr).

Some aggression consisted of physical contacts (e.g., punches and kicks), while other instances blended *noncontact* threatening (e.g., a raised arm with the intention to beat) with contact aggression. Of course, noncontact threatening is less severe than actually striking blows. In San Andrés, only about 10% of aggression simultaneously included threatening. In La Paz, however, 63% of aggression simultaneously included threatening. The mixing of noncontact threatening with physical aggression over half the time in La Paz is another indication—along with the significantly lower rate of aggression among the La Paz sample to begin with—of the La Paz children's *internal* restraint against actually engaging in physical aggression.

These findings suggest an overall reluctance on the part of La Paz children to participate in play fighting and real fighting relative to the San Andrés children, an intercommunity difference that also appears to strengthen with age. These differences in children's behavior correspond with the interpretation suggested by Fry in a chapter in Sponsel and Gregor's edited book that different beliefs and values regarding the expression of aggression are internalized in these two communities. Prevalent attitudes regarding what constitutes acceptable behavior, shared expectations about the nature of the citizenry, and overall images of the community's aggressiveness and peacefulness are all elements of a child's learning environment. It seems that through socialization, even by the 3- to 8-year-old age range, La Paz children have begun to develop internal controls against engaging in both play fighting and real fighting.

4. Psychocultural Mechanisms That Promote Peace

To shift the focus of discussion exclusively to peaceful La Paz, a variety of psychocultural features appear to contribute to a relatively nonviolent social life. O'Nell (Howell & Willis, 1989, p. 119), states that "residents of La Paz emphasize values and ideals which in their enactment stand as antithetical to a violent way of life." The social ideals that O'Nell sees as antithetical to the expression of aggression are respect, responsibility, and cooperation. Additionally, Fry recounts how members of the La Paz community hold a nonviolent image of their community, reflected, for example, in statements to the effect that we are *pacificos* (peaceful or pacifists), we don't fight, we are like one family, and so on. Fry concludes that "the citizens of La Paz maintain a self-image of themselves as respectful, peaceful, nonjealous, and cooperative" (Sponsel & Gregor, 1994, p. 140).

O'Nell discusses several psychocultural mechanisms that he sees as contributing to La Pazian peacefulness. First, he explains that persons are suspicious of witchcraft, and one check on behaving aggressively may stem from a concern that the victim might retaliate through witchcraft. Second, O'Nell points out that community life makes each person interdependent and that the necessity of reciprocity and cooperation serve to inhibit aggression. Third, O'Nell discusses how fear of gossip may check a person's aggression and/or prevent the escalation of aggression. Fourth, avoidance is noted by O'Nell as a critical mechanism for preventing aggression. He specifies that the act of removing oneself from a threatening situation is not considered cowardly by La Pazians. Additionally, the *machismo* value system with its emphasis on male fighting is not manifested in La Paz, in contrast to many other segments of Mexican society. Fifth, denial of anger or hostility is another mechanism which O'Nell emphasizes as important in maintaining the peace: "A person who feels hostile toward another will often go to great lengths to deny such feelings" (Howell & Willis, 1989, p. 126).

Fry provides an example (Sponsel and Gregor, 1994) that illustrates both avoidance and denial. When an inebriated and angry man came looking for a fellow La Pazian late one night, the fellow he was looking for simply avoided a confrontation by pretending not to be at home, letting his unmarried sister deal with the angry drunk while he remained locked in his house. The following day, the man who had verbally expressed his drunken rage the night before denied that he had ever been angry at his neighbor. Both men simply went about their business and that was the end of the matter.

5. Summary

To summarize the main points of this case study, in the first part, disciplinary practices and children's behavior were compared between San Andrés and La Paz. La Paz parents prefer positive verbal alternatives to corporal punishment. They discuss, explain, and teach their children how to behave, making frequent reference to the key value of respect. As a result of such enculturation, La Paz children tend to be more obedient, respectful, and less aggressive than San Andrés children, the latter difference being quantitatively documented through systematic observations of 3- to 8-year old children's behavior. La Paz parents, through actions and words, provide their children with methods of dealing with conflict within the family and community that do not involve physical confrontation. The La Paz case provides an example wherein parents deemphasize aggression and employ nonforceful child training techniques, and children, for their part, are generally well behaved and not very aggressive.

By adulthood, people who have grown up in La Paz have internalized certain beliefs and values that act as a first level of aggression control, contributing greatly to the overall peacefulness in the community. Thus it seems that the first level of restraint against acting aggressively comes from *within* the individuals who are the products of La Pazian enculturation. In the second part of this case study, it was suggested that certain psychocultural mechanisms operate to prevent and minimize aggression in the community. For instance, the people of La Paz regularly deny their feelings of anger and hostility, avoid conflict situations and direct confrontations, perceive their mutual interdependence with other community members, and perhaps reassure themselves, when necessary, that all the people in their community are basically good and peaceful persons. They reaffirm in daily conversations and behavior the primary social ideals of respect, responsibility, and cooperation, and, when disputes do arise, people from La Paz—again at an internal level of control—employ self-restraint to prevent the escalation or lengthy duration of the conflict.

III. SOME THEORETICAL ISSUES RELATED TO PEACEFUL SOCIETIES

A. Intracultural Variation

A consideration of peaceful societies raises several theoretical and conceptual issues. The first issue involves *intracultural* variation. There has long been a tendency within anthropology to generalize about the characteristics of a culture based on fieldwork in only one or several villages, communities, bands, and so on. When considerable variation exists among intracultural entities, generalizations may lead to misrepresentations about the level of aggressiveness, peacefulness, or other features of a culture. For example, it would be incorrect to generalize that Zapotec culture overall has a low level of aggression based solely on data from the peaceful La Paz community, or conversely, to generalize on the basis of fieldwork in a different Zapotec community than La Paz that all Zapotec communities are violent. Jean Briggs voices a similar caution that not all Inuit bands are as peaceful as the groups she describes (Sponsel & Gregor, 1994).

B. In-Group versus Out-Group Aggression

A second issue to consider in assessing peacefulness involves whether to focus on the degree of tranquility within the group, between neighboring groups, or both. Some cultures have very low levels of both in-group and out-group aggression, such as the Buid and the Semai. The Buid response to conflict both within the group or from the outside is to attempt to escape from the situation. Thomas Gibson explains that "... simple withdrawal is the preferred solution to conflict. The socially approved response to aggression is avoidance or even flight. The Buid language is rich in words for fear, fleeing, and escape from danger, none of which carries negative moral overtones" (Howell & Willis, 1989, p. 66). On the other hand, some societies with very low levels of physical aggression within the group may be willing to engage in externally directed aggression. As noted by Ross, the internally peaceful Papago of southern Arizona and northern Mexico defended themselves against raiding Apaches, although they do not themselves glorify warfare.

C. Cultural Changes in Aggressiveness/ Peacefulness Over Time

A third issue to consider in assessing the peacefulness of a culture is that the degree of internal and external aggression can change over time. Keeley writes, "With bewildering rapidity, hated enemies can become respected allies, devout pacifists can become tigers on the battlefield, peaceable societies can become belligerent, and vice versa" (1996, p. 147). For instance, Dentan (Silverberg & Gray, 1992) notes apparent shifts in levels of aggressivity among the !Kung over several decades, wherein they seem to have experienced a 2-decade period of relative peacefulness, from the mid-1950s to the mid-1970s, which was interspersed between more aggressive periods. Similarly, Thomas reports a marked shift toward violence among the previously peaceful Ju/wasi people once they gave up nomadism for a sedentary lifestyle. Sponsel (1996a, p. 106) notes that change also can occur in the opposite direction, asserting that "the transformation of warlike societies into peaceful ones has occurred repeatedly in human history." As discussed by Fry in more detail in this volume in the article entitled "Aggression and Altruism," Sponsel's point is contemporaneously illustrated with the previously warlike Waorani of Ecuador and the Chatino villagers of southern Mexico, who dramatically reduced aggression in their communities. The Waorani, for instance, while not completely transforming themselves into a nonviolent society, remarkably managed to decrease their homicide rate by *more than 90%* over several years. Thus the degree of peacefulness in a society clearly can change over time. Implications of this observation are that cultural comparisons regarding peacefulness should include a specification of the time frames involved. Also, awareness of the potential for culture change may at times account for discrepancies in descriptions of aggression and peacefulness given by different fieldworkers for the same culture but at different time periods, as seems to have occurred related to the !Kung, a point noted both by Dentan and Draper (Montagu, 1978). A final implication, relevant for reducing violence in society, is that cultural transitions toward lower levels of aggression can be both dramatic and rapid as shown by the Chatino and Waorani transformations toward more peaceful lifestyles.

D. Aggression as a Multidimensional Construct

A fourth conceptual issue related both to assessing the peacefulness of a particular society and to determining where a particular society might fall along a cross-cultural peaceful-to-violent continuum is that aggression, and more generally conflict, are multidimensional concepts. For example, possibly relevant dimensions of physical aggression might include spousal aggression, physical punishment of children, infanticide, homicide, capital punishment, interpersonal fighting with fists, clubs, sticks, or spears, and group raids, ambushes, and battles. By some such indicators a society could appear to be extremely tranquil while by other indicators the same society could appear to be more violent. This observation about multidimensionality

is relevant, of course, to any attempts to scale societies along a peaceful-to-violent continuum, an approach advocated by researchers such as James Silverberg and Patrick Gray.

Some of the challenges posed by the multidimensionality of aggression are reflected in Fabbro's comparison of seven societies. While his characterization of all seven societies as "peaceful" based on a set of criteria (e.g., no wars, no collective internal violence, little or no structural violence, little or no interpersonal physical violence) makes sense in comparison to other societies that do not meet these criteria, nonetheless the complications posed by the multidimensionality issue come into play as Fabbro notes, for instance, (1) infanticide in two cultures, but not in the other five, (2) physical punishment of children in three cultures, but not in the other four, and (3) spousal aggression in three societies, but not in one, and no explicit information on its occurrence for the remaining three societies. Furthermore, in a summary table, Fabbro classifies four societies as having "*little* physical violence" and for two of those four he notes the presence of "lethal physical violence." Fabbro classifies the remaining three societies as having "*some* physical violence" and one of these three is noted to have "lethal physical violence." Finally, Fabbro at times mentions particular cultural beliefs that may directly or indirectly relate to aggression and peacefulness—for example, noting fear of violence in one society and that violence is abhorred in another society.

Thus while all these societies are relatively more peaceful than many other cultures in the sense that they do not practice warfare, lack internal collective violence, have minimal structural violence and low levels of interpersonal violence, and so on, it is nonetheless clear that some aggressive acts—of various types, occurring at various rates, and on occasion even involving lethal violence—may happen in societies that are at or near this tranquil end of a cross-cultural peaceful-to-violent continuum. Furthermore, and related to the multidimensionality of aggression issue, arranging societies along a cross-cultural peaceful-to-violent continuum would seem to present certain challenges. For example, is fistfighting more or less violent than wife-beating? Is infanticide more or less violent than homicide intended as the capital punishment of a murderer? What importance should be given to nonviolent beliefs, attitudes, and ideals? Can different beliefs related to peacefulness and violence be meaningly compared, for example, a fear of violence versus an abhorrence of violence? It is clear that the precise criteria used to scale societies on a peaceful-to-violent continuum should be carefully considered and clearly specified in the event that such an undertaking is attempted.

IV. KEEPING THE PEACE

A. Introductory Comments

How do the members of peaceful societies manage to keep the peace? At the onset, several points should be made explicit. Recall that a peaceful society is defined as having an extremely low level of physical aggression among its members as well as having shared beliefs that devalue aggression and/or positively value harmonious interpersonal relationships. It is apparent from both the information in the literature on peaceful societies and the above discussion of aggression as a multidimensional construct that peaceful societies differ among themselves regarding exactly what constitutes "an extremely low level of physical aggression." In other words, variation exists within peaceful societies: all have extremely low levels of physical aggression, but some have lower levels than others. For instance, some societies such as the Semai and Chewong are virtually violence free, while others such as the Tahitians, !Kung, and Mbuti have rare but periodic instances of physical aggression. However, the relevant points here are that (1) acts of physical aggression are very rare and markedly less frequent than in other societies and (2) members of peaceful societies have belief systems that explicitly place a negative value on aggression and/or place a positive value on behaviors which are viewed as antithetical to aggression.

Another point to keep in mind is that although it is possible to discuss certain features often found in peaceful societies, it is critical to remember that each culture is unique. Thus there are as many different "cultural formulas" through which peaceful societies keep the peace as there are unique peaceful societies, since no two societies have identical belief systems, psychocultural mechanisms, social institutions, and so on through which the peace is maintained. The Semai "formula" for peace is different from the La Paz Zapotec "formula," for example, and both of these differ in turn from the cultural manifestations of peacekeeping in other peaceful societies.

B. The Importance of Belief Systems

Howell and Willis suggest that peacefulness "is cosmologically constructed and morally embedded in a cosmological universe of meaning" (1989, p. 25). In other words, in peaceful societies, the aspects of belief systems that devalue physical aggression and/or promote harmonious relations are integral parts of the larger cultural cosmologies, and such world views are critical to the maintenance of peace. This point is emphasized by Bonta, who concludes that a nonviolent belief system is the single most important variable for keeping the peace: "As the examination of conflict resolution in these small-scale societies proceeds, one fundamental fact emerges: the peacefulness of their conflict resolution is based, primarily, on their world-views of peacefulness—a complete rejection of violence" (1996, p. 404). The Semai and La Paz Zapotec case studies clearly show the importance, uniqueness, and multifaceted aspects of such peace-promoting belief systems or cosmologies. The Semai belief system simultaneously devalues physical aggression (e.g., the belief that hitting a child can cause its illness or death, that violence provokes feelings of terror and results in flight, the sentiment, "we don't get angry," and so on) and values interpersonal harmony (e.g., beliefs that sharing and cooperation are normal and necessary, that the unity of the band is paramount, and so on). The La Paz Zapotec also directly devalue physical aggression (e.g., the beliefs that violence might provoke retaliatory witchcraft, that one's anger should be denied, that threatening situations should simply be avoided, and so on) and, as emphasized by O'Nell, simultaneously promote harmonious values, images, and ideals that are incompatible with violence (e.g., the emphasis on respect, cooperation, reciprocity, responsibility, and interdependence; sentiments like "we are like one family," "we are *pacíficos*," and so on).

C. Egalitarianism

Although there are exceptions, many peaceful societies have an egalitarian form of social organization, including a high degree of gender equality. For example, the Buid, Canadian Inuit, Chewong, Copper Eskimo, Ju/wasi, !Kung, Mbuti, Piaroa, Semai, and Siriono, among others, are foraging societies, which tend to be highly egalitarian (nonhierarchical) and lack both centralized authority and mechanisms of superordinate social control. Peacefulness also can be found among sedentary cultivators and agriculturalists (such as the Amish, Fipa, Hutterites, Toraja, Tristan da Cunha Islanders, and La Paz Zapotec), but the foraging lifestyle, with its corresponding emphasis on egalitarianism, cooperation, and sharing, may be particularly conducive to peacefulness, a point discussed further by Sponsel in his 1996a article.

D. Avoidance, Internalization, and Social Controls

Since foragers lack centralized, superordinate social controls, peacekeeping is largely dependent upon (1) avoidance and separation of disputants, (2) the internalization of nonaggressive values and behaviors resulting in a high degree of self-restraint against expressing anger and aggression, and (3) informal social controls (such as gossip, ridicule, a high degree of interdependence within the group, and so on) as opposed to formal social controls (such as laws). Additionally, as Black proposes in his book, *The Social Structure of Right and Wrong*, the third-party dispute-resolution roles of *friendly peacemaker* and *mediator* reflect relatively egalitarian relationships between the third-party and the disputants and, especially in the case of friendly peacemakers, might be expected to be important in egalitarian, foraging societies.

Keeping in mind that each peaceful society has a unique constellation of beliefs, values, practices, mechanisms, and institutions that result in its low level of physical aggression, it is nonetheless possible to observe some frequently occurring features that seem relevant to keeping the peace. The discussion as to how peace is maintained can be organized around three basic themes: (1) avoidance, (2) internalization of self-restraint, and (3) social controls.

1. Avoidance

Black defines avoidance as "the handling of a grievance by the curtailment of interaction" (1993, p. 79). The members of many peaceful societies utilize avoidance to prevent the escalation of conflict. Relating to the Mbuti, Turnbull poetically expresses that "In later life the child will find that mobility is one of his primary techniques for avoiding a dispute or for resolving one, for once he moves elsewhere, his sphere moves with him and the dispute is discarded" (in Montagu, 1978, pp. 184–185).

Avoidance can be temporary or long-term. In the short-term, an individual can simply avoid a disputant or in some cases an angry person can remove himself or herself from the proximity of the entire group, as has been noted by Draper for the !Kung (Montagu, 1978). An example of a householder avoiding an angry, inebriated man by simply staying inside his house was given in the La Paz Zapotec case study. Hollan's descriptions of how Toraja remain emotionally "cool," or under control, also portray a series of short-term avoidance techniques. Finally, Gibson emphasizes that for the Buid, "the socially approved response to aggression is

avoidance or even flight" (Howell & Willis, 1989, p. 66). Thus short-term avoidance appears to be widely utilized and in some cases it is the culturally prescribed response to conflict.

Regarding longer-term avoidance, among the !Kung and the Ju/wasi, for instance, individuals transfer into other bands when social tensions require such a solution. Correspondingly, Bonta reports that among the peaceful Malapandaram, Birhor, and Paliyan peoples, communities can split apart in response to a conflict.

A final type of avoidance involves movement of the entire group to avoid another group, an approach practiced by the Semai and Chewong, for instance. Bonta observes that the peaceful Amish, Hutterites, and Mennonites also have moved away from conflicts with other societies on numerous historical occasions.

2. Internalization of Self-Restraint

Some peaceful societies not only devalue aggression but also inhibit the expression of anger. Supposedly, the suppression of anger also helps to inhibit aggression. Cultural values favoring the denial or nonexpression of anger can be found among the Chewong, certain Canadian Inuit groups, Ju/wasi, !Kung, La Paz Zapotec, Semai, Toraja, and other cultures. Hollan provides a thorough discussion of the individual and cultural mechanisms of anger and aggression control among the Toraja. He writes, "Standards of etiquette; fears of ridicule, supernatural retribution, and magical retaliation; and the use of culturally constituted defense mechanisms seem remarkably effective in curtailing overt displays of anger and hostility in Toraja" (1988, p. 56).

The denial of anger also has been noted in both the Semai and the La Paz Zapotec case studies. For instance, it was suggested that among the La Paz Zapotec, by adulthood, persons have internalized attitudes, values, and beliefs that serve as a self-restraining check on physical aggression. O'Nell writes that "one of the most effective and extensively used devices to prevent negative dispositions from erupting into interpersonal violence in La Paz is denial" (Howell & Willis, 1989, p. 126). Correspondingly, Briggs emphasizes that in the Inuit camps she studied, "fear of aggression was also inculcated in various ways during the process of socialization" (Sponsel & Gregor, 1994, p. 161), and that by adulthood emotional self-control was well developed, "especially denial and nonexpression of hostile and resentful feelings" (1994, p. 161).

Draper's discussion of the !Kung and Thomas' discussion of self-control among the Ju/wasi suggest that norms which run counter to the expression of anger and aggression are being internalized by persons in these societies. Thomas (1994, p. 75) explains that "self-discipline pervaded everyday life, so that people virtually never showed hunger, pain, let alone anger." Finally, self-restraint in conflict situations is noted by Bonta to occur in peaceful cultures such as the Ifaluk, Paliyan, and Tahitians.

Within the belief systems of some peaceful societies, anger and physical aggression have acquired particular cultural meanings as disgusting, frightening, or even illness provoking. It seems likely that such beliefs have an aggression-inhibiting effect once they are internalized by the individuals of a culture. Gregor explains that among most Xingu tribes, "violence is ugly, dangerous, and inhuman, while peace defines what is human and morally valued" (Sponsel & Gregor, 1994, p. 247). Fabbro notes that Mbuti abhor any violence which produces blood, because in the Mbuti belief system, an entity called *pepo* can then escape from the body through the bleeding opening, causing the death of the victim. Among the Semai and the Toraja, anger can lead to unpleasant feelings and can cause illness. Recall also that the Semai are terrified by violence. Similarly, the Chewong fear violence. Hollan quotes a Toraja mother, who in explaining how she calms herself if she begins to feel anger, alludes to both the connection between anger and illness in the Toraja belief system and the importance of exercising self-restraint: "If, for example, we are about to get angry, in order to calm/soothe/control, we must remember, 'If I get angry, what's the use?' Our bodies will be bothered. It is better, even if the children are very bad, to just reprimand them well, in order to avoid illness" (1988, p. 63). Such cultural beliefs and reactions, once they are internalized by the members of society, can be seen as having a major inhibiting influence on the expression of both anger and aggression.

3. Social Controls

In peaceful societies, acts of physical aggression—and other behaviors that violate social norms—can be met with a variety of sociocultural responses, for instance, criticism, ridicule, gossip, witchcraft, withdrawal of support, and ostracism—that is, mechanisms that can be labeled *informal* social controls, in contrast to *formal* social control mechanisms such as law. Both informal and formal types of social control operate in some peaceful societies such as the La Paz Zapotec, where both the formal legal system of courts and a host of informal mechanisms, such as concern about negative gossip or fear of witchcraft, can be seen as inhibiting physical aggression. Similarly, informal controls among the Toraja are exemplified by Hollan's descriptions of

how people are motivated to avoid expressing anger and aggression in part out of fear of social ridicule and also in part because the recipient of one's anger or aggression might retaliate through magical means. Additionally, formal aspects of social control can be seen in the posting of government civil servants in Torajan villages.

Many peaceful societies rely almost exclusively on informal social control mechanisms—a typical feature of forager social organization. One reflection of this reliance on informal social control involves the nature of third-party interventions, as practiced regularly by community members. Interventions can take many forms, most of which fall under the category of *friendly peacemaker*. The responsibility of group members to intervene is stressed by Bonta (1996, p. 407) when he summarizes for the Yanadi, Ifaluk, Malapandaram, Nubians, Paliyan and other peaceful cultures that "it is incumbent on bystanders to become involved in virtually any circumstance where controversies threaten to become serious or where a conflict situation seems to be developing." Black (1993, p. 18) provides an example of friendly peacemaking: "the only settlement agent found among the Mbuti Pygmies is the so-called camp clown, who handles conflicts primarily by making a fool of himself, thereby distracting the principals from their dispute and possibly making them join together in laughter as well." Similarly, as noted by Bonta, among the Tristan da Cunha Islanders a clever bystander might defuse a quarrel with jokes. Briggs specifies that there were no formal leaders in the peaceful Inuit camps she studied and that "every individual was equally responsible for keeping the peace" (Sponsel & Gregor, 1994, p. 156). Robarchek also emphasizes how every member of the Semai band has the responsibility to immediately bring any conflict to the attention of the headman "so that it can be brought out in the open and settled" (1979, p. 107). From Briggs' descriptions of the Inuit camps, it is clear that friendly peacemakers utilized strategies for distracting, calming, and reminding a disputant of proper behavior: "... others laughed and turned the matter into a joke; tried to reassure the angry person that 'it's nothing to get angry at, have some tea'; [or] commented disapprovingly: '*You get angry easily*'" (Sponsel & Gregor, 1994, p. 167). Instances that amount to friendly peacemaking by others are also described for the Ju/wasi by Thomas, the Toraja by Hollan, and the !Kung by Draper, who writes, for example, "Other people will intervene before a person can act in a hot rage with possible serious injury to his enemy" (Montagu, 1978, p. 43).

Third-parties who adopt the role of *mediator* go beyond the activities of friendly peacemakers by delving into the substance of a dispute in an attempt to help the disputants find an agreeable solution. Mediators attempt to be impartial, and they lack the authority or power to enforce the terms of an agreement. A statement of a Torajan villager, quoted by Hollan (1988, p. 66), suggests that persons in the community adopt mediator roles: "If we know that A has been angry with B, right away we will visit them and publicly repair [reconcile] them, so that there is peace. Because we feel that if there is a rift in the village, everything is ruined!" In the Semai *becharaa'* (examined in the above case study), the headman, assisted by the other community members who are present, adopts a mediator role, although elements of arbitration on the part of the headman also may be present. But the headman's authority is limited, as reflected in Robarchek's (1997, p. 52) characterization of the Semai headman as the "first among equals." Perhaps his role is best characterized as *mediator-arbitrator*. In a process that has some similarities to the *becharaa'*, members of Buid society may submit a dispute to *tultulan*, or collective discussion within the band, in which the group decides what compensation might be paid by one party to the other. In this case, the band members gathered at the *tultulan* function as mediators in helping to settle the dispute. Gibson explains that divorce is the most common type of dispute that is submitted to a *tultulan*, since the favored Buid approach to conflict, avoidance, cannot long be employed by spouses. Gibson writes, "No one has the authority to enforce a settlement, but through extended discussion and diffuse moral pressure, divorces are normally settled without undue disruption. The emphasis is on preserving communal harmony (*uway*) through the separation or reconciliation of the disputants" (Howell & Willis, 1989, p. 66).

V. CONCLUSIONS

While the majority of cultures tolerate, or in some cases augment, physical aggression and violence, the existence of at least several dozen peaceful societies demonstrates that a nonviolent social life also is within the realm of possibility. Bonta (1996, p. 404) suggests that "the Western world-view boils down to an acceptance of the inevitability of conflict and violence," but this is not the case within the belief systems of peaceful societies. While conflicts certainly exist in peaceful societies, the members of these societies deal with their disputes in ways other than by acting aggressively.

The first lesson to learn from the peaceful societies is that the moderate-to-high levels of violence that occur in many cultures are not inevitable features of human social life or human nature; it is possible to live in human societies with extremely low levels of physical aggression. The second set of lessons comes from a careful examination of how peaceful societies maintain their social tranquility. A key observation is that the belief systems of peaceful cultures do not accept the inevitability of violence, but to the contrary, devalue physical aggression and violence. Additionally, egalitarianism seems especially conducive to keeping the peace. Other general peacekeeping approaches seem to include (1) avoidance of antagonists, (2) enculturation processes that facilitate the development of each person's self-restraint and internalization of nonviolent values, beliefs, and behavioral patterns, and (3) a variety of psychocultural social controls, many of which are informal.

Also See the Following Articles

AGGRESSION AND ALTRUISM • AGGRESSION, PSYCHOLOGY OF • ANTHROPOLOGY OF VIOLENCE AND CONFLICT • CLAN AND TRIBAL CONFLICT • CONFLICT MANAGEMENT AND RESOLUTION • COOPERATION, COMPETITION, AND CONFLICT • NONVIOLENCE THEORY AND PRACTICE • NONVIOLENT ACTION

Acknowledgments

This chapter has benefited substantially from suggestions offered by Robert K. Dentan, C. Brooks Fry, Heikki Sarmaja, Leslie Sponsel, and Jukka-Pekka Takala. The author gratefully expresses his appreciation to these scholars.

Bibliography

Black, D. (1993). *The social structure of right and wrong*. San Diego, CA: Academic Press.
Bonta, B. D. (1996). Conflict resolution among peaceful societies: The culture of peacefulness. *Journal of Peace Research*, 33, 403–420.
Dentan, R. K. (1968). *The Semai: A nonviolent people of Malaya*. New York: Holt, Rinehart, and Winston.
Fabbro, D. (1978). Peaceful societies: An introduction. *Journal of Peace Research, 15*, 67–83.
Fry, D. P. (1992). "Respect for the rights of others is peace": Learning aggression versus non-aggression among the Zapotec. *American Anthropologist, 94*, 621–639.
Fry, D. P. (1993). The intergenerational transmission of disciplinary practices and approaches to conflict. *Human Organization, 52*, 176–185.
Fry, D. P., & Fry, C. B. (1997). Culture and conflict resolution models: Exploring alternatives to violence. In D. P. Fry & K. Björkqvist (Eds.), *Cultural variation in conflict resolution: Alternatives to violence* (pp. 9–23). Mahwah, NJ: Erlbaum.

Hollan, D. (1988). Staying "cool" in Toraja: Informal strategies for the management of anger and hostility in a nonviolent society. *Ethos, 16,* 52–72.

Howell, S., & Willis, R. (Eds.) (1989). *Societies at peace: Anthropological perspectives.* New York: Routledge.

Keeley, L. H. (1996). *War before civilization: The myth of the peaceful savage.* New York: Oxford University Press.

Montagu, A. (Ed.) (1978). *Learning non-aggression: The experience of non-literate societies.* New York: Oxford University Press.

Robarchek, C. A. (1979). Conflict, emotion, and abreaction: Resolution of conflict among the Semai Senoi. *Ethos, 7,* 104–123.

Robarchek, C. A. (1980). The image of nonviolence: World view of the Semai Senoi. *Federated Museums Journal, 25,* 103–117.

Robarchek, C. A. (1997). A community of interests: Semai conflict resolution. In D. P. Fry & K. Björkqvist (Eds.), *Cultural variation in conflict resolution: Alternatives to violence* (pp. 51–58). Mahwah, NJ: Erlbaum.

Robarchek, C. A., & Robarchek, C. J. (1996). Waging peace: The psychological and sociocultural dynamics of positive peace. In A. W. Wolfe & H. Yang (Eds.), *Anthropological contributions to conflict resolution* (pp. 64–80). Athens, GA: University of Georgia Press.

Robarchek, C. A., & Robarchek, C. J. (1998). Reciprocities and realities: World views, peacefulness, and violence among Semai and Waorani. *Aggressive Behavior, 24,* 123–133.

Ross, M. H. (1993). *The management of conflict: Interpretations and interests in comparative perspective.* New Haven, CT: Yale University Press.

Silverberg, J., & Gray, J. P. (Eds.) (1992). *Aggression and peacefulness in humans and other primates.* New York: Oxford University Press.

Sponsel, L. E. (1996a). Peace and nonviolence. In D. Levinson & M. Ember (Eds.), *Encyclopedia of cultural anthropology* (Vol. 3, pp. 908–912). New York: Henry Holt.

Sponsel, L. E. (1996b). The natural history of peace: The positive view of human nature and its potential. In T. Gregor (Ed.), *A natural history of peace* (pp. 95–125). Nashville, TN: Vanderbilt University Press.

Sponsel, L. E., & Gregor, T. (Eds.) (1994). *The anthropology of peace and nonviolence.* Boulder, CO: Lynne Rienner.

Thomas, E. M. (1994). Management of violence among the Ju/wasi of Nyae Nyae: The old way and the new way. In S. P. Reyna and R. E. Downs (Eds.), *Studying war: Anthropological perspectives* (pp. 69–84). Pittsburgh, PA: Gordon and Breach.

Peacekeeping

Alex Morrison, S.Cumner, Hanbin Park, and K.A. Zoë

Pearson Peacekeeping Centre

I. A Conceptual Framework of Peacekeeping
II. Selected Case Studies
III. Some Contemporary Issues in Peacekeeping

GLOSSARY

Bi-Polar Describing a system where there is two, relatively equal, opposing actors or coalitions.

Classical Peacekeeping A hybrid politico-military activity aimed at conflict control, which involves a United Nations presence in the field (usually involving military and civilian personnel), with the consent of the parties, to implement or monitor the implementation of arrangements relating to the control of conflicts (cease-fires, separation of forces, etc.), and their resolution (partial or comprehensive settlements) and/or to protect the delivery of humanitarian relief. (UN definition)

Humanitarian Operations Missions conducted to relieve human suffering, especially in circumstances where responsible authorities in the area are unable, or possibly unwilling, to provide adequate service support to the population.

Multifunctional Peacekeeping Actions taken by the United Nations under the authority of Chapter VI or Chapter VII of the United Nations Charter, by regional arrangements pursuant to Chapter VII of the UN Charter, or by ad hoc coalitions pursuant to a UN Security Council resolution under the authority of Chapter VI or VII of the UN Charter or consistent with Chapter VI of the UN Charter, in order to preserve, maintain or restore the peace.

NPP (New Peacekeeping Partnership) A Pearson Peacekeeping Centre term applied to those organizations and individuals that work together to improve the effectiveness of modern peacekeeping operations. It includes the military; civil police; government and nongovernment agencies dealing with human rights and humanitarian assistance; diplomats; the media; and organizations sponsoring development and democratization programs.

Peace-Building Transpires in the aftermath of conflict; it means identifying and supporting measures and structures which will solidify and build trust and interaction among former enemies, in order to avoid a relapse into conflict; often involves elections organized, supervised or conducted by the United Nations, the rebuilding of civil physical infrastructures and institutions such as schools and hospitals, and economic reconstruction. (UN Definition)

Peace Enforcement In the event that cease-fires have been agreed to but not compiled with and/or the UN has been called upon to restore and maintain order, the Secretary-General may call for the deployment of peace-enforcement units. These units would be more heavily armed than peacekeeping and would require extensive training and preparations.

Peacekeeping (PPC Definition) Actions designed to enhance peace, security and stability which are authorized by competent national and international or-

Copyright © 1999 by Academic Press.
All rights of reproduction in any form reserved.

ganizations and which are undertaken co-operatively and individually by military, humanitarian, good governance, civilian police, and other interested agencies and groups.

Peacemaking A diplomatic process of brokering an end to conflict, principally through mediation and negotiation, as foreseen under Chapter VI of the UN Charter; military contributing to peacemaking include military-to-military contacts, security assistance, shows of force and preventive deployments. (UN Definition)

I. A CONCEPTUAL FRAMEWORK OF PEACEKEEPING

A. Introduction

Those who drafted the Charter of the United Nations in 1945 did not anticipate a world in which what we have come to call "peacekeeping" would exist. However, they were determined, in the words of the Charter preamble, "to save succeeding generations from the scourge of war." To this end, they made provisions for the peaceful resolution of disputes (Chapter VI), the use of force to end conflict (Chapter VII), and the role of regional organizations in maintaining international peace and security (Chapter VIII).

Peacekeeping as we know it was invented during the 1956 Suez Crisis by Lester B. Pearson, then the Canadian Secretary of State for External Affairs. Working with UN Secretary-General Dag Hammarskjold, Pearson crafted the United Nations Emergency Force (UNEF), a lightly armed international military force that occupied an interpositional buffer zone between the belligerent parties with their consent. The purpose of UNEF, and of the other peacekeeping missions that were deployed during the Cold War, was to stabilize an international conflict and provide time and space for politicians and diplomats to work out a long-term durable solution.

Several other interpositional missions followed during the course of the Cold War. Numerous observation missions were also deployed. The main characteristics of these operations were that the vast majority were predominantly military in composition, were deployed along international frontiers between nations, operated under minimum use of force rules of engagement, and were deployed with the consent of both parties to the dispute following the successful negotiation of a truce, armistice, or cease-fire. Today these early peacekeeping

operations are often referred to as classic, traditional, or first generation peacekeeping. In the final analysis, the early missions were simply one of the many methods the international community devised to ensure that armed forces of the two superpowers, the United States and the Soviet Union, did not come into direct conflict on some remote battlefield, thus leading to potentially uncontrollable consequences.

The beginning of modern peacekeeping operations coincides with the end of the Cold War in the period of 1989–1990. With the end of superpower rivalry and the bipolar division of the globe, long-simmering ethnic and racial tensions were unleashed. Many nation-states that had been satellites of the USSR fell into severe economic decline and frequently into anarchy when their strategic importance evaporated. A new type of violent conflict came to characterize the international scene. These wars were intranational as opposed to international and involved several belligerent factions. Conflicts involved regular military forces, militias, insurgents, heavily armed organized criminals, "weekend warriors," brigand bands, thugs, local warlords, and petty criminals. Civilian elements of the population frequently became the target or the object of military operations conducted by one or more of the fighting forces. These were "savage wars of peace."

Intranational conflicts have numerous other very negative characteristics. Frequently, the conflict is associated with some natural disaster such as famine or drought which in turn precipitates huge numbers of refugees or internally displaced persons. As central governments weaken or collapse, the physical infrastructure of the country falls into disrepair. Roads deteriorate, bridges collapse, airfields and ports become inoperable. Movement into and within the country frequently becomes difficult and in some instances impossible.

In parallel with the collapse of the physical infrastructure, the social infrastructure of these countries often fails. Health systems and education systems are often the first to falter. There is also the marked tendency of a country's justice system to collapse. Established police forces are often coopted and militarized in an internal conflict and become identified with one faction or another. Judges and other members of the court system are frequently the first to be attacked. Prisons and jails often suffer a similar fate with guards vanishing and the incarceration/parole process breaking down. Gross overcrowding characterizes prisons where quasi-military forces lock up their prisoners in defiance of international humanitarian and human rights standards as some indeterminate status between prisoner of war and criminal rebel.

While the Charter of the United Nations specifically prohibits Member States from interfering in the internal affairs of other states, the vicious internal wars of the 1990s have been deemed to present a sufficient threat to international peace, security, and stability that the Security Council has frequently found grounds to authorize intervention under the provisions of Chapter VII. These modern peacekeeping missions are dramatically different from the majority of the earlier operations that preceded them during the Cold War period.

B. Definitions

The term "peacekeeping" does not appear anywhere in the UN Charter. The first major mission, the United Nations Emergency Force, was frequently referred to at the time as a "UN police force." The term "peacekeeping" came into general usage in the early 1960s following the publication of a report on UN military operations prepared by the World Court. Peacekeeping, in its original sense, was meant to signify truce, stability, observation, or interpositional operations conducted by lightly armed international military forces following the establishment of a cease-fire or truce and with the consent of both belligerents.

In the 1990s, a plethora of "peace" terms emerged. "Peacemaking" was the term applied by the international community to initiatives aimed at preventing violent conflict from breaking out in the first place by removing the root causes of conflict. (However, the term has been given other connotations: in *An Agenda for Peace,* former UN Secretary-General Boutros Boutros-Ghali defined peacemaking as: "action to bring hostile parties to agreement, essentially through such peaceful means as those foreseen in Chapter VI of the Charter of the United Nations.") When these measures failed and a situation deteriorated into violent conflict, "humanitarian operations" were frequently launched in an attempt to mitigate the severity of a conflict. The term "complex humanitarian emergency" (CHE) is used by many humanitarian organizations to describe situations involving major natural or human-made disaster coupled with violent conflict. "Peacekeeping" continues to be used in the traditional sense of interposition or observation with full consent of the belligerents. "Peace enforcement" is the term most frequently used to describe essentially military operations undertaken under Chapter VII of the UN Charter where consent of the warring factions is not complete, where a cease-fire may be tenuous at best, and where the international community is prepared to use force to restore peace

and stability. "Peace building" is the popular term used to describe actions taken by the international community to help rebuild a war-torn society.

Umbrella terms encompassing all of these activities include "peacekeeping," "peace support operations" (NATO), and "operations other than war" (USA). Japan and many other Asian nations tend to use the term "peacekeeping operations" (more frequently abbreviated as PKO). "Peace operations" is the term of choice in several academic publications. For the purposes of this analysis, "peacekeeping" is used as the umbrella term. Boutros-Ghali defined peacekeeping as "the deployment of a United Nations presence in the field, hitherto with the consent of all the parties concerned, normally involving United Nations military and/or police personnel and frequently civilians as well. Peacekeeping is a technique that expands the possibilities for both the prevention of conflict and the making of peace." The Pearson Peacekeeping Centre offers a broader definition of peacekeeping, reflective of its increasingly interdisciplinary nature: peacekeeping consists of "actions designed to enhance international peace, security, and stability which are authorized by competent national and international organizations and which are undertaken cooperatively and individually by military, humanitarian, good governance, civilian police and other interested agencies and groups."

C. Functions of Modern Peacekeeping

The functions of modern peacekeeping go far beyond traditional military stability, although stability remains one of the key elements of the equation. Generally speaking, there is almost always a requirement to separate physically the military forces of the belligerent parties. At the other end of the security spectrum, there is inevitably a need to help restore law and order in the land.

Internal violent conflicts lead to internally displaced persons as well as refugees in the surrounding nations. The international community has attempted to provide humanitarian support to noncombatants even while a bitter conflict was still raging. Providing such aid in an impartial manner has proven to be problematic in the extreme. Recent experience has shown also that immediately following a cease-fire or truce that ends an internal conflict, there is usually a continuing requirement for humanitarian assistance for some time, as a nation begins the rebuilding process.

Helping rebuild a war-torn society (peace building) is emerging as one of the major functions of the international community. The development function can be exercised in a preconflict situation in order to help remove some of the root causes of conflict and thus perhaps prevent violent conflict from breaking out in the first place. More commonly, however, the international community has not been able to effectively counter political opportunists exploiting latent communal animosities, and a discouraging number of states have turned to violence to resolve their disagreements. Military victory, mutual exhaustion, or international pressure eventually brings combatants to the negotiation table. At this point, the development function can be resumed. While development can be fostered on the shoulders of conflict, it is difficult in the extreme to conduct impartial and neutral development initiatives during the course of an on-going internal war.

Workable conclusions to violent internal conflict have proven to be difficult for belligerent parties to find by themselves. There are many reasons for this phenomenon. The savage nature of these wars tends to lead the parties to set extreme goals and objectives. Many leaders will not have had experience in the international arena and hence may be distrustful of the utility of many of the tools of modern diplomacy. External good offices are often useful in fulfilling the conflict resolution function of modern peacekeeping.

A sad characteristic of most typical internal wars is the flagrant abuse of human rights. A vital function of modern peacekeeping is the promotion and protection of human rights in a conflicted society. While human rights abuse is often thought of as a by-product of internal conflict, there is increasing evidence that it is more useful to think of human rights abuse and the cascade of retaliation–revenge–retaliation as among the fundamental causes of these wars.

The sequence of events that surrounds the end of an internal war is particularly critical if a hostile stalemate or a return to violent conflict is to be avoided. To this end, elections soon after a truce have an important role to play. While one election does not make a fully functioning liberal democracy, an election is an important symbolic event in the life of a nation moving toward/returning from anarchy. It signifies a broad attempt by the society as a whole to find nonviolent methods of resolving social conflicts. In that sense, the election support function merits the focused attention of the international peacekeeping community. Election support goes far beyond simple election monitoring and may be seen as encompassing assistance in drafting electoral laws and procedures, training election officials, managing election logistics, and the wide range of activities that are often taken for granted in societies where free and fair elections have long been the norm.

There is an information function closely linked to all stages of modern peacekeeping missions conducted as they are on the stage of instant global news coverage. The peacekeeping effort needs to be interpreted first to the various audiences that compose the host nation. Second, the information needs of the populations of the nations that are contributing people, materials, or money to the peacekeeping effort must be satisfied. Finally, the world as a whole needs to know what is being done and why. The interplay between and among the local, national, and international media and the management and public information staffs of all peacekeeping elements is a powerful and complex issue.

D. Peacekeeping Organizations

The United Nations is central to all modern peacekeeping missions. If the mission is not a UN mission per se, then at the very least, the operation would be taking place under the provisions of Chapter VIII of the Charter for regional or multilateral involvement. The principal organs of the United Nations involved in peacekeeping are the Security Council, the General Assembly, and the Secretariat (headed by the Secretary-General). Within the UN Secretariat, the Department of Political Affairs and the Department of Peace-keeping Operations are principally responsible for the planning, mounting, and support of UN-sponsored missions.

Since the UN has no standing army or standing police force, nor even a standing peacekeeping administrative organization, each peacekeeping mission must be crafted from start and may be considered to be ad hoc, even if some of them have been in existence for decades. These ad hoc missions were originally almost exclusively military in composition; modern missions incorporate civil police, civilian officials, and other components.

The main organs and bureaucratic departments of the UN do not appear as operating elements in an actual peacekeeping theater. Various agencies of the UN, however, are typically represented in virtually every peacekeeping theater. Included are the Special Representative of the Secretary-General, the High Commissioner for Human Rights, the United Nations Children's Fund, the World Health Organization, the World Food Program, the Food and Agricultural Organization, and the United Nations Department of Development.

In the early 1990s when modern peacekeeping missions began to be established, most of these agencies tended to operate independent of each other and of any large ad hoc mission on-site. By the mid 1990s, however, a much greater degree of integration had been established to the point where all UN elements of a peacekeeping mission operated under the coordination of a Special Representative of the Secretary General.

While the UN is usually the paramount international organization operating in a peacekeeping theatre, it is by no means always the only one. With increasing frequency, regional organizations will appear in-theatre, working either in conjunction with UN elements or in parallel with them. (There was an Organization of American States (OAS) presence in Haiti and there continues to be a NATO presence in the former Yugoslavia.)

The normal relations between nations do not necessarily stop when a peacekeeping mission is launched. Hence, it is not at all uncommon to discover that there are numerous bilateral (government-to-government) programs running in parallel with various United Nations and independent initiatives. These bilateral programs are most common during peace building operations but are not unknown during other phases of the peacekeeping spectrum. It is important to note that these bilateral activities are by no means limited to official development aid, but may encompass security initiatives involving troops, police, human rights initiatives, and election support: in short, any of the various peacekeeping functions previously listed. Most countries in the industrialized world have sections within their departments of foreign affairs that coordinate and fund such activities.

In addition to government organizations active in a peacekeeping theatre, there is usually a multiplicity of nongovernmental organizations (NGOs) also involved. There are several dozen NGOs active in the field of peacekeeping that are large, multidepartmental international organizations such as CARE, Oxfam, Save the Children, and Médecins sans frontières. Most NGOs, however, are much smaller and typically have only a few staff on mission. It is important to realize that NGOs are not exclusively concerned with humanitarian matters. There are NGOs in virtually every current peacekeeping theatre that specialize in human rights promotion, development, democratization, conflict resolution: almost all of the peacekeeping functions. While many NGOs operate in a strictly independent manner, many others link up with one of the UN agencies operating in-theatre on a contractual basis and provide specialized goods and services to a UN agency program as "implementing partners."

The Red Cross and Red Crescent Movement in its various guises is another major player in peacekeeping operations. Although the International Committee of the Red Cross (ICRC) could be considered a Swiss-based humanitarian NGO, the global recognition of the institution as the keeper of the Geneva Accords provides the Red Cross with unique status. The Red Cross is fiercely protective of its principles of independence and neutrality and almost always operates in a manner that is parallel to UN operations.

While this section has focused exclusively on the elements of the international community intervening in a peacekeeping situation, it must be recognized that the most important elements in any peacekeeping environment are those of the host nation. While the international community can support and assist a conflicted nation in its quest for peace, stability, and security, ultimately the will and the commitment to make peace a reality has to come from the nation itself. National military forces (in all their various configurations), government at all levels (federal, provincial, and municipal), tribal and clan structures, and civil society in general are all organizations that have a role, perhaps a key role, to play in peacekeeping.

E. Peacekeeping Disciplines

It should be evident that the multifunctional and multiorganizational dimensions of modern peacekeeping create an inordinately complex operational environment. In conceptualizing the relationships involved, the Pearson Peacekeeping Centre has identified a "New Peacekeeping Partnership": "the term applied to those organizations and individuals that work together to improve the effectiveness of modern peacekeeping operations. It includes the military; civil police; government and nongovernment agencies dealing with human rights and humanitarian assistance; diplomats; the media; and organizations sponsoring development and democratization programs."

It is important to note that many of the various peacekeeping disciplines routinely perform several ancillary functions in addition to their primary function. For example, military forces are primarily concerned with the establishment of security with respect to the military forces of the host country. Secondary military roles include support of civilian police in reestablishment of law and order; development tasks such as helping rebuild physical infrastructure; and humanitarian tasks in support of refugees, election support, and human rights protection. Virtually every partner has a role to play in the realm of election support. Most humanitarian organizations are also involved with human rights matters. Politicians and diplomats may lead in matters of conflict resolution, but equally useful parallel-track initiatives can be mounted by conflict resolution specialists and even by members of the other peacekeeping disciplines.

A complex environment involving multifunctional, multiorganizational, and multidisciplinary dimensions would appear to call for a massive effort to coordinate activities. In point of fact, the degree of coordination that has proven to be possible in modern peacekeeping is quite limited. Many individuals and organizations have repeatedly shown that preservation of their own perceived independence is more important than focused joint efforts with one group, by implication, taking primacy over the others. Perhaps the best that can be hoped for is a shared vision. The notion that peacekeeping can be conducted as a monolithic activity is as chimerical as the idea of a standing UN Army.

F. The Legal Framework of Peacekeeping

Traditional and modern peacekeeping have the common characteristic that they were, and are, conducted within a framework of international law. The various instruments that inform the legal framework of peacekeeping include the Charter of the United Nations, International Humanitarian Law, and International Human Rights Law. Chapter VI of the UN Charter provides nation states with the mechanisms for the peaceful resolution of disputes. Chapter VII was designed with the intent to permit the United Nations to bring the military resources of member states to bear against any rogue nation guilty of aggression. As the late Dag Hammarskjold once remarked when he was Secretary-General, peacekeeping fits into "Chapter Six-and-a-Half."

It is important to note that Article 2.7 of the Charter specifically forbids Member States from intervening in the internal affairs of other Member States. This creates a potential conundrum with respect to internal conflicts or intranational conflicts. Robust interpretations of the Charter have permitted the Security Council to resolve this seeming impasse by maintaining that some internal conflicts have presented such a threat to international peace and security as to warrant intervention or else that military intervention has been sanctioned on humanitarian grounds as opposed to security needs.

International Humanitarian Law has received greater emphasis in peacekeeping in recent years because of the vast number of civilians and other noncombatants affected by intranational conflicts. Refugees, internally displaced persons, and persons besieged in their own homes all require special consideration and protection as do the vulnerable populations of children, the

aged, and the handicapped. The Geneva, Hague, and New York Conventions form the basis of humanitarian law.

International Human Rights Law is also developing in conjunction with the spread of intranational conflicts. Both treaty law and conventional law have developed, making provisions for a wide range of human rights including such items as protection from cruel and inhuman punishment, standards for incarceration and for police behavior, and standards for an independent judiciary.

The issue of international response to war crimes and crimes against humanity committed in the course of these savage wars of peace remains problematic. In theory, it is the responsibility of the host nation to try its own citizens who are accused of these major crimes. In reality, political expediency or the need to effect a healing of the society leads to the award of impunity to some major criminals. *Ad hoc* war crimes commissions struck under the auspices of the United Nations have had very limited success. Support for an International Criminal Court is growing constantly stronger in the face of the inability of other legal mechanisms to deal with the problem.

Even such mundane matters as the rights and obligations of international forces operating in a second party host country are difficult when the arena of conflict is intra-national. Consent may be imperfect, and the central government authority may be weakened by a descent into anarchy. Status of Forces Agreements (SOFA) were the preferred method to outline the legal status of peacekeepers, but the negotiation of a SOFA is dependent upon the existence of an accepted and authoritative federal government with which to negotiate. It must be noted that concluding a SOFA is no guarantee that its provisions will be honored.

II. SELECTED CASE STUDIES

A. An Introduction to Traditional Peacekeeping Missions

In the aftermath of the Second World War and the establishment of the United Nations, peacekeeping emerged as a response to violent conflicts in an international situation (i.e. the Cold War) which precluded the forms of collective action which had been foreseen in the UN Charter. In the period between 1945 and 1991, a pattern of peacekeeping evolved which has come to be termed "traditional" (or "classical") peacekeeping. Peacekeeping operations in the Cold War period can essentially be divided into two types: interpositional peacekeeping missions and observer missions.

Both interpositional and observer missions rely on the central tenets of consent, impartiality, and minimal use of force. As a general rule, traditional peacekeeping operations followed the conclusion of a political agreement (usually a cease-fire), and the peacekeeping force was there, at the request of the countries involved, to oversee the observance of this agreement. Those conflicts which have produced this type of response have been predominantly inter-state, involving national, regular armies, a clear area of separation (a buffer zone), and an underlying political agreement that underpins the peacekeeping force. An observer force differs from an interpositional force in that its role involves monitoring rather than implementing a settlement or agreement.

Operations that fall into this category of interpositional missions include the United Nations Emergency Force (UNEF) on the Sinai peninsula, the United Nations Force in Cyprus (UNFICYP), the second United Nations Emergency Force (UNEF II), the United Nations Disengagement Observer Force (UNDOF) on the Golan Heights, and the United Nations Interim Force in Lebanon (UNIFIL). Observer missions include the United Nations Truce Supervision Organization (UN-TSO) which has operated in various locations in the Middle East; the United Nations Military Observer Group in India and Pakistan (UNMOGIP) on the India–Pakistan border; the United Nations Observer Group in Lebanon (UNOGIL); and the United Nations Yemen Observer Mission (UNYOM) on the border between Yemen and Saudi Arabia. In addition to UN-sponsored missions, observer missions (and indeed peacekeeping missions generally) have been mounted by other authorities. An important example is the Multinational Force and Observers (MFO) on the Sinai peninsula.

B. An Interpositional Peacekeeping Mission: UNEF

The establishment of a United Nations Emergency Force was designed to respond to the Suez Crisis of 1956. It was the first peacekeeping operation and without contemporary precedent.

The Suez Canal was nationalized by Egypt on 26 July 1956, the culmination of a period of rising tension and tit-for-tat diplomacy between Egypt and the Western colonial powers resulting largely from Cold War tensions. This nationalization of the canal threatened Western (British, French and American) profits, oil,

colonial trade and pride. In retaliation Britain, France and Israel agreed in secret to a joint attack on Egypt. Accordingly, Israel launched a full scale military attack on Egypt on 29 October 1956. Britain and France issued an ultimatum (prearranged with Israel) to the Israeli and Egyptian governments to cease fighting within 12 hours and to withdraw their forces 10 miles from the Suez canal. When the deadline expired without any cease-fire, the British and French sent troops into Egypt on the pretext of maintaining peace around the canal. The actions of the British, French, and Israelis were condemned by the UN and by world opinion, but the rivalry of the superpowers in the Security Council complicated the adoption of a firm UN resolution. On 4 November 1956, at the urging of Canada's Lester B. Pearson, the General Assembly adopted resolutions which called for the creation of an emergency force to supervise the cessation of hostilities, and an immediate cease-fire. On 5 November 1956 the General Assembly adopted resolution 1000 (ES-I) which provided for the establishment of a United Nations International Emergency Force.

The function of UNEF I was to secure and supervise the cessation of hostilities, including the withdrawal of the armed forces of France, Israel, and the United Kingdom from Egyptian territory. Once these forces had been withdrawn, the peacekeeping force was to serve as a buffer between the Egyptian and Israeli forces. A group of UNTSO military observers under Canadian General E.L.M. (Tommy) Burns was temporarily diverted from normal duties in Jerusalem and arrived in Cairo on 12 November 1956. The first units of UNEF arrived in Egypt on 15-16 November. By February 1957 UNEF was at its target strength of approximately 6000 and remained at this level until the end of 1957. From 1958 forward, numbers were gradually reduced. Military contingents were drawn from 10 countries representing a wide geographical range, with other countries providing support.

General Burns, the Force Commander, was appointed by the UN General Assembly on the recommendation of the Secretary-General. The Force Commander, responsible to the Secretary-General, was operationally responsible for all of the troops assigned to the United Nations force, and for the performance of all functions and the provision of all facilities. In carrying out this task he was required to take into account the necessity that impartiality be observed in the composition of the force as well as in its deployment. National contingents came under the operational control of the United Nations throughout the period of their deployment with UNEF. However, they remained part of their national armed forces and continued to wear their national uniforms and insignia. The blue beret and helmet—later the symbol of UN peacekeeping—came into existence during the early days of UNEF.

In May 1967 the Egyptian government requested the withdrawal of all United Nations troops from its territory. As host country consent is a fundamental principle of UN peacekeeping, UNEF was forced to withdraw once this consent had been removed. Efforts to persuade Israel to permit the stationing of UNEF troops on the Israeli side of the demarcation line were unsuccessful. The withdrawal of Egyptian consent had been part of a process of escalating tension in the Middle East over several years. Following the withdrawal of UNEF forces Egyptian President Gamal Abdel Nasser announced the closure of the Strait of Tiran: an action that Israel had previously indicated it would consider *casus belli* (a justification for resorting to war). On 5 June 1967 war broke out between Israel and Egypt. At this time UNEF troops were still in the process of withdrawing from the area and some were caught up in the fighting. Fifteen UN troops were killed. By 17 June all UN personnel had left.

That peace was preserved between Egypt and Israel for 10 years is a testament to the success of the UNEF operation. However, in some respects UNEF's success was also its downfall: support from the contributing nations and force strength had been considerably reduced by the mid 1960s, meaning that the symbolic value of the interpositionary force was diminished and making it easier for Nasser to demand its withdrawal. The crisis of 1967 and the withdrawal of UN troops demonstrates very clearly the limitations of UN peacekeeping operations in this traditional manifestation. The deployment of a force is dependent on consent. Consent is itself predicated on a number of other things, including the international political situation and the perceived impartiality of the peacekeeping force, which is an embodiment of the international political community. Many contend that when consent is withdrawn the force must leave if its moral authority, and the moral authority of the UN organization, is to be preserved. A great many others, however, are of the opinion that the UN must not be dictated to by a single national government.

C. An Observer Mission: UNMOGIP

Following the independence of India and Pakistan in 1947, a dispute arose regarding the accession of Kash-mir. In late 1947 fighting broke out between Indian and Pakistani forces. Security Council resolution 39(1948) of January, 1948 established the United Nations Commission for India and Pakistan (UNCIP) to investigate the situation between the two states and attempt mediation. Resolution 47(1948) of April, 1948 enlarged the membership of UNCIP and made suggestions as to how the fighting over the issue of Kashmir could be stopped. Among the Security Council's recommendations was the use of observers stationed between the forces to supervise any agreement that could be reached. Following the signing of the Karachi Agreement in July, 1949 a cease-fire line was established. In early 1951, UNCIP was collapsed and was replaced by the United Nations Military Observer Group in India and Pakistan (UNMOGIP)—established by Security Council resolution 91(1951) on March 30, 1951.

UNMOGIP was established on the cease-fire line between India and Pakistan in the states of Jammu and Kashmir. Its purpose was to monitor the observance of the cease-fire that had been agreed between the parties, to make reports to the Secretary-General, and to investigate complaints by either party of violations of the agreed border. Following the renewed hostilities of 1971, the cease-fire and boundary line were renegotiated and UNMOGIP's mandate renewed. However, since this time UNMOGIP has operated without India's support, although also without active opposition. India maintains that UNMOGIP's mandate expired following the changes to the cease-fire line which took place in 1971/72, as UNMOGIP was set up to monitor the observation of the Karachi Agreement of 1949 which was no longer in existence. Pakistan disagreed with this position and supported the continuation of UNMOGIP's mandate.

As a result of this disagreement, the Secretary-General has ruled that UNMOGIP will remain in place unless terminated by a Security Council decision. Meanwhile, its task remains to monitor the observance of the cease-fire line of December 1971, to report to the Secretary-General, and to investigate any complaints of cease-fire violations. Since 1972 India has not made any complaints, although Pakistan continues to make periodic representations to UNMOGIP. The activities of UNMOGIP on the Indian side of the separation line are restricted. Currently the strength of UNMOGIP stands at 44 military observers drawn from eight countries.

As with UNEF the case of UNMOGIP illustrates the importance of host country consent. UNMOGIP has not had to withdraw but its activities and authority are compromised by India's withdrawal of support.

TABLE I

UN Peacekeeping Missions: Part I (Cold War Period)

Number	Name	Location	Duration	Type[a]
1	United Nations Truce Supervision Organization (UNTSO)	Middle East	June 1948 to date	T/O
2	United Nations Military Observer Group in India and Pakistan, State of Jammu and Kashmir (UNMOGIP)	Jammu and Kashmir (India and Pakistan)	Jan. 1949 to date	T/O
3	United Nations Emergency Force (UNEF I)	Sinai Peninsula	Nov. 1956–June 1967	T/PI
4	United Nations Observation Group in Lebanon (UNOGIL)	Lebanon	June 1958–Dec. 1958	T/O
5	United Nations Operation in the Congo (ONUC)	Congo	July 1960–June 1964	T/IP
6	United Nations Security Force in West New Guinea (West Irian) (UNSF)	West Irian	Oct. 1962–Apr. 1963	T/O
7	United Nations Yemen Observation Mission (UNYOM)	Border between Yemen and Saudi Arabia	July 1963–Sep. 1964	T/O
8	United Nations Peace-Keeping Force in Cyprus (UNFICYR)	Cyprus	Mar. 1964 to date	T/IP
9	Mission of the Representative of the Secretary-General in the Dominican Republic (DOMREP)	Dominican Republic	May 1965–Oct. 1966	T/O
10	United Nations India–Pakistan Observation Mission (UNIPOM)	India and Pakistan	Sep. 1965–Mar. 1966	T/O
11	United Nations Emergency Force II (UNEF II)	Sinai Peninsula	Oct. 1973–July 1979	T/IP
12	United Nations Disengagement Observer Force (UNDOF)	Golan Heights	June 1974 to date	T/IP/O
13	United Nations Interim Force in Lebanon (UNIFIL)	Southern Lebanon	Mar. 1978 to date	T/IP

[a] Abbreviations: T, traditional peacekeeping; IP, interpositional mission, O, observer mission; M, multifunctional peacekeeping; I, in response to insurgency; C, in response to comprehensive humanitarian emergency; N, in response to national disintegration; X, others.

D. Modern Multifunctional Peacekeeping

1. Introduction

In contrast to traditional peacekeeping, situations which have involved peacekeeping forces in the post-Cold War period have changed, tending now to involve factions rather than regular armed forces. The nature of the war zone involved has itself also changed, from largely unpopulated locations to urban areas. In addition, the operational environment into which peacekeeping forces are sent is dynamic rather than stable, often due to the absence of a political agreement prior to the deployment of the force. The peacekeeping response to these complex emergencies involves not only military contingents, but also UN agencies, NGOs and humanitarian aid bodies, election supervisory bodies, political negotiators, and the media. In this type of situation, difficulties arise in the application of the essential principles of traditional peacekeeping: consent, impartiality, and minimal use of force.

It is possible to subdivide peacekeeping operations in the post-Cold War period into a number of categories based on the origins of the crisis that demanded an international peacekeeping response. Four such categories are examined and illustrated: complex humanitarian emergencies; national disintegration, insurgency, and other types of crisis situations (Tables III, IV, and V).

2. A Complex Humanitarian Emergency: Somalia

The first category of post-Cold War peacekeeping operations may be captured under the heading of Complex Humanitarian Emergencies. These situations would typically stem from a combination of human-made problems (governmental instability, war, or law-and-order difficulties) and natural crises such as famine. The result is a situation that has more than one cause and to which the solution is multifaceted, requiring cooperation between military forces, civilian agencies, and NGOs. The primary focus of such operations is likely to be humanitarian, although in a complex emergency situation the provision of humanitarian aid is

TABLE II

UN Peacekeeping Missions: Part II (Between 1988–1993)

Number	Name	Location	Duration	Type[a]
14	United Nations Good Offices Mission in Afghanistan and Pakistan (UNGOMAP)	Afghanistan and Pakistan	Apr. 1988–Mar. 1990	T/O
15	United Nations Iran-Iraq Military Observer Group (UNIIMOG)	Border between Iran and Ira	Aug. 1988–Feb. 1991	T/O
16	United Nations Angola Verification Mission I (UNAVEM I)	Angola	Jan. 1989–June 1991	T/O
17	United Nations Transition Assistance Group in Namibia (UNTAG)	Namibia	Apr. 1989–Mar. 1990	M/N
18	United Nations Observer Group in Central America (ONUCA)	Costa Rica, El Salvador, Guatemala, Honduras and Nicaragua	Nov. 1989–Jan. 1992	M/I
19	United Nations Iraq-Kuwait Observation Mission (UNIKOM)	Border between Iraq and Kuwait	Apr. 1991 to date	T/O
20	United Nations Angola Verification Mission II (UNAVEM II)	Angola	June 1991–Feb. 1995	M/I
21	United Nations Observer Mission in El Salvador (ONUSAL)	El Salvador	July 1991–Apr. 1995	M/I
22	United Nations Mission for the Referendum in Western Sahara (MINURSO)	Western Sahara	Sep. 1991 to date	M/N
23	United Nations Advance Mission in Cambodia (UNAMIC)	Cambodia	Oct. 1992–Mar. 1992	M/I
24	United Nations Protection Force (UNPROFOR)	Former Yugoslavia	Mar. 1992–Dec. 1995	M/N
25	United Nations Transitional Authority in Cambodia (UNTAC)	Cambodia	Mar. 1992–Sep. 1993	M/I
26	United Nations Operation in Somalia (UNOSOM)	Somalia	Apr. 1992–May 1993	M/C
27	United Nations Operation in Mozambique (ONUMOZ)	Mozambique	Dec. 1992–Dec. 1994	M/C
28	United Nations Operation in Somalia II (UNOSOM II)	Somalia	May 1993–Mar. 1995	M/C
29	United Nations Observer Mission Uganda/Rwanda (UNOMUR)	Border between Uganda and Rwanda	June 1993–Sep. 1994	M/I
30	United Nations Observer Mission in Georgia (UNOMIG)	Georgia and Abkhazia	Aug. 1993 to date	M/N
31	United Nations Observer Mission in Liberia (UNOMIL)	Liberia	Sep. 1993 to date	M/C
32	United Nations Mission in Haiti (UNMIH)	Haiti	Sep. 1993–June 1996	M/X
33	United Nations Assistance Mission for Rwanda (UNAMIR)	Rwanda	Oct. 1993–Mar. 1996	M/X

[a] Abbreviations: T, traditional peacekeeping; IP, interpositional mission, O, observer mission; M, multifunctional peacekeeping; I, in response to insurgency; C, in response to comprehensive humanitarian emergency; N, in response to national disintegration; X, others.

likely to require the presence of a military force to create a stable environment.

The crisis in Somalia was a combination of political and social instability and natural disaster. Following the deposition of President Siad Barre in early 1991, the country became increasingly anarchic. A split occurred between General Mohamed Farah Aidid—credited with leading the coup that deposed Barre—and Ali Mahdi Mohamed, who had been appointed by the United Somali Congress (of which Aidid was also a member) as interim President. In the autumn of 1991, fighting took place both between the supporters of Aidid and Mahdi and between the Hawiye clan (of which both Aidid and Madhi were members) and the Darod clan (of which ex-President Barre was a member). As a consequence of the breakdown of government, law, and order and in combination with a period of serious drought, 1991–1992 was a time of considerable social distress in Somalia. Figures suggest that by 1992 approximately 4.5 million Somalis, approximately half of the total population, were facing starvation and disease. In addition to this natural disaster, interclan fighting continued,

TABLE III

UN Peacekeeping Missions: Part III (Since 1994)

Number	Name	Location	Duration	Type[a]
34	United Nations Aouzou Strip Observer Group (UNASOG)	Aouzou Strip	May 1994–June 1994	T/O
35	United Nations Mission of Observers in Tajikistan (UNMOT)	Tajikistan	Dec. 1994 to date	M/I
36	United Nations Angola Verification Mission III (UNA-VEM III)	Angola	Feb. 1995–June 1997	M/C
37	United Nations Confidence Restoration Operation in Croatia (UNCRO)	Croatia	Mar. 1995–Jan. 1996	M/N
38	United Nations Preventive Deployment Force (UN-PREDEP)	Former Yugoslav Republic of Macedonia	Mar. 1995 to date	M/N
39	United Nations Mission in Bosnia and Herzegovina (UNMIBH)	Bosnia and Herzegovina	Dec. 1995 to date	M/N
40	United Nations Transitional Administration for Eastern Slavonia, Baranja and Western Sirmium (UNTAES)	Eastern Slavonia	Jan. 1996 to date	M/N
41	Unitied Nations Mission of Observers in Previaka (UNMOP)	Previaka Peninsula (Croatia)	Jan. 1996 to date	M/N
42	United Nations Support Mission in Haiti (UNSMIH)	Haiti	June 1996–July 97	M/X
43	United Nations Verification Mission in Guatemala (MI-NUGUA)	Guatemala	Feb. 1997–May 1997	M/I
44	United Nations Observer Mission in Angola (MONUA)	Angola	July 1997 to date	M/C
45	United Nations Transition Mission in Haiti (UNTMIH)	Haiti	Aug. 1997–Nov. 1997	M/X

[a] Abbreviations: T, traditional peacekeeping; IP, interpositional mission, O, observer mission; M, multifunctional peacekeeping; I, in response to insurgency; C, in response to comprehensive humanitarian emergency; N, in response to national disintegration; X, others.

TABLE IV

Other Related Missions: By OSCE and NATO

Number	Name	Location	Duration	Sponsor	Type[a]
1	Spillover Mission to Skopje (OSCE)	Former Yugoslav Rep. of Macedonia	Sep. 1992 to date	OSCE	M/N
2	Mission to Georgia (OSCE)	Georgia (South Ossetia; Abkhazia)	Dec. 1992 to date	OSCE	M/N
3	Mission to Estonia (OSCE)	Estonia	Feb. 1993 to date	OSCE	M/N
4	Mission to Moldova (OSCE)	Moldova	Apr. 1993 to date	OSCE	M/N
5	Mission to Latvia (OSCE)	Latvia	Nov. 1993 to date	OSCE	M/N
6	Mission to Tajikisatan (OSCE)	Tajikistan	Feb. 1994 to date	OSCE	M/N
7	Mission in Sarajevo	Bosnia and Herzegovina	Oct. 1994 to date	OSCE	M/N
8	Mission to Ukraine (OSCE)	Ukraine	Nov. 1994 to date	OSCE	M/N
9	Assistance Group to Chechnya (OSCE)	Chechnya	Apr. 1995 to date	OSCE	M/N
10	Mission to Bosnia and Herzegovina (OSCE)	Bosnia and Herzegovina	Dec. 1995 to date	OSCE	M/N
11	Implementation Force (IFOR)	Bosnia and Herzegovina	Dec. 1995 to date	NATO	M/N
12	Mission to Croatia (OSCE)	Croatia	Jul. 1996 to date	OSCE	M/N
13	Stabilization Force (SFOR)	Bosnia and Herzegovina	Dec. 1996 to date	NATO	M/N

[a] Abbreviations: T, traditional peacekeeping; IP, interpositional mission, O, observer mission; M, multifunctional peacekeeping; I, in response to insurgency; C, in response to comprehensive humanitarian emergency; N, in response to national disintegration; X, others.

TABLE V

Other Related Missions: By Miscellaneous Groups

Number	Name	Location	Duration	Sponsor	Type[a]
1	Neutral Nations Supervisory Commission (NNSC)	N. Korea/S. Korea	Jul. 1953 to date	Multinational	T/O
2	Multinational Force and Observers in the Sinai (MFO)	Egypt (Sinai)	Apr. 1982 to date	Multinational	T/IP
3	ECOWAS Monitoring Group (ECOMOG)	Liberia	Aug. 1990 to date	ECOWAS	T/IP
4	European Community Monitoring Mission (ECMM)	Former Yugoslavia	Jul. 1991 to date	EU	T/O
5	Moldova Joint Force	Moldova (Trans-Dniester)	Jul. 1992 to date	CIS	T/IP
6	South Ossetia Joint Force	Georgia (S. Ossetia)	Jul. 1992 to date	CIS	T/IP
7	International Civilian Mission to Haiti (MICIVIH)	Haiti	Feb. 1993 to date	UN/OAS	M/X
8	International Commission for Support and Verification (CIAV/OAS)	Nicaragua	May 1993 to date	OAS	M/I
9	Tajikistan Buffer Force (CIS)	Tasjikistan (Afghan border)	Aug. 1993 to date	CIS	T/IP
10	OAU Mission in Burundi (OMIB)	Burundi	Dec. 1993 to date	OAU	M/I
11	UN Special Mission to Afghanistan (UNSMA)	Afghanistan/Pakistan	Mar. 1994 to date	Multinational	M/I
12	CIS Peacekeeping Forces in Georgia	Georgian-Abkhazian border	June 1994 to date	CIS	T/I
13	Western European Union Police Force (WEUPF)	Bosnia and Herzegovina (Mostar)	July 1994 to date	WEU	M/N
14	Mission of Military Observers Ecuador/Peru (MOMEP)	Ecuador/Peru	Mar. 1995 to date	Multinational	T/O
15	Office of the Secretary-General in Afghanistan (OSGA)	Afghanistan/Pakistan	May 1995 to date	UN	M/I
16	Mission of the UN in El Salvador (MINUSAL)	El Salvador	May 1995 to date	UN	M/I
17	UN Office of Verification (ONUV)	El Salvador	May 1995 to date	UN	M/I

[a] Abbreviations: T, traditional peacekeeping; IP, interpositional mission, O, observer mission; M, multifunctional peacekeeping; I, in response to insurgency; C, in response to comprehensive humanitarian emergency; N, in response to national disintegration; X, others.

causing damage to infrastructure and creating large numbers of displaced persons.

Faced with this combination of famine and civil war, the UN Security Council began to take steps to address the situation in the spring of 1992. The United Nations Operation in Somalia (UNOSOM) was established by Security Council resolution 751 (1992) on 24 April 1992. Its original purpose was to enable the continued delivery and distribution of humanitarian aid to the Somali population. The mandate called for 50 unarmed, uniformed UN military observers to be deployed after consultation with the belligerent factions in Mogadishu. Two months later, agreement was reached with both principal factions and the military observers were deployed. In July 1992, in response to the continued crisis

in Somalia, UNOSOM was increased in strength. Resolution 767 (1992) of 27 July 1992 set out plans for the establishment of four operational zones: Mogadishu, Berbera, Bossasso, and Kismayo. It was proposed that each area should have a unit of 750 military personnel. Resolution 775 (1992) of 28 August authorized the increase of UN security personnel to a level of 3500. A further increase, bringing the force level to 4219 troops and 50 observers, was authorized on 8 September 1992. The first troops arrived in Mogadishu on 14 September.

The primary purpose of UNOSOM was the facilitation of humanitarian aid in Somalia. To this end a 100-Day Action Program for Accelerated Humanitarian Assistance was formulated. The program aimed both to organize food aid distribution and other emergency aid measures, and to implement more long term measures such as institution building, the provision of farming materials, and medical and immunization programs.

Throughout the autumn of 1992, UNOSOM continued to face difficulties in the application of its mandate due to continued fighting throughout Somalia, and in particular the targeting of aid convoys and ships. In October, General Aidid ordered the expulsion of the Pakistani battalion from Somalia and in early November the battalion, stationed at Mogadishu airport, was engaged in a firefight with Aidid's forces. This increasingly hostile environment precluded the carrying out of the humanitarian operation. Accordingly, in early December, 1992 the UN Security Council made provisions for a Unified Task Force to create a secure environment (Resolution 794 (1992), December 3, 1992). On December 4, U.S. President George Bush responded to the UN's request for assistance by the initiation of "Operation Restore Hope": a U.S.-led operation, the first elements of which arrived in Mogadishu on December 9, 1992.

UNOSOM II was established in March, 1993 to take over from UNITAF (Security Council Resolution 814(1993)). The UNOSOM II was intended, as was UNITAF, to establish a secure environment for humanitarian assistance, using enforcement measures if necessary. In addition, UNOSOM II was tasked to initiate moves toward the restoration of law and order and political and social reconciliation. Within this mandate were included such tasks as mine clearance, low-level disarmament, and the repatriation of refugees. The function of UNOSOM II was therefore intended to be much wider than that of a traditional peacekeeping operation and also much wider than that of the operations which had preceded it in Somalia. UNOSOM II was not a purely military operation but also encompassed humanitarian aid agencies, the international media, NGOs, and diplomatic and political negotiators.

Violent incidents and attacks on UN troops continued throughout the UNOSOM II operation. In June, 1993, 25 members of the Pakistani battalion were killed with 10 reported missing and 54 wounded in attacks in Mogadishu. Aidid's forces were blamed for the attacks and attempts were made to apprehend him. On October 3, 1993, one such attempt by United States Rangers and the U.S. Quick Reaction Force, who were deployed in Mogadishu in support of UNOSOM II but were not under UN command, resulted in the deaths of 18 U.S. soldiers with 75 wounded. The scenes of the bodies of the dead U.S. soldiers being dragged through the streets of Mogadishu displayed on international television contributed overwhelmingly to the withdrawal of U.S.

forces from Somalia by March, 1994. In October, 1994, the Secretary-General concluded that UNOSOM II's goal of facilitating the process of political reconstruction and reconciliation was increasingly "elusive," while the cost of maintaining the operation was becoming increasingly difficult to justify. It was suggested that the UN could not offer further help in the process of national reconstruction, which must emanate from the Somalis themselves.

UNOSOM II continued to operate in Somalia until March, 1995, although its mandate was scaled down after the autumn of 1993 and force levels were gradually reduced. In November, 1994, the force level was at 15,000 troops. By February, 1995, troop strength had been reduced to 7956. Withdrawal was complete by March 28, 1995.

3. National Disintegration: The Former Republic of Yugoslavia

a. Introduction

A second category of situations requiring a peacekeeping response involves crises resulting from the disintegration of states. The collapse of state authority and control has two consequences: first, the infrastructure, communications, transportation, and system of distribution of goods and services breaks down; second, such disintegration is likely to be accompanied by violence due to the loss of control over the armed forces and to communal tensions among the population. While the primary focus of the peacekeeping operation may be the provision of humanitarian aid, a military enforcement operation is likely to be necessary in order that aid can be provided. In addition, communal violence brings other tasks for peacekeeping forces: the negotiation and implementation of a peace agreement, population movement and displaced persons, disarmament, and the reconstruction of state institutions.

b. UNPROFOR

In June, 1991 Croatia and Slovenia declared their independence from the Republic of Yugoslavia. Fighting broke out because Serbs living in Croatia opposed Croatian independence and were militarily supported by the Yugoslav People's Army. Diplomatic efforts to resolve the crisis failed and the UN first became involved in September, 1991. Security Council Resolution 713(1991) (September 25, 1991) called for an arms embargo on Yugoslavia and in early October Cyrus Vance of the U.S. was appointed Personal Envoy of the Secretary-General for Yugoslavia. At this time, talks began concerning the possibility of a UN peacekeeping force being deployed if the consent of all parties could be obtained. In February, 1992, the Secretary-General recommended to the Security Council that a United Nations Protection Force (UNPROFOR) be established in Yugoslavia. The UNPROFOR was approved by Security Council Resolution 743(1992) of February 21, 1992, and established for an initial period of 12 months.

UNPROFOR was established initially in Croatia. Its mandate involved creating a secure environment within which negotiations toward the settlement of the Yugoslav crisis could take place, ensuring the demilitarization and security of the three "United Nations Protected Areas" (UNPAs) and to monitor the situation with regard to the movement of the population and levels of tension in the other areas of Croatia (the "pink zones"). In June, 1992 the conflict spread to Bosnia and Herzegovina. As a result, both the mandate and force strength of UNPROFOR were expanded with the aim of providing protection to the airport at Sarajevo and delivering humanitarian assistance in Sarajevo and the surrounding area. In September, 1992, the mandate was again expanded to include work with the UN High Commissioner for Refugees to provide (and protect) humanitarian relief throughout Bosnia and Herzegovina. UNPROFOR also monitored the "safe areas" established by the UN in five Bosnian towns and Sarajevo itself and monitored the "no-fly" zone. Subsequently, UNPROFOR also monitored the cease-fire agreement between the Bosnian government and Bosnian Croat forces, signed in February, 1994. From January, 1995 UNPROFOR also monitored the cease-fire agreement between the Bosnian government and Bosnian Serb forces. In Macedonia, where UNPROFOR had been deployed since December, 1992, UN forces were tasked to monitor and report any developments in the border regions.

c. IFOR

The NATO-led Implementation Force (IFOR) was deployed following the conclusion of the General Framework Agreement for Peace in Bosnia and Herzegovina in December 1995 (The Dayton Agreement). Its primary mission was to implement the military provisions of the agreement, in addition to giving continued military support to the civilian and humanitarian aspects of the operation. NATO had previously been involved in a variety of roles militarily supporting UNPROFOR—for example giving close air support in protection of the safe areas, undertaking Operation Deny Flight from April 1993, and preparing for air strikes.

In December 1995, following the signing of the peace agreement, IFOR commenced Operation Joint Endeavour. The tasks given to IFOR were to ensure that the cease-fire agreement was being followed and to monitor the withdrawal of belligerent forces from the cease-fire zone. IFOR was to supervise the demilitarization operation and arrange the collection of heavy weaponry into cantonment sites. IFOR was also to assume control of the airspace over Bosnia–Herzegovina. All 16 NATO nations contributed to IFOR. In addition, 18 non-NATO countries participated—largely members of the Partnership for Peace agreement. In January 1996 Russia also joined the IFOR operation—a historic cooperation which significantly increased the moral authority of Operation Joint Endeavour.

In addition to the military tasks, IFOR was important in the implementation of the civilian aspects of the peace agreement. For this purpose, cooperation was necessary with a variety of organizations including the UN High Commissioner for Refugees (UNHCR), the Office of the High Representative (OHR), the Organization for Security and Cooperation in Europe (OSCE), and the International Committee of the Red Cross (ICRC). Civilian tasks involved emergency medical treatment, provision of food and shelter for refugees and displaced persons, logistical support for aid convoys and humanitarian organizations working in the field, and support in the organization and monitoring of elections which took place in September 1996. In addition, IFOR undertook a program of redevelopment and repair including engineering work, rebuilding of bridges and roads, restoring gas, electricity and water supplies, rebuilding schools and hospitals and mine clearance. Included in the IFOR operation was a team of specialists in areas such as education, transportation, agriculture, economics, and government. This tactical- and operational-level civil/military team (CIMIC) provided advice and technical expertise to the variety of organizations working within the peacekeeping operation.

d. SFOR

Following the elections of September, 1996 the Stabilization Force (SFOR) took over from IFOR in Bosnia. This operation was also NATO-led and was formally established in December, 1996 with a mandate extending until June, 1998. The role of SFOR is similar to IFOR—to implement the military aspects of the Dayton agreement and contribute to the maintenance of a secure environment. SFOR is, however, much smaller than IFOR in terms of force size, aiming at stabilization rather than implementation. As with IFOR, all NATO nations contribute to SFOR in addition to the Partnership for Peace countries which had participated in

IFOR. Russia also continues to contribute under special arrangements. The force strength is set at 31,000 troops, around half the number present under IFOR.

In terms of involvement in civilian operations, SFOR provides support and assistance to a variety of organizations and efforts involved in reconstruction, rehabilitation, and aid (as did IFOR). SFOR was also tasked with ensuring a secure environment for the municipal elections in September, 1997 in close cooperation with OSCE. Efforts to ensure the returning of refugees also require SFOR's support, as do continuing efforts to implement the War Crimes clauses of the Dayton agreement. The implementation of the Brcko Arbitration Agreement of February 15, 1997 is also supported by SFOR. The CIMIC structure remains essentially unchanged.

4. Insurgency: Cambodia

The third category concerns situations in which the cause of the crisis is insurgency. In this situation the government may have lost control of areas of the country, rebel action may be preventing distribution of food to all areas of the country, or a breakdown in law and order may have taken place. In such situations the restoration of legitimate authority and maintenance of a stable and secure environment will be the primary aims of the peacekeeping force. Examples of such situations include the crisis in Angola, the United Nations operation in Cambodia (UNAMIC and UNTAC), and the peacekeeping operation in Mozambique, in addition to the observer missions that have taken place in South America (for example ONUCA in Costa Rica, El Salvador, Guatemala, Honduras, and Nicaragua).

Following more than 10 years of negotiations involving the United Nations, an agreement for the Comprehensive Political Settlement of the Cambodia Conflict was signed in Paris in October 1991. This agreement provided for the establishment of a United Nations Transitional Authority in Cambodia (UNTAC) and was confirmed by UN Security Council Resolution 718(1991) of October 31, 1991.

UNTAC was established with the aim of supervising the implementation of the Paris agreement. The agreement named the Supreme National Council of Cambodia (SNC) as the legitimate authority in the transitional period and the United Nations operation was designed to support the SNC. The UNTAC consisted of seven components: a military component consisting of force contingents and military observers; a civilian police component; a civil administration component; a human rights component; an electoral component; a repatriation component supported by the UN High

Commissioner for refugees; and a rehabilitation component, supported by the UN development program and other UN agencies.

In March, 1992, UNTAC took over from UNAMIC, which had been established immediately after the signing of the Paris agreement in October, 1991. Force strength was set at up to 15,547 troops, 893 military observers, and 3,500 civilian police. Provision was also made for up to 1,149 international civilian staff, 465 UN volunteers, and 4,830 local staff. During the period of the Cambodian elections, 50,000 Cambodians served as electoral staff.

The UNTAC operation contained a number of elements, both civilian and military. In terms of electoral activities, UNTAC commenced a program of civic information and education aimed at spreading information about the importance of democratic elections and building up confidence in the procedure. In particular, UN volunteers served as district supervisors and undertook the task of training Cambodian staff to be election monitors. In the area of human rights the task of UNTAC was to aid the creation of a social, political, and military climate in which human rights were safeguarded. In particular, the UNTAC human rights component was tasked to encourage the SNC to adhere to existing human rights legislation and to review institutional arrangements in the light of international human rights provisions. UNTAC also conducted a widespread public education campaign on the issue of human rights and investigated complaints of human rights abuses where possible. The aim of the military component of UNTAC was to ensure stability and to contribute to confidence-building measures. In this respect the military component was a necessary prerequisite for the other components. Tasks taken over by the UN military force included the supervision of the cease-fire, weapons control, essential engineering, logistics and communications projects, and clearance of land mines. The military component also continued to support all other components of UNTAC—for example accompanying election monitors in contested areas and aiding the repatriation process. The civilian element of UNTAC took over control of key areas of administration (foreign affairs, national defense, public security, finance and information): all administrative structures thought to be important in the electoral process. Under this umbrella, UNTAC took responsibility for the training of judges and police officers, undertook prison visits, set up road safety groups, and undertook measures designed to stabilize the economy. The UNTAC civilian police were involved in supervision and control of local police activities. UNTAC also coordinated an interagency effort to repatriate 365,000 Cambodian refugees and displaced persons from camps on the border with Thailand. In addition to assistance in returning to their communes, returnees received development assistance in the form either of agricultural land, housing plots, or a cash grant.

In September, 1993 UNTAC's mandate ended. In November, 1993, the UN Security Council considered that the primary aims of UNTAC had been successfully fulfilled (Security Council Resolution 880(1993)).

5. Others: Haiti

Finally, there are operations which do not fit into any of the above categories, as they combine elements of complex humanitarian emergency, national disintegration and insurgency. Into this group, for example, fall the peacekeeping operations in Haiti (UNMIH, UNSMIH, and UNTMIH) and the crisis in Rwanda (UNAMIR).

On 30 September 1991, the democratically elected president of Haiti, Jean-Bertrand Aristide, was deposed in a *coup d'état* headed by Lieutenant-General Raoul Cedras. Following the coup, Aristide was forced into exile and a wave of political and civil violence engulfed Haiti, largely directed at Aristide's supporters. Both the coup and the use of violence by the Cedras regime were condemned by the United Nations and the Organization of American States (OAS) and the UN called for the reinstatement of the legitimate government. Following a year of fruitless negotiations and mediation attempts, in December 1992 the UN Secretary-General appointed a Special Envoy for Haiti, Mr. Dante Caputo of Argentina. In January 1993, Mr.Caputo's role was extended to include Special Envoy of the OAS. In June 1993, as no progress had been made in negotiations, sanctions in the form of an oil and arms embargo were imposed on Haiti by the UN. In the following months two agreements designed to facilitate reconciliation in Haiti were signed between the belligerent parties. The Governors Island Agreement (3 July 1993) provided for Aristide's return to Haiti and requested a United Nations presence in Haiti to give assistance in the process of reorganizing the armed forces and police force along more democratic lines. The New York Pact (16 July 1993) provided for a six-month "cease-fire" during which respect for human rights and democratic principles in political affairs should be established. Sanctions were removed when these agreements were signed. In August 1993, the UN Secretary-General recommended the sending of a mission to Haiti.

MICIVIH, the international civilian mission in Haiti, was established in February 1993, by agreement between the UN and the *de facto* Prime Minister of Haiti, Marc Bazin. The primary function of MICIVIH was verification of human rights as laid out in the constitution of Haiti and in those international agreements to which Haiti was a signatory. The mission was to be permitted full freedom of movement and access to information in Haiti and was to organize a public information and education program to promote human rights. The mission was to be a collaboration between the United Nations and the Organization of American States. The UN provided 200 international staff, including 133 human rights observers. The OAS provided a further 133 observers. The deployment of the mission was officially sanctioned by General Assembly Resolution 47/20B on 20 April 1993. In addition to observing the maintenance of human rights, it was envisaged that MICIVIH would aid the development of civil institutions in Haiti, work toward economic and democratic political development, and assist in the reform and restructuring of national institutions such as the armed forces, the police, and the judiciary.

The United Nations Mission in Haiti (UNMIH) was authorized on 23 September 1993 for a period of six months (Security Council Resolution 867 (1993)). Its mandate was to assist in modernizing the armed forces of Haiti and establishing a new police force. UNMIH could not be fully deployed as had been envisaged in the summer of 1993, as the Haitian authorities and military refused to cooperate with the UN mission. In the autumn of 1994 a multinational force, with the support of the UN, was able to assist in the creation of sufficient stability in Haiti to enable the return of President Aristide. UNMIH was actually deployed in full in March 1995, with a mandate until June 1996.

The United Nations Support Mission in Haiti (UNSMIH) was formed in July 1996 to take over, although with a lesser role, the functions of UNMIH. The purpose of UNSMIH was to provide assistance to the Haitian authorities in the continued maintenance of a secure and stable environment and in the creation and training of a professional and democratic police force–the Haitian National Police (HNP). In August 1997 a United Nations Transition Mission in Haiti (UNTMIH) was set up to take over from UNSMIH (Security Council resolution 564 (1997)). The purpose of UNTMIH was to continue to support the Haitian government in the professionalization of the HNP. UNTMIH consisted of 250 civilian police personnel and 50 military personnel, who withdrew with the expiration of the mandate in November 1997. An international presence in Haiti continues in the form of humanitarian aid agencies and civilian police.

III. SOME CONTEMPORARY ISSUES IN PEACEKEEPING

A. Rapid Reaction Capabilities

The efficacy of UN peacekeeping missions has in the past been compromised by the differential between the adoption of a Security Council resolution to act and the preparedness of individual Member States to provide the required troops/materials in a timely manner. In the case of Rwanda, troop deployments took place months after they were committed; contingents were generally poorly equipped (if at all), and ultimately only half the required numbers were sent. The severely weakened forces present were unable to uphold the Arusha peace agreement or to contain the resultant genocide. It has been argued that if the UN had possessed a Rapid Reaction capability, this human tragedy might have been contained or averted altogether.

The argument for the formation of a Rapid Reaction Force is as old as the UN itself. Early models (developed shortly after the Second World War) envisaged an independent army, replete with nuclear weapons and under the direct control of the Secretary-General, set to uphold international law and enforce the resolutions of the Security Council. More recent conceptions have been more modest in their scope, focusing instead on improving the efficiency of existing arrangements amongst troop-contributing nations and occasionally proposing that specific national contingents be set aside and trained specifically for UN missions. Rapid Reaction proposals have fallen roughly within one of two categories: 1) the creation of a UN standing army and (2) the creation of standby forces maintained by Member States.

A UN standing army might be created in one of two ways. The first involves Member States seconding troops to the UN. While this would in theory provide the UN with a strong foundation of qualified personnel, in practice, sovereign nations are reluctant to give their citizens to third parties to do with as they will. A second possibility would be to recruit volunteers directly from the international community with the resultant forces under the direct control of the Secretary-General. While this might circumvent concerns regarding the use of national contingents, Member States have been historically unwilling to give the UN this measure of independent power. To have an army is tantamount to statehood. To enable the UN to take unilateral action is to risk having this power turned against one's own state. Further, the severe financial constraints the UN has faced since its inception (even with regard to its daily operations) render the possibility of undertaking a project of this magnitude a distant one at best.

The second category of Rapid Reaction proposals, that of creating standby forces through Member States, has gained greater currency. This involves individual countries earmarking resources and personnel for rapid deployment to UN peacekeeping missions. While the classic model has been one of immediate, unconditional political commitment, there has been a recent move to a "Standby Arrangements System" based on "conditional pledges by Member States to contribute specific resources with agreed response time into the system." These arrangements have now been realized. As of October 1, 1997, 67 member states had agreed to participate in such a system, providing a total potential force of over 88,000 personnel. While these resources are primarily military, they include approximately 880 civilian police and 240 civilian specialists and experts ranging from surgeons to procurement personnel. A peacekeeping database has been created by the Secretariat to manage these resources.

Logistics pose a problem at this early stage. Member States still must agree to participate in any given mission: the time required for political assent and administrative preparations may continue to delay response times; and indeed, given the requirement for assent, there can be no guarantee of a response at all. Still, this organization of resources represents a major step forward from previous ad hoc arrangements; its further development may see greater coordination between individual troop-contributing nations themselves, particularly regarding the matching of personnel with materiel. Also integral to the logistics of this initiative is the development of a Rapidly Deployable Mission Headquarters (RDMHQ) by the UN Secretariat. The RDMHQ, comprised of essential civilian and military personnel, would be deployed to the mission area for the first 3 to 6 months, and tasked with managing and guiding the initial phases of the peacekeeping operation. As the mission progressed, personnel would be gradually replaced by those recruited specifically for that purpose.

Whatever the details, there are certain characteristics which are generally accepted as typifying a Rapid Reaction capability. An obvious one is speed of response: forces must stand ready, as emergencies allow no training time. Decisions must be made in a timely fashion: on a political level, this necessitates a will to act; on a military level, it requires a general preparedness, including the development of generic plans that may be quickly adapted to meet situational needs. Troop deployment itself must be efficient and effective; while numbers vary, a 1995 study by the Canadian government suggests that Rapid Reaction should include: (1) the capability to deploy the minimum necessary command and control within 7 days and (2) the ability to deploy a force capable of dealing with the immediate emergency (approximately 5000 military and civilian personnel) within 3 to 5 weeks. Flexibility is also essential to the efficacy of a Rapid Reaction team; such a force must necessarily be mobile, capable of performing a wide variety of tasks, and able to handle the logistics of multiple concurrent activities. The Canadian study suggests that a "modular" organization is best suited to the constant adaptation demanded in emergency situations. Perhaps most evident (but also most neglected) is the requirement for adequate resources to be made available to the force. Rapid Reaction is no different from "regular peacekeeping" (or, indeed, from any other endeavor) in this respect, succeeding or failing on the basis of the support given. Finances are essential in order to provide for necessary personnel, equipment, and transportation: it is only when these basic needs are fulfilled that other essentials (such as creating a stable infrastructure and logistical support) may be addressed.

While the current UN initiative toward creating a "Standby Arrangements System" may fall short of a true Rapid Reaction capability (as outlined above), it constitutes an important move in this direction. Ultimately, as with all UN projects, its success or failure will hinge on the support given it by individual Member States.

B. Financing UN Peacekeeping

Deployment aside, the process of authorizing and financing a UN peacekeeping mission is itself a lengthy one. Authorization originates with a vote of the Security Council: 9 of the 15 members must assent with no negative vote (veto) cast by any of the permanent 5 (China, France, Russia, United Kingdom, and the United States). Once the initial mandate has been set, the task then passes to the Secretariat (Department of Peacekeeping Operations) to plan the operation, solicit troop contributions, and prepare a budget request. This budget is subsequently passed to the Advisory Committee on Administrative and Budgetary Questions; a revised version is finally presented to the Fifth Committee of the General Assembly, which approves it on behalf of the Assembly. Member States are then assessed by the Secretariat for their financial obligations.

There are three sources of funding for UN peacekeeping operations: (1) the UN regular budget primarily covers the daily operating costs of the organization, but at present also finances two peacekeeping missions (UNTSO and UNMOGIP); (2) voluntary contributions of cash and kind by member states supplement UN financing efforts. While payment may be demanded for goods and services, some states choose to waive reimbursement, donating these instead; (3) mission-specific peacekeeping budgets are the central source of financing, with a separate budget approved and established for each individual mission. Member state assessments are based on a scale that takes into consideration: (1) the ability of the country to meet the required payments and (2) the degree of influence held regarding the decision to implement the peacekeeping force in the first place. Permanent Security Council members are thus required to take financial responsibility for their mandates: classified as "Group A" countries, they pay roughly 22% above the regular budgetary scale (approximately two-thirds of the cost). Group B countries, consisting of other developed industrial states, pay the same share for peacekeeping as for the regular budget. Developing countries make up the balance: while the wealthier (Group C) pay one-fifth of their regular budget assessment, the poorest (Group D) pay one-tenth.

In theory, Member States are expected to pay their approved assessment within 30 days of receiving the written request. In practice, the timely payment of dues is made by only a handful of countries with the consequence that the UN finds itself in a state of perpetual financial crisis. Although peacekeeping assessments are obligations that must be honored under international law, in reality, there is little the UN can do to force payment. In 1961, France and the USSR refused to pay their peacekeeping assessments in protest of the increasing costs for missions in the Congo and Sinai. While the UN did appeal to the International Court of Justice, and while the latter did indeed rule that peacekeeping expenditures were legitimate "expenses of the Organization," the ICJ was ultimately powerless to compel the Member States to honor their obligations. Neither country paid. While Article 19 of the UN Charter authorizes the loss of a country's vote in the General Assembly for the nonpayment of dues (with the accumulation of two years' arrearages), even this is unlikely to be implemented: in the above case, the penalty was circumvented by refraining from holding votes for two sessions.

Historically, nonpayment of dues by Member States has occurred for one of two main reasons: (1) despite the "sliding scale" approach to assessment, some of the poorer states claim they are unable to provide the required financial support; others claim that the assessment procedure is itself flawed and does not reflect their fiscal reality. (However, it has been noted that many of these same states have domestic defence budgets many times in excess of what is asked of them for peacekeeping.) (2) Withholding finances has proven a favored method of certain Member States to exert political pressure on the UN. While the end of the Cold War defused the superpower rivalry, and with it the political abuse of the Security Council veto (which saw relatively few peacekeeping efforts mounted), recent efforts to force UN reform through lack of funding is proving equally crippling. Indeed, the United States bears much of the responsibility for the current funding crisis: in 1985, the U.S. Congress passed the Kassebaum–Solomon amendment, restricting funding for international organizations, pending extensive administrative reforms. As a consequence, the U.S. currently owes the UN hundreds of millions of dollars in back arrearages; the UN, lacking any borrowing authority and completely dependent on the contributions of Member States, teeters on the brink of bankruptcy.

The demand for payment "in full, on time, and without conditions" has become the catchphrase of the General Assembly. However, until it is respected, the UN will struggle to remain solvent through the creation of bonds and independent floating funds (e.g., the ongoing Working Capital Fund, the Special Accounts of 1965 and 1972, and the Trust Fund in Support of United Nations Peacemaking and Peacekeeping Activities). Yet given the unwillingness of certain Member States to honor even their legal financial obligations, it is questionable to what extent the UN may rely on such voluntary donations. At present, the UN owes troop-contributing nations alone over $1 billion. It is not unusual for funds to be diverted from peacekeeping to the regular budget, simply in the interests of keeping the secretariat afloat.

If UN peacekeeping is to continue in its present form (or indeed at all), the Member States will have to provide the financial means to support the mandates they themselves create. In this, a sense of perspective becomes critical. In 1995, $3 billion was spent on UN peacekeeping operations worldwide; this amounts to less than 0.3% of worldwide military spending. Even setting humanitarian concerns aside, it must be recognized that peacekeeping is more cost-effective than armed conflict: the 1991 Gulf War cost the U.S. over $63 billion—that is, over 100 times the cost of UN peacekeeping expenditures worldwide.

C. Role of Regional Organizations in Peacekeeping

The growth in numbers and in scope of recent demands for UN peacekeeping operations have strained the UN's ability to respond, and it has become impossible for the UN alone to deal with this enormous range of security problems. Regional peacekeeping is therefore emerging as an important addition to UN operations. Regional involvement can be beneficial in a number of ways: such efforts lead to a deeper commitment to, and understanding of, a particular conflict because the regional body is closer to the problem, and regional peacekeeping efforts can be a significant aid to the allocation and distribution of resources. In recent years much UN attention has been directed towards the conflict in the former Yugoslavia, Somalia, and Cambodia. This has left few resources for other conflicts around the world, for example, those in Africa. The UN has directed its priority towards conflicts that appear to threaten the security of dominant states within the UN (such as the threat the conflict in Haiti posed to the US) or important regions of the world (such as the Balkans). Regional peacekeeping can offer a means of rectifying this imbalance as organizations take responsibility for their own spheres of influence, without having to rely on UN initiatives.

The legal basis of regional action is established in Chapter VIII of the UN Charter. Articles 52 and 53 stipulate that efforts should be made to resolve conflicts at the regional level prior to referring them to the UN, and that the Security Council should actively encourage the settlement of local disputes through regional arrangements, provided that regional organizations act in accordance with the purposes and principles of the UN. However, the Charter deliberately leaves open, for reasons of flexibility, the interpretation of what these regional arrangements or agencies may be. Such organizations could include treaty-based organizations, regional organizations for mutual security and defense, organizations for general regional development, and groups created to deal with a specific political, economic or social issues of current concern. Nor does the Charter elaborate further on what matters are appropriate for regional action. It is for each regional organization to determine what the parameters of its role should be.

Regional bodies might be broadly divided between organizations with a peace and security role (class 1), and others created originally for other purposes but which have a potential security role (class 2). Included in the first class are the Organization for Security and Cooperation in Europe (OSCE), the West European

Union (WEU), the North Atlantic Treaty Organization (NATO), the Organization of American States (OAS), the Organization of African Unity (OAU), Organization of the Islamic Conference (OIC), and the Arab League. These organizations have an express mandate to address and respond to security issues or, in the absence of such a mandate, have developed the necessary functions through practice or need. The OAS, OAU, OIC, and the Arab League have entered into framework agreements for cooperation with the UN. The second class would include various discussion forums and newly emerging bodies such as the Commonwealth, the Francophonie, the Association of South-East Asian Nations (ASEAN), South Pacific Forum (SPF), Gulf Cooperation Council (GCC), and the Economic Community of West African States (ECOWAS). These have assumed a security role or have the potential to do so, even though playing such a role has not been their primary purpose. In addition to such region-based organizations, there are some other players, including Non-Governmental Organizations such as the International Committee of the Red Cross (ICRC), ad hoc groups of states such as the Multinational Force and Observers (MFO), and individual states.

The capacity of regional organizations for peacekeeping varies considerably. Given the differences in structure, mandate, and decision-making processes, it is difficult to try to establish a universal model for their relationship with the United Nations. Cooperation between the United Nations and regional organizations takes a number of forms, including consultation, diplomatic support, operational support, co-deployment, and joint operations.

While the use of regional organizations may circumvent the political inertia and financial crisis endemic to the United Nations, such involvement introduces potential difficulties. The potential for lack of impartiality and regional domination is a particular factor of grave concern. This can be seen in the Russian-dominated CIS efforts, and in the predominantly Nigeria-led ECOWAS operations in Liberia. In these instances it could be argued that regional peacekeeping operations were a tool used by the more powerful country in the region, prompted by motives other than the fair settlement of the conflict. If regional efforts towards peacekeeping are to be successful, they should remain impartial and must reflect the majority sentiment of all regional partners.

As modern conflicts are occurring within states, non-biased intervention is a prerequisite. This can be best ensured when the UN takes the lead in managing and resolving the conflict, and neighboring or regional states are not directly involved. The assumption that regional states know their region best, and that regional conflicts can therefore be better resolved by regional countries, is not always correct. Since the UN has been strained in its ability to deal with an enormous range of current issues, and since for the most part, regional organizations lack the UN's basic resources and experience in security matters, it is preferable for these organizations to work together to solve regional problems.

Also See the Following Articles

HUMAN RIGHTS • PEACEMAKING AND PEACEBUILDING • PEACE ORGANIZATIONS, NONGOVERNMENTAL • PEACE STUDIES, OVERVIEW

Bibliography

Boutros-Ghali, B. (1995). *An agenda for peace.* New York: United Nations Department of Public Information.

Cox, D., & Legault, A. (Eds.) (1995). *UN rapid reaction capabilities: Requirements and prospects.* Clementsport: The Canadian Peacekeeping Press.

Crocker, C. A., Hamson, F. O., & Aall, P. (Eds.) (1996). *Managing global chaos.* Washington, DC: U.S. Institute of Peace Press.

Fetherston, A. B. (1994). *Towards a theory of United Nations peacekeeping.* New York: St. Martin's Press.

Fisas, V. (1995). *Blue geopolitics.* East Haven, CT: Pluto Press.

Government of Canada (1995). *Towards a rapid reaction capability for the United Nations.* Ottawa: Department of Foreign Affairs and International Trade and the Department of National Defence.

James, A. (1990). *Peacekeeping in international politics.* New York: St. Martin's Press.

Mackinlay, J. (Ed.) (1996). *A guide to peace support operations.* Brown University, Providence, RI: The Thomas J. Watson, Jr. Institute for International Studies.

Morrison, A., Kiras, J., & Blair, S. (Eds.) (1995). *The new peacekeeping partnership.* Clementsport: The Canadian Peacekeeping Press.

Rikhye, I. J., & Skjelsbaek, K. (Eds.) (1990). *The UN and peacekeeping.* Basingstoke, UK: Macmillan.

United Nations (1996). *The blue helmets.* New York: United Nations Department of Public Information.

United Nations (1995). *General guidelines for peacekeeping operations.* New York: United Nations Department of Peacekeeping Operations.

Weiss, T. G., & Collins, C. (1996). *Humanitarian challenges and intervention.* Boulder, CO: Westview Press.

Peacemaking and Peacebuilding

Thomas Clough Daffern

International Institute of Peace Studies and Global Philosophy

GLOSSARY

Communication The most important single factor of the peacemaking process in contributing toward the transformation of negative conflict situations toward peace.

Integral Conflict Resolution One of the ultimate goals of the peacemaking process, meaning the resolution of disputes to the satisfaction of all parties.

Peacebuilding Similar to the above, but taking a more long-term view of situations of protracted conflict, which require deeper and more lasting interventions and which similarly utilize different specific strategies depending on the conflict in question.

Peace Education One of the most important long strategies for peacebuilding, involving the learning and teaching of peaceful values and ideals by drawing on all that is best in the world's educational heritage.

Peacemaking The active process of reconciliation in specific instances of immediate conflict, undertaken in various ways by various actors, depending on the situation and the temperaments of those in dispute.

Reconciliation The process whereby disputants can be brought to a genuine transformation of negative energy, ultimately through the power of truth and love, thus leading to genuine long-term peacebuilding.

Sustainable Mediation One of the most valuable resources available for peacemaking work, involving the comprehensive communication of divergent perceptions, attitudes, and feelings through the intervention of a neutral third party, leading to a reevalued perception by both parties in dispute and a sustainable reconciliation.

Copyright © 1999 by Academic Press.
All rights of reproduction in any form reserved.

THE TERMS PEACEBUILDING AND PEACEMAKING have come to be used in contemporary academic discourse, within peace studies and conflict analysis, as denoting specific processes which lead to the reduction of conflict, violence, and disagreement and which advance the development of peace, trust, confidence, and mutual accord between both individuals and social groups. As such they have a general usage within the complex studies of conflict processes that have developed in the past several decades, drawing heavily on disciplines such as psychology, sociology, group dynamics, peace research, and the like. They are also terms of common sense usage in ordinary language whose prior significance has been capitalized by academic discourse, and as such they have a deeper history, with similar terms in most world languages, denoting the active process whereby reconciliation, trust, and peace can be achieved between conflicting and warring parties. The fact that they are verbal nouns is instructive: they signify the dynamic activity that underlies the movement toward peace rather than the state of peace per se, about whose final characteristics, or whose feasiblity, people disagree. About the general need to strive and work for peace, however, there is almost universal agreement. Since time immemorial conflict, war, and violence have been part of the human condition and, as far back as records allow us to survey, thinkers have been struggling with ways to obviate this tendency toward mutual destruction that seems to be embedded in human beings. Religions, laws, social codes, educational teachings, customs, rituals, artistic activity, culture—all these at various times have been proposed and adopted by social thinkers and activists as ways to build peace out of the ruins left by destructive behavior. In recent decades, following the crescendo of violence and mass killing that has characterized much of the 20th century, there has been a growing concerted effort on the part of many groups and individuals to construct a world of social solidarity, justice, and peace beyond the frightening possibilities of nuclear apocalypse or the plethora of regional and factional interest wars. Many nongovernmental organizations have developed, often in association with the United Nations, to advance particular sectors of advocacy which bear on some dimension of the overall work of peacebuilding. Educators and scholars have also over recent decades devoted considerable thought and research to investigating the intellectual parameters of such activities, trying to articulate and analyze conceptual frameworks that can give enduring substance and purpose to what might otherwise appear as a patchwork of unrelated efforts.

It is the purpose of this article to examine some of the various strategies and methods adopted by those engaged in dynamic peacebuilding and peacemaking activities. We also consider the subject matter philosophically; that is, with proper attention to both depth and breadth, and endeavor to give an overview of the numerous methods being adopted and researched at the present time.

I. EDUCATIONAL STRATEGIES FOR PEACEBUILDING

No one single strategy available to those involved in peacebuilding and peacemaking activities is more important overall than education in its deepest and most profound senses. Against the raw instincts of competition, violence, jealousy, and aggression, which throughout human history have led to large-scale violence and warfare, there have been innumerable educational reformers and visionaries who have sought to develop the remedy of deep learning and self knowledge, cultivating instead the core values of love, altruism, compassion, service, and wisdom as a counterforce to the all-too-prevalent forces of negativity. Often if you study the personal life biographies of leading educational reformers and systematizers, such as Confucius, Pythagoras, Plato, Aristotle, Aquinas, Erasmus, Rousseau, Pestallozi, Bentham, Jefferson, Kant, Dewey, and so on, you find a deep underlying belief that it is through education that humankind can best be shaped and molded to act and think peaceably in all dealings. Yet it is also a fact that the vision of universal mass education and literacy, which is a precondition for the efforts of contemporary peace educators, is a very recent and still-fragile phenomenon. For most of recorded history formal education has been denied to the masses and instead has been the process whereby established elites perpetuate their disproportionate access to power and resources at the expense of ordinary people. Educational structures and curricula have been controlled and manipulated by specific religious or political interest groups to ensure that their particular vision of the world prevails and dominates over others. Even in the modern world, for all its sophistication and rhetorical embrace of democracy, this still remains largely the case. National governments, pyramidal in structure, set the formal agenda of schooling, with the aim of providing generations of students and graduates who are equipped to man the machinery of advanced industrial societies or to service whatever ideological or religious faction happens to be in charge of divergent educational administrations. All too often, therefore, education has itself contributed to the formation of nationalist and xenophobic attitudes, which in turn leads to war and violence between peoples of difffering belief systems. Against this sad state of affairs, the modern development of peace education, in which a small number of radical (in the true sense of going to the roots of a problem) educationists have attempted to remain true to the vision of education as being the unbiased, independent, courageous, and determined pursuit of truth, including ethical and spiritual truth, has therefore of necessity involved working for peace through education. Often, sadly, such activities, whether at the secondary school level (peace education) or at the university level, are even now largely marginalized and considered suspect—as "unpatriotic," "cosmopolitan," or some other negative designation. Notwithstanding such difficulties, enormous progress has been made in developing both curricula and resources and expertise to deliver genuine educational work that enlarges and deepens students ideational and ethical horizons. Numerous professional educational networks and organizations, in many countries and globally have come into being over recent decades to advance the vision of education as peacebuilding. In many countries of the world, academic degree programs have been established at numerous universities, providing both undergraduate and postgraduate courses in peace education and peace studies. Regular international conferences, publications, and other educational events (often of an informal "workshop" nature) supplement the formal structures that have managed to develop. Such work is still, in spite of all this, in its infancy—and too often subject to the negative pressures of marginalization and resource scarcity mentioned above, such that much still remains to be done to effectively maximize the potential that education can authentically offer to the difficult tasks of peacebuilding and peacemaking.

II. RESEARCH AS PEACEBUILDING

At the university level and beyond, it can be argued coherently that research itself can and does contribute significantly to the wider tasks of peacebuilding and peacemaking, in terms of both content and methodology. In methodological terms, at its best research implies the collegiate and cooperative search for worthwhile knowledge based on rigorous investigation, inquiry, and analysis and, as such, by bringing together scholars and researchers from many different disciplines and approaches to the common boundaries of inquiry, as providing a nexus for communication and concourse which of itself helps to break down barriers. Au contraire when states implode behind ideological barriers, as during the 1930s, their scholars usually

absent themselves from international academic forums. While the League of Nations tried to influence educators worldwide to take their responsibilities as peace-builders seriously and created a significant legacy of work in so doing, the absence of major payers from that organization and the subsequent catastrophe of World War II meant that it has been largely a result of the work of the United Nations that major progress has been made in providing institutional and intellectual support to the praxis of education as peacebuilding, particularly through the United Nations Educational, Scientific and Cultural Organization (UNESCO) and its affiliated institutions. Other international organizations, such as the Council of Europe, the European Union, and the Commonwealth of Nations, among others, have also given a high priority to the contribution of education to international and social solidarity. Between universities, The International Association of Universities, the International Association of University Presidents, and the International Peace Research Association have similarly managed to sustain a profound witness to the importance of educational peace-building. Specific courses are also being pioneered at many schools and universities, bringing together students from different cultural backgrounds to reexamine their core prejudices and assumptions about one another in innovative ways that constantly surprise and stretch the educational imagination. The long period of the Cold War, in which the clash of rival ideologies too often blocked authentic dialogue and learning and which led to a particular emphasis for peace research on the military and strategic issues associated with disarmament, has now given way to a more hopeful and yet also equally worrying period of uncertainty: nuclear Armageddon seems to have been averted and yet the world's resources are still being disproportionately channeled into militarism and organized violence. Furthermore, all too often a climate of competitiveness and ruthless psychological warfare seems to have permeated the very educational institutions that we look to as havens of moral excellence. The further challenge of increasing specialization and professionalism among academic researchers brings the danger that those seeking to synthesize interdisciplinary approaches, particularly when it comes to educational peacebuilding, have to persuade those who hold the reins of power in terms of the political economy of education on two fronts simultaneously; first, the value of education as a praxis of peacebuilding, whose investments are usually so long term that their immediate advantage escapes measurement, and second, the coherent value of the highly interdisciplinary and apparently amorphous cluster of research foci embraced by the terms "peace education" and "peace studies." Nevertheless, in spite of all this, or perhaps because of it, excellent scholarly research work is being produced in many academic and scientific educational institutions worldwide, which collectively cannot help but advance the work of peacebuilding and peacemaking in general. In what follows we explore something of these frontiers in further detail.

III. SCIENTIFIC APPROACHES TO PEACEBUILDING

The advancement of scientific knowledge has been one of the hallmarks of modernity, if not its primary defining characteristic, yet it has given the world a tragic and divided legacy as far as the contribution of science to peacebuilding is concerned. On the negative side of the balance sheet is the fact that as science and technology have advanced, they have been applied unscrupulously to the machinery of warfare and organized violence, from the invention of firearms through to nuclear missiles, "smart" bombs, and land mines. Too often scientific and technological knowledge has not been placed at the service of peacebuilding, but has been harnessed to the engine of nationalistic advancement and the military machines to serve only destruction and death. At the same time, however, there has also been a long lineage of scientists who have placed their knowledge and expertise at the service of peacebuilding. Even Alfred Nobel, who developed dynamite, of immense destructive power, placed much of the profits of his invention toward founding the Nobel Foundation, which, through its annual Nobel Peace Prize and other awards for scientific and cultural achievement, has helped considerably to raise the profile of work for peace and justice worldwide. Similarly, Pugwash, an international association of scientists initiated in the 1950s by Albert Einstein, Bertrand Russell, Joseph Rotblat, and others, continues to bring together gatherings of eminent scientists worldwide to speak out against the misuses of scientific knowledge when applied to militarism. The Royal Society and the umbrella organization of all such scientific associations worldwide, the International Council of Scientific Unions, in turn linked to UNESCO, have likewise made strenuous efforts to ensure that scientific and technological exchanges lead to useful and socially beneficial developments for the good of humanity. One of the major obstacles in the way of ensuring that scientific research and development is harnessed for peacebuilding comes from the fact that a large part of the available budget available for scientific research comes from national

defence budgets. Even the technology of modern computer systems and the Internet were originally developed for their security and intelligence potential. To counter this trend, scientists have organized in recent decades in various professional associations to campaign specifically to raise awareness of the potential contribution of their community toward genuine peacebuilding, including such organizations as Scientists for Global Responsibility and the International Network of Scientists and Engineers, who together sponsor an international week of Science and Peace in November (during the week in which November 11th falls). Events take place throughout the world during this week in which scientists work together, with the endorsement of UNESCO, to signal their commitment to the peaceful application of scientific knowledge. Medical doctors have likewise organized successfully worldwide through International Physicians for the Prevention of Nuclear War and other organizations, lending their significant professional influence to the forces of peacebuilding and opposing those voices that prefer military solutions to complex political and social problems. When the full comprehensive history of the ending of the Cold War comes to be written it will undoubtedly conclude that one of the most effective and convincing communities to urge disarmament and reconciliation on reluctant political leaders was the scientific community, in all their disparate complexity. Its work, however, could be said to have just begun—for peace-building is a long process, involving not simply the removal of the threat of immediate confrontation, but the long-term rebuilding and restructuring of societies, who for too long have associated scientific and technological expertise with advanced militarism and warfare. Scientists today therefore are working in support of the numerous organizations that are campaigning to free the world from both the threat of major nuclear catastrophe and continuing regional and intranational conflicts and to realize therefore the greater potential of science in the challenging task of peacebuilding worldwide.

IV. RELIGIOUS APPROACHES TO PEACEBUILDING AND PEACEMAKING

A. General and Interfaith Activities

At the opposite end of the spectrum from the scientific community we have the religious communities of the planet, who have likewise made significant contributions to peacebuilding, work that continues to gather momentum. From ancient times, religious visionaries and people of spiritual understanding have sought to harness the undoubted energy of faith and spirituality for building a peaceful and just world. In all the religious and spiritual traditions there are found core teachings and values which emphasize that one of the primary religious responsibilities of humankind is to live peaceably and to build conditions of social and community justice that will make it possible for man's true humanness to flourish. This has historically been true of the various divergent religious traditions of humanity, whether ancient pagan and primal faiths, Hinduism, Buddhism Jainism, Judaism, Christianity, Islam, Sikhism, Shintoism, Taoism, Zoroastrianism, or Bahai. In all these faith traditions, numerous priests, prophets, and saints have labored long and hard to awaken humankind to the full glory of peace and have spoken against warfare and violence. Unfortunately, it is also true that all too often the genuine religious traditions of the planet have been hijacked to nationalist or imperialist ends, and organized violence and oppression have often been cloaked in a veneer of religious propriety. This was and is true both in the days of organized imperialism and in the modern era of covert terrorism. To counter this misuse of the essence of religion, recent decades have witnessed a growing effort on the part of responsible religious leaders and communities to come together in witness to the power of spirituality as a force for peacemaking. In the Christian churches, many denominations have organized effective bodies to campaign for peace and justice, in the Roman Catholic tradition (e.g., *Pax Christi*), in the Orthodox Churches, and in the various Protestant churches. The Quakers and other historic peace churches (such as the Mennonites) have for many centuries worked by example to bear witness to their interpretation of the gospel as a message of radical liberation from the causes and sources of violence and oppresion. They have similarly pioneered many practical initiatives at the level of grassroots peacebuilding and nonviolence advocacy, whether with violent prisoners, in the civil rights movement, or in the peace movement per se. The World Council of Churches, which coordinates ecumenical Christian efforts worldwide in this regard, has likewise campaigned effectively over many years on peace and justice issues, sponsoring numerous meetings, publications, reports, and research projects on both the theoretical and practical dimensions of peacebuilding and peacemaking. The Pontifical Commission "Justitia et pax" has performed a similar role for the Roman Catholic tradition. Similar initiatives are underway in the other religious communities worldwide, among the

Buddhist sangha, for example, or in the Jewish faith. Among modern Hindus many have been touched by the life and witness of Mahatma Gandhi with his teaching of nonviolent resistance to oppression based on the power of the spirit. In recent decades the religious communities of the world have begun to coordinate efforts to articulate common values and to bear ethical witness to the urgent task of peacebuilding on an interfaith basis. In 1970, in Kyoto, a new international umbrella organization, the World Conference on Religion and Peace (WCRP), was formed, meeting every 5 years since and, with smaller meetings in between, bringing religious representatives from all over the world to consider together the potential that religion can offer toward healing the conflicts, wars, and violence of our time. The WCRP continues to develop both national and international work for peacebuilding in many different locations. A new international mediation service has also been launched, the Multifaith and Multicultural Mediation Service, which provides mediation and conflict resolution intervention in situations of conflict where the cause is primarily of a religious or ethnic nature and brings trained mediators and religious people together to work on problem-solving. The Fellowship of Reconciliation has another long track record in working among people of all religious persuasions to bear witness to the primacy of peacemaking. More recently, the United Religions Initiative has developed a parallel organization to the United Nations where the religious aspirations of humanity can find a common platform, a permanent assembly to speak out responsibly and wisely on solutions for the common problems facing humanity, including the urgent need for peace and reconciliation. The Chicago Parliament of the World's Religions (originally held in 1893 and then in 1993 and with a further such meeting in Cape Town in 1999) provides another venue in which peacemaking between religious communities can be significantly advanced. For Commonwealth countries a new Commonwealth Common Values Council was also established in 1997, while at the UN level, the United Nations Values Caucus has already ensured that ethical and spiritual questions are included in the largely secular approach taken to peacebuilding issues by the United Nations. In spite of all this, however, much work still remains to be done, and it could be said that the world's religious and spiritual traditions have as yet hardly begun to fully explore their true potential as peacemakers and peace-builders. All too often, in the popular eye, the theoretical contribution that religion ought to make is occluded by the failure to live up to the professed ideals or the too-zealous imposition of certain aspects of doctrine, sometimes even with force and violence, on unwilling sections of the community. Indeed, religious differences have become a growing cause of violence in recent years, leading many people to look toward secular solutions or to more heterodox spiritual systems outside the mainstream framework of religious orthodoxy per se. It is a paradox that often the main campaigners for peace within the religious paradigm have often been accused of heresy or of betrayal by their more orthodox colleagues and have paid with imprisonment or martyrdom for their views. In the contemporary era, particularly with the continuing resurgence of religiosity affecting the affairs in the Middle East, questions of religious freedom and responsibility, and the relationship between human rights law and religious laws, are leading to strenuous efforts on the part of religious leaders and intellectuals to articulate points of common values across all the major religious traditions so as to construct a sustainable peace that can be inclusive of all cultural and religious sensibilities. Religious tensions are evident in many conflicts all over the world, including: Tibet, India, Kashmir, Sri Lanka, Northern Ireland, Central Africa, the Balkans, Cyprus, North Africa, Turkey, Iran, Iraq, Israel/Palestine, the Americas, and so on. In all of these situations responsible religious representatives are working to make the voice of common sense, compromise, and peacebuilding heard effectively, but as yet there is still a long way to go before the true contribution of such approaches can be delivered in full. Let us examine some of the ways in which this work is being attempted.

B. Ritual and Ceremony

This is one of the significant ways in which spirituality can and does contribute toward peacebuilding. Ritual and ceremony is one way in which communities have since prehistoric times expressed their common sense of belonging and identity, coming together for seasonal festivities and solemn liturgies, often as sacred sites or places of numinous power. At such times, weapons were disallowed, disagreements were reconciled, and enmities forgiven or at least suspended. Throughout the world religious communities and congregations are nowadays invoking the renewed power of common patterns of worship to foster a greater sense of collective well-being and social peace and to inspire and empower their members to work tirelessly for peacebuilding and social justice. In addition to the traditional liturgies and religious rituals that have been handed down for generations, new, eclectic, and innovative rituals are being developed, often with an interfaith flavor or work-

ing in conjunction with the primal energies of nature and the landscape, calling on the spiritual world to empower and protect the work of planetary healing and peacebuilding, which is so urgently needed at this time. Such work transcends conventional logic systems or rationalist patterns of thought—yet many people in the peace movement worldwide undoubtedly find strength to go on bearing witness to the value of peace as a primary principle underpinning all else—through precisely such experimental rites and ceremonies. Primal religious traditions, whether American Indian, Australian Aborigine, Celtic European, or African, have also witnessed a flowering and rebirth, sharing their largely oral teachings and sophisticated recipes for peacemaking—in which conflicts and difficulties are dealt with through dialogue and conciliation—to a modern world full of technological wizardry, but often lacking in basic values and human spiritual sensitivities. Many of the demonstrations and manifestations of the peace movement per se, such as the ribbon of fabric panels encircling the Pentagon in 1986 or the colored ribbons and offerings for peace woven on the fences of Greenham Common airbase in Britain in the 1980s, have likewise a semi-religious ceremonial air about them and usually draw on the same reservoir of primal human emotion and spirituality.

C. Prayer, Meditation, and Silence

These remain perhaps the core remedies in the medicine chest of religious peacemakers. It is at the spiritual heart of the religious life. Muslims all over the world are enjoined to pray five times each day, that is, to enter into communion with God, the absolute source of peace; all other religions advocate a similar regimen, although varying in the details. Just as in the medical world it has now been scientifically documented that prayer can actually assist the healing process, so several organizations are promoting the power of prayer, mediation, and silence as an aid to the peacebuilding process.

V. ARTS APPROACHES TO PEACEBUILDING

Another important community that has contributed historically to the overall process of peacebuilding is the artistic community. While it is true that in some cases the arts have served the machinery of conflict by producing, for example, musical accompaniments to military parades, by fanning the flames of xenophobic nationalism, or by building great structures such as the

Triumphal arches celebrating military prowess, in overall terms, the work of creative artists has more often than not been devoted to awakening the higher sensibilities of humankind toward the more sublime affections and insights associated with peace and collective well-being. Indeed, it could even be argued that over the long haul, artistic endeavor represents the pinnacle of human creative achievement of which it is the whole purpose of peacebuilding and peacemaking to preserve and facilitate.

In the field of music, for example, many of the great composers hoped that their work would elevate the vision of humankind toward an appreciation of the universal harmony that they managed to encapsulate in tonal languages beyond ordinary speech. The very essence of music is intimately connected with the successful resolution of tonal discord and tension, through the drama of melodic interplay, toward the satisfying fulfillment of sound energies in creative and harmonic denouement. Many of the great orchestral and operatic works have been concerned with highlighting the quest for meaning, justice, and, ultimately, peacebuilding in its deepest and most transcendental sense. In recent decades, musicians have also given their expertise in an organized and methodical way toward the conscious effort of peacebuilding, whether in the world of classical music, through such organizations as the UK-based Musicians against Nuclear Arms or in the moving story of the violinist who, having experienced the horrors of life in a Nazi concentration camp during World War II, has since tirelessly traveled the world giving concerts for peace and reconciliation, or in the world of modern popular music, through such events as George Harrison's concert for the victims of the Bangladesh war in the 1970s, in John Lennon's call to "Give Peace a Chance," or, more recently, in the Live Aid concert engineered by Bob Geldof to bring relief to the victims of conflict and famine in Ethiopia and against apartheid in South Africa. Just as in ancient Egyptian mythology, as Osiris brought the values of the advanced civilization to the world through the powers of music and nonviolence, or as in ancient Greece, where Orpheus and Pythagoras performed a similar service, so too, in all cultures, music continues to play an important role in helping to lay the deep foundations for a world at peace with itself.

Dance likewise has immemorially served as a cathartic method whereby individuals and communities can experience the release of pent-up emotions and energies in a structured and healing context. Although war dances are common to most cultures, on the whole dance has been used as a means of expressing the more affective and unitive aspects of human nature. Whether in the Sufi dance tradition of the Middle East, which has recently been revived in the west as Dances for Universal Peace, in the classical traditions of ballet, or in the modern popular dance traditions, the spectacle and experience of body movement in harmony to music, swaying and pulsating with rhythm, enables those who participate to sense something of the cosmic interplay of forces whose successful and creative balancing seems to be at the very heart of the human condition. Shiva, as the Lord of the Dance, symbolizes for the Indian world this dynamic balance whose rhythm embodies the deepest secret of authentic peacebuilding: that peace is not a stasis, a mere absence of violence, but rather the creative embrace of dynamic energy, held in flux and poise, and in eternal celebration. Recently, the School of Biodanza has consciously sought to harness the potential of dance for peacebuilding, as has the Shamanic dance traditions developed by Gabrielle Roth.

In the fine arts painting has, through the power of the visual image, sought in the hands of the great masters to produce an effect of such spiritual beauty and sublimity that it stuns the viewer into a state of adoration at the beauty of the physical form. The role of the religious icon in Eastern Orthodox Christianity has played a similar, more religious role. The traditions of Japanese, Chinese, and Tibetan painting likewise convey feelings and concepts of cosmological significance in which man's place in nature and the cosmos is rendered harmonious and meaningful, leading to a profound sense of inner peace from which all true peacebuilding must proceed. Modern painters like Picasso have similarly sought to express their political commitment to peace and justice through visual creations such as the famous *Guernica* painting and to awaken, as did Goya, the conscience of the observer against warfare and its tragic effects.

The field of architecture is an interesting and important one. Indeed, the very term "peacebuilding" incorporates as its primary metaphor the idea of construction and building. It is not surprising then that as well as being responsible for the many built structures through which human habitation is rendered possible, architects have also in many instances consciously sought to construct buildings that have peace at the core of their semiotic display. From the United Nations Headquarters building, to the Peace Palace at the Hague, to the Palais des Nations in Geneva, architects have tried to construct edifices that give a sense of enduring permanence to the vital institutions that collectively are charged with the awesome responsibility of preserving peace on the planet. In religious architecture temples, churches, mosques, pagodas, and other sacred spaces have for millennia sought to bring to their visitors a sense of transpersonal peace through the interplay of light, space, structure, and symbolism; a sense of spiritual meaning whose core ethic is one of striving for peace-as-balance, peace-as-justice, and peace-as-beauty. More recently professional associations of architects have made a concerted effort, in association with town planners and urban designers, to grapple with the complex issue of the effect of the built environment on the psychological characteristics of its inhabitants. Research has now demonstrated that many of the urban jungles of modernity have a debilitating and disempowering effect on those who live and work among them, and a move is underway to reincorporate ecological principles into building design so as to inspire and restore spiritual well-being. Urban planners are also working, through their professional associations, on a process that received a great boost at the Habitat 2 Conference in Istanbul in 1996 to think through the steps needed to reclaim cities as peaceful spaces in which civilization and culture can flourish.

In the field of literature, poetry, and drama there have been highly significant contributions to peacebuilding over many centuries by many of the greatest literary figures of humanity. Poetry has served in the past both as a vehicle for military inspiration, with its tales of the heroic deeds of ancestors, as in *The Iliad* and *The Mahabarata,* but also as a vehicle for some of the most profound expressions of horror against violence and the vital need to build the structures of peace deep and fast. Sacred poetry particularly has served this purpose. The poetry of the *Bible,* of the *Upanishads,* of the *Koran,* of the *Adi Granth,* of many of the Buddhist *Sutras,* of the Bahai scriptures, of Rumi and the other Sufi poets, of Dante and Christian mysticism—all these have contributed enormously to the expression of the spiritual urge toward peace that is found deep inside the human heart, inspiring countless generations to live peaceable and virtuous lives. War poets such as Wilfred Owen and many other poets in the modern world have been inspired by the Muse to specifically pen their abhorrence of the actual brutal realities of war and to hymn instead on the need to find alternatives to violence. While epic poetry of all cultures has traditionally recorded the heroic deeds of military heroes, such as that of Homer, Virgil, Tasso, and the Norse sagas, the collected witness of humankind's poetic heritage would rather be weighted against glorification for its own sake, rather calling the reader to the moral and spiritual heroism that arises from the pursuit of justice and strength of character, which renders violence unnecessary. Addi-

tionally, novelists like Tolstoy, Pasternak, Solzhenitsyn, Hemingway, Thomas Mann, Herman Hess, J. R. R. Tolkein, and many others have taken the problems of war and peace and the challenges of peacebuilding to the heart of their work. Dramatists also, including the ancient Greek dramatists, Shakespeare, Racine, Shaw, Ibsen, Sartre, and many others have also presented the ethical dilemmas arising from war and the moral demands on character when presented with violence.

VI. PSYCHOLOGICAL APPROACHES TO PEACEMAKING

A. General Psychological Approaches to Emotional Peacemaking

While most people think of peacebuilding as an outer political process involving the building of constructive relationships, whether between social groups or nation states, there has been a growing effort among academic psychologists to understand the inner causation of violence and aggression and the parameters of achieving inner psychological peace, without which outer peace would remain an impossible dream. Freud, Jung, and the other founders of modern psychoanalytic theory were motivated in their research by a profound abhorrence of warfare and violence and the inner conflicts of drives and forces within the individual psyche that cause mental anguish and suffering, leading to psychotic states and mental illness. Many psychologists, including William James, have made a direct connection between the mental illness exhibited by unstable individuals and the collective madness that seems to overcome large social and political groups in time of war and group violence. Professional groups of psychologists have developed a large body of expertise dealing with such matters from an empirical and scientific basis. The Tavistock Clinic in London, for example, one of the world's leading centers for psychological and psychoanalytical study, originally began by examining cases of shell-shocked victims returning after World War I. The American Psychological Association has in recent years formed a special interest group dealing with the psychology of peace and conflict, and its members have published research tools for educators interested in this area, including a comprehensive bibliography of all published articles and monographs in the psychology of war, aggression, conflict, and peace over recent decades. Several universities, for example Harvard, include research units studying aspects of the psychology of conflict and peace, and most university peace studies departments include in their teaching work course options on the psychological aspects of violence and nonviolence. Undoubtedly the psychological pressures on the present generations, who have lived through the nuclear arms race, with the possibility of the wide-scale annihilation of humanity through purposeful or accidental nuclear war, is unprecedented in human history, and, not surprisingly, the situation has been reflected in the disturbed and anxious psychological condition of humankind at large. With the ending of that particular episode of east–west nuclear anxiety, research attention has shifted to more general questions of peaceful conflict resolution and the psychological dynamics of peacebuilding and peacemaking.

B. Gender Peacemaking

One key area of great importance to contemporary research into peacebuilding concerns gender relations. Feminist scholars have long argued that organized violence is primarily a functional of gender imbalance and of patriarchal social relations. They point to the fact that in those few societies where women have held significant cultural and spiritual power, organized group violence has been relatively rare. Although the details of such claims are disputed among anthropologists, historians, and sociologists, what is undeniable is that often women are the unfortunate and unwitting victims of violence and warfare, suffering death, torture, rape, dehumanization, and the loss of their homes. Whereas in earlier centuries, codes of chivalrous behavior in warfare attempted to protect the lives of women during time of war, in the 20th century, with its technological mass-scale bombings, total warfare, holocausts, guerrilla and terrorist attacks, and fratricidal civil wars blurring the distinction of battlefield and home front, such codes of chivalry seems to have broken down. Women and men alike were herded into the gas chambers of Auschwitz without distinction, or suffered in the bombings of Hiroshima, Dresden, and Coventry, or under the napalm raids of Vietnam. Many scholars argue that while male prowess at violence may indeed be a result of the time when the human species was carving out its dominant niche in the zoological pecking order, it is now an outmoded and atavistic characteristic that needs channeling and reorienting toward socially useful and spiritually beneficial activities. Women's studies as an academic discipline of recent development has made significant contributions toward the history of women as peacemakers and peace-builders, recognizing that often women have pioneered alternatives to violence and have urged their male colleagues to take routes other than violence toward the achievement of their cultural and political goals. Much of the work and successes of the peace movement would have been unthinkable without this guiding role supplied by women pioneers, in many forms and ways, from Florence Nightingale, to Bertha Von Suttner, to Fannie Andrews, and the formal structures such as the Women's International League for Peace and Freedom. Many profound studies have been made of the tragic violence that women often suffer in the domestic context, which points to an urgent need to highlight the interrelatedness of women's rights issues and those of peacemaking.

Other scholars working in the related field of men's studies are trying to analyze the pressures and dynamics of male behavior that lead them to violent behavior, be it in armed gangs and vandalism, in dysfunctional family roles, in organized military groups, or in secret fraternities of violent criminals. Those involved in the men's movement argue that it is possible to construct an alternative ethic of nurturing and generative compassion for a new masculine self-image that seeks self-worth and gender fulfillment not through violence and the desecration of the feminine, but rather in creative copartnership and responsibility between the sexes. This pioneering work is carried out both in formal academic contexts as well as in informal extracurricula workshop contexts where a number of innovative organizations have concerned themselves with peacemaking between the genders, as both men and women seek to heal the brokenness and abuse that exist around the whole issue of gender relations and sexuality and to recover the capacity for love, creativity, compassion, and mutual respect which lies at the very foundation of the covenant of human life itself.

C. Family Peacemaking

This is another closely related field of concern that has arisen in recent decades, as academics and social workers have become increasingly aware of the profound stresses and tensions that exist at the heart of many family structures, and that often lead tragically to instances of violence and abuse. Family mediation is one practical way in which this theoretical work is being translated into practical intervention, but the statistics are overwhelming in their documentation that family violence is a troubling undercurrent of social reality that cannot be ignored by those who seek to build a peaceful society. While men are often the perpetrators of violence in family contexts, there is all to much evidence that sometimes women also commit acts of tragic violence and abuse as well. Some argue that poverty, poor education, and a sense of despair and hopelessness are causal factors behind family violence, and therefore any long term constructive peace-building programs to reduce such instances of violence need to be seen as part of wider network of solutions to social and economic problems in general. Organizations such as the Economic and Social Research Council in the UK have begun to undertake large-scale funded studies into these complex issues.

D. Children

As the most vulnerable members of society, children are often the front-line victims in situations of violence, whether on the domestic front, with instances of child sexual abuse being widespread, or in actual situations of armed conflict, where children are more and more being forced to play a front-line role or are becoming victims left to wander as orphans and refugees while their elders engage in mass acts of brutality. Save the Children, UNICEF, and other international organizations have done much in recent decades to highlight the plight of children in such situations and to place the issue formally on the agenda of political decision-makers. Undoubtedly, the tragedy of what happens to children in times of violent conflict is one of the major motivating factors that fuels those engaged in peace-building initiatives, be it at the formal intergovernmental level or among NGOs and peace educators. Peace education programs aimed at giving children the tools to understand and handle conflict, including peer mediation schemes in schools, are another way of implementing practical peacebuilding initiatives in a way that impacts on children's daily lives.

VII. PEACEBUILDING AND THE ROLE OF THE MEDIA

The role of the mass media as a major player in the formation of attitudes to war, violence, and peace-building is a 20th-century phenomenon, with the paramount role played by television and, to a lesser but still vital extent, by radio, both products of advanced technological communications systems. Spreading antienemy propaganda through controlling the media has become a feature of modern warfare and was a key element of the Second World War and in the subsequent Cold War on both sides of the Iron Curtain. Democracies and dictatorships alike recognized the power of public opin-ion and the power of the media in shaping this inchoate force and therefore exerted strenuous efforts, whether by covert or explicit means, to exercise intellectual and cultural hegemony over the attitudes of the general public. Not surprisingly, therefore, many responsible voices have likewise been raised for utilizing the tremendous communication and information facilities afforded by the modern media toward peacebuilding. Television program-makers have not shrunk from their duties in exposing the horrors of war, whether in Vietnam or in subsequent conflicts, and due to such graphic accounts successfully created a public mindset that led eventually to the ending of the Cold War per se with the Treaty of Paris in 1990. The motion-picture industry has likewise played an important role in attitude formation both by churning out endless war films and films of violence that do little but glorify the more aggressive aspects of human nature and by producing the rarer but highly significant films that seek to reveal the futility and horror of warfare and the urgent need for peacebuilding in the modern era. Films like "Oh, What a Lovely War," "Gandhi," "Dances with Wolves," "The Shadowmakers," "All the Presidents Men," and many others have drawn on the powers of the medium to convey to mass audiences something of what goes on behind the scenes of organized carnage and to reveal alternative modalities for peacebuilding as being within the grasp of the human will and imagination.

The question of the negative effects of violent videos and films on impressionable minds is something that academics, media specialists, and policy-makers are actively debating. What is undoubtedly the case is that a far greater proportion of the films, videos, and television programs made and shown give a pseudo-heroic gloss to violence and warfare than their opposite, while the proportion of those that genuinely attempt to show alternative approaches, extolling peacemaking rather than conquest and victory, are few and far between. Here then is an as-yet underexplored country in which peacemakers and peace-builders would do well to colonize more effectively.

VIII. PEACEBUILDING AND THE ROLE OF INFORMATION TECHNOLOGY AND COMPUTERS

The computer industry comprises another vitally important new terrain in which the potential for peacebuilding is vast and growing. While the research and development of modern computers was partly fueled by warfare and the arms race and the search for comprehensive intelligence and encryption devices (the Internet was developed initially as an outgrowth of internal American military information exchanges funded by the Pentagon), once in the public domain, the Internet has become a tool of active peacebuilding in the hands of a growing number of peace academics, NGOs, advocacy groups, and international initiatives aimed at peacebuilding and peacemaking. One only has to "search the Web" nowadays to realize what a powerful tool the Internet is, by facilitating easy and quick international communication and information exchanges, to see the potential. Before long, perhaps, encyclopedias such as this one will be available mainly on line, with continuously updated entries giving access to the latest research and concepts at the forefront of peace thinking and peacebuilding activities. One intriguing proposal that has surfaced concerns building a "peace room" equivalent to the war game rooms available to military planners and strategic studies experts in which advanced technological communications could enable peacebuilding activities, including the provision of humanitarian relief, mediation, arbitration, and human rights violations data, to be networked among several actors and agencies worldwide, thus increasing the likelihood of successful peacemaking interventions. Many university departments of peace and conflict studies are successfully developing interfaces with leading-edge computer technologies to facilitate peacebuilding work in both theoretic and practical domains. As yet, however, it must be said that these advanced technologies are still underexplored and underdeveloped when it comes to exploiting their full potential as tools of peacebuilding and peacemaking.

IX. PEACEMAKING THROUGH JUSTICE, LAW, AND HUMAN RIGHTS

It is a simple fact of history that most conflicts, most wars, emerge when one party perceives that they have a grievance of some kind against another party. Since humankind first emerged with early tribal societies, the responsibility for peacemaking devolved onto those wise elders of the community who sought to reconcile or adjudge between conflicting parties and to ascertain the balance of justice in any given case of conflict. In preliterate communities, such judicial processes were dealt with through oral testimony and through a regime of sanctions motivated by the desire to ensure the con-

tinued functioning in harmony of the tribal collective. In historic civilizations, legal codes and practices evolved, often in concert with the religious beliefs and values of the community, since the final arbiter and dispenser of justice was felt to be the Divine Source of life itself, which communicated its dictates to humankind through religious revelation. In the modern era, as humankind has realized the full extent of the diversity of cultures and civilizations coexisting on the earth, legal thinkers have attempted to derive universal codes of behavior and conduct that would be most conducive to guaranteeing peace and stability among the population at large. Subsequently the legal profession has emerged as a highly complex and professional field of knowledge and praxis that has paramount importance when it comes to the varied modalities of peacemaking. Not surprisingly, therefore, professional lawyers and legal thinkers have been in the forefront of devising theoretical and practical ways of balancing claim and counterclaim against the dictates of reason. Legal terminology often betrays this close connection— the term Justice of the Peace, for example, is only given to legal officers in the United Kingdom, and the notion of the preservation of the peace is at the forefront of the idea of the legal process itself. Similarly, in international relations the field of international law has emerged as a governing superstructure that should theoretically determine the correct relations between divergent nations and their respective claims against one another. Sadly, the due process of international law, enshrined constitutionally at present in the International Court of Justice at The Hague and currently part of the United Nations system, has not been able always, or indeed very often, to provide suitable mechanisms to prevent aggrieved nations from trying to pursue their actions on the court of the battlefield. Professional legal associations such as the American Bar Association (Standing Committee on Dispute Resolution) have therefore been supportive of new initiatives in alternative dispute resolution and mediation, and many legal professionals also give advice or work professionally for such organizations. Academic legal institutes, such as the Harvard Law School, or centers for international legal thought, such as the Institute of Advanced Legal Studies at the University of London, have likewise developed programs and courses that focus on law as an instrument of peacebuilding, whether at the local, national, or international levels. Much more work remains to be done, however, in this area, with several outstanding problems; for example, the problem of state sovereignty in international law versus the responsibility of the international community to intervene in cases of severe human rights abuses. The international legal mechanisms of the United Nations machinery have as yet proved unable to provide clear intellectual and practical leadership in this difficult question, although the principles established by the trials of the Nazi officers at Nuremberg at the end of the Second World War did establish that individuals are also accountable before the standards and codes enshrined in international law. In the War Crimes Tribunal arising from the Bosnian War and the Rwandan conflict in the 1990s, these principles have continued to be applied. Certainly then, the clear relationship between peacemaking, peacebuilding, and justice is established both in the popular mind and also in legal precedent—however, the complex reality of legal processes often prevents the theory from becoming translated into practical reality on the ground. The Truth and Reconciliation Commission in South Africa, following the end of apartheid, is another imaginative example of the way in which legal process can sometimes extend its vision into wider peacemaking arenas. Senior authorities of goodwill realize that the provision of justice is also a psychological precondition for the successful gelling of any community of separate wills, binding them to wider loyalties than to immediate self-interest. The new International Criminal Court established by Treaty in Rome, Italy, June 15–July 17, 1998, is a new historic initiative to give teeth to all these attempts to build peace through justice.

X. MEDIATION AS PEACEMAKING

The extensive field of mediation is closely allied to the legal process and has evolved as an alternative to the formal legal system in which parties are brought into dialogue through the intermediary role of neutral third parties. Mediation as a process of active peacemaking is a field that has been present in human societies for millennia, but in its formal modern sense has been professionalized only in recent decades. At present many specialist mediation services exist in most advanced industrialized societies, helping to bring people in dispute toward reconciliation across various sectors, including divorce and family mediation, community and neighbourhood mediation, multifaith and interreligious mediation, industrial dispute mediation, environmental dispute mediation, international mediation, business mediation, and so on. In all these sectors this work could be characterized as an important mechanism of peacemaking, observing confidentiality and openness, in which parties agree to work together to-

ward the successful resolution of their disputes by brainstorming alternative solutions and examining the problem jointly, with a certain distance, and encouraged by the mediators.

XI. NATURE AND ENVIRONMENTAL PEACEBUILDING

This is one field in which mediation is developing as a necessary accompaniment to the growing realization in the world community as to how nature and natural resources should be viewed. All kinds of disputes come up here: from Greenpeace taking direct action to protest against the dumping of old oil rigs in the Atlantic ocean; to animal rights protesters who sometimes take the law into their own hands and use violence against their fellow citizens to make their point; to groups protesting against the construction of new roads or airport extensions; to aboriginal groups protesting against mineral extraction on their native lands, whether in the U.S. or in Australia; to disputes over water resources, which are growing increasingly scarce in some regions (such disputes being important, for example, in Israel's reluctance to return the Golan Heights to Syria, since they provide much of the water Israel needs); to disputes over oil such as in the Gulf War; to protesters campaigning for compensation from the effect of nuclear accidents or other industrial waste spillage, such as large oil spills in the open seas.

All these problems ideally require mediation, and some specialist mediation services have come into being to provide attempts at resolving such problems through peaceful means. What is, of course, needed is some sort of long-term global resource planning such as was attempted by the UN Conference on Sustainable Development and the subsequent international conferences on population change, global warming, urban habitats, and ozone depletion, since this would be the only really effective way of developing lasting peacebuilding measures in this sector. Unfortunately the world's political mechanisms are structured in such a way that it militates against the sort of global overview that would be necessary for peacebuilding through long-term environmental resource planning, with an emphasis rather on short-term political advantage and strategic infighting, conducted in a largely nationalist and regionalist framework, thus clouding the long-term perspective. In spite of this, international and intergovernmental organizations, such as the United Nations and the European Union, and NGOs, such as the Club of Rome, Earthwatch, Greenpeace, and so on, do continue to press home the importance of developing long-term peace-building. It would be fair to say that environmental peacemaking is an area of growing importance to the field of peacemaking and peacebuilding, and one whose significance will undoubtedly increase as resources become even more scarce in the future, including particularly water, oil, food, land, and energy.

XII. POLITICS, POLITICAL SCIENCE, AND PEACEBUILDING

A. General Observations

While Clausewitz characterized politics as war continued by other means, an observation kinder to one's moral estimation of humanity would be to say that war is what occurs when the political process breaks down. It is one of the vital characteristics of different successful political systems that they should contain, within their constitutional processes, mechanisms whereby conflicts and disputes can be successfully resolved through the nonviolent revolutions of the "wheel of fortune," (as Machiavelli termed it), of political power. The fact that this is all too often not the case and that in many countries at present, and all countries in the past, significant political change only occurs when there is accompanying violence, revolution, war, and upheaval is an indication of how far we have still to go in the true task of genuine peacebuilding through political understanding and praxis.

B. Diplomacy

Diplomacy is, of course, the formal branch of international politics whereby nation-states try to cement their relations in lasting mechanisms of concord, thus providing a context in which their differences can be resolved without recourse to violent action. Too often, however, diplomatic intrigue has in reality been used as a vehicle for the promotion of one state's interests against those of others. In the modern era there has been a continuing tendency to leave international peacemaking structures to arrangements between great powers, and recently between superpowers, in which case the hierarchy of peacemaking decisions has been arbitrated by those states which possess a plenitude of ultimate military power. Peace treaties, normally signed by parties at the conclusion of hostilities, all too often in history have failed to provide satisfactory lasting arrangements whereby the parties concerned are discouraged from resuming hostilities. Even the United Nations, formed at the end of World War II, while putting in place such a lasting mechanism, has not succeeded in preventing the outbreak of innumerable local wars ever since. Advanced observers and actors of the international diplomatic scene are united at present in the belief that more can and should be done in the way of preventative diplomacy and confidence-building to create an international climate in which recourse to violence and war could become an outmoded way of resolving disputes and grievances among nations. One of the key problem areas here is that many modern wars and conflicts involve guerrilla movements practicing terrorist strategies, whose legitimacy to engage in genuine diplomatic exchanges is questioned by official governments. As yet there are few international diplomatic mechanisms in place to effect problem-solving dialogue and negotiations between such state and nonstate parties. Academics involved in international relations and students of diplomacy are urgently continuing therefore to develop alternative models of dispute resolution and peacebuilding that can involve even such actors successfully.

C. Political Structures and Systems

The problem of peacebuilding versus political structures is not a recent one: political theorists since Plato and Aristotle have endeavored to compare the advantages of differing constitutions and polities in order to devise the optimal model of ensuring peace and justice for the community as a whole. In former times, empires and monarchies were seen as the best guarantor of overall peace, in which some one person or dynasty held absolute authority. Constitutional monarchies are felt by some to offer all that was best in these former systems while losing their worst features. Democratic and republican political structures have long been argued to present a more effective way of providing a mechanism for disputes among different rival interest groups to be acted out through electoral procedures without resulting in open violence. Modern democratic politics, it could be argued, represents the least worst available system of political peacebuilding, enabling communities to air their differences, to discuss policy and social issues, and to exercise control and accountability over their leaders without requiring citizens to turn violent in order to have their views known. It could be said, however, that we still have some way to go, even in advanced democracies, for the inherent powers of peacebuilding to really mature to their full potential—and that in the present democratic system we too often get either immature tit-for-tat oppositional mechanisms that seem to institutionalize mental violence and polarization and in which the internal micropolitics of political parties and the enormous power of the media too often prevent any real depth of vision and moral leadership from emerging or, at worst, we get corruption and nepotism in which pseudo-democratic mechanisms are used to give a gloss to ruling elites operating from behind the scenes.

XIII. SOCIAL AND ECONOMIC THOUGHT AND PEACEBUILDING

A. Economic and Social Development and Peacebuilding

Each of the sectors of peacebuilding examined previously ultimately reduces to a social dimension, since people are the final building blocks in peacebuilding. Yet people, and their societies and communities, are living, organic beings, who function autonomously and spontaneously, unlike bricks and mortar. The stresses and strains on modern societies are enormous, with all kinds of unenvisaged pressures creating conflict and violence in peoples daily lives. Economic pressures are perhaps foremost among these: the daily struggle for economic survival remains pressing for a large percentage of the earth's 6 billion inhabitants, with as yet no universally agreed-upon theories and policies as to how human societies can really guarantee social security and well-being to all citizens. Unemployment and economic insecurity in turn can lead to domestic violence and crime and in some cases to extreme revolutionary movements prepared to use violence. In 1995 the United Nations convened an epochal Summit on Social Development, which brought together over 140 heads of state and senior governmental representatives to debate policies that could end poverty, unemployment, and social conflicts worldwide. While the Declaration and Action Plan issuing from the conference sent forth a clear signal of intent on the part of those participating, the fact remains that the challenges facing those involved in developing global social and economic policies worldwide to combat the problems are awesome. Racism and racial conflict remain rampant with xenophobic attitudes recurring in many societies worldwide and racial conflicts and attacks on the increase in many quarters. Immigration and refugee movements, often caused by unrest in their countries of origin, fuel such problems, and although many mechanisms are in place at the national and international levels to combat racism, the problem remains urgent. The rapid pace of technological and industrial change has led to many pockets of permanent unemployment and hopelessness, in which whole communities feel abandoned and marginalized. Social scientists and economists continue to produce detailed analyses of the causes of social exclusion and poverty, and development studies experts have produced highly significant overviews of the in-built problems in world society whereby a small elite continue to control access to the vast majority of the earth's resources in both the material and intellectual dimensions. The grand project of communism of course tried to establish a new social system in which such problems were eradicated, but it was only able to do so at the expense of personal freedoms and human rights. The general downfall of communism as a model of human betterment and its replacement, the free market, however, has not necessarily led to an increase of social well-being on the part of many societies experimenting with newer and more liberal forms of social engineering. On the contrary, some former communist countries, including Russia, have witnessed an alarming increase of social problems in the wake of liberalization, including the rise of Mafia-style gangs and criminalization, the increase of violent crime, unemployment, and despair. The challenges facing social and economic thinkers to devise workable models for social and economic arrangements that guarantee peace-as-prosperity are therefore enormous. The danger is that if they fail there will be a return to more totalitarian-style experiments.

B. Industrial Relations, Management Science and Industrial Peacemaking

Another important area of civil conflict, and one that continues to tax the imagination of peacebuilders, concerns the arena of industrial relations. With the wide-scale impetus toward privatization and growing competition for jobs in the market place, there has been an accompanying decline in the power of trade unions in many countries. Nevertheless, trade unions continue to seek betterment for their members, organized in particular professional associations, and industrial disputes and strikes continue to cause social conflict in many instances. Organizations such as the Arbitration and Conciliation Service in the UK have been established by the government to provide mechanisms where such industrial disputes can be resolved without needless and protracted hardship and suffering on the part of those concerned. The International Labour Organisation, based in Geneva, continues to work for the rights of labor to organize and lobby for fair terms and conditions of employment worldwide. In many countries it is still illegal to form and join trade unions, and often active trade unionists are imprisoned and persecuted for campaigning even for basic employment rights. In the European Union a considerable body of industrial legislation is in force which provides protection for the rights of both workers and employers, yet this does not prevent a considerable degree of industrial unrest from taking place in that region as economic changes lead to invariable problems.

Advanced management theorists and business studies experts have similarly developed models and mechanisms whereby disputes within company management structures can be resolved without recourse to needless and protracted boardroom subterfuge and infighting. Business ethics is a growing field of study, and many successful companies are finding that guaranteeing worker satisfaction and a sense of involvement and ownership in their company is the best long-term strategy for maximizing all around success and for preventing needless disputes and dissatisfaction.

Creative negotiation techniques are one practical aspect of peacemaking that has resulted from this work, but as yet it could be said that the whole ethos of economic thinking remains embedded in outmoded models of cutthroat competition in which the basic assumption of "win–win" has failed to surface—too many actors still think in terms of "I win–you lose."

A further difficulty is associated with sudden global movements of capital and the complex arrangements of international trade and the various "trade wars" going on behind the scenes daily, which can result in considerable industrial uncertainty, insecurity, and conflict worldwide, even in economic regions once thought to be impervious to such problems. Certainly it would be fair to say that until the industrial and economic basis of general social prosperity can be assured, even in our highly complex and mobile international economic system, the effective ground plan for social and economic peace-as-prosperity will remain an illusive ideal.

XIV. CONCLUSION

Having examined in turn each of the main areas in which peacebuilding and peacemaking work is underway today, let us conclude by acknowledging that this is a hitherto under-explored terrain; the above must be regarded as sketch maps to a relatively under-explored country. At the time of writing major international conflicts are underway in the Balkans (Kosovo) and the Middle East (Iraq) along with many other parts of the world (Afghanistan, Algeria, Sierra Leone, etc.) and one

laments the fact that better peacemaking knowledge might have been used to prevent these conflicts breaking out in the first place, rather than looking to military expertise to resolve them once they have begun. All militarism and all violence is in the last analysis an admission of the failure of one's peacemaking skills, and in this most successfully warlike of centuries in human history, in which more people have perished from the industrial killing machines of modernity, we have to recognize the tragic fact that for all our technical brilliance as a species and as an emerging global civilization, modern humanity is still at kindergarten level when it comes to peacemaking and peacebuilding skills. There is a further tragic linguistic and conceptual irony to observe: the Latin terms for "peacemaking" were as follows: "pacificare," to make peace, to pacify; "pacificus," peace-making, peaceful; "pacificationem," the action of making peace; "pacifica," peace-offerings; "pacifice," peacefully; "pacifero," to keep peace; "pacificator," one who makes peace, a peacemaker; "pacificatorius," peacemaking, pacificatory. Ancient Latin then had a long linguistic recognition of the idea of "peacemaking." This same root gives us the words "pacifist," and "pacifism." Linguistically, these words descend from the Latin through French, and should simply mean "someone who believes in making peace" and "the belief in peace making." The second part of all these words, comes from Latin "facere," meaning to do, act, whence fact, facility, faculty, facilitate, face, etc. Sadly, in the whole debate over absolute "pacifism" (in the sense of absolute nonviolence) versus "peacemaking and peacemaking" as a work which sometimes needs violence in order to enforce justice, there has been overlooked the fact that a true pacifist, linguistically, is someone who advocates peace making as opposed to making war, and this is something which surely all intelligent people on this planet, in our age of super weaponry, can endorse. In other words, we cannot afford to be other than "pacifists" now—but can differ in our arguments as to how best to go about "making peace."

Many intelligent and well meaning people argue that warfare and violence are the most effective ways to "make peace" in situations of injustice. The current shift in military strategy to "peacekeeping" is accompanied by the rhetoric of using force to bring peace. This is an ancient argument which has been used to justify military force since as far back as the dawn of recorded history. The facts are somewhat different however; peace grows out of a sense of perceived justice on both sides; peace in the sense in which this article has conceived it is produced by a win–win resolution of conflict, not an imposition of perceived righteousness through superior military strength. The peace produced by military force usually leads to escalating spirals of violence, revenge, resentment, and smoldering aggression. History is littered with such spirals of violence which from time to time erupt inconflagration, such as the first and second world wars, and more recently the conflict in 1999 over Kosovo.

The challenges that lie ahead therefore are in marshaling the wisdom and intelligence of the world's intellectual, political, and religious forces to the common task of "peacemaking" on a powerful enough scale, and backed up by sufficient intelligence, knowledge, and right motivation, that the tragic conflicts of the present hour will seem in retrospect a cumbersome and barbarous way of resolving disputes which all have complex historic roots going back centuries, and which involve multi-dimensional variables, each of which requires separate attention. The fact is undeniable that warfare and violence have always been a very blunt instrument for resolving conflicts and disagreements and for "building peace" and that they are a last resort, sanctioned by some religious and ethical thinkers only in emergency and when every single other strategy has failed. But if we are not to resort to warfare and violence so swiftly, where is the knowledge and where are the skills which can ensure justice and security without the use or threat of violence?

If we are to survive as a global community of diverse human cultures living in relative harmony and peace, and to divert the resources which are so urgently needed for satisfying our social, economic, cultural and environmental needs, then there is no more urgent task facing the world's educational and scholarly community than to contribute to this ongoing debate and research as to working out the best modes of peacemaking, and educating our future "pacificators" with this vital knowledge.

Also See the Following Articles

PEACE EDUCATION: COLLEGES AND UNIVERSITIES • PEACE EDUCATION: YOUTH • PEACEKEEPING • PEACE MOVEMENTS • PEACE ORGANIZATIONS, NONGOVERNMENTAL • PEACE STUDIES, OVERVIEW • RELIGION AND PEACE, INNER-OUTER DIMENSIONS OF

Bibliography

Boulding, E. (1988). *Building a global civic culture: Education for an independent world.* New York: Columbia University, Teachers Press.

Chetkow-Yanoov, B. (1997). *Social work approaches to conflict resolution.* Binghamton, NY: Haworth Press.

Childre, D. L. (1996). *Teaching children to love.* Planetary.

Hall, L. (1990). *Negotiation strategies for mutual gain.* Beverly Hills, CA: Sage.

Higgins, R. (1990). *Plotting peace: The owls reply to hawks and doves.* London: Brasseys.

Johnston, D., & Sampson, C. (1994). *Religion, the missing dimension of statecraft.* Oxford, UK: Oxford University Press.

Liebmann, M. (1997). *Arts approaches to conflict.* London: Jessica Kingsley Publishers.

Pauling, L., Laszlo, E., & Yoo, J. Y. (1986). *World Encyclopedia of Peace.* Oxford, NY: Pergamon Press.

Smith, R. (1996). *Achieving civil justice.* Legal Action Group Education and Service Trust Limited, London.

Tannis, E. (1990). *Alternative dispute resolution.* York University, North York, Ontario: Captus Press.

Tavris, C. (1989). *Anger, the misunderstood emotion.* New York: Touchstone Press.

Unesco yearbook on peace and conflict studies. New York and Westport, CT: Greenwood Press.

Peace Movements

Robert D. Benford

University of Nebraska—Lincoln

Frank O. Taylor IV

Dana College

GLOSSARY

International Nongovernmental Organizations (INGOs) These are nonstate, nonprofit, formal organizations that operate in more than one country to achieve common objectives. Many INGOs promote institutional and policy changes in the international order related to peace, justice, and human rights

Negative Peace The absence of war. A focus on negative peace involves an emphasis on peace-restoring and peacekeeping.

Nuclear Pacifism Opposition to nuclear war. This term was sometimes used disparagingly by traditional pacifists to refer to members of the antinuclear movement whom traditional pacifists felt were not committed more fundamentally to pacifist principles.

Peace Movement A sustained, organized attempt by groups of people to prevent a war from breaking out, to end an ongoing war, to build a peaceful and just society, and/or to build a peaceful world order.

Positive Peace Generally refers to harmonious, nonexploitative social conditions that facilitate the universal maintenance of human rights and dignity. It spe-

cifically refers to the absence of conditions that lead to war. A focus on positive peace yields an emphasis on peace-building.

Religious Pacifism Opposition to war based on religious teachings and spiritual beliefs.

Secular Pacifism Opposition to war based on moral principles other than religious ones.

Social Movement An organized, sustained attempt by groups of people to promote or resist social change. Typically, social movements refer to collective, extra-institutional challenges to the status quo by those lacking power to affect change via traditional means.

THE TERM PEACE MOVEMENT has been applied to a variety of social movements that seek to affect peace between two or more countries. More precisely, a peace movement is a sustained, organized attempt by groups of people to prevent a war from breaking out, to end an ongoing war, to build a peaceful and just society, and/or to build a peaceful world order.

I. INTRODUCTION

People often clamor for social change. That is, they identify some aspect of their society, including its institutions, as problematic and in need of alteration. When people organize themselves into sustained groups and develop a set of strategies and tactics to bring about

Copyright © 1999 by Academic Press.
All rights of reproduction in any form reserved.

the desired change, they constitute a social movement. This article focuses on one particular variety of contemporary social movements, those which have sought peace in one form or another during the past 200 years.

People often speak of "the peace movement," suggesting a single, cohesive movement having continuity across time. On closer examination, the past 2 centuries have produced numerous mass-based peace movements around the world. These movements have been quite diverse with respect to goals, methods, and members. The impact of these movements has varied, too. Some have had a significant impact on people's attitudes toward war as well as on governments' willingness to wage wars and to engage in peace dialogues. Others have had virtually no apparent effect, except perhaps on their own members.

Historically, many peace movements have tended to focus on preventing an imminent conflict, stopping an ongoing war, or eliminating specific instruments of war. The general goal of these peace movements has been on achieving negative peace; that is, the absence of war. These peace movements are reactive in the sense that their mobilizations are based on reactions to events such as threats of war, actual wars, or the development of new weapons of war. Virtually every war over the past 2 centuries has spawned peace movements.

Other peace movements have focused on establishing social systems that promote positive peace and social structures and processes that facilitate harmonious and nonexploitative relations within and among human groups. The general goal of these peace movements has been to build a harmonious world by reducing and ultimately eliminating the root causes of war. In contrast to the reactive peace movements, these movements tend to be proactive. In other words, they make new claims or offer permanent solutions intended to eliminate the roots of war. Table I compares the general goals of peace movements advocating negative peace versus those advocating positive peace.

Modern peace movements not only vary in terms of

TABLE I

General Goals of Peace Movements

Reactive: negative peace	Proactive: positive peace
Stop military interventions	Establish international organizations
Prevent an imminent war	Promote human rights
Stop an ongoing war	Establish social justice
Eliminate instruments of war	Eliminate causes of war

the scope of the social change advocated, they also vary with respect to the levels at which the changes are sought. Many peace movements seek changes at the international and transnational levels. These changes can range from negative peace goals such as arms reduction and disarmament agreements among nations to positive peace goals such as developing transnational mechanisms for ensuring human rights around the globe. Peace movements may also direct their resources at the national level. For example, peace movements often lobby executive and legislative bodies to stop the funding of particular weapons systems. Peace movements also occasionally focus on the local level, as when peace activists target local industries associated with weapons production. Finally, peace movements may direct their attention on the individual or group level via consciousness-raising efforts and/or by seeking to affect people's day-to-day behaviors. Some peace movements concentrate their efforts on only one level; others pursue changes across several levels simultaneously. Table II summarizes and compares the campaigns, goals, and strategies of reactive peace movements and proactive peace movements across various levels of change.

II. CYCLES OF PEACE MOVEMENTS

Peace movements around the world have experienced cycles of mobilization. Associated with these cycles have been fluctuations in the amount of attention peace movements devote toward negative peace versus positive peace. During times of international tensions and war, peace movements tend to grow. Not surprisingly, wartime yields a disproportionate focus on the task at hand—stopping organized violent responses of the rival nations toward one another. Yet even during wars, some wings of a peace movement's focus extend beyond ending the current hostilities toward building more permanent amicable relations among societies.

Regardless of their focus, wartime peace activists are often vulnerable to accusations on the homefront that, at the very least, they are undermining the war effort by lowering the morale of their nation's soldiers. Sometimes peace activists are accused of aiding and abetting the "enemy." Hence, during popular wars the number of regular participants in peace movements may decrease as the amount of peace movement activities paradoxically increases.

Once a war ends, peace activism tends to shift toward prevention. With the horrors of war fresh on people's minds, peace activists advocating working toward posi-

TABLE II

Peace Movement Campaigns, Goals, and Strategies by Levels of Focus

Levels	Reactive: (negative peace)	Proactive: (positive peace)
International	Protests against weapons systems Arms reduction & disarmament Treaties, cease-fires Anti-intervention Witness for peace Arbitration	International organizations World federalism Social justice Human rights Liberation theology World court Environmental justice
National	Protests against weapons systems within specific nations Protest external occupations & intervening abroad Protests against joining alliances Lobbying legislative bodies & executive branch Tax resistance Draft resistance	Political changes Economic justice Economic conversion Peace studies Glasnost/peristoika Media
Local	Stop weapons deployment at sites Protest at weapons sites, defense factories	Mediation City twinning Détente from below
Group/individual	Seek to persuade individual soldiers to lay down arms	Consciousness raising Family socialization Gender socialization Conflict resolution Pacifism

tive peace are briefly granted greater legitimacy. However, even during "peacetime," many peace movements tend to concentrate on the weapons of destruction rather than on the political and economic arrangements that are conducive to war. Whether their goal is terminating a weapon system (negative peace) or eliminating the causes of war (positive peace), peacetime activists are often accused of being idealists, well-meaning but naive.

III. NEGATIVE PEACE-SEEKING

The prevalence of threats of war, ongoing wars, and weapons of mass destruction trigger the bulk of peace movement activities. Although most peace activists devoted to working toward achieving negative peace would ultimately prefer to be working for positive peace, the urgency of the threats and the severity of the suffering caused by wars commands many activists' immediate attention. Thus, most peace movements that advocate negative peace do so in reaction to specific events or conditions. Reactive peace movement campaigns, strategies, and tactics are thus organized around

the goals of preventing a conflict from becoming a war; stopping ongoing wars; or eliminating the production, testing, uses, and stockpiles of existing weapons. These goals have been pursued at various levels ranging from the international and transnational arena to the national level to local communities

A. International/Transnational Campaigns

With the possible exception of civil wars, wars, by definition, involve two or more nations engaged in sustained military hostilities toward one another. Even in the case of civil wars, additional nations typically enter the conflict on one side or the other. Hence, peace movements often focus their mobilization efforts at the international or transnational level. Initially, some peace movements seek to find alternatives to war.

1. Arbitration

Attempts to finding alternatives to war have ranged from relatively modest to sweeping strategies. All sorts of means were suggested in the early 1800s including disarmament, an international court, arbitration, and world federalism. Thus, the concept of some type of juridical-political process of arbitration was among the earliest proposals for preventing conflicts from erupting into wars. The London Peace society, founded in 1816, emphasized both arbitration and Christian principles as paths to peace. The American Peace Society, founded in 1828, combined Christian principles with the belief that all international disputes could be settled by arbitration. To this end they supported the idea of a Congress of Nations.

After the Civil War an opportunity for successful arbitration presented itself in the strained relations between the U.S. and Great Britain. The U.S. was seeking compensation for damage caused by Confederate ships built by the British. The British were smarting over Irish-American incursions into Canada. In 1871 a joint High Commission concluded the Treaty of Washington, which provided for a five-member arbitration tribunal based in Geneva, Switzerland. The tribunal successfully arbitrated the differences between the two nations. Encouraged by the success of the arbitration tribunal, peace-seekers became interested in the codification of international law and arbitration procedures. A Draft Outline of an International Code was produced in 1872 by advocates of arbitration. This was followed by an international meeting of arbitration activists in Brussels in 1873 and the establishment of the Association for the Reform and Codification of the Law of Nations. This association served as the main stimulus for the reform of international law until 1895, when it became the International Law Association.

By the end of the 19th century peace activists were generally in favor of establishing international arbitration and a world court. Another arbitration effort successfully headed off armed conflict between Britain and Venezuela when their Venezuela/British Guiana border dispute was resolved at The Hague in 1895. After World War I, such notable figures as Elihu Root, Andrew Carnegie, and Jane Addams, among a host of lawyers, feminists, educators, government officials, and industrialists, committed themselves to the establishment of some type of international peacekeeping machinery such as arbitration or world federalism. This peace movement kept pressure on Washington to join the World Court, to sign various arbitration agreements, and finally to sign the Pact of Paris in 1928.

2. Anti-Imperialism and Anti-Interventionism

In addition to arbitration, peace movements have responded with a variety of sustained campaigns aimed at preventing hostilities from erupting into wars, including isolationism, anti-imperialism, and anti-interventionism. Isolationists urged their leaders to minimize international relations as a means of avoiding getting involved in entanglements, alliances, and other situations that could lead to war. But with the development of transnational transportation systems and the resulting emergence of a global economy, isolationism became an implausible course to follow and isolationists dwindled in numbers. In contrast, anti-imperialist movements gained considerable popularity by the end of the 19th century. American anti-imperialists, for example, formed the Anti-Imperialist League in 1898 in order to voice organized opposition to U.S. expansionism in the Carribean, Samoa, Hawaii, and the Philippines.

A similar pattern of expansionism, internventionism, and public protest has marked U.S. relations with its neighboring nations to the south. For example, U.S. military interventions in Nicaragua in 1898, 1899, 1910, 1921, 1928, and 1983 were all countered with protests by various peace movements. Although U.S. intervention in Central America and South America typically followed the investment interests of U.S. businesses, the Reagan–Bush administrations turned Central America into a cold war battleground. During their administrations, the U.S. intervened in Nicaragua, Honduras, El Salvador, Guatemala, and Panama. In 1981 the U.S. began to finance a counterrevolutionary army ("Contras") in Central America organized for the purpose of overthrowing the Nicaraguan government. The Reagan administration's Central American policies gave rise to a peace movement that challenged interventionism on several fronts.

The Central American Peace Movement was composed of a broad collection of individual and collective action organizations. Of these movements, three were highly successful in promoting anti-interventionist activism: Sanctuary, Witness for Peace, and the Pledge of Resistance. Sanctuary mobilized over 70,000 U.S. citizens, who engaged in acts of civil disobedience, breaking federal immigration laws by providing shelter, food, and transportation for political refugees from Central American countries. Witness for Peace encouraged over 4,000 U.S. citizens to travel to Nicaragua to witness first-hand the death and destruction caused by U.S. policies. Over 80,000 individuals signed The Pledge of Resistance, threatening to engage in acts of mass civil disobedience if the U.S. invaded Central America.

Local and individual activism focused on candlelight vigils, establishing "twin" cities in the U.S. and Nicaragua; shipping truckloads of supplies, humanitarian aid, and materials to Central America; voting against prointervention politicians; and staging hunger strikes and war tax-resistance campaigns. Other anti-intervention social movement groups included: Veterans for Peace, Committee in Solidarity with the People of El Salvador, American Friends Service Committee, Interreligious Foundation for Community Organization, Religious Task Force on Central America, Sojourners Peace Ministry, and Nicaragua Network. Veterans For Peace, for example, lead a convoy of trucks through U.S. cities picking up supplies along the way, ultimately reaching Nicaragua. The anti-intervention coalition used a variety of tactics, such as promoting Central America weeks, educational events, the production and distribution of films to television stations and community groups throughout the nation, speakers' bureaus, and religious ceremonies. In October, 1984 these various tactics, in conjunction with sustained lobbying efforts, proved successful when the U.S. Congress voted to end military aid to the Contras. By 1989 the global movement for peace in Central America had succeeded in persuading five Central American presidents to call for the demobilization of the Contras and to agree to United Nations' supervision of the peace process.

The case of the Central American Peace Movement of the 1980s illustrates how organized opposition to interventionism and imperialism can arise within the intervening or "imperialist" nation as well as internationally. Yet the Central American Peace Movement was also comprised of grassroots, indigenous organizations; that is, locally based groups of citizens within the various Central American countries affected by U.S. interventionism. While native resistance to U.S. policies frequently took the form of armed "guerrilla" groups in Guatemala, Hondouras, El Salvador, and Nicaragua, a number of nonviolent organizations opposed to U.S. hegemony in the region were also formed in those countries.

Perhaps the largest and most successful indigenously organized movement against imperialism was the Indian Freedom Movement. Soon after World War I, Mohandas Gandhi initiated nonviolent campaigns opposing repressive British laws and policies. Although the movement was initially reactive, spawned by a collective desire to overcome various injustices associated with British colonial rule, Gandhi's method of truth-seeking or "satyagraha" was a proactive strategy based on positive peace principles of love, nonviolence, mutual respect, and self-sacrifice. In the end, the heavily armed British forces turned out to be no match against the moral, persuasive power of active, nonviolent resistance. By 1947, the nonviolent movement had not only succeeded in obtaining India's independence from Great Britain, it had also sown the seeds of the British Empire's destruction and contributed significantly to the demise of European colonialism.

3. Preventing Imminent Conflicts from Becoming Wars

From Central America to North America to the Middle East, modern history is replete with examples of peace movements attempting to prevent hostilities between nations from erupting into war. For example, on the eve of the Mexican–American War (1846), representatives from the American Peace Society and the London Peace Society urged U.S. President Polk to accept negotiation or arbitration by a third party such as Great Britain. A century later, just after the founding of Israel, a peace movement was organized there for the purpose of attempting to reduce Israeli–Arab tensions, to encourage representatives to negotiate mutually satisfactory agreements with the Palestinians, and to prevent war. Nearly another half-century later, just days prior to the 1991 Persian Gulf War, peace groups around the world sought to prevent Operation Desert Shield from being transformed into Desert Storm.

In the United States, opposition to the Persian Gulf War progressed through three stages: (1) opposition by the peace movement to the build-up of forces in Saudi Arabia; (2) attempts to prevent U.S. military action; and (3) calls for a cease-fire and negotiations once the war had commenced. In the first two stages U.S. opposition to the military build-up were largely local and spontaneous, including demonstrations in Boston, Chicago, Austin, San Francisco, New York, and Washington D.C. National Organizations, such as SANE/FREEZE and the American Friends Service Committee (AFSC) also tried to prevent the war from starting. The AFSC sent speakers on a tour of the nation and SANE/FREEZE sent legislative alerts to their members urging them to write to their elected officials. Veterans for Peace members spoke out against the use of military force. Operation Real Security produced a television ad stressing the human costs of war. The Central Committee for Conscientious Objectors and other like organizations provided draft counseling services. Peace activists in San Francisco convinced their city council to declare their entire city a sanctuary for conscientious objectors.

During the third phase the peace movement stressed negotiation and an end to active fighting. While spontaneous street demonstrations and peace rallies continued in the U.S., global opposition flourished. Massive protests and antiwar rallies took place in Paris, Bonn, Rome, Montreal, Athens, Barcelona, Buenos Aries, and numerous cities in Great Britain. These protests were largely ignored by the mainstream media. In the U.S. numerous additional national organizations came out against the war. The National Organization of Women, nine major labor unions and hundreds of their locals, Roman Catholic bishops, and the National Council of Churches all encouraged the political leaders to bring the troops home. Operation Real Security launched a major lobbying effort in Washington D.C., asking politicians if they would sacrifice their own children in order to maintain U.S. hegemony in the Middle East.

Although, for a variety of reasons, most attempts at preventing imminent conflicts from turning into wars ultimately proved unsuccessful, the preventative efforts of peace movements were remarkable. Ordinary citizens pursued an extraordinary goal: preventing a war from breaking out.

4. Stopping Ongoing Wars

Just as peace movements have enjoyed few successes in preventing hostilities from erupting into wars, their influence on existing wars has been somewhat limited. Yet, because of the prevalence of war in modern history, peace movements have frequently been tansformed into antiwar movements. As the example of the Persian Gulf War illustrates, peace groups originally organized to prevent war or to halt foreign interventions often find it necessary to shift their focus to stopping wars.

The outbreak of World War I (1914–1918) was both a tragic setback for all peace activists and a catalyst for the emergence of the modern peace movement. Initially, World War I radically split the peace movement. Existing peace societies either wavered or supported the Allied cause. As peace historian Charles Chatfield (1971) notes, the peace movement was reorganized; those who supported the war and those who adamantly opposed it aligned into two factions. Restless pacifists formed several new peace movement organizations including the Fellowship of Reconciliation (1914), the Women's Peace Party (1915), the American Union Against Militarism (1916), and the American Friends Service Committee (1917).

Women, with the exception of a few social reformers such as Jane Addams, had to this point played a relatively minor role in the peace movement. World War I prompted Addams, U.S. women's suffrage movement leader Carrie Chapman Catt, English suffragist Emmeline Pethik-Lawrence, and Hungarian suffragist Rosika Schwimmer to mobilize women to end the war. Under their leadership, nearly 3000 prominent women met in Washington D.C. in January 1915 and founded the Women's Peace Party. In the words of Charles DeBenedetti (1980, p. 94), it was a "dramatic attempt to mobilize the consciousness of international womanhood

against the war." Though they failed to end the war, the party contributed to the establishment of a neutral mediation base at The Hague, which remained available throughout the conflict. Moreover, the Women's Peace Party led to the formation of the Women's International Peace and Freedom, the first feminist-pacifist organization to emerge in the transnational drive for peace and justice.

Although it is difficult to determine the impact of antiwar movements on the leaders of the warring nations, such organized opposition has occasionally been effective in containing a war to a specific region and in limiting its duration. The Vietnam antiwar movement provides a dramatic illustration of the impact a movement can have on the course of a war. According to Charles Chatfield, the antiwar movement that "gathered in the United States between 1955 and 1975 [constituted] the largest domestic opposition to a warring government in the history of modern industrial society" (DeBenedetti and Chatfield 1990, p. 408). The movement affected the policies of Presidents Johnson and Nixon as well as the policies of North Vietnam and South Vietnam (Small and Hoover 1992). It prevented the Pentagon from expanding the war as far as envisioned, pressured the parties into negotiations, and eventually halted U.S. intervention in Vietnam.

Organized opposition to the Vietnam War came from a variety of sources including traditional pacifists, clergy, university students, civil rights movement leaders, feminist activists, politicians, ordinary citizens, and the war's own veterans. No single organization or coalition managed to assume the leadership of the movement. Rather it was comprised of numerous new and old peace movement organizations and ad hoc coalitions. The movement's tactical repertoire was equally diverse. At one time or another it employed campus teach-ins, letter-writing campaigns, lobbying, boycotts, vigils, picketing, mass demonstrations, tax protests, draft resistance, other forms of civil disobedience, and the legal system in an attempt to halt the war.

Opposition to the war emanated not only from large segments of the U.S. population but also from within Vietnam. Throughout the war, Buddhists in South Vietnam voiced opposition to the domination by either the U.S. or North Vietnam. At times their dramatic forms of antiwar protest captured the attention of the global media. On June 11, 1963 a Buddhist monk named Thich Qang Duc sat down in the middle of a downtown Saigon intersection and allowed himself to be consumed by fire. This horrific act was transmitted around the world via newspapers, magazines, and television. More self-immolations followed. Witnessing such ultimate sacrifices for the cause led some people back in the U.S. to question for the first time its government's Southeast Asian policies (DeBenedetti and Chatfield, 1990).

5. Eliminating Weapons

One recurrent solution to war advocated by peace movements has been to get rid of the guns, bullets, and other instruments of war. Numerous international disarmament movements have focused on eliminating specific types of weapons and weapons systems including conventional, chemical, biological, and nuclear.

From the dawning of the nuclear age to present international movements have sought to rid the planet of nuclear weapons. Pacifists around the world were appalled that the U.S. had used atomic weapons on Japanese civilians as a pretense to end World War II. Yet, other than a scientists' movement for international control of nuclear energy, there was little in the way of organized global opposition to nuclear weapons until the mid-1950s. In March of 1954 23 Japanese sailors were contaminated by radioactive fallout from a U.S. hydrogen bomb test in the Pacific. Objections to the testing poured in from every corner of the globe including India, Europe, and Japan. Antinuclear movements began to spring up everywhere. In Japan, the incident provoked intense public revulsion and mass demonstrations, instigating a massive antinuclear movement. In Great Britain, the response took the form of the "ban the bomb" movement. And in the U.S., a large "test ban" movement spread across the country and beyond. This movement realized a partial victory in 1963 with the ratification of the Limited Test Ban Treaty.

By the mid-1960s, peace activists increasingly turned their attention once again to opposing a hot war, the Vietnam War. Thus, the once-active nuclear disarmament movement and many of its organizations (e.g., SANE, Physicians for Social Responsibility, Campaign for Nuclear Disarmament) lay dormant for a number of years. Several factors stimulated the revival of the nuclear disarmament movement as a global movement in the early 1980s. Perhaps the most important factor was the December, 1979 U.S./NATO decision to deploy Pershing II and ground-launched cruise missiles in West Germany, Great Britain, Belgium, Italy, and the Netherlands.

By the fall of 1981, Europeans were taking to the streets in record numbers to protest the missile deployment plans. On September 5, women from Great Britain and a number of other nations established a peace encampment at the gates of the proposed cruise missile site in Greenham Common, England. Realizing that their own efforts to eliminate such weapons were limited, European peace activists challenged U.S. peace activists for assistance in their struggle.

The calls came not only from Western European movements, but from Eastern Europeans as well. In Poland, for example, a section of the Solidarity Movement, Ranks of Peace and Solidarity, initiated a nationwide peace movement. They demanded the withdrawal of all nuclear weapons and Soviet soldiers from Polish territory and the reduction of arms production and security forces. The Polish Peace Movement also called on Western peace movements to give open support to the activities of independent peace movements in the Eastern Bloc.

As the Eastern and Western European activists prodded their U.S. counterparts to take action to stop the missile deployment, newly elected President Ronald Reagan inadvertently further stimulated the movement's revival. His bellicose rhetoric and the casual way he publicly talked about "fighting and winning" "protracted" and "limited" nuclear wars frightened Americans as well as Europeans.

The movement's revival was clearly underway in the United States by the Fall of 1981. On that Veterans Day (November 11), approximately 100,000 students took part in Vietnam-era style "teach-ins" on over 150 campuses regarding the threat of nuclear war. The following summer 750,000 people from around the world marched past the United Nations during its Second Special Session on Disarmament. Two days later, over 3,000 protesters staged sit-ins at the UN missions of the five major nuclear powers. Although the movement divided over a number of issues such as whether it should pursue total disarmament, unilateral disarmament, or a bilateral freeze on nuclear weapons production, testing, and deployment, its appeal spread rapidly.

By 1984 peace movements around the world had managed to get their countries or states declared as "nuclear free zones." The nuclear free zone movement was particularly successful in the Pacific. A Nuclear Free and Independent Pacific Movement led an international campaign against the deployment of sea-launched cruise missiles by the U.S. and the U.S.S.R. The movement in New Zealand was so successful that it persuaded a new administration to refuse to allow U.S. ships from entering its ports despite intense pressure from U.S. officials. While some of the nuclear disarmament movement's campaigns were directed at international and transnational targets, the bulk of their resources were directed at national and local level targets.

B. National Campaigns

In addition to negative peace-seeking directed at a host of international and transnational targets, peace movements also frequently organize domestic campaigns. They engage in protests against the production of specific weapons, lobby political elites on matters of war and peace, refuse to pay taxes to sustain warmaking, and resist military conscription.

1. Campaigns against Weapons Systems within Specific Nations

While peace movements have occasionally called for general disarmament, many movements have sought to stop their native country from producing, deploying, or allowing other countries to deploy specific types of weapons within their borders. In the Netherlands, for example, the Dutch Interchurch Peace Council (IKV) successfully mobilized against the neutron bomb, a weapon that destroys people but preserves property. Tens-of-thousands of Dutch citizens demonstrated against the weapon's deployment on Dutch soil, and another million signed antineutron bomb petitions. The Dutch peace movement's efforts paid off in 1978 when their government announced that they would not allow neutron bombs to be deployed in the Netherlands. Shortly thereafter, U.S. President Carter decided to postpone neutron bomb production.

One of the most well-organized campaigns in the U.S. against a specific weapon was the "Stop the MX Campaign." Soon after the Carter Administration proposed a mobile basing system for Intercontinental Ballistic Missiles, a grassroots, single-issue campaign was organized. Like many narrowly focused peace movement campaigns, the Stop the MX Campaign realized successes and suffered failures. The campaign was successful in that it defeated Pentagon plans to base the missiles in a mobile system, a deployment plan that nuclear arms control advocates feared would make obtaining a verifiable treaty more difficult. The movement was also successful in that it was able to pressure the Reagan administration to negotiate with the Soviets at Geneva for arms reduction. Finally, the movement succeeded in limiting the number of MX missiles deployed to only one quarter the number originally sought by the Pentagon nuclear strategists. But, despite these important successes, the Stop the MX Campaign ultimately failed to stop the deployment of the new weapons system, one that many peace activists felt represented a

significant escalation in the nuclear arms race. Perhaps the most significant outcome of this campaign, though, was that the activists acquired considerable knowledge regarding lobbying and political processes.

2. Lobbying Political Elites

In pursuit of their goals, grassroots peace movements often seek to persuade political elites to take action. Whether the goal is stopping a weapon from being produced or deployed, reaching an arms control agreement, preventing or ending a foreign intervention, or ending an ongoing war, peace movement actors find it necessary to engage in various legislative and other mainstream political processes. The extent to which peace movements should get involved in such "normal" politics is often the subject of intense disagreement within movements. Some argue that the only way to affect the most critical decisions needed to achieve peace is to influence the elite decision-makers through established political channels. Other activists contend that the investment of movement resources in such lobbying campaigns weakens a movement, stripping it of its disruptive potential and thus diminishing its power to influence change through mass demonstrations and other tactics outside the official political process.

While concerns regarding the efficacy of peace movements shifting their tactics from the streets to the halls of parliaments are legitimate, peace movements have often found it effective to get involved in the official political processes. For example, the earliest peace societies in the U.S., such as the American Peace Society (1828), presented petitions to state legislatures and Congress calling for an end to war and slavery. Peace movements led successful lobbying campaigns to ratify various arms control agreements and to stop the deployment of specific weapons systems including the antiballistic missile system, the neutron bomb, the B-1 bomber, and to a lesser extent, the MX missile.

Perhaps the most well-organized and well-financed lobbying effort in U.S. peace movement history was organized by the Nuclear Weapons Freeze Campaign (NWFC). The NWFC employed traditional and nontraditional means in trying to persuade Congress to pass a nuclear weapons freeze resolution. They formed a political action committee that raised over six million dollars and mobilized thousands of volunteers for the Freeze Voter 1984 campaign. They held freeze referenda around the country. And they organized a "citizen's lobby," culminating in 5,000 local activists delivering petitions to Senators and Representatives containing over 800,000 signatures in favor of the freeze proposal.

In the Spring of 1983, NWFC lobbyists succeeded in persuading a majority of the members of the House of Representatives to pass a nuclear weapons freeze resolution. But the Senate tabled the motion and the freeze proposal eventually withered on the peace movement's vine. Nonetheless, the freeze campaign was successful in many respects. It raised the consciousness of many citizens regarding the dangers of nuclear war, encouraged Congress to limit the administrations's plans for deploying the Strategic Defense Initiative ("Star Wars"), restored arms control as an institutionalized policy, and contributed to ending the cold war by pushing the U.S. to the bargaining table and encouraging reformers in the Soviet Union and Eastern Europe.

3. Tax Resistance

One recurrent strategy of peace movements has been to encourage people to refuse to support war-making financially. The earliest known incidence of war tax resistance in North America occurred in 1637 when the peaceable Algonquin Indians refused to pay taxes to the Dutch to improve a fort in what is now Manhattan. But perhaps the most noteworthy case of war tax resistance involved Henry David Thoreau some 200 years later. Thoreau was jailed in 1846 for refusing to pay a poll tax he felt indirectly supported the Mexican–American War. Disappointed to learn that someone had anonymously paid the poll tax on his behalf, thereby denying him the opportunity to espouse and test his principles in court, Thoreau wrote an essay on "Civil Disobedience." He argued that citizens of a democracy must conscientiously adhere to principles of justice even if it means defying government policies and laws. Thoreau's idea of civil disobedience influenced generations of war tax resisters as well as other practitioners of nonviolent direct action such as Mohandas Gandhi and Martin Luther King, Jr.

Except for a few other isolated instances, the peace churches, particularly the Quakers, blazed the trail for modern-day war tax resisters. After the U.S. Civil War, tax resistance by the peace churches all but ceased until the second war and was only more widely revived during the Vietnam War. During the Vietnam War, thousands of citizens withheld their taxes refusing to contribute to the U.S. war effort. War tax resistance was revived once again in the 1980s by the nuclear disarmament movement. By 1985, the National War Tax Resistance Coordinating Committee claimed over 60 chapters across the United States comprised of some 20,000 citizens who refused to pay some or all of their federal income taxes.

4. Draft Resistance

For as long as records of wars have been kept, some citizens have resisted military conscription. During the Roman Empire, Christians refused military service on moral grounds, often citing their loyalty to Christ and his teachings. The penalties for such conscientious objection could be severe. For example, in 295 A.D. a Roman court sentenced Maximilianus to death in the town of Thevesta, North Africa for refusing to take the oath as a soldier. Draft resistance in the United States based on deeply held religious beliefs can be traced back as early as the Revolutionary War when Quakers refused to bear arms for the colonists' cause. But their conscientious objection bore a high price. Inflamed local patriots in Pennsylvania executed two unresisting Quakers. In another attempt to coerce them into bearing arms, Continental Army soldiers tied muskets to the backs of fourteen Quaker conscientious objectors at the Valley Forge encampment until General Washington ordered their release. Quakers also refused the payment of soldier substitutes. Thus the Colonial Quakers were both draft resisters and tax resisters.

Even during extremely popular wars, many citizens have refused to fight for their country. Such was the case in the U.S. during World War II. The bombing of Pearl Harbor by the Japanese seemed to deal a death blow to the pacifist movement. Public support for pacifist views eroded literally overnight. Yet, despite this avalanche of opposition to pacifism, a substantial core of U.S. citizens remained pacifists throughout the war. In fact the U.S. officially classified nearly 43,000 males as "conscientious objectors" who refused military induction.

C. Local and Individual Campaigns

A great deal of day-to-day peace movement activity is focused at local levels. Locally, peace activists serve as the footsoldiers for antiwar, anti-interventionist, antinuclear, and disarmament movements gathering signatures on petitions, knocking on doors, staffing phone banks, and distributing leaflets. They also lobby their city governments to pass nuclear freeze referenda, to declare their cities nuclear free zones, and to prevent defense industries from being located in their communities. And sometimes they take to the streets, demonstrating at weapons deployment sites, at the gates of defense industries, and at the offices of political leaders.

Occasionally, peace activists place themselves in grave danger by engaging in dramatic acts of civil disobedience. At the missile base near Greenham Common, England, for instance, thousands of women peace activists were arrested for a variety of acts of civil disobedience ranging from climbing over fences to chaining themselves to the gates to dancing on the missile bunkers. Perhaps the most highly publicized incidents in the antinuclear movement's history was the Plowshares Eight action of 1980. In order to express their opposition to nuclear weapons, eight protesters, including brothers Daniel and Philip Berrigan, broke into a General Electric nuclear weapons production facility in Pennsylvania. Once inside, they smashed the missiles' nosecones with hammers and poured their own blood on blueprints and tools. Other acts of civil disobedience, though less dramatic, often were just as courageous. For instance, in East Germany before the fall of the Berlin Wall, students would wear patches to school reading "Swords into Plowshares." In response, authorities sent the students home and ordered them to remove the patches only to have them to return to school the following day defiantly wearing them.

IV. POSITIVE PEACE-SEEKING

A near-universal criticism leveled at peace movements has been that they fail to offer concrete alternatives to war, that while they clearly voice their opposition to war and war-making, they fail to articulate solutions. Yet, peace movements have not only been movements of dissent, they have also been movements of advocacy. They have advocated the creation of peaceful societies and a world order based on principles of social justice, human rights, and international cooperation. From their earliest mobilizations, peace movements have fashioned and engaged in peace-building activities and campaigns.

A. International/Transnational

Perhaps the most ambitious peace movement campaigns seeking to achieve positive peace have been directed at the international or transnational level. Among these have been campaigns for world government, the establishment of international organizations, politically and spiritually based proposals for radical social change, movements for social justice and human rights, and environmental justice movements.

1. World Federalism

One idea for achieving positive peace that gained prominence among late-19th-century peace activists was the idea of world federalism. The longer secular and religious pacifists examined the problem of war, the more they came to identify national sovereignty as a major obstacle to world peace. While nearly all pacifists objected to national sovereignty, most preferred to focus on individual conversion to the ideals of peaceful coexistence. World federalists, by contrast, were impatient with a purely people-changing strategy. What was needed, they argued, was a set of international organizations through which the conciliation process could be formalized and regularized. Their proposals included establishing an international legislature, a global police force, and procedures for implementing economic sanctions against war-making countries. Despite its intermittent popularity, 19th-century advocates of world federalism were unable to overcome the predominance of national sovereignty. Most people in most counties were unwilling to consider relinquishing power to an international body, that is, to foreigners.

The embers of support for world federalism were rekindled by the devastation of two world wars and especially the unleashing of atomic energy on human populations. Many nuclear pacifists (as distinguished from traditional pacifists who opposed all war on moral grounds, not just nuclear war) came to believe that world government was necessary in order to achieve world peace. In a remarkably short period of time, the world federalist movement arose to great heights. By mid-1946, the U.S. movement garnered mainstream support from numerous Senators and Representatives as well as from Minnesota's Governor Harold Stassen, a leading contender for the Republican Presidential nomination. But like their pacifist and scientist cousins in the bourgeoning antinuclear movement, the world federalists became victims of McCarthyism. Global government was said to be nothing more than a disguised term for "communism."

Meanwhile, traditional pacifists also tended to be critical of global government. Though a few worked with the world federalists, most were suspicious of *any* form of state power. Pacifist Emily Balch epitomized their concerns: "I have a very considerable distrust of governments as such and see no reason to be sure that a world government would be run by men very different in capacity than those who govern national states." Pacifists insisted that "rather than more authority at the top" what the world needed was "greater cooperation of peoples at the bottom" (Wittner 1984, p178–179).

2. International Nongovernmental Organizations

The idea of greater cooperation among people around the world has increasingly taken the form of international nongovernmental organizations (INGOs). These are nonstate, nonprofit, formal organizations that operate in more than one country to achieve common objectives. By the 19th century, INGOs began to appear more frequently as citizens' participation in civil societies was increasingly channeled into voluntary associations. A variety of international groups emerged such as the Anti-Slavery Society (1839), the International Typographical Union (1852), the World Alliance of Young Men's Christian Associations (1855), and the International Committee for the Red Cross (1863).

Today, many of the world's expanding population of INGOs promote institutional and policy changes in the international order related to peace, justice, and human rights. By 1998, there were approximately 5000 INGOs in existence including groups such as Amnesty International, Women's International League for Peace and Freedom, Service for Peace and Justice, and Peace Brigades International. They accomplish their goals in a variety of ways. For example, INGOs can create and activate global emergency response networks as illustrated by Peace Brigades International's strategy of supplying escorts trained in nonviolent tactics to accompany activists, human rights workers, health workers, journalists, and others into repressive or conflict-ridden places such as Sri Lanka, Haiti, Columbia, and Guatemala. Another strategy is to mobilize pressure from outside states. The Service for Peace and Justice (SERPAJ), a nonviolent human rights organization in Latin America employed this strategy in its campaigns for human rights in Argentina, Chile, Uruguay, Brazil, and Ecuador. SERPAJ was so successful in bringing international pressure against the Argentine government for human rights abuses, for instance, that its campaign's founder, Adolfo Perez Esquivel, was awarded the 1980 Nobel Peace Prize.

3. Liberation Theology

As the proliferation of nongovernmental international organizations dedicated to peace, justice, and human rights suggests, pacifist ideals continue to inspire late-20th-century peace and justice movements. Similarly, religious teachings stressing peace and social justice helped ignite the activism of those opposed to intervention in Central America and South America. Particularly important were the series of papal and episcopal documents emphasizing peace and justice released during the 1970s and 1980s. These social justice doctrines defined the economic, cultural, and political arenas as important to all Christians and helped promote critical attitudes toward violence, social injustice, political oppression, and human rights violations. Liberation The-

ology became a powerful social movement in Central America and South America, emerging from the interaction between neo-Marxism and the Latin American church in the 1960s. Liberation Theology focuses on liberating humanity from spiritual, economic, cultural, and political injustice.

Thousands of North American Christians adopted the values and political viewpoints of Liberation Theology, paving the way for Christian activism in the Central American peace movement and outrage over widespread poverty and misery in Central America. Liberation Theology challenged the hierarchy of the Catholic church and its support for the power elite. Some of the "radical" proposals associated with social justice forwarded by liberation theologists included feeding the poor and providing clothing, housing, and education. Thus, the Liberation Theology movement was, in essence, a movement for social justice and human rights.

4. Social Justice and Human Rights

According to those who work for positive peace, there can be no peace without justice. This principle has been fundamental to the numerous nonviolent movements for social change inspired by Mohandas Gandhi. Yet the principle was around long before Gandhi's movement for independence in India. For example, the U.S. peace movement of the 1840s worked in coalitions with abolitionists to rid the world of slavery. Peace activists believed that peace could never be permanently achieved in societies that treated people as property and denied entire categories of people basic human rights.

More recently, the best known classification of international human rights is the United Nations "Universal Declaration of Human Rights," issued in 1948. This document outlines what are held to be universal rights, including freedom and equality; the right to life, liberty, and security of person; the right not to be subjected to slavery, torture, or cruel punishment; equality before the law; and the freedoms of movement, conscience, religion, and assembly. Several meetings of The World Conference on Religion and Peace have suggested that the United Nation's Universal Declaration of Human Rights could be the foundation for international peace.

Historically, complete human rights were granted only selectively. During apartheid in South Africa, for example, only the descendants of the English and Dutch colonists were granted full political rights; Black Africans were barred from political participation. Apartheid, a system of total segregation, was introduced in 1948 by the white supremacist Nationalist Party. Social contacts between Blacks and Whites were illegal, separate public facilities were established, areas of residence were strictly segregated, differential educational standards for Black and White students were instituted, each race had its own business sectors, and Blacks were forced to carry documents authorizing their presence in restricted areas. The entire economy, including the diamond mines worked by Blacks, was controlled by Whites.

During the 1950s and 1960s, Black African resistance to apartheid increased, culminating in the Soweto uprising in 1976. After the Soweto uprising, an international antiapartheid movement emerged, pressuring local and federal governments to adopt divestment policies toward South Africa. Meanwhile within South Africa, the South African National Congress (ANC) became the vanguard movement organization advocating civil liberties and social justice for Blacks. By the late 1980s Black activists in the South African National Union of Mine Workers and clothing workers initiated strikes and demonstrations. Blacks defied segregation laws by entering facilities reserved for Whites. On September 13, 1989 the streets of Cape Town were filled by more than 20,000 antiapartheid protestors of all races. By the 1990s, the one-million member Congress of African Trade Unions called for continued international sanctions against South Africa and the ANC adopted a nonviolent mass action strategy. These efforts were designed to keep pressure on Prime Minister de Klerk, who had instituted some reforms. Eventually, decades of activism and international economic pressure succeeded in toppling apartheid.

Other contemporary movements have focused on building peaceful societies by expanding human rights in countries where fundamental liberties have been denied. For example, prior to the fall of Eastern European totalitarian states, civil liberties and basic human rights were severely curtailed there. This situation was replicated in Central America and South America, particularly where totalitarian states existed. Many important political, economic, and military decisions excluded the involvement and participation of ordinary citizens. Human rights movements arose in response.

In Czechoslovakia, for example, human rights activism became closely associated with the independent (non-State organized) peace movement. Charter 77 was the focus of extensive human rights activism in Czechoslovakia, demonstrating that human rights and peace are inseparable. In Eastern Europe human rights demands typically focused on freedom of travel, nomination of independent candidates during elections, freedom of assembly and association, greater political democracy, abolition of military service and training, and accommodation for conscientious objectors. Activ-

ism also focused on issues of social justice, including workers' rights. Thus, peace movements, whose goal was the elimination of nuclear weapons and war, found allies in activists concerned with human rights and environmental justice.

5. Environmental Justice

Ecological activism arose in Eastern Bloc nations during the 1980s concurrent with activism around issues of peace, human rights, and social justice. It is hardly surprising that antinuclear activists and ecological activists have an affinity for each other. A nuclear holocaust and the resultant nuclear winter would certainly wreak ecological havoc. The decision by NATO to deploy nuclear weapons in Europe, and the counterdeployment by the Soviet Union, initiated ecological activism in the East Germany, Poland, Czechoslovakia, and Hungary. By the late 1970s the environmental crisis was apparent to most citizens living in these nations and included acid rain, contaminated drinking water, and ecological damage caused by rapid industrialization and the construction of hydroelectric dams.

However, it was the nuclear disaster at Chernobyl that touched off significant ecological protests in these countries. The issue of nuclear power thereby became instrumental in bringing ecological activists to the forefront of political opposition. Ecology groups had already focused on such issues as air pollution and environment destruction. Chernobyl altered the priorities of the environmental movement in the Eastern Bloc. Many ecological activists no longer uncritically accepted the ideology of technology or its promise of continual improvements in the standard of living through increased consumption. Following the model of capitalist wastefulness came to be seen as environmentally irresponsible. The Protestant Church insisted that, regardless of safeguards, nuclear power plants constituted a threat to humanity. Charter 77 released a document in May, 1986 calling the Soviet Union's response to Chernobyl completely inadequate.

Subsequently, the environmental movement became the largest nonstate-run social movement in Hungary. Environmental issues succeeded in increasing activism not only around the ecological crisis but also concerning issues of democratization. Thousands of people attended meetings and signed petitions to stop dam construction on the Danube and to improve the quality and supply of drinking water. Environmental activists took over the Austrian Embassy in Budapest in June, 1987 in opposition to dam construction.

B. National Campaigns

Only a little less ambitious than peace movements working for global changes are those that direct their positive peace-seeking efforts at the national or societal level. While a few of these movements have sought revolutionary changes in the entire structure of a society, most have focused on reforms of one or two institutions at a time.

1. Political Changes

As early as the 1790s, peace activists in the United States proposed political reforms intended to encourage positive peacemaking. Continental Army Surgeon General Benjamin Rush urged Congress to establish a cabinet-level Secretary of Peace. The proposed Peace Office was to establish tuition-free peace schools throughout the nation which would teach the principles of Christian pacifism. Additionally, the Peace Office was to distribute Bibles and work to eliminate capital punishment, military parades, titles, and uniforms. Dr. Rush's proposal thus sought to establish the institutional means to substitute a culture of peace for militarism.

More recently, peace activists in Eastern Europe and the former USSR struggled to change their political systems so they would have a voice in the politics of peace and justice. The political systems of those societies presented unique difficulties for peace movements. Whereas most peace movements around the world were grassroots, that is, organized and led by ordinary citizens who challenged the political status quo, in many of the Eastern Bloc countries the state organized, sponsored, and controlled its own "peace movements." Because only the state-orchestrated movements were officially recognized, the grassroots peace movements usually operated underground.

Unlike their Western counterparts, autonomous peace movements in Eastern Europe did not have the freedoms of expression or assembly; therefore, they could not engage in direct confrontation with the state or stage mass protests. These movements were forced to seek innovative ways of engaging in peace activities. The Berlin Appeal (1982), the first independent peace manifesto in East Germany noted the connection between human rights and calls for demilitarization and the establishment of peace. This was followed by similar appeals in other Eastern European countries and the Soviet Union. These appeals raised questions concerning war toys, the establishment of peace studies, alternatives for conscientious objectors, reforming civil defense, ending military parades, and converting military production to civil production.

Women were also active peace movement leaders in Eastern Europe. Several women's peace movements periodically issued letters and appeals to state officials. A joint East German–Czechoslovakian statement, signed by women associated with Charter 77, protested the existing nuclear facilities in those countries, militarism, and the deployment of nuclear weapons. Women for Peace appealed to the East German government to stop drafting women. In 1986, a women's peace petition, issued jointly by Eastern and West European countries entitled "Giving Real Life to the Helsinki Accords," focused on human rights.

In Hungary, the Peace Group for Dialogue, organized by university students and graduates, attracted thousands of young activists and staged numerous peace marches and public speeches. They also actively engaged the government in negotiations aimed at gaining official recognition. In the USSR, the Moscow Group to Establish Trust Between East and West, founded by scientists and intellectuals in 1982, managed to survive as an independent peace organization. This group struggled to gain recognition not only from the Soviets but also from Western peace organizations, who suspected that they were sponsored by the Soviet government. The Trust Group called for the abolition of nuclear weapons on both sides of the Berlin wall and the establishment of a peace process in which the public of both the U.S. and the USSR would have a voice equal to the politicians in the disarmament process.

Nothing symbolized the division between the East and West more concretely than the Berlin Wall. Erected in 1961, the wall stood as the symbol of a Europe divided into two armed camps. By 1987, unofficial peace and reform groups sprang up throughout the Soviet Union and other nations in Eastern Europe. The establishment of an independent press in East Germany in 1986 indicated that things were indeed changing. One of the more important publications, *Greenzfall*, was associated with Initiative Peace and Human Rights and its contents focused on environmental issues, human rights, and international peace.

A confluence of political, economic, and civic forces eventually brought the Soviet Union and its satellite nations to their respective ends, including the deepening economic crisis, Solidarity in Poland, environmental devastation, and Chernobyl. The opposition created by the independent peace and ecology movements also played a critical role in the demise of East Germany. Although the East German government tried desperately to maintain its authority, often resorting to arrests, detentions, and violence, the repressive tactics eventually failed as tens of thousands of Party members abandoned the government and thousands of others fled to West Germany. As the protests continued to grow, hundreds of thousands of protestors took to the streets of the major cities. In East Germany, speaking in front of nearly a million people, writer Christa Wolf described what was transpiring as a "revolution from below." The reunification of Germany was a major step toward positive peace-building and ending the decades-long Cold War. Gorbachev's "glasnost campaign," giving voice, interpretation, and freedom of impression to the people, was certainly part of that process.

2. Economic Restructuring

Peace movements have offered a variety of reforms directed at restructuring economies in ways that might eliminate some of the causes as well as the economic consequences of war and militarism. One strategy advocated by a variety of peace movement groups has been to focus on "economic conversion." This strategy entails persuading political leaders and captains of industry to shift from military-based economies to civilian-based economies.

A prime example of this type of positive peace-building at the national level is provided by the Jobs with Peace Campaign. Founded in 1978, Jobs with Peace launched a national reform movement that sought to redirect tax revenues away from military spending in order to spend the money locally on social programs, quality education, public transportation, health care, housing, and a host of other socially useful industries. Jobs with Peace quickly spread to dozens of cities throughout the United States. To achieve their goal they proposed reductions in nuclear weapons programs, foreign interventions, and wasteful military programs.

Campaigners wrote Jobs with Peace budgets for their communities showing the amount of tax dollars lost annually to the national military budget. Proposition X, the binding Jobs with Peace initiative, was approved by almost half a million voters in Los Angeles. The initiative required the city council to publish in local newspapers an annual report detailing local taxpayers' contributions to the federal defense budget and to identify alternative ways in which that money could be spent to produce jobs locally. It also called on Congress to spend less on defense and more on jobs, human needs, and the arts. In 1984, approximately three billion dollars left Los Angeles annually for defense purposes. Forming coalitions with many local and national labor, peace, and low-income groups, Jobs with Peace sponsored referenda throughout the U.S., many of which passed, calling for the transfer of federal defense dollars away from the military toward pressing domestic needs.

3. Peace Studies

One of the most spectacular successes of the peace movement has been the advent of peace studies on college campuses. Focusing on the causes of war and the conditions of peace, the peace studies movement arose from the ashes of World War II as an academic field of study. Initially, peace studies were limited to a few research institutes and graduate programs where scholars emphasized the role of law in world affairs and the peacekeeping potential of the newly formed United Nations. In the 1960s and 1970s faculty and student interest and participation in the civil rights and anti-Vietnam War movements lead to a dramatic expansion in the field's size and scope. During this period, numerous undergraduate programs in peace studies were established. New concepts were developed during this period such as the notion of structural violence—the idea that poverty and repression were fundamental obstacles to achieving positive peace. The most recent expansion of the field occurred during the 1980s, coinciding with the revival of the antinuclear movement. This third wave of peace studies has yielded a dramatic increase not only in the number of graduate and undergraduate courses and programs, but also a massive expansion in the amount of private and public funding of peace studies, the number of scholarly journals dedicated to the field, and, perhaps most important to peace movements, an increase in the visibility and status of peace studies. The U.S. government gave official recognition to the field of peace studies in 1984 when it established the U.S. Institute of Peace.

C. Local, Group, and Individual Campaigns

One of the most popular slogans of late-20th-century peace movements is "Think Globally, Act Locally." More and more peace activists have concluded that perhaps they can be most effective at seeking to try to build peaceful societies from the ground up, that is by focusing their efforts at the community, small group, and even individual levels.

Perhaps the most fundamental basis for achieving international peace and eliminating the causes of war is that of changing individual consciousness. One way of eradicating war and genocide is to convince people to view "the enemy" as ordinary human beings much like themselves. To this end, numerous peace movement organizations take the personal approach. They seek to provide opportunities for people from different nations to get to know each other on a personal level.

People who interact with each other are more likely to resolve their differences through peaceful negotiation when they have developed an appreciation and understanding of each other. Peace movements and organizations of this type, therefore, seek to change individuals.

Under the banner of "citizen diplomacy," many organizations have attempted to bring individuals from different cultures and nations together to experience each other's cultures and lifestyles. Such groups include churches, peace groups, foundations, and governments. The American Friends Service Committee established its Peace Service Program in the 1920s to inform public opinion on issues of war and peace. The Peace Service has sponsored peace caravans, international institutes, work camps, speakers' tours, and distributed peace literature internationally. The peace caravans sent large numbers of student volunteers both abroad and throughout rural America to stimulate thinking about peace.

Various groups have attempted to change individual consciousness by bridging the economic, political, cultural, and linguistic differences between people. Tactics employed include distribution of educational materials; cultural exchanges; student exchanges; the establishment of sister cities; peace pilgrimages; and visiting the homes, schools, churches, and communities of other cultures. Groups taking this people-to-people approach included the National Council of American–Soviet Friendship, the American Field Service, the United States Servas Committee, People to People International, the National Council of Churches, Friendship Force International, and many others. A notable example of such "détente from below" efforts is The Ulster Project Delaware, a group that arranged to bring Catholic and Protestant youths from Northern Ireland to Delaware to talk about peace and reconciliation.

V. CONCLUSION

It seems clear that there is not a single peace movement, but rather, multiple peace movements organized around various issues, with different goals and strategies for achieving those goals. Peace movements have a long history and tradition. It is also clear that peace movements go through cycles of activism as they confront the ever-changing face of violence, war, social injustice, and ecological devastation. Many peace movements that are positive in nature are split by the approach of hostilities. Thus, activists are faced with a difficult choice. If attempts to change society fail and a war is about to commence, peace activists may face

criticism for failing to support the troops. Even worse, some wars come to be defined by the public as "good" or "just" and some activists may come to accept the necessity of supporting such wars. Both World Wars exemplify this predicament.

Some peace movements, typically negative peace movements, are single-issue movements. Thus, when they fail to achieve their objectives, as happened when NATO deployed Cruise and Pershing II missiles in Europe, the movement may lapse into inactivity. Equally important is the dialectical relationship between war and peace-building efforts. As conflicts and wars erupt, peace activism tends to increase, especially negative peace activism. During long periods of relative peace, activism may subside, leaving only a handful of groups actively seeking positive peace.

It is also important to note that a nation's position in the world order shapes the type of activism occurring within its borders. For example, Eastern European grassroots peace movements were seen as a threat by their totalitarian governments. Movements in these nations were more likely to be underground movements than in the U.S., where activists enjoyed a fuller measure of human rights. Also important is the degree of absolute poverty. It is clear that peace movements that developed in South America and Central America were as concerned with issues of social and economic justice as with peace. This is likely due to the extremes of income inequality in these nations. Liberation Theology, which developed in this region, stressed an important lesson of the positive peacemakers: there can be no peace without justice.

Also See the Following Articles

ARMS CONTROL AND DISARMAMENT TREATIES • DRAFT, RESISTANCE AND EVASION OF • ENVIRONMENTAL ISSUES AND POLITICS • HUMAN RIGHTS • NUCLEAR WEAPONS POLICIES • PEACE AGREEMENTS • PEACE ORGANIZATIONS, NONGOVERNMENTAL

Bibliography

Alger, C. F. (1997). Transnational social movements, world politics, and global governance. In J. Smith, C. Chatfield, & R. Pagnucco (Eds.), *Transnational social movements and global politics: Solidarity beyond the state* (pp. 260–275). Syracuse, NY: Syracuse University Press.
Allen, B. (1991). *Germany east: Dissent and opposition.* Montreal/New York: Black Rose.
Barash, D. P. (1991). *Introduction to peace studies.* Belmont, CA: Wadsworth.
Bar-On, M. (1996). *In pursuit of peace: A history of the Israeli peace movement.* Washington, DC: United States Institute of Peace Press.

Benford, R. D. (1988). The nuclear disarmament movement. In L. R. Kurtz (Ed.), *The nuclear cage: A sociology of the arms race* (pp. 237–265). Englewood Cliffs, NJ: Prentice–Hall.

Chatfield, C. (1971). *For peace and justice: Pacifism in America, 1914–1941*. Knoxville: The University of Tennessee Press.

Chatfield, C. (1992). *The American peace movement: Ideal and activism*. New York: Twayne.

Chatfield, C. (1997). Intergovernmental and Nongovernmental Associations to 1945. In J. Smith, C. Chatfield, & R. Pagnucco (Eds.), *Transnational social movements and global politics: Solidarity beyond the state* (pp. 19–41). Syracuse, NY: Syracuse University Press.

Chatfield, C. & van den Dungen, P. (Eds.) (1988). *Peace movements and political cultures*. Knoxville: The University of Tennessee Press.

Cortright, D. (1993). *Peace works: The citizen's role in ending the Cold War*. Boulder, CO: Westview Press.

Coy, P. (1997). Cooperative accompaniment and peace brigades international in Sri Lanka. In J. Smith, C. Chatfield, & R. Pagnucco (Eds.), *Transnational social movements and global politics: Solidarity beyond the state* (pp. 260–270). Syracuse, NY: Syracuse University Press.

DeBenedetti, C. (1980). *The peace reform in American history*. Bloomington/London: Indiana University Press.

DeBenedetti, C. & Chatfield, C. (1990). *An American ordeal: The antiwar movement of the Vietnam era*. Syracuse, NY: Syracuse University Press.

Helsinki Watch Committee (1987). *From below: Independent peace and environmental movements in Eastern Europe and the USSR*. New York Washington: The Helsinki Watch Committee.

Kleidman, R. (1993). *Organizing for peace: Neutrality, the test ban and the freeze*. Syracuse, NY: Syracuse University Press.

Marullo, S. & Lofland, J. (Eds.) (1990). *Peace action in the eighties: Social science perspectives*. New Brunswick/London: Rutgers University Press.

Meyer, D. S. (1990). *A winter of discontent: The nuclear freeze and American politics*. New York/Westport/London: Praeger.

Pagnucco, R. (1997). The transnational strategies of the service for peace and justice in Latin America. In J. Smith, C. Chatfield, & R. Pagnucco (Eds.), *Transnational social movements and global politics: Solidarity beyond the state*. Syracuse, NY: Syracuse University Press.

Peace, R. C., III (1991). *A just and lasting peace: The U.S. peace movement from the Cold War to Desert Storm*. Chicago: Noble Press.

Rochon, T. R. (1988). *Mobilizing for peace: The antinuclear movements in Western Europe*. Princeton, NJ: Princeton University Press.

Small, M. & Hoover, W. D (Eds.) (1992). *Give peace a chance: Exploring the Vietnam antiwar movement*. Syracuse, NY: Syracuse University Press.

Smith, C. (1996). *Resisting Reagan: The U.S.–Central America peace movement*. Chicago/London: The University of Chicago Press.

Taylor, R. & Young, N. (Eds.) (1987). *Campaigns for peace: British peace movements in the twentieth century*. Manchester: Manchester University Press.

van der Linden, W. H. (1987). *The international peace movement 1815–1874*. Amsterdam: Tilleul.

Wittner, L. S. (1984). *Rebels against war: The American peace movement, 1933–1983*. Philadelphia, PA: Temple University Press.

Peace Organizations, Nongovernmental

Keith Suter

Wesley Mission

I. OVERVIEW OF THE ORGANIZATIONS

A. The Importance of the Organizations

Nongovernmental peace organizations often appear in the history of the struggle for peace. Meanwhile, some of the most notable individuals who have worked for peace have been members of such organizations, such as Jane Addams, Helen Caldicott, Mohandas Gandhi, and Dr. Martin Luther King, Jr.

B. Variety of the Organizations

It is impossible to create one standard definition of "nongovernmental peace organization". There is too much variety. First, "peace" itself, as this Encyclopedia shows, has many definitions. For example, the "peace" movement that opposed the Vietnam War in the 1960s and 1970s in the U.S. and allied countries was more an "antiwar" movement (opposed to a particular conflict) rather than a movement for peace. Similarly the "peace movement" of the 1980s (containing some of the same people), opposed to nuclear weapons, was more an "antinuclear weapon" movement than a peace one. There is more to peace than just the absence of war.

Second, a "nongovernmental organization" is any organization outside the government (such as the public service and the defence forces) and business. Such an organization is defined by what it is not rather than by what it is. This is like defining a "loaf of bread" as "not being a ton of coal". Additionally, some organizations which were "nongovernmental" in the western world during the Cold War were aligned to the USSR (such as the World Peace Council and the Christian Peace Conference). Similarly, the unofficial nongovernmental peace groups in Eastern Europe during the Cold War were critical of the Soviet occupation of their countries and wanted independence from Moscow. They were ostracized by the World Peace Council and its sister organizations. Ironically, members of these unofficial organizations have since become members of the governments in the post-Soviet era of their countries.

Third, organizations which have long been associated with campaigns for peace may not have "peace" in their titles. Instead, they see peace as a part of their wide spectrum of work activities. Religious bodies, such as the Christian Church's Quakers and Mennonities, have for centuries been "peace organizations" in that they have not only opposed particular wars and weap-

Copyright © 1999 by Academic Press.
All rights of reproduction in any form reserved.

ons but they have campaigned in favor of social justice. The symbol of a sword being hammered into a plowshare, which is imagery from the Jewish prophets before the common era, is a common symbol to peace groups around the world: the conversion of military equipment to effective civilian use through recycling (rather than just throwing the sword into a river to rust away).

Fourth, other organizations working for social change and the betterment of humankind have, at times of military tension, shown solidarity with the more explicit nongovernmental peace organizations by taking on their cause. For example, in the 1980s, environmental nongovernmental organizations also opposed nuclear weapons on the basis that a World War III would be the ultimate environmental disaster. Similarly, development organizations working to increase foreign aid to Third World countries criticized the high level of military expenditure in the Cold War as a diversion of resources away from helping the vast majority of humankind.

Fifth, another source of variety has been the tendency since the 1980s to create a large number of specialist nongovernmental peace organizations to mobilize particular constituencies. In the antinuclear struggle of the 1950s and 1960s, there were a few large organizations (such as Committee for a SANE Nuclear Policy in the U.S. and the UK's Campaign for Nuclear Disarmament). But in a later peace movement, whose roots go back to the December, 1979 North Atlantic Treaty Organization (NATO) decision to deploy a new generation of Intermediate Nuclear Forces (INF), SANE and CND were joined by a range of membership-specific organizations. For example, there were Lawyers Against War (LAW), Journalists Against War (JAW), Metalworkers to End the Arms Race (MEND), and even Generals for Peace. The UK Medical Association for the Prevention of Nuclear War (formed in 1951) and the U.S. Physicians for Social Responsibility (formed in 1961) had both demonstrated the value of specialist organizations dealing with their own clientele. This model was then followed by a later generation of peace organizations.

Particular mention should be made of the gender-specific peace organizations, notably those of women. The women-only camp at Greenham Common, Berkshire, England in the 1980s (opposing the Cruise missiles based there) has a long and distinguished pedigree. One survey of women's peace organizations in the UK begins at 1820, with women pioneers both in the struggle for human rights and in opposing war. Such gender-specific organizations have included: Women's International League (1915–1919), Women's International League for Peace and Freedom (from 1919), Women's Peace Crusade (1916–1918), and Women Oppose the Nuclear Threat (WONT). Women have also, of course, been disproportionately represented in all the peace organizations because they have provided the main source of labor.

Finally, although the conventional wisdom is that foreign policy is the exclusive domain of national governments, throughout the 1980s local government authorities also took an interest in opposing nuclear war. Municipal "nuclear free zones" were declared by local government authorities (with Wales and New Zealand being the first two countries to create a network linking all such authorities). In the U.S., 120 cities refused to participate in the Federal Emergency Management Agency's post-nuclear war planning arrangements, thereby obliging the Reagan Administration to scrap its civil defense program, which then undermined the Administration's war-fighting policies. This municipal diplomacy was a form of "governmental" activity—and yet to exclude such work because it was not "nongovernmental" would be to ignore an important part of the movement opposed to the fighting of a so-called limited nuclear war.

Therefore, no attempt will be made here to create a definition or typology of "nongovernmental peace organizations."

C. Similarities of the Organizations

First, all nongovernmental peace organizations are seeking a reform of some kind. They are protesting against an existing political principle, such as the overall use of war as an instrument of national policy, or a particular war (for example, Vietnam), or a weapon system (for example, the Campaign to Abolish Land Mines, which won the 1997 Nobel Peace Prize).

Second, they all believe that peace (however defined) is possible. Their members have not succumbed to a sense of fatalism that war is inevitable and that nothing can be done to stop it.

Third, all the organizations manifest, to differing extents, five common qualities: optimism (a belief that it is possible to work for a better situation); activism (a belief that it is better to be proactive rather than to just sit around and let things happen); populism (a belief that the mass of ordinary people ought to be involved in political change and not just leave decision-making to an elite); holistic vision (a belief that life consists of subtle interconnections with one component affecting others); and that the individual can make a difference.

II. ROLES OF THE ORGANIZATIONS

A. Research/New Ideas

Nongovernmental peace organizations are the nerve-endings of humanity. They highlight neglected issues and suggest new areas of action. They—rather than governments—often set the pace of change.

Additionally, it is often the governments that have created the problems in the first place and so the logic that got them into the problem cannot necessarily get them out of it. Peace activists "think outside the square", they look at issues afresh. They argued, for example, that the U.S. could not win in Vietnam several years before the Government recognized that fact.

Nongovernmental peace organizations have fraternal links across national boundaries. They have greater flexibility than national governments. For example, the Nobel Peace Prize winning anti land mine network was able to lobby governments in a way (such as through the media) that no national government could do because of the limitations of national sovereignty. These organizations can say many necessary things loudly and without inhibition. They are concerned about victims—and not about diplomatic protocol and niceties.

B. Advocates

Nongovernmental peace organizations are often on the leading edge of change because they affect the political climate in which decisions are made. For example, Greenpeace, which has a trademark that is now almost as famous as Coca-Cola's, was started in Canada in 1971 as a reaction to the prevailing view about what constituted "threats" to the environment. The environment debate was then dominated by conservationists, who were concerned about trying to preserve parts of Canadian wildlife. Greenpeace argued this was too simplistic and that there was much more involved. The entire global ecosystem was under threat (an example of holistic vision reasoning) and so there had to be a more holistic approach to saving the Earth. Greenpeace has grown in strength; it now has a larger budget than the UN Environment Program. Its activities against French nuclear testing in the South Pacific were a major factor in galvanizing international opposition to the tests.

C. Giving People an Opportunity for Involvement in Foreign Policy

Nongovernmental peace organizations give the general public an opportunity for involvement in foreign policy in four main ways. First, they have ended the governments' monopoly over foreign policy. Before World War I began in 1914, there was very limited public involvement in foreign policy. It was assumed that governments knew more about foreign policy because of their access to secret information (such as that gathered by their embassies). Also, patriotic citizens did not want to erode their government's authority in dealing with foreign governments by suggesting that there was division at home over foreign policy; as the saying went "the disputes finished where the foreign border began".

World War I shattered that complacency and the general public wanted more opportunity to be involved in foreign policy. Discussion and research organizations were created, such as the U.S. Council on Foreign Relations and the Royal Institute of International Affairs in London, to encourage public debate on foreign policy. They did not—and still do not—adopt policy statements and would not see themselves as peace organizations as such. But their role in stimulating public debate helped end governmental monopoly over foreign policy. A parallel development (often with the same people) was to establish nongovernmental peace organizations, such as the League of Nations Union (the forerunner of today's United Nations Associations), which do adopt such policy statements.

Second, the general public via nongovernmental peace organizations participate in the shaping of foreign policy decisions through public meetings, rallies/demonstrations, communications with their politicians, and letters to newspapers. These are all vital aspects of a civil society.

Third, some members of these organizations, who are recognized as having a particular expertise, are invited to serve on governmental advisory committees and governmental delegations to international conferences.

Finally, participating in this work often has an impact on the citizen through their attaining a better knowledge of current affairs. For example, they get to understand the linkage between apparently separate issues: a person may object to a particular war and through their involvement in an organization they may get to learn more about the military–industrial complex of their society and the way that the mass media report (or fail to report) issues. Similarly, by being involved in one campaign, a person can carry across the skills learned into other aspects of their life. For example, women who have become accustomed to standing up to the police at demonstrations have become emboldened to stand up their abusive husbands at home.

D. Continuity

Nongovernmental organizations survive the fads and fashions of governments; they outlive the terms of elected governments. They provide a continuity of concern and a continued focus on peace issues when governments might prefer to ignore those issues.

Additionally, some members may have a particular expertise that is lacking in their government because of the turnover of politicians and staff.

E. Personal Example

Nongovernmental peace organizations show that a good way to bring about change is to establish a model of how they would like things to be. In other words, providing warnings is not enough: it is also necessary to provide an alternative. They strive themselves to be a peaceful community.

Nongovernmental peace organizations try to ensure that they are their own peace message. They try to structure themselves in nonviolent ways, such as through allowing extensive participation in decision-making (rather than having the decisions made by only a handful of people). They try to operate in nonviolent ways (such as the way they conduct themselves at rallies and demonstrations).

F. Hope

Some people are dead at 18 but they are not buried until they are 75. In other words, there is a great emptiness in their lives and they lack a sense of purpose. Nongovernmental peace organizations provide a vehicle out of the self-absorption and self-obsession that characterize so much of life. People can get involved in a cause that is greater than themselves.

Peace activists are motivated by a belief that they can create a better world. Only the long sweep of history can ever assess whether their optimism was justified. For peace activists it is better to try something grand (and risk failure) rather than do nothing (and succeed). But the mere act of working for a more peaceful world is in itself enervating.

III. ASSESSING THE EFFECTIVENESS OF THE ORGANIZATIONS

A. Measuring Effectiveness

It is very difficult to assess the effectiveness of nongovernmental peace organizations. First, not all of the work done by these organizations is easily reduced to statis-

tics, such as the impact of their advocacy work. Indeed, there is a general problem in political science in trying to trace the chain of causation affecting the making of any decision. Just because a peace organization argued for a particular policy and a government introduces that policy does not necessarily mean that the peace movement's work caused that decision to be made. For example, did the U.S. withdraw from Vietnam because of the peace movement at home or the failure of the military to defeat the National Liberation Front in Vietnam? Also, there is a continuing debate over why the Cold War ended: to what extent can the peace movement claim credit? Or was it due more to President Reagan's decision to greatly expand the arms race or to the Soviet Union's political and economic systems tottering toward collapse?

B. Appearances can be Deceptive

The apparent decline of a peace organization may, ironically, be a sign of its effectiveness. Peace organizations are protest organizations: their members want a change in government policy or practice, etc. If a peace organization declines, it may be due to the fact that it had worked itself out of a job. The antinuclear movement in, say, 1998 was not as large or as active as it was in, say, 1988. This does not mean that there is a greater public sympathy for nuclear weapons. On the contrary, the decline has come about through the nuclear weapon governments (especially those in the U.S. and USSR/Russia) agreeing to reduce their weapons. The values of the peace movements in the 1980s had become internalized throughout a greater section of the community in the 1990s. This was also manifested in May, 1998 with the explosion of the Indian and Pakistani nuclear tests: governments were themselves in the forefront of condemning the tests and using the language of the 1980s peace movements about the dangers of nuclear proliferation.

C. Awaiting the Judgment of History

The full impact of these activities may not be assessed until some years later. This is an "instant" age. There are instant coffee and instant news reports. But the individual may not necessarily find out instantly the full impact of his or her peace activism. Here are two examples: the White Rose organization and the U.S. anti-Vietnam war peace campaign.

1. The White Rose

The White Rose was the name of a small group of students who identified with the nonmilitaristic aspects of German culture during Hitler's rise to power. They courageously distributed leaflets throughout southern Germany opposing Nazism even during the early years of the war. The key members were eventually captured and they were executed on February 24, 1943. It seemed that the White Rose's work had been in vain.

Just over half a century later, the Cold War was running hot. Various medical nongovernmental peace organizations formed to oppose nuclear weapons. Such organizations as the UK-based Medical Association for the Prevention of War and US-based International Physicians for the Prevention of Nuclear War, had new levels of membership. It was agreed that there should be an international conference of medical groups in Germany for 1986: International Year of Peace.

Some of the most active members of the organizations were Jewish and they had no desire to visit Germany. When they thought of Germany, they thought of the Holocaust and the recurring notion that there were no "good" Germans.

Then the White Rose's prophetic role was recalled. Some German students (some of whom had been studying medicine) had stood up to Hitler. Although some members still refused to journey to Germany, most of them did. The White Rose organization, half a century after all members were executed, had its finest hour.

Second, in 1969 President Nixon decided to increase the level of conflict in Vietnam to force his opponents to back down. Relevant portions of the U.S. Navy's "Operation Duck Hook" are still classified by the Pentagon. But it is clear that he intended to use some form of nuclear weapon. The deadline was November 1.

However, on October 15 there was a massive antiwar demonstration. The size of the demonstration could be quantified: its full impact could not be. As we now know, the President on that day realized that he had badly misjudged the strength of the antiwar movement. Operation Duck Hook was cancelled.

The Americans who marched that day had no idea of their impact. They were protesting against the policies already underway; they had no inkling of the proposed nuclear strike. Since the current policies remained intact, some must have thought their protest had been in vain. Only years later did they find out that they had stopped a fundamental escalation of the war.

IV. COMMON PROBLEMS FOR THE ORGANIZATIONS

If peace is such a good idea, why haven't the nongovernmental peace organizations achieved more by now? Even agreeing that it is difficult to assess the impact of individual organizations, the overall success rate seems small nonetheless. There are still, for example, nuclear weapons in existence, an increasing number of declared nuclear weapon states, and a large number of conflicts under way.

A. "Peace" Is Suspect

Not everyone does, in fact, accept that peace is a good idea. Nongovernmental peace organizations are protest movements and so they are challenging the status quo. By definition this puts them at odds with the dominant paradigm. Many people benefit from the status quo and so do not want change.

Other people may not be so supportive of the status quo but are reluctant to gamble on a change and so prefer the status quo as a less threatening risk. Therefore, for example, during the Cold War, while many people were troubled by the prospect of a nuclear war, they thought that somehow living without nuclear weapons would be an even greater risk and so they supported the concept of nuclear deterrence.

Additionally the opponents of nongovernmental peace organizations can undermine their views by eroding their legitimacy. Thus, in the western world in the Cold War such organizations were often alleged to be financed by Moscow and working to further Soviet policy. Meanwhile, in Eastern Europe, the independent unofficial peace organizations were dismissed as "dissidents" (a term of abuse) who were eroding the stability of the Warsaw Pact.

B. It Is Not Their Problem Alone

The nongovernmental peace organizations are not the sole actors. Governments, defence forces, transnational corporations, and nongovernmental political/military forces (such as the Irish Republican Army and Ulster Volunteer Force) are all in a much better position to achieve peace—after all, they are usually the ones responsible for violence. Therefore, it is important not to expect too much from the nongovernmental peace organizations.

C. No Natural Bureaucratic Allies

Nongovernmental peace organizations have no natural allies within a national government bureaucracy. Environmental or women's nongovernmental organizations, by contrast, may be able to have some tactical alliances with a department of the environment or women's affairs to create common forms of action. For example, a department may have a project that the nongovernmental organization can promote in the mass media and lobby politicians to accept or the organization has an idea and uses the department to put it into practice.

Ironically, the only governmental department that may be sympathetic to a peace organization is a department of finance because it objects to all forms of governmental expenditure and so is looking for ways to cut expenditure. It may be an "ally," but it does not share a peace organization's values. Attempts to create a national ministry for peace (which would be a natural ally within a governmental bureaucracy) have failed.

D. No Central Organization

The forces working against peace are usually better organized than those working for peace. Indeed, many are literally operating on strict, well-funded military lines.

A common complaint among new members of nongovernmental peace organizations is that the organizations ought to work together and perhaps even be amalgamated. Even the apparent national coalitions, such as the UK National Peace Council, are at most only clearing houses for common action rather than centralized bodies to direct a peace campaign. Similarly, national associations (or "sections") of an international organization (such as the Womens International League for Peace and Freedom) have a large amount of autonomy over which issues they take up and how they conduct their campaigns.

One response to this complaint is that peace organizations have a different set of values from the centralized organizations about which they are protesting. They are not defence forces or governmental departments and they are trying to show via their daily operations how people can organize themselves out of a spontaneous concern for the betterment of humankind rather than through bureaucratic regulations.

Second, too much control would erode, if not extinguish, the creative spark that initiated the organization's creation and that continues to motivate its members. These organizations operate on flexibility and spontaneity, which could be stifled by a bureaucracy.

Third, a great deal of energy would be consumed in simply holding a centralized organization together. There would be too many components straining to go in different directions. It is much better to get a general agreement for a day of action (such as August 6 events to mark the Hiroshima nuclear bombing in 1945) and let the organizations respond in their own ways to marking the day.

E. No Agreed Master Plan

In the same way as there is no agreed definition of peace, so too is there no agreed master plan for achieving it. As has already been noted, different peace organizations are seeking different goals.

Works unite and teaching divides. In other words, it is better to encourage, say, a common day of action and leave it up to individual organizations to make their own decisions as to what they will do. They will have their own motivations as to why they are involved in a common day.

Similarly, they will see the common day of action differently within their own organizational agenda. For example, a secular antinuclear organization (such as SANE or CND) would be involved in, say, an Hiroshima Day rally because it fits the organization's opposition to nuclear weapons. Meanwhile, a religious organization may be involved because its social justice agenda requires, among other things, the abolition of nuclear weapons as one of many social transformations.

F. Differences over Tactics

Even if there is an agreed goal (such as the stopping of the deployment of a particular weapon system), so there are often differences over the tactics to be used. A common difference of opinion is over the use of nonviolent confrontational tactics. At one end of the spectrum of tactics are religious services, marches through the streets (for which police permission has been obtained), movie screenings, letters to newspapers, picnics, and the distribution of leaflets.

But inevitably some peace activists think that these tactics are too restrained and so wish to have a more direct form of action. After all, they argue, these events rarely get mass media attention; they are too peaceful. The media prefer drama and confrontation. They therefore argue that it is necessary to confront head-on the forces working against peace.

Additionally, most people who get involved in an organization do so in a voluntary capacity. They are there to make a difference; not to receive a paycheck. They feel passionately about an issue; this passion makes up for the lack of pay. The risk is that because of this passion they may not be interested in working with others because they know they have the right answers.

G. Peace Organizations Are Not Always Peaceful

Peace organizations are not always peaceful (they may disagree over tactics, for example) and they may not always be expert at handling conflict within themselves. Additionally, there is a risk that such organizations spend too much time debating among themselves when their major efforts should be toward reaching others with their message. Tragically, some peace organizations have wounded themselves in factional disputes and lost many members and finances because of these feuds. They would themselves benefit from learning about conflict resolution.

V. FUTURE CHALLENGES FOR THE ORGANIZATIONS

A. Common Patterns

All protest movements rise and fall over time. Some campaigns are successful and so end (such as the campaign of the 1980s to stop the proposed mining in Antarctica and which was successful in 1991). Others are not so successful and run out of steam (sometimes only temporarily) as people despair of ever winning (such as the temperance groups who wish to stop the sale of alcohol). They may not disappear entirely but they have periods of few members and little activism. Finally, others are simply overtaken by the long sweep of history and so become irrelevant, such as the Luddite movement which opposed the introduction of technology in 19th century British factories.

The same pattern is found in nongovernmental peace organizations. Some campaigns are successful and so end (such as the campaign of the 1980s to stop the deployment of Intermediate Nuclear Forces in Europe). Others are not successful and run out of steam as people despair of ever winning (such as the campaigns for the abolition of all nuclear weapons and the ending of war as an instrument of national policy). Others have been overtaken by the long sweep of history, such as the UK Women's Peace Crusade which opposed World War I.

The middle category—those organizations which run out of steam—are important to note. These are often the foundations upon which a later generation of peace activism is based. They keep the torch alight until there is a fresh era for peace activism. They are the institutional memory.

Ironically, there is often a lack of historical perspective undergirding many newcomers to the peace organizations. They do not realize that protest movements go in cycles; they assume that their organization will continue to flourish indefinitely. They do not make sufficient plans for a downturn in media interest, membership, and revenue. Therefore peace organizations

have periodic crises, with staff being laid-off because of the downturn in the organizations' membership. Many of the membership-specific organizations of the 1980s, such LAW, JAW, and MEND, have ended while MAPW and IPPNW have had financial problems.

B. Salience of the Peace Issue

No issue has ever been constantly in the news. The mass media tire of an issue because they can find no additional "angles". Issues are tissues: they have a specific purpose but a short life; they cannot be recycled. The varying salience of an issue helps explain the cycles in protest movements. This is the major external factor determining an organization's fate.

For example, a war being opposed by a peace organization may come to an end or an issue is so protracted that the mass media leave it alone until some more angles emerge. For example, the nuclear weapon issue was a major media concern in the early 1980s; it declined in the late 1980s with the U.S.–USSR INF treaty; it emerged again in the mid-1990s with the resumption of French Nuclear testing in the South Pacific; it declined in 1996 with the completion of the comprehensive test ban treaty; it arose again in 1998 with the explosion of the Indian and Pakistani nuclear devices.

Hopefully a peace organization would want to keep a cause alive, irrespective of the mass media's interest. Indeed, it can help influence the mass media's coverage of an issue. But it has to be recognized that no matter how active an organization may be, there are limits as to what can be achieved when an issue is not then regarded as a salient one.

C. Membership and Finance

Membership and finance are perennial problems. The tasks are so large that there are rarely enough resources. Leaving aside the external problem of the salience of a peace issue, there is also the internal problem that peace organizations in western countries draw their membership disproportionately from the generation born before 1945. These people lived through the Depression of the 1930s and at least one World War; they recognize the value of community and accept that they have an obligation to contribute to it.

The postwar Baby Boomers (born 1946–1966) have had an easier life, with their parents determined to ensure that their children would not have to endure the suffering they did. The Baby Boomers are, in contrast to their parents, more selfish and less publicly committed. They can be counted on for specific tasks (such as rallies) but they lack the commitment to be involved in the day-to-day running of organizations.

The reply of the Baby Boomers is that they are so busy in their work life that they lack the time for large-scale volunteering. Given the changing nature of work, with the longer hours involved, they lack the time for the type of volunteering that their parents were able to do.

Meanwhile, a new generation has come along, born after 1966, who have fewer parental models of community involvement. Also, their employment situation is often even more precarious than that of their parents and so they may have even less opportunity or commitment for being involved in peace (and other protest) organizations.

D. Weak Conceptual Understanding of Peace

Since there is no common understanding of what constitutes "peace", so there is often a fundamental flaw in much of the work conducted by the so-called peace organizations. Most of these organizations are reacting against specific wars or weapons systems rather than providing a comprehensive program for peace. They may often recognize that there is a need for a holistic vision and they can see the interconnectedness of issues (such as a country's high level of military expenditure and the lack of government funds for economic and social reforms).

But it is difficult to convey this holistic vision. First, the general public is mainly reached through the mass media. However, the mass media, especially a television news program, wants a very short "grab" or memorable statement. The hurried news interview format is not a good opportunity to explain the intricacies of such matters as the need for multilateral disarmament under international verification systems, the introduction of techniques for the peaceful settlement of international disputes, and the need to address the underlying causes of war (such as the importance of economic and social reform). By contrast, a journalist often prefers a colorful phrase describing in abusive terms a political leader or military figure.

Second, it is also often difficult to educate even members of peace organizations on the conceptual issues. This work is best done via membership newsletters and meetings. But most of the members are, for example, at meetings for action. They want short, sharp, specific events, rather than educational seminars on such matters as disarmament, conflict resolution, and eradicating the underlying causes of conflict.

Therefore, there is a need for widespread peace education to be conducted throughout schools so that there is a common understanding of the conceptual issues of peace. This will help create a culture of peace throughout a country and provide future members of peace organizations.

Peace education will help people to have a better understanding of the importance of civil society, the work of peace organizations, and the urgency of personal commitment. Peace organizations will never die while they continue to hope and they will never perish while they continue to dare.

Also See the Following Articles

COLD WAR • CONFLICT MANAGEMENT AND RESOLUTION • NUCLEAR WARFARE • PEACE MOVEMENTS

Bibliography

Gill, A. (1994). *An Honourable Defeat.* New York: Henry Holt & Co.
Hersh, S. (1983). *Kissinger: The price of power* (pp. 118–133). London: Faber.
Liddington, J. (1989). *The long road to Greenham: Feminism and antimilitarism in Britain since 1820.* London: Virago.
Suter, K. (1983). *Ministry for peace: An Australian peace initiative.* Sydney: United Nations Association of Australia.

Peace Prizes

Peter van den Dungen

University of Bradford

Let the greatest share of honor be ever paid, not to warlike kings (the world has sorely suffered for its folly in giving them glory), but to kings who entirely reject the war system, and by their understanding and counsels, not by force and arms, restore to bleeding human nature the blessings of concord and repose (Erasmus, *Complaint of Peace*).

I. A History of Peace Prizes in Essay Contests
II. The Significance of the Nobel Peace Prize
III. An Overview of Current Annual Peace Prizes
IV. The Effects and Meaning of Peace Prizes

PEACE PRIZES are awards given to individuals or to organizations for distinguished achievements or efforts in promoting peace. This article will briefly consider the history of the subject and the importance of the Nobel Peace Prize before presenting an overview of current peace prizes. Their significance is commented on in the concluding section.

I. A HISTORY OF PEACE PRIZES IN ESSAY CONTESTS

The practice of honoring an outstanding achievement has a long tradition, particularly in the arts and sciences, and in the fields of sports and war. In modern times, probably the first award for peace was made by the French Academy in 1767. It presented a gold medal to J.-F. de la Harpe who had submitted the best treatise

showing the advantages of world peace, and inspiring horror for the ravages of war. With the formation of the first organized peace societies in the United States, Britain, Switzerland, and France in the first half of the 19th century, essay contests such as the one inaugurated by the Academy became a widespread instrument of the peace movement and have remained so to the present day. They were meant to stimulate discussion and advance knowledge about the causes of war and the best ways of achieving peace. Many of the winning contributions, which ranged from slim pamphlets to book-length manuscripts, were published and are still today regarded as pioneering analyses of the war system, providing realistic and thoughtful blueprints for a peaceful international order. *Prize Essays on a Congress of Nations* (1840) brought together the five best essays submitted to a contest organised by the American Peace Society. Each author was awarded $100, and the 700-page volume became a landmark in the literature on peace. The Society presented complimentary copies to the crowned heads of Europe and leading statesmen in America. John Quincy Adams, former president and competition jury member, argued that the publication and wide distribution of the volume would awaken and keep alive the attention of two continents on a vital subject. Many contests were organized specifically for

Copyright © 1999 by Academic Press.
All rights of reproduction in any form reserved.

schools and colleges and aimed to bring before young people the evils of war and proposed remedies.

The most successful and spectacular peace essay contest ever held was the $100,000 *American Peace Award*, which was announced in 1923 by the Philadelphia publisher and philanthropist Edward W. Bok. He offered the award for "the best practicable plan by which the U.S. may cooperate with other nations to achieve and preserve the peace of the world." The handsome sum for the winner created an enormous interest in the country—precisely what Bok had intended: over a quarter of a million citizens requested further details about the competition, and more than 220,000 submitted their plan (which had to be limited to 5000 words: excellent remuneration at $20 per word!). The winning one, by Charles Levermore, was submitted to a nationwide referendum in which the great majority of the 600,000 people who cast their ballot agreed with his proposals that the country cooperate more closely with the League of Nations and enter the Permanent Court of International Justice.

From a rich and continuing tradition, only a few instances from recent times will be mentioned. In 1985 the *Christian Science Monitor* launched its *Peace 2010* contest. Participants had to assume that world peace was a reality 25 years hence, and their challenge was to provide a coherent explanation of how the transition from war to peace had come about. The best of the more than 1300 essays submitted were published in the fascinating book, *How Peace Came to the World* (1986). The challenge of imagining a peaceful future and the process by which humanity got there unleashed the kind of creative thinking that the contest organizers believed the world needed. This, as well as the prospect of publication, stimulated the participants since no financial or other material awards were offered.

In 1989 International Physicians for the Prevention of Nuclear War (IPPNW) launched the *Appeal for Peace Contest* as part of its "Cease-Fire 89" Campaign. The aim of the contest was to generate 50,000 letters, essays, poems, songs, and other appeals for peace to the leaders of the five states that at that time were continuing nuclear weapons tests. In this way IPPNW sought to broadcast as widely as possible its concerns about the risks involved in testing and to strengthen its campaign for a ban on all nuclear tests. Participants had to send their appeal to the leader of one or more of the five declared weapons states (as well as a copy to IPPNW). The winner of the first prize traveled to Hiroshima as IPPNW's guest at its 9th World Congress there and presented the winning appeal to it.

In 1993 and 1994, world leaders themselves, in the shape of the Carlsson-Ramphal Commission on Global Governance, invited young people to submit their dreams, visions and experiences when the Commission launched its *Peace Quest International Composition Contest*. Prizewinners were invited to Geneva to meet Commission members and visit international institutions.

II. THE SIGNIFICANCE OF THE NOBEL PEACE PRIZE

Peace prizes can be divided according to the frequency of the awarding of the prize, and the purpose for which it is given. Until the end of the 19th century, virtually all awards for peace were related to occasional essay competitions, that is, the awards were made not on a regular but on an ad hoc basis and they were made only for written contributions. In both respects the Nobel Peace Prize, first awarded in 1901, was significantly different: for the first time, peace became the subject of a prize to be awarded annually (and, in effect, in perpetuity). At the same time, the nature of the peace achievement honored was not strictly circumscribed but was virtually unlimited. Alfred Nobel, the Swedish inventor who left his large fortune for the creation of five prizes, specified in his will that the peace prize should be given "to the person who shall have done the most or the best work for fraternity between nations, for the abolition or reduction of standing armies and the holding and promotion of peace congresses."

It is obvious that the Nobel Peace Prize, being the first institutionalized and general award for peace (which, moreover, remained the only such prize in existence for several decades), was bound to become the premier prize for peace. This is especially so if the following four factors are also taken into consideration: (1) The prize was one of the five prizes established by Nobel. The linkage of awards for peace with those for literature and three scientific fields (physics, chemistry, and medicine or physiology) enhanced the status not only of the award for peace but also of peace itself (which was then by no means universally regarded as being either a possible or even desirable objective); (2) The elaborate and dignified annual award ceremonies with a royal presence and growing media interest have underlined the importance of the occasion: (3) The exceptional monetary value of the prize inevitably generates curiosity and excitement and contributes to the esteem in which the prize is held; (4) The record of the Norwegian Nobel Committee in selecting laureates is an excellent one overall. The fact that many of the leading official as well as nonofficial peacemakers and peacemaking institutions of the 20th century are Nobel laureates lends further glory to the honor. (Gandhi, if he had lived, would almost certainly have been awarded the prize in 1948; the Nobel Foundation's policy does not allow the posthumous awarding of prizes. No award was made that year, the Committee declaring that "there was no suitable living candidate".)

From 1901 until 1997, the Nobel Peace Prize has been awarded to 103 laureates, comprising 85 individuals (including Le Duc Tho, who declined the prize) and 18 institutions (see Table I).

No awards were made for 19 years, 9 of which coincided with the two World Wars. The last time that no award was made was in 1972. Virtually the only conceivable reason today for withholding the annual prize would be an internal one, namely the inability of the independent, five-member Norwegian Nobel Committee to agree on a winner. The Committee's problem has never been a lack of suitable candidates, only the difficulty of deciding on the most deserving. On 23 occasions the award has been divided between laureates, with the sharing of the prize among three of them in 1994 being unprecedented.

Of the 84 individuals, only 9 (10%) have been women, which is perhaps ironic in view of the fact that it was Bertha von Suttner who inspired Nobel to create the prize for peace. She was one of the leading figures of the pre-1914 European peace movement and the first woman laureate (1905). It was not until 1950 that a non-White person was honored, Ralph Bunche. And only once before 1960 did the prize go beyond Europe and the United States, when Argentinian foreign minister Saavedra Lamas was chosen (1936). That today the prize has become truly global is indicated by the fact that the last 10 years have seen only a single laureate hailing from Europe or the United States. The list over the same period also well illustrates the multifaceted nature of peacemaking and the variety of peacemakers honored. They include statesmen, opposition leaders and human rights activists, disarmament advocates, as well as intergovernmental and nongovernmental organizations. Several awards have been made not only to honor but also to support and encourage efforts for the peaceful resolution of conflicts—in the Middle East, Central America, South Africa, and Asia.

In the course of the 20th century the Nobel Peace Prize has provided the inspiration for the foundation of many other peace prizes. The following section presents an overview of some 150 mainly annual awards in existence today.

III. AN OVERVIEW OF CURRENT ANNUAL PEACE PRIZES

Asking the question, "Who awards peace prizes, to whom, and why?" suggests at least three ways to distinguish between them. Prizes can be categorized according to the nature of (1) the awarding body; (2) the recipient; or (3) the achievement. Some awards are specifically intended either for certain kinds of recipient or for certain types of activity. Among the former are, for example, young people, students, women, journalists, authors, peace researchers; among the latter are efforts to promote disarmament (in general, or nuclear disarmament in particular), reconciliation, war resistance and conscientious objection to military service, conflict resolution, and peacemaking in general or in a specific area (e.g., the Middle East, Northern Ireland), European unity, human rights. Some organizations that award prizes may impose limitations on who or what type of activity can qualify for the award. On the other hand, no such limitations may be imposed, in which case the prize can be awarded to any type of recipient, whether person or institution, for any kind of effort on behalf of peace (this applies to the Nobel Peace Prize). Contemporary peace prizes are grouped below in accordance with the nature of the awarding body, as follows (the figures in parentheses indicate the number of prizes included in each category).

A. Intergovernmental Organizations (IGOs) (26)
  1. Awards related to the United Nations (UN) and its specialized agencies (22)
    a. UN (4)
    b. UNESCO (7)
    c. UNHCR (1)
    d. UNICEF (2)
    e. United Nations Associations (UNAs) (8)
  2. Other organizations (4)
B. International Nongovernmental organizations (INGOs) (13)
C. National official bodies (22)
  1. National governments (13)
  2. Provincial governments (2)
  3. Municipal governments (7)
D. National nonofficial bodies (90)
  1. Older, and notable, prizes (12)
  2. Prizes established before 1980 (14)
  3. Prizes established in the 1980s (39)
  4. Prizes established in the 1990s (15)
  5. Other prizes (10)

TABLE I
Nobel Peace Prize Laureates, 1901–1997

Year	Laureate	Year	Laureate
1901	H. Dunant (Switzerland)	1949	J. Boyd Orr (Great Britain)
	F. Passy (France)	1950	R. J. Bunche (U.S.)
1902	E. Ducommun (Switzerland)	1951	L. Jouhaux (France)
	A. Gobat (Switzerland)	1952	A. Schweitzer (France)
1903	W. R. Cremer (Great Britain)	1953	G. C. Marshall (U.S.)
1904	Institute for Int'l Law, Ghent	1954	Office of the UN High Comissioner for Refugees, Geneva
1905	Bertha von Suttner (Austria)	1955	None
1906	T. Roosevelt (U.S.)	1956	None
1907	E. T. Moneta (Italy)	1957	L. B. Pearson (Canada)
	L. Renault (France)	1958	G. Pire (Belgium)
1908	K. P. Arnoldson (Sweden)	1959	P. J. Noel-Baker (Great Britain)
	F. Bajer (Denmark)	1960	A. J. Lutuli (South Africa)
1909	A. M. F. Beernaert (Belgium)	1961	D. Hammarskjöld (Sweden)
	P. H. d'Estournelles-de Constant (France)	1962	L. C. Pauling (U.S.)
1910	Int'l Peace Bureau, Bern	1963	Int'l Committee of the Red Cross, Geneva
1911	T. M. C. Asser (Netherlands)		League of Red Cross Societies, Geneva
	A. H. Fried (Austria)	1964	M. L. King (U.S.)
1912	Elihu Root (U.S.)	1965	UN Children's Fund (UNICEF)
1913	H. La Fontaine (Belgium)	1966	None
1914	None	1967	None
1915	None	1968	R. Cassin (France)
1916	None	1969	Int'l Labor Organization, Geneva
1917	Int'l Red Cross, Geneva	1970	N. E. Borlaug (U.S.)
1918	None	1971	W. Brandt (Germany)
1919	T. W. Wilson (U.S.)	1972	None
1920	L. Bourgeois (France)	1973	H. A. Kissinger (U.S.)
1921	K. H. Branting (Sweden)		[Le Duc Tho (N. Vietnam) (declined the prize)]
	C. L. Lange (Norway)	1974	S. MacBride (Ireland)
1922	F. Nansen (Norway)		E. Sato (Japan)
1923	None	1975	A. Sakharov (U.S.S.R.)
1924	None	1976	M. Corrigan (Great Britain)
1925	C. G. Dawes (U.S.)		B. Williams (Great Britain)
	A. Chamberlain (Great Britain)	1977	Amnesty Int'l
1926	A. Briand (France)	1978	M. Begin (Israel)
	G. Stresemann (Germany)		A. Sadat (Egypt)
1927	F. Buisson (France)	1979	Mother Teresa (India)
	L. Quidde (Germany)	1980	A. Pérez Esquivel (Argentina)
1928	None	1981	Office of the High Commissioner for Refugees, Geneva
1929	F. B. Kellogg (U.S.)	1982	A. Myrdal (Sweden)
1930	N. Söderblom (Sweden)		A. García Robles (Mexico)
1931	N. M. Butler (U.S.)	1983	L. Walesa (Poland)
	J. Addams (U.S.)	1984	D. Tutu (South Africa)
1932	None	1985	Int'l Physicians for the Prevention of Nuclear War
1933	N. Angell (Great Britain)	1986	E. Wiesel (U.S.)
1934	A. Henderson (Great Britain)	1987	O. Arias Sánchez (Costa Rica)
1935	C. von Ossietzky (Germany)	1988	UN Peacekeeping Forces
1936	C. Saavedra Lamas (Argentina)	1989	The Dalai Lama XIV (Tibet)
1937	E. A. R. G. Cecil (Great Britain)	1990	M. Gorbachev (U.S.S.R.)
1938	Nansen Int'l Office for Refugees, Geneva	1991	A. S. Kyi (Burma)
1939	None	1992	R. Menchú Tum (Guatemala)
1940	None	1993	N. Mandela (South Africa)
1941	None		F. W. De Klerk (South Africa)
1942	None	1994	Y. Rabin (Israel)
1943	None		S. Peres (Israel)
1944	Int'l Committee of the Red Cross, Geneva		Y. Arafat (Palestine)
1945	C. Hull (U.S.)	1995	J. Rotblat (Great Britain)
1946	E. G. Balch (U.S.)		Pugwash Conference (Int)
	J. R. Mott (U.S.)	1996	C. F. X. Belo (E. Timor)
1947	The Friends Service Council (Great Britain)		J. Ramos-Horta (E. Timor)
	The Americans Friends Service Committee (U.S.)	1997	Int'l Committee to Ban Landmines
1948	None		Jody Williams

It should be noted that the above listing of organizations does not constitute a hierarchy of the awards they make. It is only a slight exaggeration to say that the world recognizes two kinds of peace prizes: those awarded by the Norwegian Nobel Committee, and others. One of the oldest and most significant of the other prizes is that of the German Booksellers' Association. Even though Germany also has official prizes awarded by provincial and municipal authorities, they do not, for that reason alone, assume greater importance than the prize awarded by this private association.

A. Intergovernmental Organizations (IGOs)

1. Awards Related to the United Nations (UN) and Its Specialized Agencies

A great number of prizes and awards are bestowed by the UN, its specialized agencies, and by the UN Associations (UNAs) in a number of member states. Although the latter organizations, strictly considered, belong to the category of national, nonofficial bodies, they are included here. Of the many specialized agencies of the UN, only three will be considered.

a. UN

The UN itself has instituted two, largely honorific and symbolic, distinctions for peace. A *UN Peace Medal* was created when U Thant was Secretary General. It is presented to heads of state in the course of customary exchanges of gifts, and to those who have served as president of the UN General Assembly. The *UN Plaque* was first awarded by the Secretary General in 1983. It is given to public officials and private persons who have made outstanding contributions to the cause of world peace. It is divided into two categories: one is given to heads of state or government, the other to cabinet ministers and nongovernmental figures.

In order to mark the 40th anniversary of the organization, the UN General Assembly proclaimed 1986 the International Year of Peace and approved a program of activities and events. Among them was the creation of an award, entitled *Peace Messenger*, presented by the Secretary General to organizations and institutions making significant contributions to the observance of the Year. Several hundred awards have been presented in subsequent years (each time on the International Day of Peace, the third Tuesday in September). More than 60 cities have received the award. They met for the first time in 1988 in Verdun (France) at the invitation of the mayor. The meeting was held as part of the

inauguration ceremonies of the World Center for Peace, Freedom and Human Rights in the city. On this occasion, the UN Secretary General received the *Peace Medal of the City of Verdun*.

b. UNESCO

Some of the prizes awarded by UNESCO are both more substantial and significant than the UN awards mentioned above; this applies especially to the two prizes for peace education and peace research. The *UNESCO Prize for Peace Education* aims to promote all forms of action designed to "construct the defences of peace in the minds of men" by rewarding "a particularly outstanding activity designed to alert public opinion and mobilise the human conscience in the cause of peace" in accordance with the spirit of the constitution of UNESCO and the charter of the UN. The prize was instituted in 1980 and first awarded the following year. It was made possible by the donation of $1 million by the Japan Shipbuilding Foundation. Its President, Ryoichi Sasakawa, has also endowed other UN prizes such as those for disaster prevention, world health, and the environment. Recent winners of the peace education prize are Ruth L. Sivard (1991), Mother Teresa (1992), Prayudh Payutto (1994), and Chiara Lubich (1996), as well as peace research centers in South Korea (1993) and Austria (1995).

In 1989, UNESCO's general conference adopted a resolution establishing a new annual prize for peace, to be named after the president of Ivory Coast: the *Félix Houphouët-Boigny Peace Prize*. It honors individuals, associations, or institutions that have made a significant contribution to "promoting, seeking, safeguarding, or maintaining" peace in the spirit of the UNESCO constitution and the UN charter. The prize was first awarded in 1991 to Nelson Mandela and F. W. de Klerk; subsequent laureates have been the Academy of International Law in the Hague (1992); Yasser Arafat, Shimon Peres, and Yitzak Rabin (1993); King Juan Carlos and former president Carter (1994); Sadako Ogata (1995). The award has been made possible through the Félix Houphouët-Boigny Foundation for Peace Research.

In 1996 the Director General announced his intention to establish the *UNESCO Mayors for Peace Prize* in recognition of exemplary action they have taken to improve living standards and to create a "citizen-friendly urban environment." The prize is to be awarded to one municipality in each of five regions of the world. It is expected that the awarding of such a prize will contribute to the establishment of regional cooperation networks among municipalities and to the creation of data banks on innovative initiatives. These promote intercommunity dialogue, urban development, the environment, cultural activities, and civic education. The first award, for the Latin America and Caribbean region, was made in September 1996 to the mayor of the city of Apartadó in Colombia during the congress "Cities and Education for a Culture of Peace" held in Rio de Janeiro. In the same year the Director-General presented the first *UNESCO-Madanjeet Singh Prize for the Promotion of Tolerance and Non-violence* to a collective of 32 women's organizations in Rwanda.

Among other relevant UNESCO prizes are the biennial *Prize for the Teaching of Human Rights*, first awarded in 1978; the *Gandhi Medal*, presented to Mandela in 1996; and the *International Simon Bolivar Prize*. The latter prize, for activity in accordance with Bolivar's ideals, was founded by the government of Venezuela. Specifically, the prize rewards an activity of outstanding merit that has contributed to the freedom, independence, and dignity of peoples, strengthened solidarity among nations, and fostered their development. It was instituted in 1983, the 200th anniversary of Bolivar's birth, and was first awarded that year to King Juan Carlos and Nelson Mandela. Later laureates of this biennial prize include the Contadora Group (1985), Václav Havel (1990), and Muhammad Yunus, "the banker of the poor" in Bangladesh (1996).

c. UNHCR

Of all the awards made by the UN's specialized agencies, the *Nansen Medal* of the Office of the UN High Commissioner for Refugees (UNHCR) is the best known. It was instituted in 1954 by Dr. Gerrit Jan van Heuven Goedhart, the first High Commissioner, and was awarded in that year to Eleanor Roosevelt (the UNHCR received the Nobel Peace Prize for the same year). The Nansen Medal is an annual reward in recognition of outstanding services rendered in the cause of refugees. In recent years the award has been presented to, for example, German President Richard von Weizsäcker (1992), Médecins sans Frontières (1993), and Graça Simbine Machel of Mozambique (1995). The award to her was for her work on behalf of refugee children. She also chaired an unprecedented UN study on the impact of armed conflict on children. The award bears the name of Dr. Fridtjof Nansen, the first League of Nations High Commissioner for Refugees (and Nobel Peace Prize laureate in 1922).

d. UNICEF

The *UNICEF Maurice Pate Award* is named after the organization's first executive director and was instituted

in 1966, the year following his death, and when the organization received the Nobel Peace Prize. The annual award is "meant to call the world's attention to progress being made for children and to methods employed, thus inspiring replication and broader support." Like other organizations, the UNICEF board regards its prestigious award "as an inexpensive means of recognition, advocacy, and inspiration which usually engenders widespread attention." In 1988, the American UNICEF Committee created a *Danny Kaye Memorial Prize*; its first recipient was Liv Ullmann for her work for the children of the world.

e. United Nations Associations (UNAs)

Prizes are also awarded by UN Associations in several countries. In Britain, the UNA awards since 1980 a *Media Peace Prize* to journalists who have used the media "for the furtherance of international understanding as a contribution to developing a more peaceful world." (An identically named prize is also awarded annually since 1980 by the Indian Federation of UNAs). UNA-UK also organizes every year the *Cecil Peace Prize*, named after the cofounder of the League of Nations, for university students in the country. Prizes are offered "for the best essay submitted on a subject falling within the field of international organization, international law, or international politics . . . and bearing upon the conditions contributing to the maintenance of peace." The Canadian UNA likewise confers two annual awards, namely the *Drayton Award* and, since 1979, the *Pearson Peace Medal* (named after the Canadian Prime Minister, 1957 Nobel Peace laureate, and strong UN supporter). In the United States, the Rochester Association for the UN has awarded its *Joseph C. Wilson Award* since 1975. Nelson Mandela, Olof Palme, and Mikhael Gorbachev have been recipients of the *Spanish UNA Peace Prize*, established in 1979 by the city council of Sabadell. Mention should here be made of the *U Thant Peace Award* instituted in 1982 by the Indian peace campaigner and sage Sri Chimnoy for promoting "peace meditation at the UN." The recipient of this annual award in 1988 was Edward Winchester, president of the Pentagon Meditation Club, for having launched the Spiritual Defense Initiative to protect humanity through individual and collective cultivation of inner peace.

2. Other Organizations

Although none of the prizes listed below (see Table II) are awarded explicitly for peace, all the organizations which have instituted them are concerned with promoting peace, international security, and human rights.

B. International Nongovernmental Organizations (INGOs)

International nongovernmental organizations of various kinds have established annual peace awards. As is also the case for other organizations that have created awards, the kind of activity and person (or organization) honored tends to reflect the general purposes and orientation of the awarding body. Religious, humanitarian, and peace organizations are all represented in the brief list below (see Table III).

The International Council of Christians and Jews awards a *Peace through Dialogue Peace Medal*; a very different organization, strongly associated with the Soviet Union, the World Peace Council, has awarded in the past a *Carl von Ossietzky Medal*.

In the broader field of human rights there are many awards, including the *Jan Palach Award for Human Rights Activism*, presented by the international committee of Charter 77 since 1980, the *Golden Dove* award of the International Federation of Human Rights since 1991, and the *Martin Ennals Human Rights Award*, first presented to the Chinese dissident Harry Wu in 1994 by the Martin Ennals Foundation. The *Africa Prize for Leadership* for the sustainable end of hunger, which is also known as "Africa's Nobel Prize" or "Africa's Peace Prize," has been awarded annually since 1987 by The Hunger Project, a New York-based INGO. Recipients include several African presidents (e.g., Nelson Mandela in 1994, Sam Nujoma in 1995) and African leaders of international or community organizations active in the continent. The prize is intended to engender a greater appreciation for and support of the effective and dynamic leadership associated with the end of hunger in Africa on a sustainable basis.

C. National Official Bodies

The fact that an increasing number of peace prizes are being awarded by a variety of national official bodies (at central, provincial, and local levels) is a reflection of the growing recognition of the importance and desir-

TABLE II

Prizes Awarded by IGOs (Other Than the UN)

1980	Human Rights Prize (Council of Europe; every 3 years)
1984	Atlantic Award (NATO)
1985	Sakharov Prize for Freedom of Thought (European Parliament)
	Prize for Journalism and Democracy (OSCE)

TABLE III

Prizes Awarded by INGOs

1976	World Methodist Peace Prize
1981	International Peace Academy Distinguished Peacekeeper Award (irregular)
1986	Caribbean Prize for Peace Through the Pursuit of Justice (Caribbean Conference of Churches, every 5 years)
1987	Red Cross and Red Crescent Prize for Peace and Humanity
1988	Pax Christi International Peace Award
1989	Lions' International Peace Poster Contest
1992	Sean MacBride Peace Prize (International Peace Bureau)

ability of peace as well as of the contribution that such authorities believe they can make in promoting efforts for peace. It is only in recent decades that such prizes have come into existence with the exception of prizes awarded in the former Communist bloc such as the *International Lenin Peace Prize* of the Soviet Union (founded in 1949 as the *International Stalin Peace Prize* but renamed in 1956), or the *Ossietzky Peace Prize* of the Peace Council of the German Democratic Republic.

1. National Governments

Many countries have official honors and awards that are bestowed on foreign dignitaries or on national citizens for all kinds of achievements, including those involving such peace-related concerns as defense and the promotion of democracy, freedom, and liberty. (In the U.S. there is, e.g., the *Presidential Medal of Freedom*). Here, only prizes explicitly awarded for peace will be considered. They are far less numerous and include those instituted by the governments of India, South Korea, and the United States. They tend to commemorate an important event or anniversary, for instance, of a prominent national citizen whose life was dedicated to the pursuit of world peace.

As part of the celebrations of the 125th anniversary of Gandhi's birth, the Indian government in 1995 created the *Gandhi International Peace Prize*. It is made "for an outstanding contribution to social, economic, and political transformation through nonviolence and other Gandhian methods," and was first awarded in 1996 to Julius Nyerere. The second Gandhi Peace Prize was awarded to Dr. A. T. Ariyaratne, who founded the Sarvodaya Shramadana rural development movement in Sri Lanka in 1958 and who has devoted his life to the elimination of poverty in accordance with Gandhian Principles, drawing also on Buddhist thought and culture. Ten years earlier, in 1986, the government had already established an annual *Indira Gandhi Prize for*

Peace, Disarmament and Development to honor the memory of the prime minister who was murdered in 1984. Her father has also a prize name after him. The Indian government's *Jawaharlal Nehru Award for International Understanding* was first presented in 1966; as far as it is possible the jury announces its decision each year on 14 November, the date of Nehru's birth.

Another national award in Asia is the *Seoul Peace Prize* established by the South Korean government following the 1988 Olympic Games in Seoul in recognition of the contributions the Olympiad has made to world peace. The prize is biennial, and is normally presented at a ceremony in Seoul on 17 September, the opening day of the Seoul Olympiad. Initially, the prize was reserved for sports-related peace activities but in view of the difficulties this created for finding suitable candidates, it was decided that from 1992 the prize should become a general one, honoring an outstanding contribution for the promotion of harmony of mankind and world peace "from any social area, including sports." The first award was presented to Juan Antonio Samaranch, president of the International Olympic Committee (1990). Subsequent recipients include the former U.S. Secretary of State George Shultz and Médecins sans Frontières.

In the United States, Congress authorized the U.S. Institute of Peace in 1990 to award annually the *Spark M. Matsunaga Medal of Peace*. It is conferred on those who "have contributed in extraordinary ways to peace among the nations and peoples of the world, giving special attention to contributions that advance society's knowledge of peacemaking and conflict management." The medal at the same time honors the senator from Hawaii who throughout his life worked for the creation of a U.S. agency dedicated to peace education, research, and training. The final passage of legislation which established the U.S. Institute of Peace in 1984 was due in no small measure to his efforts. The first awards were made in 1992 to former presidents Carter and Reagan. The United States is probably unique in also organizing an annual *National Peace Essay Contest* for secondary school students. Created by the Institute in 1987, each year it attracts the participation of some 5000 students from all 50 states. Prizes, in the form of college scholarships, are awarded to both national and state winners.

National peace prizes with an official status are also awarded in the Philippines, Turkey, and Vatican City. The *Ramon Magsaysay Award* was established to honor the late president of the Philippines (1953–1957), by giving recognition to persons in Asia who exemplify his greatness of spirit, integrity, and devotion to liberty.

"International Understanding" is one of five fields of endeavor for which an annual award can be made. The Award was made possible by a gift of $500,000 by the Rockefeller Brothers Fund of New York in 1957 and a subsequent gift of $1 million in 1963, together with support from the Congress of the Philippines. The first awards were presented in 1958. The *Ataturk International Peace Prize*, named after the founder of modern Turkey, was first awarded in 1986 to Joseph Luns, a former Secretary General of NATO. In 1992 the annual prize was awarded to Nelson Mandela, who famously declined the honor, citing Turkey's human rights record. Three years before, when still incarcerated, he had accepted the first *Gaddafi International Prize for Human Rights* and donated the prize money ($250,000) to the African National Congress (ANC). In 1991 the annual prize was given to an organization representing native Americans in the United States. Information about the above three prizes is sparse and little is known about their current status. Among the several honors and prizes awarded by the Vatican is the *Pope John XXIII Peace Prize*, which is presented triennially by the Pope for "outstanding contributions to world peace." Several other awards can be regarded as having a quasi-official status because of their significance or symbolism, and the dignity of the award ceremony (see below).

2. Provincial Governments

In the Federal Republic of Germany, a number of states and cities award their own peace prizes. The first *Hessian Peace Prize* was awarded in 1994 to Marianne Heiberg in the parliament building in Wiesbaden, capital of the state of Hesse. The institution of the prize was made possible through the generosity of Albert Osswald, a former primer minister of the state who was also responsible for the creation, 25 years before, of the first German peace research institute, the Peace Research Institute Frankfurt (PRIF, or *Hessische Stiftung Friedens-und Konfliktforschung*). Just as research at the Institute focuses on the possibility of dealing with international conflict without the application of military force, so the prize is meant to honor individuals who have distinguished themselves in the prevention or reduction of the military use of force and the introduction and application of nonviolent means for resolving international conflict. In 1995 the prize was presented to John Hume, in 1996 to Gregorio Rosa Chavez, suffragan bishop of El Salvador. Another German state, Nordrhein-Westfalen, awards an annual prize for a narrowly defined achievement in the area of peace education: the *Gustav Heinemann Peace Prize for Children's Books*. It also commemorates a German president whose efforts on behalf of international peace and reconciliation and support for peace research are well known.

3. Municipal Governments

Two famous German authors, whose peace sentiments brought them into conflict with the authorities of a previous era, are likewise commemorated in the names given to prizes which are also meant for publications dealing with peace and peaceful developments. They are awarded biennially by the cities of Osnabrück and Oldenburg. The *Erich Maria Remarque Prize* of the city of Osnabrück, where Remarque was born, honors literary, journalistic, or scholarly publications that deal in the widest sense with the themes of inner and outer peace. The institution of the prize, first awarded in 1991, symbolizes the commitment of the city to work for a more humane society in accordance with Remarque's ideas, and to nurture the legacy of its famous son whose antiwar novel, *All Quiet on the Western Front*, was publicly burned when the Nazis came to power.

The *Ossietzky Prize* of the city of Oldenburg, created in 1979, is awarded for the best publication dealing with one of three subjects: the life and work of Ossietzky (Nobel Peace laureate for 1935 while held captive by the Nazis); or with the resistance to National Socialism; or with the democratic tradition and current political situation in Germany. The prize is awarded on 4 May, the anniversary of Ossietzky's death in 1938, following years of harassment and torture.

Two other German cities have created peace prizes that are named after historic figures who have been influential in the early history of the cities concerned. The *City of Augsburg Peace Prize* was created in 1985 in order to celebrate the two thousandth anniversary of its foundation by the emperor Augustus. The prize is awarded every 3 years, and singles out efforts to promote peace and unity among different religious denominations—thus continuing an important tradition in the city: in 1555, the Religious Peace of Augsburg was concluded between Catholic and Protestant rulers. Another historic city, Aachen (Aix-la-Chapelle) has awarded its prestigious *Karlspreis* (*Charlemagne Prize*) since 1949. It fulfills the dual purpose of "commemorating Charlemagne and honoring efforts for European unity." With the Peace Prize of the German Booksellers' Association (see below), it is one of the most important awards made in Germany. Many leading figures from various European countries have been recipients of the prize. The *Aachen Peace Prize* was created in 1988 to honor special efforts for peace and human rights; it awards two prizes every year for work undertaken in Germany and abroad.

Another historic city in Germany—one whose past has been closely linked to the Nazi era—instituted in 1995 a major award as a symbol of its determination "to prevent any messages other than those of peace, reconciliation, understanding and respect for Human Rights ever to come from it." The biennial *Nuremberg International Human Rights Award* "honors individuals or groups who have, in an exemplary fashion, committed themselves to the respect of human rights, sometimes at considerable personal risk." Sergei Kovalev, who was imprisoned for 10 years in Siberia before becoming head of the new Russia's Human Rights Commission and a sharp critic of his country's military intervention in Chechnya, was its first recipient. The award ceremony (at which Václav Havel delivered the eulogy) took place in September 1995, 60 years after the proclamation of the notorious Nuremberg Race Laws.

Elsewhere, a much more modest prize, unencumbered by a historical burden, is the *Fenner Brockway Peace Prize for Literature*. The name honors the memory of Lord Brockway, a great internationalist and peace campaigner of the 20th century who was also for many years the Member of Parliament for Slough (Berkshire, England). The prize is funded by Slough Borough Council and is presented to winners of an occasional writing competition.

D. National Nonofficial Bodies

1. Older, and Notable, Prizes

The vast majority of peace prizes are awarded by nonofficial bodies of various kinds. They include, first of all, peace organizations and campaigning groups, but also religious and educational organizations, and philanthropic foundations. It is also in this category that the most famous, and longest established, prizes are to be found. Apart from the *Nobel Peace Prize* (1901) and the *Charles Sumner Prize* of Harvard University (1885, for the best annual dissertation by a student of the university on the prevention of war and the preservation of peace), they include the following two prizes.

The *Wateler Peace Prize*, first awarded in 1931 to Sir Eric Drummond, Secretary-General of the League of Nations. The prize is meant for "private persons or institutions, alternately Dutch and foreign, who have notably furthered the cause of peace by word or deed." It is the result of the testament of the Dutch banker J. G. D. Wateler, drawn up in the middle of the First World War, by which he left his considerable fortune for the creation of the annual prize. It is administered by the Carnegie Foundation and presented in the Peace Palace in the Hague.

The *Peace Prize of the German Booksellers' Association*, first awarded in 1950 to Max Tau, the editor and author who fled Germany in 1935 and made his living in Norway. Since 1951, when Albert Schweitzer was the laureate, the presentation speech has been made by the country's president, thus lending considerable prestige to the occasion. The celebrations take place in the famous Paul's Church in Frankfurt—seat of the first German parliament in 1848—and are the highlight of the annual book fair. The prize was created with a double purpose: to raise the awareness of German writers and publishers for the wider responsibility they carry in the process of the moral and cultural rebuilding of their shattered society, and to demonstrate to the outside world the new Germany's commitment to the values of peace, freedom, and human dignity. Non-Germans are also considered for the award; in recent years they have included the writers Amos Oz (1992), Jorge Semprun (1994), and Mario Varga Llosa (1996).

The next three peace prizes are instituted by foundations that, in various ways, seem to have been directly inspired by the Nobel Foundation; the monetary part of the prize in each case is considerable.

The *Balzan Prize for Humanity, Peace and Brotherhood Among Peoples* is awarded only occasionally, with an interval of at least 3 years. The International Balzan Foundation, established in 1956 in accordance with the wishes of Eugenio Balzan, formerly director of the Italian newspaper *Corriere della Sera*, also awards three annual prizes in the sciences and humanities. The laureates of the peace prize so far are the Nobel Foundation (1961), Pope John XXIII (1962), Mother Teresa (1978), UNHCR (1986), Abbé Pierre (1991), and the International Committee of the Red Cross (1996).

The *Onassis Prize for International Understanding and Social Achievement* is one of three biennial prizes awarded by the Alexander S. Onassis Public Benefit Foundation. The Greek shipping magnate Aristotelis Onassis bequeathed half of his estate to the Foundation, which was established in 1975 and is dedicated to the memory of his only son (who died in an accident at a young age). The award was presented to the UN Secretary General in Athens in 1995. Among the other prizes the Foundation awards is the *Onassis Prize for "Man and Mankind" Athinai*, which has been bestowed upon, for example, Desmond Tutu (1981), J. William Fulbright (1989), Javier Pérez de Cuéllar (1990), and Václav Havel (1993). In 1981, the Foundation introduced the award of a *Gold Medal*, which is reserved for heads of state "whose personalities and efforts have gained international acclaim." It was awarded in 1981

to Greek President Constantinos Karamanlis and in 1987 to King Juan Carlos.

The *Right Livelihood Awards* have been presented annually since 1980 in the Swedish Parliament in Stockholm on the day before the Nobel Prize presentations. The Awards, also known as "the alternative Nobel Prize," aim to support those working on practical and exemplary solutions to the real problems facing the world today. A holistic approach is a vital feature of the Awards, which bring together those who are working for peace and disarmament, human rights and social justice, sustainable economic development, and environmental regeneration. The idea and the endowment, which resulted in the establishment of the Right Livelihood Awards Foundation, came from Jakob von Uexkull, a Swedish-German writer and former Member of the European Parliament. The yearly cash award of $250,000 is shared by several recipients and is for specific projects rather than for personal use. The 1996 award was shared by the Committee of Soldiers' Mothers in Russia, the People's Science Movement in Kerala, India, and George Vithoulkas of Greece, a world authority on homeopathic medicine. A common theme in the work of the laureates is that radical reform of the structures that control people's lives is essential if the world is to offer more hopeful prospects for life in the 21st century.

The German and Greek awards mentioned above have in some respects acquired a semi-official reputation. The same applies to prizes awarded in Sweden and Spain. In Sweden, the *Olof Palme Prize* was established in 1987 for recognition of an outstanding achievement in the areas of peace and disarmament, international understanding and common security, democracy and racial harmony, goals to which the murdered prime minister had dedicated his life. The award of the prize is one of the activities of the Olof Palme Memorial Fund for International Understanding and Common Security, which was established by his family and by the Swedish Social Democratic Party to honor his memory. Among the recipients have been the United Nations Peacekeepers, Václav Havel, Amnesty International, and women peacemakers in Azerbaijan and Armenia. In Spain, the Prince of Asturias Foundation has presented annual awards since 1981 in eight areas of human endeavor. Efforts for international peace and understanding are honored by the *Prince of Asturias Award for International Cooperation* and a similar award for *Concord*. Recipients have been leading politicians and international organizations (both governmental and private).

The many other peace prizes which have been established in the period since 1950 by national nonofficial groups or by private individuals will be briefly presented and listed in chronological order.

2. Prizes Established before 1980

Whereas in the 1980s and 1990s new (mainly annual) peace prizes proliferated worldwide, their number was relatively small in the preceding period and they were largely to be found in the United States. Among the better-known are the *Jane Addams Children's Book Award* (1953), the *Gandhi Peace Award* (1960), the *SANE Education Fund/Consider the Alternatives Peace Award* (1962), the *Lentz International Peace Research Award* (1972, presented about every other year), the *Martin Luther King, Jr., Nonviolent Peace Prize* (of the King Center for Nonviolent Social Change in Atlanta, 1973), the *Ralph Bunche Award* (of the Seattle-King County Bar Association, 1973), and the *Martin Luther King, Jr., Award* (of the Fellowship of Reconciliation, 1979).

In the United States, also, two prizes launched in the 1970s were discontinued by the end of the following decade: the *Rufus Jones Award* of the World Academy of Art & Sciences (1979–1986), and the *Grenville Clark Prize* of the John Sloan Dickey Endowment for International Understanding at Dartmouth College (1975–1988). The first was established in honor of a leading American Quaker advocate of pacifism, the second in honor of a prominent proponent of World Federalism (who endowed a World Law Fund with $500,000 in the early 1960s, thereby making possible the World Order Models Project).

In Canada, the Lester B. Pearson Peace Park, which was opened in Tweed, Ontario, in 1967 as part of the country's centennial, instituted in 1969 a *Man or Woman of the Year Peace Award*. It is granted annually to a Canadian citizen who has made an outstanding contribution to world peace, Canadian unity or the humanities. In 1995 the winner was Edward Broadbent, former leader of the National Democratic Party; Larkin Kerwin won the award in 1996.

Among the diverse peace prizes instituted in the same period in Europe are the *Carl von Ossietzky Medal* of the (West) Berlin section of the International League of Human Rights (1962); the *Adolphe Bentinck Prize* (1972, France) for "an important contribution to the building of Europe, the cause of peace, or the struggle against fanaticism"; the *Ewart-Biggs Memorial Prize* to encourage peace and understanding between the peoples of Britain and Ireland (instituted in 1976 by the widow of the murdered British ambassador in Dublin); and the *Karin Grech Peace Memorial Prize* (established

in 1978 by the Center for Social Leadership in Valetta, Malta).

3. Prizes Established in the 1980s

The following prizes were instituted or first awarded in the United States during the 1980s; the sponsoring organization is also indicated (see Table IV).

To this can be added two other kinds of prizes: On the one hand, some very specialized awards such as the *Charles DeBenedetti Prize in Peace History* of the Peace History Society (1987), or the *Warren F. Kuehl Award* of the Society for Historians of American Foreign Relations (1985). The latter is for the author of an outstanding

TABLE IV

Prizes Established in the 1980s (in the U.S.)

1980	Albert Einstein Peace Prize (Albert Einstein Peace Prize Foundation)
1980	Pope Paul VI 'Teacher of Peace' Award (Pax Christi U.S.A.)
1980	Will Wittkamper Peace Award (Discipline of Christ Peace Fellowship, biennial)
1981	Adin Ballou Award (Unitarian Universalist Peace Fellowship)
1981	Peace Quilt Awards (Boise Peace Quilt Project)
1981	Rotary Award for World Understanding (Rotary International)
1981	International Peace and Tourism Award (American Society of Travel Agents)
1982	International Children's Peace Prize (Children as the Peacemakers Foundation)
1982	Peace Play Contest (Goshen College, biennial)
1982	Helen Caldicott Leadership Award (Women's Action for Nuclear Disarmament Education Fund)
1983	Beyond War Award (Beyond War Foundation)
1983	Olive Branch Awards (New York University Center for War, Peace and the News Media)
1984	Distinguished Peace Leadership Award (Nuclear Age Peace Foundation)
1984	Distinguished Contribution for Peace (Psychologists for Social Responsibility)
1984	Abraham Joshua Heschel Peace Award (Jewish Peace Fellowship)
1985	Swackhamer Prizes Student Essay Contest (Nuclear Age Peace Foundation)
1987	Joel R. Seldin Peace Award (Psychologists for Social Responsibility)
1987	Athletes United for Peace Award (Athletes United for Peace)
1987	Peace Prize (Peace Development Fund and Pacific Peace Fund)
1988	Pacem in Terris Medal (Manhattan College)
1988	Grawemeyer Award for Ideas Improving World Order (University of Louisville, KY, Dept. of Political Science)
1989	Ruth Bayley Peace Award (Peace Links)

book dealing with the history of internationalism or the history of the peace movement, including biographies of prominent internationalists or peace figures. On the other hand, there are also some general awards for human rights, such as the *Carter-Menil Human Rights Prize* of the Carter Center at Emory University (1986), or the various prizes carrying the names of such figures as Raoul Wallenberg (*Raoul Wallenberg Humanitarian Award* of the Swedish Council of America, 1982; *Raoul Wallenberg World of Heroes Award* of the Raoul Wallenberg Committee of the U.S.A., 1987), Rosa Parks (*Rosa Parks Award* for Women in Community Service, 1979), or Robert F. Kennedy (*Human Rights Award*, 1984 and *Journalism Awards*, 1980, both established by the Robert F. Kennedy Memorial Foundation).

Annual peace prizes established in the 1980s outside the U.S.A. include the following (see Table V).

4. Prizes Established in the 1990s

The present decade has seen the emergence of the following annual peace prizes (see Table VI).

5. Other Prizes

Several peace prizes have not been mentioned in the preceding pages because of a lack of sufficient information. They include the following: *Africa Peace Award, Edwin T. Dahlberg Peace Award, Film Peace Prize, Inter-*

TABLE V

Prizes Established in the 1980s (outside the U.S.)

Australia/Israel
1985	Evelyn and Norman Rothfield Prize for Education and Peace (International Center for Peace in the Middle East)

India
1983	Indian Peace Award (Indian Campaign for Nuclear Disarmament)
1988	Jamnalal Bajaj International Award for Promoting Gandhian Values Outside India (Jamnalal Bajaj Foundation)

Italy
1984	"F. Pagano" National Prize (for Peace Education) (Center for Peace Education, Naples University)
1986	Golden Dove Peace Prize (for Journalism) (Archivio Disarmo and National Consumers' Cooperative)
1988	A Truffle for Peace Prize (Promotion Committee of the Trade Fair of the White Truffle, San Giovanni D'Asso)

Japan
1983	Niwano Peace Prize (Niwano Peace Foundation)
1987	Tanimoto Kiyoshi Peace Prize (Hiroshima Peace Center)

U.K.
1984	Frank Cousins TGWU Peace Award (Transport and General Workers' Union)

TABLE VI

Prizes Established in the 1990s

Argentina
1990	Peace Prize of 'Servicio Paz Y Justicia'

Austria
1993	Kurt Waldheim Peace Prize for Conflict Resolution (Dr. Kurt Waldheim Foundation)

Belgium
1992	Peace Plume (Flemish Peace Week Committee)

Germany
1991	Clara Immerwahr Prize (German Section of International Physicians for the Prevention of Nuclear War, IPPNW)
1994	Friedrich Siegmund Schultze Peace Prize (Evangelical Working Group for the Care of War Resisters)
1996	Christiane Rajewsky Prize (for Young Researchers) (German Association for Peace and Conflict Research, AFK)

India
1993	Global Peace Award for International Understanding (Priyadarshi Academy)

Norway
1992	Mahatma M. K. Gandhi Prize for Nonviolent Peace (Mahatma M. K. Gandhi Foundation for Nonviolent Peace)

Switzerland
1994	Women's Peace Research Prize (Campaign for Peace)

U.K./N. Ireland
1993	Pat Johnston Award for Peace and Justice (Peace People and Committee for the Administration of Justice)

U.S.
1990	Pax Christi U.S.A. Book Award
1990	Peace and Justice Award (SANE/FREEZE: Campaign for Global Security)
1990	National Academy of Sciences Award for Behavioral Research Relevant to the Prevention of Nuclear War
1992	Sakharov Award (Gleitsman Foundation; biennially)
1993	J. William Fulbright Prize for International Understanding (Fulbright Association)

national Mediation Medal, George Kennan Prize, Kohl Prize for Peace, Leo and Freda Pfeffer Peace Prize, Tipperary Peace Prize, Truman Institute Peace Award, UN Albert Schweitzer Leadership Award. It remains to be seen whether the easing of international tension since the end of the Cold War will result in the disappearance or transformation of, particularly, some of the more recently established peace prizes.

IV. THE EFFECTS AND MEANING OF PEACE PRIZES

Peace prizes are frequently created with a dual purpose: to benefit not only the recipient but also the awarding body. It should not be automatically assumed that the former objective—to honor, support, and encourage a peacemaker—is always the primary one, with the latter objective playing only a subsidiary role. Nor should this necessarily be a matter for regret. Prizes are often established to honor a great peacemaker whose name is commemorated by the award. The naming of the award is meant to help keep his or her legacy alive and the award itself is meant to encourage emulation. Instituting prizes is also a means by which organizations can project themselves before a larger audience and obtain publicity for their cause. Governments, cities, and other organizations—from women's groups to churches, and from publishers to trade unions—may institute prizes as a concrete expression of their commitment to the promotion of peace from their own perspective.

The effects on laureates and their peace efforts can be profound, especially when the prize is a high profile one such as the Nobel Peace Prize. It can provide legitimacy for their activity as well as a degree of protection for their person where these were lacking before. This is certainly true for peace and human rights campaigners in societies with oppressive regimes. A Nobel laureate, and the cause he or she represents, suddenly becomes much more visible and receives extra attention from the world's media. The considerable prize money associated with several awards provides a further, concrete, stimulus for their work (see Table VII).

Many laureates have donated the funds to assist struggling peace organizations to survive and flourish, or to set up new ones. The Right Livelihood Awards are specifically designed to publicize effective, often local and small-scale, model projects (concerning harmonious living, sustainable development, peaceful economy, provision of health care) that can be replicated elsewhere. The prize money is allocated to those projects where a little help demonstrably goes a long way, thereby consolidating and developing the local initiatives while at the same time letting the world know about them. The central message that this and other peace prizes aim to convey is that there *are* alternatives—to war and violence, poverty and oppression, ecological degradation and unhealthy living—that there *is* hope, and that individuals working together *can* make a difference.

The proliferation of peace prizes in recent years raises the question of whether the creation of each new prize diminishes the value of all of them. When so many bestow and receive prizes, what distinction is gained by being a recipient? Do more awards mean less distinction? On the one hand, since value and scarcity are directly related (in market terms), the answer is

TABLE VII

Ranking of 25 Peace Prizes According to Monetary Value of Prize (1997)*

Nobel Peace Prize	US $900,000
Balzan Prize	700,000
Gandhi International Peace Prize	300,000
Seoul Peace Prize	300,000
Onassis Prize	250,000
Right Livelihood Awards	250,000
Niwano Peace Prize	160,000
Félix Houphouët-Boigny Peace Prize	150,000
Grawemeyer Award	150,000
Sakharov Award	100,000
Indira Gandhi Prize	100,000
Carter-Menil Human Rights Prize	100,000
Africa Prize for Leadership	100,000
Albert Einstein Peace Prize	50,000
J. William Fulbright Prize	50,000
Nansen Medal	50,000
UNESCO-Madanjeet Singh Prize	40,000
Olof Palme Award	40,000
Prince of Asturias Award	35,000
Hessian Peace Prize	30,000
Spark M. Matsunaga Medal of Peace	25,000
UNESCO Prize for Peace Education	25,000
UNESCO Mayors for Peace Prize	25,000
International Simon Bolivar Prize	25,000
Martin Ennals Human Rights Award	25,000

* Figures are approximate (in several cases) because of exchange rate fluctuation and rounding off, and can vary from year to year.

affirmative. In recent times newspapers have carried fewer reports on peace awards than they used to and this may be seen as confirmation of a certain devaluation in their standing. It may also be argued that the diminishing interest in peace awards (as reflected in media reporting) is a direct consequence of the post-Cold War era in which the issue of war and peace has lost its saliency. On the other hand, the opposite view can be put forward, namely, that the creation of more peace prizes indicates that society has become more interested in honoring peacemakers. In its early years the Nobel Peace Prize was not so highly regarded as it is today because the subject it honored was far less central to the preoccupations of the society of the time. The dramatic rise of the prestige of the first award for peace has encouraged the creation of subsequent awards (even though most of them are condemned to live in the shadow of the principal prize and to remain little known).

What can be unedifying is the competition between some of the awarding bodies (in particular, the aim to rival the Nobel Peace Prize), as well as the rivalry among potential recipients. The Balzan Foundation, for example, awards its prize for peace infrequently, unlike its other prizes, apparently in order that the prize money will approximate the sum attached to the Nobel prize. Thus the Foundation gives the impression that it is more concerned with securing for its peace prize the prestige of the Nobel prize—rather than with a genuine interest in honoring peacemakers. The parallels with Nobel are explicitly made by the Foundation.

Questions may also arise over the provenance of the prize money and over the wisdom of its disbursement in this fashion. Questions have been raised in this respect about a number of prizes awarded by UN agencies (including the UNESCO Prize for Peace Education) that have been sponsored by the Japanese tycoon Ryoichi Sasakawa whose World War II record has been criticized. His funding of peace and other prizes has been regarded as an instrument in the drive for rehabilitation. A similar interpretation may be attached to the Waldheim Prize, although in this case both the initiative and the endowment originated with friends of the former UN Secretary General and Austrian president. Large prizes instituted by heads of state that are also endowed by them and carry their names (e.g., Félix Houphouët-Boigny Peace Prize, Gaddafi International Prize for Human Rights) invite suspicions of megalomania and squandermania. Vanity on the part of sponsoring organizations or individuals has its counterpart in that of candidates who sometimes actively campaign to be selected.

As illustrated above, in the course of the 20th century peace awards (and related awards in the areas of human rights, justice, development, and ecology, which have all largely been ignored here) have grown in number, have been instituted by a great variety of sponsoring organizations and individuals, and have emerged worldwide. This development can be interpreted as an expression of an emerging global culture of peace at the end of a century that has witnessed the perfection of the means of global destruction and instances of unprecedented genocide. At the same time, peace awards are aiming to contribute to the nonviolent resolution of conflict in a variety of social situations and to the creation of a world society that is both just and humane.

Bibliography

Abrams, I. (1988). *The Nobel Peace Prize and the Laureates.* Boston: G. K. Hall.

Birckenbach, H.-M. et al. (Eds.) (1997). *Jahrbuch Frieden 1997.* Munich: C. H. Beck.

Holl, K. & Kjelling, A. C. (Eds.) (1994). *The Nobel Peace Prize and the Laureates.* Frankfurt: Peter Lang.

Siegman, G. (Ed.) (1989). *Awards, honors and prizes.* Detroit: Gale Research Comp.

Siegman, G. (Ed.) (1992). *World of winners.* Detroit: Gale Research Comp.

Thee, M. (Ed.) (1995). *Peace! By the Nobel Peace Prize Laureates.* Paris: UNESCO Publ.

van den Dungen, P. (1991). The prize of peace: Reflections on the awarding of efforts towards peace. *Transaktie, 20*(4), 321–341 (in Dutch).

Peace Studies, Overview

Carolyn M. Stephenson

University of Hawai'i at Manoa

GLOSSARY

Conflict Resolution The resolution of conflicts, usually including attempts to meet long-term human needs, often by the use of third parties. Some authors include conflict management and conflict settlement approaches; others distinguish conflict resolution from those.

Negative Peace The absence of war and large-scale physical violence. Concept enunciated by Quincy Wright, M.L. King, Jr., and Johan Galtung.

Peace Research Systematic research on the causes of war and violence, and the conditions of peace, and the possible relationships between them.

Peace education In British systems, elementary and secondary teaching, in American systems, teaching at any level, on peace issues.

Positive peace The absence of war and large-scale physical violence, plus the presence of social justice. Concept enunciated by Wright, King, and, more explicitly, Galtung.

Security-Community A community with dependable expectations of peaceful change among its members. Concept defined by Karl Deutsch.

Stable Peace "A situation in which the probability of war is so small that it does not really enter into the calculations of any of the people involved," and which usually encompasses perceptions of justice among its members. Concept defined by Kenneth Boulding.

PEACE STUDIES is an interdisciplinary field encompassing systematic research and teaching on the causes of war and the conditions of peace. It focuses on the causes of increases and decreases in violence, the conditions associated with those changes, and the processes by which those changes happen. While there is disagreement over the exact content of the field, and even over the definition of peace, most would agree that peace studies began to be identified as a separate field of inquiry during the first few decades after World War II.

I. PEACE STUDIES, PEACE RESEARCH, AND PEACE EDUCATION

Peace research and peace studies are generally regarded as covering research and teaching on the causes of war and the conditions of peace. The terms are sometimes used synonymously, sometimes differently. In the United States, the term peace studies tends to include both research and education. Some prefer to use the

Copyright © 1999 by Academic Press.
All rights of reproduction in any form reserved.

term peace studies to mean peace education at all levels. In British systems peace studies generally refers to research and teaching at the tertiary or university level, while the term peace education tends to be reserved for the elementary and secondary levels. One thing that is clear in both types of systems is that peace education was derived from the field of peace research several decades ago and is solidly based within it. While there has been disagreement over the exact content of the field, particularly as newcomers entered it in the 1980s without an appreciation of its academic origins, it remains clear that peace studies focuses around the causes of the increase and decrease of massive violence, the conditions associated with those changes, and the processes by which those changes happen. Peace researchers research war, peace, and conflict and the relationships between them, and peace educators teach both the findings and methods of peace research as well as examine the values and beliefs that underlie various systems of war, peace, and conflict and raise questions for peace researchers. Peace studies, at its best, incorporates the interaction of research and education, with peace education centered in the teaching of peace research.

There is general agreement on a number of elements relating to the study of peace. There seems to be agreement that the field is interdisciplinary at its best, or at least multidisciplinary, that it is international (and/or more often transnational), that it is policy oriented—meaning directed to the real-life political environment of both policy-makers and peace movements—and that it is value explicit. It is important to distinguish this last from the term value based; all work is value based, whether consciously or not, but there is an explicit commitment in the field of peace research/peace studies to making the values and the assumptions of the researcher clear. Among those values shared by the whole field is the commitment to peace as a value in itself. Generally, peace studies also includes a commitment to at least some experiential component of learning, such as an internship. Finally, there is in large part also agreement that peace research finds itself located largely within the social sciences, having begun with a positivistic and behavioral/quantitative/data-based approach, but having broadened to embrace a wide variety of research methods. Peace studies, on the other hand, seems to have a broader disciplinary base, including, in addition to all the social sciences, history, philosophy, physics, biology, religion, art, language, and linguistics and other fields as well. Table I indicates some of the ways in which the traditional disciplines relate to some of the key subfields of peace studies.

It is probably necessary to distinguish peace studies from other closely related fields such as security studies, international relations, and conflict resolution. Some would argue that these areas are totally different from peace studies, while others would argue that they are a part of it. One distinction drawn by those in the field is that peace studies covers the full continuum of violence from individual to global and the full continuum of peace, with the primary emphasis at the group level, while international relations focuses at the international level, and conflict resolution tends to find most of its practitioners and researchers in the domestic arena, in individual as well as in group conflict. The distinction drawn between security studies and peace studies is that peace studies generally focuses on the security of the whole international or global system, while the security of a single state or alliance is often the primary focus of those who identify as security studies scholars.

Since peace studies is in a sense a successor to international relations, it may be important to be more explicit about their differences. (1) While the primary difference is the difference of focus in levels of analysis (as mentioned above), both in terms of dependent and independent variables, there are others as well. (2) While international relations tends to be located within the social sciences, and especially political science (witness the membership of the International Studies Association), peace studies covers the social sciences, natural and physical sciences, and humanities, although with its focus within the social sciences. (3) Peace studies tends to focus on a longer time period than international relations, both in the past and in the future. While the study of international relations, quite logically, generally begins with the creation of the nation-state system in 1648, peace studies tends to go much farther back in history than the Peace of Westphalia, and often includes the systematic study of the future. Derivative of this difference is that even that work in international relations, which examines the structure of the system as a whole, tends to accept the nation-state as a given, while peace studies focuses on a wider variety of organizational systems, centralized and decentralized, hierarchical and nonhierarchical. (4) Peace studies is explicitly a policy science, policy oriented in the sense that it aspires to describe, explain, and recommend policy relating to the conditions of peace to both governments and social movements, while a substantial number of those in international relations see themselves as limited to description and explanation. (5) Finally, peace studies is value explicit, with both a positive valuation of peace itself and a commitment to examine trade-offs

TABLE I

PEACE STUDIES AND THE TRADITIONAL DISCIPLINES

Fields of Peace Studies	Political Science	Sociology	Psychology	Anthropology	Economics	History	Literature/ Languages	Philosophy	Religion	Art	Physics	Biology	Chemistry
Causes of War													
Competition	X		X	X	X	X	X	X		X			
Aggression	X	X	X	X		X	X	X	X	X		X	X
Weapons/ Technology	X		X	X		X				X	X	X	X
Ideology/ Culture	X	X		X		X	X		X	X			
Social/ Economic/ Political Structures	X	X		X	X	X		X					
Conditions of Peace													
Basic Human Needs	X		X	X	X			X				X	
Human Rights	X	X	X	X	X	X	X	X	X	X			
Equity	X	X	X	X	X	X	X	X	X	X			
Peaceful Processes of Conflict Resolution	X	X	X	X	X	X		X	X				
	Social Sciences					Humanities					Natural and Physical Sciences		

The Traditional Disciplines

Note: Copyright by Carolyn M. Stephenson.

between values, while values tend to be more hidden in much international relations (I.R.) research, with some I.R. scholars still claiming that research can be "value-free," a conception that social and even natural science has largely rejected for decades. Within international relations, the dominant paradigm tends in general to be more accepting of the utility of coercive power and threat systems than would be the case in peace studies. The value of conflict, of integration and disintegration, of equality, of justice, of freedom, and the relative trade-offs between these, as well as the appropriateness of various methods for achieving those valued positively, are widely debated within as well as between both fields.

II. PEACE

Probably the most serious division in the field of peace research occurs over the definition of peace. As is the case in political science for power and politics, there is no agreement over what is the central object of our study. The major question has been whether peace is to be defined simply as the absence of war and direct violence ("negative peace") or whether the concept encompasses both the absence of war and direct violence plus the presence of social justice ("positive peace"). Those who argue that peace should be narrowly defined hold that broadening the concept reduces its clarity. To some degree this division can be identified geographically; in Northern Europe and much of the "third world" the concept of positive peace is more widely accepted, while in the U.S. a larger number of peace researchers appear to limit themselves to work on negative peace. The two individual peace researchers most often associated with the two poles of this debate, Johan Galtung, who is credited with the invention of the term "positive peace" in the mid-l960s, and Kenneth Boulding, among whose "twelve friendly quarrels" with Galtung include this one, fit the geographical expectations.

This debate has been present throughout most of the development of peace studies. It comes up early with Augustine's "just war" doctrine. Quincy Wright, in a discussion of public opinion and war, distinguishes between pacifist and internationalist views of peace. Noting that "the public thinks of peace as merely the absence of war and finds it uninteresting" (p. 1097), he says that: "A negative conception of peace is self-defeating and unrealizable. Peace must be conceived positively as a universal society assuring co-operation and justice among all important groups." (p. 1098) Martin Luther King, Jr. makes a similar but not identical distinction in his 1963 Letter from Birmingham City Jail: "I had hoped that the white moderate would understand that the present tension of the South is merely a necessary phase of the transition from an obnoxious negative peace, where the Negro passively accepted his unjust plight, to a substance-filled positive peace, where all men will respect the dignity and worth of the human person." (p. 295).

There may in fact be more agreement over the definition of "peace" than the various schisms suggest. Clearly there is some relationship between the absence of war and the presence of other social values such as justice and freedom, although we may not be able to specify yet exactly what those relationships are in a general theory acceptable to the whole of the field. Most of us would not be satisfied with a notion of peace that did not imply some degree of long-term stability. As Karl Deutsch put it, a security-community is one where there are "dependable expectations of peaceful change" for the foreseeable future (1957, p. 5). Similarly, Boulding argues that "Stable peace is a situation in which the probability of war is so small that it does not really enter into the calculations of any of the people involved" (1978, p. 13). He also notes that "perceptions of justice and injustice form an important aspect of both strain and strength in a war–peace system." (1978, p. 71). Galtung's early distinction was between negative peace, not only as the absence of war, but also as the absence of organized violence between groups, and positive

peace as the presence of cooperation or harmonious living between groups. Only after the radical critique of peace research in the late 1960s did the conception of positive peace evolve to include the absence of the violence done by the structures of society to human growth and fulfillment.

Herbert Kelman, in advocating the "negative peace" definition, includes in that definition "the absence of systematic, large-scale collective violence, accompanied by a sense of security that such violence is improbable," (1981, p. 103) and makes clear that peace by this definition is an important normative concern of peace researchers in its own right. While he makes the case that peace as "the preservation of human life and the avoidance of violence and destruction are *extremely high values*" in their own right (p. 105), he also sees justice as having a strong bearing on the feasibility, stability, universality, and quality of peace (p. 109). If one accepts Kelman's definition and his ancillary advice that the study of even negative peace requires also the study of justice, as this author suspects the majority of the field does, then one is left with the notion that peace studies as a field must focus its teaching and research on the various possible relationships between "negative" and "positive" peace, rather than being doctrinaire in definitional matters. It may be perhaps clearer to *define* peace as the absence of organized violence, but to limit one's study to that would not be productive in advancing either the theory or the practice of the field.

Finally, while a commonly shared public definition of peace may be the absence of conflict, that definition is largely rejected among peace researchers. Conflict is accepted as a normal part of human life and international relations. The question is how one goes about carrying out and resolving that conflict in ways that reduce the possibility or the level of violence without reducing other values such as justice or freedom.

III. THE ORIGINS OF PEACE RESEARCH AND PEACE EDUCATION

The origins of peace research could be judged to be as far back as Thomas Hobbes' *Leviathan* (1651) or even Plato or Thucydides. Hobbes' characterization of war as originating from the combination of the greed and equality of human beings, with the solution being a social contract dependent on the creation of authoritative institutions, has been a thread in both realist and

TABLE II

Major Steps in the Development of Peace Studies, 1945–1980

Year	Journals	Research institutes	Education	Nat'l/internat'l organizations
1945		Institut Français de Polémologie		
1948			Manchester College Peace Studies Program	
1952	*Bulletin of the Research Exchange on the Causes of War*			
1957	*Journal of Conflict Resolution*	Center for Research on Conflict Resolution (Michigan)		
1959		PRIO (in Institute for Social Research) Peace Research Institute Dundas Lancaster Peace Research Centre (Richardson Institute)		
1963				Conference on Peace Research in History Peace Research Society (Internat'l)
1964	*Peace Science Society (Internat'l) Papers Journal of Peace Research*			IPRA
1966	*IPRA Proceedings*	PRIO (independent) SIPRI		Canadian Peace Research and Education Assoc.
1970				COPRED
1971			1st Chair in Peace Studies in U.S.: Colgate	
1972	*Peace and Change*			
1973			1st Chair in Peace Studies in U.K.: Bradford	Peace Education Commission of IPRA
1974				Asian Peace Research Assoc.
1975	*Alternatives*			

Note: Copyright by Carolyn M. Stephenson.

idealist strands of peace research ever since. The Lockean claim of the right of revolution against the tyranny of authoritarian institutions has been a second important strand. Yet the origins of peace research as a separate field of inquiry are probably better traced only within the 20th century. One might argue that there have been three primary waves of peace studies worldwide since its beginnings between the world wars. Table II lists some of the major steps in the early development of the field of peace studies.

A. The First Wave

Quincy Wright and Lewis Richardson, independently in the United States and in the United Kingdom in the 1930s, were among the first to do quantitative analyses of war, to some degree out of the belief that the outbreak of war was based largely on the ignorance of foreign policy makers of what might be the consequences of their decisions. Both concluded that improving the knowledge base was a necessary part of dealing with the problem of war and that evaluation and application of that knowledge would also be important. Wright, in his analysis of the causes of war, found that each of six great wars over the course of more than 12 centuries showed a combination of idealistic, psychological, political, and juridical causes. Richardson looked at the attributes of states, among other factors, and found that homogeneity in culture, language, and religion did not preclude war breaking out among them. Both Richardson's and Wright's analyses, like the more sociologically and culturally based theories of Pitrim Sorokin in the 1920s, did much to illuminate the motives for beginning war—both for men and for states—and the attributes of states and relationships between them which led to war.

While Richardson and Wright were clearly the forefathers of the field, peace studies could not be said to have begun in earnest as an academic field until the late 1940s or early 1950s. Two research institutes were founded in this period at the close of the Second World War. In France the Institut Francais de Polemologie was founded in 1945. Bert Roling was a central figure in polymologie (war research), thinking its study was essential to the development of international law, and introduced it to the Netherlands. In the U.S. in the same year, Theodore Lentz founded the "oldest continuously operating peace research center in the world," to encourage the mobilization of social scientists for a science of peace that would bring about a scientific revolution involving both changes in fact and value. The Society for the Psychological Study of Social Issues also had set up a Committee on the Psychology of War and Peace pre-World War II, but this became inactive during the war.

A letter published in April, 1951 by Arthur Gladstone and Herbert Kelman in *The American Psychologist*, arguing that pacifist challenges to the assumptions underlying conventional foreign policy deserved the systematic attention of psychologists, led to the 1952 formation of the Research Exchange on the Prevention of War and its *Bulletin*. In 1954–1955 Kelman was among the first group of Fellows at the Center for Advanced Studies in the Behavioral Sciences at Stanford, which included Anatol Rapaport and Kenneth Boulding as well as Stephen Richardson, the son of Lewis Richardson. The group was thus made aware of the writings of the late Richardson and arranged for their publication. It also split the functions of the Research Exchange, reestablishing the prewar SPSSI committee and exchanging the *Bulletin* for the more formal *Journal of Conflict Resolution: A Quarterly for Research Related to War and Peace*, which was to begin publication in 1957

at the University of Michigan, where both Rapaport and Boulding were located. The Center for Research on Conflict Resolution would also be organized here as would the Correlates of War Project, headed by J. David Singer, to look at some of the state and systemic factors thought to be associated with the frequency, severity, magnitude, and intensity of war.

In 1959 two institutes in very different traditions were founded. The Peace Research Institute Dundas (Canada) was founded by Hannah and Alan Newcombe, largely in the negative peace tradition. The Peace Research Institute Oslo (Norway) began as part of the Institute of Social Research and became independent in 1966. The radical critique of peace research was predominant here in the late 1960s and Johan Galtung's concept of "positive peace" was to be a central focus both of the Institute and of the *Journal of Peace Research*, which began publication at the Institute in 1964. It was later to be joined by the *Bulletin of Peace Proposals*. In Britain, the Lancaster Peace Research Centre, later to become the Richardson Institute, was also formed in 1959. The other major institute founded at this time was the Stockholm International Peace Research Institute, 1966, which remains a leader in the side of the field concerned with armament and disarmament.

International organizations of peace researchers also began at this time. The Peace Research Society (International), which later began to prefer the term "peace science," was set up at a meeting in Sweden in 1963 by Walter Izard of the U.S. The Polemological Institute at the University of Groningen in the Netherlands, of which Bert Roling became the first Director in 1961, became the first site of the International Peace Research Association (IPRA), which was founded in 1964 as a result of a Quaker International Conference and Seminar in Clarens, Switzerland in August, 1963. The IPRA holds meetings every 2 years in different regions of the world and publishes selected *Proceedings* of those meetings and a *Newsletter*. It is now regarded as the major international professional organization in the field of peace research.

National associations of peace researchers also began to be formed. The Conference (later Council) on Peace Research in History formed itself at the December, 1963 meeting of the American Historical Association, after the assassination of John F. Kennedy and the beginnings of heavy U.S. involvement in the Indochina War and out of the realization that the profession of history tended to focus on wars and kings and not on social movements and ordinary people. By 1972 the organization began the publication of a journal, *Peace and Change*, which was later to be jointly published with

COPRED, the Consortium on Peace Research, Education and Development. The Canadian Peace Research and Education Association was formed in 1966.

B. The Second Wave

What might be regarded as the second wave of peace studies began in the late 1960s and early 1970s. In a sense it might be regarded as the democratization of peace research; while the reaction to Vietnam led to a radical critique of peace research in Northern Europe—and then to the development of critical peace research—it led in the U.S. to peace education. If the first wave of peace studies was primarily peace research with a touch of education, primarily at the graduate level, then the second wave could be regarded as primarily a new focus on peace education, both at the graduate but especially at the undergraduate university level. In a sense it was occasioned by the realization of peace researchers that their research had a relevance for the undergraduate classroom and even more so for the troubled campuses of the era of Vietnam protests around the world.

While Manchester College in Indiana had established the first undergraduate peace studies program in the U.S. as early as 1948, stressing the interdisciplinary and cross-cultural emphasis that was to characterize later efforts as well, it was not until the early 1970s that a wave of peace studies programs was to be created. As with the Manchester program, many of these began in small religious-based liberal arts colleges. Spurred by two organizational efforts, those of the Institute for World Order (later the World Policy Institute, which cancelled its educational program, but now publishes two journals in the field, *Alternatives* and later *World Policy Journal*) and those of the new Consortium on Peace Research, Education and Development (CO-PRED), founded in 1970, a number of new programs developed, including among the earliest Colgate, where the first chair in Peace Studies in the U.S. was created in 1971, as well as Manhattan, Syracuse, University of Akron, Kent State, Juniata, and Gustavus Adolphus among others.

Unlike the earlier educational efforts of the 1950s, such as the programs at Northwestern University, Stanford, and Yale in the U.S., these were not primarily oriented to research and specialized graduate training but to teaching undergraduate students. While the number of institutions in the U.S. that taught peace studies could be counted on two hands at the beginning of the decade, by its finish there were over 100, some of them with full majors.

In Europe peace studies expanded from research institutes to teaching programs, but with a continuing research emphasis. In Sweden in 1971 Uppsala University established its Department of Peace and Conflict Research, and a professorship of peace and conflict research was established at Lund. In 1978 the Peace and Development Research Institute was established at Gothenburg. Bradford, which developed the first chair in peace studies in England in 1973, began a comprehensive graduate and undergraduate program. Founded under a Quaker initiative, Bradford struggled through an identity crisis after its first years to become a respected center in peace and security studies, conflict resolution, and social change.

The agenda of peace studies broadened in this period. If peace studies began primarily as the study of the causes and character of war, by this period it had expanded to examine other varieties of violence and injustice. The rise of the civil rights movement, the anti-Vietnam War movement, and the feminist movement in the 1960s and early 1970s led not only to a critique of hegemonic state power but to a radical critique of peace studies itself from within the field. Much of this debate took place in the *Journal of Peace Research* in the late 1960s and early 1970s. Some felt that the field's emphasis on war and direct violence caused it to underestimate the violence done by the structures of power, leading it to become the ally of the state in pacification and repression. Adam Curle, in his inaugural lecture as the first holder of the chair in Peace Studies at Bradford University in 1975 argued that "the study of peace is not the study of pacification, of suppressing dissent, of maintaining the status quo however painful it may be to the less privileged."

Other elements also broadened the field of peace studies. The increase in the power of the "third world" after decolonization and the 1973 oil crisis led to an increased focus on development in both international relations and peace studies. The increasing internationalization of peace research drew in "third world" perspectives such that IPRA's second conference in 1968 included a heavy emphasis on development, poverty, inequality, and malnutrition. The increased policy emphasis throughout the social sciences also affected peace studies, adding the studies of food, environment, oceans, human rights, and other policy areas. The questioning of scientific method, positivism, and objectivity throughout the sciences also helped to redefine some of the field.

Along with educational programs, more national and international associations developed. The COPRED had been developed to link peace research, peace education, and peace action to make each more responsive to the other and to meet the needs of both policy-makers and peace movements, primarily in the U.S. and Canada. The Peace Education Commission of IPRA was founded in 1973, specifically with the purpose of making peace research more accessible, combining the participation-action-research tradition with an emphasis on process, on experiential learning, and on democratic pedagogy. In the U.S., professional academic organizations such as the International Studies Association and the American Sociological Association began to form subsections on peace studies. International regional organizations formed, such as the Latin American Council on Peace Research, headquartered in Mexico. The Asian Peace Research Association was formed in 1974, headquartered in Japan. While the quantitative and behavioral stream continued to be important in peace research, other research traditions took their places beside it, and peace education joined peace research as an important component of the field.

C. The Third Wave

The phase of peace studies that began in the 1980s was in one sense the culmination of earlier phases and in another sense a different phenomenon. In this phase the impetus did not so much come from within the peace research/peace education community, but from peace movements all over the world and the public, who were concerned with the nuclear arms race.

Antinuclear concerns led first to the development of antinuclear organizations within professions, to organizations like Physicians for Social Responsibility, International Physicians for the Prevention of Nuclear War, Artists for Social Responsibility and the like, as well as to local referenda on nuclear-free zones and to the more familiar development of arms control and disarmament movements. Out of all of these came a concern with educating the public and eventually with educating students at all levels. Groups like Educators for Social Responsibility, United Campuses against Nuclear War, and numerous other groups joined older educational groups like the Center for the Teaching of International Relations at the University of Denver, Teachers' College at Columbia, the Center for Global Responsibility, and the Peace Education Network of COPRED in focusing not only on college level education, but on the education of teachers and the direct education of elementary and secondary students in peace studies.

Undergraduate university education expanded. New editions of the peace studies currriculum guides, which had begun in 1973, came out in 1981, 1984, and 1989,

providing guidance on syllabi for new faculty entering the field. College faculty met first at Colgate and then at the University of California at Irvine in 1987 to form the Peace Studies Association in order to further the development of college- and university-level peace studies programs. The emphasis in new programs, however, tended to be more narrow, focusing more on questions of nuclear war and international security than on the broader-based questions that the field of peace studies had asked before.

By no means did the majority of U.S. peace researchers agree with this narrow definition. Many argued that this was better classified as national security or strategic studies, closer to traditional international relations than to peace research. Some third-world scholars argued that strategic studies are increasingly irrelevant to understanding third-world conflicts. Korany (1986) argued that the power paradigm central to strategic studies overemphasized the role of the state and of (especially military) threat and thus was ethnocentric and separated third-world conflict and militarization from the global system in which they were embedded. He argued that the threats to third-world states were more often from their own internal fragility, the need for development, and cultural and religious demands. Yet the language setting up new programs like the Institute on Global Conflict and Cooperation in the University of California system explicitly excluded the study of development from its primary purposes.

Discouragement with the problems of both nuclear deterrence and military intervention led peace researchers to begin to look at the alternatives to war, such as nonviolent sanctions, nonprovocative or nonoffensive defense, and various kinds of conflict resolution. As the new field of alternative international security systems began to creep into peace studies in the 1980s, researchers began to look at the alternatives available for protecting political systems and maintaining international security with less violence. What appears to have been the first conference on the subject, the COPRED 1979 meeting, produced a book reviewing various approaches (Stephenson, 1982). UNESCO's first Disarmament Education Conference, held in 1980, included references to the need for developing alternatives as a part of disarmament education.

The work of Gene Sharp on nonviolent struggle and civilian-based defense, begun over a decade before, and the Program on Nonviolent Sanctions in Conflict and Defense at Harvard, came into public view and greater acceptance. As nonviolent struggles took place in Poland and the Philippines, and to some degree in Iran, other researchers began to give attention to this area and to transarmament, or the process of transition from violent to nonviolent struggle. Primarily in Northern Europe, in West Germany, and the United Kingdom, work began on alternative or nonoffensive or defensive defense, which spread to the U.S. in the mid-1980s.

Another component of this third wave was a tremendous increase in the emphasis on conflict resolution and particularly the use of third parties or mediation. This ranged from training in neighborhood centers in divorce mediation, through the development of new types of mediation appropriate for use in public budgetary and environmental disputes, to the development of university-level training and research programs and the development of national and international organizations in the field. In the U.S. a number of national groups emerged: the National Institute on Dispute Resolution, the Society of Professionals in Dispute Resolution, and the National Conference on Peacemaking and Conflict Resolution, which held its first conference in 1982 to try to link conflict resolution with other parts of the field and to link professional conflict resolvers with researchers and educators. As local and international mediation centers and firms were founded, joining older efforts in the labor and commercial field such as the American Arbitration Association, universities began programs of research and education, beginning largely at the graduate or postgraduate level. The Program on Negotiation, a consortium of Boston groups based at the Harvard Law School, was joined by programs at the Universities of Hawaii, Michigan, Minnesota, George Mason, Wisconsin, Colorado, Syracuse, and others. While many of these focused largely on individual or domestic conflict, some programs, including those at Hawaii, Syracuse, and Colorado, more broadly defined explicit linkages between conflict resolution and peace studies.

Since the 1980s, burgeoning research work focused specifically on international conflict resolution, as well as on that addressing the full range of conflict behavior. Pruitt and Rubin joined Kriesberg's second edition as comprehensive and thorough introductions to the field of conflict and its resolution. Fisher and Ury's *Getting to Yes*, a popular version of a larger manuscript, which puts forth a seven-point program of "principled negotiation" as an alternative to the traditional bargaining system, became probably the most widely used text for teaching and training in the field of conflict resolution.

A technique originally developed for research on conflict as well as for conflict resolution became the focus of more and more work. Originally termed "controlled communication" by John Burton, and in a modified form described as "problem-solving workshops" by

Herbert Kelman, it involves the use of academics skilled in the field of conflict studies to mediate between individual representatives of two sides of a long-standing international conflict, with a view, not to settling the conflict, but to helping the participants develop a better understanding of the other side, of the processes of conflict itself, and of the possibility for new solutions that may eventually be introduced back into the policy process.

Finally, governments began a new phase of institutionalization of peace research and education. The states of California, Ohio, and Hawaii and the government of New Zealand, among many others, began to develop peace education in the public school and university systems. National institutes were formed: the University for Peace, loosely associated with the United Nations, was formed in Costa Rica, as well as the Austrian Peace Research Institute (1983), the Canadian Institute for Peace and International Security (1984), the Australian Peace Research Centre (1984), the U.S. Institute of Peace (1984), and the Scientific Research Council on Peace and Development in the USSR (1979), followed by similar councils in Bulgaria (1981) and Hungary (1982) and a Peace Research unit in the Academy of Sciences in Czechoslovakia (1982). In at least some of these countries where peace studies was being institutionalized, the debate over whether peace studies should be policy relevant and work toward the improvement of state practice related to war, peace, and justice issues or whether peace studies should remain independent and critical of the state was rekindled by the sudden growth of resources in the field. Nor was this the only debate; the tremendous growth of peace action, peace research, and especially peace education at all levels, and the joining together of those who had long worked in the field with a large number of new individuals and organizations, was the occasion for both the reawakening of the debates discussed above and the awakening of new debates.

IV. PEACE STUDIES AFTER THE COLD WAR

While there were predictions of the end of conflict, the end of history, and the end of the need for peace research as the Cold War ended in the late 1980s, it took only a very few years for it to be apparent that conflict and violence had not abated but simply taken different forms and that research and education on the causes of war and the conditions of peace were still needed. Attention that had been focused on international conflict, and especially East–West ideological conflict backed up by nuclear deterrence, began to focus on other conflicts that had been going on all this time in other parts of the world and on new conflicts in regions where violence had been low. As demands for human rights expanded from individual civil and political, economic, and social rights to group rights, and as ethnic and national identities became the focus of conflict and often violence, peace research and other fields turned to look both at these conflicts and at the means for their control and resolution. Economic and environmental conflict also became the focus of peace research. While work on low-intensity and intranational conflict was limited during the 1980s, attention to intranational conflict and violence became a major focus in the 1990s, together with work on conflict resolution, early warning systems, and United Nations preventive diplomacy, peacekeeping, peace-making, and peace-building and enforcement. While many of the old debates that had raged since the 1930s were still present, debates over world government and enforcement power, over unilateral or multilateral control of economic and military power, over violent versus nonviolent means of carrying on and resolving conflict, the field had begun a stage of maturation marked by diversification into subfields.

It is more difficult to chronicle and to evaluate peace studies after the end of the Cold War. While some argue that the field continues to grow both in numbers and intellectually, others argue that the field has declined in numbers of participants and programs and has become intellectually fractionated. It is possible to document both of these arguments because, while the core of the field remains fairly clear, the boundaries grow ever more flexible. Certainly peace studies, broadly defined, now has more journals and more courses at the university level. Whether there is an increase in the number of programs depends on how one counts; it depends on whether a single course or individual who identifies with peace studies is defined as a program or whether a program is defined as a full-fledged major with comprehensive coverage of the field.

Funding of peace studies, defined narrowly, has declined since the early 1990s, and with it, institutions created at the peak of that funding period in the 1980s. The Australian Peace Research Centre at the Australian National University, and the Canadian Institute for Peace and International Security, both significant government-funded research institutions, as well as many others, became defunct during the mid-1990s. The Program on Nonviolent Sanctions in Conflict and Defense at Harvard lost its focus on nonviolent sanctions due

to funding difficulties and became the Program on Nonviolent Sanctions and Cultural Diversity. Some peace studies programs funded in the 1980s funding peak in the U.S., disappeared; some, especially the older ones at small liberal arts colleges, survived. The COPRED and the Peace Studies Association were both faced with financial crises, forcing them to lay off their full-time directors.

Europe, however, remained strong in its commitment to peace studies, continuing to fund solid research institutes and journals and to build some work in peace education. The traditional strength in Scandinavia was joined by other institutions throughout Western Europe and especially by the European University Center for Peace Studies, funded by the Austrian government just at the close of the Cold War, which began pilot peace studies courses in 1989 at Stadtschlaining, with faculty and students drawn from many countries. The European Peace Research Association began, with its first conference in November, 1991 in Florence.

Efforts in other regions have been more mixed. The First Latin American Conference on International Relations and Peace Research was held in April 1994. The older Asian Peace Research Association, which lost much of its original Japanese support, regenerated itself briefly as the Asia-Pacific Peace Research Association, with conferences in New Zealand and Malaysia, and then declined. A few more specialized institutes, some with a conflict resolution focus, others focused on peace and security, worked in Southeast Asia and Africa.

Journals, textbooks, and encyclopedias proliferated during the 1990s. *Peace Review* began with the intent to make peace studies accessible to the ordinary reader. *The International Journal of Peace Studies* was initiated by the Global Political Economy Study Commission of IPRA in January 1996. Several textbooks and readers were published in the UK and in the U.S. between 1990 and 1992, including Barash's widely used *Introduction to Peace Studies* (1991). While the Einstein Institution had declined in funding, it produced a landmark *Encyclopedia of Nonviolent Action* in 1997 (Powers and Vogele). Publication of the peace studies curriculum guides continued, with Klare's sixth edition, now renamed *Peace and World Security Studies*, published in 1994. Similarly, in Norway, the *Bulletin of Peace Proposals* now became *Security Dialogue*. These renamings were not incidental; they reflected a change in the direction of the field with a trend toward mainstreaming and integrating with security studies.

Tremendous diversity remained a characteristic of the field, however. Along with an increasing emphasis on social change and social movements, on ethnic and identity-based conflict, on sustainable development, and on the relationship between democracy and peace came renewed debates over the appropriateness of objective and subjective methodologies and marginalization and fractionalization of the more justice-oriented part of the field. Probably the strongest part of the field at this time is the subfield of conflict dynamics and conflict resolution, which in many ways can be regarded as a separate field.

The 1990s can be regarded, in some sense, as a period of consolidation for peace studies. The tremendous initiation of the 1970s and 1980s is gone, and there is some decline, but also diversification into separate subfields and integration into traditional fields. Many peace researchers have already gravitated to the peace studies sections that had been formed within disciplinary or interdisciplinary organizations, such as the Peace Studies Section of the International Studies Association, and similar sections in national political science and sociology associations. Peace studies can be seen either as declining or as succeeding in changing the nature of traditional fields of study.

V. CONCLUSIONS

Peace studies, as a field of research and education, has clearly come of age. Kenneth Boulding said many years ago that the definition of an academic field is whether one can give an exam in it. One does. It has research, journals, courses, and programs. By the 1990s, peace studies would still be fighting battles over whether research, education, or activism were to be priorities, but there is by this time no question that such a field exists.

What is probably important in the late 1990s is to reinvigorate the integrated search for theoretically and empirically based understandings of the underlying nature of the dynamics of conflict and its resolution and especially when and how that results in violence or peace. Diversity and creative tensions in a field are signs of health, but fragmentation may not be, and it seems that the field has splintered to such a degree that the ideological, methodological, and subfield groups are not always involved in the kind of constructive dialogue necessary for the field of peace studies to move toward its central value, peace. The complexities in the causes of war and violence and the conditions of peace were recognized by the founders of the field. A renewed effort to understand the relationships between structure and process and identities, beliefs, and the construction of

meaning, as they concern peace, is needed. Neither peace studies nor international relations were prepared for the end of the Cold War. A clear, future-oriented, theoretically and empirically based research agenda is probably necessary if peace studies is to be prepared for the next phase of the war-peace system so that it may influence it toward peaceful change.

Also See the Following Articles

CONFLICT THEORY • INTERNATIONAL RELATIONS, OVERVIEW • NONVIOLENCE THEORY AND PRACTICE • PEACE, DEFINITIONS OF • PEACE EDUCATION

Bibliography

Boulding, K. E. (1978). Stable peace. Austin, TX: University of Texas Press.

Boulding, K. E. (1977). "Twelve Friendly Quarrels with Johan Galtung." Journal of Peace Research, 14, 75–86.

Burton, J. W. (1987). Resolving deep rooted conflict: A handbook. Lanham, MD: University Press of America.

Chatfield, C. (1979). International peace research: The field defined by dissemination. Journal of Peace Research, 16 (2), 161–179.

Dedring, J. (1976). Recent advances in peace and conflict research. Beverly Hills, CA: Sage.

Deutsch, K. W. et al. (1957). Political community and the North Atlantic area. Princeton, NJ: Princeton University Press.

Fisher, R., & Ury, W. (1981). Getting to yes: Negotiating agreement without giving in. New York: Penguin.

Galtung, J. (1975). Essays in peace research, Vol. I. Copenhagen: Christian Ejlers.

Harris, I. Fisk, L. J., & Rank, C. (1998). A portrait of university peace studies in North America and Western Europe at the end of the millennium. International Journal of Peace Studies, 3(1), 91–112.

Kelman, H. C. (1981). Reflections on the history and status of peace research. Conflict Management and Peace Science, 5(2), 95–110.

Kelman, H. C. (1972). The problem-solving workshop in conflict resolution. In R. Merritt (Ed.), Communications and international politics. Urbana, IL: University of Illinois Press.

King, M. L. (1986). Letter from Birmingham City jail. In J. M. Washington (Ed.), A testament of hope, pp. 289-302 San Francisco: Harper.

Klare, M. T., & Thomas, D. C. (Eds.) (1989). Peace and world order studies: A curriculum guide. Boulder, CO: Westview.

Korany, B. (1986). Strategic studies and the third world. International Social Science Journal, 35(4), 547–562.

Kriesberg, L. (1982). Social conflicts, 2nd ed. Englewood Cliffs, NJ: Prentice-Hall.

Mack, A. (1985). Peace research in the 1980s. Canberra: Australian National University.

Powers, R. S., & Vogele, W. B. (Eds.) (1997). Protest, power and change: An encyclopedia of nonviolent action. New York: Garland.

Pruitt, D. G., & Rubin, J. Z. (1986). Social conflict: Escalation, stalemate, and settlement. New York: Random House.

Richardson, L. F. (1960). Statistics of deadly quarrels. Pittsburgh, PA: Boxwood Press.

Richardson, L. F. (1960). Arms and insecurity. Pittsburgh, PA: Boxwood Press.

Sharp, G. (1985). *Making europe unconquerable*. Cambridge, MA. Ballinger.

Singer, J. D. (1981). Accounting for international war: The state of the discipline. *Journal of Peace Research, 18*(1).

Stephenson, C. M. (Ed.) (1982). *Alternative methods for international security*. Washington, DC: University Press of America.

Varis, T. (1986). Introduction. In L. Kiuzadjan, H. Hogeweg-de Haart, & W. Richter (Eds.), *Peace research: A documentation of current research*. Moscow, USSR: European Coordination Centre for Research and Documentation in the Social Sciences.

Wiberg, H. (1983). The peace research movement. Paper delivered at the Tenth General Conference of IPRA, Gyor, Hungary.

Wright, Q. (1965). *A study of war*. Chicago: University of Chicago Press. (Originally published 1942).